The Irish Enlightenment

Michael Brown

Harvard University Press

Cambridge, Massachusetts   London, England

2016

Second printing

George Szirtes, 'Orgreave,' from *New and Collected Poems* (Tarset, Northumberland,
UK: Bloodaxe Books, 2008), reproduced with permission of Bloodaxe Books on behalf of
the author. www.bloodaxebooks.com.

Library of Congress Cataloging-in-Publication Data
Brown, Michael, 1972– author.
The Irish enlightenment / Michael Brown.
pages cm
Includes bibliographical references and index.
ISBN 978-0-674-04577-4
1. Enlightenment—Ireland.   2. Religion and politics—Ireland—History—
18th century.   3. Church and state—Ireland—History—18th century.
4. Ireland—Intellectual life—18th century.   5. Ireland—Politics and
government—18th century.   I. Title.
B802.B76 2016
941.507—dc23   2015031525

For Sandra and Daniel

Contents

∾

Introduction: Locating the Irish Enlightenment   1

PART ONE   **The Religious Enlightenment, 1688–ca. 1730**

1   The Presbyterian Enlightenment and the Nature of Man   23
2   The Anglican Enlightenment and the Nature of God   60
3   The Catholic Enlightenment and the Nature of Law   106

PART TWO   **The Social Enlightenment, ca. 1730–ca. 1760**

4   Languages of Civility   161
5   The Enlightened Counter Public   210
6   Communities of Interest   252

PART THREE   **The Political Enlightenment, ca. 1760–1798**

7   A Culture of Trust?   307
8   Fracturing the Irish Enlightenment   345
9   An Enlightened Civil War   405

Conclusion: Ireland's Missing Modernity   459

Notes   475
Acknowledgements   589
Index   593

The earth could keep
its darkness. It was the end of the century right now,
the end of the war. A new kind of peace would creep
out of the atom with pale hands, its brow
unlined and vacant. There was something deadly
about its frivolity, which would allow
Anything at all except fire and memory

—'Orgreave', George Szirtes, 2001

Introduction

Locating the Irish Enlightenment

∾

Many of our gentry seem to think learning not only a needless but an impertinent qualification; and it has been made a remark that the state of conversation among us is such as to require a well-furnished wine cellar much more than a library for its support.

—[James Arbuckle], *The Tribune*, Dublin, 1729

CONTEMPORARIES thought little of Ireland's pretentions to Enlightenment. The Scot David Hume denigrated the Irish national character by pronouncing 'the common people in Switzerland have probably more honesty, than those of the same rank in Ireland', even before he composed a notorious passage on the Ulster Rising of 1641 as part of his *History of England* (1754–1762).[1] There he described a 'conspiracy' among the native Irish to destroy a settler plantation in the province, and recounted how, in October of that year,

> an universal massacre commenced of the English, now defenceless and
> passively resigned to their inhuman foes. No age, no sex, no condition
> was spared . . . destruction was everywhere let loose, and met the
> hunted victims at every turn. In vain was recourse had to relations, to
> companions, to friends: All connexions were dissolved, and death was
> dealt by that hand, from which protection was implored and expected.[2]

This view of the Ulster Rising as an assault on basic human decency held some currency in the period, and not just in Britain. The industrious contributor to Diderot and d'Alembert's *Encyclopédie* (1751–1772), Louis, chevalier de Jaucourt, in writing on Ulster's Plantation by James I, described how the native population was

> taught farming and other skills. They were put into fixed dwelling for their security. Punishments were imposed for pillaging and robbery. Thus from being the most savage and unruly of Irish provinces, Ulster soon became the province where the rule of law and a favourable culture seemed most established.[3]

Irish civility here depended on English authority, a fact underlined by Jaucourt when he proposed the king had 'introduced humanity and justice to a nation which had never previously risen above the utmost barbarity and the most terrible ferocity.'[4] Voltaire also largely accepted the story of 1641 as a meaningless slaughter, associating it with the Saint Bartholomew's Day massacre in exemplifying the needless destruction incurred by religious motivations. The Irish were connected in his mind with the condition of colonisation, for as he remarked of the Battle of the Boyne: 'The Irish, whom we have seen as such good soldiers in France, have always fought badly at home. There [are] some nations which seem to be made to be subject to another. The English have always had over the Irish a superiority of genius, wealth and arms.'[5] Given his Anglophile attitude, expressed at length in his *Letters on the English Nation* (1733), it was to be expected that Voltaire viewed the Anglo-Irish connection as beneficial. However, he finessed this view in the *Essai sur les moeurs* (1756), arguing that

> this land has always remained under the domination of England, but uncultivated, poor and unproductive, until finally in the eighteenth century, agriculture, manufacturing, the arts, the sciences, everything has been perfected there; and Ireland, though subjugated, has become one of the most flourishing provinces in Europe.[6]

Voltaire even contended in the *Treatise on Tolerance* (1763) that sectarian massacres would no longer occur in Ireland as an age of tranquillity was now established. This was evidenced elsewhere, in the *Précis du Siècle de Louis XV* (1768), which took notice of the peaceful relations during the 1745 Jacobite rising in

Scotland.[7] But despite the hints that Voltaire offers of a counter narrative, Irish history was largely constructed by eighteenth-century writers as a record of barbarism, colonisation, and superstition.[8] This did not give hope for the fortunes of Enlightenment ideas of civility, autonomy, and secularism.[9] Ireland was the Enlightenment's antinomy.

Historians have followed suit for, as A. T. Q. Stewart has pointed out of Enlightenment scholars, 'It is almost as if authors inhabiting so rarefied an intellectual atmosphere dread some kind of devaluation if they mention the homeland of [Hans] Sloane, [George] Berkeley, [John] Toland, [Jonathan] Swift and [Francis] Hutcheson. Nor', Stewart then bewails, 'do the Irish take much interest in the Enlightenment; they prefer to remember the Age of the Protestant Ascendancy, the penal laws and the 1798 Rebellion.'[10] For example, readers as sensitive as Toby Barnard have written of how 'at the same time, something akin to the Enlightenment, but more practical than speculative, flourished among the Protestants who crowded into the Irish capital.'[11] Similarly restrictive in its purview is the remark of Thomas Bartlett that 'Irish Protestant society, or at least the upper reaches of it, shared in this enlightened mood, much of which seemed to emanate from France', although admitting that, given the sectarian quality of political life in the country, 'Enlightenment had some way to go in Ireland'.[12] Even Ian McBride in a chapter on 'The Irish Enlightenment and Its Enemies' is unable to subscribe to the idea that the Enlightenment was untroubled in Ireland's environment, writing 'we have seen repeatedly . . . that feature which more than any other defined Irish resistance to England, loyalty to Counter-Reformation Catholicism, was regarded as the antithesis of everything the enlighteners stood for. Even [the Catholic antiquarian Charles] O'Conor could not openly contest the basic assumption that English colonisation was ultimately a beneficial, essentially modernising force in Irish history.'[13] Here issues of Enlightenment are connected to questions of 'modernisation' only to be sublimated into matters of ethnic and religious identification, returning Irish history to the traditional paradigms of Anglo-Irish colonial control and sectarian dispute.

What little other work that has been done directly on the intellectual history of Ireland in the period has pointed towards a brief, if as yet inexplicable, flurry of philosophical writing, which occurred circa 1688–1730; a period usually considered as coming before the great Enlightenments of continental Europe.[14] Configuring this generation of thinkers has proven to be a difficult task; David Berman has suggested in a series of seminal essays that the Irish supplied a

Counter-Enlightenment, without having had, and before the event of, a positive 'Enlightenment' in Europe.[15] While he has identified 'a line of thinkers' active 'between the 1690s and the 1750s,' he notes 'their bent was theological'.[16] For Berman, author of a *History of Atheism in Britain* (1988) and a student of early eighteenth-century free thought, this excludes the Irish thinkers from the process of Enlightenment, constituted for him by a capacity to reject religious orthodoxies and explore the limits of heterodoxy.[17] As he remarked elsewhere of George Berkeley, quoting A. A. Luce, 'you think he is building a house, you find he has built a church.'[18] That, for Berman, is to reject Enlightenment practicality in favour of superstition. He does accept that this early collection of Irish thinkers acted 'in the interplay of Enlightenment with Counter-Enlightenment.'[19] However, Berman concludes that the tenor of the school was predominantly conservative, Counter-Enlightenment, and intolerant. Ireland was philosophical but not enlightened.

One historiographical trend which enables scholars to look at the question afresh is that of examining the Enlightenment in the peripheries of Europe. This work rests on the suggestion that the traditional focus on Paris, London and Berlin occludes as much as it illuminates. To examine Enlightenment elsewhere raises questions about the elite character of the intellectual movement; its geographic spread; and most significantly its relationship to concepts of historical change that cannot be answered by examining the work of a scant number of authors, however innovative.[20] Daniel Roche has examined how far Enlightenment ideas penetrated rural France; Peter Borsay has looked for its influence in urban renewal in the urban centres of England; Bob Harris has sought to identify Enlightenment in the towns of Scotland.[21]

Moreover, this trend has complemented an examination of how national context shaped regional articulations and applications of Enlightenment ideas.[22] Commonly associated with the work of Roy Porter, who sought to map out the influence of Enlightenment ideas on British thought, it also provides a framework for the relationship between the English and Scottish Enlightenments in a fashion that sets the second in positive relief.[23] Although Nicholas Phillipson has controversially argued that the Scottish Enlightenment is largely a consequence of the exportation of English concepts of politeness, urbanity, and economic progress to Scotland, this view is hotly contested.[24] The idea of a national Enlightenment has provided David Allan, Christopher Berry, and Alexander Broadie, for example, a means of conceptualising the Scottish Enlightenment on its own terms, with its own origins, its own developmental mechanisms, and its own local application.[25]

Taken together, these perspectives inform Sean Moore's recent confidence in his ascription of the concept of Enlightenment to Ireland. He asserts that the country 'was not just a consumer of Continental ideas, but a producer of its own brand of Enlightenment.'[26] These Enlighteners Moore describes as being 'liminal in the best sense: they may have been on the outskirts of a European metropolitan Enlightenment, but produced their own peripheral Enlightenment that could, by virtue of its more distant perspective, see things that metropolitan intellectuals could not.'[27] However this location also made the Irish objects of the Enlightenment as much as they were its actors. In a postcolonial fashion, 'Ireland and the Irish are significant to the international movement because, in the philosophical imagination, they served as some of the colonized, dialectical "Others" helping to define the enlightened subject.'[28] Moore is here caught between a model of Ireland as integrated into the European mainstream and one which places it on its imperial edge. While the Enlightenment is present, its character is indeterminate and contested.

The imperial aspect of the Irish Enlightenment might be better captured by seeing it as one venue in a broader Atlantic Enlightenment. In reflecting upon rapid economic, commercial, and social change, communities around the ocean's edge conducted a vibrant conversation about questions of cultural difference, personal autonomy, and political recognition.[29] This Enlightenment prompted enquiry about the value of civility, tolerance, and democracy, bringing such transoceanic figures as John Witherspoon, Mathew Carey, and Thomas Jefferson into new focus; it also makes sense of the career of Thomas Paine. Moreover, as Susan Manning and Frank Cogliano recognise,

> the Atlantic was not just the space in which debates and circulation
> took place but . . . shaped the contours of debate and informed the
> 'enlightened' profile of the (northern, Protestant) Atlantic world . . .
> [It was] a world of exchanges and relationships, whose political and
> cultural events cannot be understood apart from the dynamic physical
> and geographical environments in which they were determined.[30]

As Ned Landsman has vividly shown it was also a world constructed by the antimony of metropolitan vice and provincial virtue; one in which London was thought of as a den of iniquity and Scots, Irish, and ultimately Americans deemed themselves more capable of moral conduct than their corrupt English masters. If in Scotland this propensity was sublimated into overrepresentation in the institutions of imperial outreach—the military, or the East India and Hudson Bay Companies for instance—and if Americans transformed themselves across the century from provincials to nationals, the Irish experimented in a variety of modes of limited autonomy institutionalised in the Dublin parliament house.

The Irish Enlightenment, in the work of James Livesey for instance, is rendered as a subset of both a cultural debate about virtue in civil society and a political debate about the locus of power in a commercial imperium.[31] In his work the decisive dilemma is political. The crucial context was the restrictive conditions under which the Dublin parliament operated, being hampered by the mechanism of Poynings's law (1495)—which ensured that 'Heads of bills' were sent to the English Privy Council for amendment or veto before they could be formally passed by the assembly—and hamstrung by the Declaratory Act of 1720, that formalised the position of the English House of Lords as the final court of appeal in Irish legal cases. Added to by trade restrictions emanating from the Westminster Parliament to favour English trade, these measures ensured that Ireland (even Anglican Ireland crucially) was unable to play a full participatory role in the emergent British Empire. Livesey argues that the response was to create forms of local patriotism and new ways of thinking about economic activity. The Irish rejected the central conceit of mercantilism that wealth was a consequence of a positive balance of trade, and instead developed an economic model which depended on domestic demand, productivity, and agricultural improvement. As Livesey pithily explains: 'Agriculture was being used and imagined . . . not as an element in the political economy of the nation, but as the core of the nation itself . . . Technological change [in this sector of the economy] offered the possibility of flourishing without challenging the political parameters that defined Ireland's role in an imperial economy.'[32] If this model posits a close connection between the provincial patriotism of the Irish and the Americans in the run-up to the Revolution of 1776, it also provides Ireland with a distinctive application of Enlightenment ideas in the face of the country's economic and political condition. The striking difference between Ireland and America, the abiding fact of a Catholic majority population residing in Ireland, is not ignored by Livesey; rather the political defeat of the Catholic community and their resultant loss of political autonomy is read as a microcosm of the country's condition.[33]

Taking its lead from the move to peripheral, national, and Atlantic Enlightenments, the twin ambition of this study is to reconstruct the role Irish thinkers, writers, and actors (of all sorts) played in the Enlightenment project and to delineate an explicitly Irish Enlightenment, thereby situating the country's intellectual heritage within the broader context of British, European, and Atlantic history. Ireland was not trapped by the sectarian politics of the seventeenth century and was not in a moribund catatonic state in the eighteenth century. Rather it was a vigorous and controversial participant in the transcontinental experiment of creating a modern world, defined by the reimaging of the universe based on the premise that man, not God, was the starting point of understanding. In telling the story of that engagement this book traces an Irish contribution to the European Enlightenment. But it also makes clear how the identification of the Enlightenment's Irish variant inflects and reconfigures our received narrative of penal era and golden age, and the intersections between politics, society, and faith.

Thinking about Enlightenment

The term 'Enlightenment' identifies a crucial change in the understanding of the world. It is both a movement and an idea—in Vincenzo Ferrone's memorable analogy it is 'a kind of conceptual Centaur'.[34] In the first sense it is sometimes used as a shorthand term for progressive eighteenth-century thought; and this leads to a form of social history. Used in the second sense, the Enlightenment as a philosophical category has involved defining it through reference to a set of progressive principles such as toleration, cosmopolitanism, or democracy.[35] But rather than try to maintain that certain political, philosophical, or religious tenets constitute a definition, the Enlightenment is perhaps better conceived of as an idea with various applications. It offers a method of approach to the universe; a means, not a set of preordained ends.

Crucially, it begins, not by assuming the existence of a deity as a starting point for philosophical reflection, but by an assertion that at the core of human understanding of the world is humanity itself.[36] This approach allows for the possibility that the Enlightenment methods might provide a satisfactory proof for God's existence, and hence it is not inherently antagonistic to religious belief.[37] However, it does set the Enlightenment in opposition to the traditional

Scholastic approach of the Enlightenment's opponents. For Enlightenment thinkers, humans are the measure of all things, and they constitute the basic unit of analysis.[38] The movement, in this broadest of senses, originates with Descartes's thought experiment, stripping away the accretions of experience until the residue of essential existence became clear in the aphorism 'I think therefore I am'.[39] Enlightenment was in this precise meaning a 'science of man' implying not that man was always the object of the investigation but rather that the better treatment of humanity was the determinant, inspiration, and ultimate intended outcome of the investigative process.[40] Where the end was once the glory of God the Enlightenment pursued the welfare of mankind.

If the Enlightenment is commensurate with a prose of humanity, the movement also had its own internal dynamic, its own history. It developed in a series of phases across the eighteenth century; three broad chronological spans which might be termed as the periods of secularisation, sociability, and subversion. Each of these episodes had a specific centre of gravity. In the case of the first, Religious Enlightenment, phase, the focus was Holland where émigré communities interacted with Dutch theological debates. Jonathan Israel has sourced the impetus of the radical Enlightenment to the writings of Benedict Spinoza; John Locke's interaction with the environment was prompted by retreat from the Rye House Plot and focussed on the circle of the Quaker Benjamin Furly; there also existed a vibrant Huguenot exile community personified by John Toland's companion Pierre des Maizeaux.[41] The period of the Social Enlightenment was grounded in the English experience of Enlightenment, with a flourishing civil society that encompassed the discursive practices of politeness and improvement; an extensive public sphere of coffeehouses and taverns; and an institutional subculture of clubs and associations.[42] The final phase, the Political Enlightenment, was centred in France where revolution made explicit the consequences of the shift from subject to citizen, as well as the implications of conducting a public debate on the foundational questions of the state's legitimacy and the value of maintaining a religious establishment.[43] Ireland was never a central locus of the Enlightenment but Enlightenment was central to solving the interweave of problems—sectarianism, economic underdevelopment, and political dependency—that confronted the country through the century.

This historical dynamic was a consequence of another important aspect of the Enlightenment. From the basic assumption that the human being is the basic unit of analysis can be derived a range of approaches to knowledge creation. In other words a spectrum of philosophical methods existed within the Enlightenment encompassing three kinds of thought process: an intuitive approach, dwelling on personal insight and projecting hidden esoteric meanings into the external world that might only be revealed by an inspired adept or cunning observer; a rationalist approach which deduced general laws from preordained principles, drawing holistic theories about human behaviour or the natural world; and an empirical method of reflection which collated incremental observations of the external world to develop general theories about their subjects.[44]

Identifying this spectrum has the advantage of allowing for variation both within the Enlightenment as a whole and within the thought of any given individual. It is easy to see how certain questions—about natural philosophy for example—might best be answered by empirical research, while others—legal injunctions, perhaps—relied more on deductions from general principles being applied to specific cases. So too some metaphysical and theological questions might suggest delving into the realms of speculative free thought and mysticism to search for transcendent meaning.

Identifying a spectrum of Enlightenment thought also allows us to distinguish the Enlightenment from its opponents. Scholasticism in all its varieties, from Ramism to neo-Aristotelian thought presumed the potency of preexisting authority. The characteristic rhetorical strategy for Scholastics was one to cite competing authorities in pursuit of resolution, namely dialectics. By the late seventeenth century the reliance on established authority, had evolved into a series of competing schools of thought.[45] The Irish made a distinct contribution to a number of these. The Irish Franciscan Luke Wadding for instance wrote within a Scotist framework, while the Anglican Archbishop of Armagh, James Ussher, was influenced by Ramism while working in the domain of biblical chronology—leading to his calculation of the date of creation as 4004 BC.[46] In the emergent Presbyterian church system, the Westminster Confession of Faith, which acted as a determinant of orthodoxy, expressed a form of Calvinist Scholasticism, with biblical learning combined with knowledge drawn from church elders to provide a repertoire for citation and disputation.[47]

As this diverse ecosystem suggests, the scholastic worldview did not simply disappear, but has a distinct intellectual history of its own. While it began as either indifferent to the Enlightenment or resolute in rejecting its methods, as the century progressed Scholasticism came into conflict with the Enlightenment, and was reshaped accordingly. In particular, there emerged a self-conscious

Counter-Enlightenment that articulated an expressly anti-*philosophe* rhetoric, and which identified modern thought with anticlericalism, libertinism, atheism, amorality, and republicanism.[48] The pre-Enlightenment intellectual world slowly transformed itself into the anti-Enlightenment right wing, culminating in a thesis that damned the Enlightenment for inspiring the Jacobin Terror either indirectly or through the conduit of a Masonic or philosophic plot.[49] The Counter-Enlightenment had its Irish advocates, such as John Thomas Troy, Roman Catholic archbishop of Dublin, who deeply opposed the United Irish movement as an atheistic radical aberration.[50]

Delineating the Irish Enlightenment

This book offers a narrative of the Irish Enlightenment. Its ambition is to trace the full spectrum of enlightened thought—the empirical, rationalist, and freethinking elements—as it developed across the three phases of the Enlightenment's life span—the religious, social, and political. In doing this it keeps in mind how Enlightenment thought was related to and shaped by pre-Enlightenment, un-Enlightened, and Counter-Enlightenment idioms of thought. In other words, to make sense of the nature and form of the Irish Enlightenment the wider culture of public debate needs to be examined. In effect the study of one aspect of Irish intellectual life provokes a wider cultural history of the country. That is an intended consequence of this work, albeit keeping in focus the central conceit of the Enlightenment as a way of understanding the stakes of particular discussions.

I quote extensively from the sources. This has two distinct advantages. First, it allows the reader to hear the voices in the debate directly. Even if the prose is often distant from the sparse clean style of a twenty-first-century writer, and can sound rather alienating to the contemporary ear, the immediacy of the issues being confronted and the passion of the protagonists in the discussion are best conveyed by quoting them. Second, much of the argument made here depends on a reading of the rhetorical structures being deployed, and the methodological presuppositions they entail. As such, each text requires a kind of double treatment, to understand the polemical intent of the composition, and to reveal how the argument is being constructed. Both elements, taken together, identify the text as indebted to Enlightenment ideas.

This formulation of the book's ambition has an additional consequence. In tracing the history of the Enlightenment as a public debate, it is largely understood that issues of reader reception, of private correspondence, and personal biography are, of necessity, set aside. That is not to say that the questions such approaches raise are of no import; rather this book intends to analyze the public discussion as a prelude to those questions, which it is hoped future historians of the period might elucidate. What is offered here is a necessary starting point for just such interrogations.[51]

One further introductory remark: it is the central contention of this book that the Irish Enlightenment was characterised by a concern for the issue of confession, by which is meant the public articulation of faith. If the Scottish Enlightenment was prompted by the parliamentary Union of 1707 with England, and the resultant decay in the possibility of enacting civic virtue, and the American Enlightenment was concerned with issues of dependency, the Irish focus was on how to allow a variety of contending faith communities to worship freely. The Irish Enlightenment engaged in an extended debate about which faith or faiths were sufficiently civil as to be permitted to publicly engage in religious, social, and political discourse. The question at stake was less who was Irish—a nineteenth-century question—than who was enlightened. Who could be trusted to engage impartially in the conversation about the common good, and who was excluded as a result of preexisting religious (or atheist) convictions.[52] The ambition amongst all the literati—whatever their persuasion and disposition—was to answer this question in either a restrictive or expansive fashion and to thereby create a stable basis for civil society on the island (here intended to imply both the modern sense of the term as a community of apolitical actors, and in its early-modern sense encompassing what is now thought of as society and the state). This book tracks precisely the rise and fall of that debate—as the community moved away from the religious conflict at the end of the seventeenth century; as a vision of cross-confessional society became a practical, if limited, reality; and as the question of inclusion of Catholics and dissenters in an explicitly Anglican state fractured and eventually destroyed the possibility of sustaining a civilised discussion. The net result of this fracture was the civil unrest of 1798.

Part One, which examines the Religious Enlightenment, examines the intellectual character of the three dominant faiths in the country in the generation after the War of the Two Kings (1688–1691) which replaced Catholic James II with Protestant William III as head of the composite monarchy of England, Scotland, and Ireland. While the full spectrum of methodological approaches was used by members of each faith, there was a tendency for each of the faiths to concentrate their energies in a particular direction. The Presbyterians availed of rationalism to rethink their condition in the early decades of the eighteenth century; the Anglicans adopted an empirical outlook to explain their circumstance; and for reasons of political necessity, Catholics retained a deep commitment to Scholastic methods, and remained largely suspicious of Enlightenment novelty. While adherents of all three faiths experimented with speculative free thought, it was not the dominant approach in any of these communities.

Chapter 1 contends that Presbyterians found themselves debating how best to petition for tolerance from the Anglican state, with one faction arguing for the need to evince order within the confession and another proposing the best route was to show intellectual latitude within the church while making a rational case that tolerance be exercised by others. Chapter 2 then examines the Anglican condition of confessional supremacy, examining how that expressed itself in the development of an empirical argument for the vitality of the church-state settlement. Chapter 3 proposes that the Catholic community faced a rather different problematic, namely how to restate intellectual legitimacy in the wake of military defeat, with writers predominately using Scholastic forms of argument to rehearse the continuing pertinence of traditional doctrine and worship.

While the confessional divisions remained acute in the generation after the Battle of the Boyne, by around 1730 the War of the Two Kings was fading from living memory and was commensurately less divisive. The second part of the study, which attends to the Social Enlightenment, traces how in the middle decades of the eighteenth century various figures reached out across the confessional divides to confront the economic problems which beset the country. Availing of a creative blend of rationalist and empirical methods, the High Enlightenment period saw the development of a broad discourse of civility, which contained four distinct languages of analysis: politeness, improvement, aesthetics, and political economy. As is shown in Chapter 4, these languages of civility were inherently and oftentimes explicitly nonconfessional in content: behaviour, not belief, was the crucial criteria deciding inclusion.

The debates these languages encouraged were conducted in a wide range of social venues, evidenced in Chapter 5. While there remained an extensive confessional, and officially recognised, public sphere of churches, libraries, and state-sponsored theatre, there emerged an unofficial public sphere of coffee-houses, taverns, bookshops, and theatres that ran counter to the proscribed confessional categorisation of the populace. This counter-public sphere supported forms of social interaction that crossed confessional divides, generating friendships and fertile collaboration. Threatened by the possibility of disorderly conduct and subversive fraternisation, the state moved in the 1780s to limit the counter-public sphere's capacity and to regulate its behaviour.

As Chapter 6 illustrates, the impulse towards cross-confessional sociability was quickly institutionalised in a wide range of clubs and associations. Religious sodalities and speculative Freemasons encompassed the extremes of bonding and bridging societies; strengthening group identity on the one hand and encouraging the dissolution of identities into fraternal fellow feeling on the other. Yet the vast bulk of these clubs merged the empirical realities of Irish circumstance with a rational desire for improvement in arguing for civil ends: the polite reform of behaviour, the raising of educational standards, the extension of charity to the deserving poor, and the creation of commercial opportunity in mercantile associations.

However, the cross-confessional socialisation found in a number of clubs and societies in the middle of the century cut across the spiritual character of the ancien régime state and posed critical questions of the ruling elites' formative assumptions.[53] In the final quarter of the century, the political consequences of the new modes of thought became increasingly problematic as the un-confessional nature of the Enlightenment project posed a structural challenge to a state administration which rested its legitimacy on a claim to confessional supremacy. Ironically, the very power of the Enlightenment to posit political questions tore apart the Enlightenment settlement, grounded as it was on the presumption of social tolerance and the collaboration of empirical and rationalist methodologies. Hence the period of Political Enlightenment foreshadowed the movement's close.

The final part of this study tracks that declension into violence. It examines how the third generation of the Irish Enlightenment, which became active around 1760, struggled to make sense of the issue of political identity. In Chapter 7 disparate genres—the legal tract, the antiquarian history, the novel of sentiment, and the comedy of manners—are shown to articulate a persistent problem of trust within Irish society. The instability this uncovered related precisely to the inability or unwillingness of the Anglican polity to incorporate the Catholic and dissenting communities into its formal political deliberations. This failure of the Irish

Enlightenment to project a political analogue of the social collaboration that had flourished since the 1730s slowly ruptured the movement. Chapter 8 depicts the problems the Irish Volunteer movement of the late 1770s and early 1780s experienced in finding a way to speak on behalf of the whole people of Ireland. The reform movement held within it two contending groups: those who on rational grounds argued for the extension of the electoral franchise to propertied Catholics and those who, providing empirical evidence drawn from Ireland's contested past, argued that Catholics were inherently untrustworthy and that the polity should continue to exclude them. This intellectual division between those favouring a rationalist methodology and those availing of an empirical approach laid the ground for a conflict between advocates of a rationalist politics that would overturn the Irish administration and empiricists who favoured its retention. The result, as documented in the final chapter, was an unseemly and violent civil war which exposed the failed nature of the Enlightenment's ambitions to settle the confessional question and reframed the debate for the nineteenth century.

While the seeds of the 1798 Rebellion germinated in the soil of the Irish Enlightenment, the conclusion will propose that 1798, and the Act of Union of 1800 which followed swiftly on from the Rebellion, altered the question from one of confession and civility to one of sectarianism and nation. Confessionalism became sectarianism. The question 'Who is Enlightened?' gave way to the toxic query 'Who is Irish?'

Three Books

To begin, it is appropriate to turn our attention to three books which suggest that Ireland and Enlightenment were not mutually exclusive terms. Their existence proposes that there was an active Enlightenment within Ireland in the eighteenth century, making significant contributions to European-wide discussions concerning the limits of religious orthodoxy, the possibility of economic improvement, and the development of political opinion. The books serve as initial case studies of the impact of the Enlightenment on the cultural life of the island, raising questions about the Enlightenment's reach and depth that this study intends to address. Intentionally, the chosen texts come respectively from the phases of Religious, Social, and Political Enlightenment, underlining the duration of Ireland's engagement with the movement of ideas.

Published in late 1695, *Christianity not Mysterious* is an attack on clerical authority. Written by the controversialist John Toland, the book revolves around a definition and rejection of 'priestcraft'.[54] A term of abuse since the 1660s, this word was given kinetic energy by Toland's philosophical ability.[55] Developing the consequences of the theory of knowledge expounded by his contemporary and acquaintance John Locke, Toland explored the vexed relationship between faith and human reason. His conclusions were starkly deflating: the gospels were to be understood within the light of human comprehension; they did not stand above and apart. 'All the doctrines and precepts of the New Testament (if it be indeed divine)', he observed,

> must consequently agree with Natural Reason, and our own ordinary
> ideas. This every considerate and well-disposed person will find by the
> careful perusal of it. And whoever undertakes this task will confess the
> Gospel 'not to be hidden from us, nor afar of, but very nigh us, in our
> mouths and in our hearts.'[56]

There was no source of understanding beyond the human mind. Revelation had to accord with reason, for as he put it 'the doctrines of the gospel are not contrary to reason'.[57] Any attempt to argue otherwise was no more than malicious obfuscation, motivated by a lust for power. That obfuscation was condemned as priestcraft, or the setting up of an unwarranted authority by claiming false expertise. Ceremonial was identified as the central mechanism whereby the faith was corrupted for

> the decrees or constitutions concerning ceremonies and discipline, to
> increase the splendour of this new state [the Roman Catholic
> Church], did strangely affect or stupefy the minds of the ignorant
> people; and made them believe they [priests] were in good earnest
> mediators between God and men, that could fix sanctity to certain
> times, places, persons or actions. By this means the clergy were able to
> do any thing; they engrossed at length the sole right of interpreting
> scripture, and with it claimed infallibility to their body. This is the
> true origin and progress of the Christian mysteries.[58]

Christianity not Mysterious offended churchmen across Britain. Condemned by the Middlesex jury for its heretical contents, it was burnt by the public hangman in Dublin by order of the Irish parliament. Toland was, for a time, a pariah.[59] Yet his work resonated: it fed a controversy over the relationship between faith and reason that lasted through the first half of the eighteenth century as Deists who rejected special revelation, Socinians who rejected the divinity of Christ, and Arians who rejected the doctrine of the Trinity openly criticised the orthodoxy of the Anglican faith.[60] Toland was a cause célèbre in this early Enlightenment theological debate.[61]

In contrast to Toland's jutting argumentative prose, *The Querist* (1735–1737) reads like a work of philosophical poetry. Written by the Anglican Archbishop of Cloyne, George Berkeley, it addressed the primary question of the Social Enlightenment: the issue of economic development. By availing of the hypnotic repetition of the interrogative 'whether' Berkeley provided the work with a rhythm and a cadence while highlighting the Spartan nature of the prose. And through the device of listing hundreds of questions, he gave the text a rigid formal structure while preserving an open-ended quality to his meditations on the economic condition of the country. It was the tension between these two aspects that enabled the work to treat closely the specific nature of the Irish condition while ranging widely on the material wants and imaginative desires of mankind. The queries were concise and epigrammatic in their individual parts, yet accumulated to give the work an architectural solidity that belied its theoretical splendour. At times the questions asked for specifics; others were merely rhetorical. The book was hardheaded yet often allusive. It was at once viscerally physical and fluidly allegorical.

At the centre of *The Querist* was a concern for Ireland's economic underdevelopment. Query 418 raised the issue of infrastructure, lamenting how 'it be . . . a new spectacle under the sun, to behold, in such a climate and such a soil, and under such a gentle government, so many roads untrodden, fields untilled, houses desolate and hands unemployed.' Shortly after this, Berkeley acknowledged 'we are . . . the only people who may be said to starve in the midst of plenty' (Q446). The kind of improvement he sought was articulated in a series of proposals which, taken together, constitute one of the two registers that dominated the *Querist*.[62] Most famous of these proposals involved the creation of a national bank for the country, a scheme he described as the 'philosopher's stone in a state' (Q459).[63] This rhetoric of improvement and the specific and descriptive quality of many of Berkeley's proposals stood in tension with a second, moral register.[64] He demanded a personal reformation from his readership and condemned the fashion for foreign goods and luxurious expenditure he saw as endemic within the upper echelons of Irish society. Women in particular earned his opprobrium for ostentatious display. 'Whether it would not be a horrible thing to see our matrons make dress and play their chief concern?' he asked in Query 452, and, in Query 175, 'Whether a woman of fashion ought not to be declared a public enemy?' In an extraordinary rhetorical question (Q326), Berkeley mused: 'Whether it would not be better for this island, if all our fine folk of both sexes were shipped off, to remain in foreign countries rather than that they should spend their estates at home in foreign luxury, and spread the contagion thereof through their native land?'

Crucially Berkeley's condemnation of luxury was not directed at expenditure as such.[65] Rather he was opposed to the preference for foreign goods, which retarded the development of indigenous industry and drained resources from the country. In his system, wealth was produced by emulation and the satisfaction of consumer demand, rather than the simple increase in production.[66] Indeed, the second would only occur when there was a clear and obvious demand for the goods to be produced. As he noted in Query 20, 'the creating of wants be . . . the likeliest way to produce industry in a people.' Given this, he then asked 'whether, if our peasants were accustomed to eat beef and wear shoes, they would not be more industrious?' Demand would be created by emulation, for he believed 'mankind [to be] . . . more governed by imitation rather than reason' (Q280). In describing this cumulative effect, he wondered 'whether as industry produced good living, and in proportion thereunto, whether there would not be every day more occasion for agriculture? And whether this article alone would not employ a world of people?'—an analysis which could be easily extended to any trade imaginable (Q403).

The psychological underpinnings of this thesis were revealed when Berkeley reversed the terms of analysis. In Query 423 he asked, 'Whether there be not two ways of growing rich; sparing and getting? But whether the lazy spendthrift must not be doubly poor?' What was required for industry to flourish was a population of diligent labourers motivated by a desire for the possession of the rewards of hard work.[67] In this, Berkeley's interest in labour and wealth creation foreshadowed that of the Scottish school of political economy headed by James Steuart and Adam Smith.[68] It also shared in the wider rejection of mercantilism of his contemporary John Law and the Physiocratic school of economic thought that flourished in France.[69] In that, Berkeley's work addressed an Enlightenment concern with improvement and political economy, the latter of which is identified by John Robertson as sitting at the very core of the European Enlightenment's endeavour.[70]

Significantly, there was nothing inherently confessional about Berkeley's desire for an economically vibrant society. Although the 1735 edition offered a series of observations on the practicality of converting the Catholic population to Protestantism, these were omitted from later editions.[71] However, even here Berkeley drew a distinction between 'papists' on the one hand and 'recusants' on the other: 'Whether the case be not very different in regard to a man who only eats fish on Fridays, says his prayers in Latin, or believes transubstantiation, and one who professeth in temporals a subjection to foreign powers, who holdeth himself absolved from all obedience to his natural prince and the laws of his country? Who is even persuaded, it may be meritorious to destroy the powers that are? (OQ298). Given this, he inquired 'Whether in granting toleration, we ought not to distinguish between doctrines purely religious and such as affect the state?' (OQ297).

'Granting toleration' was the central concern of Arthur O'Leary. A Capuchin friar hailing from Dunmanway in west Cork, who had been educated in St Malo, France, he was an active pastor, helping to build a chapel on Blackamoor Lane in the city, and authoring a sequence of pamphlets favouring civil obedience and defending the Catholic Church from accusations of subversion and revolt.[72] Yet in the *Essay on Toleration, or Plea for Liberty of Conscience* (1780) he did not argue his case on the foundations of Christian ethics, or through any ontology of human creation, but from the pragmatic grounds of political utility.[73]

Inspired by an anxiety born in the heart of an anti-Catholic campaign that culminated in the Gordon riots of 1780, described as 'scandalous scenes . . . exhibited . . . last year in Scotland and England', the *Essay* posited that the origins of government lay in a social contract.[74] 'The authority with which you are invested', O'Leary informed the government, 'is delegated by the people, and while you enjoy it, you claim the sanction of Heaven. But neither Heaven nor man', he then determined, 'has granted you a power to punish any but malefactors. And', he concluded crucially, 'no man is less liable to the imputation, than one who follows the dictates of his conscience.'[75]

What this implied, O'Leary contended, was that 'faith is a gift of God'; one 'which is not in the power of the state either to give or to take away.'[76] The grounding of this faith was in the manifested nature of the individual as created by God, placing it safely beyond the reach of the secular state. As he explained:

Faith, then, depending entirely on the interior dispositions of the mind, the quantity of grace, and the measure of spiritual science, which it is in the power of God either to increase, or, from a just but hidden judgement, to diminish; the want of it cannot be punished by any earthly tribunal: because the magistrate's power extends only to outward crimes that disturb the temporal peace of society, but not to the hidden judgements of God, not to the interior dispositions of the mind, nor to the disbelief of divine truths.[77]

It followed that the polity could not punish someone for what they believed so long as they did not commit crimes or disturb the society in which they lived. The mistake made by oppressive states was that rulers intervened in spiritual matters that were beyond their capacity. In the light of this distinction, 'the most monstrous absurdity . . . that ever met with apologists in church and state is the misdirected zeal that punishes the body for the sincerity of an erroneous conscience'.[78] The tolerance of speculative errors which O'Leary was espousing consisted of the recognition that 'error in faith is not a crime' and that the sanguinary laws that purported to insist on orthodoxy emanated from 'an abuse of power, and an error of fact, as well as of right'.[79] In practical terms, this involved allowing religions other than that of the magistrate to practise, albeit while simultaneously restricting their access to the offices of state. This was to reduce the contest between competing religious communions to a question of political order, not doctrinal rigour. In turning his attention to Ireland, O'Leary gently mocked the preposterous nature of the anti-Catholic legislation as a misguided effort to direct the spiritual affairs of the populace. Were this penal code to be dismantled, he suggested 'the kingdom would soon flourish, and the brilliant example, set to such princes as have not as yet thrown open the gates of toleration would rescue mankind from the heavy yoke which misconstrued religion has laid on their necks.'[80]

If O'Leary's *Essay* accords with a broad characterisation of the Enlightenment as promulgating modes of political tolerance, the books by Toland, Berkeley, and O'Leary all share a substantial turn away from a poetics of divinity and towards the prose of humanity. That shift in intellectual presuppositions, from assuming the existence of God as the start of meaningful philosophical reflection to an assertion that at the core of human understanding of the world is humanity itself, is constitutive of the revolution in thought historians demarcate as the Enlightenment.

Each of these three books avails of Enlightenment methodology to interrogate a question of concern to Ireland in the eighteenth century. Toland's freethinking raises questions about church authority that were subversive of the political settlement that positioned the Church of Ireland within the establishment. Berkeley's rationalism was being put to pragmatic use to confront a crisis of economic performance that engulfed the country in food dearth sporadically from the 1720s to the early 1740s and haunted the imagination of a generation. And O'Leary's empirically grounded plea for tolerance asks questions about the possible extent of political reform as the state became increasingly potent and the populace ever more politicised. In each case the authors wrestled with the implications of their ideas for the vexed question of the public articulation of faith. Confession was for Toland a limiting objective which paraded the interest of the clergy as metaphysical truth; for Berkeley confession was a problem to be overcome in seeking economic development; for O'Leary it was to be set aside in search of a humanitarian settlement of inherently political differences. For none of these writers was confession a determining facet of their intellectual ambition, but a strategic and specific problem encountered when applying Enlightenment methods to the context of eighteenth-century Ireland.

Taken together, the books by Toland, Berkeley, and O'Leary ask us to reimagine Irish cultural life in the eighteenth century in a way which is at odds with the image of the country as barbaric and superstitious. They propose that a commitment to a life of the mind was shared across the confessional divides which marked out the religious politics of the period, suggesting the possibilities of social discourse and fraternisation. They also supply an initial outline of Enlightenment politics, indicating a way to re-narrate the country's history removed from the tropes of sectarian blood feuds and ancient hatreds. To map an Irish Enlightenment is to reframe the history of Ireland in the eighteenth century a fashion that ultimately raises questions about the country's long-term development and modern-day problems.

PART ONE

The Religious Enlightenment,
1688–ca. 1730

෯

I

The Presbyterian Enlightenment
and the Nature of Man

∾

The poor creatures we meet in the streets seem to know the avenues to the humane
breast better than our philosophers.
—Francis Hutcheson, 'Reflections on the Common Systems of Morality', 1724

THE ENLIGHTENMENT had a shaping influence on all the Christian
confessions in Ireland. The shift in foundational assumption—that the
human being and not God was the starting point for meaningful philosophical
reflection—raised questions about the source of religious learning and the character and condition of humanity. Thus, to comprehend the Irish Enlightenment
it is necessary to examine the debates within each of the major confessions of the
island; to examine in turn how Enlightenment methodologies were appropriated and utilised by Presbyterians, Anglicans, and Catholics. This leads to three
observations: First, it is necessary to look to debates within the confessions, and
not between them, to understand the first generation of the Irish Enlightenment.
Second, it is important to recognise that the full spectrum of Enlightenment
methodologies—empiricism, rationalism, and free thought—can be identified
as operating in each of the confessions. Third, it can be shown that one methodology is more dominant than the others in each particular confession. While
none was inclined to entertain the adherents of speculative free thought, the
Presbyterian church was the most open to rationalist methods of justifying

human knowledge, the Church of Ireland depended for political reasons on the empirical method to articulate its legitimacy, and the Catholic Church remained largely wedded to Scholastic learning that helped make sense of its political defeat at the Battle of the Boyne in 1690. This chapter and the two which follow will identify how Presbyterianism, Anglicanism, and Catholicism mediated the impact of the Enlightenment.

In the case of Presbyterianism, there was a convoluted controversy over subscription to the Westminster Confession of Faith in the 1720s, in which the stakes were marked out by commitments for and against the Enlightenment. Those who wished to defend the Confession broadly maintained a commitment to Scholastic readings of the Bible; the non-subscribers who opposed them were intent on developing rationalist approaches to scriptural interpretation. At question was the issue of how to justify the public articulation of the Presbyterian faith when the confession was faced with legal restrictions imposed by an Anglican state.

In other words, the Presbyterian encounter with the Enlightenment was largely the result of theological revisions conducted by non-subscribers using a rationalist methodology to pose a vocal challenge to the Scholastic worldview of the subscribing tendency. This challenge was tempered by a small faction that articulated a moderate Presbyterian vision grounded on empirical assumptions, while the Presbyterian faith also harboured a few figures who dallied with heterodoxy and free thought, giving further heat to an already divisive dispute. That dispute, and its pro- and anti-Enlightenment character, is the subject of this chapter.

The Depravity of Man

Humanity was irredeemable. Among the five basic tenets of the Presbyterian faith, enunciated at the Synod of Dort in 1619, was the presumption of total depravity. This belief underpinned and informed all the theological assertions that followed: the unconditional election of the chosen; the limited power of atonement; the irresistible nature of God's grace; and the perseverance of the saints. It defined a pessimistic vision of man's moral nature and set in dramatic relief the gift of God's grace. Calvinism denied the human capacity for virtue without the intervention of divine will. Good behaviour was a gift from God.

Elect or reprobate, the intrinsic qualities of humanity were to be despised, not celebrated; repressed, not reformed; controlled, not liberated.

This assumption of moral inability informed the doctrine of British Presbyterians in the seventeenth century. Coming together in 1643, a gathering of divines at Westminster met in the shadow of civil war in England and an intra-communal conflict within the three-kingdom dynastic holdings of the Stuart line. Their purpose was clear: to delineate a shared doctrinal position among English and Scottish Presbyterian adherents that would provide a church settlement in the archipelago as a whole. The document they drafted, the Westminster Confession of Faith, was the last great flower to bloom in the covenanting strand of Presbyterian theology in the British Isles, which had begun with the 'First Bond' of 1559, and it provided a benchmark for measuring orthodoxy among the faithful.[1]

Of particular pertinence to the conflicts that lay ahead was chapter two, 'Of God and the Holy Trinity', which asserted not only that 'there is but one only, living and true God, who is infinite in being and perfection' but that 'in the unity of the godhead there be three persons of one substance, power and eternity; God the Father, God the Son and God the Holy Ghost. The Father is of none, neither begotten nor proceeding, the Son is eternally begotten of the Father, the Holy Ghost eternally proceeding from the Father and the Son.'[2] Chapter twenty was also relevant to the debates of the 1720s, for under the rubric 'Of Christian Liberty and Liberty of Conscience' the Confession pronounced: 'Under the New Testament the liberty of Christians is further enlarged, in their freedom from the yoke of the ceremonial law to which the Jewish church was subjected . . . God alone is the Lord of the conscience and hath left it free from the doctrines and commandments of men which are in this thing contrary to his Word, or beside it in matters of faith and worship'.[3]

Although Calvinism was the established confession in Scotland, in Ireland the Presbyterian Church was a minority faith. Adhered to by Scottish migrants in the northern province of Ulster, and by a southern community of English origin congregating around Dublin, the faith was in a deeply anomalous position. Part of the Reformed tradition, it could play a part in a pan-Protestant front when confronting the Roman Catholic Church. Yet, it was not an established church like Anglicanism, and its membership shared an experience of legal discrimination with Catholic contemporaries.

In particular, the ambiguity surrounding marriage caused deep personal anxiety and resentment.[4] The dilemma was that, as the state tended to treat marriage solely in terms of its status as a religious ceremony, the sacrament came under the remit of the Anglican Church courts. Ecclesiastic lawyers therefore tended to treat only those weddings that had been conducted by an established minister as valid, leaving the matrimonies of Presbyterians of questionable value. The legal implication was that the children of these unions were illegitimate, and hence unable to inherit property from their parents. It equally left the couple open to prosecution for fornication. An occasional campaign of prosecution appears to have been conducted by the Anglican bishops in the period from 1697 to 1702, but its formalisation was delayed until 1711, when the Irish Convocation passed a canon preventing the recognition of any wedding that had not been conducted by a clergyman of the Church of Ireland. The pressure did not alleviate with the death of Anne and the accession of George I in 1714. Prosecutions continued, despite a failed attempt to gain legislative redress in 1723, when, under the direction of the Whig lord lieutenant, Lord Grafton, heads of a bill recognising Presbyterian marriages were sent to London for sanction by the Privy Council but rejected upon its return to the Irish House of Commons. In the years that followed, persecutions became less frequent, and less successful, making the Relief Act of 1737 which legalised Presbyterian marriage a recognition and not an alteration of the practical reality.[5]

Less intimate but just as galling was the passage of a bar to Presbyterian participation in the public life of the country.[6] The test clauses of 1704 enacted that every candidate to 'bear any offices civil or military or who shall receive any pay, salary, fee or wages' from the state had publicly to take the oaths of supremacy and abjuration before receiving 'the sacrament of the Lord's supper, according to the usage of the Church of Ireland'.[7] These provisions ensuring the conformity of the state's officers with the church-state settlement disqualified dissenters from the political pursuit of the common good in Ireland; identifying their status as second-class subjects. Particularly insulting was the test's inclusion in the Act to Prevent the Further Growth of Popery, thereby equating the Presbyterians with the Catholic community and separating them from their fellow Protestants. Their removal from the political nation was rhetorical as much as practical.

Yet, the legal circumstance was not clear-cut. Alongside these hindrances, the Anglican state provided some relief. At its most limited and halfhearted, this took the form of a Toleration Act sanctioned by the Irish parliament in 1719.[8] The Act for Exempting the Protestant Dissenters of this Kingdom from certain

Penalties, to which they are now Subject removed the necessity to take the oath of uniformity from Protestant dissenters, leaving only the oath of abjuration, which declared against papal power and stipulated that 'the person pretended to be prince of Wales during the life of the late King James, and since his decease pretending to be, and taking upon himself the style and title of King of England, by the name of James the third, or of Scotland, by the name of James the eighth, or the style and title of king of Great Britain, hath not any right or title whatsoever to the crown of Great Britain.'[9] Those who subscribed in front of justices of the peace at either general or quarter sessions were, by clause VIII, released from the threat of prosecution under the Act of Uniformity or as clause XVIII rendered it: from being 'prosecuted in any ecclesiastical court, for or by reason of his or their nonconforming to the Church of Ireland, as by law established.'[10] Dissenting ministers and teachers were formally exempted from the duty of jury service, giving limited state recognition to their status within nonconforming communities.

More constructively, the state provided a grant to help in the material support of Presbyterian ministers. Originating with Charles II, the *regium donum*, or king's grant, had been suspended by James II before its reintroduction under William.[11] The donation was stipulated to be £1,200 in 1691—some £15 for every minister in the country—and remained at this level throughout William's reign. Queen Anne renewed the grant upon her accession in 1702 and, despite the protest lodged by the House of Commons in Dublin in 1703 that 'the pension of £1,200 per annum granted to the Presbyterian ministers in Ulster is an unnecessary branch of the establishment', payment continued unabated until, under pressure from High Church Tories, it was suspended in 1714.[12] By the summer of 1715, the situation once again favoured the Presbyterians: the Hanoverian accession in 1714 had ensured a change in political tack, as George I declared in favour of the grant's resumption. Payment started by mid-1715, at the same rate as before. The amount was increased in 1718 to £1,600, alongside a new grant of £400 set aside for the Protestant dissenters of the south of Ireland, recognising the cultural difference between those of Scottish extraction who were loyal to the Synod of Ulster and those of English origin who made up a looser Southern Association. Equally importantly, the grant was moved to the English Civil List, removing it from the remit of the Dublin parliament. George II and George III both confirmed its existence upon their accession, and the payment remained at a total worth of £2,000 until its final removal in 1784, a measure in line with the wider policy of limiting state interference in the unestablished churches of the country. In all this, the *regium donum*'s history encapsulates the peculiarities of the Presbyterian position in the early eighteenth century: paid yet persecuted, tolerated when not tormented, considered Protestant but restricted for being Presbyterian.[13]

Alongside the practical difficulties caused by living this political half-life, the Presbyterian community was perplexed by new theories concerning the moral ability of man that infiltrated their confession in the early eighteenth century. As they confronted the problem of minority status, some turned towards a philosophy of human aptitude, of the value of philosophical independence, and of the virtue of rational reflection. They began to tease out the consequences of a view of human endeavour, at once anthropomorphic and optimistic; a shift in perspective towards seeing mankind as morally capable, which contradicted the Westminster Confession of Faith. And it tore the community apart.

'Expedients for Peace'

The crisis began in 1719 with an intemperate sermon, preached by the fiery non-subscribing minister John Abernethy.[14] Addressing a congregation in Belfast, he offered observations on Romans 15.5: 'Let every man be fully persuaded in his own mind', which impinged on the issue of church government. Instead of seeing the church as a body deliberating on, and defining, theology, he declared its role to be exhortatory, imploring his congregants to look instead to their own conscience in seeking God. 'A power for edification', he wrote, 'is a power to promote truth and sincere religion, which can never be promoted by men's being obliged to act contrary to the inward conviction of their own minds, or without it . . . From hence we may see the just limits of church power: Its decisions bind the conscience as far as men are convinced and no farther.'[15]

The challenge Abernethy set down was to affect Presbyterianism from the General Synod of Ulster to the local congregation. If the Synod could not impose theological orthodoxy upon the ministry, and was restricted to offering guidance to tender consciences, its institutional integrity was undermined. This radical reassessment of the purpose and limits of church discipline appalled adherents to the ecclesiology enunciated in the Westminster Confession of Faith, which had been made the test for ministerial office in 1698.[16]

So controversial was the assertion of personal convincement over confessional orthodoxy that individual congregations began to reject the guidance of ministers who took the opposing side in the dispute.[17] Even in a set of non-subscribing 'Expedients for Peace' the depth of the split on the ground was recognised. The authors acknowledged that 'new congregations of such as have separated from their own pastors are erected; all possible means are used by many to break the congregations of some ministers, to cool and alienate the affections of their people from them, and to render their ministry useless, their persons contemptible and their characters odious; and the same persons have been for some years attempting to make an open synodical rupture'.[18] This was not just rhetorical hyperbole. In 1723, for instance, upon the erection of a congregation at Bellynure under the care of the Presbytery of Antrim, local representatives gave notice to the General Synod that 'they have scruples of conscience against submitting to the ministry of a non-subscribing minister.'[19] The suggestion was that Mr Wilson, the minister at Bellycare, from which Bellynure had emerged, was of the non-subscribing faction; hence there was a need for a second, subscribing meeting. The erection of 3rd Belfast was similarly the result of subscribing discomfiture at the theological tendencies of that city's ministers. At the Synod of 1723, the nascent congregation complained of how 'the two other sessions in Belfast refused to give dismisses to some persons who think they have right to join with the said 3 congregation . . . [and] that they [the orthodox] have been branded with the odious name of schismatics by their neighbours'.[20]

Within the Synod, the matter came to dominate proceedings to the detriment of much regular business. In 1723, at the height of the controversy, numerous items had to be deferred or delegated, with the meeting determining that 'all business which ought to have come before this Synod and cannot now be issued, is referred to the next General Synod, unless the parties agree to refer their cause to their own presbyteries or Sub-Synods, or to the General Synod's fixed committee.'[21] The torturous debates concerning the impact of rationalist methods of reading scripture on a doctrine wedded to Calvinist Scholasticism were now destroying the harmony of the community, and were soon to destroy its very communion.[22] The conundrum of man's moral capacity in confronting and interpreting scripture had, paradoxically, incapacitated the Presbyterian Church.

It was clear that something overarching was required were the dispute finally to end. The General Synod of 1725, held at Dungannon, saw a dramatic initiative.

It followed a suggestion by the Commission of Overtures that 'the subscribing brethren and their elders, and the non-subscribing brethren and their elders may each of them meet by themselves to consider and condescend upon such expedients as may tend to heal the divisions of this church.'[23] The subscribing grouping was the first to avail of this opportunity.[24] At first, they appeared to recognise the views of both sides acknowledging that 'there are several ministers and others who scruple communion with ministers of non-subscribing, or non-declaring principles . . . Such [should] be allowed peaceably to follow the light of their own consciences in that particular . . . If any person shall scruple communion with subscribing ministers, the same liberty shall be allowed them.'[25]

The second overture proposed a practical means of dealing with disputes arising when non-subscribers were called to congregations. The subscribers proposed submitting to the General Synod in any contested calls; yet this asserted the central power of the Synod over the presbytery and effectively placed control of the matter in the hands of the subscribing majority. In rebuttal, the non-subscribers defended the capacity of the presbytery, arguing 'no power of Synods can suspend the exercise of their right to proceed; for that would be in effect the assuming of a power to suspend their obedience to the law of Christ, that they might obey a synodical law.'[26] The Synod ought instead to trust the presbytery to adjudge the calibre of its ministry.

Finally, in light of the dilemma posed by communion in a divided church, the third overture proposed restructuring the Sub-Synod of Belfast, to which most non-subscribers were affiliated, by rearranging the presbyteries. Henceforward the church was to have new presbyteries at Bangor, Killyleagh, Templepatrick, and Antrim, with the various ministers and congregations newly affiliated within these structures. The non-subscribing ministers were to associate within the Presbytery of Antrim.[27] Yet even this organisational rearrangement did not suffice to conclude the row. A further and final breach came with the presentation of 'Expedients for Peace' to the Synod of 1726 by James Kirkpatrick, non-subscribing minister of 2nd Belfast.

The document was presented as though it was a conciliatory move, providing 'a gospel cure' to the 'disease' that had so racked the Presbyterian body.[28] First, it placated the subscribing faction by appealing to scripture as a final judge of the dispute, asking that they 'consider the many clear gospel precepts which settle the terms of religious communion and enjoin Christian forbearance, notwithstanding of differences in judgement and practice in lesser matters.'[29] Upon this, the authors of the 'Expedients' built the subsidiary expedients they deemed desirable, namely, that 'we should carefully avoid all questions which tend to strife and contention'; that 'we take care, on all sides, not to lay stumbling blocks in one another's way, or in the way of any good people'; that 'we study the vigorous exercise of these Christian virtues of charity, humility and impartial justice'; and, finally, 'that ministers and people on every side of the questions debated amongst us, should fervently and frequently pray for the "peace of Jerusalem"'.[30] Although there was much here that those committed to the Synod's ecclesiastical authority and the Westminster Confession's doctrinal position could agree with, the thrust of the pamphlet was to outline how those regulatory systems could be challenged. Indeed, a set of subclauses to the first expedient provided propositions that supported the non-subscribers' stance. The 'Expedients' therefore quickly changed character, from being an act of conciliation to one of self-justification.

These propositions centred on the liberty of the communicant to determine freely and sincerely the content of doctrine, vocalising a commitment to a rationalist ethos. Indeed, the document provided a clear statement of the value of individual sanction, stating that 'candidates for the holy ministry may give clear and sufficient evidence of the soundness of faith without subscribing or professing an assent to any one imposed uninspired form of articles or confessions of faith.'[31] The very next proposition asserted provocatively: 'We are humbly of [the] opinion that the great head of the church [Jesus Christ] hath given no power to the church to make any canon or religious law by which an entrant into the ministry who gives sufficient proof of his soundness in the faith, and of having all the other ministerial qualifications and abilities required in the gospel, shall be refused licence to preach the gospel, ordination or instalment, merely because he refuses to give his assent or subscription to the Westminster Confession.'[32]

Later in the pamphlet, the non-subscribers outlined how far the General Synod might exercise lawful authority over the ministers and communicants of the faith. In what was by 1726 a typical reduction and redefinition of the difficulties, it was argued that 'whether church power in general be properly authoritative or only consultative is a controversy, which, if it be managed according to that essential Protestant principle which asserts the rights of private judgement, must dwindle into a mere logomachy, and debate about words.'[33] In the terms of the non-subscribers' argument, the limitations of the General Synod's jurisdiction were clear: 'If by authority be meant a power in the church to make new laws, superadded to the laws of Jesus Christ; or (which is the same thing) the power of making authoritative explications of his laws . . . Christ hath given them no such authority.'[34] Rather, synods 'ought to inform the conscience but they have no dominion over our faith and consciences'.[35] All that could be granted to the General Synod was what was here termed 'a lower . . . secondary notion of authority, which consisted solely of 'a power of Christian discipline; in the due exercise whereof, scandalous persons clearly convicted of their offences ought to be cast out of the church'.[36]

Any attempt to extend the authority of the Synod over tender consciences was described scathingly as 'the setting up in the church [of] an exorbitant and arbitrary power, contrary to the essential rights of natural equity' and as 'a snare to the conscience' equivalent to, in a heavily freighted analogy, the establishment of an 'Inquisition'.[37] Indeed, the propensity of churchmen to centralise power and create 'too high an idea of church authority' was expressly associated with the Catholic Church. In a brief historical overview, it was asserted that from the principle of absolute submission to higher authority might be traced the origins of 'prelacy', 'for it was thought inexpedient to leave every minister to choose his own expressions in the public devotions of the church. All the ceremonies of Popery were introduced and are chiefly supported by the same claim to power.'[38] In other words, the demands of the subscribers were commensurate to establishing Roman Catholicism within the kirk.

Predictably, given such abuse, the terms of settlement laid out by the non-subscribers were rejected out of hand by the Synod. Moreover, in dismissing the 'Expedients', the subscribing majority expressed concern at the continuing disavowal of the Synod's governance by non-subscribers and, in an incendiary passage, they declared:

> our steady adherence to our own principles, and that it is matter of
> the deepest concern to us, that by these their principles and their
> declared resolution to adhere to them they put it out of our power to
> maintain ministerial communion with them in Church Judicatories as
> formerly, consistently with the faithful discharge of our ministerial
> office as the peace of our consciences.[39]

The events of 1726 only underlined how divided the church had become. The final vote on the excommunication of the Presbytery of Antrim was passed by thirty-six votes to thirty-four. Eight members of the Synod abstained from the vote and two, both with non-subscribing leanings, were absent.[40]

What had emerged across the 1720s was a pronounced tension between the governing authority of the Synod in doctrinal and temporal matters and the desire by individual ministers to answer only to scripture and to preach as they saw fit. Within this division about church government was a second debate revolving around the capacity of the individual to reason upon theological concerns.[41] And it is this second debate, about the nature of humanity and its relationship to the public confession of faith, which allows the subscription controversy to be configured within an Enlightenment context, with the subscribers adopting a Scholastic stance on the matter while being challenged by a non-subscribing faction who were relying on rationalist method to render scripture meaningful.[42] Between these two warring parties stood a moderate cluster of irenic Presbyterians who were intrigued by the possibilities of empiricism, while on the extreme edges resided some individual freethinkers. These positions will now be elucidated in turn.

Subscribers and Scholasticism

The Synod held in Antrim in 1705 had confronted a problem of orthodoxy raised by the inability to confirm that the influx of ministers from abroad, notably Scotland, were correctly prepared for duty. In response, they introduced a formal process to manage contested claims: 'That those who come amongst us, profess to be our Communion, give account of themselves by their testimonials, and if they be suspected that they are not authentic, to be brought to the minister and session, and if need be, the minister shall report to his presbytery, who are to appoint one of their number to write to the place from whence the said testimonials are dated.'[43] Significant in the light of the Irish parliament's introduction of the test clause excluding dissenters from the state administration the previous year, the Synod turned to the state to help police their decisions: 'It shall thereby be known whether [it is] a true testimonial. If the person or persons refuse to give a testimonial, these in the bounds were they came are prudently to apply to the civil magistrate to relieve the place of such vagrants.'[44]

While this offered the Synod a disciplinary mechanism to police its institutional boundaries, the formal content of the exiles' faith had still to be determined. Thus, the next overture enunciated the demand 'that such as are to be licensed to preach the Gospel subscribe to the Westminster Confession of Faith, and promise to adhere to the doctrine, worship, discipline and government of this church.'[45] The aim of using this highly structured, legalistic doctrinal statement to test the convictions of prospective candidates for the ministry was to ensure they would not embarrass. Subscription was therefore a central measure in a determined policy to reassure the Irish state of the Synod's control over its membership. The issue at stake was the capability of the church to decide the terms for the public articulation of the Presbyterian faith.

The adoption of the Westminster Confession was based on a scholastic mode of thought, drawing on an established statement of orthodoxy to police the behaviour of the Synod's adherents. This habit of mind, dismissed by the non-subscribers as 'a great many metaphysical salvos (the very worst method divinity can take for resolving cases of conscience)', deeply informed the theological approach of the subscribers.[46] Mr Stirling, for example, in dissenting from the Synod's determination to 'exercise Christian forbearance' towards non-subscribing ministers, cited scripture to defend his intransigence. Ironically, given Abernethy's use of Romans in *Religious Obedience Founded on Personal Persuasion*, Stirling drew his argument from the same book, contending that

> the great harm done to religion by these unnatural heats, divisions and
> animosities that are amongst us . . . is very much owing to the carriage
> of these brethren who differ from the Synod; there ought to be a mark
> put upon those who cause divisions. (Rom. 16.17) 'Now I beseech you
> brethren, mark them which cause divisions and offences contrary to
> the doctrine which we have learned, and avoid them, for they that are
> such serve not our Lord Jesus Christ but their own belly, and by good
> words and fair speeches deceive the hearts of the simple.'[47]

A similar dependence on the sanction and sanctity of scripture can be located in the work of John Malcome, who articulated the subscribing stance in a lengthy rebuttal of Abernethy's polemical sermon.[48] Ordained in 1687 and the minister for Dunmurry since 1699, Malcome was an elderly, orthodox man who, despite sharing an education at Glasgow with many of the non-subscribers, remained wedded to scriptural methods. 'Our faith and obedience', he wrote, 'must be founded on Christ Jesus speaking by his prophets and Apostles', for 'if we build upon another foundation we'll be like the man that built his house upon the sand.'[49] Malcome further denied the optimistic anthropology that underpinned Abernethy's claim that reason guided correct religious conduct: 'I do not deny but conscience being enlightened by the word of God directs the man to his duty ... By no means can it be justly called the foundation of our obedience ... unless we fall in with the cursed Socinians, who tell us plainly that humane reason is our rule and guide even in points that directly relate to our eternal salvation; and with them our author plainly agrees.'[50] As well as associating Abernethy with the heresy that Christ was wholly human, however divinely inspired, Malcome also accused his antagonist of replacing authority with the play of reason and grace with free will, and chastised him in saying he 'ought first to have shown us how this doctrine is founded on the text, before he had attempted to show that religious obedience is founded on personal persuasion'.[51]

To Malcome's mind, the only solution to Abernethy's challenge was the separation of communions. 'What if some differ from us in points that are essential?' he asked. 'Shall we then allow them the tokens of Christian communion? And what if their light be darkness? Must we not refuse the token of communion to them? ... And if I should give them all the tokens of Christian communion; what sort of communion will it be, betwixt them and me? Even such as is between light and darkness, Christ and Belial, a believer with an infidel.'[52]

Malcome's pessimism about human nature was in accordance with the theological worldview outlined by the Westminster Confession, and left him with little choice when faced with the stubbornness of his opponents. As he asserted in a passage that rested on the erroneous character of the non-subscribing thought for its purchase:

> I'm for charity to all those who differ from us in smaller things, so as to
> love them, and look upon them as brethren; but as for such as are
> carried away with gross errors, let them pretend what reason and
> sincerity they please. God forbid that I should have any more charity to
> them, while they continue such, than to pray to God that they may be
> brought from the error of their ways. You may enlarge your charity as
> far as you please, but at that rate, in the strength of Christ, I shall never
> be one of your Society, for I'm sure this is not the good old way.[53]

This 'good old way' Malcome identified as the essential doctrines of the faith, namely 'the blessed Trinity in the godhead, the incarnation of the son of God, the satisfaction he gave to the justice of God; for the elect, the necessity of repentance towards God, and faith toward our Lord Jesus Christ &c, all of which are much undervalued in this degenerate age, when scepticism prevails so much.'[54]

Matthew Clerk, whose response to a letter from the non-subscribing Belfast Society provided a clear exposition of the subscribers' position, displayed a similar religiosity. In a passage that highlights how the subscribers began their philosophical investigations with the assumption of God, and not man, Clerk remarked of how 'I am confident in God's strength that though you deny subscribing [to] the Confession, and we that have subscribed should all concur to throw it at our heels, yet there will be as many zealous Christians of our hearers, as will continue to have a regard for our *Confession of Faith* and still hold Presbyterian principles.'[55] Indeed, this was only the opening for a sharp rebuke provided by Clerk to the non-subscribers. 'Nobody can call you Presbyterians', he remarked, 'till you subscribe [to] our Confession of Faith, they may call you as their fancy leads them, that is either Episcopal, Papist, Quaker, Anabaptist, Latitudinarian, Seeker, Muggletonian, Bangorian . . . But they cannot call you Presbyterians.'[56] Rather than assent to the proposition that the defence of individual conscience was the central tenet of the reformed tradition, Clerk argued that it induced theological chaos: 'It is a prop [that] will bear all religions and opinions equally, there being as many heathens in the world as Mohometans, as many Mohometans as Christians, as many papists as Protestants, with a great many Jews; every distinct people exercising their judgement both private and public upon the articles and constitutions of each other, and all of them judging themselves in the right.'[57] 'Until you sign a confession,' he declared, 'none can tell your religion, nor pass judgement on it.'[58]

A fear of free thought and religious anarchy clearly haunted Clerk, for he returned regularly to it throughout his attack on the non-subscribers. A central passage reveals the heterodoxy that he perceived existing between the lines of his opponents' writings. 'There is', he believed, 'no less need of a Confession of Faith when heresies are spreading and increasing, so that every person's private judgement may be known by their own hand.'[59] Immediately after this, Clerk associated the non-subscribers with the Arian heresy—the denial of the Trinity— writing of how 'only the Arians refused to subscribe the canons of Nice [*sic.*] Council, and our New Light men refused to subscribe our Westminster Confession . . . Never any refused to subscribe what they believed to be true, except our bairns [children], that pretend to be wiser than their fathers, as all petted bairns are apt to do.'[60]

Clerk's fear was shared by many subscribers, including Malcome, who rhetorically flourished in *The Good Old Way Examined* (1720), 'I leave it then to all men of learning and sense whether your author [Abernethy] in that point does not fall in with the cursed Socinians'.[61] Indeed, subscribers suspected that under the demand for individual autonomy rested a lurking Arianism which intruded upon the integrity of the Christian community altogether. While the non-subscribing faction was provocative in denying church authority, what conditioned the subscribers' refusal to come to a settlement was their antipathy to free thought. Echoing Malcome's comments about Socinians, Mr Stirling's statement to the Synod of the subscribing position expressed a concern 'that their refusing to subscribe [to] the Westminster Confession of Faith does arise from a dissatisfaction with the doctrines therein contained, for though they say they own the important essential articles, I know not what articles they judge to be such; they have been pleased to declare themselves with respect to the deity of the Son of God, why may they not declare themselves with respect to all as well as that?'[62] This suspicion was understandable, even if the non-subscribing position was technically sustainable within the parameters of orthodoxy.[63]

The general sense of the Synod was expressed in the reasons supplied for holding a fast day on the first Wednesday of August 1725. Although undertaken because of poor weather, and the demoralising nature of recent foreign events, the prayers offered included 'that he [King George I] may preserve us with the neighbouring islands from the danger of Deism, the Arian heresy, popery, Quakerism and other errors, drawing aside from the grace of God, faith of Jesus Christ and practical Godliness, and that sound doctrine, pure ordinances and brotherly love may be the lasting blessing of this Church.'[64] Here they coupled the fate of the confession with a profound fear of the freethinker. The ordering of their desires is revealing. 'Sound doctrine' was to be valued before 'brotherly love', and they were connected through the workings of 'pure ordinances'. For the scriptural faction in the Synod, the only way to secure the faith was to defend its borders from enemies without and to expel the heretics within. But that was not the view of every member of the faith.

Irenic Presbyterianism

Despite the polarised nature of the debate, a moderate irenic faction sought peace between the competing factions within the church. Predominantly southern in origin, they emerged not from the tradition of Scottish churchmanship but the independent congregationalism that had infiltrated Dublin from England in the 1650s. Indeed, the prime exponents of this approach were the correspondents from the Dublin Presbytery who had observer status at the General Synod. In 1721 these representatives were Nathaniel Weld, Richard Choppin, and Joseph Boyse. Despite their unofficial standing at the Synod they presented 'a letter from Sir Alexander Cairns, Mr Henry, Dr Cumming and several other gentlemen of Dublin' in which they recommended 'in the most pressing manner . . . peace, charity and mutual forbearance.'[65] In 1723 they advocated 'mutual forbearance to all members of this Synod.'[66]

Central to the enunciation of their position was the pamphleteer Joseph Boyse. Born in Leeds in 1660, he was educated in dissenting academies at Kendal and Stepney and, by 1679, was preaching in Kent before acting as chaplain to the Countess of Donegal. He also spent six months ministering in Amsterdam before answering the call of the congregation in Wood Street, Dublin, which came in 1683. While Boyse was Calvinist, he had an awareness of the characteristics of Christianity that were shared by those in the Anglican Church. This had its limits, however. Heterodoxy, Quakerism, and the Roman Catholic creed were excluded from his vision of a tolerant society.[67]

The generous definition Boyse offered of Protestantism, and his comprehension of Presbyterianism as part of a greater Reformed tradition, was paralleled by his formulation of the Calvinist creed. He overtly drew on both the subscribing concentration on scriptural truth and the non-subscribing concern for sincerity of faith to develop a third, irenic, form of Presbyterianism. This position utilised an empirical methodology, rejecting both the Scholasticism and rationalism of the two great antagonistic parties within the Synod of Ulster.

This characteristic mediation of the two positions—scriptural and rationalist—can be seen operating in Boyse's sermon 'On Love to Our Neighbour' (1708), which interrogated the vital question of human worth. At its surface, his remarks agreed with the subscribers in their estimate of human fallibility. In particular, the sermon focussed on the sin of selfishness, identified as 'the fundamental corruption of the will of man', which he held responsible for 'all those unjust and uncharitable actions that render this earth so like to hell; such a scene of confusion and disorder; such a theatre of wars and contentions, such a vale of tears and of misery'.[68]

Boyse here unveiled a vision of the world as dissolute and depraved, a moral landscape wracked with violence and warped by human evil. Onto his compelling canvas he painted 'the perverse blindness of the infidel world; the woeful corruptions of the greatest part of the Christian Church; the sufferings or declensions of the Reformed Churches themselves; the daring insolence of profligate sinners; the shameful falls of professed Christians, and the woeful decays of piety too visible among the best.'[69] And at the vanishing point of this dark vista stood the figure of the philosopher, the epitome of the absorbed, aggrandising egoist, who claimed knowledge and insight where only prideful self-deceit existed. According to Boyse, it was even in the full awareness of 'this vile and corrupt maim of degenerate nature, [that] some confident *Pretenders* to *Philosophy*, [have] cried [selfishness] up as it were the most undoubted dictate of our unprejudiced reason. And 'tis easy to imagine what kind of morality those must teach us that thus make the radical corruption of our nature an innocent and harmless thing.'[70]

Into this bleak tableau Boyse inserted a small, yet glistening sliver of hope. Against the grain of the subscribers' acceptance of the intractable nature of human depravity, he asserted that humanity was capable of moral improvement. Love of others might overcome selfish passions, for 'as one member does in some degree feel the ease that another enjoys, so should we (though we cannot relish a sensible) yet find a rational complacency and satisfaction in the good of others.'[71]

Akin to the position of the non-subscribers, Boyse enjoined his congregation to use their mental faculties in pursuit of Christian wisdom. In speaking of how each individual needed to keep to the injunction to love one another, he observed: 'And here we have great occasion to descend into our own hearts and observe the most secret workings and motions of them towards our neighbour.'[72] In adopting rationalism as an ethical tool, he shared in the ontological optimism that characterised the stance of the non-subscribers. He repeatedly swooned over the godly aspect of human nature, exclaiming that 'every man hath the same natural faculties and powers, and is thereby capable of being restored to the moral holy image of God, and of being for ever happy in the enjoyment of Him.'[73] This divine countenance could be found in any individual, countering the ugly depiction in the first part of the sermon. To Boyse, 'there's none but we may behold in them the beautiful image of God enstampt [*sic*] on their rational nature. There is in every man a heaven born spirit, resembling the father of spirits'.[74]

In resolving the tension between these two contrasting portrayals of human nature—the depraved and the divine—Boyse appealed to the contradictory cacophony of everyday experience, and to the empirical reactions of his congregation.[75] This appeal to experience was coupled with a rhetorical dependence on the sensory responses of his congregation to the visions of distress they met with on the streets of the capital. Notice how he here refers his listeners to sight and sound and to the physical responses induced in the observer: 'The deplorable objects of human misery which we behold, or the tidings of it which we hear, should deeply affect our hearts, and move the bowels of our compassion towards our suffering fellow creatures.'[76]

Out of this empirical register, Boyse compiled an argument for social tolerance and religious latitude; a thesis founded upon an understanding that human nature was vexed by the competing demands of a prideful nature and an impulse for compassion. In a revealing statement of his social empathy, he asserted, 'We should . . . esteem every man, looking on none as despicable, and below our consideration and regard'.[77] This ethos found succinct expression in a remarkable passage, surprising in its open-ended definition of the applicability of Christian charity and in its use of natural law ideas to legitimate a scriptural precept. According to Boyse, it was incumbent on people to offer their love to 'every one that's near and allied to us, either as a Christian, or as a man, by the bonds of graces or of nature it self, our enemies themselves not excluded.'[78] He was realistic however, and did not demand a totalising, holistic, and ineffectual love of all. Rather, he identified a series of ever-expanding circles of care:

> We must first extend our beneficent love to those that are under our immediate care, and whom providence has placed in a dependence thereon. But yet, it must not be so confined unto them as to hinder us as we have an opportunity from doing good to all we converse with, especially to them 'that are of the Household of Faith' (Gal. 6.10). And we should when such proper objects and occasions of charity occur, promote the good of others, with the like cordial affection and zeal as we would our own.[79]

This passage drew directly on scripture and on the sense of human weakness on which the subscribers insisted; yet it balanced these with an understanding that humans could act for the good, supporting the optimism of the non-subscribers. In creating this interplay of the competing registers, it effected a third mode of speaking. It cordoned off the aggravation caused by these disputes, and proposed that Christian charity was the right response. In a clear statement of his irenic take on Christianity, Boyse asserted that love is 'busy and active, 'tis a communicative and diffusive principle, and will therefore render us liberal benefactors to others in proportion to our real abilities.'[80] Belief in Christianity would lead to sociability and sympathy, not to division and discord.

That this approach might have had a direct practical application in the dissensions and divisions of the 1720s is suggested in Boyse's sermon of 24 June 1722, delivered during the sitting of the General Synod at Londonderry. His intention was to salve the wounds caused by the dispute; a mission which involved him in the office of a 'peacemaker . . . [who] endeavoured the preservation both of truth and love among you.'[81] To this end the sermon promoted 'our Saviour's new command of mutual love among his disciples.'[82] As he observed in the prefatory note, he believed that Christ 'put no bar in the way of our communion by imposing such terms of it' as would lead to the exclusion of others.[83] He told the congregation of how 'we have here in this part of the kingdom [Dublin] a different method for the admission of entrants into the ministry from what your General Synods have appointed. (And what we have found by the divine blessing a sufficient barrier against heresies and dangerous errors.) But God forbid that we should declare non-communion with you, or you with us on the account of that difference.'[84]

It was not that Boyse was surprised that differences had emerged over minor matters of theology. This was to be expected while man lived 'in this present state of darkness and imperfection.'[85] Yet he was convinced 'there is . . . an easy and safe expedient that would entirely remove that embarrassing difficulty, viz. allowing the entrant . . . to make a declaration of his faith in his own words, in which if anything be found contrary to sound doctrine and the wholesome words of our Lord Jesus Christ, the Presbytery that are to concur in his ordination may refuse to admit him.'[86] This was a satisfactory compromise for Boyse for two reasons: it allowed latitude for those of tender conscience and ensured the rules of entry into the church if the Presbyterian faith were upheld. Both tyranny and licentiousness were avoided. The church remained a broad organisation built on a coherent doctrine.

The philosophical foundations for this stance were made explicit in the writings of Francis Hutcheson.[87] Born in Drumalig, County Down, in 1694 to John Hutcheson, a minister who was to take the side of the subscribers in the dispute, Francis was educated at Glasgow University where he took theology under the direction of John Simson.[88] During the 1720s, he taught at a dissenting academy in Dublin sponsored by Boyse's Wood Street congregation.[89] In his writings from this period, Hutcheson offered an analysis of human nature grounded upon empirical assumptions.

An Inquiry into the Original of Our Ideas of Beauty and Virtue, published in 1725, emerged during the heart of the subscription controversy. The volume was in no direct sense a contribution to that debate, however. This is indicated by Hutcheson's choice of genre: the polite literary essay, not the sermon, and an argument favouring human moral capacity that, while optimistic, rejected the rationalistic certainties of the non-subscribing faction. In this, he was addressing the Anglican inhabitants of Ireland in a delicate and understated plea for toler-ance of religious dissent in a self-consciously confessional state.[90]

Nonetheless, Hutcheson was caught up in the subscription controversy, and was careful to navigate a cautious route between the two factions in the church.[91] In doing so, Hutcheson reached for the rhetorical constructions of John Locke's *Essay concerning Human Understanding* (1690) to develop a system of aesthetic and moral philosophy. The opening chapter was deeply indebted to the rubric and definitions offered by Locke, with Hutcheson proposing that ideas could be 'compounded' by an active mind in a process he termed abstraction and which generated simple and complex ideas, all terms he drew from the *Essay*.[92]

But the real purpose of this brisk synopsis of an empirical epistemology was to lay the groundwork for Hutcheson's central contentions: that there exists within mankind an inbuilt capacity to identify beauty; and that there is a con-comitant moral function. These internal senses were explicitly described as prerational, separating Hutcheson from the rationalist non-subscribers. With regard to beauty, which Hutcheson treated as analogous to the more significant moral sense, he contended that 'this superior power of perception is justly called a sense, because of its affinity to the other senses in this, that the pleasure does not arise from any knowledge of principles, proportions, causes or of the useful-ness of the object, but strikes us at first with the idea of beauty: nor does the most accurate knowledge increase this pleasure of beauty, however it may super-add a distinct rational pleasure from prospects of advantage or from increase in knowledge.'[93]

The moral sense was similarly conceived as operating prior to the interven-tion of human rationality and Hutcheson was at pains to disavow the idea that this reaction could be altered by any prior perception of self-interest. To do so, he offered the following corporeal analogy:

> Should any one advise us to wrong a minor, or orphan, or to do an
> ungrateful action toward a benefactor; we at first view abhor it: assure
> us that it will be very advantageous to us, propose even a reward; our
> sense of the action is not altered. It is true, these motives may make us
> undertake it; but they have no more influence upon us to make us
> approve it, than a physician's advice has to make a nauseous potion
> pleasant to the taste.[94]

In a later passage, he considered the merits and use of reason in the moral domain, observing: 'Men have reason given to them to judge of the tendencies of their actions, that they may not stupidly follow the first appearance of public good, but it is still some appearance of good which they pursue.'[95] In other words, reason was a tool to help direct the individual in their pursuit of goods identified by the moral sense. It was a mechanism for determining means, not choosing ends.

From these prerational origins in the senses, Hutcheson developed definitions of both beauty and virtue that underlined his commitment to an empirical philosophy. In the first case, he argued that 'what we call beautiful in objects, to speak in the mathematical style, seems to be in compound ratio of uniformity and variety: so that where the uniformity of bodies is equal, the beauty is as the variety; and where the variety is equal, the beauty is as the uniformity.'[96] In his moral theory Hutcheson formulated the thesis that 'that action is best which accomplishes the greatest happiness for the greatest numbers'—a phrase which he coined.[97] In both cases, the worth of an object resided in the empirical response it generated in the observer; a form of subjective realism, grounded in the consistency of human responses when confronted with similar circumstances.

The rhetoric of the book supported Hutcheson's empirical credentials, for in both the treatise on beauty and that on virtue, the text was absorbed by numerous apparently anecdotal expositions of his theses. For instance, in treating of the question of the moral sense's relationship to education, Hutcheson dwelt on his own experience as a teacher in Dublin, writing: 'The universality of this moral sense, and that it is antecedent to instruction, may appear from observing the sentiments of children, upon hearing the stories with which they are commonly entertained as soon as they understand language. They always passionately interest themselves on that side where kindness and humanity are found; and detest the cruel, the covetous, the selfish or the treacherous.'[98] In a typical appeal to his readers to examine their own empirical development, he concluded one passage dealing with intellectual pursuits by confidently asserting that 'we may leave it in the breast of every student to determine whether he has not often felt this pleasure without such prospect of advantage from the discovery of his theorem'.[99] In the treatise on virtue Hutcheson passed the task of illustrating his assertions over to the reader: 'That the perceptions of moral good and evil are perfectly different from those of natural good, or advantage, every one must convince himself by reflecting upon the different manner in which he finds himself affected when those objects occur to him.'[100]

This trust in the right-minded nature of the reader was an indication of Hutcheson's empirical epistemology and his optimism about the human condition. Vice in the *Inquiry* was oftentimes equated with misinformation, or a deformity of character, commensurate with colour blindness in relation to aesthetics. Indeed Hutcheson, in his equable fashion, argued that 'human nature seems scarce capable of malicious, disinterested hatred, or a sedate delight in the misery of others'.[101] Rather he perceived 'the ordinary springs of vice . . . among men must be a mistaken self-love, made so violent as to overcome benevolence, or affections arising from false and rashly formed opinions of mankind, which we run into through the weakness of our benevolence'; a suggestion he illustrated by proposing an everyday situation:

> When men who had good opinions of each other, happen to have
> contrary interests, they are apt to have their good opinion of each
> other bated, by imagining a designed opposition from malice; without
> this they can scarcely hate one another. Thus two candidates for the
> same office wish each other dead, because that is an ordinary way by
> which men make room for each other; but if there remains any
> reflection on each other's virtue, as there sometimes may be in
> benevolent tempers, then their opposition may be without hatred;
> and if another better post, where there is no competition, were
> bestowed on one of them, the other shall rejoice at it.[102]

Note here the use of the word 'ordinary' to emphasise how mundane observation of the world's dealings supported Hutcheson's more general moral contentions.

This pragmatic, empirical attitude also underpinned Hutcheson's theological approach, notably his belief in a benevolent God. He suggested, in an explicitly enlightened mode, that 'it has often been taken for granted in these papers, "that the deity is morally good"; though the reasoning is not at all built upon this supposition.'[103] He then continued:

> If we enquire into the reason of the great agreement of mankind in
> this opinion, we shall perhaps find no demonstrative arguments à
> priori, from the idea of an independent being, to prove his goodness.
> But there is abundant probability, deduced from the whole frame of
> nature, which seems as far as we know, plainly contrived for the good
> of the whole; and the casual evils seem the necessary concomitants of
> some mechanism designed for vastly prepollent good. Nay, this very
> moral sense, implanted in rational agents, to delight in and admire
> whatever actions flow from a study of the good in others, is one of the
> strongest evidences of goodness in the author of nature.[104]

Not assuming God's existence, Hutcheson was offering empirical proof of his benevolent presence.

In turning this system of moral philosophy to practical account, Hutcheson directed his attention to the controversies surrounding church governance in a letter to his subscribing father. He did 'not imagine, that either government or the externals of worship are so determined in the Gospel as to oblige men to one particular way in either; [but rather think] that all societies may, according to their own prudence, choose such a form of government in the church, and agree upon such external order of worship, as they think will do most good to promote the true end of all real piety and virtue—but without any right of forcing others into it'.[105] As Hutcheson remained a Presbyterian, and had no intention of converting, he would bow to the wishes of his community and subscribe to the Westminster Confession of Faith; he also recognised the power and cogency of the non-subscribing argument. Given the context of the letter, with his father anxious about reports that he might embrace Anglicanism, Hutcheson extended his reflection on the power of custom in denoting religious ritual, suggesting: 'in King Charles the first's reign in England, had I lived then, I would only have enquired whether an actual separation would have probably done more good than the contrary, and practised accordingly.'[106] This pragmatic, empirically grounded test of the utility of confessional distinction was a far cry from the subscribing Presbyterians' convincement concerning scriptural truths, and from the non-subscribing commitment to individual conscience. Hutcheson evinced a middle way between the two contesting camps. Like Boyse, he enunciated a modest empirical enlightened Presbyterianism.

The Optimism of the Belfast Society

While the irenic Presbyterianism of the Dublin ministers drew on Enlightenment ideas of human capacity, and in this shared something with the non-subscribers, they adopted an empirical methodology. The non-subscribers, in contrast, took a rationalist approach to their faith, arguing that humans had a faculty through which, with due attention, they could understand God's will and purpose. The practice of developing a rational exposition of scripture was the central purpose of the Belfast Society, a Bible reading club that became a central locus of non-subscribing theology. Cofounded by John Abernethy in 1705, the society started as a polite reading group for preachers, students of divinity, and prospective candidates for the ministry, intent on developing their knowledge of scripture in the light of natural philosophy.[107] Members included Michael Bruce of Holywood, Thomas Nevin of Downpatrick, the Belfast physician Dr Victor Ferguson and, later, Samuel Haliday, all prominent non-subscribers in later years.[108] Minister James Duchal recalled the proceedings as follows:

> At every meeting, two were appointed to read and seriously consider
> three or four chapters of the Bible, or more, according to the nature
> of the subjects contained in them, and to present to the next meeting
> the doubts that should occur to them, or that they should find in
> commentators, about the true meaning of difficult passages, with the
> best solutions of them; the one beginning with the Old Testament,
> the other with the New. These doubts and solutions were canvassed by
> the meeting, to whom they were presented . . . Another branch of our
> business was what we called a communication of studies; that is that
> every member should at every meeting communicate to the whole the
> substance of everything he had found remarkable in the books he had
> read since the former meeting. By this means a bookish disposition
> was encouraged and kept up by all; every man's reading came to be
> better digested by his talking it over to his friends; new matters and
> questions were often started on these occasions that issued in some
> very agreeable eclaircissement of the subject at hand.[109]

In the 1720s, the Belfast Society was to be an explicit target of the traditionalists' ire. Matthew Clerk, for instance, saw the society behind Abernethy's campaign against subscription, for 'they act all by concert, and what one does, all do; if it were but voting in a synod, what he that's cashed first votes, they all follow in a string, like wild geese, no discord among them.'[110] And when Clerk fell into dispute with them, he wryly remarked, 'Methinks it strange that a society of people should agree to allow every man his private judgement, and yet cavil at any body that makes use of the grant they have so freely given. This is to throw down with one hand what's built with the other.'[111] So too, John Malcome took issue with the nature of the organisation, in his case dwelling on its foundation in which he saw the shadow of independency. 'As for your joining in a voluntary society', he wrote, 'I do not quarrel the thing, but of the manner of it; viz. that you set up a society, as you call it, without consulting your respective presbyteries before. Sure it became you to do so, seeing you profess to be Presbyterians.'[112]

In contrast, the society, in a pamphlet refuting Malcome's negative depiction of its operations in *Personal Persuasion no Foundation for Religious Obedience*, emphasised the innocent and well-meaning nature of its activities: 'The unnatural contentions and animosities among Christians being one great cause of the lamentable decay of Christian piety, we made choice of such subjects as we believed most conducive to revive and encourage the vigorous exercise of that noble grace and charity, the bond of perfectness.'[113] Far from according with Malcome's perception of the society as a haven for heretics and schismatics, the society highlighted the learned, spiritual nature of their ambitions: 'We being sensible of many difficulties arising from our personal circumstances, as well as the common condition of the brethren of our persuasion in this kingdom, which have hampered us in our pursuit after learning, could not think of a better expedient for promoting Christian knowledge and for stirring up the gift of God in us, than by joining in a voluntary Society where we communicate to one another our Christian experience, the fruits of our reading, meditation and prayer, and confer upon those points, which we judge to be the most necessary for rendering us faithful in the service of our great Lord and master.'[114]

For the Belfast Society, toleration on doctrinal matters was justified by reference to the status of Christ in the Christian Church. The non-subscribing Christology placed Jesus in the sole position of eminence, arguing that Christ, and He alone, was the head of the church. In the *Vindication of the Presbyterian*

Ministers of the North of Ireland, for instance, James Kirkpatrick repeatedly avowed the primacy of Christ in the ecclesiology of the non-subscribing faction. 'Christ is the sole king, head and lawgiver to his church,' he bluntly declared, 'and if He be, then no set of uninspired men have a legislative authority over the Church of Christ in matters of conscience, for if they have, they are kings in His Kingdom, and He is not the sole king of it Himself. Our blessed redeemer', he proceeded, 'had not delegated this authority to any of His subjects. It is his incommunicable royalty and none can be qualified for it, without infinite perfection.'[115] Indeed, in a passage pointedly linking the demand for subscription in the Presbyterian Church to papal authority in the Catholic Church, he observed, 'had the royalty of the Lord Redeemer in settling the terms of Communion (as a peculiar branch of his kingly power) been asserted always in the Christian church, the man of sin had never been able to trouble and poison the world with the heresy, idolatry, superstition and tyranny of the mystical Babylon: Popery must have been nipped in the bud.'[116]

So too, the non-subscribing 'Expedients for Peace' offered to the Synod in 1726 expressly asserted the centrality of Christ in their religious formulations, pronouncing that 'our Lord Jesus Christ, the only head, king and lawgiver to his church, hath by his invaluable laws, recorded in the New Testament, perfectly and sufficiently determined all the conditions and terms which the Christian Church, or any part of [it] . . . ought to comply with'.[117] Earthly authorities ought to defer to Christ, and any attempt to propose laws that were not evidently espoused in scripture was to impose upon Christ and to set oneself up as a false God and heretic.[118]

It was this understanding of the purity of Christian doctrine that informs the following passage from the non-subscribing manifesto *The Good Old Way*:

> That Christ Jesus, as head of the church, hath the uncommunicable prerogative of making laws to bind the consciences of his subjects in matters of religion and eternal salvation. That by his decisions alone they are to stand and fall. That he alone hath settled the terms of Communion which are contained in the Holy Scriptures. And that it is unwarrantable for any church or society to make new terms of Communion. That the terms of communion settled by our Lord Jesus Christ are the true and only centre of unity in the Christian Church. That a close adherence to them is the most effectual way to promote

charity and love among all true Christians, and a departing from them
the way to promote and perpetuate schism.[119]

This turned the charges of schism back on the subscribers. It was the device
of subscribing to the Westminster Confession that was the great theological
novelty and the stumbling block to unity within the Confession. The non-
subscribers chastised the subscribing ministers for failing in their Christian duty
towards their fellow Presbyterians. This charge riled Malcome greatly. Writing in
the *Good Old Way Examined*, he asserted that 'you have set up a society distinct
from your presbyteries, and without the knowledge of several presbyteries to
which you belong; and yet you would make the world believe you have made
no separation.'[120]

   Yet, despite such quibbling over words, and the pedantic slurs as to which
faction was to blame for the controversy, there were significant philosophical
issues at stake. In particular, the theological stance of the Belfast Society relied on
an optimistic view of human nature that was directly at odds with the pessimism
of the Westminster Confession and the subscribing faction. As a consequence the
society adopted a rationalist methodology instead of the traditional reliance on
Scholastic learning. As *The Good Old Way* made plain, it was the considered view
of the society that individuals could determine the meaning of the Bible for
themselves, without relying on the pronouncements of church authorities, however eminent. A crucial passage undermined the claim of such gatherings as the
Westminster Assembly to dictate doctrine to believers. Restating a commitment
to latitude, it ran: 'Infallibility is justly disclaimed by all Protestant churches.
That therefore all the decisions of councils and synods in matters of religion
ought to be examined according to the Word of God. And that every private
Christian hath an essential unalienable right of judging for himself whether they
are right or wrong.'[121] This evinced a confidence in the ability of every individual
to apply reason to matters of faith. While misreading scripture could have profound consequences for salvation, the society remained convinced that it was a
necessary burden, enriching the relationship between God and the believer, and
ensuring that each communicant took care of their personal religious condition.

   It was in that light that the Belfast Society's reproof of Malcome for his interpretation of Abernethy's sermon was to be read. Underlying the politics of
reading that informs the following passage was, first, a belief in the sanctity of
individual interpretation; second, a belief in the rational capacity of individuals

to determine truth; and third, the deeply personal and abusive implication that in misinterpreting Abernethy, Malcome had shown himself to be an incompetent reader: 'The doctrine contained in this sermon you have misunderstood: drawn false consequences from it, disowned by him and us: and put these consequences, of your own drawing, upon us; contrary to the express words of the sermon, and the most obvious evident sense of which they are capable, in the judgement of any unprejudiced reader.'[122] The interlocking assumptions and arguments beneath this passage were the heart of the subscription controversy, for it indicates how the Belfast Society was philosophically committed to the idea that individuals, through the careful exercise of their powers of reasoning, might successfully interpret the word of God. The implication was that subscribers were too deferential to worldly authority to ascertain the wishes of divine authority. Enraptured by the worldly power they wielded, they were in danger of losing their eternal souls.

At the heart of the question of subscription therefore lay the twin issues of human mental ability and 'sincerity'.[123] A capable and honest reader of the Bible could divine the basic tenets of the faith. To underline this apparent truth, itself dependent on an optimistic human ontology and a rationalist methodology, the Belfast Society confirmed their belief that 'it is the duty of Christians to forebear one another in love, and not to urge a rigid uniformity in points of doubtful disputations and that are not the plain essentials of religion. And to help Christians to judge of fundamental articles, we have taught that every fundamental article of faith hath two essential characters, viz. 1. that it be so clearly propounded and opened in some place of scripture or other, that not only the learned, but the unlearned, in a due use of the ordinary means, may all attain unto a sufficient understanding of it. 2ly that the Holy Scriptures make it necessary to salvation.'[124] In this light, the Bible was an open book, permitting each reader to ascertain the will of God. Human reason and scripture was all that was required to live a Christian life.

In generating a distinction between the essential and inessential tenets of faith, the Belfast Society was consciously following the lead of their arch-polemicist, John Abernethy. Indeed, the whole controversy dated back to 1719 and his decision to contest a transfer from Antrim to a congregation gathered at Usher's Quay in Dublin. This was a substantial snub to the authority of the Synod, for this meetinghouse was something of pet project and a lynchpin of a wider strategy of expansion. Alongside the congregation at Capel Street, it was associated with

Presbyterians of Ulster and Scottish extraction, rather than of an English or southern Irish heritage. Moving to Usher's Quay in 1707 from an earlier location in the Coombe, it was a bellwether of the Synod's power in the city.[125]

Yet, as Abernethy explained to the Synod held in Belfast in 1719, 'he acquiesced in that act loosing his relation from the north, and that it needed no other execution; but as to the other act transporting him to Usher's Quay, he said that not being now a member of the Synod, he thought that they could not call him to account.'[126] While the committee charged with examining the affair recognised that Abernethy had 'spoken in the integrity and simplicity of his heart', they determined that the Presbytery of Dublin had first claim on his services, thereby upholding the transfer and the authority of the Synod.[127] They explicitly blocked any attempt by Antrim to reclaim him, describing any approach as 'a dangerous breach of all good order.'[128]

Thus, from the start the controversy concerned the Synod's authority. The sermon in which Abernethy argued his case, *Religious Obedience Founded on Personal Persuasion*, was preached in December 1719 to the Belfast Society. Within the oration, he twinned his recalcitrance over church government with a rejection of the doctrinal capacity of the Synod. By highlighting personal conviction in the shaping of faith, he formulated the challenge rationalism supplied to the Synod's Scholastic claim to define the interpretation of scripture. Meek submission to a human authority in the face of personal belief was, he declared, 'in effect to say we may be saved by a mere profession and a course of external actions; that is by hypocrisy.'[129]

For Abernethy, inessential tenets were those elements in which disagreement was conscionable without rending the fabric of the faith. While he admitted that the excuse of individual conscience could not be offered in defence of those sins for which biblical injunction could be identified, he inquired:

> Will it at all follow, that because we ought to deny the tokens of
> Christian Communion to those who sin against the light, and are
> self-condemned, therefore we should also deny them to such as walk
> according to the Light, though different from ourselves, in points that
> are not essential? Because the rules of the Gospel direct us to separate
> from those who are openly scandalous and profligate in their lives,
> doing those things which the common sense of mankind condemns,
> therefore we may also separate from such as differ from us in things

wherein the reason of man and the sincerity of Christians permit
them to differ . . . Can it be justly inferred that mere ecclesiastical
authority is sufficient to determine points of conscience, so that any
thing shall commence good or bad, duty or sin, only by its declarations, and a man may rest satisfied in them without the persuasion of
his own mind?[130]

He coupled this with a blurry sense of the distinction, effectively collapsing the
gap just as he was creating it. He wrote of how 'the things wherein our full persuasion is required are things of an inferior nature, not fundamental doctrines
and precepts of Christianity; yet in matters of the highest importance we cannot
possibly be accepted without persuasion.'[131]

Abernethy conceived of the individual as a competent truth seeker, and highlighted how the discovery of any insights depended on rational procedures. In
being persuaded the individual had to 'be deliberate, for sudden and rash conclusions without duly weighing the reasons upon which they were founded, and
what evidence there may be on the opposite side, are the reproach of intelligent
natures, such as ours'.[132] Deliberation 'ought to be unprejudiced, free from passion or the influence of any consideration except that which should rationally
determine us, that is in the present case anything but the pure evidence of the
mind and will of God.'[133] Abernethy effectively placed the burden of truth on
the faculty of reason, believing that it alone could justify man's acceptance of
ethical norms and positive values.

This rationalism subsumed doctrinal orthodoxy to an individualistic account
of knowledge formation. Every God-fearing man had to engage in the struggle
to overcome the human passions which thwart the search for truth. Through
deliberate rational inquiry humanity approximated the divine good in conducting a personal exploration of scripture. In return, God demanded that
people remain true to their own convictions. 'He is a sincere person and may
enjoy the comfortable assurance of his sincerity', Abernethy averred, 'who, in
opposition to his worldly interest and the sinful inclinations of his heart, faithfully endeavours to do the will of God and to abstain from every known sin,
who willingly, and with a ready mind, embraces every discovered truth and
renounces every discovered error and who continually labours to find out his
remaining sins and mistakes, that he may reject them.'[134] Equally, with its
implicit conception of man's perfectibility, rationalism left little room for the

communal nature of faith and its concomitant coordination by church govern-ment. It devolved responsibility for defining the content of moral behaviour to each individual, leaving Abernethy open to accusations of inciting anarchy and destroying the structure of the church.

The non-subscribers' challenge might extend to considerations of political, as well as spiritual, control. In contrast to the policing of doctrinal orthodoxy exer-cised by the Synod of Ulster, when confronted with the threat of heterodoxy and the Irish state's intolerance of dissent the Belfast Society favoured using the vocabulary of natural rights in pleading for state recognition.[135] They proposed this tactic in the belief that if Presbyterians were to request tolerance by seeking the unhampered public articulation of their faith they had to be exemplary in their exercise of it towards others. This was in direct conflict with the subscribers' tactic of entrenching church authority as a means ensuring social discipline, as a route to the same end of gaining acceptance of the public practice of their belief.[136] Ironically, while both camps wanted to legitimate the public confes-sion of Presbyterianism, their inability to determine the best mode of appeal resulted in a split within the church. Unable to decide how best to petition for toleration from the Church of Ireland, they ultimately failed to exercise it amongst themselves.[137]

The Trial of Thomas Emlyn

Whether they adopted the assertion of a social order policed by subscription to the Westminster Confession, or exemplified religious latitude in their for-bearance of disagreement, there were limits to the toleration Presbyterians could expect from the Irish state. In this, they accepted that the public articulation of faith had to be regulated in some fashion, even if the restrictions they desired would encompass the free practice of their own particular confession. The freethinker Thomas Emlyn crossed these boundaries to his personal cost. On 14 June 1703, the Court of the Queen's Bench convened in Dublin to con-sider a charge of heresy against him, despite his position as the longtime Presbyterian minister at the Wood Street congregation. He had also served for five years, from 1683, as the personal chaplain of the Countess of Donegal and of Sir Robert Rich from 1685 until 1691. For a decade, he had enjoyed 'the great esteem' of his congregation, 'and all others that knew him for his learning, piety, industry and exemplary life.'[138] Trouble emerged when a perplexed layman, Dr Duncan Cuming, queried him about the nature of his faith.[139] To the shock of Cuming, Emlyn acknowledged his scepticism about the divinity of Christ. He later recalled how 'I fully owned myself convinced that God, and Father of Jesus Christ, is alone the supreme being and superior in excellency and authority to his Son (or to that effect), who derives all from Him.'[140] Having said of his fellow ministers that 'they were Trinitarian and he was not' he had effectively admitted to heresy.[141]

Matters took an untidy and unsatisfactory turn when Emlyn, having left for London, was removed from office. His co-minister at Wood Street, the irenic empiricist Joseph Boyse, denounced him in print.[142] Boyse explained that the punitive action was a direct consequence of Emlyn's heterodox beliefs, expressed in a series of sermons on a verse from Paul's epistle to the Philippians (Phil 2:8): 'And being found in a fashion as a man, he humbled himself, and became obedient unto death, even the death of the cross.' Boyse recalled that ''twas not till after such apparent and repeated grounds of suspicion as these, that he was desired to declare his judgement in this important point; and in such circumstances the said ministers think there was very just reason to put him upon it, to prevent the danger of the people's being perverted from the common faith.'[143]

Emlyn responded in *The Case of Mr E*, which he published in August 1702. Therein, he argued that 'Mr E conceived it more for the honour of J[esus] Ch[rist] to suppose the complete deity in its full conception to be united to, to dwell and operate in him than to suppose it only a portion of God but partially considered.'[144] Despite the obscurity of this intricate theological point—that God was inherent in Christ, but that Christ was not himself God—at the argument's heart was a debate about what to call the divine aspect of Christ. As he viewed the matter, 'on both sides the worship terminates on the same object, viz. that divine nature which is united to and dwells in the man J[esus] Ch[rist] and which may be worshipped absolutely, or as related to and being in him: only they think this divine nature may be called Christ; he, that it must rather be called God.'[145] This seemingly dealt with the problem, turning it from a question of substance to a matter of semantics. Yet, words were important, and when Emlyn amplified this position, publishing *An Humble Inquiry into the Scripture Account of Jesus Christ: Or A Short Argument concerning his Deity and Glory according to the Gospel* (1702), he paradoxically provided his opponents with the opportunity to silence him more effectively.

In a closely argued text, Emlyn marshalled an array of scriptural evidence to validate his view that Christ was 'Lord of Lords, but that notes an inferior character, compared with that of God of Gods.'[146] In other words, Christ, while an agent of God, and sharing in his divine essence, was not identical or commensurate with God. In this, Emlyn was clearly, if anonymously, complicit with a notorious heresy: Arianism. This tenet dated from the fourth century, when Arius challenged his bishop over the divine character of Jesus. Arianism proposed that while Christ shared in the spiritual nature of God, he was dependent on God's will and was not self-creating. In that, he was not God, but rather an inferior, subordinate manifestation of God's essence: a part of the deity, but not identical to nor an embodiment of God. As Emlyn put it: 'It appears that Christ is so God, as to be under a superior God, who has set him over all'.[147] And in propounding this view, condemned by the Council of Nicaea in 325 AD, Emlyn was prompting wider trouble than a local dispute with his congregation and co-minister.

Emlyn undeniably drew upon the Bible in defending his stance. In line with freethinking practice, the *Humble Inquiry* relied deeply on the deployment of scripture, even as it sought to critically subvert orthodox readings. Even on the title page quotation was used to polemical effect. Two items jostled for attention. The first derived from 1 Corinthians, reading 'to us there is but one God, and he is the father, of whom are all things; and one Lord, viz. Jesus Christ, through whom are all things.'[148] In reproducing this on the cover sheet, Emlyn was openly signalling the theological contention his text was supporting, that God and Christ were distinct beings. Beneath it, suggesting something of the hierarchy of authority Emlyn was prepared to accept, lay a quote from Augustine: 'Thou shalt not urge me with the Council of Arminum, nor I thee with the Council of Nice [*sic*.], but let us decide the cause by scripture authority.' As well as advertising Emlyn's scholarly ability, these quotations indicated the method he was using, the scholastic deference to scripture, albeit put to subversive ends in rejecting the council's adjudications.

Emlyn was thereby not only challenging the theology of his opponents but also undermining the methods they used to derive their interpretations. He was attacking them on the very ground of their claim to legitimacy: their capacity to read text correctly. The freedom to read for oneself, which Emlyn conceived of as being at the heart of the Reformation, was to become a central plank of his defence for publishing this Arian tract. As he subsequently protested:

When it is considered that the Reformation itself began upon this
very principle, 'that all persons ought to search the scriptures and
study the sense and meaning of them with diligence and integrity, as
their only rule of faith and manners': and that has been the case and
conscientious practice of Mr E for above twenty years, which his
greatest enemies cannot deny. How comes it that that very thing must
be criminal and deserve to be punished in him which is highly and
justly commended and applauded in Cranmer and Ridley here and
Luther and Calvin abroad?[149]

Unfortunately, some of his readers did not share the view that Emlyn was a
late product of the Reformation. Instead, the publication prompted the legal
pursuit of its author for the public promulgation of heresy. The case, held before
the Queen's Bench with Church of Ireland bishops sitting in judgement, tested
the limits of confession as it was accepted in Ireland in the period. Despite some
difficulties in formulating the charges—up to three drafts were made before
being settled—he soon stood before the court under three counts. First, the jury
declared in the grinding prose of legal contestation that

Thomas Emlyn of the city of Dublin Gent. not having God before his
eyes, nor yielding reverence to the true and orthodox holy Christian
religion, established in the kingdom of Ireland; but being wholly moved
by the instigation of the devil, and presumptuously treating of the
divinity of our saviour and redeemer, Jesus Christ, did on the eighth
day of February, in the first year of the reign of our sovereign Lady
Anne by the grace of God, of England, Scotland, France and Ireland
queen, defender of the faith &c. at Merchant's-Key [sic], in the parish of
St Owen, in the ward of St Owen, in the county of the city of Dublin
aforesaid, by force and arms, namely by sword, stick &c. write and
cause to be printed a certain infamous and scandalous libel entitled *An
Humble Inquiry into the Scripture Account of Jesus Christ, or a Short
Argument concerning His Deity and Glory according to the Gospel.*[150]

Second, as was a necessary element in the prosecution of seditious libel, the
jury identified and presented a particular passage in the text they deemed offen-
sive. In this case, and again in the stifling terminology of the law court, they
contended that

he the said Thomas Emlyn did impiously, blasphemously, falsely and maliciously assert, affirm and declare in these English words following, namely, 'I' (meaning him the said Thomas Emlyn) 'see no reason there will be to oppose those Unitarians who think him' (meaning Jesus Christ our saviour and redeemer) 'to be a sufficient saviour and prince; though he' (meaning Jesus Christ our Lord aforesaid) 'be not the only supreme God' . . . 'So then Jesus Christ in his highest capacity being inferior to the Father' (meaning God the Father) 'how can he (meaning Jesus Christ our Lord aforesaid) 'be the same God to which he' (meaning Jesus Christ our Lord aforesaid) 'is subject, or of the same rank and dignity? So that I' (meaning him the said Thomas Emlyn) 'may safely say thus much, that the blessed Jesus has declared himself not to be supreme God or equal to the Father, as plainly as words could speak or in brief express'.[151]

Finally, and most damaging for Emlyn's position, the jury determined that his motives in publishing the pamphlet could only be construed as malicious. Both ignorance of his fault and mere good intent were dismissed as grounds for a defence. Instead, they pronounced that 'the said Thomas Emlyn did . . . publish the said infamous and scandalous libel with intention to disturb the peace and tranquillity of this kingdom, to seduce the pious, true and faithful subjects of our said lady the queen, from the true and sacred Christian faith and religion, established in this kingdom of Ireland; to the evil and pernicious example of others and against the peace of our said lady the queen.'[152]

The trial, which took a mere day to conclude, saw him found guilty. Emlyn did not ingratiate himself with his prosecutors, claiming it was implausible that a 'jury consisting of citizens and laymen should so readily take upon themselves to determine in one of the greatest controversies in divinity, and requesting, instead of 'twelve tradesmen', a 'more learned jury.'[153] Found guilty of authoring a seditious tract, the next day the judges returned to sentence him. Fined £1,000, he was imprisoned until 21 July 1705. He may have been lucky in that, for 'some [judges] we hear were for a corporal punishment'.[154] Testing the limits to which the public articulation of faith could be put had punitive consequences.

Emlyn represents an extreme wing of the newly emergent Enlightenment. It was his case, and the ignominy that the Presbyterian community perceived itself to be under as a result, and alongside the test clauses of 1704, that prompted in 1705 both the reimposition of subscription to the Westminster Confession of Faith and the foundation of the non-subscribing Belfast Society. On the one hand, faced with the problem of free thought within its ranks, the Synod of Ulster tried to maintain theological orthodoxy through the mechanism of the Westminster Confession; on the other, the Belfast Society advocated tolerance while interrogating the Bible using individual reason and contemporary learning in seeking new foundations for old orthodoxies.[155] The tension between these two tactics for coping with Emlyn's heterodoxy ultimately split the church asunder.

That Emlyn was aware of the poisonous consequences of the Westminster Confession's dictation of orthodoxy is evident in an appendix to the narrative of his case. There, he took issue with the dissenting ministers of Dublin over his expulsion from the active ministry. As he observed bitterly, 'the dissenters, in rejecting me, and others who willingly accept the scripture, for not assenting to human articles, phrases, and creeds, stand chargeable with the spirit of imposition and with narrowing the scripture-terms of communion'.[156] In a scathing rebuke, he spat: 'what God would leave in a latitude, they will have more restrained, and so require more than he has required . . . thus while they cry out of human inventions in worship, themselves urge human inventions in creeds.'[157] This was the nub of the issue; whether the Synod of Ulster might dictate on Scholastic grounds a reading of scripture, or whether individual reason could engage with the Bible unhindered by worldly authorities.

Moreover, while few Presbyterians were prepared to follow him into freethinking ways, Emlyn's case highlights how the full spectrum of the Enlightenment could and did manifest itself within Ireland. Alongside his heterodoxy, the Irish Presbyterian community produced advocates of rationalism and empiricism, as well as retaining devotees of traditional scriptural religiosity. That they divided over the application of human reason to the Bible only emphasises the implications of the Enlightenment for the confessional organisation of the country as a whole.

What the Emlyn case illustrates, furthermore, is that although he generated an immense reaction within Presbyterianism, the subversion inherent in his ideas was not limited to the church in which he practised. That the representatives of the Anglican state church deemed it necessary to fine and imprison a dissenter for espousing his views indicates that the perceived threat of free thought was widespread within Irish religious life.

Rethinking Non-Subscription

In confronting the twin dilemmas of the challenge of free thought and the supremacy of Anglicanism in the confessional politics of the early 1700s, the Presbyterian Church became exposed to the antagonism between Scholastic church authority and rationalist individual convincement. The non-subscribers held an optimistic view of human nature that differentiated their anthropology from that of the Scholastic subscribers. While Abernethy accepted the revelatory nature of the Bible, he drew a crucial distinction between what he termed 'essential' and 'inessential' articles of faith and failed to precisely demarcate the two aspects, falling back on such generalised assertions as 'faith in our Lord Jesus Christ and repentance towards God.'[158] It was this very imprecision about doctrine that antagonised the subscribers.

In sum, the sphere of faith, defined, guarded, and imposed by the church authorities through the General Synod of Ulster, was challenged by an emergent rationalism and an emphasis on moral autonomy, which subscribers associated with the heterodoxy and anarchy of free thought. And at the heart of that confrontation was the question of human capacity. In their optimism about human endeavour the non-subscribers' aligned themselves with the central philosophical assumption underpinning the rationalist movement inside the European Enlightenment: that man was a moral agent, and that the good life could be discerned by his intelligence.

2

The Anglican Enlightenment
and the Nature of God

∾

Undoubtedly, philosophers are in the right when they tell us, that nothing is great or little other wise than by comparison.

—Jonathan Swift, *Gulliver's Travels*, 1726

O N 12 JULY 1691, on the battleground of Aughrim, 7,000 soldiers died in combat, more than on any other day in Irish history.[1] Although the early auguries were positive for the forces of the Catholic king, James II, the battle was won decisively by the forces of the stadtholder of Holland, William III. Thereafter, James's campaign disintegrated and the army began to dissolve. The end came with the second siege of Limerick and the articles of surrender that followed. The Treaty of Limerick, as it was to become known, saw the remaining Jacobite forces join the ranks of the French army of Louis XIV.[2] The vision of a Catholic polity, briefly glimpsed at the Jacobite parliament of 1689, dissolved with the retreating ranks of the decimated troops. Power was now in Protestant hands.

Unlike in England, where the change in monarch could subsequently be celebrated as a bloodless revolution, the transition of power had come at an immense cost of life. And nor could the revolution be narrated as the clear abdication of James and the peaceful choosing of a new monarch.[3] Military resistance in Ireland had begun on 7 December 1688, with the closing of Derry's city gates to the royal army of the Earl of Antrim by thirteen apprentice boys, four days before James fled London.[4] With the arrival of James at Kinsale in March 1689, the context changed, although the supporting French landing of May 1689 was aborted following a defeat by the English navy. The military tensions implicit in the confrontation at Derry were drawn to the surface as James made for the northwestern corner of the country, determined to break the resistance of local Protestant militias. The focal point of the conflict was the city itself, which James placed under prolonged siege. It lasted over 100 days, only being lifted when the boon that blocked the city's reprovisioning by river was broken on 28 July. In the same period, west Ulster showed itself ready to fight, for at the Battle of Newtownbutler Protestant frontiersmen familiar with the rolling topography of the Drumlin landscape killed 2,000 Jacobite troops.

In early August, the English Williamite forces finally landed, determined to claim the country for their new king. Led by the Duke of Schomberg, 14,000 men were ferried across the Irish Sea unhindered, landing at the northern town of Bangor. While the Jacobite forces beat a hasty retreat south towards Dublin, the duke failed to press home this tactical advantage, allowing James's forces time to regroup. Across the traditional winter break in military campaigning, which both sides observed, the antagonists drew upon foreign troops—French in the case of James, Danish and Dutch in the case of Schomberg—further internationalising the conflict. When William intervened personally, landing at Carrickfergus in June 1690, the stakes were raised again, for now the conflict was clearly between two warring monarchs, with claims to the same dominion. The religious subtext added a further frisson to the European quality of the contest.

On 1 July 1690 the two armies finally clashed in the Boyne valley. William's force of 37,000 men faced James's army of 25,000. The defeat of James opened the way to Dublin, which the Jacobites quickly abandoned as lost, and hence to a Williamite victory in the war as a whole. James fled to France, leaving his troops to continue fighting. They managed, due in large part to the tactical skill of Tyrconnell, to fend off a siege at Limerick late in the season, but their fate seemed bleak, particularly given the arrival of the Earl of Marlborough, who in September 1690 took the helm of the Williamite troops, William having departed for London. Marlborough slowly took the towns of south Munster, with Kinsale falling after a two-week siege in October. The winter break then deferred further hostilities until 1691, although Jacobite 'rapparees' harried the Williamite troops in an extended guerrilla campaign.

Once campaigning resumed, the Williamites, led by the Dutchman Godert de Ginkel, took Athlone, before being confronted by the main Jacobite force, now led by the French commander Marquis de St Ruth. In the Battle of Aughrim the death of St Ruth and the failure of his lieutenant, Patrick Sarsfield, to take command swung the battle to the Williamites. Within a week, the Jacobites had lost Galway. Only Limerick now offered significant resistance and it was soon besieged. The city might have held out for some time, but the cause was increasingly forlorn, and the conflict concluded when on 3 October 1691, Ginkel, William's lords justices, and the Jacobite commanders in the city signed the articles of surrender.[5]

The death toll in the War of the Two Kings (1688–1691), which amounted to around 25,000 men in combat, many more in disease-ridden camps, and as a consequence of food shortages and the economic dislocation of the population, raised a philosophical spectre that haunted the ensuing Protestant hegemony. How was it that the reign of the chosen people could be grounded on military usurpation at a cost of human suffering? What kind of deity might indulge in blood lust to ensure the rule of the faithful? How could a Christian God permit such carnage and yet be considered a just and benevolent father? How could God found righteous dynasties upon human heartache? How could the confession of a faith founded on violence be justified? The answers to these questions were enunciated in a range of ways between 1690 and 1730. Many of these responses were consciously to draw upon, reinterpret, refashion, and skillfully deploy the methods of the Enlightenment.

Within the established Anglican Church of Ireland the full spectrum of methodologies was deployed. A number of Scholastic thinkers argued that God was unknowable and that only the special revelation of scripture provided any glimpse of the divine nature. This fideism was indicative of an unenlightened, occasionally anti-Enlightenment, attitude to questions concerning man's moral capacity and the religious foundations of truth. However, not all members of the Anglican faith were willing to accept this view. There were those who chose to experiment with the methodologies of either empiricism or rationalism, believing they could shed light on the conundrum of God's character and motivations. So too the Anglican community produced freethinkers who, in their determination to reveal God's truth for themselves, decided to test the comprehension offered by the Church of Ireland by promulgating heretical views. The dilemma for all these thinkers was how to understand the peculiar nature of their political supremacy and legitimate the church establishment.[6]

The weight of interest in the Enlightenment amongst Anglican thinkers fell on the empirical methodology, leaving rationalist deduction to a small cluster of clerics and the extremes of free thought to eccentrics and provocateurs. Thus the central debate within the Church of Ireland was between Scholastics such as Jonathan Swift, the dean of St Patrick's Cathedral, who thought the Enlightenment confidence in the capacity of man to know the world wholly misplaced, and empiricists like his immediate church superior, Archbishop William King of Dublin, whose work espoused a conviction that the divine order and God's will were on the side of the Anglicans. It is to the character of that difference of approach that this chapter now turns, looking at Swift's Scholastic commitments before identifying the wider culture of Anglican empiricism articulated in a series of historical essays on the condition of nations. The chapter will then identify the rationalist character of Latitudinarian theology and of George Berkeley's immaterialist epistemology, before concluding with the heretical free thought of the Robert Clayton, bishop of Clogher.

The Distortions of Gulliver

By the end, Lemuel Gulliver was a creature to be pitied. His epic voyages, strange adventures, and surreal experiences had left him disjointed and disconnected from his rural home in England. Traumatised by encounters with foreigners so exotic as to distort his sense of selfhood, he admitted, 'When I happened to behold the reflection of my own form in a lake or a fountain, I turned away my face in horror and detestation of myself'.[7] He was equally distraught, upon his return home, to have to keep the company of his old companions:

> At the time I am writing it is five years since my last return to
> England. During the first year I could not endure my wife or children
> in my presence, the very smell of them was intolerable; much less
> could I suffer them to eat in the same room. To this hour they dare
> not presume to touch my bread, or drink out of the same cup, neither
> was I ever able to let one of them take me by the hand.[8]

Turning away from his spouse, his family, his friends, and his community, Gulliver remained close to those strangers in whom he saw a noble bearing and a moral virtue. Indeed, he closed his wayward narrative by telling readers that his newly purchased horses 'understand me tolerably well; I converse with them at least four hours every day. They are strangers to bridle or saddle, they live in great amity with me, and friendship to each other.'[9] Estranged from humanity, who he denounced as uncouth Yahoos, Gulliver's ontological crisis was completed by his adoption of the Houyhnhnms, or horses, as his solace in a debauched world.

In *Gulliver's Travels*, which first appeared under the authorship of Lemuel Gulliver in 1726, Swift offered readers a perplexing, aggravating, and subversive rendition of a favourite genre: the travelogue. The narrator, a ship's physician and soon-to-be captain, recounted his adventures on a series of voyages into different regions of the globe. 'Faithfully' recounting the events of 'sixteen years and above seven months', Gulliver's volume presented a bestiary of wonders: dwarfs and giants; projectors and eternals; talking horses and depraved humanoids.[10] It distorted the map of known geography, finding uncharted islands and lost coastlines, flying landmasses and unknown peninsulas, entering the blank realms on the map more timid men had left unexplored.

At the heart of the tale is the dreadful deconstruction of Gulliver which, when it arrives, is terrifying, precise, and brutal. Across the four books that make up the saga of Gulliver's expeditions his confidence in his own sense of perspective is destroyed. The persistent dilemma which torments him is how to find an acceptable standard from whence to judge his surrounds. His failure to appropriate, or perhaps to imperialise, his experience causes his dissolution. He is a traveller at home only on the sea, caught between fearful places where his failure to acclimatise, go native, or dominate the host community unravels his indistinct personality.[11]

In the first book, Gulliver finds himself washed up on a land of tiny people, the Lilliputians, who take him prisoner, then adapt to his presence, and finally use him as a machine of war against their archenemy: the neighbouring country of Blefuscu. Throughout, the comedy is one of scale, as when the conflict's origin is traced back to a dispute over which end of an egg to break open:

> The primitive way of breaking eggs before we eat them was upon the
> larger end: but his present majesty's grandfather, while he was a boy,
> going to eat an egg, and breaking it according to the ancient practice,
> happened to cut one of his fingers. Whereupon the emperor his father
> published an edict, commanding all his subjects, upon great penalties,
> to break the smaller end of their eggs. The people so highly resented this

law, that our histories tell us there have been six rebellions raised on that account; wherein one emperor lost his life and another his crown.[12]

In Lilliput Gulliver is too large to perceive the intricate dealings of his hosts. This is both a physical and moral blindness. He is repeatedly in need of his spectacles to bring objects into focus, while he also gets entrapped in the court politics that sees him slandered, impeached, and threatened with blinding; a fate he only avoids through withdrawing to Blefuscu.[13] The reasons for all of this he has to have explained to him by a friend in the court, for 'I had been hitherto all my life a stranger to courts, for which I was unqualified by the meanness of my condition. I had indeed heard and read enough of the dispositions of great princes and ministers; but never expected to have found such terrible effects of them in so remote a country, governed, as I thought, by very different maxims from those in Europe.'[14] The import of this passage is heightened by the pun on the meanings of 'mean' and 'great'; indicating a social rank but also a physical size; irony being added by the fact that it was Gulliver's girth which had gained him entry into the highest echelons of society amongst the miniscule Lilliputians.

Book two reverses the perspective of the first, with Gulliver shipwrecked in Brobdingnag, a land of giants, where he is as small to them as the Lilliputians had been to him. While there, he is systematically reduced, his status overlooked and person demeaned. Treated as an animate doll, he becomes a pet for the daughter of the household in which he finds himself. Even worse treatment occurs when the father seizes the commercial opportunity Gulliver's presence accords:

> He hired a large room between three and four hundred feet wide. He
> provided a table sixty foot in diameter, upon which I was to act my
> part, and palisaded it round three foot from the edge and as many
> high, to prevent me falling over. I was shown ten times a day to the
> wonder and satisfaction of all people . . . The frequent labours I
> underwent every day made in a few weeks a very considerable change
> in my health: the more my master got by me, the more unsatiable he
> grew. I had quite lost my stomach, and was almost reduced to a
> skeleton. The farmer observed it and, concluding I must soon die,
> resolved to make as good a hand of me as he could.[15]

While Gulliver becomes a public spectacle, a curiosity to be examined and observed, his own sight reveals too much, with every pore and blemish on the skin of his hosts being revealed to his exacting vision. When a nurse breastfeeds an anxious child, Gulliver confesses, 'no object ever disgusted me so much as the sight of her monstrous breast, which I cannot tell what to compare it with, so as to give the curious reader an idea of its bulk, shape and colour. It stood prominent six foot, and could not be less than sixteen in circumference. The nipple was about half the bigness of my head, and the hue both of that and the dug, so varied with spots, pimples and freckles, that nothing could appear so nauseous.'[16] Note how here Gulliver fails to find a suitable analogy to convey his displeasure, underlining man's inability to measure and weigh his surrounds adequately; a reflection that extends to his homeland: 'This made me reflect upon the fair skins of our *English* ladies, who appear so beautiful to us, only because they are of our own size, and their defects not to be seen but through a magnifying glass, where we find by experiment that the smoothest and whitest skins look rough and coarse and ill coloured.'[17] The perception of beauty is wholly dependent on an appropriate sense of scale, and 'experiment'; the iconic tool of the natural philosopher, the magnifying glass, demeans the object it examines. Beauty here is literally in the eye of the beholder, for it depends on the viewpoint of the observer; a fact Gulliver then emphasises by noting the changes in perspective offered to the diminutive Lilliputians:

> I remember when I was in Lilliput, the complexions of those diminutive creatures appeared to me the fairest in the world, and talking upon this subject with a person of learning there, who was an intimate friend of mine, he said that my face appeared much fairer and smoother when he looked on me from the ground, than it did upon a nearer view when I took him up in my hand, and brought him close, which he confessed was at first a very shocking sight. He said he could discover great holes in my skin; that the stumps of my beard were ten times stronger than the bristles of a boar, and my complexion made up of several colours altogether disagreeable.[18]

Note how the measurement, 'ten times', depends on comparison, and how Gulliver himself is made the subject of the searching gaze, destroying his personal vanity. Gulliver's vantage point gives him both a physical and a moral perception of his hosts, offering a close view of their blemishes. In this, Swift was literalising his imagery, a common tactic within his satire.[19]

The perspective offered by his travelling also allows Gulliver to reflect upon his own community; in the interviews with the king of Brobdingnag for example the confusions generated by the connections between physical scale and moral perception become increasingly apparent. This is notably the case when the monarch rejects Gulliver's offer of gunpowder:

> The king was struck with horror at the description I had given of those terrible engines, and the proposal I had made. He was amazed how so impotent and grovelling an insect as I (these were his expressions) could entertain such an inhuman idea, and in so familiar a fashion as to appear wholly unmoved at all the scenes of blood and desolation which I had painted as the common effects of those destructive machines.[20]

The first half of the book is therefore grounded upon a simple optical conceit, in which Lemuel Gulliver is first too big, overwhelming the Lilliputians, before being dwarfed by the inhabitants of Brobdingnag.[21] The second half of the book depends on a similar conceit, albeit an ontological one, in which Gulliver first encounters people who are overly intellectual and abstracted from their environment, before having humanity revealed to him as horrifically physical and animalistic in their selfish sating of desires.

The central episode in the third book—in which Gulliver traverses a number of islands supposedly off the coast of Japan—brings him to Laputa. This island in the air is populated by a collection of philosophers, whose concentration on abstract ideas is so intent that to gain their attention they need to be physically accosted by a servant. As Gulliver relates:

> The business of this officer is, when two or three or more persons are in company, gently to strike with his bladder the mouth of him who is to speak, and the right ear of him or them to whom the speaker addreseth himself. This flapper is likewise employed diligently to attend his master in his walks, and upon occasion to give him a soft flap on his eyes, because he is always so wrapped up in cogitation, that he is in manifest danger of falling down every precipice, and bouncing his head against every post and in the street of justling others, or being justled himself into the kennel.[22]

Again the comedy of scale plays a part, with Gulliver remarking on how the Laputian tendency towards theory and deduction resulted in the mismanagement of getting clothes made for him: 'Those to whom the king had entrusted me observing how ill I was clad, ordered that a tailor come the next morning, and take my measure for a suit of clothes. This operator did his office after a different manner from those of his trade in *Europe*. He first took my altitude by a quadrant, and then with rule and compasses, described the dimensions and outlines of my whole body, all of which he entered upon paper, and in six days brought my clothes very ill made and quite out of shape, by happening to mistake a figure in the calculation.'[23] With this last phrase, Gulliver highlights the inadequacy of any such dependence on abstract thought in dealing with a physical object. During his account of the Academy of Lagado, itself a thinly disguised parody of the activities of the Royal Society in London, he witnesses an array of bizarre experiments, from distinguishingly colours by 'feeling and smelling', building houses from the roof down, and the cultivation of naked sheep.[24] The twinning of academic and political folly is mocked in his account of the school of political projectors housed within the institution, in which barbaric experiments are conducted in the name of progress:

> When parties are violent, he offered a wonderful contrivance to
> reconcile them. The method is this. You take an hundred leaders of
> each party, you dispose them into couples of such whose heads are
> nearest of a size; then let two nice operators saw off the *Occiput* [the
> back of the head] of each couple at the same time, in such a manner
> that the brain may be equally divided. Let the *Occiputs* thus cut off be
> interchanged, applying each to the head of his opposite party-man. It
> seems indeed to be a work that requires some exactness, but the
> professor assured us that if it were dextrously performed, the cure
> would be infallible. For he argued thus; that the two half brains being
> left to debate the matter between themselves within the space of one
> skull, would soon come to a good understanding, and produce that
> moderation as well as regularity of thinking much to be wished for in
> the heads of those who imagine they come into the world to watch
> and govern its motion.[25]

The crazed abstract thinkers in the academy stand in contrast to the Yahoos Gulliver encounters during the final excursion. These are depicted as barbaric, driven solely by their appetites and predatory instincts. Unlike the absorbed academics of Laputa, the Yahoos appear to be the most unteachable of animals, their capacities never reaching higher than to draw or carry burdens. Yet I am of opinion this defect ariseth chiefly from a perverse, restive disposition. For they are cunning, malicious, treacherous and revengeful. They are strong and hardy, but of a cowardly spirit, and by consequence, insolent, abject, and cruel.[26]

Gulliver finds comfort among the Houyhnhnms, rational and profound horses by whom he is taken in. They are initially puzzled by the fact that he wears clothes, and hence does not appear to be a Yahoo. This raises a central theme in this book, the ability of humans to deceive; something Gulliver insisted was beyond the comprehension of the horses: 'In frequent discourses with my master concerning the nature of manhood, in other parts of the world, having occasion to talk of lying and false representation, it was with much difficulty that he comprehended what I meant, although he had otherwise a most acute judgement. For he argued thus; that the use of speech was to make us understand each other, and to receive information of facts; now if anyone said *the thing that was not*, these ends were defeated.'[27] Gulliver repeatedly extols the moral worth of the Houyhnhnms:

> *Friendship* and *benevolence* are the two principal virtues among the Houyhnhnms, and these not confined to particular objects, but universal to the whole race. For a stranger from the remotest part is equally treated with the nearest neighbour, and wherever he goes, looks upon himself as at home. They preserve *decency* and *civility* in the highest degrees, but are all together ignorant of *ceremony*. They have no fondness for their colts or foals, but the care they take in educating them proceeds entirely from the dictates of *reason*. And I observed my Master to show the same affection to his neighbour's issue that he has for his own. They will have it that *nature* teaches them to love the whole species, and it is *reason* only that maketh a distinction of persons, where there is a superior degree of virtue.[28]

Reason, virtue, and benevolence are thus not found among intractable humans, but rather in horses: they are qualities beyond the capacity of Gulliver and his fellow men.

Yet, while Gulliver holds up the Houyhnhnms as an ideal, the narrative tells of how their freethinking society dissolves his sense of selfhood, so much so that he can coolly report on the debate within the Houyhnhnm ruling assembly over the one decision that vexed them: namely, 'whether the *Yahoos* should be exterminated from the face of the earth.'[29] Gulliver has his own complicity in this discussion revealed when his master recalls his description of how horses are treated in England: 'Among other things, I mentioned a custom we had of castrating Houyhnhnms when they were young, in order to render them tame . . . This invention might be practised upon the younger *Yahoos* here, which besides rendering them tractable and fitter for use, would in an age put an end to the whole species without destroying life.'[30] Gulliver had fallen foul of trusting the benevolence of his hosts, although the truth that underlies their treatment of him is merely a momentary tolerance, not total acceptance. The Yahoos are to be destroyed by a means proposed by one of their own. Deceived by apparent virtue, Gulliver has become, in this act, a traitor to his species.

Indeed, the entirety of *Gulliver's Travels* offers a meditation on the failure of human beings to appreciate their surrounds. To take humanity as the fundamental unit of analysis, by which everything else can be assessed, categorised, and defined is an exorbitant folly, Swift contended, and Gulliver became his vehicle for asserting the paucity of anthropomorphic thought. Human pride was the central ethical problem upon which all other human frailties were founded and the book constituted a vigorous assault on hubris, teaching distrust in the notion that man is the measure of all things. Swift revealed this moral purpose in the final passage of the book. Note the list, which again avails of comparison to highlight the perceived identity of respectable and reproachful professions: 'My reconcilement to the *Yahoo* kind in general might not be so difficult, if they would be content with those vices and follies only, which nature hath entitled them to. I am not in the least provoked at the sight of a lawyer, a pickpocket, a colonel, a fool, a lord, a suborner, an attorney, a traitor or the like: this is all according to the due course of things: But when I behold a lump of deformity, and diseases both in body and mind, smitten with *pride* it immediately breaks all the measures of my patience; neither shall I ever be able to comprehend how such an animal and such a vice could tally together.'[31]

But the attack on human pride was not merely internal to the text itself. Swift skilfully opened the book out to reflect upon the readers of the tale, even as they worked through the narrative. Through constant use of allusion, Swift suggested that a key would unlock the real meaning of the story.[32] The place-names of the mythical lands Gulliver visited constantly played on those of Dublin or London, England or France, while incidents echoed contemporary political divisions, scandals, and affairs.[33] For example, the history of the civil commotions and the conflict between Lilliput and Blefuscu recalled the religious conflicts which tore apart England in the sixteenth and seventeenth centuries and the enduring conflict with France. The articles of impeachment that threatened Gulliver in Lilliput consciously echoed those that drove Swift's Tory allies from power in 1710.[34] So too there appears to be a sustained analogy with events in Ireland, informing passages in book three that were so politically charged Swift withheld them for fear of censure.[35]

However, there is no sustained analogy, no narrative drive behind these echoes; they are there for the subtle reader to uncover, but when stripped back, add little to the comprehension of the overarching scheme of the book.[36] They serve only to highlight the reader's own desire to be seen as clever, knowing, and insightful, to be able to read the text in a different light, to see more in it than other, more naïve readers. The puns and wordplays thus become a satiric comment on the act of reading itself, offering an inner text that is less meaningful than the outer shell that encases it. Pride, through the reader's pursuit of knowledge, was again the target of Swift's mockery.

Despite the vehemence of his mockery of the Enlightenment's presumption of human centrality, the positive quality of Swift's religious sensibility in contrast is clouded in uncertainty.[37] His few constructive writings suggest he was a traditionalist in terms of churchmanship and ecclesiology, and not given to theological speculation. In his sermon considering the doctrine of the Trinity, he worried that in the rush to defeat the Arian heresy which asserted Christ was not divine, churchmen had muddied the issue:

> This heresy, having revived in the world about a hundred years ago,
> and continued ever since; not out of a zeal for truth, but to give a
> loose to wickedness, by throwing off all religion; several divines, in
> order to answer the cavils of those adversaries to truth and morality,
> began to find out farther explanations of this doctrine of the Trinity
> by rules of philosophy; which have multiplied controversies to such a
> degree, as to beget scruples that have perplexed the minds of many
> sober Christians, who otherwise could never have entertained them.[38]

Indeed, the whole project of offering a philosophical defence of theological doctrine was wrongheaded to Swift, placing the dispute onto the terrain of the speculative freethinkers.[39] It also denied the possibility of appealing to the sole plausible defence for religion: faith. For Swift 'this union and distinction [of the three elements of the Trinity] are a mystery and utterly unknown to mankind. This is enough for any good Christian to believe on this great article, without inquiring any farther: And this can be contrary to no man's reason, although the knowledge of it is hid from him.'[40] Scripture was not answerable to man's humble faculty of reason, for the divine purpose was not fully expressed in the Bible. As he informed his congregation, 'it is impossible for us to determine for what reasons God thought fit to communicate some things to us in part, and leave some part a mystery. But so it is in fact.'[41]

In his positive belief system Swift was therefore a Scholastic thinker, whose understanding of the world was based on a spiritual faith. He relied on the injunctions of the Bible and of established authority, rather than the new methods of empirical, rational, or speculative procedure. In his sermon on the 'Testimony of Conscience' he cautiously revealed his dependence on an external and preordained moral system, speaking of how 'the word *conscience* properly signifies that knowledge which a man hath within himself of his own thoughts and actions. And because if a man judgeth fairly of his actions by comparing them with the law of God, his mind will either approve or condemn him according as he hath done good or evil; therefore this knowledge or conscience may be called both an accuser and a judge.'[42] God was inscrutable to human reason, existing beyond the rules of ordinary existence.[43] He chose only to supply occasional glimmers of His purpose and of the world to come. This fideism, presupposing the inability of man to comprehend the divine nature through an act of reason, produced in Swift the deep pessimism over human pride evidenced in his creative ironic productions. He retreated from speculative thought, advocating instead a pragmatic religion of ritualistic observance and social activism.[44] Moreover, for Swift the Enlightenment, with its assumption of human centrality, held the threat of moral disintegration. Only acceptance of the rigours of the church, informed by prescribed doctrine and established authority could hold the crisis of Lemuel Gulliver at bay. The curious and the intrepid, the clever and the intelligent were tempting destruction.

The State of Nations

Archbishop William King of Dublin shared Swift's perception of God as inscrutable, unknowable, and distant. Yet unlike Swift, he adopted an empirical approach to the problem of identifying God's will in the workings of the world and accepted the central Enlightenment proposition that man was a self-creating, self-determining, and self-satisfying agent, who through a sequence of choices created his own fate.[45] In a form of theological representationalism that was characteristic of an Irish school of Anglican philosophical thought, he argued that man approximated the divine nature of God, who King depicted as singular, infinite in nature and power, conscious, intelligent, purposeful, and good.[46] This likeness was only limited by humanity's mediocre understanding and feeble competency, while God's benevolence and generosity was underscored by his grant of free will to such humble creations. God was wholly independent of influence. Hence, as King concluded, 'He is . . . wholly indifferent to all external things, and can neither receive benefit nor harm from any of them. What then should determine his will to act? Certainly nothing without Him; therefore He determines Himself, and creates to himself a kind of appetite by choosing.'[47]

That God is free to choose and that he had chosen to create the world implied, for King, an immediate and active involvement in its affairs. As he explained: 'Since God is perfect in Himself, since all things subsist by His providence, and stand in need of Him, but He of none; and since He can neither be profited or incommoded by His works, nor affected by their good or evil; it follows that He made these things for no advantage of His own'.[48] Given such intrinsic disinterest, that God had voluntarily created the world constituted evidence of his benevolence. His goodness was not compromised by the existence of evil; rather it was ratified by the decision to encompass free human agency in the workings of the world. The very fact that God chose to create the world as it is, when he could have held his hand or acted differently, suggests that 'God, by willing, makes those things pleasing to Him which were before indifferent.'[49]

While at a macro level, this accounts for the value of the creation itself, its microcosmic parallel implies that the political vista of early eighteenth-century Ireland was pleasing to God. Through particular divine providence, Protestant hegemony had been accomplished, and its existence was transformed into 'agreeableness'. Thus, where Swift had counselled leaving the status quo unexamined, trusting in faith, King's argument for Anglican supremacy rested on the contention that the empirical evidence of history pointed towards their hegemony. King's polemic, *State of the Protestants of Ireland* (1691), mustered the evidence for special providence in Irish Anglican history, surveying the events of the War of the Two Kings to reveal how God's personal intervention accounted for the tribulations and triumph of Protestantism in the face of the Catholic threat. At the heart of his concern was the need to justify the Anglican community's actions in allying themselves with William having once been loyal to James. This act of infidelity was deeply unsettling for King, having advocated passive obedience before the revolution.[50]

Yet, King overcame his theoretical qualms by enacting a neat sleight of hand. In focussing attention not on the Williamite intrusion into English, Scottish, and Irish affairs, but on the policies of James in the period from his accession in 1685, King manoeuvred blame for the event away from the Irish Anglicans and towards the Catholic monarch and his administration. The events of 1688–1691 did not constitute a revolution in the modern sense—a dramatic alteration in the social, economic, and political fabric of the country—but in its traditional understanding of a return to origin. The coming of William was less a palace coup than it was a restoration of the natural order of things, disrupted by the accession of James to the Protestant confessional kingdoms of England, Scotland, and Ireland. The real trauma, therefore, occurred in 1685 and not in 1688. It was the Catholic community that was guilty of usurpation and rebellion, not against the king but with his connivance. By documenting the mistreatment of the Protestant community by the sovereign, King argued that James had declared war on his subjects, forcing them to resist. As he observed of the Roman Catholic community James had favoured, 'I do not see how they can condemn us for what we have done; or what else they could have expected from us; except they would have held up our throats till they cut them; which no man had a reason to expect from a whole body of a people, and they least of all, who designed to be actors in it.'[51] The purpose of the treatise was to compile evidence of the perfidy of James in his treatment of his realm. These empirical evidences King subdivided under nine distinct heads, each of which offered proof of James's malicious intent towards the Protestant community in Ireland.

King revealed the polemical thrust of his argument in a passage assessing the treatment of the Irish army. While he emphasised their traditional loyalty to the monarch, he despaired of how

no sooner was King James settled in his throne but he began to turn
out some of the officers that had been most zealous for his service, and
had deserved best of him, merely because they had been counted firm
to the Protestant religion and the English interest. The first who were
made examples to the rest were the Lord Shannon, Captain Richard
Coote and Sir Oliver St George . . . He took their troops from them
and gave them to men of mean or broken fortunes, who must do
anything to keep them; some of them unqualified by law. It is fit their
names should be known that the reader may the better observe what
kind of change the king began with, when he substituted Captain
Kerney, if I remember right, one of the ruffians, Captain Anderson, a
person of no fortune, Captain Sheldon, a professed papist, and
Captain Graham in the places of the Lord Shannon, Captain
Fitzgerald, Captain Coote and Sir Oliver St George.[52]

In this early passage the specificity of the charge was accentuated by the naming
of particular individuals who suffered, who in turn were made emblematic of a
general policy of persecution. This was a rhetorical structure that informed the
whole of King's narrative, with individual events becoming symptomatic of a
generally applicable moral lesson. When it came to the malaise in manners in
the Catholic treatment of the Protestants, he moved from the general to the
specific, illustrating his point with one carefully chosen episode:

They everywhere insulted over the English, and had their mouths continually full of oaths, curses and imprecations against them; they
railed on them, and gave them all the opprobrious names they could;
and if any chastised them for their sauciness, though ever so much
provoked, they had the judges and juries on their side. They might
kill whom they pleased without fear of law, as appeared from Captain
Nagle's murdering his disbanded officer in the streets of Dublin; but if
any killed or hurt them they were sure to suffer; as Captain Aston
found to his cost, who was hanged for killing a papist upon his
abusing the Captain's wife in the street.[53]

Here one incident of each sort stands for an endemic, structural problem in
the politics of the country, a disparity in power that was revealed through the
insolence with which Catholics treated their Protestant counterparts.

The antagonism between Protestants and Catholics informed King's political analysis from the conception of his text through to its completion. It was revealed in the very title of the work, in which *The State of the Protestants of Ireland* implied a contrast with the competing condition of the Catholics of the country. If one side is well treated, it follows in King's polarising approach to politics that the other community must necessarily suffer. Thus, when it came to perpetrating a character assassination upon the Catholic leader Tyrconnell, accusing him of cruelty to his troops, of dissembling his intentions to cashier Protestant officers, and of bankrupting those who endeavoured to serve him, King concluded that his motives were to advance 'the popish Irish interest in Ireland, which everybody knows cannot be done without the utter ruin of the English Protestants.'[54]

Paradoxically, King's argument also implied that a Catholic rebellion against a Protestant monarch imposing tyrannical restrictions on their freedoms was legitimate.[55] To defend himself from this deduction, he offered a dialectical contrast; one grounded in the natural order. In King's view, Catholics were intrinsically barbaric and the Protestant community was cultivated. King argued that the nature of the Catholic Irish tended them towards primitive emotional responses, such as anger and rage, which made them ill-suited for civil society. He found supporting evidence for this by placing the crisis of 1685–1691 in historical context. It was to this end that King drew upon his intellectual progenitor, John Temple, whose *Irish Rebellion* of 1646 had offered an analysis of the 1641 uprising in similarly anti-Catholic and dehumanising fashion.[56] Indeed, King contended that

> most of them were the sons or descendants of rebels in 1641, who had murdered so many Protestants. Many were outlawed and condemned persons that had lived by Torying and robbing. No less than fourteen notorious Tories were officers in Cormuck O'Neale's Regiment; and when forty or fifty thousand such were put into arms, without any money to pay them, we must leave the world to judge what apprehensions this must breed in Protestants, and whether they had not reason to fear the destruction that immediately fell on them; they saw their own enemies in arms and their own lives in their power.[57]

The rhetoric of this passage emphasises the precision of King's efforts. The initial 'many' who were outlawed is soon clarified, with 'fourteen' individuals being chosen to stand for a wider group, while the rapid transition to the 'forty or fifty thousand' who were armed suddenly swells the numbers to a frightening degree. At that point, having been in turn ambiguous, accurate, and approximate in his assessment of the numbers involved, King leaves the matter to the reader, whose imagination is asked to fill in the consequences of the arming of the descendants of 'rebels'. The disorientation of the shift up and down the numerical scale accentuates the sense of uncertainty and panic induced by the militarisation of the enemy.

His anxiety to number and document the atrocities and cruelties was shot through the text as a whole, with King at times despairing of his inability to get the information required to assess properly the magnitude of the damage that James had inflicted on the country. He bewailed of how 'there were some very barbarous circumstances in their sufferings, which I must leave to the persons themselves to relate, having not yet had the full information.'[58] Yet he also compiled a vast appendix of documents, running for almost the same length as the main body of the book, offering letters, lists, proclamations, official memoranda, and other supporting evidence of James's premeditation in the destruction of his Protestant people. The effect was to instil a sense of authority in the case that had preceded it, turning the book into a legal file, in which the charges brought were supported by items of evidence for the prosecution.

In effect, King translated the narrative of history into empirical evidence of God's will. He saw history as working along providential lines, which translated the Anglican success from pragmatic and actual to purposeful and moral. The de facto power of the community became, through the providential interpretation of the events, de jure. As King concluded in a sermon of thanksgiving at St Patrick's Cathedral in December 1690, 'we had not, neither have we yet in our utmost view another chance to save us, our liberties, estates or religion, but this one, of his majesty's coming to the rescue of these kingdoms: and his undertaking it has been carried on by such a miraculous chain of providences, that we must acknowledge that it is by the grace of God, that William and Mary are now our king and queen.'[59] In other words, God had chosen the Anglican confession to rule in Ireland and its political superiority was evidence of the favour bestowed on their faith.

As King's polemic suggests, if Presbyterian Ireland was deeply imbued with the methodological assumptions of rationalism, Anglican Ireland was similarly infused with empirical practices. If Presbyterianism was concerned with the need to differentiate its confession from both the established church and Roman

Catholicism, the Anglicans required a justification for their confession's supremacy over the others. This necessity produced a genre of writing that explored the state of nations, with Ireland either to the fore, as in King or later in the writing of William Molyneux, or as an unstated shadow text, as in Robert Molesworth's 1694 *Account of the Kingdom of Denmark*. Just as King used the evidence of the recent past to bolster the Anglican claim to supremacy in his present, so the Viscount of Swords, Molesworth, combined a comparative analysis of economic practices with political observation at home to justify the Williamite Revolution, even while arguing for a series of practical reforms.

In line with the empirical methodology Molesworth adopted, his rhetorical emphasis was upon the compilation of observational evidence. He filled many pages with statistical tables, documenting, for example, the import customs which applied, or the structure and form of state revenue.[60] He listed the 'horse and foot in the service of the king of Denmark', calculated the cost of running one regiment in detail, and identified the names of the general officers and the ships in the fleet.[61] He also assessed the country's geography and climate, the latter of which he described as having 'but two seasons of the year, winter and summer; those two other more agreeable ones of spring and autumn not being commonly known'.[62] In sum the Danish king's dominions constituted little more than 'a very large, disjoint and intermixed [territorial holding] producing but a moderate plenty of necessaries for the inhabitants, but few commodities for the merchant and no manufactures, if we except a little iron.'[63]

As in this passage, so throughout his treatment of individual provinces and regions, Molesworth had an eye on the economic consequences of the qualities he described. Developing a negative portrayal of the country, he disparaged the country as infertile and without utility, writing, for example, of how 'the Baltic sea near this city [Copenhagen] is very ill stored with good fish; neither did I ever know any sea town of that consequence worse served with it: Whether it be that the sea wants its requisite saltness (being rather to be esteemed brackish than salt) or that the people are not industrious enough to take them; but I rather believe the former.'[64] Note how Molesworth here compared Copenhagen to other towns of which he had personal knowledge, highlighting his worth as a worldly traveller and reliable guide. It is this position that enabled him to be so dismissive of the other regions under his purview. Even more disparaging is his account of Iceland and Faroe which he proclaimed to be 'miserable islands in the North ocean; corn will scarce grow in either of them, but they have good stocks of cattle.'[65] So too he dismissed Funen as 'second to Zealand, whether its bigness or the goodness of the soil be considered; it has plenty of corn, hogs, lakes, and woods; the chief town of it is Odensee, a well-seated and formerly a flourishing little city, but at present much fallen to decay. This island produces nothing for the merchant to export, except some few horses, the inhabitants usually consuming their own commodities.'[66]

His depiction of economic activity was drawn directly from his experience and depended entirely for its authority upon Molesworth's credibility as an observer. Indeed, as the opening passages of the book related, 'My design is to acquaint you with the present state of these countries and to offer nothing but what I have either collected from sensible grave persons, or what my own knowledge and experience has confirmed to be the truth.'[67] Molesworth had been in Denmark from 1689 to 1692 as an envoy of William III to the court of Christian V, charged with threatening Denmark with war if they did not accede to British demands to settle a dispute with Sweden and unravel a developing Franco-Danish alliance. The Treaty of Altona was signed before Molesworth arrived, resolving many of these tensions, so he turned his attention to hiring a Danish force to fight on behalf of William in the conflict in Ireland.[68]

It was this voyage that gave Molesworth the authority to render Denmark's recent history as a moral fable. The country's political revolution in 1660 had pertinence for the British Isles for, as Molesworth asserted, the British system and Denmark drew their constitutional structure from the same historic root:

> The ancient form of government here was the same which the Goths
> and Vandals established in most, if not all parts of Europe, whither
> they carried their conquests and which in England is retained to this
> day for the most part . . . Denmark therefore was still within these
> two and thirty years governed by a king chosen by the people of all
> sorts, even the boors had their voices . . . The estates of the realm
> being convened to that intent were to elect for their prince such a
> person as to them appeared personable, valiant, just, merciful, affable,
> a maintainer of the laws, a lover of the people, prudent, and adorned
> with all other virtues fit for government, and requisite for the great
> trust reposed in him; yet with due regard to the family of the
> preceding kings . . . Frequent meetings of the estates was a part of the
> very fundamental constitution: In those meetings all matters relating
> to good government were transacted, good laws were enacted, all
> affairs belonging to peace or war, alliances, disposal of great offices,

contracts of marriage for the royal family &c. were debated . . . [As
for the king], his business was to see a due and impartial administration of justice executed according to the laws; nay, often to sit and do
it himself; to be watchful and vigilant for the welfare of his people, to
command in person their armies in time of war, to encourage
industry, religion, arts and learning: and it was his interest, as well as
duty, to keep fair with his nobility and gentry, and to be careful of the
plenty and prosperity of his Commons.[69]

Yet, as chapter seven of his book narrated, 1660 witnessed a dramatic alteration
in Denmark's governance, with the monarch taking advantage of divisions between
the Commons and the nobles to destroy the delicate balance on which the mixed
constitution depended. Thus 'the kingdom of Denmark in four days time changed
from an estate little differing from aristocracy to as absolute a monarchy as any is
at present in the world'. Denmark was a warning that manners, morals, and mores
could be destroyed by political malpractice. Yet in drawing this lesson, Molesworth
intriguingly renounced the idea that the conflict was, as King for example had
formulated it, a conflict between Catholicism and Protestantism. Indeed,

whoever takes the pains to visit the Protestant countries abroad who
have lost their liberty ever since they changed their religion for a
better, will be convinced that it is not popery as such, but the doctrine
of a blind obedience in what religion soever it be found that is the
destruction of the liberty, and consequently the happiness of any
nation. Nay, I am persuaded that many are satisfied the late King
James' attempts to bring in popery was the principle thing which
rescued our liberties from being entirely swallowed up; there seeming
in his reign through the interest and dishonesty of some, the disso-
luteness, laziness and ignorance of others, to have been (in many
men's opinions) a general tendency towards slavery which would
scarcely have been vigorously enough opposed, had he left the
business of religion untouched.[70]

In other words, the dilemma facing the Protestants of Ireland was not the confrontation with Catholicism, but the choice between liberty and slavery.
    This assessment fitted Molesworth's own rather lax religious attitudes—he was
once chastised by the Irish parliament for insulting the Lower House of the

Convocation of the Church of Ireland.[71] Yet it also suggested that the empirical register struggled to comprehend the political conundrum the Anglicans faced in the wake of the War of the Two Kings. If the conflict was not a providential one fated to be determined by God's favour, hence supplying a de facto legitimacy based on religious identity and actual power, Molesworth had to redefine it in a fashion that did not undermine the Anglican community's position in Ireland. While a political rendition of the Williamite Revolution suited the current biases of an audience confronting Louis XIV on the battlefield, the internal threat posed by Irish Catholicism was not negated by Molesworth's political fable.[72] There was, therefore, a need to confront Irish history head on, narrating it in such a way as to accommodate and account for the fact of Anglican supremacy. The Anglican Enlightenment required an urtext, and William Molyneux provided it.

Molyneux's politics was informed by a deep interest in Irish antiquity. His involvement in the plans of Moses Pitt to create a universal atlas brought him the friendship of Roderick O'Flaherty, a Catholic scholar who wrote a description of West Connaught for the project. Despite the collapse of the scheme, the two men remained in touch and Molyneux arranged for the publication of O'Flaherty's magisterial rendition of Irish history from the ancient period to 1684, *Ogygia*.[73] Molyneux himself made use of medieval history to argue against Irish subjugation to the English Parliament in his seminal study *The Case of Ireland being Bound by Act of Parliament in England Stated*, published in 1698, the year of his death at the age of forty-two.

Molyneux's treatise emerged directly from his participation in Parliament.[74] Its composition was prompted by the controversy surrounding efforts to regulate the Irish woollen industry, which Westmidlands farmers in England perceived to be in direct competition with their own produce.[75] A bill tabled by Sir Edward Seymour was proceeding through Westminster which intended to proscribe Irish exportation of wool. In light of this threat to Irish industry, and the perceived usurpation of power by Westminster over Dublin, Molyneux asserted the independence of the Irish parliament and denied the legislative jurisdiction of Westminster.[76]

In *The Case*, Molyneux utilised the historical evidence of ancient charters and acts of Parliament to show how the English had never militarily conquered Ireland. He argued instead that the great chieftains of the country had, in the twelfth century, willingly adopted Henry II of England as their overlord. Quoting extensively from the testimonies of Giraldus Cambrensis, Roger

Hoveden, and Mathew Paris, he illustrated how 'all the archbishops, bishops and abbots of Ireland came to the King of England, and received him for King and Lord of Ireland, swearing fealty to him and his heirs forever. The Kings also and Princes of Ireland, did in like manner receive Henry King of England for Lord of Ireland, and became his men and did him homage, and swore fealty to him and his heirs against all men.'[77] This argument was further substantiated by a lengthy account of the development of the kingdom since that date. Molyneux particularly stressed an episode of independence, when Ireland had constituted a separate kingdom under the power of King John, while the dominion of England remained under the jurisdiction of Henry II. 'By this donation of the Kingdom of Ireland to King John', Molyneux concluded, 'Ireland was most eminently set apart again, as a separate and distinct kingdom by itself from the Kingdom of England; and did so continue until the Kingdom of England descended and came unto King John after the death of his brother Richard the First, King of England, which was about twenty-two years after his being made King of Ireland.'[78] This implied that had Richard had a successor other than John, and John himself produced children, the kingdoms of Ireland and England would have developed in parallel but not in tandem. In other words, Ireland could claim equal status with England as a fully cohered kingdom and the legislature of England could not claim authority over the country.

This led Molyneux to argue, in a far from fully accomplished attempt to prove a negative, that Ireland had never been subjected to English legislation without its parliament having granted explicit, prior permission. Much of the book was taken up with this exercise, documenting how, on occasion, the Irish parliament had willingly taken upon itself to adopt the laws of its neighbour.[79] He tracked the development of legislation across the centuries; drawing on the *Annals of Ireland* (compiled in the seventeenth century from medieval records) as well as such legal treatises as indicated the status of Ireland as understood by the English assembly. Rather than indicate subordination, the history Molyneux reconstructed suggested the power of the Irish assembly to adopt English legislation as it saw fit, but also, by inference, to reject or ignore those acts which appeared inadequate or irrelevant when transposed to local circumstance.

Rhetorically, the pamphlet abounded with scholarly detail, the purpose of which was as much to convince its readers by empirical compilation as it was to confound Molyneux's antagonists by legal citation of authority. The book was awash with quotation, left in its original Latin—inferring both a learned readership and an erudite author—and lengthy lists of legislation. For example, in defence of his assertion that Ireland had explicitly enacted that English legislation which did hold sway, he compiled the following history of due process:

> In the 12th of Henry the 8th, an Act was made in England making it a felony in a servant that runneth away with his masters or mistresses goods. This Act was not received in Ireland till it was enacted by a parliament held here in the 33rd of Henry the 8th. C.5. See. 1.
>
> In the 21st of Henry VIII. C. 19. there was a law made in England, that all Lords might distrain on the Lords of them holden, and make their avowry not naming the tenant, but the land. But this was not of force in Ireland till enacted here in the 33rd of Henry VIII. C. 1. Ses. 1.[80]

The list ran to seventeen items in this instance, and the repetition of form and structure in its compilation added a bludgeoning effect to the passage. The evidence was marshalled to command assent, building a deep and broad evidential case from practical legal episodes. The aim was to reveal a general truth about the circumstance of the country: a law of nations, if not of nature.

Yet when his argument was in danger of falling into gaps in the historical record, Molyneux changed tack, appealing suddenly, and apparently in contravention of his more precise empirical procedure, to wider first principles in the form of a universal natural law.[81] In doing so, he shifted his approach from an inductive to a deductive register, suggesting how Enlightenment methodologies might become fruitful allies in the development of new learning. Thus in the opening pages he wrote, "Tis the cause of the whole race of Adam that I argue: Liberty seems the inherent right of all mankind; and on whatsoever ground any one nation can challenge it to themselves, on the same reason may the rest of Adam's children expect it.'[82] Towards the end of the tract he opined,

> All men are by nature in a state of equality, in respect of jurisdiction or dominion: this I take to be a principle in it self so evident, that it stands in need of little proof. 'Tis not to be conceived that creatures of the same species and rank, promiscuously born to all the same advantages of nature, and the use of the same faculties, should be subordinate and subject one to another; these to this or that of the same kind. On this equality in nature is founded that right which all men claim, of being free from all subjection to positive laws, till by

their own consent they give up their freedom by entering into civil
societies for the common benefit of all the members thereof.[83]

In particular, Molyneux suspended his empirical progression to tease out a
counterfactual alternative. Testing the consequences of his opponents' assertions, he briefly dwelt on the repercussions of accepting that Ireland had been
subject to an English conquest. In so speculating, he explicitly inquired, 'What
title conquest gives by the law of nature and reason?' In answering, he showed
his dexterity as a deductive thinker. He first differentiated between the rights
bestowed by an unjust and a just conquest, contending that the first of these
gave the intruder no title of supremacy. In the latter case, ''tis plain he get by his
conquest no power over those who conquered with him; they that fought on
his side, whether as private soldiers or commanders cannot suffer by the conquest, but must at least be as much freemen as they were before.'[84] So too those
who remained unopposed to the invasion were released from any subsequent
claim of authority. Having thus parsed the case to its essentials, Molyneux
asserted that, according to natural law, those who had actively fought the invader
'by putting themselves in a state of war by using an unjust force, have thereby
forfeited their lives. For quitting reason (which is the rule between man and
man) and using force (which is the way of beasts) they become liable to be
destroyed by him against whom they use force, as any savage wild beast that is
dangerous to his being.'[85] In this central passage Molyneux revealed the purpose
of his adoption of natural law. By opposing the king unreasonably, by abandoning dialogue and adopting brute force, the aggressors had transformed from
men into animals, relinquishing any claim to the universal rights of man or a
civilised dispensation by the monarch. They had reverted to the status of rabid
beasts, to be destroyed because they were dangerously beyond the bounds of
rational arbitration. In other words, natural law indicated that they were not
merely rebelling against just order in politics, but against the natural laws of
society itself.

Both aspects of Molyneux's construction, his use of historical citation and his
avowal of natural law, testified to his desire to normalise the country. The natural law extended to Ireland as it did to England, while the history of the civil
constitution indicated the Irish capacity for self-governance. Molyneux's politics of knowledge lent itself to a defence of Ireland's constitutional independence without and Protestant supremacy within, for both were to be considered

products of a historical development placed squarely within the bounds of the normal development of society. Instead of Anglican supremacy being a miraculous gift of God, or a result of legitimate resistance to arbitrary rule, Molyneux positioned it as a temporal fact, a result of the evolution of society over time. Irish parliamentary independence and the concomitant Anglican confessional supremacy emerged organically from the nature of things.

The underlying rationale for this concentration of effort on the empirical investigation of the state of nations by Anglican writers was to effect a form of sublimated political reasoning. The Williamite Revolution had been far from bloodless in Ireland and had left a residual population of adherents to the minority Church of Ireland as owners of the majority of the land and in a position to extend monopolistic control over the political institutions of the country. In this, they found themselves, by dint of historical accident, in a position of unlikely confessional supremacy. The obvious and most recurrent method of justifying this peculiar circumstance was by appeal to history, for it made Anglican privilege appear natural.

Empiricism did not gain total assent within the Anglican faith, however. If some Anglicans, like Swift, sustained a Scholastic commitment to the mystery of divine motives, there were also those who availed of a rationalist method to solve the conundrum of Anglican supremacy. While Molyneux pointed the way towards this mode of argumentation by filling the gaps in his empirical model with natural law deductions, there were clerics whose work engaged more consistently with the rationalist method. In particular, there were a small number of Low Church clerics, known as Latitudinarians, who accepted a rationalist mode of reading scripture—while in George Berkeley the Church of Ireland had an exponent of rationalism of European significance.

The Reasonableness of Faith

The Latitudinarian movement propounded a version of Anglicanism that was sympathetic to the doctrinal deductions of Presbyterian logic.[86] Within Ireland, the most complete exponent of this theological trend was Edward Synge the younger. Son of an archbishop of Tuam (also Edward), Synge eventually rose to be bishop of Elphin from 1740 until his death in 1762.[87] It was as prebendary of St Patrick's, Dublin, that he preached a sermon before the Irish House of

Commons outlining his ecclesiology. In particular, he considered the extent to which either the church or the state could legitimately coerce a population into accepting a faith as their own.

According to Synge's dissection of the issue, two extreme forms of argument had to be avoided. In the first case, the church had the right to determine orthodoxy and to demand that the state punish heretics by death. This was the stance Synge associated with the Catholic Church. The alternative was that the state could determine the limits of the faith, and that it could demand the absolute allegiance of its population to that institution, the position articulated by the freethinker Thomas Hobbes.[88] Yet both of these contentions were to Synge's mind erroneous, and on similar grounds, for neither the church nor the state could legislate the faith within an individual's heart:

> The only good of such severities must be to reclaim men from their errors. And in order to this, an alteration of judgement, an inward conviction of the mind is plainly necessary. Now this cannot be wrought by external force or compulsion. Racks and torments may indeed extort from those who are not able to bear up against the extremity of pain and anguish an outward profession of anything however false or extravagant. And those which are speciously termed wholesome severities may make men hypocrites and tempt them to dissemble their opinions. But neither one nor the other can make any one a true convert because they cannot make him believe that true, which he thinks to be false, or think that practice innocent, or agreeable to the will of God which his own reason and conscience tells him is not so.[89]

Synge instead emphasised convincement, the personal acceptance of the truth of a doctrine. The only grounds for this were, he opined, 'of a very different kind: calm reasoning, persuasion, explaining our own opinions, showing the falsehood and absurdity of other men's, proofs from the Holy Scripture, to show the conformity of our tenets with the Christian law, and these proposed in the spirit of meekness, without gall, bitterness or invective'.[90] In sum, he proposed that 'all persons in a society, whose principles of religion have no tendency to hurt the public, have a right to toleration. By a toleration I mean a liberty to worship God according to their consciences.'[91]

Synge did impose some restrictions on the civil behaviour of the community espousing dangerous doctrines however. He argued that the state could and should limit active participation in the state to those who ascribed to the established church. Concerning adherents of other creeds it followed that the state 'may make laws to limit their property, to divide it into several hands, and to hinder their making new acquisitions which either in kind or degree may be dangerous to the public peace . . . As a further means to the same end, some moderate restrictions may be put on their civil liberty. They may be excluded from fortresses, or other places where their dwelling or meeting in any great numbers may be really dangerous to the public.'[92] In this, Synge was constructing a defence of many of the penal code's measures, albeit exempting those that directly hampered the Catholic community's freedom of worship, which he adjudged unacceptable. Moreover, in the face of the political threat posed by the Catholic community, Synge was willing to propose one final and extraordinary sanction: expulsion of the populace. 'It is in itself lawful', he opined,

> for all society being founded in some contract express or tacit between the members, and the end and design of this contract and of the social union being the common good of all, whenever any one or more persons are found utterly unqualified to promote this end, but on the contrary are disposed to do their utmost to defeat it, the contract, with respect to him or them, may and ought to be dissolved. The society may refuse such persons any further benefit of that protection which arises from the union of their forces, and at the same time absolve them from that submission which they had stipulated or were bound to pay the civil government. But then, when this resolution is taken with regard to any members of a civil society, 'tis plain they ought to be allowed full liberty, with their persons to transport their effects, or if these cannot be removed, to exchange them for others that may . . . If a convenient time be allowed for this, and he afterwards continues to dwell in the land, he may be treated as an alien and an enemy, he has no right to the protection of the laws and whatever force is necessary to drive him away may be used against him.[93]

As in this passage, rhetorically Synge displayed the full flourish of a rationalistic method, parsing each subject into its constituent parts, numbering them and dealing with each in turn. He deduced his conclusions not through the examination of history, but from first principles—notably the Anglican community's right to self-defence and the conflicting Catholic right to the free expression of religious sentiments. Only after he had dissected and debated his speculative, theoretical argument did he apply the theory to a specific circumstance, namely the religious demography and political climate of the country. That the final proposals were intolerant does not detract either from the logical deduction used to derive them or from the shock the sermon produced in the audience, given the context of it being delivered on the anniversary of the Ulster rising of 1641.[94] The idea that Catholics might enjoy any toleration of their confessional expression was startling.[95]

Certainly, Latitudinarianism as espoused by Synge was not a popular trend within the Church of Ireland.[96] If Synge's primary concern was to protect Anglicanism from the political threat of Catholicism, he also recognised the challenge of free thought, personified for him by Hobbes. In this, Synge was chiming with the anxieties evinced in the work of the idiosyncratic clergyman George Berkeley.[97] Berkeley's career was characterised by a fear of the enemy within, the freethinking sceptic whose work tended towards atheism and social disorder. Indeed, a middle-period study by Berkeley, published in 1732, *Alciphron: or the Minute Philosopher* was subtitled 'an apology for the Christian religion against those who are called free thinkers' and was structured as a series of refutations of their systems. So too the earlier *Three Dialogues* of 1713 was written 'in opposition to sceptics and atheists'. The subtitle of his major work of epistemology *Treatise concerning the Principles of Human Knowledge* conceded the text was intended to expose 'the grounds of scepticism, atheism and irreligion'.[98]

Published in 1710, a year after he has been ordained (he was elevated to the bishopric of Cloyne in 1734), the *Treatise* appeared while Berkeley was a junior fellow at Trinity College, teaching Greek, Hebrew, and Divinity. His religious convictions permeated his philosophy and informed his choice of subject matter for he was convinced that it was the misapprehensions built into empiricism that made freethinking speculations plausible. At the heart of this analysis lay his distaste over the concept of abstraction. Where the English empiricist John Locke had posited the existence of general ideas, derived from the shared common characteristics of particular items, Berkeley dismissed the possibility of imagining abstractions at all.[99] In every case, the individual had to imagine something concrete, be it an object in motion or a specific geometric shape. In constructing this thesis, Berkeley alluded to his awareness of his own interior processes of cogitation:

Whether others have this wonderful faculty of abstracting their ideas,
they best can tell: for myself I find indeed I have a faculty of imagining, or representing to myself the ideas of those particular things I
have perceived and variously compounding and dividing them. I can
imagine a man with two heads or the upper parts of a man joined to
the body of a horse. I can consider the hand, the eye, the nose, each
by itself abstracted or separated from the rest of the body. But then
whatever hand or eye I imagine, it must have some particular shape or
colour. Likewise the idea of man I frame to myself, must either be of a
white, or a black or a tawny, a straight or a crooked, a tall, or a low, or
a middle-sized man.[100]

In Berkeley's view the danger of accepting the concept of abstraction was that
it gave ground to materialist philosophy, by proposing that external objects had
a form of independent existence which was imperceptible and hence inexplicable to the human mind. Conceding to this kind of materialism was to impose
a brand of nonsense on the reader of such tracts, speaking of qualities as being
inherent in objects which could not be seen. For example, of the idea of extension he observed how

it is said extension is a mode or accident of matter, and that matter is
the substratum that supports it. Now I desire that you would explain
what is meant by matter's *supporting* extension: say you, I have no idea
of matter, and therefore cannot explain it. I answer, though you have
no positive, yet if you have no meaning at all, you must at least have a
relative idea of matter; though you know not what it is, yet you must
be supposed to know what relation it bears to accidents, and what is
meant by supporting them. It is evident *support* cannot here be taken
in its usual or literal sense, as when we say that pillars support a
building: it what sense therefore must it be taken?[101]

In rejecting the concept of extension and the materialist thesis that matter
exists independently of humanity and has qualities which are beyond the sensory
range of humanity, Berkeley reduced the external world into what was observable, or as his dictum pronounced: 'esse is percipi'; 'to exist is to be perceived'.[102]
Unless seen, the object, quality, or substance could not be assumed to be there.
In this, he argued that his immaterialist philosophy, rather than contradicting

Locke, was a logical extension of his system. Although he rejected Locke's division between the primary abstract qualities of objects such as extension, and the secondary, perceptible qualities such as colour, where Locke had rightly shown secondary qualities to be dependent on the senses, this premise was now generalised to apply to existence as a whole.

Berkeley underpinned his argument that existence depended solely on perception by constantly shifting the perspective of the writing. For example, in an early passage attacking the concept of an independently existing matter he repeatedly changed the identity of the speaker, ventriloquising the assumed objections of the reader, alluding to the attitudes of an unnamed community of materialists, as well as asserting ownership over his own thesis. Thus, in paragraph eight the perspective begins with the reader—'But say you'—before moving to the author—'I answer'. The pattern is then repeated—'but if you say'; 'I appeal to anyone'— before moving in paragraph nine to another broader vantage point, a community of thinkers who accept the distinction between primary and secondary ideas— 'some there are'. In opposition to these new antagonists Berkeley constructs a commonality between the author and the reader, revising the initial opposition between the author and the reader—'the ideas we have of these they acknowledge'; 'an unthinking substance they call *matter*. By matter therefore we understand'.[103]

This microcosm of his rhetorical strategy found fuller exposition in the series of thirteen objections to immaterialism with which Berkeley dealt in paragraphs thirty-four to eighty-four and which generated an imagined argument between the writer and the reader. Only in paragraph 118 of the text, where he was dealing with the advantages inherent in his scheme of thought did Berkeley complete the process of convincement, indicated by the sudden shift from personal pronouns to the assertion of a shared understanding: 'we hold' and 'we suspect'.[104]

While his deconstruction of the material world was consciously conceived of as an attack on the supposed mystifications of the materialists, it was imperative that Berkeley replace their system with another. Thus, *The Principles* was not merely a negative, critical text; rather it contained a reconstructive epistemological project. In particular, in the place of matter, which he condemned as esoteric and unknowable, he conceived of a universe filled with ideas and spirits.

At the kernel of Berkeley's system lay the notion of an idea, which he understood as the object of the senses. All he could accept within his philosophical system were those things which produced sensations. At its most extreme, when individuals closed their eyes, the world no longer existed. As he wrote,

It will be objected that from the foregoing principles it follows, things
are every moment annihilated and created anew. The objects of sense
only exist when being perceived: the trees therefore are in the garden,
or the chairs in the parlour, no longer than while there is somebody
by to perceive them. Upon shutting my eyes all the furniture in the
room is reduced to nothing, and barely upon opening them it is again
created . . . For my part after the nicest inquiry I could make, I am
not able to discover that anything else is meant.[105]

Quite simply, there was no evidence to prove the continued existence of ideas
without an agent being present to sense them.

It was by so reducing ideas into the perceptions of the mind that Berkeley
established the primacy of mental facilities. As he observed of all knowledge,
'either we must know it by sense or by reason' and if sense was dependent on,
and a product of the mind's reasoning, it was the capacity for thought that produced all awareness.[106] In a world in which all knowledge depended on the
production of ideas, the facility of perception was foundational.

The power of perception was, for Berkeley, identical with the possession of a
spirit: 'All the unthinking objects of the mind agree, in that they are entirely
passive, and their existence consists only in being perceived: whereas a soul or
spirit is an active being, whose existence consists not in being perceived, but in
perceiving ideas and thinking.'[107] The spirit he defined as 'one simple, undivided
active being: as it perceives ideas, it is called the *understanding*, and as it produces or otherwise operates about them, it is called the *will*.'[108] Yet it was essentially unknowable, for as he admitted 'there can be no idea formed of a soul or
a spirit . . . They cannot represent unto us, by way of image or likeness, that
which acts. A little attention will make it plain to anyone, that to have an idea
which shall be like that active principle of motion and change of ideas, is absolutely impossible. Such is the nature of *spirit* or that which acts, that it cannot
be of itself perceived, but only by the effects which it produceth.'[109] Crucially,
therefore, other spirits could not be known from empirical evidence; rather their
presence was deduced from the fact that only the will of an active spirit might
have caused the alterations in the ideas we perceive. The existence of other spirits
was suggested by the unwilled nature of much of an individual's perception. As
Berkeley concluded, 'When in broad daylight I open my eyes, it is not in my
power to choose whether I shall see or not, or to determine what particular

objects shall present themselves to my view; and so likewise as to the hearing and other senses, the ideas imprinted on them are not creatures of my will. There is therefore some other will or spirit that produces them.'[110]

In place of the materialist world of objects, Berkeley had generated a philosophical phantasmagoria, filled with unknowable spirits. The human being was, in effect, the ghostly presence at the heart of all existence, shaping it in accordance with its will and responding to the will of other sentient, active spirits. The external world became an illusion, a conceit of the mind. And this extravagant reduction of the universe to the imagination, the will, and the understanding— to the mental exertions of the spirit—centralised the power of reason. In this, Berkeley subscribed to the methodology of deduction and the Enlightenment predicate of the ontological autonomy of the human being. It was in this sense a wholly enlightened register. It accepted the central Enlightenment premise that the human being was the basic unit of analysis, for Berkeley appeared to deny the knowable existence of anything else. It deduced from the assumption of human centrality an epistemological system that renarrated the external world as the product of our ideas. This was achieved by the exercise of the faculties of the mind: through the understanding, the imagination and the will.

Yet Berkeley was not done. To leave the system like this might be to reopen a door through which his stated enemies, the sceptics and freethinkers, might reenter, and as Berkeley averred, 'we are not for having any man turn sceptic'.[111] To defend his system it was necessary to show that within the phantasmagoria one spirit presided and made the system cohere. That spirit was divine.

Berkeley began alluding to this final deduction early in the *Principles*, preparing the reader for a defence of God, even as his text became increasingly reductive and apparently secular in its manner. As early as paragraph six he highlighted how the complexity and intricate beauty of the world suggested the existence of a higher, more powerful mind. 'Some truths there are so near and obvious to the mind', he asserted,

> that a man need only open his eyes to see them. Such I take this
> important one to be, to wit, that all the choir of heaven and furniture
> of the world, in a word all those bodies which compose the mighty
> frame of the world, have not any subsistence, without a mind, that
> their being is to be perceived and known; that consequently so long as
> they are not actually perceived by me, or do not exist in my mind or

that of any other created spirit, they must either have no existence at all, or else subsist in the mind of some eternal spirit.[112]

What here appeared as an option was soon stated with certainty, as when he depicted visible ideas—or our capacity to see things in advance of being accosted by them—as constituting 'the language whereby the governing spirit, on whom we depend informs us what tangible ideas he is about to imprint on us, in case we excite this or that motion in our own bodies.'[113]

Ultimately, just as the unwilled nature of many of our ideas argued for the existence of external spirits, so the complexity and benevolence of the world proposed the existence of a divine creative force. Towards the conclusion of the treatise, he placed the capstone on this philosophical construction:

> But if we attentively consider the constant regularity, order, and concatenation of natural things, the surprising magnificence, beauty, and perfection of the larger, and the exquisite contrivance of the smaller parts of the creation, together with the exact harmony and correspondence of the whole, but above all the never enough admired laws or pain and pleasure, and the instincts or natural inclinations, appetites and passions of animals; I say if we consider all these things, and at the same time attend to the meaning and import of the attributes, one eternal, infinitely wise, good and perfect, we shall clearly perceive that they belong to the aforesaid spirit, who works all in all, and by whom all things consist.
>
> Hence it is evident that God is known as certainly and immediately as any other mind or spirit whatsoever, distinct from ourselves. We may even assert that the existence of God is far more evidently perceived than the existence of men; because the effects of nature are infinitely more numerous and considerable than those of human agents . . . We need only open our eyes to see the sovereign Lord of all things with a more full and clear view, than we do any of our fellow creatures.[114]

In effect, God exists to produce reality. He is the all-seeing eye; the great perceiver, and without his benevolent observance our world would come to an end.

What this revealed was how the whole of Berkeley's intellectual endeavour was directed to defending faith from within the Enlightenment's terrain. He used enlightened methods for a divine purpose, building his religious argument from the deductive tools of rationalism.[115] It was Berkeley's contention that if you assumed the human being was the primary unit of analysis, so long as you were true to the logic of the argument, the existence of God became a necessary conclusion. Those who denied such a truth were deceitful or imbued with philosophic pride.

It is for this reason that Berkeley rejected the sermon and the theological tract in favour of the essay form and the formal philosophical treatise. And it is why he targeted the freethinkers, deriding them as 'minute philosophers', unable to see the bigger, divine picture. Trapped by their perceptions of reality, they were incapable of seeing through the glass darkly and perceiving the enabling power that ordained and sustained the very existence they extolled as sufficient. God became, in Berkeley's hands, a necessary cause.

The Blasters and the Humanity of Christ

Berkeley's only recorded intervention in Parliament was in defence of the established confession. It was inspired by reports of a freethinking society in the city of Dublin. In March 1738, the Committees in Religion reported to the House of Lords

> that an uncommon scene of impiety and blasphemy appeared before
> them; that they have sufficient grounds to believe that several loose
> and disorderly persons have erected themselves into a Society or Club,
> under the name of Blasters, and have used means to draw into this
> society several of the youth of this kingdom; that what the practices of
> this society are (besides the general fame spread through the kingdom)
> appears by the examination of several persons taken upon oath in
> relation to Peter Lens, painter, lately come into this kingdom, who
> professes himself a Blaster. By these examinations it appears that Peter
> Lens professes himself to be a votary of the devil; that he hath
> offered up prayers to him, and publicly drank to the devil's health;
> that he hath at several times uttered the most daring and execrable
> blasphemies against the sacred name and majesty of God; and often
> made use of such obscene, blasphemous, and before unheard-of
> expressions, such as the Lords Committees think they cannot even
> mention to your Lordships.[116]

The Blasters reappeared as a concern in Berkeley's *Discourse addressed to Magistrates and Men in Authority occasioned by the Enormous Licence and Irreligion of the Times* (1738), wherein he described them as an 'execrable fraternity of blasphemers, lately set up within this city of Dublin'.[117] Indeed, according to the bishop of Cloyne, the society was not merely guilty of simple blasphemy, nor 'simple cursing or swearing: it is not the effect of habit or surprise; but a train of studied, deliberate indignities against the divine majesty; and those of so black and hellish a kind as the tongues alone which uttered them can duly characterise and express. This is no speculative heresy, no remote or doubtful inference from an author's tenets. It is a direct and open attack on God himself.'[118]

Yet despite the novelty of their extreme articulation of heresy Berkeley interpreted the Blasters' presence as the virulent product of a wider moral decay. At the heart of his diagnosis lay the view that 'men's actions are an effect of their principles' and that the 'licentious habits of youth give a cast or turn to age: the young rake makes an old infidel; libertine practices beget libertine opinions; and a vicious life generally ends in an old age of prejudice not to be conquered by reasoning'.[119] The Blasters indicated a malaise in the moral health of the community, being a specific symptom of a more generally rooted disorder.

Linking the heterodoxy and heresies of the freethinkers with the potential for collapse in the authority of the state as much as the Anglican confession itself, he opined, 'It is manifest that no prince on earth can hope to govern well, or even to live easy and secure, much less respected by his people, if he do not contribute by his example and authority to keep up in their minds an awful sense of religion . . . Religion is the centre which unites, and the cement which connects the several parts or members of the political body.'[120] This was why he addressed his *Discourse* to those 'magistrates and men in authority' who were responsible not just the established Church of Ireland but the civil order of the state. Yet it was paradoxical that those in authority, to whom the society would normally look to in times of trial, were most prone to the disease of licentiousness. This was a peculiarly dangerous circumstance, for

> if men of rank and power, who have a share in distributing justice,
> and a voice in public councils, shall be observed to neglect divine
> worship themselves, it must needs be a great temptation for others to
> do the same . . . Fashions are always observed to descend, and people
> are generally fond of being in the fashion; whence one must would be

apt to suspect the prevailing contempt of God's word, and estrangement from his house, to a degree that was never known in any
Christian country, must take its rise from the irreligion and bad
example of those who are styled 'the better sort'.[121]

The idea of religious belief as a fashion, open to trends and shifts in taste, might initially seem disconcerting and subversive. Yet, in suggesting it, Berkeley was enabling a second thesis; one that would defend the establishment from the very critics who saw the church as depending on unexplained and self-interested authority. The argument required a prior assumption, however. It had to be recognised that people were oftentimes unable to spend the time, or merely did not have the intellectual ability, to divine the speculations upon which religion rested.[122] What these people relied on instead were the basic principles of their education and the early ideas which first informed their development. In this, Berkeley was contending that most people acted on prejudices, a term he defined as 'notions or opinions which the mind entertains without knowing the grounds and reasons of them, and which are assented to without examination.'[123] This open definition allowed for both good and bad prejudices:

> It may not be amiss to inculcate that the difference between preju-
> dices and other opinions does not consist in this—that the former are
> false and the latter true; but in this—that the former are taken upon
> trust, and the latter acquired by reasoning. He who hath been taught
> to believe the immortality of the soul may be as right in his notion as
> he who hath reasoned himself into that opinion. It will then by no
> means follow that because this or that notion is a prejudice, it must be
> therefore false. The not distinguishing between prejudices and errors
> is a prevailing oversight among our modern freethinkers.[124]

In redefining prejudice in this way, Berkeley was freeing the church from the criticism that it promulgated ideas without explaining their origin and grounds. However, if actions depended on opinions, as he asserted, the importance of 'a proper education' in maintaining the virtue of the population could not be understated. So too, the threat posed to the state by the misjudged demands of freethinkers made the society vulnerable to vice, villainy, and violence. For Berkeley, 'if you strip men of these, their notions, or, if you will, prejudices, with regard to modesty, decency, justice, charity and the like, you will soon find them so many monsters, utterly unfit for human society.'[125] The choice was therefore between 'the savage state of undisciplined men, whose minds are nurtured to no doctrine, broke by no instruction, governed by no principle' and 'a society of persons educated in the principles of our church, formed betimes to fear God, to reverence their superiors, to be grateful to their benefactors, forgiving to their enemies, just and charitable to all men.'[126] In the careful formation of the children of the age lay the future sanctity of the church-state relationship, and the security of the confession.

Certainly the energy of Berkeley's prose gained greatly from his fear that the freethinkers posed an internal threat to Anglicanism as coherent and dangerous as Jacobitism posed to the political order. However, Berkeley did not have to look to cabalistic rituals of secret societies or to the idiosyncrasies of enthusiasts to perceive heterodoxy undermining the confessional stance of the Church of Ireland. His close friend of the late 1720s, Robert Clayton, was to declare himself to be a freethinker in the 1750s.[127] Clayton had held the lieutenancy in the Bermuda Project to Berkeley's generalship, and had been translated in 1745 to Clogher, considered the second best bishopric in Ireland.[128] Indeed, his early career as an Irish cleric, in the sees of Killala and Cork and Ross, was remarkable only for his successful use of marital connections in hurrying his rise.[129] His cultural endeavours, which included historical and scientific investigations, were of a piece with the empirical register adopted by the bulk of the church, and saw Clayton nominated to fellowships in the Royal Society and the Society of Antiquaries.[130] Yet he had, by the 1730s, come to embrace the Arian heresy, which Thomas Emlyn had earlier espoused, that denied the divinity of Christ.[131] And in 1750, he issued the text that declared his intellectual apostasy: *An Essay on Spirit*.[132]

Daringly, Clayton dedicated it to the Primate of All Ireland and archbishop of Armagh, George Stone, guaranteeing that its contents would provoke notice and controversy. Moreover, the dedicatory preface openly proclaimed the heterodoxy of the author. As Clayton recalled, 'Before I could be admitted [to religious office], I was obliged to subscribe the four first canons, which include my assent to the Articles of our religion, and also to declare publicly my unfeigned assent and consent to all and everything contained in *The Book of Common Prayer*. And, as I have not been so much employed about my temporal affairs, but that I have found leisure to apply some time to my books and to think as well as read; I find that I do not now agree exactly in sentiment either with my former opinions, or with those persons who drew up the Articles of our religion, or with the compliers of our liturgy, and in particular, with the Athanasian creed.'[133]

In admitting this, Clayton mimicked Berkeley's rhetorical strategy in confronting heresy in the 1730s. Just as Berkeley had neutralised criticism of church authorities by redefining prejudice, so Clayton in the preface redefined the concept of 'heresy' in such a way as to make it acceptable, even virtuous. He treated it, but as a public fault not a private feeling, being a wilful perseverance in the unrestricted articulation of a condemned opinion. Clayton defended the right to individual conscience, and to personal disagreement with the stated dogmas of the national church. In each nation the established church took on a different hue and colour, so much so indeed that 'a person may be esteemed as very orthodox in England or Ireland who would be deemed a heretic at Rome or in other countries'.[134] Equally, historical changes might account for a redefinition of orthodoxy, so that, for example, Christianity itself might move from being a heretical religious trend within the Roman Empire to supplying the definition of orthodoxy. In this, Clayton was at once domesticating and defusing heresy as a conceit, a process that culminated in a further redefinition: 'Since it appears that a man's being of a wrong opinion is not that which properly denominates him a *heretic*, but rather his being of a different opinion from the majority; one would be apt to wonder why that word, in general, should have so bad an idea annexed to it; but that the answer thereto is obvious, *viz.*, that it arises from our having too great a fondness for ourselves, and our own opinions; and too great an aversion to those who differ in opinion from us.'[135] The polemical effect of this when addressing an audience within the reformed Church of Ireland was clear: heresy lay at the origin of the faith. Yet the law was not accommodating to vagaries of view. 'Every person is liable to be punished by the laws of the land', Clayton admitted ruefully, 'who shall preach, declare, or speak to the derogation or depraving any Act of Parliament.'[136]

As though the preface was not provocative enough, the treatise to which it was attached laid out the grounds upon which Clayton chose to reject the consubstantiality of Christ with God. Or as he summarised the content: 'From the consideration of the nature of spirit, by the light of reason, it appears there can be but one God, that is, one supreme intelligent agent; which one God may however create an infinite series of spiritual agents, in subordination, one to another.'[137]

This vision of the supernatural edifice of the world was built upon two premises, from which he was to reason, through speculative reading and extensive, if
selective, citation of scripture that Christ was a special envoy from God designated with the task of saving mankind from themselves. The first assumption
was that there existed throughout all of God's creation a natural hierarchy of
existence.[138] Just as human beings enjoyed dominion over the unthinking world
of brute matter and the instinctual world of the animals, so there existed a
higher order of beings exercising authority over mankind.

Clayton's view of the nature of this higher order, and of God himself,
depended upon his second presumption. This was that the world could be
divided into two distinct categories of existence, namely, 'of a thinking, active,
powerful existence; and a dull heavy, inactive existence. One of which, to wit,
the active, we will for distinction sake, without entering into any further metaphysical disputes about words, call the spiritual existence, subsistence or substance; and the other, *viz.* the inactive, we will call the material or bodily existence; and sometimes for brevity's sake, we will call one spirit and the other
matter or body.'[139] Just as mankind had a more spiritual existence, and was freer
from the material aspect of their lives than were the animals, thus Clayton speculated that there must exist creatures so ethereal in nature as to be almost always
imperceptible to humans. Mankind's limited sensory ability was simply incapable of attending to their presence: 'Hence it is that human beings may be
surrounded with myriads of spiritual agents without ever being sensible thereof;
unless those superior beings are pleased to condescend to furnish themselves
with such qualifications as are capable of making an impression on the human
spirit from within, or the human senses from without.'[140] These creatures
Clayton identified as the angels spoken of in the Bible, whose spiritual aspect
was only surpassed by the deity, the nature of which Clayton described as purely
spiritual and wholly self-creating. And while God was the final source of
authority, it was designated that the angels would have a realm akin to that of
human kings. Each of the many peoples of the past had their guardian angel, the
most significant of whom watched over the people of Israel. This was the angel
known as Jehovah by the Jews, who was made manifest in the person of Jesus,
taking on material form to do the will of God.

This ontology, dependent on and a completion of a cosmology of the material and spiritual worlds, placed Christ in a dependent relationship with God.
Rather than understanding Jesus as a manifestation of God and hence as sharing

his nature and substance, he was imagined as an envoy doing the bidding of God; at once more spiritual in kind than man and more material than the divine power. Jesus became, as Clayton termed it, 'a secondary essence': 'And as that secondary essence was by the Jews called the Image of God, so is the Lord Jesus Christ called in the language of the New Testament "The image of the invisible God": that is the visible image, or delegated representative in power of the invisible God.'[141]

To sustain this analysis of Christ's distance from God—in contradiction of the Trinitarians who asserted their consubstantial nature—Clayton replicated the Scholastic method of the theologians, constructing his narrative by integrating and juxtaposing scriptural quotations to subvert the orthodoxy he denied. For example, he could quote and cite the Gospel of St John in arguing that Jesus

> acknowledges in numberless places that it was the Father who sent
> him, and gave him a commandment what to do. 'For, says he, I must
> work the work of Him that sent me'; and again he says, 'The Father
> which sent me gave me a commandment, what should I say, and what
> I should speak'. And again, 'As the Father gave me commandment, so
> do I'. We may therefore fairly argue, as our saviour himself does upon
> another occasion, that 'as the servant is not equal to his Lord, neither is
> he that is sent equal to him that sent him'. He therefore also acknowl-
> edged, that all the power he was possessed of, not only natural but
> supernatural, was received from the father, and was 'given unto him'.[142]

Through this mocking mimicry of the scripturalism of the clerics he opposed Clayton built a multifaceted and deeply heterodox theology. In his later *Vindication of the Histories of the Old and New Testaments* (1752/1757), he explained how in reading the scriptures it was necessary to treat 'the Hebrew language, as most of the oriental languages are, as being more figurative, bold and elevated in its style, than those of the Western climates; and not to be tied down in its interpretation to the severer rules of modern criticism.'[143] The Bible might be safely treated as at times allegorical, symbolic, or poetic. Thus, 'although the title of God is in the language of scriptures given to men and angels, and in particular to the Messiah or Christ the son of God . . . this must nevertheless be understood to be in subordination to that supreme God, who is our God and their God, and his God.'[144]

Clayton had in sight a specific pragmatic end: the redefinition of the Anglican confession to accommodate his tender conscience. As the preface had already made plain, the *Essay on Spirit* was motivated by a desire to remove the Nicene and Athanasian creeds as fundamental tests of orthodoxy, given their espousal of the doctrine of consubstantiality of Christ with God. In protesting against the fashion in which 'this metaphysical dispute should be made a part of the public service of the church, which is an assembly composed not only of quick-sighted philosophers, but of the lowest of the people', he 'expect[ed] some of the right reverend members of the Protestant Church of Ireland, either to account for this, or to exonerate their consciences, by joining in a humble remonstrance against it.'[145] Yet, Clayton was dissatisfied by the response to his book, a copy of which he had sent to each of the Irish episcopacy and a number of prominent politicians. Given their apparent apathy towards his reforming tract, he decided to forward his unusual views in the most prominent venue available to him: the House of Lords.

On 2 February 1756 Clayton proposed a bill of his own devising, offering amendments to the Act for the Uniformity of Public Prayers, passed under Charles II and altered under James II. Clayton envisioned one inclusion and two deletions, and each of these followed as a consequence of the other. At the foundation of his proposal lay a precise distinction: 'As there is a wide distance between being certain of the truth and certain of the falsehood of some propositions' he concluded that 'it is no way inconsistent with the strictest honesty, for persons to give their consent, for peace and uniformity sake, to the use of some particular forms of worship, either in doctrine or discipline, though they may not thoroughly approve of the things themselves, and to try to get them amended.'[146]

The initial purpose of highlighting this public/private distinction was to target the Act for the Uniformity of Public Prayers for ignoring the difference between public acquiescence and private reservation. In the preamble to the act, as Clayton pointed out at some length, the ministers of the Church of Ireland were required merely to give their assent 'to the use of all things in' the Book of Common Prayer. However, in the oath itself assent expressed intellectual conformity, for consent was given 'to all and every thing prescribed in, and by the book entitled the Book of Common Prayer'.[147] Ecclesiastical ordering had given way to intellectual bullying.

It was a similar line of attack with which Clayton approached his next target, the Council of Nicaea, observing that 'I think we may safely say, it seems unreasonable, that we, at this distance of time, should be tied down to their determinations.'[148] The creed of faith with which the council was associated made the belief in the Trinity a matter of doctrine, and in raising questions about the creed's validity, he was consciously undermining the stature of that tenet. Once again intellectual freedom was his concern.

To Clayton, using the creed as a test of orthodoxy clearly overstepped the line between faith and freedom, by designating as integral to doctrine a dogma that could not be clearly ascertained from scripture. As he observed to the assembled House of Commons, the Nicene Creed was a man-made folly: 'as far as it differs from the Apostles creed, [it] is nothing else but the determination of a number of number of bishops in the fourth century.'[149]

In turning to the Athanasian Creed, which articulates belief in the Trinity and the Incarnation, Clayton utilised another line of assault, asserting that it was 'a known forgery'.[150] Yet, even if it were granted that it was a genuine document, Clayton still abhorred its presumption in determining doctrines without a clear derivation from the Bible: 'For as it searches and mines further into that which is not revealed, than even the Nicene creed does, it is so much the more faulty as a creed, which ought to contain nothing that is not plainly and clearly revealed in the scriptures.'[151] Once again, Clayton was levelling accusations of intellectual browbeating and of intruding into the necessarily private thoughts of the minister through the device of creedal formulations.

Clayton appealed to the Protestant desire to purify the church of Roman Catholic accumulations, and argued that by removing the two creeds from the Book of Common Prayer, as his bill proposed, the Anglicans might accommodate and encompass the Presbyterians. The rubric of the speech was undeniably suspicious. The attack on the creeds could hardly be read as anything other than an attack on Trinitarian Christianity. In leaving open for disputation and personal convincement a doctrine Anglicans saw as a cornerstone of their faith, Clayton was doing more than purifying the Church; he was altering its composition.

At the heart of Clayton's challenge lay a radically different vision of the nature of God. Unlike the fideism of Swift, the ordinary providence supported by King and Molyneux, or the special providence embedded in the occasionalism of Berkeley, Clayton transgressed over the boundary of acceptable speculation on divinity within the Anglican confession. In propounding his Arianism, he implicitly questioned the veracity of the church settlement derived from the War of the

Two Kings. Indeed, he explicitly treated religious differences of opinion as on a par with natural inequalities of strength or intellect:

> If it pleases the Almighty to endow one man with a better under-
> standing, or greater natural abilities of any kind, than his neighbour, to
> appoint the place of his birth, where he has better opportunities of
> being informed in true religion, or to produce him from such parents as
> will take care that he is better educated in the paths of virtue; these are
> blessings for which he ought to be thankful to his Creator; but are far
> from being any reason why he should bear an ill will to those persons
> who have not received the same advantages from providence; or why he
> should not live in a kind and neighbourly manner with them, though
> he thinks them in an error with regard to their religious principles.[152]

This implied that the treatment of the Roman Catholic population by an anxious Anglican community was as illegitimate as its mistreatment of those within
its faith that queried the fundamental tenets upon which its claim to authority
and righteousness rested.[153]

That Clayton's theories about the nature of Christ were deeply unorthodox was
clear. However, he had carefully kept his name from the title page of the *Essay on
Spirit* and cautiously kept his argument about the creeds distinct from a statement
of personal opinion.[154] Rather he treated Christ's consubstantiality with God as 'a
metaphysical point of theology not fully revealed, not plainly revealed in the scriptures'.[155] But when Clayton published the third part of his system, *A Vindication
of the Histories of the Old and New Testament*, in 1757, in which he defended 'the
scriptural account of the fall', he boldly placed his name on the cover.[156]

The text once again rehearsed the theology outlined in the *Essay on Spirit*,
arguing for the hierarchy of existence, the existence of guardian angels, and the
identification of Christ with the Archangel Michael who, while 'the ruling or
guardian or archangel of Daniel and the Children of Israel', was a being inferior
to God himself.[157] As a consequence, the Old and New Testaments became the
tale of Michael's confrontation with the evil archangel, Satan, and the salvation
of man through his sacrifice in compromising his angelic nature and suffering
the lesser nature of man by becoming Jesus Christ.

As a consequence of placing his name of the title page Clayton was attacked in
pamphlets and threatened with legal removal from office for heresy, something
he had clearly envisaged.[158] He told the unidentified noble lord to whom the

seven letters composing the text were addressed that 'in answer to your query, whether I am not afraid of being branded with the odious name of heretick, for talking so freely about mysteries, and the Athanasian doctrine of the Trinity? I will truly and honestly answer that I am not, it is a term of reproach, who designing men, who have no other merit but their reputed orthodoxy, are fond of giving to those whom they would have excluded out of the Church because thereby there would be more room made for themselves, and others as ignorant as them.'[159] Despite such bravura, it seems that the threat of legal punishment disheartened him greatly, although he died in February 1758, before the matter could be processed.

The Irish Anglican Enlightenment

The Anglican experience of Enlightenment was defined by the uneasy grasp the community had on its power. The origins of the Protestant state resided in the violence and expropriation of the late seventeenth century, raising questions concerning the legitimacy and sustainability of the revolutionary settlement in the country. But it also prompted queries about the religious aspect of the church-state equation. How was it that God could permit such human suffering as that experienced on the battleground of the Boyne or Aughrim? Why was it that God had chosen to punish the Protestant people and yet save them at the final hour? What was the actual nature of this wilful, judgmental deity?

Robert Clayton's case suggests that well into the eighteenth century the Church of Ireland remained insecure about its political, social, and intellectual status in the country. At the heart of that insecurity rested a deep-seated sense that the survival of the church rested upon the continuing enjoyment of divine pleasure. Heterodoxy of the kind Clayton espoused threatened the special relationship between God and his chosen community. His sanction always loomed over the Anglican sense of supremacy, prompting explanations of the country's condition that emphasised their sanctity and reinforced the need to renounce sin and subdue heresy.

Certainly some Anglicans chose, like Swift, to rest their hopes in an unfathomable God, and rely on the dictates of scholastic authority. Many others turned to the Enlightenment methodology of empirical investigation to ascertain how God's will legitimised their power, couching their arguments in de facto terms, not in the language of not de jure certainties. The hold on power was too recent, too unstable, too weak, and too clearly founded on the expropriation of land and the usurpation of office to be founded on principles of conscience. What was required was not the citation of authority, which had to be distorted and editorialised were it to be fashioned satisfactorily, but a language forged from the methods of empirical examination of the world as currently constituted. This was the tactic of King, Molesworth, and Molyneux who each provided a close examination of the state of nations to provide justification for political and confessional dominance. This empiricism, with its pragmatic bent, was the most common stance of educated Anglicans, wary to pry too deeply into the origins of their political privilege.

Some others applied deductive rationalism as a means of finding comfort in, and assurance about, the continuing favour of God. Latitudinarians such as Synge drew on rationalist methods to defend Anglican orthodoxy from the perceived dangers of speculative heterodoxy. Berkeley mobilised an idiosyncratic rationalism to negate the threat he perceived free thought posed to the established church. Only a few reached out like Clayton to the speculative extremes of heterodoxy, reimagining the religious settlement as a consequence.

One reason why the fear of free thought intruded so deeply into Anglican minds was their numerical weakness in the religious demography of the country. Internal backsliding was capable of inflicting serious psychological damage. Just as converts from Catholicism to Anglicanism were publicly lauded, and parochially cherished, so any dissidence caused private consternation and personal shame.[160] Freethinkers were however, despite their prominence, in a distinct minority among the Anglican population, and the real threat lay beyond the confines of the Anglican community, in the throng of Catholic adherents. In the first third of the century, the dominant Protestant nightmare was of Catholic renewal.

Roman Catholicism may have been militarily defeated in the War of the Two Kings, but the numerical predominance of adherents to the faith was to affect every aspect of life in the realm. Protestants employed many domestic servants, while even the heartland of Anglicanism, the capital city of Dublin, had by midcentury a Catholic majority within the city walls. Yet, what Irish Anglicans were slow to recognise was that Catholicism too was changing. The political, social, and economic fallout from the War of the Two Kings had left many Catholics questioning the nature of their circumstance. And in so doing they too turned to Enlightenment methods to explain their condition.

3

The Catholic Enlightenment
and the Nature of Law

∽

Many gentlemen, who formerly made a considerable figure in the kingdom are now a days, when they walk with canes and sticks only in their hands, insulted by men armed with swords and pistols, who of late rose from the very dregs of the people.
—Cornelius Nary, *The Case of the Roman Catholics of Ireland*, 1724

As was the case for the Anglicans, the overarching context of the intellectual life of the Catholic community in the early eighteenth century was the War of the Two Kings (1688–1691). In contrast to the Anglican community, the consequence of the conflict was an immense psychological pressure caused by military defeat and cultural repression. Defeat traumatised the intellectual and spiritual leadership, as much as it displaced social and political authorities. The response, paradoxically, was to fall back on traditional verities. The poets developed a trope of restoration, imagining a reversal of the Williamite settlement and the renewal of a Jacobite regime. The priests retained their loyalty to forms of Scholastic philosophy, heightened by their commitment to papal authority. Both forms of cultural leadership were shaped by a desire to retain the foundational assumptions of the Catholic confession. Intellectually, the Irish Catholic community therefore remained largely committed to the Scholastic method. The Enlightenment was attractive to only a few thinkers who reimagined the Catholic condition by using empirical methods to seek an accommodation with their Anglican rulers, or availing of rationalist approaches to knowledge to explain God's distance from his earthly community of believers. Speculative freethinking was deeply unusual, with only idiosyncratic figures dabbling in the possibilities such an approach provided.

The prognosis for Irish Catholicism had not been so gloomy in 1685, when the coreligionist James II succeeded to the thrones of England, Scotland, and Ireland. Indeed, the accession ushered in a brief high noon of political influence, culminating in the Jacobite parliament held in Dublin in 1690. On 24 March 1690, a day after he arrived in Dublin, the monarch called for the assembly to convene on 7 May.[1] The elections resulted in only six Protestant members being returned, including two for the University of Dublin, among an assembly of 230 notables. Five lay Protestant peers also apparently took their seats, alongside four Church of Ireland bishops, one of whom, Anthony Dopping of Meath, became a vocal opponent of the administration's measures. These were to include a twin-track assault on James's enemies, namely the retrieval of land lost as a consequence of the Restoration in 1660, and the attainder of those who had joined William in the current conflict. The first of these generated opposition, not only amongst the Protestants but also within the 'new Catholic interest' that had made land purchases since 1660. Compromise was reached and efforts were started to renew the pre-1641 pattern of landholding. The recent proprietors were to be compensated with land forfeited by Williamite supporters. These included 2,000 individuals named in the Act of Attainder, including 1,340 sentenced to death for high treason if they did not surrender to Jacobite justice by 10 August. The legislation also limited James's power to exercise leniency, stating that royal pardon had to be achieved by 30 November 1689.

More constructively, the parliament made provision for James's financial requirements, with the Commons earmarking specific expenditure for the army, although collection became increasingly problematic as the war turned sour. Even less popular in the countryside than the new imposition was the introduction of the 'brass money': minted coins made of a bewildering variety of metals and nominal values. The value of these coins fluctuated with the tidal shifts in the fortunes of the regime that underwrote the experiment.

The real contention between James and his parliament arose with regard to the religious policy of his administration. Catholics were anxious to see their church reestablished, but James was profoundly wary of upsetting those English Protestants he hoped to convince of his legitimate status as monarch. The result was a kind of stasis whereby Anglican vacancies were not filled and the resources were diverted to support their Catholic counterparts. This inaction was coupled with a bill articulating the principle of liberty of conscience, and permitting the meeting of all Christian faiths whose activities did not threaten public order. While the Act of Uniformity remained untrammelled and James later made efforts to halt the spoiling of Protestant churches by his army, he attended Catholic Mass at Christ Church Cathedral, Dublin, recently reclaimed from the Church of Ireland.[2]

Yet the king's presence among the peers and commoners of the realm was indicative of a weakness as much as it was a symbol of the importance Irish Catholicism held for the monarch. After all, James was in the country as a result of his failure to ensure order in England.[3] This was driven home by the passage of an act declaring the English Parliament's inability to legislate for Ireland, although James deflected an attempted renunciation of Poynings's law.[4] The military debacle that followed in 1690–1691 underscored the interconnected nature of political power within the three kingdoms of the archipelago, and left the Catholic community of Ireland distraught.

In physical terms, the reverse at the Boyne in 1690 and the slaughter at Aughrim in 1691 prompted the removal of many active soldiers to the Continent.[5] The Articles of Limerick contained a stipulation whereby the Dutch Williamite general Ginkel would transport the remaining Jacobite forces to France. Upward of 12,000 availed of the opportunity, regrouping around James II's court-in-exile, which was initially located at St Germain-en-Laye under the protection of the French monarch, Louis XIV. These exiles joined a contingent of 5,000 soldiers who, as part of the Franco-Jacobite alliance, had sailed from Kinsale to Brest in 1690, filling three foreign regiments in the French army under Justin MacCarthy, Viscount Mountcashel. In 1698, prompted in part by the Peace of Ryswick the previous year, under the terms of which Louis XIV recognised the legitimacy of William of Orange, the Jacobite army were co-opted into the French army proper. Yet they maintained a distinctive Irish regimental character and leadership. Numbering 5,600 individuals, these eight infantry regiments were flanked by two squadrons of cavalry. This structure persisted until the 1715 general reform of the French military structure, when the infantry regiments were reduced to five.

Certainly, these regiments took in non-Irish soldiers; the 1729 troop inspection of the Rothe regiment suggested that Irishmen made up 55 percent of their total. But recruitment predominantly drew on the communities of north Munster and south Leinster, a core region for the production of Irish-language poetry in the period. Up to half the Irish-language poets active between 1690 and

1760 resided in the region.[6] Despite the entrenched nature of Jacobite sympathies within the Catholic population, squabbles within the Stuart court prevented the option of an Irish invasion ever progressing beyond the planning stage. Instead, Scottish advisors remained in the ascendant, so that in both 1715 and 1745 it was there Jacobite forces first made landfall.[7] In both years, the Irish political scene remained peaceful. Indeed Lord Chesterfield, the lord lieutenant at the time of the 1745 Rebellion in Scotland, was so phlegmatic about the matter that he resisted pressure to harass the Catholic population, apparently remarking that the only dangerous papist of his acquaintance was the noted beauty Miss Ambrose.[8]

Even if the hoped-for invasion never materialised, exile at the Jacobite court offered an escape from the experience of degradation and poverty in the home-land. For those who remained in Ireland, the military defeat ensured a sense of internal exile. This found expression in the vivid verse of the Irish-language poets. One such was Seán Clárach Mac Domhnaill, a farmer and teacher from County Cork, whose poetry combined a sense of abandonment with one of persecution. In a portrayal of the lacerating poverty experienced by Jacobite loyalists he condemned the traitors to the cause, and offered only a modicum of hope that the Stuart line might yet be restored:

Atá mo chóraid gan fuithin
Is mo chuingir gan fear gan fás
Atá anshógh ar mo mhuirear
Is a n-uilinn gan éadach slán;
Atá an tóir ar mo mhullach
Go minic ó thiarna an stáit
Atá mo bhróga-sa briste
Is gan pinginn dá bhfiacha im láimh[9]

Since the Royal buck quitted the field, I'm lett [sic] alone,
And my countrymen left without pleasure or sport to moan:
For the wolves unrelenting soon drove him from house and home
And the timorous fugitive through foreign lands did roam
My kin shelterless on the blake [sic.] hill in winter lie,
My charges naked with badges of real poverty;
My tyrannical landlord is frequently driving me
And tho' I'm ill-shod, a new pair of shoes I cannot buy.
In the fatal field many brave heroes welt'ring lay
And some disloyal men from the Boyne basely ran away:

> By good fortune our hero may come once more and free
> The true Milesians from the sad yoke of slavery.[10]

For Dáibhí Ó Bruadair, a prolific poet based in County Limerick, who died in 1698, defeat presaged an age of barbarism and degradation, an epoch in which learning, scholarship, and erudition were despised and denigrated. In a bitter disavowal of his contemporaries he declared:

> Mairg nach fuil 'na dhubhthuata,
> Gé holc 'na thuata,
> I ndóigh go mbeinn mágcuarda
> Idir na daoinibh duarca
>
> Mairg nach fuil 'na thrudaire
> Eadraibhse, a dhaoine maithe,
> Ós iad is fearr chugaibhse,
> A dhream gan iúl gan aithne.
>
> O it's best to be a total boor
> (though it's bad to be a boor at all)
> if I'm to go out and about
> among these stupid people
>
> It's best to be, good people,
> A stutterer among you
> Since that is what you want,
> You blind ignorant crew.[11]

So too, in the case of Aogán Ó Rathaille, from County Kerry, the desolation of the period evoked in his poetry a lament of profound emotional purchase.[12] He characteristically expanded his vision away from the personal, offering a panoramic diagnosis of the crisis.[13] He painted a landscape of startling decay, sapped of its nutrient, and starved of replenishment.

> Monuar-sa an Chárrth-fhuil tráighte, tréith-lag
> Gan rígh ar am gcóip ná treorach tréan-mhear
> Gan fear cosnaimh ná eochair chum réit igh
> Is gan sciath dín ar thír na saor-fhlaith
>
> Tír gan triath de ghrian-fhuil Éibhir,
> Tír fá ansmacht Gall do traochadh,

Tír do doirteadh fá chosaibh na méirleach
Tír na ngaibhne—is treighid go héag liom.

Woe is me! Weak and exhausted is the race of Carthach [McCarthy], without a prince over the hosts, or a strong nimble leader, without a man to defend, without a key to liberate; without a shield of protection for the land of noble chieftains.

A land without a prince of the sun-bright race of Eibhear, a land made helpless beneath the oppression of the stranger; and a land poured out beneath the feet of the miscreants; a land of fetters—it is sickness to me unto death.[14]

Laid waste by oppression, the 'tír'—the land, or country—provides the poem's rhythmic beat—repeating at the start of each line—bringing the audience back to the poet's central concern and continuously confronting them with their suffering, dynastic and domestic, spiritual and secular, moral and material:

Tír gan eaglais chneasta ná cléitigh,
Tír le mioscais, noch d'itheadar faolchoin,
Tír do cuireadh go tubaisteach, traochta
Fá smacht namhad is amhas is méirleach.

Tír gan tartha gan tairbhe i nÉirinn,
Tír gan turadh gan buinne gan réiltean,
Tír do nochtadh gan fothain gan géaga,
Tír do briseadh le fuirinn an Bhéarla.

A land without a meek church or clergy, a land which wolves have spitefully devoured; a land left placed in misfortune and subjection beneath the tyranny of enemies and mercenaries and robbers.

A land without produce or thing of worth of any kind; a land without dry weather, without a stream, without a star; a land stripped naked, without shelter or boughs; a land broken down by the English prating band.[15]

Note the equation of English oppression and the decline of the Catholic Church, creating an imbalanced binary opposition that fused religious and ethnic conflict.

Yet despite its political misfortune, Catholicism remained the expression of scriptural truth recognised by the bulk of the populace. Those who lived in Ireland remained aware that, unlike other confessional states, the established faith was not that professed by the majority of the people. This truth, repeatedly underscored by the demographic plumb lines sent down by Anglican clergy to measure the depth of the religious sympathy they elicited, confronted the Catholic connection in the country with a profoundly unsettling series of intellectual, as well as political, challenges.[16] In particular, the question of loyalty, to faith and to king, was scrutinised closely in that environment. The competing claims of the Stuart and Hanoverian lines forced Catholics to articulate their sense of righteous rule. As Donnchadh Caoch Ó Mathúna expressed it, the dilemma was that 'Ós ceart a cheart ina ceart go dtaga go luath'—'since his right [claim] is right [lawful], to his right [entitlement, patrimony] may he come soon'.[17] And in this articulation, some, if by no means all, turned to the enlightened assumption that the human being is the starting point of philosophical analysis, and to the methods of empiricism and rationalism, in composing their response. These thinkers turned to the Enlightenment to help address a profound question concerning the legitimacy of the Catholic confession and the dictates of the law, be it spiritual and natural or secular and positive; a challenge encapsulated by the presence of the penal code on the statute books of Ireland.

Penal Purgatory

Given the overwhelmingly Catholic adherence of the Irish population, the Anglican community had to determine how they would treat their obstinate subjects. At the heart of the answers they supplied lay a persistent fear of Catholic renewal. The initial response of the Anglican elite was to assert the confessional nature of the state. This they did through the institution of parliament, in the drafting and passage of acts intended to hinder the practice of the Catholic faith and undermine the residual foundations of its political power.[18] Partly informed by a need to overcome the latitude granted under the Treaty of Limerick, to which the parliament had not been party, the penal code was as much about exercising political autonomy in the face of English interference as it was about keeping the Catholic power bloc safely neutered.[19] From 1695 until 1715, the

Irish parliament passed at least one penal measure in every session. So frequent were the demands for anti-Catholic action, and so determined was the House the Commons on seeing its safe passage into the statue book, that the Dublin administration and English Privy Council quickly realised the penal code's worth as a bargaining chip in the convoluted negotiations surrounding the granting of financial support for the state.[20] The penal code was largely granted in exchange for the continuation of taxes and the funding of the pension list. That the deal in each case was for a two-year supply ensured the penal code's continuing expansion: the consistent turning of the tourniquet blocking the lifeblood of Catholic cultural and political life.

Despite the intricate nature of the penal code's origins, the intent of the collective body of legislation was clear: to humiliate the Catholic community, to effect their social degradation, and to humble their leadership in the eyes of their confreres. Within that remit, the laws identified four distinct targets: Jacobite power; the institution of the Catholic Church; landed Catholics; and Catholics in the professions. In its enactment the code assumed a connection between Catholicism and Jacobitism and, instead of trying to break it, attacked the first as a signifier of the second. At the dark heart of the two great compendia of penal legislation, the 1704 Act to Prevent the Further Growth of Popery and the parasitic 1709 Act to explain and amend an Act entitled An Act to Prevent the Further Growth of Popery, resided then, not the Jacobite supporter, but the monstrous 'papist'. The aim was to negate the visceral, primitive urges the figure presented to the Protestant imaginary.

Throughout the 1704 act, Roman Catholicism was occluded by its knavish counterpart, popery, offering a rhetorical concentration on the political connotations of the faith: a subservience to hierarchy and a belief in the pope's capacity to sanction the slaughter of heretical sovereigns, known as his deposing power. In its central measures, moreover, the act articulated the intersection of Catholic social and political power. It legislated in suffocating detail for the management of landholding, making it illegal for Catholics to inherit property or to hold anything more than a tenancy of thirty-one years' duration. It further discriminated against Catholics by reinforcing a ban on the foreign education of children, first introduced in 1695. And it deployed the oath of abjuration that rejected the claims of the Jacobite line to the throne as a qualification for office holding, and for exercising the franchise.

Indeed, the penal code repeatedly made recourse to oath taking as a means of demarcating those willing to accept the established faith from its antagonists. The oath of supremacy and the oath of abjuration became central criteria for identifying the membership of the confession. At stake was a willingness by the oath takers to make a public declaration of their faith, bearing witness to their acceptance of doctrinal norms. Akin to the Presbyterian reliance on subscription to the Westminster Confession of Faith which antagonised John Abernethy, or the Anglican communion's continued adherence to the Athanasian and Nicene Creeds to which Robert Clayton took exception, here the penal code used an oath to determine the membership of a religious community.

The litany of measures in the 1704 act pursued two distinct, if dependent ambitions: overturning the Catholic social order and removing Roman Catholicism from the legal record. In line with the first desire, Article III determined, in a notorious clause, that 'in case the eldest son and heir of such popish parent shall be a Protestant, that then from the time of enrolment in the high court of chancery of a certificate of the bishop of the diocese, in which he shall inhabit, testifying to his being a Protestant, and conforming himself to the Church of Ireland as by law established, such popish parent shall become, and shall be, only tenant for life of all the real estate whereof such popish parent shall be then seized in fee tail or fee simple, and the reversion of fee shall be vested in such eldest son being a Protestant.'[21]

In line with the second ambition, legal guardianship of minors was limited to Protestants, even in the case of a child born Catholic. So too, wilful refusal to take the oaths as qualifiers for office, if coupled with a continuing exercise of the powers vested therein, led to the legal death of the miscreant, as Article XVIII specified: 'Every such person and persons shall be disabled from thenceforth to sue or use any action, bill, plaint, or information in course of law, or to prosecute in any suit in any court of equity, or to be guardian of any child, or executor or administrator of any person, or capable of any legacy or deed of gift, or to bear any office within this realm.'[22] A convert was defined in such a way as to allow a return from legal invisibility. Marking out the limits of the ban on the Catholic inheritance of land and property, for instance, Article VIII determined that 'if any papist or papists . . . shall after become Protestant and conform as aforesaid . . . such conforming person and his heirs shall be entitled as he would have been if he had been a Protestant'.[23] A similar limitation arose with regard to the practical application of the test clause, the use of which underscores the importance of oath taking in monitoring the public confession of faith. The act declared that

any person who by any neglect and refusal shall lose and forfeit any
office, may be capable of a new grant of the said office or of any other,
and have and hold the same again, such person taking the said oaths
and subscribing the same, and the said declaration, in such manner as
aforesaid, and producing such certificate as aforesaid, and proving the
same at the time of taking the said oaths as aforesaid, of his having
received the sacrament according to the usage of the Church of
Ireland within three months then last past.[24]

Throughout these articles the intrusion of administrative formulae, the constant need to cross-reference the act with other measures, the recognition of exceptions, and the means to alleviate the law they introduced, inoculated the act of much of its confessional cadence. Details overwhelmed desires and normalised the language of the penal enactments. Yet the bill was framed by a set of articles that made plain the insecurities that prompted them. In the very first article of the act, legislating against Catholic missionary work, converts from Anglicanism were described as subject to 'the extreme sickness and decay of their reason and senses'.[25] Only such degradation could account for a desire to become a Catholic. In the same article, Catholics were depicted as evincing a 'hatred and aversion to the said true religion', suggesting an inherently atavistic nature.[26] The 'cunning devices and contrivances' they used to avoid the penal laws informed their 'evil practices'.[27] The malevolence and otherworldly quality of the papist was further highlighted when the act drew attention to how 'many persons professing the popish religion have it in their power to raise a division among Protestants by voting in elections and also have it in their power to use other ways and means tending to the destruction of the Protestant interest in this kingdom.'[28] The peculiar echo of witchcraft that informs this passage contrasts with the banality of the use of 'elections' to ferment discord: pointing up the hyperbolic nature of the register being applied in formal legal prose. Such unnatural qualities were illuminated by the act's accusation that 'many of the said persons, so professing the popish religion on this kingdom, have refused to make provision for their own children, for no other reason but their being of the Protestant religion': an unnatural overthrowing of parental emotions which was given real motive in the measure to reduce the father of a convert to the status of a tenant.[29]

At the close of the act, the language dissolved into an effusion of accusatory vitriol, this time sparked not by the threat of the supernatural papist, but by the throng of the popish mob. Article XXVI warned of how 'the superstitions of Popery are greatly increased and upheld by the pretended sanctity of places, especially of a place called St Patrick's Purgatory in the county of Donegal, and of wells to which pilgrimages are made by vast numbers at certain seasons; by which not only the peace of the public is greatly disturbed, but the safety of the government greatly hazarded by the riotous and unlawful assembling together of many thousands of papists.'[30] These 'superstitious, dangerous and unlawful assemblies' were outlawed, and those who gathered subjected to a ten-shilling fine, a punishment raised to being 'publicly whipped' if defaulted on.[31] Here the fear of public violence was countered by the incorporation of just such an event into the law of the polity.[32]

Similarly ironic implications characterised the 1709 act, which closed a series of loopholes inside previous penal legislation. For example, in restating the demand for the registration of Catholic priests, first enacted in 1704, the 1709 bill gave legal sanction to the very faith it was endeavouring to extinguish. Indeed, restating the terms of registration suggested that the 1704 act had failed: the penal code was inscribing on itself its own failures, advertising its ineffectiveness and highlighting its disjuncture with reality. Similarly, raising the stipend a convert priest might demand of his community, from the £20 first legislated for in the same 1704 Act for Registering the Popish Clergy, to £30, stipulated in Article XVIII, indicated how such figures were special cases within the ranks of the Anglican clergy. It was their origin among the Catholic seculars that now determined their income, and not the role they played within the established church. The final clause, which proposed the payment be made 'until he or they are otherwise provided for by some ecclesiastical benefice or curacy of the like or greater value', recognised that many Anglican clerics were eking out a living on a more meagre sum.[33] But their income was not to be enhanced; hence the act created a subset of enriched clerics whose financial comfort entirely depended on their recusant past. So too, the seven-year limitation on the taking up of this offer suggested that there was a realisation among the parliamentarians that the conversion of the Catholic clerics might not be a swift accomplishment. So it proved, with a mere 105 Catholic priests being recorded as having changed their confessional allegiance on the Convert Rolls.[34]

The cumulative effect and rhetorical integrity of the penal code makes it appear more coherent in intent then it was in application.[35] In many ways it was expressive of an ungainly balance of interests; as a result it was often little more than a collection of desires and anxieties, neither of which had any strong relationship to the lived experience of the Catholic community. The evidence strongly suggests that its implementation was patchy and sporadic, and the intentions of the legislators may have been as much to enact a symbolic domination over their Catholic neighbours as it was to materially discommode them.[36] That is not to underestimate the psychological pressure which the code placed on Catholic adherents, rather it is to realise that that was its very purpose.[37] In writing into the statute book an understanding of Catholicism as superstitious, barbaric, and proximate to witchery, and by summoning the papist as a subject of legal paranoia, the Anglican community inscribed their victory into the very architecture of the state, thereby reminding the Catholics at every turn of their political defeat.

The only difficulty was that the Catholics seemed in large part to ignore this truth, and continued to practice both their faith and culture regardless of the inducements to conform offered by the penal code, and the energies expended to induct them into the imaginary of the Anglican world.[38] Catholicism continued to function as a faith community, and began slowly to repair its political fortunes. The Catholic clergy remained a prominent, if legally disabled, force, giving spiritual sustenance to their congregations. They grew in numbers from a low point in 1704 of about 1,100 to around 2,000 by midcentury.[39] Equally, the communities of North Munster and South Ulster sustained a culture of poetic endeavour and scholarship that articulated the sense of disorientation caused by the war, and projected the political and cultural hopes for renewal felt by the defeated.[40] The *fili* composed poetry and acted as receptacles for the wisdom of the community through their work as scribes.[41]

While both groups felt the stresses of the political defeat, through the withdrawal of many of their patrons and the debilitating presence of the penal code in the statute books, Gaelic Catholic Ireland remained curiously resilient, not only socially and culturally, but intellectually and spiritually. In the wake of the War of the Two Kings, and the resultant beheading of the social structure effected by the exile of the Jacobite soldiery, the *fili* and clerics led the remnant, despite the fracture lines within and between these groups.[42] The project of cultural conservation and protection on which *fili* and the clerics had embarked—saving the faith or saving the culture—was in many ways intellectually conservative, driven towards sustaining what was left rather than creating anew. Hence there was a tendency within both groups towards a continued assertion of scholasticism.

The Poetics of Scholasticism

In 'An Aisling', one of a series of vision-poems written by Aogán Ó Rathaille, his fairy maids

> 'fachain na dtrí gcoinnle do lasadh ar gach cuan,
> in ainm an rí dhíograis bheas again go luath
> I gceannas na dtrí ríochta, 's dá gcosnamh go buan'

> had cause to light three candles above the harbours:
> in the name of the faithful king who is soon to come
> to rule and defend the triple realm for ever.[43]

In a typical gesture towards the displacement articulated in these poems, this particular vision comes to the poet while out walking in the half-light before dawn. Yet the despondency induced by the barren landscape in Ó Rathaille's poem is replaced in the dream by an image of a natural cornucopia, cast in a golden glow by the early morning light:

> Fearastar scím dhraíochta nár dhorcha snua
> ó Ghaillimh na líog lí-gheal go Corcaigh na gcuan:
> barra gach crainn síorchuireas toradh agus cnuas,
> meas daire ar gach coil, fírmhil ar chlochaibh go buan.

> A film of enchantment spread, of aspect bright,
> From the shining boulders of Galway to Cork of the harbours:
> Clusters of fruit, appearing in every treetop,
> Acorns in woods, pure honey upon the stones.[44]

This description of this-worldly fecundity finds immediate echo in the encounter with otherworldly eroticism, personified by his informant, the Lady Aoibhill, described with the phrase 'nár dhorca snua' ('of aspect bright'); an encounter that leaves the poet sated and exhausted:

> As m'aisling do shlímbhíogas go hachomair suas
> Is do mheasas gurbh fhíor d'Aoibhill gach sonas dár luaigh;
> Is amhlaidh bhíos tímchreathach doilbhir duairc,
> Maidean sul smaoin Totan a chaos do luaill.

> I started up—soft, sudden—out of my dream
> Believing the good news Aoibhill told me was true

But found that I was nerve-shaken, downcast and morose
That morning 'ere Titan had thought to stir his feet.[45]

The poem is driven forward by an immense internal tension: the vision of political and economic hope is personified by Aoibhill, yet it is the satisfying of the
sexual desire she evinces in the poet that returns him to his actual, depressing
circumstance.

A similar polarity informs Ó Rathaille's masterpiece of the genre, 'Gile na Gile'
('Brightness most Bright'). Here the poet recounts a vision of the fairy world generated by lust for a beautiful woman encountered on his peripatetic travels:

> Gile na gile do chonnarc slí in uaigneas,
> Criostal an chriostail a goirmroisc rinn-uaine,
> Binneas an bhinnis a friotal nár chríonghruama,
> Deirge is finne do fionnadh 'na gríosghruannaibh.

> Brightness most bright, I beheld on the way, forlorn.
> Crystal of crystal her eye, blue touched with green
> Sweetness most sweet her voice, not stern with age
> Colour and pallor appeared in her flushed cheeks.[46]

This image of physical beauty is slowly transfigured, into something much less
certain, as Ó Rathaille recognises his maiden's ethereal nature:

> Caise na caise I gnach ribe dá buí-chuachaibh
> Bhaineas an cruinneac den rinneac le rnnscuabadh
> Iorra ba ghlaine ná gloine ar a broinn bhuacaigh,
> Do gineadh ar ghineamhain di-se san tír uachtraigh.

> Curling and curling, each strand of her yellow hair
> As it took the dew from the grass in its ample sweep
> A jewel more glittering than glass on her high bosom
> —created, when she was created, in a higher world.[47]

Her ambiguity is here introduced by referencing her power to take dew from the
grass, at once a symbol of her astonishing beauty, and a suggestion that her
appeal may be underscored by a dangerous capacity to expend the natural vigour
of the world. This blend of eroticism and danger is made apparent in the fourth
verse, where her beauty literally captures the poet. He tells of being 'bound
tightly, her prisoner' until he speaks the name of Christ, whereupon 'do bhíog

uaimse, / is d'imigh an bhruinneal 'na luisne go bruin Luachra ('she started from me / and vanished like light to the fairy dwelling of Luachair').[48] That the ambivalence of Ó Rathaille's attraction to the fairy woman is resolved by a religious invocation hints at the tension between popular and elite spiritual beliefs, for the fairy world had been officially exiled by the Catholic Reformation, yet remained an active quality within devotional life in Ireland throughout the eighteenth century.

The verse then becomes political, when the poet follows the woman to the ring fort, having traversed a liminal landscape redolent of the marginal land onto which the Catholic community had been displaced by their military enervation: 'trí imeallaibh corraigh, trí mhongaibh, trí shlímruaitigh' ('by the margins of marshes, through swamps, over bare moors').[49] The woman is here being mistreated by 'a gang of goblins' one of whom ''s mo bhruinneal ar broinnibh ag broinnire broinnstuacach' ('a lumbering brute took hold of my girl by the breasts').[50] The analogy is clarified when, at the culmination of this voyage into a fairy Hades, the rescuer has to remind the rescued of her duty:

D'iniseas di-se, san bhfriotal dob fhíor uaimse,
Nár chuibhne di snaidhmeadh le slibire slímbhuartha
's an duine da ghuile ar shloicht chine Scoit trí huaire
ag feitheamh ar ise bheith aige mar chaoin-nuachar

I said to her then, in words that were full of truth,
How improper it was to join with that drawn gaunt creature
When a man the most fine, thrice over, of Scottish blood
Was waiting to take her for her tender bride.[51]

That she responds to this admonition by weeping 'goileann go fíor-uaibhreach / is sileadh ag an bhfliche go life as a gríosghruanniabh' ('in high misery / and flowing tears fell down from her flushed cheeks') shows how far the country had fallen, in the poet's mind, under England's sway, giving itself over to harsh treatment and tolerating the rough manner and misshapen visage of the goblin/English.[52]

The structural tensions inside the *aisling* genre were produced by an ambiguity that informed their constituent nature. Just as it represents a generic development highlighting the vibrant quality of the tradition of Irish-language composition, it is a lament for the decay of that tradition, brought on by a change in the political and economic circumstances that supported its creation. The point of the *aisling* is to bemoan the collapse of the environment that is conducive to its existence, while simultaneously projecting an imaginative deliverance. That the deliverance is cast in the mode of a vision echoes the traditional status of the poet as a Gaelic shaman, a keeper of knowledge, while it identifies the ethereal, intangible quality of the hope it tries to provide.[53] The *aisling* is at once a haven of hope and a reflection of present paralysis.

More prosaically, this poetry was imbued with an elegiac yearning for the return of the Stuart line. At a stylistic level, the *aisling*, or 'vision', was indicative of a trend away from formal, highly intricate verse structures, intended to display the skills of the composer, to a less complex, more rhythmic sentence structure that could be set to music. This shift was commensurate with a downward trajectory in the social status of the imagined audience, away from the great house and into the farmland beyond, which combined with a second trend also found in the *aisling*. The poetry moved away from the parochial celebration of particular families towards a wider communal vision of the polity: the poet no longer spoke of the caste or the clan, but spoke increasingly of the people and the kingdom.[54]

This change was intrinsic to the *aisling* in its articulation of Jacobite sympathy, and in providing it with a futurity that offered hope to the poet and his audience, despite the collapse of their cause. Born near Killarney around 1675, Ó Rathaille was acutely aware of the collapse of social order induced by the War of the Two Kings. His family was relatively prosperous, being tenant farmers working on the lands of the Old English, Catholic planter Sir Nicholas Browne. They also claimed some affiliation with the MacCarthys whom Browne had displaced. Browne was displaced in turn, with his estate being confiscated by the Dublin government as punishment for supporting James II in the field of battle. The knock-on consequence for the aspiring poet was migration and poverty, with Ó Rathaille leaving the district and moving to Castlemaine Harbour, County Kerry. The economic hardship implied in this relocation found expression in his lament for the MacCarthy chieftains, 'Is Fada Liom Oíche Fhírfhliuch' ('The Drenching Night Drags On'), in which his descent is evoked by his changing diet: 'anfa ar toinn taobh liom do bhuair mo cheann, / 's nár chleachtas im naíon fíogaigh ná ruacainn abhann' ('This storm on the waves nearby has harrowed my head / —I who ate no winkles or dogfish in my youth!').[55] In contrast the poet recalls the generosity of the MacCarthys, described as 'na seabhaic nár frith cinnte' ('never-niggardly lords').[56]

Yet despite the deep decline in his personal fortunes Ó Rathaille remained convinced of Jacobite legitimacy, and the potency of the Gaelic aristocracy, personified by the MacCarthy clan. Even in 'Is Fada Liom Oíche Fhírfhliuch' he celebrated the character of the clan chieftain, and yearned for the Pretender's return:

> Ar Carathach groí fíochmhar lér fuadh an mheang
> Is Carathach laoi I ndaoirse gan fuascladh fann
> . . . .
>
> A thonnsa thíos is aired géim go hard
> Meabhair mo chinnse cloíte ód bhéiceach tá;
> Cabhair dá dtíodh arís ar Éirinn bhán,
> Do ghlam nach binn do dhingfinn féin id bhráid.
>
> Great Carthy, fierce and fine, who loathed deceit;
> With Carthy of the Laoi, in yoke unyielding, faint;
> . . . .
>
> You wave down there, lifting your loudest roar,
> The wits in my head are worsted by your wails.
> If help ever came to lovely Ireland again
> I'd wedge your ugly howling down your throat![57]

Once again ambiguity intrudes on the poetic expression, however. As before, the poem's structure is informed by the conditions of its creation, which in turn undermine its longevity. Poetry becomes a defiant gesture, just as it recognises its own diminution. So, elsewhere Ó Rathaille made plain his nostalgia about the old aristocracy, at the same time as being forced to admit their inability to reclaim the status on which the poet depended:

> Níl Ua Dotharta I gcomhthrom ná a chaomh-shliocht;
> Níl Síol Mórdha treon ba thréanmhar;
> Níl Ua Flaithbheartaigh i gceannas ná a ghaolta
> Síol mBriain dearbh n-a nGallaibh le tréimhse.
>
> O'Doherty is not holding sway, nor his noble race, the O'Moore are
> not strong, that once were brave; O'Flaherty is not in power, nor his
> kinsfolk, and sooth to say, the O'Briens have since become English.[58]

In the face of this social degradation, Ó Rathaille found himself retreating, not into fairy visions, but into faith, and pleading for providential restitution:

Guidhim an Tríonóid fhíor-mhór naomhtha
An ceo so do dhíochur díobh le chéile,
De shleachtaibh Ír is Chuinn is Éibhir
Us aiseag do thabhairt n-a mbeatha do Ghaedhealaibh.

Aiseag do Ghaedhealaibh déin, a Chríost i n-am
N-a mbeatha go léir ó dhaor-bhruid daoithe Gall.
Smachtuigh na méirligh, féach ár gcríoch go fann!
Is dalta na hÉireann faon lag claoidhte thall.

I beseech the Trinity, most august, holy, to banish this sorrow from
them altogether—from the descendants of Ir, of Conn, of Eibhear—
and to restore the Gaels to their estates.

O Christ, restore betimes to the Gaels all their estates, rescued from
the dire bondage of foreign churls; chastise the vile hordes, behold,
our country is faint, and Erin's nursing, weak, feeble, subdued,
beyond the sea![59]

Ó Rathaille's invocation of the deity as a final source of redemption for the
Pretender, the Gaelic aristocracy, and, lower down the privilege system, the poet,
highlights two key aspects of this form of verse utterance. First, it emphasises
how it depended on traditional modes of social organisation, which were disrupted, if not destroyed, by the intrusion of English manners and mores into the
Irish countryside.[60] In the hands of Aindrias Mac Craith, a rakish peddler-poet
from County Limerick who, as a schoolmaster, had taught John Hely-Hutchinson,
provost of Trinity College Dublin, this trope of yearning for the renewal of ancient
practices of hospitality took a comic and libertine turn.[61] Note the religious appeal
to providence, petitioning to enhance his chances for sexual adventure:

I travelled all the nations and raking I lived astrole
Kissing willing females that pleasingly loved the sport
Loving, drinking, gaming, thus daily I spent my store,
With comely loving ladies still raising their petticoats

If providence proves graceful to wear off this English yoke
And fix our Scottish heroes with safety on the English throne
Our frolics then increasing and earnestly we can then rove
It's but rolling, kissing, raking, and raising their petticoats.[62]

Secondly, Ó Rathaille's plea to God to reestablish the ancient order of Ireland emphasises how the bardic community remained deeply indebted to traditional, Scholastic, modes of thought. The clergy and the aristocracy were both looked to for social instruction and models for emulation; authority remained top-down and the citation of past precedent offered important guide ropes for intellectual life. This found full expression in the rhetorical conceit of the prophecy, wherein the future was imagined as a return to past order through the restoration of rightful authority, and the unpleasant present was wished away. One example exemplifies its form in foretelling the return of the Stuarts:

The Druids and sages unfold it—
The prophets and saints have foretold it,
That the Stuart would come o'er the water with his legions,
And that all Éire's tribes should behold it![63]

Prophecy depended for its very existence on the ability of ancient prophets to have predicted the problems being experienced, and their future resolution.[64] This found full expression in the *aisling*, where the woman representing Ireland projected the future salvation of the country, reinforcing the insights of the prophecies and reasserting the authority of their promulgators. In one such, the 'spouse of Charles' appears to the poet and assures him:

As ancient seers and prophets tell,
Who can and read the omens well,
A fleet will brave the ocean swell
On Saint John's day.
From Munster's land 'twill put to rout
Each portly, thieving English lout,
They'll one and all be driven out
And swept far away.[65]

Note here how ancient authority is associated with an assertion of faith in the Catholic form and how the coming invasion is dated to 'Saint John's Day', underlining the Scholastic assumption that God, not man, lies at the heart of worldly affairs. This was underlined in a passage that combined providential and millennial faith with political optimism and ethnic anger:

But God is good and, by the road in which He died for men,
He soon will chase the foreign race from out our land again.

> I'll pity not the treacherous horde
> When once they're smitten by the Lord
> My harp will sound a joyful chord
> For the Gaels will be free.[66]

The dilemma faced by advocates of such Scholastic methods was that the possibilities of sustaining this highly technical culture of authority were dwindling, alongside the social structures that it legitimated. Despite the generic innovation witnessed in the *aisling*, the problem was that it germinated in soil that was increasingly fallow, as Ó Rathaille keenly realised.

The leadership of the community had been exiled and their authority reduced. The possibilities of upholding a Scholastic worldview increasingly relied on help from abroad, in the intellectual life of Irish Colleges, where training clergy for the Irish mission took place and the old authorities and verities found sanctuary, sustenance, and salvation. In the disputes surrounding the University of Paris in the 1730s the Irish clerics tended towards an ultramontane, regalist position, rejecting the reforming impulses of those associated with Jansenism and Gallican concillarism.[67] In this, the Irish clerics were dictated to by political circumstance. It was the political aspect of Jansenism, with its Gallican emphasis on regional diversity and its concillar downgrading of papal authority, which made it profoundly unattractive to Irish Catholic clerics. Crucially, in the wake of the collapse of Catholic political ambition in 1690, a concillarist system could not flourish, particularly once the Bishops' Banishment Act of 1697 had made the overt presence of the hierarchy a punishable offence in the country. This legislation may have resulted in the exile of up to 500 regulars, as well as the loss of the vast majority of the bishops.[68] In other words, concillarism was practically, if not theoretically, impossible in Ireland because of the legal limitations and political character of the state in Ireland.[69] Catholic clerics had to rely on the central authority of the pope to ensure the maintenance of group identity in what had been reduced to mission status within the church structure. One of the ironies, therefore, of the penal code, was it made Irish Catholicism more 'papist' in character, stunting the growth of the Gallican alternative; one that, to Anglican eyes at least, was more enlightened and less politically threatening.[70]

One such Scholastic voice speaking from aboard was Michael Moore, who taught at the seminary at Montefiascone and at the Collège de France. He was a noted educationalist, enacting reforms at the seminary and at the University of Paris, where he took up the position of rector.[71] He served as principal of the arts students for the Collège de Navarre. His career was also shaped by a brief and untidy intervention into public affairs in his native country.[72] His academic life at the University of Paris was interrupted by his return to Ireland in 1686, where he was vicar-general for the archdiocese of Dublin under James II. He may have briefly taken up the provostship of Trinity College in 1689, although a dispute with James and the requirements of the Jacobite army, which ensured the college was transformed into a barracks for the duration of the occupation, led to his removal and some sense of disenchantment. Yet the Irish episode fed Moore's desire for a restoration of ancient order, both in the political and intellectual sphere; a desire which found expression in his subsequent publications.

The kernel of Moore's work as a philosopher and educationalist was a rejection of the writings and ideas of René Descartes.[73] As he wrote in *De Existentia Dei* ('Of the Existence of God'; 1692), the title of which is itself a declaration of the primacy of the deity in philosophical reflection: 'I have no doubt but that in due time posterity will be amazed that Descartes should have attained so much fame and have so many followers—a man who never really saw what constituted a genuine philosophical demonstration nor what real "scientia" or "knowledge" could be. This was so serious for Descartes that he could not possibly have any genuine concept of rational knowledge.'[74] Moore wished to restore the supremacy of Aristotle, regarding him as the preeminent thinker of the ancients. 'No other philosopher', he wrote, 'has ever treated more accurately, more fully or more fruitfully of moral law or civil law, of the natural discipline of a rational being, of metaphysics itself, or of rhetoric or of poetry. All these studies Aristotle either invented or perfected to the highest degree.'[75] In contrast to this holistic and all-encompassing genius, Descartes was an irksome irritant, a small-minded contender in the realm of metaphysics. Yet the very reach of Aristotelianism was also its greatest weakness for if one element of the structure collapsed under the stress of modern argumentation the whole edifice would be destabilised.[76] Moore's perception that he had witnessed the dawning of a new and destructive philosophical age was evidenced in his concluding remarks to *De Existentia Dei*. Deeply troubled, he observed how 'men have appeared in our present age who have grown accustomed to despising Aristotle. They have never sufficiently understood Aristotle; perhaps they have never read his works. They are not only unjust to Aristotle but they are also censors of the greatest intellects of many generations which they condemn along with Aristotle.'[77]

Thus the danger of the new learning was greater in Moore's mind than the loss of one guide, however profound. Aristotle's name was an emblem for the broad European tradition of Scholastic investigation; a tradition these self-regarding moderns were actively denigrating. The depth of their folly was worrying, although there was hope for a revival in the future for 'certainly they are exposing themselves to accusations of no trivial recklessness and negligence. All posterity will get to know that these changes in philosophy, though plausible, are quite suspect.'[78]

In his *Hortatio ad studium linguae Graecae et Hebraicae* (*Oration on the Study of the Greek and Hebrew Languages*; 1700), Moore diagnosed the cause of the rise of Cartesianism, and its associated heterodoxy and irreligion.[79] As became an educationalist, he argued for the centrality of a properly informed curriculum in fending off the twin evils of the unbelief of heretics and the false faith of Protestants. In particular, he contended that a failure to inculcate basic linguistic skills in Greek and Hebrew left the officers of the Catholic Church unable to access the wisdom of the ages. At one level, the inability to comprehend the ancient languages precluded proper engagement with scripture, although this was alleviated by the church's sanction of the Vulgate Bible. More significant was that this linguistic ignorance limited access to the writings of the church fathers who 'are neglected because they are not understood.'[80] In the case of Hebrew, the significance of the rising tide of linguistic ignorance was profound for it was the divine language, spoken by God to the Jews when communicating Mosaic law. As Moore expressed it, 'The divine law was not written by ink, pen or pencil, but by God himself, by his hand and finger . . . in tablets of stone.'[81] In other words, it was only through a return to origins and a recognition of early authority that the church might maintain its vision of truth in a world blighted by philosophical pride and irreligion founded on a wilful misuse of biblical scholarship left unchallenged by the ignorance of the churchmen. As he observed, 'The Jews alone recognise the Hebrew text, the heretics always challenge the sources in Greek and Hebrew, they do not respect our Vulgate, they do not approve it, they diligently choose these languages; they make exertion in them by day and night; it is so much the opinion among themselves, that Luther did not hesitate to agree.'[82]

Moore yearned for an intellectual restoration to parallel a political revival of the Catholic cause in Ireland. The parlous condition of Roman Catholicism and the collapse of Stuart pretensions of power he had witnessed in Ireland resulted in a rejection of intellectual, as well as political, challenges to the Catholic

Church and Stuart court-in-exile. Maintaining the orthodoxy of the curriculum was the sublimation of a desire to sustain the political and ecclesiastic cause to which he had committed himself in a period of general crisis and personal danger.[83] The final sentence of *De Existentia Dei* expressed this intellectual loyalty: 'In the first position of importance, however, I state that in all these things said and written by me, I wish to be submissive to the Catholic Apostolic and Roman Church which I have always recognised as master of all doctrine and morals and which I have tried to follow; but this has not been without the divine help and grace of our Lord Jesus Christ to whom, with the Father and the Holy Spirit, let there be praise and glory.'[84] In characteristic Scholastic fashion, Moore here placed God at the centre of his reflections, and derived authority from the mediation of his truths by established, here specifically clerical, authorities. In this, he was typical of the majority of Catholic clerics in and from Ireland and was similar in kind to the Irish-language poets who looked to the old nobility to defend their position.

Yet within Irish Catholicism there were more maverick figures who rejected this Scholastic stance, deeming it inappropriate to their social conditions after the Boyne. While they were products of the same culture as Moore, they were open to Enlightenment ideas concerning man's centrality and the methods of empiricism and rationalism, and co-opted them in shaping new arguments concerning the legitimacy of the law, both spiritual and secular. And in exploring their ideas, the impact of the Enlightenment on Catholic Ireland can be assessed.

Empirical Accommodations

Not every Catholic writer was as committed to formal doctrinal rigidity as Michael Moore. His privileged vantage point, as a leading administrator and educator abroad, may have precluded a fully empathetic understanding of the travails of churchmen in penal era Ireland. They were faced with a more troubled situation than the Scholastic certainties of Moore allowed and, in the light of their experience in the country, some were disposed to accommodate themselves to the new dispensation. In their attempts to do so, they co-opted the empirical methodologies that prevailed within Anglican intellectual culture.

Perhaps the most striking figure to emerge in Catholic Ireland in the first three decades of the century who advocated a rapprochement with Anglican authority was Dublin priest Cornelius Nary.[85] In many ways, he was a typical Scholastic, a product of the church culture of deference to ancient authority. In his major work of scholarship, he committed himself to a defence of biblical chronology and to the philosophical assumption that examining the heart of human affairs might illuminate God's presence.

The *New History of the World* (1720) constituted a vast exercise in scriptural criticism, being at once a synthesis of Scholastic learning and an exercise in compilation and recitation.[86] The project was aimed at resolving the discordances which existed between a variety of ancient historical chronologies—spiritual and secular. To accomplish this, as Nary explained, it was necessary to divide the history of the pre-Christian era into six manageable time periods, before setting down 'a chronological table in two columns, in which the years of the patriarchs from the days of Phaled and those of the rulers, judges, kings, and governors of the Children of Israel are paralleled with Nimrod, with the kings of Babylon and Assyria; with the kings of the Medes and Persians, with Alexander the Great, and his successors in the line of the Seleucidae, and with Pompey, Julius and Augustus Caesar, where the reader may see what kings were contemporaries with the said Patriarchs, rulers, kings and governors in each age.'[87]

The import of this academic labour was moral, with Nary 'flatter[ing] myself that in the whole . . . I have scarce omitted any remarkable passage which I judged proper for the instruction or edification of youth.'[88] He was restating the accuracy of biblical chronology and, it followed, defending scripture as a truthful account of the coming of Christ, thereby reinforcing the lessons taught therein. Didacticism and historical exposition were crafted together in his hands. In this light, Nary was an exemplary exponent of the scholastic treatment of history, searching it for ethical axioms and moral exemplars, while upholding the veracity and authority of the ancient authors.

The first chapter of the book underscored Nary's Scholastic credentials, discussing at length the decision to rely on the Septuagint rather than the Hebrew text of the Bible.[89] So too, his opening assertion revealed a Scholastic perception of divine intervention in history, suggesting that human experience might be best studied not for its insights into human nature, but the character of God. 'There is nothing that conduces more to the improvement of mankind than universal history', he declared, 'because men may therein see the omnipotent power of a supreme being displayed in the creation of the world.'[90] Yet if by training he was a Scholastic, by temperament he was an empiricist, whose polemical endeavours evinced a realist streak. In doing so, Nary appropriated aspects of the Enlightenment project. It was in all probability Nary who scripted the anonymous *Case of the Roman Catholics of Ireland*, applying therein a tough-minded empirical methodology to the current condition of his communicants.[91] This brief pamphlet was prompted by a parliamentary proposal that no unregistered Catholic priest could say Mass in Ireland without risking prosecution for high treason. The terms of registration were, in a reiteration of earlier penal legislation, set down as the taking of the oath of abjuration which renounced the Jacobite claimant to the throne.[92] Yet, despite its specific origins, the pamphlet took issue with the presence of the penal code as a whole, which as the author recalled had bloomed in the epoch of Queen Anne.

At the heart of Nary's *Case* lay a deeply embedded concern for the legitimacy of the state. He contended that the penal code represented a profound breach of the Articles of Limerick, and hence, in a phrase that was to echo throughout the text, a break in the 'public faith' that the administration of the country might otherwise enjoy.[93] This issue of trust had its direct counterpart in the requirement of the state that the Catholics take public oaths to ensure their political probity. This demand was, to Nary's mind, demeaning, for the oaths intruded beyond the necessary safeguards that any administration might insist upon. Writing of the oath of allegiance, which demanded that subscribers desist from plotting against the king, Nary inquired: 'Is not any government the most tyrannical or the most unjustly acquired in the world, safe under such a tie, from men whose love and affections they suspect, if this oath be kept? Or if it be not, what other oath will they keep?'[94]

Yet this did not suffice to quiet the doubts festering in Protestant minds, for they chose to depend on the oath of abjuration. For this legal sanction, Nary reserved particular opprobrium. The terms declared James II to have been illegitimate from the start; Nary conceived of this as running counter to the basic principles of Roman Catholicism. Moreover, he conceived of it as a fatuous rejection of the empirical truth of the matter, a flight from political reality. As he wryly inquired, 'Could I in conscience violate my Oath of Allegiance to them [the Jacobite claimant] and to my power be aiding and assisting in dethroning them for doing that which it is my opinion and belief they ought to do? No, surely!'[95]

Yet, more than just hampering the legitimate activities of the Catholic community, the breach in 'public faith' by the administration opened up a terrifying vista of social disintegration and atavistic violence, for if the recantation of the

Articles of Limerick was accepted as an adequate standard of behaviour, 'well may then any general who comes to besiege a town offer their own terms to the besieged . . . and break them when the besieged are in his power, if he can dispense with these sacred ties. Well might men break their vows, oaths and promises, when it is convenient for them, if public faith [again note the use of the term here] may be broken upon any consideration . . . In a word, loose that sacred band, and all the world will be a chaos, an Haceldama, or a field of blood.'[96]

This chimed with Nary's more general charge against the penal code: that in its concern for religious order it had enacted an unintended revolution in the social structure. He observed how 'many gentlemen, who formerly made a considerable figure in the kingdom are now a days, when they walk with canes and sticks only in their hands, insulted by men armed with swords and pistols, who of late rose from the very dregs of the people.'[97] Note how the religious persuasion of the two categories is not stated. Religion is here occluded by the ordering of rank. This despair at the social disruption generated by this uncouth body of legislation continued into Nary's complaint that, in limiting the nature of Catholic landholding, 'all encouragement for natural industry is taken away from them, and [they] are left under an impossibility of being other than slaves.'[98] The danger was that the enemies were irredeemably committed to just such a catastrophe, for 'it is plain the design of those our enemies who had no regard to the sacred bands by which all nations are in a manner tied together, was to destroy and exterminate us from off the face of the earth.'[99]

In the face of this threat to their existence, Nary mounted a pragmatic, empirically contrived defence of his community, emphasising their decency and highlighting their utility to the Protestant regime. This began by Nary offering a counternarrative of the War of the Two Kings to that of the penal code's advocates, espousing the political trustworthiness of the Catholic community. In a pointed reversal of Protestant political discourse, Nary noted how the Catholics had remained committed to their original political principles until overcome by the events around them. They 'did conceive, and believe it to be undeniably true, that by the ancient and fundamental laws and statutes of England and Ireland, the imperial crown of England was monarchical [and] hereditary, lineally gradually descending by inherent indefeasible and unalienable right of *primo geniture* and proximity of blood, to the next true heir upon the death or voluntary abdication of the preceding lawful monarch, without any intervening formality, call, authority, recognition, coronation oath or other ceremony whatsoever.'[100] Siding with James II in the conflict was in line with these principles of loyalty and service. In disavowing the argument that James had abdicated, they had done their duty until 'they had King James's consent upon his departure from Ireland to make the best condition they could for themselves.'[101] This record of political fealty was then, paradoxically, precisely the guarantee needed by the new administration. Once the new government was recognised, the Catholics would uphold its legitimacy steadfastly: 'The said Roman Catholics . . . have ever since to this day, lived peaceably and quietly under the government of the respective kings and queens of Great Britain, without ever attempting to molest or disturb, or raise any rebellion or tumult in it, as is evident to all the world.'[102]

Sometime in 1727 or 1728 Nary attempted to actualise this understanding of Catholic quiescence by drafting an oath of allegiance to the newly crowned Hanoverian king, George II, which Catholics could take in good conscience. As well as containing a basic statement of fealty, it specifically proclaimed that the oath taker would 'make known all treasons, traitorous conspiracies and plots against his person' thereby renouncing the Jacobite cause, and contained an overt denial of the idea that 'the Pope hath power to depose princes.'[103] The ambition to establish a satisfactory Catholic oath in recognition of Hanoverian legitimacy was a necessity if the public confession of the faith was to be separated from the implication of Jacobite loyalty that was assumed in much of the penal legislation passed by the Irish parliament. And in this attempt to ingratiate Catholics with the Anglican elite and create a common bond between the two communities Nary was not alone. Individuals from both sides of the confessional divide sought at times to identify the right form of words.[104] Edward Synge, author of *The Case of Toleration Considered*, defended his position in a *Vindication of a Sermon* which contained his favoured formulation. And Nary's proposal was also contemporary with a direct address to monarch led by Lord Devlin.[105] Signed at the Lion in Werburgh Street by around twenty prominent Dublin Catholics, it reassured George II of the community's 'steady allegiance and most humble duty to Your Majesty's person and government.'[106]

Despite the failure of these initiatives in the late 1720s the idea of a Catholic oath and the drafting of a Catholic address to the king were expressive of a renewed desire to find a way for the two communities to live side by side, untroubled by the politics of religious confession. Similarly, just as Nary articulated a desire for tolerance of the Catholic confession grounded upon an empirical recognition of the power politics of the Irish ancien régime, so Irish-language scholars began to realise that their pragmatic interests were on occasion served by treating with the Anglican cultural elite. The process of rapprochement with the Anglican community was slow, and depended on goodwill on both sides, but found a means of expression through a shared investment in empirical methodology and the investigation of the past. The work of the scribes of Gaelic Ireland was central to this process of cultural initiation.

The position and prestige of scholars in Gaelic culture remained high in the first half of the eighteenth century, particularly as print was slow to take up Irish as a medium of expression—partly because differences in orthography required a special, and expensive, type font, and partly because the market did not seem to justify the initiative required.[107] Aside from a few grammars, religious works, and two dictionaries, virtually nothing made it through the press in the course of the century.[108] In contrast, the survival of around 4,000 Irish-language manuscripts from the course of the century suggests something of the scale of the scribal culture Ireland housed.[109] Cork and Clare remained vibrant centres, with Cork alone having at least 227 scribes active in the period. In County Limerick, the poet Aindrias Mac Craith was an adept scribe, his activities including transcribing the important fourteenth-century account of dynastic conflicts in Thomond from 1276 to 1318, *Caithréim Thoirdhealbhaigh*, in 1721.[110] In Armagh, poets such as Peadar Ó Dornín contributed to the maintenance of knowledge through scribal activity; among other works he produced was a now lost manuscript of the great Ulster cycle, the *Táin Bó Cuailnge*.[111] The purpose of such scribal activity was to record and transmit the learning of the community to future generations.[112] Scribal activity was thus primarily a Scholastic activity, retaining and celebrating ancient lore, through acts of retrieval and transcription.

In conducting this work, the scribe could rely on a remarkably interlaced culture of support and interest, which enabled the dissemination of the conserved material.[113] The intersections across the regions are well illustrated in a long poem written in the 1720s by Tadhg Ó Neachtain. Therein, he dwelt on the circle of friends and fellow scribes who had informed his own development and shaped his practice. Some twenty-six scribes are mentioned as among 'Sloinfead scothadh na Gaoidhilge grinn / dá raibhe rém rae a Nduibhlinn' ('the best scholars of the keen Irish language that / were in Dublin in my time').[114] Notable, however, is that in the brief pen sketch offered within the poem—a verse devoted to each practitioner—attention is almost always given to the geographic origin of the scribe. And in each of these cases, the subject has his roots located someplace other than Dublin itself. Scribes are drawn to the city from specific locales, such as 'Calláin thaiobhe Teamhrach' ('Callan beside Tara') or 'ó Fhine Gall' ('from Fingal'), or from more general regions—from Longford for example, or from Munster.[115] Only in the verse devoted to William Lynch was the capital city in which the network had been forged actually mentioned, and only to observe that 'áth na Gcliath char an chuim, / mar [a] ndearnadh sé an Ghaoidhilg dfóghluim' ('he loved Dublin, where he learned Irish').[116] The religious affiliation of the community was also occasionally noted; with 'Proinnsias feartach' ('miraculous Francis') being described as 'an bráthair bocht, / gidh saidhbhir a n-eagnadh 's a n-inntlacht' ('the poor friar rich in wisdom and intellect'), while Peter Mulligan was simply 'pearsadh a n-eagluis Dé' ('a member of the church of God').[117] Equally, ethnic identity was the source of some observations: 'bu Gaedhul an fear' ('He was an Irishman') while of Dermot O'Connor it was remarked: 'bhá a threabh do m[h]acaibh Míleadh' ('his family were Milesians'), an allusion to the supposed originators of the Irish kingdom.[118]

The work of this coterie of scholars crossed numerous disciplines, notably historical labours and linguistic endeavours.[119] Indeed, the group understood themselves to be the natural inheritors of the learned families who maintained the *seanchas*, or traditional knowledge of the Gaels. Importantly, the preservation of *seanchas* involved more than the assertion of pedigrees, although that provided a lucrative sideline, creatively exploited by at least member of the coterie, Dermot O'Connor.[120] Nor did it limit itself to the compilation of documents, although that too was a necessary function. Rather it implied the explication of literature and myth, leading the group to engage with hagiography, place-name lore, romances, and praise poetry.[121] This all imposed a precise sense of the language and Ó Neachtain, among others, regularly included lexicographical insight into his manuscripts, compiling at least two dictionaries, notably drawing up a fair copy of a lengthy Irish/English version. Indeed, within the corpus of linguistic material left by the community of scholars was a manuscript Irish grammar, composed in English and entitled the *Grammatica Anglo-Hibernica* (circa 1713). Compiled by the Franciscan Francis Walsh, it seems to have been intended for publication, although this was not a necessary outcome for many of the scholars in the group. The production of manuscript copies sufficed, enabling like-minded workers to trade knowledge and resources, swap verse epigrams and missives, trade texts, and offer scribal emendations on a shared copy.[122]

The empiricism evident in the linguistic work conducted by the Ó Neachtain circle both complemented and confused the essentially Scholastic task of preserving ancient lore, something to which they devoted a great deal of their energies. Between 150 and 200 manuscript books still exist which can be accredited to their hands; often the finished artefact shows evidence of more than one contributor.[123] One of Ó Neachtain's compilations shows how interconnected all this activity was; in documenting his loans to other scribes in the city, he recalled twenty-one different beneficiaries and a range of printed and manuscript offerings.[124] The work involved the copying of exemplary texts, drawn from the private collections of the regional landowners or fallen gentry. Equally, some manuscripts were owned by the scribes, for their familial lineage back into the bardic culture of the sixteenth century often ensured such legacies. Manuscripts were also avidly sought out in Dublin itself, and in the regions from where the scribes originated. Religious orders were approached, and the private and institutional collections extant in the city were scoured for their riches. Ó Neachtain travelled as far as France to hunt for such resources.[125] This was a two-way traffic, for many of the collectors in the city were tempted to pay for copies of material not in their possession, the scribe being relied on to provide a trustworthy version.

The activities of the Dublin scholarly community thereby indicate the kind of structural pressures and commercial opportunities transforming scribal life.[126] Indeed, the shift away from Scholasticism indicated by the preservation of ancient lore and towards an empirical accommodation with the postwar circumstances, suggested by the translation of that material into English, is personified by two figures in Ó Neachtain's network.[127] On the one hand, there was the magisterial presence of Seán Ó Neachtain, Tadhg's father. On the other, there was a native of County Clare named Aobh Buidhe Mac Cruitín. Of his father Tadhg wrote: 'Seán Ua Neachtuin, niamh na scol, / seanóir ársaigh a chrích Connacht, / ughdar fír-ghlic an Ghleacuidh Luinn / 's mórán staradh oile dá shamhuil' ('Seán Ó Neachtain, the shining light of the poets, the old veteran from Connaught, author of the *Ardent Champion* and many similar stories'); of the latter he remarked: 'Aodh Mhac Curtáin, an crann os coill, / ailgm-heasach Mumhain 'nois chanuim, / an file faobhrach [a] bhfhriotal Fáil, / feas a bhreath bheith [a] measg na mórfháil' ('Now I mention Hugh MacCurtin, the highest tree in the wood, a sharp poet in Irish and one whose judgement is acceptable in the great assemblies').[128] Yet, despite sharing the admiration of

Tadhg Ó Neachtain, their work looked in different directions, Ó Neachtain senior to the past, Mac Cruitín to the future.

Seán Ó Neachtain was a native of the barony of Athlone, County Roscommon, where he may have suffered expropriation under the Restoration land settlement.[129] He became a teacher in Dublin, having spent time in County Meath, before suffering further disruption when the profession of teaching was debarred to Catholics under penal legislation passed in 1695, resulting in a brief exile to the Wicklow Mountains, south of the city. He returned, however, and lived his remaining days out around Thomas Street in the Liberties neighbourhood of Dublin, devoting much of his scholarship to the translation and transcription of works of piety in Latin, English, Italian, and Portuguese, although for the latter two he may have worked from extant English versions. In this, he followed in the tradition of gathering, preserving, and disseminating material by way of manuscript transcription: in sum, a Scholastic pursuit that relied on the recitation of past authority to confront present circumstance.

In his poetic effusions, Ó Neachtain was similarly in line with the tropes of his day. His commitment to Catholicism—he may have been related by marriage to the Catholic archbishop of the city, John Carpenter—and his sympathies for the Jacobite cause found expression in a large body of verse. But his place within, and sense of possibilities for, the Irish-language tradition found fullest expression in a sequence of prose tales.[130] And of these, *Stair Éamoin Uí Chléire* (*The History of Éamonn O'Clery*) was by far the most perplexing.

Therein, Ó Neachtain recounted the tale of the eponymous Éamonn and his fight with alcoholism. The story was recounted in a series of short humorous episodes, more akin to traditional European romances than the novel then forming in Britain. Ó Neachtain made ample use of archetypes, such as the woman 'Decency, daughter of Fortune' who accompanied Éamonn on his mock-heroic progress. Moreover, given the social leadership offered to Gaelic Ireland by the Catholic clergy, it is significant that O'Clery finds salvation from his alcohol dependency through the intervention of a priest. He initially adopts religion to save himself from a beating, but he becomes increasingly fervent and convinced. This prompts his old friend Father Aogán to plead with the fairy queens on his friend's behalf. Heeding his plea, they provide O'Clery with a magical potion to ease his woes, but not before they inform him plainly that "'the reason for our visit here today is that Aogán the Miraculous, in his wisdom and erudition, has summoned us.'"[131]

Just as the first part revolves around the power of faith and the redemption offered by the priesthood, so the second part, although significantly less accomplished than the first, indicates sympathy for the other lost leaders of the community, the Jacobite exiles. In recounting the marvels of a fairy arcadia called Mullarney, the narrator, Cormac MacSharry recollects Cybele, the mother of Jupiter saying,

'O child of my heart . . . since you have the obligation of keeping the rights of every land in order, it amazes me that you don't come to the deliverance of the poor Gaels who are dying of hunger while their wealth, their land, their patrimony, and the rest of their rightful due is in the possession of Foreigners, at whose hands their elders and ancestors were banished by perfidy, pogrom and persecution.'

'Dear mother', he said, 'all you have said is so; nevertheless, at times I scourge the one who is dear to me, consecrating him to myself. But they will find deliverance when I deem the time is right. As for the Foreigners, their own time is yet to come, despite the fact that I have used them as a scourge.'[132]

This episode captures the essence of Ó Neachtain's intellectual commitments. He at once articulated his sense of the cultural and material loss suffered by his Gaelic community, and looked to the future for divine restitution, in that Jupiter offers a prophecy akin to those found elsewhere in the Jacobite canon. Additionally, it is the Gaels' religious zeal and purity which result in favour being shown, albeit a deferred favour, while they are themselves offered as a kind of sacrifice—an act of consecration recalling Christ's sacrifice on the Cross. So at once the passage expresses grief for past glories and a continued assurance about the efficacy of the leadership that involved them in that defeat. Commensurate with this is a contempt shown to the foreigners, whose actions are at once a necessary purge, and so despicable in themselves as to bring divine displeasure and punishment in the future. The hopes, fears, and cultural assumptions of Ó Neachtain are here laid bare.

Yet one thing clearly perplexes this Manichean view of the divisions between Gaelic saints and foreign demons, for Ó Neachtain's narrator then admits that '"when I heard Jupiter speaking to his mother on this occasion, it terrified me, for I was afraid he would prosecute all he promised against the Foreigners during my own time; for I was a Foreigner by ancestry and all my relations were in the service of the king, and no two of them sharing the same religion.'[133] Acculturation was therefore in Ó Neachtain's terms both a reality—the history of sexual attraction and marital ties between the two communities ensured this—and profoundly disruptive of his foundational political and religious assumptions. This passage tells of his awareness of cultural interchange, and his worries at its consequences. How might the community be treated by its God when in their midst resided those whose ancestry or religious commitments did not accord with the picture of ethnic and spiritual purity on which Jupiter's prophecy of restoration depended?

Ó Neachtain's awareness of cultural liminality found further expression in his fictive rendition of the linguistic turmoil of the period. In a remarkably adept episode, filled with complex punning and the layering of double and triple meanings, O'Clery encounters a young boy who, being taught at an English-language school, has been instructed not to speak Irish. This results in him talking in a nearly incomprehensible pidgin dialect which brings together English words and Irish sentence structures, often relying on direct translations from the Irish. The following excerpt may be taken as typical of Ó Neachtain's extravagant wordplay. O'Clery asks the boy as to the whereabouts of the 'woman of the house' ('mban an tí'). The boy replies:

> 'The house is not married to any woman.'
> 'To any woman, then?' Éamonn said.
> 'Yes,' he said.
> 'But where is the woman that used to be in the house?'
> 'She is go 'pon market', said the little fellow.
> 'What market?' said Éamonn.
> 'The Market of Newford', he said.
> 'Indeed! What market is that? said Éamonn.
> 'The market Nua-Áth in Irish', he said.
> 'What business had she there?' said Éamonn.
> 'To buy trout going', he said.
> 'What is that?' said Éamonn.
> ''Tis breacán in Irish'.
> 'Really! How is it breacán?' said Éamonn.
> 'Breac is "trout" and fán is "going"', said the little fellow.[134]

Breacán was a type of plaid cloth, although the transformation of the term by the young boy into 'trout going' seems, in its literalness, logical enough. This linguistic confusion is threateningly turned on O'Clery when, at the end of this encounter, O'Clery asks after the boy's father only to be told:

> 'By my soul, he be gone to kill man for money,' . . .
>
>   'By the hokey', said Éamonn, 'this is a dangerous place I've come upon. Now then, where is he gone you say?'
>
>   'To kill man' for money', said the little fellow.
>
>   The word had hardly left his lips when Éamonn saw a large, sallow, gaunt man coming to the door. He had a bloody knife in his hand, and his hands moreover, were drenched in blood, and there was a huge streak of blood on his face . . . The sight of him and the fact that the little boy had said that his father 'went to kill man for money', filled Éamonn's heart with so much fear and trembling that he was convinced that the big man had just killed someone, and this prompted him to shout 'Murder! murder!'[135]

Running away, O'Clery then meets with a 'big man carrying a cow's hide on his back' who informs him that the blood on the householder's face is nothing but 'the blood of the cow who wore this skin. Kilmany is the village I live in.'[136] Linguistic confusion, it transpires, can lead to dangerous misunderstandings.

   Further evidence of Ó Neachtain's discontent at intersections between the Irish- and English-speaking communities in the city can be drawn from his poetic oeuvre.[137] A poem exists attacking Charles Lynegar, the professor of Irish at Trinity College from 1708 until at least 1715. Dated 1712 it began in traditional fashion, lamenting the passing of the traditional orders of Ireland, before turning Ó Neachtain's ire fully on the charlatan upstart Lynegar:

> If all the stories his crooked mouth now tells are to be believed, there never was in all Ireland since the Flood any artist fit to be compared with him.
>
>   I would advise the descendants of Conn—all of them who still live—not to listen to his false pedigrees since his knowledge is very scanty.[138]

   While the reason for this resentment is left unexplained, in keeping with the strong sense of faith that imbued much of his work Ó Neachtain hinted that his antagonism towards Lynegar had its origins in disapproval of the latter's conversion to Anglicanism. The poem snarls:

> He forsook the law and faith of the Lord for the folly of the world
> and false illusion, therefore whoever believes him is akin to Cain.
>   People who attend to the words of any man who deceives God for
> the sake of the wealth of the world, whose treasures are evil, shall
> suffer great oppression forever more.[139]

The vitriol evinced here is subsequently leavened by Ó Neachtain's use of a pun, characteristic of his poetic style. Here it plays on the Irish version of Lynegar's name, Ó Luinín, which literally means 'little blackbird'. Yet in making mock, Ó Neachtain got to the heart of his displeasure:

> Sweet is every blackbird that frequents a wood, in music pleasing and
> decorous. Not so Ó Luinín who makes music in praise of foreigners,
> drinking in their company.[140]

As in the prose tale, Ó Neachtain shows how he was distressed by what he perceived as cultural treachery: trading heritage for worldly favour. Yet, within the circle centred on his son Tadhg, this does not seem to have been the prevalent view. For example, Aobh Buidhe Mac Cruitín took a rather less abstemious view of the question of cultural interaction.

Akin to Tadhg Ó Neachtain, Mac Cruitín was an able poet, writing a range of verse that accorded with many of the standard themes of the period: the loss of native patronage and hopes for a Jacobite recrudescence, a cause for which he apparently served in the armies of the Continent. For example, in 'Do Chlann Tomáis' ('For Clan Thomas') he railed against the uncultured upstarts who replaced the traditional landed elite in the wake of the War of the Two Kings, while claiming a status and lineage to which they had no right:

> Déarfaidh an braobaire is buartha 'en chóip:
> 'Is mé féin is mo chéile is uaisle ar bord,
> Is ó from Éibhear mac Éibhir do ghluais mo phór
> Is tá gaol ag Ó Néill thoir, dar Duach, le Mór.'

> The most feverish boor in the crowd will declare:
> 'Myself and the wife are the best at this table.
> My line is descended from Éibhear Mac Éibhir
> And by Damn but Ó Néill is connected with Mór!'[141]

Yet Mac Cruitín's work accommodated interests in three other elements that differentiated him from Ó Neachtain: print, polemic, and the past. While his scribal labours included a collection of poems composed by his ancestors, he also aided in the compilation of an English-Irish dictionary, published by Father Conor Begley in Paris in 1732; having himself compiled and published an Irish grammar, *Elements of the Irish Language*, which emerged in Louvain in 1728.[142] In 1717, he published a *Brief Discourse in Vindication of the Antiquity of Ireland*, which in contrast to Ó Neachtain's expressions of anxiety concerning cultural interchange, expressly climbed into the battle by accosting the Anglican Sir Richard Cox for his perceived mistreatment of Irish history in *Hibernia Anglicana* (1689–1690). While Cox was quick to dismiss the writings of Geoffrey Keating and other manuscript accounts of the pre-Norman period as nothing more than, in Mac Cruitín's words, 'an ill-digested heap of very silly fictions', Mac Cruitín now set about dismantling Cox's assertions and rendering the narrative of the period anew.[143] Where Ó Neachtain's wariness of the English language led to a retreat, Mac Cruitín's umbrage prompted him to advance into the print culture, taking the battle to the fields of his enemies.

This process of accommodation to the new world of post-Boyne Ireland extended to the incorporation into scribal circles of those Protestants who expressed a desire to comprehend the locality in which they lived. For example, the group around Tadhg Ó Neachtain was able to collaborate in the project for a new history of Ireland envisioned by Anthony Raymond, the Church of Ireland vicar of Trim, County Meath. Despite a commitment to the fashionable idea that Irish was related to Phoenician, and that it was thereby directly connected to Greek and Latin, at the heart of Raymond's interest was not language but history.[144] As he expressed it:

> A notion . . . generally prevails that . . . the Irish were a rude unci-
> vilised people governed by barbarous laws and customs and that no
> notice is taken of them by any historians but their own who
> are . . . partial and fabulous. I must confess I was of this opinion till I
> had read some of their approved histories and found their accounts
> generally agreed with the writings of other authors of undoubted
> credit. Having communicated my observations to some persons on
> whose judgement I could rely and finding they approved of them I
> was persuaded to undertake the general history of Ireland from the
> first peopling of the kingdom to the coming of the English.[145]

To this end Raymond engaged a number of scribes to transcribe and translate Irish-language manuscripts, among which were a number by Tadhg Ó Neachtain, Aobh Buidhe Mac Cruitín, and Dermot O'Connor.[146] He borrowed the fourteenth-century *Book of Ballymote* from the library at Trinity College, which ended up in the permanent possession of Tadhg Ó Neachtain following Raymond's early death in 1726. Raymond also broached the idea of travelling to France to reclaim the medieval *Book of Lecan*, which had been removed from Trinity College's holdings by a Jacobite soldier, identified by Raymond as John Fitzgerald, during its occupation by James II's troops in 1688–1689.[147] Although Dermot O'Connor's ill-received translation of *Foras Feasaar Éirinn* (Foundation of the History of Ireland) trumped his own endeavours—Raymond was to carry out a bitter campaign of abuse against the man he had once employed as a scribe and now demeaned as his 'servant'—he maintained a deep commitment to Irish-language scholarship throughout his life.[148]

Raymond's open-mindedness was clearly reciprocated by a number of the scribes in the city, most notably Tadhg Ó Neachtain himself. Indicative of this close connection and mutual esteem was a lengthy doggerel praise poem scripted by Ó Neachtain in honour of Raymond's exertions. Once again, the poem began by grieving for the fate of the traditional orders of Ireland, seeing their loss in the decay and aridity of the natural world. Yet

> Now Anthony has taken on himself to set her free because of the pity he has for her not wickedly desiring wealth he has scattered her dark clouds and her cry [of despair].
>
> He showed her to herself and to her people, he blew away the heavy cloud of sorrow, he left her like the bright morning sun after the hoar frost of a spring morning.
>
> He told her about her line of kings, the majesty of her sons and their eternal fame. He revived (a true saying) her law, her customs and her genealogies.
>
> He enlightened her darkness regarding knowledge giving new life to her smooth breast. He applied the healing to the wounds of her body and put his hands under her head to help her.
>
> Even though it was difficult, he reawakened her arts, her speech, and her good manner of life. He showed the majesty and vigour of her ancestors, and her bondage under a foreign yoke.[149]

This in praise of a personification of just such a 'foreign yoke'; Raymond was, after all, English by ancestry and Anglican by conviction. The Ó Neachtain family was clearly diverging, with the father and son differing in their perception and evaluation of the merits of Anglican interest in Gaelic culture and lore. A generational shift was apparently under way.

Perhaps the most symbolic moment in this accommodation came not through poetry or antiquarian interest in the past, both of which required mediation through language, but in the sensory realm of music, which needed no specific skills in its transference beyond an open mind and an attuned ear. In 1724, a compilation of traditional Irish airs was published under the title *A Collection of the Most Celebrated Irish Tunes proper for the Violin, German Flute or Hautboy*. As the specified instruments indicate, this collection was aimed at a genteel audience who nonetheless held some sympathy for the culture around them; although this was tempered by the fact that the volume was part of a series, the publishers having already offered 'a quarto book of the best Scotch tunes and another of the finest English ayres [*sic*] and newest minuets.'[150] The volume published by the Protestants John and William Neal marked a significant cultural détente between the Gaelic world and the English-speaking community. The collection drew inspiration from the success of the harpist Turlough Carolan, who had recently entranced the polite society of Dublin with his skill and charismatic presence.[151] Tunes such as 'Grace Nugent' were explicitly credited to him, while the presence among the compilation of such Jacobite airs as 'Patrick Sarsfield'—named after James II's Irish general—suggests that music could infiltrate politically suspect sentiments into inclement regions and that the War of the Two Kings and its concomitant culture of mutual suspicion was loosening its grip on the imagination of Ireland's inhabitants. That John Neal was to rise to the presidency of the Musical and Charitable Society in the 1730s underscores the changing complexion of Dublin's cultural scene.

At first glance, the Catholic intellectual culture was intrinsically Scholastic in its method. It depended on the survival of ancient knowledge, protected by clerics and scribes. However, that gloss obscures the subtle shifts occurring within the community. As we can see in the case of Nary, some priests were concerned to reach an accommodation with the Anglican regime; so too the circle around Tadhg Ó Neachtain illustrates the potential for cooperation between Gaelic scribes and Anglican patrons, and the slow integration of Gaelic culture into Anglican taste. In this, the political bent of Nary's empirical methodology found

its social corollary, for it implied a recognition of the realities of cultural production in the early eighteenth century, the demise of the Gaelic patronage system
and the need to acclimatise to Anglican supremacy if the scribal community was
to survive.

The Distance from God

In contrast to the extensive cultural architecture that maintained the scribal
pursuit of history and its concomitant empirical interrogation of the world,
there was no support network for those few Catholic writers who availed of a
rationalist method in defence of their faith. For some, however, neither a continuing confidence in Scholastic authority nor a pragmatic recognition of empirical actualities was sufficient to justify the confession. The problem the rationalist reimagining of Catholicism confronted was the apparent abandonment
by God of his chosen people. Why, if Catholicism was the legitimate expression
of divine truth, had it suffered such a resounding defeat on Irish soil? For
thinkers of this hue, a Jansenist attitude towards the Bible and faith became
attractive, with its perception of God's restraint in exercising special providence,
and in its treatment of the world as a vale of suffering.

Irish involvement in Jansenism can be dated back into the seventeenth century, but it was to cause particular controversy in 1720s in the wake of the papal
condemnation of the Montpellier catechism.[152] Originally authored in French
by François Pouget, and appearing in 1702, the Montpellier catechism supplied
a compendium of Catholic doctrine from a distinctly Jansenist angle. Although
probably intended as a reference book for the clergy it was placed on the Index
in 1721; the Spanish translation followed suit, being condemned in 1727. The
Irish repercussion of this condemnation was to be found in the difficulties
encountered by Father Sylvester Lloyd upon embarking on an English-language
translation of the French-language original. A committed Jacobite and opponent of any formulation of a Catholic oath to the Hanoverians, he began his
career as a Hieronymite friar, before transferring to the Franciscans. Rising
rapidly from preacher to confessor of the laity in 1716, he was elevated to the
office of deputy provincial in 1723, possibly as a result of the impression made by
his 1712 translation which was initially well received in Dublin. That the condemnation of 1721 altered this perspective is apparent from the declaration on

the cover page of the second, 1723, edition. There he confirmed that while this new treatment had been 'translated from the French' it had also been subjected to close scrutiny whereby it was 'carefully compared with the Spanish approved version'—a translation which had not yet drawn the admonition of the papacy. In the unseemly haste to chime with the new circumstances, however, the editor of the new edition made one major error of retention, leaving unaltered a passage praising the original, now-condemned French publication. 'This Catechism', Lloyd had written on the opening page of his preface,

> was first published in France, in the diocese of Montpellier, by order
> of Mr Colbert, bishop of that see, in the year 1702. It was everywhere
> received with the greatest applause, and there were a great many
> editions of it in a very little time . . .
>
> It is a history of all the errors, schisms and heresies that troubled
> the church from the beginning of Christianity to this very day . . . and
> it is an explanation of the Christian morality, sacraments, prayers,
> ceremonies and rites of the church, in which her doctrines are
> faithfully delivered without entering into those nice disputes, which
> rather puzzle the understanding than mend the heart . . .
>
> Those who are in error or wavering in their faith, may in this book
> find sure and incontestable principles whereby to clear their doubts
> and satisfy their scruples; those who are true believers will find certain
> and infallible rules for living holily in every state and condition of
> life, and for avoiding a thousand evils that men daily fall into either
> through ignorance or superstition; . . . so that the reader will on a
> serious perusal find that he never read a book more proper to
> strengthen his faith and compose his manners, or to instruct him in
> every good word and work.[153]

Immediately upon its publication, the 1723 edition of the catechism was sent by Archbishop Byrne of Dublin to three separate committees to study its doctrinal quality. All three found in favour of Lloyd, arguing for the dexterity with which he had purged the catechism of any suspect tenets. As the 'theologicans [sic] of the diocese of Dublin', a gathering which included Cornelius Nary, expressed it: 'They have found nothing in Lloyd's translation which is contrary to faith and morals; indeed, they remark that Lloyd's skill is especially noticeable in the way he ingeniously omitted whatever was superfluous or dubious in the original French or emended such passages to bring them into line with Catholic teaching; consequently they consider this translation, which took so much study and hard work, suitable to provide knowledge of salvation to those who sit in darkness and in the shadow of death.'[154] The members of the Dominican order called to adjudicate were even more effusive in their commendation, stating that 'they have found nothing in the translation which is opposed to faith and morals, and that the doctrine outlined in it is in keeping with the sacred scripture and the teaching of the fathers'.[155]

Yet despite these acclamations, suspicions clearly remained. In publishing the second part of the translation's new edition, Lloyd felt it necessary to vocalise his concerns at the rumours of heterodoxy his endeavour was creating. He freely recognised that it had 'been industriously given out since the publication of the first volume of this translation that it contained some of the pernicious errors of Jansensius and Quesnelle and it having been further insinuated that this work was never translated by any Catholic hand into the Spanish language.'[156] In response he assured the suspicious reader 'that it has been approved by most of the eminent divines of this city, as they have attested by instruments under their hands, and are ready to acknowledge when required: and, secondly, that it has been carefully compared with the Spanish translation now in the printer's hands, a translation which is in the greatest esteem in Spain, where it was published by authority.'[157] He further appended an approbation of the Spanish text, significantly written by a Jesuit, Joseph Casani, who was also the qualificator of the Supreme Council of the Inquisition in Madrid.

Even with such assurances Lloyd's translation quickly became an instrument in the arguments over translation and elevation to the see of Dublin which followed Archbishop Byrne's death in February 1724.[158] The central church authorities charged with overseeing the Irish mission were confused as to the doctrinal clarity of Lloyd's efforts, arguing that the condemnation of the French-language version extended to the English-language translation until it had been determined otherwise by the Holy Office. To this view, the vicar capitular—the de facto head of the diocese in the interregnum before a successor to Byrne was nominated—cautiously deferred. An examination of the translation was subsequently held in Rome, with the cardinals deciding on 15 January 1725 to place Lloyd's text on the index alongside the French-language original. Although the rationale for this decision remains imprecise it does seem that, despite the author's best efforts to cleanse the text of the errors inherent in the Montpellier version, new and significant errors had been brought in, leading to the fresh censure. Lloyd had to suffer the ignominy of announcing the ban from his own pulpit, publicly retracting the fruit of many years work. It delayed his elevation to a bishopric, which, when it finally occurred in 1732, was a repercussion of his political efforts on the part of the Pretender and not a tribute to his clerical career.[159]

Equally emblematic of the difficulties into which Irish clerics might run for evincing Jansenist sympathies is the case of Matthew Barnewall. Although active in France, his fate—he was imprisoned in the Bastille from June 1712 to November 1713 for distributing Jansenist literature—highlights the obstacles sympathisers encountered in proselytising for the movement. Apparently unfazed by this period of incarceration, in 1719 he published a French translation of the New Testament. By the early 1730s he was attached to the *convulsionnaires*, an extreme Jansenist community. He was rearrested on 12 January 1736 for a final time, while processing to the old Jansenist centre of Port Royale. Although he died in prison in 1738, he availed of his time there to compose a *Profession de Foy*, in which he characterised himself as 'a prisoner for Jesus Christ'.[160] In a truculent Jansenist gesture, he condemned the papal bull Unigenitus as the toxic 'fruit of Molinisme'. In contrast, Jansen's work was 'a manifestation of the doctrine of Saint Paul, of Saint Augustine, of Saint Thomas [Aquinas] and all the other saintly defenders of grace.'[161]

Caution is required in ascribing these figures to a rationalist wing of the Enlightenment, however, for Jansenism in its theological form had little similarity with the Enlightenment, of whatever variety. Jansenism was grounded on a belief in original sin and the intrinsic depravity of man—much as scriptural Presbyterianism inculcated. In this, it shared with Jonathan Swift a deep distrust of any philosophical system that was centred on humanity, and not on God; it rejected the primary assumption of the Enlightenment, that humanity was the starting point of philosophical reflection. Despite this crucial caveat, the relationship between the Enlightenment and Jansenism remained close. This proximity was partially derived from the Jansenist sensibility that God had withdrawn from direct action in the universe, allowing history to unfold according to natural laws. They rejected the claims of secular and spiritual authority to represent and speak for the divine power. In particular, Jansenists dismissed the papal claim to be a conduit of truth, seeing it only as a necessary practical authority in a chaotic and sinful world. That perception of authority as legitimated solely in human terms was something that was shared by Enlightenment thinkers anxious to dispute any claim to supernatural wisdom.[162] Nor was this merely a proximity born of a shared dissent towards the nexus of church and state as it existed under the divine right monarchy enunciated by the Bourbon crown. Rather, Jansenism developed a complex political philosophy that focussed attention on the role of the *parlements* and church councils as necessary bulwarks against absolutism—be it monarchical or papal in character. And in as much as these figures gestured towards a radical reform of the church, grounded on the exercise of power by church councils and not the monarchical central authority wielded by the papacy, and on a natural law understanding of the mechanics of the world, they chime with a rationalist Enlightenment view.

The Trajectory of Bernard Connor

If the rationalist methodology that underpinned Jansenist theology was largely unattractive to Irish Catholics, the speculative modes indicative of free thought were even less appealing. The infrequency of such daring and the deep suspicion it evinced in most Irish Catholic observers indicates something of the failure of the Enlightenment project in Ireland to stretch deeply into the Catholic universe in the early years of the eighteenth century. Yet some radical voices did emerge, enunciating a deep distrust in the clerical leadership that had led the community to political disaster in the War of the Two Kings.

One example of an anticlerical freethinking attitude being adopted by an Irish Catholic is provided by Bernard Connor, even if his story of intellectual experimentation saw him move across the whole spectrum of the Enlightenment. He dabbled with empirical observations of a foreign country and rationalist deductions about the natural world, as well he accepted a form of freethinking materialism in speculations on the soul.[163] Born in County Kerry in 1666, Connor was a student of the college at Reims, where he appears to have encountered the new science of Cartesianism. He trained as a medic, and it was in that capacity he travelled to Poland in 1694, taking up the post of physician to the monarch, John III. He stayed less than a year, finding the intellectual conservatism of the court too stifling for his ambitions. He settled in London in early 1695, where he converted to the established church. He seems to have marked this transition by altering his surname, from the Irish sounding O'Connor to the more neutral

Connor. His travels paid significant dividends in gaining him entry into the capital's literary society: he donated Polish material to the Royal Society, and was soon a member of its august ranks. Alongside lecturing at Oxford on anatomy he penned a *History of Poland*, published in two volumes in 1698.

As a medical practitioner Connor was marked by a commitment to empirical observation and practical experimentation. His central achievement came in the field of anatomy, where he was the first to identify the back condition ankylosing spondylitis.[164] He also developed a 'new plan of animal economy', 'being a natural account of the fabrick and operations of the human body, grounded on experiments of chymistry and dissections of live and dead animals', which he 'demonstrated at Oxford in the Spring Anno 1695, in London in the Winter following, and at Cambridge in the year 1696'.[165] This schema centred on the importance of blood in supplying life to an organism and paradoxically introducing disease. In summarising his views, he described how 'after having examined the different parts of the world, and the elements of the body by chemistry, I have divided the human body into solid and fluid parts. Before I considered the solid parts in particular, I thought it necessary by way of chemistry to be acquainted with all the humours, and specially with the principles and motions of the blood, which is the *Primum Mobile* of the whole machine.'[166] Note here how the account offers a narrative of Connor's personal intellectual interrogation, a biographical expression of the empirical method, something which also underpins his remedial conclusions:

> I have likewise examined and endeavoured to explain the nature and
> different effects of alterating medicaments, which operate in the mass
> of blood without any evacuation, such as sweeten the blood when
> sowr [*sic*], that thin it when gross and thick, that hasten its too slow
> circulation, that stop its too rapid motion, as in fevers; that cool the
> blood, that heat it and raise the spirits, as cordials; that calm the
> spirits, as narcotics; that strengthen the tone of the parts, as Styptics
> and Astringents; that open obstructions, as asperitives.[167]

Indicative of this commitment is where Connor lays claim to the 'several years fervent application [needed] for anyone to attain a tolerable knowledge of' the topic, which itself 'cost me some months labour to demonstrate at Oxford.'[168]

Equally empirical in its tenor was his work on Poland, itself a contribution to the 'state of nations' genre which Anglican Ireland developed in the 1690s.

Drawing explicitly on his experiences while living there, Connor documented a wide array of issues relating to the kingdom, from its constitutional structure to its geography and economic power. Moreover, he was anxious to discern from these observations the play of institutions and character, dwelling on the temper and manners of the Poles. As he summarised his impressions, 'they exceed all the nations in Europe in vivacity of spirit, strength of body and living long, which cannot be occasioned by their climate, because the Swedes, Muscovites and Germans live all under the same parallel, and yet enjoy not the like vigour and health.'[169] Instead Connor connected these characteristics to the diet and their habit of 'living hardily', the popularity of hunting and other exercises, their preference for hard beds, and to political culture.[170] With regard to this last element, he argued that 'their health, vigour and vivacity may reasonably be augmented by their great freedom and privileges; for where slavery hebetates and blunts the mind, and consequently enervates the body, liberty exhilarates the one, and by that means strengthens the other.'[171]

This political culture had a further consequence in making the Poles, 'generally open-hearted and honest . . . more apt to be deceived than to deceive and not so easily provoked as appeased.' Indeed, Connor identified as their greatest fault

> that they run mad after liberty, and rather drive than invite their kings
> to observe their laws. They not only hate the name of slavery, but
> likewise abhor a just and hereditary monarchy. The gentry claim
> prerogatives that will scarce give them leave to be guilty of any crime,
> and whenever they happen to acknowledge any such, the prince has
> seldom the power to punish it. They are not only licentious in their
> morals and civil life, but likewise in religion and sacred observances,
> for without fear of ecclesiastical censures, they will both talk and act
> as they please against that function, affirming themselves self-suffi-
> cient to be their own guides in those matters.[172]

Connor's proximity to the subjects of his portraits was illustrated through the domestic specificity that he brought to bear. In dealing with their appearance, he was able to observe how 'their present fashion is a vest that reaches down to the middle of their legs, not unlike our morning gowns, lined with fur'; a detail that added little to his central argument, but which built up the reader's image of a well-informed and acute social observer.[173] So too, he regularly highlighted exceptions to his general trends, which argued for his competency as a guide and for the overarching validity of his more general assertions. He noted how 'some few of the Poles imitate the French fashion and wear linen and lace, point, perukes, and swords', at once telling the reader of the general applicability of his first description and informing them of the intrusion of foreign fashions and modes into the Polish psyche.[174]

The recounting of intimate detail exposed how heavily Connor drew on personal experience to compile his account; a conceit underlined by his structuring of the text as a series of epistles to a variety of grandees. So for example, in dealing with funereal practice, he protested to John Lord Marquis of Normandy that

> it may not be improper to entertain your Lordship with the manner
> of her [Queen Mary Ludovica, wife to Sir John Casimir] death, there
> being something observable in it. She died of a defluxion upon her
> lungs, or of a consumption, occasioned by an excess of passion, on
> account of a contest she had had with the Chancellor Patz about
> something she had proposed to him which he would not consent to.
> This princess loved so dearly to intermeddle with, and to govern the
> state solely according to her fancy, that she was not a little jealous
> when the king, her husband, spoke to other women, and that chiefly
> for fear that he might incline to be governed by another more than
> herself. This your Lordship may imagine gave him no great cause to
> be concerned at her death, for at the very instant of her expiring, he
> posted away to a mistress he had formerly loved, but whom he durst
> not of spoke to during his queen's life.[175]

The passage combines the intimacy of a letter, and the possibility of transmitting salacious tittle-tattle, with an assertion of Connor's privileged position—his acquaintance with the intricacies of power—and his professional competency in giving a view as to the cause of the queen's demise, all within the context of a philosophically minded section devoted to detailing the Polish manner of mourning.

Yet all this was completed in the wake of Connor's removal from the court, a departure caused by a contretemps when dining at the court of King John III. He had been quizzed concerning his view of the location of the soul and answered,

> I might perhaps differ from the divines then present, and conse-
> quently oppose the common doctrines of the Schools, for they hold,
> with Aristotle, that the soul is entire with all the body, and wholly in

every part of the body, which was impossible to conceive; for if the soul was entire in every part of the body, there would be as many souls in the body as there are parts, since it is impossible that the self-same substance, though an indivisible spirit, can ever be in two places at the same time; besides the soul can't be but where it does think, and everyone finds by experience, that his thoughts is not in his hands nor feet, but is conscious to himself that his thoughts are in his head, and that consequently the soul must be only in the brain, which is the seat of sensation, and the origin of all the nerves, which are the organs of perception and motion.[176]

This overt rejection of Aristotelian doctrine did indeed provoke the feared negative response, with one dinner guest, Father Vota, arguing that 'if the soul was only in the head, the rest of the body would be dead'.[177] Matters became more heated when the king enquired of Connor as to the nature of death. Once again, Connor was plainspoken in his rejection of the Scholastic thesis: 'The School divinity maintains that death was a separation of the rational soul from the body . . . I could not allow that separation was the cause of death, but that the death of the body was the cessation of the motion of the heart, of the blood, and of the spirits . . . by which it appears that the separation of the soul is not properly the cause of death, but that the death of the body is the cause of the separation.'[178] This materialist position led Connor to an avowal of his general methodological approach, alongside a general critique of the Catholic clergy for their attachment to Aristotelian modes of thought:

By this you may plainly see how fond the divines are of their old opinions, relying upon the doctrine of Aristotle, whom we can't suppose to be so thoroughly acquainted with the structure, springs and motion of the human body, nor indeed with all other natural causes, as the modern physicians are; yet it is the policy of the divines, not only in Poland, but in Spain, Italy and most other countries where their power is very great, not to let any opinions creep in among them, that would seem to contradict those of Aristotle; for having built their systems of divinity upon the principles of this pagan philosopher, they are justly afraid that if experience and reason should shake the foundation, the superstructure would fall to the ground, as doubtless it would for the most part.[179]

In this passage Connor explicitly twinned 'experience and reason' in accounting for his method, and while empiricism informed his medical work, rationalism was more prominent in his treatment of miracles.

That this encounter in Poland provided an initial spur to reflections on miracles was hinted at when, in recalling the origins of the book, he observed, 'I had formerly discoursed with others, both in this and in other countries, upon the same subject, and had some years ago drawn up a rude scheme of an essay towards the clearing of this point.'[180] In the same volume, Connor's English-language version of his ideas concerning miracles was set in the context of a series of appended letters on animal economy and the principals of physics. In 'A Letter to his reverend Dean J. R., concerning *Evangelium Medici*', Connor broached the controversial core of his views.[181]

This letter indicates that just as his physical peregrinations did not end at the Polish court—removing himself via Holland to London—nor were Connor's intellectual voyages complete, for the Latin text *Evangelium medici; seu medicina mystica; de suspensis naturae legibus, sive de miraculis*, published in two editions in 1697, dwelt at length on that central, and highly controversial, question of faith: the existence and explicability of miracles. In contrast to the empiricism so evident in his description of Poland, Connor's treatment of the topic was intrinsically rationalist in approach, dealing with the deductive consequences of a central assumption. For example, note the emphasis on first principles in his stated ambition: 'My design therefore, Sir, is to endeavour to make it no longer a difficulty to conceive, and make evident by reason, and the principles of physic, I mean the principles of nature, all the supernatural effects authentically delivered to us concerning bodies chiefly, but particularly the humane.'[182]

The central principal upon which Connor then built his thesis was that 'motion is the only true cause of all natural phenomena; and [by logical deduction] the suspension of the laws of this motion are the only causes of all supernatural effects.'[183] From this, he postulated that 'the laws of motion can be suspended . . . and by one or more of those laws of suspension, it is easy to solve all supernatural effects.'[184] Such a suspension, effected by God, was a standard defence of the concept of miracles, and in this Connor was well within the bounds of orthodoxy. What was striking about his work was thus not its content, but its tenor. Particularly startling was his assertion of status within the debate; a claim founded upon his position as a physician. As Connor construed the matter, it was evident that 'since it is on all sides acknowledged that miraculous effects are above natural causes, no people can better judge whether any effect is really supernatural than those that make it their business and profession to know how far the activity of natural causes can reach.'[185] Connor was here proclaiming that it was the physician and the natural philosopher, not the theologian and cleric, who occupied a privileged position of authority when it came to adjudicating over the presence of the divine in the natural world. Nor did he limit himself to self-aggrandisement. In a brusque attack on such authorities he proposed it was 'for want of sufficient insight in this matter [of natural phenomena, that] several divines of the latter ages have given very gross ideas of the supernatural effects they have pretended to explain; and in several places where I have been, I saw them either through ignorance or for interest give out for miracles phenomena that were only surprising effects of natural causes, which has given so great an occasion to scepticism and increase of Deism.'[186]

The anticlerical streak within his text was sharpened by an empirical example drawn from Connor's personal history. In a telling anecdote, he recalled how

> at Rome some years since, passing by chance through the Strabo del Popolo, I saw a multitude of people hurrying a man to St Mark's Chapel, which belongs to the Venetian Ambassadors; they told me he was possessed with the devil, and that they were carrying him there to be exorcised. I crowded through the throng into the church, and felt the man's pulse; I found him in a fever, making hideous grimaces and motions with his face, eyes, tongue and all his limbs, which were nothing else but a fit of convulsive motions all over his body, occasioned by a disorder of his blood and spirits, being a hypochondrical [sic] person. The clergy began very devoutly to fright the pretended devil out of him, and in a little time his disorderly motions ceased, which, as they thought to be the miraculous effect of their prayers, I attributed to the natural abatement and usual cessation of such fits.[187]

In this, Connor was giving vent to anti-Catholic as well as anticlerical feelings, yet his awareness of the sensitivities required in treating the topic was clarified when he disavowed any desire to intrude on theological questions. In a rather disingenuous passage at the start of the missive, given what was to come, he reassured his addressee that 'the learned and judicious gentlemen of your gown can have no reason to complain that I have invaded their province, or encroached upon their prerogatives. For I do not undertake to prove that there were ever any supernatural effects produced, that matter I think belongs entirely to divines to make evident from authentic testimony; I only endeavour to demonstrate the possibility of them, and if there ever were any to demonstrate the *mode* and *mechanism* with which we may conceive how they might have been performed.'[188] In this, Connor was apparently drawing clear demarcation lines around his project. In a similar and not entirely convincing fashion, he repudiated any implication that his project was theologically subversive or conducive to free thought. Rather he asserted that 'I hope to convince our sceptics, the Deists, who must give their assent when they have the same evident reason to conceive of the possibility, and consequently to believe the truth of such miraculous effects that are authentically related as they have to conceive that straw can burn in a flaming fire.'[189]

Despite such assurances and protective denials, Connor's commitment to the Enlightenment project can be summarised by his declaration of intellectual independence. 'Since therefore experience and reason are our only guides', he wrote, 'no body is to take it amiss if I censure such as wrote before me, with as much justice as they did their predecessors: for I'm sworn to no master.'[190] This at once expressed his disdain for the scholastic method, in which the citation of past authority is granted status as a mode of proof, and his concomitant adoption of the empirical and rationalist methods of procedure.

Yet Connor clearly was anxious to repudiate any suggestion that he had fallen beyond the limits of orthodoxy by adopting materialism. The reality of this border in his mind is further suggested by the rumour of his deathbed return to the faith of his birth. Although his conversion to the Church of England had proven professionally wise, the Anglican cleric William Hayley who attended Connor on his deathbed in October 1698 deemed it necessary, when offering solace, to 'put several questions to him, as whether he believed in the gospel? Whether he gave credit to the miracles that are there recorded and looked upon them as attestations of the truth of the Christian religion? Whether he believed that Jesus Christ was the saviour of the world, and that he came to be our propitiation, and to satisfy divine justice for the sins of mankind?'[191]

Having sought this assurance concerning the suspicions of holding 'some heterodox opinions, which his censurer imputed to' Connor, Hayley pronounced him 'sufficiently purged [of] the imputation of deism, Socinianism and popery' and 'a true penitent member of the Church of England'.[192] However, Hayley then sheepishly reported how, after he departed, and 'partly on occasion of an accident', 'a certain person, who it seems was a Romish priest, came to the doctor's lodgings, and desired very earnestly to see him, declaring that he was his countryman, his friend and his relation'.[193] An eavesdropper reported how the priest, having gained admission to the invalid, had given Connor 'absolution and then asked him whether he would have extreme unction, and the doctor [Connor] said yes, after which it was suspected it was given to him.'[194] To Hayley this apparent prevarication 'both with God and man' was little more than evidence of how 'his judgement was now quite decayed and that he did not know what he did'.[195] Yet it seems that at the last Connor had reverted to O'Connor, the Anglican thinker had renewed his faith in Catholicism, and the polemicist had fallen silent.

Religious Enlightenment in Ireland

The Enlightenment in Catholic Ireland had its limits; albeit ones that, in rejecting free thought and overt heresy, were broadly shared by the Anglican community and by the Presbyterian communion. The need to maintain a confessional identity under the immense psychological pressure of the penal code forced the Catholic community to hold fast to the orthodoxies and belief systems that defined them. For the Anglicans, it was the need to uphold a claim to political power and God's favour that ensured heterodoxy was not to be tolerated. And for Presbyterians, the adoption of Arianism was anathema, for it undermined the complex relationship between the rational believer and his deity, as well as drowning out any pleas for toleration from the state they might utter.

Yet experimentation with the empirical and rational methods was a shared feature of the intellectual life that emerged across the religious spectrum in the wake of the War of the Two Kings as they sought novel ways to justify the continuing public articulation of their faith. While Scholasticism retained its hold on the vast bulk of the Irish population, whatever their denominational identity, the chaos and confusion brought by the armies of James II and William III induced in parts of the cultural elite the desire to rethink their condition and to reassess the problems facing their communities. They brought a crucial new assumption to the task, turning away from the initial premise of God's existence, and replacing it with the rather more mundane, if immodest, proclamation that philosophical reasoning must begin with the recognition of the human being's centrality. Only then might a truly human understanding be broached and a 'science of man' articulated. So too, they brought to bear approaches that differentiated the Enlightenment into different forms and colourings: the inductive reasoning of those of an empirical bent; the deductive procedures of those of a rationalist temper; and the speculations of the freethinkers at the limits of the Enlightenment spectrum.

In other words, while Ireland was still a God-fearing and Christian country, and the vast majority of its inhabitants remained uninspired by the paths explored by the cultural elite treated here, the early decades of the eighteenth century witnessed the emergence of a Religious Enlightenment in Ireland: at once an Enlightenment in that it assumed the same starting point and many of the same approaches to problems as was to be found in Enlightened thought elsewhere in Europe, and yet religious, in that the issues to which the thinkers put their energies into solving were conditioned, if not determined, by the question of confession—the public articulation of faith. The responses they devised depended on the religious demography and political history of the country. The unstable position of the Presbyterians, a minority faith and politically occluded, prompted in some dissenters a rethinking of the very nature of humanity, choosing to assert the essential value of human endeavour in a subtle plea for state toleration of their condition. The political supremacy enjoyed by the minority Anglican communion shaped their Enlightenment towards an empirical acceptance of the world as they found it. In direct contrast, the political repression of Catholicism pushed Catholic thinkers towards the rearticulation of Scholastic verities.

Yet despite the variations in topics and themes, the bedrock of Enlightenment assumptions and practices are locatable beyond the rubric and rhetoric of individual cases. John Abernethy, George Berkeley, and Sylvester Lloyd share an intellectual heritage grounded on rationalism, just as much as they differ in their confessional allegiance. So too, there are identifiable similarities, generated by the empirical methods they employ, in the thought patterns of Francis Hutcheson, William Molyneux, and Cornelius Nary. Just as significantly, John Malcome, Jonathan Swift, and Michael Moore approached philosophical questions from a shared Scholastic standpoint, while Thomas Emlyn, Robert Clayton, and Bernard Connor all explored the possibilities of heterodox free thought. The confessional differences between these thinkers have done much to occlude their intellectual similarities, but they are there nonetheless.

In fact, the Enlightenment intruded early into Ireland, and took on a religious hue from the debates in which it intervened. Yet that was not the end of the story, for by its very involvement, it came to reshape and redefine the very problems it encountered. The Enlightenment may have emerged within a religious dialogue, but it did not remain there. By 1730 it was starting to transform itself, and with it the intellectual life of the country as a whole. The transformation from a phase of Religious Enlightenment to one of Social Enlightenment was under way, and it was to open up possibilities and reframe problems in startling new ways in the half century before 1780.

PART TWO

The Social Enlightenment,

ca. 1730–ca. 1760

∾

4

Languages of Civility

∾

Whether the bulk of our Irish natives are not kept from thriving by that cynical content in dirt and beggary, which they possess to a degree beyond any other people in the kingdom?
—George Berkeley, *The Querist*, 1752

THE MAJOR PROBLEM facing Ireland's political nation by the 1730s was the parlous condition of the economy.[1] Following a period of growth in the immediate wake of the 1688–1691 war, decay set in during the late 1710s. Although this was followed by a brief recovery, the late 1720s saw a devastating series of harvest failures.[2] In 1725 and 1726 Ireland experienced extremely bad summer weather and scarcity. The harvest failed again in 1727 and 1728. By the spring of 1729, even the relatively unaffected Munster region saw food riots prompted by the exportation of scarce commodities to the other provinces.[3] The crisis produced a flood of beggars into the capital. Conditions there were exacerbated by the weather preventing coal ships from docking at the port. So concentrated was the influx of the poor into Dublin that proposals were floated for their treatment. This culminated in the 1730s with the notorious proposition by Jonathan Swift that beggars be badged to enable identification of which parish was responsible for their upkeep in accordance with the poor law.[4]

Even when the subject was not directly relevant, the profusion of the poor insinuated itself into Irish consciousness. Francis Hutcheson could remark, in a discussion of Thomas Hobbes, 'the poor creatures we meet on the streets seem to know the avenues to the humane breast better than our philosophers'.[5] Swift alluded to the problem in the opening of his *Modest Proposal* (1729), observing 'it is a melancholy object to those who walk through this great town, or travel in the country, when they see the streets, the roads, and cabin doors, crowded with beggars of the female sex, followed by three, four or six children, all in rags, and importuning every passenger for an alms.'[6] David Bindon fretted in 1729 that

> among us there is not any care taken to prevent the people's falling
> into extreme poverty, nor to relieve them when they are in that
> condition. It is no wonder therefore to see our streets crowded with
> beggars of all sizes, and such objects of compassion exposed to public
> view, as makes a good-natured man's heart bleed to behold his fellow
> creatures reduced to such misery. Yet it would be inhumane to prevent
> their begging in the streets, until better provision is made for their
> sustenance.[7]

Arthur Dobbs was clearly thinking of contemporary circumstance when in 1729 he contended that 'by such methods our numerous poor must increase, for want of money and trade to employ them, and become a burden to the remainder; the values and rents of lands must fall, and the whole community be turbulent and uneasy, wishing for any change to alter their condition'.[8]

Both the grassland economy of the south and the proto-industrial landscape of Ulster were depressed, the latter situation resulting in the migration of large numbers of Presbyterians from Ulster to the American colonies.[9] This was a matter of official concern. In 1729 Lord Carteret, the lord lieutenant, expressed his 'regret to hear that such great numbers of Protestants have left the north of Ireland' while Anglican churchmen feared that the depletion of Ulster of its Calvinist population made the Protestant task of reformation all the more difficult.[10] Primate Hugh Boulter of Armagh wrote to the Duke of Newcastle on 23 November 1728 apologising that

> I am obliged to give your Grace so melancholy an account of the state
> of this kingdom, as I shall in this letter, but I thought it my duty to
> let his Majesty know our present condition in the north. For we have
> had three bad harvests together here, which has made oatmeal, which
> is their great subsistence much dearer than ordinary . . . The whole
> north is in a ferment at present, and people every day engaging one

another to go next year to the West Indies. The humour has spread
like a contagious distemper, and the people will hardly hear any body
that tries to cure them of this madness. The worst is that it affects
only Protestants, and reigns chiefly in the north, which is the seat of
our linen manufacture.[11]

The following March he detailed how 'the humour of going to America still
continues and the scarcity of provisions certainly makes many quit us: there are
now seven ships at Belfast that are carrying off about 1,000 passengers thither.'[12]
At the end of the month, still despairing, he summarised the bleak circumstance
in a letter to British Prime Minister Robert Walpole: 'With scarceness of corn in
the north and the loss of all credit there, by the numbers that talk of going to
America, and with the disturbances in the south, this kingdom is at present in a
deplorable condition.'[13]

An even deeper crisis engulfed the country in late 1739, when a sequence
of extraordinary climatic occurrences tipped Ireland into full-blown famine.
Beginning in December 1739 with a deep and resilient frost, which drastically
reduced the potato crop in the spring, a long-lasting drought followed which,
among other detrimental effects, resulted in widespread fires in the urban centres of Carrick-on-Suir, Thurles and Moate, and Wexford. The lack of rain decimated tillage, resulting in the widespread death of livestock due to lack of feed.
Bread prices soared and riots ensued. In April 1740 Drogheda flared into violence, prompted by the exportation of grain, and the port closed. May saw disruption in Cork and Dublin, where a bread riot disturbed the city for several
days. Belfast, which seemed to have escaped much of the trauma, saw demonstrations over the price of food. While the August harvest alleviated some of the
suffering, the autumnal weather was again distressingly bitter, with snowstorms
in September and November followed by flooding and frost in December. Deep
snow accentuated the crisis, and although this was to be brief—ten days duration before the ice started to break and melt—the cumulative effect of the year
of want was to weaken the populace and prime it for disease. In the spring of
1741 smallpox, dysentery, typhus, and relapsing fever took hold, and food shortages rapidly accelerated the mortality rates as summer arrived, even as, in early
July, food prices finally started to fall. The last great weather event of the crisis
occurred when Leinster suffered extensive flooding, but food had largely been
harvested. Through the dark months of famine and disease somewhere between

310,000 and 480,000 people died; signifying between 13 and 20 percent of the island's population.[14]

Something of the reach of the famine can be evidenced in the response of the Irish-language poets.[15] The Dublin-based Tadhg Ó Neachtain captured the quality of emotional distress felt across the country, while subtly hinting at the political context in his opening refrain:

> Má bhí brón ró-mhór gan téimheal
> 'Na chinnteacht daoirse i gCrich Fhéilim,
> Fulang fada gan neach do réiteach
> Bhus so am an chantail phréachta
>
> Ochón ochón ochón m'éagnach!
> Ochón i mbrón is ochón déarach!
> Mo chreach chráite bás déanach,
> An photáta dílis croí na féile!
>
> Má bhí gan cháidh diachair Éireann,
> má bhí gach dearc 'na sreabh déara,
> gach ceann má bhí i ndaoirse daorbhroid,
> bhus so am an chantail phréachta.
>
> If there was great unremitting sorrow
> as certain evidence of oppression in Ireland
> Continual suffering unrelieved by anybody
> This will be the time of the frozen sorrow.
>
> Alas alas alas, my cause of grief!
> Alas in sorrow, and alas in tears
> My bitter loss for the recent death
> Of the faithful potato, the heart of generosity!
>
> If the sorrow of Ireland was unremitting
> If every eye was a stream of tears
> If every head was depressed in woe
> This will be the time of frozen sorrow.[16]

From the heart of the crisis, in Munster, a poem emerged in the hand of Seaghán Ó Dálaigh which placed the dearth directly into a political frame.[17] The Jacobite resonance of the opening stanza was coupled with an appeal to God's special providence for salvation, in a standard Scholastic trope of the genre:

M'atuirse ghéar, mo phéin, mo bhrón, mo bhroid,
Flatha na nGael i ngéibhinn chruaidh anois,
A mbeatha go léir gur léirscrios uatha an sioc,
Is gan carthannacht Dé níl gaor a bhfuascalta.

My great sorrow, my pain, alas, my worry
The leaders of the Gaels are now in a harsh prison
All their food is destroyed by the frost
And without God's charity there is no hope of saving them.[18]

Immediate blame was heaped on those landlords who Ó Dálaigh deemed guilty of failing in their humanitarian duty: 'Is daor na heaspaithe chleachtaoid in ardchríoch Mhogha, / Glaoch ar airgead fearainn is fataí ag lobhadh' ('Cruel are the exactions they are imposing in Ireland / Demanding rent while the potatoes are rotting').[19]

Yet the poet also recognised that relief could be found in unlikely places; one such was the leadership offered by Bishop George Berkeley of the Church of Ireland in Cloyne, who garnered resounding praise:

Tá déirc is daonnacht in easpag Chluanach,
Agus glaofad go haerach i bhflaitheas thuas air.

Is air do scríbhfidhear go fírinneach gach text tig uaidh,
Is gur chríochnaigh go fínis an léann go suairc,
Maoifeadsa ar dhraoithibh 's ar éigsibh suaigh,
Gur fírinneach do ghníthear an déirc i gCluain.

Charity and humanity imbue the bishop of Cloyne
And I will cheerfully call on him in heaven above.

Every text from him will be truthfully written in his honour
That he brought scholarship to completion civilly
I will boast to poets and composers of song
that alms are genuinely given in Cloyne.[20]

Berkeley's initiative in giving alms and soup was needed given the inability of the state to intervene adequately to alleviate the suffering.[21] Indeed, the work of the churches more generally was vital, and a number of schemes were devised to help. Anglican clergy in Dublin organised a public relief fund, for instance, while the Catholic Church reduced the number of fast days, allowing their congregants to take nutrients when available. Individuals also acted. Prior to his appointment as Grand Master of the Freemasons of Ireland in 1741, Charles, Baron Moore of Tullamore spent time in 1740 collecting money in the city for the poor. Katharine Conolly gave over £300 to build an obelisk on her estate at Castletown, County Kildare, the folly serving as a private works scheme for the labourers.[22]

The Presbyterian James Arbuckle certainly understood the nature of the crisis. In *The Tribune*, he bore witness to how 'the people . . . are a generation of half-starved, half-naked, half-dead animals, and a nursery for nothing else but the whipping post, the plantations and the gallows.'[23] His pessimistic view drew upon his image of the cotters, who, as he described closely,

> live in little huts, or cabins, much in the same form and capaciousness
> with swine-sties, and move, with their families, like the Tartars, from
> place to place, as they can get out of debt with their landlords or into
> employment elsewhere. Their choicest food is potatoes, cabbage and
> milk, which they enjoy only one part of the year. For during the rest of
> it they must content themselves with such herbs as they can pick up in
> the fields, and make themselves merry with a plug of tobacco and a
> cup of pure elements . . . They generally lie upon dirty straw, with a
> coarse cadew over them; and their habit is no more than merely a
> covering for their nakedness . . . The wife has four or five ill-looking
> children, who all pig together on the ground, in one of those swine-
> sties aforesaid, which is filled with smoke, filth and vermin.[24]

Despite the animalistic imagery and the apparent lack of sentiment this passage evinced, Arbuckle attested this was 'a wretched, but true representation of the misery of these poor people'.[25]

Writing in the midst of a dearth, the rest of the essay was spent identifying the causes of this economic failure. The stringent blame he levelled in the first instance on the landlords, who rented out land on harsh terms. This was coupled with additional costs for grazing and a percentage taken for every bushel of grain sold. 'In these circumstances', he asked, 'how is it possible for them to be better fed or clothed, or instructed than we see them?'[26] Secondly, while he proposed that 'the children . . . must be taken wholly out of the management of their parents [and] . . . kept constantly to some kind of work', the next issue articulated a complaint he had with the economic structure.[27] As he explained: 'In Ireland . . . besides the proprietor of the soil, the land maintains three or four, and in many parts, a greater number of intermediate landlords, who must all be supported out of the produce of the ground, and the labour of the poor creatures who immediately occupy or manure it.'[28] To Arbuckle's mind the middlemen were no more than a 'motley generation of half landlords, half tenants [who] fill the country with a sort of idle half gentry, half commonalty, who abound at all races, cock-fights, and country fairs; and are the very pest and bane of the nation.'[29] Their hybrid economic stature confused Ireland's social order, providing a false sense of power to a group of mimics and fops, 'in constant emulation with our gentry to keep up a rank and character, to which they are in no ways entitled; and for that purpose, are perpetually running into the most expensive and extravagant methods of living.'[30] A burden on the honest farmer, middlemen caused a general distrust in the code of manners and appearances.[31] An economic blight and moral threat, in response, Arbuckle used the artifice of a tribune to propose sumptuary laws so that 'no person for the future should hold more land of another, than he could sufficiently occupy, that is manure by himself and servants.'[32]

Arbuckle's economic proposals were intimately connected with his vision of an Irish civil society that contained aspirational, descriptive, and deliberative elements. While the economic crisis of the late 1720s was the prompt for *The Tribune* and accounted for much of its content, he did not limit its reforming zeal to the material well-being of the community. Instead, as the first issue of the periodical set out, the title of the new publication was derived from the Roman adjudicator who acted as a public moralist:

> Their whole authority consisted in controlling the decrees of the
> Senate, by the Latin word VETO; that is to say, *I forbid it*, by which
> they gave their negative to any public resolutions, whenever they
> judged them contrary to the interests of their constituents . . . These
> magistrates, as they were only designed for the protection of the
> distressed so for a long time were they the chief rampart of the public
> liberty against the usurpations of the great and the rich.[33]

Arbuckle's *Tribune* thus struck a didactic tone. Issue five, for example, consisted of a letter taking up the perennial concern of eighteenth-century Irishmen, the linen industry and the importation of foreign cloths. Arbuckle followed a conscientiously patriotic line, with the 'Tribunes of the People of Ireland . . . prohibit[ing] the use and wear of lustring scarves and Cypress hatbands at all funerals in this Kingdom.'[34]

The ethical content of *The Tribune* became clear in issue ten which documented a debate about why landlords absented themselves from Ireland and removed to England.[35] Perplexity was expressed that Ireland could not retain its local ruling elite; exasperation was voiced at the idea that England could tempt them away through a blend of entertainments and attractions. Even with regard to 'the affair of gallantry', it was mused that 'we had much the same opportunities as the rest of the world, being supplied with sufficient supplies of sinners who might be kept very cheaply in clean linen, provided our wild sparks would stay at home and encourage their country-wares.'[36] Delinquency was directly attributed to a

> luxurious and expensive manner of living which has of late years
> grown so upon us . . . Men of elegant taste are naturally lovers of
> retirement; and for that reason would chose to spend the best part of
> their time at their country seats, to enjoy the pleasures of temperance,
> contemplation, study and exercise. But, at present, this delightful way
> of life seems to be banished the country and those places which ought
> to be the retreats of wisdom and virtue, are become the principle
> scenes of riot and debauch.[37]

Here the image of the countryside as the rural idyll, a haven from the corrupting influence of the city, was overthrown and replaced with one in which 'the whole business of the day is to course down a hare, or some other such worthy purchase; to get over the most enormous and immoderate dinner; and guzzle down a proportionable quantity of wine'.[38] Violence, gluttony, and drunkenness—'the real pleasures of country are forgotten; tranquillity and ease [are] made to give way to tumult and uproar; and those beauties of nature [are left] unattended to, which are so refreshing both to body and mind.'[39] By setting up this opposition between the reality and the ideal, the essay contended for an ethical life, conceived in term of politeness, self-control, and moderation. With Dublin suffering from its proximity to the neighbourhoods they had left behind, it was to London the landed gentry flocked, for 'they have the opportunity there of living according to their own inclinations, either by shutting themselves up in the utmost privacy, or going into the soberest and politest company.'[40]

'Soberest and politest', Arbuckle was here subscribing to the ideology of civility and turning a moral tradition upside down by locating the imaginative landscape of virtue in an urban space and away from the supposed indecency of rural life.[41] He also predicated a life within the urban world filled with associational activity; with company, conversation, and conviviality. In issue two, he described a set of gentlemen acquaintances helping him to compose the periodical. They included an Irish gentleman, Sir Humphry Thorowgood, and his literary son, Mr Edward; a medic, Dr Hartshorn; a spendthrift esquire, Richard Marygold of Kerry; a parsimonious high Tory, Thomas Verger; and an English republican of the commonwealth variety, William Truman.[42] While these men were ciphers, allowing Arbuckle to comment on a range of local issues, the conceit was ideologically loaded, mimicking Joseph Addison's invented coterie of Sir Roger de Coverley, the knight-errant; Andrew Freeport, the merchant; Captain Sentry the military man; and William Honeycomb, the gallant who appeared in *The Spectator* series.[43] In other words, Arbuckle was stating his commitment to the commercial civility that informed Addison's venture, and was translating it to Irish circumstances.[44]

This civility was made explicit in concocting the figures. Sir Humphrey who, having made his fortune in the wool trade, 'when in town . . . usually takes his morning's walk around St Stephen's Green and adjourns from thence to the Anne Coffee House'. His son, while not yet forty and too young to be a tribune, was similarly polite, for 'his travels have mightily improved his taste of books, men and manners. And a certain softness of behaviour, which never fails to distinguish the fine gentleman from the mere scholar, makes him the most delightful as well as the most instructive companion.'[45] If this seems rather bland, spice and grit were added to the company by Thomas Verger, whose 'notions of government are fitter to direct a good prince than to preserve a nation from an ill one', and Mr Trueman, 'by birth an Englishman and, as his father had a considerable command under the Rump parliament, this his son became of course very early devoted to the republican notions.'[46] Social tolerance prevailed in the virtues of the medic Dr Hartshorn, including how 'he reasons strongly and has a clear and beautiful expression', and Richard Marygold, who was complimented 'for that just taste which he has in poetry and all the other species of polite writing.'[47] By allowing these men to contribute to the imaginative history of the periodical, and by drawing such a varied constellation of characters from the Irish social scene, Arbuckle was developing a conception of Enlightenment which was constituted by and contributing to civil society.[48]

Arbuckle had a wide view of the project of civility, and *The Tribune* captured the multivalent nature of this programme of personal refinement and cultural amelioration. In forwarding these ideas, Arbuckle was not a lone voice, for his writing fits into a wider discourse of civility that can be identified across the Irish Enlightenment of the middle decades of the century. For instance, in the advertisement by the author for the 1752 edition of the *Querist*, George Berkeley opined that

> as the sum of human happiness is supposed to consist in the goods of mind, body and fortune, I would fain make my studies of some use to mankind with regard to each of these three particulars, and hope it will not be thought faulty or indecent in any man, of whatever profession soever, to offer his mite towards improving the manners, health and prosperity of his fellow creatures.[49]

Berkeley was signalling his intention of contributing to the discourses of politeness and improvement; two languages which can be identified as operating within the Social Enlightenment in midcentury Ireland.

Politeness dealt primarily with people, and their modes of behaviour, their adoption of certain norms, and their moral purview. It proposed an internal reformation. Improvement focussed on objects, projecting an external amelioration of the conditions of life. It offered a programme of estate improvement, architectural accomplishment, and industrial advancement.[50] These two languages within the discourse of civility which were concerned with individual circumstance were coupled with two further concerns, namely those of aesthetics and political economy, which dealt with the themes of beautification and economic advancement on a general level. Both levels involved rejecting the confessional divisions of Irish society to the extent that they emphasised the need for all parties in the country to commit to creating a civil society. The middle years of the century thereby saw the emergence of a moderate, high Social Enlightenment in which rationalist and empirical methods took central stage, promulgating critical approaches and models for action.[51] The methodologies of Scholasticism and freethinking speculation made lesser contributions to these languages, although their contribution can be occasionally isolated in the broad discourse of civility. In this chapter the four languages within the discourse of civility—of politeness and aesthetics, improvement and political economy—are surveyed to capture the polyvocal and occasionally discordant debate that developed within the Social Enlightenment about how best to develop the country in moral and material terms in the shadow of hunger and want.

The Ethos of Refinement

The middle decades of the century saw the articulation of a distinctively Irish approach to the issue of politeness, one bound up with the understanding of rhetoric. This school of thought was decisively positive about rhetoric, evincing scant scepticism about artificial speech and deceptive appeals to emotions. An appeal was instead made to the natural modes of speech, suggesting that the country was capable of polite behaviour despite its reputation as a rude nation. In that, it spoke to the possibilities of cross-confessional communication.

The concern that Ireland was habituated to uncouth behaviour was expressed in a series of projects for inculcating civic decency and cultural refinement that emerged in the immediate aftermath the War of the Two Kings (1688–1691). For instance, the Society for the Reformation of Manners, founded in the wake of a 1695 act of parliament, was established 'for the more effectual suppressing of profane cursing and swearing'.[52] The society utilised standard presentment forms, brought over from a sister body in England, to help members to bring miscreants to court. Its aim was to enforce the legislation by managing civic activism, and was notable for its interdenominational Protestant membership, with dissenters' prominence worrying the Church of Ireland hierarchy. Despite an initial flurry of enthusiasm, which saw similar associations spring up in Drogheda, Kilkenny, and Maynooth, the impetus was soon lost and the society disbanded.[53]

Despite an apparent revival in attempts to convert the native Irish symbolised by the charter school movement of the 1730s, the trend was towards improvement within the confines of the established church. Thus the Anglican clergy concerned themselves with maintaining the church buildings, while the bishops and archbishops devoted themselves to improving their residences and in discouraging absenteeism among their clerical charges. In their drive to develop their estates, and the buildings upon them, however, they differed little from lay landowners.[54] As this introversion took hold, the religious foundations for this activity gave way to a more secular version, registering the shift from religious to social phases of the Enlightenment.

The drive to cultivate manners was to find fresh expression in a literature devoted to outlining and recommending particular forms of etiquette to the reader. The Irish picked up on the models for polite, urbane living offered within the pages of Joseph Addison and Richard Steele's *Spectator* periodical (1711–1712), refashioning the directives to the dilemmas of living in a religiously divided and economically less-developed society. Notably, Irish mirrors of the *Spectator* took on a rather more prescriptive tone, as befitted a society where much of the population were considered by the intellectual elite to be degenerate in their religion and ethnicity, as well as in their manners. Arbuckle's vehicle, *The Tribune*, characteristically described as its purpose

> to prohibit from time to time, whatever is hurtful to the peace or happiness of any of my fellow creatures, as far as it comes to my knowledge. For this purpose, my paper shall be constantly open to receive the complaints of the distressed and the innocent. When particular ones do not offer, I shall apply myself to rectify such general disorders as are incident either to the human species or to particular societies.[55]

Or as a letter to the Edmund Burke–edited periodical, *The Reformer* (1748), aptly observed: 'you, sir, are a reformer, I am a humble spectator.'[56]

A formal tradition of rhetoric also emerged, evincing a deep concern for the affect of language on an audience, and the connection between utterance and decorum.[57] In arguing for the value of the rhetorical arts, this Irish school of oratory was set in opposition to an English discourse which rejected the value of rhetoric and reduced it to a system of deceit and pretence; a means of enabling hypocrites and promoting demagogues. This sceptical approach to rhetoric dated back at least as far as the works of Thomas Hobbes, with his concern for a plain style and clear speaking, and his antagonism to the refined mode of ornate literariness he associated with the republican populism of the 1650s and the emergent cultural Whiggery of the Royal Society.[58] In this distrust he found an unlikely ally in John Locke, whose *Essay Concerning Human Understanding* (1690) provided a succinct expression of the anti-rhetorical strand of thought extant in the period.[59]

Irish thought about rhetoric was far more positive about the attributes of oratory.[60] For instance, the first professor of oratory at Trinity College Dublin, John Lawson, appointed in 1750, authored a sequence of *Lectures concerning Oratory* which he published in 1758, the year before his death.[61] Openly antagonistic to the Lockean understanding of language, he used the opening lecture to defend the value of rhetoric. As he explained,

> Mankind, however curious and lovers of truth, will seldom give admission to her, if presented in her own natural, unadorned shape. She must soften the severity of her aspect, must borrow the

embellishments of rhetoric, must employ all the charms and address
of that to fix, conquer, and win over the distractions, prejudice and
indolence of mankind. If because reason is natural to men, they were
to be left to the power of simple unassisted reason, the minds of the
multitude would be in a state as destitute as their bodies, if abandoned equally to nature alone, without raiment, without houses.
Eloquence, we may therefore style the clothing of reason, which at
first coarse and plain, a defence merely against the rigours of the
seasons, became at length a source of beauty.[62]

Its utility lay precisely in the assistance it gave to the cultivation of knowledge,
in contradistinction to Locke's notion that rhetoric obfuscates the transmission
of learning. For Lawson,

in the several liberal professions for which all who now hear me are
intended, the power of speaking well qualifies the professor to be
eminently useful. Whether you deliver your sentiments concerning
the measures most beneficial to your country, and seek to abrogate
hurtful, or erect wise laws. Whether you do right to injured innocence, or bring guilt to due punishment, recover or defend property
usurped or attacked. Or whether lastly, you lay before men their duty
as reasonable creatures and Christians, paint the charms of religion
and virtue, or display the horrors of infidelity and vice. In all these
important offices of what mighty efficacy is eloquence? Without this,
knowledge proceedeth faintly, slowly, like unassisted strength in
manual works, which may at length obtain its end, but with much
clumsy labour. Oratory, we may compare to the mechanical arts,
which by furnishing engines, and well adapted instruments, produce
the same effects with ease, and finish with elegancy.[63]

Far from being a dubious attribute, rhetorical proficiency was a virtue, for

those that understand the nature of society will not, I believe, esteem it
a paradox if we assert that the orator, who employs his talent aright, is
one of the most useful members of the community. Infusing principles
of religion, humanity, and virtuous industry in all who hear him,
contributing to preserve peace, justice and harmony among men.[64]

The orator, in Lawson's hands, became the paradigm of the virtuous citizen.

Thomas Sheridan concurred.[65] His *Lectures on Elocution* (1762) which laid out the basic principles of how to speak in public was predicated on the veracity of natural modes of speech and gesture.[66] The reason why 'good public reading, or speaking, is one of the rarest qualities to be found in [this] country' was because of an educational system which, akin to the binding of women's feet in China, held 'a custom far more fatal, that of binding up and contracting from early childhood and moulding into unnatural forms, the faculties of speech, which are amongst the most noble, useful and ornamental that are possessed by man'.[67] Morality, utility, and politeness; the three constituent parts of the civil persona were here highlighted.

Far from being anxious about the artificiality of speech acts, Sheridan saw in this the possibility of amelioration by education. In effecting this paradox—the development of an educational scheme to help people be natural—he placed great store on the idea of habit as a form of second nature; one which might be altered by repeated practice.[68] The ambition of the course was to shape a virtuous second nature,

> that he may be acquainted with the method of attaining what is right, in order that a good habit may succeed to a bad one. For as habit only can get the better of habit, and as a man when he has parted with one manner, must necessarily acquire another, unless he knows what is right, he many only change one bad manner for another, or perhaps for one that is even worse.[69]

Whereas Locke was concerned by the caprice and instability of speech acts, Sheridan was optimistic about directing them to polite and sociable ends, themselves thought to be natural to humankind. He identified the cause of the malformation of speech in how 'we are taught to read in a different way, with different tones and cadences, from those we use in speaking, and this artificial manner is used instead of the natural one, in all recitals and repetitions at school'.[70] He therefore argued for a retreat from artifice and a retrenchment of the natural speech patterns of people.

This prompted in Sheridan a pronounced antipathy to classical rhetoricians; he actively sought to overthrow their authority, seeing in their retention of pronunciation and accent marks, the meaning of which had been lost, mere 'inanity' caused by formal conservatism.[71] 'This practice', he declared with an echo of *Gulliver's Travels* resonating in the analogy,

is just as wise as if the same term which signified man amongst the
Greeks, signified horse amongst us, and we were to reason from
names to things, and conclude therefore that a horse was a rational
creature. For whoever read Greek in that way necessarily destroyed all
quantity and measure; and therefore they were obliged to read the
same individual words in a different manner in verse, from what they
did in prose. Amazing! That such an absurdity did not at once
convince them of their error.[72]

It was instead the modern manner of speaking that was Sheridan's central concern, as befitted a theorist of polite behaviour and education. Elocution was
being defined generously as 'the just and graceful management of the voice,
countenance and gesture in speaking'.[73] It was the effect that the words made on
a listener that was Sheridan's test for propriety, for he proposed 'no utterance can
be agreeable to the ear, which is void of proportion and as all quantity, or proportion of time in utterance depends upon a due observation of the accent, it is
a matter of absolute necessity to all who would arrive at a good and graceful
delivery to be master of that point.'[74] 'Good and graceful', the chiming of ethics
and etiquette; Sheridan enunciated the cornerstone of the discourse of civility in
three simple words.

The third part of his triumvirate, utility, could be added to the virtues of
natural speech for the confidence Sheridan expressed in natural rhetoric
extended to the presumption that an individual speaking authentically would
convince more effectively than the finest mannered orator:

When we reflect that the end of public speaking is persuasion (for the
view of everyone who harangues in public is to bring his hearers into his
way of thinking) and that in order to persuade others to the belief of
any point, it must first appear that the person who attempts it is firmly
persuaded of the truth of it himself; how can we suppose it possible that
he should effect this, unless he delivers himself in the manner which is
always used by persons who speak in earnest? How shall his words pass
for the words of truth, when they bear not its stamp?[75]

In this emphasis on the natural speaker, Sheridan was effectively democra-
tizing the possibility of polite speech, something which made the habits of eloquence available for those of any religious confession. However committed his
politics was to the Castle administration, the consequences of his conception

to polite behaviour was that his theory was open to all, so long as they spoke authentically and transparently.[76] That the natural speaker was convincing and deceit and falsity were not was a common conceit within this optimistic line of Irish oratorical thought; a school of thinking that culminated in James Usher's *Clio; A Discourse on Taste* (1767).

Usher defined taste as 'a clear sense of the noble, the beautiful, and the affecting, through nature and art. It distinguishes and selects, with unerring judgement, what is fine and graceful from the mean and disgusting; and keeping a strict and attentive eye on nature, never neglects her, but when nature herself is in disgrace.'[77] He insisted this taste was a 'natural sense', a term which located his work in both the Irish school of politeness and the tradition of moral sense philosophy that emerges from Francis Hutcheson's contention that morality was grounded on an internal sense, akin to the sense of sight or hearing.[78] Rather than being the consequence of learning, education, and social training, these affectations hampered the development of a refined taste, with transitory social norms and fashionable trends warping the natural inclinations. For Usher, taste, despite its natural origins, was

> attained by very few. I have already intimated the reason: true taste
> and sentiment lie deep in the mind; and it requires vast judgement to
> bring the beauteous ore to light, and to refine it. I should not be
> impartial and candid if I had not owned to you that learning, in
> much the greater part of mankind, distorts the genius as much as
> laced stays do the body, oppresses the natural seeds of propriety and
> beauty in the imagination, and renders men ever incapable of writing
> or even thinking well.[79]

Hence, 'ladies write and speak better than scholars' while 'the enslaved pupils of colleges and schools in tender youth are forced into awkward imitations . . . and the mind[s] unmercifully swaddled in prejudices and regular impertinences that distort it for life'.[80]

In making this case, Usher rejected the criticism that the judgement of taste was related to time and place. Taste had not only to be natural, but also universal in time and democratic in its participants.[81] While he admitted that the lower orders of society did not evince evidence of the wide spread of refined taste, this he ascribed to social circumstances, not a natural disinclination. A despoiled environment could warp the natural development of an individual's capacity for discernment for,

in the present situation of the world, the necessaries and comforts of
life are procured by vast labour and hardships, which fall to the lot of
the common herd of mankind in all countries, and labour requires
harsh, forced, and violent motions, which, therefore, along with the
labour become habitual to the crowd . . . Their low station, their
wants and employments give them a sordidness and ungenerosity of
disposition, together with a coarseness and nakedness of expression
from whence it happens that their motions and address are equally
rude and ungraceful.[82]

He asked that the reader consider the condition of the higher orders, 'who by
their fortunes are disengaged from wretchedness and poverty, and are at liberty
to follow the bent of human genius'.[83] It was they who, counterintuitively,
revealed the real natural state of man, by fulfilling their inclinations; expressing
their understanding, and revealing their motivations, all without the need to
curry favour or find comfort.

In this, Usher equated aesthetics with a mode of life; one he delineated
through the concept of personal elegance. He argued that it was in life that we
find the basic principles expressed in art,

of unaffected justness, the same easy grace and simple grandeur [that]
will animate our thoughts, and dispose of them in our writings, like the
lights and shades of nature, with a careless propriety, and will enlighten
our judgements in literature, in sculpture, architecture and painting.[84]

When it came to defining the object of taste, then, the notion of personal elegance became significant. Beginning with the notion that 'elegance is the natural habit and image of the soul beaming forth in action' he expanded on its
content in three distinct ways.[85] 'The first and most respectable part that enters
into the composition of elegance', he argued

is the lofty consciousness of worth or virtue, which sustains a habitual
decency, and becoming pride. The second and most pleasing part is a
display of good nature approaching to affection, of gentle affability
and in general, of the pleasing passions . . . The third part of elegance
is the appearance of a polished and tranquil habit of mind that softens
the actions and emotions, and gives a covert prospect of innocence
and undisturbed repose.[86]

Personal elegance thus involved self-confidence, sociability, and sensitivity, or comportment, conversation, and compassion.[87] And, as with taste, Usher accepted that elegance was open to everyone, for

> nature, that bestows her favours without respect of persons, often denies to the great the capacity of distinguished elegance, and flings it away in some obscure villages. You sometimes see it at a country fair spread amiableness over a sun-burnt girl, like the light of the moon through a mist.[88]

The way in which taste and elegance were connected was through the signals sent through gestures and expressions. Taste was able to read into these signs the modulation of the passions, thus gaining an insight into the nature of the person under observation. In this regard, Usher was germinating a theory of sensibility when he argued that elegance resulted in 'a union of the fine passions but so delicate that you cannot conceive of any one of them separate from the rest, called sensibility, which is requisite in an elegant deportment.'[89] Sensibility, the thesis that the inner character of a person might be read from their comportment, appearance, and facial expressions, was vividly expressed when Usher concluded:

> The face is the mother country, if I may call it so, or the habitation of grace, and it visits the other parts of the body only as distant provinces, with some little partiality to the neck, and the fine basis that supports it; but the countenance is the very palace in which it takes up its residence; it is there it reveals through its various apartments; you see it wrapped in clouded majesty upon the brow, you discover it about the lips hardly rising to a smile, and vanishing in a moment, when it is rather perceived than seen; and then, by the most engaging vicissitudes, it enlivens, dissolves and flames in the eye.[90]

In this way, politeness became identical to virtue, and virtue became a quality to be learnt by rote. This explains why the pursuit of polite living resulted in a number of fashionable social trends in midcentury, such as the sudden popularity of dancing masters. Dance was valued for teaching posture and coordination as much as for its social cachet and its ability to bring members of the opposite sex into close proximity without offending propriety. Ballrooms and dance halls were built in many of Ireland's leading towns and were the regular haunt of the *beau monde*. Dance masters opened schools for the sons and daughters of the lesser nobility. For example, Lawrence Delamain taught the skill in Cork, and built a highly successful career there. Among the ninety-two names that are recorded to have availed of his services are numerous members of the leading families of the region, with women outnumbering men by two to one. So famous was he for his work that the district of the city in which his school was located was renamed 'Hop Island'.[91] Even Trinity College Dublin found a place for dance within its programme of education, with a master of the art being employed by the gallant provost John Hely-Hutchinson. During Hely-Hutchinson's twenty-year tenure beginning 1774, he also employed a teacher of fencing and made unsuccessful moves to found a riding school.[92]

The Irish School of Aesthetics

If Irish writers on politeness and rhetoric were concerned with the issue of personal comportment, and with articulating the national capacity to exercise restraint in behaviour, the amelioration of the environment was the concern of a second language within the discourse of civility: aesthetics.[93] As with politeness, this language projected ideas about beauty, but here the object of concern was not the individual, but the material world. Just as an Irish school of rhetoric emerged, so the middle decades of the eighteenth century saw the emergence of a domestic school of aesthetics, concerned precisely with the definition of beauty and its relationship to an Irish world thought of as desolate and ugly.[94] In doing so it essayed a concern for the environment in which all the confessions lived, and the consequences of material disfigurement on the moral landscape; a connection directly made by the Presbyterian thinker Francis Hutcheson.

Hutcheson drew an analogy between the sense of beauty, a faculty he argued was inherent in all individuals, and a corresponding moral sense. His *Inquiry into the Original of our Ideas of Beauty and Virtue* (1725) defined beauty as 'uniformity amidst variety', and outlined a psychology of observation grounded on an adoption of Lockean epistemology.[95] In particular, Hutcheson proposed the existence of a series of internal senses, one of which accounted of human aesthetic responses.[96] The most profound and influential expression of this concern for developing cultural sensibility was, however, a treatise by Edmund Burke.

A Philosophical Enquiry into the Origin of our Ideas of the Sublime and Beautiful (1757) offered definitions of two competing aesthetic categories, the beautiful and the sublime. Akin to Hutcheson, Burke argued that these qualities were pre-rational and instinctual.[97] Beauty, for example, 'is no creature of reason,' he wrote, 'since it strikes us without any reference to use, and even where no use at all can be discerned.'[98] Instead it was constituted by 'some quality in bodies, acting mechanically upon the human mind by the intervention of the senses.'[99] Specifically, he located beauty in objects containing some or all of a series of qualities.

> First, to be comparatively small. Secondly, to be smooth. Thirdly, to
> have a variety of the direction of parts; but fourthly to have those
> parts not angular, but melted as it were into each other. Fifthly to be
> of a delicate frame, without any remarkable appearance of strength.
> Sixthly, to have colours clear and bright; but not very strong and
> glaring. Seventhly, or if it should have any glaring colour, to have it
> diversified with others.[100]

All of these qualities instilled in the observer a sense of attraction and consequently an emotion of love. Physically this resulted in a series of bodily reactions, which Burke described in sentimental fashion: 'The head reclines something on one side; the eyelids are more closed than usual and the eyes roll gently with an inclination towards the object, the mouth is a little opened and the breath drawn slowly, with now and then a low sigh: the whole body is composed. All this is accompanied with an inward sense of melting and languor.'[101]

Although beauty might be found in inanimate objects, it was fundamentally based on humanity's social instincts, for,

> where women and men, and not only they, but when other animals
> give us a sense of joy in beholding them (and there are many that do
> so), they inspire us with sentiments of tenderness and affection
> towards their persons; we like to have them near us, and we enter will-
> ingly into a kind of relation with them.[102]

Thus, while beauty directed humanity's procreation, it was not restricted to this function. Platonic friendships, as well as romantic love, were animated by the desire for its presence.[103] At beauty's heart was a desire for order and refinement. It was found where the human controlled the environment, neutralising danger and allowing individuals to relax and take their ease.[104]

More influential in subsequent thought was Burke's definition of the sublime. This was the sense of awe that imposed itself on the viewer when confronted with a circumstance that threatened harm. As Burke wrote: 'Whatever is fitted in any sort to excite the ideas of pain, and danger, that is to say, whatever is in any sort terrible, is conversant about terrible objects, or operates in a manner analogous to terror, is a source of the sublime.'[105] These sources were, by their nature, diverse, from the fear of solitude to the vast architectural grandness of mountains, and the frightening cries of animals.[106] What they shared was an awareness of an external power that held the potential to destroy the observer, for Burke acknowledged that he knew 'of nothing sublime which is not some modification of power'.[107] As proof, he observed that

> pain is always inflicted by a power in some way superior, because we never submit to pain willingly. So that strength, violence and terror, are ideas that rush in upon the mind together. Look at a man, or any other animal of prodigious strength, and what is your idea before reflection? Is it that this strength will be subservient to you, to your ease, to your pleasure, to your interest in any sense? No; the emotion you feel is, lest this enormous strength should be employed to the purposes of rapine and destruction.[108]

The sublime had its foundations in the instinct of self-preservation, for it involved a close proximity to danger and an awareness of possible oblivion:

> As pain is stronger in this operation than pleasure, so death is in general a much more affecting idea than pain; because there are very few pains, however exquisite, which are not preferred to death; nay, what generally makes pain itself, if I may say so, more painful, is, that it is considered as an emissary of this king of terrors.[109]

The sublime therefore required a distance to be placed between the source of the threat and the observer. Too close and sublimity turned to terror, as Burke recognised: 'When danger or pain press too nearly, they are incapable of giving any delight, and are simply terrible; but at certain distances, and with certain modifications, they may be, and they are delightful.'[110] A sense of the sublime, then, was produced when the external environment threatened to overwhelm the human but did not do so—the thrill was voyeuristic. Unlike the sense of beauty, the sublime represented a world beyond the control of the human observer; it was a world in which the chaotic and the capricious were commonplace. It was a malicious world, full of violence and horrifying agonies. It was a world of illness and death.

Binding beauty and the sublime together was the power of sympathy. While beauty dwelt upon the drive for procreation, and the sublime was generated by man's instinct for self-preservation, it was by sympathy, Burke contended, 'that we enter into the concerns of others; that we are moved as they are moved, and are never suffered to be indifferent spectators of almost anything which men can do or suffer.'[111] It accounted for human responses to both the successes and the suffering of others. Sympathy, Burke wrote,

> must be considered as a sort of substitution by which we are put into the place of another man, and affected as in many respects he is affected; so that this passion may either partake of the nature of those [ideas] which regard self-preservation, and turning upon pain may be a source of the sublime; or it may turn ideas of pleasure.[112]

It enabled one person to empathise with the terror and agonies of another, bringing social passions and personal preservation into agreement.[113] In sum, aesthetics became a mechanism for mediating between the desire for order, structure, and form and the oftentimes confusing, multifarious, and disorienting reality. It bound together society in a mutually beneficial cycle of sympathetic emotions.

A similar programme was articulated by James Barry, the neoclassical artist, in a self-promoting gallery guide published in 1783.[114] *An Account of a Series of Pictures in the Great Room of the Society of Arts, Manufactures and Commerce* provided the reader with a strict interpretation of Barry's finest artistic sequence, a series of six large-scale works devoted to the cultivation of the arts.[115] The underlying ambition was patriotic: he wanted to produce a work of historical art that might stand against the great treatments rendered in Italian or French art, rectifying the condition of English art as bereft of works of timeless splendour.[116]

The failing was due, Barry believed, to a mutual failing on the part of the artist and the patron, for 'from our too eager attention to the trade of portraits, the public taste for the arts has been much depraved, and the mind of the artist often shamefully debased.'[117] Thus, the challenge was to raise the ambition of the artist and cultivate the taste of the connoisseur. Barry was clear-headed in his depiction of the artist he was hoping for, suggesting

> when the man shall arrive, who from intense and vigorous applica-
> tion, is fundamentally skilled in the various parts of this very extensive
> art, possessing also the additional advantages of a cultivated and
> capacious mind, enriched with those treasures from the superior

sciences that alone can invigorate and give an extension and value to
the art; if further he should from moderation, self-denial, and
estrangement, from the weakness, vanities, and impertinence of life,
be enabled to employ his whole time and attention in this way,
everything will be possible to him.[118]

In collaboration with this new man, there would be a new audience, capable of
cultivated reflection and filled with admiration for his achievements. 'The higher
exertions of art', for Barry, 'require, for the developing of all their beauties, not
only some degree of information in the spectator, but also that he considers
them with some attention and study.'[119] Bereft of such intermediaries the public
in England were little more than a 'thoughtless rabble,' a 'mere herd'.[120]

At the heart of this revivified discussion between historical artist and cultivated
public lay the work of art itself, which Barry understood to have a very precise
moral purpose. Unlike the exactitudes of portraiture, or the beauties of landscape,
historical painting was instructive. 'The principal merit of painting as well as of
poetry', he avowed, 'is its address to the mind; here it is that those Arts are sisters,
the fable or subject, both of the one and the other, being but a vehicle in which are
conveyed those sentiments by which the mind is elevated, the understanding
improved, and the heart softened.'[121] It was this achievement that Barry was
aiming for in his historical series, the moral of which he rather portentously
declared to be 'that the obtaining of happiness as well individual as public, depends
upon cultivating the human faculties'.[122] In this sequence he was illustrating the
developing relationship between the arts and society, a story which began with
the gift of the arts by Orpheus and was currently encapsulated by the work of the
Society of Arts in London.[123] Thus the fifth painting was devoted to his argument
that patronage was a necessary element in the proper progression of the arts, and
was simultaneously a celebration of the Society, for, as he observed:

The distribution of premiums in a Society founded for the patriotic
and truly noble purposes of raising up and perfecting those useful and
ingenious arts in their own country, for which in many instances they
were formerly obliged to have recourse to foreign nations, forms an
idea picturesque and ethical in itself.[124]

The subject also gave Barry the opportunity to insert portraiture into his historical panoply; allowing him to court prospective patrons. Indeed, he was quick to
highlight how the study included an image of

my former friend and patron Edmund Burke Esq. To the conversation of this truly great man I am proud to acknowledge that I owe the
best part of my education. Providence threw me early in his way; and
if my talents and capacity had been better, the public might have
derived much satisfaction and some credit from the pains he bestowed
upon me. It was he that maintained me whilst I was abroad, during
my studies, and he did discontinue his very salutary attentions until
my return, when it might be supposed I could no longer stand in any
need of them.[125]

In making this connection public Barry was highlighting his own social
cachet. While he had risen to heady heights within English social circles—
Samuel Johnson and even the Prince of Wales sat for portraits, the latter attired
as St George—and was elected professor of painting at the Royal Academy in
1782, he later gained notoriety as the only member of the Royal Academy to be
expelled from its membership. While his relationship with academy's President
Sir Joshua Reynolds was never strong, it quickly deteriorated into animus. The
trigger to Barry's ejection was, however, the election of Reynolds's replacement
to the office of president upon his death in 1792. Barry took umbrage at the
choice of Benjamin West, and claimed that a plot was being laid to alienate him
from the academy. He in turn made public his criticisms of the academy in his
intemperate and ill-judged *Letter to the Dilettanti Society* (1798), wherein he laid
out his criticisms of the academicians for greed and gullibility.[126]

This assault continued into his next series of lectures at the academy itself,
pushing the general assembly in April 1799 to take action against its vitriolic
internal critic. Charges were drawn up by' to an internal committee filled with
Barry's enemies; he was expelled for

> making unallowable digressions form the subject, on which he is
> bound exclusively to discourse. Hinting to his auditors that the
> Academy's money was disposed of in a mysterious and secret manner,
> in pensions for themselves.
>
> And proclaiming to many strangers then present, particularly to
> the students, that the Academy possessed sixteen thousand pounds—
> But alas! Alas! He lamented, and feared that no part thereof would
> ever be employed in the purchase of a few pictures, for their advance-
> ment in the arts—Thus encouraging them to licentiousness and to

deprecate the manifest advantages which they have long enjoyed and continue to receive from the bounty of this noble institution.[127]

While Barry was not his own best advocate, nor was his expulsion entirely motivated by the politics of art; it was also informed by formal political tensions. By 1798 Barry was frequenting the circle of William Godwin and Mary Wollstonecraft and he had acted as a teacher to William Blake.[128] His republican instincts were coming to the fore, and his sympathy for the Irish rebellion of that year found expression in 'Passive Obedience'—a private pen-and-ink drawing composed around 1802–1805.[129] His unease as an Irish Catholic embedded in the higher echelons of Anglican Britain's ruling caste was unsettling his posture as an adjudicator and creator of taste.[130] His final years were to be spent in disconsolate exile from the sphere of life he once yearned for and briefly enjoyed.[131]

The complexity of Barry's position was articulated in *An Inquiry into the Real and Imaginary Obstructions to the Acquisition of the Arts in England* (1775). It concerned the failure of English art to develop a school of moralistic historical painting. In the central chapter of the book, chapter four, Barry refuted any suggestion that the failure of the English to develop the highest art form was a consequence of geographic determinism. Instead the failure was laid at the door, once again, of the patrons who were prepared to pay for portraiture and landscape (oftentimes of their own estates) but were unwilling to be instructed in their duties by the classical subject matter of history painting.

However, this was only a symptom of a profounder malaise, namely that the artistic development of England had been halted by the Protestant reformers:

> The accidental circumstance of the change of religion, which happened just at the time we should have set out in the arts, gave us a dislike to the superior and noble parts; the subjects of Christian story, which might generally be understood and felt, were then prohibited, so that, except landscape, portrait and still life, everything else was either unintelligible or uninteresting in the people at large: the artists were then naturally led to practice only the lower and the baser arts. The farther they advanced in these the wider they wandered from the truth and dignity of art.[132]

Far from being a patriotic British text, as the passages about the intrinsic capacity of indigenous artists and a lengthy celebration of English-language poetry suggested, Barry was suggesting that history painting expressed a Catholic aesthetic which Anglicans could not emulate. Making plain his artistic commitments, he drew a stinging, and politically inexpedient, comparison with France:

> Painting and sculpture, which were grown to a state of maturity in
> Italy, were in this state introduced into France in the same manner as
> the good taste of architecture was into the state of Venice, which is the
> reason why in those places there have been so few intermediate artists
> between their states of barbarism and perfection. Whilst Francis was
> thus taken up with introducing the arts into his kingdom, our Henry
> was engaged with warm controversies with Luther, afterwards with
> the pope.[133]

The implication of this passage—that England was still in a state of barbarism— was then confirmed as Barry discussed how the Reformation prompted 'the pulling down of pictures, images &c, and the setting fire to them by public authority.'[134] This iconoclastic antagonism to art persisted in England until the Interregnum, which itself 'showed but too convincingly how little the public in general were disposed to cultivate national art until this zeal for religious canting and reformation had spent itself.'[135] By implication, Catholic countries, like that from which he hailed, were more fertile for artistic expression, more cultivated, more civilised; more enlightened.

Theorising Improvement

If the languages of politeness and aesthetics expressed optimism that Ireland could meet the standards of European civility, this was undercut by an awareness of the economic malaise that marred the country in the second quarter of the century. The repeated shocks to the food supply in the period generated amongst commentators a concern with Irish economic performance. This expressed itself in two languages of analysis: improvement was concerned with the specifics of agricultural estate management and the spread of best practice; political economy with the general legislative and social infrastructure of trade. Apparently these were antithetical: the first language was weighted towards an analysis that saw moral culpability, and the possibility of reform, as located within Ireland itself; the second was engaged in rethinking the Anglo-Irish relationship and petitioning the administration to establish the instruments of economic management.[136] However, both languages contributed to the discourse of civility by projecting a possible future in which Ireland escaped poverty and became a vibrant civil society.

The micromanagement of landed estates generated a broad pragmatic literature concerned with dispersing the language of improvement across the agricultural community.[137] Oftentimes piecemeal in its application and entangled with other social ambitions—the expansion of the Church of Ireland or the promulgation of patriotic political ideas—the discourse of improvement nonetheless generated a thoughtful analysis of Ireland's economic condition, and posited an agenda to ameliorate the problem.[138] Crucially the project gave agency to a landed class that commonly felt inhibited by the political dependency of the kingdom on British decision making. Its fundamental argument, that the country had the capacity to develop on its own account, enabled estate managers to contribute to the general weal while also tending to their own interests, even if the initial investments involved could be debilitating. Moreover, the movement towards agricultural improvement rehearsed a discussion about how extensive a form of latitude could be exercised in involving Catholics in the project of civility. The practical issue of dealing with Catholic tenants concentrated the minds of ambitious improvers on the issue of confessional identity and participation in Irish civil society.

Close empirical observation was clearly required to diagnose Ireland's economic woes as was evident in George Rye's *Considerations on Agriculture* (1730).[139] This began with a remarkable description of County Cork—from where Rye was writing—which revealed an economic imagination in his treatment of the landscape and resources:

> The Barony of Musketry [Muskerry] on the south west is about twelve
> miles distance from Bantry Bay on the eastern part about five miles
> distance from Cork, and on the south, about two miles distant from
> the navigable part of the Bandon river at Inishannon. But in its own
> bosom it hath a fine vale of limestone land and sufficiency of turf for
> burning of lime; so that the very common labourers are so expert at
> burning lime with turf, that they furnish the neighbouring baronies
> and towns with lime, all to the southward at twenty miles distance.[140]

The central issue with which Rye tussled was the impact of the market on the food supply, a problem given fatal energy by the 'calamities of last quarter of 1728 and the first quarter of 1729' where, despite the good quality of the land in

Cork, allowing 'the north of Ireland and Dublin [to be] supplied from thence with barley, oats and potatoes . . . covetousness and the desire of gain drew off so much from thence that at last a violent famine raged in Cork, the metropolis of that fruitful County'.[141]

In contrast to such swings in fortune, 'it is a certain market that makes the husbandman industrious: the reward must equal his toil'.[142] Having no control over the fluctuations of price, the farmer could only use best practice to ensure sufficient foodstuffs to fend off famine. That was the task to which Rye turned his pen, arguing that, while 'our own market is not a sufficient encouragement to the husbandman', knowledge could still be valuable and ought to be diffused as widely as possible: 'It's my opinion that wherever anything suiting this design may be taken, it ought to be collected together; the more opportunely to fall into everyone's hands.'[143] This involved him in compiling recent agricultural ideas, primarily drawn from the pages of the Royal Society's *Philosophical Transactions*. Indeed, he openly admitted halfway through the pamphlet, that in turning from manure to crops, 'I shall still follow the same method of producing what authority I can find in the *Philosophical Transactions* to support my reasonings.'[144] This reliance had its limits, however, for it did not extend to customary knowledge. Instead Rye expressed scepticism about the value of adages that expressed the inherited lore of agriculture, observing acerbically 'it is the common husband-man's neglect, superstition'—a loaded and dismissive term—'and giving himself up to old sayings that gives us bad wheat'.[145] In this light, it is significant that the authorities he turned to were themselves advocates of the empirical method; he observed succinctly 'experience is the touchstone of all speculations'.[146]

Throughout, Rye fleshed out the text with reminiscences and anecdotes, as in this passage concerning a kind of soil type he had seen:

> In the barony of Fermoy, in that fine limestone vale which lies between the Blackwater and the Ballyhaura Mountains, of at least six miles in breath; they find amongst the limestone, quarries of a rotten limestone; the husbandmen of that country esteem it above lime, and they tell wonders of its performances; I have heard often of ten or twelve crops running. When I have been on the lands in that Barony where the pits are, I have examined the superficial nature of that manure, and what was above on the land thrown out of the pit, appeared a brown round grained unctuous sand; but when I descended into the pit, I saw no

sand but a seeming limestone quarry. I made the workman take out a
stone and it looked as any other limestone, but when it was on the
ground, he gave it two or three strokes and it fell all to sand; the people
of the country carry it four or five miles for manure. I searched our
limestone vale but could not find any of it, neither have I heard of any
but in that barony of Fermoy.[147]

This extract circles around Rye as an observer, actor, and reporter. It situates
him as an authority whose observations can be relied on, whose reportage is
valuable and whose reflections are worth considering. The text begins with him
hearing reports ('I have heard often'), sees him attend to the site of interest
('when I have been on the lands in that Barony'), interrogating the evidence
('I have examined'), searching out confirmation ('when I descended into the
pit'), observing ('I saw'), querying ('I made the workman'), and then trying
to find corroborating evidence ('I searched our limestone vale'), but admitting as an honest broker that he had been unable to find corroboration ('neither
have I heard'). This passage illustrates the methodology of the new scientist—
moving from reports to empirical investigation, through active experimentation to glean confirmation through corroboration and repetition.[148] It is as
a validation of this practice that the phrase 'I have seen' peppers the text so
frequently.[149]

It is this process of overturning the Scholastic reliance on cited authority in
favour of personal empirical exploration that the pamphlet enacts. In this, Rye
personified the moving away from the traditional modes of thought towards an
adoption of the Enlightenment assumption that individuals could improve their
own circumstance in the face of established practice. This commitment to
improvement was made plain in his assertion that 'I have thus declared the best
method yet known for the culture of potatoes and the reducing our wild barren
uncultivated hills to arable land, and employing our poor to the bettering our
country; which sort of culture was not known with us till within these five
years.'[150] The new methods were, almost literally, bearing fruit.

In 1725 in *The Present State of the Tillage in Ireland Considered*, Kildare estate
owner and improver Samuel Pierson expressed a similar concern to Rye for the
national economy and the deprivations experienced by the penurious. Yet while
his proposals were energised by a desire for improvement, they were also expressive of confessional anxieties. The central tension emerged from the polarity

between the enlightened agriculturalists, to whom Pierson could defer judgement, and the fool who remained entrapped by his traditional practices. While
Pierson readily admitted that

> as in most things, so in this, both farmer and plough-holder are so
> much wedded to their long-accustomed methods, that to conquer
> that prejudice will be the greatest difficulty in conveying to them
> knowledge of the recommended one: When the prejudice of the
> farmer is removed we can best apply a remedy to that disease in his
> servant. To remove the famer's prejudice, a conviction of the greater
> gain and less expense will be sufficient.[151]

To overcome this Enlightenment bugbear, prejudice, Pierson tried to convince
the farmer that his interest was best served by improvement and reform. In particular, he suggested that model farms be established, allowing the new methods
to be observed and studied. As for the theoretical ammunition deployed in his
pamphlet, he admitted his ambition was 'to convey to everyone the best instructions he can to forward the design, so he has chosen the most plain address,
without regard to censure for the meanness of its style.'[152]

The pamphlet provided a new method of ploughing fields and advice concerning the best kinds of grass to grow to maintain and enhance crop yield. All
of this instruction, densely delivered, drew on Pierson's practical experience.
'This experiment', he stated,

> was made, by observing on the top of the ridge, the only good corn
> grew, and that the greatest part on both sides the ridge was very thin;
> and what did grow was but a weak straw, with a small, light ear. It was
> further observed on measuring with the largeness of the furrow which
> bears nothing and the void spaces on the ridge, a third part of the
> land lay waste . . . It's evident by experience in this country, that the
> recommended method of ploughing will remove these objections; and
> that there is a certainty of the great produce.[153]

'Experiment', 'observing', 'observed', 'measuring', 'experience': this passage is
peppered with the terms of the empirical practitioner's art and proposes an
authority granted by personal endeavour and bitter lessons. Elsewhere he
answered an objection that his method might waterlog the land by reflecting on
how the drainage had proven itself 'by this year's experience, by the heavy rains

in Winter and the excessive bad weather in the months of May, June and July, and [there was] not so much prejudice'—that key term reappears here—'done the corn sown in this method, as to the corn in the former method.'[154] His empiricism was buttressed by the provision of account tables comparing the expenses incurred by the two modes of ploughing, and a page of illustrations comparing different machinery.[155]

Monetary self-interest, combined with an appeal to patriotic improvement, also informed Pierson's *Farther Considerations for the Improvement of the Tillage in Ireland* (1728). This too was laced with statements of authorial integrity and the anxiety to prove his theories empirically. Pierson interwove these concerns into his credo concerning agriculture. 'Success in husbandry', he asserted, 'depends on an exact and regular management in every part, and as in mechanical movements, art and skill must here direct the work. A miscarriage gives everything a disrepute and by unskilful trials many useful improvements have been lost and rejected.'[156] This reveals at once an anxiety that his best efforts might be dismissed as fanciful speculations, at the same time as highlighting the schematic and orderly nature of his progress in the art. To counter his insistent fear of rejection, Pierson used the opening of the pamphlet to announce the utility of his previously made proposals concerning the tillage of wheat; which the subtitle asserted had been 'since proved on trial'. He averred how, in pursuit of knowledge and to provide 'fuller information to the public, I put this improvement on trial to an open view at the lands of Ardrass, about ten miles from Dublin, in the middle of the county of Kildare. A known corn country . . . this work was done by people bred in that country and but then newly instructed.'[157] This statement deserves parsing, for it emphasises at once the Enlightenment values of publicity and transparency, while being balanced by an underlying concern over the ability of the indigenous peoples to make the necessary changes. It worries about Ireland's readiness for reform, at the same time making a patriotic assertion of that capacity. Finally, it raises the stakes by supplying a validation of the author's authority, drawing on his advertised experience of the labours involved.

A second tier to this layered assertion of legitimacy came by calling 'neighbouring farmers' as witnesses who 'frequently viewed and made their observations of the growing crop, and agreed that its appearance promised well'.[158] Indeed, Pierson claimed that it was their judgement that underwrote any claim he held to success, for while 'the crop at Ardrass produced something more than eight barrels and a half an acre, as appeared after threshing; the grain was large, and far exceeded any in the neighbourhood in colour, fullness and weight', what really strengthened his case was that 'the neighbours so much coveted it for seed, that they carried it from the barn as fast as it could be threshed.'[159]

A third stratum to his claim to authority surfaced with his appeal to independent validation:

> A little time after publishing my former treatise, I prevailed in some
> farmers about Newcastle in the County of Dublin to plough about
> two acres in each of their farms into setts . . . They immediately
> discovered that it made the land work much finer and that the
> draught on their cattle was easier, by giving the first thorough
> ploughing; and that all the other ploughings were sooner done, than
> they could any way expect, and I have had the satisfaction since to
> find by them that the land so ploughed (though of equal goodness
> with the rest) produced this last harvest considerably more and better
> corn, than any part of their land ploughed in the old method, and
> several others on that conviction have ploughed all their wheat land
> this year in the recommended method.[160]

Their 'conviction' stood in for the convincement of the readership, and was to assuage any residual doubts as to the authority of the author in making his recommendations.

Pierson was experimenting with an eye to the betterment of estates across Ireland, being more of a patriotic than a self-interested improver. That patriotism had its limits, however. As was typical for a man of his caste, confession, and context, he revealed how the kingdom he spoke of and for was coterminous in his mind with 'the Protestant interest'—a term he used.[161] His final recommendation for the improvement of tillage argued that Charity School Boys, reared in the Church of Ireland, ought to be apprenticed to Protestant estates: 'In each of the various employments of the country, some of these boys will be made useful members of the community, and by this means in some years there will, be a supply of Protestant servants and cotters.'[162]

Less evidently confessionally demarcated was the work of the solicitor and architect Gorges Edmond Howard. And while *Some Scattered Pieces upon Agriculture* (1770) shared a view of the achievable nature of agricultural improvement his work was more in line with a rationalist methodology than the heavy-handed empiricism of Pierson's projecting. Written in 1770 as letters to the *Dublin Journal* under the agnomen Agricola, Howard offered two central proposals. First, he argued for the creation of a vast apprenticeship scheme. He asked the reader to imagine how

> if 200 boys were to be bound as apprentices in each of the four
> provinces, 150 to skilful husbandmen and farmers, and the remaining
> fifty to artificers of the machines and instruments of husbandry in the
> several branches thereof, for seven years, at 12l yearly each, for their
> entire maintenance, diet, lodging and clothing, during their service,
> and to keep up a succession of them, what a populous wealthy
> kingdom might we not expect to see ere many years would pass.[163]

This scheme would be financed by the state; a position in keeping with Howard's support of the administration at Dublin Castle. Secondly, he posited how

> if certain portions of land were also to be taken at the public expense
> in every of the said provinces, for no other purpose but the making of
> experiments in husbandry, and they were to be annually published,
> the knowledge as well scientifical as practical, which must then arise
> of course would without any other profit, largely overpay the expense
> of the rent.[164]

Despite such optimism concerning the self-financing of the schemes, this vast outlay was justified by asserting the primacy of the agricultural sector in the economy, something upon which he waxed as lyrically as he was able. 'Cultivation under creation' he wrote,

> is the business of the highest importance and advantage to society; it
> is the natural, the only root, from whence all manufactures, and all
> improvements in crafts, with their various materials, all arts and all
> sciences can arise; these are the branches, the flowers and the fruit; but
> culture is the root and trunk which yields nourishment, sap and
> growth for the whole.[165]

More prosaically, he constructed a simple hierarchy of activities which ran 'agriculture; manufactures; wealth; luxury; fine arts', set out with each category given a line in a stark descent down the page.[166] The placing of this last item was significant since the purpose of Howard's intervention was to complain about the expense of training artists in schools, depriving the country of much needed resources in the mundane and necessary art of husbandry.

Howard was arguing for the reengagement of the nobility and landed gentry in the daily management of their estates. He regretted 'that mankind seems to apply itself more to the productions of art than those of nature, and hence it happens that the primitive source of wealth, and the vital support of no less than the whole human species are both consigned to the management of mean, ignorant people.'[167] This perception drove Howard into print and determined his rhetorical stratagem. Admitting freely that he was a victim of this erroneous attitude and that his knowledge of the art of agriculture was limited to what he was able to draw from books, he was determined to draw general lessons that would entice his readership—he imagined them as enjoying a similar elite social standing—to divert energies into the practicalities.

This approach accounts for the most intricate rhetorical moment in the text, where Howard explained why it was that agriculture, despite its stated importance, was so undervalued:

> But this grand object is not attended to near so as much as it ought to
> be, nor could anything (as a late ingenious author says) make us
> forget these truths but because they are common ones, mankind being
> naturally fond of novelty, and too apt to prefer the showy to the
> useful, or overlook what is near, in order to speculate upon that which
> is distant; yet it is better to prefer plain, obvious and simple truths as
> proving in the end most useful, as well as most universal.[168]

This passage encapsulates Howard's distrust of human nature—drawn as it is to folly and 'novelty'—and his preference for the unadorned over the decorative, the obvious over the obscure. This conservative temper fits his establishment politics; but that is not all the passage does. In it, Howard is turning the idea of agricultural improvement, or reform, into a cause for the elite, for the socially significant. To be distracted by the baubles of art and architecture was to succumb to moral corruption and luxury. The passage, in other words, captured the language of improvement for the elite, making it an integral part of their cultural politics. It argues that the solution for the poverty and distress that animated Rye and Pierson could only come from the top down, and was not found amongst the poor and the distressed. That these forerunners of Howard might have had some sympathy for that stance does not detract from the fact that

Howard had made his social presumptions so obvious. His was a commitment to a hierarchy of social order; one in which each member of society worked as befitted their place for the benefit of all.

If Howard saw the state as a reservoir of wisdom, the anonymous author of *Some Thoughts on the General Improvement of Ireland* (1780) thought rather differently. While averring a commitment to the 'Protestant interest' akin to Pierson, in contrast to Howard's reliance on the aristocracy, *Some Thoughts* argued that the state's capacity to impose its rational will on the citizenry should be mobilised in support of improvement.[169] The text supplied a series of proposals concerning the economic infrastructure of the country that relied on the potency and legitimacy of institutional systems. State-created and often state-run, these institutions of improvement included workhouses, foundling hospitals, and granaries.

The second part of the pamphlet proposed a 'national society' under which the charitable societies already existing might either 'be subordinate' or 'dissolve . . . entirely', having had their purpose replaced by the overarching structure.[170] This new body was envisaged as being 'subject to no control, or impediment, from the selfish views of private proprietors; nor accountable for its orders, or actions, to any inferior tribunal, court, or jurisdiction, save only to the supreme court of the nation in parliament assembled'.[171] From this centralisation of effort, the author predicted that 'the utmost improvement of ourselves, and our country'—note the twin aims here stated—'might be expected to arise', an expectation described as 'rational and probable'.[172] This new society was to be supplied by the funds once granted to the voluntary societies it superseded, by a 'tax upon luxuries' and imports, and 'the whole profits . . . of a national bank'.[173] This final proposal, contentious since the 1720s, exemplified the confidence the author invested in the capacity of the state.[174] Indeed, according to the ambitious improver, a national bank simply could not fail, 'unless we suppose the whole constitution overturned, the country laid waste and the kingdom depopulated.'[175]

Having outlined his schemes for national improvement, the author concluded by envisioning a utopian future for the country, in line with a rationalist ambition to inaugurate a beneficial system of benevolent governance:

> Husbandry, trades and manufactures would be every day multiplying among us, as well as carrying on to still greater degrees of improvement; so this national gain would be every year increasing. The merchant would find vent for more goods, these would employ more

hands, people would flock into our country, till the whole became a
land of villages and gardens; our ports would be crowded with ships,
importing and exporting all kinds of commodities; our rivers and
canals would be covered with flats and lighters, carrying from our
ports the various materials for our different manufactures, and
bringing down the same again curiously wrought up, and made eight
times more valuable by the labour of our people.[176]

This expressive optimism concerning the character of humanity imbued *Some
Thoughts* with a hope the individual might be reformed. That was the real power
that resided in the state, for if the authorities of the church failed, the state could
step in: 'Will it not then be incumbent on the gentlemen of the legislature to
exert their authority, and either spirit them [people, ministers, and bishops]
up to their duty by suitable rewards, or compel them to it by condign punish-
ments?' he asked.[177]

In this ambition to regenerate the populace within the spiritual realm, *Some
Thoughts* slides over the bounds of rational deduction and into the realm of
freethinking speculation. Specifically, the proposal to recast the thirty-nine articles that underlay Anglicanism recalled the Arianism of the heretic bishop
Robert Clayton, and was expressive of an extreme tolerance concerning confessional diversity. Recognising that the diversity of human opinion made it 'morally impossible to bring all men to one way of thinking, with respect to so many
different doctrines and tenets as are contained in our liturgy and articles of
religion' he wrote, in a cautious third person voice:

> It has been alleged that such abstruse, speculative, disputable doc-
> trines might more prudently be left out of a general liturgy, so as to
> find no place in a form of prayer composed for the constant and
> ordinary use of common people, which should rather consist of
> unfeigned confessions of our sins, earnest supplications for pardon,
> holy resolutions of amendment and ardent petitions of grace and
> strength to fulfil the same, with heavy acknowledgements for public
> and private blessings, both temporal and spiritual, and a humble
> dependence on providence for a continuance of his favour and
> protection against every evil.[178]

At the heart of the pamphlet, however, was not a theological ambition but a
temporal one: to bind together the personal virtues of politeness and the social

considerations of economic practicality to invigorate the country. And at the heart of this scheme was a reform of education, rejecting defunct and unnecessary learning like the 'two dead languages', Latin and Greek, and replacing them with utilitarian courses in political economy and linen manufacture.[179] These would be coupled with university chairs devoted to polishing the personal attributes of students so that 'even dancing, fencing, riding ought to find a place in a university. And the study of oratory and civil polity should be principally inculcated upon all those who hope one day to have the honour of representing their country in the great assembly of the nation'; once again the focal point of the author's thought was parliament.[180]

While this concentration of attention on parliament was unusual in its intensity, in combining politeness and improvement the author of *Some Thoughts* gave expression to the central issue facing the avid improver in search of a polite and productive world. This was less a practical concern with outcomes of individual proposals than a problem with binding together the twin demands for personal polish and environmental development into a coherent scheme. Was primacy to be granted to the regeneration of the individual or the refashioning of the surroundings? This further raised the question of the confessional limits of the project. The discourse of politeness had its origins in a desired reform of the individual while the improvement of estates and urban settlements depended on a concern with the external environment. If the personal programme of politeness had as its general counterpart the language of aesthetics so the particular project of estate improvement had a social extension. The language of political economy constitutes the fourth element in the discourse of civility, and again a distinctive Irish contribution can be identified, and here too issues of confession loom large.

The Irish School of Political Economy

The debate concerning political economy flourished in the critical conditions of Ireland of the 1720s and early 1730s. While the language of improvement was concerned with remedying economic distress through reforming particular practices, the writers on political economy were inclined to draw general laws and postulate systemic transformations. In this way, the language of political economy parallels that of aesthetics, with its concern for identifying universal laws of social ordering.

The writers on political economy were profoundly concerned with matters of currency and trade, and this required descriptive accuracy and the accumulation of statistical data, something in which they excelled. However, their concern was not simply one of precise documentation and realist description of circumstance. In particular, the Irish school of political economy was motivated—indeed arguably brought into existence—by the critical dilemmas facing the country in the bleak decade of the 1720s.[181] From the publication of Swift's *Proposal for the Universal Use of Irish Manufactures* (1721) to the economic meltdown of the early 1740s, the central concern was the economics of development, and the solution for endemic poverty. This prompted, ultimately, a rapprochement with a Catholic population whose wealth-generating capacity needed to be mobilised.

Two schools of understanding, with concomitant approaches as to how to rectify the country's ailing economy, presented themselves and Irish writers were torn between them. On the one hand, the mercantilist creed proposed that development relied on the pursuit of national wealth; on the other, a civic humanist inheritance suggested that national virtue would suffice. This tension between wealth and virtue resulted in alternate futures for the country. In the first system Ireland had to become a vibrant and successful exporter of produce into foreign markets, thereby matching the central criterion of the mercantilist creed, that wealth, measured through the national deposits of specie, was generated through a positive balance of trade. In the civic humanist vision, the country ought to be inherently self-sufficient: able to resist the lure of foreign trinkets and baubles. The effect of a Stoic national virtue was to ensure that desire was tamped down and the needs of the country thereby reduced, allowing it to flourish despite limited material goods.

In one particular aspect, both understandings of political economy agreed: Ireland had to develop its own goods, either to export into the foreign markets or to provide for the population directly. However, where much mercantilist thought was concerned with industrial manufactures, civic humanist writing celebrated agricultural produce. In one vision, Ireland engaged with the burgeoning imperial, urbanised environment; in the other, it retrenched as a pastoral idyll. The difficulty was that Ireland's condition did not make either school of thought the obvious best route to take. Whereas in England, this division was resolved by the political reduction of the rural Tories and their replacement by the self-consciously urban Whigs after 1714 and the accession of George I, the Irish political caste found that both proposals had limitations. In the case of the mercantilist system, the whole edifice relied on the notion that trade was viable and that the country had something to sell to foreign competitors. Yet, with the woollen industry exemplary, Ireland found its capacity to trade hampered by political restrictions emerging from its relationship to England (and then Britain). Similarly, the civic humanist schema relied on an internal market to operate, allowing goods within the country to find their place in the homes and bellies of the population. This, however, required a satisfactory circulation of money for trade to occur. But Ireland simply did not meet this requirement: there was an inadequate amount of coinage circulating, and no national bank to underwrite the private banking system that had emerged in an ad hoc fashion, and which was highly unstable throughout the period.

In the face of such dilemmas, Irish political economists focussed their energies on trying to resolve the twin problems of the monetary system and Irish trade. In relation to monetary matters, in the late 1720s David Bindon projected a number of solutions to the vexed issue of the circulation of both copper coinage and specie. A member of parliament for Ennis County Clare, he was agitated by the poverty the economic crisis of the last years of the decade had created.[182] His solution to the problem of raising people out of poverty lay in understanding how the circulation of money, through the multiplier effect, harnessed and enhanced the energy of commerce. Money was, he explained, 'the universal commodity of the trading world, the value whereof especially ought to be lowered in the hands of tradesmen and such sort of people who are the riches of the country, and the needy part too.'[183]

With regard to the scarcity of coin, Bindon understood that allowing foreign coins such as the Portuguese Moyd'or to circulate required the rounding off of values or constantly measuring the weight of coins to estimate the content of gold or silver therein.[184] Even were the coins to be exchanged in proportion to their actual specie content, he raised the question of

> whether a man must not acquire a perfect skill in the receipt of
> money, and learn a good part of the silver-smith's trade, before he
> undertakes to receive any considerable sum, in such intricate species.
> As for lesser sums and small payments, which are the life of trade and
> whereon the maintenance of the common people depends, they must
> of course be attended with proportional, if not more inextricable
> difficulties. The ill consequences of this would be at first a general
> diffidence and confusion, which of course must end in an entire

confidence in the credit of a few persons, who would acquire skill
enough to undertake the difficult and hazardous task of receiving
money, in lieu whereof their notes would circulate in all manner of
business.[185]

In place of just such an imagined cabal, Bindon turned to the state. His understanding of monetary value was stable, with gold and silver holding their value
'only . . . according to the purity and weight of the mass, be it wedge, dust,
ingot, bullion or the coin of a particular country'.[186] The state's task was to
validate a coin's real content, for

there is another quality which gold and silver have obtained in
particular countries. This proceeds from the authority of the state
whereby such and such particular portions of either metal, bearing
certain stamps, which are warrants of their fineness and quantity, are
ordered to be accepted in payments by certain denominations. And
this is what is properly called money.[187]

Given this, the solution to Ireland's monetary crisis was obvious: the creation of
a national mint. This institution could 'regulate all the jarring pieces of different
nations, and bring them into a proper mass of money to answer the business of
a trading country.'[188]

Thomas Prior's *A List of the Absentees of Ireland* was similarly motivated by
Ireland's monetary distress. However, he feared it was less an institutional failing
that created the problem than a moral one. In particular he distrusted the
penchant amongst the Irish landowners for foreign luxuries and disdained their
habit of spending extensive periods of time in England. Foreign trade thus generated a problem. He estimated that

the balance of our whole trade for the year 1726, instead of being in
our favour, was 12,000*l* against us, occasioned by a great importation
of foreign commodities.

'Tis melancholy to observe that now we are labouring under great
disadvantages in trade, and struggling with penury and want; the
humour of living and spending abroad still increases among our men
of quality and station, and has even infected our ladies, who may be
sooner found out at London, Paris, Rome or any foreign place of
expense than at home.[189]

Unlike Arbuckle, who argued that the nobles were escaping a degraded and depraved rural backwater for the urban civility of England, Prior here proposed that the moral failure was that of an absentee nobility, and their removal of crucial economic resources from the country:

> If we enquire into the motives of this conduct of our gentlemen, so
> injurious to their own and their country's interest, we shall find that a
> luxurious manner of living, an affectation of imitating the nobility
> and gentry of other countries in their expenses, together with the
> largeness of their fortunes are the principal motives of their spending
> all their estates abroad . . . We can justly date the ruin of several great
> families from the fatal period of their going to live abroad.[190]

The corruption, through emulation, extended into Ireland's domestic life:

> We are apt to complain of the hardships laid upon us by England in
> respect to our trade, and when we are pinched and in distress charge
> our misfortunes to the account of other people; but if we truly
> examine all circumstances, we shall find that to our selves we owe
> most of the misfortunes and inconveniences we labour under; we owe
> them to our immoderate consumption of foreign commodities at
> home, and extravagant spending abroad.[191]

The corrective proposal he proffered relied again, as with Bindon, on legislative action, this time to staunch the flow of money out of the realm. He suggested that

> a tax of four shillings in the pound on the estates of absentees would
> in all likelihood remove the evils complained of by stopping in a great
> measure those wasteful drains of our money; and would in all respects
> answer the occasions of the government . . .
>
> An act of gavelkind, whereby all estates above 500*l* per annum
> should descend, and be divided in equal proportion among all the
> sons, as co-heirs (with certain reservation, in favour of those who have
> titles of honour, of all present family settlements, and of eldest sons, if
> it should be thought advisable) would, in a great measure, prevent so
> much living and spending abroad, and induce all the sons to sit down
> on their own respective patrimonies and improve them.[192]

This mercantilist concern for money—described by Prior as 'the measure of all commerce'—was coupled in his thought with patriotic sentiment. This concern emanated from residence, for

> the love of one's country is seldom found in any remarkable degree
> but in those who live long in it, agreeable to the intention of nature,
> which disposes all men and other creatures to a fondness for those
> places in which they live; if this be the case, I fear we can expect but
> little good from those who by forsaking their country must have lost
> almost all natural affection towards it.[193]

It was this complaint that prefaced his remarks on trade, for in attending to that issue, he again found Ireland to be beholden to its neighbour, this time through the exchange of raw materials for manufactures:

> England receives a vast benefit by all the goods we send them, for the
> wool, woollen yard and worsted, which they have from us yearly to
> the quantity of between two and 300,000 stones at eighteen pound
> weight the stone, and for which they pay us about 13,000*l*, when fully
> manufactured by the people of England will sell for 500,000 at least
> in foreign markets, which is a benefit that would otherwise accrue to
> the people of Ireland had England not reserved the manufacture and
> profit thereof to themselves.[194]

This was thought to be the result of the restrictions England had placed on Irish trade. As he admitted, despite his worries over absenteeism, 'for my own part, as I have some small estate in both countries, I am persuaded as an Englishman that a proper use of the labour and industry of the people of Ireland is the best and surest fund to increase the wealth of England.'[195] While he offered a series of practical improvements that Ireland could make to its economic practice—in line with the self-sufficiency civic humanism celebrated—Prior's ultimate object of concern was the wider British polity and the need for Ireland to contribute to its welfare. Thus he concluded his observations with the self-effacing plea:

> If the people of England will still keep us under the same restrictions
> of trade let them send home our gentlemen, or if they will have our
> gentlemen live and spend their fortunes among them, it is to be

hoped that they will give us a greater liberty of trade to enable us to
maintain them there; one or other of these expedients seems to be
absolutely necessary at present for the support of the kingdom.[196]

The solution to Ireland's woes, it seemed, was ultimately out of its hands.[197] In that, Prior exemplified precisely the limitations of the economic thought systems he inhabited, for domestic patriotism and local expenditure was simply irrelevant to the geopolitics of international trading systems that placed Ireland at a distinct competitive disadvantage.[198]

The nature and form of this international trade was the concern Arthur Dobbs, who argued precisely that the solution to Ireland's difficulties was greater integration into the British imperial system, not the augmentation of local autonomy.[199] Indeed, he spent much of his career in the imperial theatre: searching for the Northwest Passage; maintaining an extensive estate in North Carolina; and investing his efforts in the Ohio Company, eventually becoming the governor of North Carolina in 1753.[200]

It was in *An Essay on the Trade and Improvement of Ireland* (1729) that Dobbs first articulated the vision that would motivate this transoceanic career. It began with an encomium of the moral and material value of trade. 'Trade and commerce', he observed,

> unites in interest and affection the most distant nations. As the soul
> animating the natural body, makes all the members of it useful to
> each other, in subservience to its maintenance and more comfortable
> subsistence: so trade, in the body politic, makes the several parts of it
> contribute to the well-being of the whole and also to the more
> comfortable and agreeable living of every member of the community.
> Every nation, every climate from the equinox almost to the very poles,
> may partake of the produce of all the rest, by means of a friendly
> intercourse and mutual exchange of what each has to spare.[201]

Despite this generosity of understanding, Dobbs recognised that 'by reason of the divisions, animosities and distractions which are now in the world' this was a utopian ideal which was little practised.[202] Given such truths, he fell back on local patriotic sentiments, for

> it is . . . every man's duty, more immediately to promote the happiness
> of the nation wherein he lives, and by such means as are lawful to

increase its power and wealth, that it may be better able to defend its people from violence, to redress injuries, to punish crimes, to protect the oppressed and relieve such as are in want and distress.[203]

When it came to 'Great Britain and Ireland' it was necessary to comprehend that their 'interests are inseparable'.[204] Yet he contended that English legislation hampered Irish commercial and industrial development, a fact he illustrated through a lengthy and closely documented survey of Irish trade. As befitted the empirical strain of his thinking, Dobbs produced a series of tables quantifying the nature and extent of the country's imports and exports.[205] Indeed, he was anxious to defend the quantity and quality of his compilations for he perceived 'how apt people are to err in calculations when they have not facts to build upon.'[206] This entire endeavour was, however, put to a polemical end, for,

> having plainly shown of what consequence Ireland is to Britain, whilst
> increasing in wealth and numbers, and protected in the enjoyment of
> our religious and liberties, I shall here, to fully convince those in
> Britain, who have run away with a contrary notion, show the danger
> they must be in from Ireland, and the expense they must necessarily be
> at, in case at any time hereafter such dangerous politics should prevail
> there as to foment jealousies and misunderstandings between us and
> oppress us in our taxes and trade to make us poor and dispirited.[207]

Far from being 'of the greatest benefit . . . the choicest jewel and acquisition of the crown and people of England', interference with Irish trade risked making the country 'a perpetual charge to England . . . or so turbulent as to be apt to join with any prince who should invade us.'[208] This line of reasoning culminated with Dobbs projecting how 'I am confident in time . . . they [English ministers] will think it convenient to enlarge the bottom at home and incorporate us with them, there being trade and commerce abroad sufficient to employ and maintain all the lands in Britain and Ireland were they double what they are now.'[209]

This external union of Britain and Ireland found an internal resonance in Dobbs's thesis that the country could improve its condition by mobilising the skills and intuitions of its Catholic population. In a carefully tempered passage, he envisioned a rapprochement between the confessional disputants that would produce economic improvement for the country:

I could wish, for the good of religion and our public benefit, that so wide a breach were not kept up between us and the papists: for I am fully convinced nothing retains them more obstinately in the persuasion than an impression that they are suffering for religion. Were there a free intercourse between us, and no stain fixed upon Protestants, who through curiosity might sometimes be present at their sermons, or celebration of their mass, we might more easily expose their errors and superstition to the vulgar, who are kept in ignorance, than we can now. The chief reason we can have to discourage popery by the penal laws . . . arise from the three follow-ing tenets or doctrines they hold, viz. a foreign jurisdiction in the pope over kings to dethrone and murder them; their keeping no faith with heretics; and their maintaining an inquisition over conscience . . . Now should any part of the popish secular clergy be brought to abjure these, and expose their tenets to their hearers, and endeavour to discover and suppress those who taught them, and at the same time take the oath of allegiance to his majesty, I would freely give my voice for a toleration of them and their religion, and distin-guish the laity, who adhered to this less erroneous part of the Church of Rome, by giving them tenures, and an interest in the country, sufficient to promote their being industrious and assisting to increase the wealth of the kingdom.[210]

Dobbs was here expressing a view that political economy was inherently blind to confessional difference (and that a Catholic oath of allegiance to the Hanoverian crown was an achievable objective). Successful economies utilised the productive value of all its citizens. If the political reasons that lead Anglicans to distrust Catholics could be overcome, there were sound economic reasons to incorporate them into the operations of civil society.

Despite Dobbs's ecumenism, the vast majority of writers on the problem of Irish underdevelopment remained wedded to a confessionally restrictive and mercantilist model of political economics, fretting over the lack of specie, vaunting a national bank or mint, or decrying British legislation which ham-pered Irish industry. When it came to treating of the indigenous economy they often did little more than complain of the Irish population's moral laxity illumi-nated in an aversion to domestic produce and a desire to parade foreign luxuries.

It was this reliance on piecemeal moralistic reforms to general structural problems that prompted the disgust of Jonathan Swift.

A Modest Proposal

A Modest Proposal is a work of savage genius. Published in 1729, the pamphlet suggested that the solution to Irish poverty was to make produce out of the poor. The idea, simple in its grimness, was to supply the offspring of the peasantry for consumption by the higher ranks of polite society, for, as the proposer recalled, 'I have been assured by a very knowing American of my acquaintance in London, that a young healthy child, well nursed, is at a year old a most delicious, nourishing, and wholesome food, whether *stewed, roasted, baked* or *boiled*, and I make no doubt that it will equally serve in a *fricassee* or a *ragout*.'[211] Adopting the persona of a projector, Swift went through the details of this proposal in coldhearted detail. Utilising the discourse of political arithmetic, he offered calculations concerning the oversupply of children in relation to Ireland's economy. Twinning children with other herds kept for their meat, thereby dehumanising and commodifying them, he recommended that 'twenty thousand may be reserved for breed, whereof only one fourth part to be males, which is more than we allow to sheep, blackcattle or swine.'[212] The remainder could be butchered, sold and eaten.

The advantages such a scheme embodied were explored in a tone of equanimity by the proposer. It would disproportionately affect the Roman Catholic population for they were 'the principal breeders of the nation'.[213] But confessional concerns aside, the entire country would benefit from the reduction in population and gain a new, reliable food supply, albeit rather a refined and expensive dish, suitable only to the palates and purses of '*persons of quality and fortune*.'[214] This was advantageous in the mind of the proposer for 'the poorer tenants will have something valuable of their own, which by law may be made liable to distress, and help to pay their landlord's rent, their corn and cattle being already seized and money a thing unknown.'[215] On the part of the landlords, he punned, 'as they have already devoured most of the parents, [they] seem to have the best title to the children.'[216]

Although it drew for inspiration upon the biblical verse Jeremiah 19.9, 'And I will cause them to eat the flesh of their sons, and the flesh of their daughters', what gave this pamphlet its macabre potency was how closely it mimicked the improving schemes common in the Irish press at the time. It also ironically accorded with the strictures of Irish patriotic discourse, which campaigned for Irish people to consume domestic produce; the projector wryly remarked that 'this product will not bear exportation, the flesh being of too tender a consistence to admit a long continuance in salt.'[217] He further ingratiated himself by adding as a bitter aside, 'perhaps I could name a country which would be glad to eat up our whole nation without it.'[218]

Swift's pamphlet constituted a profound assault on the concept of progress that underpinned many patriotic schemes. For the *Modest Proposal* was immodest in its targets. It revealed the dark logic at play in the programmes for refinement of the person and improvement of the environment by desecrating the language of political economy. This was the clear import of the title, with its three concerns. The *Modest Proposal for Preventing the Children of Poor People from being a Burthen to the Parents or the Country, and making them beneficial to the Public* identified the personal (parents), the broader society (the country), and the economy (beneficial to the public) as intrinsic elements within a wide programme of intellectual and practical activity.

Swift's *Modest Proposal* can be understood as a satire on the discourse of the Social Enlightenment, of personal embellishment and material enhancement. Notably, it cruelly mocked the demand for the Irish population to adopt more refined manners and polite modes of behaviour, tying it to the desire for economic gain, and hence self-interest. Swift described how material concerns would produce a desire for healthy offspring, thereby increasing 'the care and tenderness of mothers towards their children'.[219] So too would it help mothers, for 'men would become as fond of their wives during the time of their pregnancy, as they are now of mares in foal'.[220] Starkly, economic interest would proscribe the beating of pregnant women.[221] He predicted his scheme would 'prevent those voluntary abortions, and that horrid practice of women murdering their bastard children, alas! too frequent among us, sacrificing the poor innocent babes, I doubt, more to avoid the expense than the shame, which would move tears and pity in the most savage and inhumane breast.'[222] For this projector at least, a market for, and an economy of, infanticide was preferable to occasional unregulated murder prompted by hardship.

The *Modest Proposal* also mocked the improvers, whose schemes were derided as futile. 'Let no man talk to me of other expedients', the proposer enjoined, before listing a series of proposals Swift had suggested across the course of the 1720s of taxing our absentees at five shillings a pound: Of using neither clothes, nor household furniture, expect what is of our own growth and manufacture: Of utterly rejecting the materials and instruments that promote foreign luxury: Of curing the expensiveness of pride, vanity, idleness, and gaming in our women: Of introducing a vein of parsimony, prudence and temperance: Of learning to love our country, wherein we differ even from the Laplanders and the inhabitants of Topinamboo: Of quitting our animosities and factions, nor act any longer like the Jews, who were murdering one another at the very moment their city was taken: Of being a little cautious not to sell our country and consciences for nothing: Of teaching landlords to have at least one degree of mercy towards their tenants. Lastly of putting a spirit of honesty, industry and skill into our shopkeepers, who, if a resolution could now be taken to buy only our native goods, would immediately unite to cheat and exact upon us in the price, the measure and the goodness, nor could ever yet be brought to make one fair proposal of just dealing, though often and earnestly invited to it.[223]

'Honesty, industry and skill.' Again we find a concern for 'a broad Enlightenment programme concerned with politeness and improvement. But here, by twinning the concern with personal morality with the necessity for social amelioration, Swift revealed the twisted logic of economic theory. In a world in which polite civility, enjoined by many economists, had reduced the Irish economy to rubble, it appeared the only option was to reverse the equation. Swift envisioned a world of rapacious and greedy economic animals, ready to consume their children in the pursuit of material comfort.[224] The *Modest Proposal* underlined the savage consequences of accumulation, treating humanity as a raw material and not as the market for wares.

What the Irish discourse of civility ultimately asked—and what it sought to propose—was whether societal advancement was dependent not on the accumulation of goods but on the stimulation of desire. However, this need to create desire would hasten the demise of a form of confessional economic protectionism within Ireland: for the country to flourish, Catholic and dissenter, as well as the establishment Anglican had to contribute to the productivity of the economy. So long as the Catholic and dissenter were mannerly and productive, it mattered little that they did not adhere to the established faith. In that, the discourse of civility helped de-confessionalise Irish social life, advancing a tolerant programme for interaction, which was to find social expression in the coffeehouses and taverns of urban settlement, and institutional expression in the fraternities, clubs, societies, and lodges of the mid-eighteenth century.

Thus, despite Swift's concerns, the intricate discourse of civility, which combined politeness, aesthetics, improvement, and political economy, achieved two things. First, it constituted the programmatic ambition of the Social Enlightenment of mid-eighteenth-century Ireland. Civility offered a broad diagnosis of the ailments of the country and a means to ameliorate its condition, providing a varied and interlocking vocabulary for articulating the dilemmas of Irish life. It did so by answering the question of how the satisfaction of multiple personal desires on the part of disparate individuals might enhance the prospect of social cohesion and the amelioration of the shared environment. It forged a bond between private virtues and public benefits.

Secondly, and dependent on this first achievement, civility supplied the Irish Enlightenment with a discourse for discussion and a project of activity that crossed the confessional divides that had so scarred the country's recent history. It enabled Presbyterians, Anglicans and Catholics to combine creatively in the development of their society, sharing technical know-how and discussing recent theoretical propositions. It provided a discursive mode in which those committed to rational and empirical methodologies could collaborate in ameliorating the social environment in which everyone lived. The ambition was to create a civil society where people of differing views, differing creeds, and differing methods could contribute to the common weal. When this debate was held within the coffeehouses and taverns of Ireland, and when the propagation of the values of civility was institutionalised in clubs and associations, the Irish Enlightenment found full creative expression. Subsequent chapters examine these twin domains—the public sphere and associational life.

5

The Enlightened Counter Public

෨

I happened to go into one of our coffee houses the other morning, and meeting there a friend of mine, asked him if he had read the *Mercury* of that day . . . A person in good clothing who stood by me, and it seems was an acquaintance of my friend's, immediately said with some warmth; he hoped my friend would never read such a rascally paper.

—*Dublin Mercury*, 22 December 1770

THE DECADES between 1730 and 1780 constituted the apogee of the Social Enlightenment. As the previous chapter documented, the half century witnessed an extensive debate concerning the discourse of civility. Conducted through the languages of politeness, aesthetics, improvement, and political economy, the discourse of civility drew on rationalist and empirical methodologies to imagine a future in which Presbyterians, Anglicans, and Catholics could play a constructive, progressive role in reforming the moral character of individuals and replenishing the material condition of Ireland. Yet talking about civility was not sufficient. It required answering an old question— that of the legitimacy of participation.

This half century saw the emergence a literary public sphere marked by novel modes of communication (newspapers), changes in old mechanisms for divulging information (the culture of the theatre for instance), and new locations (the coffeehouse) where people could perform in public.[1] This amounted to a dramatic change in the concept of the public itself, away from its connotations with the state—as in notions of the public good or the public purse—and towards those venues which neither emanated from the domestic world nor from the establishments of church, state, and corporation. Instead the public sphere occupied that space in which individuals unrelated by blood or kinship might socialise beyond the surveillance of the state bureaucracies. An ecosystem of taverns, coffeehouses, theatres, and bookshops was introducing a new mode of life for Irishmen and women; one which contained a dialogue that encompassed participants in Dublin, Limerick, Cork, Belfast, and the hinterlands of those urban centres.

This was as much a challenge and a threat as a blessing. It demanded new kinds of behaviour even as it upset long-held preconceptions about what qualified as civility. It forced urban dwellers to renegotiate how they might jostle along on their busy streets, and refashioned the ways in which the different denominations of the island might conceive of life together. The physical proximity in which people debated, argued, fought, and reconciled posed problems as much as it generated solutions.[2] And those dialogues were to be conducted in depoliticised languages dramatically different from the confessional categories in which the languages of the Religious Enlightenment expressed themselves.

Indeed, the decades across the midcentury seem bereft of political interest— little of the violence of 1690 or 1798, or the social turbulence associated with either the Wood's halfpence affair of the 1720s or the Volunteer movement of the 1770s, trouble their apparently placid waters.[3] Yet this impression of a country becalmed and at ease with itself from the 1730s to the 1760s is deceptive. The political mask hides a ferment of a different sort, for as the religious chaos subsided and the rules of engagement settled, an experiment in living in civil society, tolerant of confessional difference, and open to participation by all faith was under way.[4] The Religious Enlightenment was giving way to the Social Enlightenment.

The Sleeping Sister

The public sphere of the Social Enlightenment lived alongside, and in tension with, an official public world, constituted by the privileges it enjoyed from the state. This is to recognise that the term 'public' can allude both to matters relating to the people and to matters relating to the state. There was no clear and obvious distinction between the literary public sphere in which the discourse of civility emerged, and the official public sphere in which the dictates of the administration were issued to the populace.[5] There is clearly no ideal type. Political clubs were founded early in the century and regularly used taverns to host their meetings. The Oxmantown Coffeehouse on Church Street, run by the printers Edward Lloyd and Richard Pue, was a noted Tory enclave, with Whigs offering their custom to the Union Coffeehouse on Cork Hill, an establishment that became known as the Hanoverian in 1714.[6] Nonetheless, midcentury saw the power of the privileged public sphere weaken and the development of a new informal public sphere.

Theatre provides a microcosm of the movement from official to counter public sphere.[7] The playhouse was a central institution in the traditional, hierarchical public sphere. With actors speaking set lines, it provided a highly didactic mode of oration and performance. And drama's origins in Ireland lie precisely in the state's view that such entertainments might be instructive as well as diversionary.[8] The first theatre in the country, Smock-Alley, was founded by royal patent in 1662, under the watchful eye of the Master of the Revels. It was located within a few yards of Dublin Castle. The theatre soon became a central venue for the dramatisation of royal authority, both within the plays themselves and through the appearance at performances by the lord lieutenant and his Castle administrators. The playwright Charles Shadwell, for instance, remarked of Lord Bolton, the lord lieutenant, 'plays and players are by him approved', stating he was 'the great supporter of the stage'.[9]

However, the 1740s marks a decline in the attendance of the lords lieutenant and of Castle command performances. In the epoch between Lord Carteret in the 1720s and Lord Chesterfield during the 1745 Jacobite rebellion, lords lieutenant attended frequently and requested performances of politically apt plays. The Duke of Dorset commanded thirty performances and the Duke of Devonshire as many as fifty-four during the 1730s.[10] Yet with the Jacobite defeat in 1745, and the recall of Chesterfield, who used all the arts as propaganda tools to protect his regime, the habit changed, and patronage of the theatre slowly dissipated as political tensions eased.[11]

Just as the stage was witnessing a withdrawal of state support, a central institution of the official public sphere underwent a period of relative indolence. Trinity College was so moribund it garnered the nickname the sleeping sister. So stagnant was the institution that between 1722 and 1753 not a single publication was offered to the public gaze by a fellow of the college, a run which was finally broken by Thomas Leland's edition of the *Phiippics* by Demosthenes.[12] So too the curriculum had a dusty feel, with all texts under consideration by an undergraduate in 1736 (the earliest date for which there is a record) dating back to the previous century. The most contemporary mind on display was Samuel Pufendorf, whose *Whole Duty of Man* (1673) was a prescribed element in the final year's study of ethics. It stood alongside the *Ethics* of Father Eustace de Paul, a Cistercian who died in 1613; a metaphysical textbook by Robert Baron of Marischal College, Aberdeen, *Metaphysica genralis*, again composed in the first half of the seventeenth century; and Bishop Robert Sanderson of Lincoln's *Prelections* which date from 1646–1647.[13]

The inertia of the college can be tracked through its vexatious relationship with practitioners of medicine in the city. Until 1711 there was no significant formal attempt to inculcate the subject in the college, although the physicians had convened a trade organisation as early as 1654. Nominally connected to Trinity College, this was effectively self-governing. Given a Royal Charter under Charles II and again under William in 1692, the Royal College of Physicians worked as an examining and regulatory body during the eighteenth century, breaking with the university in 1761 over the granting of a degree to Fielding Ould, the author of *A Treatise of Midwifery* (1742) and master of the Rotunda lying-in hospital in the city, having succeeded the founder Bartholomew Mosse upon his death in 1759.[14] So too, the relationship with the surgeons was one of distance and disdain. While a Dublin Society of Surgeons met regularly in the Elephant Tavern in Essex Street, the King's Arms in Smock Alley, the Eagle Tavern in Eustace Street, or the music hall in Fishamble Street, Trinity did not engage with efforts to regulate and reform the practice.[15] Ultimately it was petitioning by the society itself that led to the grant of a Royal Charter, establishing a College of Surgeons in 1784.

Structurally, Trinity College was not quite as conservative; for by midcentury the faculty had increased from nineteen in 1700 to twenty-eight.[16] Yet this is somewhat deceptive because the chairs and lectureships created between 1730 and 1774, those in medicine, chirurgery, and midwifery, that were filled in 1749, depended on a bequest from Sir Patrick Dun which dated back to 1717.[17] These King's Professorships were delayed because Dun's widow had the effrontery to live for twenty-two years after the demise of her generous spouse. More creative was the establishment of a chair in music in 1764, under the provostship of Francis Andrewes and first held by the Earl of Mornington. His position was mainly honorary, however, composing trifles for official functions about the college before he decamped to London in 1774.[18]

Books devoted to the college fretted over the condition of the institution.

Samuel Madden, for instance, offered *A Proposal for the General Encouragement of Learning in Dublin College* in 1730. While the scheme was not overtly critical of the college, the need to encourage learning through a series of awards or premiums was indicative of a general failure to generate a culture of learning within its walls. Madden projected a fund raised through the imposition of a graduate tax which would provide monies for an annual award to those most successful in the quarterly examinations. While the scheme met some opposition—the author himself predicted that 'some might censure even this [one shilling] as too severe a tax' even though he 'hoped no parent will think it unreasonable, since by the paying this small sum all the whole expense of his child's education is rendered abundantly more secure'—the university adopted it and began to nominate scholars of the college to sit alongside the fellows.[19] To Madden, who provided an initial start-up gift of £300, the idea was 'easy, plain, useful and practicable, and has no views but the general good of our country, and the advancement of those almost inseparable things, diligence, learning, virtue, good sense and religion amongst us'.[20]

Less constructive and more scathing about the state of the college was Patrick Duigenan, the lawyer and polemicist. His *Lachrymæ academicæ* (1777) was a compilation album of his attacks on his bête noir, John Hely-Hutchinson, and on the college which had had the temerity to appoint him as provost in 1774, in what was widely perceived to be victory for ministerial corruption over proper protocols.[21] In Duigenan's embittered assessment—he resigned his fellowship of the college in protest—Hely-Hutchinson was not fit for the post, failing almost every category of qualification. As well as having married Christina Nickson in 1751 in contravention of the laws of college fellowship which dictated remaining a bachelor, he listed the following accusations:

> That he is not a man of exemplary life or unblemished reputation is
> well known to the world . . . that he is not provident, nor economical;
> that he does not manage the estate, nor transact the business of the
> College, and not his own, but in a manner directly contrary; that in
> adjudging causes he does not follow the rules of equity and that he is
> not capable of doing so; but follows the dictates of the most inveterate
> malice, extravagant folly and unbridled fury; being totally under the
> guidance of the most turbulent and malignant passions . . . It appears
> that the Provost ought to be a man of learning . . . but I shall show

also that Mr Hutchinson is ridiculously illiterate, even more than
could be expected considering his profession.[22]

This was substantiated with reference to the provost's apparent ignorance of the
classics, for 'he is quite unacquainted' Duigenan claimed 'with the two learned
languages of Greek and Latin'.[23] Moreover Hely-Hutchinson was prone to
'petulance and [had a] disposition to mountebanking' leaving the only conclusion to Duigenan's jaundiced eye to be that 'he has not the slightest tincture of
learning, even in that branch to which he pretends a knowledge'.[24] This view was
inspired by Duigenan's political differences with the provost, and his criticism of
the managerial style as officious.

Yet, paradoxically, it was with the installation of Hely-Hutchinson that the
college undertook a coherent programme of renovation and reform. A pamphlet
dated 6 January 1775 which offered *An Account of Some Regulations Made in
Trinity College Dublin since the Appointment of the Present Provost* admitted 'that
composition and elocution were not sufficiently cultivated among us' and suggested that 'the first object of the provost was to encourage attention to those
long neglected subjects' to which end he established 'premiums for compositions in Greek, Latin and English, and for elocution in Latin and English' to be
awarded to new entrants.[25] So too,

> it would be highly beneficial to have professors of modern languages,
> namely Spanish, French, Italian and German established in this
> college; he has applied to government to grant a moderate fund for
> this purpose, and has declared his intentions, if that application
> should fail, to give an annual sum of two hundred pounds out of his
> salary as provost for that useful purpose.[26]

In line with these measures to support the inculcation of polite manners, the
provost 'proposed, and the board has agreed, that there should be a riding house
in the college for the use of students only', although this did not come to pass.[27]
Investment in law books and scientific instruments and a revamp of the broader
curriculum were also undertaken.

Nor were these innovations presented to a disinterested student body, for a
further regulation obliged 'the bachelors to attend the lectures directed for that
profession for which they have declared and punishing them for not attending
or for negligence, by private admonishment for the offence of the first term,

public admonishment for the second and removal from the college for the third.'[28] The wider social discipline of the student body was a central pillar of Hely-Hutchinson's vision, for

> in a great and numerous University, situated in a metropolis, disci-
> pline is a most important object; as such he has attended to it with
> the utmost care and solicitude. A moderate but exact discipline is
> established, the statutable regulation of not going into the city
> without a written permission from the tutor is strictly attended to; the
> number of tardes, or coming in too late for night roll, restrained and
> determined . . . He has increased and fixed the number of chapels in a
> week, and divine worship was never better known to be better
> attended in this college.[29]

Here the provost of Trinity College connected themes of faith, discipline, and learning in a project to serve the confessional state. It was a restatement of orthodoxy concerning the priorities of the official public sphere.

Challenging Monopoly

If the official public sphere was in decline in the middle of the eighteenth century, only resuscitating itself in the 1770s, this process was compensated for by the emergence of an unofficial realm of debate, dialogue, discussion, and deliberation. Again, theatre acts as a barometer of developments. The 1730s and 1740s saw a rise in command performances by private individuals and by chari-table organisations, filling the void left by the absentee viceroy. Alongside ben-efit performances for individuals, often debtors, these occasions underpinned the finances of many of the city's new charitable institutions, notably Mercier Hospital (founded 1734), the Hospital for the Incurables (established 1744), the Lying-In Hospital (opened 1745), and Swift's legacy, St Patrick's Hospital which was finally completed in 1749. All of these received at least one benefit night within three years of opening.[30] This symbiosis culminated in the creation of the Rotunda which opened to the public in 1757. Completed a decade later, and the brainchild of Bartholomew Mosse, the project combined a hospital with a pleasure garden and assembly rooms large enough to host concerts, balls, and other fashionable gatherings. Located to the northwest of Sackville Mall and housing a lying-in hospital (Mosse had opened the first such institution in the British Isles on George's Lane in 1745), the five-acre site was the venue for a fashionable promenade, access to which involved the purchase of a ticket, with profits going to the hospital.[31]

Laid out in 1750, alongside the hospital grounds, Rutland Square became a centre for modish and elite sociability, as suggested by *An Accurate List of the Several Persons for whom Tickets have been Issued for the Annual Assemblies at the Public Rooms, Rutland Square* (1793). It provided a virtual parade of Irish high society, with the original subscribers appearing in order of precedence. At each of the six nights of the specific card assemblies there had been a minimum of 154 luminaries present—at the first noted event in 1791—and a high mark of 627 on the third such night in 1792. The average of a fluctuating number was 292, with women in the majority on all but one occasion, the fourth night in 1792.[32] These events were self-consciously intended as worthy forms of entertainment for the duration of the social season, for the *List* warned:

> The entertainments at the public rooms are calculated to occupy every
> Tuesday from the meeting of parliament to the 1st of May, and will
> invariably be adhered to. With the preoccupancy of a year it is almost
> impossible that Ladies will persist (by late supper or musical parties
> on these nights) to destroy the objects here proposed; elegant public
> society, and relief for the most wretched of their own sex—No friend
> to humanity can hesitate this sacrifice to public duty and should any
> (through inattention) be announced, requisitions in the daily prints,
> and every other possible method will be used to point out the glaring
> impropriety.[33]

The rising private demand for theatrical performances and other modes of entertainment helped prompt the emergence of competition for attention, time, and interest, which in turn implied neutralising the privileges enjoyed by the Theatre Royal. While the 1720s saw the emergence of booths for theatricals in the city (notably that of the puppeteer Randall Stretch), it was the 1730s which saw the most vibrant activity. Upon her second visit to the city, in 1730, Madame Violante, whose brand of tumbling, dance, and stagecraft had enthralled the city when she appeared in the Theatre Royal the previous year, set up an independent Theatrical Booth on Dame Street. She vacated this space in 1733, moving to another custom-built booth on George's Lane. Despite this investment, the booth was empty by early 1734, perhaps because of the financial costs of mounting the performances.[34] Concurrent with Madame Violante's booth was a second, also located on Dame Street, known as the 'Great Booth', perhaps the structure in which Stretch had displayed his puppets the decade before. Stretch had moved his business to a booth on Capel Street; by 1736 there is evidence that the lot was used occasionally for theatrical performances. So other spaces also supplied the desire for entertainment.[35] The 1738 *Dublin Directory* notes the existence of 'Geminiani [*sic*] Great Room' on Dame Street where Franseco Geminianui played music.

The first full challenge to the monopoly held by the Theatre Royal came during their sojourn in Aungier Street, where they opened on 9 March 1734 following the collapse of part of the old Smock-Alley construction. A second troupe, led by Luke Sparks, John Barrington, and Miss Mackay, had been working out of Violante's booth on Dame Street until the Theatre Royal flexed its wasting muscle by successfully petitioning the Lord Mayor to uphold their privilege to the exclusive performance of theatricals promised within their royal patent. The rogue troupe spent a couple of years under the patronage of the Earl of Meath, performing within his Liberty on Ransford Street, near St James's Gate. The removal of the Theatre Royal to Aungier Street gave this company an opportunity to move in and rebuild the Smock-Alley theatre entirely, eventually opening on 11 December 1735.[36] The new Smock-Alley provided for more sophisticated staging, although the mode of acting remained classical for some time to come. Managed by William Phillips and then by Samuel Foote, a further theatre was erected in 1745 on Capel Street, and ran in overt, sometimes political, competition with Smock-Alley until, in 1750, Thomas Sheridan took up a twenty-one-year lease on the property with a view to closing it down, and reopening the old Aungier Street venue in that February to give the appearance of competition to the city.[37] Another theatre opened on Crow Street in 1758, directed by the Dublin actor Spranger Barry, while in 1784, Fishamble Street, which was one of two music halls constructed in the 1730s—Dame Street opening in 1731 and Crow Street the year following—took on Robert Owensen as its manager and turned its hand to drama.[38] By this time, the royal patent which the Theatre Royal had tried to assert as late as 1733 was well and truly spent credit.

The monopoly that Smock-Alley held over musical culture beyond the official sites of the Castle and the Cathedral choirs was challenged just as effectively as its hold over acting. By 1731 Crow Street housed Mr Johnston's Great Room which had been built at the request of the Musical Academy. The Great Hall on Fishamble Street followed a decade later, across from the Philharmonic Room where it seems smaller concerts were conducted from at least 1742. Fishamble Street was the hub of Dublin's musical culture until the opening in 1767 of a concert hall connected to the Rotunda complex, capable of holding an audience of 2,000. Crow Street was active through to midcentury, hosting charitable and benefit nights of music and song, until it was taken over as a theatre and rebuilt for that purpose in 1754, opening in 1758. The challenge posed by the Rotunda also affected Fishamble Street, although in 1777 it innovated by hosting a full season of Italian opera. Slow decline culminated in its closure in 1798. The Rotunda's open-air concerts found competition of their own when William Hollister opened a formal garden in Ranelagh, which hosted events until he gave up the struggle to bring people out of the city centre and closed the operation in 1777.[39]

Even the reserved and sheltered retreat of the library saw a sudden burst of competition around the 1730s. Narcissus Marsh's Public Library, which had stood alone as a public place for learning upon its opening in 1707, had by this time been joined by the Edward Worth collection, which catered to the tastes of the city's medical fraternity, while the law library was developing its holdings.[40] More public competition came in 1737, with the introduction of a circulating library administered by the Catholic printer and bookseller James Hoey. He launched his scheme in the *General Advertiser*, announcing he held

> a large collection of histories, romances, novels, memoirs etc con-
> taining the greatest variety that has been seen in this kingdom . . . The
> conditions are that the persons who borrow, are to have one book at a
> time, and leave the value thereof in hand: the hire of large books at
> 8d., small and middling at 6d. per week, and to have as many books
> as they please in a week.[41]

This appears to have been the first such establishment, but another venture was created at the Bible on Skinner's Row by Richard Watts in 1754.[42] Thomas Armitage followed suit in 1762; James Williams established a collection in 1765 and the Butler Circulating Library was operational in 1774.[43] In the final two decades of the century four collections were available for curious Dubliners to peruse, namely those of the Universal Circulating Library (from 1775), Colbert's

Circulating Library (founded by Samuel Colbert in 1778 and continued by his widow Harriet from 1788), Jackson's Circulating Library (which was in existence from 1786 to 1799), and the Apollo Circulating Library, run by Vincent Dowling from 1792 and containing 2,000 volumes according to a 1794 catalogue.[44] This establishment was in line with the other such circulating libraries in housing a large number of novels. However, Dowling also offered a number of nonfiction works to his subscribers, making a virtue of this in an advertisement in the *Hibernian Journal*:

> The fund of information and amusement which this establishment presents, must strike every discerning mind, friendly to the improvement of knowledge and refined taste, especially in the rising generation, while the terms of subscription unite those advantages with the strictest economy, and point out a rational and most advantageous source of amusement to this who prefer 'The Feast of Reason and the Well-Stored Mind' before recreations of a much more expensive and less advantageous nature.[45]

Other ventures were less long-lived, with Charles Brown's establishment lasting from 1786 to 1794, while John Archer's 1788 foundation, the General Book Repository, acted more like a club than a library. The century's last foundation in the city was the Hope Circulating Library, created in 1796 and located on Exchequer Street.[46] Although these establishments were often ephemeral and limited in their scope, they represented a challenge to the market which Marsh's initially monopolised; a common experience for the official public sphere in midcentury.

The Unofficial Public Sphere

The informal public sphere originated with the hosting of salons within private houses. Jonathan Swift was engaged in a poetic coterie at Gaulstown House, home of the Rochforts, in the 1720s.[47] In the early 1720s a constellation of writers and thinkers also encircled Robert Molesworth's estate at Brackenstown in Swords County Dublin.[48] Later, a similar grouping emerged around Bishop Rundle.[49] And showing how the political public sphere could be hinted at within the literary one, there was patriotic debate conducted in the soirees hosted by the Kildare and Conolly families.[50] It even occurred within a form of personalised state patronage, with John Carteret, the lord lieutenant from 1725 to 1730, inviting literary notables to the Castle in an attempt to alleviate the boredom induced by his enforced sojourn in the provincial capital. Later in the century, the celebrated actress Peg Woffington brought together a circle of wits and conversationalists who gathered at her house in Dublin.[51]

Women dominated elsewhere, as with the coterie gathered around Martha Perceval in St Stephen's Green or Elizabeth Vesey at Lucan House.[52] Vesey was an associate of Samuel Johnson when in London. Her second husband, Agmondesham, was a member of the Club and she was considered part of the bluestocking circle which included Elizabeth Montagu, Hannah More, and Fanny Burney. She eventually retired to London after the death of her husband in 1785.[53] More committed to the country was Elizabeth Rawdon, Lady Moira.[54] She held a salon in Moira House on Usher's Island which included Thomas Dermody, Maria Edgeworth, and Joseph Cooper Walker. Dermody dedicated his *Poems Moral and Descriptive* (1800) to her, while Edgeworth used her as the basis of a number of fictional creations, and Walker admitted that his *Historical Memoirs of the Irish Bards* (1786) had benefitted from her critical eye.[55] She acted as patron to Irish-language scribes, notably Muiris Ó Gormáin. He was an amanuensis for Charles O'Conor who transcribed at least four manuscripts for the Moiras and provided Walker with a translation of 'The Adventures of Farbhlaidhe, Daughter of the King of Scotland, and Cerbhaill, son of Donnchaid Mhoir Uí Daluigh'.[56] She patronised a number of poetesses including Mary Tighe and Henrietta Battier.[57] She was also a writer of note, publishing in the *Proceedings of the Royal Dublin Society* in 1773 on the cultivation of flax and an account of a skeleton found in a bog in *Archaeologia* in 1783. A committed political advocate, she described herself as

> an aristocrat of the genuine brand . . . I loved the people and thought
> my duty to protect and serve them, I should not, nor do I choose to
> be tyrannised by the mob, having never had the least inclination to
> practice tyranny over those who were subject to my influence. I am
> loyal and national—but I sigh when I behold those who never had a
> great grandfather to whom the noble feudal feelings of grateful
> attachment to a faithful follower and the indulgence of power to
> protect and serve are unknown.[58]

In the 1790s her circle took in a number of active United Irishmen, including Wolfe Tone, Thomas Russell, and Edward Fitzgerald.[59]

Perhaps the most prestigious of these coteries was that run jointly by Patrick Delany and his wife, Mary. Their house in Glasnevin played host to Jonathan Swift and their circle also included Thomas Sheridan the elocutionist, Thomas Helsham the natural philosopher, the printer Constantia Grierson, and the poet Laetitia Pilkington.[60] As this list suggests, and in contrast to those held in France, these gatherings provided decidedly mixed company: women were not merely confined to the role of hostess but were active participants in the creation of literary artefacts.[61] Something of the affective quality of the connections made in the circle, as well as the intellectual ambitions of the circle can be found in Mary Barber's poem 'To Dr Richard Helsham upon My Recovery from a Dangerous Fit of Sickness':

> The wise and wondrous Laws you clearly know,
> Which rule those Worlds above, and this below.
> The World of Life, which we obscurely see,
> In all its Wonders, is survey'd by thee:
> And thou in ev'ry Part canst something find,
> To praise thy Maker, and to bless thy Kind:
> Quick to discern, judicious to apply,
> Your Judgment clear, and piercing, as your Eye.[62]

The occasionality of this kind of verse—situated precisely in relation to a person and an event—highlights not the biographical quality of Barber's writing but the way in which she chose to situate her work within a broad social context. She availed of poetry to embroider her network of associations with personal and literary meaning.[63] Occasionality allowed her to express herself as a poet and revealed the value she put on close intimacies and intellectual friendships; a theme Barber deployed again when reflecting 'On Imagining a Friend had Treated the Author with Indifference':

> Go Jealousy, Tormentress dire;
> On lovers only seize:
> In Love, like winds, you fan the flame
> And make it a higher Blaze
>
> But Friendship's calmer, purer joy
> Thou dost not heighten, but destroy.[64]

This modest paean to friendship was playing with the trope of calm and violent passions, integral to much moral philosophy in the period of its composition, and in projecting her entanglement with a friend as proximate to that of two lovers, she was intimating that the affection between intellectual companions came close to that which informed the deepest emotions of humanity.[65]

Despite the significance of the salon in eighteenth-century Ireland and regardless of the vital outlet it provided for women to articulate cultural expression, the key institutions of the public sphere were not housed in private homes, but rather were located in a public domain. Nor were they so clearly mixed in their company, but were predominantly homosocial in character. While the salon culture can be understood as emanating from the patronage offered in the big houses to the cultural life of their hinterland—connected in that sense to the traditions of Irish hospitality—the unofficial public sphere of this period was novel and was founded on the availability of exotic goods, notably coffee.[66] Indeed, the three main venues for this new public sphere were the coffeehouse, the tavern, and the bookshop, all of which came to prominence in the period following the War of the Two Kings (1688–1691).

In the case of the coffeehouse, its development was in part a repercussion of links with imperial trade, and occurred in imitation of English trends.[67] Similarly, taverns emerged as part of a broader change in the habits of the Irish populace, away from drinking outdoors, as was predominately the case in the seventeenth century, and towards imbibing indoors.[68] This may imply a change in etiquette, and certainly the coffeehouse and tavern appear to have proliferated from a central point in Dublin, spreading into the countryside beyond the Pale. As for the bookshops, they benefitted from a loophole in the Licensing of the Press Act (1662), which enabled the emergence of a copying market. This broke the monopoly over printing enjoyed, until then, by the holder of the king's patent—a privilege held by the Grierson family.[69] An efflorescence of printers accounts for the emergence of the newspaper as a form, which at once reported on and created a public; this in turn frequented the coffeehouses, taverns, and bookshops.

Newspapers help to date the phenomenon. The first sustained title dates back to the 1690s, when the lapse of the licensing law in 1695 freed up the market. Since 1690 the government had sponsored a newspaper, the *Dublin Intelligencer*, highlighting how the official public sphere foreshadowed the emergence of a literary public sphere. Below its masthead it even declared that it was 'published by authority.'[70] This monopoly eroded rapidly, for between 1700 and 1760 at least 160 news imprints were founded, flourished, or foundered in the city.[71] The *Flying Post* started the flood, launching in 1699 under the guidance of Cornelius Carter, competing with the *Dublin Intelligencer* which was now the responsibility of the gifted Francis Dickson. The same period saw the launch of the Tory-inclined *Pue's Occurrences*, highlighting how quickly political debate emerged. By 1716, the number of titles had increased to twelve, with thirty-three introduced between 1714 and 1727.[72] This inundation was not to abate in the decades that followed.

As for literary periodicals, the 1730s was the crucial decade. Following James Arbuckle's pioneering 'Hibernicus's Letters' of 1725–1726—which were inserted into the *Dublin Weekly Journal*—two were founded in quick succession.[73] The *London and Dublin Magazine, or Gentleman's Monthly Intelligencer* ran from 1734 to 1745, but was little more than a reprint of the *London Magazine* with local news items added. In contrast, the short-lived *Weekly Miscellany* of 1734–1735, published by Edward Exshaw, contained three distinct sections: 'Discourses: Political and Moral', 'Literary News', and 'An Exact Summary of the News of the Week' aimed directly at a Dublin audience. These titles were followed by the *Compendious Library: or Literary Journal Revived* of 1751–1752; the *Magazine of Magazines* of 1751–1769; the *Grand Magazine of Universal Intelligence* of 1758–1760; the *Dublin Magazine* of 1762–1765; and the *Young Gentleman's and Ladies Magazine* of 1770 marvellously subtitled *The Repository of all Entertaining, Useful and Polite Knowledge*. In the case of the *Literary Journal* of 1744–1749, edited by the Huguenot émigré Jean-Pierre Droz, the vehicle was explicitly used to disseminate empirical knowledge drawn from the new sciences, to house debate between divergent correspondents, and to foment a politics of confessional toleration.[74]

Dublin's Public Sphere

How did these new institutions reshape the social environment of the capital? First it is important to take stock of the existing shape of the city's official public sphere.[75] Plotting the placement of the Anglican churches in the city affords a brief guide to the conduits through which official Ireland passed information to the populace. The parochial system ensured that each neighbourhood of the city had a focal point, wherein sermons could instruct, choirs could entertain, and ministers could direct. An axis of power also ran east to west, from the basin of College Green where parliamentarians gathered and the fellows of

Trinity College congregated, up Dame Street and past the centre of administrative power, Dublin Castle, to the twin peaks of Anglican confessional authority, Christ Church and St Patrick's Cathedrals. In this way the westerly location of Marsh's Library mirrored the learning found in Trinity, itself the eastern extremity of this line. So too the location of Theatre, along the northern fringe of this power line and close to the quays of the city, connected its semiofficial status to the clustering of official Ireland along the rise of Cork Hill. As for the theatre on of Aungier Street, its challenge was geographically articulated by its relationship to this flow of power; it acted as a wellspring at one remove from the central power system, and from which might flow alternative views and critical attitudes to the desired cultural politics of the central hub.

When the tolerated dissenting churches are accounted for, the city remains rather open, for unlike Belfast where the Presbyterian congregations huddled together in a small complex—the first and second congregations met side by side in Rosemary Street—the capital provided a range of possible locations for worship sprinkled through the streets and neighbourhoods. This may, paradoxically, have been a consequence of the city's mixed Presbyterian heritage, for the church was culturally split between those with roots in Ulster Presbyterianism and those who traced a lineage to English congregationalism. Thus the desire of an English congregation like Wood Street to fraternise with the Ulster mission church established at Usher's Quay was rather limited. Again though, this is to suggest that the population of the capital did not have far to go to hear the word of a minister and to listen to a sermon.

In contrast, what is noticeable is the proximity of the city's eleven coffee-houses with each other.[76] Far from serving distinct areas of the city, they were cheek by jowl with each other.[77] Five ran along Essex Street, and three others gave their address as Essex Bridge. If nothing else their connection to the quays underlines how these shops traded in an import. Still, they were to become emblematic of a form of urban gentility and merchant mobility that signified a social cachet which belies their small number. Indeed, so central were coffee-houses to the elite culture of the city that when the Rotunda was planned in 1745 (it opened in 1757) Bartholomew Mosse included a coffee stall within his pleasure gardens. In the 1760s, the Wide Streets Commission displayed its plans for urban improvement in the coffee room of the Royal Exchange for public debate.[78] Of those listed in 1738, Lucas's on Cork Hill was perhaps the most socially preeminent. Founded in 1690, in 1725 the Presbyterian philosopher

Francis Hutcheson wrote in the 'Hibernicus's Letters' of how 'free wits', fops attracted to a disreputable materialism made fashionable by Bernard Mandeville's *Fable of the Bees* (1714), used it as a haunt.[79] In 1747, during theatre riots, Thomas Sheridan's ally Charles Lucas was upset by the way in which Edward Kelly's Catholic allies were colonising Lucas's for themselves and displacing the typically Protestant clientele.[80] It was removed by the Wide Streets Commission in the late 1760s because, as James Malton recalled in 1799, 'the site of the Exchange was formerly occupied by a range of old houses, and a particular one called Lucas' Coffee-House, which so narrowed the passage to the Castle that two carriages could scarcely pass abreast, there not being more than twenty feet from house to house.'[81]

Yet despite the prestige such establishments garnered, the precarious nature of the business is indicated by comparing the 1738 list with one drawn up by Richard Lewis in 1787.[82] Reporting in *The Dublin Guide* he identified nine coffeehouses within the city, which he listed along with their location.[83] Although Daly's might have served the same uptown market as Lucas's had done earlier in the century, the memory of its fashionable conviviality was fading. In 1760 Peter Wilson noted in *The Dublin Directory* one Ed. Tyrell who was the 'Master of Norris's Coffeehouse' which he located on Essex Street, and which was not mentioned by Richard Lewis.[84] Certainly Norris's Coffeehouse had functioned for some time, being mentioned again in the *Directory* for 1768.[85] However, only two establishments survive from 1738—the Globe Coffeehouse and the Custom House Coffeehouse—both on Essex Street, suggesting the significance of this artery to the flow of information around Dublin's urban body.

The need to secure a firm future for the business caused many owners to diversify. The coffeehouse keeper John Barnett dabbled in the sale of alcoholic beverages, for example, being described by William Wilson in the *Dublin Directory* for 1780 as a 'spirit and wine-dealer' alongside his coffeehouse concern.[86] Similarly, the *Freeman's Journal* on 7 April 1764 announced that

> Owen Gallagher, master of the Custom House Coffee House in Essex
> Street, has by the advice of many of his friends, opened a new coffee
> room, in the next house, up one pair of stairs, where gentlemen will
> be supplied, as usual, with tea, coffee and chocolate every day. And
> has likewise fitted up his late coffee room in the most elegant manner
> for a tavern and chop house.[87]

Although taverns were located throughout the capital, their clustering around Essex Bridge and just south of the Liffey is remarkable. There were a number of taverns that served the needs and appetites of the parliamentarians, priests, and paper pushers of official Ireland—they too needed a drink and a meal. Yet the taverns were frequently a part of this new, unofficial public sphere. This may be a result of the status required to be identified as a tavern.[88] Taverns differed from public houses in that they usually implied overnight accommodation was available. In contrast public houses solely served alcohol and remained in large part just that, unlicensed houses opened to neighbours and friends in which ale and whiskey might be found. The Liberties certainly had their share: by the 1790s it is estimated that Dublin housed over 1,300 of them, with Thomas Street alone containing around 50. So too dram-houses filled up the vacuum, with the traveller Richard Twiss reckoning Dublin had 1,200 brandy shops alone.[89] These connected to older forms of sociability where people drank out of doors from illicit stills, and as such did not contribute to this novel public sphere. That the presence of taverns implied accommodation, also, by default highlights how traders might be journeying into the city, with news and information, which might eventually make it into the newsprints of the city.

A similar clustering of location informs the distribution of bookshops. First of all an array of institutions trickle down from Cork Hill, through Dame Street, and wash up at the University in College Green. These serviced the needs of official Ireland. So too did the second large cluster, located on High Street and Skinner's Row, close to both the Castle and the Anglican Christ Church Cathedral. This accounts for the three bookshops situated next to St Patrick's Cathedral on Patrick Street. Yet there was a third major grouping, which is connected to the port area around Essex Bridge, particularly on the streets of the southern bank, where the coffeehouses and taverns already existed. So it is that Skinner's Row, Essex Street, and Fishamble Street again created a knot of cultural activity, beyond which Dublin looked rather desolate of such sociable and communal communication. This places the centre of the bookselling trade in the same areas of the city as the coffee shops and the taverns, making these closely connected streets a hive of argument and debate.[90] Virtually every building in these alleyways and thoroughfares must have contained a bookshop, a coffeehouse, or a tavern, and its beating heart was located on the stage of the Smock-Alley Theatre. Information washed through this area with immense speed, as the post-boats landed or merchants drew up to the doors of the coffeehouses and taverns.

Dublin was as much a port town as it was an administrative centre. The official public sphere which ran from Trinity College, through College Green and the parliament building, up Cork Hill, past the Castle and the corporation to the church bastions of Christ Church and St Patrick's Cathedrals, faced competition from its squatting neighbour. Moreover, a new north-south axis through the city opened up across Essex Bridge, displacing the east-west axis that ran along Dame Street. The laying down of Parliament Street in 1753 only firmed up this shift in perspective.

For this new sphere of debate and dialogue, economics was the fuel, not politics. Indeed, the provision of newspapers and periodicals aided and abetted the use of the coffeehouse as a locus for trade. The information necessary for informed investment was to be found in the newsprints, and the coffeehouse provided salubrious and comfortable lodgings while business deals were struck. That the coffeehouse was open to all ensured that suitable partners for business ventures could be met there. Advertisements in the *Dublin Weekly Journal* noticed Dempster's Coffeehouse in Essex Street, where Doctor Patrick Anderson sold his 'angellical pills, and Merchant's Coffeehouse where John Frezell took orders for shipping freight abroad.[91] Peter Wilson in *The Dublin Directory for the year 1760* observed of John Burns that although he was 'born deaf and dumb; [he] sells haberdashery ware; and may be heard of at the Globe and Dublin Coffeehouse, Essex Street.'[92] The same directory for 1766 described how George Cannon, a self-proclaimed 'transactor of law business between London and Dublin', availed of Norris's Coffeehouse, Essex Street, as a commodious site from which to conduct his affairs.[93] Dick's Coffeehouse on Skinner's Row, where the estate of James Stevenson esquire was auctioned on 1 November 1725, was the site for the majority of book auctions that occurred in the capital.[94] Another such event occurred in 1746 when the *Dublin Journal* advertised:

> By judgement given in his Majesty's High Court of Admiralty in
> Ireland, the good ship the le [*sic.*] Port of Bordeaux, and the good
> ship the St Philip of Isle Dieu, with all their rigging, tackle, apparel
> and furniture, and all and singular the goods wares and merchandise,
> taken on board them were condemned as lawful prize, to Captain
> Luke Mezeer, commander of the Bessborough, a private ship of war.
> This is to give notice that the said ships, with all their riggings, tackle,
> apparel and furniture will be sold by auction to the highest bidder on
> the 20th last at the Dublin Coffee House in Essex Street.[95]

The *Freeman's Dublin Journal* reported in 1747 how the coffeehouse acted as a convivial place in which to conduct legal business, for 'the creditors of Robert Hawkins Magill esquire, deceased are desired to meet on Wednesday the 6th of May next at the Custom-House Coffeehouse, Dublin, at six o'clock in the evening to order to fix on some method for the speedy recovering of their demands from the executors.'[96] In a similar vein, the *Freeman's Journal* recorded a lengthy anecdote of another form of transaction in 1770, whereby

> about this time twelvemonth, a country gentleman purchased at a
> coffee house in this city, a few lottery tickets in the exchange scheme,
> for a joint account of himself and a lady . . . Soon after the drawings
> of the state lottery were finished, the lady sent up the tickets to a
> friend in Dublin to be informed of her success: he advised her that
> one of them was a prize of 100*l*, and in due time handed her the said
> sum, which she divided with her partner. A few days ago, the country
> gentleman came to Dublin, and was surprised at being wished joy by
> the master of the coffee house, in his good fortune at having received
> 1000*l*, Irish, in the last lottery . . . He applied to the faithful agent
> who insisted he had received but 100*l*. He then applied to the person
> who paid the prizes who offered to procure the identical ticket with a
> receipt thereon for the full sum of 1000*l*. The trusty friend, finding
> himself detected beyond a possibility of coming off, confessed the
> knavery and paid the 900*l* of which he had so infamously attempted
> to defraud his friend. The gentleman tells the fact, but does not name
> the treacherous agent, who is thus left under the cloak of a fair
> character to exercise his talents on his unsuspecting acquaintance.
> However this undoubted fact may serve as a caution to lottery
> adventurers for the future.[97]

Trade and trust were not commensurate, even though the coffeehouse keeper came away as the unintentional hero of the tale.

In many ways, the coffeehouses, taverns, and bookshops of the capital city identify the heart of the Irish Enlightenment. If the culture of Enlightenment can be found anywhere in midcentury, it is to be found in the handful of streets between Dame Street and the Liffey, and from Fishamble Street down the Hill to Eustace Street.[98] It was here that the clearinghouse for information and ideas was centred. Ideas flooded in from the port or were carried in from the countryside, to be weighed, measured, and redistributed in the coffeehouses, taverns, and bookshops of the neighbourhood. The international flavour of this exchange was captured in the doggerel squib which purported to be a 'Letter from the Quidnuncs at St James Coffee-House and the Mall' in London, and addressed to 'their brethren at Lucas's Coffee-House'. In the poem the London beaus bemoan the lack of any recent news worth gossiping over, admitting that

> Having nothing else to do
> We send these empty lines to you:
> To you, these empty lines we send,
> For want of news my worthy Friend:
> In hopes, ere long, some Spirit kind
> Will either raise a storm or wind,
> Or cause an earthquake, or in the air,
> Embattled troops will make appear:
> or Produce, somewhere, something new:
> Cause stories, whether false or true,
> To flie about.[99]

In this bereft state, the Quidnuncs beg those in Dublin to offer up some small morsel to sate their hunger for news, asking for any small piece of tittle-tattle they thought worthy to mention:

> When on dry ground, shall people tread
> From Howth's high hill to Holly Head?
> Wide as the Thames, shall Liffey flow?
> Amidst your bogs shall spices grow?
> Say can a better V[ice] R[egent] grace
> The D[uke] of G[rafton]'s ardous place?
> Than him, who'll station more despise?
> And will the factious ere be wise?[100]

Lucas's reputation as the epicentre of Dublin fashion was highlighted by a rather different verse, inscribed by 'Luke Lively, Gent' and contained in a short-lived periodical entitled *The Merry Fellow or Entertaining Magazine* (1757). Printed by James Hoey in Skinner Row, the poem recorded a conversation between the head and the heels of a city fop. The head demanded that the heels carry him about the town, expostulating:

Ye insolent dogs! Do you dare refuse
So little a walk in a new pair of shoes?
My legs too, methinks, might have gratefully gone,
Since a new pair of claves I this morning put on.[101]

To this outburst, the Heels retorted:

Do you call us ungrateful? The favours you prize,
Were design'd not to gratify us, but your eyes;
Is the footman oblig'd to his lordship or grace,
Who to feed his own pride, has equipped him in lace?[102]

Victory in the dispute went to the heels, and a chair was summoned to bring the beau the short distance, saving his new shoes and his appearance. The trumping argument comes when the Heels remind the Head of how 'we danc'd with the wives', hinting at how the coffeehouse was a venue for the fashionable to parade and perform, practising the polite arts of conversation and learning the rules of sociability and seduction; rules that had application in the parties, balls, and banquets with which the life of a city beau was taken up.[103]

A similar set of associations embedded in coffeehouse culture is made explicit in a pithy poem written by John Winstanley, a fellow of Trinity College, which celebrated the beauty and charms of a Mrs Cartwright, wife of the owner of the Custom House Coffee Shop. Writing of her rivalry with a Mrs Joyce, which a footnote to the poem records 'then kept the Globe Coffee-House', Winstanley admitted that many beaus were torn between the two. He recalled how they admitted of Mrs Cartwright:

Her goods, we own, are choice, and sweet
Her vessels neat, and clean, and meet,
Her Coffee's fresh, and fresh her Tea
Sweet is her Cream, Ptizan and Whea,
Her drams, of ev'ry sort, we find
Both good and pleasant, in their kind
And what of these? Hadn't we are choice,
As sweet and good from Mrs Joyce?[104]

Yet for Winstanley the choice was easy for

> Next her Barr's a magick chair,
> Oft I am charm'd in sitting there;
> Oft observe, when ere I rise
> Many watch, with longing eyes,
> Prompt to seize that happy place,
> Nearest to her lovely face
> Pleas'd to gaze on beauties there,
> Wond'rous Charming, Sweet and Fair.[105]

This blend of information gathering with social and sexual fraternisation was an intoxicating brew, heady with financial and amorous promise. It made the coffeehouse a site of intellectual and sensual pleasure, mixing the exotica of international news and strange tastes with local gossip and homely fare.

Enticing though this was, its appeal worried observers of a Scholastic and religious inclination. The Anglican curate of Donaghendry, County Tyrone, and a graduate of Trinity College, John Anketell penned a poem offering a 'Description of Sunday Evening Spent in a Coffeehouse in the City of Dublin' in which he fretted over how

> . . . when pray'rs are done,
> Straight to the coffeehouse crowds thronging run,
> Where from their minds they utterly discard
> Texts which in church they heard without regard.
> Calls for the news, and 'is the packet come?'
> With waiters' 'Here, sir!' echo thro' the room.[106]

Predictably it was the fashionable nature of the clientele and the easy social mixing enjoyed by those of low rank that caused his greatest consternation:

> The tawdry fops, with sneering, vain grimace,
> Adorn'd with ignorance—and flimsy lace,
> Strut in mock majesty, and view with scorn
> The *lower* creatures who this scene adorn
> . . . .
> The spruce apprentice, from his master free
> In his best cloaths hastes here with merry glee;

With powder'd hair resolv'd to cut a dash,
And treat of money—tho' he has no cash:
While the coxcomb will not want his tea.
He must be trusted as he cannot pay.[107]

The coffeehouse was a venue which at once appealed and appalled. It was also ripe for imitation across the island, not just in the other cities, but in the market towns and villages of the countryside.

The Provincial Public Sphere

The counter-public sphere certainly operated throughout the provinces. One indicator of this was the existence of circulating libraries that provided novels and histories in exchange for a subscription. Cork, for instance, was home to the Cork Library (established 1792), John Connor's Circulating Library (established 1794), and the more exotic French and Italian Circulating Library run by the language teacher M. Jacquottin which was operational before the century closed.[108] Similarly, the Belfast Circulating Library, organised by John Hay, was open by 1775 and Hugh Warrin's competitor lasted from 1772 until at least 1792, holding almost 2,000 volumes.[109] Armagh was the site of a public library when the Anglican Archbishop Richard Robinson's bequest came to fruition in 1774.[110]

Another indicator of the rise of a provincial public sphere was the spread of regional newspapers. The *Belfast News-Letter* was founded in 1737 by Francis Joy as part of a burgeoning print trade centred on Bridge Street in the city.[111] The *Limerick Journal* followed two years later; the *Sligo Journal* was launched in 1752; and the *Connaught Journal* (based in Galway) arrived in 1754. In 1765 the *Waterford Chronicle* appeared, while *Finn's Leinster Journal* was run in Kilkenny by a Catholic family from 1766. The situation was similar in Cork, where the first long-lasting publication, *The Corke Journal*, was launched by the Catholic printer Eugene Swiney in 1753. He had been an apprentice to a Limerick printer, Andrew Welsh, who had run the *Munster Journal* from 1749. A city rival to Swiney's vehicle, *The Cork Evening Post* appeared two years later under the stewardship of Phineas Bagnell.[112] The north of the country soon caught up, when the *Newry Journal* launched in 1761 was challenged by the *Newry Chronicle* in 1777. The *Strabane Journal* emerged in 1771, while the *Londonderry Journal* arrived in the same year, 1772, as the *Hibernian Gazette* based in Clonmel. The *Drogheda Journal* was founded in 1774, was the *Kerry Evening Post*. In 1778 the *Clare Journal* emerged, and by 1784 the *Ennis Chronicle* was active.[113]

A similarly staggered pattern accompanied the rolling out of a theatre culture, in part prompted by the competition in the capital in the 1730s which ensured that the two troupes had to expand the market for their wares. The peregrinations by Dublin companies saw the Aungier Theatre troupe going south, setting up a route that took in Kilkenny, Waterford, Cork, and Limerick, while the New Smock-Alley went north, staging summer performances in Drogheda, Newry, Belfast, and Derry.[114] Cork opened the Theatre Royal in 1736, a development which was followed in 1770 with permanent constructions devoted to drama opening in Limerick and Belfast. The latter city had its own resident company, the Theatre Royal troupe, by the 1770s, which themselves spent the summers touring Ulster, taking in Derry and Newry.[115]

Crowds in the countryside were similarly entertained by smaller strolling companies, who used barns and similar venues as makeshift theatres. Far from being events at which country folk were instructed in the culture of the capital these improvised theatricals provided opportunities for negotiation and exchange.[116] Even in the county towns, a vibrant localism could find expression on the stage. For instance, in Waterford Thomas Ryder flattered his audience's sensibilities in 1767 by producing *Harlequin in Waterford, or The Dutchman Outwitted*, a new pantomime in which the scenery consisted of flats painted to illustrate local sights, such as 'a view of Tramore, the Quay of Waterford, Christendom Church and churchyard, Form-yard, tombs, Church, Pump &c'.[117] Similarly, in 1771 Ryder had to make a public apology for his absence from the town, one which provides an insight into the place of the theatre in the city's social season:

> Mr Ryder with infinite pleasure informs the ladies and gentlemen of
> the city and county of Waterford, that he has obtained permission
> from the present worshipful mayor to open a theatre in the said
> city . . . He embraces this opportunity of assuring them that the
> highest attention shall be paid to their amusement and entertainment
> in the exhibition of the newest and most moral theatrical pieces that
> have been performed at the theatres of London and Dublin the last
> two winters. And as he had the ill fortune to displease some of the
> ladies and gentlemen of Waterford by not coming at the former

appointed times, he declares in this public manner, it did not proceed
from the want of a proper respect, he ever did and ever will retain for
them, but a chain of concurring disappointments which totally
deprived him of the means for undertaking so long a journey, being
then nearly two hundred miles from Waterford.[118]

The role of Waterford corporation in facilitating theatre was underlined when
the original playhouse, built in the 1730s and considerably too small for requirements, was replaced in 1784, with the urban government resolving that 'the sum
of £200 be granted . . . for the purpose of carrying on the building of the new
play house and assembly rooms'.[119] Typically, this new edifice was large and
centrally located, and provided boxes for the urban elite to set themselves apart
from those attending in the pit, all developments indicative of theatre's cachet.

Social mixing perplexed the more unstable theatrical culture of Kilkenny.
Operating without a custom-built playhouse until 1795, Ryder's touring troupe
made its way across from Waterford from at least 1767 to stage performances in
the assizes hall. This edifice was hampered by the demand it made on the audience, for Ryder found it necessary 'to lay the pit and gallery into one', discom-
moding 'persons of consequences'.[120] On occasion, as on 13 February 1768, privileged audience members—on that night the president and brethren of the
Friendly Brothers of St Patrick—were allowed to sit on the stage. By the time
Ryder returned in 1770, the plays had been moved to the Thosel where space
permitted side boxes to be erected and the seats sold at a shilling higher than the
2s asked for a place in the pit. Still, difficulties cropped up, with space being
such a premium that servants were not allowed to keep seats for their masters,
and had to be paid for were they to be admitted at all.[121]

The sporadic nature of the city's theatre culture was emphasised by the failure
of a 1784 scheme to provide a permanent home for the players. The aim was to
supply 'two substantial houses as wings to the theatre; the rent of which houses
will nearly repay, it is presumed, the expense of the entire building, and at all
times ensure an annual income to the subscribers.'[122] When it arrived, the playhouse was a statement of overheated ambition, with a footprint of fifty feet by
ninety feet and having boxes encircling the pit, as well as a second set of lesser
side boxes.[123]

In the case of Derry, a similar trajectory from transient to resident and up the
social spectrum can be identified. The Smock-Alley troupe seems to have first

played in the city in 1741, and certainly performed there in the spring of 1755. These early theatricals were housed in the great hall on the peer floor of the Town House and Exchange, the centre of Derry's social whirl, before removing in 1774 to a custom-built theatre on Ship Quay outside the northeast gate of the city's walls. As with many regional playhouses there were no boxes. Yet it was clearly a success, for opening in race week, in early August, the run lasted right through until Christmas, and was repeated the following year. When theatre manager Michael Atkins removed to Dublin in 1778, the theatre halted abruptly; from 1779 to 1782 the city was bereft of this mode of entertainment. This paucity was dramatically amended when Atkins indicated his desire to return, just as Myrton Hamilton, a one-time member of the Atkins troupe, declared that he too wished to establish a playhouse in the city. While Hamilton ran a season in June and July 1782, Atkins was to begin his show in August, with the season again running until December. A further season under the direction of Atkins's deputy manager John Bernard followed in 1783, and in 1784 a determined investment in the city was made by Atkins with his decision to raise a new play-house, a scheme which took until 1789 to complete. An edifice of eighty feet by forty feet, the new establishment was at the heart of the city, located near to St Columb's Cathedral in the southeast quadrant of the conurbation. The gala opening in January 1790 was enacted before the Derry Independent Volunteers regiment, and the following season, on 6 April, the Orange Lodge 132 attended in full regalia.[124]

In availing of the theatre for entertainment, the clubs and societies of Derry were by no means peculiar. For instance, *Finn's Leinster Journal* recorded how

> by command of the Master, Wardens and Brethren of the Ancient and Honourable Society of Free and Accepted Mason, belonging to No. 96 Clonmel and 484 of Fethard. On Monday the 15th of Feb. instant, at the theatre in Cashel, will be presented a tragedy called *The Revenge* with a farce called *The Virgin Unmasked*. Before the play, a prologue in character of a Master Mason, by Brother Hall. With the original Mason songs, choruses &c, &c.[125]

So too, in the heated atmosphere of the late 1770s, members of a local Volunteer regiment attended the opening night of Waterford's 1778 season and were regaled with a prologue by local author Dr Houlton, filled with militaristic fervour:

But would you ladies be as kind as fair,
Often to grace out scene of action here,
And you, good sirs, deign frequent to review
The little corps I've solely raised for you,
Soon should I boast your generous acts to me,
Made mine an Independent Company![126]

Theatre was not the only aspect of the public sphere enjoyed in the provinces. Limerick had two coffeehouses in operation through much of the century— Bouchier's and Gloster's; a fact which highlights how important competition was to the culture of commerce, but also the ways in which a contest over public space could brew even within a small urban space.[127] The earliest coffeehouse outside of Dublin was possibly the Mercantile in Cork, which dates from 1710 and the city had two operating by midcentury.[128] As early as 1722, the landlord Richard Edgeworth of Edgeworthtown estate in County Longford described how he regularly frequented a coffeehouse in Kinsale while conducting his legal duties as a justice of the peace.[129] Kildare also had a coffeehouse, the Curragh, which opened in 1759 and which was bought out from its proprietor and founder, Thomas Pasley, in 1761 by three former presidents of the Jockey Club which had regularly met within its walls: Sir Ralph Gore, Charles O'Hara, and Robert Clements.[130] The *Leinster Journal* was sold in Nixon's coffeehouse in Waterford in the 1770s, while around 1784 William Drennan complained to his sister from Newry that 'our coffee house is closed up here, so that I am obliged to get a peep of a paper when I can.'[131] In contrast, Cork sustained its interest in this kind of sociability, for in 1795 a proprietor named D. Manley opened the Merchant's Coffeehouse at the corner of Castle Street and North Main Street, offering twenty newspapers and broadsheets from across the British Isles for prospective customers to peruse.[132]

Two years earlier, in 1793, an Associated Society was established in Cork to 'raise a fund for erecting a coffee-house'. The deed of foundation detailed at considerable length the community of interest behind the project, and gives an insight into the kind of clientele these institutions attracted: the list of investors provided 116 names covering 140 shares. The mechanism they used to arrange the investment—a tontine scheme whereby each share was allocated to a child and the last one living inherited everything—suggests they thought it likely the venture would thrive. Indeed, the list suggests that hard heads were involved, for

fifty-three of the names described themselves as 'merchants', while others specified the nature of their trade more precisely. Julius Bernard was a sailcloth man-
ufacturer, for instance, while John Power and William Roberts were woollen
drapers, and John Litchfield and Henry Terry both dealt in linen. Even an iron-
monger purchased a share. Given the importance of the trade to the local
economy, it is little surprise to find one subscriber, Daniel Callaghan, describe
himself as a butter merchant. The names of the bankers James Bonwell and
Thomas Roberts on the list must also have been reassuring, coming as they did
just above Richard Fitton Esq, counsellor at law, and the attorney at law Thomas
Chatterton, who shared his occupation with James Gregg. Perhaps no name
reassured the others so much as that of Austin Skinkwin, who as an insurance
broker must have had a notion of the risk implied in the venture. Cork's local
elite was equally tempted by the scheme: Sir Robert Warren, a baronet, bought
two shares, while Sir Samuel Rowland, 'Knight and Alderman', bought one.
There were ten names for which the only occupation descriptor used was that of
esquire, while the fact that John Shaw, the 'Mayor of Cork', and two burgesses,
Richard Lane and Robert Hutchinson, were listed suggests that the imagination
of the urban elite was also fired. Lower down the social scale, clerk Rev. Francis
Orpen and grocer Daniel White were not precluded from investing their hard-
earned money. Even the relations of a number of bankrupts were able to invest
money on their behalf, perhaps in the forlorn hope of digging their estates out
of the mire. A widow put money forward, with Elizabeth Wills naming her son
James, a student at Trinity, as her nominee, while Miss Hannah Miller seems to
have been unmarried, if monied, when she named her eldest daughter, Susanna
Maria Frances Orpen, as her inheritor. Bookseller Thomas White and doctor of
physic Thomas Westropp may have had a more direct interest in the establishment of a coffeehouse, for both may have materially benefited from the venue as
a place of business.[133]

    While provincial cities like Cork could sustain venues of this kind, it was an
uncomfortable truth that convening together in the countryside could be more
difficult than to do so in an urban setting.[134] Yet this did not dissuade the sociable.
In particular, and despite an initial declension in the event's importance within
the rural economy, the continuance and ultimate expansion of the fair ensured
a vibrant focus for conversation, commerce, and conviviality. Certainly the fair
was in decline in the first half of the eighteenth century, at least in terms of
crude numbers, with patents running at their lowest level since the start of the

seventeenth century.[135] Those that did emerge were linked to regional urban centres which were attracting the trade of their hinterland with increased voracity. The average number of patents for fairs granted was less than ten per county, although Cork with sixty-seven, Tipperary with twenty-seven, and Limerick with twenty-six are significant outliers.[136] The vast bulk of the countryside saw active fairs in retreat, with the density falling in the first half of the century. The latter half of the century saw this trend reversed as economic conditions improved, with 200 new markets being brought to life. Few places in Ireland beyond the extreme western edges of the country were further than twenty kilometres from a market by century's close. Fairs similarly rose in density in the final decades, with there being few places in the county where there was not a fair held at some point in the year within forty-three square kilometres.[137]

Similar expansion was under way in the rural pastime of the hunt, an activity which, while dependent on the patronage of the local landlord, involved a variety of people from the lower ranks such as groomsmen and dog handlers, and which brought an array of local observers out onto the byways and fields of rural Ireland.[138] Moreover, the physical exertion was followed by a visit to a hostelry where conviviality turned to intoxication. The Belfast Hunt, for instance, met in the Donegall Arms, while the Kilkenny Hunt availed of the Garter Inn, and their rivals the Merry Harriers met at the Wheatsheaf.[139] Participation at these extracurricular events was not limited to the memberships, for women regularly joined their partners for the evening repast. Again the Kilkenny Hunt Club was exemplary with many other social activities interjected into the days of hunting.[140]

However, the cost of hunting was undeniably prohibitive for most; making it a distinctly elite pastime.[141] Oftentimes, the costs were defrayed by the gentry themselves by adopting a subscription system and moving the pack of dogs from household to household. The Kildare Hunt demanded a fee of £5 13s 9d in 1760, although this may have included the costs of entertainment when the hunt itself was not in season.[142] The time of the hunt was another bar to wider appreciation, with Irish hunts tending to begin in the early morning—perhaps off-putting to those who might have wished to travel to witness the spectacle.[143]

The spread of associations devoted to the hunt suggests something of its regularity and popularity as a sporting and festive occasion. In Limerick there is evidence of a club consisting of twelve squires from 1734, and the Croom Hunt which gathered between 1785 to 1791 was part of a wider fad for the sport which saw six other hunts in existence at some point between those dates, including the Rathkeale Hunt which was active from 1791 to 1794. In Clare the years of activity were broadly similar, with the County Clare Hunt occurring between 1786 and 1790, followed by the new County Clare Hunt which occurred in 1793 if not in other years, and the Milltown Chase happening in at least 1787 and 1788. Tipperary had a hunt in 1769 and again in 1779, and the Nenagh Hunt was active between 1786 and 1788, before being overtaken by the County Tipperary Hunt Club that held an event in 1789. As for Cork, one of the most durable hunts in Munster ran in Timoleague from 1769 to 1777, and the 1770s saw hunts gather in Doneraile, Carrigaline, and Castlecor from 1773 to 1777 and Imokilly from 1777 to 1788. The Duhallow Hunt persisted through the 1790s, beginning in 1786 and running to the close of the century.[144]

In a similar fashion hurling may have engaged the interest of some element of the landed gentry, albeit only in the southern counties where it was a summer game, associated with fairs and gambling, and not in Ulster where a winter version presided.[145] Wexford, for instance, had its elite exponents of the game. The Carews of Castleboro, the Devereuxs of Carrigmannon, and the Clocloghs of Duffray all provided notable participants, with this last family leaving a poetic reminder of their ability in 'The Hurling at Mohurry' wherein

> Squire Cloclough, our patriot, threw up the ball
> And Dick Doyle from Marshallstown gave the first fall
> Our men being trained in the hurling School
> Like a shot from a cannon they sent the ball cool.[146]

Members of the Butlers of Kilkenny were similarly renowned for their prowess in the game, while John Cuffe, Baron Desart was the subject of a lament upon his death in 1766 inspired by his ability at the game, having garnered the nickname Sean a'Chapin ('Jack of the Cap') among local admirers.[147] This elite participation ensured hurling played its part in genteel sociability as when a spa in Kilkenny advertised how 'horse racing, dancing and hurling will be provided for the pleasure of the quality'.[148] A similar array of sociable entertainments were laid on in County Galway, according to *Pue's Occurrences* in 1746, when

> for the better accommodation of the ladies and gentlemen and the
> benefit of a good road for carriages, it is agreed to remove the famous
> match of hurling from Ballinduffe to the turlough of Newtown

within a quarter mile from Gort. This is therefore to give notice that on Friday 14 August there will be on the turlough of Newtown a match of hurling where married men are to hurl against bachelors, to the number of twenty-one men a side, for a bett [*sic*.] of forty guineas where all sportsmen who are inclined to that diversion are required to give their attendance.

   NB: there will be a bridle and sweep stakes run for before the hurling and a ball at night at Mr Edmund Ruberry's in Gort, for the entertainment of the ladies, where all possible care will be taken for their reception. Also a buck hunt the next morning.[149]

Despite the polite nature of this social whirl, hurling could involve participants in courting some danger—as indeed could the hunt; in 1744 one player whose opponent 'stuck him with his hurl on the head' died as a consequence, while in Dunmore, County Kilkenny, a man named James Kelly died from a similar 'stoke of a hurl'.[150] Even with the dangers, the spectacle of both the hunt and the hurling match suggests the vibrancy of the rural public—witnessing the event before socialising across the lines of social rank and privilege in the wake of the excitement.

Social Mixing

Theatre again acts as a barometer for the development of this type of informal sociability. The playhouse was as much a place for social mixing as it was for displays of elite status. Indeed, without the presence of the lower ranks to gasp at, admire, and emulate the performances of the fashionable young men of the city, the theatre would have lost its audience and much of its social purpose.[151]

An illustration of the New Smock-Alley Theatre from 1789, which contains the renovations conducted in the summer of 1747, shows three entry points to the building, marking out the social divisions inside. To the left-hand side and up a short stairwell is the door to the upper gallery, where servants and the lower orders congregated. To the right-hand side and straight off the street is the 'passage to the pit and middle gallery' where the 'beaus, coquettes and prostitutes' resorted.[152] The elite went to the boxes through the front door, which stood at the middle of the building.[153] That contemporaries were aware of this physical manifestation of social segregation can be seen in the anonymous description offered by *The Tricks of the Town Laid Open* (1746). 'In our playhouse in Dublin', the author observed,

> besides an upper gallery for abigails, serving men, journeymen and apprentices, we have three other different and distinct classes. The first is called the boxes, where there is one peculiar to the lord lieutenant, and the rest for persons of quality and for ladies and gentlemen of the highest rank, unless some fools who have more money than wit or perhaps more impudence than both, crowd in among them. The second is called the pit, where sit the judges, wits and censurers, or rather the censurers without either wit or judgement . . . In common with these sit the squires, sharpers, beaus, and bulliers, and here and there an extravagant male cit. The third is distinguished by the title of the middle gallery, where the citizens' wives and daughters etc. commonly take their places.[154]

These divisions were maintained by the pricing policy, with a box costing some 5s 5d, a place in the pit 3s 3d, access to the gallery costing 2s 2d, and the upper gallery 2 pence.[155] This social gradient presented aesthetic problems, however, with playwrights anxious to keep the entire audience satisfied with the production. This unease found expression in Charles Shadwell's epilogue to *Irish Hospitality* (1717/1718) where he noted the different perspectives of the gathered assembly:

> Ladies will smile if scenes are modest writ
> Whilst your double entendres please the pit.
> There's not a vizard sweating in the gallery
> But like a smart intrigue, a rake and raillery.
> And were we to consult our friends above,
> A pert and witty footman 'tis they love.
> And now and then such language as their own,
> As 'Damn you dog, you Lie!' and knock him down.
> Consider then how hard it is to show
> Things that will do above and please below.[156]

This seems to have been a recurrent concern for Shadwell, the failure of whose final play, *Roderick O'Connor* (1720), he in part blamed on the complexity of managing diverse custom in the theatre house:

Now 'tis observed, out friends two story high
Do always laugh when other people cry,
And murdering scenes to them are comedy.
The middle regions seldom mind the plot
But with a Vizard chat of you know what,
And are not bettered by the play one jot.[157]

Shadwell's anxieties were well justified because theatre houses were highly combustible locations in the eighteenth century, with riots repeatedly breaking out as social, political, and confessional differences were performed, contested, and disputed through the medium of audience reaction.[158] On such episode, the Kelly riot which took place in 1747, revolved precisely around the issue of who might appear in public and who might ascribe to themselves the epithet of 'gentleman'. As Edmund Burke subsequently reported in a letter after attending a performance of *Aesop* (1697) by John Vanburgh:

> During the performance Mr Kelly comes in flushed with liquor, and
> going into the greenroom where the players dress—and began to
> entertain the actresses in the most nauseous bawdy and ill language,
> calling them bitches and whores, put his hand under their petticoats
> and would have forced some of them if his ability had answered his
> inclinations. This was represented to Mr Sheridan, who is the
> manager of the Theatre. Upon which he ordered Kelly out of the
> house, who, enraged at this, goes into the pit, and as soon as
> [Thomas] Sheridan comes on the stage, pelted him with oranges etc
> and called him a thousand ill names, bidding him go off the stage and
> tells him that unless some gentleman takes care of him, he would be
> obliged to turn him out of the house. Ten times more enraged at this,
> he goes after the act to Sheridan's room and insults him again.
> Sheridan represented calmly to him his abuse of the female players,
> and of himself, and he persisted in his ill language, Sheridan gave him
> a flogging, which he bore with Christian patience, not however,
> without vowing vengeance.[159]

The affidavits drawn up later confirm the initial intrusion, and Edward Kelly's attempt to, as it was politely put by one actress Mrs Dwyer, 'do what her husband Mr Dwyer had done to her, using the obscene expression'.[160] Sheridan's physical assault on Kelly occurred on the street, however, not backstage, for the evidence points to Kelly making recourse to a coffee shop to recover, where he claimed Sheridan's servants held him down while Sheridan beat him with a stick. More contentious was the assertion that where Burke thought Sheridan merely asked for Kelly's removal from the pit—the part of the theatre house where gentlemen sat during performances—Sheridan had in annoyance asserted to Kelly or the audience that 'I am as good a gentleman as you are'.

A second act occurred on 21 January when Kelly sought recompense. During Sheridan's next appearance on stage, a charity performance of Nicholas Rowe's *The Fair Penitent* (1703), a clique in the audience started shouting 'out with the ladies and down with the house'. A riot ensued, with the troublemakers seeking out Sheridan unsuccessfully to enforce retribution. They prodded swords into closets and then accosted the actress George Ann Bellamy, only leaving once they had been 'permitted to lift the covering of my toilette to see whether the manager [Sheridan] was there.'[161] The third and final act came on 11 February, with a charity performance of *The Fair Penitent* for the Dublin Hospital of Incurables. The stage was filled with ladies, as was the custom on such occasions, but this did not dissuade thirty gentlemen rising up upon Sheridan's entry and breaking up the performance.[162] Upon news of this discord reaching the streets, a mob of students trapped those they deemed the leading culprits, at least three of whom had to make a public apology, on their knees, in the front square of Trinity College Dublin, while being doused with water from the pump.

The trial that resulted saw Sheridan acquitted of assault and Kelly jailed. During its progress, the apparent nub of the matter was stated in an exchange between Kelly's lawyer and Sheridan. The lawyer sneered, 'I have often seen a gentleman soldier, and a gentleman tailor, but I have never seen a gentleman player.' It seemed that the judgement proved Sheridan right when he rebutted, 'Sir, I hope you see one now.'[163] The paradox was that it was Thomas Sheridan, a player, and therefore not a gentleman, who was victorious in the 'gentleman's quarrel'. As such, the subsequent 'clearing of the stage' of gentlemen seems to be a victory for the status of actors, and professional and aesthetic quality.[164]

Yet the drama also spoke to a rather different, older, revolution, in which the Protestant community had supplanted the Catholic aristocracy.[165] Kelly was, apparently, a convert from Catholicism who originated in Galway. This transformed the drama from a contestation over notions of hierarchy within the Protestant community into a contest between old and new elites. Kelly was at once an arriviste on the Dublin scene and a throwback to an older order. That was the purchase of Sheridan's assertion that he was as much a gentleman as Kelly, for both were playing at being a gentleman: neither Sheridan as a player nor Kelly as a Catholic convert could lay claim to such a title. However, that the contest took place over access to the Smock-Alley stage also turned the contest into a struggle over who could be seen to perform in public. Smock-Alley was at the epicentre of the liminal landscape between the privileged and unofficial public spheres.

Yet the problem of social mixing was not contained within the walls of the theatre house; as in the gentleman's quarrel, it spilt out into the coffeehouses and taverns of the town. The difficulty was that on occasion people did not get along. The coffeehouse and more potently the tavern were locations for social mixing, but equally, and concomitantly, were venues for the rubbing together of people who held different views, behaved differently, and who could come into conflict with each other. The addition of alcohol did not lend itself to tranquillity and politesse. Rather, the public sphere was often rude and dangerous.

The ideal of civility was difficult to live by.[166] The Social Enlightenment promulgated the virtue of tolerance but sociability often involved encountering people who differed over controversial issues of the day or whose behaviour was not of an expected form. This promoted argument and, on occasion, interpersonal violence. This is to accept that the discourse of civility remained largely an aspiration, with the reality of life in Irish cities and towns being frequently confrontational.

Certainly much of the conviviality was innocent, even when it was conducted to excess and resulted in inebriation. The practice of many clubs and societies to engage in toasting usually only ensured that fraternal gatherings resulted in the intoxication of celebrants.[167] And so long as the group remained united, the escapades the event inspired were largely confined to boisterous singing and lively carousing. Complications arose however, when the standards of propriety were loosened and those beyond the group began to be imposed upon, or took offence at the antics of the drinkers. One correspondent of the *Freeman's Journal* took umbrage at the behaviour of soldiers who had had a night on the town. He opined to the newspaper:

> An old officer, who is an admirer of exact military disci-
> pline . . . desires to know why the officers from the different guards in

the city are allowed to frequent Coffee Houses and to appear publicly in all streets in towns, in defiance of a standing order, and the scandal of the army on the Irish establishments.[168]

Nor were the complaints about behaviour solely about people who had fallen below expected standards; the same issue of the newspaper that denounced 'the clandestine malice of some discontented coffee house politician' also complained about how one establishment was courting a disreputable clientele. The correspondent highlighted how a venue on Essex Street had introduced a hazard table

in the house near where the cockpit is kept that is frequented by the most notorious gamblers in this city, from eight o'clock in the evening till morning, to the great detriment and annoyance of the public . . . His Lordship's [the mayor's] attention to redress the many grievances in this city, especially the suppressing of billiard tables in the said street, must ever claim the thanks and regard of the citizens of Dublin.[169]

Violence could result from the mingling of different types of people in a confined space. Thus a drunkard was reported as having attacked waiters in a Dublin assembly in 1769, while a month later a public breakfast in Dublin was pillaged by a 'rude mob of genteel participants who left silver coffee pots and teapots strewn around'.[170] The extreme case of this kind of fracas could be the instigation of a murder, as when in October 1781 in Cork, a 'Lieutenant Robert Hickson, a soldier home on leave, was challenged by Mr Brereton of the Duhallow Rangers'. They did not wait until the morning and instead conducted a duel in a coffeehouse on Brown Street. Breteton was killed as a result.[171] More fortunate was Robert Martin who in 1735 was acquitted of the murder of Lieutenant Henry Jolly in a Galway billiard room.[172] The court, however, had heard graphic details of the fatal assault and the circumstances preceding it:

The next evidence called was Captain Edward Southwell, who swore that Mr Jolly and he were diverting themselves in a billiard room at a coffee house in Galway, and that the prisoner Martin furiously came into the room, drew his sword and instantly demanded satisfaction of the rascal who spit upon him as he was passing by; that Mr Southwell answered, it was he that did it, but through no affrontful design, and in the most humble manner asked his pardon. Such humility little availed, for Mr Martin insisted upon further satisfaction, and being in

a very great passion, Mr Southwell said let me go to my Barrack for a
sword, I will very speedily return and comply with your request (there
being no sword between either Mr Southwell or the deceased Mr
Jolly). The prisoner asked Mr Southwell was the first attack by the
deceased with any instrument, not a sword, at the billiard table,
before the prisoner drew his sword, Mr Southwell answered no. The
next evidence was Robert Watson the coffee-boy who swore that there
was four yards distance at the billiard table between Mr Martin and
Mr Jolly, Mr Jolly standing by the window, and Mr Martin at the
door with his sword drawn, and approached Mr Jolly; that Mr Jolly
took up a chair to defend himself, through the frame of which the
prisoner made several thrusts at the deceased.[173]

Lucas's Coffeehouse was renowned as a location for duels, with the backyard
being the site of a number of bloody resolutions to slights of *amour propre*. The
earliest duel recorded dates from 1725, when Nicholas Jones, an army captain,
killed the Honourable Colonel Nugent; a case ensued in which political inference was decisive in getting the charge reduced to manslaughter, which effectively
acted as a reprieve.[174] A further seven duels occurred in the decade from 1748 and
1758. At least two of these resulted in the death of a participant, with Francis
Hamilton being killed by Arthur Mervyn in January 1748, and Patrick Kerwin of
Creggs, County Roscommon, slain in a swordfight with Edward Brereton, the
deputy serjeant of arms at the Irish House of Commons. Nor was Lucas's alone
in hosting such contretemps: at least four other assignations were conducted
within the coffeehouses and taverns of the city between 1754 and 1763, with a
fatality resulting from gunfire in June 1763.[175] Even as late as December 1774, a
Dublin coffeehouse hosted a duel in which a Lieutenant Franquefort was killed.[176]

Regulation and Retreat

Just as the ritual of duelling abated in the last decades of the eighteenth century, so too the vibrant public sphere began to dissolve from the late 1770s.[177]
This began with the increasingly obvious intrusion of oppositional politics into
the content of the papers, stages, and discussion housed by the institutions of
conviviality that powered the Social Enlightenment. In December 1770, the

Dublin Mercury cited a heated discussion in a coffeehouse, as a correspondent informed the publisher James Hoey,

> I happened to go into one of our coffee houses the other morning, and meeting there a friend of mine, asked him if he had read the *Mercury* of that day, on the true promoters of the prorogation, and plainly showing that our worthy c[hie]f g[overno]r was not in the least to be blamed for it; he made answer, not yet. A person in good clothing who stood by me, and it seems was an acquaintance of my friend's, immediately said with some warmth; he hoped my friend would never read such a rascally paper . . . This strange declaration and the manner in which it was uttered satisfied me that to enter into contest with such a charterer, would be like fighting a flame: I immediately enquired who he was, and was told he was a virulent republican.[178]

As this indicates, debate within the coffeehouse was becoming more politicised and radical. Fashionable exchange was slipping into the vortex of political contestation. Moreover as the dismissal of the *Dublin Mercury* suggests, the newspapers themselves were becoming increasingly partisan, with such organs as the *Volunteer's Journal* promulgating one view and government organs such as the *Volunteer Evening Post* another.[179] So too, the theatre entered a more confrontational phase, while the bookstores poured forth the vitriol of the public debate.

Once the reforms associated with Grattan's parliament of 1782 were granted, and the Volunteer movement faded momentarily from the scene, the government took the chance offered by the lacunae to enact a series of legislative measures that attempted to tame the counter-public sphere.[180] First of all they went about prosecuting those printers who would not come to heel, which involved a systematic attack on unsympathetic press titles, with lawsuits being pursued against the *Volunteers Journal* (edited by the Catholic Matthew Carey), the *Dublin Evening Post*, and the *Hibernian Journal*.[181] This coincided with the passage in 1784 of the Act to Secure the Liberty of the Press, by Preventing the Abuses arising from the Publication of Traitorous, Seditious, False, and Slanderous Libels by Persons Unknown. It stipulated that, in the face of a fine of £100,

> no person whatsoever shall print, or cause to be printed, publish or cause to be published any newspaper, intelligencer or occurrences . . . before he, she or they shall have first given into the

commissioners for managing his Majesty's Stamp duties, or their
proper officers in the respective towns . . . an affidavit setting forth
his, her or their true name and names of the proprietor or proprietors
of such newspaper . . . and of all and every person or person receiving
or sharing, or entitled to share the profits thereof, together with the
place or places of abode of every such printer, publisher or other
person aforesaid.[182]

Further parliamentary energy raised the stamp duty, making it increasingly
uneconomic to run a newspaper, while offering covert financial support to
those editors who followed a government line.[183] The most prominent title
seduced by these inducements was the *Freeman's Journal*, which was to run as a
government vehicle in the 1790s under the stewardship of the spymaster
Francis Higgins.

Moreover, in a seven-year period after 1784 this Press Act was followed by a
raft of other legislation imposing order on an unmannerly public sphere, most
notably the Act for Regulating the Stage in the City and County of Dublin,
initially mooted in 1779 but eventually placed on the statute books in 1786.[184]
Article one stated by justification that 'the establishing of a well regulated theatre in the city of Dublin, being the residence of the chief governor or governors
of Ireland, will be productive of public advantage and tend to the improvement
of the morals of the people'.[185] This simple sentence stated the government's
sense that the theatre was their domain and that its role was to inculcate proper
political sentiments, not to be a venue for discussion.

Article two prohibited the performance of any 'interlude, comedy, prelude,
opera, burletta, play, farce, pantomime, or any part or parts therein on any stage,
or in any theatre, house, booth, tent, or any other place within the said city of
Dublin, or the liberties or suburbs, or county thereof, or within the county
of Dublin, under any colour or pretence whatsoever, save or except in such a
theatre or playhouse as shall be established or kept by letters patent.'[186] The
message was clear: only officially sanctioned performances were permitted.
The patriot-leaning Fishamble Street theatre shut its doors while the bill was
passing through the legislative stages.[187] The act marked a return of a didactic
understanding of theatre.

This measure was built on in 1790 with the Act for Regulating the Coffee
Trade. This was lengthy piece of legislation, which alongside renewing the

standard duty of six pence for each pound of coffee imported, determined that 'every person who shall sell by retail, or otherwise deal in coffee . . . shall take out a license from the collector of the district in which such person shall reside and shall pay for the same a duty of twenty shillings.'[188] This left the coffee-houses in the hands of reliable proprietors, minded to inform on potential troublemakers. Certainly in the 1790s, coffeehouses were places over which the United Irishmen and the government might challenge each other for control over the population's allegiance. Coffeehouses in Waterford, for example, sub-scribed to the *Northern Star*, while those in Dublin were often frequented by spies loyal to the Castle.[189]

The introduction of this regulatory regime continued in 1791 with the Act for Regulating the Sale of Licenses for the Sale of Spirituous Liqueur by Retail, and a tranche of later legislation aimed at curbing the alcohol trade. This chimed with a growing concern over public health, something the bill asserted as a motive, relating how 'the use of spirituous liquors prevails to an immoderate excess, to the great injury of the health, industry and morals of the people.'[190] These were to be restored through the mechanism of dramatically raising the tariff for a licence to between £4 and £20.

All this legislative energy amounted to a concerted campaign to recolonise the public sphere by the state. At the same time the United Irish movement was being concocted in the minds of disaffected opponents of the regime. They were to compete, through newspapers, ballad sheets, plays, and conversation for the allegiance of the public sphere, generating an oppositional landscape that con-fronted, both overtly and subversively, the claims to hegemony by the Castle and its functionaries. In effect, the last quarter of the century saw the politicisa-tion of the public sphere and its shift away from a literary mode. This alteration was given legislative expression in the 1787 Act to prevent Tumultuous Risings and Assemblies, and for the more effectual Punishment of Persons guilty of Outrage, Riot and illegal Combination, and of administering and taking unlawful Oaths. Assemblies implied sedition and riot, while illegal combination was con-nected in the mind of authority with oath-bound conspiracy, two years before the French Revolution was to further radicalise the Irish climate.

Despite the anxieties evinced in the state's response to its development, the emergence of a counter-public sphere in Ireland in the decades from 1730 to 1760 was a vital component of the Social Enlightenment. It supplied a social context for the discourse of civility mapped in the previous chapter. Its existence suggests that there were places in which interconfessional sociability was accept-able practice, in which ideas circulated, and affective ties developed. Once poli-tics and faith were set aside, commonalities were identified which resulted in fraternisation and friendship. These connections were oftentimes formalised and institutionalised in the clubs and associations which flourished in the period of the Social Enlightenment.

6

Communities of Interest

∾

Whilst thus in unity we join,
Our hearts still good and true;
Inspired by the grace divine,
And no base ends in view;
We friendly meet, ourselves employ,
To improve the fruitful mind;
With blessings which can never cloy
But dignify mankind.

—Laurence Dermott, Song XLII, *Ahiman Rezon: Or, A Help to All that Are
(or Would Be) Free and Accepted Masons*, 1764

CLUB LIFE constituted the central praxis of the Enlightenment. It institutionalised the debate that emerged in midcentury concerning how
Ireland might best meet the challenges of dearth and was the outcome of a
public sphere that emerged in the salons, coffeehouses, taverns, and theatres of
Irish society. The club was an ambition and a location; an agenda and a rendezvous.[1] Clubs provided the Enlightenment with a means of determining and
implementing a course of action. They provided the Enlightenment with
social capital, bringing together unrelated actors for shared, commonly nonpo-
litical, ends.[2] The ambition of many of these heterogeneous associations was the
common weal, beginning with the desire to make Irish society a more pleasant
community in which to live; allowing the divisions of the political past to be

softened and the wounds of confessional conflict to be healed by mutual correspondence, collaboration, and cooperation. This chapter examines the emergence of a realm of associational life that emerged from the deployment of
Enlightenment methods, reflected the discourse of civility, and often cut across
traditional confessional demarcation lines.

The desire to create a club was elusive and personal. The motivation for many
of them was little more than the desire for select society, finding entertainment
and hospitality to one's taste, or a retreat from the noise of the city street. Thus
the Dublin Florists' Club, which was active between at least January 1747 and
September 1766, was the excuse for a great deal of convivial eating and drinking.
Supposedly devoted to the promulgation of ornamental gardening, the society
awarded premiums for the cultivation of flowers. Yet many of its members did
not have a substantial garden, and the purpose was the cultivation of each other's company, with the group gathering at the Phoenix Tavern on Werburgh
Street to drink a series of toasts. The florists were a self-selecting elite; solidifying
and sharing social connections through membership. Men such as John Putland,
a recidivist presence in associations of this kind, wined and dined there with
Bishop Richard Pococke and the Earl of Moira.[3]

A similar function of mutual companionship and affective ties brought
together those at the opposite end of the social spectrum. In 1754 a beggars' club
was apparently meeting in the Cow's Head of Liffey Street. Made up of 'the
cripples, the blind, and the aged, established and badged beggars of the parish
of St Mary's' their toasts included 'prosperity to begging'; 'may no foreign beggar
ever find the benefit of this parish'; and 'confusion to all those in the worst of
times quitted our ancient and honourable occupation for any mean servile
trade'.[4] With 'Peter Ivers in the chair' they enacted the standard forms of club
life etiquette, mixing conviviality with a concern for sharing problems and bol-
stering self-esteem.[5]

Some of the joy involved in establishing a society came in drafting and
administering the rules governing the association. A typical example of such
legislation underpinned a gentleman's club convening in Shaw's Court in Dublin
during the 1770s. The institution granted a cheap place to take breakfast and
imbibe 'tea and coffee in the evening', albeit 'other things there called for [were]
to be at the established prices in coffee houses'.[6] Membership was granted
following a process of publicity as 'a person proposed to be a member of this
club must have his name put up in the coffee room a fortnight before he can be

balloted for, along with the name of the person who proposed him'.[7] On the occasion of the ballot—held overnight from Monday night to Tuesday morning, with a quorum of twelve of the 200 members—'one black ball excludes'.[8] The cost of entry was substantial: 'three guineas, and likewise the annual subscription prior to his being admitted, which is two guineas more.'[9] The fraternal ethos was articulated in rules surrounding the main meal, which was 'on the table at eleven o'clock, at three shillings a head, which every member then in the house is to pay whether they sit down to supper or not'; a clear indication that sociability was presumed.[10] Yet there was also an exclusivity implied for 'none but members [are] to be admitted into any part of the house, under any pretext whatsoever, excepting into that room which is allotted for the reception of such as may have business with some of the members of the club.'[11]

While convivial sociability was a primary attraction, membership was often dictated by the interests that the association claimed to represent. Nor was Ireland in the mid-eighteenth century lacking in options. To take only William Burton Conynham and John Putland as examples, the first was not merely a founding member of the Kildare Street Club, and a reject from Daly's, but he was heavily invested in both the Dublin Society, of which he became a member in 1758, and the Royal Irish Academy, being a founder member in 1785. In the first of these he served on the Antiquities Committee and the Committee of Commerce, having an interest in fisheries and the uses of salt. In the RIA he was treasurer in 1785 and vice-president in 1792. A government MP, he was made a trustee by parliament for the proposed academy of the Society of Artists in Dublin in 1765. He also founded the Hibernian Antiquarian Society in 1779, with himself as president, to replace the by-then defunct Royal Dublin Society committee.[12] Putland was similarly voracious. As well as being a member of the Dublin Florists he was involved in the Dublin Society and the Physico-Historical Society, being treasurer of both in the 1740s. A Freemason, he was junior grand warden in 1737, senior grand warden five years later, and deputy grand master repeatedly from 1747 to 1750 and again from 1763 to 1764.[13] He was invested in charitable activity, as a governor of St Mercier's Hospital between 1736 and 1756, and in the life of the wider public sphere, holding shares in the Smock-Alley Theatre run by Thomas Sheridan.[14]

The foremost contemporary theorist of an Irish associational life was the physician Samuel Madden.[15] In his *Letter to the Dublin Society* (1739), he understood the institution as mobilising the nascent Irish civil society. Expressing an ethos of self-help he praised the society for agreeing that 'the remedies of all our evils, must begin from ourselves, rather than our neighbours, and chiefly from our own increase of industry'.[16] Acknowledging their commitment to a programme that blended rationalism and empiricism, or 'knowledge and experience' as he termed it, he postulated that an apolitical association such as the Dublin Society could best devote its energies to the pursuit of utility.[17] 'Next to being eminently good and virtuous', he suggested,

> to be truly and generally useful to others is the great and honest glory
> of a man and a citizen; and he who, by his writings can lend us one
> important hint, purpose and thereby hereafter occasion one excellent
> law, whoever overturns a wrong turn of thinking, or acting in his
> country, is to be encouraged and approved, though his style, or his
> method, his manner or even his arguments be ever so censurable.[18]

This was an appeal not just to the landed and the Protestant community, for in his contention that national utility should be privileged Madden was explicit that 'all ranks and orders of men among us will throw in their mites to this treasury of our Jerusalem, and scorn to support their country with only their wishes and their prayers.'[19] Confessional purity was to be trumped by patriotic commitment.

The primary difficulty the Dublin Society faced was how to energise their prospective audience to pursue their aims and ambitions. As Madden accepted 'many gentlemen who live in the country will be less inclined to subscribe, as their distance and absence make them almost incapable of any share'.[20] To counter this, he proposed that the membership turn the potential enthusiasm for the project kinetic through personal connection. In a passage which speaks of his ambition to mobilise civil society he informed members:

> I am satisfied if every one of your present numbers was desired to
> name a worthy friend, who should enter into the Society, like the
> Roman Senators, *Vir virum legens*, you might at once by this very
> method, with a little care and consideration double their numbers and
> perhaps treble your fund. Among so general an acquaintance, and so
> many friendships and intimacies, as they must have entered into the
> world, it is impossible but every gentleman must have one, if not
> several in his view, whom he can engage in so worthy a cause.[21]

This vision of an activated civil society extended to the running of the Society itself, for Madden proposed that all the critical decisions within the body be taken 'by plurality of voices, by balloting'—the term 'voices' hints at how he had in mind the conversational world of the public sphere.[22] Proxies overcame the problem of distance.[23] In establishing this due process, the Society effected the ideal of a rational-critical discussion, in which everyone retained their autonomy, for 'whoever subscribes becomes from that moment a judge, how the money he gives is employed.'[24] Indeed, the Society was instrumental in the creation of public discourse, for

> among the other services you have done us, you have taught many of
> our Irish gentlemen the honest courage to venture to lay useful
> thoughts before the public; and as our country has been generally cen-
> sured for being almost a mute in the commonwealth of letters, it is to
> be hoped it will appear that we have at least improved our thinking by
> our silence now we begin to publish our reflections.[25]

While the *Letter* was addressed to the Dublin Society, Madden's instructions were not directed to it alone. He offered a vision of a broad-based associational culture, for there was, he claimed, in the activities of the Linen Board,

> indisputable evidence for the use and efficacy of such societies . . . and
> as I shall show hereafter, that there are a number of very difficult,
> though most useful improvements, which want as much to be nursed
> up and encouraged in Ireland, it will, when that is proved, be as
> demonstrable, that is in the highest manner incumbent on us, as our
> duty, as our interest, to set up such Societies; and when set up, to
> support, by larger contributions (adequate to such great and gen-
> erous designs) every attempt they shall make, of new improvements
> among us.[26]

The first meeting of the Dublin Society was held in Trinity College Dublin on 25 June 1731.[27] Quickly, however, it shed its privileged origins, moving away from the college to Shaw's Court and then to its own premises on Grafton Street. Beginning with fourteen founders, as early as 1733 there were 267 members, sug-gesting the society had tapped into a vein of interest in the local community in a manner that made membership faddish.[28] If so, the fashion waned quickly for by the late 1730s the society was close to extinction; a fate which exemplifies the problem of sustaining the engagement requisite to ensure longevity in the world of voluntary association.[29] Joiners rapidly turned into miscreants, failing to pay their dues or attend meetings. Indeed, the Dublin Society highlights how, were clubs to flourish, they required constant injections of fresh blood.

The early 1740s saw just such a resuscitation of the institutional body, with the introduction in 1741 of weekly meetings—the decision to publish the minutes had to wait twenty-three more years. That same year also saw an overhaul of the internal structure, a standing committee of twenty-one being established (later reduced to fifteen) and annual elections for the offices of the society. It also subdivided the concerns of the Society into three subcommittees, with respective remits covering experiments, publications, and the accounts.[30] In 1740 membership had been limited to 100, but this was quickly relaxed, for in 1750 a published list of members included 119 names, including the lord lieutenant, William Earl of Harrington, who was the nominal president, two dukes, three archbishops, four earls, five bishops, and seven lords.[31] Beyond this top tier of entitled figures, the list was largely made up of lesser clergy and numerous esquires, suggesting something of the demography of the voluntary sector in eighteenth-century Irish society. The membership continued to climb, with 420 members identified in 1770, although active participation was scant. The laws of the Society dictated that it only took five members to make a quorum and a mere seven to elect a new member.[32] Attendance seems to have hovered around forty in the 1760s, with a falling off occurring in the 1770s when thirty-two was the norm. This slackened even further in the 1780s as the fashion for voluntarism faded generally in Ireland, and a mere eighteen to nineteen members could be expected, although on occasion only five or six arrived.[33]

Despite the decline in the activism of members, in a number of ways the Dublin Society remained the emblematic institution of associational life in eighteenth-century Ireland.[34] First, it exemplified the cooperation of two Enlightenment methods, rationalism and empiricism. It insisted that, according to the nineteenth rule governing its activities,

> every member of this society at his admission is desired to choose
> some particular subject either in Natural History, or in Husbandry or
> Agriculture or Gardening or some species of Manufacture or other
> branch of improvement and make it his business by reading what has
> been printed on that subject, by conversing with them who made it

their profession or by making his own experiments, to make himself master thereof and report in writing the best account they can get by experiment or inquiry relating thereunto.[35]

But it was not only book learning that was used by the Dublin Society.[36] Money was used to buy land near the city in 1733 to run experiments and, later, to buy a factory for making implements in Celbridge.[37] From 1795 there was a botanical garden founded in Glasnevin with the support of parliament. The Society also collated data drawn from its members across the countryside and established a series of schools employing, as the by-laws of 1765 make clear, masters in the teaching of 'drawing human heads and figures', 'ornamental drawing', and 'drawing in architecture', and a school of mineralogy that employed the notable Irish chemist Richard Kirwan.[38] Kirwan was to use this platform to convince the Dublin Society to purchase a noted mineral collection, known as the Leskean Cabinet, and this became the inspiration for *Elements of Mineralogy* (1784), the first systematisation in English of the subject.[39]

The practical purpose of all this activity was to defend against a repeat of the economic crisis that had befallen Ireland in the 1720s and again in the early 1740s.[40] This ambition was given focus by Madden's suggestion that the Dublin Society use its monies to ameliorate specified sectors of the Irish economy through the award of premiums.[41] A list from 1765 requisitioned money to disperse to those who furthered the technology and practice in manufactures of silk, woollens, leather, iron and steel, copper and brass, paper, glass, earthenware, mixed fabrics, gold and silver threads, and the printing of cloth, with funds totalling almost 10,000*l* set aside for the awards.[42]

In this activity the Dublin Society aimed to be a clearinghouse for ideas. How far this was achieved is difficult to ascertain. Certainly there were obstacles imposed by the persistent problem of distance. The drive to corral activism in agriculture in the provinces of Munster and Connaught in particular was fraught with difficulty. The need to send central communications out and the connected requirement that members spend time in Dublin attending the weekly meetings ensured that dialogue was haphazard. There were, for example, only twenty Munster members in 1770.[43] Efforts were made to overcome the natural limits of the Society's catchment, with printed copies of what premiums were available produced in large numbers—around 1,000 pamphlet copies and 2,000 broadsides.[44]

The second way in which the Dublin Society might be considered emblematic of Irish associational life was its willingness to overlook confessional concerns. Presbyterians could become full members, such as Andrew Caldwell, the barrister and MP for Knocktopher in County Kilkenny, whose interests extended into urban improvement—he was a member of the paving board and Wide Streets Commission, and helped to develop the planned town of New Geneva.[45] He may have written the 'Observations on Architecture' that appeared in the *Freeman's Journal* between December 1768 and February 1769 and his interest in plants, being a fellow of the Linnean Society, helped in the purchase of the land that made up the Botanical Gardens in Glasnevin, Dublin.[46] While Catholics could not be full members, premiums awarded by the society for best practice repeatedly found their way into their hands.[47] For instance, Thomas Wyse, cofounder of the Catholic Committee, won prizes for handsaws and scythes.[48]

Madden made this commitment to democratic engagement in the scheme of improvement explicit when he argued in the close of his *Letter to the Dublin Society* that what was being proposed was not a projecting frenzy

> but plain and obvious rational designs for the general service of every landlord and tenant, tradesman, merchant or manufacturer, nay, every labourer and beggar (if there be any difference betwixt those two callings) in this nation.
>
> This might seem a daring and presumptuous way of speaking, if what I am saying was not so evident a truth; and as it will be as practicable as praiseworthy in our countrymen to join hands, one and all, for the good of all, I will be as confident they will let nothing divert them from espousing it. As there is no faction, no partial views, no private interests carried on or thwarted by it, as it is neither Papist nor Protestant, Whig or Tory, nor can any ways hurt the general good of England, where all we can gain or save must go at last, I think there is no opposition to be feared from any quarter. All ranks and orders of men are interested in it, even our clergy, are as much obliged to wish well to it as our landlords, or our tradesmen, since all improvements of this kind will naturally be productive of civility, good sense and taste, or arts and industry, and consequently of religion and virtue, which are more essentially united to them than some people conceive.[49]

'Neither Papist nor Protestant, Whig or Tory' were excluded from a project for 'all ranks and orders of men'; what Madden here envisaged was a broadly based collaborative society pursuing the progress of civility in all its forms—'good sense' or politeness; 'taste' or aesthetics; 'arts' or improvement; and 'industry' or political economy. In this, the Dublin Society was emblematic of a wide culture of club life that emerged in the decades either side of 1750.

The third significant way in which the Dublin Society was characteristic of wider associational life concerns the process whereby it came to be sustained by the political administration. The dilemma for the Dublin Society was that its more ambitious plans required financial muscle that could only be offered by the state; yet the very attraction of the Society was that its membership was able to ignore the limits of active citizenship imposed by a confessional state. Civil society was, after all, intentionally apolitical, with arguments concerning power supposedly set aside in pursuit of shared concerns.[50] Yet the process of politicisation undergone by the Dublin Society foreshadowed a wider fate whereby the civil society of Ireland was, in the late eighteenth century, politicised, polarised, and radicalised.

In the specific case of the Dublin Society this process can be tracked through reference to the granting of parliamentary funds to the institution. This followed in the wake of Madden's suggestion that the Society tap 'a greater resource' than personal voluntarism and charitable inclination,

> namely our representatives in parliament who are the great guardians
> of our fellow subjects and countrymen, and all that is near and dear to
> them and us as a nation. Whatever appears evidently to affect the
> public welfare will never want encouragement and protection from
> them; and if your cares and labours to serve us shall seem to need (as
> undoubtedly they will ever deserve) their assistance, there is little
> reason to fear you will be refused either their votes or their purses.[51]

Madden's optimism proved accurate, for the earliest parliamentary grant, given in 1749, was for £500 with the annual supply rising to £8,000 in the 1763 session.[52] In that of 1765 the MPs also supplied £8,000.[53] The grant fell to £7,000 in 1767, but in 1785 a further two statutes provided £2,500 and £5,000 respectively.[54] In 1786 the grant settled down to the level of £5,000 annually until 1794 when the grant was increased to £5,500.[55] While this act also made some provision for the Royal Irish Academy, that body was not named in 1795 when a bill renewing the £5,500 grant failed to be enacted; this glitch was ironed out the following year when two acts were passed granting £5,500 each.[56] The final years of the century—and of the parliament—saw the legislative support pass into law without further trial or tribulation.[57]

Moreover, through 1749 and 1750 a process of gaining state recognition was undergone, with the Society being incorporated by a Royal Charter granted by George II on 2 April 1750. Again, this followed on from Madden's express wish that 'your Society should make it one of your first cares to be embodied into a corporation, by a charter and letters patent under the broad seal' for only by doing so might the institution 'be a perpetual [rather] than a lasting society'.[58] When it came, the charter recognised the previous voluntary work of the Society whereby members

> have at their own expense made many experiments, and published
> useful observations and instructions for raising flax, draining bogs,
> and improving unprofitable lands; and distributed considerable sums
> of money in premiums, to the most deserving, whereby a spirit of
> industry and emulation hath been raised, and great hopes conceived
> that much greater effects might arise there from tending farther to
> civilise the natives of our said kingdom, and render them well affected
> to us, and our royal family, and more able to contribute to the
> increase of our revenue, and the support of the establishment of our
> said kingdom.[59]

Across the course of this description the Society was rhetorically, as well as legally, incorporated into the state. The economic voluntarism that initially inspired members was sublimated into ends applicable to the wider political culture—the civility of the populace—and then to more narrowly institutional ambitions—the improvement of the revenue of the state. Whatever advantages the Society gleaned from the charter, and the survival of the body may well have been one, the cost was a submission to political fortune and a loss of institutional flexibility. So too, in relation to the parliamentary grants, indebtedness for generosity paved the way for more open intervention by well-meaning parliamentarians, often themselves members of the Society.[60] The wider cost to civil society may have been greater still, with politics creeping into the crevices of cultural life and inflecting the informal, sociable relations that had been enabled by the clubs and associations of the mid-eighteenth century. So even as the Dublin Society struggled to retain its autonomy, it set the coordinates for the rest of the clubs that flourished in the half century from 1730 to 1780, and which constituted a wider experiment in the possibility of human coexistence. In its attempt to generate social commitment to a failing country, the associational flowering at midcentury represents the high point of the Irish Enlightenment and its broadest impact on the cultural life of the country.

At the heart of the club life of the period rested a new conception of the human being as a social actor first and a spiritual soul second. It was informed by an intricate discourse of civility that encompassed the interlocking languages of politeness, aesthetics, improvement, and political economy. Associational life emanated from and relied on the facilities provided by the new public sphere—clubs met in coffeehouses and assembled in taverns. The social mixing such places encouraged was in turn formalised and institutionalised in the body of the club. In this, the clubs embodied Enlightenment theory in action: a praxis that emerged from, was embedded within, and articulated the value of civil society. This chapter offers a taxonomy of these institutions as they emerged across the spectrum of the Enlightenment methodologies and through the component languages of the discourse of civility, emphasising how confessional mixing occurred in many of these organisations, before turning towards the issue of the eventual politicisation of associational life. This process was prompted by controversies within the state over parliamentary autonomy and the definition of citizenship encapsulated in the question of legislative Catholic relief.[61]

Not all voluntary associations were enlightened in purpose, however. Religious fraternities remained wedded to a Scholastic worldview and other legitimate and illegitimate societies emerged which were more political or criminal than civil in their intent. So too, the Freemasons constituted an extreme wing of the spectrum of thought, which, while freethinking, was less interested in the vector of debate that constituted the broad centre ground of the Enlightenment. Those societies which were devoted to making Ireland more polite, more materially successful, more beautiful, and more efficient shared a general commitment to an empirical or a rational methodology or, more typically, an uneven blend of both. The ambition was to help Ireland flourish through public engagement. An Enlightened civil society was to bloom at midcentury in a colourful, boisterous, and convivial culture of association.

Scholastic Solidarities

The legislative universe of eighteenth-century Ireland did little to fragment, and much to solidify, the sense of group cohesion within confessional communities. Faced with state antagonism articulated in the penal code, Catholics developed lay associations to provide strong social support to co-religionists. Fraternities existed on Werburgh Street in Dublin, for instance, where two had a brief existence. Records also indicate that in 1743 the Confraternity of Our Blessed Lady of Mount Carmel was active, while four years later, a Confraternity of the Brown Scapular was meeting there.[62] In Wexford, the Confraternity of the Cord of St Francis held a membership roll of 681 members for the period 1763–1789, of which 609 were women. The Sodality of the Blessed Virgin Mary was active in the region, spreading through Waterford, Cork, Clonmel, and Dublin, while the Confraternity of Christian Doctrine, at the end of the century, garnered members in Wexford, as well as in St Micham's parish in Dublin where it provided an outlet for female spirituality and educational endeavour.[63] Similarly, amongst Presbyterians in Ulster, fellowship societies were a feature of the Reformed Presbyterians from the 1740s and, from the 1790s, of the evangelical wing in the Synod of Ulster.[64]

Reading societies across Ulster, emerging from the 1770s onwards, helped to ground religious sentiment in biblical scholarship, as well as to open up the possibilities of secular learning.[65] The first book club of which there is evidence was located in Doagh village in County Antrim, with thirty members meeting in 1770 with the local schoolmaster William Galt at its helm.[66] Subsequently County Down was the location for two politically divergent clubs, founded in 1786, with the Newry Book Society having Volunteer and later United Irishman William Drennan as a member and the Portaferry Literary Society boasting a young Lord Castlereagh, later Chief Secretary for Ireland, as an alumni.[67] If this division was symbolic of a wider breach in the public sphere that occurred in the final decades of the eighteenth century, the social mixing that occurred within the confines of the Belfast Reading Society, founded on 13 May 1788 and evolving into the Linen Hall Library, was a residue of the generous sociability of earlier decades. Working under the title of the Belfast Society for the Promotion of Knowledge from 1792, the association brought together the improving plebeians of Belfast with the worthy middle ranks. It provided access to a wide range of Enlightenment texts, including work by David Hume and William Robertson and a complete set of the

Encyclopaedia Britannica (1768–1771).[68] This society was at the apex of a wider phenomenon, with book clubs forming throughout County Down in 1789 and the early 1790s. These included the Newtownards Society for Acquiring Knowledge, the Ballygoskin Reading Society and clubs in Ballynahinch, Dromore, Hillsborough, and Banbridge.[69] Two others in County Antrim—in Lowtown and Templepatrick—have left traces.[70] The middle of the decade also saw the foundation of an Artisan's Reading Society in Belfast (circa 1795), the Down Literary Society (1793), and the Banbridge Reading Society (1795).[71] The Shan Van Vocht [*sic*] Club of Newtownards, founded in 1795, was indicative of a turn towards political discussion that moved the book clubs well away from their religious roots.[72] Ultimately, many of them became the object of suspicion within loyalist circles and in the 1798 Rebellion the collections of the Doagh Book Club and the Newry Literary Society (founded 1797) were destroyed, while the United Irish secretary of the Belfast Society for the Promotion of Knowledge, Thomas Russell, was arrested for republican activism.[73]

Within Anglicanism, the need to buttress the identity of lay devotees was lessened by state sponsorship, with energy directed instead to bringing recusants into the fold. As early as 1730, Henry Maule, then bishop of Cloyne, later Dromore and subsequently Meath, composed *An Humble Proposal for Obtaining His Majesty's Royal Charter to Incorporate a Society for Promoting Christian Knowledge among the Poor Natives of the Kingdom of Ireland.* Partially inspired by his experience with the Shandon Charity School founded in Cork in 1717, and a tour of Europe where Maule took cognisance of educational establishments, the *Humble Proposal* contended that 'it has been the sense of our parliaments ever since the Reformation that the erection and maintenance of English Schools in all convenient parts of this kingdom must be of excellent use towards bringing the people both to truth in religion and civility in their manners.'[74] This preceded a characteristically Scholastic list of the legislation 'now in force for the erection and due regulation of schools within this kingdom' before a regretful acknowledgement that 'for the erection and support of *English* schools ... sufficient provision has not yet been made'.[75] Although he recalled the voluntarism that fuelled the Shandon School experiment, Maule deferred to the state in a fashion that marked him, and the incorporated society, out from the wider associational impulses of the central decades of the century.[76] He deemed that his ambitions could not be achieved by personal activism, but required the benevolent hand of the polity to realise his vision of a reformed community. He humbly admitted, while composing yet another list,

The purchasing of ground in all proper places; the building thereon
school houses and dwelling houses for the masters; the engaging fit
persons to teach, and upon such terms that the children of the poor
may be instructed without any charge or expense to their parents, the
sending of bibles, common prayers and other proper books to these
schools; the giving of premiums, if not of clothes also, that the poor
popish natives may be the more easily induced to suffer their children
to be brought up in a religion different from their own; and the
providing fit materials for the children of every such school to work
upon, that they may receive an early turn to labour and be sent out
into the world with the impressions of an industrious, as well as a
religious education, are things which a few gentlemen, meeting in a
private capacity, will not be able though never so well disposed to
execute to any considerable purpose.[77]

Here Maule retreated to the traditional powers of church and state to effect his
programme of reform. Indeed, he requested that 'his Majesty be sued to in a
proper manner for his royal charter to incorporate certain of the nobility, clergy
and gentry'—note the emphasis placed on the established leaders of society—
'with a fund of about one thousand pounds per ann[um].'[78]

A formal petition to the king through parliament occurred in 1731, although
the charter was not issued until 6 February 1734.[79] Through it a society was
established to correct the lamented fact that 'in many parts of the said kingdom,
there are great tracts of land almost entirely inhabited by papists, who are kept
by their clergy in great ignorance of the true religion, and bred up in great disaffection to the government.'[80] The connection between the state and the society
was personified by 'the lord lieutenant, and some of the chief nobility, gentry
and clergy' who were 'constituted a corporation or body politic'. The society, in
other words, was legally recognised by the state.[81] This relationship was strengthened through the 1745 enactment of a tax on hawkers and peddlers that provided
it with 'twenty shillings per annum for each horse, ass or mule he trades with'
and fines of £3 if a peddler was found to be without a license.[82]

Thus was created by royal edict and parliamentary legislation a powerful engine
for supporting the Church of Ireland, an Incorporated Society for Promoting
English Protestant Schools in Ireland, which was purposed with the task of rearing
the children of Catholics as industrious Anglicans. The society was composed of a
committee in charge of schools, which looked to the Dublin central committee,

eventually based at the house of its secretary John Hansard on Grafton Street.[83] The initial ambition was to create four schools, one in each province, and this was quickly achieved. The Earl of Kildare donated monies for an institution in Castledermot in Leinster, and Minola in Connaught; Ballynahinch in Ulster and Shannon Grove in Munster were all set up the following year, 1735.[84] Each of these thrived, for in 1762 Castledermot was described in society records as having been expanded by the son of the original donor; Minola as having 'twenty-four children'; Ballynahinch as containing 'thirty children'; and Shannon Grove as holding as many as 'eighty children'.[85] By March 1738 there were nine schools established, five under way, and a further fifteen awaiting approval. By the turn of the decade, fifteen schools were active, construction for another three was under way, and fourteen plans had been submitted to the central committee and were pending decisions. Two years further on, sixteen schools were open, the society was building four more, and another two had been proposed.[86] By midcentury, there were forty schools with 1,600 children enrolled; a decade later, in 1760, the society encompassed forty-four schools: nine in Ulster, thirteen in Munster, sixteen in Leinster, and six in Connaught.[87] The 1750s also saw the development of a provincial nursery system, beginning in 1743 in York Street, Dublin, and expanding to Monivea (Connaught), Shannon Grove (Munster), and Monasterevan (Leinster). There was also to be one in Armagh which was never built.[88]

The aim of all of this construction was to develop a network of schools which would act as the engine of a renewed conversion campaign on the part of the Church of Ireland. The simple ambition was to evangelise Catholic children, inducting them into the rigours and rituals of the Anglican faith. The rules of the society were thus decidedly confessional. The very first regulations proposed that 'the most eligible place for every such first school to be erected will be some very popish and extended parish, in or near which there is some country town, or other principal town; that the good effects of such school may be the more conspicuous' and that 'no person be a master or mistress of a charter school who is not a known and approved Protestant'.[89] In 1749 this exclusivity was extended to include women servants, who again had to be Protestant, and in 1757 it was further determined that no goods were to be bought from Catholic traders.[90]

Within the schools themselves a confessional regimen existed, in which prayer began the day and service was attended at least weekly.[91] The curriculum was similarly inflected, for reading and writing exercises drew from scripture and the catechism, while *The Whole Duty of Man* (1658) was a central text, alongside

James Talbot's *The Christian Schoolmaster* (1707), and, from 1740, *The Protestant Catechism*, of which the Society sponsored an edition in 1742.[92]

The central plank of the conversion campaign was the removal, or 'transplanting', of Catholic children from their locale, separating them from the influence of family and kin. The *Dublin Courant* in October 1745 reported on a visit by a select committee of the society to the school in Santry, County Dublin, established by Hugh Boulter, where they found twenty boys of popish parents from distant counties. Another press report in the *Freeman's Journal* two years later described the opening of Ardbraccan School in County Meath with forty children of 'popish parents, transplanted from distant parts'.[93] The policy was adopted uneasily, however, for it provided a strong source of grievance from Catholic families whose children were peremptorily moved outside of the parish, and of complaint from English supporters of the general idea of the society for its inhumanity. In defence the society accentuated how

> the transplanting of children in order to put them quite out of the
> influence of their popish relations has been kindly and justly
> demanded by the gentlemen of this kingdom, and the Society saw the
> necessity of it from the beginning, but could not in prudence attempt
> it upon the first opening of the charter for fear it might discourage
> parents from giving up their children to be disposed of by the Society,
> for the priests would not have failed to represent this as a sort of
> kidnapping, and that they would never hear more of their children,
> but since they have learnt that their children are safe and kindly
> treated, those apprehensions are removed.[94]

The policy was to glean parliamentary backing in an act 'to provide for begging children, and for the better regulation of charity schools'. It determined that 'those persons enticing children to elope from charity schools or apprenticeships' were punishable by six months hard labour.[95]

The capstone of this confessional edifice was the hosting of sermons at Christ Church Cathedral in Dublin before the General Committee of the society; a practice which began in 1736 when Bishop Thomas Rundle of Derry delivered his reflections on false and truthful zeal.[96] To Rundle, the Anglican faith was trapped between the excesses of popery and the licentiousness of free thought, and he warned the congregation of how 'infidelity would break the cup and spill the cordial; superstition dash it with poison and turn the remedy to inflame the

fever. But indifference to religion sees its excellence, yet neglects to take it.'[97]
This vision of a church surrounded by enemies prompted a call for repentance.
True zeal, he contended, recommended the work of the Incorporated Society for
'if men love the honour of God, and the good of their neighbour . . . what can
advance those more than educating the unhappy in the nurture and admonition
of the Lord?'[98] Sharing in Henry Maule's pessimistic assessment of civil society,
he observed that

> the only objection which frightens some into a coolness about it
> seems to be that the design is too great to be managed by private
> wisdom, or supported by private bounties. 'Tis true, voluntary
> contributions will never make it a universal blessing, but the example
> of the great benefits which will arise from the care and charity of a few
> may prevail on, and associate the whole nation by the influence of the
> lawgivers, to undertake it for the common good.[99]

On this basis Rundle defended the policy of removing children from their parents and wider family, arguing

> there can be no pretence that we violate the rights of conscience by
> snatching those who are yet unable to guide themselves from the
> slavery and manacles of early terrors when done by the consent of their
> parents and no other force than that of charity and persuasion . . . And
> such prudent care can alone overcome, among us, the vanities of the
> present education of the poor natives, in what is worse than ignorance,
> in a belief of the most superstitious falsehoods: Falsehoods which fetter
> them in slavery to monks and foreigners, and make them rebels to the
> natural authority of the laws that protect them.[100]

A similar combination of pessimism over the human condition, Scholastic
trust in established authority, and paranoid fear of a Catholicism associated with
moral turpitude and intellectual degeneracy was articulated by James Trail,
bishop of Down and Connor as late as 1779, when he reminded the society of
how 'by the divine decree, virtue and duty consist in the cultivation and perfection of our several faculties; and by the same appointment, the cultivation and
perfection of these necessarily constitute our happiness.'[101] In an apparent adoption of Enlightenment rubric, he concluded, 'benevolence must be the source
of all our social offices'.[102] However, he equally accepted that 'the empire of

ignorance is wide and extensive' and 'if the understanding is dark through ignorance, if warped by prejudice, or perverted by error, in vain shall we look for
uniformity, consistency or propriety in conduct.'[103] In a fashion characteristic of
Scholastic thought, he relied on 'the informed mind' which he thought 'acts
equally with coolness and with vigour'.[104] In a use of the term which referenced
established authority, and not the notion of intellectual autonomy, he spoke of
'the mind enlightened by instruction'.[105] In this interpretation, imparting
ancient knowledge was not priestcraft, but rather 'co-operating with God, and
promoting the purpose of his Gospel'.[106] 'How sunk we are in ignorance', Trail
despaired, 'and therefore how feeble in improvement! A ray of knowledge hardly
glimmers in our land'.[107] Lacing the sermon with fear for the consequences of
the Catholic Relief Act of 1778, Trail contended that 'the barbarity that so hid-
eously deforms too many of our countrymen' was particularly to be found
among 'our Popish fellow Christians'.[108] 'How sincerely', he protested, 'how
affectionately, do I lament their civil degeneracy; their religious delusion!'[109] The
only source of optimism in this vision of a reprobate land was the work of the
society, for its charter schools 'have proved a most beneficial nursery to true
religion and to civil virtues; for to them we owe a number of rational Christians
and of industrious citizens'.[110]

Over forty years after the granting of the Royal Charter the results of all this
zeal were dispiriting, however. The devotion of numerous members of the
Anglican hierarchy to the movement had not changed the confessional demography of the country.[111] Indeed, a meeting of the General Committee of the
society held on 3 November 1773 effectively admitted defeat, for it conceded

> that in general the children have not been instructed to the satisfac-
> tion of the Society in reading and writing and that in many of the
> schools the instruction of the children is much neglected to the great
> injury and discredit of the institution and contrary to the rule and
> general orders and committee of fifteen upon that essential subject.[112]

The dilemma for the Scholastic communities of faith was precisely that the
faith that ensured their internal vitality and mobilised their activists limited their
ability to cross the dividing lines of religious life in the country. While faith might
bring a sense of purpose to a believer, it was not easy to impart that sensibility to
someone with a similar commitment to different doctrines. Yet there was another
strand to Irish associational life, one that drew upon a less rigorous approach to

supernatural questions and was able to overcome confessional divergences. This stood at the other end of the spectrum of Enlightenment methodologies, namely the freethinking speculative fringe of the movement. Although it attracted suspicion it was significant site of cross-confessional fraternisation and, despite its commitment to secrecy within its meetings, in its marches and charitable activities provided a public challenge to the norms of eighteenth-century Ireland's official public sphere.

Freethinking Rituals

The relative openness of the Society of Freemasons to religious mixing was expressed in the regulations that governed the lodges. In *Ahiman Rezon* (1756), the text that governed English, and by default Irish, Masonic practice for much of the century, Laurence Dermott, an Irishman living in London, enjoined that

> the craft, instead of entering into idle and unnecessary disputes
> concerning the different opinions and persuasions of men, admits
> into the fraternity all that are good and true; whereby it hath brought
> about the means of reconciliation amongst persons, who without that
> assistance, would have remained at perpetual variance.[113]

With origins dating back at least to 1725, the Masons spread quickly throughout the country.[114] There were around 300 lodges extant in the 1770s, 20 percent of which operated in Dublin, 40 percent in Ulster, and a further 30 percent in Munster.[115] By 1735 there were thirty-five lodges in the capital, and by 1745 another ten had been organised.[116] The increase then accelerated with nine founded in 1747 alone, and a further eight just two years later. In the 1750s seventeen were formed. Eight more followed in the 1760s, and six in the 1770s. Two were created in the early years of the 1780s but by then the spread had stalled and no more were warranted in the course of the century.[117] While this suggests that eighty-two lodges were created in total, they suffered from decay, disrepair, and abandonment: only twenty-nine were active in 1794.[118] Similarly, although there was an admission of about 5,300 members in the period between 1758 and 1799, probably no more than 1,500 Masons were active at any one time.[119]

In Ulster the first lodge warranted by the Grand Lodge of Ireland was Number 17 at Enniskillen, followed by a lodge in Cavan the following year and four more in the south Ulster region in the 1730s.[120] The decade of the 1740s saw fourteen further lodges recognised, including the first two in Belfast, numbers 182 and 183, warranted in 1748.[121] Following Dublin's lead, but with a slight time lag, the 1750s saw the most dramatic expansion, with twenty-nine lodges formed, although some of these apparently closed before 1760 when forty-two lodges were meeting. Of these, one third were active in County Antrim while only three were to be found in Tyrone.[122] This expansion seems to have continued and in 1781 there was a sudden flurry of new members with upwards of 300 memberships registered at the Grand Lodge, as well as an average of ten new lodges created annually during the rest of the century; an enthusiasm possibly tied to a wider process of politicisation in the province.[123] By 1792 there were about 276 lodges active in Ulster, with between 12,000 and 14,000 members.[124]

In the other heartland of the movement, Munster, the first warrants were issued by the Grand Lodge of Ireland in 1732, and the movement grew steadily until the 1760s, with a total of fifty-eight lodges founded in the province.[125] The Masons had a presence in every county of the region by 1737.[126] The 1730s as a whole saw twenty-two lodges warranted; a growth which tapered off in the 1740s when eleven were founded.[127] Although the movement was streamlined by the Grand Lodge, the 1750s saw a further increase in the number of lodges in the region, with an additional twenty-four gaining recognition in the decade, producing around 341 additional members.[128]

On the national stage, in the early period, Catholic involvement in the society was peculiarly prominent; Henry Benedict Barnewall, Viscount Kingsland, acted as grand master in 1733 and 1734, with another Catholic, James Brennan, serving as his grand warden during his first year of office, taking over from Robert Nugent who had been appointed in 1732. Brennan then succeeded to the position of deputy grand master in 1734, a role he fulfilled until 1737.[129] Yet this cluster of Catholic members did not have any legacy, for there were no other national officeholders associated with Catholicism through the century.

In Dublin some twelve lodges appear to have contained a substantial number of Catholics in their ranks, constituting around 40 percent of the membership of the society in the city in the decade 1758–1769.[130] It is likely Lodges 348 and 319 were set up by Catholics, while Lodge 54, founded in 1736, was largely Catholic in its intake. Lodge 137 and Lodge 324 drew support primarily from that confession, being located in Catholic neighbourhoods. Lodge 241, founded in 1753, and Lodge 263, founded two years later, as well as Lodge 382, created in 1762, were mixed in their intake.[131]

By contrast, in Ulster there were some lodges which ignored the injunction to share social space and Protestants monopolised membership. Of the four of these for which detail exists, three were clustered within ten miles of each other, being located in Lurgan, Tandragee (both County Armagh), and Banbridge, County Down. The fourth was in Downpatrick, County Down, sharing something of the frontier town quality of the other lodge locations. Strangely given wider social trends in the region, the 1765 injunction barring Catholics in Downpatrick was dropped by the time of the 1783 byelaws, with the lodge supporting Catholic parliamentary representation in 1792—an example of how a club might alter its character over time.[132] Alongside religious intransigence, Ulster also provided a home for predominately Catholic lodges. Lodge 405 in Ballyconnell and 451 in Ballymagaveran (both in County Cavan) and 434 in Killygordon and 569 in Lifford (both in County Donegal) appear to have had a majority of members professing the Roman Catholic faith.[133] Lodges could also be confessionally mixed, as was Lodge 502 in Aughnacloy, County Tyrone. Lodge 266 in Lurgan welcomed Catholic Masons, generating an argument over religious affiliation with its more doctrinaire cousin Lodge 394, which excluded them.[134]

Munster rates of Catholic participation were rather less than those found in Dublin—possibly unsurprising given the segregated character of parts of the province's cultural life. Certainly the evidence suggests that Lodge 1 in Cork was entirely Protestant, although it does not appear to have passed any discriminatory byelaws like its overtly confessional Ulster cousins.[135] The sketchy records that survive suggest that around 20 percent of Masons were Catholic, representing a substantial minority of the society in the region.[136] Indeed, some of the founding figures in the early lodges were probably Catholic, in line with the prominence of fellow communicants on the national stage. Arthur Collins and John Dalton at Lodge 13 in Limerick in 1732, Clarke and Keane Mahoney at Lodge 28 in Cork in 1734, and Thomas Burke and Charles McCarthy at Lodge 84 in Bandon in 1738 were all founding members of their respective enclave.[137] Anecdotal evidence drawn from the membership list of Lodge 27 in Cork in the 1740s suggests that Catholic involvement continued in that decade, but the peak in membership came with a wider expansion in the society's reach in the late 1750s.[138] The membership lists from the six Tipperary lodges active in that decade suggest that as many as sixty-eight of 104 Masons may have been

Catholic. Similarly in Clare twenty-two of forty-five members had traditionally Catholic surnames.[139] Beyond these two counties, however, Catholic membership was rarer with only a further twenty-seven names added to the Munster lists, thirteen of which were to be found in the regional capital of Cork. Kerry, for instance, did not register a single Catholic Mason in the 1750s, and had to wait until the 1770s for the sole possible Catholic to enter the lists.[140]

If the 1750s was a golden age for Catholic incursions into the Speculative Freemasons, the 1760s, 1770s, and 1780s saw a falling off of this membership. In Dublin this can be partially attributed to the elevation of John Carpenter to the Catholic see in 1769, as he may have enforced the long-ignored papal bull against the Masons, issued by Clement XII in 1738 and confirmed in a second bull from Pope Benedict XIV in 1751.[141] In contrast, and despite the wider politicisation of civil society which might have had something to do with the Catholic retreat, patchy evidence for Ulster suggests that the 1780s marked a high point for Catholic membership in the society, perhaps riding a wave of enthusiasm for civil engagement generated by the repeal of substantial parts of the penal code.[142] In the heady days of the mid-1790s, ecumenical attitudes could be highly praised, as when in 1795 the *Northern Star* reported approvingly of how 'on St John's Day, 24 June, the freemason lodges consisting of Crossgare near Downpatrick, No 343; Lisnod, No 659 and Saintfield, no. 425; and constituted of different religious persuasions, walked yesterday in our town, made a most respectable appearance, and spent the day in the greatest harmony.'[143] Munster was more in line with developments in Leinster, and if anything may have experienced decline as early as the 1760s. Arguably a consequence of the Whiteboy agrarian unrest, but also a result of a politicised society that was reluctant to entertain beyond known social circles, the number of possible Catholic members fell from 117 to sixty-seven across the course of the decade.[144] Although there was an anomalous increase in the Catholic participation in Cork during the 1770s, which accounts for 102 of the 139 possible Catholic Masons on the membership rolls, the 1780s saw a collapse in participation to a low of fifty-five. This trajectory may be a result of the activism of the Volunteers and the enthusiasm and despondency generated by successive campaigns for Catholic relief.[145]

Yet all of these attempts to calculate the confessional composition of the Freemasons begs a question, for was not the attraction of the Masons intimately connected to their freethinking character? How far does registering Catholic or Protestant involvement make sense when the content of Masonic ritual was apparently contrary to Christian doctrine? The Masons were, after all, connected in contemporary minds to the spread of irreligion, deism, and heterodoxy.[146] The methodology they promulgated was intuitive and speculative.[147]

Masonic structures and rituals imitated and parodied the practices of Christian ceremony. There were typically three levels of Mason (mirroring the Catholic Church's structure of priest, bishop, and cardinal), termed degrees: apprentice, fellow craft, and master mason.[148] While not encouraged, lodges often introduced intermediate or higher ranks, with ever more esoteric names—such as the knight templar or the royal arch—and elaborate initiation rituals became widespread in the 1780s.[149] These rituals were a means of binding the initiate to the community in a close parallel to communion.[150] Yet they also availed of the power of embarrassment to ensure that members would not divulge the events which occurred when the door closed and the meeting began.

Indeed, at the heart of this antagonism towards organised religion was a commitment to secrecy. For this alone Clement XII could instruct Catholics to desist from joining. Yet according to Laurence Dermott, the commitment to keeping quiet about lodge activities was a fundamental pillar of the society's integrity:

> One of the principal parts that makes a man be deemed wise is his
> intelligent strength and ability to cover and conceal such honest
> secrets as are committed to him, as well as his own serious
> affairs . . . Before all other examples, let us consider that which excels
> all the rest, derived ever from God himself . . . Whereby we may
> readily discern that God himself is well pleased with secrecy.[151]

In the eighteenth century, however, the Masons had a strong public presence which belied the secret nature of their foundational ideas. While what happened in the lodge remained within doors, members were happy to identify themselves as such to the wider public through participating in a twice-annual parade. These celebratory events fell on the Saints Days of St John, namely 27 December and 24 June, considered to be the red-letter days of the Masonic calendar.[152] Great effort went into organising and advertising parades which were showcases for Masonic imagery, allusion, and arcana. They were, as a lengthy report from *Faulkner's Dublin Journal* on a parade held in Youghal, County Cork, in December 1743 illustrates, a means of displaying to the public the structure and spiritual form of the movement:

Impris, the first salutation of the Quay of Youghal, upon their coming out of their Lodge chamber, was the ships, firing their guns with their colours flying.

Secondly, the first appearance was a concert of music with two proper sentinels with their swords drawn.

Thirdly, two Apprentices, bare-headed, one with twenty-four gage, the other a common gavel.

Fourthly, the Royal Arch carried by two excellent Masons.

Fifthly, the Master with his proper instruments, his Rod gilt with gold, his Deputy on his left with a square and compass.

Sixthly, the two Wardens with their truncheons gilt in like manner.

Seventhly, the two Deacons with their rods gilt after the same manner.

Eighthly, the excellent Masons, one bearing a Level, and the other a Plum Rule.

Ninthly, then appeared all the rest most gallantly dressed, followed by couples, each of them leaving a Square hanging around his neck to a blue ribbon.[153]

Here the ranks within the Masonic movement take precedence over normal social status, providing a bacchanalian release from daily life, while underpinning the legitimacy of hierarchy as a natural outcome of sociability. The elaborate display suggests that the parade was an articulation of the power and wealth of the Masons, while simultaneously providing a vehicle for young men to dress up in ravishing clothes and impress onlookers—strutting and preening as a socially potent expression of privilege and power. The esoteric symbolism hinted at the arcane knowledge held by members and provided a splendid set of baubles to adorn outfits.

While St John's Day was an excuse to party, it created an uneasy blending of two systems of thought: Christian and Masonic. Some variants of the origin myth of the masons rested on an association with biblical figures. Laurence Dermott, for example, thought he could provide

a long and pleasing history of masonry from the creation, to the time
of their writing and publishing such accounts, viz. From Adam to
Noah, from Noah to Nimrod, from Nimrod to Solomon, from
Solomon to Cyrus, from Cyrus to Seleucus Nicator, from Seleucus

Nicator to Augustus Caesar, from Augustus Caesar to the havoc of the Goths, and so on until the revival of the Augustan style.[154]

Yet in doing so, and in line with the deistic concern for design and order, the precise purpose of these histories was

> to give us an account of the drawing, scheming, planning, designing, erecting and building of temples, towers, cities, castles, palaces, theatres, pyramids, monuments, bridges, walls, pillars, courts, halls, fortifications, with the famous lighthouse of Pharos and Colossus at Rhodes, and many other wonderful works performed by the architects, to the great satisfaction of the readers and edification of freemasons.[155]

A similar tension between the Christian and the deistic elements within the thought of the Masons gave a nervous energy to the forty-ninth song appended to Dermott's text. Opening with a set of classical references, to Jove and Atlas, the verse then pursued the theme of order when envisioning God as the first Freemason:

> By Masonry, this stupendous ball
> He [the Almighty] poised on geometry, and measured all
> With lines east and west; also from north to south;
> This spacious lodge he measured out
> And adorned precious jewels three
> As useful lights in masonry.[156]

Yet the very next verse incorporated the Christian story, with its appeal to the content of Genesis within a Masonic paradigm:

> To rule the day, the Almighty made the sun,
> To rule the night he also made the moon
> And God-like Adam, a master-mason free
> To rule and teach posterity;
> Sanctity of reason, and majesty of thought
> Amongst freemasons should be sought.[157]

If there was a tension within the Masons between their Christian environment and deistic commitments, there was no such anxiety underlying the shadier, licentious Hell Fire Clubs. The first of these was founded around 1737 by the one-time grand master of the Freemasons in Ireland, Richard Parsons, the first Earl of Rosse.[158] Joined by the English portrait miniaturist James Worsdale, Rosse's satanic society included Jack St Ledger; Harry Barry, Lord Santry; Simon Luttrell, Lord Irnham; Colonel Henry Bessborough; Richard St George; and Colonel Clements amongst its florid reprobates.[159] Meetings occurred in the Eagle Tavern on Cork Hill—which also hosted the Freemasons in the same years.[160] The club was associated with a range of excesses including orgies, sado-masochism, and animal sacrifice. Members actively pursued the virtue of women who had been left unattended, with the poet Laetitia Pilkington locking herself in her dining room on one occasion to avoid rape by Rosse and others who had broken in.[161] Luttrell was a libertine of heroic proportions, and the subject of William Coombe's satirical *The Diaboliad* in 1777.[162] Lord Santry was anecdotally the perpetrator of a vicious murder of a sedan chairman whom he plied with brandy in a tavern on Fishamble Street before laying him out on a table. He then 'set fire to the sheets &c the wretch lay in, who soon expired in the most excruciating manner.'[163] Whether other members of the club were involved is unclear, but Santry's violent impulses were not sated, for he was convicted in 1739 of the unprovoked murder of Laughlin Murphy during an altercation in Patrick Corrigan's tavern at the Palmerstown Fair the previous year.[164]

The Dublin Hell Fire Club seems to have been active until the lodge burnt down in the 1740s; it was briefly revived in the 1770s under the auspices of the notorious rake Thomas 'Buck' Whaley.[165] A similarly debauched club assembled in Limerick, meeting at Askeaton, and was the subject of a group portrait by Worsdale, who may have moved his attention to the southwest following the dissolution of the Dublin assembly.[166] It was described in the verse of Daniel Hayes, himself a member:

> Eternal scenes of Riot, Mirth and noise
> With all the thunder of the Nenagh boys
> We laugh, we roar, the ceaseless bumpers fly
> Till the sun purples o'er the morning sky
> And if unruly Passions chance to rise
> A willing Wench the Firgrove still supplies.[167]

Wine, women, and song were undeniably attractive to the rich men who made up the membership of these rakish societies, and the chance to snub established clerical authority must also have been a source of their magnetic charm. It was equally the cause of lurid public speculation. For instance, *An Ample Discovery of the Damnable Cabal Commonly Known by the Name of the Hell Fire Club* (1738) imagined a 'society of gayest modern libertines' engaged in 'sacrificing a maid' (probably taking her virginity), meeting only 'where brightest nymphs do constantly abound to satiate our constantly craving appetites' and 'when our lusts run high, and nature rallying gives new force to love.'[168] Yet they also encapsulated the limits of fraternalism. In the case of the Masons the chance to mix with social superiors, or slum it with mercantile neighbours in the safety of the lodge, was vital in generating connections across confessional and social divides. So too, clubs gave men the chance to relax, to eat, to drink, and in the case of the Hell Fire Clubs to masturbate and fornicate in each other's company. Add to the mix the claim to esoteric knowledge and the boyish game playing involved in secret codes and messages, and the libertine societies encapsulated a peculiar outcome of the enlightened notion of brotherhood.[169]

Politeness and Cooperation

Neither the Scholastic fraternities nor the freethinking Masonic lodges and iconoclastic Hell Fire Clubs were characteristic of associational life in the mid-century. Rather, the great majority of societies were devoted to one or another aspect of the project of civility. Indeed, the clubs of eighteenth-century Ireland can be examined through a taxonomy that mirrors that of the languages of Enlightenment discussed in Chapter Five: politeness, aesthetics, improvement, and political economy. What they shared was a commitment to the fraternal ethos of associational life; what might be termed the morality of association. Membership in a society simultaneously involves a submission to shared rules and regulations and a level of interpersonal cooperation. This is grounded in the reciprocity upon which club life depends—membership is a social criterion—one cannot be the only member.[170]

Yet it is not a given that associations necessarily pursue the common weal, or indeed virtuous ends. Criminals and violent subversives congregate in organisations just as much as law-abiding and peaceable individuals. However, there was a pronounced concern within the Irish Enlightenment for the promotion of politeness. Far from inhabited by genteel, learned, and civilised men, Irish society was thought by contemporaries to be corroded by an addiction to interpersonal violence.[171] This trait found elite expression in the continued practice of the duel, which, while claiming a connection to the etiquette of the nobility and the upholding of decorum and decency, was increasingly thought to be a reprehensible reflection of the failure of Ireland to develop a polite civil society. Indeed, duelling increased in popularity during the decades after 1745. Thirty-six recorded incidents occurred in the decade 1745–1755, and another twenty-eight in the decade 1755–1765. This contrasts with twenty-one duels noted in the press during 1725–1735, and fifteen between 1735 and 1745.[172] While this increase may be an illusion caused by the nature of reportage, the impression that duelling was endemic prompted an association to lead a campaign to alter perceptions of polite behaviour.

With hazy origins around the War of the Two Kings, the Friendly Brothers of St Patrick was devoted to rejecting the duel as an acceptable recourse of honourable men. Emerging in Athenry, County Galway, in 1750, by 1754 there were twenty-one Knots (the term for a local meeting) in the country, and Dublin was the acknowledged headquarters.[173] There was a Principal Knot created in each major city, with subsidiary knots across each county. This regional structure was capped by the General Grand Knot which coordinated activity nationally, and which was headed by a grand president, annually elected on 17 March, St Patrick's Day.[174] The characteristic statute of the society articulated opposition to duelling and instructed the members that

> no Friendly Brother shall affront or quarrel with a continued member
> of the order. But as the best of mankind in their unguarded moments
> are subject to passions, if any member of this order, through the
> frailty of human nature, should have the misfortune so far to forget
> the love he owes his brother, and the obedience due to these statutes,
> and proceed to anger with a continued friendly brother, and disturb
> the peace and tranquillity of the order, he shall not presume to decide
> his own quarrel, according to the laws of pretended honour, by the
> barbarous practice of duelling, unknown to the politest and bravest
> nations, but shall peaceably and with due deference, submit his
> differences to the decision of his Knot.[175]

Although this provided the central rationale for the society, it was far from the only element in their understanding of polite behaviour. Statue twenty reminded members that 'all profane cursing and swearing shall at all times be avoided by the Friendly Brothers'.[176] Alongside this determination to eliminate impolite behaviour, the Knot was held together by the typical activities of numerous clubs—convivial imbibing and fraternal dining. The main activity of the Kildare Knot was hosting dinners at a public house—in this case typically either Vousden's, where the Knot erected a room for the purpose of society meetings by September 1781, or Maxwell's, both of which were in Maynooth. Less frequently, they convened at Read's in Lexlip or Toole's in Kilcock. Attendance could reach a high of fifty or a low of six, but averaged around twenty-five in 1777–1779, fourteen in 1780–1784, and nineteen in the years 1785–1791.[177] As well as these intimate male gatherings, the Knot sponsored and hosted balls for members and their relatives, and these were opened up to paying guests, defraying costs and advertising the select social cachet of the club.

This sociability was underlined in statute fifteen, which enjoined that 'no new admitted brother shall be permitted to treat or feast the Knot, into which he is admitted; but on the contrary, every new Brother, at the time of his being admitted a novice, shall be treated by the Knot.'[178] The technical terms used by the society similarly infused a sense of affective affinity among members. Each individual was a brother, a group was a Knot, and the society was self-declared to be 'friendly'. The theme of friendship was a recurrent trope in the society, a process which began within their *Fundamental Laws* (1751). There, friendship was understood to be a natural and necessary quality of human existence. In an imagined prehistory of the species, the author postulated how

> man being in his natural state, the most naked and helpless of all
> creatures, is forced to fly to society for assistance; where, by means of
> the benefits mutually paid and received, his weakness is protected, his
> infirmities relieved, and all his wants comfortably supplied. He
> therefore that is the best member of society is consequently the
> best man.[179]

So too, friendship was the subject of reflection by John Kenney, the prebend of Kill Brittain, when he preached at Bandon before the Principal Knot of the society in Cork on St Patrick's Day 1756. Friendship was 'a strong and habitual inclination of virtuous persons to promote the good and welfare of each other', being based on esteem and love, albeit with the simple caveat that 'esteem and love must be mutual. It must also be mutually professed and known; otherwise it will be no more than benevolence'.[180]

The focus on friendship allowed the Friendly Society Brothers to remove themselves from the ugly behavioural norms of Irish society; a characteristic accentuated in statute nineteen of the *Fundamental Laws*: 'No person whatsoever shall be admitted into this order who does not profess himself a Christian: nor shall any religious debate be admitted in any Knot'.[181] Certainly this statute was phrased in terms of social categories it debarred from membership. And it was this statute which led to the expulsion of Achmet Borummadal from the Knot in Kildare. The owner of a Turkish bathhouse on Bachelor's Walk, Dublin, he had been elected in October 1777 only to have his membership vetoed by the General Grand Knot by June 1778 on the grounds that he was a Muslim. In fact he was an Irish conman, Patrick Joyce, hailing from Kilkenny.[182] Yet what is really significant about the statute is that in allowing all Christians entry, it was enabling Roman Catholics and dissenters a place at the table alongside members of the established Anglican faith. Within the bounds of the Christian tradition, the society was confessionally blind.

The meeting book of the Kildare Knot that excluded Joyce allows for detail to be offered on this point. In the period from 1758, when the Knot was apparently founded, to 1775 when the record begins, there were forty-one members. The year 1776 saw a renewal of energy in the society, with twenty-six new brothers, and the record then picks up in 1777, when a further thirty-one were elected, and runs from 1778 to the closure of the Knot in 1791, during which period eighty-nine men entered the society.[183] While the Knot had the prestige of having William Fitzgerald, the second Duke of Leinster, as its president, membership was typically drawn from the local gentry and commercial ranks. This was offset by the presence of twenty-seven Protestant clergymen. It was also open to Catholics, and the Kildare Knot welcomed John Lock, a Catholic landlord at Blanchardstown, and Thomas Wogan Browne who, despite his conversion to Anglicanism in 1785, was a member of the Catholic Committee and was still thought of as a member of that confession.[184] The society was, within the limits of social hierarchy, confessionally diverse, suggesting the power of sociability to overcome traditional antipathies.

Aesthetic Amelioration

In contrast to the language of politeness, with its concern for personal behaviour and appearance, the Irish school of aesthetics was devoted to the propagation of fine taste and the creation of beautiful environments. This found its practical expression in a series of clubs promulgating select entertainment and encouraging the education of a fine-grained artistic sensibility.

The most prestigious of these clubs was the Charitable and Musical Society, which provided diversions for the upper echelons of Irish society and offered succour to those of the merchant community who had failed in their labours. Founded by Patrick Beghan in Dublin's Bull's Head Tavern in 1710 as a musical society, the early meetings were recalled by the poet Laurence Whyte as occasions on which 'we shook off our domestic cares, / By Irish, English or Italian Airs'. The title altered as a result of a newly found impetus in 1723, for after a move to the Bear Tavern in Christ Church Lane the society was reconstituted as a benefit society for confined debtors.[185] As Whyte rendered it:

> But then amidst our harmony and mirth,
> Some pious thoughts gave Charity a birth
> And fill'd each head with these exalted notions
> For her support, to make new laws and motions
> To Christ Church Yard we removed for sake of room
> . . . .
> 'Twas there our charity first took its rise,
> 'Twas there we did the scheme and plan devise,
> To free the captive debtors from a jail,
> Compound, or pay their debts upon a nail
> And by subscription annually set free
> So many souls from want and misery.[186]

As verse celebrations suggest, the social intake of the society was broadly based and confessionally blind. In the year of its reorientation, one poem lauded:

> There lawyers met and eke physicians,
> Attorneys, proctors, politicians,
> Divines and students from the college
> Men full of speculative knowledge,

Captain's and coll'nel's all in red,
Who in school of Mars were bred.
Some beaux and prigs, with nice toupees,
With wast-coats lac'd down to their knees.
Some poets, painters and musicians,
Mechanicks, and mathematicians,
For tradesmen there gave no offence
When blessed with manners or good sense;
Some gentlemen, lords or squires,
Some Whigs and Tories and Highflyers;
There Papists, Protestants, Dissenters,
Sit check and jole at all adventures.[187]

Whyte, writing in 1740, made a similar point: 'There you might see old Alderman M[a]l[o]ne, / Who cou'd relate the feats of Forty-one / There sat his nephews, Ne-lls, Ree-s, T-gg, / With papists, Tories and some honest Whigs.'[188] Or as he later expressed the same sentiment:

The goddess her at length her anchor fixt
Both Sexes blended and all parties mixt
She without schism has brought them to agree,
To join and set the captive debtor free.[189]

The society was financially successful for it was involved in the building of a new music hall, custom designed by Richard Cassels (who also designed the Dublin home of the Duke of Leinster), providing the largest auditorium in the city. An estimated 700 people could congregate on gala nights, so long as the men left their swords at home and the women desisted from donning hooped skirts. Built by a consortium of the three principal charities of the city, and managed by the secretary of the Dublin Charities' Commission, John Neal, alongside his son William, it was described by Whyte, the poet laureate of the society, as

Adorn'd with all that workmanship can do
By ornaments and architecture too
. . . .
At th' eastern end the awful throne is plac'd,
With fluted columns and pilasters grac'd,

Fit for the noblest President to rest,

Who likes the arms of Ireland for his crest.[190]

The hall was to be the venue for Lord Mornington's Musical Academy in the 1750s and 1760s, but its apogee came earlier, when it was host to two brisk series of performances by George Frideric Handel in the winter of 1741 and spring of 1742, apparently following an invitation by the lord lieutenant, the Duke of Devonshire.[191]

On 21 November 1741, *Pue's Occurrences* announced that 'Wednesday last, arrived from London the celebrated Dr Handell [*sic.*], universally known by his excellent compositions in all kinds of music, he is to perform here this winter, and has brought over several of the best performers in the musical way.'[192] His round of appearances began with a charity event at St Andrews (or the Round Church) Dublin, on 14 December 1741.[193] By 23 December he had begun a series of subscription concerts, which were sufficiently successful to induce him to stay on in the city and perform a second sequence from February 1742. In March, the production of a recent composition, *Messiah*, was announced in *Faulkner's Dublin Journal*:

> For the relief of the prisoners in the several jails, and for the support
> of Mercer's Hospital in St Stephen's Green, and of the Charitable
> Infirmary on the Inns Quay, on Monday the 12th of April, will be
> performed at the Music hall in Fishamble Street, Mr Handel's new
> grand Sacred Oratorio, call'd the Messiah, in which the gentlemen of
> the choirs of both cathedrals will assist, with some concertos on the
> organ, by Mr Handell [*sic.*]. Tickets to be had at the Music Hall and
> at Mr Neal's in Christ Church, at half a guinea each.[194]

The performance raised £400; 142 debtors were released; and money went to the Charitable Infirmary and Dr Steevens's Hospital, with a second evening following on 3 June, two months before the composer departed for London.[195]

The visit was an inspiration to the Dublin musical scene by setting in train an annual production of *Messiah* from 1743 in support of Mercer's Hospital, and Whyte again caught the atmosphere in a poem:

> When at the organ, or the trembling wire [the harpsichord]
> Both hand employ'd, and more it might require
> In different parts, and diff'rent spheres they move,
> And both conduce to harmony and love.
> His fingers fly with universal sway,
> Whilst hundreds stand amazed to hear him play.[196]

Equally it informed subsequent Irish engagement in the classical tradition; culminating in the oeuvre of John Field, who was a child performer at the Rotunda Assembly Rooms in the 1790s before turning his hand to composition and developing the nocturne form in the early decades of the nineteenth century.[197]

A similar engagement with the classical tradition was under way in the realm of art, where artistic education and training in mechanical drawing dovetailed in the Dublin Society–sponsored student premiums, such as that awarded in 1746 to Jane Tudor for her drawings after Raphael and Titian.[198] The following year, the premiums were won by a group of eight boys who all attended a drawing school in George's Lane kept by Robert West. As the Dublin Society's plans became more ambitious, they co-opted the establishment as the most illustrious and able of the Dublin art schools, and West was appointed as drawing master for the society in 1750, and the students were hence forth selected by the society.[199] This school for figure drawing was later accompanied by one for landscape and ornament—which involved the 'art of drawing ornaments in foliages, flowers and scrolls, and patterns and designs proper for the several manufactures' under the direction of James Mannin, which appears to date from 1756— and in March 1764, a school of architecture under the tuition of Cork-born Thomas Ivory.[200]

A Fine Arts Committee was formalised in November 1766, with the antiquarian Charles Vallancey as its first chairperson, having as one responsibility the duty 'to visit the schools in the hours of drawing'.[201] It organised a public exhibition of the work of the 'schools of figure and ornamental drawing' in March 1764, in which 'all painters, carvers, chasers, goldsmiths, carpet-weavers, linen and paper strainers, damask and diaper weavers, their journeymen and apprentices and others whose professions depend on design, may have free admission to view the drawings of said schools in Shaw's Court, Dame Street.' In this fashion it inculcated best practice and raised artistic standards beyond the confines of the schoolroom.[202]

Responding to Frailty

Fear concerning the educational standards of the country was one aspect of a broader commitment to a culture of improvement, and it found focus in the Hibernian Society. Established in 1757, the wellspring of the society were the ideas expounded in *British Education* (1756), a treatise by the Smock-Alley actor and manager Thomas Sheridan who despaired about the general quality of teaching, and asked for a reformation in the methods used to inculcate spelling, pronunciation, diction, and idiom; advocated the study of rhetoric; and encouraged public speaking and reading. Inspired by the proposals, and with the possible ambition of creating an office and income for Sheridan, a number of Dublin notables convened at Fishamble Street Music Hall on 6 December 1758. This intention of supporting Sheridan was the cause of much opposition among schoolteachers already at work. An anonymous *Address to the Hibernian Society* (1750) argued,

> You have entered into compact with this orator, ye have made him the object of fools' admiration; dubbed him a teacher who was now but a player, as if they were kindred studies; transplanted him from the theatre of lewdness and folly to the school of virtue and understanding.[203]

Nonetheless the notables proposed that 'they should form themselves in a society for the improvement of education, and particularly for examining and carrying out Mr Sheridan's scheme into execution, if, when explained and considered, it should appear to deserve encouragement'.[204] A committee of forty-one was nominated to adjudicate on the proposal and, with John Tickell in the chair, it was decorated by such august names as the Earl of Shelborne, and the Anglican bishops of Derry, Clogher, and Killala, as well as educationalists like the rhetorician Thomas Leland.[205] The deliberations progressed weekly, leading to a series of resolutions adopted on 27 January 1757 to the effect that 'it is the opinion of this committee that the present mode of education is very defective and erroneous in the most essential points' and that 'the plan proposed by Mr Sheridan for the improvement of the education of the youth of this kingdom . . . is exceedingly well calculated to answer that purpose.' This resulted in a final decision, 'that it is the opinion of this committee that the carrying the said plan into execution will be highly advantageous to the education of the youth of this kingdom and deserves public encouragement.'[206]

A subscription fund was created, and on 8 February 1757, a standing committee was created which included Thomas Adderley of Jervis Street as treasurer, meeting 'every Wednesday' at Sheridan's home. A deputation was sent to petition the lord lieutenant 'on the next levee day in order to lay before him the proceedings of the society and request his countenance and encouragement to the scheme.'[207] This involved the foundation of 'a public school' which, despite the 'approbation of persons of distinguished worth and eminence, who are known to be above little private views and whose judgement cannot be easily imposed upon in matters of this nature', did not come to fruition until Samuel Whyte opened a school on Grafton Street in which Sheridan was noticeably absent.[208]

The existence of a subscription for this scheme and the appeal to 'persons of distinguished worth and eminence' suggest the pronounced connection that existed between improving projects and charitable activism.[209] Education was understood to be a key mechanism for the inculcation of civility, and hence was a suitable outlet for the benevolent impulses of Irish high society. That most schooling was intended for children and hence was targeted on a category of the populace that could be depicted as both necessarily dependent and part of the deserving poor, made efforts to establish schools even more edifying.

Amongst Catholics the blend of charitable impulse and educational initiative was often found among female lay religious, who located an outlet for their social ambitions that accorded with expectations of their sex as tender and nurturing, while evading the controls that limited their autonomy when they joined the closed orders that monopolised Irish convent life in the period.[210] Thus Sister Nano Nagle of Cork began her career in philanthropy by establishing a school for poor children in 1755, and expanded the project to encompass seven schools in the city by 1769, five of which intentionally reared girls for useful and virtuous futures. Her frustrations with convent life were such that she established the Society of the Charitable Instruction, a congregation that took as its burden 'solely . . . works of charity among the poor . . . seek[ing] them out in their hovels of misery and want and woe.'[211] The work of Dublin-based educationalist Theresa Mulally was similarly motivated, with her desire to improve the lot of children prompting her to found a Catholic school for poor girls in Mary Lane around 1769, gaining eighty-four subscribers to her project, of which sixty-five, or 77 percent, were women.[212]

If education gave much of the culture of improvement a specific focus as an outlet for social activism, the wider material condition of the country also promoted collaborative action. For instance, it was a broad portfolio of interests that brought together clerics, gentry, medics, and merchants in 1744 under the rubric of the Physico-Historical Society.[213] The energising force of the association was produced by a combination of the Waterford-born apothecary and topographer Charles Smith and the lawyer and antiquary from Offaly Walter Harris. Together they compiled *The Ancient and Present State of the County of*

Down (1744), which was a template for the projected survey of the country from the perspective of natural philosophy and historical investigation.[214] With an initial membership of 226 in 1745 and regular monthly meetings, the society produced two further surveys, covering Waterford and Cork, before subsiding into inactivity in 1752. Another pair of studies, addressing Kerry and Dublin, emerged in the wake of its demise. Nominally headed by a figurehead president—the privy councillor Lord Southwell was followed in the chair by the lord lieutenant, Lord Chesterfield, and then the lord chancellor, Lord Newport—the labour was largely undertaken by a central committee that acted as an editorial board for the county surveys, alongside a number of local informants and, from 1745, paid itinerant investigators who collected and collated the data. Twinned with a survey of the book holdings of Trinity College and Marsh's Library, this commitment to empirical research was evinced in the surveys which emerged, for they were filled with what was proudly asserted to be 'natural, civil, ecclesiastic, historical and topographical description'.[215]

The study of Waterford, for instance, offered observations on the topography of the county, alongside a history of the city and its surrounds. Chapters were devoted to the mountains and the bogs, to the rivers and the medicinal quality of the waters, to the air, and the plant life and insects that populated the place. The chapter on 'the feathered tribe', for example, subdivided birds into the categories of 'terrestrial and aquatic, which again were subdivided into carnivorous, phytiverous, fissipedes, palmipedes &c.' before providing the varieties that lived in the region:

> Motacilla, Johnst, the water swallow, or water wag tail
> Lutia Avis, the yellow hammer
> Alauda Vulgaris, the lark, of which we have many kinds
> Aurivtis, the gold-finch or thistle finch
> Turdus, the thrush
> Merula Vulgaris, the common blackbird,
> Rubecula, the robin red breast.[216]

The staggering task of inductive compilation that the county surveys represented was inspired by a commitment to the culture of improvement, as the introduction made plain, speaking of how 'it must be a great pleasure to every well wisher of his country to observe that a spirit of improvement begins to appear' while simultaneously lamenting that 'this kingdom is not above a fourth peopled . . . It might maintain eight times its present number of inhabitants.'[217]

The harsh truth was, as Smith accepted, that the famine conditions of the 1740s had posed a substantial challenge to this notion, which 'has induced the author to say something of agriculture in the following sheets, which may be equally useful to every part of the kingdom.'[218]

Despair in the futility of the task was not far away, for Smith acknowledged his frustration that

> the generality of our farmers are apt to conceive that they have already
> brought the business of tillage to the greatest perfection. But were
> they so knowing as they imagine, or would put into practice such
> hints as might be communicated, we should not have such frequent
> complaints of the miscarriage of their experiments. But what can be
> expected from a set of people who, out of an ignorant obstinacy, will
> not be beaten out of their old tracks by the most powerful arguments,
> founded upon reason, and backed by the experience of wise and
> faithful persons?[219]

So it proved: the society folded, with Harris and Smith falling out over the profits of the Waterford volume.

Frustration did not get the better of Smith, though, for he established the Medico-Philosophical Society in 1756, drawing together men of the medical profession to deliberate both the theoretical foundations of their learning and its practical application. Although, or perhaps because, the new society was limited in its membership to medics. It was active in Dublin for over a quarter of a century, only ceasing its endeavours in 1784. Attention was now lavished on practical and medical matters, looking to halt herb sellers passing off fake cures to Dubliners, and creating a viable Irish pharmacopeia that would stop frauds and decrease the importation of foreign cures.[220] It extended the Physico-Historical Society's interest in spa waters, for the Medico-Philosophical Society supported John Rutty's examinations of river and lake waters that culminated in the publication of *An Essay towards a Natural, Experimental, and Medicinal History of the Mineral Waters of Ireland* (1757).[221] The Quaker Rutty was a central figure in this society for it was his broad curiosity that drew the organisation into a consideration of electricity, inoculation, and the campaign to reduce the intake of alcohol amongst the poor. A graduate of Leiden University, his diligence encompassed the keeping of a weather diary which he tried to connect to his compilation of mortality rates in the city.[222]

As Rutty's Quakerism suggests the medical profession was not demarcated by the penal code as a haven for Anglican professionals, yet the membership of the Medico-Philosophical Society was resolutely Protestant in its confessional colour. Only Sylvester O'Halloran breached the spiritual divide by corresponding formally with the society.[223] Yet the availability of medical practice to ambitious Catholics ensured that the voluntary sector that emerged in this arena was not confessional in its character.[224] The Charitable Infirmary, founded in 1718, was the brainchild of six Catholic medics: the surgical brothers George and Francis Duany, Patrick Kelly, Nathaniel Handson, John Dowdall, and the anatomy teacher Peter Brennan.[225] Located on Cook Street, Dublin, it accommodated the 'maimed and wounded poor of the city' and quickly expanded to provide beds at a house in Anderson's Court, before moving in 1786 to Jervis Street upon the city's decision to locate the Four Courts on the site it occupied.[226] In *Wilson's Almanack* for 1740, the institution was described as housing

> great numbers of maimed, wounded, and diseased poor, [who] are
> constantly relieved. There are above thirty-six beds, with provision
> and all necessaries for interns, who are received into the house, and
> constantly attended; as well as medicines and advice gratis for all
> externs, who flock in numbers thither daily. This charity is altogether
> supported by the voluntary contributions of the well disposed. The
> physicians, Dr R[ichar]d Weld and Dr John Fergus, attend every
> Tuesday and Friday from nine to eleven o'clock and the surgeons daily
> in their turns. All without fee or reward.[227]

The Charitable Infirmary was not the only monumental foundation that catered to the sick and the needy. Indeed, the middle decades of the century were a fertile phase for the voluntary philanthropic infrastructure of Dublin. The Foundling Hospital was founded in 1703 in a forlorn attempt to limit the practice of infanticide.[228] In the first year 260 children were admitted, and the numbers rose by midcentury to 1,468. Yet of these, 420 died within twelve months from diseases such as measles and smallpox that racked the institution. In 1752, 365 deaths occurred from the intake of 691. What was intended as a charitable refuge was acting as a death trap, and accusations of foul play circulated in 1757. The policy of transportation that the hospital adopted also had its casualties, and while it buttressed the Protestant proselytisation that was part of the hospital's mission it caused misery and distress as children were parted from their familial network. Equally, the farming out of children to paid nurses led to the peculiar abuse of children entering the facility in the hope that parents could then successfully 'foster' their own children and receive a payment for doing so. While the treasurer, Joseph Pursell, was cleared by the governors of the sexual abuse of one inmate, Margaret Hayden, in 1748, a parliamentary inquiry conducted in 1758 uncovered evidence of physical brutality and corruption.[229]

This inquiry may have prompted the concern of Lady Arbella Denny (herself an honorary member of the Dublin Society) who successfully petitioned the governors to allow ladies to visit and improve the environment; she was the sole woman to continue visitations. She also provided premiums to encourage nurses in medical provision and for the children to pursue lace making; supplied the financing to enlarge and improve the buildings; and founded the Magdalen Asylum in Leeson Street, Dublin, in 1767 as a means of dealing with the women who abandoned their children. It was in turn supplied with monies by the services held at the attached chapel that became a fashionable rendezvous for Dublin's polite society.[230]

Not all such endeavours were such pronounced failures as the Foundling Hospital. Dr Steevens's Hospital, which opened in 1733 following the bequest of Richard Steevens, a physician, in 1710 and the labour of his twin sister, Griselda, in seeing his wishes enacted, provided care to the sick of the city. This was a year after a similar bequest, from Mary Mercer, who had run a shelter for poor girls, led to the creation of Mercer's Hospital, for which Jonathan Swift served on the board of governors. Patrick Kelly and Peter Brenan, founders of the Charitable Infirmary, were agitators, alongside Thomas Mercer, James Dillon, and Edward Walls, for St Nicholas Hospital, which became the Meath Hospital. It functioned from 1753, finding a permanent site in the Coombe in 1770. As the *Gentleman's and Citizen's Almanack* explained in 1754:

> The Meath Hospital in the Coombe was opened on March 3 1753, supported hitherto by a benefit play, some benefactions and annual subscriptions of several of the principal inhabitants of the earl of Meath's Liberty and other well-disposed persons who judged that an institution of this nature was much wanted in a part of the town remote from city hospitals and greatly thronged with the industrious poor. Messrs Alexander Cunningham, Redmond Boat, David McBride and Henry Hawkshaw, surgeons, attend daily in their turns and all serve without fee or reward.[231]

Indeed, Dublin was the epicentre of radical revision of medical care in the 1740s. The Royal Hospital of Incurables, which began operation in 1744 in a small building in Fleet Street, was the first such institution in the British Isles, as was the Rotunda maternity hospital, opened by Bartholomew Mosse a year later. A similar first was achieved when Swift's bequest for the creation of an asylum for the mentally ill was made manifest in the opening of St Patrick's Hospital for Imbeciles in 1747.

From the 1720s onwards, however, there was a determination to reject such paternalistic aid and to rely instead on self-help. Alongside the grander initiatives of institutional charity a number of mutual benefit societies linked to trades emerged, including Societies of Undertakers, Journeymen Broad-Cloath Weavers, and the Society of Journeymen Dyers.[232] The sense of self-worth with which these societies infused their members, the degree of personal autonomy and fraternal reliance, was expressed vividly in *An Historical Poem in Honour of the Loyal Society of Journeymen Shoemakers* (1727) composed by a member, Robert Ashton. His verse extolled the society for its social egalitarianism and charitable instincts:

> Or where's that trade on earth dare be so free,
> To bear a lady's small upon their knee
> For we alone support the Lady's pride
> And find access where kings are oft denied;
> Such radiant glorys grace this shining train
> Who comfort widows and the sick maintain
> And now united do to church repair
> As if the highest race of Gods were there.[233]

This sense of pride in artisanal fraternity was commonplace, as is evidenced in the verse concerning the Society of Journeymen Smiths penned by Henry Nelson, a self-described bricklayer:

> Let it be repeated by every tongue
> And their great merits round the globe be sung
> Who widows do support and orphans young
> Their sick relieve, likewise their dead inter
> What actions greater can the world prefer?[234]

So too, the charitable purpose of the Journeymen Tailors was given the stamp of approval by the artisan writer. In offering *A New Poem on the Ancient and Loyal Society of Journey-Men Tailors* (1726), Nelson versified,

Let time their actions write in books of fame,
Who age supports and orphans young maintain,
Their sick relieve, likewise their dead inter
What actions greater can the world prefer.[235]

This kind of fraternal self-help was not met with universal approval, how-ever. The guild system that existed in the city, and which had state recogni-tion, took some umbrage at this show of autonomy by those of low ranking within the structure. A sense of this disdain was captured in a satire of the parade of the Society of Journeymen Tailors through the streets of Dublin, which was circulated in 1726. The author protested, 'I must needs satirise a vicious band / Of hungry prick-lice who in pomp appear / Like crawling mag-gots each revolving year.'[236] Some forms of sociability were clearly not to be encouraged.

Mercantile Ambition

Despite provoking anxiety at the challenge voluntary self-help societies posed to the established institutions of Ireland, the Society of Journeymen Tailors was expressive of a belief that sociable associationalism was conducive to economic productivity. In this, it points towards an array of merchant organisations which provided the social capital underpinning material advancement. The origins of the public sphere owed much to the mercantile need for reliable information and the circulation of news and produce. The coffeehouses and taverns of the urban centres allowed this community to congregate and converse, and one consequence of fraternisation was the creation of partnerships, merchant houses and mercantile associations.

Although it quickly metamorphosed into a drinking club for the rich traders of the capital, the Ouzel Galley Society is indicative of this inclination. With hazy origins resting in a legal dispute over the ownership of goods imported into Ireland on a ship that had been given up for lost, and on which the insurance had been paid out, the Ouzel Galley episode of 1705 gave rise to a social club that nominally provided an arbitration mechanism for Dublin's merchants.[237] In 1787 Richard Lewis, writing in *The Dublin Guide*, described the society as 'extremely laudable' as it 'supersedes the necessity of persons going to law, and perhaps ruining themselves and families in litigating matters that are of little moment.'[238] So too, they engaged in limited philanthropic support of distressed merchants as when they recorded in their minutes how

> Mr Sutton applied for William Byrne a distressed sailor—five guineas paid, Mr Pim made a motion for widow Green—five guineas paid, Mr Sutton made a motion for Mr Bianabe, a distressed citizen—ten guineas paid, Mr Byrne made a motion for Mrs Oulton, a widow— ten guineas.[239]

The society's structure mirrored the ranks and offices of a ship, with membership limited to forty and each holding a title from captain and lieutenant, to master, bursar, boatswain, and on down to the ship hands.[240] In abeyance for much of the first half of the century, it was re-formed in February 1748 at a meeting in the Phoenix Tavern in Werburgh Street, Dublin; activity increased with the arrival of banker and alderman John Macarell in the post of captain, with the club convening four times yearly, in February, June, August, and November.[241] Initially meeting in the apposite location of the Ship Tavern in Chapelizod, the Ouzel Galley Society was a highly exclusive association with links to the aldermanic faction in the Dublin Corporation who were resistant to Charles Lucas's programme of administrative reform.[242] Yet, despite this political bent, the Ouzel Galley was diverse, with Peter Barré, a French Huguenot among the newly constituted crew.[243] By 1756 Quaker John Pim Joshua was brought on board, followed by his co-religionist banker Joseph Fade a year later. The 1760s saw a number of Quakers join up: Hosea Coates in 1763, Joseph Pike in 1768, and Edward Strettell in 1769; with Joseph Pim arriving in 1776. The successful Presbyterian merchant Travers Hartley joined in 1762, the same year that he entered the Dublin Corporation committee; he was later elected a Patriot MP for the city in 1782.[244] Yet it was not until 1783 that Anthony McDermott, a wealthy trader, became the first Catholic to join.[245]

Similar religious latitude shaped the character of the Dublin Committee of Merchants, which was established in 1761 as a counterweight to the monopolistic attitudes of Dublin Corporation. Hartley was a founding figure, and his co-religionist Robert Black was also a member, while a further six of its twenty-one-man membership were either Quaker or Catholic. John Pim Joshua and Edward Strettell again appear in the lists, with Anthony and Owen MacDermott, Michael Cosgrove, and John Connor co-opted by the late 1760s.[246] Indeed, the *Case of the Merchants of Dublin* (1768) made a distinct virtue of this attribute, arguing that 'the choice of that Committee has been made on the same liberal principles on which the Society was originally formed, no regard being had in it to any difference of party, or opinions, but merely to consideration in trade or capacity, and active disposition to be useful.'[247]

The activities of the committee were largely taken up in the two decades of its existence with the construction of the Royal Exchange building on the southern end of Parliament Street, strategically situated next to Dublin Castle. Built to a design by Thomas Cooley, it was located on the site of Lucas's coffee-house. It was funded by a series of fourteen lotteries which were organised by the committee from 1766 to 1779, generating a profit of £49,441.[248] The 100 square foot location was provided with a domed building under which was the central hall, and which was supported by a ring of columns forty-six feet in diameter.[249] The grandeur and location of the edifice was an intentional snub to the Dublin Corporation, which the committee regularly sidelined in its proceedings.

As early as 1761, however, the committee was being pressured by the factions of landowners who had a vision of the city as an urban playground for the winter season and wished to displace the smells and sounds of trade and industry from the centre of the conurbation. The author of *An Address to the Committee of the Merchants Society* (1761) complained of its timidity in the face of these rural stakeholders in the city.[250] Matters came to a head with the operation of the Wide Streets Commission, which was run by the grandees without reference to the Committee of Merchants. The tinderbox was lit in 1769 by the proposal to move the Custom House downstream and away from the rising Royal Exchange. This disrupted the axis of trade that the committee envisioned as running down Parliament Street to the riverfront, and was thought to be an arrogant refusal on the part of the Wide Streets Commission to comprehend the wealth generated on the city's quays and in its warehouses.[251] It prompted a characteristically direct address to the lord lieutenant, pointedly bypassing the intransigent corporation and unsympathetic parliament from whence the Wide Streets Commission was staffed. The petition made plain the divisions of rank and status that lay at the heart of the conflict, and laid out the likelihood that the unintended consequence of the gentry's scheme was the opposite of what they desired. 'Your petitioners are thoroughly convinced', it asserted,

> that no argument can be adduced in support of this measure which
> has any meaning in it, unless the convenience of the nobility and

gentry, by affording them more direct and quick passage from and to
the north-east and south-east quarters of the town. Your petitioners
sincerely wish every accommodation to people of their rank, that
could be obtained without so expensive a sacrifice of the navigation
and trade of this city . . . Your petitioners beg leave further to observe
that in consequence of building a bridge and custom house in the
situation proposed all the hurry, crowd and annoyance which
necessarily attend trade, will be brought even to the doors of our
nobility and gentry, and many of those elegant streets in which they
now reside will become the common passages for porters and carts,
loaded with the necessaries of life and all kinds of merchandise, to be
diffused through the whole city.[252]

The Custom House was eventually built to a design by James Gandon as his first
large-scale commission. Spirited into Dublin in April 1781 by his sponsors, Lord
Carlow and John Beresford, in the face of the opposition of the merchants, Gandon
quickly acquired other public commissions, from the renovation of the parliament
building on College Green and the King's Inns, to the development of the Four
Courts, again on a river location.[253] The Custom House was completed by 1791.

Regardless of the committee's failure to stop the scheme, they remained optimistic about the possible shape of the city's commercial future. By 1783, with
new opportunities emerging in the wake of parliamentary independence, the
Committee of Merchants reconstituted itself as the Chamber of Commerce,
declaring as it did so that it was aware of

the present important situation of this country, its lately renewed
constitution, its fond hopes of rising commerce and consequently
increasing opulence, the variety of commercial regulations necessarily
incident to this change of circumstance and particularly requisite from
the late revolution in the political system: every consideration appearing
to demand a general union among traders and a constant unwearied
attention to their common interests; from a view whereof to promote
these laudable objects in this particular district and to hold forth an
example for imitation and cooperation to the rest of the kingdom.[254]

The chamber did not last long.[255] Elected on 18 March 1783 in a wave of enthusiasm among the merchant community, and containing on its council six Catholics

and a Quaker (Travers Hartley was its first president), the pulse of excitement rapidly weakened.[256] Its activism extended into the political realm with their opposition to William Pitt's Commercial Propositions bringing them to the floor of the Irish House of Commons through the involvement of Hartley in his office as MP for Dublin.[257] Yet economic depression and political uncertainty took its toll, and by 1788 the chamber was defunct.[258]

Yet despite its brief life span, the Chamber of Commerce represents a high-water mark for the voluntarism of the merchants of the country. The formality and institutional solidity of its title; the popular election that created its central committee; the mustering of 293 initial members; the desire to engage in political debate concerning the national management of commerce—all spoke to the ambition of the association.[259] Yet in its broad remit and its desire to intervene in political discussions normally reserved for College Green and the Castle, the Chamber of Commerce was pushing the limits of civil society's definitional limits as a realm of voluntary association for apolitical purposes, and encapsulated a novel phenomenon: the politicisation of civil society.

The Catholic Challenge

The project was ambitious: to defend an acceptable mode of confession for Catholics while accommodating the faith to the political realities of Anglican ascendancy. Established in July 1756, the Catholic Association, renamed the Catholic Committee four years later, was devoted to phrasing an acceptable oath allowing Catholics to articulate publicly their loyalty to the Hanoverian monarchy.[260] If the words were correct, the members reasoned, the matter would be simple enough: separating Romanists—or papists—from their Gallican confreres. Populated by merchants of the city of Dublin, the Catholic Committee was led by the physician John Curry and the gentleman farmer Charles O'Conor. Their ambition was to generate an intellectual ambiguity, a form of Catholicism that could be loyal to the Hanoverian succession and the papacy. What was required was a civil oath of allegiance which did not recognise the king as the head of the church; a difficult task given the confessional and sacerdotal character of the British monarchy.[261]

This difficulty did not dissuade the committed activists. In particular, Viscount Limerick moved to put an oath on the statute book in 1756, with a second foray made the following year by the Catholic noble Robert Barnewall, the twelfth Baron Trimleston, albeit in opposition to the Catholic Committee who fretted over the capturing of the agenda by the gentry. While the first of these twin assaults failed in parliament, the second progressed as far as the Irish Privy Council. Yet in rallying support Trimleston, a genteel, educated man usually engaged in the study of botany and birds, mobilised the city's Catholic community by having public prayers said for the king. Occurring in the context of the opening salvoes of the Seven Years' War (1756–1763), a rapprochement from Ireland's Catholic subjects was desirable but an invasion scare scuppered plans for reconciliation.

Two years later, a similar scare was used constructively to produce an address of loyalty signed by 400 Catholics. Anthony McDermott and John Cromp, two Catholic envoys, presented it to the Speaker of the House of Commons, John Ponsonby, who then passed it to the lord lieutenant, the Duke of Bedford. Intending to use the loyalty address as the springboard to push for another Catholic oath, nine individuals formed a small subcommittee from the Dublin parishes and held their first meeting at the Elephant Tavern on Essex Street in Dublin on 2 April 1760. The subcommittee included John Curry and the industrialist Thomas Wyse, who had made money in smelting iron and copper in the late 1740s.[262] Wyse put a formal committee structure in place, wherein matters would be decided by ballot and a simple majority.

Following a petition of around 600 names to the newly crowned George III and the narrowly focused ambition, the effort dwindled away, and the Catholic Committee, such as it was, was moribund by 1763, having been ripped apart by dissensions over money and tactics.[263] Charles O'Conor told Curry, 'You have acted your part honourably, warmly and honestly, and now have nothing to do, but give up your political patient'.[264] Yet despite the apparently ineffective history of the first Catholic Committee, this ill-fated spurt of confessional organisation was significant in one unexpected way: it was the first occasion the Catholic community established an institution of their own within the voluntarist world of associational life that was directed towards the achievement of a political aim. Its significance lay in the means applied: Catholics were deploying the resources of civil society to change their political condition. The consequences would be revolutionary.

When the committee resuscitated in 1767, meeting regularly in rooms supplied by the Custom House Coffeehouse on Essex Street, owned by Owen Gallagher, it was once again a defensive organisation.[265] It had been given new life by the anxiety of the Catholic merchant community of Dublin that a measure might pass parliament to legislate for the much-hated, if still customary, quarterage payments—made in exchange for commercial privileges in a city levied on non-freemen—which by definition Catholics were, as the Dublin Corporation was Anglican by law since the Test Act of 1704. While the initial heads of bill were rejected at the English Privy Council, the proposal frightened the potential subjects of the measure into drafting a petition expressing their sense of injustice.[266]

The persistence of the Irish parliament in pleading this case kept the Catholic Committee alive. There were repeated attempts to introduce a measure 'for confirming and ascertaining the aids and contributions of intrusion money and quarterage in the city of Dublin, and other cities and towns corporate therein mentioned' into statute in 1771, 1773 (three times), 1775 (twice), and 1777.[267] This mobilised the merchant community of the capital to engage in political petitioning, and as the threat reared up the committee responded by commissioning legal advice from Owen Hogan, their local representative, and a London agent, Daniel MacNamara, later replaced by Richard Burke, son of Edmund, and then, Wolfe Tone.[268] In 1773, for example, the first year for which a full record exists, the Catholic Committee met thirteen times from April to December, and almost all of these meetings were involved in coordinating the campaign against a proposed quarterage bill.[269] This was successful for each attempt to introduce the measure stalled.

Even given its practical successes, the committee was rather less grand than its self-advertising indicated. Operating under the bloated title of the General Committee of the Catholics of Ireland, attendance at meetings rarely rose above twenty, and there only forty-six names appear in the minutes before 1775; indeed, the committee often lapsed into desuetude when parliament was not in session. Moreover the committee was composed predominately of Dublin merchants: brewers, grocers, ironmongers, sales masters, woollen drapers, an apothecary, a chandler, a haberdasher, a hatter, a livery stable keeper, a peruke maker, a saddler, and a skinner.[270]

The claim to national status was not entirely without merit, however, for the intended structure of the committee was to draw two members from all the Dublin parishes and a series of urban centres of the country—certainly including Carrick-on-Suir, Cashel, Clonmel, Cork, Drogheda, Dungarvan, Enniskillen, Limerick, and Waterford.[271] While this gave the committee a modicum of representative power, it was hampered even here by the ability of one person to hold a berth for multiple constituencies. James Reynolds, a Dublin-based wool merchant, was the epitome of this trend, speaking for the Catholic constituencies of Cashel, Drogheda, Limerick, and Waterford, while also serving as treasurer until his resignation was prompted by ill health in June 1778.[272]

The dilemma the committee faced was that it could not approach the legislature directly, or as Catholics. Thus it had to commission Anglicans to act on its behalf, and to transmit petitions that were claiming to speak for all the 'non-freemen' of a city, and not merely the Catholic community. As they elegantly expressed it in the petition against the 1773 quarterage bill, they spoke for 'the several persons who are hereunto subscribed, in behalf of themselves, and the rest of the merchants, manufacturers, and artists, inhabitants of the city of Dublin, and of all the other cities in this kingdom; and of the towns of Drogheda, Carrickfergus and Youghal who are not free of any of the guilds, or corporations of the said cities and towns.'[273] In other words, for all the rhetoric of the committee claiming to speak for all the Catholics of the Irish polity, the members were acutely aware of their limited and uncertain status.

This modesty belies the significance of the Catholic Committee, which lay in how it mobilised and politicised Catholicism. It raised the spectre of a reinvigorated and revitalised Catholic community, subverting not the state, but the civil society that provided the polity's lifeblood and gave it health. The Catholic Committee embodied a challenge to the social and political premises of the Anglican state; emerging from the apparently neutral zone of the civil society of the Enlightenment.[274] In that, it foreshadowed developments in the last quarter of the century as the Enlightenment itself became political in nature.

The Royal Irish Academy

The apogee of the politicisation of associational life came in 1785 with the foundation of the Royal Irish Academy. Far from being a society determined to exercise political influence, it was a society political forces were anxious to influence. Much of the academy's early character pointed towards a close affiliation to Patriot politics.[275] In the person Lord Charlemont, its first president and the leader of the Volunteers, for instance, the academy was closely tying itself to a brand of patriotism that had recently been in the ascendant. As the preface to the first volume of *Transactions* (1787) asserted, 'every qualification, natural and acquired concurred in pointing out a president whose zeal for the interests of Ireland could only be equalled by his zeal for the interests of learning'.[276] So too the preface treated the contentious intervention of Henry II into Ireland with evasive phrasing: 'the important changes which took place in the government upon the invasion of Henry the second were not carried on with so little disturbance as to permit the nation to apply itself immediately to the peaceful employments of literary enquiry'. According to the author of this prefatory essay, Robert Burrowes,

> the connection of this kingdom with England, instead of teaching
> Ireland the many valuable acquisitions of English industry, tended
> rather to entice away its men of genius to a country in which, as
> learning was more fashionable its professors might be certain of
> enjoying more at ease the advantages of rational communication and
> of receiving more ample encouragement.[277]

Yet, the academy was also the product of an apolitical determination to coordinate and institutionalise intellectual life; the progeny of the associational impulse that had shaped Irish life since the 1730s. In its earliest manifestation, the academy 'consisted of an indefinite number of members, most of them belonging to the university, who at weekly meetings read essays in turn.'[278] This group was either the Palaeosophers, who were particularly concerned with patristic history, or the Neophilosophers, another coterie, headed by Robert Perceval, a professor of chemistry, which debated scientific conundrums.[279] These two societies merged in March 1785, and were then sponsored by Charlemont in their ambition to 'make their labours redound to the honour and advantage of their country', sketching a constitution for a wider academy of learning.[280] The first meeting of this new body took place at Charlemont's house on Rutland Square in Dublin on 18 April 1785.[281]

As well as being the site of intellectual encounter, with Charlemont embodying connoisseur curiosity as much as patriotic passion, the academy was the subject of wider political pressures.[282] Established in the midst of a political backlash against constitutional reform and against a backdrop of renewed agrarian unrest being read as Catholic insurgency, the academy was in need of a protective screen against accusations of political bias.[283] The heady days of the grant of parliamentary independence in 1782 was already long behind the

Patriots and the political pendulum had swung back in favour of the Castle administration.

In that light the speedy application of the grant of a Royal Charter made sense. Issued in January 1786, the charter provided the academy with the 'Royal' in its title, with legal recognition, and with a specific power to purchase of land worth up to £1,000.[284] The charter thus supplied the academy with a powerful status in society and the financial security it required to ensure—unlike many of its associational compatriots—long-term survival.[285]

If the rationale for the academy's application is clear, less certain given its apparently patriotic hue was the reasoning behind the government's support for the measure. In his preface, Burrowes alluded to one possible explanation:

> It has been instituted too at a time when it can enjoy the protection of
> a monarch, whose patronage of the liberal arts has made his reign an
> illustrious era in the annals of literature; at a time when two of the
> sciences have had advantages hitherto unknown in this country held
> out to them, in the establishment of a medical school and the
> foundation of an observatory astronomical purposes.[286]

Certainly George III might have been minded to support this cultural venture, but that is to rest a heavy burden on the monarch to cultivate Ireland's cultural life.[287] Moreover, the charter had to pass through the due channels of Castle administration and Irish Privy Council before it was placed before the king for his attention.[288]

The origins of Lord Lieutenant Rutland's determination to forward the project are opaque, but one hint emerges from within the specifics of the Charter, which stipulated that

> it is our further will and pleasure, and we do by these presents for us,
> our heirs and successors, ordain, constitute and appoint that if any
> abuses or differences shall at any time hereafter arise and happen
> concerning the government or affairs of the said Academy, whereby
> the constitution, progress, improvement or business thereof may
> suffer or be hindered, then and so often, we do by these presents
> nominate, assign and constitute that our lieutenant general or other
> our chief governor or governors of our said kingdom of Ireland for the
> time being, shall be visitors of the said corporation with full power to

reconcile, compose and redress any such differences and abuses, and
with all other powers to the said office of visitor of right belonging.[289]

This was to grant a level of oversight to the lord lieutenant in the activities of the
academy that mirrored his role in the political life of the nation. It enabled the
state to step in if the society was deemed to be detrimental to the political process and the health of the nation as they defined it. In other words, the measure
effected de jure, if not de facto, the politicisation of the academy, recognised in
the adoption of 'Royal' in its title. The actions of the academy reflected glory,
not only on the nation but also on the person of the monarch. The king, as well
as the kingdom, was celebrated in the achievements of members. In exchange
for patronage and protection, the academy had placed itself under the umbrella
of the state.

This is to read the grant of the Royal Charter in the light of a wider concern
on the part of the Irish administration over the burgeoning public sphere of
mid-eighteenth-century Ireland. The charter was of a piece with the legislation
that effected disciplining controls over ale houses, coffee shops, and the stage.[290]
In this, the academy represents a key shift in the dynamics of the Irish
Enlightenment. The academy had its origins in the informal associationalism
and club life documented in this chapter. It was committed to the languages of
politeness, aesthetics, improvement, and political economy. Indeed, the preface
to the *Transactions* averred the academy was interested in

> whatever . . . tends, by the cultivation of useful arts and sciences, to
> improve and facilitate its manufactures; whatever tends, by the
> elegance of polite literature, to civilize the manners and refine the
> taste of its people; whatever tends to awaken a spirit of literary
> ambition, by keeping alive the memory of its ancient reputation for
> learning.[291]

The contents of the first volume had essays devoted to political economy, aesthetics, and scientific improvement.[292] The more general origins of the academy
lay in the emergence of a discursive space which did not discriminate on the
grounds of confessional identity. This was evident in the academy's broad initial
membership, which was akin in its intake to the Freemasons or the Knots of the
Friendly Society of St Patrick. Within the group of thirty-eight founders there
was an Anglican archbishop (Richard Robinson of Armagh), four bishops and

three peers, and the provost and ten fellows of Trinity College.[293] Shortly there-after a further fifty members were co-opted which included, alongside twenty-three MPs and clergymen, two Roman Catholics—the medic John Purcell and the antiquarian Charles O'Conor.[294] Subsequently, with further expansion Theobald MacKenna, the Catholic pamphleteer, was included as was the Presbyterian medic and activist William Drennan.[295]

Yet, while the Royal Irish Academy pointed back to the second phase of the Irish Enlightenment—the Social Enlightenment—so too it was embedded within a final phase, the period termed here the Political Enlightenment. The anxiety of the Castle administration to oversee the activities of the academy was indicative of nervousness about the public sphere, and their answer was inter-vention and oversight. The wider process, of which this was a part, was one of a general politicisation of social exchange.

PART THREE

The Political Enlightenment,
ca. 1760–1798

7

A Culture of Trust?

∾

Lady Sneerwell: I'll go and plot mischief, and you shall go and study sentiment.
—Richard Brinsley Sheridan, *School for Scandal*, 1777

THE WRITINGS OF CHARLOTTE BROOKE imagined many of the possibilities that eluded Irish life in the last quarter of the century.[1] Her compilation of Gaelic poetry 'translated into English verse', *Reliques of Irish Poetry* (1789), posited the vision of a harmonious coexistence between the Irish- and English-speaking worlds.[2] The text illustrated this desire by providing Irish-language 'originals' of each of the seventeen poems she had translated for the volume in an extensive appendix to the collection.[3]

The intention of the sequence was to capture a picturesque image of a Gaelic past as civilised, decorous, passionate, and virtuous. Brooke made use of the idea of a picture when she wrote of the language, 'it is . . . possessed of a refined delicacy [note the emphasis on refinement] of descriptive power, and an exquisitely tender simplicity of expression [the virtue of tenderness is here appropriated, in contrast to the standard Protestant depiction of the native Irish as heartless and cruel]; two or three artless words [underlining the authenticity of the sentiments the poetry conveyed] or perhaps only a single epithet, will sometimes convey such an image of sentiment, or of suffering to the mind, that one lays down the book to look at the picture.'[4]

However, while Brooke accommodated the ancient Irish past to the cultural tastes of her audience, she also used strikingly recent material.[5] This included an elegy to Turlough Carolan, the Meath-born, blind harpist who died in 1738. While a selection of his compositions had been published as early as John and William Neale's *A Collection of the Most Celebrated Irish Tunes* (1726), it was still an important signifier of Brooke's ambition that she celebrated the Irish-language compositions of a figure who postdated the War of the Two Kings (1688–1691). She even included two songs attributed to Carolan, 'for Gracey Nugent' and 'for Marble Kelly'.[6] The importance of this gesture was emphasised when in her 'Thoughts on Irish Song' she wrote,

> Besides the two following songs, there are more of the compositions
> of Carolan possessed of considerable merit; but as it was not in my
> power to give them all a place in my collection, I have selected, for
> translation, two that appeared to be the best amongst them; which,
> together with some other songs of modern date, I give to show of
> what the native genius and language of this country, even now, are
> capable; labouring as they do, under every disadvantage.[7]

In this light, Brooke's appropriation of Irish-language poetry had an ecumenical subtext, for her own background as an Anglican did not deter her from seeking beauty and virtue in the poetic canon of Catholic Irish-speaking countrymen and women.

Brooke's difficulty in effecting this project arose because she recognised the defining political disjuncture that complicated confessional relations: the sentiments of legislators did not mimic the manners of the people.[8] The first were self-consciously Anglican, the second predominantly Catholic; a mismatch between the institutional life and demographic reality of the country which shaped the Irish Enlightenment in the last phase of its history. The consequences of this disaggregation of ideal and reality had ramifications across Irish cultural life, bleeding into a wide range of creative forms and undergirding many of the central achievements of the generation of thinkers and writers who flourished in the 1760s, 1770s, and 1780s.

In the case of each of the four languages of Political Enlightenment—law, history, sentiment, and manners—the foundational problematic of the connection between the sentiments of the legislators and the manners of people generated kinetic, often discordant, cultural energy. Ireland was herein configured as a location of anxiety. This took multiple forms, but the question of trust remained central.[9] In legal tracts the issue was the extent to which the Irish state could be trusted by its Catholic subjects; in history writing this was reversed and the question of the trust the Anglican state could repose in the Irish population was raised. In novels and dramas the questions were less specific, more generic: the first raised the problem of undisciplined sentiments and the necessity for good government; the second of deceptive manners and the requirements for maintaining social order. And in both these imaginative forms of literature, Ireland was a venue in which the problem was perceived as peculiarly acute, either as a disorienting eddy in the stream of the plot, or as a dangerous under-current threatening to overturn the audience's expectations.[10]

In other words the politicisation of Irish life shaped intellectual expression. Indeed, the period from 1760 to 1790 saw an intense politicisation of Irish cul-tural production; by which is indicated how politics took up a central posi-tion in the the thinking of the citizenry. Politicisation identifies the rise of the realm of politics within the cultural imaginary, with people increasingly pre-suming that 'political' contexts explain events and provide guidance for future action. The process of politicisation reduces other realms of human activity—private, economic, social—to subsidiary, dependent domains, offering a sim-plification of those arenas and a false presupposition that the difficulties inherent in them might be resolved through an identification of their political premises.[11]

That the politicisation of Irish cultural life was coupled with a perception that the polity and the people were at odds ensured Ireland remained in an unsettled state. As this final part of the book, which treats of the Political Enlightenment, will document, the potential problem identified by writers in the 1760s and 1770s turned kinetic in the late 1770s. As the Irish Volunteers transformed from a Protestant defence organisation into a campaigning body, two wings of the movement emerged: one committed to an empirical politics that limited reform to the relationship between Ireland and Britain; the other a rationalist wing that thought this was just the first stage of a more radical reor-ganisation of the polity, which would culminate in the granting of Catholic relief and franchise reform. By the 1790s, the disjuncture between the two wings of the Irish Enlightenment—the empirical and the rationalist—was becoming insurmountable. The polarisation of the 1780s gave way to a process of radicali-sation, as the means to effect political change moved from argument and debates to physical force. Both sides radicalised and the 1790s was to see a low-grade civil conflict become an overt rebellion in 1798.

The *Reliques of Irish Poetry* was a landmark in the politicisation of Irish culture in the late eighteenth century, one that marks the last vestige of an imagined shared project for the Irish Enlightenment. In harbouring a veiled critique of the prevailing system of governance, Brooke's project of retrieval was also a political gesture of rapprochement. The *Reliques* constituted a reimagining of the ancient Irish polity, a contribution to an Enlightenment discussion of political culture and an imaginative reconciliation of the disjuncture between the sentiments of the legislators and the manners of the people. Speaking of her decision to offer renditions of Irish-language poetry to an English-speaking audience, Brooke made use of a legal metaphor to articulate the problem of translation:

> I know not how far those rules might censure, or acquit me. I do not
> profess to give a merely literal version of my originals, for that I
> should have found an impossible undertaking—Besides, that spirit
> which they breathe, and which lifts the imagination far above the
> tameness, let me say, the injustice of such a task,—there are many
> complex words that could not be translated literally without great
> injury to the original.[12]

Yet given the nature of her enterprise, history and hence empirical accuracy were central to the project, and Brooke placed great store on how she had garnered help from many of the country's leading antiquarians, naming '[Charles] O'Conor, [Sylvester] O'Halloran and [Charles] Vallencey [*sic*]' in capitals at the bottom of the first paragraph.[13] She argued moreover that the compositions she had translated were to be valued not simply because of the 'merit they possess with the historian and Antiquary', but as they 'breathe the true spirit of poetry'.[14] The capacity of verse to transmit sentiments was vital, for the project relied on the assumption that poetry was 'for ages, the vital soul of the nation'.[15] Poetry, in other words, was more than just a vehicle for high emotion; it spoke of 'nations in general' and recollected the manners of the people that had long since become the shades that populate her text. She valued the poems precisely because they provided 'so many faithful delineations of the manners and ideas of the periods in which they were composed.'[16] Law, history, sentiment, and manners: all caught within the many-tiered, multilingual, composite creation composed by Brooke's 'comparatively feeble hand'.[17] In the *Reliques*, Ireland found an imaginative homeland which harnessed the idealism inherent in the Enlightenment's vision of the polity and people.

Yet for this idealisation to have imaginative purchase, it was necessary that the state held cultural power. It had to be a central and unavoidable part of the mental imaginary of the populace, making cultural production a political act, and one which could reflexively reflect on political issues by mobilising apparently unconnected genres. This was by no means obvious in Ireland, where the state did not have an absolutist character, and the population over which it ruled largely did not share its confessional character. However, Charlotte Brooke's verse collection came at the culmination of a period in which the Irish state burgeoned, a process that began with an apparently arcane argument over the expenditure of state revenues: the money bill crisis of 1753.

The Resurrection of the State

The relationship was beginning to sour. Harry the coachman, who had long enjoyed the favours of the housekeeper Mrs Dorothy Major, now suspected her affections were being directed to a younger rival. John, the rival and another coachman, was of lowly origins, being the son of a juggler, Presto. Dorothy's morals were lax, and she was known to be flirting with John, even though he was the beau of the serving girl Mrs Jenny Minor. This new love match was being overlooked by the chaplain, who 'idled away his time in playing Scotch-hop and Shuttlecock with schoolboys'.[18] Meanwhile, the Overseer had resisted the demand of the lovelorn Harry that he be granted access to the larder, and rumours were rife that the house itself was to be condemned and knocked down. Patrick's home was a hotbed of avarice and sexual ambition.

This intricate political allegory offered by Henry Brooke, father of Charlotte, captures the knotted nature of the political arguments within the Irish political caste in the early 1750s.[19] Patrick (a personification of Ireland) found the running of his demesne challenged by uppity servants and a demanding brother, George (England), who sent across an Overseer (the lord lieutenant) to tend to his interests. Patrick's 'winter residence' (parliament) was descending into chaos, caused by the illicit and uncontrolled passions of his servants (the MPs). Harry, a cipher for Henry Boyle, the manager of the government's agenda in the chamber of the House of Commons, was losing the affections of Mrs Dorothy Major (the parliamentary majority) who was in turn being wooed by John Ponsonby, leader of the minority (itself allegorised as Mrs Jenny Minor). This was being winked at by the leader of the court interest in the House of Lords, Primate George Stone of Armagh, whose rumoured homosexuality was alluded to by Brooke ('playing . . . with schoolboys'). Into this mix of loyalties and ambitions came the twin dispute of a proposal to unite the parliaments of Ireland and Britain (knocking down the winter residence) and the money bill dispute (access to the larder).[20] All the while Patrick's tenants, the Irish population, were left to struggle and starve, helped only by the labours of Farmer Goodman, keyed by Brooke as signifying the Dublin Society.[21]

At the heart of Brooke's diagnosis of the crisis were not the details of personal likes and hatreds, ambitions and frustrations, but a failure to connect appearance to reality. Harry could not rely on Dorothy Major to show her true feelings, while simultaneously determining to hide his low esteem for her virtue:

> He had no reliance upon her constancy; he knew that her virtue and reputation had been long upon a level; that in her temper she was grown luxurious and mercenary, and therefore had some reasonable doubts of her fidelity to him, if the perfect restraint upon her pleasures was not speedily removed.
>
> He carefully concealed from her the disrespectful sentiments he had of her, and she on her part being secretly pleased to think the Overseer had designs upon her, as carefully concealed her sentiments from him, so that in all outward appearance they kept up a good correspondence with each other.[22]

Brooke's squib was perceptive, for at the heart of the money bill dispute of 1753 resided, not the vagaries of personal chemistry and political manoeuvring, although they were factors in its progress, but the fundamental question of trust. It was the trust between parliamentarians, parties, communities, and countries that was to structure Irish politics and culture through the second half of the eighteenth century. Might MPs trust each other to act for the common good? Did the court party assembled around the Dublin Castle administration, which looked to England, act in good faith? Was the oppositional Patriot faction that claimed to speak for Irish autonomy within the British Empire actually driven by a self-interested desire for place and profit? Might the Protestant community trust that the Catholics had foresworn Jacobitism and posed no threat to their security? Might the Catholics believe that the Protestants had given up their ambition to destroy their faith?

The origin of all this anxiety, paradoxically, was a moment of strength. Leaving behind an epoch of state impotence, pockmarked by famine and want, the late 1740s had seen the reorganisation of the revenue of the state and a recovery in its financial standing.[23] In particular, it was now able to repay the capital on its national debt that had been a staple entry in the state's budget since 1716.[24] Following payments in 1749 and again in 1751—both of which had been mediated by Boyle in his role as the Undertaker of the Castle administration's parliamentary business—in 1753, a surplus of £328,000 was estimated to exist on the books. This allowed parliament to let certain taxes lapse—namely renewable supply legislation—and prompted them to draft a bill giving over £120,000 to reduce the national debt. This action raised the question of the right of parliament to set money bills in motion.

While the proposed money bill was not technically a supply bill, as it raised no revenue, instead disposing of cash already garnered from the country, it returned from London with the king's imprimatur inserted into the wording—effectively claiming that the monarch, not parliament, had the right to dispense with the surplus. This was prompted in part by an irate King George II, whose status as the fount of all finance bills was stated in the Act of 1749 and that of 1751 (although in the latter year the altering of the phrase 'previous recommendation' to 'previous consent' by the English Privy Council had perturbed Boyle's following).[25] When in 1753 the bill was reworded in London to state the monarch's original authority in the matter, the Patriot opposition took offence. A two-day debate in the Commons saw the Castle's view of the monarch's prerogative challenged by an articulation of parliamentary power. The vote, on 17 December, saw the bill voted down by 122 to 117, with twenty officeholders amongst the opposition.[26]

The issue was a device in a party political conflict between a court interest surrounding Primate Stone and the Speaker, Henry Boyle who, while long an Undertaker of the administration's parliamentary business, was now adopting the Patriot rhetoric of the opposition.[27] The viceroy, the Duke of Dorset, availed of Boyle's failure to process the bill to dismiss him from the position of lord justice and the office of Chancellor of the Exchequer, as well as to remove a number of Patriot allies from their posts.[28] In this, the episode was also one chapter in a long-term strategy of displacing Boyle from a position of preeminence held since the early 1730s, and building a court party within the parliament on which the Dublin Castle administration might more easily rely. A standoff ensued which appeared to break in the Patriots' favour in March 1755 when Dorset was recalled to London. Stone was then removed as lord justice in April and Boyle was restored to office in May.[29] The pyrrhic nature of this victory became clear the following year when Boyle was elevated to the House of Lords as the Earl of Shannon and took a court pension, reneging on his Patriot avowals during the crisis and renewing his support of the Castle administration.

Although the personalities were unreliable, the money bill dispute had two structural features of importance. First, the immediate cause of the argument was the sudden resuscitation of the state's financial capacity; this altered the balance of power between the various factions within the political nation. The Castle administration in Dublin and the British officials in London were now inclined to intervene in the running of the Irish polity, as larger resources were in place and the stakes commensurately heightened. In this, Irish policy fell within the broader remit of imperial governance and the desire to centralise power at Westminster. As was the case in America also, this action caused an equal and opposite reaction, forcing the local elite to adopt a defensive posture—a recalcitrance that found expression in Patriotic utterances. In the 1750s, this stance was taken opportunistically; by the 1770s, as the next chapter will show, the Patriotic constituency in Ireland was both more consistent in its commitment and radical in its ambitions.

Secondly, the public sphere was freshly and extensively engaging in political debates, and was finding its independent voice, even at a time when the Duke of Dorset was using the politics of display, consumption, and emulation to assert his authority.[30] The public's willingness to engage was partly prompted by a contraction of available credit—the Dublin-based bank of Dillon and Ferrall suspended payments in March 1754—and there were fears expressed that the money bill's assertion of the monarch's prerogative might imply specie being withdrawn from the country. A poor harvest in the summer of 1752, followed by a harsh winter and another poor crop yield in 1753, generated inflation in food prices that added to the urgency with which the public invested in events in parliament. The highly symbolic linen industry was contracting, adding to the sense of crisis.[31] Intellectual dependency was also slowly giving way to a limited autonomy, with a transition in the tone of public debate implying a distinct, if unfinished, move from a world of patronage to one of criticism.[32] This criticism relied on anonymity, allegory, and allusion to sustain its freedom of expression.[33]

Any slippage might result in prosecution for libel and/or high treason; Dorset issued a proclamation against the printing of seditious libels in February 1754.[34]

In effect, the money bill dispute politicised the populace—evidenced in a brief florescence of political clubs that occurred in the period.[35] It was indicative of the resonance of the debate that on 2 March 1754 Smock-Alley Theatre was once again the cockpit for a conflict between rival factions within the public sphere.[36] Unlike the gentleman's quarrel of the 1740s, however, the riot that destroyed much of the building and left manager Thomas Sheridan determined to exile himself in London was openly political in its content. A faction within the audience was fired into anger during a production of Voltaire's 1741 drama, *Mahomet, ou le fanatisme*, recently adapted by James Miller and John Hoadley as *Mahomet the Imposter* (1744). A month earlier, during an evening performance on 2 February, the day that the parliament was prorogued by Dorset, the opening night of the play had been disrupted when a claque in the pit demanded that a speech be repeated.[37] Asked about the moral calibre of the senate, the actor West Digges's character, Alcinor, replied:

> If, ye powers divine!
> Ye mark the movements of this nether world,
> And bring them to account, crush, crush these vipers
> Who, singled out by a community
> To guard their rights, shall, for a grasp of oar
> Or paltry office, sell them to the foe![38]

When the same call came in March, Digges would not comply, saying that 'his compliance would be greatly injurious to him'. This implied that he was not being permitted by the theatre manager to endorse the Patriot cause, a reading informed by Sheridan's open espousal of the Castle line. 'A Youth in the Pit stood up', Victor Cousin reported, 'and cried out, *God bless his Majesty King George*, and three Huzzas! And at the end of the last huzza, they all fell to demolishing the house, like lions devouring their prey; and the audience part was all in pieces in five minutes.'[39]

Anger at Sheridan's Castle loyalties, epitomised by his involvement in the Beefsteak Club, created friction when placed alongside the Patriot rubric of the passage, turning a French play mocking superstition into an attack on the Castle administration of Primate George Stone.[40] That the members of the Beefsteak club, which included the lord lieutenant, the Duke of Dorset, and had the only female member, actress Peg Woffington, as president, were suspected of having managed a confrontation with the Patriots by restaging the play, drawing the Patriots into an act of civil disorder and giving a reason for Sheridan to be bailed out financially by a state pension, captures the thicket of subplots and anxieties that generated the riot.

As this suggests the fact that the state held badly needed resources ensured that politics was thought to hold the answer to many of Ireland's problems. In other words, the questions of political economy that had energised the generation of the Social Enlightenment into private activism were increasingly thought of as having a political kernel. The Irish polity, its nature, its power, and its limitations, became the focus for the third generation of the Irish Enlightenment: the Political Enlightenment. The reform or retrenchment of the Irish parliament became the dominant dilemma debated in the last decades of the eighteenth century.

Crucially, this resurgence in the state system posed a fresh problem for Enlightenment thinkers—the dilemma being that the state's relationship with the public sphere was implicitly challenged by the Catholic issue, and the capacity of Catholic society to participate (even if only to a limited extent) in the wider public sphere that had emerged since the late 1720s. This potential, and the challenge it implied, was given substance and voice by the Catholic Committee, which organised itself in 1756. In the face of this challenge the Irish polity continued to articulate its legitimacy by emphasising confessional identity, placing the Catholic community beyond the bounds of full citizenship. That fact, coupled with an understanding of power as top-down, not bottom-up, complicated any appeal to public opinion that politicians, of any religious hue, might make. But all of this rested on a legal definition of citizenship that was by no means uncontested. Indeed, the foundations of the Irish polity in the War of the Two Kings were the subject of persistent Catholic complaint, forcing Anglican writers to become explicit about their understanding of the constitution they were determined to defend.

A Protestant Constitution?

The legal dispute revolved around the Articles of Limerick. Signed at the conclusion of the War of the Two Kings, they constituted one of a set of terms of surrender which returned a kind of normality to the ravaged island.[41] In setting out the terms upon which King William could establish uncontested jurisdiction over the island, the nature and application of the articles became a legal foundation of the state. Yet, as Catholics had come to point out, the articles were never ratified by the parliament of 1692, or by any of its successors, and many of the details of the treaty had been ignored. The Dublin assembly had developed a penal code in, the Catholics claimed, direct contravention of the peace accord. Catholic Committee activist John Curry wrote in 1786 of how

> the conditions they had by that surrender obtained (I may say sealed
> by their blood), though agreed upon and signed by both parties in the
> most solemn manner, and afterwards ratified and approved by both
> their majesties King William and Queen Mary, under the great seal of
> England, were soon after basely infringed contrary to the law of
> nature, the law of nations and the public faith.[42]

Eight years before, a *Humble Remonstrance for the Repeal of the Laws Against the Roman Catholics* (1778) drew attention to the status of the articles as a cause of just complaint, paralleling their history to the possible resolution of the then burgeoning conflict with the American colonies. Ominously, the anonymous author reflected,

> If that capitulation, for which valuable consideration viz., the imperial
> crown of these realms and empire, was ceded for the rights mentioned
> in that treaty is neglected, how can colonies that are deemed rebels by
> law confide to a treaty. But if the capitulation of Limerick is reli-
> giously observed, they will have no reason not to confide to a
> proclamation of general oblivion by the king's royal mercy on a
> cessation of arms by land and sea, which should be immediately, and
> to a treaty for the renewal of the union of these realms and their
> colonies.[43]

Earlier in the decade, Curry, with the antiquarian Charles O'Conor, had deployed similarly empirical methods to argue for the repeal of the penal code. With only one mention of 'natural rights', *Observations on the Popery Laws* (1771) was constructed so that 'history and stubborn facts shall be my guide'.[44] The argument rested on the view that Ireland under King William was materially, socially, and politically in a better state than that which Queen Anne had subse-quently bequeathed to the Hanoverians, for in erecting the penal code she had allowed her legislature to give vent not merely to their fears of Catholic revenge, but to their desire for preemptive retribution. 'It should seem therefore', he suggested,

> that Queen Anne's penal laws had their source, not so much in the
> fear of a remote and possible danger, as in the resentment of former
> injuries, when Protestants and papists (the two great parties on our
> stage) contended about the mighty stake of power and property.
> However natural our fears may be, or however just our resentments;
> yet neither should hurry us out of the line of our true interests.[45]

Moreover, as he bluntly asserted, 'the extirpation of popery is not to be effected by those penal laws.'[46] Given that to Curry's mind 'the reason of every law should be tried by its utility', this condemned the penal code as ineffectual and absurd.[47]

The use of term *utility* was weighty, for Curry deemed that the real impact of the penal code was to remove Catholics from the general interest, and to trap the island in an economic crisis. Given the natural resources of the island, the failure of the economy suggested that 'the inhabitants could not be miserable without some defect in our laws'.[48] Co-opting the persona of a liberal-minded Protestant, Curry suggested that his motivation for writing was the material condition of the people, and not a partisan attempt to remove restrictive legislation. This placed him squarely within the rubric of the language of improvement which had been popular since the 1730s. It allowed him to provide a pessimistic portrait of the country: 'our fields [are] uncultivated, our wastes un-reclaimed, our labouring people destitute of food and raiment; our roads and villages infested by vagrant beggars; in many parts houses abandoned; in most no houses built, no improvements made.'[49] This was the pernicious result of a legislative system in which 'the papists of this kingdom have for seventy years past been an insuperable obstacle to its prosperity. Cut off from the principal benefits of its free constitution, they necessarily became a disease within its bowels.'[50]

The pamphlet argued for the removal of the restrictions on the Catholic community that hampered the free practice of their faith, and for their reintegration into the economic life of the country.[51] Only in the realm of explicitly political liberties, Curry conceded, might the penal code remain in force. In suggesting this he recognised the potency of the distinction drawn between civil and spiritual parts of the confession—between the church and the faith, between papists and Catholics. Yet he turned this argument about-face, pronouncing on how

the metaphysics of any established religion should never be imposed
upon dissenters from it, because civil government being concerned
only about their civil fidelity, a test drawn from the principles of the
religion they profess is the most proper for them; indeed no other can
be proper.[52]

Given this particular set of circumstances, and Catholic quiescence since 1691,
the time was propitious for 'a legal toleration of all sects' to be implemented
with 'a test of fidelity to the civil government from each'.[53] This revised oath of
allegiance would bind the Catholic community to the polity, allowing it to contribute its portion to the material circumstance of the country. Appealing to 'our
humane legislators', Curry was optimistic that as

we know our distemper, both in kind and degree . . . the remedy is
easy from the present disposition of the legislature, from our present
state of repose, from the soundness of our constitution, from the good
intentions of the executive government, under the best of kings, from
our natural advantages and in fine, from the power of uniting the
hearts and hands of all our people, to avail ourselves of almost every
earthly happiness that God and nature intended for us.[54]

The text began with a recitation of Curry's theorisation of the state as
embodying a particular local sentiment which informed the legislation and
which emanated from the manners of the people:

In every constitution, political as well as natural, there are original
springs and principles by which the economy of the whole is conducted: some communicate vigour, and promise longevity; others
seemingly performing the functions, and occasionally promoting the
purposes of life, tend ultimately to its dissolution. They are the several
components of a complicated machine, acting and acted upon
alternately; now co-operating, now counter-working, as events favour,
or accidents affect their several powers. Hence therefore the great
strength of attention, and the great exertion of skill, necessary to
produce all the good, and remedy every evil which such a constitution
is capable of producing. This is properly the province of the legislature
in every country . . . In our own [country] where power becomes
either a remote or an immediate delegation from the people, this task

of managing the springs, or correcting the deviations of the machine
of government will be the more difficult.[55]

It was clear that Ireland suffered from a peculiar gap between the sentiments of
the legislators and manners of the people. The effect of the state's determination
to exclude Catholics from this Protestant preserve was to hamper the opportunities of the community to develop in harmony, and to mutual benefit. The
self-evident need was a toleration of confessional difference.

Arthur Browne disagreed. Although himself of American birth and education (he attended Harvard) he was, since 1772, the holder of Trinity College
Dublin's chair in civil and canon law, and professionally, as well as politically (he
was an MP), this ecumenical reading of Irish legal history irritated him. His
rejection of the Catholic narrative of grievance came in *A Brief Review of the
Question whether the Articles of Limerick have been Violated?* (1788); a query he
bluntly answered in the negative.

While most of the terms pertained to specifics, either in relation to the sur-
rendering community in Limerick or named persons, the crucial and highly
contested first article had stipulated

> the Roman Catholics of this kingdom shall enjoy such privileges in
> the exercise of their religion as are consistent with the laws of Ireland,
> or as they did enjoy in the reign of King Charles the second; and their
> majesties as soon as their affairs will permit them to summon a
> parliament in this kingdom, will endeavour to procure the said
> Roman Catholics such further security in this particular as may
> preserve them from any further disturbance upon the account of the
> said religion.[56]

It was this statement that Browne decided to parse.

The pamphlet took two key elements from the article and demonstrated how
in each case the demands had been met. First Browne observed that the circumstances of the Roman Catholic community under Charles II were far from ideal;
secondly he showed that the delay in ratification and the modifications in the
1697 bill that reduced its efficacy was not a breach of the treaty. In the first case,
Browne provided a recital of the history of persecutions under Charles II to
validate the idea that the penal code erected in the wake of the War of the Two
Kings was within the bounds of normal government for the island. Pages of case

law were mustered to demonstrate empirically the illiberal nature of life in the 1660s and 1670s.[57] This led to the harsh conclusion that

> it cannot be denied that in the reign of Charles II the free exercise of
> the popish religion was so far from being permitted in Ireland that it
> laboured under very severe penalties which were often rigorously
> enforced. The penal laws were not before the Revolution (as they have
> usually been since) a dead letter, suspended over their transgressors
> *in terrorem* and seldom carried into effect. They were really and
> severely felt.[58]

With regard to ratification, Browne argued that the king could only bring the articles before the parliamentarians and support their introduction on the statute book. Such an outcome was, as he made clear, a consequence of a constitution in which 'parliament retains the privilege of showing both by word and deed its approbation or disapprobation of the royal mode of exercising this power, by addresses; by refusing supplies; by not following up the treaty with such acts as may be necessary to complete it, and which are at the same time wholly within its province'.[59] In the case of the Catholic supplicants, 'they acceded to the articles at their peril' with the knowledge that parliament might well reject the specifics of any deal struck.[60] Critical to the shape of Browne's argument, he further contested that

> if it be said that they confided in the king, and that he deceived them
> by persuasions that he had more influence with his parliaments than
> he really possessed, it may throw a stain on the memory of King
> William, but never can discredit the public faith. That was the
> conduct of the individual, not of the nation.[61]

This was to raise the question at the very kernel of the debate over the articles: Was the failure to observe their terms or to ratify them punctually in the first parliament after the Revolution—that of 1692—indicative of a wider failure of the strands of trust that knitted the state and the people together? In other words, could Catholic subjects rely on Protestant legislators? Browne's case was that in neither area had there been a failure of the 'public faith' residing in the state: in the ratification process and the erection of a protective penal code the parliament had acted within the bounds of equity and in recognition of the specific terms of the surrender.

The vocabulary of trust and public faith was mobilised throughout *A Brief Review*, beginning with the statement of the author's intention

> to examine the truth of an opinion which has, as far as my observation extends, very generally pervaded the nation, that the penal laws were a breach of public faith; and that the abolition of them is not so much to be considered in the light of bounty as of just restitution to the privileges set forth in the Articles of Limerick.[62]

Similarly, in his treatment of the penal code, trust was to the fore of Browne's rendering of the history of the legislation:

> Granting, say they [the Catholic critics], that parliament might consistently with honour and good faith have made new laws if the public exigencies required them, still the public word had been broken, because no such necessity existed. Much has been said of the uniform loyalty and peaceable disposition of the Catholics ever since the accession of the Hanoverian family. Far be it from me to deny the truth of this encomium. But it must be observed that in demonstrating these assertions of loyalty, they labour under peculiar disadvantages. Their enemies might impute this quietness to the very laws which they condemn.[63]

The question of trust could cut both ways.

As a member of parliament Browne was inclined to rest his trust in the state, and to rely on the honourable sentiments of his fellow legislators. In what amounted to an axiom for the text, he announced in an empiricist strain that 'laws must vary with manners and with times. Covenants must be interpreted agreeably to common sense, and mutual benefit.'[64] Moreover, he proposed that 'immutability is not consistent with the laws of Ireland'.[65] The penal code was empirically justifiable given the potential threat posed by the Catholics in the wake of the War of the Two Kings. They, not the Protestant legislators, were untrustworthy. As he concluded, the pamphlet was 'not an attack on Catholics, but a defence of Protestants', yet in the polarising world of 1780s Ireland, the achievement of the second came by way of the first, and Catholics were quick to take offence.[66]

If, for Browne, the dynamic was for law to express a moral ideal of civic harmony which was threatened by the people, Curry suggested otherwise. He proposed the fault lay with the dishonesty of the state in acknowledging its responsibilities to the people. Either way both agreed that however plausible the connection between the sentiments of the legislators and the manners of the people might be in a French or English context—Montesquieu famously celebrated the English legal settlement as conducive to and expressive of the population's spirit of liberty—the Irish settlement was malformed and misshapen by the Catholic issue.[67] In Ireland, law constituted a significant intellectual puzzle, being at once an implement for intentional social engineering, notably in the confessional realm where attempts to mould the manners of the people by legislation were pronounced, and the cause of significant political strain as the state, because of its own particular historical development, was unresponsive to the condition of the people, resulting in political agitation and subversion. This question of the historical condition of the country was to spark a culture war in the unlikely realm of antiquarianism.[68]

A Barbarous Populace?

Thomas Leland, professor of oratory at Trinity College and author of *A Dissertation on the Principles of Human Eloquence* (1764), was profoundly concerned with the nature of Irish development. His *History of Ireland from the Invasion of Henry II*, published in 1773, was an attempt to write a national narrative, albeit in certain facets a failed one.[69] Prompted from very different directions by Edmund Burke and Charles O'Conor, Leland intended to compose a version of the country's past that could sit with credit alongside the philosophical histories penned by the Scottish luminaries William Robertson and David Hume.[70] Burke admitted that 'I really thought our history of Ireland so terribly defective that I did, and with success urge a very learned and ingenious friend of ours in the University of Dublin to undertake it.' Similarly, O'Conor deemed Leland an appropriate candidate as he was 'a philosopher as well as a Christian' and one of those 'writers in a superb orb who do not permit religious zeal to extinguish the lights of philosophy'. In undertaking the history of Ireland, O'Conor predicted, Leland would 'through his philosophical knowledge render us wiser than we are, and no nation ever wanted the true knowledge of their interests more than ours. History in such hands would reform us much.'[71]

Leland rather self-importantly thought himself up to the task, and openly declared his objective neutrality in the 'Preliminary Discourse' affixed to his work. He contended that

> the circumstances of Ireland were a still more dispiriting obstacle to
> the historian of this country. Prejudices and animosities could not end
> with its disorders. The relations of every transaction in times of
> contest and turbulence were for many years dictated by pride, by
> resentment, by the virulence of faction, by the obliquity of particular
> interests and competitions. It was scarcely possible for a writer not to
> share in the passions and prejudices of those around him: or however
> candid, dispassionate and accurate, still he must have done dangerous
> violence to their opinions and prepossessions . . . Even at this day the
> historian of Irish affairs must be armed against censure only by an
> integrity which confines him to truth, and a literary courage which
> despises every charge but that of wilful or careless misrepresentation.[72]

Having accounted himself as being in possession of 'integrity' and 'literary courage', Leland then progressed to the issue of ethnic origins, in a manner that suggested the Irish had found their philosophical historian.

In accordance with a predominantly Catholic school of interpretation, Leland accepted the thesis that the Irish were descendants of the Milesian peoples who had constructed a great pre-Christian civilisation. In a careful passage, he proposed that 'it is generally asserted'—note the distancing effect of this phrase—

> that about a thousand, or to speak with the more moderate [with
> whom he clearly wished to associate himself] about five hundred years
> before the Christian era, a colony of Scythians, immediately from
> Spain, settled in Ireland, and introduced the Phoenician language and
> letters into this country; and that however it might have been peopled
> still earlier from Gaul or Britain, yet Heber, Heremon and Ith, the
> sons of Milesius, gave a race of kings to the Irish, distinguished from
> their days by the names of Gadelains and Scuits, or Scots.[73]

This Phoenician model for the migration into Ireland accentuated the difference between that country and its nearest neighbour and was in contradistinction to a Nordic myth history in which Ireland was colonised from the east, and which understood Ireland and Britain as emerging from similar ethnographic stock.[74] In accepting the story supplied by the Gaelic tradition, Leland was openly reaching across a confessional and ethnic divide and setting up the possibility of a fair-minded historical narrative. This was then cemented by his celebration of the civilisation which the Milesians had erected on the island, enjoying 'a regular form of government . . . a grand seminary of learning and . . . the Fes, a triennial convention of provincial kings, priests and poets at Teamor, or Tarah in Meath, for the establishment of laws and regulation of government.'[75]

Granted, and again in line with much Gaelic scholarship, Leland contended that the bards had become corrupted by power, and the contest between the provincial kings had repeatedly descended into civil war, the structure of elected monarchy being inherently unstable. Yet he was generous in bestowing praise on the manners of the people who lived in this distant age. On his reading of the evidence—albeit mediated by Irish-language translators for he had no skill in the tongue—

> we have a lively picture of manners, more worthy of attention than the events which they deliver, with so profuse a mixture of giants, necromancers, obscure allegorics and extravagant fables. They describe a brave people driven from their native land in search of a new settlement, establishing themselves by their valour in a fair and fertile island: the chieftains parcelling out lands to their attendants, and the whole collection of adventurers, from the moment of their peaceable establishment, deriving means to give stability to their acquisitions . . . They have rights independent of the monarch, and frequently indicate them by arms against his invasions . . . In this state of things, a robust frame of body, a vehemence of passion, an elevated imagination were the characteristics of the people. Noble instances of valour, generous effusions of benevolence, ardent resentments, desperate and vindictive outrages abound in their annals.[76]

This Montesquian overview of the manners of the people, then informed a guarded if broadly positive assessment of the laws:

> Reflection and the gradual progress of refinement convince them of the necessity of settled laws. The principles of equity and independence implanted in the human breast receive them with delight; but

> the violence of passion still proves superior to their restraint. Private
> injuries are revenged by force; and insolent and ambitious chieftains
> still recur to arms.[77]

This passage proved central, for it prepared the reader for Leland's treatment of one of the most controversial and vivid episodes of the recent Irish past, namely the rising in Ulster that occurred in October 1641.

In the chapter devoted to the outbreak of the Ulster Rising, Leland focussed attention on the perfidy of individual conspirators, and laid out the malice aforethought with which they dreamt up the insurrection. Foremost of these men was Roger Moore, who held a 'hereditary hatred of the English . . . irritated as he was by the sufferings of his ancestors, his own indigence and depression, and the mortifying view of what he called his rightful inheritance possessed by strangers.'[78] He was abetted by such men as Richard Plunkett, adjudged to be 'vain in his temper, indigent in his fortune and bigoted in religion'.[79]

Leland coupled such individual poison-pen portraits with a condemnation of the manners of the Catholic Irish, prompted into 'the violence of passions' by 'private injuries'. While it had been the determination of the rebellion's leadership to minimise bloodshed, leaving the Scots of Ulster 'totally unmolested, as if with peculiar favour and indulgence to the old allies and kinsmen of the Irish', once the rising occurred the leadership were unable to restrain their troops.[80] In the first phase, as the rebellion spread,

> parties of plunderers multiplied; by force or artifice they possessed
> themselves of the houses and properties of their English neighbours.
> Resistance produced some bloodshed; and in some instances private
> revenge, religious hatred and the suspicion that some valuable
> concealment enraged the triumphant rebels to insolence, cruelty and
> murder. So far however was the original scheme of the conspiracy at
> first pursued, that few fell by the sword, except in open war and
> assault; no indiscriminate massacre was yet committed. The English
> were either confined in their prisons, in perpetual terror of destruc-
> tion; or driven from their habitations, naked, destitute exposed to the
> rigours of a remarkably severe season, fainting and dying in the
> highways, or crawling to some place of refuge in the ghastliness of fear
> and famine.[81]

While this horror was accorded the title of restraint by Leland, that moderation slipped away as the rebels were facing defeat. In a noxiously detailed passage, Leland recounted how

> the defeat of Lisburn [County Antrim] provoked this savage [the rebel leader, Sir Phelim O'Neill] and his barbarous followers to a degree of rage truly diabolical. Lord Caulfield, who had been conveyed to one of the houses of O'Nial, was wantonly and basely murdered. Fifty others, in the same place, fell by the poniards of the Irish. Their miserable prisoners, confined in different quarters, were now brought out under pretence of being conducted to the next English settlements. Their guards goaded them forward like beasts, exulting in their sufferings, and determined on the destruction of those who had not already sunk under their tortures. Sometimes they enclosed them in some house or castle, which they set on fire, with a brutal indifference to their cries, and a hellish triumph over their expiring agonies. Sometimes the captive English were plunged into the first river, to which they had been driven by the tormentors. One hundred and ninety were, at once, precipitated from the bridge at Portadown. Irish ecclesiastics were seen encouraging the carnage. The women forgot the tenderness of their sex; pursued the English with execrations, and imbrued their hands in blood; even children, in their feeble malice, lifted the dagger against the helpless prisoners.[82]

The pornography of violence in which Leland here indulged antagonised and alienated his Catholic readers—O'Conor in umbrage declared that Leland 'resigns his literary merit and all credit with impartial men, in favour of present advantage either within his grasp or within his expectation'.[83] It was a contentious lapse in the objective stance that he had claimed for himself in the preliminary discourse. As he discovered, the arguments of history were not merely antiquarian, but came freighted with immensely heavy ideological baggage.[84] The events of 1641 were a particular lodestone for arguments about the legitimacy of the state, and the manners of the Catholics. Repeatedly Leland applied the terms 'barbarous' or 'barbarities' to the rebels and their actions, suggesting that they stood outside of civilisation; a far cry from his vision of a pre-Christian civilisation created by the native Irish.[85] Thus, just as much as his project evinced a desire for a shared narrative, so too it pointed up the pressures under which such a project operated. The distrust of the Catholic confession amongst Anglicans implied a need for them to establish their credentials as civil actors and ensured the empirical record of rebellion and civil disorder came repeatedly under examination, and cross-examination.[86]

For all the social and sympathetic connections that existed, the language of privilege through which the Irish state operated overtly excluded the Catholic community and drove them into political as well as religious opposition. Yet in so doing they lost the sympathy of the Protestants and announced themselves to be violent malefactors who needed the stern hand of government to temper their cruel and disordered passions. English rule, in this paradigm, saved the Irish from themselves, and the country from the continuous cycle of civil unrest Leland documented in treating of pre-Christian times.

Paradoxically it was the recent divisive past that underscored the emotional need for an imagined community of the past which could extol the unity of Irish purpose in a shared developmental narrative—however spurious, as the capture and promulgation of St Patrick for Protestant polemical purposes underlines—and the existence and visceral power of the antiquarian culture wars.[87] The genre of historical writing was perceived by its practitioners as illuminating the manners of the community; and if the recent past did not provide evidence of the civility of the Irish, then a sober and successful civilisation had to be projected into the distant past. The imagining of just such an Edenic polity was precisely the task taken up by the Catholic Committee pamphleteer Charles O'Conor.[88]

In the first edition of his *Dissertations on the Ancient History of Ireland* (1753), O'Conor invested the pre-Christian epoch of Irish history with immense psychological importance, developing a picture of the ancient people as enjoying the benefits of a substantially developed civilisation.[89] 'Grandeur', he claimed, 'was sustained without pageantry; dignity without pomp; and power without terror.'[90] The manners of the people were those befitting a rural landscape in which 'the whole land was one continued village, where the inhabitants did not encroach too much to incommode, nor separate too far to be able to assist and assemble upon any extraordinary emergency.'[91] Alongside a tradition of hospitality and benevolence that such proximity bestowed, the product of their labour was sufficiently bounteous as to allow Ireland to begin to trade with other countries, 'and such a beginning soon removed the seat of northern commerce from Britain to Ireland.'[92] This commercial civilisation was imagined as a country in which the favours of nature were so gloriously improved; where the wealth of the state was great and solid, while that of individuals was restrained within moderate bounds; where luxury, the parent of private opulence and public indigence, found no entrance; and consequently where liberty could never be merely nominal.[93]

Indeed, it was to Ireland's credit that the Roman Empire had never effected an incursion for, far from bringing civilisation, O'Conor proposed, in a self-conscious reversal of terms, the 'frank, humane and rational way of living' enjoyed by

the original Celts . . . continued longer than in any country; because ever free from the inroads of the nations we call polite, particularly the Romans . . . These were the very people who first imported luxury and false refinements into Europe; who spoiled the morals, as they destroyed the liberties of many great nations, whom without distinction, they very civilly styled barbarians.[94]

This linguistic reclamation was integral to a wider rhetorical ploy; that of setting Ireland's past apart from, and morally above, that of England.[95] Whereas Ireland could boast of being at that time 'the emporium of science and literature to the western world', O'Conor carefully placed in a footnote the snide remark that 'the Saxons, who doubtless were a very brave people, yet neglected the cultivation of their minds, as well as the Normans.'[96]

In contrast, O'Conor was decided in his opinion that the Irish had ancestors of noble character and learned intellect. 'Of the Scythian or Celtic Nations' he opined,

the ancient Spaniards were certainly the most martial and free, the most humanised by letters, and the most conversant with the Egyptians, Phoenicians, Persians and Grecians. From that nation our Gadelian or Scottish colony derive their original. All foreign authorities on this subject concur in the same account; the genius of our poetry and peculiar disposition of our letters confirm it, and the identity of customs and language prove it.[97]

This projection of an independent lineage and the supposition of direct connection to the great Middle Eastern civilisations resulted, O'Conor contended, in the early use of letters, while the subsequent history 'preserved the druidic theology in greater purity here than in any other Celtic country: Philosophy came to its early assistance' while 'religion to have its proper influence, borrowed its arms from reason.'[98] History thus suggested that far from being backward and a burden on its neighbour, Ireland could, if adequately governed, become a net contributor to Britain's burgeoning commercial empire.

O'Conor's history spoke to a Patriot party that was rising in influence across the second half of the eighteenth century, and which sought to rescind the legislative restrictions on the Dublin parliament's autonomy, found in the twin bars of Poynings's law and the Declaratory Act. Socially, as well as intellectually, O'Conor found himself feted by the antiquarians of that bent. Indeed, despite their differences of interpretation, Leland and O'Conor became interlocutors, with the university don relying on the Catholic polemicist for source material in the writing of his history. From 1761 Leland also facilitated O'Conor's use of the manuscript holdings in the Protestant bastion of Trinity College.[99] This courting of the Catholic antiquary culminated with O'Conor being nominated in 1773 as a corresponding member of the Select Committee for Antiquaries of the Dublin Society, and, in a personal coup for O'Conor, he was then able to nominate a similar honour for the Catholic archbishop of Dublin, John Carpenter. To O'Conor, this optimistically represented 'a revolution in our moral and civil affairs the more extraordinary, as in my own days such a man would only be spoken to through the medium of a warrant and a constable'.[100] Yet despite the optimism that these informal ties evinced in O'Conor, the tide was running against collaboration. In fact, Irish intellectual life was becoming increasingly polarised as the century drew to its close, as the tensions embedded within the novels and the plays of the period imaginatively display.

Novel Sentiments

If the dichotomy between the sentiments of the state and the manners of the people inspired debates within Irish jurisprudential and antiquarian circles in the third quarter of the century, that concern also manifested in other modes of cultural expression. In particular Irish writers made significant contributions to the development of the sentimental novel and of the comedy of manners.[101] In both genres, Ireland was to act as a significant locus for anxiety and the question of combining honest sentiments with decent manners came to the fore. In the case of the novel, the primary concern was with good government; within drama, focus fell on the nature of social order.

The question of good government and the capacity of repression to warp honourable sentiments was the central theme of the *Memoirs of Miss Sidney Bidulph* (1761) by Frances Sheridan. The wife of Thomas Sheridan, and herself a playwright of note, Sheridan had been born in Dublin and was a close friend of Samuel Richardson, having met the English author on her enforced sojourns in London in the aftermath of the various Smock-Alley riots that had engulfed her husband. Prompted by Richardson to write, she had helped recuperate her family's finances by penning the novel which struck a chord with an audience increasingly invested in sentimental tales of female suffering—a trend Richardson's own works had inaugurated.[102]

Sidney Bidulph constituted a rigorous test of someone whose moral failing was her submissive, pacific acceptance of fate.[103] Sidney herself is introduced as a character who is commonly spoken for and who submits happily to this condition, admitting to her correspondent Cecelia: 'I have been accustomed from my infancy to pay an implicit obedience to the best of mothers; the conforming to this never yet cost me an uneasy minute, and I am sure never will.'[104] When an arranged match is mooted, her brother George chastises his sister for accepting their mother's scheming: 'I know that you will urge your perfect submission to your mother's will; and I know too, that *will* is as absolute as that of an Eastern monarch. I therefore repeat it, I do not mean to reproach you with your compliance, but I am vexed to the heart, and must give it vent.'[105]

In due course, George is proved correct. The humility Sidney espouses is indeed a fateful sentiment, for the novel is built upon a recitation of the unease and distress caused by her biddable nature.[106] Thus, when married to the adulterous Mr Arnold, she is willing to set aside her own impulses and insights in favour of her new director, her husband. As she admits, 'But that I have laid it down as a rule never to oppose so good, so indulgent a husband as Mr Arnold is, in any instance wherein I do not think a superior duty requires me to do so, I should certainly shew some disapprobation of what he now purposes doing.'[107] This martyrdom complex leaves her acknowledging how 'I sicken at the very thought of Mr Arnold entertaining a doubt of my true affection for him! I would rather he should treat me roughly—if I discovered that to be his humour, though it would frighten me, yet should I patiently conform to it.'[108] Even at the central moment of the plot's origin, it is the quiescent and demure nature of her personality that results in a fateful misjudgement, the rejection of her true love, Orlando Faulkland.[109] When it is revealed that he has sired a child out of wed-lock with a Miss Burchell, Sidney is emotionally distraught and falls back on her mother's guidance:

> I was ready to melt into tears; my spirits, exhausted by sickness, were
> not proof against this unexpected blow; a heavy sigh burst from my
> heart, that gave me a little relief. You know my mother is rigid in her
> notions of virtue; and I was determined to shew her that I would
> endeavour to imitate her. I therefore suppressed the swelling passion
> in my breast, and with as much composure as I could assume, told
> her, I thought she acted as became her and that, with regard to
> Faulkland, my opinion of his conduct was such that I never desired to
> see him more. This answer, dictated perhaps by female pride (for I will
> not answer for the feelings of my heart at that instant), was so
> agreeable to my mother, that she threw her arms about my neck, and
> kissed me several times; blessing and calling me by the most endearing
> names at every interval.[110]

When Sidney marries, then, it is an arranged match with Mr Arnold, for whom she has no feelings.[111] While in anguish she protests 'I could cry of very vexation to be made such a puppet of', in keeping with her character it is society's view of her predicament that brings her to heel.[112] As her overbearing mother reports:

> Lady Grimston has put your affair in such a light to me as I never
> considered it in before. How mortifying must the reflection be my
> dear, to think that it may be said Mr Faulkland perhaps flew off, from
> some disadvantageous circumstance he discovered in regard to you.
> The world [a key term in this passage] wants not envious malicious
> tongues enough to give it this turn. Your unlucky illness and your
> brother's ill-timed assiduity in going so often to him when he was at
> Richmond, looks as if we had been endeavouring to recall him.
> Everyone knows that the marriage was almost concluded and Lady
> Grimston, though she thinks our reasons for breaking it off were
> extremely cogent, yet as she knows the world well, thinks it has not
> virtue enough to believe those to be the true reasons, and that it will

be much more apt to put an invidious construction on the affair, that may be very detrimental to you in your future prospects.[113]

In a brief moment of self-awareness, Sidney then regrets how 'I have no will of my own.'[114] Yet despite this illumination, the match with Mr Arnold proceeds, leaving Sidney 'trying to like Mr Arnold as fast as I can.'[115]

This was clearly a warning against marrying without love—the ultimate act of false sentiments—and the novel examines the consequences of such folly. Once the match is complete, and two children are born, libidinous male urges disrupt Sidney's contentment, for Mr Arnold becomes infatuated with Mrs Gerrarde. Sidney has therefore simply moved from the social authority exercised by her mother to the sexual authority of Mr Arnold. In neither case has her own sentiments been well served by her choice of government. The book thus offered a trenchant defence of exuberant adolescent sexuality by exploring the tear-stained consequences of loveless marriage and the fatuous demands of social niceties and ethical etiquette.

In drawing out these moral lessons Sheridan conformed to a fashionable notion that the effect of events mapped onto the human face in miniscule reflexes that the acute spectator could observe and read.[116] As Sidney explained:

> There are little minute touches on the countenance sometimes, which are so transient they can hardly be overtaken by the eye, and which from the passions being strongly guarded that give rise to these emotions, are so slight that a common observer cannot discover them at all. I am sure my mother did not, but my sensibility was particularly roused at her relating a story that I did not then wish to have divulged; and I was too much interested in the narrative not to attend precisely to its effects on the hearer.[117]

The difficulty was that though much of this sensibility was involuntary, it could be wilfully imitated. Actors lied about the impact of events on their affective bearing, and emotional disguise was not uncommon. As Sidney instructed Miss Burchell:

> All disguises must now be thrown aside, depend upon it, your candour will more effectually recommend you to Mr Faulkland's esteem . . . [A] variety of passions discovered themselves on her face while I spoke, but shame was predominant . . . She burst into a flood

of tears: oh madam, you read my very soul! What disguise can I make
use of before such penetrating eyes as yours?[118]

Much of the novel's action revolves around the revelation of various characters'
real intentions when social circumstance suggest other motives: Faulkland is
honourable despite siring a child out of wedlock; Miss Burchell is not the injured
party so much as a conniving seductress and libertine; Mr Arnold is a foolish
lover, not a stable partner; and Lady Bidulph is an emotional bully, not a cautious protectress. Only Sidney herself remains wedded to her initial character—
submissive but stultified.

Fashionable sentimentalism also shaped the work of Hugh Kelly whose
novel *Memoirs of a Magdalen* (1767) tussled with the relationship between emotional honesty and good government. Born in Killarney, Kelly had moved to
London in 1760 and taken up hack journalism as a means to make a living. He
was to find his way into theatrical circles through an association with the renown
actor David Garrick, and was to pen a number of moderately successful plays.[119]
His sole prose fiction, *Memoirs*, predated this turn in his fortunes, but was itself
well received. Unlike the earlier work by Frances Sheridan, however, that by
Kelly was more concerned with the control of emotions than expressing fear at
their irresponsible repression.[120] While this attitude befit his wider establishment politics it also separated him from Sheridan's attack on neo-Stoic attitudes, offering instead a meditation on how to manage the passions without
smothering them. Rationalist optimism about the creative power of passionate
impulses here gave way to an empirical resignation that they are always likely to
threaten social happiness unless properly monitored. As one character expresses
it, 'Women, like ourselves [men], are only flesh and blood [and] desires are as
natural to them as to us'.[121]

Memoirs of a Magdalen tells the tale of Louisa Mildmay of Oxfordshire, a
noted beauty who by twenty-one had already, on her introduction, had 'four
duels, in which two hot-headed block-heads were actually killed'.[122] She is
described as having 'a voluptuous fleshiness through her person, which keeps
the imagination constantly on fire, and would kindle the bosom of an anchorite
into an instant flame of sensuality'.[123] She is courted by Sir Robert Harold while
at Bath, who, while allowing himself to be a 'libertine', assumes as 'a fixed principle that the same woman who suffers even the man she doats upon to distraction to take advantage of an unguarded moment, will have her unguarded

moments with other people'.'[124] Louisa ultimately succumbs to him a few days before their marriage, when they are left unattended late into the evening at the Mildmay home.[125]

Spurred by this act of passion into fearing for his wife-to-be's future fidelity, Robert effects a cancelation of the marriage. He adopts the same reserve that had initially brought him to Louisa's attention, but while before his disinterest had piqued her curiosity she now reads it as rejection, given that he had succeeded in bedding her. He protests that she was putting 'a strange interpretation upon looks' which contrasted with her own 'wildness of look' as the relationship unravelled.[126] In line with the theory of sensibility, Robert's ability to govern his emotions is crucial in allowing him to modulate and control the relationships he is engaged in; Louisa in contrast is incapable of managing her sentiments. Whereas he admits 'reason and reflection may on particular occasions, oblige me to resist its emotions', he laments 'did these women but know how we worship them [for refusing to gratify our wishes . . . yet] they constantly betray their own cause, and oblige them in a manner to despise and desert them'.[127]

Louisa's response to the crisis is to ensconce herself at her aunt's London abode and then apparently elope with another fashionable suitor. Yet when she reemerges into society after an eleven-month absence, it is to reveal that her aunt 'is a fiend of darkness, an instrument of hell, a priestess of destruction' and her elopement was in fact an abduction by the rake Sir Harry Hastings, facilitated by her greedy relative.[128] Escaping from her imprisonment during a fire, Louisa finds refuge in the well-run home of Deborah Dobson, who possesses the 'uncultivated benignity of [a] worthy rustic'.[129] It was she who brings Louisa to 'that admirable institution called the Magdalen' House.[130] The good government she encounters there enables the recuperation of Louisa's physical health, and ultimately her social standing.[131] She sacrifices herself to government over her sensibility, accepting that 'it is true, if my imagination had not been disturbed, I had never dreamed of entering into a place particularly dedicated to the public penitence of prostitution. Yet . . . how am I better than the unhappy poor creatures, whom the pinching hand of necessity, or the poignant stings of remorse have brought to the same salutary yet humiliating habitation?'[132]

While built around a structure of virtue—shame—redemption, the novel is energised by moving Louisa through a series of households that offer different models for managing the passions. One contrast to the redemptive Magdalen

House is the mother's lax government of Louisa. Faced with the consequences of leaving two amorous youths unattended, she accepts mournfully that

> I am more to be blamed for leaving Sir Robert and Louisa so fre-
> quently together than either is for abusing the confidence which I
> reposed in their discretion. Young people, where they tenderly love
> each other, and where a day is set apart for their marriage, are very
> dangerous companions . . . Oh my sweet Louisa! Your doating
> mother's extravagant fondness has been the cause of all our calamities;
> and your indiscretion was nothing more than the natural result of her
> mistaken partiality.[133]

The other contrast to the Magdalen House is the harsh treatment Louisa experiences in the house of the tyrannous Sir Harry Hastings. Both his housekeeper and his sister admit that 'their lives would not be safe if they acted in the least contrary to the will of their master.'[134] 'Absolute' in his power, Hastings was himself ruled by his passions; when Louisa fell into a fever he became 'absolutely frantick; . . . he frequently tore his hair and stamped upon the ground with all the agitation of a bedlamite.'[135] Only by freeing herself and submitting to the healthy environ of the Magdalen House is Louisa made fit for a return to society and enabled to reengage with her true love, Sir Robert Harold.

The reformation of character is not limited to Louisa, however, for Robert too has altered since the fateful moment when he and Louisa gave way to lust. Robert starts the novel by striking a rakish pose. In the first letter he brags to his older friend Charles Melmoth, 'You may recollect what a propensity I have to be particular with every woman who is fool enough to admit of my familiarity.'[136] While he soon accepts 'it is high time for me to think of getting sons and daughters for myself instead of wasting my time increasing the families of other people', he still finds it hard to give up a licentious lifestyle and settle down to matrimonial commitment.[137]

After he rescinds his engagement with Louisa, he is sorely admonished by Melmoth for 'breaking off with a lady merely because she has given you the most convincing proof of her affection [; this] is what, in my opinion, savours considerably more of romance than of real understanding.'[138] The lesson Robert needs to learn is to recognise real emotions and to honour them. Faced with the consequences of his actions, Robert finally tells Melmoth that he now under-stands how 'thoughtless . . . I have been in many connections with the sex; the consequences which have resulted from this affair with Miss Mildmay make me detest what I formerly esteemed the principal source of felicity, and convince me that a man of gallantry is no less a contemptible than a dangerous character'.[139] Reformation complete, he is willing to settle down with Louisa and honour his promise of matrimony; a state projected by Kelly as the one venue in which desire may be legitimately expressed and the passions produced by lust ably governed.

Both Sheridan and Kelly were thus engaged in a debate over whether and how sentiments should be controlled. Sheridan distrusted the repression of sentiments and attacked neo-Stoic attitudes accordingly; Kelly insisted on the government of passions, and used his moral tale to explore what kind of regimen might work best in managing them. For both the issue at stake was whether an individual's personal sentiments might be trusted and considered honourable; Sheridan's rationalist view was that they could be, whereas Kelly, an empiricist, thought the social context was vital in hemming in dangerous impulses. Sheridan was to evince this optimism about human nature in adopting a liberal stance on the passions; Kelly found support for his anxiety about social control in his establishment politics. Sentiments could send people in either direction.

Staged Manners

If the *Memoirs of Miss Sidney Bidulph* and of *A Magdalen* are concerned with questions of how to govern disruptive sentiments, the awareness of how social manners and polite appearance might hide a false heart was the focus of much of the drama produced in these decades.[140] The comedies of manners produced by Charles Macklin and Oliver Goldsmith debated the question of good social order. Macklin, or Cathal MacLaughlin, was a famed actor of the London stage and an unsuccessful entrepreneur, setting up a tavern in which he offered public lectures on theatrical matters called the British Inquisition.[141] Goldsmith, who hailed from County Longford, was a jobbing author and translator, who made his way into Samuel Johnson's literary circle.[142] But despite their similar standing as Irish literary men on the make in England, in *Love à la Mode* (1759) and *She Stoops to Conquer* (1773) they offered differing understandings of how personal intentions related to the performative demands of social etiquette. In both plays marriage plots serve as key moments of negotiating this relationship, as it is in the making of a good match that honouring sentiments and maintaining social order comes into most immediate conflict. For Macklin, the gap between synthetic and sincere sentiments was resolved by connecting honest sentiments to social order; for Goldsmith, sincere sentiments subverted public standing.

The opening line of Macklin's most successful play, *Love à la Mode* (1759), establishes the question of the relationship between government and sentiment. Charlotte opines that 'there can be no harm in a little mirth, guardian; even those who happen to be the objects must approve the justice of it'.[143] Her father and governor, Sir Theodore, cautions her, asking her to consider 'what the world [again a key term] will say of me?' Sentiment here is placed in tension with manners, and good governance is tested by measuring the correspondence of the two. Charlotte's riposte to her father's warning is that 'the world will applaud the mirth, especially when they know what kind of lovers they are', suggesting that their social appearance does not accord with their personal merit.[144] She proceeds to dismantle each suitor as inadequate. One is ridiculed for pretending to be 'a wit, and a man of taste; another for having 'ruined his finances by dogs, grooms, cocks, horses and such polite company'; a third for his lack of social niceties in having a 'tongue, like the dart of death [which] spares neither sex nor age'.[145] The last, Sir Theodore's nephew Callaghan, is introduced as a military man 'born in a siege'.[146] She slyly admits that she 'like[s] his character extremely' and that 'I am in love with his warlike humour—I think it highly entertaining', suggesting that it is here, with a plainspoken masculine presence, that her heart lies.[147]

While each of these men represents a crudely drawn stereotype—the foppish Jewish moneylender (Macklin was himself celebrated for acting the role of Shylock[148]), the uncultured English squire, the vituperative Scot, and the Irish sword for hire—the purchase of these thumbnails sketches is to indicate how far the social order of the British Isles is implicated in the story of Charlotte's sentimental attachments. At stake is also the relationship between virtue and social standing, for each suitor in turn asserts his eligibility by addressing his rank and status. Indeed, the Scot MacSarcasm and the Irishman Sir Callaghan O'Brallaghan fall into a fight over the fashionable antiquarian dispute as to whether Scotland colonised Ireland or vice versa, personified by Sir Callaghan's brusque claim that 'the Scots are all Irishmen's bastards'—destroying any claim to social recognition for MacSarcasm's countrymen. Callaghan himself claims an ancient lineage which 'by my fader's side, are all the true old Milesians, and related to the O'Flaherty's, and the O'Shocknesses and the MacLaughlins, the O'Donnegans, O'Callaghans, O'Geogaghans, and all the tick blood of the nation'.[149]

When Charlotte apparently becomes poor, and lowers herself to the social standing enjoyed by Sir Callaghan, his awe of her is removed and he can finally court her. As he explains:

> When she was computed to have a hundred thousand pounds I loved her, 'tis true, but it was with fear and trembling, like a man that loves to be a solider, yet is afraid of a gun, because I looked upon myself as an unequal match to her—but now she is poor, and that it is in my power to serve her, I find something warm about my heart here, that tells me I love her better than when she was rich.[150]

The other suitors, who intend to raise their social standing by making a connection with a rich heiress, are dissuaded from pursuing their suit. MacSarcasm directly links his withdrawal of affection to the influence marrying beneath his station would have, citing how 'I hai had letters frai the dukes, the marquis, and aw the deegnetaries of the family remonstrating—may axpressly pro-heebeting my contaminating the blood of MacSarcasm wi' anything sprung frai a hogsheed, or a counting hoose.'[151] Hearing Charlotte's protest that there is 'no virtue in man', he reveals the fundamental connection he is devising between sentiments and social standing by responding 'nor in woman neither that has no fortune'.[152] That connection is integral to the play, but it is the sentiments that need to be tested not the social status, hence Charlotte's ruse. Only the Irishman comes through the test, relying on his open articulation of true sentiments: 'I know I can't talk fine courtship, and love and nonsense like other men' he admits to Charlotte, 'for I don't speak from my tongue but my heart: so that if you can take up your quarters for life with a man of honour, a sincere lover, and an honest Prussian solider, now is your time.'[153] Honour, sincerity, and honesty are the virtues of true sentiment, and enough to woo Charlotte away from her deceiving suitors.

If maintaining social order is effected while honouring true sentiments in *Love à la Mode*, in Oliver Goldsmith's masterpiece of social observation, *She Stoops to Conquer*, the concluding marriages equally and happily resolve the comic negotiations of status and sentimentality. The marriage of the two young men Marlow and Hastings to Miss Hardcastle and Miss Neville, respectively, brings a sentimental, romantic, and restorative close to this drama of dislocation and upset identities; as Mrs Hardcastle observes, 'this is all but the whining end of a modern novel'.[154] Yet unlike in Macklin's work, where Charlotte pretends to lower her standing to drive false suitors away, in Goldsmith's drama the heroine's deceit is contrived to attract a nervous lover to declare himself. Social standing is ultimately reinforced in Macklin, for a match of equals is effected by Charlotte and Sir Callaghan before they are both raised up to her real station by the revelation that she never actually lost her fortune. In contrast it is creatively subverted by Goldsmith whose moral is that love should overcome social boundaries. Far from sustaining the power of rank and social duty, the play consciously subverts it.

Indeed, the comedy in Goldsmith's drama is generated from the gradations of behaviour expected between the ranks of society. Led by the mischievous Tony Lumpkin to believe that the Hardcastle household was an inn, young Marlow treats his potential father-in-law with disdain, and chases his bride-to-be, Miss Hardcastle, as if she was a servant. This predictably leads to annoyance on the part of Mr Hardcastle who, sick of being treated like as servant in his own house and seeing his daughter being roughly wooed, makes to throw out his guest for his 'insolence'.[155] The offence caused by Marlowe's unthinking rudeness to those beneath him is contrasted to the discomfiture and reserve he exhibits whilst amongst his peers. Instead of grasping the hand of Miss Hardcastle, and trying to gain a kiss when he thinks her to be a serving maid, Marlow's approach when he sees her as a heiress and prospective mate is, as he self-righteously protests to Mr Hardcastle, distinctly less impulsive:

> *Marlow:* Sure, sir, nothing has past between us but the most profound respect on my side and the most distant reserve on hers. You don't think, sir, that my impudence has been past upon all the rest of the family.
>
> *Hardcastle:* Impudence! No I don't say that—not quite impudence— though girls like to be played with, and rumpled a little too, sometimes. But she has told no tales, I assure you.
>
> *Marlow:* I never gave her the slightest cause.
>
> *Hardcastle:* Well, well, I like this modesty in its place well enough. But this is overacting, young gentleman. You *may* be open. Your father and I will like you the better of it . . .
>
> *Marlow:* But why won't you hear me? By all that's just and true, I never gave Miss Hardcastle the slightest mark of my attachment, or even the most distant hint to suspect me of affection. We had but one interview, and that was formal, modest, and uninteresting.[156]

Two characters are here talking at cross-purposes; one convinced his daughter has been wooed, the other thinking he was seducing a serving girl. Marlow's awkwardness amongst women of his own rank—a source of friendly jibes from his friend Hastings—is dispatched with as an act, underlining the tension that existed between manners and morals. Which is the true Marlow, and which the performance? Is he the reticent young man who gets tongue-tied before a girl of his own station, or the boisterous lad in search of sexual favours from a social inferior? In complicating Marlow's character in this way, Goldsmith raised questions concerning the consistency of personality and the effects of polite society in which people parade.

Goldsmith added a further layer of comic irony to the situation by positioning Marlow at the nexus of another sequence of exterior demands. He gets caught between the different expectations of the discommoded Mr Hardcastle and the feisty bride-to-be, for whom his show of spirit is more appealing than any stately diffidence. The contrast emerges when Mr Hardcastle and his daughter compare notes on their rather different first impressions:

Miss Hardcastle: Sure sir, you rally! I never saw anyone so modest.

Hardcastle: And can you be serious! I never saw such a bouncing, swaggering puppy since I was born . . .

Miss Hardcastle: Surprising! He met me with a respectful bow, a stammering voice, and a look fixed on the ground.

Hardcastle: He met me with a loud voice, a lordy air, and a familiarity that made my blood freeze again . . .

Miss Hardcastle: One of us must certainly be mistaken.

Hardcastle: If he be what he has shown himself, I'm determined he shall never have my consent.

Miss Hardcastle: And if he be the sullen thing I take him, he shall never have mine.

Hardcastle: In one thing then we are agreed—to reject him.[157]

In the central conceit of the play, Miss Hardcastle is required to stoop socially and pretend to be a servant to open up the sexual energy and loquacious lust of her potential lover. As she explains to her maid, 'In the first place I shall be *seen*, and that is no small advantage to a girl who brings her face to market. Then I shall perhaps make an acquaintance and that's no small victory gained over one who never addresses any but the wildest of her sex.'[158] Ironically, it is only by deciding to 'keep up the delusion' that Marlow is in an inn that she can actually

get to be seen, and it is only in the midst of this encounter that the stage directions note that Marlow 'looks full in her face'.[159] He is instantly smitten—'I vow
child you are vastly handsome'—and makes his amorous approach.[160]

Goldsmith's target is social appearance and the folly of mistaking socially
determined manners for interior sentiments. So, at crucial moments in the
incipient romance, the play scrutinises and criticises the word 'sentiment' and
its derivative 'sentimental'. In the awkward first interview between the two
lovers Miss Hardcastle observes: 'I have often been surprised how a man of
sentiment could ever admire those light airy pleasures where nothing reaches
the heart'. Anxious to please, Marlow concurs, stuttering 'it's—a disease—of
the mind madam.'[161] This failed encounter is dismissed by the disappointed girl
as 'a sober, sentimental interview.'[162] Unknowingly, Marlow echoes this assessment when he muses within her earshot that 'as for Miss Hardcastle, she's too
grave and sentimental for me.'[163] Finally, at the crucial moment in which
Miss Hardcastle reveals her true identity and makes her own emotions plain,
she recalls how she had been addressed by her lover both 'as the mild, modest,
sentimental man of gravity, and the bold forward, agreeable Rattle of the
ladies' club.'[164]

What irked Goldsmith was 'the old pretence of a violent passion', wishing to
replace it with the 'simplicity [which] bewitches me'.[165] Marlow is caught
between the demands of society and the demands of his interior self, as he
explains to the disguised Miss Hardcastle: 'Your partiality in my favour, my dear
touches me most sensibly, and were I to live for myself alone, I could easily fix
my choice. But I owe too much to the opinion of the world, too much to the
authority of the father, so that—I can scarcely speak it—it affects me!'[166] What
Goldsmith values above all is 'sincerity', a word that is used twice in quick succession. When Marlow retreats in embarrassment as his misapprehensions are
made plain, Mr Hardcastle remarks, 'I'm astonished at the air of sincerity with
which he parted'.[167] In the same scene, this redeeming feature is reiterated and
associated with Miss Hardcastle when she asks of her father, 'Then what sir, if I
should convince you to your face of my sincerity?'[168] Two 'sincere' lovers ought
not be kept asunder, for if they came together redemption was nigh. As Marlow
tells his soon to be wed friend Hastings, 'I give you joy sincerely', blessing the
match with the highest praise Goldsmith could muster.[169]

The debate in drama thus revolved around how social rank related to true
sentiments with Macklin's concern for decorum set against Goldsmith's high

valuation of sincerity. Just as this subgenre of drama, concerned with the connection and contradiction between individual sentiments and social manners, intruded into the broader traditions of Irish theatrical composition, so too Ireland leached into these comedies of manners. Goldsmith's plot for *She Stoops to Conquer* apparently draws on a youthful blunder made at the house of the Featherstone family in Longford, and the dilemmas of behaviour generated by the distance between Anglicised travellers and their Gaelic hosts.[170] Equally, in making a hero of a stage Irishman, Macklin dramatized the condition of the Irish adventurer in England.[171] In both texts, Ireland is a signifier for a cultural anxiety about the difficulty of managing social order; just as from a different direction, Frances Sheridan and Hugh Kelly had used the genre of the novel to interrogate the question of good government.[172]

In this, the novels and sentiment and comedies of manners parallel on a microcosmic level some of the questions of trust that inflect the legal and historical writings of the period. From the 1760s to the 1780s, therefore, as the Irish state became more potent, the culture that it oversaw became increasingly concerned with the question of trust. It was a question with a stark political resonance, which was to become increasingly apparent as the issue of Catholic relief from penal impositions became kinetic in the late 1770s.

Languages of the Political Enlightenment

The ancien régime political ideal saw the four languages of law, history, sentiment, and manners combining in a holistic vision of human society, and each of the four concerns generated distinct genres of literature. The legal treatise burgeoned in the third quarter of the century, with its formal philosophical treatment of the occasional decisions of lawmakers, and its systematisation and standardisation of the accumulated determinations of society concerning good behaviour. So too the period saw an explosion in historical writing, from regional antiquarianism, concerned with the history of counties or towns, to the collation of threads of evidence—treatises on coins, household objects, or architecture—to grand narratives of reigns, epochs, or societies. Similarly, individual sentiments were explored in the new bloom, the novel, which provided space for the explication of individual viewpoints and offered meditations on how to moderate, manage, and govern disruptive desires. The delineation and deceptive capacity of social manners was a feature of late eighteenth-century drama, high-lighting the hypocrite, decrying the dissembler, and capturing the charlatan.

Ireland produced work in all these fields, attempting to comprehend the historical development of the community and the individual's role within it. The problem not only informed the writing of jurisprudence and antiquarianism, it simultaneously leached into such imaginative genres as novels of sentiment and comedies of manners. This was a consequence of how the Irish circumstance was profoundly complicated by the religious divisions within the population, and the way the confessional demography shaped the relationship between the individual, the society, and the state. In a successful system, law, history, sentiment, and manners acted in concert, with rationalism and empiricism working in harmony. The dilemma was that in Ireland the sentiments of the avowedly Anglican legislators were not in alignment with the manners of the predominantly Catholic people; a fact which heightened the politicisation of these modes of cultural production as writers struggled to integrate diverse elements into a holistic vision of the Irish condition.

This conflict was exacerbated by the improved condition of the state's finances in the 1750s, and the trend towards greater engagement by the British administration, culminating in the permanent presence of the viceroy from Lord Townsend in 1767 onwards.[173] This prompted a reaction within the Irish political nation, which resorted to the Patriots' language of opposition as they were increasingly deprived of the spoils of office and the power of patronage. They were also able to draw upon support out-of-doors constitutive of a political public sphere.

In each of the four languages of the late Irish Enlightenment, these political trends and tensions were sublimated into creative utterance. Yet the central issue remained unaddressed until the Catholic question came sharply into focus in the 1770s, as Ireland's political leadership struggled to claw back some of the power it had lost in the 1750s and 1760s and as Ireland's relationship with Britain and the state's relationship to its populace were redesigned. The last quarter of the eighteenth century saw numerous attempts to resolve this dilemma on amicable grounds. It was only in the 1790s, with the radicalisation of Irish society, the conflict irredeemably moved towards a violent conclusion.

8

Fracturing the Irish Enlightenment

∾

Who would make slavery the shield of Protestantism?
—Peter Burrowes, *Plain Arguments*, 1784

THE REFORM of the franchise stumbled to its death. It ended ignominiously, with the decision by the House of Commons, 158 votes to 49, not to discuss the matter.[1] Tabled by Henry Flood, an eighteen-point plan to reinvigorate the constitution of the country drafted by the Grand National Convention of Volunteers was, under the guiding hand of Chief Secretary Thomas Pelham, refused an airing in parliament in the early hours of 30 November 1783, on the grounds that it had originated in an armed assembly.

The vote made public a split in a broad reform movement that within parliament was articulated by the Patriot party and was embodied by the Volunteers in the country beyond. The issue of the franchise was a proxy for a debate within the reform movement about how far the polity ought to integrate the Catholic community that had been excluded since the War of the Two Kings (1688–1691). The fracture that was exposed was between rationalist thinkers who wished to extend the franchise to Catholics and those of an empirical bent who sought to stabilise the Protestant polity as it was then established.

The reform movement broke asunder, in other words, over how to integrate the sentiments of the legislators with the manners of the people. As the previous chapter explored, the ideal was for the two to act in harmony, with state legislation being drafted in accord with the habits and prejudices of the populace; Ireland, however, did not chime with this ambition because the legislators were predominantly Anglican, while the people were typically Catholic. This confessional disjuncture made any attempt by the state to represent the people a form of legal fiction and generated the gap in which reforming ambitions were articulated. Those who favoured Catholic relief wanted the law to better reflect the people; those who rejected it thought the manners of the people ought to mirror the confessional identity of the state.

As this chapter will document the attempt by the Volunteers to speak for the Irish nation as a whole failed when the matter of Catholic relief polarised views. The rationalists campaigned for an alteration in the state while the empiricists sought to maintain the status quo. This disagreement about the ambitions of the Volunteer movement was articulated through two modes of political rhetoric. The rationalists tended to adopt a commercial republicanism that favoured free trade and understood politics as an articulation of natural rights inherently held by humanity; the empiricists in contrast relied on a classical republicanism which despised luxury and viewed political power as a consequence of positive grants of privilege to loyal citizens.[2]

Despite the tensions within the Volunteers, the auguries for reform in 1783 had been propitious. The National Convention was held in the immediate aftermath of a sequence of successes for the Patriot party over the Dublin Castle administration. With the backing of the Volunteers, the Patriots had argued successfully for a Free Trade Act in 1779 and, in 1782, under the leadership of Henry Grattan and Henry Flood, the parliament had removed the Declaratory Act of 1720 and amended Poynings's Law of 1494. This 'constitutional revolution' established some limited autonomy for the Irish parliament within the British imperial system, allowing parliamentarians to initiate legislation and removing the veto previously held by the British Privy Council over Irish domestic policy. When the third Dungannon Convention met on 8 September 1783 it was thought that a fresh opportunity had arisen to review the internal workings of the Irish political system, freed from the restrictions imposed by the British administration. While the intention was 'that a committee (of five persons from each county) be now chosen (by ballot) to represent his province in a Grand National Convention, to be held at noon in the Royal Exchange of Dublin, on the twelfth day of November next', the response was so overwhelming that it was necessary to remove to the Rotunda as delegates swamped the location.[3] Amongst their number were fifty-nine MPs and six peers.[4]

The provincial meetings which were convened in preparation of the convention expressly supported a fundamental reform of the franchise. The gathering in Ballinasloe of the Connaught Volunteers committed itself 'to persevere to the utmost of our power to obtain a parliamentary reform' while that at Waterford, at which Munster regiments met, asserted that 'when abuse of representation has deprived the people of their share of the legislature they have a right to demand of parliament a reform of such abuse and to restore to the constitution its true balance and original purity', before adding tersely: 'resolved unanimously, that the present state of the representation of this kingdom evinces such abuses.'[5]

The Leinster meeting went further. While they agreed with the other meetings that reform was needed, not every delegate left it to the National Convention to dictate the content of any necessary alterations. Peter Burrowes, a Dublin lawyer and a delegate from the Irish Brigade, 'called the attention of the assembly to the rights of the Roman Catholics of this kingdom'.[6] In a lengthy intervention, he argued not for a return to the 'original purity' of an ancient constitution, but for a refashioning of the Anglican nature of the state. Instead of arguing on grounds of religious tolerance, he asked, 'Was the right of election to be decided by numbers or by property?' Tactically rejecting the first option as giving 'the right of election to the mob', he then observed how even on more limited grounds, the Catholic community was entitled to consideration, for 'the Roman Catholics now had a property in the kingdom, and a power of acquiring more'.[7] On this basis he moved 'that the attachment to the rights of the constitution, manifested by the Roman Catholics, merited some extension of the election franchise to that respectable body'.[8] Carefully chosen though his terms of reference were, Burrowes had overestimated the dynamic of reforming zeal in the chamber. Opposition was voiced to his proposition on the grounds that instructions over the matter had not been issued to the delegates by the regiments, and that the content of the reforms should be deferred to the National Convention. Burrowes demurred and withdrew his motion, 'as he wished for unanimity in everything.'[9]

This retreat foreshadowed events in the Grand National Convention, for it was quickly apparent that the delegates had little appetite for Catholic relief.[10] It was with relief that they latched upon the spoiling tactics of George Ogle, who on the second day informed 'the Convention that he had received a letter from a Roman Catholic peer'—the implication was that it was the influential Valentine Browne, Viscount Kenmare—'expressive of the sentiments of the Roman Catholics in general; and that they had relinquished the idea of making any claim further than the religious liberty they already enjoyed, through the lenity and goodness of the legislature'.[11] Although this assertion was met with astonishment and disbelief by many of the delegates—Counsellor Blosset protested that 'I have the honour of being a member of the most respectable Roman Catholic corps in this kingdom . . . In the county of Galway the number of Roman Catholics preponderate more than in any other county, and I assert that it is not their wish to remain in their unfranchised state'—it provided a pretext for the convention to shelve a divisive issue.[12] This determination survived an appeal for the matter to be reopened by a meeting of the Catholic Committee, which denied all knowledge of Ogle's communication and claimed that the convention had been led astray by a tactical ploy. Flood, rather disingenuously, regretted how 'time might not have been lost in fighting with phantoms'.[13]

While the question of Catholic relief which had divided the Volunteers throughout their existence was thus deflected, the matter of constitutional reform remained to be determined. Here too, those who looked to the convention for a fundamental alteration were outmanoeuvred. Giving responsibility for drafting the plan of reform to a subcommittee on which the moderate Flood was influential, the radical Volunteers, headed by the colourful Earl-Bishop Frederick Hervey (4th Earl of Bristol and bishop of Derry), were unable to get their ideas onto the floor of the convention proper. What emerged from the committee, and was adopted by the National Convention, was a plan of reform drafted largely by Flood that explicitly limited the franchise to 'every Protestant in every city, town, borough or manor (not decayed) seized of a freehold within the precincts' and to 'any Protestant possessed of a leasehold interest in any city, town, borough or manor (not decayed) . . . of the clear yearly value of ten pounds, which at its original creation was for thirty-one years, or upwards'.[14] Other, more general reforms included measures against absentee voters, resolutions against the abuse of pension lists and patronage, and restriction of the duration of parliament to three years.[15] The limited temper of these measures was made apparent when it was expressed 'that it is the opinion of this committee that all suffrages be given *viva voce*, and not by ballot', overturning the traditional mechanism used by Volunteer regiments in selecting their officers in favour of a method associated with maintaining landowners' influence over their tenant electors. But not all the resolutions conferred power on the bastion of the Irish polity, for in resolving that 'all decayed, mean and depopulated cities, towns, boroughs and manors, which have hitherto returned members to serve in parliament, by an extension of the franchise to the neighbouring barony or baronies, parish or parishes, be enabled to return representatives agreeable to the principles of the constitution' the opportunity was provided for the convention, under the guise of restoring the spirit of the ancient constitution, to produce evidence of patriotic sacrifice.[16] The self-denying quality to this ordinance was illustrated by Lord Charlemont, who from the chair of the convention averred:

> Though his attendance on the Grand Convention might be sufficient
> to manifest his disposition in favour of a reform, and though he had
> always held the patronage of a borough in trust for his country, and
> had only returned such men as he thought most capable of serving it,
> yet he would now most willingly relinquish it, and not one act of his
> life ever gave him half so much pleasure.[17]

Sir Vesey Colclough concurred, although he rather spoiled the effect by hoping he would be reimbursed for his loss of property in the franchise:

> I have the honour, for the fourth time, to be returned for one of the
> most independent, popular, and respectable counties in this kingdom.
> I have ever held it as a principle of my political creed, to obey
> faithfully the instructions of my constituents. They, Sir, desire that
> retribution should be made to the holders of boroughs. Every person
> who knows me, knows how little estimation money is in my sight;
> and as I never considered it in the common transactions of private
> life, I cannot be thought to bring it in competition of the general and
> real welfare of my country . . . And if here or elsewhere I should
> appear for retribution, believe me, Sir, that though my voice if for it,
> my heart is against it.[18]

The essence of this debate did not concern property rights, however, although the convention's vote of thanks suggested that what had occurred was a 'generous sacrifice of private property at the altar of public virtue'.[19] The underlying tension was between the claim to loyalty made by the state and that made by the people. If the first was preeminent, there was either no need for the gesture of relinquishing influence in the boroughs, or the patron should indeed be properly reimbursed for his loss. If, however, the real basis of political legitimacy was the people, the gesture was not empty, but nor should it be rewarded. It was a matter of doing what was right and necessary to bring the constitution to its senses. In fact, this decision was vital, for it was the claim of the Grand National Convention that it was a finer representation of the wishes of the people than the corrupt parliament that sat in session across the river Liffey at College Green. And by prompting peers and commoners to act on that understanding it was offering itself as an alternative source of legitimate power in the realm.

Yet precisely because it had MPs within its membership, the contest could be determined by the decisions of certain personifications of the problem. William Brownlow, MP for County Armagh, found his loyalties torn, but sided with the National Convention averring, 'I have neglected my attendance in the House of Commons, merely to do my duty here, and am on that account held as a delinquent, and ordered into the custody of the Serjeant of arms'; similarly,

> the Earl of Bristol, Mr Warburton, Sir Edward Newenham and Mr Edgeworth, who contended that their first duty should be their attendance on a Convention to which they had been delegated by the real voice of the people; [argued] their attendance in the House of Commons was but a secondary consideration.[20]

The ultimate sanction to the National Convention's work was to walk away and rejoin the parliament, as occurred when the issue of the reduction of the length of parliament arose in debate, and

> Mr George Ogle said he was an advocate for the octennial bill, that he had not received the instructions of his constituents (the freeholders of the county of Wexford)—that he thought he had no right to vote on this question till he received their instructions, and should retire till the question was disposed of. Four or five members of parliament, upon the same principle, followed him.[21]

There were also some gestures towards striking a diplomatic balance; as Christopher Lyster, delegate for County Roscommon, explained when arguing about the exclusion of revenue officers from the franchise, 'he conceived that that meeting was not convened for the purpose of disqualification'—itself a revealing resume of what the convention deemed to be its purpose—'it was their business to draw the great outlines of a reform, but to leave the investigation and the arrangement of the minuter parts to another assembly.'[22] In this, the National Convention was committing itself to a rationalist mode of proceeding, leaving the empirical practice to the House of Commons; a decision also evident in

Flood's assertion that 'it is better for the Convention to adopt a general plan for the whole kingdom at present, a general principle'.[23]

Flood's optimism that the convention could monitor the passage of a reform bill through the Irish parliament by supplying 'a resident committee of delegates to attend its progress' proved foolish for the plan of reform never got that far.[24] The final contest over the supremacy of the two assemblies was not fought on the floor of the convention, but on that of the House of Commons. Despite reservations about the timing of the action, late in the evening of 29 November 1783 Flood and the other MPs in the convention attended parliament and presented the plan of reform. Yet the House of Commons peremptorily refused to discuss the matter, dismissing the convention as a sham assembly.[25]Although Flood reintroduced the reform bill in March 1784, hoping that a different context might allow the parliament to consider the measures afresh, that effort too was frustrated, going down by 159 votes to 85.[26] Reform had its limits and the problem of combining the sentiments of the legislators with the manners of the people remained unresolved.

Conventions and Conviviality

As the events in Dungannon in February 1782 indicate, the Grand National Convention was not the first time that the Volunteers had gathered in public. The Volunteers were initially a defence force, designed to thwart the imperial ambitions of absolutist France and its confederal ally, America.[27] It became a pressure group arguing for the reshaping of the administrative context of the state and the political culture of the people. In this process the Volunteers became addicted to conventions as a means of conducting their business, with units repeatedly sending delegates to provincial meetings to debate and deliberate.

Indeed, the name of the site of the Ulster meeting—the town of Dungannon— became a signifier for a kind of reforming attitude, and for an aggressively assertive politics; the result of three provincial meetings of Ulster Volunteer delegates held in the Presbyterian meetinghouse there. The first convention, held on 15 February 1782, received representation from 143 companies (there were around 400 in Ulster at the time).[28] The second, hastily arranged for 21 June 1782 in the wake of the constitutional revolution, represented 306 regiments, while the third, which opened on 8 September 1783, a vigorous rebuttal of the quiescence of the second, attracted delegates from 272 companies, drawing particularly from Antrim and Londonderry, which sent representatives from almost all companies. In contrast, Fermanagh sent delegates from only eight companies and Cavan from four.[29]

The purpose of these assemblies was to draft resolutions concerning the affairs of the nation. Alongside a statement concerning Catholic relief, the first event denounced the use of Poynings's law to block the parliament's desires and the British claim to legislative sovereignty over the country, asserted the need for free trade and an independent judiciary, and proclaimed that the Volunteers had a right to intervene in political debates.[30] The second adopted a draft acceptance of the constitutional settlement; while the third decided to campaign for annual parliaments, election by secret ballot, abolition of rotten boroughs, and the extension of the franchise, calling for a national Volunteer convention to meet in Dublin in November 1783.[31]

Yet the effect was not merely to forward a set of political ambitions. The conventions provided a mechanism for the Volunteer movement to coordinate its actions on a provincial level and provided a counterweight to the decidedly localist character of many of the units. The meetings permitted sociability and fraternisation across the regiments—if only at the personal level of the delegates—generating wider camaraderie and a sense of affiliation. Moreover, the resolutions and the resulting publicity created a public persona for the Volunteers and added gravitas to the act of joining their ranks. To commit yourself to their cause was to confirm your determination to defend and restore the liberties of the country and, more controversially, reform the constitution. This had its limits: while Catholics were slowly entering the Volunteer ranks, there were none present at any of the conventions.

These large-scale deliberative meetings were not the only way the Volunteers displayed their commitment in public.[32] Units regularly gathered at an Anglican Church or Presbyterian meetinghouse to receive admonition and encouragement while displaying their Christian ethics and military order. The incongruous nature of these occasions, in which a paramilitary movement received the blessing of a minister of the church, was oftentimes acknowledged by the preacher, as when Samuel Butler of the prestigious St Michan's parish in Dublin averred, 'In truth, to insinuate the incompatibility of the duties of war and religion, approaches nearly to blasphemy'.[33] Discussing Nehemiah 4.14, 'Be not afraid of them: remember the Lord which is great and terrible, and fight for your brethren, your sons and your daughters, your wives and your houses', he argued, 'a man may be enlisted at once under the banners of Christ and the banners of his country; stand forth in the field to defend all that is dear to him on earth, and in the service of the Lord of Heaven, who will be his strength, and cover his head in the day of battle.'[34] Far from criticising the men in uniform, he castigated those who resisted their allure. 'But how dare any young man', he fulminated, 'in the vigour of life, presume to partake of the benefits of society and decline joining in the defence of it; hugging himself up in his prudence, good sense, economy, and I know not what other names he is complacent enough to give his real cowardice and want of spirit'.[35]

A similar note was struck by the Presbyterian minister William Steel Dickson when preaching to the Echlinville Volunteers, County Down, on the same verse of scripture chosen by Butler.[36] 'Thank God', he prayed, 'wide as corruption hath spread her baneful flood, the spirit of the nation is not quite overwhelmed! The numerous associations which have been formed through the kingdom, and trained to the use of arms, afford so many examples of prevailing patriotism'.[37] The cause of this corruption he located, in line with the tropes of classical republicanism, in the decadence inherent in commercial gain. In contradistinction to the siren call of abundance and leisure, he recalled his audience to the virtuous circles of affection. 'As men', he reminded them,

> we have rights and privileges, wives and children; as members of
> society we have a country and brethren; and as Christians, a God,
> who is great and terrible, whom we ought to remember, and a
> religion, which we owe to his goodness, by which we hope to be
> saved. These are the only valuable concerns in human life.[38]

The defence of these connections was the purpose and pleasure of Volunteering, 'designs' which he thought 'correspond with the great purposes of providence'.[39]

Andrew Alexander, a New Light Presbyterian, concurred.[40] In preaching to four Strabane corps—itself evidence of the role of the sermon in generating sociable fraternity within the Volunteers—he argued in accordance with classical republicanism's argumentative line that the corroding effect of luxury in modern commercial society could be corrected by Volunteering, explaining optimistically that the time involved 'is only a relaxation for youth from their usual occupations, to which, it is well known they return with fresh pleasure and keenness.'[41] While he admitted 'young men are too prone to spend [vacant hours] in idleness, perhaps in guilty pursuits, where a taste for arms prevails among them, [they] are usually employed in improving and perfecting themselves in the military art; and this in place of corrupting, tends to improve their morals.'[42]

Thomas Drought agreed heartily with this assessment of the social and moral consequences of Volunteering, and dismissed the economic argument marshalled against the movement. He observed with pride how

> everybody is so inquisitive into the designs and intentions of Ireland,
> that young persons, who are not lost to all sense of honour and public
> spirit, quit the roads of dissipation, adventure and gambling; and
> instead of being the nuisance and terror of English families, their
> company is sought for and respected.[43]

So too Francis Dobbs ventured 'to assert that there is not a poor man in the kingdom the poorer for being a Volunteer. The exercise of arms becomes his recreation. He substitutes it in place of cockfighting, horse racing and the various amusements to which he was formerly addicted, and finds a saving in the change.'[44]

Not everyone was so convinced of the social benefits of the movement, however. The social mixing that occurred within a Volunteer unit—in which the tenant and the landlord appeared in a shared uniform—caused some consternation in a hierarchical society. Uniforms gave, critics fretted, a veneer of respectability to dubious characters who might abuse the admiration the movement enjoyed. Amyas Griffith, for instance, wrote in appalled tone of how

> the Ladies are ruined by this unlucky spirit's prevailing: for, as the
> gentlemen of the army were the chief objects of their attentions, it
> may happen now that in walking, or in public meetings, Miss may be
> engaged in small chat with a good military cobbler, in regimentals,
> whom the dear innocent had taken for a major, and whom she would
> not so much as look at, were he not *en garb militaire* from head to
> foot. It is really astonishing to see quondam ragged wretches, who
> would formerly no more wear ruffles and cue-wigs, than they'd wear
> halters, now strutting in regimentals, sword or bayonet, tailed wig,
> edged ruffles.[45]

The social kudos of donning a dashing uniform, signifying one's bravery and patriotism, was clearly an attraction; the admiration of women and elders was an additional desideratum. The Volunteers spent a lot of their inventive energy on their insignia, their equipment, and their flags. The last of these items held

special affection in the heart of a regiment, for it was the symbol of the individual unit's existence and character, and was the centrepiece of many of the
social functions in which the Volunteers publicly stated their patriotism and
garnered social approbation. It was a common occurrence for a local beauty, or
the wife of a local notable, to be honoured with the task of presenting the flag
to the regiment, as when 'at a meeting of the True Blue Horse, August 1st, 1782,'
it was 'resolved that our thanks of this corps be given to Mrs Monsell for the
elegant standard presented by her to them this day.'[46]

A similar set of ambitions inform the attention lavished on their uniforms.[47]
Units made careful choices concerning the colour of the two sides of their
jackets, the cut of their helmet, and the decorations that would adorn their belts
and weapons.[48] Indeed, as a complaint in the *Londonderry Journal* on 20 August
1779 had it, a number of units managed to commission their uniforms but not
their weapons: 'Is it not incumbent on those gentlemen who are their officers,
who really wish these people to be serviceable', the writer inquired, 'to relieve
them from such a ridiculous predicament, and exert their influence towards
procuring them guns?'[49] In the Grand National Convention, the matter of the
appearance of delegates was taken so seriously that one representative, Mr
Cullen, 'was going to speak but, not being in his uniform, would not be heard.'[50]

The politics of appearance culminated in the mustering of troops, usually for
inspection by an officer. John Moore described to Arthur Annesley on 14 August
1780 his recollection of a recent event in Downpatrick:

> We had twenty-one companies reviewed two days ago near Downe,
> making a body of about 1,800 men. Their entire performance was
> infinitely superior to what I expected or indeed . . . conceived
> possible: the men in general young and handsome, and their appoint-
> ments much more expensive than the regulars.
>
> On each day after the review was over the troops rested for over
> about an hour when a detachment of 400 men was thrown into the
> old abbey at Down and it was then attacked by the remainder of the
> body in three columns. On the first day after a constant fire had been
> kept up for three hours on both sides, the assailants were beat off; on
> the second day the citadel surrendered. The whole was conducted
> under the direction of two gentlemen who served in the last war and
> were chosen generals for the day. I presumed there were not fewer

than twenty thousand spectators present on these two days, and much
to the honour of the people not a single person appeared in liquor nor
did the slightest accident happen.[51]

Not every military manoeuvre was so civilised. Two weeks after Moore wrote, a
Mr Stewart reported to the Earl of Abercorn about how a reenactment of the
siege of Londonderry held in the town had dissolved into disorder. 'I understand', he explained, 'the gallant lads attacked the walls with such material ardour
that they burned the faces of their opponents, who were so much enraged, that it
was with the utmost difficulty that they were restrained from returning real shot,
and many now bear the honourable wounds of that glorious day.'[52]

Easier to effect was a simple parade, and the Volunteer calendar was peppered
with reasons to convene, march, and celebrate.[53] These events allowed units to
create a shared purpose and display to their locality their presence in the community, their military prowess, and their numerical strength.[54] It was also a chance
to dress up and show off in public. This practice culminated at the Grand
National Convention, when the need to move out of the Royal Exchange became
apparent: 'They then walked in procession through the ranks of the Volunteers of
the city and county, who lined the streets and received the delegates who presented arms and colours flying, and proceeded amidst the acclamations of many
thousands of admiring spectators to the Rotunda.'[55] Such public events were in
contrast to the intimate social gathering of Volunteers in taverns and ale houses
that percolated through the movement's existence, in which boisterous evenings
often culminated in the proposing of numerous toasts that blended alcoholic
inebriation, fraternal bonding, and political exhilaration.[56] On 1 August 1778, for
instance, the Londonderry Independent Volunteers and the Derry Fusiliers
held a dinner in which the toasts included, in a list of twenty-five, 'King and
Constitution', 'the representatives of Derry and success to them in their intended
opposition to the popery bill', 'a free trade to Ireland' and 'the supporters of the
Irish bills in the British House of Commons'.[57]

As all of this celebratory activity suggests, the incentive to join in the
Volunteers was as much to cut a dash as it was to defend the nation.[58] The fun
of appearing in uniform at a ball, of impressing women with one's commitment
to patriotic ideals, and of having the chance to decamp to a tavern with friends
were motivating factors that had little to do with the potential to do battle with
possible enemies. This intimate connection to the practices of sociability is

highlighted by the pattern of clubs and associations either joining en masse or making available the location for Volunteer meetings to occur. For example,

> at a meeting of the Gentlemen of Ballymoe Club, at the Club-room
> at Ballymoe in the County of Galway on Wednesday the 22nd of
> September 1779, Sir John Burke, Bart, in the chair resolved that those
> men who have already frequently assembled at Glinsk, and voluntarily
> offered their service for the protection of their King and Country, be
> forthwith embodied under the title of the Glinsk Loyalists, and be
> formed into eight companies, of thirty privates each, with one troop
> of light horse.[59]

The Volunteers thus depended on, and emerged out of the array of practices of sociability that had shaped the Social Enlightenment. They provided a mechanism for the associational life of the country to offer itself in defence of the nation.[60] In that, they could claim their activism was a product of civil society— it was this understanding that ensured they maintained a sturdy independence when offered the chance to gain state commissions in the militia.[61] Indeed, Francis Dobbs was ignominiously turned away from the Dungannon Convention in September 1783 precisely because he had availed of just such an opportunity.[62] This paramilitary circumstance and independent status—both closely guarded— provided them with the chance to claim that they, and not a state they repeatedly denounced as malformed, spoke on behalf of the people.[63] In the tension that was shaping the cultural life of the country, between the sentiments of the legislators and the manners of the people, the Volunteers claimed to be against the former and for the latter. The only difficulty was how to determine the content of that most ambiguous of terms, 'the people', implicit in which was the need to resolve how the majority Catholic population might be incorporated into the workings of the Anglican state.

Enacting Reform

The atmosphere was changing. The mid-1760s saw a rearticulation of the penal code's provisions for the conversion of Catholicism, and a hardening of attitudes among Anglicans in defence of their status. In 1758 there was a revival of the incentive to convert, which had gone into abeyance in 1716—with the state offering Catholic clergy £30 for their compliance; an act which was renewed in 1772, with the incentive then rising to £40 per annum. Yet in the decade after its reentry on the statue book, only seventeen clerics were entered on the convert rolls; only the act's renewal in 1769 seems to have prompted anything like a flurry, with six names noted that year.[64] The Catholic community was not as quiescent as it once had been, however.[65] The pressure of economic upheaval prompted a spate of agrarian outrages under the nomenclature of the Whiteboys. While this could be read as a continuing echo of the confessional conflicts of the 1690s, it could just as easily be comprehended through the prism of a moral economy.[66] In an urban setting, moreover, self-assurance was also burgeoning, with a campaign for the privileges of quarterage to be extended to Catholic merchants gaining ground. So while Catholics were still anxious to secure their land tenure through registering conversion, they were not as compliant or publically cautious as before. Yet the Catholic community was now openly avowing its position in society as a commercially successful, competent, and confident component of Irish life.[67]

Catholic middlemen were increasingly given to social display and activism.[68] Nowhere was this more the case than in the mixed territory of Cork—where Protestant enclaves and Catholic bastions delineated a confessionally divided landscape. This performativity was to have tragic consequences on occasion, as documented in the elegiac and angry *Lament for Art O'Leary*, for it was O'Leary's confidence that caught the eye of Eibhlín Dubh Ní Chonaill. Witnessing him promenading after his return from the Continent, her heart was captured, and she married him in 1767. She was smitten by his flamboyance, and erotically charged by his fearlessness:

> Mo ghrá go daingean tú,
> Agus nuair théiteá sna cathracha
> Daora daingeana,
> Bhíodh mná ceannaithe
> Ag umhlú go talamh duit,
> Óir do thuigidís ina n-aigne
> Gur bhreá an leath leapa tú
> Nó béalóg chapaill tú[69]

> Husband,
> when you rode your gallantry

into a fortress town
the shopkeepers' wives
in their frippery
would practically fall over.
They could see as well as I
what their husbands could never,
that you'd be a masterful lover
with the reins in your hands,
leading them on through secret thickets
into the wild country.[70]

O'Leary, in his vitality, presented a fresh, optimistic, outlook for the Irish polity, one in which cross-confessional cooperation was a viable option. In that, he represented a possible outcome of the Social Enlightenment's experiment in mutual toleration.

Yet, as Eibhlín Dubh Ní Chonaill recognised, this display made O'Leary a target for the resentment and fear of others. It was a feud with a Protestant neighbour that resulted in his untimely demise, prompted by racing, and a mix of social and sexual jealousy.[71] The immediate cause was the resuscitation of the penal code. O'Leary's neighbour and a member of the influential Shannon political interest, Abraham Morris had given him a mocking offer of the requisite fee of 5l.5d for O'Leary's horse. Refusing to part with his steed, the encounter turned violent, when one of Morris's servants fired a gun at O'Leary. He duly disarmed the servant, but holding a gun, let alone one stolen from a Protestant, was a further criminal act. Morris, working under the umbrella of the Muskerry Constitutional Society, then lodged bills of indictment to the Munster assizes, but they were not forwarded to the Grand Jury and were therefore notionally held back under the assize of March 1772. At no point in fact did the threat of prosecution materialise. Instead, two years after this incident—in 1773—O'Leary, living under the permanent threat of prosecution from his avowed enemy, decided to end the matter. Riding forth to hunt down and kill Morris, O'Leary was ambushed by Morris's men. Distraught and forlorn, Ní Chonaill turned her vitriol into impassioned invective, destroying Morris rhetorically:

Órrú a *Mhorrison* léan ort!
Fuil do chroí agus t'ae leat!
Do shúile caochta,

Do ghlúine réabtha,
Do mhairbh mo laosa,
Agus gan aon fhear in Éirinn
Do ghreadfadh na piléir leat![72]

Morris, you treacherous lout,
I hope your body will suffer
a thousand wounds even worse
than your wounding of Art.
I hope your liver shrivels
and your blood congeals,
your eyeballs itch
and your kneecaps split asunder.
You have taken my husband from me
and I see no one in Ireland
with the guts to make you pay.[73]

But here the keen took an unusual twist, for in seeking revenge, she did not imagine turning to her immediate family, as she had fallen out with them over the marriage to her reckless lover. Instead, she dreamt of taking her complaint to the monarch, George III:

Tá fhios ag Íosa Críost
Nách mbeidh caidhp ar bhaitheas mo chinn
Ná léine chnis lem thaoibh
Ná bróg ar thrácht mo bhoinn
Ná trioscán ar fuaid mo thí
Ná srian leis an láir ndoinn
Ná go gcaithfead féin le dlí,
Is go rachad anonn tar toinn
Ag comhrá leis an rí,
Is mura gcuirfidh ionam aon tsuim,
Go dtiocfad tar n-ais arís
Go bodach na fola duibhe
A bhain díom féin mo mhaoin.[74]

God knows, the very cap on my head,
the silk on my thigh,

the buckle on my shoe,
the sheets in my bed
and the brown mare's bridle —
I will spend the lot,
if I have to, at law,
and I will sail across the sea
to make my case to the King.[75]

This turn towards the established authorities was twinned to disaffection with
the old verities, for Ní Chonaill also disavowed the Catholic Church. She dis-
dainfully recalled how, upon finding the body of her husband:

Gan pápa gan easpag,
Gan cléireach gan sagart,
A léifeadh ort an tsailm,
Ach seanbhean chríonna chaite
A leath ort binn dá fallaing[76]

No priest was on hand
to whisper prayers,
no monk to sing your praises,
only a dry-eyes, sorry old woman
to throw a bare coat over you.[77]

Her grief acute, her anger embittering and eloquent, Ní Chonaill's *Lament*
speaks of two conflicting narratives of interconfessional relationships in the early
1770s. On the one hand, the immediate context of its composition and utterance is evidence of a hardening of attitudes, a part of the reflexive retreat into
confessional camps that the Whiteboy agitation of the late 1760s sparked and
promoted. The *Lament* is informed by fear and by anger. Yet in the failure to
bring O'Leary before a court of law—despite the charges being levelled—Morris
was implicitly accepting that the anti-Catholic vendetta on which he had
embarked might not receive the legal sanction required to bring his malice to
fruition.[78] So too, it marks a shift in Catholic perceptions of their condition.
The confidence and pride O'Leary emitted in his public persona may well
have discommoded Morris, but it was a personification of the possibilities for
social advancement opening to Catholics in the country. So also, Ní Chonaill's
reaction—to reject her social connections and her confessional identity and

instead petition the king to whom Morris might have expected to have sole claim—was indicative of a shift in the register of the relationship between the Catholic community and the Irish Hanoverian state.

This trend towards practical coexistence was formalised in 1774 when, after a lengthy campaign and proposals dating back to the 1720s, an oath of allegiance was finally formulated that was broadly acceptable to the Catholic community. Articulating a desire to 'promote peace and industry among the inhabitants', the act was intended 'to enable his Majesty's Subjects of whatever persuasion to testify their allegiance to him'.[79] Drawn up by antiquarian and Catholic Committee activist Charles O'Conor and amended by the Anglican Earl-Bishop, Frederick Hervey, the motives behind the declaration were various. To O'Conor, it articulated loyalty to Hanover and disabused Protestants of any scaremongering concerning the political consequences of Catholic religious tenets. Hervey's ambitions, in contrast, lay in dissecting the Catholic community between Gallicans, with whom he could treat, and Romanists, who he believed should remain resolutely outside the domain of political life.[80] Proposed in the House of Commons by the independent-minded member for Roscommon, John French, the act stipulated that to receive recognition by the state Catholics would declare:

> I, A. B., do take Almighty God and his only Son Jesus Christ my Redeemer to witness that I will be faithful and bear true allegiance to our most gracious sovereign lord, King George the third, and him will defend to the utmost of my power against all conspiracies and attempts whatsoever, that shall be made against his person, crown and dignity; and I will do my utmost endeavour to disclose and make known to his majesty, and his heirs, all treasons and traitorous conspiracies, which may be formed against him or them; and I do faithfully promise to maintain, support and defend, to the utmost of my power, the succession of the crown in his majesty's family against any person or persons whatsoever.[81]

This oath was of crucial importance to a self-consciously Anglican state faced with a Catholic majority, serving as the first breach in the barricades erected after the War of the Two Kings. It positioned the Catholic community to accept the status quo that had emerged. It constituted a political abjuration of the Jacobite claim to the British multiple monarchy; a renunciation that echoed the 1766 decision of the pope not to recognise Charles III as a legitimate claimant after the death of his father, James III. That allowed the Catholic constituency in Ireland to discard the Jacobite court by 'utterly renouncing and abjuring any obedience or allegiance unto the person taking upon himself the style and title of prince of Wales in the lifetime of his father and who since his death is said to have assumed the style and title of king of Great Britain and Ireland by the name of Charles the third'.[82] In this, the oath enabled the Catholic community to find a form of legitimacy for the public articulation of their faith under the auspices of an Anglican state.

While the Catholic hierarchy in Munster broadly backed the idea and welcomed its success, and a contemporary estimate suggested that by 1780 some 6,500 Catholics had subscribed to the declaration, not everyone was content.[83] In particular, a number of the bishops in Leinster were uncomfortable, in part because they had relied on the Jacobite claimant for patronage. More significantly, their discomfort was also caused by the declarations concerning doctrine. The lay origins of the oath left them anxious that a precedent was being set that would allow noncommunicants like Hervey to impose regulations, and that the hierarchical order of the Catholic Church was being undermined by figures like O'Conor.[84] This was accentuated by act's rejection of the deposing power of the pope and the assertion that 'I do not believe that the Pope of Rome or any other foreign prince, prelate, state or potentate hath or ought to have any temporal or civil jurisdiction, power, superiority, or pre-eminence, directly or indirectly, within this realm'.[85] Yet for all the distrust the oath engendered, it was the foundation for a series of measures that would ameliorate the relationship between the Catholic people and the Anglican state in the twenty years that followed its passage. In particular it effected a distinction between Catholics who discriminated between their religious affiliation and their political loyalties and to whom the state could afford some limited recognition, and 'papists' or Romanists who retained a political as well as a religious loyalty to the papacy, and whom the Irish polity continued to distrust and persecute.

These measures were set in train by the passage in 1778 of 'An Act for the Relief of his Majesty's Subjects of this Kingdom Professing the Popish Religion'. While the title of the measure reiterated the abusive term 'popish' in describing its subject, this was due to an amendment insisted upon by the British Privy Council. The first reference in the act was to 'Roman Catholics of Ireland' only reverting to the diminutive 'papist' in subsequent clauses.[86]

The preamble justified the measure through a conciliatory blend of Enlightenment empiricism and improvement ideology, hinting at a pragmatic concern over the conflict with America. It contended that 'from their [the Catholics] uniform peaceable behaviour for a long series of years, it appears reasonable and expedient to relax the same [penal laws], and it must tend not only to the cultivation and improvement of this kingdom, but to the prosperity and strength of his majesty's dominions'. Certainly the last stated element carried immense weight in prompting the measure's introduction, for Catholic Relief was to be introduced in conscious exchange for Catholic recruitment into an imperial army which was facing turbulence in North America.[87] While this parallel had to be handled sensitively, for it could be read as arming Irish Catholics to repress American Protestants, it was considered by well-wishers to be substantively different from the question of a Catholic militia as the army was to be sent abroad and was not a direct danger to the Irish polity.

However, the first two justifications in the preamble—the empirically verifiable history of quiescence and the desire for economic improvement—carried equal weight within the bill's formulation, with the second element in particular echoing the 1774 act providing a Catholic oath. This imperative was more visible in the proposed bill, which would have granted the Catholic community the right to purchase land in fee simple. That would have facilitated Catholic investment in the countryside, ensuring commercial wealth did not drain abroad, and providing secular leadership for the confession.

All of this was decidedly controversial and Prime Minister Frederick North's caution concerning the safe passage of the bill through its legislative stages was clearly indicated by the choice of the independent MP for County Dublin, Luke Gardiner, to introduce it in College Green. As with the 1774 act, the independent origin of the relief act was insisted on to avoid turning it into a party issue. Yet the bill was extensively debated in the Commons, with the result that it was effectively hamstrung. The chamber altered the terms so as to allow only a leasehold of 999 years. While this effectively ceded perpetual leaseholds on land, Catholics remained excluded from direct property ownership and hence from any claim to political rights. If, as the act proclaimed, the motive was to help the economy, the MPs clearly deemed that aim could be achieved without transforming the confessional character of the state.

The parliamentarians did give ground in relation to the first ambition—that of recognising quiescent social and civil relations since 1691—despite the provocations of repeated Jacobite risings across the Irish Sea. Whereas the penal code had intentionally disturbed Catholic family relations by providing for the removal of a recusant father by a convert son, the relief act altered the terms of legal dependency so as to normalise familial relationships.[88] Moreover, the act permitted Catholics to purchase leases and to pass them on to their eldest son, shifting the practice of inheritance from the gavelkind desired by the penal code to the primogeniture preferred in Anglican Ireland. Again, normalisation was worked towards, if not fully effected.

The stated aim of these measures was to create a material connection between the Catholic people and the Anglican state, but the consequence of the House of Commons redrafting the legal ground of possession from property to lease undermined the act's efficacy. So too, the chamber was determined to irritate the British administration. While the Westminster Parliament passing a relief act in 1778 in favour of Catholics was taken to be a sanctimonious precedent for the Irish parliament, the Irish parliament took revenge by mimicking their display of tolerance and benevolence, only shifting the subject of their attentions to the Presbyterian community. The British government did not wish to extend civic recognition to dissenters, yet the Irish relief act had a clause tacked on which proposed a repeal of the test clause of 1704 which excluded Presbyterians from civic office. The idea garnered the support of anti-Catholic MPs as a destructive rather than a constructive tactic. They believed the measure would be removed in London, and hence the bill rejected upon its return to Ireland on the grounds that the English Privy Council had tampered with it; or that the High Church bishops sitting in the Irish House of Lords would reject the bill if the clause remained. Either way, Catholic relief would be stymied.[89]

If so, the anti-Catholic MPs had their bluff called, for the English Privy Council accepted the change concerning property, but not that concerning the test clause, forcing the Irish MPs to decide how far they were prepared to lose face over a clause favouring dissenters. The decision to remove the clause also ensured that the act was now known to be of government design. This forced the Dublin Castle administration to back the bill. Yet despite the partisan nature of the proposal, the amended measure passed through the Irish parliament with barely a whisper about the alterations that had been made. Although a committee for comparison was established and the differences between the original draft and resultant measure identified, the demand for Catholic relief far outweighed the principled umbrage taken at the bill's editing and the measure was voted through by 129 votes to eight-nine in the Commons, with the upper House dividing forty-five for and twenty-nine against.[90]

The issue of relief for the dissenters did not dissipate and was revived as soon as the next session of parliament.[91] The author of the original 1778 clause, Edward Newenham, had Presbyterian sympathies, and was determined to revisit the matter.[92] Moreover, by 1779 circumstances outside parliament favoured Newenham's original idea—that of a separate measure to relieve dissenters of the burdens of the penal code. Two things had decisively shifted. First, the enthusiasm of Ulster Presbyterians for the Volunteers had made the Castle administration distinctly wary, and the relief bill was now considered a necessary sop to their sensibilities. Second, within the Anglican elite there was an emerging perception that it was invidious to have passed relief measures for Roman Catholics while fellow Protestants, however truculent and enthusiastic, remained under the code's sanction. If confessional diversity, even of a limited kind, was to be accepted, it was to be extended to dissenters within the Reformed tradition as much as to the unreformed Roman Catholic populace. When parliament reassembled on 12 October 1779, Newenham presented a bill scrapping the test clause by enacting

> that all and every person or persons, being Protestants shall and may have, hold, and enjoy any office or offices civil or military and receive any pay, salary, fee, or wages belonging to or by reason of such office or place, notwithstanding he shall not receive or have received the sacrament of the Lord's Supper.[93]

Despite continuing anxiety caused by the British administration's reluctance to grant Irish dissenters freedoms their English counterparts did not enjoy, the bill passed the Privy Council and was returned to the Irish parliament. Once there, four Anglican bishops were sufficiently angered by the measure that they registered their disapproval in the records, but the effect was negligible and the proposal received royal assent on 2 May 1780.[94]

As in the 1778 Catholic Relief Act, so in this act the target was the all-encompassing Act to Prevent the Further Growth of Popery (1704) which was steadily being unpicked. While no justification was offered for this sudden liberty—the act is extremely terse in its phrasing—the clarity of purpose was revealed in the 1782 Act for the Relief of Protestant Dissenters, which regularised the legal status of Presbyterian marriages, and hence their capacity to bequeath and inherit land.[95] It intended to provide for 'the peace and tranquillity of many Protestant dissenters and their families'; a rallying of Reformed feeling which resulted in 1784 in the raising of the *regium donum* from £2,000 to £3,000.[96] The confessional state was slowly retreating under social pressure.

Ironically, it was the 1778 Relief Act which created the context for the further grant of tolerance. Grattan and other MPs reasoned that if the government could trust Catholics, so too could the Patriots. This renewal of confidence was stated in the first Relief Act of 1782, for it declared that those who had taken the oath stipulated in 1774 'ought to be considered as good and loyal subjects to his majesty' and that 'a continuance of several of the laws formerly enacted and still in force in this kingdom, against persons professing the popish religion, is there-fore unnecessary . . . and is injurious to the real welfare and prosperity of Ireland'.[97] This view was even more pithily expressed in the second Catholic relief measure, in recognising how 'several of the laws made in this kingdom . . . are considered too severe'.[98] It was on those grounds that the subsequent 1782 acts were justified, gathering support as the Patriots were outflanked by the government allying with the Catholic voice.[99]

Again Luke Gardiner was the vehicle for the policy of Catholic relief in parliament. He proposed three distinct bills. The first permitted Catholics to hold land on the same terms as Protestants, and freed registered priests (those who took the oath of allegiance) from penal restrictions; the second allowed Catholics who had taken the oath of allegiance to act as guardians to Catholic children, and to open and teach at schools—higher education was explicitly safeguarded—as long as no Protestants attended; the last, in line with relief being granted to the Presbyterians, permitted mixed marriages. Gardiner was effecting a dramatic transformation in the state's self-understanding, positing the possibility of a rapprochement with the Catholic community it governed.

While the first two measures passed into law without significant opposition, the last proposal failed by a narrow margin to leave the House. The toleration of Catholics and their active social acceptance were still decidedly different for some parliamentarians. This sensitivity surrounding the social status of those beyond the Church of Ireland also explains one of the detailed subclauses inserted into the broad brushstroke of the first relief act, one of a number of restrictive exclusions the later clauses of the bill insisted on. Alongside stated anxieties concerning Catholic proselytisation and the presence of regular clergy (exempted from the provisions of the bill in its entirety), paragraph eight insisted

> that no benefits in this Act contained shall extend, or be construed to
> extend, to any popish ecclesiastic who shall officiate in any church or
> chapel with a steeple or bell, or at any funeral in any church or
> church-yard, or who shall exercise any of the rites or ceremonies of

the popish religion, or wear the habits of their order, save within their usual places of worship or in private homes, or who shall use any symbol or mark of ecclesiastic dignity or authority, or assume or take any ecclesiastic rank or title whatsoever, but that all the pains and penalties which now subsist according to the laws now in being, shall remain in full force against such popish ecclesiastic.[100]

It would seem that Catholicism might be tolerated, so long as it remained a private affair; the public profession of faith was still anathema. Publically accepting the practice of faiths other than that of the established Church of Ireland was yet too much for the confessional state to encompass.

Representing the People

Writing on the eve of the National Convention in Dublin, Andrew Doria asserted 'the right and competency of the people to effect' parliamentary reform.[101] This was justified by the principle that 'the aim of civil government, confessedly, is public good', and that 'the disposition of it therefore must ever be subject to the control of the people, by whose authority at first it was framed, and on whose acquiescence ultimately it relies for support'.[102] Doria was here drawing a strong distinction between the people and the state. On the first, he rested the authority for determining the nature of government: 'the legislature which in the hands that are appointed to conduct it is strictly a trust, is with the public a property, and a property is always at the disposal of the owner.'[103] The parliament, in contrast, was a mirror of the people:

> Is it not an assembly of persons nominated by the people to represent them in the Great Council of the Nation, there to express the public mind of and to act as the people themselves would act? Is it not an abstract merely from the community, which at large would be too numerous for effective deliberation?[104]

The parliamentarians were little more than delegates of the people, as a consequence of which 'representation, which is a trust, is ever in its nature responsible and the representation of a community, which is the most important of all trusts, should be called to account as frequently as is compatible with the efficient discharge of its functions.'[105] On this elaborate theoretical basis, Doria called for annual parliaments, and argued for the reconstruction of the constituency system to abolish rotten boroughs.

In doing this, the people were placed into a rationalist system of politics that was set in contradiction to what Doria perceived as a corrupted and illegitimate reality. Pitching the theory of government against the reality of governance, the latter was found wanting, for 'it is reasonable to conclude that our applauded system is perverted, that practice has been warped from theory, and that while a specious appearance is delusively preserved, the spirit, health and energy of the constitution is destroyed.'[106] History was a tale of Gothic decay and dissolution: 'Antiquity is a word of sacred use and mystical implication' he averred, 'it prevails like religion, and sanctifies contradictions.'[107] He emphasised in its stead 'the plain discernment of every man', or 'plain reason'.[108] In the conflict between the sentiments of the state and the manners of the people, the people took precedence: 'When the rights which freemen prize above existence become a question between the servants of the state and the community at large, the delegated power of the legislature is superseded, and the robe of veneration wherewith it was invested plucked away.'[109]

Francis Dobbs concurred, proclaiming that 'a free people must be their own protectors'.[110] The Volunteers were the embodiment of just such a sentiment, for in their capacity to bear arms they protected themselves from foreign and domestic despotism, and confirmed their liberties. As with Doria, Dobbs viewed government as an instrument of power, but legitimacy resided with the people:

> To the people at large I would say—'consider the knowledge of arms
> as the first and greatest of your acquisitions, your glorious constitu-
> tion is framed on that just idea that government is formed for the
> people, not the people for government. If ever you admit a power
> distinct from and superior to you, you will cease to be free.'[111]

The Volunteer movement was, in this analysis, necessary because of the failure of the state. Not just a self-defence association, they were a force for reconfiguring politics; an ambition which was justified by portraying parliament in the winter of 1781 as

> more venal than ever sat before it:—those who conducted public
> business thought only of numbers, and how to secure a majority in

the Senate—corruption on system took place, and certain obedience waited on the nod of the Minister;—but however this might suit a nation that had no military power, but was immediately under the control of government, it was ill calculated for the then state of Ireland. The people had power—had arms—and knew their use.[112]

In this dark hour the state and the people stood in opposition, and 'the just demands of the people were treated with scorn and contempt.'[113]

Given the desire that the sentiments of the legislators and the manners of the people correlate, and the assumption that the people took precedence over the polity, the intrusion of the Volunteers into parliamentary politics became necessary, justifiable, and laudatory. And when success was achieved, Dobbs made plain that what had been accomplished was a reconnection of the state with the people; a return to the natural relationship between administration and community. Of the passage of the Free Trade Act he exclaimed: 'Parliament was in rapture, the *people* were in rapture; Dublin was almost on fire; and a sort of frantic joy pervaded the nation.'[114] Recalling when the Declaratory Act had been repealed, he reminisced about how 'addresses to the Lord Lieutenant, expressing in their warmest terms their gratitude to him were voted unanimously—the nation resounded with joy and congratulation and universal happiness for once seemed to pervade a kingdom.'[115]

The harmonious connection was grounded in righteous representation and the virtue of the parliamentarian. 'A legislator', Dobbs surmised,

> should have an excellent head, and an undoubted heart: his knowledge should be extensive, and every form of government should be his study. He should have read the history of the world and minutely studied that of his own country; and the happiness and prosperity of the people should be his greatest object.
>
> But who is to judge of these qualifications? I answer the people. This leads me to that glorious constitution which we have regained, and which I also hope Ireland is to bring to its perfection.[116]

Yet despite the role of the Volunteers in effecting an alteration in the constitutional arrangements of the country, Dobbs was cautious. He issued the movement with a stern warning, admonishing that 'the Volunteers should, and I dare say will, consider that they are not the people of Ireland. Should they, because they have power, act contrary to the sense of the majority of the people, they become tyrants'.[117]

Not everyone agreed. Andrew Doria, for instance, was happy to blur any distinction between the movement and the country at large, writing:

> To the Volunteers—In addressing you I speak to the people of
> Ireland, to all the virtue, spirit, strength and independence in the
> nation. The ties which unite and the principles that actuate you,
> embrace and animate the whole community. Whatsoever of patriotism,
> whatsoever of genius, whatsoever of experience and ability this kingdom
> could produce, is leagued in you; and every lover of his country, every
> honest Irishman is in act or sentiment, a Volunteer.[118]

As a correspondent to the *Belfast News-Letter* put it in February 1782, 'the Citizen and Volunteer are not different characters, but one and the same character under different titles'.[119]

The extent to which the Volunteers could justify this claim to speak for the nation emerges from a secret assessment of the strength of the movement, taken by the Castle administration in the summer of 1784, when moves were afoot to replace the Volunteers with a government-organised militia.[120] The Volunteers were then undergoing their final spasm of expansion, under the direction of Dublin radicals desirous of organising a nonconsumption agreement to complement parliamentary reform. While the list was admittedly incomplete—'there are no returns from the counties of Monaghan, Fermanagh and Mayo' the compiler notes—the review, alongside other evidence that fills in gaps in the picture, provides a snapshot of a movement that had found resonance in every part of the country.[121]

The return estimated that there were 18,500 active Volunteers—about 2,000 of which were mounted—yet the compiler was downbeat about the likely future of the movement. It was the considered opinion that there was 'an evident decline' in the activism of the movement and its claim to loyalty.[122] This view also emerged in the comments on individual counties, where repeated reference was made to how 'these Corps are all very much on the decline' (Wexford) and that 'these corps have not been lately assembled, are supposed to be very much on the decline' (Waterford).[123] Even when dealing with the Ulster heartland, the compiler synthesised his numbers, observing 'it is generally allowed that the spirit of Volunteering has been long on the decline in many of the northern counties.' The official then adduced a cause for this collapse, namely 'the late Belfast resolutions in favour of Roman Catholics have contributed to its almost total extinction.'[124]

The return's information on Catholic involvement provided a mixed view.[125] Note was taken when Catholics were thought to be enlisted. So, 'the Raphoe battalion has a company of fifty Roman Catholics under the direction of the Revd Mr Hervey at Mullinhall', while in Carlow it was observed how 'these corps have full as many Roman Catholics as Protestants in them and one corps (Mr Cavanagh's) is entirely composed of Catholics; he is himself one.'[126] But it was also clear that their presence in the ranks was not always met with approbation by Protestant comrades. Tensions became apparent, as when 'the Royal Boyle Protestants actually refused the Barrony Cohort Catholics to pass through the town of Boyle with Arms', while in Cork the report remarked how 'no new corps have been embodied in this County since the year 1779 except the Youghall Horse who were rather a defection from the Midleton Horse last year on account of admitting Roman Catholics, that corps being entirely composed of Catholics.'[127]

The return also noticed how the Volunteers were not homogenous in their political views.[128] A degree of residual Castle loyalty was identified, as when, in discussing Antrim, it was recognised that 'the two last of these corps were raised as were also the Carrickfergus Royals in favour of the government'. Elsewhere, 'the Naas Corps . . . is commanded by the Honourable John Bourke, a zealous friend of the government.'[129] The national reach of the Volunteers involved accepting dissention within the movement, and accommodating delicate religious, social, and political sensibilities. Yet, for the Volunteers, the claim to speak for the nation as a whole was a desirable rhetorical ploy, and a necessary aspect of extraparliamentary legitimacy. It was at the heart of the movement's ambition, and its decline.

Crucial to the idealisation of the movement as representative of national sentiment was the extent of Presbyterian and particularly Catholic participation. Certainly most of the rank and file in the Ulster Volunteers were dissenters, with Anglicans often taking officerships, in recognition of their landed status and as a cover for the regimental composition.[130] Indeed, Volunteering had its origins in the northern province, when the citizens of Belfast banded together into a military unit on St Patrick's Day 1778.

Catholic engagement was much more problematic.[131] The Volunteers had been created as a paramilitary defence force for the Anglican state; yet right from the start some Catholics showed an inclination to support the locality in their efforts to muster regiments. In Limerick, Catholics supplied £800 for national defence in the wake of the 1778 Repeal Act, while in Waterford attempts to establish a regiment of their own in 1779 had to be quietly discouraged by authorities.[132] In Ulster, as William Steel Dickson ruefully admitted,

> amidst the pleasing circumstances which surrounded this institution,
> one equally shameful and impolitic occurred. The Catholics in great
> numbers and with great zeal offered themselves as Volunteers in
> common with their Protestant and Presbyterian fellow-countrymen.
> Throughout the greater part of Ulster, if not the whole, their offers
> were rejected, and in some cases not without insult. In my neighbour-
> hood this was universally the case.[133]

Not everywhere was so dismissive of the offer of aid. In 1779 an independent Volunteer company was founded in Wexford which included Catholics. It was financed by prominent Catholic figures, including Bishop Sweetmen, the gentry Robert Devereux and Michael Sutton, the middlemen Patrick Roche and John Scallan, and four merchants from the city, Richard Hayes, Patrick Rossiter, Patrick Scallan, and John Boggan, along with another, Patrick Sutton, from Enniscorthy.[134]

Through 1780 and 1781 the tenor of the relationship changed, with Catholics taking up an increasing number of berths in Volunteer regiments. In Dundalk, in August 1780, the *Hibernian Magazine* reported that 'this company is partly composed of Roman Catholics, and there is not a Volunteer corps in the kingdom assembles with more cheerfulness and harmony'.[135] A Carrick Volunteer observed that a 'tide of good sense, moderation and liberal sentiment is rushing in strongly on the public, and Sligo is too little to resist the torrent.'[136] Less circum-spect was the anonymous author of *Thoughts on the Conduct and Continuation of the Volunteers of Ireland* who, in 1783, reflected back on the ameliorative effect of the fraternisation that had occurred across religious divide:

> Having united the two religions by the bonds of common interest, it
> proceeds to bind them still closer, by the softer ties of social intercourse.
> The papist, with an orange cockade fires in honour of King William's
> birthday. He goes to a Protestant church, and hears a charity sermon.
> He dines with his Protestant associates and perhaps a Popish chaplain
> says grace . . . Volunteering has done what the law could not do.[137]

While this rather condescending passage captures something of the shift in thought amongst Protestants, the change in attitude towards the Volunteers within the Catholic constituency can also be tracked through the shifting register of the Irish-language poets at work through the 1770s and early 1780s. Within their oeuvre can be identified a distinct shift in perspective towards Grattan and the other Patriot leaders, and in relation to the American crisis. During the first months of the conflict, Uilliam an Chreatháin Ó Dábhoireann, from Country Clare, drafted the following poetic reflection:

> Is trua liom na scéalta do chuala go déanach
>   im' chluasa do chéas me le sealad
> ar scuaine seo an Bhéarla do ghluais uaim le tréimse
>   as cuanta na hÉireann go Boston,
> le fuadar le faobhar dá bhuadach le chéile
>   is dá scuabadh ins na spéarthaidh 'na gceathaibh
> le fuaim torann piléaraibh ag slua Prebytérian
>   cé gur mhór ar féasta iad 's ar bainis

> Grieved I am by the stories I've lately heard that have pained my ears
> for some time, about this English-speaking herd which set out some
> time ago, from the harbours of Ireland for Boston, with energy and
> arms being driven together, and being blown into the sky in showers
> to the sound of roaring bullets by a Presbyterian army—though they'd
> be great at a feast or banquet.[138]

This is very much a case of a plague on both your houses—the fate of the 'English-speaking herd' and the 'Presbyterian army' are both ironically lamented. But this view was not indicative of every poet reflecting on proceedings. Séamus Ó Dálaigh, a tailor from Mungret, near Limerick, could write:

> 'Ós cantar', ar sí, 'leatsa díogras mo scéala,
> is aithris mór-thimpeall do chloinn Scoit na soar-bheart,
> go bhfuil fáistine fíora na ndraoithe is na n-éigse,
> de dhearbhthoil Íosa á síorchur ar mhéirligh.
>   Súd Washington calma treallúsach thiar,
>   Mar Hannibal Carthage I dtreasaibh ba dhian,
>   Ag leagadh 's ag leadradh na nDanar sa ngliadh,
> Is tré loscadh 'na gceallaibh beidh daltaí an phoic adharcaigh
> Is a maireann dá gcaraid gan fearann, gan feadhmas'.

'Since', she said, 'the import of my story is being recited to you,
spread it around among the children of Scot of the noble feats, that
the true prophecy of the druids and the poets, by the settled will of
Jesus is being continually enacted on the villains. There in the west is
brave, daring Washington, like Hannibal of Carthage in fierce battles,
felling and thrashing the Danes in combat, and having been scorched
in their churches the disciples of the horned back and their surviving
friends will be without property and power'.[139]

'Brave, daring Washington': the political attitude towards the American conflict
had shifted. The discomfiture caused by the colonists was becoming a reason to
rejoice, whatever the shared origins of the protagonists in the conflict.

Remarkably, this choosing of sides in the American argument had repercussions closer to home, for by November 1779 Thomás Ó Míocháin, a poet from
County Clare, wrote a song 'ar bhfuascailt na nÉireannach ó dhaorchuing na
Sacsan le saorarm gáirmhianach na Banban, dá ngoirtear Volunteers' ('on the
liberation of the Irish from England's oppressive yoke by the glory-seeking free
army of Ireland, called Volunteers'). In it, the Patriot leaders were extravagantly
celebrated as heroes of the nation:

> Ar Ghrattan ba náir gan trácht go taitneamhach,
> cáidhfhear ceanamhail, cáilmhear, ceannasach,
>   seol scóip is trealamh gan tím;
> is ba dheacair dá bhfágfainn bláth-Bhurgh beachtaithe,
> ráib le'r tagaradh cás na Banda,
>   i nglór beoil ba bheannaithe binn.
> Ligeam 'na ndiaidh go dian gan dearmad
> Yelverton fial ag fiach na bhfealladh-chon,
> sciath gheal-tseasamhach, íodhan acmhainneach,
> rialach, rabairneach, triathach, teanga-chlis,
>   lann óir is luiseag na nGaoidheal.

Grattan it would be shameful not to mention with affection, an
excellent amiable man, reputable and commanding, a spirited
well-equipped guide without timidity; and harsh would it be were I to
omit polished and precise Burgh, a champion by whom Ireland's case
was asserted, in diction that was blessed and sweet. Let us admit
quickly after them without fail, generous Yelverton hunting the

> treacherous dogs, a bright and steadfast shield, a sturdy spear, regular,
> unstinting, lordly, quick-tongued, the golden blade and the knife-
> point of the Gaels.[140]

This material suggests that the Catholic constituency was, through the course of the conflict, coming into line with the political nation within Anglican Ireland, largely by supporting the Patriot faction. In particular, the Volunteers were, in their overt criticism of the Irish polity and its practices, providing a rubric of political participation which Catholics could use. The Volunteers, by claiming to speak on behalf of the society beyond the state, were utilising a language of politics in which the Catholics were, often openly, included. Catholics were reciprocating by binding the Volunteers into their political worldview, and praising the Patriot leadership in the Dublin parliament. The Volunteer ambition to speak for society as a whole facilitated the participation of the Catholic community in the politics of the state.

Given such a disparate catchment for Volunteer support, it was necessary to clarify where the movement stood in relation to the question of who constituted the people. It was this issue which informed Peter Burrowes's *Plain Arguments in Defence of the People's Absolute Dominion over the Constitution* (1784), in which he asserted that 'the un-contradicted sense of the Volunteers ought to be considered as the sense of the community'.[141] Yet as the community was not commensurate with the political nation, this involved him in a more inclusive vision. 'I do not mean by the people the electors only' he admitted, for

> when the rights of the people are talked of, the whole community is
> understood, under which term is comprehended not only the electors,
> but every individual who owes natural allegiance to the state,
> contributes to the expenses of government, or is a natural born
> subject thereof, or admitted to the rank of one by naturalisation,
> denization or whatever established mode of communicating a right of
> citizenship exists therein.[142]

Indeed, 'it would be absurd in the highest degree to take the electors for the people. They bear a very small proportion to the mass of the community.'[143] This was to redraw the concept beyond the traditional limits of property-bearing, adult, male Protestants as this definition of the people explicitly included Catholics: 'I allude to the enfranchisement of the Roman Catholics, who are a majority of those to whom I have addressed myself', he wrote.[144] He was, how-ever, anxious to distance himself from any association with the Church of Rome. In a passage replete with condescension and contempt he adduced:

> For my part I think the present state of representation so great an evil
> and the danger of popish pre-eminence so mere a bugbear, that, as
> much as I despise the Roman Catholic religion as a mode of
> Christianity, and as reluctant as I would be (and no man could be
> more reluctant) to see it the established religion of the land, I do not
> hesitate between the alternatives. I think it can scarcely be doubted
> that we have no alternative but to associate the Roman Catholics in
> our pursuit, or at once to abandon it.[145]

The allusion to a bugbear—a fantastical creature who scared and disciplined children—set Catholicism in opposition to enlightened, rational thinking, to which Burrowes laid claim. This opposition was elsewhere developed into a thesis that enlightenment and toleration would trump the 'superstition' that gave life to bugbears and hobgoblins. Roman Catholicism was historically des-tined to lose its sublime capacity for 'terror':

> No thinking man of reading and experience can doubt but that
> popery is decaying, and likely to decay all over Europe, and that in
> our country it will wear out faster than the possessions of the Roman
> Catholics will accumulate, unless we prop their superstition with their
> resentment, and keep their prejudices by maintaining our own. But
> what is it we have to fear? The idle hobgoblin rumours of popery and
> the Pretender have lost their terror.[146]

The potency of these monsters resided in their imaginative power over juve-nile minds, prone to listening to authority and disregarding criticism. Capacious thought was rare, with most people merely considering their own particular interests. Sadly, 'the bulk of mankind are neither deep politicians nor abstruse reasoners. They judge of forms of government by their effects and estimate their own rights by instinctive feeling.'[147] Yet precisely this reliance on instinct and self-interest made the need for reform self-evident to the people. Only the people could bring the state back into the desired symbiotic relationship with the community it governed, as 'whatever is the form of government, whether monarchical, aristocratical, democratical or mixed, the legislature that obtains therein derives its authority from the consent of the people, either directly or indirectly given, to be governed by laws enacted in such a legislature.'[148] The law was expressive of the community; the hope was to blend the sentiments of the legislators with the manners of the people in a mutual harmony for, with regard to reform, 'the parliament may do it with the approbation of the people, or the people through the medium of parliament'.[149]

This hope for systemic reform of the polity was stymied, Burrowes believed, by the recalcitrance of the state. The unsavoury truth was that where parliamentary independence served the interests of the MPs, franchise reform threatened their power, and self-preservation dictated that many of them would turn against the Volunteers now that the agenda had moved beyond removing the fetters of trade restrictions, Poynings's Law, and the Declaratory Act. Nor did Burrowes rest any hope in the electorate. In line with his analysis that those in power wished to retain their privileges, he pessimistically acknowledged how 'constituents of a great majority would instruct against reform.'[150] The privilege of voting was a property which few would willingly extend, for fear of watering down its political, social, and material value. Only by appealing beyond the electorate might the reform agenda glean the kind of support which would legitimate taking action. This was to understand politics not as the domain of particular privilege but as the expression of communal rights, written into the nature of things and not historically situated. Thus, 'the inalienable rights of a people depend not upon precedents and cannot be abridged by any earthly authority', while the constitution

> whatever may be its origins, age or growth, the people are its owners.
> The present race of men, by adopting it have made it their own, and
> the experience of all ages and countries corroborates every man's
> reason and uncorrupted feelings in proving that they have a right to
> make whatever alterations in it shall appear necessary to their
> happiness and security. Instances of an exercise of this right are
> innumerable, but unnecessary; for the inalienable rights of a people
> depend not upon precedents and cannot be abridged by any earthly
> authority.[151]

Burrowes here buttressed the authority he granted elsewhere to the operation of reason. History was demeaned as a negative force, blocking progress and forestalling the recognition of universal rights, as when he asked his readers 'can we then answer it to our Roman Catholic brethren to let groundless antiquated apprehensions obstruct the free progress of an enlightened toleration?'[152] In the face of historic privilege Burrowes erected rational rights, deducing from first principles a code of political action and rejecting arguments grounded on empirical practice. This was, he admitted, not to every reader's taste, for

> I know original principles have always had an uncouth appearance to
> men, who viewing objects in the glass of fashion, and accustomed to
> see them adorned according to the taste that prevails amongst the
> great, are shocked with the naked unornamented truth . . . Liberty is
> too precious to be sacrificed to ceremony.[153]

It was this compulsion to question the principles of political activity, and to follow the argument whence it led, that forced Burrowes to circle back to the issue of Catholic engagement with the state. And it was his optimism about the reform movement which gave him confidence in the capacity of the Volunteers to effect change. 'Do the Roman Catholics wish to be enfranchised?' he enquired, before answering: 'I will not answer I know they do—But I will say I know they are men—they are Irishmen—they live in a period of liberation—have caught the love of freedom—and would disgrace you, themselves, and their country if in this moment of universal expectation they were indifferent or hopeless.'[154] This was at once a simple expression of a shared common humanity and of a view of the late eighteenth century as a period of progressive enlightenment and toleration. Burrowes was subscribing to the radical reforming agenda of the Volunteers and was placing it into an understanding of society as rational and civil.

Burrowes's position was too optimistic for some within the Volunteer ranks, and his definition of the people too broad. One—possibly John Johnson—felt sufficiently moved that he offered up a series of *Strictures* on the text. The defence placed Johnson as a moderate voice within the wider Volunteer movement—happy to celebrate the achievements to date, but wary of any extension of the agenda towards franchise reform.[155] Johnson queried whether the National Convention was voicing the will of people, asking, 'Is not the silence of the Volunteers the sense of the nation too? On the subject of the Popish franchises they were silent; but their silence has a peculiar emphasis.'[156]

Indeed, in Johnson's case, it was the decision to reject proposals for Catholic voting reform that was to be celebrated in the National Convention's deliberations. The idea that the Catholic community could be included in the working of the state was, for him, anathema. Appalled at the thought, he turned to history for his defence of their exclusion, asking: 'Are the people whose arbitrary principles, bloody zeal, treachery and rebellion, in England and Ireland, drove us to form this constitution, are they to be entitled to a share in the legislation with us?'[157] This drew Johnson towards an understanding of politics as enunciating privileges, not as recognising rights. In that, the core of his commitment to the Volunteer movement was closer to its origins as a Protestant defence association than to the radical reform organisation it had metamorphosed into, and to which Burrowes gave his allegiance. And the nub of the distinction could be found in competing definitions of the term 'people'.

While to Johnson it was commensurate with those who had been granted the privilege of citizenship—those in the political nation—he saw in Burrowes's 'a certain ambiguity in his use of the word . . . With him it sometimes means the whole aggregate body, sometimes it is the National Convention of last year; then it is the Volunteers.'[158] This eroded the power of parliament to represent and legislate for the community, and set up in contradistinction an unstable, illegitimate, and temporary government: 'The representatives of the nation are no more; the National Convention speaks the sense of the people, unless some more extended class, the Papists or the Plebs *infima*, the Canaille of the streets should differ from them and call a convention of their own. Where will this marvellous chain of argument cease?'[159]

In this argument between Burrowes and Johnson, the basic sketch of a wider division within the Volunteer movement was drawn. On the one side, there was a broad definition of the people as those within the community at large, and a concomitant commitment to the view that the people should shape the state in their image; on the other, a narrower notion of the people as those granted the privilege of participation, and a view of politics as shaping the society. To one, the manners of the people trumped the sentiments of the state; to the other, the sentiments of the state directed the manners of the people. And behind this debate lay a further difference of worldview. Burrowes was committed to a rationalist view of politics in which states should recognise and reflect the natural rights of the people; Johnson held fast to an empirical understanding of the state as shaped by experience, which understood politics as reliant on historical privilege. And this division, between rationalist activists who viewed politics through the prism of rights and empirical thinkers who spoke the language of privilege, slowly prised the movement apart. The hope that the Volunteers might ventriloquise the nation was fated to fail.

Fracture Lines

Ironically, because the Volunteer movement had come to embody the wider reaches of the political community it was fissiparous. Moreover, in terms of the languages of the late Enlightenment, the Volunteers were just as inarticulate. The ambition was to coalesce the sentiments of the legislators with the manners of the people, but whether it was the state or society which required reform was unclear. It was equally uncertain as to whether a new polity might be conceived as emergent within the old, drawing on the imaginative ambitions of the reformers, or if the proper mode of procedure was through cumulative reform, informed by historical precedent and a retrieval of an ancient constitution. The first presumption forwarded its Enlightenment ambitions through the projection of a possible future grounded on first principles; the latter on an empirical methodology that looked to the past for guidance. In political terms this also involved a divergence between a commercial Whiggery that saw opportunities in wealth creation, and a true, or Old Whig position that distrusted commerce and the financial instruments of paper money, the national debt, and speculation on the stock market in London.[160] In other words, while the Volunteers claimed to speak on behalf of the whole nation, its membership ensured that its political practice and theoretical statements were unable to achieve this. Whereas the Social Enlightenment had flourished through the collaboration of these modes of procedure, the politicisation of the populace implicit in the relief acts and the inclusion of the wider community into the realm of public opinion by the Volunteers fragmented the Political Enlightenment into two distinct camps.

An example of the problem can be found in two pamphlets which contemporaries saw as articulating the central dogmas of the Volunteers. Here is Francis Dobbs celebrating them: 'At this period a number of well written and spirited writings filled the newspapers, and drew the attention of the people to their situation: Guatimozin's and Owen Roe O'Neill's letters deservedly caught the public eye, and patriotism began to diffuse itself through every breast.'[161] This association in the public's eye might have come about because both series were published in the pages of the Volunteer organ, the *Freeman's Journal*, and as the later publication, *The Letters of Owen Roe O'Nial*, notices the earlier work: 'Can Guatimozin himself even in the generous ardour of his zeal and the fire of his consuming indignation, can he restrain a tear for the weakness of humanity.'[162]

Yet the two authors were from rather different backgrounds, and the texts they penned of different colouration. Frederick Jebb, was an Anglican and a member of Dublin's civic and charitable elite. He was the fourth master of the Rotunda and an author on midwifery, as well as a proponent of a national bank.[163] He wrote under the name of the last Aztec emperor, Guatimozin, who was noted for his stoicism when tortured by the Spanish, refusing to reveal the location of his gold. Owen Roe O'Neill, the leader of the Ulster Irish in the Confederate Wars of the 1640s, was the adopted pen-name of Joseph Pollock, a Presbyterian from Newry.

Both men were members of the Monks of the Screw, a Patriot social club that met in Dublin, and Jebb and Pollock shared the polemical ambition of reworking the Anglo-Irish relationship through the establishment of free trade; the central aim of the Volunteer movement in 1779.[164] Moreover, they shared certain tropes, for instance the blame they apportioned the Scots in thinking through the dilemmas faced by the Irish political nation.[165] But, despite such similarities, the central method adopted by the two polemicists in constructing their argument for free trade was fundamentally different.

The slogan 'free trade' covered a number of different possibilities, allowing Jebb and Pollock to agree that it was required without necessarily agreeing as to its formal content. There were broadly three versions of the thesis.[166] The first—a national free trade concept which accorded broadly with a constitutional analysis of the problem—continued to have imaginative purchase. This view contended that the legislative restrictions which persisted in the management of Anglo-Irish trade with England were unfairly detrimental to the domestic economy, and that Ireland should be allowed to compete with the British manufacturers and companies. This implied that limited reforms might suffice to sate the demand for free trade; it was co-opted by those parliamentarians who were anxious to limit the ambitions and activism of the Volunteers. A second rhetoric, drawing on Old Whig sources deemed the relationship between Ireland and Britain was largely exploitative, with Ireland serving as a source of natural resources, taxation, and manpower for a British imperial venture. This approach contended that free trade was a matter of commercial equality within the empire and Ireland should therefore have the ability to sell its produce in the markets of the colonies.[167] More extensive was a neo-mercantilist model of the economy, a form of free trade which was informed by Adam Smith's recently published *Inquiry in the Origins and Nature of the Wealth of Nations* (1776) that promoted commercial legislative independence in which the context for foreign imports would be governed by the Dublin parliament. This was co-opted by the modern commercial Whigs who contended that free trade involved unrestricted access to imperial connections and that the Irish trading community had a right to engage in trade unhampered by British self-interest.[168]

Jebb followed in the path of William Molyneux by offering an analysis of the country's ancient constitution. He shared with his progenitor the classical republican conceit concerning liberty; that it was a positive quality, recognised by the state in cognisance of the citizens' participatory virtue, and which the citizens played an active role in formulating:

> What are the liberties of Englishmen? To be governed by laws to which
> they have given consent, either by themselves or their representatives in
> parliament. Have the Irish consented to the several British Acts, by
> which they are now restrained? . . . In short we are to understand that
> liberty means one thing in England and another in Ireland.[169]

Ireland was here understood to share a similar grant of privilege to that which underpinned English liberties, for 'Henry III who succeeded his father John in the government of both kingdoms granted to Ireland a Magna Charta [sic], which is preserved in the Red Book of the Exchequer, in the first year of his reign, eight years before he granted the Magna Charta [sic] of England, and the one is a copy of the other.'[170]

Given this historical circumstance, Jebb argued that Britain had subsequently overstepped its legitimate authority, becoming tyrannical in its dealings with Ireland. This he dated to 1641, 'when the exceeding confusion of the government in Ireland, and the impossibility of holding a parliament there laid the foundation of a precedent which was monstrously built upon in the reign of Charles II.'[171] Since that time, with the Woollen Act of 1698 and the Declaratory Act of 1720, Jebb maintained 'you may trace Ireland, through the [legislative] code as you track a wounded man through a crowd, by blood'.[172] He hoped that while 'the age of tyranny does not greatly exceed a century . . . it may not live to be much older.'[173]

This recent history of exploitation left active citizens with little option but to resist, exercising a privilege that was embedded within British (and by extension Irish) constitutional arrangements:

> It is the privilege of a subject living under the British constitution to
> act, to speak, and to publish every thing which is not forbidden by

law; and till the illegality of combining in favour of our own manufactures shall be unquestionably demonstrated I will take the liberty
to reject all assertional doctrine upon this head, and to put my fellow
citizens on guard against the ill tendency of such.[174]

While this passage defended the Volunteer movement, it is worth noting not
just its polemical intention, but its rhetorical construction. Jebb here relied on
an empirical rubric found in the notion of demonstration; the collation and
ordering of data would prove his contention.

Jebb depended on empirical argumentation to such an extent that by the
fifth letter he was admitting that 'I have in my former letters nearly gone over
the extent of ground laid down in my chart', while yet continuing to write,
solely so that he might, through repetition, be prompted into 'the recollection
of some materials which have escaped the first enquiry.'[175] He duly provided
readers with a lengthy analysis of Ireland's political economy, an empirically
inclined subject and argued that 'experience shows that the greatest advantages
of soil, climate and situation and the most inexhaustible proliferation in the
fishing coasts of a country will not accomplish the purposes of national prosperity without manufactures.'[176] Indeed, 'the idea of a nation of farmers is completely absurd'.[177] In its place he offered a synergetic, holistic image of the
economy in which fisheries, farms, and factories produced national wealth.

The power of political economy to ameliorate Ireland's condition was underlined when 'our condition exempts us from the necessity of doing such things for
our deliverance as our tyrants would call rebellion. We have only to unite in the
plain system of consuming, exclusively, the manufactures of this country and the
work is done.'[178] Thus, in the movement for Irish manufacture the sentiments of
the state and manners of the people—which currently stood at variance—could
be harmonised. But this relied on a transformation in the character of the Irish
people; all too habituated to the inferior status political history had inculcated
them: 'if men will think themselves inferior, they will certainly become so', he
admitted.[179] Jebb looked then to the free press, and his own writings, to alter the
manners of his countrymen, and to invigorate the cause of free trade:

If the conductors of the free press will give me a corner, I intend (God
willing) every Saturday, to publish an essay until I shall have roused
my countrymen, universally to a sense of their condition, or convinced myself that the expectation is in vain. I will not apply the

match to the tinder, which I hope lies concealed in the breast of every virtuous Irishman; before I shall have convinced his reason.[180]

As with Jebb, Joseph Pollock argued that it was only through free trade that 'the interest of the governors and of the people, now so opposite, would be reconciled'.[181] But unlike Jebb, with his emphasis on empirical support and inductive accumulation, this conclusion was reached through deductive reduction, as Pollock first rejected the proposition of a union as emaciating the country, and then dismissed the idea of protest on individual issues through associations as ineffectual. So, while sharing conclusions with Jebb, Pollock did not deploy anything like the same rhetorical stratagem. Instead of understanding politics as predicated on privileges, Pollock deployed a rights-based register; as he said in relation to the construction of European geopolitics, 'it is fixed in the nature of things'.[182] Moreover he founded his political analysis on what he took to be a self-evident principle:

I must beg leave to premise . . . a principle upon which I intend to build much . . . the principle is this, that political bodies whether sole or aggregate, whether composed of a person or a multitude, act uniformly from the narrowest kind of selfishness and are totally incapable of a steady or uniform principle of generosity.[183]

This was particularly the case when colonial territories were considered, for Pollock contended

that those nations who enjoyed most liberty themselves have been ever the greatest tyrants of others, and provinces of a despotic king have been generally treated more kindly than those of free states. The reason is that in a free state every man is in a degree one of the government and few men in power like to part with it. Most are willing to abuse it. The proud cannot bear spirit in others, and they are more men of pride than of dignity. To a despotic king all his subjects are pretty equal, provided they pay him his taxes; and if his government is rather mild the provinces will share it. The free citizen of a free state will hardly put *his* subject in the province on a footing with himself, their Lord and governor in his capital.[184]

Here each sentence encompasses a deduction from the statement of principle contained in the preceding statement. So too the passage is laden with a priori assumptions concerning the nature of man, of politics, and of national rivalry. The passage is populated by abstract personages—'every man', 'the proud', 'a despotic king', and 'free citizens'—all of whom have actions and reactions presumed upon an assessment of their supposed nature. The consequence of this process was revealed when Pollock wrote, 'from this proximity of England, I would deduce this truth, which I wish to be engraven on the heart of every Irishman: England is the only power that can either enslave us farther or keep us as we are.'[185] Here a deductive methodology is twinned with a concern for the sentiments of the people to reject a history of slavery and project a possible future of liberty.

This is a rationalist rhetoric, and only after his argument is asserted does he look to empirical justification: 'but to facts.'[186] These are deployed to support his conclusions, at least so far as the reality is evidence of the warping of principles. As he colourfully claimed, 'the steps of nations have been ever planted in selfishness, marked with injustice and may be traced in blood. Their monuments are desolation. Their glory is the stain of humanity—Let us compare facts with reasoning.'[187] The second letter provided comparisons to Ireland's condition, highlighting how the rebellious history of Holland, Switzerland, and America provided evidence that Ireland's fate was not determined by dependence on England. In these three cases, 'each of them was once oppressed by all the rigours of slavery. Each of them burst her shackles and baffled the most inveterate attacks of enemies whose power seemed to approach them with the irresistibility of fate.'[188] History, to Pollock, only displayed that there was no predetermined fate for a country or a people. The condition of Ireland could be altered by the courageous. The past did not dictate to the present; as Pollock averred, 'I shall not then war with the dead.'[189]

If he rejected an empirical rhetoric, Pollock remained wedded to a vision of the right-functioning polity that blended the sentiments of the state with the manners of the people. For him, 'morality is felt. Politics must be studied. The conscience of the man is natural. That of the politician is artificial. The habit of reasoning only is not favourable to feeling. The habit of being cunning is not favourable to strictness of principle'.[190] This structuring of oppositions, between morality and cunning, feeling and reasoning, nature and artifice, spoke to Pollock's fundamental distrust of the state and his favouring of the people. Yet he accepted that 'some however can feel for the little community to which they belong. A few for their country. But how many are they', he enquired sceptically, 'who are born for the universe?'[191] The elevation here from community to country to cosmos bespoke an anxiety that men of virtue were rare and frequently slow to act: 'selfishness is eternally in arms, while benevolence often sleeps on her post'.[192] It was into this vacuum that the Volunteers stepped:

> Have we not men in arms already? Men whom England, and the
> slaves of England, would long ere this have disarmed, had they dared
> to do so! Men whose spirit they now affect to approve, because they
> find their approbation is indifferent to them! . . . Men who may yet
> teach England that the soil of their own country benumbs not their
> courage; that it is not on the plains of Flanders or America alone that
> Irishmen can conquer![193]

At the heart of the Volunteer project was, for Pollock, the rejection of a national dependency he saw as 'the very malignity of corruption', for while 'honour may support the individual . . . the abjection of a nation is infamy indeed'.[194] Just as virtue could rise from the individual to the community and the universe, so corruption interacted at the individual and corporate levels. Yet this was also grounds for limited optimism, for if the reforms Pollock was petitioning for came to pass, he was confident that 'the interest of the governors and of the people, now so opposite, would be reconciled' and that 'public virtue would have an object, and private virtue, the virtue of the people, would at once be the spring, the effect and the cement of the government'.[195] He hoped to create a 'community of interest' from which 'would naturally arise a mildness of government and a benevolence of toleration which is unknown to the laws of any other country in Europe'.[196]

As this passage suggests, the desire to identify the people with the state committed Pollock to a politics of religious toleration.[197] Only by extending the right (crucially here considered a right not a privilege) of political participation to the Catholic community might the Irish polity reflect the manners of the people it claimed to govern: 'Unless we entertain for each other a mutual and general confidence, unless we lay aside all rancour of prejudice on account of distinctions either political or religious, or attempt such a relief from those shackles, would be only to solicit confusion.'[198] Instead of favouring a sectional interest, Pollock was enunciating a general principle of confessional liberty.

Far from being a shared platform, the two pamphlets by Jebb and Pollock articulated different agendas, using different methods and proceeding from different premises. That the Volunteers could contain such opposing ideas spoke not just to the broad intake of the movement, but the uneasy coalition that this engendered within its ranks. Yet it was through an uneasy merger of two distinct vocabularies that William Drennan rallied the troops as the movement faded, in 1784 in the *Letters of Orellana, an Irish Helot*.[199]

The level of conceptual confusion Drennan's text embodied was clear from his Janus-faced treatment of the Catholic issue Pollock has so clearheadedly confronted. In the first instance, it appeared that Drennan was in favour of Catholic relief, and their inclusion in the political nation—an inclusion he extended to his fellow Presbyterians. In this vein, he was to write an extended panegyric of national unity; one that lamented that it was religious animosity that stood against an imagined futurity of plenty and pleasure:

> I call upon you Churchmen, Presbyterians, and Catholics to embrace
> each other in the mild spirit of Christianity and to unity as a secret
> compact in the cause of your sinking country—For you are all
> Irishmen—you are nurtured by the same maternal earth. The hand of
> Heaven has broken off this island from the continent, as if to preserve
> one fragment free, and has made it your common habitation. That
> same hand has scooped out your capacious harbours, deepened your
> ports, and sheltered them from the storms. It has chained down the
> hurricane least it should ravage the land. It has commanded the power
> which shakes the earth and terrifies its guilty inhabitants to be still. It
> has stifled the raging volcano and forbids the dreadful visitation of the
> pestilence. The gentle dews of Heaven drop fatness on your fields, and
> not even one venomous animal ventures to contaminate their verdure.
> Dare not abuse the gifts of God, and show that it is your religion to
> be free.[200]

This passage was laden with natural imagery, underwriting the idea that confessional freedom and national unity were inscribed by God into the order of things. Yet Drennan swiftly moved to discredit the idea that the Roman Catholic population should be allowed full access to the franchise; an opposition based on fear of the lower orders. Catholics, he recalled, were predominantly poor, and he reasoned that

> it is chiefly on this account that the Catholics of this day are abso-
> lutely incapable of making a good use of political liberty, or what is

the same thing, of political power. I speak the sentiments of the most
enlightened amongst them, and I assert it as a fact that the most able
men in that body are too wise to wish for a complete extension of civil
franchise to those of their own persuasion; and the reason is because
they well know that it must require the process of time to enlarge
their minds and meliorate their hearts into a capability of enjoying
the blessing of freedom.[201]

In contending this, Drennan made use of the Scottish Enlightenment trope of
stadial history. This metanarrative of human development read societies as
having four stages marked by different economic activities, culminating in commercial society. Those lower down the developmental scale required—in some
versions of the tale—a different kind of governance, with democratic practice
being reserved for those in the commercial stage. Applying this narrative to
Ireland, Drennan noted with relief that 'the Catholics, I again repeat it with
exaltation, have declined all share of the contest', and postulated that

conscious that the plurality among them are placed as it were in an
earlier stage of society than the rest of the island, they submit in
silence to the necessity of situation and circumstance—waiting with
patience until time has given them maturity of strength, and ability
equal to the arduous object they wish to attain.[202]

In contrast to this static rendition of Irish Catholic history—locked in a
lower stage of history than their Protestant counterparts—Drennan envisioned
the English constitution as a constitutional inheritance worth saving. Here he
readjusted his rhetoric away from the commercial republican language of progress towards an ancient constitutional conceit that was reminiscent of an older
generation of true Whigs: one that understood the modern age not as progressive but as corrupt and sought to reestablish eternal verities found embodied in
the original settlement of government. But this celebration of the ancient constitution only created a further tension within the *Letters*, for Drennan rejected
the prescriptive power of history and law in another passage where he once again
forwarded the benefits of reform:

Why entangle your understandings with researches into the musty
records of antiquity? Why perplex yourselves with the professional
subtlety of the law? Here is the origin of evil; you hear of it abroad—
you see it at your doors—the people are lost, if they do not at present

speak and write and act with all the energy which the spirit of the
constitution warrants. It is not the temporizing expedient of repealing
this or that law, or removing this or that minister which can yield
substantial and enduring redress to the ills of the nation; and if I be
asked who are the agents powerful enough to effect the work of
reform, I lay my hand upon my heart and I answer, yourselves.[203]

This espouses not the politics of the past, but the present power vested in the
people. If this implied a distrust of the state, and a commensurate celebration of
the people, this position could equally be set aside when the moment required.
In an open letter 'To the King of Great Britain and Ireland', Drennan wrote
lyrically of the wisdom and beauty of the state, drawing as it did on the three
orders of society, in a complex balancing of power.[204] Associating the constitution with a sublimity of design, he described it as

a pyramid of matchless workmanship, founded on the broad base of
democracy, and ascending with due gradation, until the image of the
sovereign is exalted upon its height and terminates its elevation. No
overhanging part ought to endanger its stability: No enormous power
ought to destroy its just proportion.[205]

But in the very first letter in the series, Drennan had already dismissed the efficacy of the balance of powers within the British constitution:

I know no idea which has been productive of more harm than one
which took its rise from the speculations of some fanciful foreigners,
that there was something of superhuman excellence in the frame and
contexture of what is called our political constitution. National
partiality, or more properly national bigotry, has adopted this idea with
enthusiasm and superstitiously adhered to it. The same sanctified veil
of mystery has been thrown over civil and religious matters, and the
same timidity in questioning the supposed perfection of this complex
sort of being, called king, lords and commons, has bound down its
votaries into a sort of political bondage unworthy of free men.[206]

Such contradictions were necessary in covering over cracks in the coherence
of his argument. All of these many convolutions—arguing for and against Catholic
relief; switching from stadialism to ancient constitutionalism; celebrating and

criticising the constitutional separation of powers—indicate how Drennan was struggling to hold together a Volunteer movement that contained—or had contained—people for whom each approach was motivational. In trying to revivify the movement—then in a phase of steep decline—he was availing of every rhetorical stratagem he thought might prompt action in his readers. The difficulty was he had too many audiences; he was trapped by the Volunteers' previous success in mobilising a disparate alliance of interests. And the conceptual chaos this engendered in the movement was placing enormous rhetorical strain on his writing.

Underlying this literary conjuring was a fundamental dichotomy in the movement. It was the same polarity that drove Jebb and Pollock into different understandings of the Volunteer movement's significance: namely, whether the state provided privileges to the citizens, or whether politics should be rendered in a rights-based vocabulary that prioritised the people's generative power over the state. In the second letter, Drennan was clear: politics was grounded on rights.

> Constitutional rights are those rights respecting life, liberty and property without which we cannot be free; and an assemblage of those rights I call free constitution. Every art and science has its fundamental axioms, which, by their intrinsic evidence become worthy of universal acceptation; which if not expressed are always understood in every deduction of reasoning, and to whom, in all dubious cases, there must be made a last appeal. The science of politics [the phrase echoes David Hume], not less demonstrative than others, has its first principles and self-evident truths, which are axioms in their nature, the source from whence all reasoning must spring, and distinguished by the name constitutional rights. It is upon the solid basis of these rights that every system and plan of government, however various in form, must be erected.[207]

This was buttressed by his adoption of a deductive mode of reasoning, which connected his postulations on politics—as noted above comprehended as a 'science'—to the science of mathematics: 'As the propositions of Euclid are deduced from the self-evident axioms prefixed to the work, the laws in a free country are so many political thermos or problems derived from a ground of certainty equally uncontrovertible [sic]—the rights of human nature'.[208]

This grounded Drennan in one line of argumentation. But the thorny nature of his position, and the competing demands the problematic circumstances of composition were placing on him, drove him even then to express anxiety that a rationalist politics might be insufficiently inspiring to call out the lost Volunteers that the moment now needed. He fretted: 'I pity the man who can discuss such a question as a problem in mathematics, and when he triumphs in his argument walks off convinced and contended. This nation will never achieve its object till it joins the ardour of love to the composure of political philosophy'.[209] And so, even on this most fundamental of questions—the basis on which politics operated—Drennan was inconsistent. Despite the avowal of rationalism and rights, in the fourth letter he celebrated the exercise of a classically understood civic virtue. 'The genius of reform must be attended', he pronounced,

> with a certain gallantry of soul which pushes forward in the field of virtuous glory. It is this gallantry of soul, like the white plume on the helmet of Henry the fourth of France, always seen in motion among the thicket of the enemy—which will inspire those who follow with confidence, and those who oppose you with despair.[210]

It was in despairing of that spirit in his countrymen, who he saw falling away from the Volunteers for fear that parliamentary reform would be acrimonious and ruinous, that he set up the central trope in the text, one which contrasted the adult manliness of the patriot—he wrote of how 'despondency is a poor, weeping, whimpering quality of mind, unfit for bearded men'—with the status of children, incapable and undeserving of the liberties of free citizens.[211] Writing of the possibility that a reform bill might be granted by the administration as a sop to the Volunteers, Drennan admitted that it would stick in his craw: 'Did the concession of the ministry at this moment present the nation with a reform bill in a gold box, I should accept it, as an Irishman with a reluctance bordering on disgust: when I reflected that my countrymen might only divert themselves for a little time with the blessing as children with a toy'.[212] Repeatedly the image of children playing at adult affairs came to his mind as he assessed the state of affairs in the Volunteer movement: 'You looked indeed at Dungannon as if you were not making game, and we recollect that your redcoats had the same effect on us as the terrific terms of raw-head and bloody-bines had upon us when children.'[213] Equally he saw the scant hope left in the chance that they could petition the king as coming 'to pour out our complaints as children to a parent, and by the prevailing power of this pathetic appellation, we think ourselves secure of your favourable attention'.[214] This sequence culminated in the transference of the image onto the nation as a whole:

> Ireland is yet a child. There is sometimes seen in rickety children an
> extraordinary forwardness of mental powers, which surprises everyone
> with its strength, acuteness and comprehension. The nurse wonders
> and the parents expect that the little one will turn out a prodigy.
> Everything seems learned by instinct and intuition—Gradually, its
> powers weaken, its faculties shrivel up. It loses all its fiery spirit, its
> glowing ambition; and the little wonder of the world at length lives a
> simpleton and dies a sot.[215]

Ireland imagined as a sickly and stupefied child—a tragic vision which accorded with Drennan's medical background.[216]

The image of children also allowed Drennan to deploy an empirical register which was at odds with the avowed rationalism of his rights-based rubric. For instance he deployed the language of associationalism—in which he was conversant from his time in Edinburgh University—to dismiss religious animosities by associating them with childish fears: 'Is this a time to summon up those dreadful ideas which had impressed themselves on our minds when children, and of consequence became associated with the first principles of education, to make these spectres ascend in gloomy resurrection before our eyes and make us children again?'[217] This language also appeared in his rejection of the historical connection of the Irish and the British in constitutional development:

> Your boyhood and your youth were led astray by false associations;
> and blinded by the refined delusion of history: you claimed relation-
> ship with the Saxon Alfred, who established juries, crushed corruption
> and laid the foundation of the English constitution; with Hampden,
> who had a head to contrive, a heart to conceive, and a hand to
> execute; and Sidney, who shook the scaffold with his undaunted tread,
> was to be sure, one of your great progenitors! 'Tis all the fairy tale of
> infancy.[218]

Drennan's *Letters of Orellana, An Irish Helot* mark a watershed. While the Enlightenment methodologies of empiricism and rationalism had been creatively combining since the late 1720s, the confusion their application was inserting into his attempts to animate the Volunteer movement indicate that by the mid-1780s, the collaboration was becoming volatile. The twin language of moderate Enlightenment was now fracturing into its component halves under the pressure caused by their political mobilisation. When the discourse of Enlightenment ran up against the reality of politicisation, it bifurcated, leaving two parties standing across a conceptual chasm. On the one side, figures who adopted the empirical language favoured by Jebb found themselves deploying the discourse of history, understanding politics through privilege and seeing the state as the bastion of order. To them, the achievement of free trade and the renunciation of Britain's claim to legislate for Ireland were sufficient. It was now time for the Volunteers to depart the stage. In contrast, figures like Pollock who adhered to a rationalist methodology in approaching political issues placed hopes for the future in a recasting of the law. They thought of politics as the exercise of preexisting, naturally ordained rights and contended that the people were the originators of the state. To them the Volunteers were valuable because they rethought the possibility of the Irish state, freeing it from dependency on Britain and suggesting a substantial reformation grounded on franchise reform. They were also edging towards a rapprochement with their Catholic coun-trymen. While Drennan endeavoured to keep these two positions in harmony, contextual pressures were systematically driving them apart, for these different understandings of the political present produced different historical narratives and future ambitions. They ultimately were to conflict with each other, leading initially to the demise of the Volunteers, the reassertion of confessional divi-sions, and the provisional defeat of the rationalist Enlightenment.

Entrenchment

The ecumenism articulated by the rationalist wing of the Volunteers prompted fear in certain sections of Irish society. This became apparent when the privileges of the Church of Ireland were contested by the Rightboy move-ment, which emerged in Mallow, County Cork, in 1785.[219] Motivated by the demand to rescind or reduce the payment of the tithe to church ministers, although it also extended to a demand to relieve payments towards the Roman Catholic clergy, the Rightboys engendered terror through their campaign of intimidation and violence.[220] During 1785 and 1786 all the counties of Munster, and many in Leinster, were disturbed. This was in part, paradoxically, a consequence of agrarian success—with the improvement in conditions the value of the tithe also escalated in real terms, if not as a proportion of the farmer's income. Yet the economic safety net provided by the buoyancy in prices also gave farmers a sense of security. Confidence led to confrontation and conflict. But while there was sympathy for the programme of the Rightboys, particularly amongst a coterie of landed Protestant families that would have gained if the tithe payment were to be reduced, attempts in parliament to address the issue were derailed by the fear that it was a cover for a confessional argument and that the Anglican Church was in danger.

In 1787 the tide turned against those of a placatory attitude, and a backlash emerged; prompted in part by the propaganda efforts of the Anglican bishop of Cloyne, Richard Woodward. His publication *The Present State of the Church of Ireland* (1787) self-consciously drew attention to the perceived crisis in church and state, giving it form and offering it some evidentiary substance. As he averred in stark terms, 'No man of reflection can doubt but that the situation of the established church is dangerous in the extreme'.[221] He saw in the Rightboys' activities a general plot to breach the battlements of the Anglican Church. To his anxious mind, 'the outrages of the Whiteboys in the south supposed to be confined to tithes (which alone would be a matter of no little moment to the Protestant religion . . .) do by no means stop there. They extend to the persons of the established clergy who are hunted from their parishes.'[222] This nightmare was exacerbated by how the church was vitally linked to the polity, for it transformed the Rightboy campaign into a scheme of political subversion, turning them from agrarian protesters to Catholic ultras and thence to social bandits intent on undermining the 'Protestant interest'.[223] Woodward warned 'I need not tell the Protestant proprietor of land, that the security of his title depends very much (if not entirely) on the Protestant Ascendancy'.[224]

In this construction, Woodward configured the people's manners as commensurate with their religious denomination. From this it followed that

> despotic states, whether the supreme power were lodged in one or a few,
> have found in the papal authority, a congenial system of arbitrary
> dominion; and of course have regarded popery as a powerful ally, or at
> least a useful engine of state. Republics, proceeding with a like consis-
> tency, have adopted the levelling principle of the Presbyterian church;

while the several monarchies of the north, and almost all the principalities of Germany, which embraced the reformation of Luther, still retained episcopacy, as congruous to their form of civil government.[225]

Using this schema besmirched the political reputation of both the Catholic community and the Presbyterians of Ulster.[226] 'Of the three persuasions', he concluded, 'the members of the established church alone can be cordial friends to the entire constitution of this realm with perfect consistency of principle.'[227] Catholics and Presbyterians were beyond the realm of formal politics—excluded by their predilection to support a church that was antagonistic to that recognised by the Irish state. This fear of the people was a recurring trope within the pamphlet, with Woodward repeatedly remarking on the capacity for destruction embodied by the 'popish mob', casting aspersions on the 'the prejudices of the people', and commenting on how Catholic priests benefited from 'rooted prejudice, strong in proportion to the ignorance of the people, and by the habits of obedience from his flock'.[228] This was set against a concern for the maintenance of the 'Protestant Ascendancy' or 'Protestant interest', either term denoting a narrow definition of the people—he admitted that 'in Ireland the Protestants are not one fourth of the people; the members of the establishment little more than an eighth'.[229]

Despite this clear preference for confessional adherence over demographic proportions, Woodward's text was peppered with numbers, a rhetorical device he used to defend his political theories. For instance, he provided a table of the clergy's incomes for the province of Munster and supplied close detail for his emblematic anecdotes, as when he recounted in a footnote how

> the parish of Ballyvourney in the diocese of Cloyne (the church of which is in ruins) will be an instance in proof, if proof were necessary, how effectual the reduction in tithes would be to prevent the building of churches, and the progress of the Protestant religion. The tithes of this parish were let many years ago for £60 per annum as I am informed and are supposed now to be worth between £200 and £300 according to the usual rate of setting tithe. In consequence of a combination in that extensive parish the tithes are now reduced so low that the late incumbent did not receive from it £10 per annum and resigned it into my hands.[230]

This numerical display was indicative of a methodological commitment to empiricism that found further expression in his compilation of lists and the provision of extensive footnotes, often containing supporting evidence but equally supplying the page with a sturdy, scholarly, appearance, suggesting authorial competence and a sustained analysis of a mass of material. Typical of this use of the note was this extended remark supporting his assertion that the Rightboys intimidated and suborned jurymen:

> The effect of this is proved by the proceedings at the last assizes in
> Munster; where after the multitudes of instances of breaking-open
> houses, robbing the inhabitants of firearms, ammunition and money,
> of incendiary letters, of maiming inoffensive and helpless persons and
> other capital crimes [note here the compilation of another list]
> notoriously committed in every quarter of the province, by many
> different parties of men, each amounting to several hundreds, so that
> the number of persons guilty of capital felonies must have amounted
> to thousands, only two person were capitally convicted; and not one
> in the extensive county of Cork, where the outrages were at least as
> flagrant and general as in any other. The cause is obvious, the
> witnesses did not dare to appear.[231]

Woodward made explicit his commitment to the empirical methodology in his remarks on his approach:

> Facts are the only sure groundwork for the discussion of this point:
> that is, facts of so general a nature as to support political conclusions.
> For the inquiry must be taken upon a large scale, not by the price of
> the tithe of a single acre, not by the rates of a single parish, nor by the
> amount of a few livings, which makes their incumbents conspicuous;
> but on the proportion, which the whole sum, raised for the parochial
> clergy shall be found to bear to the number, and station, of the
> persons employed. Such only are the proper researches of those who
> are to make national regulations.[232]

He repeatedly informed the reader of the source of his information—'an extract from an essay on the right of the clergy to a maintenance, published in London in 1726 by Mr William Webster curate of St Dunstan was communicated to me by a member of the House of Commons in this kingdom, on whose accuracy I can rely, but who does not answer for the goodness of the author's information', he carefully enunciated for instance—admitting modestly to his own limitations—'I shall with the greatest deference', he supplicated, 'submit to the public judgement such [remedies] as have occurred to me on a very mature consideration; hoping that their very defects might be of some use by inducing persons of greater penetration and more extensive knowledge of the subject to exert their abilities in supplying them'—and making recourse to the knowledge of the readership—'let the experience of every parish decide this matter'.[233] He also appealed to the conclusions drawn by a 'judicious man' in offering a 'plain account', which rested on 'common sense'.[234]

The weight such terms carried in the text contrasted with the value given to the term 'innovation', which throughout was used as a scare word. In the first section of the pamphlet, Woodward fretted over how the tithe movement might prise open a demand for wider constitutional change, seeing in

> the consequent temporary subversion of the provision for the
> established clergy . . . the extinction of the order; and what is still
> more to be feared, because it creates less public alarm, a rash spirit of
> innovation in ecclesiastical matters, too general an indifference to all
> religion, and the influence of the two great bodies of dissenters
> [Catholics and Presbyterians] on future arrangements.[235]

He feared innovation for its destructive power. Section six was revealingly entitled 'Of the bad effects of innovation on either plan'.[236] Indeed, Woodward was perplexed as to what might be envisioned by the anti-tithe campaigners as the future of the church, writing, 'What scheme, if any, may be in the contemplation of the present favourers of innovation, the writer cannot decide'.[237] This uncertainty led him to ask, 'What a chaos of confusion will such an innovation create?'[238] As his antagonism to innovation grew across the pages of the aptly named *Present State of the Church of Ireland*—for he was afraid of the future tense—he filled in the spaces in his understanding of his opponents' position with nightmarish speculations about their ambitions. In a revealing footnote he wrote:

> Of course nothing is left for the author but to draw his conjectures of
> the species of innovation which may be intended, from the projects
> suggested in common conversation—the several plans hereafter
> mentioned are not, however, mere phantoms of his own creation but
> schemes which he has heard men of good judgement on other
> subjects endeavour to support; and the least absurd . . . which have
> come to his knowledge. The judicious reader therefore, when tired of

attending to the detection of such absurdities as are obvious to a good
understanding, will pardon a trespass on his patience necessary to an
author, who is reduced . . . to the necessity of obviating the prejudices
of the ignorant and anticipating the whimsies of projectors.[239]

Here he brought together many of the rhetorical conceits that drove forward his
argument: his fear of innovation, his reliance on information drawn from conversation, his appeal to a 'judicious reader', and his contempt for 'the prejudices
of the ignorant'. These were combined with the denial of 'phantoms' and the
assertions of 'whimsies' projected onto his opponents, who were condemned as
'projectors'.

'Innovation' was set in opposition to 'improvement', which denoted careful,
considered, stately change. Yet the one could become the other, and Woodward
was determined to warn of the potential for an ill-thought alteration to unleash
uncontrollable forces of change:

The fairest prospect of improvement will not justify the risk of
innovation in a system which, in a religious view, has no equal and in
a political one, is essential to the preservation of the best constitution
that was ever framed. But in the case before us, the reverse of
improvement presents itself, at the first glance, and the more you
extend your view to the distant effects, the wider field is displayed of
national confusion and ruin, such as nothing but the necessity of
alarming the public could induce me to delineate.[240]

Faced with such 'confusion and ruin', Woodward found succour in the law,
upon which the claim for the tithe itself rested as he carefully delineated in section two of his text. In examining the charge of extortion he reasserted the legal
basis for the tithes, arguing that as the cleric

is entitled by law to take his own tenth, after it is separated from the
other nine parts . . . The terms therefore of extortion, exaction,
oppression and the like, lavished with such profusion on the clergy are
clearly as inapplicable in law as they are undeserved in fact. They
come naturally enough indeed from the mouth of a peasant, vexed at
his disappointment of a good bargain; but they fall with an ill grace
from men of a liberal, and with great inaccuracy from men of legal
education.[241]

This reliance on the law was coupled with a confidence in the operations of the state, shown when in his search for 'remedies' Woodward argued that 'from the poverty of the bulk of the people, the first impediment [the 'want of churches'] can be removed only by the bounty of parliament'; so too of the second such barrier to improvement, 'in respect of glebes, it were to be wished that a further parliamentary bounty might be extended to parishes under £60 per annum'.[242] He proposed 'that a law be enacted empowering the incumbent to exchange a portion of his tithes for a quantity of land not less than ten, or exceeding twenty acres, with the consent of the patron and the bishop'.[243] Less specific but similarly dependent on the state was his suggestion that the third and final impediment he identified, that of the language barrier between the minister and his flock, be rectified by an act of parliament. He lamented how 'sufficient care has not been taken to change the regulations of law in conformity to the alteration in circumstances'—his empiricism once again evident—'but I shall not enlarge on this subject' he submitted, 'as it will probably be under the consideration of parliament in the ensuing session.'[244]

In placing trust in the legal system, Woodward effected an alteration in the vocabulary of politics as significant as his developing of the term 'Protestant Ascendancy'. He self-consciously recast the term 'rights', so valuable to Volunteers like Drennan, as a metonym for privileges. Indeed, he favoured the complex idea 'legal rights' as a means of placing the language of rights strictly under the control, and within the grant, of the state.[245] He viewed the Rightboys as challenging the tithe payment in such a way as to have the clergy 'despoiled by violence of their legal rights', and this was in turn 'a species of attack on the legal rights of one class of the subjects of this realm, hitherto unprecedented, [which] constitutes a new grievance, for which it cannot be doubted that the justice of the legislature will provide a suitable remedy'.[246] Modestly he ascribed to the clergy, 'no further wish than to be replaced in the situation in which they stood before this new plan was devised to strip them of their legal rights', therefore, they 'think they are entitled, as one class of his majesty's subjects, to look up to the legislature for that protection.'[247] This was to translate rights into privileges and to rework the vocabulary of the reform-minded Volunteers into a language favouring the conservation of the 'present state'.

A stark polarity was thereby drawn between those reformers who favoured a rights-based politics and those defenders of the Protestant Ascendancy who considered a rights-based understanding of politics to be defective and causally connected to anarchy, and wished to reinforce the potency of privilege and the power of the polity. That the Volunteers were themselves divided on the correct approach to politics ensured that when Catholic relief—the crucial issue to which a rights-based politics was to be applied—came to the fore, the movement was prone to splitting apart.

As the poles of privilege and rights—of empiricism and rationalism—were drawing the political dialogue apart the support of the middle ground for Volunteering waned dramatically. Even as early as 1783 there were murmurs about the desirability of continuing with the movement. As one anonymous pamphlet, which raised the question of the 'conduct and continuation of the Volunteers' admitted, 'I hear it argued the Volunteers have effected their purposes, and are no longer necessary; that it is absurd to infer their future from their past discretion . . . that the superintending power of an armed and unbridled democracy is incompatible with law, commerce or tranquillity'.[248] Yet this author did not conclude that the movement was now unnecessary; he instead proposed that they adopt a self-denying ordinance removing themselves from political activity. Given their history of reforming achievement, surveyed in brief, the danger they faced that their ambition would outreach propriety: 'If they appear in ordinary political questions [they] must appear with less dignity and less effect . . . I deny that the resolutions of Volunteers are, upon ordinary questions, the most efficacious. The sacred fire should not be brought forth upon common occasions, and if it be it will not be reverenced.'[249]

A Series of Letters Addressed to the Volunteers first published in the government-sponsored *Volunteer Evening Post* in the summer of 1784 concurred, arguing that the movement was becoming the stronghold of 'abandoned ruffians' intent on radical reform.[250] The 'Volunteer' pleaded that 'we must be constantly on our guard against the insidious suggestions of desperate incendiaries and also against our own passions and prejudices', and warned against meddling in 'any speculative political question'.[251] Although foreseeing darker days ahead, he staked out the incremental reform position that would be the preserve of the Whig party in years to come. Indeed, he here petitioned for the Volunteers to reassess their judgement on Grattan for having accepted a pension, writing of how 'there is a tyranny and absurdity in our self-denying ordinance, in our wishing to exclude from all honours and emoluments those who are most worthy, and in whom we have most reason to confide. Is it possible', he asked, for 'anyone seriously to believe that Grattan, Yelverton Foster &c. are transformed from champions into betrayers by the single circumstance which ought and does attach them, if possible, more strongly to our interest, to wit, by their receiving the just reward of their merited services?'[252] The problem was, as this apologia suggests, support for moderation was unstable, and the polarities of the contest were drawing people away from the centre ground. The consequence for the Irish Enlightenment—as well as for the political system and individual citizens— was to be fatal.

The Volunteers and the Enlightenment

In the wake of the Grand National Convention, parliament pressed for a proper state militia.[253] The reform movement had failed and the Volunteers withdrew completely from political activity in 1785, resuscitating briefly in the early 1790s before being formally banned by parliament in 1793. The year before, the Dublin radical James Napper Tandy, the secretary of the United Irishmen, tried to involve them again in politics; a move which hints at how the Volunteer movement foreshadowed the conflict of the 1790s.

By 1785 the radicalisation of the two wings of the Volunteer movement was complete, and the overarching administrative structure had, effectively, broken down. On the one side lay those whose primary concern had been to enact an explicit renunciation of power by the Westminster Parliament; on the other stood those for whom the primary post-1782 issue had been the extension of the franchise through the incorporation of the Catholic populace. The first grouping resided their trust in the state; the second placed it in the people. The first party were largely content with things as they were, embodied in the privileges of the freeborn Irishman, and were empirical reformers; the second were still envisioning a restructuring of the polity deduced from natural rights and were radical rationalists. What the Grand National Convention in Dublin evidenced was that the two factions within the Volunteers were now incompatible with each other. They saw different possible futures and were committed to different principles of proceeding.

Inherent in the radicalisation of the movement that occurred in the post-1782 epoch was therefore an earlier polarisation, driven by these fundamental differences in Enlightenment methodology. For the moderates, the adoption of an empirical approach to political questions, and their acceptance that they were working within preexisting structures, resulted in an acceptance of the politics of privilege and hence an emphasis on the sentiments of the state. The state's task was to instil and encourage civilised manners in the populace it governed. In this analysis Irish political life had been misshapen because of its dependency on Britain. The desired result from the Volunteer activism was to liberate Ireland's political system from such intrusions and oversight. Privilege would be enhanced as a consequence. The focus of attention was on the state system and the Patriot party's battle with a corrupt, ineffective, and immoral administration.

In contrast, the radical wing of the Volunteers adopted a rationalist methodology in their understanding of Ireland's political plight; a method that drew on a discourse of natural rights, not on a language of privilege. This ensured that the radicals placed their focus, not on the state, but on the manners of the people, arguing for their inherent civility and the need for the state to be recast so as to better reflect the desires and wishes of the populace. The state's duty was to adequately reflect the mores of the populace, and the people were to hold politicians to account. In this analysis Irish political life was tarnished and deformed by the exclusion of the Catholic community; the Anglican state failed to reflect the manners of a Catholic people. The ambition of the radicals was to extend the franchise and recognise the claims of the people. The focus was thus on extraparliamentary involvement in the political debate and in the granting of relief to those from whom rights had been withheld. Ultimately, the Volunteer campaign in the decade from 1775 to 1785 gained independence for the parliament from British influence, but not, despite a number of relief acts, the identification of the state with the people. On the demand that it do so, the Volunteers tore themselves apart.

This was a split between those who worked from an empirical understanding of political life—they remained within the confines of a classical republican understanding enunciated in a vocabulary of privilege—and those who brought to bear a rationalist approach to the practice of political thought—they veered towards a commercial republican stance grounded in a vocabulary of rights. This was not a split between reactionaries and revolutionaries; it was a fracture within a reform movement, and an intellectual movement: the Irish Enlightenment. Since at least the 1730s the two registers, an empirical discourse and a rationalist one, had coexisted without any significant disharmony. Now it was collapsing under the strain of political consequence.

Crucially, by engaging in issues of reform, the Volunteers drew Catholic and dissenting communities into a broad debate about the future of the state, and this was not a discussion that could easily lapse. In the United Irish programme, enunciated on the movement's foundation in 1791, the aim was explicitly to overcome the confessional divisions that had shaped Irish society through the century. That might have been the agenda of the Volunteers, but they could never construct a coherent and comprehensive programmatic statement of ambitions.

Nonetheless, Catholic and Presbyterian enlistment in the Volunteer regiments marked a watershed in the political experience of many Anglicans, who for the first time stood alongside their confessional opponents in a common cause. What had begun as a Protestant defence association had morphed into a national movement, before it fragmented again on the rock of confessional recognition. Equally, the Volunteer regiments were often the first place that Catholics and Presbyterians could serve the interest of an Irish polity from which they had been excluded. Politicisation was being inculcated at the same time as public opinion formed in the ranks of the movement. The problem was that the shared process of politicisation did not result in a shared view of what the political problems were and how they ought to be solved. In fact, the opposite was the case. Once the distribution of political power was at stake, the schisms and divides within the Irish Enlightenment became increasingly intractable.

Projecting forward into the 1790s, the Volunteer movement seeded the ground for the conflict of that decade. But instead of seeing the United Irishmen as the sole inheritors of the Volunteers mantle, it is necessary to widen the lens, and realise that both sides, the republicans and the reactionaries, were upholding the legacy of militarised citizenship inherent in the Volunteers. The men of the 1790s, both in the United Irish cells and in the militia that opposed them on the battlefields of Vinegar Hill and Wexford Town, were indebted to the earlier movement, just as the philosophical stakes of the argument of the 1790s had its roots in the debates and discussions that had grown within the Irish Enlightenment in the 1770s and 1780s. The 1790s forced those disagreements into the open, ripping the Enlightenment project, and the society that housed it, apart.

9

An Enlightened Civil War

∾

We are free in theory, we are slaves in fact.
—Theobald Wolfe Tone, *An Argument on behalf of the Catholics of Ireland*, 1791

THE DECADE of the 1790s in Ireland was characterised by strange alliances. While the Volunteers in the 1770s and early 1780s attempted to speak for the nation as a whole, the difficulty of incorporating the Catholic community into the polity fractured the movement and polarised the Political Enlightenment between those whose rationalist commitments led them to argue for Catholic relief and those whose empiricism led them to fear the consequences of a dramatic reform in the confessional state. With the French Revolution, the two camps radicalised, becoming increasingly inclined to use violence in achieving their ambitions and to see their enemies as irredeemable and incomprehensible. The Enlightenment cohabitation of rationalists and empiricists ended and a civil war broke out between the two approaches to problems of politics, society, and religion. Significantly, the conflict did not map onto confessional identities.[1] Rather it was the Irish Enlightenment which unravelled across the 1790s and collapsed in the first half of 1798, when the argument turned violent.

The United Irish Rising which began on 23 May 1798 took in Dublin and the surrounding counties; Wexford; Antrim and Down; and Mayo; and left 20,000 dead. It also destroyed the possibility of a shared vision of the country emanating from the Irish Enlightenment. The initial, failed, plan was for Dublin to fall to the rebels in the first days, although fighting occurred across the province of Leinster. The Rising in Ulster was also bloody, culminating in the Battle of Ballynahinch on 12 June 1798. The most extensive United Irish military campaign occurred in County Wexford. After initial successes, which resulted in the effective control of the county ceding from the authorities, the momentum shifted. A sequence of defeats beginning at New Ross on 5 June and ending at Vinegar Hill on 21 June sealed the rebellion's fate. The intervention by 1,000 French troops into Connaught in August acted as a depressing coda to a violent season, with their final defeat occurring in Ballinamuck, County Longford, on 8 September 1798. Both sides were guilty of committing atrocities. Between 300 and 500 United Irish prisoners were massacred on the Curragh in County Kildare on 29 May, while in the immediate wake of their defeat at New Ross, the United Irish burnt to death more than 100 civilians in a barn at Scullabogue, County Wexford, on 5 June.

While the fate of the Irish Enlightenment was determined in that turbulent year, the decade which preceded it had set the terms of its demise. During those years a fissure existed in the bedrock of ontological attitudes, created by two different methodological approaches to political questions. The United Irish movement had at its heart a vision of politics as amenable to alteration. The United Irishmen offered up an ambitious vision of the country as unified by fraternal feeling, unhindered by the connection with Britain. They tended towards a rationalist approach to politics, deducing conclusions from high-minded first principles concerning civic virtue and natural rights. The consequence of this was to see current political circumstance as unacceptable and in need of radical adjustment. It prompted a visionary politics of renewal and regeneration, in which authority might legitimately be undermined, upturned, and overthrown. The temperament that inclined towards such politics contained a confidence in human ability. Paradoxically, partly because this political outlook emphasised universal rights, opponents were understood, not merely as expressive of a different social interest, but as wrongheaded and ill-informed, suffering from false consciousness. For the rationalist, the political vision offered was not merely reasonable, but an accurate analysis of circumstance, and if the opposition was not irrational, more probably corrupt, they would recognise this to be so. At the core of this political vision was a pathology of social control.

In contrast, the loyalists tended to be aware of the limitations social and political realities imposed on action. As a consequence of this intellectual modesty they leaned towards an empirical methodology. This in turn produced a pragmatic

approach to problems and a conservative temperament, which accepted the legitimacy of the establishment and defended the administration for fear of unsettling society by pursuing the fictitious abstractions of freedom, equality, and
national independence. The politics of these figures emphasised the particularity of circumstance and the need for law to recognise individual circumstance
through the grant of specific privileges; opponents were thought of as foolish
or naïve. The ultimate outcome was a technocratic approach to politics that
demanded authority be respected and obeyed. For such figures the central threat
faced by Irish society in the 1790s was political enthusiasm. At the epicentre of
this view was a pathology of political power.

Ireland descended into a civil conflict over these two visions of politics. At its
simplest, it was a contest between what one side saw as the inalienable 'rights of
man' and the other perceived as 'common sense'. It was the consequence of this
division within the Enlightenment, between rationalist utopians, who were set
on imposing their ideas of a finer, better society on the community in which they
lived, and empiricists who favoured the status quo. In Ireland, the attractions of
these visions of order destroyed the Enlightenment in the hysteria of the 1790s.

The Death of Whiggery

The 1790s saw a spectacular failure of nerve. The middle ground of Irish
intellectual and social life, where the rationalist and empirical wings of the
Enlightenment had collaborated, disintegrated as the political environment
polarised into opposing republican and loyalist camps. This process of fracture
and contestation can be observed by tracing the fate of the Irish Whigs and the
decline of the politics of constitutional reform. From the foundation of the
Whig Club in 1789, the contextual pressures produced by the French Revolution
subverted their attempts to triangulate the republican and loyalist factions. The
decision to criticise the Irish administration for its corrupt use of place and
pension gave too much ground to the republican critique for the Whigs to be
comfortable upholders of the constitution. At the same time as facing loyalist
assertions that they were guilty of subversion, the Whigs were damaged by the
republican challenge that they were not radical enough and the solution they
offered—stealthy, slight reform of the electoral franchise—was insufficient in
the face of the constitutional malaise they highlighted.[2] The difficulty they confronted shaped the 'Letters on the British Constitution', which appeared in the

pamphlet *Belfast Politics* (1793). Penned by William Bruce and Henry Joy, this series of letters, which were originally contributed to the pages of the reform-minded *Belfast News-Letter* which Joy edited in late 1792 into early 1793, articulated the dilemmas of moderate men in a rapidly radicalising political context.

At its simplest, the 'Letters' restated Whig orthodoxy concerning the utility of a mixed constitution. Outlining the three primary classical systems of government—democracy, monarchy, and aristocracy—the letters evidenced the failures of each in its pure form.[3] This paved the way for an encomium on the British constitutional settlement for encapsulating the virtues of each type, and containing the potential to correct their vices.

> It is now near two thousand years since Polybius, in contemplating the various defects to which governments were subject, conceived a mixture of the elements of each that was to avoid the errors of all. He probably did not entertain a hope that the bold flight of his fancy would be realised in the revolution of time; that the system would prove as excellent in practice as it was in theory; and that its pre-eminence would be placed beyond the possibility of doubt by its having among its other virtues the valuable one of stability.[4]

Yet despite the confidence of this ode to the British polity, the authors were concerned that this blend of theory and practice was now under threat:

> This publication was occasioned by an apprehension that some fanciful and dangerous opinions were gaining ground among the multitude. The splendid success of the French Revolution, the popular nature of its principles and the imperfect state of our representation had excited serious apprehensions that the affection of the people would be alienated from the form of government under which we live.[5]

The 'Letters' offered a damning portrait of the radicals, seeing them as motivated by speculative fancies and theoretical delusions to reject and destroy a constitution which had run the gauntlet of historical experience:

> There are persons who endeavour, in their speeches and actions, to drive things by precipitate and premature violence, to a greater extremity than one thought of before them; who seem to pay little

regard to peace and order; but speak familiarly of bloodshed and
devastation; who laugh at a government that has stood the test of
ages, and secured the domestic comfort, the internal quiet, and the
personal liberty of the people, as well as extended the power and
supported the dignity of the country abroad, better than any other
that has ever been heard of. These men trusting to, and insulting your
ignorance, throw out certain crude and fantastical ideas, which
instead of being justified by experience, are nothing more than
guess-work and conjecture.[6]

Despite this appeal to historical experience, Bruce and Joy were not dis-
counting the alternative threat posed by the advocates of unthinking loyalism.
Their Whig affiliation saved them from any sense that the constitutional liberties they held dear did not require endless vigilance to uphold. As they remarked
in a flight of lyricism,

Persecution in politics, as well as religion, is absurd. It rivets error,
while it vainly attempts to check the progress of truth: But a mild
administration of government disarms the violent, and confirms the
zeal and influence of its friends. When we imagine we are forging
fetters for human thought, we open new regions to its flight, enlarge
the sphere of its action and excite energies that were latent before.[7]

The second threat to the political balance thus came from those who might
usurp liberty in the name of order. Advocates of extensive authority were just as
threatening to the peace and tranquillity of the country as the speculators of
rational liberty.

For Bruce and Joy, a healthy median lay between a rationalist desire for
improvement and an empirical insistence on the actual state of affairs. As they
made plain, the balance to be struck was to 'anticipate evils . . . by timely reform.'[8]
The ultimate injunction was that

it is the part of every good patriot never to despair of the country, but
in every situation to act for the best; and he must be a bad citizen or a
shallow observer, who wishes that our political lethargy should
increase with the hope of being roused by a French reform. Such a
man admits no medium between slavery and revolution; the loss of
liberty and the subversion of all government. Amid ten thousand

chances of despotism and anarchy, there is scarcely one of rational freedom.[9]

Despite such intellectual energy being invested in the cause of the political centre ground, the parliamentary history of the Irish Whigs from 1789 to 1798 reads like a tragic drama, falling into three distinct acts: the period of success, the emergence of hubris, and the final fall.[10] The early period, to 1793, saw the Whigs organise and, in that year, see through a significant portion of their programme of reform. Founded in the maelstrom of the regency crisis, the intention of the Whig Club was to coordinate activity between the Irish Whigs and their British counterparts, led by the mercurial Charles James Fox. The illness and resultant mental disturbance of George III in late 1788 had, however, rather different repercussions on either side of St George's Channel. For the British Whigs, the matter was clear: there was an immediate and desirable duty to empower the Prince of Wales as regent, and to do so without the imposition of parliamentary restraint. This would result in the removal of royal favour from William Pitt and the dissolution of his administration. The prince would then distribute patronage among his confidants at the Whig bastion, Holland House.

In Ireland, the regency crisis cut across the religious issue. The Prince of Wales had long harboured an interest in Irish affairs, going so far as to risk his father's displeasure—which was liberally given and frequently expressed—by proposing himself for the office of lord lieutenant. In particular, he favoured a policy of concessions to the Roman Catholics. During the crisis, the Irish Whigs briefly gained the upper hand in the House of Commons in Dublin, with noted trimmers such as Lord Shannon moving towards support of Henry Grattan and the proponents of unhindered regency. Pitt's administration was, in contrast, determined to limit Grattan's ministry by passing an act to delimit the regent's remit and hinder his exercise of power. Crucially, Pitt was to retain control over Westminster, while his Irish administration lost control over events. According to Pitt's supporters in Ireland, the country had to accept any limits placed on a British regency without hesitation or alteration. Grattan, in contrast, contended that the Dublin parliament had a procedural role to play in recognising the incumbent. This assertion of Irish Patriot sentiments was favoured by the regent himself, who would have preferred not to be encumbered by the kind of legal restrictions on his power of patronage and policy on which Pitt was insisting. The difference highlighted the continuing dilemmas embedded in Anglo-Irish legal relations, and although the Irish Whigs passed a motion inviting the Prince of Wales to take up the office of regent without restrictions in mid-February 1789, the matter was to become moot with George III's recovery in early March.[11]

Despite such inauspicious beginnings, the Irish Whigs remained a coherent force through their adoption of a reform programme, one element of which they had proposed in the Commons in the midst of the crisis: a bill to reduce the Crown's influence by restricting the distribution of patronage. Other proposals included the reform of Dublin's constabulary, the foundation of an Irish Treasury Board to monitor expenditure, and minor reforms to the electoral franchise. All these and more were to be realised when, in 1793, the political climate once again favoured them and office beckoned.

Worn down by the persistence of the Catholic question and having already fought an extensive rearguard action the year before, the Castle party made do with speeches and grand gestures when the British government mooted the question of the Catholic franchise. This decision, and the limited tactics adopted by the Castle men, was dictated by outbreak of hostilities between Great Britain and revolutionary France in February 1793. Although willing to accept the extension of the vote to propertied Catholics, the Castle drew the line at granting the privilege of entering into the chamber itself. Catholic emancipation was to remain a live issue for a further thirty-six years.[12]

The disaffection caused by the Relief Act generated movement within the austere intransigence of the Castle party. Suddenly, in light of the act, the Ascendancy men who had long enunciated the validity of the extant constitution found value in the concept of reform, albeit directed at removing the influence of the British administration that had imposed Catholic relief. The Whig platform, for long the preserve of righteous opposition, was now the rallying cry of all Dublin politicians. The Castle party proposed a pension bill, which mimicked previous proposals made by the Whigs in capping the cost of this outlay. In a further bill the hereditary revenue of the monarch was appropriated in exchange for a parliamentary grant, offered through the mechanism of a civil list. Even more significantly, a Treasury Board, which mirrored that in Britain, was established, while all of the administration's revenue was brought under parliamentary purview. The aim of these measures was to provide the Irish parliament with a financial independence to parallel the legislative independence gained in 1782. However, the attempt to reduce government placemen was not entirely successful and parliamentary autonomy was still fundamentally limited by the fact that the lord lieutenant served at the pleasure of the British cabinet—as the Whigs were to be harshly reminded two years later.[13]

Ironically, the victories of 1793 held within them indications of Whig weakness. The Catholic Committee had significantly altered their stance towards the administration in the course of negotiations around the Repeal Act. The committee had abandoned a deferential attitude, by which they remained neutral towards the vagaries of party politics, adopting instead a more activist position. This was twinned with an articulation of the wrongs of the penal code expressed in terms of natural rights, rather than seeking a grant of toleration based on the good will of the Irish government. And this alteration was personified by the removal of Richard Burke, son of Edmund, as the committee's agent, and his replacement with Theobald Wolfe Tone.[14]

However, with the 1793 Catholic Relief Act, all that seemingly remained to quarrel over was the issue of Catholic parliamentary representation—or emancipation. This appeared at the outset a minor affair, for property restrictions suggested that even if Catholics were to be granted the freedom to sit at College Green, their numbers would remain exceptionally low—perhaps as few as three. However, for both camps the principle was more important than the technicalities. The oath of supremacy remained a security for the Protestant establishment and its continuing existence was of symbolic, as well as practical, concern. And it was this, apparently minor, concession upon which the Irish Whigs were to flounder in the four years that followed.

The second act of their drama, which saw the Irish Whigs overreach their power, was connected to the fate of the ill-fated lord lieutenancy of Earl Fitzwilliam. Appointed in late 1794 as part of the compact that drew the Duke of Portland into the orbit of William Pitt's British administration, Fitzwilliam acted too hastily in removing the traditional protagonists of Irish power, notably John Beresford, first commissioner of the revenue, and undersecretaries Cooke and Hamilton, and replacing them with those more sympathetic to his views. Indeed, in advocating the promotion of the Ponsonby faction within the Dublin government, the lord lieutenant was flouting an agreement made in London between the composite elements of the new administration. He was equally guilty of overexuberance in permitting a Catholic relief bill to be proposed by Grattan on the floor of the House of Commons on 12 February 1795, granting, amongst other concessions, parliamentary representation. His recall, decided on by the British cabinet on 21 February, after a mere two months in the country, was an ignominious retreat for Portland and a personal disaster for Fitzwilliam. It was just as significant for Grattan and the Irish Whigs who had very publicly gathered around his now-extinguished flame.[15] In particular, their brief support of the continuation of the war with France during his tenure was to haunt them with charges of political opportunism throughout the evensong of their political career. Symbolic of this defeat was the fate of the bill proposing Catholic emancipation: it fell on its second reading, on 4 May, by 155 votes to eighty-four.

Finally, in 1797, the Whigs imploded, withdrawing from parliament in recognition of their political impotency. The final blow was the defeat, in the early hours of 16 May, of W. B. Ponsonby's bill forwarding reform of the boroughs in parliament and Catholic emancipation. With defeat looming, Grattan announced to the chamber that 'we have offered you our measure—you will reject it; we deprecate yours; you will persevere; having no hopes left to persuade or dissuade, and having discharged our duty, we shall trouble you no more and after this day shall not attend the House of Commons.'[16] He defended this action in a pamphlet publication in July 1797, drawing attention to the three foundational principles on which he opposed the administration: Catholic emancipation, political repression and parliamentary reform.[17]

That Grattan appealed to the public sphere only underlines how the Irish Whig stock had fallen, for it was no safe place from which to assert moral supremacy, and a flood of criticism rebuking his actions soon spilled from rival presses.[18] Having rejected parliament, Grattan was soon associated by his antagonists with the sedition inherent in the United Irish movement; in the words of a one-time ally, Charles Francis Sheridan—brother of the dramatist Richard Brinsley Sheridan—with regard to the constitution, 'its determined enemies are close at the heels of its discontented friends.'[19] While this was to misrepresent Grattan's position, the perception of his sympathy for the Rising deprived him of the status of Irish privy councillor on 8 October 1798, and saw him struck off the membership rolls of the capital's Guild of Merchants and Corporation. Trinity College Dublin, although itself a seedbed of student activism on behalf of the United Irish movement, had a deeply loyalist community of fellows and they too took umbrage, removing Grattan's portrait from its place in the Examination Hall's gallery of worthies, symbolically replacing his image with depictions of Edmund Burke and John FitzGibbon.[20] The high tide of moderate reform had retreated, revealing the battleground on which more extreme forces would soon fight.

Empirical Realists

The dissolution of the Irish Whigs granted the field to the more extreme exponents of the Protestant Ascendancy. Indeed, as Grattan predicted, the administration lost no time in pressing on with their policy of repression. The day following the withdrawal, 17 May 1797, the government proscribed the United Irish movement. This policy was advocated by the Beresford faction that Earl Fitzwilliam had tried to sideline, and by John FitzGibbon, Earl of Clare, whose antipathy to the United Irishmen was visceral. Although himself of Catholic stock, his father having converted to Anglicanism to enable a career at the bar, FitzGibbon became an articulate exponent of the establishment in church and state.[21] While his careerism and scathing tongue earned him few friends, he was grudgingly admired and advanced to positions of power. His central political insights drew from his experience on the Munster legal circuit in the aftermath of the Whiteboy agrarian outrages of the 1760s, namely his awareness of Irish political dependence on British military and fiscal support and of how radical politics was a toxic cause of social disaggregation. While the first insight saw him mocked and disdained by his parliamentary colleagues as a mere creature of British politicians—no less a figure than Lord Lieutenant Westmorland observed that 'he has no God but English government'—his second perception led him into the vanguard of opposition to the forces of United Irish republicanism.[22]

The intellectual basis of this outlook originated in a deeply realist philosophical temperament. FitzGibbon was little given to abstract speculation or metaphysical meditations. He dealt in the uncomfortable detail of existence, recognising the intractable imperfection of particular circumstance. This did not imply a simpleminded acceptance of the status quo, however. It is significant that FitzGibbon was an active agricultural improver and prone to giving lengthy homilies on the subject in the chamber of the House of Commons. This tendency to exhort his fellow parliamentarians to attend to such mundane matters is indicative less of a pedestrian mind than of an instinctively pragmatic response to political and social problems, a tendency which was expressed in his response to the Catholic demands for relief from the penal code. When, on 10 January 1793, the king's speech proposed that 'the situation of his majesty's Catholic subjects' be attended to with 'wisdom and liberality', FitzGibbon used the occasion to express his opposition to any remedial measures.[23] He targeted a pamphlet on the legal status of the Catholic community, which had contended that the penal code constituted a retrograde bulwark, retarding the economy and prompting political disaffection; a breach in faith with regard to the Articles of Limerick which contravened the natural rights of man to self-defence. In each case, FitzGibbon responded by declaring that the breach of faith was on the part of the authors of the pamphlet who he accused of misstating the actual circumstance.

The structure of the rebuttal was established when FitzGibbon addressed the charge that Catholics were unable to own weapons and hence were 'exposed to the violence of burglary, robbery and assassination'. In response to this general charge, he considered the specifics of the legal case, countering a broad principled accusation with precise contradictory evidence:

> The prohibition is stated as general and without exception . . . In
> these laws there is an exception for every man of that persuasion who
> shall obtain a licence from the lord lieutenant and privy council to
> carry arms; and that such a licence has never in any instance within
> the memory of man been denied to a Catholic whose rank and
> education entitled him to it.[24]

In dealing with the charge which, he admitted, were it true 'would be an outrage upon every principle of natural justice', he delved into the context and application of the enactment.[25] He first highlighted how the measure had been prompted, not by a fear of rebellious Catholicism, but by the agrarian outrages perpetrated by the Whiteboys, before reminding his audience that there was within the act a clause ensuring 'that no person shall be convicted, or incur any penalty, for any offence, upon any confession, or discovery made on such examination'.[26] Confession did not lead to criminal proceedings thus negating the charge levelled by the Catholic pamphleteers.

Indeed, for FitzGibbon, the real danger lay in Catholic activists undermining the shared interests of the Anglican and Catholic elite. The danger of arming the population at large came not from the Catholic community as such, but from the disaffected and mobilised lower ranks of society. As he explained,

> I am sorry to say, that at this hour, such is the rude state of the lower
> order of the people of all religions in Ireland, that if offensive weapons
> are to be put into their hands, every man of property who lives in the
> remote districts, whether Catholic or Protestant, will quickly feel to his
> cost, that he is daily exposed to the violence of burglary and robbery.[27]

This identification of economic interests offered FitzGibbon a practical reason why the landed Anglican elite would not, indeed could not, eject their Catholic tenantry as his antagonists claimed, namely, that 'there are not enough Protestants in the country to occupy the soil'.[28]

In noting how, in one of his occasional tirades on the state of Irish agriculture, the real problem was the free and open resale of the lot at the end of each lease, leaving the tenants insecure and unwilling to invest in improvements, FitzGibbon revealed the cornerstone of his methodological approach to political dilemmas: personal experience. As he recalled, 'It happened to me in the year 1783, to canvas the county in which I live, and on an estate which had been newly set at 26,000*l.* a year, as I recollect, I found but five Protestant tenants.'[29] This reminiscence followed hard on a wider claim to authority, for he asserted 'so far as my experience goes, and I think that few men are better acquainted with the South of Ireland than I am, where a great majority are of the Popish religion.'[30]

The speech ended with a forceful declaration of precisely this practical, first-hand approach to politics. In the case of the Catholic question, FitzGibbon asserted that

> I do most solemnly protest, that as an individual, I have never, nor will
> I ever enquire what may be the religion of any man.—If he be an
> honest man, whatever his religion may be, it shall never influence me
> in my private dealing, and the more zealously any man is attached to
> any religion which he professes, the greater confidence I will be
> inclined to place in him . . . If there be a clause in the statue book
> which restrains their religious worship—if there be a clause which
> renders their characters, their persons, or their property less secure than
> the characters, persons or properties of Protestants, let it be repealed,
> but if any man can be so wild as to look to a total repeal of the Popery
> laws of this kingdom—if any man can be so wild as to desire to
> communicate the efficient power of a free Protestant government to a
> great majority of the people of Ireland, professing the Popish religion, I
> do not scruple to say, that it is an absurd and wicked speculation.[31]

Confessional tolerance here found its limits.

Moreover, it is certain that FitzGibbon was intellectually, as well as emotionally, opposed to the abstract schemes of reform proposed by the United Irishmen. Less obvious perhaps, because well-guarded by his public persona, was a pragmatic bent of mind which saw Irish interest as best served by the English connection, but also prompted piecemeal answers to structural problems. An empirical temperament, at home among particularities, was confronted in the 1790s with esoteric challenges to structures that had been relied on throughout his career. He responded with a fervour born of fear.

In this, FitzGibbon shared something with the most violent and extreme exponent of the empirical faction within the Irish Enlightenment. Sir Richard Musgrave was a hard-line voice of anti-Catholic bigotry and a reactionary defender of the establishment; a product of the heartland of hard-line ultra-Protestantism: Munster.[32] Musgrave was the member of parliament for the pocket borough of Lismore from 1778 to 1800, having held office as the sheriff of County Waterford, from which vantage point he may have first formulated his view of the intractability of the Roman Catholic character.[33] Although he was allied by marriage and patronage to the Whiggish Ponsonby faction, his opinion of the desirability of Catholic emancipation diverged from their tolerant outlook. In particular, the resurgence of agrarian unrest in north Munster in the shape of the Rightboys may have played upon his mind, although west Waterford, the location of his parliamentary seat, remained relatively tranquil. Inactive as an MP for much of the late 1780s and 1790s, through financial constraints upon his autonomy, Musgrave wrote in favour of war with revolutionary France in 1794, and again in 1796. His antipathy to the growing radicalism in Ireland was galvanised by the presence of a Roman Catholic bishop, Thomas Hussey, in the region in 1797, for in his criticism of government policy Musgrave detected a religious dimension to the political tensions crowding in on him. When a tithe war ensued late that year, in the wake of collapsing grain prices, Waterford remained relatively calm; but when the Castle, under Cornwallis, chose to adopt a lenient response to the Rising of 1798, Musgrave's ire reached boiling point.

In January 1799, in response to a pamphlet by Veritas defending the reputation of the Catholic clergy of Wexford, Musgrave published *A Concise Account of the Material Events and Atrocities which Occurred in the Late Rebellion*.[34] This laid out the central conspiracy theory which, for Musgrave, accounted for the crisis in the Irish polity in the previous decade. He asserted that Catholicism had a despotic character, and that the Rebellion was the consequence of the inveterate Roman Catholic hatred of Protestantism, defending this thesis through an examination of events in Wexford.[35] There, and across the uprising as a whole, Musgrave found consistent and damning detail that the clergy were responsible for the virility of the conflict. He asserted that 'it has appeared from many collateral facts, that they seldom exerted that authority which they unquestionably had to save the lives of the unfortunate Protestants.'[36] Nor, he recalled, had 'the Popish prelates . . . in a body, exhort[ed] the Roman Catholics to loyalty and a peaceable deportment until the 26th of May, and few, if any of them did so previous to that period.'[37] Worse than this immoral indifference was the activism of numerous individual clergy—he took the time to list them—who were implicated in the insurgency. As he observed,

> the town of Wexford and all the rebel camps were constantly attended
> by great numbers of priests, who animated and exhorted the rebels by
> inflammatory and sanguinary harangues, and daily said Mass for
> them. The truth is they believed a rising was general all over Ireland,
> that Dublin was in the hands of rebels, and that a complete subver-
> sion of the Protestant state, and a separation from England, which
> they meditated, must take place.[38]

The implication of this clerical support was that the Rebellion was considered a sacred mission; a confessional conflict; a war of religion.

Musgrave acknowledged that the Rebellion was far more widespread and more ecumenical than this suggested. Yet while the Rising in Ulster complicated his simplistic, monocausal analysis, he was quick to dismiss Presbyterian sympathisers and even Anglican advocates of the United Irish cause as stooges, taken in by the malicious machinations of their Catholic counterparts.

> The first leaders consisted of a motley list of Protestants, Presbyterians
> and Papists, but it is notorious that the latter artfully concealed their
> secret design of extirpating the former till the rebellion broke
> out . . . That monster Popish fanaticism lurked behind the curtain
> and meditated the destruction of all Protestants without distinction.[39]

Of the Presbyterians, potentially fellow members of a pan-Protestant front, Musgrave offered compensatory praise of their character, highlighting how the rebellion in the north of the country was more orderly and better conducted than elsewhere, which he understood as involving the barbaric disintegration of social ties:

> It is observable that Presbyterians were almost exclusively concerned
> in the conspiracy and rebellion in the counties of Down and Antrim;
> and though they have more intellect, more courage and were better

supplied with arms, than the inhabitants of the former, the destruction of property in them was but small compared to it in the counties
of Mayo, Kildare, Wicklow and Wexford, where the rebels were
impelled by Popish fanaticism; and in the former there was no general
massacre and but few if any assassinations.[40]

Yet the centre of Musgrave's thesis was not that the Catholic rebellion was an
ill-formed, undirected, atavistic upheaval of a mob. Rather he attributed the
ferocity and venom of the violence in Wexford to Roman Catholic despotism;
quite simply, 'the spirit of Popery is equally destructive in all times and
places.'[41] From this position he expanded beyond the parochial concerns of specific events in Wexford to find in history empirical evidence of his conceit. In a
lengthy prelude to his treatment of 1798, he recounted how the origins of
Catholic tyranny lay in the Lateran Council's decision of 1215 to extirpate heresy.
This determination, which gave the pope power to police thought, expanded his
remit into the secular domain, for as Musgrave made clear, the intention was to
destroy the heretic. It was this claim over the secular world that differentiated
Catholicism from Anglicanism: 'The Romish bishops, in their oath of inauguration, promise to persecute and impugn the persons of heretics, the Protestant
bishops merely that they will banish and drive away erroneous *doctrines*.'[42] The
Lateran Council had inaugurated an era of religious persecution, in which
Catholic prelates could renounce secular laws, excommunicate monarchs, and
exonerate murder.[43]

In documenting this, Musgrave differentiated between Catholicism and the
pure form of Christianity which was enunciated by Anglicanism, but which was
not, intriguingly, necessarily encompassed by it. This rather unexpected ecumenism on his part enabled him to comprehend the actions of Catholic loyalists: 'many of the Popish noblemen and gentlemen were loyal during the rebellion and why? Because though they conformed to a few idle ceremonies and
believed in a few speculative doctrines of their church, they were in their moral
conduct Christians, and not Papists.'[44]

In Musgrave's view, at the Lateran Council Catholicism had absented itself
from the Christian tradition. It had set aside the vocabulary of love and the
message of mutual comprehension preached by Christ. In turning away from
the gospel message, it had chosen secular power over spiritual glory; indeed, in
pursuing the baubles of political splendour, the Roman Catholic Church had

become a force for atheism. As he summarised his stance, the rebels were 'Catholics in profession, but Deists in religion.'[45]

This analysis of the Rebellion as the confrontation between the constant spiritual power of Protestantism and the malignant secular atheism of Roman Catholicism was given full voice in his next publication, *Memoirs of the Different Rebellions in Ireland from the Arrival of the English* (1801).[46] This put bones on Musgrave's basic thesis of Catholic perfidy, Presbyterian false consciousness, and peasant atavism. Termed a memoir, which underlined the historicity and the immediacy of the text, it replayed the personal experience of numerous actors within the cauldron of the Rebellion, and highlighted the long historical record of rebellious activity among Irish Catholics, particularly since the Whiteboy agitations of the 1760s. This documentary approach was in line with a deep methodological empiricism.

Published in the immediate wake of the union—a measure he supported—Musgrave defended his intolerant thesis by providing an atrocity album.[47] Page after page of macabre and ghoulish detail built up an inventory of barbaric torture, illustrating the intrinsic sadism of the Catholic community in their treatment of the Protestant bystander and the loyal servant of the state.[48] Musgrave provided, through a series of set pieces, or attitudes, a drama of cruelty and satanic malevolence. In the case of the notorious massacre at Wexford Bridge, in which retreating rebels summarily killed their prisoners, he described with clinical, gruesome precision how individual after individual died, an atrocity so extensive that

> when the rebels retreated from the bridge . . . [Thomas] Dixon and
> his wife attempted to follow them; but their horses started at the
> immense quantity of blood which was shed on the bridge, and refused
> to pass through it; on which they dismounted, and led their horses
> over the bridge; she at the same time, holding up her riding habit, lest
> it should be stained with blood. She was heard to desire the rebels not
> to waste their ammunition, but to give the prisoners plenty of
> piking.[49]

Even nature baulked at scenes the rebel sympathisers merely adjudged an inconvenience to their fashions.

To depict the physical nature of this crime, Musgrave offered his readers a series of direct quotations from witnesses, described as 'some respectable persons', who by recounting their immediate experience lent veracity to his account.[50] As one lady diarist exclaimed, 'I thought some alarm induced them to leave the town, and sat eagerly watching, till I beheld, yes I saw, absolutely saw, a poor fellow cry for life, and was then most barbarously murdered.'[51] These honourable, and therefore trustworthy, witnesses stood in stark contrast to the rebel insurgents who committed the crimes. According to one James Goodall, 'the assassins on the bridge were like a pack of starving hounds rushing on their game.'[52] Again, the lady diarist captured the inferiority of the rebels and the empirical nature of the evidence; note her emphasis on sound, sight and touch:

> No savages ever put their prisoners to more deliberate torture . . . I
> saw the horrid wretches kneel on the quay, lift up their hands,
> seeming to pray with the greatest devotion, then rise and join, or take
> the place of other murderers. Their yells of delight at the sufferings of
> their victims will ever, I believe, sound in my ears. To describe what
> we all suffered would be impossible. I never shed a tear, but felt all
> over in the most bodily pain.[53]

This empirical register was supported by the citation of other accounts, as well as the compilation of intimate, if anecdotal, detail. Indeed, the cumulative effect of chapters recounting 'the attack upon Naas', 'the attack on the town of Prosperous', 'the attack upon Clane by the rebels', the 'insurrection near Dunlavin', 'the attack upon Monastereven' and so forth, was to insist on the extent of the rebellious conspiracy, the insidious nature of the plot, and the profound psychological impact it had upon a loyal, respectable, Protestant people. This was further shown by the inclusion of numerous maps of the battlefields, making visible the geographic reach of the insurgency.

The sense that Musgrave was marshalling a vast quantity of empirical evidence in favour of his case was accentuated by the addition of a vast appendix, containing numerous contemporary documents. The second and third editions underscored the importance of this buttress to the architecture of the main text by providing further appendices containing yet more documentation. Most significant, however, was a series of headings under which 'a list of Protestants massacred' in particular events or regions was supplied. Drawn from affidavits given to the parliamentary committee appraising damages and compensation, the effect of these lists was to put a human face on the suffering and, paradoxically, to overwhelm the reader with the sheer quantity of the data indicting the

Catholic community of sadistic brutalism. For example, the entry on the fate of the Protestant community in the diocese of Ferns began:

> Samuel Atkin, tide waiter at Wexford, massacred at the bridge of Wexford.
> James Austin of Ballyadams, murdered; left a wife and six children.
> James Aston of Kilmuckridge, murdered there.
> Reverend Thomas Troke, curate, murdered on Vinegar Hill, first of June, his widow in a state of derangement from her misfortunes; one of her children was starved to death, and another died from the same cause.
> William Daniel, surveyor, murdered on the bridge at Wexford twentieth of June 1798, left a widow and seven children in the utmost distress.[54]

This inventory of suffering covers twenty-two pages.

A desired policy of state-sponsored reprisal against the rebels was empirically justified in Musgrave's view given the record of political untrustworthiness and the immediate evidence of criminal aggression on the part of the Catholic community. The Catholics' attitude to the state, for Musgrave, was no more than a manifestation of their intrinsic political disaffection and a consequence of their barely suppressed tyrannical ambition. The text was thereby telling the Protestant readership that their immediate fate, and their ultimate salvation, was dependent on their comprehension of Catholicism as a carnivorous, elemental force within Irish society.[55]

In Musgrave's account there are the dark prognostications of a religious enthusiast; in FitzGibbon's response, the anxiety of a pessimistic legislator. Yet in both, the Rebellion was comprehended through the exercise of empirical compilation and analysis. What this suggests is that there existed a spectrum of loyalist thought from devotees of the establishment like FitzGibbon to the apocalyptic enthusiasm of Musgrave. It was a distinctly mixed alliance, drawn together by a pragmatic approach to political problems and an empirical methodology in their dealings with the world.[56]

Rationalist Idealists

The politics the loyalists feared was built upon a deductive rationalism that drew radical and utopian conclusions from first principles its advocates asserted in terms of inalienable rights and universal laws. To loyalists, this seemed unnatural and hallucinatory in imagining a fantastical world at odds with the truths of existence. To Musgrave, for example, the United Irish movement drew in the unsuspecting, idealistic Presbyterian middling sort and the muddleheaded Catholic peasantry, and guided them maliciously to their doom. For many of the most committed activists, however, it was moral principle and ethical independence that committed them to a reformist and, ultimately, revolutionary cause. It was precisely that it offered a future other than the corrosive drudgery of current circumstance that won people over and inspired them to sacrifice their lives.

The foundational document of 1791, penned by Theobald Wolfe Tone, made many of the United Irish movement's intellectual commitments clear.[57] Twice in the space of a few hundred words Tone made reference to the rights of man, describing the era as one in which for Europe 'the rights of man are ascertained in theory and substantiated in practice' and desiring 'the equal distribution of the rights of man through all the sects and denominations of Irishmen.'[58] This outcome was thwarted by confessional squabbles within Irish society, although hope was drawn from the European trend whereby 'religious persecution is compelled to abjure her tyranny over conscience.'[59] In Ireland, this ambition was further frustrated by an external despotism, darkly served by a system of internal corruption. According to Tone,

> We have no national government; we are ruled by Englishmen, and the servants of Englishmen, whose object is the interest of another country, whose instrument is corruption, and whose strength is the weakness of Ireland; and these men have the whole power and patronage of the country as a means to seduce and to subdue the honesty and the spirit of her representatives in the legislature.[60]

In the face of this system of political degradation, the United Irishmen appealed to public opinion—'We submit our resolutions to the nation'—promising to remove the influence of England from Irish affairs, reform the representative system of a discredited parliament, and reunite the religious communities of the island in fraternal love.[61]

Within the ranks of the United Irish movement was a similar spectrum to that found on the loyalist side of the argument. And just as moderate loyalist voices were drowned out by demands for decisive action, so too the United Irish movement tried unsuccessfully to contain a variety of radicalised opinions. William Drennan and similar moderates became disillusioned by the increasingly insurgent quality of the movement, and with its developing fascination with the politics of violence.[62] Among those who remained there were still significant differences of emphasis over policy, which even survived the Rebellion and divided the movement during their incarceration in Fort George. While there, the factionalism and personal animosity between Arthur O'Connor and Thomas Addis Emmet reached such a pitch they intended to duel upon their release.

This incident suggests that a residual influence of the mores of aristocratic republicanism stirred in the breasts of the United Irish leaders. O'Connor, a case in point, was the offspring of a landed family in Cork, and so born into this cultural outlook. So connected was he that, when on trial for sedition in England in April 1798, he was able to call Henry Grattan and Charles James Fox as character witnesses. Yet his life reveals an increasingly rapid slide towards violent political endeavour.[63] His central political tenets were laid out in their most theoretically articulate fashion in *The State of Ireland* (1798), published in the immediate run-up to the Rebellion. Therein, O'Connor's viciously condemned the corruption he saw as corroding the health of the country:

> If, then, this sacred fund [the capital assets of the country] has been
> squandered by the government and legislature of Ireland—if every
> means by which Irish industry could acquire Irish capital has been
> sacrificed to sell the funds, and to promote the industry, of Great
> Britain, I do not hesitate to assert that the government and legislators
> of Ireland have been the most prostitute hirelings, that they have
> committed the foulest treason against the people of Ireland that ever
> government or legislature committed against a people.[64]

While this thesis echoed the harangues of many Irish Patriots, in the structure of his argument O'Connor revealed his rationalist, and radical, colours. The argument moved repeatedly from theoretical assumption to observable fact. It was a deductive methodology, which set up an ideal type, a norm, or a standard, through which the 'state of Ireland' was measured and assessed. Take, for example, an early passage in which O'Connor reflected on the freedom of religion. It began by making fundamental, unverifiable, and deistic assumptions about the nature of God:

> When I contemplate the various attributes of that mighty power, which has created and moved the myriads of worlds I see floating around me—when as an inhabitant of this globe, which the same power has created and animated, I attempt from the contemplation of his works, to collect the numerous laws by which he ordained that his creatures should be directed and governed—when I consider the difficulty of knowing which to admit, and which to reject, of those writings which in so many ages, and in so many nations, have been received and accredited as coming from God, for the rule and direction of man—when I consider how many various interpretations the mind of man has given to those scriptures, received and accredited among Christians, written in trope, in metaphor, in figure, in parable and in allegory—I cannot conceive how any two thinking men (and I hold those who think not for themselves, but who leave it to others to think for them of no account) could form the same opinion on such an extensive and difficult subject.[65]

From here, the passage asserted the right of individuals to a free conscience, again a philosophical assumption and one at variance with the perception of a zealous believer who might wish to extirpate heresy. For O'Connor, however, the issue was clear:

> What possible right can one man set up to interfere with the faith and belief of another? What standard do those who do not agree, use by which they settle their difference? Or without such a standard, how can the controversy ever be decided? These considerations and a thousand others, with imperious mandate, consecrate the right of the individual in his religious opinions against the whole world beside. It is a concern between him and his God.[66]

Only then, once these assumptions were proposed, could the condition of the country be properly diagnosed:

> If a whole nation has no right to interfere with the most insignificant citizen in his religious opinions, so as to do him the slightest injustice

for the freest exercise of the imprescriptible right, by what title does
one class of Irish Protestants, not one tenth of the nation, arrogate the
power of appropriating such exorbitant funds for the ministers of its
religion, to which the other nine tenths are not only made to
contribute, but to pay their own religious instruction besides?[67]

This structure of argument, from the statement of initial axioms, through the
assertion of universal rights, to concluding with a critique of the current circumstance was repeated time and again. The wastage caused by the legal system's profligacy, the expense of education, the imposition of land tax to failing national
industries and the financial burden of government were discussed in relation to
the corruption of principle as much as the inefficiency of practice. This last topic,
the cost of administration, suggested a sublime alternative, binding together the
sentiments of the legislators and the manners of the people in a utopian daydream:

When they [the laws] are such as to secure every member equally the
fullest enjoyment of his natural rights, the freest expression of his
industry, and the most undisturbed fruition of its produce—when
they open to him every means of acquiring the most ample and liberal
wages, by which he may procure the necessaries and comforts of
life—when by securing to his industry the most extensive markets for
the work he has wrought, it ensures him constant employment—
when he suffers no peculation—when no deductions are made from
his earnings but what his own interest tells him he should readily and
willingly grant—trust me, fellow citizens, a government founded on
principles like these would require no expense to support it. In such a
government, every citizen would find a protection for every blessing,
for every comfort, human society was meant to afford. Here the laws
would be held in veneration, and the legislators would be respected,
revered and beloved. In this state no military execution, no bastilles,
no gibbets, no burning of houses, would be required to protect and
uphold usurpation, corruption and treason![68]

As in this passage, what O'Connor's rhetorical structure of principle-right-
criticism produced was a shadow text at which the actual writing only hints. In
this alternate version the ideals and principles O'Connor assumed to be universal truths were actualised in a reformed, regenerated Ireland. This hidden

Ireland remains, however, a ghostly, ethereal paradise that haunts the book, filled instead with the grubby detail of a fetid reality, enabling O'Connor to forward his demands for the reform and renewal of the country, namely 'Catholic emancipation and a restoration of popular representation'.[69]

Through the consistent device of contrasting the ideal with the actual, the pamphlet pointed towards the potential of the country. Yet despite his theoretical ambitions and the impassioned nature of his prose, O'Connor remained within the middle ground of reformist thought. He never veered from accepting the essential legitimacy of social and property relations within the country. However, at the most extreme edges of the United Irish movement resided people who were prepared to see the whole system of property holding unsettled. The most prominent example of this wing of the movement was Thomas Russell.[70] An outspoken advocate of social radicalism, including a policy of land redistribution, his thought was infused with a premillennial religious vision of the saintly life.[71] That he failed to live up to the ethos of his own philosophy, often sinking into sexually induced guilt (he frequented prostitutes) and drunkenness, only hurried his activism when sated and sober.[72]

While Russell never produced a concrete proposal for land reform or a study of Irish economic circumstance, his attraction to social revolution was clearly indicated in *A Letter to the People of Ireland, on the Present Situation of the Country* (1796). The aim of this publication was to forward the sentimental unification of the Irish people, fragmented by religious disagreement and vested economic interests:

> It is obvious that the interests of some of these landholders will in
> small matters clash with each other; though in the main object, that
> of holding in their hands the power of the country against the people
> at large, they will agree. In proportion then as the people show any
> desire to assume political consequence, these gentlemen will all unite
> with the English party against the common enemy—the people—and
> in proportion as the people are crushed and torpid, the separate
> interest of these gentlemen in counties and boroughs, making of
> roads, canals, excisemen, commissioners, bishops, judges &c. &c. &c.
> will be considered.[73]

Positioning the people in the role of 'common enemy' to the Irish gentry and English administration enabled Russell to extol the virtue of unity while highlighting the civic decency of the peasantry. Russell's social radicalism thus informed his economic treatment of the country. In line with Physiocratic theory, he began with the contention that 'agriculture is the basis of all riches, commercial as well as others; the earth was given to man by he who alone had a right to give it, for his subsistence'; a premise which led him to propose an alteration in social attitudes to 'let not those then who raise the fruits of it among us be despised.'[74] In contrast to the celebration of the landed gentry which underpinned much loyalist thought, Russell followed a Lockean labour theory of value to undermine their political pretensions:

> The fact is, the rich men (those whose wealth derives from commerce excepted) derive their wealth from the labours of the poor. The possession of land without cultivators is of no value to a man, except so much as could support himself, and that several of these gentlemen who vilify the mob would be but ill qualified to do. It is not here intended to question the right of landed property; but merely to show . . . the mass of the people are entitled to a share in the government as well as the rich.[75]

However, the moral character of the common people had been eroded by the turpitude of social superiors, who alternated between abstaining from ethical leadership and aggressive maladministration. In exculpation of the peasantry's sins he wrote 'that the lower orders, thus left to themselves, conceiving that they were oppressed and without people of knowledge or consequence to advise or protect them, should at times commit unjustifiable actions is not surprising.'[76] He further argued that

> great pains have been taken to prevent the mass of mankind from interfering in political pursuits; force and argument, and wit, and ridicule, and invective, have been used by the governing party, and with such success that any of the lower, or even the middling rank of society who engage in politics have been and are considered not only as ridiculous, but in some degree culpable; even those who are called moral writers, employed their talents on the same side, so that at last it became an indisputable maxim that the poor were not to concern themselves in what related to the government of the country in which they lived; nevertheless, it is an error of the most pernicious nature.[77]

Redemption was grounded upon Russell's further assumption that 'the God of Heaven and earth endowed these men with the same passions and the same reason as the great, and consequently qualified them for the same liberty, happiness and virtue.'[78] Aware as he was that rational deduction to universal solutions might be open to dismissal as foolish speculation Russell underlined the practicality of his visionary politics by availing of lengthy historical exegesis to suggest empirical foundations for his theoretical analysis. Indeed, in a critical passage he declaimed: 'Whenever an Union of the people takes place—when they once consider all Irishmen as their friends and brethren, the power of the aristocracy will vanish' adding immediately 'nor is this abstract reasoning: let the facts be appealed to.'[79] Nonetheless, despite ceding ground to his antagonists, Russell's fundamental approach was in line with a rationalist methodology, deducing conclusions from first principles, each based on a vision of man as personally responsible for his own opinions and actions. The conclusion was drenched in optimism about the human condition, asserting the power of human autonomy:

> The great object of mankind should be to consider themselves accountable for their actions to God alone, and to pay no regard or obedience to any men or institution which is not conformable to his will. It is on this account that liberty should be sought and is truly estimable; by breaking and destroying those prejudices and institutions that made man bow down before man, or his law; and to those idols of his own making, offer up the sacrifice of his abilities, his conscience, and his eternal happiness.[80]

Unlike the loyalists, for whom the legitimacy of the establishment was empirically proven by the passage of time, for Russell reason and morality pointed to revolution.

In the 1790s, therefore, through a process of continuing political radicalisation, the Enlightenment was slowly breaking asunder. The consequence of the political discord was the tearing apart of the modest settlement of empiricism and rationalism that had enabled so much social interaction, intellectual endeavour, and practical change to occur across the century. With the rapid disintegration of the middle ground, the Enlightenment began to divide as empirical caution and rational flights of fancy contended against each another. The Enlightenment was heading into war with itself.

Cultural Conflict

While imprisoned in Fort George after the Rebellion, Arthur O'Connor composed a neat intellectual squib. Apparently loyal in sentiment, it revealed a covert polemical charge when the first line of the second verse was read immediately after the first line in the first, alternating back and forth in a subversion of the traditional method of reading:

> The pomp of courts, and pride of kings
> I prize above all earthy things;
> I love my country, but the King
> Above all men his praise I sing;
> The royal banners are display'd
> And may success the standard aid.
>
> I fain would banish far from hence
> The 'Rights of Man' and common sense;
> Confusion to his odious reign,
> That foe to princes, Thomas Paine!
> Defeat and ruin seize the cause
> Of France, it liberties and laws![81]

What this radical revision of reading practices suggests is that the United Irish project was more than a political programme of reform or renewal. It also contained a novel cultural order, which in turn required a new kind of man.[82] Rationalism demanded the demise of superstitious and illogical cultural formations and attitudes and their replacement with a fresh community of independent cultural creators. Because of the extent of this agenda, the United Irishmen did not restrict themselves to political production. The need to regenerate society ensured that their remit included works of literature, art, and music. And in confronting the threat, the loyalist cause responded in kind, asserting the validity of an organic theory of culture, and defending it from the interventions of the projectors. The conflict of the 1790s was therefore not merely political: it involved a struggle over public opinion and wider cultural production.[83]

It is indicative of United Irish concerns that the movement contained a number of notable poets.[84] Most prominent of these was the society's founding father, William Drennan. The one-time Volunteer, and author of the *Letters of Orellana, An Irish Helot* (1784), he also penned a slew of sentimental verse, making heroes of those who were to sacrifice themselves to the Society's cause. Typical of these compositions was 'Erin', the first poem to be printed in the United Irish vehicle *The Star* (on 5 October 1797) and included afterwards in *Paddy's Resource*, the United Irish songbook. It is in this poem that Drennan coined the term 'the emerald isle'. Beginning with the image of an island, independent by dint of geography, the verse offered a mournful depiction of the woes of the country, torn by civil strife and oppressed by British rule, before a rousing finale calling for a political struggle. During this arc Drennan shifted the emotional register from pride in the country, through despair and sorrow at its condition, before ending with a steely note of defiance—producing patriotic ardour in a by now emotionally primed reader:

> The cause it is good, and the men they are true
> And the green shall outlive both the orange and blue;
> And the daughters of Erin her triumph shall share
> With their full-swelling chest, and their fair-flowing hair.[85]

In 'The Wake of William Orr', published in *The Star* on 13 January 1798, Drennan celebrated the life and death of a young member of the United Irishmen, the first to be executed for inciting sedition under the terms of the 1796 Insurrection Act. He evoked an emotional response by comparing the hero's fate with his many merits, instilling a sense of outrage that Orr had been treated so disgracefully by the Irish administration. Orr's fate was then transfigured into a microcosm of the macrocosmic crisis engulfing Ireland, becoming a harbinger of change and a stimulus to action:

> Write his merits on your mind,
> Morals pure and manners kind;
> On his head, as on a hill,
> Virtue placed a citadel
> . . . .
> Hapless nation, hapless land,
> Heap of uncementing sand!
> Crumbled by a foreign weight,
> Or by worse, domestic hate![86]

This sentimentalisation of the Irish country and the lamentation over the fate of its people was again intended to inspire the readers to political action.

While the United Irish movement had within its ranks numerous versifiers, the poems they penned were not merely pastoral odes or romantic laments. The polemical charge of these works derived from the fact that they inculcated political values—notably republican virtue—and articulated demands for constitutional and social change. In this, the United Irishmen engaged an intensely instrumental theory of culture; the poems, the songs and the prose satires they composed were literary means to achieving political ends. They were not, in any meaningful sense, culture for the sake of culture.[87] This broad agenda involved the United Irishmen in co-opting all modes of cultural production and investing them with political resonance.[88] In particular, though not exclusively, they drew on specifically Irish forms of culture in asserting the political capacity their programme depended on.[89] They flirted with the use of the Irish language as a means of disseminating propaganda, briefly publishing the Gaelic newspaper *Bolg an tSolair* in 1795 under the direction of Patrick Lynch.[90] They dabbled in the country's music; the society sponsored the Belfast Harper's festival in 1792, while Thomas Russell worked hard to become a serviceable player of the instrument.[91] They also drew upon the artistic symbols of the country, notably that of the harp, which they refashioned by removing the Crown.[92] Other gestures included cutting their hair short, as was the fashion in revolutionary France, and composing popular ballads such as the following squib, sung to the tune of 'God save the king':

> Long live our gracious king,
> To him our treasure bring,
> Generous and free!
> His feelings are so tough,
> You ne'er can bring enough;
> Why keep you back the stuff,
> Rebels you be.[93]

This programme culminated in the repeated publication, in 1795, 1796, and again in 1798, of a collection of songs and ballads entitled *Paddy's Resource*, which, redrafted on each occasion, moved from celebrating high ideals to an increasingly demotic and violent image of the struggle upon which the Society had embarked.[94] However, the central literary form in which the United Irishmen excelled remained the political pamphlet. O'Connor's *State of Ireland* and Russell's *Letter to the People* are elements of an extended campaign of pamphleteering which sought to alter, through the management of public opinion, the law of the country.

For the loyalists, this agenda was dangerously subversive of decency and nor-mality. Empirical assumptions led them to think about culture as an organic product of the community, the outcome of the endless accretion of particular agreements. The intention of the loyalists was therefore to reflect the Irish society in its legal and cultural framework, drawing them not towards poetry and polit-ical polemic but to the historical study of the emergent manners of the people. Indicative of this cultural output was the series of 'observations' concerning Irish counties compiled under the auspices of the Dublin Society in this period.[95] That of William Tighe, who treated of Kilkenny, is typical of the kind.[96] Across two lengthy volumes he offered maps of the environment, an anecdotal history of the region, lists of charitable foundations, and accounts of selected curiosities. This text was clearly the result of personal knowledge and inquisitive probing of contacts, with Tighe including letters from correspondents and supplying accounts of his own observations. Illustrations of antiquities jostled with infor-mation about the economy and industry, and the whole supplied an eclectic, ragbag of documentation. It was an unmanaged and unmanageable effusion of empirical labour.[97]

The outcome of this division between two approaches to cultural politics was a competition to appropriate cultural production. This produced varied attempts by both sides to use the medium of newsprint, for both the Castle and the Society of United Irishmen made the publication and distribution of editorially sympathetic titles a priority in conducting their war over public opinion.[98] Most prominent on the loyalist side was the figure of John Giffard, at one time a sup-porter of James Napper Tandy and a long-term advocate for the Protestant Ascendancy, a term Jonah Barrington even mistakenly attributed to him.[99] An apothecary by trade, by the 1790s he was a leading member of Dublin Corporation and at the head of the Orange Order. He was also an employee of the state, a 'Castle-Scribbler' known as 'the dog in office', acting as the parliamentary recorder from 1781 to 1801 and producing seventeen volumes of proceedings. Through his imprint, *Faulkner's Dublin Journal*, which he had taken over in 1788—in the midst of the regency crisis—from an increasingly ill George Faulkner, Giffard produced the closest Ireland had to an official government press organ. For this service the Castle secretly rewarded him a £300 pension, alongside £1,000 in annual support for the paper itself through advertising and subventing £300 of the £500 annual payment that Giffard owed the Faulkner family for leasing their title.[100] He was also involved in coordinating a spy ring, being the handler of

Thomas Collins, a Dublin-based United Irishman and regular informant.[101] Giffard served as sheriff in 1794, suppressing the United Irish movement in the city and forcing it underground. Increasingly erratic in his behaviour, he was imprisoned for a month in 1795 for assaulting a fellow newspaper editor, James Potts, the owner of *Saunder's News-Letter*. Despite his support of the Crown, and his subsequent support of the union, Giffard was a troublesome ally for the administration.

Equally stalwart, just as surreptitious, and even more pecuniary in his defence of the established authorities was Francis Higgins, colloquially known as the 'shamsquire' after his impersonation of gentility when wooing his wife came to light in the fraud trial that followed. A protean half-life figure, Higgins was both a handler like Giffard and a valuable informer, with his letters being a vital source of insight for the Castle. His agent Francis Magan was responsible for turning over a transient Lord Edward Fitzgerald to the authorities.[102] As the proprietor of the *Freeman's Journal*, Higgins pursued a vigorous Castle line, serving up a flow of vitriol against the United Irish cause, and turning the title away from its oppositional roots as his influence waxed. This editorial stance drove the circulation of the title ever downwards, and Higgins repeatedly demanded the injection of cash from his allies in the Castle. Although the title received as much as £1,500 per annum in advertising, and Higgins accepted a £300 pension before his reward for informing was calculated, he remained disconsolate and demanding.[103]

In the face of the administration's efforts to commandeer the public sphere, the United Irish movement financed the publication of newspapers to promulgate their vision of Ireland.[104] Notable amongst these was the Belfast-based *Northern Star* edited by Samuel Nielson.[105] Founded in late 1791, the first issue appeared on 2 January 1792. As it recalled in 1794: 'A reform of parliament was the great end of our establishment; the union of Irishmen the means.'[106] The paper provided its readership with international and national news, slanted to accentuate the achievements of the republican forces in France and to highlight the civic purpose of the reform movements at home. It supplied a locus where information concerning the radical movement could be discovered, from meetings in taverns to demonstrations and rallies. It also provided a course of political instruction through intellectual essays, brief maxims, and long prose polemics. In this, it was a central vehicle in the dissemination of the United Irish cultural agenda, housing such significant literary achievements as the satires of William Sampson and James Porter's *Billy*

Bluff and the Squire (1796).[107] It also offered readers a selection of poems and songs, which drew attention to the high ideals of the United Irish movement. Circulation was large, dwarfing its local competitor, Henry Joy's Whig vehicle, *The Belfast News-Letter*, with 4,000 copies sold of each of its twice-weekly offerings. Despite constant government harassment it only halted publication when the presses were destroyed by the Monaghan regiment in May 1797.

In Dublin, the *National Journal*, an unsuccessful title hampered by dull content and editorial wrangling, flickered in 1792 and a later venture, *The Press*, sparked briefly into life between September 1797 and March 1798. While *The Press* supplied a more sophisticated diet of political reflection than the *Northern Star*, its poetic output was demotic and populist. As the movement radicalised and broadened its intake, the high ideals of the *Northern Star* made way for the impeding insurgency. The atrocities of the government and the sufferings of the people became a regular theme for both its news section and its literary contributors. Drennan complained that it was 'vulgar for the vulgar.'[108] It certainly had its share of horror and melodrama. For instance, on 19 October 1797 it reported in lurid detail of how 'the chastity of an innocent virgin of a respectable family was forcibly violated in the presence of her bound, gagged and agonised brother' by a Scottish regiment.[109] The poetry was often maudlin and macabre, celebrating United Irish martyrs and demonising the administration and its agents.

In this, it was complemented by the furious, demagogic production *The Union Star*, which during its brief efflorescence from the early summer to the end of 1797 supplied, on single sheets designed for prominent display on hoardings around the city, a list of potential assassination targets and other incitements to violence. Whether the mercurial and unstable editor, the gunsmith and Freemason Walter Cox, was a pawn of the Castle, providing such inflammatory matter to excuse the heavy-handed governmental crackdown on the liberty of the press, was unclear to contemporaries. Certainly it drew down the ire of many United Irish leaders, who feared it would hinder their work by antagonising their opponents. Cox finally turned himself in, striking a deal with the Castle for clemency for his own seditious actions in exchange for revealing the identity of the editor—himself as it turned out to the administration's immense chagrin.[110]

The cultural conflict these newspapers encapsulated also occurred at street level, with the ritualistic and theatrical politics of marches and festivals staking out claims over territory. The United Irishmen, in the early stages, availed of significant dates, such as Bastille Day or St Patrick's Day, to provide a show of strength and proclaim their ownership of the streets. Later, once the movement had been proscribed, they held false funerals to cover for military training and underline their threatening presence within the community. In the countryside, they held communal potato diggings, usually for an imprisoned member, combining political and charitable intent.[111] On the loyalist side, similar attempts were made to use a calendar of commemoration to rally support and provide a statement of power. In particular, the Williamite anniversaries, of military victories at the Boyne and at Aughrim, and the celebration of William's birthday, 4 November, were utilised to express loyalism and the defence of the Crown and constitution.[112] This street politics of ritual and symbol was to become central in the thinking of the Orange Order. They availed of the vocabulary of marches, oaths, and secret cabals to threaten their opponents, creating a repertoire of cultural references infused with political meaning. From their very first march, held on 12 July 1796, they blended military formations and Masonic paraphernalia with declarations of loyalty to the state.[113]

The central paradox within the exercise of this cultural politics is that for both parties, the theory of culture they avowed and their actual practice were in significant tension. In the case of the United Irishmen, while their cultural approach was primarily instrumental, in that it desired to effect a change in the manners of the people in support of a preordained vision of a healthy, rational, and muscular republican system, they drew so directly on the manners of the people as to appear to be an organic growth from the preexisting environment. In practice, in other words, the United Irish cultural agenda took on the complexion of the people. In trying to change the nature of the community, they inadvertently celebrated and reaffirmed the vibrancy of popular culture. In contrast, despite their theory of culture proclaiming it to be an organic and natural growth from within the community, to be tended as little as possible and allowed to flourish freely, the loyalists imposed a politically instrumental culture from above. In their repeated use of parliamentary grant, in the promotion of 'Royal' foundations (the Royal Dublin Society and the Royal Irish Academy), and, most controversially, in their sporadic sponsorship of the street theatre of the Orange Order, the devotees of the Castle generated cultural manifestations of political loyalty in contravention of their own supposedly laissez-faire approach to culture. The effect of this extended competition over the question of cultural representation of the people politicised the populace in the decade of the 1790s. The knock-on consequence of this was to make the conflict all the more intractable, for more was at stake than the particularities of individual political proposals; it was a vision of the cultural life of the community. That in turn made the Rebellion, when it arrived, all the more violent.

Regions of Rebellion

The Rebellion broke out, in stuttering fashion, on 23 May 1798.[114] Just before the call to arms was issued, a number of significant arrests were made in Dublin. Edward Fitzgerald, for instance, was captured, suffering mortal wounds during the incident, a loss that severely hampered the movement's preparations. The signal for the United Irish to rise was the halting of the mail coaches out of Dublin. This was only partially accomplished, although John Giffard's son, Lieutenant William Giffard, was among the first casualties; an unfortunate passenger on a waylaid mail coach bound for Limerick, he was piked by insurgents in Kildare town.

The conflict was concentrated in four main areas: the counties around Dublin; the region of North Down and Antrim; Wexford; and, eventually, Connacht.[115] Dublin was the spark for the conflagration but, paradoxically, the uprising within its urban boundaries barely materialised.[116] Although the United Irish had a strong presence within the city—membership is estimated at 10,000 concentrated in the relatively poorer western districts—the rising was aborted quickly.[117] The hinterland did come out, however, with rebels being sighted in numerous outlying villages. The counties surrounding Dublin also rose, with Kildare notably active and the rebels gaining a minor victory at the town of Prosperous. Elsewhere the violence was notable only for its brevity and ferocity, with large numbers of rebel causalities being attributed to loyalist forces, a death toll dramatically exacerbated by a massacre of 300–500 prisoners on the Curragh on 29 May.

A similar configuration emerged in Ulster, with Belfast, which had been the birthplace and long provided the intellectual heartbeat of the United Irish movement, failing to rise, under the explicit direction of the leadership and in the face of deeply felt criticism from other members. New men rose to prominence and Antrim rose up on 7 June, but the rising there was quickly suppressed. Local political divisions on the Ards peninsula prompted a more significant insurrection. In both regions, though, the Rebellion was hampered as much as inspired by the preceding history of governmental repression and the cowing of the populace through arbitrary arrest and physical intimidation.[118] On 12–13 June the rebel forces in Down were routed at the Battle of Ballynahinch, ending the brief insurgency.

The central basin of the summer's turmoil was in Wexford, with the wellspring located in the north of the county, where the official clampdown had been conducted with such ferocity by the North Cork militia that it prompted active resistance rather than sullen compliance.[119] The real catalyst, however, was a rebel victory at Oulart Hill on 27 May. Enniscorthy was assailed by the insurgents two days later and gutted, with numerous people being put to the pike under suspicion of being Orange sympathisers. Wexford town fell with the rebels commandeering artillery from relief forces who were early victims of the carnage. Yet the retreat of the Crown forces, and the decision by the rebels not to harass them, gave the loyalists time to regroup. The capture of Wexford was the crescendo of the rebel song.

The decision to divide the United Irish forces in three, taken to spread the disaffection as wide as possible, weakened the rebels' position. Two portions of their army were easily defeated while the third was broken at New Ross on 6 June. Despite fewer numbers, the time the loyalist forces had to prepare their defences proved decisive. Following a lengthy and vicious battle, the rebels were turned back, having suffered a catastrophic defeat, both strategically and numerically. They regrouped on Vinegar Hill only to be finally run from the field on 21 June. In the aftermath of the battle, some seventy Protestant prisoners were murdered on Wexford Bridge, but the defeat marked the end of rebellion proper. Mopping-up operations were initially bloody and looked likely to aggravate unrest. Lord Cornwallis rapidly put a halt to military unruliness. About 1,500 rebels were brought before a court—military or civil—by the end of 1799.

The final crucible of conflict was the Mayo-Longford region, and was the result of the belated landing of a French expeditionary force under General Humbert, rather than any internal combustion of society in the region, which had remained quiescent throughout the summer and where the United Irish organisation was thinly populated.[120] A veteran of a failed, chaotic attempt to land at Bantry Bay in 1796, Humbert put to sea on 6 August, in advance of the main French force, which was itself defeated by the forewarned British navy in October near Lough Swilly; a reverse that resulted in the capture and subsequent suicide of Theobald Wolfe Tone. The French force disembarked near the town of Killala on 22 August. Victory at the 'Castlebar Races' on 27 August was followed by procrastination and vacillation, and a forlorn attempt to join up with indigenous rebels. The final conflict came on 8 September, at Ballinamuck, County Longford, from which an unconditional surrender resulted.

Even where the Rising did not overtly take hold, where intense political division emerged at the local level it was accompanied by a series of repressive and counterrevolutionary measures. In the case of Munster, for example, the political constellation favoured the loyalist camp, so although society was divided, the outcome was rowdy repression, rather than violent upheaval. While Cork city's United Irish organisation had been successfully decapitated by arrest and imprisonment, the surrounding countryside was only dissuaded from overt activity by the presence of the military. In Tipperary, where the United Irish had found fertile soil, the atmosphere was more charged, but the liberal use of the whip by the circuit judge Thomas Judkin Fitzgerald and the forcible disarming of the county by the army kept the balance in favour of the existing authorities. So too, in Limerick city an extensive army presence and a policy of corporal punishment for seditious activity tamed the urban conurbation.[121]

Moreover, the impact of the fighting was not delimited to those immediately under threat and was psychological as well as physical. Indeed, the diaries and letters of the summer are strewn with the anxieties of those whose sole encounter with the Rebellion came through rumour and anecdote.[122] And for those directly confronted with the impact of social combustion, the horror was by no means sublime; rather it was viscerally immediate. The violence of the summer of 1798 was unprecedented on Irish shores. One day alone, 5 June, saw the death of 1,500 people in a battle over the town of New Ross, and the massacre of over 100 men, women, and children in a blazing barn in nearby Scullabogue.[123] By the end of the military operations, the Rebellion had cost around 20,000 lives, dying in defence of one cause or another, or simply caught up in the brutality of local antipathies and grievances.[124]

The Collapse of Civil Society

Given the death toll it is not surprising that attention has been focused on the events of the summer of 1798. However, the Rebellion needs to be situated within the broader context of life in the 1790s. In the first place, it should be recognised that the success of the United Irish movement in mobilising was a kind of victory, given the history of harassment and oppressive countermeasures conducted by the government forces. The amputation of much of the leadership further restricted any action on their part. In some senses, the Rising was a dying gesture of defiance in the face of the overwhelming victory of the state-sponsored campaign of attrition.

An agrarian crisis in 1795 had culminated in a policy of repression under Viceroy Camden. Habeas corpus was suspended and an Insurrection Act passed in early 1796, allowing disorderly counties, and indeed whole provinces, to be proclaimed and put under military rule. It further sanctioned the taking of illegal oaths with the punishment of death specified for miscreants; it was under these terms that William Orr was executed in October 1797. Following the scare produced by the appearance of a French invasion force off Bantry Bay, the government adopted a policy of politically directed brutality. Early in 1797 General Lake was given a free hand over counterinsurgency measures in Ulster. As Camden informed Lord Portland, 'The general has orders from me not to suffer the cause of justice to be frustrated by the delicacy which might possibly have actuated the magistracy.'[125] With the proclamation of the province on 13 March, this campaign to restore order was put onto a secure legal footing, and the army energetically dismantled the United Irish organisation. By June 1797, 103 of the province's United Irish leaders, including such notables as Arthur O'Connor, were imprisoned. The *Northern Star* had been silenced. Numerous military excesses occurred as order within the ranks broke down in the face of a civilian threat. John Giffard, on service in the region, wrote of the actions of the Ancient Britons:

> I was directed by the smoke and flames of burning houses and by the dead bodies of boys and old men slain by the Britons, though no opposition whatever had been given by them and, as I shall answer to almighty God, I believe there was nothing to fire at, old men, women and children excepted. From ten to twenty were killed outright, many wounded and eight houses burned.[126]

In a notorious incident four United Irishmen who had infiltrated the Monaghan militia were identified and executed on 14 May before the troops on Blairis Moor outside Belfast. Across the summer months, house burning, floggings, and mass arrests all became frequently used tactics of military intimidation. In the winter assizes of 1797, fifty people were condemned for capital crimes.[127]

Secondly, the 1798 Rebellion has to be seen as the highpoint of an interminable low-grade uncivil war within Irish society in the decade as a whole, which had involved agrarian conflict in the north Leinster and south Armagh region since the late 1780s. This culminated in the Armagh Outrages, the flight of numerous Catholics into Connacht and, in 1795, the emergence of the Orange Order.[128] The polarisation of the country into two deeply distrustful camps was coupled with, and exacerbated by, a profound failure within civil society, indicated by the growth in politically motivated violence and intimidation. The Rising was the consequence and culmination of a period of social disintegration and disaffection on both sides of the intellectual and cultural divides. The casual attitude of the government towards its people was combined with an aggressive policy of assassination, disorder, and the imposition of terror by the United Irish elements within the society. Particular targets of the symbolic violence of intimidation were agents of the government and church, although it could spill over into general social disobedience, as with the riots that attended the arrival of Lord Camden as the replacement of the ill-starred Fitzwilliam.[129] Moreover, the traditional agencies of the maintenance of order, the local justices of the peace and the courts, suffered a systems failure, with jury intimidation endemic and the magistracy remaining supine in the face of insolent behaviour. Three magistrates were killed in Ulster in this period—two of whom were also clerics of the Anglican Church. Others, such as the Reverend Philip Johnson of Lisburn and Reverend John Cleland, servant of Lord Londonderry, survived assassination attempts. Homes were destroyed and women and children threatened in United Irish efforts to thwart the arbiters of justice. Symbolic violence was also deployed, with gallows erected in front of the homes of targeted members of the community. The result was that many of those whose task it was to enforce order left for the anonymity of the capital. Others chose inactivity or compliance with the wishes of the aggressors.[130] The declaration of martial law nationwide in March 1798, weeks before the outbreak of the Rebellion, was indicative of weakness, not strength in the administration. Only local martial law, the suspension of habeas corpus, and the draconian actions of the army kept a semblance of control over the festering chaos of 1796 and 1797.

Ultimately, neither side could claim an honourable record in this dirty war. Both parties to the intracommunal conflict were guilty of an array of misdemeanours, such as the breaking of windows when recalcitrant or ignorant citizens failed to illuminate their homes in honour of one event or another.[131] Both sides were guilty of mental and physical intimidation. Both factions committed murder. In other words, what the widespread and prolonged political violence of Ireland in the 1790s suggests is that two cultural outlooks came into conflict in that decade, and that civil society did not act as a buffer. The Rebellion itself was only the most extreme manifestation of a much wider phenomenon, the breakdown of social order and civil tranquillity from around 1794. This social disaggregation generated a spiral of tit-for-tat retributions that culminated in the fires of the summer of 1798.

Why did civil society fail? In part, the disaster may have been an unintended consequence of the politicisation of civil society, which had been ongoing since the money bill crisis and had accelerated in the late 1770s.[132] While newspapers had always been an important political signifier, their reach into cultural enclaves accelerated in the 1790s. And once the clubs and associations that had bloomed in the placid waters of the midcentury had been taken up by the tides of political public opinion, the potential for their destruction in a flood of vituperative polemic was raised. The division of civil society into politically distinct associations was deeply corrosive. At its simplest, it became easier to demonise a political antagonist once the club life that had identified and strengthened other apolitical common interests was now used as a marker of difference. The associations that had brought people together in civil association were now harnessed to political ends, and divided citizens from each other.

As previously argued, in the middle decades of the century civil society in Ireland encompassed a broad cultural debate concerning civility, a vibrant and vocal public sphere, and a diverse spectrum of clubs and associations. But in the last four decades of the eighteenth century, as the public sphere became a matter of government concern and societies of all kinds became politicised, the discourse of the Enlightenment was complicated by the evident difference between the sentiments of the legislators and the manners of the people. This difference ultimately bifurcated the Volunteers. That movement began by representing the centre ground of the Enlightenment: the blend of empirical and rationalist attitudes that inspired much of the Social Enlightenment of midcentury. As the centre ground in Irish political life dissolved, the Volunteers came under increasing structural pressure, particularly over the issue of confessional recognition: the Catholic question. The disintegration of the Irish Whigs was echoed in the public sphere by the suppression of the Volunteers in 1793. In their place arose two oppositional forces that at once co-opted the Volunteering impulse and radicalised the means they were willing to avail of in pursuit of their ambitions: the yeomanry and the Society of United Irishmen.

First mooted by Thomas Knox, member of parliament for Tyrone, the yeomanry was intended to harness the residual strength of the defunct Volunteers.[133] However, when Camden finally sanctioned its formation, in September 1796, the local impetus that had characterised the earlier foundation was now tempered by a directional role exercised in Dublin, ensuring the yeomanry did not turn on central authority, as had its illustrious predecessor. Akin to the Volunteers, the yeomanry, at least initially, consciously tried to attract members from across the confessional spectrum, and enabled Volunteer regiments to reform under the new banner. The purpose of the muster was twofold. First, it was to augment the national defences in a period when French invasion threats and war on the Continent were overstretching the resources of the military establishment. Secondly, the yeomanry increasingly engaged in counterinsurgency measures within the country, first participating in the disarming of Ulster and then, with the Orange Order increasingly swelling the ranks of its corps, in confronting the Rising itself.

The political divide between the rationalists and the empiricists was captured by the emerging chasm between the United Irish and the yeomanry. The difference between them was symbolically encapsulated by the taking of the oath of allegiance by the yeomanry and the secret oaths of the United Irish, but went far deeper than that.[134] While the Society of United Irishmen was intent on the reformulation of the state, the yeomanry was the creation of the polity. The United Irish also drew from Volunteering roots, tapping into the residual desire for the reform of the constitution. Indeed, the United Irishmen can be understood as a radical and vibrant offspring of the earlier organisation, as they hijacked the Volunteer parades and rituals in the early 1790s.[135] Only following the suppression of the Volunteers in 1793 and the subsequent outlawing of the United Irishmen themselves did the movement turn fully secretive. Even then, the structure of the society, with its flotilla of fraternal cells and its illicit musters, recalled the Volunteer past as much as it pointed towards a revolutionary conspiracy. And the existence of shadowy clubs under the banner of which the United Irish continued to meet, such as the Strugglers Club of Struggler's Tavern in Cook Street, Dublin, or the United Society of Pill Lane in the same city, only underlines the intrusion of politics into the apparently fraternal and apolitical activities of civil society.[136]

On the outer edges of the spectrum of club life resided a diverse set of societies, Defenders, the Orange Order, and the Freemasons. Both the Defenders and the Orange Order were products, and purveyors, of a traditional mode of politics, the moral economy on the one hand and church-and-state loyalism on the other. Although by lending their support to the United Irishmen and the yeomanry respectively, they ended up on either side of the central divide, it was not by chance that the emergence of the one was prompted by the actions of the other. Both organisations emanated from a vocabulary of deference and dues. Inspired by economic grievance, the Defenders emphasised the privileges of the tenantry and the injustice of many of the administration's actions when measured against a preexisting moral universe, while the Orange Order cried up the duties of the subject in upholding the legitimate Protestant polity.

The Defenders, who emerged in the drumlin country of north Leinster and south Down/Armagh, conducted an economic conflict over land with an immigrant Presbyterian community, a similar jostle for power in the linen industry of the region, and a political campaign for Catholic relief in the early 1790s.[137] It was this last aspect that gave the Defenders a positive agenda, moving beyond the defence of local privileges. In this, they were radically different to those agrarian societies that had gone before, the Whiteboys or the Rightboys for example. In the summer of 1792 the movement fused with the Catholic Committee's campaign for the repeal of penal legislation and the Defenders moved out of their traditional heartland, setting up cells in Louth, Leitrim, and Meath. The 1793 militia riots further accelerated this process, with their consequent weakening of the bonds of the moral economy.[138] By the later 1790s, the Defenders were merging with the United Irishmen, completing a process of radical political engagement. A movement that had been a vehicle for a traditional mode of social protest was now articulating a progressive form of political and social radicalism.

Forming in Armagh in 1795 from a Protestant defence association, the Peep O'Day Boys, and a contested election, the Orange Order was at once a loyal antidote to the threat of unrest coordinated by the Defenders, and a counterpart to them in their complicity with agrarian and industrial unrest in Armagh and Tyrone.[139] However, the order soon evolved away from this narrow, traditionalist remit. By 1797 the first lodge had been founded in the capital, and the Orange Order soon became synonymous with church-and-state loyalism. Following the foundation of the Grand Lodge in Dublin in March 1798, and with the tepid encouragement of certain members of the nobility—John Giffard, who was to become acting grand master in 1814, managed to tempt the Duke of Cumberland into flirting with the movement in the early 1800s—it spread south. By the Rebellion it had set down roots in the Wexford area, significantly exacerbating confessional tensions there.[140] However, the administration remained wary of the unruly and unmannerly element to the order; only at the very last did they seriously encourage members to defend the country from insurrection. Even in Ulster, the nobility favoured the unsuccessful tactic of encouraging mixed associations—defence organisations in which both Catholic and Protestant could participate—before bowing to the pragmatic sponsorship of the rival, more spontaneous, Orange Order.[141] By 1798 it is estimated that the order contained nearly 12,000 men drawn from seventeen counties. Armagh remained the stronghold, but it had spread as far afield as Longford, Westmeath, and Limerick. Dublin had five warrants issued to found lodges.[142] Although the Grand Lodge was not in a position to coordinate the movement's response to the crisis of that summer, only issuing a declaration of loyalty, many Orangemen served with crown forces in repelling the rebels. They acted under the banner of the yeomanry, however, and not as a distinctively Orange force. Yet they were a vital part of the propaganda war, with the United Irish regularly raising the spectre of an Orange mob.

A similar potential for profit in the propaganda war was offered, this time to the loyalists, by the organisation at the other end of the civil society spectrum: the Freemasons. Conspiracy theories on the Continent and in Britain identified the movement as complicit in the French Revolution.[143] Strangely, Richard Musgrave did not have much to say on the Freemasons, and it seems that no one in Ireland availed of the potential to bind them in with a conspiracy theory concerning the Rebellion.[144] The lack of a conspiratorial thesis concerning the Freemasons is made even stranger when it is recognised that the United Irishmen had drawn on the Freemasons in drafting their foundational documents. William Drennan had written to his brother-in-law Samuel MacTier, of how

> the new society should have much of the secrecy and somewhat of the ceremonial of freemasonry, so much secrecy as might communicate curiosity, uncertainty, expectation to [the] minds of surrounding men, so much impressive and affecting ceremony in its internal economy as, without impeding real business, might strike the soul through the senses.[145]

Moreover, the two associations shared similar aspirations. The Freemasons, of which there were approximately 800 lodges in 1800 containing as many as

50,000 members, espoused a creed that overcame social and economic inequalities in favour of cross-confessional conviviality. The union of minds and hearts of the United Irish vision was already theoretically pursued inside the Masonic lodge, and in the summer of 1795 it would appear that the society tried to subvert the system of Masonic lodges and bring them over to their cause.[146] In Dublin, approximately thirty lodges operated during the 1790s, primarily with an industrial membership found in the convivial taverns of the city's Liberties. About half of these experienced infiltration by the United Irishmen. Although the total dual membership may have amounted to only 350 of the Freemasons' total presence in the capital of 1,500, most of the members who joined in the years immediately preceding the Rebellion were committed to the United Irish cause.[147]

Yet the Freemasons did not become revolutionary. Just as the traditionalists split between the Orange Order and the Defenders, so too did the freethinking Freemasons divide into two distinct political camps. Caution is required, for although a number of United Irish leaders can be identified as Freemasons the lodges did not act as fronts for the political subversives. Indeed, many Freemasons were active in promoting the cause of the loyalists, through membership of the yeomanry or through ties with the Orange Order. Local factors played an important part in determining the complexion of individual lodges, with Tyrone predominately leaning to the United Irishmen, and Armagh swaying towards the loyalist cause, supplying an important context for the creation of the Orange Order there.[148]

As early as December 1792, the Freemasons in Ulster had split into two distinct camps. Twenty-six of Armagh's thirty-five lodges declared that 'whatever defects may exist in it [the constitution], we are adverse to see the rude hand of innovation attempt to correct what it can only by the endeavour deform'; a statement which in the context implied a rejection of Catholic relief and franchise reform.[149] The radical camp within the Freemasons countered with an explicit statement of principle, emanating from Lodge 534 at Maghera:

> Resolved—That we shall no longer suffer the tools of corruption, the mercenary slaves of power to extinguish in our breasts the fire of patriotism, the pure benevolence of brotherhood, but by that happy union of power and sentiment with our virtuous brethren of every religious description, we shall do all that in us lies, in perfect consistence with liberty and loyalty to establish the rights of the nation.[150]

This tendency was further pronounced at a meeting of thirty of the fifty-six active lodges in County Tyrone on 7 January 1793, in which revolution was only set aside as impractical, if not unprincipled. They appealed 'let every lodge in the land become a company of citizen soldiers. Let every Volunteer company become a lodge of masons.'[151]

In each case, and across the spectrum, therefore, the associations and societies that emerged from, or were dependent on the cooperation of, civil society experienced politicisation during the 1790s. While the United Irishmen and the yeomanry were by definition political organisations, both drew upon the Volunteering impulse and were indicative of aspects of the Enlightenment spectrum of thought: rationalist improvement in the case of the United Irishmen and the defence of the empirically given status quo in the case of the yeomanry. At the edges of the spectrum the situation was even more problematic. The conflict between rationalist republicanism and empirical loyalism produced deep divisions within the associations that had emerged from within civil society itself. In the case of the traditionalists, the consequence of the crisis of the centre was to exacerbate local and visceral infighting between Defenders and the Orangemen caused in turn by economic distress. In the case of the other wing of the civil society spectrum, the Freemasons, the movement disagreed within itself. Ultimately, with the polarisation of the 1790s, civil society no longer restrained people within acceptable practices, for there were no agreed terms of reference from which society as a whole might begin to negotiate a peaceful settlement of their differences.[152] In a climate of increasing tension, of immediate fear of crime, and of government severity, the mediation of political, social, economic, religious, and cultural differences of opinion was charged with the potential for violence. The mechanisms that had generated social ties, soothed tempers, and overcame disagreements were now markers of parochial affiliation. Through its politicisation, civil society had effectively become part of the problem, not the instrument of its solution.

The conditions of the Rebellion were therefore threefold. First, a significant fracture line emerged within the Irish polity typically expressed as a conflict between loyalists and republicans. Philosophically, however, the division can be conceived as one between those temperamentally inclined to empiricism and rationalists, and was most fully expressed in urban centres with highly developed public spheres, notably Dublin and Belfast, although Cork and Limerick also had progeny. The second condition depended on the first as the partition of the Enlightenment into these two feuding camps resulted in a charged atmosphere in which differing cultural agendas were laid out and pursued. Thus the organic theory of the loyalists faced the instrumental ideas of the United Irishmen, which had the important consequence of politicising the population as a whole. Thirdly, while the Irish state suffered a catastrophic collapse of political legitimacy, caused in part by economic stress and the conditions of external warfare, what ensured that these difficulties resulted in intracommunal violence was that the civil society of clubs and associations which had flourished in mid-century had been effectively politicised, making mediation or sublimation of conflict impossible. Civil society was eroded by politicisation. Militaristic violence resulted in the summer of 1798 where these conditions were met and where local political conditions made the ideological fracture acute, as was the case in Wexford or on the Ards Peninsula. However, it should be underlined that this was just as true in regions where the counterrevolutionary forces quickly gained the upper hand and rebellion was effectively and efficiently quenched, as in Armagh or, more strikingly still, in Munster. In other words, the Rebellion of 1798 was the consequence, as well as the cause, of the destruction of the Irish Enlightenment.

Reflections on the Revolution in France

Often overlooked but vital to comprehending Edmund Burke's view of the Revolution are those passages of the *Reflections on the Revolution in France* (1790) which are deeply critical of the Bourbon regime. Burke recognised that the monarchy had stored up problems by exercising a dictatorial handling of politics and in failing to accommodate itself to the manners of the people. Yet he also concluded that these abuses could be reformed:

> I am no stranger to the faults and defects of the subverted government
> of France; and I think I am not inclined by nature or policy to make a
> panegyric upon any thing which is a just and natural object of
> censure. But the question is not now of the vices of that monarchy,
> but of its existence. Is it then true that the French government was
> such as to be incapable or undeserving of reform; so that it was of
> absolute necessity the whole fabric should at once be pulled down,
> and the area cleared for the erection of a theoretic experimental edifice
> in its place?[153]

The calling of the Estates-General and the soliciting of *cahiers des doléances* had provided an opportunity for the French state to reform in line with the ancient constitution: 'Your constitution, it is true, whilst you were out of possession, suffered waste and dilapidation; but you possessed in some parts, the walls, and in all the foundations of a noble and venerable castle. You might have repaired those walls; you might have built on those old foundations.'[154]

But the Revolution took another course, one in which the ancient edifice was abandoned, condemned, and demolished. The Revolution's rejection of the system that brought together individuals into a harmonious unity caused profound alienation, according to Burke, and condemned them to a vicious present:

> By following these false lights, France has bought herself undisguised calamities at a higher price than any nation has purchased the most unequivocal blessings! France has bought poverty by crime! France has not sacrificed her virtue to her interest; but she has abandoned her interest, that she might prostitute her virtue.[155]

Burke despised the idea of building a constitution from scratch, and condemned the French for attempting such a feat. In articulating his disdain, he squarely placed himself on the empirical wing of the Enlightenment, denouncing the rationalist methodology as worthless and unwholesome:

> The science of constructing a commonwealth, or renovating it, or reforming it, is, like every other experiment, not to be taught *à priori*. Nor is it a short experience that can instruct us in that practical science; because the real effects of moral causes are not always immediate; but that which in the first instance is prejudicial may be excellent in its remoter operation; and its excellence may arise even from the ill effect it produces in the beginning. The reverse also happens; and very plausible schemes, with very pleasing commencements, have often shameful and lamentable conclusions.[156]

Instead of rationalist deduction, he offered a celebration of manners, and notoriously of prejudice, albeit of a kind that was commensurate with the stately increment of shared social experience and wisdom:

> In this enlightened age, I am bold enough to confess that we are generally men of untaught feelings; that instead of casting away all

our old prejudices, we cherish them to a very considerable degree, and, to take more shame to ourselves, we cherish them because they are prejudices; and the longer they have lasted and the more generally they have prevailed, the more we should cherish them.[157]

This respect given to the manners of the people was complemented by a profound deference towards the sentiments of the legislators, for 'if civil society be the offspring of convention, that convention must be its law.'[158]

Taken together these passages offer an intricate vision of the right running of a community as grounded in a partnership between law and history, sentiment and manners; and one which should not swiftly be cashed in for passing fancies or hazardous future gains:

> Society is indeed a contract. Subordinate contracts for objects of mere occasional interest may be dissolved at pleasure—but the state ought not to be considered as nothing better than a partnership agreement in a trade of calico or tobacco, or some other low concern, to be taken up for a little temporary interest, and to be dissolved by the fancy of the parties. It is to be looked on with other reverence; because it is not a partnership in things subservient only to the gross animal existence of a temporary and perishable nature. It is a partnership in all science; a partnership in all art; a partnership in every virtue, and in all perfection. As the ends of such a partnership cannot be obtained in many generations, it becomes a partnership not only between those who are living, but between those who are living, those who are dead, and those who are to be born.[159]

While this peroration paints a grand vista of human development, bringing together the past, the present and the future in seamless, harmonious progression, just as powerful is the repetition of the notion of a partnership. The word appears seven times in those 156 words, and acts like a mantra, drumming out the human rhythm of procreation and death. It suggests how this version of the social contract, unlike its abstract counterpart found in the minds of the revolutionaries, was enabled by a communal ethic, grounded in a Christian moral code. As Burke stressed, 'We know, and what is better, we feel inwardly, that religion is the basis of civil society, and the source of all good and of all comfort.'[160]

The National Assembly, in Burke's mind, were rebels against this architecture of civilization. Their agenda was filled with pride in that they declared themselves at war, not just with civility, but with reality. In place of empirical acceptance the National Assembly expressed rationalist ambition, abandoning the connection between law and history:

> First of all, the science of jurisprudence, the pride of the human
> intellect, which, with all its defects, redundancies and errors, is the
> collected reason of ages, combining the principles of original justice
> with the infinite variety of human concerns, as a heap of old exploded
> errors, would no longer be studied. Personal self-sufficiency and
> arrogance (the certain attendants upon all who have never experienced
> a wisdom greater than their own) would usurp the tribunal.[161]

Empirical experience and social connections would be abandoned in favour of individual autonomy; an act which would pitch Europe back into an age of 'barbarism with regard to science and literature . . . and thus the common-wealth'—a key term which articulates for Burke a vision of a flourishing social collectivity—'would, in a few generations, crumble away, be disconnected into the dust and powder of individuality, and at length dispersed to all the winds of heaven.'[162]

Burke countered this threat with an extended defence of particularity, empha-sising the empirical grounds on which his position was taken and drawing a stark contrast to the rationalist speculations of the National Assembly and their allies. Indeed, 'circumstances (which with some gentlemen pass for nothing) give in reality to every political principle its distinguishing colour and discriminating effect. The circumstances are what render every civil and political scheme benefi-cial or noxious to mankind.'[163] For this reason he went to great lengths to become informed about the precise nature of events in France and fleshed out his study with data concerning the country's condition before the Revolution. His survey included discussions of the finances of the realm, fiscal policy, demographic trends, the wealth of the nation, and the state of various orders.[164]

Burke's empiricism was intrinsic to his thesis, and made sense of the structure of the pamphlet. Three hundred and fifty six pages in its original edition, the book is a holistic whole, undivided into chapters, sections, or parts. This was a structural mimicking of the organic content of his argument and a subtle sug-gestion that the varied elements he examined within were so fully intercon-nected as to be incapable of analytical separation. This similarly accounted for his peculiar choice of genre. Begun as a private letter on public matters, Burke was contending that the two were intimately conjoined, in contradistinction to the revolutionary espousal of a division of public and private spheres of activity.

At the heart of the *Reflections* is a diagnosis of the trauma of the Revolution as generating a schism in the historical development of Europe and an anatomy of the parasitic creatures he had identified as its cause. The public and personal are here again combined. The Revolution was brought on by a disintegration of the affective ties that bound together the sentiments of the legislators with the manners of the people. Symptoms included a disavowal of the history of the community, which had shaped the manners, and an instrumental view of law as a mechanism for the regeneration or refashioning of the people. The revolutionaries were individualists who favoured law and sentiments over history and manners, forcing Burke to articulate the value of those elements in his defence of the whole. Faced with an illness of this sort, Burke determined to effect a cure by medicating with a surfeit of empiricism, trying to recalibrate the balance between law and history, sentiments and manners. And, where the revolutionaries were depicted as a 'cabal' or a 'faction' or a 'party', in each case a group term suggestive in Burke's parlance of noxious organisms within the body politic, the values he enunciated could be identified with the fate of a single individual, Marie Antoinette:

> It is now sixteen or seventeen years since I saw the queen of France, then the dauphiness, at Versailles; and never surely lighted on this orb, which she hardly seemed to touch, a more delightful vision. I saw her just above the horizon, decorating and cheering the elevated sphere she just began to move in,—glittering like the morning star, full of life, splendour and joy. Oh! What a revolution! And what an heart must I have, to contemplate without emotion that elevation and that fall! Little did I dream when she added titles of veneration to those enthusiastic, distant and respectful love, that she should ever be obliged to carry the sharp antidote against disgrace concealed in that bosom; little did I dream that I should have lived to see such disasters fallen upon her in a nation of gallant men, in a nation of men of honour and of cavaliers. I thought ten thousand swords must have leaped from their scabbards to avenge even a look that threatened her with insult.—But the age of chivalry is gone.—That of sophisters, oeconomists and calculators, has succeeded; and the glory of Europe is extinguished forever.[165]

Here the queen is portrayed as prompting sentiments and focussing manners. In doing so she becomes the personification of the values of an age. She is an idealisation of those virtues; and the inactivity of her countrymen to spring forth in her defence indicative of the enervation of the moral code that protects her. The tragedy of her circumstance is then used to give a more general prognosis for France, and indeed Europe. Her death—foreseen in this purple passage—foretells the death of a civilisation and is a harbinger of a cruder, harsher, harder epoch. The Revolution in France is understood as having catastrophic consequences; the National Assembly having released a moral pandemic which was to eradicate European society.

The ethical foundations of European civilisation were identified in a passage which blended together manners and sentiments, law and history, by undergirding them with an ethic of chivalry: 'This mixed system of opinion and sentiment had its origins in the ancient chivalry; and the principle, though varied in its appearance by the varying state of human affairs, subsisted and influenced through a long succession of generations, even to the time we live in.'[166] Gallantry was configured as conjoining the various interests and individuals in society in a system of mutual esteem and sympathy. This ethic

> without confounding ranks, had produced a noble equality, and
> handed it down through all the gradations of social life. It was this
> opinion which mitigated kings into companions, and raised private
> men to be fellows with kings. Without force or opposition it subdued
> the fierceness of pride and power, it obliged sovereigns to submit to
> the soft collar of social esteem, compelled stern authority to submit to
> elegance, and gave a domination, vanquisher of laws, to be subdued
> by manners.[167]

This was Burke's eulogy of the system he defended, and was a central passage in the *Reflections*. The manners of society here informed the sentiments of legislators in a historical evolution that served the whole community. The sublime majesty of the monarchy was softened into beauty by the chivalric ethos, while the society was gently goaded into legal submission by the understanding of the code of gallantry.

Into this holistic, organic entity intruded the purveyors of revolution:

> Now all is to be changed. All the pleasing illusions, which made
> power gentle, and obedience liberal which harmonized the different

shades of life, and which, by a bland assimilation, incorporated into
politics the sentiments which beautify and soften private society are to
be dissolved by this new all-conquering empire of light and reason.[168]

Note how here Burke twice articulated a synchronicity of sentiments of the state
and manners of the people—connecting politics with the sentiments that 'soften
private society', and seeing power as gentle, and obedience liberal; reversing the
categorisations of power as sublime and submission as beautiful first made in the
Philosophical Enquiry into the Origin of Our Ideas of the Sublime and Beautiful
(1757). The interplay of law, history, sentiments, and manners is intricately
evoked, while this intimate network is set in direct opposition to the austere
rationalist 'empire of light'.

The Revolution destroyed the interweave of sentiments, manners, history,
and law by atomising the society and instrumentalising the law:

On the scheme of this barbarous philosophy, which is the offspring of
cold hearts and muddy understanding, and which is as void of solid
wisdom, as it is destitute of all taste and elegance, laws are to be
supported only by their own terrors, and by the concern which each
individual may find in them, from his own private speculations, or
can spare to them his own private interests. In the groves of their
academy, at the end of every visto [*sic*], you see nothing but the
gallows.[169]

This was a morbid vision of society as held together by communal fear and judicial murder. And in place of the gallantry that had forged the values of the
civilisation which was being lost, Burke pointed to a mechanistic rationalism
that prioritised self-interest and severed the connection between the state and
society: 'On the principles of this mechanic philosophy, our institutions can
never be embodied, if I may use the expression, in persons; so as to create in us
love, veneration, admiration or attachment. But that sort of reason which ban-
ishes the affections is incapable of filling their place.'[170]

Yet where did this threat emanate from? How had France come to this
impasse? To understand how the ancient value system of French civilisation had
suffered such a catastrophic failure Burke began by postulating the basis for the
ethic of chivalry. 'Nothing is more certain', he avowed, 'than that our manners,
our civilization, and all the good things which are connected with manners

and with civilization, have in this European world of ours, depended for ages upon two principles; and were indeed the result of both combined; I mean the spirit of a gentleman and the spirit of religion.'[171] Yet in the revolutionary decade, it was precisely these social groups—the nobility and the churchmen—who were targeted and assailed most virulently by the revolutionary cadres, whom Burke identified as the sophists, or intellectuals, and the economists, or 'monied interest'.

The tragedy of the French circumstance was that it was the pursuit of the noble virtue of grandeur which had poisoned the system and set the context for the rise of the mercantile men of malice. The contest between Britain and France for global military power had driven France into an ever-spiralling national debt. The revelation in May 1789 by Jacques Necker that the state was bankrupt had prompted the calling of the Estates-General that had precipitated the chaos that ensued. More ironic and devastating was the use of the national debt as a means of exculpating a programme of expropriation and desecration. At the hub of this was a novel moneyed interest that was not connected by any sympathy or shared history to the rest of society:

> By the vast debt of France a great monied interest had increasingly
> grown up and with it a great power . . . The monied property was
> long looked on with rather an evil eye by the people. They saw it
> connected with their distresses, and aggravating them. It was no less
> envied by the old landed interest, partly for the same reasons that
> rendered it obnoxious to the people, but much more so as it eclipsed,
> by the splendour of an ostentatious luxury, the un-endowed pedigrees
> and naked titles of several among the nobility.[172]

Embedded in this sociological analysis was a series of value-laden assumptions. Emphasising the national debt as a route to power for this revolutionary cadre construed their influence as primarily fictive—a spectral power based on false credit and superstition. So too the weight given to luxury situated Burke's rhetoric in a long-standing language of denunciation. The modern affectation, luxury, was then contrasted to the 'pedigree' of history, that was perceived as 'naked' and unsullied by the fopperies and trivialities of fashion.[173]

Yet despite the insubstantial nature of the moneyed interest's potency, they had been bolstered by a nefarious alliance with another novel social category, whose malicious intent was, for Burke, even more despicable and deadly.

> Along with the monied interest, a new description of men had grown
> up, with whom that interest soon formed a close and marked union; I
> mean the political Men of Letters. Men of Letters, fond of distin-
> guishing themselves, are rarely adverse to innovation . . . The literary
> cabal had some years ago formed something like a regular plan for the
> destruction of the Christian religion.[174]

The corrosive nature of the revolutionary plot was thereby exposed. The moneyed
interest was eroding the power of the nobility, while the men of letters were targeting the religious orders. Between them, the ambition was to overturn the
moral foundations of European civilisation and introduce a mechanical, instrumental code grounded on self-interest. This demonic alliance of the moneyed
and the literati was contracted through the device of the *assignat*, a paper, and
hence fictive, money introduced by the National Assembly to service the national
debt. It was backed by confiscations from the church, hence coupling the attack
on the landed with an attack on the religious establishment:

> As these two kinds of men appear principal leaders in all the late
> transactions, their junction and politics will serve to account, not
> upon any principles of law or of policy, but as a *cause*, for the general
> fury with which all the landed property of ecclesiastical corporations
> has been attacked . . . On what other principle than that which I have
> stated can we account for an appearance so extraordinary and
> unnatural as that of the ecclesiastical possessions, which had stood so
> many successions of ages and shocks of civil violences, and were
> guarded at once by justice and by prejudices, being applied to the
> payment of debts, comparatively recent, invidious, and contracted by
> a decried and subverted government.[175]

At the centre of the revolutionary project, therefore, lay a devious scheme to
destroy the church and the values it articulated. This was intended to corrode from
within the European civilisation that was founded on chivalry and gallantry. Once
this ethic had been dissolved and the institutions which upheld it desecrated,
the interlocking network of sentiments, manners, law, and history would come
crashing down. Burke's fear was that the rationalist politics of the revolutionaries had lit an unquenchable fire that would burn down the whole edifice of
Enlightenment Europe. 'We are now in a condition to discern', he wrote,

with tolerable exactness, the true nature of the object held up to our imitation . . . The beginnings of confusion with us in England are at present feeble enough; but with you, we have seen an infancy still more feeble, growing by moments into a strength to heap mountains upon mountains, and to wage war with Heaven itself. Whenever our neighbour's house is on fire, it cannot be amiss for the engines to play a little upon our own. Better to be despised for too anxious apprehensions, than ruined by too confident a security.[176]

His anxiety was justified; his native country was to be engulfed in the blaze less than nine months after his death.

Conclusion

Ireland's Missing Modernity

∾

Discord is indeed, our natural element; . . . we are comfortable only in a tempest.
—Thomas Moore, *Memoirs of Captain Rock*, 1824

DANIEL CORKERY famously described the Catholic community of the eighteenth century as living in a 'Hidden Ireland'; hidden from legal view by the proscriptions of the penal code and hidden from subsequent historiography by the linguistic barrier established by the nineteenth-century adoption of English as the primary tongue. While a great deal of work has been done since his provocative essay of 1924 to create a bifocal view of the period, there remain blind spots.[1] One such is the impact of the Enlightenment across the confessional divides of the country. As this book has argued, the concern amongst historians of Ireland for the vertical history of the three major confessions has occluded a horizontal understanding of a shared encounter with Enlightenment methods.[2] The Enlightenment was not a phenomenon that transfigured one or other of the Christian faiths, rather it transformed them all.

The impact of the Enlightenment shaped the intellectual life of the Presbyterian, Anglican, and Catholic churches respectively. In each case the shared problematic was to overcome the troubles of the seventeenth century and bring the wars of religion to a close. Rejecting Scholastic authority, the shared Enlightenment presupposition was that intellectual debate could begin by considering the human being as the basic unit of analysis. From this further knowledge could be developed, either by using empirical induction or rationalist deduction. In a small number of cases speculative freethinking was also engendered. In this sense, the Religious Enlightenment was prompted by a redefinition of the notion of religion, dissecting the confession, or a set of public practices and rituals, from the faith, or the set of individual doctrinal beliefs held by individuals. The first of these was to then become a question of social order; the second a matter of private persuasion.[3] Confession was a matter for the state; faith for the individual. In doing so, the Religious Enlightenment acted to usher in a secular age.[4]

The movement bore particular fruit by germinating the idea that confessional difference was less important in social relations than shared interests and ambitions. This understanding laid the groundwork for the emergence of a Social Enlightenment. In the decades from 1730 to 1760, the focus of intellectual concern shifted away from religious division to economic failure, and the requirements of wealth creation.[5] This involved the collaboration of the empirical and rationalist parts of the Enlightenment spectrum in a shared endeavour to inculcate civility in the populace. The emergent discourse of civility, which held within it languages of politeness, aesthetics, improvement, and political economy, comprehended religious differences and proposed a counter-public sphere to that sponsored by the state; theoretically open to all, conceptually transparent, and intellectually democratic. The outcome of this apolitical fraternisation was the blooming of a diverse ecology of clubs in which people associated to pursue enjoyment and economic favour beyond the confines of legal discrimination.

However, this mode of apolitical sociability was a standing challenge to a state system that presumed the identity of social and religious personalities and which, given the economic recovery of the country, was increasingly potent. Conflict erupted between the nascent civil society and the confessional state in the final decades of the century. The consequence of the politicisation of civil society—caused both by the emergence of political associations and the desire of civil associations to reform the state—was the bifurcation of the Enlightenment into its constituent parts. The empirical wing of the Enlightenment defended the status quo, whereas the rational wing was drawn towards reformist politics. At the close of the century, the divide widened as political circumstances polarised the two factions. The denouement saw a radicalisation of the situation and the acceptance of violence by both groups to achieve their ambitions. The tragic irony of the Enlightenment was that the ambition of defusing religious tensions to escape civic conflict eventually provided the energy for a civil conflagration.

The victory of the Castle administration over the United Irish movement in 1798 signified an empirical retrenchment, rather than inaugurating a rationalist reimagining of the state. The Anglo-Irish Act of Union of 1800 appeared to place a capstone on this settlement.[6] In this, the kind of modernity Ireland encountered was conservative and loyalist, akin to Scotland where issues of religious identity also became kinetic in the nineteenth century.[7] It also has similarities to that settlement found in America, where the Revolution was as much prompted by a defence of privilege as by a demand for natural rights.[8] In Ireland, Scotland, and America, indicatively, religious observance has remained high in comparative terms, particularly when set against the French example where the rationalist wing of the Enlightenment won out.[9] This is also why Irish historiography has been trapped between ancien régime comparisons with Britain, which suggest that Ireland was fundamentally hierarchical, and colonial models which propose a connection to America, which are informed by the continuing power of ethnic and religious imagining.

A Failed Enlightenment?

Despite the apparent victory of the empirical wing in the Enlightenment's civil war, the bookending of the Enlightenment with the spasms of intercommunal conflict—the War of the Two Kings (1688–1691) and the United Irish Rising (1798)—suggests that the story of the Irish Enlightenment is actually one of failure. In this reading, it constituted a failed project to inoculate Irish religious identities of their fratricidal qualities and to embellish the country by participating in a pan-European civilising project: the Enlightenment. Thus the ambition of the religious phase of the Enlightenment was to discover a means of living with ontological difference; the Social Enlightenment endeavoured to embed practices and norms which allowed for fruitful collaboration; the Political Enlightenment registered the consequences of that project on the organisation of the state. However, the relapse of political debate into physical violence marked a conclusion to the Enlightenment project which in turn raises questions about the movement's efficacy in an Irish context. In particular, the Enlightenment's collapse into civil war begs the question of whether Irish religious hatreds were peculiarly resistant to the cures deployed on the European continent. This would be to connect the wars of religion of the seventeenth century with the social exclusivities exercised in the nineteenth century. It reads Irish history as immutable.

Despite these apparent continuities, something had changed. The intimate balance between church and state had been renegotiated. In the seventeenth century the fundamental concern was the relationship between confession and monarchy. Yet if the fundamental demographic character of the country had remained unaltered, and Catholicism was still a majority faith, the question of the kingship was effectively settled in 1688. While this retained some valence into the eighteenth century, amongst Jacobite loyalists most obviously, the Irish Enlightenment instead debated the relationship between confession and civility. This debate was concerned with identifying which faiths were legitimate social constituencies, which could be entrusted to participate in the public sphere, and which had a voice in discussions over the nature and content of the common good.

The Anglo-Irish Act of Union of 1800 reset the question once again, in part by dividing the confessions internally. Some Catholics supported the Anglo-Irish Act of Union to facilitate their entry into parliament, while others saw in the measure the reification and calcification of the Protestant Ascendancy.[10] Equally, part of the Anglican community rejected the measure as a stepping-stone to Catholic emancipation, while other communicants supported the inclusion of Ireland into a greater Protestant polity, thereby ensuring confessional demographic superiority, even with the entry of Catholics into full civic activity. The union subsumed the Dublin parliament into Westminster, and in so doing destroyed the desired continuity of practice the defence of which mobilised the empirical wing of the Enlightenment. Yet the failure of the newly constituted union parliament in Westminster to countenance the repeal of the final penal laws, and to integrate Catholics fully into the polity, ensured it also failed to meet the hopes of the rationalist Enlightenment for a politics grounded in natural rights and universal laws.[11] Despite the commitment of Prime Minister William Pitt to the measure, the opposition of the Lords and, more potently, George III ensured the Catholic emancipation remained a dead letter until 1829.[12] The desideratum for religious conformity jostled uneasily with broader conceptualisations of the national community.[13] Indeed, the reordering of the state system raised a series of questions about confession and nationhood. Who was to participate in the state? Who was to be recognised by it? Who was to be given the full rights and responsibilities of citizenship? Or, to contract the question further: Who was Irish?

The denouement of the Enlightenment project revealed the primary structural weakness in the programme: it was unclear who was and who was not a social actor or indeed a moral subject. It was unclear to whom the term 'Irish' really belonged. In a very simple sense, the Irish Enlightenment failed, not because there was no Enlightenment, but rather because there was no agreed community of the Irish.

A Successful Enlightenment?

Certainly the Romantic debate concerning the relationship between confessional and national identity emerged from within the Enlightenment question of citizenship. The campaign for Catholic emancipation was a residue of the Enlightenment's vigorous concern for political rights, and was a diminuendo of the symphony played from the 1770s to the 1790s on the theme of dismantling the penal code; it was concerned with order, form, and harmony. But, in contrast, the campaign to repeal the union and establish a Dublin Home Rule assembly, conducted from the 1840s to the 1910s, was a Romantic composition: it was concerned with issues of authenticity, belonging, and autonomy. The resulting tune was a nationalist air in which authenticity was measured through proximity to the peasantry, belonging was to be found through Catholic observance, and autonomy was to be exercised in a Home Rule assembly or a separated national parliament.

In this, Ireland chimed with other nineteenth-century nation-state building projects, albeit one in which religion acted to identify fraternal fellowship.[14] Irish confessional devotion was thus a consequence of embracing modernity, not a form of resistance to it. It was complicit with issues of social disciplining and of political order.[15] The Catholic hierarchy at times was vexed by separatist demands from the radical reaches of the nationalist movement, denouncing the Young Irelanders and the Irish Republican Army as secular forces. At the same time, priests and congregants often overlooked such theological niceties and involved themselves in the provision of emotional support, material aid, or active engagement.

The connective tissue that linked religious to national identity in the nineteenth century helps us to identify how, in one sense, the Enlightenment had succeeded. It had reset the terms of religious conflict away from ontological dispute and towards social discord. By no means an unmixed blessing, this achievement suggests how the term 'sectarianism' had changed meaning since the seventeenth century.[16] Once used to identify small dissenting groups that have broken from the broad churches traditions, by the nineteenth century the word was deployed to register political antipathy to religious communities of any size. Crucial in this transition was the use of public oaths of political quiescence; from Quakers to Covenanters to Roman Catholics, the oath ensured that private belief was understood to have no public consequence. Coupled with an end to the state-sponsored conversion projects, oaths indicated that the confessional state was no longer seeking conformity but compliance. The problem of religious difference was transmuted from a question of intellectual orthodoxy to one of social order.[17]

This suggests that Ireland was not premodern. In fact, one of the consequences of identifying an Irish Enlightenment is to reset the puzzle of Ireland's confessional conflicts and economic woes within a decidedly modern frame.[18] If the Irish encountered the Enlightenment, they entered modernity with the rest of Europe in the eighteenth century. The nineteenth- and twentieth-century debates concerning Catholicism, land ownership, and nationalism, and the intracommunal conflict that has sprung from these debates, cannot be designated as throwbacks to an earlier, less sceptical and less tolerant age. They cannot be hidden behind the rhetoric of primordial antagonism, ancient hatreds, and narrow ground. The Irish Question is a modern question.

Three Tales

The emergence of a defined constituency of the Irish and the concomitant development of ideas of sectarian difference can be traced in the novels of the first quarter of the nineteenth century.[19] Three tales help to identify the contours of this national and confessional bildungsroman.[20] Maria Edgeworth's *Castle Rackrent* (1800) suggests an optimistic version of the future by situating cultural antagonisms decidedly in the past. In contrast, Sydney Owenson's *The Wild Irish Girl* (1806) proposes that the future can be ensured by holding fast to an expressly Irish cultural expression. Thomas Moore's *Memoirs of Captain Rock* (1824) is less sanguine, articulating the power of recidivistic national antipathies and the potency of sectarian animosity. The elective affections were redirected through the trajectory of these novels away from union with Britain and towards a recast religiously homogenous vision of the Irish nation, precisely as the union settlement was finally effected with the passage of Catholic emancipation in 1829.

First, *Castle Rackrent* enacts a distancing from the Irish past.[21] It is the saga of the decline of the Rackrent family, and the eventual loss of their estate through neglect, high living, and moral turpitude. It is also the story of a conflict between two families, the Rackrents and the Quirks, the decay of the first culminating in the usurpation by the second of the deeds to the property. Consciously set 'before the year 1782'—which was the year of Grattan's parliament and, more prosaically, when the Edgeworth family moved from England to their County Longford estate, Edgeworthstown—the tale was temporally removed from readers, enabling them to explore the exotic universe the book presented.

The text was from the start intrinsically and elementally unstable, even composed on at least two separate occasions.[22] The glossary, in which numerous explanations and pieces of factual information were offered to direct the reader through the plot, was included at the last moment, resulting in its appearance before, rather than after, the actual narrative. And even once, in the second edition, this was rectified, the glossary only added to the dialogic nature of the book. So disjointed is the tale being told, so disruptive is the transition from one discourse to the other, that the narrative itself is ruptured, and the concentration is not on the historical, comic decline of the Rackrents but on the denouement, their defeat by their legalistic, materialistic adversary, Jason Quirk. In this way it marked the displacement of the Irish ancien régime and the inauguration of a new political dispensation. It was an obituary for the world of Irish Enlightenment.

Indeed, a major theme of the novel is the incommensurability of the new world with the old. Edgeworth emphasised that the reader should treat the book as containing

> 'tales of other times' . . . The manners depicted in the following pages
> are not those of the present age; the race of the Rackrents has long
> since been extinct in Ireland, and the drunken Sir Patrick, the
> litigious Sir Murtagh, the fighting Sir Kit and the slovenly Sir Condy,
> are characters which could no more be met with at present in Ireland
> than Squire Western or Parson Trulliber in England.[23]

Yet there remains the intrinsic problem of communication generated by the changes that have occurred. The new world can now only comprehend the old by seeing it as exotic and strange, different and difficult, humorous and bucolic, and it is this which the notes and glossary that surround the novel self-consciously reveal. Repeatedly, these use terms such as 'formerly', 'some years ago', and 'by antient usage'.[24] The Editor frequently wrote in explanation of certain usages that 'it was customary' to explain their apparent lack of social or economic utility.[25] Indeed, part of the power of Edgeworth's novel, and a large part of its ambiguity, emanates from its concern with the insubstantial and situational nature of language, how hard it is to capture, define, and decode.

In all of this, Edgeworth's 'Hibernian tale' is resonant of the conflicts in Irish society that broke to the surface as the tale was being composed: the desire for a legal egalitarianism and the disintegration of the Protestant Ascendancy's world of rank, order, and deference.[26] Edgeworth was personally and acutely conscious of the dramas played out in the fields and towns around her. Making her position in the dispute clear, she concluded *Castle Rackrent*'s preface with an avowal that

> there is a time when individuals can bear to be railed for their past
> follies and absurdities, after they have acquired new habits and a new
> consciousness. Nations as well as individuals gradually lose attach-
> ment to their identity, and the present generation is amused rather
> than offended by the ridicule that is thrown upon their ancestors.[27]

The context of this commitment was, however, specific and frightening. While within the text there is little allusion to the intracommunal violence of the 1790s, which sprung in turn from the disentanglement of empirical and rationalist politics, the preface made her awareness of this circumstance plain. That her commitment to modern manners depended on a historical method was shown by her prediction that 'probably we shall soon have it in our power, in a hundred instances, to verify the truth of these observations'; a commitment at once in line with the antiquarian 'memoir' she had chosen to create and in sympathy with the empirical faction within the rapidly fragmenting Enlightenment.[28] So too, in the preface she asserted her support for the Anglo-Irish Act of Union. Yet in this measure she saw the opportunity for Ireland to break finally and successfully with the world of *Castle Rackrent*: 'When Ireland loses her identity by an union with Great Britain, she will look back with a smile of good-humoured complacency on the Sir Kits and Sir Condys of her former existence.'[29]

While this suggests some commitment to a progressive Enlightenment, in the figure of Jason, Edgeworth created a deeply unsympathetic representative of that future.[30] Jason is the Rackrents' nemesis, for in his knowledge of the law, and of Sir Condy's imperilled finances, he is given the ability to take over the estate. He is a schemer, a rapacious, acquisitive, and manipulative lawyer; in that, he was as frightful and duplicitous as the Rackrents were dissolute and unthinking. So too, the final lines of the book are deeply ambiguous about the promise of a union with Britain, raising the possibility that incomers might adopt the slovenly manners of their adopted home:

> It is a problem of difficult solution to determine, whether an Union would hasten or retard the amelioration of this country. The few gentlemen of education who now reside in this country will resort to England: they are few, but they are in nothing inferior to men of the same rank in Great Britain. The best that can happen will be the introduction of British manufacturers in their places. Did the Warwickshire militia [stationed in Ireland in the 1790s], who were chiefly artisans, teach the Irish to drink beer, or did they learn from the Irish to drink whiskey?[31]

If Edgeworth's tale involves distancing herself from Ireland's past, Sydney Owenson's *The Wild Irish Girl* is a saga of domestication. It tells the story of Horatio, a son of Lord M–, who is obliged to retreat to his father's Irish estates—situated on the west coast—having dissipated his reputation and fortune in London. Once arrived, his sense of ennui leads him to explore the surrounds of the estate. A fateful encounter brings him into the orbit of Glorvina, the daughter of the Catholic chieftain whose forefather Lord M–'s father had displaced. Adopting the identity of a migrant artist, Horatio insinuates himself into the household and falls in love with Glorvina. Resolution comes with their marriage, signifying the binding together of England and Ireland in fecund harmony.[32]

The trajectory in this tale is one of having Irish exotica adopted by an English noble. The two lovers first meet when Horatio overhears Glorvina playing a harp. Transfixed he climbs a rocky outcrop, but when the ground gives way he tumbles, falls, and is carried unconscious into the chieftain's abode. As with the accumulated representation and translation of Thady's dialect in *Castle Rackrent* and with Thomas Moore's later *Irish Melodies* (1808–1834), the attractions of Ireland are here transmitted not by the eye so much as the ear. Ireland resonates with the reader as much as it is represented, generating a sympathetic, romantic reaction at odds with any analytical, empirical, or rational response.[33]

Yet unlike Thady's vocabulary, which the Editor annotates for a presumed English readership, the effect of Glorvina's music is not to alienate but to entice.

For instance the Editor of *Castle Rackrent*, whose voice is that of an Enlightenment empirical collector and classifier, offers supplemental footnotes to the tale, supplying clarification and identification, as when the identity of the banshee is explained in a mock naïve manner:

> The Banshee is a species of aristocratic fairy, who in the shape of the a little hideous old woman has been known to appear, and heard to sing in a mournful supernatural voice under the windows of great houses, to warn the family that some of them are soon to die. In the last century every great family in Ireland had a Banshee, who attended regularly, but latterly their visits and songs have been discontinued.[34]

In contrast, Horatio in *The Wild Irish Girl* responds to an early encounter with native Irish music by emphasising the emotional response it engendered:

> Almost every word of Murtoch's lamentation was accompanied by the sighs and mournful lamentations of his auditors, who seemed to sympathize as tenderly in the sufferings of their progenitors, as though they had themselves been the victims to the tyranny which had caused them. The arch-policy of the 'ruthless king' who destroyed at once the records of a nation's woes, by extirpating the 'tuneful race', whose art would have perpetuated them to posterity, never appeared to me in greater force than in that moment.[35]

Where Edgeworth used sounds to separate the reader from the native Irish and they from their past—the banshee's song is now little heard—Owenson availed of music to generate proximity, both allowing Horatio to connect sympathetically with his hosts and they to collapse the difference between the past and the present.

The outcome of this sympathy is the appropriation of the English lord by the Irish lady; again running in the contrary direction to the Rackrents' tale of the Irish inculcation of English modes and manners. Horatio begins his courtship of Glorvina by symbolically relinquishing his identity: to sustain it would be to admit himself to be a pariah to her family for historical reasons of colonisation and desecration. He equally gives up his expressed prejudices against the Irish. He begins by vocalising the traditional image of the 'barbarity of the Irish', recognising how 'I feel the strongest objection to becoming a resident in the remote part of a country which is still shaken by the convulsions of an anarchical spirit'.[36]

At the close, following Glorvina's emotional education, he commits himself to spending the majority of his time in Ireland—'eight months out of every twelve on that spot from whence the very nutrition of your existence is to be derived'—a geographic shift that physically represents his change of view.[37] The location of domestic virtue is thereby moved from England to Ireland, and the colonial character of the regime ameliorated by affective ties. As Lord M— instructs Horatio, he is to 'remember that you are not placed by despotism over a band of slaves, creatures of the soil, and as such to be considered; but by Providence, over a certain portion of men, who in common with the rest of their nation, are the descendants of a brave, a free, and an enlightened people.'[38] From being symbols of 'barbarity' to being recognised as an 'enlightened people', Owenson's novel translated Ireland for the English by transforming the status of their culture.

Finally, while Owenson's work concerns domestication (specifically that of the English by the Irish), Thomas Moore's hybrid of historical study and robber tale, *The Memoirs of Captain Rock*, performs a narrative of disruption. Moore himself, who was to find fame in London with his sequence of *Irish Melodies*, enacted a form of double existence that mirrors that which Horatio settles on, residing in England but spending sojourns in Ireland.[39] Yet despite centring his activity in London, his politics was decidedly more aggressive than that enunciated by Edgeworth or even Owenson.[40] His poetry was often intentionally subversive, layering in allusions to Irish concerns and complaints, and romanticising the island's recent history of protest and resistance.[41] But far from generating an emasculating distance from a heroic past, Moore dabbled in more immediate political campaigns and related his poetic utterance to the current condition of the country.[42] In relation to *Captain Rock*, the immediate energy for Moore's disruptive narrative was a trip to Ireland in 1823 which uncovered for him the nature of recent Rockite agrarian disturbances and the continuing campaign for Catholic emancipation.[43]

The book renders the Rockite agitation as one episode in an extended narrative of Irish resistance to English colonial intrusion, written in a declamatory mode that hectors as much as it instructs. Here the sound of Ireland is not melodious so much as clamorous.[44] The sound of declaratory law and strident rebellion emanate from the pages. In Queen's Mary's reign, 'the Irish were from the very first declared "enemies" by the English law, and it is only declaration of the English law by which they have very cordially abided ever since'; in that of Queen Elizabeth, 'the plan of pacifying Ireland by exterminating the Irish . . .

was tried on a grand scale . . . Never had the Rocks a fairer harvest of riot than during this most productive reign.'[45]

The story begins in earnest with the incursion of Henry II in 1171, which allows for Moore's projection of an idyllic pre-English Irish past in the *Irish Melodies*.[46] Yet once the English had begun to interfere, the Rock family made it their concern to engage in continual retaliatory resistance.[47] This episodic saga was taken down to the Rising of 1798, read as being the predictable result of the mishandling of the country by the British government. Highlighting the parallels to the events of 1641, Moore's account suggested how far Irish history was trapped in a repeating cycle of maladministration and rebellion, tyranny, and civil unrest; slavery and bloodshed:

> I have already had occasion, in remarking upon some extracts from the journal, kept by one of my ancestors in the great Rebellion of 1641, to compare briefly the events of that period with those of 1798, and to show the family resemblance that existed between the two rebellions. Both born in the perfidy of the government, and both nurtured into strength by its cruelties, they each ran the same career of blood, and each in expiring left an unburied corpse to poison the two parties that still sullenly contended over it.[48]

As for the United Irish violence, while not wished away, it was excused by reference to the context of oppression in which it had occurred:

> With respect to the atrocities committed by some members of my families, during the paroxysm of that re-action which the members of the government had provoked [note how the primary agency for the violence still resides with the government], it is far from my intention to enter into any defence of them. I will merely say, that they who, after having read the preceding pages, can still wonder at such events as the even the massacre at Scullabogue, have yet to learn that simple theory of the connection of events with their causes, which is the sovereign cure for wonder on all such occasions.[49]

What Moore effects is a conjectural history of Irish violence, connecting the secondary outcome (interpersonal violence) to a primary cause (colonial intrusion). Irish history is immutably connected to conflict so long as its neighbour persists in being an actor in its affairs. The account of bloodletting in 1641 'contain[s] the concentrated essence of Irish history.'[50] The *Memoirs* are a transcript of national pride and a counsel of despair.

But by taking his history right up to near-contemporary affairs, Moore does something more than tether current politics to a despairing history of disruption. Part two, which deals with the life of the Captain Rock born in 1760, takes a peculiar detour from its declension of Irish history to provide a chapter offering 'the Captain's opinions on tithe matters' and 'civil rights to tithes'.[51] Of this practice he is dismissive, suggesting that far from having scriptural authority its origins were more prosaic, less edifying:

> It was not till the fourth century that this mode of providing for the
> clergy was introduced into the church; and even then the priest was
> entitled to but a third part of the tenths, the remaining two portions
> being apportioned to the repair of churches and relief of the poor. In
> the course of time, however, the priest contrived to monopolize all to
> himself and from that moment the struggle between the laity and the
> clergy began—the former paying reluctantly, if at all, and the latter
> cursing them with all the flowers of church eloquence in consequence.[52]

This injects a decidedly sectarian aspect into the national issue, for what might be worse than an unenlightened tax propping up superstition is a tax which supports a church to which the population do not pledge any allegiance. In chapter eight, Moore again effects a detour, but this time Captain Rock illuminates a peculiarly Irish aspect to the grievance:

> I consider a church establishment eminently calculated to serve the
> cause of discord, in whatever form it exists, and as it exists in Ireland
> supereminently so. In all other countries the laws of reason and nature
> are so far consulted in this institution, that the creed of the majority
> of the people has been the religion adopted by the state . . . In Ireland,
> however, where everything is done (as astronomers say) *in anteced-
> entia*, or contrary to the order of the signs, so completely has this
> obvious policy been reversed, that the church of about 500,000
> persons out of population of seven millions is not only crowned as the
> sole Sultana of the state, but the best interests of the state itself are
> sacrificed to its pride, and a whole people turned into slaves and
> beggared for her triumph.[53]

If Edgeworth proposed assimilation and Owenson suggested appropriation, Moore highlighted the antagonism that marred Anglo-Irish affairs. Captain Rock's own fate is entangled with the Irish insurrection, for the memoir concludes with an account of his arrest and deportation to Australia, a geographic dislocation which stymied his actions on behalf of Ireland.[54] This final portion of the text is supposedly written by the owner and editor of the manuscript; the obligatory English observer. The introduction, conclusion, and editorial matter is thus attributed once again to a foreign eye; in this case not a nobleman but a missionary, given the unenviable task of proselytising the Irish. Moore emphasised how little foreknowledge the cleric brings to his venture, admitting that 'I little thought at one time of my life, that I ever should be induced to visit Ireland' and that he was chosen by his fellow evangelicals 'as knowing more of Catholic countries than the rest, from having passed six weeks of the proceeding summer at Boulogne'.[55] By the close, and unlike Horatio, he does not physically relocate, but his emotional commitments have decidedly shifted, announcing that the *Memoirs of Captain Rock* have taught him 'that it is the rulers, not the people of Ireland who require to be instructed and converted.'[56] The mission had ironically made the cleric a proselytiser for the Irish cause in England; just like Moore himself. What *Captain Rock* thus brings home, and what Moore's own biography indicates, is that by the first quarter of the nineteenth century, Irish Catholicism was inside the British body politic and the issue of how to handle this discordant body of citizens was shaping and remaking the possibilities of British identity.

The final grant of Catholic emancipation in 1829, following the successful mobilisation of the Catholic community by Daniel O'Connell, effectively opened up a new question into which the Irish condition was to be comprehended, namely, Who was British?[57] Intersecting with sectarian animosities and an ongoing land question that took a despairingly fatal turn in the 1840s, the Irish community was now reductively read as devotedly Catholic and irremediably peasant in its constitution. The confessional complexity of the eighteenth century was transmuted into the binary codes of Catholic-Protestant, tenant-landlord, and, crucially, Irish-English. Ireland remained a truculent, disaffected, abrasive, and unamenable addition to the British polity, now awkwardly termed the United Kingdom of Great Britain and Ireland.[58] As the subsequent parliamentary and political history of the nineteenth century indicated, the Irish Question was to be a British problem.

Notes

Acknowledgements

Index

Notes

∾

Introduction

1. David Hume, 'Of National Characters', in idem, *Essays Moral, Political and Literary*, Eugene F. Miller (ed.) (Indianapolis: Liberty Fund, 1987), 197. This was first published in 1742.
2. David Hume, *The History of England from the Invasion of Julius Caesar to the Revolution in 1688*, 6 vols. (Indianapolis: Liberty Fund, 1983), V, 342. See also David Berman, 'David Hume on the 1641 Rebellion in Ireland', *Studies*, 258 (1976), 101–112.
3. Quoted in Éamon Ó Ciosáin, 'Attitudes towards Ireland and the Irish in Enlightenment France', in Graham Gargett and Geraldine Sheridan (eds), *Ireland and the French Enlightenment* (Houndmills: Palgrave, 1999), 129.
4. Ibid.
5. Quoted in Graham Gargett, 'Voltaire's View of the Irish', in Gargett and Sheridan, *Ireland and the French Enlightenment*, 159.
6. Ibid., 166.
7. Ibid.
8. The superstition ascribed to the Irish informs the brief allusion to Irish clerics in Paris by Montesquieu: 'Those who I have mentioned argue in the common tongue, and are to be distinguished from another kind of disputant, who uses a barbarous language which seems to increase the fury and obstinacy of the combatants. In some parts of Paris you can see a dense black mob, as it were, of this class of person; they feed on distinctions; they live on unclear arguments and false conclusions. They might have been expected to die of hunger at this business, but it is profitable all the same. A whole nation, expelled from its country, was observed to cross the seas and settle in France, without anything to assist in providing the necessities of

life except a redoubtable talent for debate.' Montesquieu, *Persian Letters*, C. J. Betts (trans) (London: Penguin, 1973), 90. See also Darach Sanfey, '"Un redoubtable talent pour la dispute": Montesquieu and the Irish', in Lise Andries, Frédéric Ogée, John Dunkley, and Darach Sanfey (eds), *Intellectual Journeys: The Translation of Ideas in Enlightenment England, France and Ireland* (Oxford: Voltaire Foundation, 2013), 177–194.

9. For the defence against such caricatures offered by one Irish writer, see Hilary Larkin, 'Writing in an Enlightened Age? Charles O'Conor and the Philosophes', in Luke Gibbons and Kieran O'Conor (eds), *Charles O'Conor of Ballinagare: Life and Works* (Dublin: Four Courts Press, 2015), 97–115.

10. A. T. Q. Stewart, *The Shape of Irish History* (Belfast: Blackstaff, 2001), 110.

11. Toby Barnard, *The Kingdom of Ireland, 1641–1760* (Basingstoke: Palgrave Macmillan, 2004), 11. While the confessional and geographic limits this draws might be tested, more immediately noticeable is the way this observation delimits the Enlightenment to speculative philosophy. In that, it fails to recognise the shift towards the doing of Enlightenment, rather than the thinking of it, that has characterised scholarship in the past twenty years. For a recent and useful survey, see Thomas Munck, *The Enlightenment A Comparative Social History, 1721–1794* (London: Arnold, 2000).

12. Thomas Bartlett, *The Fall and Rise of the Irish Nation: The Catholic Question, 1690–1830* (Dublin: Irish Academic Press, 1992), 67, 70.

13. Ian McBride, *Eighteenth-Century Ireland: The Isle of Slaves* (Dublin: Gill and Macmillan, 2009), 51–99. The quote is on 98.

14. One exception to this general observation is the work of Ultán Gillen in which the chronology is helpfully extended to the second half of the century, taking in the radical political ideas mooted by the United Irishmen. See for instance, Ultán Gillen, 'Varieties of Enlightenment: The Enlightenment and Irish Political Culture in the Age of Revolutions', in Richard Butterwick, Simon Davies, and Gabriel Sanchez Espinosa (eds), *Peripheries of the Enlightenment: SVEC* (Oxford: Oxford University Press, 2008), 163–182; idem, 'Constructing Counter-Revolutionary History in Late Eighteenth-Century Ireland', in Mark Williams and Stephen Paul Forrest (eds), *Constructing the Past: Writing Irish History, 1600–1800* (Woodbridge: Boydell Press, 2010), 136–154.

15. David Berman, 'The Irish Counter-Enlightenment', in Richard Kearney (ed.), *The Irish Mind: Exploring Intellectual Traditions* (Dublin: Wolfhound Press, 1985), 119–140; idem, 'Irish Philosophy and the American Enlightenment during the Eighteenth Century', *Eire-Ireland*, 24 (1989), 28–39. Collected in David Berman, *Berkeley and Irish Philosophy* (London: Continuum Press, 2006).

16. Berman, 'The Irish Counter-Enlightenment', 119.

17. David Berman, *A History of Atheism in Britain: From Hobbes to Russell* (London: Croom Helm, 1988).

18. David Berman, *George Berkeley: Idealism and the Man* (Oxford: Clarendon Press, 1996), v.

19. Berman, 'The Irish Counter-Enlightenment', 119.

20. See Richard Butterwick, Simon Davies, and Gabriel Sanchez Espinosa (eds), *Peripheries of the Enlightenment: SVEC* (Oxford: Oxford University Press, 2008), passim.

21. Daniel Roche, *France in the Enlightenment* (Cambridge: Harvard University Press, 2000); Peter Borsay, *The English Urban Renaissance: Culture and Society in the Provincial Town 1660–1770* (Oxford: Clarendon Press, 1991); Bob Harris, 'The Enlightenment, Towns and Urban Society in Scotland c.1760–1820', *English Historical Review*, 126 (2011), 1097–1136.

22. This trend is encapsulated and inspired by the essays in Roy Porter and Mikulás Teich (eds), *The Enlightenment in National Context* (Cambridge: Cambridge University Press, 1981). See also Marie-Christine Skuncke, 'Was There a Swedish Enlightenment?' in Svavar Sigmundson (ed.), *Norden och Europa, 1700–1830: Synvinkalr på ömsesidigt kulturellt inflytande* (Reykjavík: Félag um átjándu aldar fræði Háskólaútgáfan, 2003), 25–42. I would to thank Marie-Christine Skuncke for a copy of this article.

23. See also Porter, *Enlightenment: Britain and the Creation of the Modern World* (London: Penguin, 2000).

24. See, for example, Nicholas Phillipson, 'Politics, Politeness and the Anglicisation of Early Eighteenth-Century Scottish Culture', in R. A. Mason (ed.), *Scotland and England, 1286–1815* (Edinburgh: John Donald, 1987), 226–246. See also the appreciative reflections in Colin Kidd, 'The Phillipsonian Enlightenment', *Modern Intellectual History*, 11 (2014), 175–190.

25. David Allan, *Philosophy and Politics in Later Stuart Scotland: Neo-Stoicism, Culture and Ideology in an Age of Crisis, 1540–1690* (East Linton: Tuckwell Press, 2000); Christopher J. Berry, *The Idea of Commercial Society in the Scottish Enlightenment* (Edinburgh: Edinburgh University Press, 2013); Alexander Broadie, *The Scottish Enlightenment: The Historical Age of the Historical Nation* (Edinburgh: Birlinn, 2001).

26. Sean Moore, 'Introduction: Ireland and Enlightenment', *Eighteenth-Century Studies*, 45 (2012), 347.

27. Ibid.

28. Ibid., 348.

29. Susan Manning and Frank D. Cogliano, 'Introduction: The Enlightenment and the Atlantic', in idem (eds), *The Atlantic Enlightenment* (Aldershot: Ashgate Press, 2008), 1–18.

30. Ibid., 18.

31. James Livesey, *Civil Society and Empire: Ireland and Scotland in the Eighteenth-Century Atlantic World* (New Haven: Yale University Press, 2009). For a trenchant

critique, see Ian McBride, 'The Edge of Enlightenment: Ireland and Scotland in the Eighteenth Century', *Modern Intellectual History*, 10 (2013), 135–151.

32. James Livesey, 'A Kingdom of Cosmopolitan Improvers: The Dublin Society, 1731–1798', in Jani Marjanen and Koen Stapelbroek (eds), *The Rise of Economic Societies in the Eighteenth Century: Patriotic Reform in Europe and North America* (Houndmills: Palgrave Macmillan, 2012), 67–68.

33. Livesey, *Civil Society and Empire*, 90–127.

34. Vincenzo Ferrone, *The Enlightenment: History of an Idea* (Princeton: Princeton University Press, 2015), 4.

35. John Marshall, *John Locke, Toleration and Early Enlightenment Culture* (Cambridge: Cambridge University Press, 2010); Anthony Pagden, *The Enlightenment, and Why it Still Matters* (Oxford: Oxford University Press, 2013); Jonathan Israel, *A Revolution of the Mind: Radical Enlightenment and the Intellectual Origins of Modern Democracy* (Princeton: Princeton University Press, 2011).

36. 'The end purpose of freed human deeds [was] . . . brought down to earth and focussed on human beings rather than on God. In this sense the Enlightenment was a form of humanism, or if preferred, anthropocentrism. It was no longer considered necessary, as theologians had maintained, to always be willing to sacrifice the love of creatures for the love of the Creator: it was henceforth enough to love other human beings. Whatever was waiting for us in the hereafter, human beings had to impart meaning to their earthly lives. The quest for salvation was replaced by the search for happiness.' Tzvetan Todorov, *In Defence of the Enlightenment* (London: Atlantic Books, 2009), 12. 'This picture puts man firmly at its centre, with his capabilities and his limitations, his growing and ever more tragic and acute awareness of his dramatic finitude, his need to constantly redefine the very foundations of the religious question, of social, political and economic order, so as to give rise to what we now see as our modern civil society.' Ferrone, *The Enlightenment*, ix.

37. The revision of the relationship between the Enlightenment and religion has been a central concern of much recent study. For useful reflections on this historiographical turn, see Jonathan Sheehan, 'Enlightenment, Religion and the Enigma of Secularisation: A Review Essay', *The American Historical Review*, 108 (2003), 1061–1080; Simon Grote, 'Review Essay: Religion and Enlightenment', *Journal of the History of Ideas*, 75 (2014), 137–160. See also the special issue devoted to 'Religion(s) and the Enlightenment': *Historical Reflections*, 40.2 (2014).

38. It should be borne in mind that while 'it is true that the [Renaissance] introduced one fundamental characteristic of modern culture, namely the creative role of the person . . . that idea did not imply that the mind alone is the source of meaning and value, as Enlightenment thought began to assume.' Louis Dupré, *The Enlightenment and the Intellectual Foundations of Modern Culture* (New Haven: Yale University Press, 2004), xi.

39. René Descartes, 'Discourse on the Method of Rightly Conducting the Reason', in idem, *Philosophical Works*, 2 vols, Elizabeth S. Haldrene and G. R. T. Ross (trans.) (Cambridge: Cambridge University Press, 1975), I, 79–130.

40. The term 'science of man' is taken from David Hume, *A Treatise of Human Nature*, David Fate Norton and Mary J. Norton (eds) (Oxford: Oxford University Press, 2000), 4.

41. See Jonathan Israel, *Radical Enlightenment: Philosophy and the Making of Modernity, 1650–1750* (Oxford: Oxford University Press, 2001); Richard Ashcraft, *Revolutionary Politics and Locke's* Two Treatises of Government (Princeton: Princeton University Press, 1986), 338–467; Anne Goldgar, *Impolite Learning: Conduct and Community in the Republic of Letters* (New Haven: Yale University Press, 2001).

42. From an extensive literature, see Lawrence E. Klein, 'Gender, Conversation and the Public Sphere in Early Eighteenth-Century England', in Judith Still and Michael Worton (eds), *Textuality and Sexuality: Reading Theories and Practices* (Manchester: Manchester University Press, 1993), 100–115; idem, 'Politeness for Plebs: Consumption and Social Identity in Early Eighteenth-Century England', in Ann Bermingham and John Brewer (eds), *The Consumption of Culture 1600–1800: Image, Object, Text* (London: Routledge, 1995), 362–82; idem, 'Coffeehouse Civility, 1660–1714: An Aspect of Post-Courtly Culture in England', *Huntington Library Quarterly*, 59 (1996), 30–51; Philip Carter, *Men and the Emergence of Polite Society: Britain, 1660–1800* (London: Routledge, 2001); Brian Cowan, *The Social Life of Coffee: The Emergence of the British Coffeehouse* (New Haven: Yale University Press, 2005); Steve Pincus, '"Coffee Politicians Does Create": Coffeehouses and Restoration Political Culture', *Journal of Modern History*, 67 (1995), 807–834; Borsay, *The English Urban Renaissance*; Peter Clark, *British Clubs and Societies, 1580–1800: The Origins of an Associational World* (Oxford: Oxford University Press, 2000).

43. On these issues see for instance Keith Michael Baker, *Inventing the French Revolution: Essays on French Political Culture in the Eighteenth Century* (Cambridge: Cambridge University Press, 1990); Robert Darnton, *The Forbidden Bestsellers of Pre-Revolutionary France* (London: Fontana Press, 1996); and Dale Van Kley, *The Religious Origins of the French Revolution* (New Haven: Yale University Press, 1994). See also Roger Chartier, *The Cultural Origins of the French Revolution* (Durham: Duke University Press, 1991).

44. This idea draws on that of Jonathan Israel who identified a difference between a Spinozean and moderate Enlightenment, the latter of which was divided between Malebrachian and Lockean schools of thought. I am less confident about the impact of individual authors but accept the suggestion that different languages of analysis grew up within the Enlightenment discourse. See Israel, *Radical Enlightenment*. Israel's wider project of reconstructing a progressive, freethinking Radical Enlightenment that lies at the base of modern democratic society has been the

subject of extensive critique. See for instance, Anthony J. La Vopa, 'A New Intellectual History? Jonathan Israel's Enlightenment', *The Historical Journal*, 52 (2009), 717–738; Annelien de Dijn, 'The Politics of Enlightenment: From Peter Gay to Jonathan Israel', *The Historical Journal*, 55 (2012), 785–805.

45. Liam Chambers, 'Irish Catholics and Aristotelian Scholastic Philosophy in Early Modern France, c. 1600–c. 1750', in James McEvoy and Michael Dunne (eds), *The Irish Contribution to European Scholastic Thought* (Dublin: Four Courts Press, 2009), 212–230.

46. Alan Ford, *James Ussher: Theology, History and Politics* (Oxford: Oxford University Press, 2007).

47. Robert S. Paul, *The Assembly of the Lord: Politics and Religion in the Westminster Assembly and the Grand Debate* (Edinburgh: T & T Clark, 1985). See also Crawford Gribben, *God's Irishmen: Theological Debates in Cromwellian Ireland* (Oxford: Oxford University Press, 2007). More generally on the scholastic tradition within Calvinism, see Richard A. Muller, *After Calvin: Studies in the Development of a Theological Tradition* (Oxford: Oxford University Press, 2003).

48. Darrin McMahon, 'The Counter-Enlightenment and the Low-Life of Literature in Pre-Revolutionary France', *Past and Present*, 159 (1998), 77–112; idem, *Enemies of the Enlightenment: The French Counter-Enlightenment and the Making of Modernity* (Oxford: Oxford University Press, 2001).

49. For the conspiracy theory linking the French Revolution with freemasonry, see Abbé Augustin Barruel, *Memoirs Illustrating the History of Jacobinism*, 4 vols (London: T. Burton, 1798), and John Robison, *Proofs of a Conspiracy Against all the Religions and Governments of Europe* (Edinburgh: T. Cadell, 1797). See also Peter Campbell, Thomas Kaiser and Marisa Linton (eds), *Conspiracy in the French Revolution* (Manchester: Manchester University Press, 2010).

50. See John Thomas Troy, *To the Reverend Pastors, and Other Roman Catholic Clergy, of the Archdiocese of Dublin* (Dublin: H. Fitzpatrick, 1798).

51. A further restriction of this study is the limited attention given to developments in the history of science and the history of art. Again further studies might integrate developments in these fields into the narrative offered here, or serve to challenge these findings.

52. The question of how to include those of strong religious convictions continues to perplex thinkers whose work relates to the legacy of Enlightenment public discourse. For instance, Jürgen Habermas, in *Between Naturalism and Religion: Philosophical Essays* (Cambridge: Polity Press, 2008), argues that claims based on spiritual authority must be relinquished in public debate and that religious citizens must translate their ideas into secular terms if their views are to be given merit in the wider community; see particularly 'Religion in the Public Sphere: Cognitive Presuppositions for the "Public Use of Reason" by Religious and Secular Citizens', 114–148, and 'Religious

Tolerance as a Pacemaker for Cultural Rights', 251–270. See also Habermas, 'On the Relations between the Secular Liberal State and Religion', in Hent de Vries and Lawrence E. Sullivan (eds), *Political Theologies: Public Religions in a Post-Secular World* (New York: Fordham University Press, 2006), 251–260. More generally, see Martha C. Nussbaum, *The New Religious Intolerance: Overcoming the Politics of Fear in an Anxious Age* (Cambridge: Harvard University Press, 2013).

53. See Keith Michael Baker, 'Public Opinion as Political Invention', in idem, *Inventing the French Revolution*, 167–199.

54. John Toland, *Christianity not Mysterious*, in Philip McGuinness, Alan Harrison, and Richard Kearney (eds), *John Toland's* Christianity not Mysterious: *Text, Associated Works and Critical Essays* (Dublin: Lilliput Press, 1997), 100.

55. See Mark Goldie, 'Priestcraft and the Birth of Whiggism', in Nicholas Phillipson and Quentin Skinner (eds), *Political Discourse in Early Modern Britain* (Cambridge: Cambridge University Press, 1993), 209–231.

56. Toland, *Christianity not Mysterious*, 43, quoting Deut 30.14.

57. Toland, *Christianity not Mysterious*, 31.

58. Ibid., 97.

59. For details of his peregrinations, see Michael Brown, *A Political Biography of John Toland* (London: Pickering & Chatto Press, 2012), which offers a reading of *Christianity not Mysterious* at 21–39.

60. Robert E. Sullivan, *John Toland and the Deist Controversy: A Study in Adaptations* (Cambridge: Harvard University Press, 1982).

61. See for instance Israel, *Radical Enlightenment,* 609–614; and Margaret Jacob, 'John Toland and the Newtonian Ideology', *Journal of the Warburg and Courtauld Institute,* 32 (1969), 307–331; and idem, *Living the Enlightenment: Freemasonry and Politics in Eighteenth-Century Europe* (Oxford: Oxford University Press, 1991). His intellectual habits and preoccupations are well covered in Justin Champion, *Republican Learning: John Toland and the Crisis of Christian Culture, 1696–1722* (Manchester: Manchester University Press, 2003).

62. For an example of his commitment to this programme, see George Berkeley, *The Querist,* in Joseph Johnston (ed.), *Bishop Berkeley's Querist in Historical Perspective* (Dundalk: Dundalgen Press, 1970), Queries 412–414.

63. Patrick Kelly, 'Berkeley and the Idea of a National Bank', *Eighteenth-Century Ireland,* 25 (2010), 98–117.

64. For a similar reading, see Scott C. Breuninger, 'Berkeley and Ireland: Who are the "We" in "We Irish Think Otherwise"', in David A. Valone and Jill Bradbury (eds), *Anglo-Irish Identities, 1571–1845* (Cranbury: Bucknell University Press, 2008), 114–121.

65. On the philosophical conception of luxury, see Christopher J. Berry, *The Idea of Luxury: A Conceptual and Historical Investigation* (Cambridge: Cambridge University Press, 1994).

66. Patrick Kelly, 'Ireland and the Critique of Mercantilism in Berkeley's *Querist*', *Hermathena*, 139 (1985), 101–116.

67. 'Self-interest, at least among the most wretched and desperate, was a latent, rather than an active principle which needed awakening from its dormant state before it could serve an economic purpose.' Patrick H. Kelly, '"Conclusions by No Means Calculated for the Circumstances and Condition of *Ireland*": Swift, Berkeley and the Solution to Ireland's Economic Problems', in Aileen Douglas, Patrick Kelly, and Ian Campbell Ross (eds), *Locating Swift: Essays from Dublin on the 250th Anniversary of the Death of Jonathan Swift, 1667–1745* (Dublin: Four Courts Press, 1998), 58.

68. Nicholas Phillipson, *Adam Smith: An Enlightened Life* (London: Penguin, 2011); John Dwyer, *The Age of Passions: An Interpretation of Adam Smith and Scottish Enlightenment Culture* (Edinburgh: Tuckwell Press, 1998); Ronald L Meek, 'The Rehabilitation of Sir James Steuart', in idem, *Economics and Ideology and Other Essays* (London: Chapman and Hall, 1967), 3–17; Andrew A. Skinner, 'Sir James Steuart: Economic Theory and Policy', in Peter Jones (ed.), *Philosophy and Science in the Scottish Enlightenment* (Edinburgh: Edinburgh University Press, 1988), 117–144 .

69. Antoin E. Murphy, *John Law: Economic Theorist and Policy Maker* (Oxford: Clarendon Press, 1997); Liana Vardi, *The Physiocrats and the World of the Enlightenment* (Cambridge: Cambridge University Press, 2012).

70. John Robertson, *The Case for the Enlightenment: Scotland and Naples, 1680–1760* (Cambridge: Cambridge University Press, 2005); idem, 'The Scottish Contribution to the Enlightenment', in Paul Wood (ed.), *The Scottish Enlightenment: Essays in Reinterpretation* (Rochester: University of Rochester Press, 2000), 37–62.

71. Omitted Queries, 289–306.

72. For an account of his life and writings, see James Kelly, '"A Wild Capuchin of Cork": Arthur O'Leary (1729–1802)', in Gerard Moran (ed.), *Radical Irish Priests, 1660–1970* (Dublin: Four Courts Press, 1998), 39–61.

73. James Kelly describes the pamphlet as 'one of the most radical statements in favour of religious and political forbearance published in eighteenth-century Ireland'. Ibid., 46.

74. Arthur O'Leary, *An Essay on Toleration, or Mr O'Leary's Plea for Liberty of Conscience* (1780) in Arthur O'Leary, *Miscellaneous Tracts*, 2nd edn (Dublin: Tho McDonnel, 1781), 391.

75. Ibid., 333.

76. Ibid., 375.

77. Ibid., 377.

78. Ibid., 347.

79. Ibid., 366, 367.

80. Ibid., 392.

1. The Presbyterian Enlightenment and the Nature of Man

1. For the central place of the covenant in Calvinist theology see Quentin Skinner, *Foundations of Modern Political Thought*, 2 vols (Cambridge: Cambridge University Press, 1978), II, 236–238. On its place in English Presbyterianism, see Christopher Hill, *The English Bible and the Seventeenth-Century Revolution* (London: Penguin, 1994), 271–283. On Scottish thinking in this direction, see T. F. Torrance, *Scottish Theology* (Edinburgh: T & T Clark, 1996), 125–156.

2. Church of Scotland, *The Confession of Faith: and the Larger and Shorter Catechisms. First agreed upon by the Assembly of Divines at Westminster* (Edinburgh: T. Lumisden and J. Robertson, 1744), 8–9.

3. Ibid., 44. See also S. D. Fratt, 'Scottish Theological Trends in the Eighteenth Century: Tensions Between the Head and the Heart' (PhD thesis, University of California, 1987; reprinted Michigan, 1994), 17–32.

4. Detail in this paragraph is drawn from J. C. Beckett, *Protestant Dissent in Ireland, 1687–1780* (London: Faber, 1946), 116–123.

5. Controversy arose again in 1782 when an act attempted to extend this provision to all dissenting faiths.

6. The origins of the test clauses are obscure. They were introduced by the English Privy Council, whose motives are unclear, but were soon adopted by the Irish parliament as a bulwark of the church-state settlement. The parliament repeatedly refused to follow the suggestion of Whig lord lieutenants to remove the test. See ibid., 40–53. See also D. W. Hayton, 'Exclusion, Conformity and Parliamentary Representation: The Impact of the Sacramental Test on Irish Dissenting Politics', in Kevin Herlihy (ed.), *The Politics of Irish Dissent, 1650–1800* (Dublin: Four Courts Press, 1997), 52–73.

7. 'An Act to Prevent the Further Growth of Popery', *Statutes at Large Passed in the Parliaments held in Ireland*, 20 vols (Dublin: George Grierson, 1786–1801), IV, 24.

8. Again the precise origins of this measure are obscure. See Beckett, *Protestant Dissent in Ireland*, 71–82.

9. 'An Act for Exempting the Protestant Dissenters of this Kingdom from Certain Penalties, to which they are now Subject', *Statutes at Large*, IV, 509–510.

10. Ibid., IV, 510.

11. Detail in this paragraph is drawn from Beckett, *Protestant Dissent in Ireland*, 106–115.

12. Quoted in ibid., 108.

13. As Beckett states of the idiosyncrasies and contradictions involved, 'neither the claims of the Presbyterians nor the laws of the country could be completely ignored or completely carried out. So the existence of organised Presbyterianism was connived at, and Presbyterian ministers were paid by the government to perform functions that had been declared illegal by an act of parliament.' Ibid., 114.

14. See R. Finlay Holmes, 'The Reverend John Abernethy: The Challenge of New

Light Theology to Traditional Irish Presbyterian Calvinism', in Kevin Herlihy (ed.), *The Religion of Irish Dissent* (Dublin: Four Courts Press, 1996), 100–111; A. G. W. Brown, 'John Abernethy 1680–1740: Scholar and Ecclesiast', in Gerard O'Brien and Peter Roebuck (eds), *Nine Ulster Lives* (Belfast: Ulster Historical Foundation, 1992), 125–147; R. B. Barlow, 'The Career of John Abernethy (1680–1740), Father of Non-Subscription in Ireland,' *Harvard Theological Review*, 78 (1985), 399–419.

15. John Abernethy, *Religious Obedience Founded on Personal Persuasion* (Belfast; James Blow, 1720), 36.

16. I. R. McBride, *Scripture Politics: Ulster Presbyterians and Irish Radicalism in the Late Eighteenth Century* (Oxford: Clarendon Press, 1998), 43.

17. For examples of congregational loyalty to the non-subscribers, see Patrick Griffin, *The People with No Name: Ireland's Ulster Scots, America's Scots Irish, and the Creation of a British Atlantic World 1689–1764* (Princeton: Princeton University Press, 2001), 57–58.

18. 'Expedients for Peace among the Protestant Dissenters in the north of Ireland, humbly offered to the Consideration of the Presbyteries and of the next Synod by the Non-Subscribing Ministers', in *A Narrative of the Proceedings of Seven General Synods of the Northern Presbyterians in Ireland* (Belfast: James Blow, 1727), 184.

19. Presbyterian Church of Ireland, *Records of the General Synod of Ulster from 1691 to 1820*, 3 vols (Belfast: Archer and Sons, 1890), II, 49.

20. Ibid., II, 45. See also ibid., II, 33.

21. Ibid., II, 66.

22. For a contemporaneous account, see *A Narrative of the Seven General Synods*. The standard account is J. S. Reid, *History of the Presbyterian Church in Ireland*, 3 vols (Belfast: Whittaker, 1867), III, 174–185.

23. *Records of the General Synod of Ulster*, II, 88.

24. *Narrative of the Seven General Synods*, 138.

25. *Records of the General Synod of Ulster*, II, 95.

26. Ibid., 150–151.

27. Under this rubric, they listed the prospective ministerial members as 'Mr Michael Bruce, Mr Kirkpatrick, Mr Haliday, Mr John Mairs, Mr Harper, Mr Abernethy, Mr Tho Wilson, Mr Clugston, Mr Henderson, Mr Thomas Shaw, Mr Will Taylor Junr, Mr John Orr of Comber if he please and Mr John Elder, left at liberty to join this new presbytery of Antrim or continue if he please, and Mr Pat Simson is left at liberty to join with the presbytery of Antrim or continue where he please.' Ibid., II, 96.

28. 'Expedients for Peace', 184.

29. Ibid.

30. Ibid., 219, 220, 221, 228.

31. Ibid., 186.

32. Ibid., 187.

33. Ibid., 206.

34. Ibid., 207.

35. Ibid., 206.

36. Ibid., 207.

37. Ibid., 188.

38. Ibid., 211.

39. *Records of the General Synod of Ulster*, II, 105.

40. McBride, *Scripture Politics*, 46.

41. 'Christology thus served as the basis for the liberty of individual conscience, the corresponding right of private judgement, and it ultimately grounded the spiritual nature of Christ's kingdom . . . While the congregation's right to choose its own pastor was defended, it was not a major part of this debate.' James E. Bradley, 'The Religious Origins of Radical Politics in England, Scotland and Ireland', in James E. Bradley and Dale K. Van Kley (eds), *Religion and Politics in Enlightenment Europe* (Notre Dame; Notre Dame University Press, 2001), 225.

42. 'New Light theology was peculiarly attractive to the emerging *bourgeois intelligentsia* of eastern Ulster, who, like their counterparts elsewhere in western Europe, were susceptible to Enlightenment influences and were critical of what appeared to be artificial restrictions upon freedom in business, politics and ideas. A rational form of religion, eschewing mysterious and metaphysical dogma, and emphasising duty and responsible behaviour, "polite Presbyterianism" was popular among them'; Holmes, 'The Reverend John Abernethy', 109.

43. *Records of the General Synod of Ulster*, I, 100.

44. Ibid.

45. Ibid.

46. 'Expedients for Peace', 202. Both McBride and Griffin argue that the subscribers came predominately from lower down the socioeconomic scale than their non-subscribing brethren. See McBride, *Scripture Politics*, 58; Griffin, *People with No Name*, 39–41.

47. *Records of the General Synod of Ulster*, II, 48.

48. John Malcome, *Personal Persuasion no Foundation for Religious Obedience: or some Friendly Reflections on a Sermon Preach'd at Belfast, December 9, 1719, by John Abernethy* (Belfast: Robert Gardner, 1720).

49. Ibid., 8–9. The reference is to Matt 7.26.

50. Ibid., 10. On Socinianism, see Sarah Mortimer, *Reason and Religion in the English Revolution: The Challenge of Socinianism* (Cambridge: Cambridge University Press, 2010). I would like to thank Catie Gill for sending me a copy of this work.

51. Malcome, *Personal Persuasion no Foundation*, 8. For examples of biblical citation in Malcome's rebuttal of Abernethy, see ibid., 17, 27.

52. Ibid., 26–27.

53. John Malcome, *The Good Old Way Examined, being an Answer to the Belfast Society* (Belfast: Robert Gardner, 1720), 14–15.
54. Ibid., 8.
55. Matthew Clerk, *Letter from the Belfast Society to the Reverend Matthew Clerk with an Answer to the Society's Remarks* ([Belfast], 1723), 8.
56. Ibid., 15.
57. Ibid., 16.
58. Ibid., 19.
59. Ibid., 21.
60. Ibid., 20–21.
61. Malcome, *Good Old Way Examined*, 10.
62. *Records of the General Synod of Ulster*, II, 47.
63. 'On the question of the orthodoxy of the non-subscribers, modern scholarship has come down decisively on the side of the non-subscribers . . . Even in the case of John Abernethy, the most advanced non-subscriber thinker, there is no positive evidence that he actually embraced Arianism, though the tendency of his thought towards Arminianism and nomism is unmistakable.' Bradley, 'Religious Origins', 224. See also ibid., n165. The orthodoxy issue is fully teased out in M. A. Stewart, 'Rational Dissent in Early Eighteenth-Century Ireland', in Knud Haakonssen (ed.), *Enlightenment and Religion: Rational Dissent in Eighteenth-Century Britain* (Cambridge: Cambridge University Press, 1996), 51–64.
64. *Records of the General Synod of Ulster*, II, 101.
65. Ibid., II, 7.
66. Ibid., II, 35, 57.
67. This paragraph is informed by A. W. G. Brown, *The Great Mr Boyse: A Study of the Reverend Joseph Boyse* (Belfast: Presbyterian Historical Society of Ireland, 1988) and Sandra M. Hynes, 'Mapping Friendship and Dissent: The Letters from Joseph Boyse to Ralph Thoresby, 1680–1710', in Arial Hessayon and David Finnegan (eds), *Varieties of Seventeenth- and Early Eighteenth-Century Radicalism in Context* (Farnham: Ashgate Press, 2011), 205–220.
68. Joseph Boyse, 'On Love to Our Neighbour: Sermon II', *Sermons Preach'd on Various Subjects*, 2 vols (Dublin: S. Powell, 1708), II, 385.
69. Ibid., II, 396.
70. Ibid., II, 383.
71. Ibid., II, 393.
72. Ibid., II, 387.
73. Ibid., II, 390.
74. Ibid., II, 389.
75. Ibid., II, 388.
76. Ibid., II, 396.

77. Ibid., II, 391.

78. Ibid., II, 380.

79. Ibid., II, 400, quoting the Epistle of Paul to the Galatians, 'as we have therefore opportunity, let us do good unto all men, especially unto them who are of the household of the faith'. Boyse's passage is clearly related to the views expounded by his friend and coreligionist Francis Hutcheson in his *Inquiry into the Original or Our Ideas of Beauty and Virtue* (London: J. Darby, 1725). Therein Hutcheson outlined a sequence of lower and higher attachments to which the moral agent was committed. These began with the family, the emotional connection to which was 'antecedent to all acquaintance'; ibid., 196. Yet, it expanded out to a general love of all humankind, which he termed 'universal benevolence'; ibid., 197.

80. Boyse, 'On Love to Our Neighbour: Sermon II', II, 400–401. Again, this statement seems to emerge from an engagement with Hutcheson.

81. Joseph Boyse, *A Sermon preached at Londonderry, 24 June 1722*, in idem, *The Works of the Reverend and Learned Mr Boyse of Dublin*, 2 vols (London: John Gray, 1728), I, 377.

82. Ibid., I, 377–378.

83. Ibid., I, 378.

84. Ibid. The sermon was on Christian brotherhood and is of more theological than polemical interest. The polemical component is made plain in the preface and it is this I have concentrated on here. For the full sermon, see ibid., I, 379–385.

85. Ibid., I, 334.

86. Ibid.

87. The standard work remains W. R. Scott, *Francis Hutcheson: His Life, Teaching and Position in the History of Philosophy* (1900; Bristol: Thoemmes Press, 1992).

88. For the relationship between Francis Hutcheson and his father, John, see James Moore, 'Presbyterianism and the Right of Private Judgement: Church Government in Ireland and Scotland in the Age of Francis Hutcheson', in Ruth Evelyn Savage (ed.), *Philosophy and Religion in Enlightenment Britain* (Oxford: Oxford University Press, 2012), 141–168. I am grateful to James Moore for allowing me to see a copy of this paper in advance of publication. On the colourful career of John Simson, see Anne Skoczylas, *Mr Simson's Knotty Case: Divinity, Politics and Due Process in Early Eighteenth-Century Scotland* (Montreal: McGill-Queens University Press, 2001).

89. M. A. Stewart notes that the *Dictionary of National Biography* entry on Boyse suggests that Boyse initially acted as Hutcheson's assistant when the academy was opened. Stewart, 'Rational Dissent', 46 n10.

90. For a full version of this interpretation of the *Inquiry*, see Michael Brown, *Francis Hutcheson in Dublin, 1719–1730: The Crucible of His Thought* (Dublin: Four Courts Press, 2002), 25–74.

91. Hutcheson was not wholly successful in this, for both contemporaries and subsequent

commentators have associated him with the non-subscribing position despite taking the Confession in 1730 upon his appointment as professor of moral philosophy at the University of Glasgow.

92. Francis Hutcheson, *An Inquiry into the Original of Our Ideas of Beauty and Virtue*, Wolfgang Leidhold (ed.) (Indianapolis: Liberty Fund, 2004), 19–23.

93. Ibid., 25.

94. Ibid., 95.

95. Ibid., 140.

96. Ibid., 29.

97. Ibid., 125.

98. Ibid., 145–146.

99. Ibid., 40.

100. Ibid., 89.

101. Ibid., 105.

102. Ibid., 121–122.

103. Ibid., 196.

104. Ibid., 196–197.

105. Francis Hutcheson to John Hutcheson, 4 August 1726, PRONI D/971/84/G/1.

106. Ibid.

107. This trajectory is documented in Thomas Witherow, *Historical and Literary Memorials of Presbyterianism in Ireland*, 2 vols (Belfast: William Mullan and Son, 1879), I, 156–162.

108. Holmes, 'The Reverend John Abernethy', 104.

109. [James Kirkpatrick], Appendix to James Duchal, *Sermon on the Occasion of the Death of the late Reverend John Abernethy* (Dublin, S. Powell, 1741), 36ff, cited in Witherow, *Historical and Literary Memorials*, I, 162–164.

110. Clerk, *A Letter from the Belfast Society*, 11.

111. Ibid., 29.

112. Malcome, *The Good Old Way Examined*, 5.

113. Belfast Society, *The Good Old Way: or a Vindication of some Important Scripture-Truths and all who Preach Them from the Imputation of Novelty* (Belfast: James Blow, 1720), 5–6.

114. Ibid., 4–5.

115. [James Kirkpatrick], *A Vindication of the Presbyterian Ministers in the North of Ireland* (Belfast: James Blow, 1721), 21.

116. Ibid., 27.

117. 'Expedients for Peace', 185.

118. This paragraph is informed by Bradley, 'The Religious Origins of Radical Politics in England, Scotland and Ireland', 224–230.

119. Belfast Society, *Good Old Way*, 6–7.

120. Malcome, *Good Old Way Examined*, 15.

121. Belfast Society, *Good Old Way*, 6.

122. Ibid., 4.

123. Ibid., 12.

124. Ibid., 7–8.

125. See Steven ffeary-Smyrl, '"Theatres of Worship": Dissenting Meeting Houses in Dublin', in Kevin Herlihy (ed.), *The Irish Dissenting Tradition, 1650–1750* (Dublin: Four Courts Press, 1995), 51.

126. *Records of the General Synod of Ulster*, I, 489. Technically he was correct as the Usher's Quay congregation affiliated with the Southern Association, not the Synod. This was discussed at the Synod of 1720. Ibid., I, 523–524.

127. Ibid., I, 492.

128. Ibid., I, 493. Antrim's protest about this judgement is on ibid., I, 506.

129. Abernethy, *Religious Obedience*, 20.

130. Ibid., 37–38.

131. Ibid., 20.

132. Ibid., 12–13.

133. Ibid., 13.

134. Ibid., 14–15.

135. For the shift in Presbyterian rhetoric, see Ian McBride, 'Ulster Presbyterians and the Confessional State, c.1688–1733', in D. George Boyce, Robert Eccleshall, and Vincent Geoghegan (eds), *Political Discourse in Seventeenth- and Eighteenth-Century Ireland* (Houndmills: Ashgate Press, 2001), 169–192.

136. On the subscribers' position see Griffin, *People with No Name*, 48–49.

137. 'In other words, if church judicatories should not impose subscriptions of faith, neither should the state obtrude in matters of conscience.' Bradley, 'Religious Origins', 226.

138. [Thomas Emlyn], 'Advertisement by Another Hand', *An Humble Inquiry into the Scripture Account of Jesus Christ: Or a Short Argument Concerning His Deity and Glory According to the Gospel* (1702), in David Berman and Patricia O'Riordan (eds), *The Irish Enlightenment and Counter-Enlightenment*, 6 vols (Bristol: Thoemmes Press, 2002), I, 3.

139. Emlyn made much of this sequence of events in his subsequent defence, for example, writing that 'he desires it may be known that he never voluntarily published matters, nor desired to make any disturbance among the people about them. But his opinion was curiously pried into and this declaration of his judgement was wrested from him by an importunate repeated enquiry and demand, which he could not well resist; and since he must speak, he durst not but speak with all

sincerity'; Thomas Emlyn, *The Case of Mr E. in Relation to the Difference between Him and some Dissenting Ministers of the City of D which He supposes is Greatly Misunderstood*, in [Emlyn], *An Humble Inquiry*, 2.

140. George Mathews, *An Account of the Trial on 14 June 1703, Before the Court of the Queen's Bench, Dublin, of the Revd Thomas Emlyn for a Publication Against the Doctrine of the Trinity* (Dublin: John Robertson and Co and W. M'Combrin, 1839), 11.

141. Ibid., 7.

142. Joseph Boyse, *The Difference between Mr E and the Protestant Dissenting Ministers of Dublin Truly Represented* (Dublin, [1703]).

143. Ibid., 10.

144. Emlyn, *The Case of Mr E*, 1.

145. Ibid., 1–2.

146. [Emlyn], *An Humble Inquiry*.

147. Ibid., 4.

148. 1 Cor 8.5.

149. Thomas Emlyn, *A Brief Account of the Prosecution and Imprisonment of Mr Tho Em, an Eminent Divine in Dublin in Ireland*, in [Emlyn], *An Humble Inquiry*, 4.

150. Thomas Emlyn, *A True Narrative of the Proceedings Against Mr Thomas Emlyn* in idem, *The Works of Mr Thomas Emlyn*, 3 vols (London: John Noon and John Whitson, 1746), I, 27.

151. Ibid., 27–8. The passage is found in [Emlyn], *An Humble Enquiry*, 4.

152. Emlyn, *A True Narrative*, 28.

153. Emlyn, *A Brief Account*, 2, 3.

154. [Emlyn], 'Advertisement by Another Hand', 4.

155. For an outline of these two approaches, see Griffin, *People with No Name*, 38.

156. Thomas Emlyn, 'Appendix to the *Narrative*' in idem, *Works*, I, xlvi.

157. Ibid., I, xlviii.

158. Abernethy, *Religious Obedience*, 17.

2. The Anglican Enlightenment and the Nature of God

1. J. G. Simms, *Jacobite Ireland* (1969; Dublin: Four Courts Press, 2000), 227. The account that follows draws on this standard account, and on David Dickson, *New Foundations: Ireland 1660–1800*, 2nd edn (Dublin: Irish Academic Press, 2000), 31–42.

2. In fact, its legal status was little more than a military cessation and was to have its terms virtually ignored in the Protestant parliament seated in Dublin in the 1690s.

3. J. P. Kenyon, *Revolution Principles: The Politics of Party, 1689–1720* (Cambridge: Cambridge University Press, 1979) remains a useful summary.

4. This point is made in Tim Harris, 'Incompatible Revolutions? The Established Church and the Revolutions of 1688–9 in Ireland, England and Scotland', in Allan

I. MacInnes and Jane Ohlmeyer (eds), *The Stuart Kingdoms in the Seventeenth Century* (Dublin: Four Courts Press, 2002), 207.

5. For an examination of the range of articles of surrender that brought the conflict to a close, see Eoin Kinsella, 'In Pursuit of a Positive Construction: Irish Catholics and the Williamite Articles of Surrender, 1690–1701', *Eighteenth-Century Ireland*, 24 (2009), 11–35.

6. This issue has been examined primarily in relation to political ideas. See Robert Eccleshall, 'Anglican Political Thought in the Century after the Glorious Revolution', in D. George Boyce, Robert Eccleshall, and Vincent Geoghegan (eds), *Political Thought in Ireland since the Seventeenth Century* (London: Routledge, 1993), 36–72; Robert Eccleshall, 'The Political Ideas of Anglican Ireland in the 1690s', in D. George Boyce, Robert Eccleshall, and Vincent Geoghegan (eds), *Political Discourse in Seventeenth- and Eighteenth-Century Ireland* (Houndmills: Ashgate Press, 2001), 62–80; S. J. Connolly, 'The Glorious Revolution in Irish Protestant Political Thinking', in S. J. Connolly (ed.), *Political Ideas in Eighteenth-Century Ireland* (Dublin: Four Courts Press, 2000), 27–63.

7. Jonathan Swift, *Gulliver's Travels*, Robert Demaria Jr. (ed.) (London: Penguin, 2001), 255–256.

8. Ibid., 265–266.

9. Ibid., 266.

10. Ibid.

11. For a sensitive postcolonial reading of the text, see Clement Hawes, 'Three Times Around the Globe: Gulliver and Colonial Discourse', in Jonathan Swift, *Gulliver's Travels and Other Writings*, Clement Hawes (ed.) (Boston: Houghton Mifflin, 2004), 438–464. See also Jill Marie Bradbury, 'Domestic, Political and Moral Economies in Swift's Irish Writings', in David A. Valone and Jill Marie Bradbury (eds), *Anglo-Irish Identities* (Lewisburg: Bucknell Press, 2008), 165–180, for a postcolonial reading of *Gulliver's Travels* within the corpus of his wider Irish interventions.

12. Swift, *Gulliver's Travels*, 48.

13. Ibid., 64–68.

14. Ibid., 64.

15. Ibid., 94–95. On the historical context of this passage see Claude Rawson, *God, Gulliver and Genocide: Barbarism and the European Imagination, 1492–1945* (Oxford: Oxford University Press, 2001), 92–182.

16. Swift, *Gulliver's Travels*, 87.

17. Ibid., 87. See also ibid., 105.

18. Ibid., 87.

19. Ian Higgins, 'Language and Style', in Christopher Fox (ed.), *The Cambridge Companion to Jonathan Swift* (Cambridge: Cambridge University Press, 2003), 148.

20. Swift, *Gulliver's Travels*, 124–125.

21. The term 'optical conceit' is used by Robert Demaria Jr., introduction, ibid., xiv. See also Deborah Needleman Armintor, 'The Sexual Politics of Microscopy in Brodbingnag', *SEL: Studies in English Literature 1500–1900*, 47 (2007), 619–640.

22. Swift, *Gulliver's Travels*, 148–149.

23. Ibid., 151.

24. Ibid., 167–179; quote is at 168.

25. Ibid., 176–177. This is a macabre pun literalising the idea of being in two minds. My rendition of this passage is indebted to Claude Rawson, 'The Injured Lady and the Drapier: A Reading of Swift's Irish Tracts', *Prose Studies*, 3 (1980), 24–27.

26. Swift, *Gulliver's Travels*, 244.

27. Ibid., 221.

28. Ibid., 246.

29. Ibid., 249. Again, an intriguing series of cultural contexts is supplied by Rawson, *God, Gulliver and Genocide*, 256–310.

30. Swift, *Gulliver's Travels*, 250.

31. Ibid., 271.

32. On the use of keys in eighteenth-century literature, and the complexity of using one, see Robert Darnton, *George Washington's False Teeth: An Unconventional Guide to the Eighteenth Century* (New York: Norton, 2003), 49.

33. For a range of contemporary analogies, see J. A. Downie, *Jonathan Swift: Political Writer* (London: Routledge and Kegan Paul, 1984), 274–281. Downie argues Swift was a consistent Old Whig in his political engagements.

34. Swift, *Gulliver's Travels*, 65–66.

35. Ibid., 160–162. See also ibid., 286n30. These included the Wood's halfpence affair, on which see, Robert E. Burns, *Irish Parliamentary Politics in the Eighteenth Century*, 2 vols (Washington DC: Catholic University of America Press, 1989), I, 134–216; Paddy McNally, 'Wood's Halfpence, Carteret and the Government of Ireland', *Irish Historical Studies*, 30 (1997), 354–376; Alfred Goodwin, 'Wood's Halfpence', in Rosalind Mitchison (ed.), *Essays in Eighteenth-Century History* (London: Longmans, Green, 1966), 117–144.

36. In a slightly different interpretation, F. P. Lock has written: 'His method in *Gulliver's Travels* was to create types or paradigms, whether of individuals, institutions or societies. These paradigms are based, of course, on his knowledge of actual examples. But it is misleading to search for originals or prototypes: history illustrates *Gulliver's Travels*, it does not explain it.' *The Politics of Gulliver's Travels* (Oxford: Clarendon Press, 1980), 35.

37. For a useful assessment, see Marcus Walsh, 'Swift and Religion', in Fox, *The Cambridge Companion to Jonathan Swift*, 161–176.

38. Jonathan Swift, 'On the Trinity', in *The Prose Writings of Jonathan Swift*, Herbert Davis (ed.), 16 vols (Oxford: Basil Blackwell, 1939–74), II, 129–30.

39. See Daniel Carey, 'Swift among the Freethinkers', *Eighteenth-Century Ireland*, 12 (1997), 89–99.
40. Swift, 'On the Trinity', 131.
41. Ibid.
42. Jonathan Swift, 'On the Testimony of Conscience', in *The Prose Writings of Jonathan Swift*, II, 380.
43. 'What comes across most strongly in Swift's references to God is a sense of his remoteness and unknowability'. Michael DePorte, 'Swift, God and Power', in Christopher Fox and Brenda Tooley (eds), *Walking Naboth's Vineyard: New Studies in Swift* (Notre Dame: University of Notre Dame Press, 1995), 89.
44. As DePorte notes, 'Swift talks about God as the ultimate authority for doctrines of imperative social importance, about crimes against social order being crimes against God, but about individual relationship to God he says remarkably little. Indeed, there is a great deal in Swift's writings to suggest that he found the whole matter of a personal relationship with God disquieting.' Ibid., 88. The connection between fideism and a pragmatic faith is clearly identified in Christopher J. Fauske, *Jonathan Swift and the Church of Ireland, 1710–1724* (Dublin: Irish Academic Press, 2002), 63–73, 110.
45. William King, *Essay on the Origin of Evil*, Edmund Law (trans.) (London: R. Knaplock, 1731), 180–183. For a different reading, see Raymond Whelan, 'An Irish Scholastic: The Public Identity of Archbishop William King, 1650–1729' (PhD thesis, University of Aberdeen, 2015).
46. King, *Origin of Evil*, 45–51. On theological representationalism, see David Berman, 'The Irish Counter-Enlightenment', in Richard Kearney (ed.), *The Irish Mind: Exploring Intellectual Traditions* (Dublin: Wolfhound Press, 1985), 119–140. On its application to King, see David Berman, 'The Irish Pragmatist', in Christopher Fauske (ed.), *Archbishop William King and the Anglican Irish Context, 1688–1729* (Dublin: Four Courts Press, 2004), 123–134.
47. King, *Origin of Evil*, 185.
48. Ibid., 52.
49. Ibid., 187.
50. See Philip O'Regan, *Archbishop William King of Dublin (1650–1729) and the Constitution in Church and State* (Dublin: Four Courts Press, 2000), 19–25. See also Christopher Fauske, *A Political Biography of William King* (London: Pickering & Chatto Press, 2011), *passim*.
51. William King, *The State of the Protestants of Ireland under the late King James' Government* (London: Samuel Roycroft, 1691), 5.
52. Ibid., 52–53.
53. Ibid., 55.
54. Ibid., 54.
55. This logically coherent outcome of King's argument is used to argue for the intrinsic

instability of the Anglican community's supremacy in Jarlath Killeen, *Gothic Ireland: Horror and the Irish Anglican Imagination in the Long Eighteenth Century* (Dublin: Four Courts Press, 2005), 62.

56. Joseph Richardson, 'Political Anglicanism in Ireland 1691–1801: From the Language of Liberty to the Language of Union', in Michael Brown, James Kelly, and Patrick M. Geoghegan (eds), *The Irish Act of Union, 1800: Bicentennial Essays* (Dublin: Irish Academic Press, 2003), 58–67.

57. King, *The State of the Protestants of Ireland*, 56.

58. Ibid., 93.

59. William King, *Europe's Deliverance from France and Slavery* (Dublin: Tim Goodvin, 1691), 21.

60. Robert Molesworth, *An Account of the Kingdom of Denmark as it was in the Year 1692* (London: printed for Timothy Godwin, 1694), 96–102, 114. For a modern edition, see idem, *An Account of Denmark, With Francogallia and Some Considerations for the Promoting of Agriculture and Employing the Poor*, Justin Champion (ed.) (Indianapolis: Liberty Fund, 2011).

61. Molesworth, *An Account of the Kingdom of Denmark*, 119–123, 124–125, 127–128, 131–132.

62. Ibid., 10.

63. Ibid., 37–38.

64. Ibid., 11.

65. Ibid., 36.

66. Ibid., 26.

67. Ibid., 2.

68. On Molesworth's diplomatic mission, see Hugh Mayo, 'Robert Molesworth's *Account of Denmark*—its Roots and its Impact' (PhD thesis, Odense University, 2000), 316–382. I would like to thank Hugh Mayo for providing me with a copy of his thesis.

69. Molesworth, *An Account of the Kingdom of Denmark*, 38–42.

70. Ibid., 235–237.

71. Upon their presentation of a petition to the lord lieutenant, Molesworth apparently remarked: 'They that have turned the world upside down have come hither also.' The House of Lords, led by the bishops, demanded some retribution but although Molesworth was removed from the Privy Council no further action resulted. On this, see *Journals of the Irish House of Lords*, 8 vols (Dublin, 1779–1800), II, 441–442.

72. Molesworth's awareness of the Irish condition was briefly alluded to, but only to highlight the gap between the ruler and the ruled in both Denmark and Ireland. Writing of the Danish tongue, he observed, 'The language is very ungrateful, and

not unlike the Irish in its whining, complaining tone. The king, great men, gentry and many burgers make use of the High Dutch in their ordinary discourse and of French to strangers. I have heard several in high employment boast that they could not speak Danish.' *An Account of the Kingdom of Denmark*, 91.

73. J. G. Simms, *William Molyneux of Dublin, 1656–98* (Dublin: Irish Academic Press, 1982), 35–38.

74. It also drew extensively on a tract written at the Restoration by Molyneux's father-in-law, Sir William Domville. See Patrick Kelly, 'Recasting a Tradition: William Molyneux and the Sources of *The Case of Ireland . . . Stated*', in Jane Ohlmeyer (ed.), *Political Thought in Seventeenth-Century Ireland: Kingdom or Colony* (Cambridge: Cambridge University Press, 2000), 83–106.

75. See Eoin Magennis, 'The Politics of Economics: The Case of the Woollens Industry in Ireland and England, 1690–1750', unpublished paper delivered to the Annual Conference of the British Society of Eighteenth-Century Studies, University of Oxford, 5 January 2007. I would like to thank Eoin Magennis for a copy of this talk.

76. In point of fact, Molyneux was incorrect; for Westminster did occasional legislate directly for Ireland. This supremacy was finally asserted in the Declaratory Act of 1720. On the practice, see Isolda Victory, 'The Making of the Declaratory Act of 1720', in Gerard O'Brien (ed.), *Parliament, Politics and People: Essays in Eighteenth-Century Irish History* (Dublin: Irish Academic Press, 1989), 9–30.

77. William Molyneux, *The Case of Ireland's being Bound by Acts of Parliament in England Stated*, J. G. Simms (ed.) (Dublin: Cadenus, 1977), 29–30.

78. Ibid., 47–48.

79. Ibid., 62–92.

80. Ibid., 68.

81. 'The language of natural or abstract right, evidently influenced by John Locke's *Two Treatises of Government* (1689), cropped up occasionally in *The Case*, but mainly to justify the claim that it was an inherent right of mankind to be ruled by consent: there was no suggestion of an appeal (past or future) to the right of resistance in the event of a tyranny on the part of the ruler.' Jacqueline Hill, 'Ireland without Union: Molyneux and his Legacy', in John Robertson (ed.), *A Union for Empire: Political Thought and the British Union of 1707* (Cambridge: Cambridge University Press, 1995), 285.

82. Molyneux, *The Case of Ireland . . . Stated*, 3.

83. Ibid., 117.

84. Ibid., 34.

85. Ibid., 35–36.

86. For discussion of the English movement, see John Spurr, '"Latitudinarianism" and the Restoration Church', *Historical Journal*, 31 (1988), 61–82; Martyn Fitzpatrick,

'Latitudinarianism at the Parting of the Ways: A Suggestion', in John Walsh, Colin Haydon, and Stephen Taylor (eds), *The Church of England, c.1689–c.1833: From Toleration to Tractarianism* (Cambridge: Cambridge University Press, 1993), 209–227.

87. See David Berman, 'Edward Synge the Younger', in Thomas Duddy (ed.), *Dictionary of Irish Philosophers* (Bristol: Thoemmes Press, 2004), 322.

88. Thomas Hobbes, *Leviathan*, Richard Tuck (ed.) (Cambridge: Cambridge University Press, 1991). See also Quentin Skinner, *Visions of Politics, Volume III: Hobbes and Civil Science* (Cambridge: Cambridge University Press, 2002).

89. Edward Synge, *The Case of Toleration Considered* (Dublin: A. Rhames, 1725), in David Berman and Patricia O'Riordan (eds), *The Irish Enlightenment and Counter-Enlightenment*, 6 vols (Bristol: Thoemmes Press, 2002), II, 15–16: Notice how close Synge's treatment of hypocrisy is to that of the Presbyterian rationalist John Abernethy; see chapter one above.

90. Ibid., 17. Notice here how the argument rests on 'persuasion', again echoing Abernethy's rhetoric.

91. Ibid., 21. It is from this assertion that the positive and sympathetic reading of Synge as a liberal derives. See Marie-Louise Legg, 'The Synge Family and the Limits of Toleration', in Fauske (ed.), *Archbishop William King*, 160–176.

92. Ibid., 27.

93. Ibid., 27–28. It is from this proposition that the negative, unsympathetic reading of Synge as an authoritarian derives. 'Synge's famous sermon concerning the toleration of Catholics is a masterpiece of doublespeak: he argues that the Catholics could and should be legitimately punished very severely because they were Catholics as long as it was made clear that they were being punished for the political implications of their religion rather than for their purely religious beliefs'; Killeen, *Gothic Ireland*, 86. It should be said that Synge really steered between the poles of toleration and coercion, offering an oath to enable Catholic participation in the state by discerning the difference between religious Catholics and political papists—a common distinction among Protestants in the period.

94. The anti-Catholic content of this officially sponsored ritual is examined in Toby Barnard, 'The Uses of the 23rd of October 1641 and Irish Protestant Celebrations', in idem, *Irish Protestant Ascents and Descents, 1641–1770* (Dublin: Four Courts Press, 2004), 111–142. For a reading of Synge's sermon that accords with the one offered here, as offering a very limited version of tolerance, see Richard Holmes, 'James Arbuckle: A Whig Critic of Irish Penal Laws?' in John Bergin, Eoin Magennis, Lesa Ní Mhunghaile, and Patrick Walsh (eds), *New Perspectives on the Penal Laws: Eighteenth-Century Ireland Special Issue 1* (2011), 93–112.

95. Synge, *Case of Toleration*, 37.

96. The reasons for this dearth are considered in Joseph Richardson, 'The Missing Moment: The Absence of Latitudinarianism in Eighteenth-Century Ireland',

unpublished paper, 2001. I am grateful to Joseph Richardson for providing me with a copy of this essay.

97. For overviews of his life and thought, see Scott C. Breuninger, *Recovering Bishop Berkeley: Virtue and Society in the Anglo-Irish Context* (New York: Palgrave Macmillan, 2010); Kenneth P. Winkler, *Berkeley: An Interpretation* (Oxford: Clarendon Press, 1994); David Berman, *George Berkeley: Idealism and the Man* (Oxford: Clarendon Press, 1996).

98. George Berkeley, *Principles of Human Knowledge* in idem, *Philosophical Works*, Michael R. Ayers (ed.) (London: Everyman, 1993), 71.

99. John Locke, *An Essay concerning Human Understanding*, P. H. Nidditch (ed.) (Oxford: Clarendon Press, 1975).

100. Berkeley, *Principles of Human Knowledge*, 78.

101. Ibid., 94–95.

102. Ibid., 90.

103. Ibid., 91–92.

104. Ibid., 137.

105. Ibid., 105.

106. Ibid., 95.

107. Ibid., 146.

108. Ibid., 99.

109. Ibid.

110. Ibid., 100.

111. Ibid., 103.

112. Ibid., 91.

113. Ibid., 107. Note here that Berkeley is giving priority to the sense of sight over the other senses.

114. Ibid., 148–149.

115. The debt he owed to Malebranche is crucial here, for Berkeley's ingestion of the Christianised Cartesianism of his precursor offered him immense sustenance in his polemical battles. On this, see A. A. Luce, *Berkeley and Malebranche: A Study in the Origins of Berkeley's Thought* (1934; Oxford: Clarendon Press, 1967).

116. Alexander Campbell Fraser (ed.), *Works of George Berkeley*, 4 vols (1901; Oxford: Clarendon Press, 1994), IV, 480.

117. Ibid., IV, 502. The context of this pamphlet is explored in George C. Caffentzis, 'Why did Berkeley's Bank Fail? Money and Libertinism in Eighteenth-Century Ireland', *Eighteenth-Century Ireland*, 12 (1997), 100–115.

118. Fraser, *Works of George Berkeley*, IV, 502–503.

119. Ibid., IV, 484, 485. This highlights the link between this text and *Alciphron* where Berkeley took to task a range of freethinking opinions.

120. Ibid., IV, 492–493.

121. Ibid., IV, 505.

122. Ibid., IV, 487.

123. Ibid., IV, 486.

124. Ibid., IV, 487–488.

125. Ibid., IV, 487.

126. Ibid., IV, 489.

127. David Berman, 'Berkeley, Clayton and *An Essay on Spirit*', *Journal of the History of Ideas*, 33 (1971), 367–378. Berman argues that the philosophical dispute between Clayton and Berkeley was based on the pluralist occasionalism of the former and the monist variant preferred by the latter.

128. On the Bermuda Project, see Breuninger, *Recovering George Berkeley*, 95–115.

129. A brief biography is offered in A. R. Winnett, 'An Irish Heretic Bishop: Robert Clayton of Clogher', in Derek Baker (ed.), *Schism, Heresy and Religious Protest*, *Studies in Church History*, 9 (1972), 311–21.

130. For the context of this activity and Clayton's contribution, see Macdara Dwyer, 'Sir Isaac Newton's Enlightened Chronology and Inter-denominational Discourse in Eighteenth-Century Ireland', *Irish Historical Studies*, 39 (2014), 221–229.

131. Clayton's Arianism is usefully put in wider British context in C. D. A. Leighton, 'The Enlightened Religion of Robert Clayton', *Studia Hibernica*, 29 (1995–1997), 157–184.

132. Robert Clayton, *An Essay on Spirit* (Dublin: S. Powell, 1750), reprinted in Berman and O'Riordan, *The Irish Enlightenment and Counter-Enlightenment*, VI.

133. Ibid., iii–iv.

134. Ibid., xxiv.

135. Ibid., xxxii.

136. Ibid., lx.

137. Ibid., 130–131.

138. Ibid., 97–98.

139. Ibid., 7.

140. Ibid., 35–36.

141. Ibid., 103, quoting Col 1.15.

142. Ibid., 111–112, citing Jn 13.16; Jn 5.26, 12.2, 7, 8, 9, 11.

143. Robert Clayton, *A Vindication of the Histories of the Old and New Testament, Part III; Containing Some Observations on the Nature of Angels and the Scriptural Account of the Fall and Redemption of Mankind* (Dublin: George Faulkner, 1757), 89.

144. Ibid., 114.

145. Ibid., 170, 171.

146. Robert Clayton, *The Bishop of Clogher's Speech made in the House of Lords, in Ireland* (London, 1757), reprinted in Berman and O'Riordan, *The Irish Enlightenment and Counter-Enlightenment*, VI, 7–8.

147. Ibid., 5.
148. Ibid., 14.
149. Ibid., 12–13.
150. Ibid., 18.
151. Ibid., 21.
152. Clayton, *Essay on Spirit*, xxxvii–xxxviii.
153. Clayton, *Speech*, 3, 7.
154. Berman, Leighton, and Winnett all discuss and dismiss the rumour that Clayton did not write the *Essay on Spirit* and that it was actually authored by a young clergyman in his diocese. The similarities in idiosyncratic thought between the *Essay* and the acknowledged *Speech* and *Vindication* certainly suggest that Clayton was indeed responsible for the *Essay*. See Berman, 'Berkeley, Clayton and *An Essay on Spirit*', 367–371; Leighton, 'The Enlightened Religion of Robert Clayton, 182–184; Winnett, 'An Irish Heretic Bishop', 312–314.
155. Clayton, *Speech*, 9.
156. Clayton, *Vindication of the Histories of the Old and New Testament*, title page.
157. Ibid., 149.
158. The pamphlet attacks are listed in Winnett, 'An Irish Heretic Bishop', 320–321.
159. Clayton, *Vindication*, III, 33.
160. See Michael Brown, 'Conversion Narratives in Eighteenth-Century Ireland', in Michael Brown, Charles Ivar McGrath, and Thomas P. Power (eds), *Converts and Conversion in Ireland, 1650–1850* (Dublin: Four Courts Press, 2005), 237–274.

3. The Catholic Enlightenment and the Nature of Law

1. This account draws on J. G. Simms, *Jacobite Ireland* (1969; Dublin: Four Courts Press, 2000), 74–94.
2. Ibid., 86–89.
3. 'The legislation and proceedings of the parliament are significant as demonstrations of what Catholics wanted, and of the limits to which they could push an unwilling king'; ibid., 93.
4. Ibid., 77–81.
5. The analysis in the next three paragraphs draws from Colm Ó Conaill, '"Ruddy Cheeks and Strapping Thighs": An Analysis of the Ordinary Soldiers in the Ranks of the Irish Regiments of Eighteenth-Century France', *Irish Sword*, 24 (2004–2005), 411–426. I am very grateful to Colm Ó Conaill for supplying me with a copy of this paper prior to publication and discussing its contents with me.
6. David Dickson, 'Jacobitism in Eighteenth-Century Ireland: A Munster Perspective', *Éire-Ireland*, 39 (2004), 62. It should be noted that the other basin of high-level activity, in and around County Armagh, was not productive of French mercenaries.

See A. J. Hughes, 'Gaelic Poets and Scribes of the South Armagh Hinterland in the Eighteenth and Nineteenth Centuries', in A. J. Hughes and William Nolan (eds), *Armagh, History and Society: Interdisciplinary Essays on the History of an Irish County* (Dublin: Geography Publications, 2001), 505–547. R. A. Breatnach writes that 'the poets of South East Ulster and North Leinster appear to have followed a simpler stylistic tradition . . . In Munster, on the other hand, the poet was expected above all else to speak eloquently.' 'The End of a Tradition: A Survey of Eighteenth-Century Gaelic Literature', *Studia Hibernica,* 1 (1960), 146.

7. Murray Pittock, *Jacobitism* (Houndmills: Palgrave Macmillan, 1998).

8. See Kevin Berland, '"Chesterfield Demands the Muse": Anglo-Irish Poets Publishing the "Irish" Voice, 1745–6', *Eighteenth-Century Ireland,* 17 (2002), 136n42.

9. Quoted in Éamon Ó Ciardha, *Ireland and the Jacobite Cause, 1685–1766: A Fatal Attachment* (Dublin: Four Courts Press, 2002), 157.

10. This English-language version was composed by Philib Ua Giobúin of Killhyle, County Wexford, in 1740. It is an extremely loose rendition of the ideas expressed. It is reproduced in Diarmaid Ó Muirithe, '"Tho' not in Full Stile Compleat": Jacobite Songs from Gaelic Manuscript Sources', *Eighteenth-Century Ireland,* 6 (1991), 96. I would like to thank Colm Ó Conaill for discussing this with me.

11. Seán Ó Tuama and Thomas Kinsella (eds), *An Duanaire, 1600–1900: Poems of the Dispossessed* (Dublin: Colin Smythe, 1981), 112–115.

12. Ó Ciardha describes Ó Rathaille, in a succinct phrase, as 'the Dryden of Munster' and as 'the Jacobite poet *par excellence*'. *Ireland and the Jacobite Cause,* 157.

13. This point is made in Joep Leerssen, *Mere Irish and Fíor Ghael: Studies in the Idea of Irish of Nationality, its Development and Literary Expression prior to the Nineteenth Century* (1986; Cork: Cork University Press, 1996), 228–229.

14. Cited in ibid., 229.

15. Ibid., 229–230.

16. See, for example, Marie Louise Legg (ed.), *The Census of Elphin, 1749* (Dublin: Irish Manuscripts Commission, 2004).

17. Quote (and translation) in Breandán Ó Buachalla, 'The Making of a Cork Jacobite', in Patrick O'Flanagan and Cornelius Buttimer (eds), *Cork, History and Society: Interdisciplinary Essays on the History of an Irish County* (Dublin: Geography Publications, 1993), 477, 493n32.

18. For a list of the major pieces of anti-Catholic legislation, see Appendix I in John Bergin, Eoin Magennis, Lesa Ní Mhunghaile, and Patrick Walsh (eds), *New Perspectives on the Penal Laws: Eighteenth-Century Ireland Special Issue 1* (2011), 275–277. For its significance in historical treatments of the period, see James Kelly, 'The Historiography of the Penal Laws' in ibid., 27–52.

19. The Protestant discontent created by the Treaty of Limerick is highlighted by

Patrick Kelly, 'Ireland and the Glorious Revolution: From Kingdom to Colony', in Robert Beddard (ed.), *The Revolutions of 1688* (Oxford: Clarendon Press, 1991), 181.

20. On the role of the Irish financial system in generating an Irish parliamentary tradition, see Charles Ivar McGrath, *The Making of the Eighteenth-Century Irish Constitution: Government, Parliament and the Revenue, 1692–1714* (Dublin: Four Courts Press, 2000).

21. 'An Act to Prevent the Further Growth of Popery', *Statutes at Large Passed in the Parliaments held in Ireland*, 20 vols (Dublin: George Grierson, 1786–1801), IV, 15.

22. Ibid., 25.

23. Ibid., 18.

24. Ibid., 25–26.

25. Ibid., 12.

26. Ibid.

27. Ibid., 13.

28. Ibid.

29. Ibid., 12–13. As late as 1777–1779, the antiquarian Charles O'Conor was challenged by his brother using this device in a legal case concerning the inheritance of their father. See Claire O'Halloran, '"A Revolution in our Moral and Civil Affairs": Charles O'Conor and the Creation of a Community of Scholars in late Eighteenth-Century Ireland', in Luke Gibbons and Kieran O'Conor (eds), *Charles O'Conor of Ballinagare: Life and Works* (Dublin: Four Courts Press, 2015), 82.

30. 'An Act to Prevent the Further Growth of Popery', 29.

31. Ibid., 30.

32. The discordance and self-contradictory nature of the penal code more generally is discussed in Jarlath Killeen, *Gothic Ireland: Horror and the Irish Anglican Imagination in the Long Eighteenth Century* (Dublin: Four Courts Press, 2005), 77–85. He argues that 'what we see in the generalized shape of the penal laws, the nebulous, interstitial and provisionary quality of the whole process of their administration, implementation and legislation, is an expression of the complications and contradictions of the Irish Anglican mind in this period.' Ibid., 81.

33. 'An Act for Explaining and Amending an Act Entitled An Act to Prevent the Further Growth of Popery', *Statutes at Large*, IV, 200.

34. See appendix to Thomas P. Power, 'The Conversion of Catholic Clergy to Anglicanism', in Michael Brown, Charles Ivar McGrath, and Thomas P. Power (eds), *Converts and Conversion in Ireland, 1650–1850* (Dublin: Four Courts Press, 2005), 209–213.

35. As S. J. Connolly puts it, 'these were compromise measures, drafted and amended to achieve maximum support in a House in which opinions differed on how best to deal with the problem of Catholicism. From this point of view a certain vagueness as to

ultimate purposes was an advantage.' *Religion, Law and Power: The Making of Protestant Ireland, 1660–1760* (Oxford: Oxford University Press, 1992), 275.

36. See the surveys offered in Patrick J. Corish, *The Catholic Community in the Seventeenth and Eighteenth Centuries* (Dublin: Helicon, 1981), 82–115; L. M. Cullen, 'Catholics Under the Penal Laws', *Eighteenth-Century Ireland*, 1 (1986), 23–36; James Kelly, 'The Impact of the Penal Laws', in James Kelly and Dáire Keogh (eds), *History of the Catholic Diocese in Dublin* (Dublin: Four Courts Press, 2000), 144–174; Eamon O'Flaherty, 'An Urban Community and the Penal Laws: Limerick, 1690–1830', in Bergin et al., *New Perspectives on the Penal Laws*, 197–225.

37. For one form of cultural response to this legislation, see Vincent Morley, 'The Penal Laws in Irish Vernacular Literature', in Bergin et al., *New Perspectives on the Penal Laws*, 173–195.

38. D. W. Hayton, 'Did Protestantism Fail in Early Eighteenth-Century Ireland? Charity Schools and the Enterprise of Religious and Social Reformation', in Alan Ford, James McGurie, and Kenneth Milne (eds), *As By Law Established: The Church of Ireland since the Reformation* (Dublin: Lilliput Press, 1995), 166–186.

39. Estimates are taken from Tomás Ó Fiaich, 'Irish Poetry and the Clergy', *Léachtaí Cholm Cille*, 4 (1975), 30–31.

40. Important differences in tone and texture emerge when the two regions are compared. The Munster poetry was typically more aristocratic in tone than the Ulster variant, while the texture of the poetry produced in the northern region was less political and more domestic. These are differences of degree and not in type. On Munster, see Daniel Corkery, *The Hidden Ireland: A Study of Gaelic Munster in the Eighteenth Century* (1924; Dublin: Gill and Macmillan, 1989); and Cornelius G. Buttimer, 'Gaelic Literature and Contemporary Life in Cork, 1700–1840', in O'Flanagan and Buttimer, *Cork, History and Society*, 585–653. On Ulster, see Tomás Ó Fiaich, 'The Political and Social Background of the Ulster Poets', *Léachtaí Cholm Cille*, 1 (1970), 23–33; Hughes, 'Gaelic Poets and Scribes of the South Armagh Hinterland', 505–549.

41. An important clarification is offered by R. A. Breatnach, namely, 'We equate "poetry" with *filíocht* and "poet" with *file*, whereas *file* in the Irish tradition at this stage is rather a man of letters who composes *filíocht*, which is simply metrical discourse.' 'End of a Tradition', 146.

42. For splits in the Catholic Church, see Eamon O'Flaherty, 'Indiscipline and Ecclesiastical Authority in Ireland', *Studia Hibernica*, 26 (1991–1992), 65–106.

43. Ó Tuama and Kinsella, *An Duanaire*, 154–155.

44. Ibid., 154–155.

45. Ibid., 154–155.

46. Ibid.

47. Ibid.
48. Ibid.
49. Ibid.
50. Ibid. This may be a personification of George I; a suggestion made to me by Eamon Ó Ciardha.
51. Ibid., 152–153.
52. Ibid.
53. On the connection between poets and shamans as found in the *aisling*, see Leerssen, *Mere Irish and Fíor Ghael*, 238–239.
54. As David Dickson writes, 'Two tendencies in the formal character of the poetry have been identified which have a wider relevance. There was a move away from syllabic verse and intricate literary construction to an accentuated poetry that was intended primarily to be sung; and in the political verse there was a broadening of the poetic voice from an inward-looking caste-bound perspective to one that sought to speak collectively and inclusively.' 'Jacobitism in Eighteenth-Century Ireland', 67. He notes that Ó Rathaille was indicative of both trends. For a study of the second trend, see Leerssen, *Mere Irish and Fíor Ghael*, 229–230. There was however a tradition of 'caste' or 'clan' poetry dating from at least the 1620s and 1630s. I would like to thank Éamon Ó Ciardha for raising this with me.
55. Ó Tuama and Kinsella, *An Duanaire*, 140–141.
56. Ibid.
57. Ibid.
58. Leerssen, *Mere Irish and Fíor Ghael*, 230.
59. Ibid.
60. On hospitality, see Toby Barnard, 'Public and Private Uses of Wealth in Ireland, c.1660–1760', and L. A. Clarkson, 'Hospitality, Housekeeping and High Living in Eighteenth-Century Ireland', both in Jacqueline Hill and Colm Lennon (eds), *Luxury and Austerity: Historical Studies XI* (Dublin: UCD Press, 1999), 66–83 and 84–105.
61. On Mac Craith's relationship with local notables, see David A. Fleming, 'Affection and Disaffection in Eighteenth-Century Mid-Munster Gaelic Poetry', *Eighteenth-Century Ireland*, 27 (2012), 90. He concludes 'MacCraith's [poetry] displays a mentality that alters as Jacobitism declines as a political ideology.' Ibid., 95.
62. Ó Muirithe, '"Tho' not in Full Stile Compleat"', 103.
63. Quoted in Breandán Ó Buachalla, 'Irish Jacobitism and Irish Nationalism: The Literary Evidence', in Michael O'Dea and Kevin Whelan (eds), *Nations and Nationalisms: France, Britain, Ireland and the Eighteenth-Century Context, Studies on Voltaire and the Eighteenth Century*, 335 (Oxford: Voltaire Foundation, 1995), 107.
64. As Ó Buachalla writes, 'Inherent in the idea of prophecy is the assumption that the

sages of the past were aware of present-day problems, thus an unbroken continuum between past and present is presupposed and an obvious link between them is established'. Ibid., 107.

65. Quoted in ibid., 109.

66. Ibid.

67. See Priscilla O'Connor, 'Irish Students in the Paris Faculty of Theology: Aspects of Doctrinal Controversy in the *Ancien Régime*', *Archivium Hibernicum*, 52 (2003), 85–97; idem, 'Irish Clerics and French Politics of Grace: The Reception of Nicholas Madgett's Doctoral Theses, 1732', in Thomas O'Connor and Mary Ann Lyons (eds), *Irish Migrants in Europe after Kinsale, 1602–1820* (Dublin: Four Courts Press, 2003), 182–202.

68. The estimate is offered in Ó Fiaich, 'Irish Poetry and the Clergy', 30. See also Ciarán MacMurchaidh, '"My Repeated Troubles": Dr James Gallagher (Bishop of Raphoe, 1725–37) and the Impact of the Penal Laws', in Bergin et al., *New Perspectives on the Penal Laws*, 149–170.

69. Thomas O'Connor observes that 'because of the complexity of the political situation in Ireland and the precariousness of the position of the [Catholic] Church the Paris Irish [and therefore by default most Irish clerics] were not as attached to the Gallican articles as their French confreres. Irish students would return to a mission where the Roman connection was essential to the maintenance of identity, and where any Gallican tendency was only too likely to be encouraged by the Dublin régime to the detriment of that identity.' 'The Role of Irish Clerics in Paris University Politics 1739–1740', *History of Universities*, 15 (1997–9), 198–199.

70. For a fuller version of this argument, see Michael Brown, 'Ultramontane Ultras: The Intellectual Character of Irish Students at the University of Paris', in Allan I. Macinnes, Kieran German, and Lesley Graham (eds), *Living with Jacobitism, 1690–1788: The Three Kingdoms and Beyond* (London: Pickering & Chatto Press, 2014), 111–123.

71. Liam Chambers, 'Knowledge and Piety: Michael Moore's Career at the University of Paris and the Collège de France, 1701–20', *Eighteenth-Century Ireland*, 17 (2002), 9–25.

72. Detailed in Liam Chambers, *Michael Moore, c.1639–1726: Provost of Trinity, Rector of Paris* (Dublin: Four Courts Press, 2005), 41–60.

73. See in particular, Liam Chambers, 'Defying Descartes: Michael Moore (1639–1726) and Aristotelian Philosophy in Ireland and France', in Michael Brown and Stephen H. Harrison (eds), *The Medieval World and the Modern Mind* (Dublin: Four Courts Press, 2000), 11–26. For the spread of Cartesianism in Europe in this period, see Jonathan Israel, *Radical Enlightenment: Philosophy and the Making of Modernity, 1650–1750* (Oxford: Oxford University Press, 2001), 23–38.

74. Michael Moore, *De Existentia Dei* (1692) quoted in Seamus Deane (ed.), *Field Day Anthology of Irish Writing*, 3 vols (Derry: Field Day Theatre Company, 1990), I, 966.

75. Ibid.

76. This point is well made in Chambers, *Michael Moore*, 78.

77. Moore, *De Existentia Dei*, in Deane, *Field Day Anthology*, I, 965.

78. Ibid., 965–966.

79. This paragraph derives from Chambers, *Michael Moore*, 91–95.

80. Quoted in ibid., 92n59.

81. Ibid., 93n61.

82. Ibid., 93–94n66.

83. 'Personal and national insecurities combined to produce such a strident critique of Cartesianism in which there could be no room for compromise'; ibid., 81.

84. Moore, *De Existentia Dei*, in Deane, *Field Day Anthology*, I, 966.

85. On his expansive career, see Patrick Fagan, *Dublin's Turbulent Priest: Cornelius Nary, 1658–1738* (Dublin: Royal Irish Academy, 1991).

86. Cornelius Nary, *A New History of the World, Containing an Historical and Chronological Account of the Times and Transactions from the Creation to the Birth of Jesus Christ* (Dublin: Edward Waters, 1720).

87. Ibid., iii.

88. Ibid.

89. Ibid., 5–11.

90. Ibid., 5–6.

91. [Cornelius Nary], *The Case of the Roman Catholics of Ireland* (1724), in Hugh Reily, *The Impartial History of Ireland* (London, 1768), 115–146.

92. The proposal is detailed in Fagan, *Dublin's Turbulent Priest*, 114.

93. For example the phrase occurs on [Nary], *The Case of the Roman Catholics*, 123, 130, 131, 137 (twice), and 144.

94. Ibid., 125–126.

95. Ibid., 129.

96. Ibid., 131. Haceldama is the 'field of blood' purchased with the price paid to Judas for his treason .

97. Ibid., 121.

98. Ibid., 122.

99. Ibid., 133.

100. Ibid., 116.

101. Ibid., 118.

102. Ibid., 120.

103. The full text of the oath is reprinted in Fagan, *Dublin's Turbulent Priest*, 139.

104. The long history of attempts to negotiate a form of words is recounted in Patrick Fagan, *Divided Loyalties: The Question of an Oath for the Catholics in the Eighteenth Century* (Dublin: Four Courts Press, 1997).

105. See Ian MacBride, 'Catholic Politics in the Penal Era: Father Sylvester Lloyd and the Devlin Address of 1727', in Bergin et al., *New Perspectives on the Penal Laws*, 115–147.

106. Quoted in Fagan, *Dublin's Turbulent Priest*, 129.

107. The interactions between scribal and print cultures are discussed in Meidhbhín Ní Úrdail, *The Scribe in Eighteenth- and Nineteenth-Century Ireland: Motivations and Milieu* (Münster: Nodus Publikationen, 1997), 199–225. See also Gerard Long (ed.), *Books Beyond the Pale: Aspects of the Provincial Book Trade in Ireland before 1850* (Dublin: Rare Books Group of the Library Association of Ireland, 1996).

108. Brian Ó Cuív, 'Irish Language and Literature, 1691–1845', in T. W. Moody and W. E. Vaughan (eds), *New History of Ireland*, Volume 4: *Eighteenth-Century Ireland, 1691–1800* (Oxford: Clarendon Press, 1986), 390.

109. Ibid., 391.

110. Ní Úrdail, *The Scribe in Eighteenth- and Nineteenth-Century Ireland*, 144–145.

111. Hughes, 'Gaelic Poets and Scribes of the South Armagh Hinterland', 515.

112. It was an occupation that often passed down the family line, as with the Limerick-based Ó Longain family, where Mícheál mac Peattair Ó Longain was succeeded by Mícheál Óg Ó Longain. See Ní Úrdail, *The Scribe in Eighteenth- and Nineteenth-Century Ireland*, 35–100.

113. This point is well made in Pádraig A. Breatnach, 'Oral and Written Transmission in the Eighteenth Century', *Eighteenth-Century Ireland*, 2 (1987), 60–63.

114. The Irish-language version is to be found in T. F. O'Rahilly, 'Irish Scholars in Dublin in the Early Eighteenth Century', *Gadelica: A Journal of Modern Irish Studies*, 3 (1913), 158. The English-language translation is to be found in Alan Harrison, *The Dean's Friend: Anthony Raymond 1675–1726, Jonathan Swift and the Irish Language* (Dublin: Edmund Burke Publisher, 1999), 165.

115. O'Rahilly, 'Irish Scholars in Dublin', 159; Harrison, *The Dean's Friend*, 166.

116. O'Rahilly, 'Irish Scholars in Dublin', 158; Harrison, *The Dean's Friend*, 165.

117. Ibid.

118. O'Rahilly, 'Irish Scholars in Dublin', 160; Harrison, *The Dean's Friend*, 167.

119. For an overview of the group's activities across the genres see Harrison, *The Dean's Friend*, 25–66.

120. N. J. A. Williams, 'Dermot O'Connor's Blazons and Irish Heraldic Terminology', *Eighteenth-Century Ireland*, 5 (1990), 61–88.

121. This is underlined by Harrison, *The Dean's Friend*, 53–54.

122. In that, it was akin to the English-language poetic circles that have been identified in Dublin in the Restoration period, on which see Marie-Louise Coolahan, '"We Live by Chance, and Slip into Events": Occasionality and the Manuscript Verse of Katherine Philips', *Eighteenth-Century Ireland*, 18 (2003), 9–23.

123. Harrison, *The Dean's Friend*, 46, 49.

124. The list is reproduced in ibid., 46–47.

125. Ibid., 52.

126. For an overview of developments in the field across the century, see Nessa Ní Shéaghdha, 'Irish Scholars and Scribes in Eighteenth-Century Dublin', *Eighteenth-Century Ireland*, 4 (1989), 41–54.

127. For a complementary reading of the transformative efforts of the Ó Neachtain circle, see Liam Mac Mathúna, 'Getting to Grips with Innovation and Genre Diversification in the Work of the Ó Neachtain Circle in Early Eighteenth-Century Dublin', *Eighteenth-Century Ireland*, 27 (2012), 53–83.

128. O'Rahilly, 'Irish Scholars in Dublin', 159, 158; Harrison, *The Dean's Friend*, 165, 166.

129. Biographical information comes from Mary H. Risk, 'Seán Ó Neachtain: An Eighteenth-Century Writer', *Studia Hibernica*, 15 (1975), 47–60; Seán Ó Neachtain, *The History of Éamonn O'Clery*, William Mahon (trans.) (Indreabhán: Cló Iar-Chonnachta, 2000), 15–22. On Ó Neachtain's translations, see C. G. Ó Hánile, 'Neighbours in Eighteenth-Century Dublin: Jonathan Swift and Seán Ó Neachtain', *Éire-Ireland*, 21 (1986), 115.

130. For an overview of his work, see Ó Hánile, 'Neighbours in Eighteenth-Century Dublin', 115–120.

131. Ó Neachtain, *The History of Éamonn O'Clery*, 73–74.

132. Ibid., 93.

133. Ibid.

134. Ibid., 59–60.

135. Ibid., 60–61.

136. Ibid., 61.

137. Two further examples take the scribe Diarmaid Ó Conchubhair (Dermot O'Connor) to task. These are reproduced in Irish in M. H. Risk, 'Two Poems on Diarmaid Ó Conchubhair', *Éigse*, 12 (1967), 38. O'Connor translated Geoffrey Keating's *Foras Feasa ar Éirinn* ('Foundation of the History of Ireland') (circa 1634) into English, which he rendered under the title of *A General History of Ireland*, a text that met with deep contempt among other Irish-language scholars. See also, Diarmaid Ó Catháin, 'Dermot O'Connor, Translator of Keating', *Eighteenth-Century Ireland*, 2 (1987), 67–88. Ó Neachtain's criticisms may well have been fair. A modern judgement reads: 'O'Connor's translation was careless and defective, even by the relaxed standards of the day, and the mistakes were then attributed to Keating and used in the attack against him later in the century.' Clare O'Halloran, *Golden Ages and Barbarous Nations: Antiquarian Debate and Cultural Politics in Ireland, c.1750–1800* (Cork: Cork University Press, 2004), 21.

138. Quoted in M. H. Risk, 'Charles Lynegar, Professor of the Irish Language, 1712', *Hermathena*, 102 (1966), 24.

139. Ibid., 24–25.

140. Ibid., 25.

141. Ó Tuama and Kinsella, *An Duanaire*, 168–169.

142. Ó Cuív, 'Irish Language and Literature', 396–397.

143. Hugh MacCurtin [Aobh Buidhe Mac Cruitín], *Brief Discourse in Vindication of the Antiquity of Ireland* (Dublin: S. Powell, 1717), x. For an assessment of the text, see Harrison, *The Dean's Friend*, 59–62.

144. For his linguistic theories, see Anthony Raymond, *A Short Preliminary Discourse to the History of Ireland* (London, 1725).

145. Cited in Harrison, *The Dean's Friend*, 100.

146. The evidence for these connections is surveyed in ibid., 67–74. Another connection made by Harrison is that between Raymond and Cornelius Nary, who gathered materials for the scholar while sojourning in France, notably passages from the *Book of Lecan*. See ibid., 97, 125.

147. Ibid., 93, 52.

148. Ibid., 122. The controversy is treated at length in ibid., 104–148.

149. Cited in ibid., 70–71.

150. *A Collection of the Most Celebrated Irish Tunes Proper for the Violin, German Flute or Hautboy* (Dublin, 1724; reprinted Dublin, 1986), title page.

151. On Carolan, see Donal O'Sullivan, *Carolan: The Life, Times and Music of an Irish Harper*, 2 vols (London: Routledge and Kegan Paul, 1958).

152. On this early history see Thomas O'Connor, *Irish Jansenists, 1600–70: Religion and Politics in Flanders, France, Ireland and Rome* (Dublin; Four Courts Press, 2008).

153. Sylvester Lloyd, *General Instructions by Way of Catechism*, 1. Quoted in Patrick Fagan, *An Irish Bishop in Penal Times: The Chequered Career of Sylvester Lloyd OFM, 1680–1747* (Dublin: Four Courts Press, 1993), 25.

154. Cathaldus Giblin, 'Catalogue of Material of Irish Interest in the Collection *Nunziatura di Fiandra*, Vatican Archives, Part 4, volumes 102–22', *Collectanea Hibernica*, 5 (1962), 107, 108.

155. Ibid., 108–109.

156. Lloyd, *General Instructions*, part 2, advertisement, quoted in Fagan, *An Irish Bishop in Penal Times*, 28.

157. Fagan, *An Irish Bishop*, 28–29.

158. This paragraph draws on ibid., 30–32.

159. Lloyd's career as a Jacobite activist is fully explored in ibid., passim. For his critique of a Catholic attempt to accommodate to Anglican rule, see McBride, 'Catholic Politics in the Penal, 115–147.

160. Liam Chambers, 'A Displaced Intelligentsia: Aspects of Irish Catholic Thought in *Ancien Régime* France', in Thomas O'Connor (ed.), *The Irish in Europe, 1580–1815* (Dublin: Four Courts Press, 2001), 168.

161. Ibid., 167; my translation.

162. 'Both the Jansenist accentuation of original sin and the *philosophe*'s rejection of it, and the ambivalent attitude of both movements to authority can ultimately be interpreted as expressions of a fundamental uncertainty, not just about the nature of truth but its accessibility. Whether the concept of original sin is rejected, or interpreted as man's definitive separation from God, it represents our total alienation from the source of truth and value, and also results in the distrust of any authority which itself claims to embody them'; Geoffrey Bremner, 'Jansenism and Enlightenment', *Enlightenment and Dissent*, 3 (1984), 11. This paragraph draws on this insightful article.

163. Liam Chambers, 'Medicine and Miracle in the Late Seventeenth Century: Bernard Connor's *Evangelium Medici*' in James Kelly and Fiona Clark (eds), *Ireland and Medicine in the Seventeenth and Eighteenth Centuries* (Farnham: Ashgate Press, 2010), 53–72. I am indebted to Liam Chambers for a copy of this paper prior to publication.

164. See Davis Coakley, *Irish Masters of Medicine* (Dublin: Town House, 1992), 20.

165. Bernard Connor, *The History of Poland in Several Letters to Persons of Quality*, 2 vols (London: D. Brown, A. Roper and T. Leigh, 1698), I, 293.

166. Ibid., I, 297.

167. Ibid., I, 299–300.

168. Ibid., I, 300.

169. Connor, *History of Poland*, II, 189–190.

170. Ibid., II, 190.

171. Ibid., II, 191.

172. Ibid., II, 193–194.

173. Ibid., II, 196.

174. Ibid., II, 197.

175. Ibid., II, 207–208.

176. Ibid., I, 180–181.

177. Ibid., I, 181.

178. Ibid., I, 183.

179. Ibid., I, 184.

180. Ibid., I, 313.

181. Davis Coakley tentatively identifies J. R. as Dean John Richards of Ardfert, Connor's former Irish teacher, giving the letter an added and specifically Irish context. *Irish Masters of Medicine*, 22.

182. Connor, *History of Poland*, I, 313.

183. Ibid., I, 314–315.

184. Ibid., I, 315.

185. Ibid., I, 317.

186. Ibid., I, 314.

187. Ibid., I, 317–318.

188. Ibid., I, 316–317.

189. Ibid., I, 314.

190. Coakley, *Irish Masters of Medicine*, 20.

191. William Hayley, 'The Character of Bernard Connor MD', in *Memorials and Characters together with the Lives of Divers Eminent Persons* (London: John Wilford, 1741), 346.

192. Ibid., 346–347.

193. Ibid., 347.

194. Ibid.

195. Ibid.

4. Languages of Civility

1. David Dickson describes the period as 'an historic trough'; idem, *New Foundations: Ireland 1660–1800*, 2nd edn (Dublin: Irish Academic Press, 2000), 115.

2. Detailed in James Kelly, 'Harvests and Hardship: Famine and Scarcity in Ireland in the late 1720s', *Studia Hibernica*, 26 (1992), 65–105.

3. Ibid., 88.

4. Jonathan Swift, *A Proposal for giving Badges to Beggars, April 22, 1737*, in idem, *The Prose Writings of Jonathan Swift*, 16 vols, Herbert Davis (ed.) (Oxford: Basil Blackwell, 1939–1974), VI, 127–141. See also Mary Carter, 'Swift and the Scheme for Badging Beggars in Dublin, 1726–1737', *Eighteenth-Century Life*, 37 (2013), 97–118.

5. Francis Hutcheson, 'Reflections on the Common Systems of Morality', in Thomas Mautner (ed.), *Francis Hutcheson: Two Texts on Human Nature* (Cambridge: Cambridge University Press, 1993), 103.

6. Jonathan Swift, *A Modest Proposal*, in idem, *Major Works*, Angus Ross and David Wooley (eds) (Oxford: Oxford University Press, 1984), 492.

7. [David Bindon], *Scheme for Supplying Industrious Men with Money to Carry on Their Trades* (Dublin: Thomas Hume, 1729), 12.

8. Arthur Dobbs, *An Essay on the Trade and Improvement of Ireland* (Dublin: J. Smith, 1729), 68.

9. On migration out of Ulster in this period, see Patrick Griffin, *The People with No Name: Ireland's Ulster Scots, America's Scots Irish, and the Creation of a British Atlantic World, 1689–1764* (Princeton: Princeton University Press, 2001), 65–97.

10. The quote is taken from ibid., 65. For the Anglican churchmen's concerns, see T. C. Barnard, 'Improving Clergymen' in Alan Ford, James McGuire, and Kenneth Milne (eds), *As by Law Established: The Church of Ireland since the Reformation* (Dublin: Lilliput Press, 1995), 150.

11. Hugh Boulter, *Letters to Several Ministers of State in England*, 2 vols (Dublin: George Faulkner and James Williams, 1770), I, 209–210.

12. Ibid., 231.

13. Ibid., 237. See also the letter to the bishop of London, 13 March 1728/9, ibid., 231–236, which details the thesis of the Presbyterian community that the cause of emigration was the distress caused by requiring them to pay tithes to the established church. See also the petition to the Lord Justices, signed by Francis Iredell and Robert Craghead, that tenders this analysis, alongside broader complaints about the state of the country and the detrimental effect of short-term leases. Reprinted in W. T. Latimer, 'Ulster Emigration to America', *Transactions of the Royal Society of Antiquarians of Ireland*, 32 (1902), 389–392. I would like to thank Patrick Walsh for pointing out this petition.

14. Details in this paragraph are drawn from David Dickson, *Arctic Ireland* (Belfast: White Row Press, 1997). For the death rate estimate, see ibid., 69.

15. Some English-language sources that indicate the crisis was 'countrywide' are collated in James Kelly, 'Coping with Crisis: The Response to the Famine of 1740–41', *Eighteenth-Century Ireland*, 27 (2012), 103.

16. Quoted in Cormac Ó Gráda and Diarmuid Ó Muirithe, 'The Famine of 1740–41: Representations in Gaelic Poetry', *Éire-Ireland*, 45(2010), 55 and 57.

17. Kelly writes: 'If the combination of geography, demography, hunger and disease account for the twenty per cent mortality that devastated Munster, the greater range of institutional, individual and general charity available in Dublin helped to ensure the excess death rate was significantly lower in the capital.' 'Coping with Crisis', 115.

18. Quoted in Ó Gráda and Ó Muirithe, 'The Famine of 1740–41', 50 and 52.

19. Ibid.

20. Ibid., 51 and 53.

21. Kelly, 'Coping with Crisis', 118–119.

22. Details here are taken from ibid., 104–107.

23. I have followed Richard Holmes in attributing this periodical to Arbuckle, despite the assertion of Bryan Coleburne that it was in fact written by Patrick Delany. See Richard Holmes, 'James Arbuckle: A Whig Critic of the Penal Laws', in John Bergin, Eoin Magennis, Lesa Ní Mhunghaile, and Patrick Walsh (eds), *New Perspectives on the Penal Laws: Eighteenth-Century Ireland Special Issue 1* (2011), 93–112; Bryan Coleburne, 'Jonathan Swift and the Dunces of Dublin' (PhD thesis, National University of Ireland, Dublin, 1982), 254.

24. [James Arbuckle], *The Tribune* (Dublin: S. Powell, 1729), issue seventeen, 122–123.

25. Ibid., 123.

26. Ibid., 124

27. Ibid., 125. In this, and in his view that 'under this regulation many of them would become Protestants', he was echoing his patron Robert Molesworth. Ibid., 125.

28. [Arbuckle], *The Tribune*, issue eighteen, 127.

29. Ibid., 128. On this social category, see David Dickson, 'Middlemen', in Thomas Bartlett and D. W. Hayton (eds), *Penal Era and Golden Age: Essays in Irish History, 1690–1800* (Belfast: Ulster Historical Foundation, 1979), 162–185.

30. [Arbuckle], *The Tribune*, issue eighteen, 128.

31. For a discussion of about the moral standing of middlemen, see Kevin Whelan, 'An Underground Gentry: Catholic Middlemen in Eighteenth-Century Ireland', in idem, *The Tree of Liberty: Radicalism, Catholicism and the Construction of Irish Identity, 1760–1830* (Cork: Cork University Press, 1996), 3–56; and T. C. Barnard, 'The Gentrification of Eighteenth-Century Ireland', *Eighteenth Century Ireland*, 12 (1997), 137–155.

32. [Arbuckle], *The Tribune*, issue eighteen, 128.

33. [Arbuckle], *The Tribune*, issue one, 4.

34. [Arbuckle], *The Tribune*, issue five, 35.

35. See A. P. W. Malcomson, 'Absenteeism in Eighteenth-Century Ireland', *Irish Economic and Social History*, 1 (1974), 15–35.

36. [Arbuckle], *The Tribune*, issue ten, 66.

37. Ibid., 67–68.

38. Ibid., 68.

39. Ibid.

40. Ibid., 69. This is despite the fact that as Richard Holmes argues Arbuckle was personally committed to a form of British identity. See Richard Holmes (ed.), *James Arbuckle: Selected Works* (Lewisburg: Bucknell Press, 2014), xv–xl.

41. From a large literature see Markku Peltonen, 'Politeness and Whiggism, 1688–1732', *The Historical Journal*, 48 (2005), 391–414; Lawrence E. Klein, *Shaftesbury and the Culture of Politeness: Moral Discourse and Cultural Politics in Early Eighteenth-Century England* (Cambridge: Cambridge University Press, 1994); idem, 'Liberty, Manners and Politeness in Early Eighteenth-Century England', *The Historical Journal*, 32 (1989), 583–605; idem, 'Gender, Conversation and the Public Sphere in Early Eighteenth-Century England', in Judith Still and Michael Worton (eds), *Textuality and Sexuality: Reading Theories and Practices* (Manchester: Manchester University Press, 1993), 100–115; idem, 'Politeness for Plebes: Consumption and Social Identity in Early Eighteenth-Century England', in Ann Bermingham and John Brewer (eds), *The Consumption of Culture 1600–1800: Image, Object, Text* (London: Routledge, 1995), 362–382; idem, 'Politeness and the Interpretation of the British Eighteenth Century', *The Historical Journal*, 45 (2002), 869–898; Jenny Davidson, *Hypocrisy and the Politics of Politeness: Manners and Morals from Locke to Austen* (Cambridge: Cambridge University Press, 2004); Nicholas Phillipson, 'Politics, Politeness and the Anglicisation of Early Eighteenth-Century Scottish

Culture', in R. A. Mason (ed.), *Scotland and England, 1286–1815* (Edinburgh: John Donald, 1987), 226–246.

42. [Arbuckle], *The Tribune,* issue two, 7–16.

43. Joseph Addison and Richard Steele, *The Spectator,* 5 vols, Donald F. Bond (ed.) (Oxford: Oxford University Press, 1965). For a thoughtful treatment of Addison's cultural politics, see Brian Cowan, 'Mr Spectator and the Coffeehouse Public Sphere', *Eighteenth-Century Studies,* 37 (2004), 345–366.

44. For the changing character of Whig political ideas in this period towards a commercial ethos that encompassed civility and rejected the austerity of neo-Stoic anxieties about luxury, see J. G. A. Pocock, 'The Varieties of Whiggism from Exclusion to Reform: A History of Ideology and Discourse', in idem, *Virtue, Commerce and History* (Cambridge: Cambridge University Press, 1985), particularly 215–230.

45. [Arbuckle], *The Tribune,* issue two, 10.

46. Ibid., 13, 14–15.

47. Ibid., 11, 12.

48. For an extended discussion of Arbuckle's deployment of the language of civility, see Michael Brown, 'The Biter Bitten: Ireland and the Rude Enlightenment', *Eighteenth-Century Studies,* 45 (2012), 393–407.

49. George Berkeley, *The Querist,* in Joseph Johnston (ed.), *Bishop Berkeley's* Querist *in Historical Perspective* (Dundalk: Dundalgen Press, 1970), 124.

50. These broad approaches were by no means exclusive of each other and regularly blended in the minds of individual theorists and practitioners. However, the demand for personal refinement and good morals could be, and on occasion was, seen to stand in contradiction to the pursuit of material goods. In other words, there was a tension between the pursuit of wealth and the demands of virtue. The contrasting demands of wealth production and virtuous living posed the puzzle of how to square self-interest with civility, sociability with social development. For an important theoretical discussion of this in a Scottish context, see Istvan Hont and Michael Ignatieff (eds), *Wealth and Virtue: The Shaping of Political Economy in the Scottish Enlightenment* (Cambridge: Cambridge University Press, 1985).

51. This might be related to Norbert Elias, *The Civilizing Process* (Oxford: Blackwell, 1994), See also theoretical descriptions of Irish modes of behaviour in David Hayton, 'From Barbarian to Burlesque: English Images of the Irish, c. 1660–1750', *Irish Economic and Social History,* 15 (1988), 5–31.

52. 7 William III, c.9.

53. See T. C. Barnard, 'Reforming Irish Manners: The Religious Societies in Dublin during the 1690s', in idem, *Irish Protestant Ascents and Descents 1641–1770* (Dublin: Four Courts Press, 2004), 143–179.

54. On this see Barnard, 'Improving Clergymen', 136–151.

55. Arbuckle, *The Tribune*, issue 1, 5.

56. Edmund Burke, *The Reformer*, in Paul Langford (ed.), *The Writings and Speeches of Edmund Burke*, 9 vols (Oxford: Clarendon Press, 1981–), I, 110.

57. See in particular, Paddy Bullard, *Edmund Burke and the Art of Rhetoric* (Cambridge: Cambridge University Press, 2011), 52–78.

58. Quentin Skinner, *Reason and Rhetoric in the Philosophy of Hobbes* (Cambridge: Cambridge University Press, 1996).

59. See Edward P. J. Corbett, 'John Locke's Contributions to Rhetoric', *College Composition and Communication*, 32 (1981), 423–433.

60. This section is partially indebted to Katherine O'Donnell, 'Burke and the School of Irish Oratory', *Studies in Burke and His Time*, 21 (2007), 70–87. However, where O'Donnell reads the 'Trinity rhetoricians' as deriving their inspiration from Aristotle, the reading here suggests they were early proponents of a theory of sensibility.

61. David Murphy, 'John Lawson', *Dictionary of Irish Biography*, http://dib.cambridge.org (accessed 2 January 2011).

62. John Lawson, *Lectures concerning Oratory Delivered in Trinity College, Dublin* (Dublin: George Faulkner, 1758), 5–6.

63. Ibid., 8–9.

64. Ibid., 9.

65. For a helpful summary of Sheridan's work on elocution, see Paul Goring, *The Rhetoric of Sensibility in Eighteenth-Century Culture* (Cambridge: Cambridge University Press, 2005), 91–113.

66. Philippa M. Spoel, 'Rereading the Elocutionists: The Rhetoric of Thomas Sheridan's "A Course of Lectures on Elocution" and John Walker's "Elements of Elocution",' *Rhetorica: A Journal of the History of Rhetoric*, 19 (1001), 49–91.

67. Thomas Sheridan, *A Course of Lectures on Elocution* (London: W. Strahan, 1762), 3.

68. 'Sheridan investigates the notion of natural or authentic speech and considers how the blessing of such primal authenticity can be recreated . . . The only thing that can cure education it seems is more education, albeit of a radically altered kind, designed to cultivate a heightened self-consciousness.' Conrad Brunström, *Thomas Sheridan's Career and Influence: An Actor in Earnest* (Lewisburg: Bucknell University Press, 2011), 68–69.

69. Sheridan, *Lectures on Elocution*, 6.

70. Ibid., 4. Both M. Wade Mahon, 'The Rhetorical Value of Reading Aloud in Thomas Sheridan's Theory of Elocution', *Rhetoric Society Quarterly*, 31 (2001), 67–88, and Conrad Brunström, 'Thomas Sheridan and the Evil Ends of Writing', *New Hibernia Review*, 3 (1999), 130–142, accentuate the importance of the spoken word over the written word in Sheridan's hierarchy of communication; predictable for an actor and elocutionist.

71. Sheridan, *Lectures on Elocution*, 40.

72. Ibid.

73. Ibid., 19.

74. Ibid., 44.

75. Ibid., 5.

76. Sheridan's place in the wider development of the form of English spoken by the Irish is considered in Martin J. Croghan, 'Swift, Thomas Sheridan, Maria Edgeworth and the Evolution of Hiberno-English', *Irish University Review*, 20 (1990), 19–34.

77. James Usher, *Clio: Or a Discourse on Taste* (London: T. Davies, 1767), 2–3.

78. Ibid., 7.

79. Ibid., 38.

80. Ibid., 38, 39.

81. This democratic universalism was lived out by Usher not only in arguing for the removal of the penal laws against Catholics but also by converting to their faith. See James Usher, *A Free Examination of the Common Methods employed to Prevent the Growth of Popery* (London, 1766), and Daniel Beaumont, 'James Usher' in *Dictionary of Irish Biography*, http://dib.cambridge.org (accessed 4 January 2011). See also Kevin Barry, 'James Usher (1720–77) and the Irish Enlightenment', *Eighteenth-Century Ireland*, 3 (1988), 115–122.

82. Usher, *Clio*, 18–19

83. Ibid., 20.

84. Ibid., 37. For Usher on the fine arts, see Kevin Barry, *Language, Music and the Sign* (Cambridge: Cambridge University Press, 1987), 57–65.

85. Usher, *Clio*, 31.

86. Ibid., 60–62.

87. Usher further contends that 'from the combination of these fine parts arise the enchantments of elegance; but the two last, are oftener found together and then they form politeness'. Ibid., 70.

88. Ibid., 71–72.

89. Ibid., 30.

90. Ibid.

91. Details of this career are drawn from T. C. Barnard, 'The Languages of Politeness and Sociability in Eighteenth-Century Ireland', in D. George Boyce, Robert Eccleshall and Vincent Geoghegan *Political Discourse in Seventeenth- and Eighteenth-Century Ireland*, (Houndmills, Palgrave Macmillan, 2001), 213–214.

92. Constantia Maxwell, *A History of Trinity College, Dublin, 1591–1892* (Dublin: The University Press, 1946), 124. McDowell and Webb note that this trend towards polite education was already in motion before Hely-Hutchison's appointment as Provost. In 1759, under the tenure of Francis Andrews, Thomas Sheridan, Thomas Leland FTCD, and Gabriel Stokes FTCD proposed a postgraduate/finishing

school, while from 1764 to 1774, a professor of music was employed, although the incumbent, the Earl of Mornington had no official teaching duties and seems to have only been required to compose the occasional tune. R. B. McDowell and D. A. Webb, *Trinity College, Dublin, 1592–1952: An Academic History* (Cambridge: Cambridge University Press, 1982), 56, 58.

93. Luke Gibbons, *Edmund Burke and Ireland: Aesthetics, Politics and the Colonial Sublime* (Cambridge: Cambridge University Press, 2003), 39–79; idem, '"Into the Cyclops Eye": James Barry, Historical Portraiture and Colonial Ireland', in Fintan Cullen and John Morrison (eds), *A Shared Legacy: Essays on Irish and Scottish Art and Visual Culture* (Aldershot: Ashgate Press, 2005), 35–59.

94. This idea of an Irish school of aesthetics is indebted to the insight of Gibbons, *Edmund Burke and Ireland*, 239–240n5. See, however, Liam Lenihan, 'James Barry and the Aesthetic of an Irish Enlightenment?' *Studies in Burke and His Time*, 21 (2007), 58–69, which contests the idea that there was a specifically Irish aesthetic, at least as constructed by Gibbons.

95. For a reading of this work as related to his social circumstances, see Michael Brown, *Francis Hutcheson in Dublin, 1719–30: The Crucible of his Thought* (Dublin: Four Courts Press, 2002), 25–50.

96. Peter Kivy, *The Seventh Sense: A Study of Francis Hutcheson's Aesthetics and Its Influence in Eighteenth-Century Britain* (New York: Burt, Franklin, 1976).

97. How indebted Burke was to Hutcheson is contested. Suggestive of a formative relationship is a juvenile poem by Burke. Edmund Burke, 'To Dr H————n', *Writings and Speeches*, I, 30–38. Yet Lock notes that Burke dispensed with Hutcheson's idea of an internal sense. *Edmund Burke*, Volume I: *1730–1784* (Oxford: Clarendon Press, 1998), 93–94. Hutcheson and Burke both supplied a psychological portrait of the aesthetic sensibility, identifying the mental origins of these responses within the human makeup. This shared concern was suggested in the intriguing echo of Hutcheson's work that is to be heard in the title of Burke's publication.

98. Edmund Burke, *Philosophical Enquiry into the Original or Our Ideas of the Sublime and Beautiful*, Adam Phillips (ed.) (Oxford: Oxford University Press, 1990), 102.

99. Ibid., 102.

100. Ibid., 107.

101. Ibid., 135–136.

102. Ibid., 39.

103. On Burke's capacity for friendship and romance see Elizabeth R. Lambert, *Edmund Burke of Beaconsfield* (Newark: University of Delaware Press, 2003).

104. Burke highlights the importance of relaxation in *Philosophical Enquiry*, 139–140.

105. Ibid., 36.

106. Ibid., 40, 66, 77. The inclusion of solitude as a source of the sublime underlines Burke's foundation of beauty upon social passions.

107. Ibid., 59.

108. Ibid., 60.

109. Ibid., 36.

110. Ibid.

111. Ibid., 41.

112. Ibid.

113. This centralisation of sympathy in a reflexive ethical system foreshadows the theories of Adam Smith, *The Theory of Moral Sentiments* (1759; Indianapolis: Liberty Fund, 1984). On the personal relationship that developed between the two men, see Donald Winch, *Riches and Poverty: An Intellectual History of Political Economy in Britain, 1750–1834* (Cambridge: Cambridge University Press, 1996), 125–220.

114. See particularly William L. Pressly, *The Life and Art of James Barry* (New Haven: Yale University Press, 1981); idem, *James Barry: The Artist as Hero* (London: The Tate Gallery, 1983).

115. James Barry, *An Account of a Series of Pictures in the Great Room of the Society of Arts, Manufactures and Commerce* (London: William Adlard, 1783).

116. On this theme see Tom Dunne, 'James Barry's "Moral Art" and the Fate of History Painting in Britain' in Tom Dunne and William L. Pressly (eds), *James Barry, 1741–1806: History Painter* (Farnham: Ashgate Press, 2010), 1–10.

117. Barry, *An Account of a Series of Pictures*, 11; for his practice in this regard, see William L. Pressly, 'Barry's Self-Portraits: Who's Afraid of the Moderns?' in Tom Dunne (ed.), *James Barry, 1441–1806: 'The Great Historical Painter'* (Cork: Gandon Editions, 2005), 60–117.

118. Barry, *An Account of a Series of Pictures*, 28–29.

119. Ibid., 23–24.

120. Ibid., 13.

121. Ibid., 31–32.

122. Ibid., 40.

123. On this sequence, see William L. Pressly, 'Barry's Murals at the Royal Society of Arts', in Dunne, *James Barry, 1441–1806*, 46–55; David G. C. Allan, '"A Monument to Perpetuate His Memory": James Barry's Adelphi Cycle Revisited' in Dunne and Pressly (eds), *James Barry*, 233–245.

124. Barry, *An Account of a Series of Pictures*, 71.

125. Ibid., 76–77. For the details of the relationship, see Liam Lenihan, 'History Painting and Aesthetics: Barry and the Politics of Friendship' in Dunne and Pressley, *James Barry*, 145–160.

126. Details here are drawn from Pressly, *The Life and Art of James Barry*, 133–141.

127. Quoted in ibid., 139.

128. N. F. Lowe, 'James Barry, Mary Wollstonecraft and 1798', *Eighteenth-Century Ireland*, 12 (1997), 60–76.

129. How far this all amounted to a real republican commitment on Barry's part is contested in Tom Dunne, 'Painting and Patriotism', in Dunne, *James Barry, 1741–1806*, 119–121.

130. For a thoughtful reading of Barry's writings through the lens of his liminal status as an Irish Catholic in Britain, see Liam Lenihan, 'Arguing for Art: James Barry's Cultural Strategy', *Eighteenth-Century Ireland*, 29 (2014), 85–107.

131. 'Barry's perception of himself as a lone champion battling a corrupt world led him increasingly to withdraw from society . . . He practised an austerity, which to many of his contemporaries bordered on madness'; Pressly, *Life and Art of James Barry*, 187.

132. James Barry, *Inquiry into the Real and Imaginary Obstructions to the Acquisition of the Arts in England* (London: T. Beckett, 1775), 64–65.

133. Ibid., 67–68.

134. Ibid., 68.

135. Ibid., 70.

136. This desire for local organisations found focus in the debate over a national bank. See Michael Ryder, 'The Bank of Ireland, 1721: Credit, Land and Dependency', *The Historical Journal*, 25 (1982), 557–582.

137. The efficacy of this literature in altering agricultural practice is challenged in a British context in Pamela Horn, 'The Contribution of the Propagandist to Eighteenth-Century Agricultural Improvement', *The Historical Journal*, 25 (1982), 313–329. Her sceptical assessment does admit, however, that 'if the role of the propagandists was less significant than some earlier supporters have claimed, it was certainly not without its effects. By focussing repeatedly on the need for agricultural improvement, by reporting on the best practices, and encouraging the establishment of agricultural societies and shows, they played a part in keeping the subject before the farming public.' Ibid., 326.

138. The piecemeal nature of improvement in Ireland is emphasised in Toby Barnard, *Improving Ireland? Projectors, Prophets and Profiteers, 1641–1786* (Dublin: Four Courts Press, 2008). The religious origins of the improvement impulse are highlighted in Andrew Sneddon, 'Bishop Francis Hutchinson: A Case Study in the Culture of Eighteenth-Century Improvement', *Irish Historical Studies*, 35 (2007), 289–310. The relationship to politics is explored in Gordon Rees, 'Sir Richard Cox, 1702–66: Patriotism and Improvement in mid-Eighteenth Century Ireland', *Eighteenth-Century Ireland*, 29 (2014), 47–62. For an account that relates the improvement agenda to an antiquarian concern for the country, see Macdara

Dwyer, 'Historical Cultures and Political Ethnographies in Early Modern Ireland, 1690–1760' (PhD thesis, King's College London, 2015).

139. For Rye, see David Dickson, *Old World Colony: Cork and South Munster, 1630–1830* (Cork: Cork University Press, 2005), 172.

140. [George Rye], *Considerations on Agriculture* (Dublin: George Grierson, 1730), ix.

141. Ibid., v–vi.

142. Ibid., vii.

143. Ibid.

144. Ibid., 40.

145. Ibid., 53–54.

146. Ibid., 4.

147. Ibid., 23–24.

148. See Simon Schaffer and Steven Shapin, *Leviathan and the Air-Pump: Hobbes, Boyle and the Experimental Life* (Princeton: Princeton University Press, 1985).

149. See for example, Rye, *Considerations on Agriculture*, 22, 23, 32, 51, 57, 60.

150. Ibid., 53. The historical irony of his reliance on the potato as a staple crop cannot be overlooked, particularly given his remark that 'when either our oats may be destroyed by high winds, as they were in the year 1728, in the north of England or Ireland: or our wheat bad from a moist, cold season: yet that the potato may be a certain relief to us'; ibid., xi.

151. S.[amuel] P.[ierson], *The Present State of the Tillage in Ireland Considered and some Methods offered for its Improvement* (Dublin: George Grierson, 1725), 31.

152. Ibid., 30.

153. Ibid., 9.

154. Ibid., 12.

155. Ibid., 26–27, 36.

156. Samuel Pierson, *Farther Considerations for the Improvement of Tillage in Ireland* (Dublin: George Grierson, 1728), 33.

157. Ibid., 4.

158. Ibid.

159. Ibid., 5.

160. Ibid., 8–9.

161. Ibid., 37.

162. Ibid., 36–37.

163. Gorges E. Howard, *Some Scattered Pieces upon Agriculture and the Improvement of Husbandry* (Dublin: Elizabeth Lynch, 1770), 30.

164. Ibid., 31.

165. Ibid., 24.

166. Ibid., 35.

167. Ibid., 33–34.

168. Ibid., 33.

169. Anonymous, *Some Thoughts on the General Improvement of Ireland*, 2nd edn (Dublin: Like White, 1780).

170. Ibid., 34. The plan is outlined on ibid., 35–44.

171. Ibid., 34.

172. Ibid., 34, 35.

173. Ibid., 41.

174. For the controversy around the national bank proposal in the 1720s, see Sean D. Moore, 'Satiric Norms, Swift's Financial Satires and the Bank of Ireland Controversy, 1720–1', *Eighteenth-Century Ireland*, 17 (2002), 26–56; Patrick Kelly, 'Berkeley and the Idea of a National Bank', *Eighteenth-Century Ireland*, 25 (2010), 98–117; Jill Marie Bradbury, '"Interest" and Anglo-Irish Political Discourse in the 1720–21 Bank Pamphlet Literature', *Eighteenth-Century Ireland*, 29 (2014), 31–46.

175. Anonymous, *Some Thoughts on the General Improvement of Ireland*, 15.

176. Ibid., 48.

177. Ibid., 27.

178. Ibid., 28.

179. Ibid., 25.

180. Ibid., 10.

181. Studies of the Irish school of economics include James Kelly, 'Jonathan Swift and the Irish Economy in the 1720s', *Eighteenth-Century Ireland*, 6 (1991), 7–36; Salim Rashid, 'The Irish School of Economic Development, 1720–1750', *The Manchester School of Economic and Social Studies*, 54 (1988), 345–369; Patrick Kelly, 'The Politics of Political Economy in Mid-Eighteenth-Century Ireland', in S. J. Connolly (ed.), *Political Ideas in Eighteenth-Century Ireland* (Dublin: Four Courts Press, 2000), 105–129.

182. J. T. Gilbert, revised Paul Caffrey, 'Francis Bindon', *Oxford Dictionary of National Biography*, www.oxforddnb.com (accessed 11 January 2011).

183. [Bindon], *A Scheme for Supplying Industrious Men with Money*, 20.

184. On the issue of the circulation of foreign coins in Ireland, see Johnston, *Bishop Berkeley's* Querist *in Historical Context*, 52–71.

185. David Bindon, *An Essay on the Gold and Silver Coin Currant in Ireland* (Dublin: E. Dobson, 1729), 14.

186. Ibid., 2.

187. Ibid., 3.

188. Ibid., 18.

189. Thomas Prior, *A List of the Absentees of Ireland* (Dublin: R. Gunne, 1729), 22.

190. Ibid., 25.

191. Ibid., 28.

192. Ibid., 33–34.

193. Ibid., 18, 36.

194. Ibid., 59–60.

195. Ibid., 72.

196. Ibid., 80.

197. Livesey, 'The Dublin Society in Eighteenth-Century Irish Political Thought', *The Historical Journal*, 47 (2004), 630–631. 'While they might not have much chance of persuading England to re-describe itself in such a way that Irish Protestants could be acknowledged as full partners in the polity, they could, potentially, find a manner of re-describing themselves that eliminated or reduced the baleful effects of dependency . . . They had to find a way of explaining how one might enjoy all one's rights without sharing in sovereignty, a way of describing a community in which identity was not political. Irish thinkers were being invited to discover and describe civil society.'

198. 'The dependent nature of Ireland even turned trade and labour into slavery. A kingdom dependent on another could pervert the incentives to work offered to its population. Even Prior acknowledged this and concluded that if the kingdom of Ireland was not allowed to trade freely then the people should not work.' Ibid., 630.

199. 'An Ireland free to determine its own interests would naturally form part of a virtuous British commercial empire . . . Dobbs saw the possibility of an internally free trading commercial empire, rather than an English commercial monarchy surrounded by more or less dependent satellites. On the other hand, an Ireland which was denied the means to develop itself would be a genuine threat to the peace and safety of the "British dominions" since its poverty would produce rebelliousness.' James Livesey, 'The Dublin Society in Eighteenth-Century Irish Political Thought', Ibid., 47 (2004), 624.

200. Eoin Magennis, 'Arthur Dobbs', *Dictionary of Irish Biography*, http://dib.cambridge .org (accessed 11 January 2011).

201. Dobbs, *An Essay on the Trade and Improvement of Ireland*, 1.

202. Ibid., 2.

203. Ibid.

204. Ibid., 3.

205. See for example, ibid., 36–41.

206. Ibid., 61.

207. Ibid., 68.

208. Ibid., 66, 69.

209. Ibid., 69.

210. Dobbs, *An Essay on the Trade of Ireland, Part II* (Dublin: A. Rhames, 1731), 91–92.

211. Swift, *A Modest Proposal*, 493–494.

212. Ibid., 494.

213. Ibid., 496.

214. Ibid., 494.

215. Ibid., 496. This last clause is a reference to the lack of specie in the Irish economy at the time.
216. Ibid., 494.
217. Ibid., 498. See Martyn Powell, *The Politics of Consumption in Eighteenth-Century Ireland* (Houndmills: Palgrave Macmillan, 2005), passim.
218. Swift, *A Modest Proposal*, 498.
219. Ibid., 497.
220. Ibid.
221. Ibid.
222. Ibid, 493. On the prevalence of this crime see James Kelly, 'Infanticide in Eighteenth-Century Ireland', *Irish Economic and Social History*, 19 (1992), 5–26.
223. Swift, *Modest Proposal*, 497–498.
224. For a treatment of the food image, see Robert Mahony, 'Protestant Dependence and Consumption in Swift's Irish Writings', in Connolly, *Political Ideas in Eighteenth-Century Ireland*, 83–104.

5. The Enlightened Counter Public

1. See Jürgen Habermas, *Structural Transformation of the Public Sphere: An Inquiry into a Category of Bourgeois Society* (Cambridge: Harvard University Press, 1989), 29. The applicability of the concept of a public sphere is cogently disputed in J. A. Downie, 'How Useful to Eighteenth-Century English Studies Is the Paradigm of the Bourgeois Public Sphere?' *Literature Compass*, 1 (2003), 1–19. In contrast, the uses made of the concept have been helpfully summarised in Harold Mah, 'Phantasies of the Public Sphere: Rethinking the Habermas of Historians', *Journal of Modern History*, 72 (2000), 153–182. For the argument that the coffeehouses constituted a challenge to the power of the state, see Steve Pincus, '"Coffee Politicians Does Create": Coffeehouses and Restoration Political Culture', *Journal of Modern History*, 67 (1995), 807–834. See also idem, 'The State and Civil Society in Early Modern England: Capitalism, Causation and Habermas's Bourgeois Public Sphere', in Peter Lake and Steven Pincus (eds), *The Politics of the Public Sphere in Early Modern England* (Manchester: Manchester University Press, 2007), 213–231.
2. It is necessary to recall the cramped and intimate way in which eighteenth-century town dwellers lived. It is easy to overestimate the level of privacy which an urban dweller might enjoy; private space was at a premium. The notable thing about the elite in this regard was precisely that they could choose how and when to appear in public. See, for instance, the description of Paris in Arlette Farge, *Fragile Lives: Violence, Power and Solidarity in Eighteenth-Century Paris* (Cambridge: Polity Press, 1993).
3. See, however, Eoin Magennis, *The Irish Political System 1740–65: The Golden Age of Undertakers* (Dublin: Four Courts Press, 2000).

4. According to John Keane, 'civil society . . . is an ideal-typical category that both describes and envisage a complex and dynamic ensemble of legally protected non-governmental institutions, that tend to be non-violent, self-organising, self-reflexive and permanently in tension with each other and with the state institutions that "frame", constrict and enable their activities.' *Civil Society: Old Images, New Visions* (Cambridge: Polity Press, 1998), 6. Michael Walzer offers the following definition of the term: 'The words "civil society" name the space of un-coerced human association and also the set of relational networks—formed for the sake of family, faith, interest and ideology—that fill this space.' 'The Civil Society Argument', in Ronald Beiner (ed.), *Theorizing Citizenship* (New York: SUNY Press, 1995), 153. Edward Shils similarly highlights the values inherent in the domain: 'A civil society is a society of civility in the conduct of its members of the society towards each other. Civility regulates the conduct between individuals and between individuals and the state; it regulates the conduct of individuals towards society. It likewise regulates the relations of collectivities towards each other and the relations between collectivities and the state.' 'The Virtue of Civility', *The Virtue of Civility: Selected Essays on Liberalism, Tradition and Civil Society* (Indianapolis: Liberty Fund, 1997), 322.

5. From an examination of very different evidence, in *Hidden Ireland, Public Sphere* (Galway: Arlem House, 2002), Joep Leerssen suggests that the 1780s are the critical decade in the politicisation of the public sphere. See also Ultán Gillen, 'Varieties of Enlightenment: The Enlightenment and Irish Political Culture in the Age of Revolutions', in Richard Butterwick, Simon Davies, and Gabriel Sánchez Espinosa (eds), *Peripheries of the Enlightenment* (Oxford: Voltaire Foundation, 2008), 163–182. This is not to underplay the potential exhibited in Swift's 'Drapier pamphlets' which Sean D. Moore identifies with the origin of an Irish public sphere. See Sean D. Moore, 'Satiric Norms, Swift's Financial Satires and the Bank of Ireland Controversy, 1720–1', *Eighteenth-Century Ireland*, 17 (2002), 26–56. So too, the 1730s seem to have shown some indication of political public opinion; see Sean D. Moore, *Swift, the Book and the Irish Financial Revolution: Satire and Sovereignty in Colonial Ireland* (Baltimore: Johns Hopkins University Press, 2010), 190–213.

6. Patrick Walsh, 'Club Life in Late Seventeenth- and Early Eighteenth-Century Ireland: In Search of an Associational World, c.1680–1730', in James Kelly and Martyn Powell (eds), *Clubs and Societies in Eighteenth-Century Ireland* (Dublin: Four Courts Press, 2010), 43.

7. Michael Warner, *Publics and Counterpublics* (New York: MIT Press, 2002).

8. 'The eighteenth-century Irish theatre was probably the second most important political stage after the parliament on College Green', asserts Martyn Powell, 'Political Toasting in Eighteenth-Century Ireland', *History*, 91 (2006), 520.

9. Cited in Desmond Slowey, *The Radicalisation of Irish Drama, 1600–1900* (Dublin: Irish Academic Press, 2008), 73.

10. John C. Greene and Gladys L. H. Clark, *The Dublin Stage, 1720–1745: A Calendar of Plays, Entertainments and Afterpieces* (Bethlehem: Lehigh University Press, 1993), 45.

11. On Chesterfield's use of propaganda, see Kevin Berland '"Chesterfield Demands the Muse": Anglo-Irish Poets Publishing the "Irish" Voice, 1745–6', *Eighteenth-Century Ireland*, 17 (2002), 121–145; and Helen Burke, *Riotous Performances: The Struggle for Hegemony in the Irish Theater, 1712–1784* (Notre Dame: University of Notre Dame Press, 2003), 126–127.

12. R. B. McDowell and D. A. Webb, *Trinity College Dublin, 1592–1952: An Academic History* (Cambridge: Cambridge University Press, 1982), 39, 60.

13. The whole curriculum is surveyed in ibid., 45–49.

14. Eamon O'Flaherty, 'Medical Men and Learned Societies in Ireland, 1680–1785', in Judith Devlin and H. B. Clark (eds), *European Encounters: Essays in Memory of Albert Lovett* (Dublin: UCD Press, 2003), 255; Helen Andrews, 'Sir Fielding Ould', *Dictionary of Irish Biography*, http://cambridge.org.dib (accessed 9 October 2010).

15. Eoin O'Brien, *The Charitable Infirmary Jervis Street, 1718–1987* (Monkstown: Anniversary Press, 1987), 11.

16. McDowell and Webb, *Trinity College Dublin*, 43.

17. Ibid.

18. Ibid., 58.

19. Samuel Madden, *A Proposal for the General Encouragement of Learning in Dublin College* (Dublin: George Faulkner, 1732), 14.

20. Ibid., 24.

21. James Kelly, 'John Hely-Hutchinson', *Dictionary of Irish Biography*, http://dib.cambridge.org (accessed 29 December 2010).

22. Patrick Duigenan, *Lachrymæ Academicæ; or, the Present Deplorable State of the College of the Holy and Undivided Trinity, of Queen Elizabeth, near Dublin* (Dublin: printed for the author, 1777), 50–51.

23. Ibid., 63.

24. Ibid., 76.

25. *An Account of Some Regulations Made in Trinity College Dublin since the Appointment of the Present Provost* (Dublin, 1775), 1, 2.

26. Ibid., 4.

27. Ibid.

28. Ibid., 6.

29. Ibid., 9.

30. Susan Harris, 'The Tender Mother and the Faithful Wife: Theatre, Charity and Female Subjectivity in Eighteenth-Century Ireland', *Éire-Ireland*, 37 (2002), 208 f2.

31. For a contemporary description of the 1745 lying-in hospital, see Desmond Clarke, *Thomas Prior 1681–1751: Founder of the Royal Dublin Society* (Dublin: Royal Dublin Society, 1951), 41–42.

32. *An Accurate List of the Several Persons for whom Tickets have been Issued for the Annual Assemblies at the Public Rooms, Rutland Square* (Dublin, 1793), 9.

33. Ibid., 23.

34. Nollaig P. Hardiman and Máire Kennedy (eds), *A Directory of Dublin for the Year 1738* (Dublin: Dublin City Public Libraries, 2000), 38; Grainne McArdle, 'Signora Violante and Her Troupe of Dancers, 1729–32', *Eighteenth-Century Ireland*, 20 (2005), 55–78.

35. See Greene and Clarke, *The Dublin Stage*, 24–28.

36. Ibid., 26–30.

37. See Burke, *Riotous Performances*, 214, 216. Sheridan soon reopened Capel Street as well; see ibid., 225.

38. David A. Fleming, 'Diversions of the People: Sociability among the Orders of Early Eighteenth-Century Ireland', *Eighteenth-Century Ireland*, 17 (2002), 106.

39. Information in this paragraph is drawn from Brian Boydell, 'Venues for Music in Eighteenth-Century Dublin', *Dublin Historical Record*, 29 (1975), 28–34.

40. See Muriel McCarthy and Ann Simmons (eds), *The Making of Marsh's Library: Learning, Politics and Religion in Ireland, 1650–1750* (Dublin: Four Courts Press, 2004); Muriel McCarthy and Ann Simmons (eds), *Marsh's Library, A Mirror on the World: Law, Learning and Libraries, 1650–1750* (Dublin: Four Courts Press, 2009).

41. Cited in Robert Munter, *The History of the Irish Newspaper 1685–1760* (Cambridge: Cambridge University Press, 1967), 49.

42. Ibid.

43. Richard C. Cole, 'Community Lending Libraries in Eighteenth-Century Ireland', *The Library Quarterly*, 44 (1974), 112.

44. Ibid., 113–114.

45. *Hibernian Journal*, 13 June 1793, quoted in ibid., 115.

46. Ibid., 115–116.

47. On the poetry this group generated, see Moyra Haslett, 'Swift and Conversational Culture', *Eighteenth-Century Ireland*, 29 (2014), 19–23.

48. How far this constituted a formal circle is disputed. See Michael Brown, *Francis Hutcheson in Dublin: The Crucible of his Thought* (Dublin: Four Courts Press, 2002); M. A. Stewart, 'John Smith and the Molesworth Circle', *Eighteenth-Century Ireland*, 2 (1987), 89–102.

49. T. C. Barnard, '"Grand Metropolis" or "The Anus of the World": The Cultural Life of Eighteenth-Century Dublin', in Peter Clark and Raymond Gillespie (eds), *Two Capitals: London and Dublin, 1500–1840* (Oxford: Oxford University Press, 2001), 189.

50. Martyn Powell, *The Politics of Consumption in Eighteenth-Century Ireland* (Houndmills: Palgrave Macmillan, 2004), 84.

51. Burke, *Riotous Performances*, 224.

52. This section is informed by Amy Prendergast, 'A French Phenomenon Embraced:

The Literary Salon in Britain and Ireland', unpublished paper. I would like to thank the author for providing me with a copy of this essay.

53. Bridget Hourican, 'Elizabeth Vesey', *Dictionary of Irish Biography*, http://dib .cambridge.org (accessed 29 December 2010).

54. Amy Prendergast, '"The Drooping Genius of Our Isle to Raise": The Moira House and Its Role in Gaelic Cultural Revival', *Eighteenth-Century Ireland*, 26 (2011), 95–114.

55. Rosemary Richey, 'Elizabeth Rawdon', *Dictionary of Irish Biography*, http://dib .cambridge.org [accessed 29 December 2010].

56. Lesa Ní Mhunghaile, 'Anglo-Irish Antiquarianism and the Transformation of Irish Identity, 1750–1800', in David A. Valone and Jill Marie Bradbury (eds), *Anglo-Irish Identities* (Lewisburg: Bucknell Press, 2008), 190–191.

57. Janet Todd, 'Ascendancy: Lady Mount Cashell, Lady Moira, Mary Wollstonecraft and the Union Pamphlets', *Eighteenth-Century Ireland*, 18 (2003), 105.

58. Ibid., 46, quoting *Proceedings of the Royal Dublin Society*, vii (1773), 324–333.

59. Richey, 'Elizabeth Rawdon'.

60. Andrew Carpenter, 'Patrick Delany', *Dictionary of Irish Biography*, http://dib .cambridge.org (accessed 29 December 2010).

61. Dena Goodman, *The Republic of Letters: A Cultural History of the French Enlightenment* (Ithaca: Cornell University Press, 1994).

62. Mary Barber, *Poems on Several Occasions* (London: Samuel Richardson, 1734), 31.

63. For similar activity see Marie-Louise Coolahan, '"We Live by Chance, and Slip into Events": Occasionality and the Manuscript Verse of Katherine Philips', *Eighteenth-Century Ireland*, 18 (2003), 9–23.

64. Barber, *Poems on Several Occasions*, 194.

65. '*Poems on Several Occasions* can be seen as the culmination of informal conversations and epistolary exchanges'; Aileen Douglas, Review of Bernard Tucker (ed.), *The Poetry of Mary Barber, Eighteenth-Century Ireland*, 7 (1992), 189. On Barber, see Bernard Tucker, '"Our Chief Poetess": Mary Barber and Swift's Circle', *Canadian Journal of Irish Studies*, 19 (1993), 31–44.

66. On the exoticism and novelty of the coffeehouse, see James Livesey, *Civil Society and Empire: Ireland and Scotland in the Eighteenth-Century Atlantic World* (New Haven: Yale University Press, 2009), 24–53.

67. Brian Cowan, *The Social Life of Coffee: The Emergence of the British Coffeehouse* (New Haven: Yale University Press, 2005).

68. Elizabeth Malcolm, 'The Rise of the Pub: A Study in the Disciplining of Popular Culture', in James S. Donnelly and Kerby A. Miller (eds), *Irish Popular Culture, 1650–1850* (Dublin: Irish Academic Press, 1999), 50–77.

69. Lisa-Marie Griffith, 'Mobilising Office, Education and Gender in Eighteenth-Century Ireland: The Case of the Griersons', *Eighteenth-Century Ireland*, 22 (2007), 64–80.

70. Munter, *The History of the Irish Newspaper*, 13–14.

71. Ibid., 16.

72. Ibid., 132.

73. For a brief discussion of the 'Hibernicus Letters', see Richard Holmes, 'James Arbuckle and Dean Swift: Cultural Politics in the Irish Confessional State', *Irish Studies Review*, 16 (2008), 436.

74. Allison Neill Rabaux, '*A Literary Journal:* A European Periodical in Eighteenth-Century Ireland' (PhD thesis, University of Ulster, 2013).

75. The following section draws on maps of the public sphere contained Michael Brown, 'The Place of Learning in Eighteenth-Century Dublin', in McCarthy and Simons, *Marsh's Library*, 104–126. They rely in turn on the map of the city provided in Kennedy and Hardiman, *A Directory of Dublin for the Year 1738*.

76. These are Lucas's Coffeehouse, Cork Hill; the Anne, Essex Bridge; the Cocoa Tree, near the Custom House, Essex Bridge; St James's Coffeehouse, on the upper part of the Great House, Essex Bridge; Bacon's Coffeehouse, Essex Street; the Custom House Coffeehouse, Essex Street; Dempster's Coffeehouse, Essex Street; the Globe Coffeehouse, Essex Street; the Merchant's Coffeehouse, Essex Street; the Post Office Coffeehouse, Fishamble Street; Dick's Coffeehouse, Skinner Row. This compares to 551 coffeehouses listed for London in the directories of 1734. See Cowan, *The Social Life of Coffee*, 154.

77. In London 'the famous coffeehouses [are] clustered around the Royal Exchange and its environs; they are also significantly located in or near some of the wealthiest sections of the city'; ibid., 157.

78. Edel Sheridan, 'Dublin and Berlin: A Comparative Geography of Two Eighteenth-Century European Capitals' (PhD thesis, University College Dublin, 1993), 129.

79. Francis Hutcheson, *Remarks upon the Fable of the Bees* (Glasgow, 1758; London: Thoemmes Press, 1998), 119.

80. Tickets for performances at Smock-Alley were on sale in Lucas's. See *Faulkner Dublin Journal*, 22 February 1746, where a benefit night for Sheridan is advertised with 'tickets to be had at Lucas' and the Custom House Coffeehouse.'

81. Sheridan, 'Dublin and Berlin', 131.

82. The social status and economic power of the coffeehouse keeper is discussed in Cowan, *The Social Life of Coffee*, 161–167.

83. Richard Lewis, *The Dublin Guide: or, a Description of the City of Dublin, and the Most Remarkable Places within Fifteen Miles* (Dublin: printed for the author, 1787), 113–114. These were Daly's, Dame-Street; the Dublin Coffeehouse, Crampton-Court; Royal Exchange on Cork Hill; the Old Exchange on Crampton-Court; the Four-Courts Coffeehouse on Christ-Church Lane; the Globe in Essex Street; Hughes's Club on College Green; the Constitutional Club in Kildare Street; and Sam's or the Custom House Coffeehouse on Essex Street.

84. Peter Wilson, *Wilson's Dublin Directory, for the Year 1768* (Dublin: printed for the author, 1768), 43

85. Ibid., 94.

86. William Wilson, *Wilson's Dublin Directory, for the Year 1780* (Dublin: printed for the author, 1780), 23.

87. *Freeman's Journal*, 7 April 1764.

88. Peter Clark, *The English Ale-House: A Social History 1200–1830* (London: Longman, 1983).

89. Powell, *Politics of Consumption*, 8. In *The Social Life of Coffee,* Cowan notes that in London 'there was at least one alcohol-serving watering hole per thirteen households in the City', 159.

90. There was also an ephemeral trade in chapbooks, ballads, and single-sheet squibs centred on Mountrath Street on the north bank of the Liffey, and further west. Padhraig Higgins, *A Nation of Politicians: Gender, Patriotism and Political Culture in Late Eighteenth-Century Ireland* (Madison: University of Wisconsin Press, 2010), 50.

91. *Dublin Weekly Journal*, 15 May 1725, 28; ibid., 11 December 1725, 150.

92. Peter Wilson *The Dublin Directory for the year 1760* (Dublin: printed for the author, 1760), 7.

93. *Wilson's Dublin Directory, for the year 1766* (Dublin: printed for the author, 1766), 34.

94. Ibid., 23 October 1725, 120. See also James W. Phillips, *Printing and Bookselling in Dublin, 1679–1820* (Dublin: Irish Academic Press, 1998), 82.

95. *Dublin Journal*, 14 January 1746. See also *Faulkner's Dublin Journal*, 15 March 1746 and 6 October 1747 for advertisements for auctions to be held in the Dublin coffeehouse.

96. *Faulkner's Dublin Journal*, 28 April 1747.

97. *Freeman's Journal*, 29 September 1770.

98. Dublin accords with the pattern whereby urban improvement had generated 'a cultural *quartier*, usually in the central area of town, distinguished by paved streets and rebuilt civic buildings, joined with assembly rooms, coffee houses and other drinking premises, and adjacent closed walks and private pleasure gardens; a continuum of premises which enabled the better-off classes to move easily from one venue, and one entertainment, to another'; Peter Clark, *British Clubs and Societies, 1580–1800* (Oxford: Oxford University Press, 2000), 169.

99. *A Letter from the Quidnuncs at St James's Coffee-House and the Mall, London, to their Brethren at Lucas's Coffee-House in Dublin* (Dublin, 1724?), 1.

100. Ibid., 2.

101. [Luke Lively], 'A Dialogue Between a Beau's Head and his Heels: taken from their mouths as spoken at Lucas's Coffee-House', in idem, *The Merry Fellow; or Entertaining Magazine*, 2 vols (Dublin: James Hoey, 1757), I, 83.

102. Ibid.

103. Ibid.

104. 'An Anacreontic, Upon Mrs Carterwright, at the Custom House Coffee-house, in 1730', in John Winstanley, *Poems written Occasionally by John Winstanley, Interspers'd with many others by Several Ingenious Hands* (Dublin: S. Powell, 1742), 96.

105. Ibid., 97.

106. John Anketell, *Poems on Several Subjects* (Dublin: William Porter, 1793), 132. This poem is discussed in Higgins, *A Nation of Politicians*, 33–34.

107. Anketell, *Poems on Several Subjects*, 132–133.

108. Cole, 'Lending Libraries in Eighteenth-Century Ireland', 116–117.

109. Ibid., 117.

110. Ibid., 118.

111. Raymond Gillespie, *Early Belfast: The Origins and Growth of an Ulster Town to 1750* (Belfast: Ulster Historical Foundation, 2007), 142–143.

112. For Cork's development, see David Dickson, 'Jacobitism in Eighteenth-Century Ireland: A Munster Perspective', *Éire-Ireland*, 39 (2004), 94.

113. This list draws on Higgins, *A Nation of Politicians*, 29.

114. Christopher Morash, *A History of Irish Theatre, 1601–2000* (Cambridge: Cambridge University Press, 2002), 44.

115. Helen Burke, 'Eighteenth-Century Theatrical Touring and Irish Popular Culture', in Nicholas Grene and Christopher Morash (eds), *Irish Theatre on Tour* (Dublin: Carysfort Press, 2005), 119.

116. Ibid., 125–138.

117. William Smith Clark, *The Irish Stage in the County Towns* (Oxford: Clarendon Press, 1965), 149. Quote taken from ibid, citing *Limerick Journal*, 21 November 1767.

118. *Waterford Chronicle*, 9 August 1771, cited in ibid., 149–150.

119. Quoted in ibid., 153.

120. Ibid., 165, quoting *Leinster Journal*, 16 January 1768.

121. Ibid., 166, 167.

122. Ibid., 178, quoting *Leinster Journal*, 15 December 1784.

123. Ibid., 185.

124. Information in this paragraph is drawn from ibid., 198–215.

125. *Finn's Leinster Journal*, 12 February 1771, quoted in Lisa Meaney, 'Freemasonry in Munster, 1726–1829' (MA thesis, Mary Immaculate College Limerick, 2005), 154.

126. Ibid., 152, quoting *Exshaw's Gentleman's and London Magazine*, February 1779, 118.

127. Martyn Powell, 'Convivial Clubs in the Public Sphere, 1750–1800', in Powell and Kelly, *Clubs and Societies*, 359.

128. Walsh, 'Club Life in Late Seventeenth- and Early Eighteenth-Century Ireland', 37; Livesey, *Civil Society and Empire*, 29.

129. T. C. Barnard, 'The Cultures of Eighteenth-Century Irish Towns', in Peter Borsay and Lindsay Proudfoot (eds), *Provincial Towns in Early Modern England and*

Ireland: Change, Convergence and Divergence (Oxford: Oxford University Press, 2002), 220.

130. James Kelly, 'The Pastime of the Elite: Clubs and Societies and the Promotion of Horse Racing', in Kelly and Powell, *Clubs and Societies*, 420.

131. Cited in Powell, *Politics of Consumption*, 94. Nixon's coffeehouse is mentioned in Higgins, *A Nation of Politicians*, 33.

132. Máire Kennedy, 'Eighteenth-Century Newspaper Publishing in Munster and South Leinster', *Journal of the Cork Historical and Archaeological Society*, 103 (1998), 83. The titles are listed on ibid., 88n124.

133. The data in this paragraph is drawn from the *Copy of the Deed or Charter, entered into by the Associated Society to Raise a Fund for Erecting a Coffee House and other Buildings in the City of Cork; for the Government of the Said Society . . . dated 21st January 1793* (Cork: Anthony Edwards, 1794).

134. Peter Clark suggests 'it was difficult to organise newer forms of fashionable sociability there. Apart from churches, villages had few public facilities (inns or coffeehouses) for smart social gatherings . . . Rural socialites also had to contend with poor by-roads, darkness, robbers and bad weather'; Clark, *British Clubs and Societies*, 183.

135. Patrick O'Flanagan, 'Markets and Fairs in Ireland, 1600–1800: Index of Economic Development and Regional Growth', *Journal of Historical Geography*, 11 (1985), 372.

136. Ibid., 373.

137. Ibid., 373, the map on ibid., 374.

138. Martyn Powell remarks 'hunting clubs were regarded benignly; they were perceived as a medium through which the order of the urban world was transmitted to the countryside and thus as source of welcome refinement.' Martyn Powell, 'Hunting Clubs and Societies' in Kelly and Powell, *Clubs and Societies*, 394. He also notes that Catholic participation was limited; ibid., 405.

139. Ibid., 400.

140. Ibid., 401.

141. For a similar view of horse racing, see Kelly, 'The Pastime of the Elite', 409–424.

142. Powell, 'Hunting Clubs and Societies', 397 and 398.

143. Ibid., 398–399.

144. David A. Fleming, 'Clubs and Societies in Eighteenth-Century Munster', in Kelly and Powell, *Clubs and Societies*, 440 and the table on 441.

145. Kevin Whelan, 'The Geography of Hurling', *History Ireland*, Spring (1993), 27. See also the maps on ibid., 28, 29, and the list of gentry patron families on ibid., 29.

146. This quote and the details about Wexford are drawn from Eamon Doyle, 'The "Yellow Bellies" and the Hurling Men of Cornwall', *History Ireland*, Summer (2002), 8.

147. Donnelly and Miller, *Irish Popular Culture, 1650–1850*, 13. The lament is in Dáithí Ó hÓgáin, *Duanaire Osraíoch* (Dublin: An Clóchamhar Tta, 1980), 51–53.

148. Whelan, 'The Geography of Hurling', 28.

149. *Pue's Occurrences*, 5 August 1746, quoted in ibid.

150. Powell, 'Hunting Clubs and Societies', 392.

151. Christopher Morash observes that 'there were not many places in early eighteenth-century Ireland in which the "broom man" and "the greatest peer" could hiss and cheer in the same room and the theatre was one of them.' *A History of Irish Theatre*, 35.

152. Harris, 'Outside the Box', 46.

153. See Smock-Alley Theatre in 1789, National Gallery of Ireland which adorns the cover of *Eighteenth-Century Ireland*, 20 (2005).

154. Quoted in Sean Connolly, 'An Déanamh *Commanding:* Élite Responses to Popular Culture, 1650–1850', in James S. Donnelly and Kerby A. Miller (eds), *Irish Popular Culture, 1650–1850* (Dublin: Irish Academic Press, 1999), 11.

155. Ibid.

156. Quoted in Slowey, *Radicalisation of Irish Drama*, 75.

157. Ibid., 113.

158. Burke, *Riotous Performances*, passim.

159. Quoted in Victor Power, 'The Kelly Theatre Riot', *Eire-Ireland*, 7 (1972), 67.

160. Ibid., 68.

161. Ibid., 70.

162. Women attended more frequently on charity nights when they could sit on stage instead of being confined to the boxes. Susan Cannon Harris, 'Outside the Box: The Female Spectator, *The Fair Penitent,* and the Kelly Riots of 1747', *Theatre Journal*, 57 (2005), 46.

163. Victor, 'Kelly Riot', 73.

164. Conrad Brunström, *Thomas Sheridan's Career and Influence: An Actor in Earnest* (Lewisburg: Bucknell Press, 2011), 31–36.

165. Burke, *Riotous Performances*, 117–148.

166. Michael Brown, 'The Biter Bitten: Ireland and the Rude Enlightenment', *Eighteenth-Century Studies*, 45 (2012), 393–407.

167. Powell, 'Political Toasting in Eighteenth-Century Ireland', *passim.*

168. *Freeman's Journal*, 18 December 1770.

169. *Freeman's Journal*, 6 December 1770.

170. *Dublin Mercury*, 10–13 March 1769; *Dublin Mercury*, 22–25 April 1769, both quoted in Clark, *British Clubs and Societies*, 188.

171. James Kelly, *That Damn'd thing Called Honour: Duelling in Ireland, 1570–1860* (Cork: Cork University Press, 1995), 179.

172. Ibid., 55–56 for a discussion of the political context of this trial.

173. *The Whole Tryal and Examination of Mr. Robert Martin* (Dublin: E. Waters, 1735).

174. Kelly, *That Damn'd thing Called Honour*, 51.

175. Information in this paragraph is drawn from ibid., 77–78.

176. Ibid., 161.

177. This dates the political public sphere a decade later than is proposed by Douglas Simes: 'In the late 1760s and early 1770s this situation changed. The rise of a Wilkes-style charismatic politician—in the shape of Charles Lucas—willing to appeal to the public by means of the newspaper press, coincided with the tenure in office of a lord lieutenant, Lord Townsend, whose policies offended much of the politically significant population, politics in the press moved from being occasional and slightly peripheral to being a central and continual concern.' 'Ireland, 1760–1820s', in Hannah Barker (ed.), *Press and the Public Sphere in Europe and America: 1760–1840* (Cambridge: Cambridge University Press, 2002), 116.

178. *Dublin Mercury*, 22 December 1770.

179. Volunteering radicalism is described in Higgins, *A Nation of Politicians*, 45–46. However, see the revision to this polarised reading offered in Martyn Powell, 'The *Volunteer Evening Post* and Patriotic Print Culture in Late Eighteenth-Century Ireland', in Mark Williams and Stephen Paul Forrest (eds), *Constructing the Past: Writing Irish History, 1600–1800* (Woodbridge: Boydell Press, 2010), 113–135.

180. 'In the 1780s the government became increasingly concerned with the politics of the press. Officials saw newspapers as a pernicious influence on the public and took a keen interest in their contents.' Higgins, *A Nation of Politicians*, 46.

181. Brian Inglis, *Freedom of the Press in Ireland, 1784–1841* (London: Greenwood Press, 1954), 19–45.

182. *The Statutes at Large, passed in the Parliaments held in Ireland*, 20 vols (Dublin: George Grierson, 1786–1801), XII, 666.

183. Ibid., XIII, 122–148.

184. Irish Legislation database, www.qub.ac.uk/ild/ [accessed 6 September 2010].

185. *Statutes at Large*, XIII, 938.

186. Ibid., 939.

187. Burke, *Riotous Performances*, 289. Burke relates the Stage Act to the politicisation of theatre in this period, and to a concern on the part of the government that there existed a general 'Dublin problem' which manifested itself in mob disturbance and political criticism; see ibid., 281–290.

188. *Statutes at Large*, XV, 66.

189. Gillian O'Brien, '"Spirit, Impartiality and Independence": The *Northern Star*, 1792–1797, *Eighteenth-Century Ireland*, 13 (1998), 14.

190. *Statutes at Large*, XV, 560.

6. Communities of Interest

1. Associational life is the subject of a large, mainly sociological, literature. See, for instance, the contrasting conclusions of Robert D. Putnam, *Bowling Alone: The Collapse and Revival of American Democracy* (New York: Simon and Schuster, 2000), and Theda Skocpol, *Diminished Democracy: From Membership to Management in American Civic Life* (Norman: University of Oklahoma Press, 2003). For the historical development in Britain, see Peter Clark, *British Clubs and Societies, 1580–1800: The Origins of an Associational World* (Oxford: Oxford University Press, 2000).

2. See, however, the essays in part three of James Kelly and Martyn Powell (eds), *Clubs and Societies in Eighteenth-Century Ireland* (Dublin: Four Courts Press, 2010), which deals with political clubs in this period.

3. E. Charles Nelson, 'The Dublin Florists' Club in the Mid Eighteenth Century', *Garden History*, 10 (1982), 142–148.

4. *The Beggars (of St Mary's Parish) Address to their Worthy Representative, Hackball, President of that Ancient and Numerous Society* ([Dublin]: Lord Hackball's Printer, 1754), 3-6.

5. Ibid., 4. Martyn Powell suspects that this report 'might have been more a reflection of newspapers' excitable interest in club life . . . But these inventions are important as they reflected the key role that club life was beginning to play in Dublin's public sphere.' *The Politics of Consumption in Eighteenth-Century Ireland* (Houndmills: Palgrave Macmillan, 2005), 84.

6. *Rules for the Club in Shaw's Court* (Dublin, 1770), 7.

7. Ibid., 4.

8. Ibid., 4, 3.

9. Ibid., 3.

10. Ibid., 7.

11. Ibid.

12. Patrick M. Geoghegan and Linde Lunney, 'William Burton Conyngham', *Dictionary of Irish Biography*, www.dib.cambridge.org/ (accessed 29 August 2010). See also C. E. F. Trench, 'William Burton Conyngham (1733–1796)', *The Journal of the Royal Society of Antiquaries of Ireland*, 115 (1985), 40-63.

13. Turlough O'Riordan, 'John Putland (1709–73)', *Dictionary of Irish Biography*, www.dib.cambridge.org/ (accessed 29 August 2010).

14. T. C. Barnard, '"Grand Metropolis" or "The Anus of the World": Cultural Life in Eighteenth-Century Dublin', in Peter Clark and Raymond Gillespie (eds), *Two Capitals: London and Dublin, 1500–1840* (Oxford: Oxford University Press, 2001), 199. See also A. C. Elias, 'Richard Helsham, Jonathan Swift and the Library of John Putland', in Muriel McCarthy and Ann Simmons (eds.), *Marsh's Library, A Mirror*

on the World: Law, Learning and Libraries, 1650–1750 (Dublin: Four Courts Press, 2009), 251–278

15. 'Madden's originality was to perceive that an un-virtuous, self-interested society could still have a distinctive set of moral qualities'. James Livesey, 'The Dublin Society in Eighteenth-Century Irish Political Thought', *Historical Journal*, 47 (2004), 640.

16. Samuel Madden, *A Letter to the Dublin Society on the Improving their Fund* (Dublin: R. Reilly, 1739), 8. As James Livesey puts it, the Dublin Society was 'the late off-spring of a genealogy of failure.' 'A Kingdom of Cosmopolitan Improvers: The Dublin Society, 1731–1798', in Jani Marjanen and Koen Stapelbroek (eds), *The Rise of Economic Societies in the Eighteenth Century: Patriotic Reform in Europe and North America* (Houndmills: Palgrave Macmillan, 2012), 53.

17. Madden, *A Letter to the Dublin Society*, 11.

18. Ibid., 6.

19. Ibid., 16.

20. Ibid., 23.

21. Ibid., 15.

22. Ibid., 21.

23. Ibid., 23.

24. Ibid., 17. This passage hints at a concern for transparency, again a virtue of the public sphere, and in monetary matters Madden was adamant, for he instructed the Society that 'no sum over two or three pounds should be laid out but by the appointment and hand writing of at least ten members' and that 'besides this, quarterly accounts also of your disbursements should still be laid before the whole Society, on the oaths of those who manage them.' Ibid., 22, 23.

25. Ibid., 5.

26. Ibid., 13.

27. Kieran R. Byrne, 'The Royal Dublin Society and the Advancement of Popular Science in Ireland, 1731–1860', *History of Education*, 15 (1986), 81.

28. A brief sketch of the founding members can be found in Desmond Clarke, *Thomas Prior 1681–1751: Founder of the Royal Dublin Society* (Dublin: Royal Dublin Society. 1951), 25–26.

29. The capacity of the Dublin Society to endure is a central theme in T. C. Barnard, 'The Dublin Society and other Improving Societies, 1731–1785', in Kelly and Powell, *Clubs and Societies in Eighteenth-Century Ireland*, 53–88.

30. This draws on the account in ibid.

31. *A List of the Members of the Dublin Society Named in the Charter, Also of the Members Elected since the Opening of the Charter* (Dublin: printed for Henry Hawker, 1750).

32. *The Royal Charter of the Dublin Society to which are Added the Society's By-Laws and Ordinances* (Dublin: S. Powell, 1766), 16.

33. Barnard, 'The Dublin Society and other Improving Societies', 83.

34. James Livesey records, 'In 1761 Bertin, head of the maison du Roi, tried to inspire a network of societies in the French provinces based on the model of the Dublin Society. In Britain, the Board of Agriculture and the Royal Agricultural Society admitted their inspiration from the Dublin exemplar.' 'The Dublin Society in Political Thought', 616.

35. Quoted in Byrne, 'The Advancement of Popular Science', 83.

36. Barnard neatly states that to the Society 'example worked better than books'. 'The Dublin Society and other Improving Societies', 60.

37. Byrne, 'The Advancement of Popular Science', 83.

38. *The Royal Charter of the Dublin Society to which are Added the Society's By-Laws*, 10–11; Livesey, 'The Dublin Society in Political Thought', 615.

39. Duncan Thorburn Burns, *Richard Kirwan, 1733–1812: 'The Philosopher of Dublin'* (Dublin: Royal Irish Academy, 2003), 13.

40. For the Dublin Society, 'the key issue was productivity'. Livesey, 'A Kingdom of Cosmopolitan Improvers', 66.

41. Madden, *A Letter to the Dublin Society*, passim.

42. *The Application of the Money Granted By Parliament in the Year 1765 to the Dublin Society* (Dublin: S. Powell, 1766), 3. A similar outlay, albeit for 5,477*l*, is recorded in *Parliamentary Premiums offered by the Dublin Society, 1770* (Dublin: S. Powell, 1770).

43. Barnard, 'The Dublin Society and other Improving Societies', 81. His conclusion is that the Dublin Society only represented activism in the capital, or at best, within Dublin's extended hinterland.

44. Ibid., 79.

45. See Herbert Butler, 'New Geneva in Waterford', *Journal of the Royal Society of Antiquaries of Ireland*, 77 (1947), 150–155.

46. Jane A. Meredith, 'Andrew Caldwell', *Oxford Dictionary of National Biography*, www.oxforddnb.com (accessed 5 September 2010).

47. T. C. Barnard reads this circumstance more pessimistically: 'Catholics might receive premiums but, not being members, could not allocate them'. This emphasises a lack of status over the granting of recognition. Barnard, 'The Dublin Society and other Improving Societies', 70.

48. Woods, 'Thomas Wyse', *Dictionary of Irish Biography*.

49. Madden, *A Letter to the Dublin Society*, 53.

50. This is understood as a novel development in Livesey, 'The Dublin Society in Political Thought', 618: 'The Dublin Society was the model for a nation organized neither around virtue, the core notion of citizenship for the civic humanists, nor justice, the equivalent for the natural jurisprudential tradition. Instead the Society incarnated an ideal of a community self-consciously organized around utility.'

51. Madden, *Letter to the Dublin Society*, 18.

52. 3 George III, c.14.

53. 5 George II, c.12.

54. 7 George III, c.15; 25 George III c.61; 25 George III, c.27.

55. 26 George III, c.48. 34 George III, c.15.

56. 36 George II, c.16; 37 George II c.41.

57. All the information in this paragraph is drawn from the Irish Legislation Database, www.qub.ac.uk/ild/ (accessed 6 September 2010).

58. Madden, *Letter to the Dublin Society*, 20.

59. *A Copy of His Majesty's Royal Charter for Incorporating the Dublin Society* (Dublin: printed for Henry Hawker, 1750), 4.

60. Barnard accepts that the Dublin Society 'channelled a well-meaning but often inchoate patriotism into practical measures' but warns that 'to single out the Dublin Society as the principal vehicle for constructive patriotism ignores its limitations'. 'The Dublin Society and other Improving Societies', 76, 87.

61. The following sections make no claim to comprehensive coverage, but offer a broad conceptual map of the club life of the country onto which associations that are not mentioned might be plotted.

62. Information drawn from Irish Confraternities, 1775–1965 database, http://www .forasfeasa.ie/index.php?option=com_content&view=article&id=83:irish -confraternities-1775–1965&catid=48:projects&Itemid=78 (accessed 28 August 2010).

63. This information is drawn from Rosemary Raughter, 'A Discreet Benevolence: Female Philanthropy and the Catholic Resurgence in Eighteenth-Century Ireland', *Women's History Review*, 6 (1997), 471–472.

64. Andrew R. Holmes, *The Shaping of Ulster Presbyterian Belief and Practice, 1770–1840* (Oxford: Oxford University Press, 2006), 290–291.

65. Ibid., 279.

66. Johanna Archbold, 'Book Clubs and Reading Societies in the Late Eighteenth Century', in Kelly and Powell, *Clubs and Societies in Eighteenth-Century Ireland*, 143.

67. Ibid., 145.

68. This is discussed in ibid., 146–147.

69. Ibid., 148.

70. Ibid., 149.

71. Ibid., 149–150.

72. However, Johanna Archbold notes that 'members of the dissenting community played a crucial part in the establishment of Ireland's reading societies in the late eighteenth century'; ibid., 161.

73. Ibid. On Thomas Russell, see chapter nine below.

74. Seán Patrick Donlan, 'Henry Maule', *Dictionary of Irish Biography*, http://dib .cambridge.org/quicksearch.do (accessed 2 October 2010); [Henry Maule], *An*

Humble Proposal for Obtaining His Majesty's Royal Charter to Incorporate a Society for Promoting Christian Knowledge among the Poor Natives of the Kingdom of Ireland (Dublin: George Grierson, 1730), 17.

75. [Maule], *An Humble Proposal for Obtaining His Majesty's Royal Charter*, 26.

76. For information on the early charity schools of which Maule's establishment in Shandon was a part, see Karen Sonnelitter, '"To Unite Our Temporal and Eternal Interests": Sermons and the Charity School in Ireland', *Eighteenth-Century Ireland*, 25 (2010), 62–81.

77. [Maule], *A Humble Proposal for Obtaining His Majesty's Royal Charter*, 28.

78. Ibid., 29.

79. Kenneth Milne, *The Irish Charter Schools* (Dublin: Four Courts Press, 1996), 23.

80. Richard Pococke, *A Sermon Preached at Christ Church, Dublin, on the 27th of June 1762 before the Incorporated Society . . . with a Continuation of the Society's Proceedings* (Dublin: S. Powell, 1762), 15.

81. Ibid., 16.

82. 19 Geo. II c.5. Milne, *Irish Charter Schools*, 41.

83. Ibid., 24.

84. Ibid., 24, 35. 'Minola was given a House especially built for the purpose by George and John Brown, who endowed the school with ten acres forever. Shannon Grove was built on William Bury's land at his expense (£80) and he also gave one acre in perpetuity and a further nineteen at a low rent. The bishop of Dromore, Maule, gave two acres for the school at Ballynahinch, the society farming eight additional acres from a tenant of Sir John Rawdon.' Ibid., 35.

85. Pococke, *A Sermon Preached at Christ Church, Dublin*, 23.

86. All this information is drawn from Milne, *Irish Charter Schools*, 28.

87. Ibid., 46, 35.

88. Pococke, *A Sermon Preached at Christ Church, Dublin*, 42.

89. *Rules established by the Incorporated Society in Dublin for Promoting English Protestant Schools in Ireland* (Dublin: George Grierson, 1734), 3–4, 5.

90. Milne, *Irish Charter Schools*, 136, 135.

91. Ibid., 137.

92. Ibid., 127.

93. Ibid., 143.

94. Letter to English Charter School Society in 1740, quoted in ibid., 140.

95. Ibid., 142. 23 Geo II c.11.

96. A list of the preachers up to 1762 can be found in Pococke, *A Sermon Preached at Christ Church, Dublin*, 77–78.

97. Thomas Rundle, *A Sermon Preached in Christ Church Dublin on the 25th day of March 1736 before the Incorporated Society* (Dublin: R. Reilly, 1736), 8.

98. Ibid., 21.

99. Ibid., 20.

100. Ibid., 21–22.

101. James Trail, *A Sermon Preached at Christ Church Cathedral Dublin on the 7th of February 1779 Before the Incorporated Society* (Dublin: G. Perrin, 1779), 2.

102. Ibid., 3.

103. Ibid., 5.

104. Ibid.

105. Ibid., 6.

106. Ibid.

107. Ibid., 14.

108. Ibid., 16. 'A law was lately framed for the relief of the Roman Catholics of this kingdom. It is certainly the duty of a good subject to acquiesce in the determination of the legislature of his country: and God grant that the consequences of this law may even exceed the fond hopes of its warmest advocates! Yet after an alteration in our constitution so sudden and so important, can we, in this time of trouble and public confusion, can we look forward to the dark and doubtful transactions of succeeding years without the most painful apprehensions?' Ibid., 18. On the Relief Act, see chapter eight below.

109. Ibid., 16.

110. Ibid., 17.

111. For a treatment of earlier failed attempts to use education as a conduit to conversion, see David Hayton, 'Did Protestantism Fail in early Eighteenth-Century Ireland? Charity Schools and the Enterprise of Religious and Social Reformation, c. 1690–1730', in Alan Ford, James McGuire, and Kenneth Milne (eds), *As by Law Established: The Church of Ireland since the Reformation* (Dublin: Lilliput Press, 1995), 166–186.

112. Quoted in Milne, *Irish Charter Schools*, 119.

113. Laurence Dermott, *Ahiman Rezon: or, a Help to a Brother. Shewing the Excellency of Secrecy, and the First Cause of the Institution of Free-Masonry*, 2nd edn (London: Robert Black, 1764), 14; see also Philip Carter, 'Laurence Dermott', *Oxford Dictionary of National Biography*, www.oxforddnb.com (accessed 31 August 2010).

114. The accuracy of this data in discussed in Petri Mirala, *Freemasonry in Ulster, 1733–1813* (Dublin: Four Courts Press, 2007), 43n. On wider issues of the origins and spread of Speculative Freemasonry in the British Isles, see David Stevenson, *The Origins of Freemasonry: Scotland's Century, 1590–1710* (Cambridge: Cambridge University Press, 1998), and Clark, *British Clubs and Societies*, 309–349.

115. Patrick Fagan, *Catholics in a Protestant Country: The Papist Constituency in Eighteenth-Century Dublin* (Dublin: Four Courts Press, 1988), 131. Lisa Meaney states that there were ninety-nine lodges in the province in 1771, 109 the next year, forty-eight in 1773, seventy on 1774, and 103 in 1775. This provides an average of

eighty-five active in any given year in the early 1770s and this makes up 28.3 percent of the estimated total of 300 lodges. See Lisa Meaney, 'Freemasonry in Munster, 1726–1829' (MA thesis, Mary Immaculate College Limerick, 2005), 98.

116. Fagan, *Catholics in a Protestant Country*, 127.

117. Ibid., 129. Fagan suggests that both the Barristers Lodge and the Medical Lodge were really units of the United Irishmen.

118. Ibid.

119. Ibid., 132.

120. Mirala, *Freemasonry in Ulster*, 56.

121. Ibid., 56–57.

122. Ibid., 57.

123. Ibid., 63, 64, 65.

124. Ibid., 68.

125. Meaney, 'Freemasonry in Munster', 38.

126. Ibid., 39.

127. Ibid., 41.

128. Ibid., 43.

129. Fagan, *Catholics in a Protestant Country*, 127–128.

130. Ibid., 139.

131. Ibid., 134–137.

132. Mirala, *Freemasonry in Ulster*, 139.

133. Ibid., 137.

134. Ibid.

135. Meaney, 'Freemasonry in Munster', 208–222.

136. Ibid., 168.

137. Ibid., 170.

138. Ibid., 171.

139. Ibid., 173.

140. Ibid., 174.

141. Fagan, *Catholics in a Protestant Country*, 128–129, 138.

142. Mirala, *Freemasonry in Ulster*, 138.

143. Quoted in ibid., 138.

144. Meaney, 'Freemasonry in Munster', 176.

145. Ibid., 177. Lisa Meaney is sceptical about this however, noting that 'the Volunteer years coincided with a marked decline in new registered Masons.' Ibid., 178.

146. A recent version of this thesis is deployed in Margaret C. Jacob, *Living the Enlightenment: Freemasonry and Politics in Eighteenth-Century Europe* (Oxford: Oxford University Press, 1991).

147. Moreover, as James Van Horn Melton contends, 'Freemasonry's affirmation of its own inviolability and autonomy expressed an idea that was basic to the emergence

of the enlightened public sphere: the idea of civil society as a realm of association whose members defined and asserted their interests separately from the state.' *The Rise of the Public in Enlightenment Europe* (Cambridge: Cambridge University Press, 2001), 253.

148. Mirala, *Freemasonry in Ulster*, 97.

149. Ibid., 97.

150. Also as James Van Horn Melton notes of Freemasonry, 'its ceremonial, hierarchical and mystical elements were deeply embedded in the symbolic universe of the Old Regime'. *Rise of the Public*, 263.

151. Dermott, *Ahiman Rezon*, 1–2.

152. For an able reading of these events, see Pertri Mirala, '"A Large Mob Calling Themselves Freemasons": Masonic Parades in Ulster', in Eoin Magennis and Peter Jupp (eds), *Crowds in Ireland, c.1720–1920* (London: Palgrave Macmillan, 2000), 117–138.

153. *Faulkner's Dublin Journal*, 10–14 January 1744, quoted in Meaney, 'Freemasonry in Munster', 137.

154. Dermott, *Ahiman Rezon*, i.

155. Ibid.

156. Ibid., 172.

157. Ibid.

158. Turlough O'Riordan, 'Richard Parsons', *Dictionary of Irish Biography*, www.dib .cambridge.org (accessed 31 August 2010).

159. George C. Caffentzis, 'Why Did Berkeley's Bank Fail? Money and Libertinism in Eighteenth-Century Ireland', *Eighteenth-Century Ireland*, 12 (1997), 106. There is a painting by Worsdale in the National Gallery of Ireland (Catalogue Number NGI 134) depicting Colonel Henry Clements, Henry Ponsonby of Ashgrove County Kilkenny, Baron Barry of Santry, Simon Luttrell, later first Earl of Carhampton, and Colonel Richard St George. See David Ryan, 'The Dublin Hellfire Club', in Kelly and Powell, *Clubs and Societies in Eighteenth-Century Ireland*, 337.

160. Ryan, 'The Dublin Hellfire Club', 337.

161. Ibid., 340.

162. William Coombe, *The Diaboliad, a Poem: Dedicated to the Worst Man in His Majesty's Dominions* (London: printed for S. Kearsly, 1777).

163. Quote taken from Ryan, 'The Dublin Hellfire Club', 341.

164. Ibid., 347–349. See also Neal Garnham, 'The Trials of James Cotter and Henry, Baron Barry of Santry: Two Case Studies in the Administration of Criminal Justice in Early Eighteenth-Century Ireland', *Irish Historical Studies*, 31 (1999), 328–432.

165. Patrick M. Geoghegan, 'Thomas Whaley', *Dictionary of Irish Biography*, www.dib .cambridge.org (accessed 31 August 2010).

166. Ryan, 'The Dublin Hellfire Club', 350. The painting is catalogue number NGI 4523.

167. Denis Hayes, 'Eclogue III', in idem, *The Works in Verse of Daniel Hayes, Esq; Late of the Middle-Temple, London* (Limerick: Andrew Watson, 1785), 26.

168. *An Ample Discovery of the Damnable Cabal Commonly Known by the Name of the Hell Fire Club,* [Dublin: G. F., 1738], 1. This is discussed further in Ryan, 'The Dublin Hellfire Club', 338–339.

169. For the wider context, see David Stevenson, *The Beggar's Benison: Sex Clubs of Enlightenment Scotland and their Rituals* (East Linton: Tuckwell Press, 2001).

170. This paragraph draws on Nancy L. Rosenblum, *Membership and Morals: The Personal Uses of Pluralism in America* (Princeton: Princeton University Press, 1998), 47–53.

171. See, however, Neal Garnham, 'How Violent was Eighteenth-Century Ireland', *Irish Historical Studies*, 30 (1997), 377–392.

172. Statistics drawn from James Kelly, *'That Damn'd Thing Called Honour': Duelling in Ireland, 1570–1860* (Cork: Cork University Press, 1995), 80, Table 2.1.

173. See ibid., 65.

174. *The Fundamental Laws, Statutes and Constitutions of the Ancient and Most Benevolent Order of the Friendly Brothers of St Patrick* (Dublin, 1751), passim.

175. Ibid., 12.

176. Ibid., 11.

177. Patrick Guinness, '"Man Being in his natural state the most naked and helpless of all creatures": The Meeting Book of the County of Kildare Knot of the Friendly Brothers of St Patrick, 1758–1791', *Journal of the County Kildare Archaeological Society*, 19 (2000–1), 126, 124.

178. Ibid., 10.

179 *Fundamental Laws*, 3.

180. John Kenney, *Private Friendship consistent with Universal Benevolence: A Sermon* (Dublin: M. Williamsons, 1756), 5.

181. *Fundamental Laws*, 10.

182. Guinness, 'The Meeting Book of the County of Kildare Knot', 126–127.

183. Ibid., 122.

184. Ibid., 149, 131.

185. Walsh, 'Club Life in Late Seventeenth- and Early Eighteenth-Century Ireland', 47.

186. Laurence Whyte, 'An Historical Poem on the Rise and Progress of the Charitable and Musical Society', *Original Poems on Various Subjects* (Dublin: S. Powell, 1742), 223–224. On this edition, see T. C. Barnard, 'The Gentrification of Eighteenth-Century Ireland', *Eighteenth-Century Ireland*, 12 (1997), 137–155.

187. Quoted in Walsh, 'Club Life in Late Seventeenth- and Early Eighteenth-Century Ireland', 48.

188. Whyte, 'An Historical Poem on the Rise and Progress', 218.

189. Laurence Whyte, 'A Poetical Description of Mr Neal's New Music Hall in

Fishamble Street Dublin', in Andrew Carpenter, *Verse in English from Eighteenth-Century Ireland* (Cork: Cork University Press, 1998), 279.

190. Ibid.

191. Hugo Cole, 'Handel in Dublin', *Irish Arts Review*, 1 (1984), 28. David Hunter, 'Inviting Handel to Ireland: Laurence Whyte and the Challenge of Poetic Evidence', *Eighteenth-Century Ireland*, 20 (2005), 156–168, suggests that an official invitation was unlikely.

192. Quoted in Tom Fredell, 'Handel in Ascendancy Dublin', *Éire-Ireland*, 20 (1985), 6.

193. Cole, 'Handel in Dublin', 28.

194. Quoted in Fredell, 'Handel in Ascendancy Dublin', 9. There is some controversy as to whether *Messiah* was composed for the Dublin venture, with Cole, for instance deeming it unlikely that the work was written for the Dublin charities, while Fredell suggests that '*Messiah* was written in London in a space of twenty-four days in late summer 1741, most likely after the composer received the lord lieutenant's invitation . . . Handel would not have dared such a work for his usual audience' for it 'gave a concrete beginning and direction to Handel's new departure' namely a decision 'to concentrate his energies toward reinvigorating the moribund English oratorio'. Ibid., 9, 11.

195. Cole, 'Handel in Dublin', 29–30. The importance of this charitable context is underlined in Harry Whyte, 'Handel in Dublin: A Note', *Eighteenth-Century Ireland*, 2 (1987), 182–186.

196. Laurence Whyte, 'A Poem on the General Effect and Excellency of Music, but now more Particularly on the Famous Mr Handel's Performance and Compositions', *Original Poems on Various Subjects*, 4.

197. Michael Murphy, 'John Field', *Dictionary of Irish Biography*, http://dib.cambridge.org (accessed 8 October 2010).

198. John Turpin, *A School of Art in Dublin since the Eighteenth Century: A History of the National College of Art and Design* (Dublin: Gill and Macmillan, 1995), 13.

199. Ibid., 15.

200. Ibid., 43, 49.

201. Ibid., 27, 23.

202. The eighteenth-century history of the schools is surveyed in Turpin, *A School of Art*, 32–55.

203. *An Address to the Hibernian Society with a Plan of Education in a Letter to the Provost and Fellows of Trinity College Dublin* (Dublin, 1758), 5.

204. *The Proceedings of the Hibernian Society drawn up by their Order* (Dublin: George Faulkner, 1758), 4.

205. The full membership is listed in ibid., 5–6.

206. Ibid., 9.

207. Ibid., 11, 10.

208. Ibid., 14. Conrad Brunström observes 'Dublin society . . . could not stomach the concept of a jobbing actor taking charge of the education of polite youth'. *Thomas Sheridan's Career and Influence: An Actor in Earnest* (Lewisburg: Bucknell University Press, 2011), 21.

209. A survey of charitable activism in the period is offered in James Kelly, 'Charitable Societies: Their Genesis and Development, 1720–1800', in Kelly and Powell, *Clubs and Societies in Eighteenth-Century Ireland*, 89–108. This notes a rise in their popularity in the 1750s.

210. 'The conventional eighteenth-century moral ideal of womanhood' as 'predisposed . . . to charitable activity' is examined in Rosemary Raughter, 'A Natural Tenderness: The Ideal and the Reality of Eighteenth-Century Female Philanthropy', in Mary O'Dowd and Maryann Valiulis (eds), *Women and Irish History* (Dublin: Wolfhound Press, 1998), 71–88; quote is on 74.

211. Presentation Annals, quoted in Raughter, 'A Discreet Benevolence', 479. This paragraph follows the argument of this significant article.

212. Ibid., 469.

213. Information from this paragraph is drawn from Eoin Magennis, '"A Land of Milk and Honey": The Physico-Historical Society, Improvement and the Surveys of Mid-Eighteenth-Century Ireland', *Proceedings of the Royal Irish Academy*, 102 C (2002), 199–217.

214. In this it was an endeavour to complete a project that had origins in the Hartlib circle and the work of the Dublin Philosophical Society in the seventeenth century. See Eamon O'Flaherty, 'Medical Men and Learned Societies in Ireland, 1680–1785', in Judith Devlin and H. B. Clark (eds), *European Encounters: Essays in Memory of Albert Lovett* (Dublin: UCD Press, 2003), 261–262, and Toby Barnard, *Improving Ireland? Projectors, Prophets and Profiteers, 1641–1786* (Dublin: Four Courts Press, 2008), 114–115.

215. Charles Smith, *The Ancient and Present State of the County and City of Waterford* (Dublin: A. Reilly, 1746), title page.

216. Ibid., 335, 340.

217. Ibid., viii, ix.

218. Ibid., xiii. The utility of Smith's objectives is underlined in O'Flaherty, 'Medical Men and Learned Societies in Ireland, 1680–1785', 264.

219. Smith, *The Ancient and Present State of the County and City of Waterford*, xiii. Note how this passage avails of a blend of empirical and rational methods to effect change in agricultural practice.

220. Toby Barnard, 'The Wider Cultures of Eighteenth-Century Irish Doctors', in Fiona Clark and James Kelly, *Ireland and Medicine in the Seventeenth and Eighteenth Centuries* (Farnham: Ashgate Press, 2010), 187.

221. Ibid., 188.

222. O'Flaherty, 'Medical Men and Learned Societies in Ireland, 1680–1785', 265–266.

223. Barnard, 'The Wider Cultures of Eighteenth-Century Irish Doctors', 191, 192.

224. This is highlighted in ibid., 191–195, where the medical writings of John Curry (the antiquarian member of the Catholic Committee) and the connection of this Dublin apothecary (through experiments in chemistry conducted with James Tassie) to the development of the paste for cameos are both used as evidence for a wider cultural engagement open to Catholic medics. See also O'Flaherty, 'Medical Men and Learned Societies in Ireland, 1680–1785', 254–255.

225. Maurice Craig, *Dublin, 1660–1860: The Shaping of a City* (1952; Dublin: Liberties Press, 2006), 162 and note.

226. Quoted in Eoin O'Brien, *The Charitable Infirmary Jervis Street, 1718–1987* (Monkstown: Anniversary Press, 1987), 2.

227. Quoted, ibid., 3. By 1749 Fergus was paired with Dr John Curry, the physician and antiquarian.

228. See James Kelly, 'Infanticide in Eighteenth-Century Ireland', *Irish Economic and Social History*, 19 (1992), 5–26.

229. Details in this paragraph are drawn from Fred Powell, 'Dean Swift and the Dublin Foundling Hospital', *Studies: An Irish Quarterly Review*, 70 (1981), 162–170, particularly 166.

230. Detail in this paragraph draws on Beatrice Bayley Butler, 'Lady Arbella Denny, 1707–1792', *Dublin Historical Record*, 9 (1946–7), 1–20. This also provides a summary of the operation of the Magdalen Asylum.

231. Quoted in Peter Gatenby, 'The Meath Hospital, Dublin', *Dublin Historical Record*, 58 (2005), 122.

232. Mel Doyle, 'The Dublin Guilds and Journeymen Clubs', *Saothar*, 3 (1977), 6–14.

233. Robert Ashton, *An Historical Poem in Honour of the Loyal Society of Journeymen Shoemakers* (Dublin: Thomas Walsh, 1727), 1.

234. Henry Nelson, *Poem on the Procession of Journeymen Smiths on May the First 1729* (Dublin: printed for Theophillis Musgrove, 1729), 1. Nelson is part of a tradition of artisan labourers who composed verse. See Thomas Gogarty, 'Henry Jones: Bricklayer and Poet', *Journal of the County Louth Archaeological Society*, 2 (1911), 363–374.

235. Quoted in Clark, *British Clubs and Societies*, 164. The repetition of the final two lines suggests that Nelson may have been cannibalising his own poetry.

236. Ibid., 264.

237. Lisa Marie Griffith, 'The Ouzel Galley Society in the Eighteenth Century: Arbitration Body or Drinking Club?' in Michael Brown and Seán Patrick Donlan (eds), *The Laws and Other Legalities of Ireland* (Farnham: Ashgate Press, 2011), 165–186. See also more briefly, idem, 'Dublin's Commercial Clubs', in Kelly and Powell, *Clubs and Societies in Eighteenth-Century Ireland*, 111–117.

238. Richard Lewis, *The Dublin Guide: or, a Description of the City of Dublin, and the most Remarkable Places within Fifteen Miles* (Dublin: printed for the author, 1787), 198.

239. Ouzel Galley Transactions Book 15 February 1748–18 December 1823. RIA, Ouzel Galley, MSS 12 F 48E, 4 September 1777, quoted in Griffith, 'Ouzel Galley Society', 174.

240. L. M. Cullen, *Princes and Pirates: The Dublin Chamber of Commerce, 1783–1983* (Dublin: Dublin Chamber of Commerce, 1983) 27.

241. Griffith, 'Ouzel Galley Society', 172; Cullen, *Princes and Pirates*, 27.

242. Later meetings took place elsewhere: 'from November 1755 to November 1767 they met at the Rose and Bottle but returned to the Phoenix from 1769, the Eagle Tavern on Eustace Street was their primary residence from November 1769 to 1797'; Griffith, 'Ouzel Galley Society', 173.

243. Ibid., 172–173.

244. Desmond McCabe, 'Travers Hartley', *Dictionary of Irish Biography*, http://dib.cambridge.org (accessed 5 October 2010).

245. Membership details taken from Cullen, *Princes and Pirates*, 28–29.

246. Ibid., 35. See also Lisa Marie Griffith, 'Dublin's Commercial Clubs', 119–120.

247. *Case of the Merchants of Dublin*, quoted in Cullen, *Princes and Pirates*, 35–36.

248. Ibid., 38–39.

249. Craig, *Dublin, 1660–1860*, 221–222.

250. *An Address to the Committee of the Merchants Society* (Dublin, 1761).

251. Cullen, *Pirates and Princes*, 41–42.

252. Petition to the lord lieutenant, quoted in ibid., 42–43.

253. Gandon's career is quickly sketched in Craig, *Dublin, 1660–1860*, 260–282. Craig proposes that 'Four Courts and Custom House must be considered together, for they stand for the two aspects of Gandon's mind. The Four Courts is masculine in feeling, built on cubical if not vertical theme: the Custom House is feminine and predominately horizontal.' Ibid., 274. This resonates with eighteenth-century ideas concerning the masculine quality of public deliberation and a feminine aspect to commercial activity.

254. Quoted ibid., 45.

255. A brief history is offered in Griffith, 'Dublin's Commercial Clubs', 120–123

256. Cullen, *Pirates and Princes*, 46–47.

257. Griffith, 'Dublin's Commercial Clubs', 122–123.

258. Cullen, *Pirates and Princes*, 52–53.

259. Ibid., 46.

260. This account draws on Thomas Bartlett, *The Fall and Rise of the Irish Nation: The Catholic Question, 1690–1830* (Dublin: Irish Academic Press, 1992); Patrick Fagan, *Divided Loyalties: The Question of an Oath for Irish Catholics in the Eighteenth*

Century (Dublin: Four Courts Press, 1997); and Maureen Wall, 'John Keogh and the Catholic Committee', in Gerard O'Brien (ed.), *Catholic Ireland in the Eighteenth Century: The Collected Essays of Maureen Wall* (Dublin: Geography Publications, 1989), 163–170.

261. On this, see Paul Kleber Monod, *The Power of Kings: Monarchy and Religion in Europe, 1589–1715* (New Haven: Yale University Press, 1999).

262. C. J. Woods, 'Thomas Wyse', *Dictionary of Irish Biography*, www.dib.cambridge .org (accessed 3 May 2011).

263. Thomas Wyse, *Historical Sketch of the Late Catholic Association of Ireland*, 2 vols (London: Henry Colburn, 1829), I, 73–84. This Thomas Wyse was the great-grandson of the activist.

264. James Quinn, 'John Curry', *Dictionary of Irish Biography*, www.dib.cambridge.org (accessed 5 September 2010).

265. See R. Dudley Edwards (ed.), 'Minute Book of the Catholic Committee, 1773–92', *Archivium Hibernicum*, 9 (1942), 3, 26.

266. Maureen MacGeehin, 'The Activities and Personnel of the General Committee of the Catholics of Ireland, 1767–1784' (MA thesis, University College Dublin, 1952), 9.

267. Details taken from Irish Legislation Database, www.qub.ac.uk/ild (accessed 29 September 2010).

268. Edwards, 'Minute Book of the Catholic Committee', 28; MacGeehin, 'The Activities and Personnel', 7. MacNamara was a lawyer with expertise in convey-ancing and was, at least nominally, an Anglican.

269. Bartlett, *Fall and Rise of the Irish Nation*, 76.

270. The list is taken from MacGeehin, 'The Activities and Personnel', 31.

271. These are all mentioned in Edwards, 'Minute Book of the Catholic Committee', passim.

272. Ibid., 13, 3, 9, 12, 30.

273. Ibid., 14.

274. Thomas Bartlett argued: 'The organisation that did emerge during the late 1750s and early 1760s was for long distinguished more by its long periods of inertia (punctuated by bitter internal wrangling) than by its forceful statement of Catholic grievances. In the period before 1790 one would be hard pressed to point to any indubitable, concrete achievement can be attributed to it. None the less, the emer-gence of a Catholic association or committee, its very existence over a period of time, its tentative nationwide structure and its function as a forum in which the concerns of all Catholics could be discussed . . . were all of vital importance. For Catholics to meet together publicly, in a representative guise and in an ordered fashion with a secretary, membership lists, minutes and, later, funding, was a striking development . . . The Catholic Committee (its title for most of this period) educated Catholics to the realities of power, put the Catholic question on the

political agenda and, through its petitioning efforts, helped in the politicisation of the Catholic people of Ireland.' *Fall and Rise of the Irish Nation*, 60.

275. This is to follow the analysis offered by Claire O'Halloran who writes of 'the Patriot agenda of the Academy', of the 'overall political focus of the academy', and of how 'recent political developments, notably the achievement of legislative independence, were equally important in providing its members with a sense of purpose'. *Golden Ages and Barbarous Nations: Antiquarian Debate and Cultural Politics in Ireland, c1750–1800* (Cork: Cork University Press, 2004), 167, 167, 166–167.

276. Robert Burrowes, preface to *Transactions of the Royal Irish Academy: Volume One* (Dublin: Royal Irish Academy, 1787), xvi.

277. Ibid., x.

278. Ibid., xiv.

279. R. B. McDowell, 'The Main Narrative', in T. Ó Raifeartaigh, *The Royal Irish Academy: A Bicentennial History 1785–1985* (Dublin: Royal Irish Academy, 1985), 8–9.

280. Burrowes, preface to *Transactions of the Royal Irish Academy*, xiv.

281. McDowell, 'The Main Narrative', 9.

282. James Kelly, 'Lord Charlemont and Learning', *Proceedings of the Royal Irish Academy*, 106 C (2006), 395–409.

283. For this context, see chapter eight below.

284. *Charter and Statutes of the Royal Irish Academy for Promoting the Study of Science, Polite Literature and Antiquities* (Dublin: Luke White, 1786), 5.

285. The other important contemporary survivor is the Dublin Society, which was itself granted a royal charter in 1750. Walter D. Love has premised that 'it may be that the Academy succeeded where the Antiquarian Society failed because the Academy devoted itself to a wider range of interests.' 'The Hibernian Antiquarian Society', 419.

286. Burrowes, preface to *Transactions of the Royal Irish Academy*, xv–xvi.

287. R. B. McDowell accepted this reasoning, arguing 'ex-officio patrons, though decorative, can be somewhat incongruous; but George III, who was encouraging Herschel and building up the great royal library which was to form the nucleus of the British Museum, was eminently suited to be the first patron of a learned society.' 'The Main Narrative', 10.

288. *Charter and Statutes*, 3–4.

289. Ibid., 9–10.

290. For the details of these measures see chapter five above.

291. 'Burrowes, preface to *Transactions of the Royal Irish Academy*, xi.

292. Michael Brown, 'Configuring the Irish Enlightenment: Reading the *Transactions of the Royal Irish Academy*', in Kelly and Powell, *Clubs and Societies in Eighteenth-Century Ireland*, 163–178.

293. McDowell, 'The Main Narrative', 10.

294. Charles O'Conor's circle of acquaintance included notably Edmund Burke and

Robert Clayton. See Walter D. Love, 'Charles O'Conor of Belanagare and Thomas Leland's "Philosophical" History of Ireland', *Irish Historical Studies*, 13 (1962), 1–25; Macdara Dwyer, 'Sir Isaac Newton's Enlightened Chronology and Inter-denominational Discourse in Eighteenth-Century Ireland', *Irish Historical Studies*, 39 (2014), 222–229.

295. McDowell, 'The Main Narrative', 12, 13.

7. A Culture of Trust?

1. On Brooke, see D. A. R. Caird, 'Charlotte Brooke', in *Dictionary of Irish Biography*, www.dib.cambridge.org (accessed 12 May 2011); Lesa Ní Mhunghaile (ed.), *Reliques of Irish Poetry* (Dublin: Irish Manuscripts Commission, 2009), xxi–xliv.

2. On Brooke's management of the relationship between Irish and English, see Lesa Ní Mhunghaile, 'The Intersection between Oral Tradition, Manuscript and Print Cultures in Charlotte Brooke's *Reliques of Irish Poetry* (1789)', in Marc Caball and Andrew Carpenter (eds), *Oral and Print Cultures in Ireland, 1600–1900* (Dublin: Four Courts Press, 2010), 14–31.

3. Charlotte Brooke, *Reliques of Irish Poetry* (Dublin: George Bonham, 1789), 265–324.

4. Ibid., 230.

5. For examples of how she bowdlerised some of the compositions to accord with eighteenth-century ideas of propriety, see Ní Mhunghaile, 'The Intersection between Oral Tradition, Manuscript and Print Cultures', 24–26.

6. For a considered treatment of Brooke's use of the form, see Leith Davis, 'Charlotte Brooke's *Reliques of Irish Poetry:* Eighteenth-Century "Irish Song" and the Politics of Remediation', in John Kirk, Andrew Noble, and Michael Brown (eds), *United Islands? The Languages of Resistance* (London: Pickering & Chatto Press, 2012), 95–108.

7. Brooke, *Reliques of Irish Poetry*, 245.

8. For a treatment of this theme from a legal vantage point, see Michael Brown and Seán Patrick Donlan, 'The Laws in Ireland, 1689–1850: A Brief Introduction', in Michael Brown and Seán Patrick Donlan (eds), *The Laws and Other Legalities of Ireland, 1689–1850* (Farnham: Ashgate Press, 2011), 1–32.

9. From a large literature on the sociological idea of trust, see Niklas Luhmann, *Trust and Power* (Chichester: Wiley, 1979); Adam B. Seligman, *The Problem of Trust* (Princeton: Princeton University Press, 1997); Piotr Sztompka, *Trust: A Sociological Theory* (Cambridge: Cambridge University Press, 1999); and Geoffrey Hoskins, *Trust: A History* (Oxford: Oxford University Press, 2014).

10. This was the heyday of the stage Irishman. See, for instance, Sir Lucius O'Trigger in Richard Brinsley Sheridan, *The Rivals* (1775), in Richard Brinsley Sheridan, *The School for Scandal and Other Plays*, Eric Rump (ed.) (London: Penguin, 1988), 29–124.

11. Jacques Ellul, 'Politicisation and Political Solutions', in Kenneth S. Templeton Jr (ed.), *The Politicization of Society* (Indianapolis: Liberty Fund, 1979), 209–247.

12. Brooke, *Reliques of Irish Poetry*, v–vi.

13. Ibid., iii. On the social circle that helped and supported her work, see Lesa Ní Mhunghaile, 'Charlotte Brooke, her Political and Literary Connections and the Genesis of *Reliques of Irish Poetry* (1789)', *Breifne* 12 (2011), 245–261.

14. Brooke, *Reliques of Irish Poetry*, v.

15. Ibid., iv.

16. Ibid., v.

17. Ibid., iii.

18. [Henry Brooke], *A Fragment of the History of Patrick* (London [Dublin], 1753), 12.

19. A useful treatment of this pamphlet is to be found in Jacqueline Hill, '"Allegories, Fictions and Feigned Representations": Decoding the Money Bill Dispute, 1752–6', *Eighteenth-Century Ireland*, 21 (2006), 72–74. For a full treatment of Henry Brooke, see Michael Brown, 'Farmer and Fool: Henry Brooke and the Languages of Enlightenment', in Brown and Donlan, *The Law and Other Legalities of Ireland, 1688–1848*, 301–324.

20. The proposal to unite the parliaments was uttered by Lord Hillsborough in 1751, and met with strong opposition. A discussion was also held in 1753 between Arthur Dobbs and Lord Pelham, the British prime minister. See Martyn Powell, *Britain and Ireland in the Eighteenth-Century Crisis of Empire* (Houndmills: Palgrave Macmillan, 2003), 26.

21. [Brooke], *A Fragment of the History of Patrick*, 14n.

22. Ibid., 11.

23. Declan O'Donovan cites 'more prosperous economic conditions and . . . improvements in revenue collection' as the source of the surplus: 'The Money Bill Dispute of 1753', in Thomas Bartlett and D. W. Hayton (eds), *Penal Era and Golden Age: Essays in Irish History, 1690–1800* (Belfast: Belfast Historical Foundation, 1979), 59.

24. The history of the Irish national debt is discussed in Charles Ivar McGrath, 'The Irish Experience of "Financial Revolution", 1660–1760', in Charles Ivar McGrath and Christopher Fauske (eds), *Money, Power and Print: Interdisciplinary Studies on the Financial Revolution in the British Isles* (Cranbury: University of Delaware Press, 2008), 157–188.

25. See Eoin Magennis, *The Irish Political System 1740–65: The Golden Age of the Undertakers* (Dublin: Four Courts Press, 2000), 37, 67–68.

26. Powell, *Britain and Ireland in the Eighteenth-Century Crisis*, 29; O'Donovan, 'The Money Bill Dispute', 64. Magennis states the division was 123 to 118. See Magennis, *The Irish Political System*, 82

27. On the vagaries of this political rivalry in this period, see Magennis, *The Irish*

Political System, 62–92. See also Powell, *Britain and Ireland in the Eighteenth-Century Crisis*, 16–47, who emphasises the intrusion of Britain into the mechanics of Irish domestic politics.

28. This took some time, with parliament having been prorogued on 5 February 1754, before the administration finally got the permission of London to remove Boyle himself from post, which occurred on 19 April 1754. He was replaced as lord justice by Lord Bessborough, father of John Ponsonby. Some allies were dismissed as early as February.

29. Magennis, *The Irish Political System*, 93–100.

30. On Dorset's use of the politics of display, see O'Donovan, 'The Money Bill Dispute', 77–78. Helen Burke notes that 'the rise in the number of viceregal command performances at the playhouse during the tenure of this viceroy (for example from four during the 1749–50 season to twenty-four during the 1751–2 season) can be read in a similar ideological light; as in earlier periods of crisis, the administration was turning to the playhouse to court the Irish élite and to showcase its presence and power'. *Riotous Performances: The Struggle for Hegemony in the Irish Theater, 1712–1784* (Notre Dame: University of Notre Dame Press, 2003), 222.

31. On this context, see O'Donovan, 'The Money Bill Dispute', 74–79.

32. Unfinished in that encomiums were certainly still composed. See, for example, the verse prologue with which Thomas Sheridan greeted the Duke of Dorset's first visit to Smock-Alley in October 1751: 'Parent *Hibernia*, heav'n protected isle / Thro' time's dark cloud what joyful prospect smile? / Just is the loud applause that fills thy land, / When *George* commits the reins to *Dorset's* hand.' Quoted in Burke, *Riotous Performances*, 222. See also ibid., 223. It should also be noted that the political aspect of the public sphere may well have been spluttering into life since the Wood's halfpence affair at least. Swift's political satires, including 'The Legion Club', are sufficient evidence to suggest this. See also Sean Moore, *Swift, the Book and the Irish Financial Revolution: Satire and Sovereignty in Colonial Ireland* (Baltimore: Johns Hopkins University Press, 2010), 190–213.

33. A pamphlet war broke out over the money bill following its rejection, with the government side being advertised in [Christopher Robinson], *Considerations on the Late Bill for Payment of the Remainder of the National Debt* (Dublin: R. James, 1754). The Patriot stance is enunciated in [Sir Richard Cox], *The Proceedings of the Honourable House of Commons of Ireland in Rejecting the Altered Money Bill* (Dublin: Printed for Peter Wilson, 1754). In *The Irish Political System*, 86, Magennis describes this pamphlet as being 'crucial to the politicisation' of the public. A précis of the pamphlet war can be found in O'Donovan, 'The Money Bill Dispute', 70–74.

34. *By the Lord Lieutenant and Council of Ireland, A Proclamation* (February, 1754).

35. See the maps of Patriot activity presented in Bob Harris, *Politics and the Nation: Britain in the Mid-Eighteenth Century* (Oxford: Oxford University Press, 2002),

222–223. There is a list of the fifteen 'known clubs' offered in Bob Harris, 'The Patriot Clubs of the 1750s', in James Kelly and Martyn Powell (eds), *Clubs and Societies in Eighteenth-Century Ireland* (Dublin: Four Courts Press, 2010), 233.

36. This account draws on the thoughtful reading of this event in Burke, *Riotous Performances*, 209–240.

37. Burke suggests this disruption was a 'continuation of [a tradition] of Patriot counter-theatre'. *Riotous Performances*, 229.

38. Quoted in ibid., 230.

39. Victor Cousin quoted in ibid., 209 and 210.

40. For a similar turning of a Voltaire piece attacking superstition into an attack on Stone and the Castle, see Tim Conway and Graham Gargett, 'Voltaire's *La Voix du sage et du peuple* in Ireland: Or Enlightened Anticlericalism in Two Jurisdictions?' *Eighteenth-Century Ireland*, 20 (2005), 79–90.

41. For a discussion of the other terms, see Eoin Kinsella, '"In Pursuit of a Positive Construction": Irish Catholics and the Williamite Articles of Surrender, 1690–1701', *Eighteenth-Century Ireland*, 24 (2009), 11–35.

42. John Curry, *An Historical and Critical Review of the Civil Wars in Ireland*, 2 vols (Dublin: Printed for Luke White, 1786), II, 225.

43. Anonymous, *Humble Remonstrance for the Repeal of the Laws Against the Roman Catholics* (Dublin: Printed for B. Corcoran, 1778), 12.

44. [John Curry, with Charles O'Conor], *Observations on the Popery Laws* (Dublin: T. Ewing, 1771), 16, 9.

45. Ibid., 17.

46. Ibid., 37–38.

47. Ibid., 22.

48. Ibid., 12.

49. Ibid.

50. Ibid., 14.

51. In this, the pamphlet supports Thomas Bartlett's assertion that 'the historical writings of Curry and O'Conor signalled the end of Catholic quiescence and the beginnings of a Catholic challenge to the intellectual props of the penal laws'. *The Rise and Fall of the Irish Nation: The Catholic Question, 1690–1830* (Dublin: Irish Academic Press, 1992), 52. It also links to a growing confidence in the Catholic community discussed in chapter eight.

52. [Curry, with O'Conor], *Observations on the Popery Laws*, 23.

53. Ibid., 19.

54. Ibid., 40–41.

55. Ibid., 5–6.

56. Arthur Browne, *A Brief Review of the Question whether the Articles of Limerick have been Violated?* (Dublin: William M'Kenzie, 1788), 70–71.

57. Ibid., 22–24, for example.

58. Ibid., 26.

59. Ibid., 39.

60. Ibid., 46.

61. Ibid.

62. Ibid., 4.

63. Ibid., 59.

64. Ibid., 56.

65. Ibid., 57.

66. Ibid., 66. For a direct rebuttal, see [An Unbiased Irishman], *The Question Considered Have the Articles of Limerick been Violated, being Strictures on Mr Browne's Brief Review* (Dublin: J. Chambers, 1783),

67. See Ursula Haskins Gonthier, *Montesquieu and England: Enlightened Exchanges, 1689–1755* (London: Pickering & Chatto Press, 2010).

68. Writing of a division in the Hibernian Antiquarian Society in the 1780s, Clare O'Halloran observes, 'Clearly, the main tension was political and not simply a matter of personality. The enduring colonial debate was being played out in an ostensibly scholarly arena; projected onto the remote past, in which imagination was allowed full rein, and political opinion could be voiced in a coded way.' '"A Revolution in our Moral and Civil Affairs": Charles O'Conor and the Creation of a Community of Scholars in late Eighteenth-Century Ireland', in Luke Gibbons and Kieran O'Conor (eds), *Charles O'Conor of Ballinagare: Life and Works* (Dublin: Four Courts Press, 2015), 90.

69. See Walter D. Love, 'Charles O'Conor of Belanagare and Thomas Leland's "Philosophical" History of Ireland', *Irish Historical Studies*, 13 (1962), 1–25.

70. On Scottish history writing in this period, see David Allan, *Virtue, Learning and the Scottish Enlightenment: Ideas of Scholarship and Society in Early Modern Scotland* (Edinburgh: Edinburgh University Press, 1993); Colin Kidd, *Subverting Scotland's Past: Scottish Whig Historians and the Creation of Anglo-British Identity* (Cambridge: Cambridge University Press, 1993); Nicholas Phillipson, *Hume* (London: Weidenfeld and Nicolson, 1989); J. G. A. Pocock, *Barbarism and Religion*, Volume Two: *Narratives of Civil Government* (Cambridge: Cambridge University Press, 2001).

71. Both Burke and O'Conor are quoted in Love, 'Charles O'Conor of Belanagare and Thomas Leland', 2, 3.

72. Thomas Leland, *The History of Ireland from the Invasion of Henry II*, 3 vols (Cork: D. Donnoghue, 1775), I, iv–v.

73. Ibid., I, x.

74. See Claire O'Halloran, *Golden Ages and Barbarous Nations: Antiquarian Debate and Cultural Politics in Ireland, c.1750–1800* (Cork: Cork University Press, 2004), 14–15. As she notes, the Nordic myth had significant support in Scotland and was

given influential voice by James Macpherson in the Ossian texts, and more stringently by the Scottish antiquary John Pinkerton, who further replaced a Celtic origin with a Pictish one.

75. Leland, *The History of Ireland*, I, x.

76. Ibid., I, xv–xvii.

77. Ibid., I, xvii.

78. Ibid., III, 96.

79. Ibid., III, 98.

80. Ibid., III, 107.

81. Ibid., III, 122.

82. Ibid., III, 131–132.

83. Quoted in Love, 'Leland's "Philosophical" History of Ireland', 15.

84. For a useful disentanglement of these polemical controversies that engulfed Irish history writing in this period, see O'Halloran, *Golden Ages*, 41–70 (on the controversy of origins), and 141–157 (on the 1641 rebellion).

85. Leland, *History of Ireland*, III, 130, 131.

86. See, for instance, the debate which developed about the number of casualties involved in the Ulster Rising of 1641; on which see Eoin Magennis, 'A "Beleaguered Protestant"? Walter Harris and the Writing of *Fiction Unmasked*', *Eighteenth-Century Ireland*, 13 (1998), 86–111. The key statements of the two positions are [John Curry], *Brief Account from the Most Authentic Protestant Writers of the Causes, Motives and Mischief's of the Irish Rebellion on the 23rd Day of October 1641* (London, 1747); and Walter Harris, *Fiction Unmasked . . . in a Dialogue Between a Protestant and a Papist* (Dublin: printed for William Williamson, 1757).

87. On the polemical uses of St Patrick, see Clare O'Halloran, '"The Island of Saints and Scholars": Views of the Early Church and Sectarian Politics in Late Eighteenth-Century Ireland', *Eighteenth-Century Ireland*, 5 (1990), 7–20.

88. For an overview of his career, see Diarmaid Ó Catháin, 'Some Account of Charles O'Conor and Literacy in Irish in His Time', in Gibbons and O'Conor (eds), *Charles O'Conor of Ballinagare*, 28–51. For his intellectual engagements with European thought, see Hilary Larkin, 'Writing in an Enlightened Age? Charles O'Conor and the Philosophes', in ibid., 97–115.

89. For some thoughtful remarks about the themes on which O'Conor focussed, see John Wrynn, 'Charles O'Conor as a "Philosophical Historian"', in ibid., 72–80.

90. Charles O'Conor, *Dissertations on the Ancient History of Ireland* (Dublin: James Hoey, 1753), 122.

91. Ibid., 133–134.

92. Ibid., 138.

93. Ibid., 139–140.

94. Ibid., 123–124.

95. For a postcolonial reading of O'Conor's *Dissertations*, see Thomas McLoughlin, *Contesting Ireland: Irish Voices Against England in the Eighteenth Century* (Dublin: Four Courts Press, 1999), 135–160. See also Luke Gibbons, '"A Foot in Both Camps": Charles O'Conor, Print Culture and the Counter-Public Sphere', in Gibbons and O'Conor, *Charles O'Conor of Ballinagare*, 116–132.

96. O'Conor, *Dissertations*, 140, 125n.

97. Ibid., 11.

98. Ibid., 12.

99. Love, 'Leland's "Philosophical" History of Ireland', 6.

100. Quoted in O'Halloran, *Golden Ages and Barbarous Nations*, 38. O'Conor later became a member of the Royal Irish Academy.

101. 'Consider a clutch of names associated with the mid-eighteenth century English movement of sensibility and sentimentalism: *Steele*, Hume, Ferguson, Burns, *Goldsmith*, Adam Smith, Mackenzie, Hugh Blair, *Frances Sheridan*, Sterne, *Charlotte Brooke, Henry Brooke, Hutcheson*, Macpherson, *Burke, Macklin, Hugh Kelly*, David Fordyce. All of these authors are either Irish or Scottish'. Terry Eagleton, 'The Good-Natured Gael', *Crazy John and the Bishop and Other Essays in Irish Culture* (Cork: Cork University Press, 1998), 68. I have placed the Irish writers in italics.

102. Ian Campbell Ross, 'Sheridan, Frances (1724–1766)', *Dictionary of National Biography*, www.odnb.com (accessed 20 July 2014).

103. The novel is read as an exploration into the demands of Christian Stoicism in Susan Staves, *Women's Writing in Britain, 1660–1789* (Cambridge: Cambridge University Press, 2006), 346. In this, it is akin to the Stoic parable written by Oliver Goldsmith, *The Vicar of Wakefield*, Stephen Coote (ed.) (1766; London: Penguin, 1982). For a discussion of the formal relationship between the two novels, see Morris Golden, '*Sidney Bidulph* and *The Vicar of Wakefield*', *Modern Language Studies*, 9 (1979), 33–35.

104. Frances Sheridan, *Memoirs of Miss Sidney Bidulph* (1761; Oxford: Oxford University Press, 1999), 28.

105. Ibid., 91.

106. As Patricia Meyer Spackes has observed, 'In the harrowing narrative of women's experience that constitutes *Memoirs of Miss Sidney Bidulph* . . . each refusal of utterance entails sequences of imposed suffering'. Yet, the central problematic of the text was that, Spackes further contends, 'if Sidney causes her own suffering, she does so by being too good, in the most orthodox female fashion', raising the question 'is female goodness an inevitable agent of suffering?' 'Oscillations of Sensibility', *New Literary History*, 25 (1994), 509, 510. This paradox is equally understood by Janet Todd in writing more generally of the trope of female suffering that 'the implication of misery in sensibility was a particular concern of women since, by the late eighteenth century, their perceived identity was inseparable from the quality.' *Sensibility: An Introduction* (London: Methuen, 1986), 61.

107. Sheridan, *Memoirs of Miss Sidney Bidulph*, 120.

108. Ibid., 130.

109. For the role of the thwarted lover, see Kathleen M. Oliver, 'Frances Sheridan's Faulkland, the Silenced, Emasculated, Ideal Male', *Studies in English Literature, 1500–1900*, 43 (2003), 683–700.

110. Sheridan, *Memoirs of Miss Sidney Bidulph*, 48–49. For a treatment that concentrates on the role of Miss Burchell, see Anna M. Fitzer, 'Mrs Sheridan's Active Demon: *Memoirs of Miss Sidney Bidulph* and the Sly Rake in Petticoats', *Eighteenth-Century Ireland*, 18 (2003), 39–62.

111. As Susan Staves notes, 'Sidney's marriage becomes simultaneously an act of obedience to a beloved parent and a generous gesture towards an unfortunate woman: it has nothing to do with the gratification of her own desires'. *Women's Writing in Britain*, 348.

112. Sheridan, *Memoirs of Miss Sidney Bidulph*, 84.

113. Ibid., 85.

114. Ibid.

115. Ibid., 88.

116. See Todd, *Sensibility*; G. J. Barker-Benfield, *The Culture of Sensibility: Sex and Society in Eighteenth-Century Britain* (Chicago: University of Chicago Press, 1996).

117. Sheridan, *Memoirs of Miss Sidney Bidulph*, 154.

118. Ibid., 304.

119. Beverly E. Schneller, 'Kelly, Hugh (1739–1777)', *Oxford Dictionary of National Biography*, www.odnb.com (accessed 20 July 2014).

120. 'Throughout the novel Kelly's sentimentalism corresponds more to sentiment—to moral thought that is—than it does to the more modern notion of sentimentalism as excessive emotion'. Robert R. Bataille, *The Writing Life of Hugh Kelly: Politics, Journalism and Theatre in Late Eighteenth-Century London* (Carbondale: Southern Illinois University Press, 2000), 33.

121. Hugh Kelly, *Memoirs of a Magdalen; or the History of Louisa Mildmay* (London: Printed for W. Griffin, 1782), 18.

122. Ibid., 6.

123. Ibid., 7.

124. Ibid., 18.

125. Susan Staves, 'British Seduced Maidens', *Eighteenth-Century Studies*, 14 (1980–1981), 109–134, studies the wider genre in which Hugh Kelly's *Memoirs* operates.

126. Kelly, *Memoirs of a Magdalen*, 23.

127. Ibid., 24, 26.

128. Ibid., 62.

129. Ibid., 71.

130. Ibid., 73.

131. The regimen under which she lived is not described in the novel; a point made in Bataille, *The Writing Life of Hugh Kelly*, 32–33. However, see Sarah Lloyd, '"Pleasure's Golden Bait": Prostitution, Poverty and the Magdalen Hospital in Eighteenth-Century London', *History Workshop Journal*, 41 (1996), 50–70.

132. Kelly, *Memoirs of a Magdalen*, 73.

133. Ibid., 42.

134. Ibid., 67.

135. Ibid., 70.

136. Ibid., 5.

137. Ibid., 14.

138. Ibid., 27.

139. Ibid., 38.

140. For an important construction of this broader tradition of self-consciously Irish drama performed within the country, see Christopher J. Wheatley, *Beneath Iërne's Banners: Irish Protestant Drama of the Restoration and Eighteenth Century* (Notre Dame: University of Notre Dame Press, 1999); for an analysis more informed by changes in the rank and class of audience and characters, see Desmond Slowey, *The Radicalisation of Irish Drama: The Rise and Fall of Ascendancy Theatre* (Dublin: Irish Academic Press, 2008).

141. On Charles Macklin, see J. O. Bartley (ed.), *Four Comedies by Charles Macklin* (London: Sidgwick and Jackson, 1968), 1–33; Robert R. Findlay, 'The Comic Plays of Charles Macklin: Dark Satire at Mid-Eighteenth Century', *Educational Theatre Journal*, 20 (1968), 398–407; Paul Goring, '"John Bull, pit, box and gallery said No!" Charles Macklin and the Limits of Ethnic Resistance on the Eighteenth-Century London Stage', *Representations*, 79 (2002), 61–81.

142. See Michael Griffin, *Enlightenment in Ruins: The Geographies of Oliver Goldsmith* (Lewisburg: Bucknell Press, 2013), for an informative treatment of Goldsmith's writings.

143. Charles Macklin, *Love à la Mode*, in Bartley (ed.), *Four Comedies by Charles Macklin*, 45.

144. Ibid., 45.

145. Ibid.

146. Ibid., 46.

147. Ibid., 46.

148. Bartley (ed.), *Four Comedies by Charles Macklin*, 16–17.

149. Macklin, *Love à la Mode*, 59.

150. Ibid., 75.

151. Ibid., 73.

152. Ibid.

153. Ibid., 72.

154. Oliver Goldsmith, *The Collected Works of Oliver Goldsmith*, 5 vols, Arthur Freidman (ed.) (Oxford: Clarendon Press, 1966), V, 215.

155. Ibid., 181. 'Insolence' is a central term within the play and is used repeatedly throughout.

156. Ibid., 198–199.

157. Ibid., 159–160.

158. Ibid., 169.

159. Ibid., 168, 170.

160. Ibid., 170.

161. Ibid., 146.

162. Ibid., 148.

163. Ibid., 169.

164. Ibid., 212.

165. Ibid., 176, 186.

166. Ibid., 186.

167. Ibid., 199.

168. Ibid., 201.

169. Ibid., 216.

170. Situating *She Stoops to Conquer* in a similarly allegorical light, but one which offers a colonial rather than a religious reading, Michael Griffin writes of how 'Marlow's chauvinism is, in the end, problematized by the realisation that his supposed superiority is no more than a fiction of the scenario into which he has been fooled. Thus he earns, through the mistakes of a night, a greater critical self-awareness, a quality which, cumulatively, Goldsmith's writings try to instigate at the level of the nation. In the place of chauvinism, Goldsmith recommends that other societies be viewed, as far as possible, from below, so that a greater cultural empathy, and a better understanding of how societies function, or fail to function, might be made available.' *Enlightenment in Ruins: The Geographies of Oliver Goldsmith*, 84. I would like to thank Dr Michael Griffin for discussing this.

171. Writing of the stage Irishman, Desmond Slowey remarks on how 'the internal opposition that is captured within these Irish characters, between their mercenary brains and the quixotic gallantry of their hearts, is repeated in the comparable tension articulated between them and the society that spawned them. They are outcasts from that society, removed from it spiritually as well as spatially. This duality reaches its highest expression in the work of Oliver Goldsmith and Thomas Sheridan's son, Richard Brinsley Sheridan. Though none of their plays are set in Ireland, in them the idea of alternate selves is almost a commonplace.' *The Radicalisation of Irish Drama,* 146. This is a reference to Sheridan's *The Rivals*, in which Sir Lucius O'Trigger appears.

172. Ireland appears in Sheridan when Mr Arnold retreats to his estate there; Hugh

Kelly has an Irish servant appear, described as an 'honest Hibernian' working for Louisa's brother. His sensibility is evidenced by having him say, 'The honour of a good family is a very nice affair; I am come from as good a family myself as any in Ireland and know how to feel for such a misfortune as has happened to my master's', even as his temerity in equating the rank of servant and master is dismissed as 'egotism'. *Memoirs of a Magdalen*, 40.

173. Thomas Bartlett, 'The Townshend Viceroyalty, 1767–72', in Bartlett and Hayton (eds), *Penal Era and Golden Age*, 88–112. I would like to thank Professor Patrick Griffin for discussing the importance of this episode.

8. Fracturing the Irish Enlightenment

1. I. R. McBride, *Scripture Politics: Ulster Presbyterians and Irish Radicalism in the Late Eighteenth Century* (Oxford: Oxford University Press, 1998), 142.

2. From a vast literature on classical republicanism, see Caroline Robbins, *The Eighteenth-Century Commonwealthman: Studies in the Transmission, Development and Circumstance of English Liberal Thought from the Restoration of Charles II to the War with the Thirteen Colonies* (Cambridge: Harvard University Press, 1959) and J. G. A. Pocock, *The Machiavellian Moment: Florentine Political Thought and the Atlantic Republican Tradition* (Princeton: Princeton University Press, 1975). On natural law traditions of political thought, see Richard Tuck, *Philosophy and Government, 1572–1651* (Cambridge: Cambridge University Press, 1993). For the emergence of commercial republicanism, see Knud Haakonssen, *Natural Law and Moral Philosophy: From Grotius to the Scottish Enlightenment* (Cambridge: Cambridge University Press, 1996). On the place of Ireland in these discussions, see James Livesey, *Civil Society and Empire: Ireland and Scotland in the Eighteenth-Century Atlantic World* (New Haven: Yale University Press, 2009); Stephen Small, *Political Thought in Ireland 1776–1798: Republicanism, Patriotism and Radicalism* (Oxford: Oxford University Press, 2002).

3. *History of the Proceedings and Debates of the Volunteer Delegates of Ireland on the Subject of a Parliamentary Reform* (Dublin: W. Porter, 1784), 11. The convention actually opened on 10 November.

4. McBride, *Scripture Politics*, 142.

5. *History of the Proceedings and Debates of the Volunteer Delegates*, 24, 25.

6. Ibid., 19.

7. Ibid., 20.

8. Ibid., 21.

9. Ibid., 23.

10. A useful narrative account of the Grand National Convention can be found in

Patrick Rogers, *The Irish Volunteers and Catholic Emancipation 1778–1793: A Neglected Phase of Ireland's History* (London: Burns, Oates and Washbourne, 1934), 113–133.

11. *History of the Proceedings and Debates of the Volunteer Delegates*, 30.

12. Ibid., 35.

13. Ibid., 78. The extent to which Ogle was put up to the affair by the Castle administration, or acted independently, is contested. See Thomas Bartlett, *The Fall and Rise of the Irish Nation: The Catholic Question, 1690–1830* (Dublin: Irish Academic Press, 1992), 107.

14. *History of the Proceedings and Debates of the Volunteer Delegates*, 50.

15. See ibid., 49–51.

16. Ibid., 49.

17. Ibid., 76.

18. Ibid., 77.

19. Ibid., 78.

20. Ibid., 57, 69.

21. Ibid., 93.

22. Ibid., 97.

23. Ibid., 72.

24. Ibid.

25. Rogers, *The Irish Volunteers*, 130–131.

26. McBride, *Scripture Politics*, 143.

27. On this theme, see Neal Garnham, *The Militia in Eighteenth-Century Ireland: In Defence of the Protestant Interest* (Woodbridge: Boydell Press, 2012), 101–122.

28. Smyth, 'The Volunteers and Parliament', 123n44.

29. Ibid., 131n74.

30. Rogers, *The Irish Volunteers and Catholic Emancipation*, 69–70.

31. Danny Mansergh renders the narrative of the three conventions as a tragic tale of the rise and fall of Francis Dobbs, acting as the 'conductor' of the first, enacting a 'tactical error' by holding the second, and being excluded mortifyingly from the third. *Grattan's Failure: Parliamentary Opposition and the People in Ireland, 1779–1800* (Dublin: Irish Academic Press, 2005), 27–105, quotes at 65, 81.

32. Volunteer 'public festivities' date back to at least 4 November 1779 when on the anniversary of William III's birthday College Green was the site of a protest demanding free trade. From the start this intrusion into the political public sphere was contested by the government. See Padhraig Higgins, *A Nation of Politicians: Gender, Patriotism and Political Culture in Late Eighteenth-Century Ireland* (Madison: University of Wisconsin Press, 2010), 70–81.

33. Samuel Butler, *A Sermon Preached in the Parish Church of St Michan, Dublin. . . . Before the Goldsmith's Company of Volunteers in Dublin* (Dublin: M. Mills, 1779), 8.

34. Ibid., 9.

35. Ibid., 12–13.

36. The corpus of Presbyterian Volunteer sermons is surveyed in Michael O'Connor, '"Ears Stunned with the Din of Arms": Belfast, Volunteer Sermons and James Magee, 1779–1781', *Eighteenth-Century Ireland*, 26 (2011), 51–79.

37. William Steele Dickson, *A Sermon on the Propriety and Advantages of Acquiring the Knowledge and Use of Arms, in Times of Public Danger* (Belfast: James Magee, 1779), 22.

38. Ibid., 19.

39. Ibid., 8.

40. Both Dickson's sermon and that of Alexander are treated within a wider Presbyterian tradition of war sermons in Allan Blackstock, 'Armed Citizens and Christian Soldiers: Crisis Sermons and Ulster Presbyterians, 1715–1803', *Eighteenth-Century Ireland*, 22 (2007), 81–105.

41. Andrew Alexander, *The Advantage of a General Knowledge of the Use of Arms* (Strabane: James Blyth, 1779), 22.

42. Ibid.

43. Thomas Drought, *Letters on Subjects Interesting to Ireland and Addressed to the Irish Volunteers* (Dublin: W. Colles, 1783), 7.

44. Francis Dobbs, *Thoughts on Volunteering* (Dublin: M. Mills, 1781), 11.

45. Amyas Griffith in *Dublin Evening Post*, 4 August 1778, cited in Martyn Powell, *The Politics of Consumption in Eighteenth-Century Ireland* (Houndmills: Palgrave Macmillan, 2005), 91.

46. *Limerick Chronicle*, 1 August 1782, cited in Stephen O'Connor, 'The Volunteers, 1778–1793: Iconography and Identity', (PhD thesis, National University of Ireland Maynooth, 2008), 77.

47. See Higgins, *A Nation of Politicians*, 166–170, for a reading of the uniform as carrying 'symbols of a heroic masculinity'. Ibid., 167.

48. O'Connor, 'The Volunteers, 1778–1793', passim. I am very grateful to Stephen O'Connor for supplying me with a copy of his thesis, on which I rely for much of my understanding of the Volunteers' politics of display.

49. Cited in Breandán Mac Suibhne, 'Whiskey, Potatoes and Paddies: Volunteering and the Construction of the Irish Nation in Northwest Ulster, 1778–1782', in Eoin Magennis and Peter Jupp (eds), *Crowds in Ireland c.1720–1920* (London: Palgrave Macmillan, 2000), 60.

50. *History of the Proceedings of the Volunteer Delegates*, 47.

51. Cited in Peter Smyth, '"Our Cloud Cap't Grenadiers": The Volunteers as a Military Force', *The Irish Sword*, 13 (1978–1979), 199–200.

52. Ibid., 204. For a full description of this event, held on 10–12 August 1780, which contradicts the sense of disorder and instead describes it as a 'resounding success', see Mac Suibhne, 'Whiskey, Potatoes and Paddies', 72–74, quote at 72.

53. On the 'spectacle of Volunteering', see Higgins, *A Nation of Politicians*, 170–173.

54. See, for instance, Pádraig Ó Snodaigh, 'Class and the Irish Volunteers', *The Irish Sword*, 16 (1984–6), 168–169

55. *History of the Proceedings and Debates of the Volunteer Delegates*, 26.

56. Martyn Powell's study of the phenomenon concludes that it was 'a means of uniting a political grouping in an atmosphere of conviviality and camaraderie.' 'Political Toasting in Eighteenth-Century Ireland', *History*, 91 (2006), 508–529, quote at 529.

57. Mac Suibhne, 'Whiskey, Potatoes and Paddies', 58. Mac Suibhne makes the astute point that 'these dinners enabled officers, particularly captains, to assert their authority; given that the initiative to establish companies had not come from these men and that they had been chosen by the rank and file, this was a matter of considerable consequence.' Ibid.

58. This causal connection could also run the other way, with patterns of consumption allowing for the expression of political opinions. See Higgins, *A Nation of Politicians*, 82–105.

59. *Dublin Evening Post*, 19 October 1779, cited in O'Connor, 'The Volunteers, 1778–1793', 21–22.

60. The connection to associational life is also drawn in Higgins, *A Nations of Politicians*, 107–115.

61. This despite the fact that the Volunteers originated from a failure of the state to be able to provide the money to embody a militia envisioned in the Militia Act of 1778, (19–20 Geo. 13 in *Statutes at Large*, XI, 109) and the granting of arms to the Volunteers by the state in July 1779 when Spain entered the Anglo-American War. Maurice O'Connell, *Irish Politics and Social Conflict in the Age of the American Revolution* (Philadelphia: University of Pennsylvania Press, 1965), 74–75, 86–87.

62. Mansergh, *Grattan's Failure*, 82–83.

63. For a comparable discussion concerning the value of paramilitarism in upholding civic virtue, see John Robertson, *The Scottish Enlightenment and the Militia Issue* (Cambridge: Cambridge University Press, 1985). I would like to thank Padhraig Higgins for reminding me of the parallel.

64. Details on conversion rates and the legislative amendments are taken from Thomas P. Power, 'The Conversion of Catholic Clergy to Anglicanism', in Michael Brown, Charles I. McGrath, and Thomas P. Power (eds), *Converts and Conversion in Ireland, 1650–1850* (Dublin: Four Courts Press, 2002), 190.

65. For an example of this confidence and the consequence of its expression in poetic form, see Vona Groarke, *Lament for Art O'Leary from the Irish of Eibhlín Dubh Ní Chonaill* (Oldcastle: Gallery Press, 2008). For a more formal translation, see Angela Bourke, 'Lamenting the Dead', in Angela Bourke et al. (eds), *The Field Day Anthology of Irish Writing*, Volume IV: *Irish Women's Writing and Traditions* (Cork: Cork University Press, 2002), 1378–1384.

66. For a study of the Whiteboys that highlights the economic quality of their motivation, see James S. Donnelly Jr, 'The Whiteboy Movement, 1761–5', *Irish Historical Studies*, 21 (1978–1979), 20–54. For the debate about any residual Jacobitism, see Vincent Morley, '"Tá an cruatan ar Sheoirse"—Folklore or Politics?' *Eighteenth-Century Ireland*, 12 (1998), 112–120; Vincent Morley, 'George III, Queen Sadhbh and the Historians', *Eighteenth-Century Ireland*, 17 (2002), 112–120; and S. J. Connolly, 'Jacobites, Whiteboys and Republicans: Varieties of Disaffection in Eighteenth-Century Ireland', *Eighteenth-Century Ireland*, 18 (2003), 63–79.

67. See Cormac Begadon, 'The Renewal of Catholic Religious Culture in Eighteenth-Century Dublin', in John Bergin, Eoin Magennis, Lesa Ní Mhunghaile, and Patrick Walsh (eds), *New Perspectives on the Penal Laws: Eighteenth-Century Ireland Special Issue 1* (2011), 227–247.

68. In a critique of Kevin Whelan's work, Toby Barnard pointedly says, 'A paradox in Dr Whelan's study is that his gentry—if indeed they were such—so far from being hidden were highly visible.' 'The Gentrification of Eighteenth-Century Ireland', *Eighteenth-Century Ireland*, 12 (1997), 155.

69. This Irish variant is taken from Angela Bourke, 'Lamenting the Dead', in Angela Bourke et al., *The Field Day Anthology of Irish Writing*, Volume IV, 1376.

70. Vona Groarke, *Lament for Art O'Leary from the Irish of Eibhlín Dubh Ní Chonaill* (Oldcastle, 2008), 34. This translation is perhaps less faithful than others, but captures well the emotion and sexual attraction, without which the keen or lament can seem overwrought and garish in English. For a more precise translation, see Bourke, 'Lamenting the Dead', 1378–1384.

71. Details in this paragraph are taken from L. M. Cullen, 'The Contemporary and Later Politics of *Caineadh Airt Uí Laoire*', *Eighteenth-Century Ireland*, 8 (1993), 7–38.

72. Bourke, 'Lamenting the Dead', 1374.

73. Groarke, *Lament for Art O'Leary*, 26.

74. Bourke, 'Lamenting the Dead', 1376.

75. Groarke, *Lament for Art O'Leary*, 34–5.

76. Bourke, 'Lamenting the Dead', 1373.

77. Groarke, *Lament for Art O'Leary*, 24.

78. A point well made in Cullen, 'The Contemporary and Later Politics of *Caineadh Airt Uí Laoire*', 21.

79. *The Statutes at Large, passed in the Parliaments held in Ireland*, 20 vols (Dublin: George Grierson, 1786–1801), X, 589.

80. The origins of the act and the motive of the two authors are quickly sketched in Bartlett, *Fall and Rise of the Irish Nation*, 77–81.

81. *The Statutes at Large*, X, 589–590. See also Vincent Morley, 'Catholic Disaffection and the Oath of Allegiance of 1774', in James Kelly, John McCafferty, and Charles

Ivar McGrath (eds), *People, Politics and Power: Essays on Irish History, 1660–1850 in Honour of James McGuire* (Dublin: UCD Press, 2009), 122–143.

82. *The Statutes at Large*, X, 590.

83. Bartlett, *Fall and Rise of the Irish Nation*, 80.

84. Ibid., 78.

85. *The Statutes at Large*, X, 590.

86. O'Connell, *Irish Politics and Social Conflict*, 120.

87. Thomas Bartlett argues this ensured that the British government was anxious to shore up support at home, from any quarter: the war against America, and by default against the French, meant they had to be wary of internal disquiet. Also they needed manpower urgently, and Irish Catholics, with a long tradition of military involvement in Europe were, since the Seven Years' War (1756–1763), seen as an untapped source. See Bartlett, *Fall and Rise of the Irish Nation*, 58–59. See also Robert Kent Donovan, 'The Military Origins of the Roman Catholic Relief Programme of 1778', *The Historical Journal*, 28 (1985), 79–102. This situates the Irish Relief Act in a wider British context and relates it to the Gordon riots of 1780.

88. *Statutes of Ireland*, XI, 300.

89. This paragraph is based on James Kelly, '1780 Revisited: The Politics of the Repeal of the Sacramental Test', in Kevin Herlihy (ed.), *The Politics of Irish Dissent* (Dublin: Four Courts Press, 1997), 74–92.

90. These figures are found in Bartlett, *Fall and Rise of the Irish Nation*, 90.

91. This paragraph and the next draws on Kelly, '1780 Revisited', 74–92.

92. For a treatment of his idiosyncratic career see James Kelly, *Sir Edward Newenham MP, 1734–1814: Defender of the Protestant Constitution* (Dublin: Four Courts Press, 2003).

93. 19–20 Geo, c.6. *The Statutes at Large*, XI, 373.

94. O'Connell, *Irish Politics and Social Conflict*, 208. In contrast, Bishop William Newcombe of Waterford supported the bills so as not to antagonise citizens of the king. Ibid., 209.

95. *The Statutes at Large*, XII, 243. It enacted 'that all matrimonial contracts or marriages heretofore entered into, or hereafter to be entered into, between Protestant dissenters, and solemnized or celebrated by Protestant dissenting ministers or teachers, shall be, and shall be held and taken to be good and valid to all intents and purposes whatsoever.'

96. *The Statutes at Large*, XII, 243. A further £500 was granted to the Seceders. Details are drawn from anonymous, *The Irish Regium Donum: Its History, Character and Effects* (London: Arthur Miall, 1865), 10.

97. *The Statutes at Large*, XII, 237.

98. Ibid., 388.

99. See Bartlett, *Fall and Rise of the Irish Nation*, 100–101.

100. *The Statutes at Large*, XII, 240.

101. Andrew Doria, *A Letter to the Volunteers upon the Subject of a Parliamentary Reform* (Dublin: D. Graisberry, 1784), 19. This is a pseudonym, as Andrew Doria was, as Stephen Small notes 'the ruler and mediator of the Genoese republic in the mid-sixteenth century'. He further comments, 'Doria is perhaps a strange icon for a radical Irish Patriot. For although he presided over a prosperous expansion of Genoese commerce and banking, he did so by reinforcing the power of the old nobility and by bringing Genoa under the influence of the great imperial power of his day—Hapsburg Spain.' *Political Thought in Ireland 1776–1798: Republicanism, Patriotism and Radicalism* (Oxford: Oxford University Press, 2002), 121n28.

102. Doria, *A Letter to the Volunteers*, 20.

103. Ibid., 22.

104. Ibid., 9.

105. Ibid., 16.

106. Ibid., 5.

107. Ibid., 11.

108. Ibid., 8, 9.

109. Ibid., 24.

110. Dobbs, *Thoughts on Volunteers*, 16.

111. Ibid., 15.

112. Francis Dobbs, *A History of Irish Affairs from the 12th of October 1779 to the 15th September 1782* (Dublin: M. Mills, 1782), 44.

113. Ibid., 45.

114. Ibid., 13.

115. Ibid., 83.

116. Ibid., 158–159.

117. Ibid., 154.

118. Doria, *A Letter to the Volunteers*, 3.

119. Cited in Vincent Morley, *Irish Opinion and the American Revolution, 1760–1783* (Cambridge: Cambridge University Press, 2007), 287.

120. Garnham, *The Militia in Eighteenth-Century Ireland*, 123–141.

121. James Kelly (ed.), 'Select Documents XLIII: A Secret Return of the Volunteers of Ireland in 1784', *Irish Historical Studies*, 26 (1989), 292. Pádraig Ó Snodaigh, *The Irish Volunteers: A List of the Units* (Dublin: Irish Academic Press, 1995), notes that in 1784 two units were noted in the Irish press as active in Fermanagh, seven in Mayo, and five in Monaghan. None of the counties was a heartland of Volunteer activity.

122. Kelly, 'Secret Return', 292.

123. Ibid., 287.

124. Ibid., 279.

125. This picture accords with the anecdotal evidence that while many units took in

Catholic members, other parts of the Volunteer movement were less accommodating. In both Armagh and Wexford, it is asserted, no Catholics were recruited.
For Wexford, see Ó Snodaigh, 'Class and the Irish Volunteers', 173.

126. Kelly, 'Secret Return', 278, 286.

127. Ibid., 281, 291.

128. For a survey of the fissures within the movement, see James Kelly, 'The Politics of
Volunteering, 1778–93', *The Irish Sword*, 22 (2000), 139–157.

129. Ibid., 285.

130. McBride, *Scripture Politics*, 123.

131. A cautious assessment of their involvement during the early years of the movement
is offered in Higgins, *A Nation of Politicians*, 146–150.

132. Rogers, *Irish Volunteers and Catholic Emancipation*, 63.

133. Cited in ibid., 64.

134. Kevin Whelan, 'The Catholic Community in Eighteenth-Century Wexford', in
Thomas P. Power and Kevin Whelan (eds), *Endurance and Emergence: Catholics in
Ireland in the Eighteenth Century* (Dublin: Irish Academic Press, 1990), 156. The academic confusion over the extent of Catholic participation can be illustrated by juxtaposing this information on Wexford, with James Kelly's assertion that 'by July 1781
they [Catholics] were so far accepted that only the gentlemen of counties Meath
and Wexford refused to associate in arms with them'. 'The Parliamentary Reform
Movement of the 1780s and the Catholic Question', *Archivium Hibernicum*, 43 (1988),
96. The most recent study of the movement concludes by lamenting that 'despite at
least two attempts at the beginning of the twentieth century, the question of religion
in relation to Volunteering has been neglected in recent times. The issue of the religious composition of Volunteer companies is one that has raised many questions, but
has received few answers.' O'Connor, 'The Volunteers 1778–1793', 299.

135. Cited in Rogers, *Irish Volunteers and Catholic Emancipation*, 66.

136. *Finn's Leinster Journal*, 23 September 1780, cited in Morley, *Irish Opinion*, 235.

137. Anonymous, *Thoughts on the Conduct and Continuation of the Volunteers of Ireland*
(Dublin: D. Graisberry, 1783), 20–21.

138. Morley, *Irish Public Opinion*, 107.

139. Ibid., 184–185.

140. Ibid., 229–230.

141. [Peter Burrowes], *Plain Arguments in Defence of the People's Absolute Dominion over
the Constitution* (Dublin: Thomas Webb, 1784), 15.

142. Ibid., 9.

143. Ibid., 10.

144. Ibid., 32.

145. Ibid., 41.

146. Ibid., 53.

147. Ibid., 3.
148. Ibid., 7.
149. Ibid., 13.
150. Ibid., 37.
151. Ibid., 5.
152. Ibid., 54.
153. Ibid., 21.
154. Ibid., 44.
155. [John Johnson], *Strictures on a Late Pamphlet entitled* Plain Arguments (Dublin: P. Byrne, 1784), 21.
156. Ibid., 22.
157. Ibid., 23.
158. Ibid., 11–12.
159. Ibid., 19.
160. For a useful genealogy of these developing views, see J. G. A. Pocock, 'The Varieties of Whiggism from Exclusion to Reform: A History of Ideology and Discourse', *Virtue, Commerce and History: Essays on Political Thought and History, Chiefly in the Eighteenth Century* (Cambridge: Cambridge University Press, 1985), particularly 215–230. For the development of ideologies of commercial Whiggism in Scotland, see Christopher J. Berry, *The Idea of Commercial Society in the Scottish Enlightenment* (Edinburgh: Edinburgh University Press, 2013).
161. Dobbs, *History of Irish Affairs*, 11. Historians have agreed in placing these two pamphlets together. See, for example, Danny Mansergh, *Grattan's Failure*, 41, or Small, *Political Thought in Ireland*, 75.
162. [Joseph Pollock], *The Letters of Owen Roe O'Nial* (Dublin: printed for W. Jackson, 1779), 9.
163. Frederic Jebb, *A Physiological Enquiry into the Process of Labour, and an Attempt to Ascertain the Determining Cause of It* (Dublin: printed for Richard Moncrieff, 1770).
164. See David Lammey, 'The Free Trade Crisis: A Reappraisal', in Gerard O'Brien (ed.), *Parliament, Politics and People: Essays in Eighteenth-Century Irish History* (Dublin: Irish Academic Press, 1989), 69–92, which at once highlights how the term 'free trade' was capable of multiple meanings, and illustrates how a variety of constituencies in Ireland, from the administration itself, the Patriots in parliament, and the southern elements of the Volunteers could all be in favour of its introduction.
165. [Pollock], *The Letters of Owen Roe O'Nial*, 35; [Fredrick Jebb], *The Letters of Guatimozin* (Dublin: printed for Henry and Robert Joy, 1779), 41. This seems to be part of a more general trope. See Martyn Powell, 'Celtic Rivalries: Ireland, Scotland and Wales in the British Empire, 1707–1801', in Hugh Bowen (ed.), *Wales and the British Overseas Empire: Interactions and Influences, 1650–1850* (Manchester: Manchester University Press, 2012), 62–86, for further examples and the proposition that it was generated

both by an anxiety about Scottish enthusiasm for centralising imperialism and by a modicum of 'Celtic one-upmanship, as each region sought to demonstrate its loyalty—and by extension its whiggery—to the crown.' I would like to thank Martyn Powell for a copy of this paper prior to its publication.

166. On these modes of free trade, see James Livesey, 'Free Trade and Empire in the Anglo-Irish Commercial Propositions of 1785', *Journal of British Studies*, 52 (2013), 103–127.

167. On the imperial context for this debate, see Anne Crerar, 'Commerce and Constitutionalism: The English East India Company and Political Culture in Scotland and Ireland' (PhD thesis, University of Aberdeen, 2013), chap. 4.

168. On the political languages that underpinned these different registers, see Small, *Political Thought in Ireland*, 75–82. He also notes that 'in the heat of the moment most Patriot pamphleteers simply did not perceive a contradiction between their Country critiques of British commercial self-interest and their praise for commerce in general . . . The volatile political environment of the free trade agitation lent itself to clear forceful rhetoric rather than anxious classical republican warnings about the dangers of commercial society. Ibid., 75–76.

169. [Jebb], *The Letters of Guatimozin*, 14.

170. Ibid., 14.

171. Ibid.

172. Ibid., 57.

173. Ibid., 16.

174. Ibid., 9.

175. Ibid., 33.

176. Ibid., 34.

177. Ibid., 35.

178. Ibid., 18.

179. Ibid., 17.

180. Ibid., 5. In this he was, it seems, partially successful, for Robert Johnson, under the pen-name Causidicus (pleader of causes), was to enter the lists in a letter to the *Freeman's Journal*, where he admitted, 'if what I have said' about the nature of rebellion 'shall rectify the opinion of one man who reads it, let him owe his knowledge to Guatimozin. I read his essay with unusual attention. If it did not convince me, it roused me. If it did not direct me what to think, it instructed me how to think.' Ibid., 65.

181. [Pollock], *The Letters of Owen Roe O'Nial*, 42.

182. Ibid., 32, 23.

183. Ibid., 7.

184. Ibid., 10.

185. Ibid., 24.

186. Ibid., 10.

187. Ibid., 8.

188. Ibid., 17.

189. Ibid., 13.

190. Ibid., 7.

191. Ibid.

192. Ibid., 8.

193. Ibid., 28.

194. Ibid., 34.

195. Ibid., 42.

196. Ibid., 26, 27.

197. Indeed, in the assessment of Patrick Rogers, while 'a number of other far seeing men shared [William Steele Dickson's] views . . . the most prominent of them was also a Presbyterian from County Down—the barrister and political writer, Joseph Pollock'. *Irish Volunteers and Catholic Emancipation*, 64.

198. [Pollock], *The Letters of Owen Roe O'Nial*, 24.

199. For a survey of the influences on Drennan, see Ian McBride, 'William Drennan and the Dissenting Tradition' in David Dickson, Dáire Keogh, and Kevin Whelan (eds), *The United Irishmen: Republicanism, Radicalism and Rebellion* (Dublin: Lilliput Press, 1993), 49–61.

200. [William Drennan], *Letters of Orellana, An Irish Helot to the Seven Northern Counties Not Represented in the National Assembly of Delegates Held at Dublin, October 1784*, in William Drennan, *Selected Writings*, Volume One: *The Irish Volunteers, 1775–1790* (Belfast: Belfast Historical and Educational Society, 1998), 208.

201. Ibid., 210. This stood at odds with Drennan's comments elsewhere in the *Letters* on how the Volunteers ought to reject any call for them to show patience and perseverance: 'I look in the dictionary for the exact meaning of this puzzling polysyllable, perseverance, and I find that it implies steadiness in pursuit, and constancy in progress. Can we pursue and stand still—at the same time? A cessation of all active power in the people cannot surely be perseverance.' Ibid., 223.

202. Ibid., 210–211.

203. Ibid., 201.

204. Ibid., 217.

205. Ibid., 218.

206. Ibid., 194. The foreigners are later identified as Montesquieu and Jean de Lolme at 196. Note the religious language here employed; yet elsewhere Drennan asserted that 'the question of reform is therefore to be considered merely as a political question,' 210.

207. Ibid., 195.

208. Ibid., 196.

209. Ibid., 204.
210. Ibid., 206.
211. Ibid., 226. There is also a strong gender distinction being drawn, with Drennan arguing in another letter that 'the breath of corruption will then blow like the spirit-sinking Sirocco across the land. The sternest patriot will feel himself emasculated; and the sinewy strength of manly integrity will relax into the weakness of the woman', 213. So also he wailed, 'My eyes grow womanish when I think of thy situation', 201.
212. Ibid., 202.
213. Ibid., 215.
214. Ibid., 218.
215. Ibid., 217.
216. See, for instance, 'this progression ought to move on with a velocity accelerated in proportion as the nation approaches the object which attracts it'; or, 'the love of country and mankind warms and dilates the youthful breast'; and also, 'I do not think there is any radical defect in the heart of Irishmen, which is the cause of this wonderful stoppage in the circulation of public spirit, nor do I think there is such a derangement in your understanding as not to comprehend the perils of your present situation'. Ibid., 203, 206, and 207.
217. Ibid., 208.
218. Ibid., 193–194. In yet another contradiction, Letter VI states how the Irish 'approach him [the King] with the honest confidence which becomes us as the brethren of Britons, and the co-heirs of Magna Charta'. Ibid., 217.
219. On this spasm of agrarian unrest, see James S. Donnelly Jr., 'The Rightboy Movement', *Studia Hibernica*, 17/18 (1977–1978), 120–202; Maurice J. Bric, 'Priests, Parsons and Politics: The Rightboy Protest in County Cork 1785–1788', *Past and Present*, 100 (1983), 100–123.
220. On the assault on Catholic clergy, see particularly R. E. Burns, 'Parsons, Priests and the People: The Rise of Irish Anti-Clericalism, 1785–1789', *Church History*, 31 (1962), 151–163.
221. Richard Woodward, *The Present State of the Church of Ireland*, 2nd edn (Dublin: W. Sleater, 1787), 16.
222. Ibid., 14.
223. Woodward repeatedly used the term. See ibid., 14, 54, and 77 for instance.
224. Ibid., 17. For other uses of this phrase, see ibid., 20, 21, 47, 56, and 77. The ideological freight carried by the term 'Protestant Ascendancy' at any one time in this period has been the subject of an extended controversy. W. J. McCormack sites the creation of a social legitimation for sectarian supremacy primarily in the response of Dublin Corporation to the Relief Act of 1792. James Kelly suggests that the origin of the ideological resonance of the term lies slightly earlier, in the response

of ultra-Protestants to the Rightboy disturbances discussed above. This is to shift the focus away from a mercantile and urban origin towards a clerical invention, emerging from a cluster of alumni of Trinity College Dublin. What is being argued in this section is less about the development of a political ideology and more about the polarisation of debate in the 1780s, with a fissure emerging between those who adopted an empirical rationalist methodology and those who preferred a rationalist approach. Whether the former developed a coherent perspective glossed by the term 'Protestant Ascendancy' in 1785 or 1792 is not at issue. For the debate, see W. J. McCormack, 'The Genesis of the Protestant Ascendancy', in Francis Barker et al. (eds), *1789: Reading, Writing, Revolution* (Essex: University of Essex Press, 1982), 302–323; W. J. McCormack, *Ascendancy and Tradition in Anglo-Irish Literary History from 1789 to 1939* (Oxford: Clarendon Press, 1985), 61–96; W. J. McCormack, 'Vision and Revision in the Study of Irish Parliamentary Rhetoric', *Eighteenth-Century Ireland*, 2 (1987), 7–36; James Kelly, 'Inter-Denominational Relations and Religious Toleration in Late Eighteenth-Century Ireland: The Paper War of 1786–88', *Eighteenth-Century Ireland*, 3 (1988), 39–67; James Kelly, 'Relations Between the Protestant Church of Ireland and the Presbyterian Church in Late Eighteenth-Century Ireland', *Éire-Ireland*, 23 (1988), 38–56; James Kelly, 'The Genesis of the "Protestant Ascendancy": The Rightboy Disturbances of the 1780s and their Impact upon Protestant Opinion', in O'Brien, *Parliament, Politics and People*, 93–127; W. J. McCormack, 'Eighteenth-Century Ascendancy: Yeats and the Historians', *Eighteenth-Century Ireland*, 4 (1989), 159–181; James Kelly, 'Eighteenth-Century Ascendancy: A Commentary', *Eighteenth-Century Ireland*, 5 (1990), 173–187.

225. Woodward, *Present State*, 9–10.

226. For his comments on Presbyterians, see ibid., 18–19.

227. Ibid., 19.

228. Ibid., 15, 93, 34, 53.

229. Ibid., 84.

230. Ibid., 55. For the table see ibid., 42.

231. Ibid., 16. The note proceeds: 'And the repetition of like offences since the assizes, when all the disputes about tithes were at an end for the current year; the continuance of assembling in numerous well-armed bodies and passing winter-nights in levying money and taking fire-arms forcibly and feloniously from the Protestants, a proceeding which now extends to the province of Leinster, within less than fifty miles of the capital, are proofs too pregnant of the effect of their impunity of their associates and of their future intentions.' Ibid., 16.

232. Ibid., 40–41.

233. Ibid., 45, 87, 30. The pamphlet referred to is William Webster, *The Clergy's Right of Maintenance Vindicated from Scripture and Reason* (London: printed for John Brotherton; Samuel Belingsley, and James Crockatt, 1726).

234. Woodward, *Present State*, 58, 32, 17.

235. Ibid., 16.

236. Ibid., 76.

237. Ibid., 63–64.

238. Ibid., 70.

239. Ibid., 64.

240. Ibid., 76.

241. Ibid., 28–29.

242. Ibid., 87, 88.

243. Ibid., 89.

244. Ibid., 90–91.

245. Only once is this coinage not availed of, when in a footnote on the connection between despotism and Catholicism he wrote, 'The author is so far from justifying this alliance that he thinks it a combination against the natural rights of mankind'. Ibid., 10.

246. Ibid., 93, 98.

247. Ibid., 99.

248. *Thoughts on the Conduct and Continuation*, 2–3.

249. Ibid., 27 and 29.

250. Anonymous, *A Series of Letters Addressed to the Volunteers of Ireland* (Dublin, 1785), 5.

251. Ibid., 5, 6.

252. Ibid., 4–5.

253. Garnham, *The Militia in Eighteenth-Century Ireland*, 137–143.

9. An Enlightened Civil War

1. Archbishop John Thomas Troy of Dublin, for example, articulates a version of Counter-Enlightenment thought that comes close to that examined in Darrin McMahon, *Enemies of the Enlightenment: The French Counter-Enlightenment and the Making of Modernity* (Oxford: Oxford University Press, 2001). Indeed, he cites Abbé Augustin Barruel, *Memoirs: Illustrating the Antichristian Conspiracy* (Dublin: William Watson and Son, 1798). See John Thomas Troy, *To the Reverend Pastors, and Other Roman Catholic Clergy, of the Archdiocese of Dublin* (Dublin: H. Fitzpatrick, 1798), 6. I would to thank Ultán Gillen for discussion of this matter, and for pointing out Troy's text to me. See also Dáire Keogh, 'Archbishop Troy, the Catholic Church and Irish Radicalism, 1791–3', in David Dickson, Dáire Keogh, and Kevin Whelan (eds), *The United Irishmen: Republicanism, Radicalism and Rebellion* (Dublin: Lilliput Press, 1993), 124–134, for Troy's difficulties in confronting radicalism. On the Catholic clergy's involvement in the Rising, see Dáire Keogh, *The French Disease: The Catholic Church and Radicalism in Ireland 1790–*

1800 (Dublin: Four Courts Press, 1993). For similar differences within the Presbyterian church, see I. R. McBride, *Scripture Politics: Ulster Presbyterianism and Irish Radicalism in the Late Eighteenth Century* (Oxford: Oxford University Press, 1998), 186–206, 232–236.

2. This assessment draws on Nancy J. Curtin, '"A Perfect Liberty": The Rise and Fall of the Irish Whigs, 1789–1797', in D. George Boyce, Robert Eccleshall, and Vincent Geoghegan (eds), *Political Discourse in Seventeenth- and Eighteenth-Century Ireland* (Houndmills: Ashgate Press, 2001), 270–289. Curtin pronounces that the Whigs were 'the party of reform, but not too much reform', 275.

3. See letters II, III and IV, in William Bruce and Henry Joy, *Belfast Politics* (Dublin: UCD Press, 2005), 56–72.

4. Ibid., 77.

5. Ibid., 30.

6. Ibid., 89–90.

7. Ibid., 40.

8. Ibid., 94–95.

9. Ibid., 38.

10. A useful overview is provided in Denis Kennedy, 'The Irish Whigs, Administrative Reform and Responsible Government, 1782–1800', *Éire-Ireland*, 8 (1973), 55–69.

11. This paragraph draws on Denis Kennedy, 'The Irish Whigs and the Regency Crisis in Ireland, 1788–89', *Éire-Ireland*, 18 (1983), 54–70.

12. On the passage of the 1793 Relief Act and the question of emancipation, see Thomas Bartlett, *The Fall and Rise of the Irish Nation: The Catholic Question, 1690–1830* (Dublin: Irish Academic Press, 1992), 146–172.

13. Detail in this paragraph is drawn from Kennedy, 'The Irish Whigs, Administrative Reform and Responsible Government', 64–66.

14. On this shift in Catholic opinion, see Eamon O'Flaherty, 'Irish Catholics and the French Revolution', in Hugh Gough and David Dickson (eds), *Ireland and the French Revolution* (Dublin: Irish Academic Press, 1990), 52–67.

15. For contrasting assessments of these events, see R. B. McDowell, *Ireland in the Age of Imperialism and Revolution, 1760–1801* (Oxford: Clarendon Press, 1979), 445–461; Deirdre Lindsay, 'The Fitzwilliam Episode Revisited', in Dickson, Keogh, and Whelan, *The United Irishmen*, 197–208; David Wilkinson, 'The Fitzwilliam Episode, 1795: A Reinterpretation of the Role of the Duke of Portland', *Irish Historical Studies*, 115 (1995), 315–339.

16. Quoted in Robert Mahony, 'The Pamphlet Campaign against Henry Grattan in 1797–99', *Eighteenth-Century Ireland*, 2 (1987), 151. In this, Grattan preempted the actions of his British Whig allies, for on 26 May 1797 Charles Fox and his faction also withdrew, again in the wake of the defeat of proposals for parliamentary reform.

17. Henry Grattan, *Mr Grattan's Address to his Fellow-Citizens. Corrected from the Original Copy* (Dublin: Campbell and Shea, 1797).

18. Mahony, 'The Pamphlet Campaign against Henry Grattan', 162–166, lists the responses.

19. Quoted in ibid., 153.

20. For this act of symbolic counterrevolution, see Fintan Cullen, 'Radicals and Reactionaries: Portraits of the 1790s in Ireland', in Jim Smyth (ed.), *Revolution, Counter-Revolution and Union* (Cambridge: Cambridge University Press, 2000), 194.

21. For the complexity of FitzGibbon's religious origins and some remarks on its consequences for his own career, see David A. Fleming, 'Conversion, Family and Mentality', in Michael Brown, Charles Ivar McGrath, and Thomas P. Power (eds), *Converts and Conversion in Ireland, 1650–1850* (Dublin: Four Courts Press, 2005), 295–300.

22. Quoted in Ann C. Kavanaugh, 'John FitzGibbon, Earl of Clare', in Dickson, Keogh, and Whelan, *United Irishmen*, 120.

23. See Bartlett, *The Fall and Rise of the Irish Nation*, 159.

24. John FitzGibbon, *Substance of the Speech of the Rt. Hon. Lord FitzGibbon, Lord Chancellor of Ireland, on the 10th of January 1793, respecting the Catholic Delegates and the Popery Laws of Ireland* (London: W. Miller, 1793), 3–4. I would like to thank Patrick Geoghegan for bringing this speech to my attention.

25. Ibid., 5.

26. Ibid., 6.

27. Ibid., 4.

28. Ibid., 10.

29. Ibid.

30. Ibid.

31. Ibid., 16–17.

32. The conceptualisation of the Protestant Ascendancy dates back to Richard Woodward, bishop of Cloyne, *The Present State of the Church of Ireland* (1786), which includes 'a general account of the progress of the insurrections in Munster'. On this see chapter eight above.

33. This paragraph draws on David Dickson, foreword to *Memoirs of the Irish Rebellion of 1798*, by Sir Richard Musgrave (Enniscorthy: Duffy Press, 1995), i–xiii.

34. An account of this debate is to be found in James Kelly, *Sir Richard Musgrave, 1746–1818: Ultra-Protestant Ideologue* (Dublin: Four Courts Press, 2009), 71–83.

35. [Richard Musgrave], *A Concise Account of the Material Events and Atrocities which Occurred in the Late Rebellion, with the Causes which Produced Them; and an Answer to Veritas's Vindication of the Roman Catholic Clergy of the Town of Wexford. By Veridicus*, 3rd edn (Dublin: J. Milliken and J. Wright, 1799); Veritas, *A Vindication of the Roman Catholic Clergy of the Town of Wexford, during the Late Unhappy*

Rebellion, from the Groundless Charges and Illiberal Insinuations of an Anonymous Writer, signed Verax (Dublin: H. Fitzpatrick, 1798).

36. [Musgrave], *A Concise Account*, 25.

37. Ibid., 64.

38. Ibid., 27. For the list of the disloyal and the threatened loyal clerics, see ibid., 60–64.

39. Ibid., 42.

40. Ibid., 71.

41. Ibid., 20.

42. Ibid., 11.

43. Ibid., 19.

44. Ibid., 43.

45. Ibid., 42.

46. For treatments of this work, see Kelly, *Sir Richard Musgrave*, 103–120, and Jim Smyth, 'Anti-Catholicism, Conservatism and Conspiracy: Sir Richard Musgrave's *Memoirs of the Different Rebellions in Ireland*', *Eighteenth-Century Life*, 99 (1998), 62–73.

47. In building an analysis of the country's history as blighted by the perfidy of igno-rant and untrustworthy Catholics, Musgrave shared a political perception previ-ously articulated by Sir John Temple in his treatment of the 1641 Rising in Ulster and William King in his analysis of James II's Irish administration. For an analysis of this trilogy of sectarian histories, see Joseph Richardson, 'Political Anglicanism in Ireland, 1691–1800: From the Language of Liberty to the Language of Union', in Michael Brown, Patrick M. Geoghegan, and James Kelly (eds), *The Irish Act of Union, 1800: Bicentennial Essays* (Dublin: Irish Academic Press, 2003), 58–67. Importantly, Musgrave's work differed from that of Temple, in that the former, published in 1646, built upon biblical paradigms in line with the scripturalism prevalent in its period, whereas Musgrave's work was wholly empirical in its method. They did, however, share a Gothic quality in their imagining of atrocity. On both the biblical and Gothic aspects to Temple's history, see Jarlath Killeen, *Gothic Ireland: Horror and the Irish Anglican Imagination in the Long Eighteenth Century* (Dublin: Four Courts Press, 2005), 36–47. I would like to thank Nicholas Canny for discussion of this issue.

48. As Siobhán Kilfeather puts it, 'Sir Richard Musgrave recruited witness statements that focussed on rebel atrocities against women, children, the elderly and the saintly.' 'Terrific Register: The Gothicization of Atrocity in Irish Romanticism', *boundary 2*, 31 (2004), 58. For Musgrave's concern to collate evidence, see Kelly, *Sir Richard Musgrave*, 91–103.

49. Musgrave, *Memoirs of the Irish Rebellion of 1798*, 457.

50. Ibid., 454. Siobhán Kilfeather argues that 'much of the writing that appears in the fifty years after 1798 is much more akin to what in the twentieth century was identified

as survivor guilt—a form of trauma experienced by people who have escaped life-threatening situations and whose experience of the existence of their consciousness in time is fractured by repeated intrusive memories of the time of danger, memories in which visual images of horror predominate.' This suggests one way to comprehend Musgrave's determination to supply empirical accounts: this is the literature of memory as much as it is of atrocity, and the two are intimately linked, as 'an attempt to come to terms with things that had been seen and that could neither be fully remembered nor completely forgotten within the various genres available for narrating experience'. 'Terrific Register', 67.

51. Musgrave, *Memoirs of the Irish Rebellion*, 455.

52. Ibid., 456.

53. Ibid., 455–456.

54. Ibid., 734–735.

55. For Jim Smyth, 'disjointed facts are compiled in the manner of a medieval chronicle without any attempt to integrate them into the flow of the narrative.' 'Anti-Catholicism, Conservatism and Conspiracy', 65. My interpretation is that this was intentional on Musgrave's part, providing both a sense of the chaos of war and a rhetorical buttress to his claim over a truthful and accurate presentation of events.

56. For a rather different treatment of this conservative school of thought, see James Kelly, 'Conservative Protestant Political Thought in Late Eighteenth-Century Ireland', in S. J. Connolly (ed.), *Political Ideas in Eighteenth-Century Ireland* (Dublin: Four Courts Press, 2000), 185–220.

57. On Tone as a political thinker see Tom Dunne, *Theobald Wolfe Tone, Colonial Outsider* (Cork: Tower Books, 1982); Thomas Bartlett, 'The Burden of the Present: Theobald Wolfe Tone, Republican and Separatist', in Dickson, Keogh, and Whelan, *The United Irishmen*, 1–15; Marianne Elliott, 'Wolfe Tone and the Republican Ideal', in Cathal Póirtéir (ed.), *The Great Irish Rebellion of 1798* (Cork: Mercier Press, 1998), 49–57. For a reading of Tone as an early Romantic, see Declan Kiberd, *Irish Classics* (Cambridge: Harvard University Press, 2000), 221–242.

58. 'Declarations and Resolutions of the Society of United Irishmen of Belfast', in T. W. Moody, R. B. McDowell, and C. J. Woods (eds), *The Writings of Theobald Wolfe Tone, 1763–98*, Volume 1: *Tone's Career in Ireland to June 1795* (Oxford: Oxford University Press, 1998), 140, 141.

59. Ibid., 140.

60. Ibid.

61. Ibid., 141.

62. The case of Drennan is particularly interesting. A founding figure in the United Irish ranks, he withdrew his overt support after he was put on trial in 1794 for seditious libel. Following the demolition of a key government witness, the turncoat William Carey, he was acquitted. See Ian McBride, 'William Drennan and the

Dissenting Tradition', in Dickson, Keogh, and Whelan, *The United Irishmen*, 49–61; John Larkin (ed.), *The Trial of William Drennan* (Dublin: Irish Academic Press, 1991).

63. Jane Hayter-Hames, *Arthur O'Connor, United Irishman* (Cork: Collins Press, 2001) provides a romanticised version of his life. A similar trajectory can be traced for Lord Edward Fitzgerald, who came from equally august stock. For a similar account of his life, see Stella Tillyard, *Citizen Lord: Edward Fitzgerald, 1763–1798* (London: Chatto and Windus Press, 1997).

64. Arthur O'Connor, *The State of Ireland*, James Livesey (ed.) (Dublin: Lilliput Press, 1998), 34–35.

65. Ibid., 40. Note here that this passage contains in microcosm the typical structure of O'Connor's argumentation, from assumption about God, through the assertion of right of interpretation, to tragic conclusion in which the statement of doctrine is denounced as hubristic. Note also the statement in brackets, which is reminiscent of Immanuel Kant's definition of Enlightenment as commensurate with thinking for oneself.

66. Ibid., 40–41.

67. Ibid., 41.

68. Ibid., 53–54.

69. Ibid., 66.

70. The standard biography is James Quinn, *Soul on Fire: A Life of Thomas Russell, 1767–1803* (Dublin: Irish Academic Press, 2002). See also C. J. Woods, 'The Place of Thomas Russell in the United Irish Movement', in Dickson and Gough, *Ireland and the French Revolution*, 83–108.

71. The prominence of Russell in this regard is highlighted in James Quinn, 'The United Irishmen and Social Reform', *Irish Historical Studies*, 31 (1998), 188–201.

72. Evidence of his sexual profligacy can be found strewn through his notebooks. See C. J. Woods (ed.), *Journals and Memoirs of Thomas Russell: 1791–5* (Dublin: Irish Academic Press, 1991).

73. Thomas Russell, *A Letter to the People of Ireland, on the Present Situation of the Country* (Belfast: printed at the *Northern Star* office, 1796), 5.

74. Ibid., 17.

75. Ibid. John Locke proposed that value, and hence property rights, depended on the investment of time and energy in a given object by an individual. See John Locke, *Two Treatises of Government*, Peter Laslett (ed.) (Cambridge: Cambridge University Press, 1988). This idea was also adapted to revolutionary aims by the French revolutionary theorist Emmanuel Sieyès, and subsequently by Karl Marx in his concept of the alienation of labour.

76. Russell, *A Letter to the People of Ireland*, 12.

77. Ibid., 15.

78. Ibid., 18.

79. Ibid., 8.

80. Ibid., 23.

81. *The Monthly Mirror*, VII (February 1799), 127. The author was identified as Arthur O'Connor in a letter to the editor of *Drakard's Paper* (later *The Champion*) on 14 April, 1813. This version is sourced from Hayter-Hames, *Arthur O'Connor, United Irishman*, 206.

82. On this theme in the French Revolution, see 'Regeneration', in François Furet and Mona Ozouf (eds), *A Critical Dictionary of the French Revolution* (Cambridge: Harvard University Press, 1989).

83. For a provocative assessment of one medium in which this conflict took place, see Cullen, 'Radicals and Reactionaries', 161–194.

84. For discussions of a selection of these, see Ann C. Kavanaugh, 'Henrietta Battier: Poet and Radical, 1751–1813', in David Dickson and Cormac Ó Gráda (eds), *Refiguring Ireland: Essays in Honour of L. M. Cullen* (Dublin: Lilliput Press, 2003), 172–183; Liam McIlvanney, *Burns the Radical: Poetry and Politics in Late Eighteenth-Century Scotland* (East Linton: Tuckwell Press, 2002), 220–240.

85. William Drennan, 'Erin', reproduced in Mary Helen Thuente, *The Harp Re-strung: The United Irishmen and the Rise of Irish Literary Nationalism* (Syracuse: Syracuse University Press, 1994), 239–241.

86. William Drennan, 'The Wake of William Orr', reproduced in ibid., 241–242.

87. This point is made by Kevin Whelan, 'The Republic in the Village: The United Irishmen, the Enlightenment and Popular Culture', in Kevin Whelan, *The Tree of Liberty: Radicalism, Catholicism and the Construction of Irish Identity 1760–1800* (Cork: Cork University Press, 1996), 62: 'One can claim that they were simply not interested in popular culture *per se*, but only in politicising it'. For sceptical comments on the success of United Irish efforts at politicising the populace, see Tom Dunne, 'Popular Ballads, Revolutionary Rhetoric and Politicisation', in Gough and Dickson, *Ireland and the French Revolution*, 139–155.

88. A useful survey of their efforts is James S. Donnelly Jr., 'Propagating the Cause of the United Irishmen', *Studies*, 69 (1980), 5–23.

89. In her survey of the cultural materials upon which the United Irish drew, Mary Helen Thuente notes English literature, British Antiquarianism, the Volunteers' cultural output, and traditional music. She also points up the international debt to French and American Revolutionary culture. *The Harp Re-strung*, 17–63.

90. Ibid., 94–96. The deployment of Irish-language material in *Bolg an tSolair* has been described by Niall Ó Ciosáin as 'an engagement with Gaelic culture but not an engagement with Irish-language speakers' containing as it did little or no political content. 'Popular Song, Readers and Language: Printed Anthologies in Irish and Scottish Gaelic, 1780–1820', in John Kirk, Michael Brown, and Andrew Noble

(eds), *Cultures of Radicalism in Britain and Ireland* (London: Pickering & Chatto Press, 2013), 130.

91. On the Harpers' Festival, see Charlotte Milligan Fox, *Annals of the Irish Harpers* (London: Smith Elder and Co., 1911), 97–122. Luke Gibbons uses the event to argue that the United Irishmen were 'opening up the Enlightenment itself to its "others", and to a prospect of genuine multiculturalism in an age of cosmopolitan ideals'. This construction depends on the thesis that 'racism and cultural intolerance were not incidental but major components of the Enlightenment', thereby allowing the United Irish a privileged position. Indeed, Gibbons remarks, 'What is remarkable about the United Irishmen is that though firmly wedded to Enlightenment principles, they refused to buy into such hierarchical concepts of culture.' 'Towards a Postcolonial Enlightenment: The United Irishmen, Cultural Diversity and the Public Sphere', in Clare Carroll and Patricia King (eds), *Ireland and Postcolonial Theory* (Cork: Cork University Press, 2003), 84, 88, 88. On the Belfast Harpers' Festival, see ibid., 89. This, however, is to ignore the Enlightenment critique of imperial ambition and the injurious treatment of indigenous cultures found in such writers as Diderot, Raynal, and Condorcet.

92. Barra Boydell, 'The United Irishmen, Music, Harps and National Identity', *Eighteenth-Century Ireland*, 13 (1998), 44–52.

93. Quoted in Nancy J. Curtin, *The United Irishmen: Popular Politics in Ulster and Dublin 1791–1798* (Oxford: Clarendon Press, 1998), 197.

94. This is the analysis offered by Thuente, *Harp Re-Strung*, 125–169. On the importance of song as a vehicle for the communication of news in Paris, see the remarks of Robert Darnton, *George Washington's False Teeth: An Unconventional Guide to the Eighteenth Century* (New York: Norton, 2003), 53–67.

95. This point is also made in Tadhg O'Sullivan, 'Burke, Ireland and the Counter-Revolution, 1791–1801', in Seán Patrick Donlan (ed.), *Edmund Burke's Irish Identities* (Dublin: Four Courts Press, 2006), 171–182. For a broader context for this kind of local study, see Rosemary Sweet, *Antiquaries: The Discovery of the Past in Eighteenth-Century Britain* London: Hambledon, 2004).

96. William Tighe, *Statistical Observations Relative to the County of Kilkenny made in the years 1800 and 1801*, 2 vols (Kilkenny: Grangesilvia Publications, 1988).

97. Others in this series include Sir Charles Coote, *Statistical Survey of the County of Armagh, with Observations on the means of Improvement; drawn up in the years 1802, and 1803, for the Consideration, and under the Direction of the Dublin Society* (Dublin, 1804; reprint, Ballynahinch: Davidson, 1984); Horatio Townsend, *Statistical Survey of the County of Cork, with Observations of the Means of Improvement: Drawn up for the Consideration, and by Direction of the Dublin Society* (Dublin: Graisberry and Campbell, 1810); George Vaughan Sampson, *Statistical Survey of the County of Londonderry, with Observations of the Means of Improvement:*

Drawn up for the Consideration, and by Direction of the Dublin Society (Dublin: Graisberry and Campbell, 1802); John McEvoy, *Statistical Survey of the County of Tyrone, with Observations on the Means of Improvement, Drawn up in the years 1801 and 1802 for the Consideration, and under the Direction, of the Dublin Society* (Dublin: Graisberry and Campbell, 1802); Thomas James Rawson, *Statistical Survey of the County of Kildare, with Observations on the Means of Improvement* (Dublin: Graisberry and Campbell, 1807). Rawson was an informant of Musgrave and commented on the Rebellion from a loyalist perspective within this text (ibid., v–xxiv). See Liam Chambers, 'Patrick O'Kelly and the Interpretation of the 1798 Rebellion', in William Nolan and Thomas McGrath (eds), *Kildare History and Society: Interdisciplinary Essays on the History of an Irish County* (Dublin: Geography Publications, 2006), 439–459.

98. A survey of the newspaper scene is provided by Brian Inglis, *Freedom of the Press in Ireland, 1784–1841* (London: Greenwood Press, 1954), 52–112.

99. Jacqueline Hill, 'John Giffard', *Dictionary of Irish Biography*, www.dib.cambridge .org (accessed 17 May 2011). I would like to thank Jacqueline Hill for a copy of this essay for the prior to its publication.

100. Inglis, *Freedom of the Press*, 61.

101. See Thomas Bartlett, *Revolutionary Dublin 1795–1801: The Letters of Francis Higgins to Dublin Castle* (Dublin: Four Courts Press, 2004), 101.

102. For an assessment of Higgins's career, see ibid., 23–30.

103. Ibid., 57. Bartlett also notes that two other editors-cum-spies were actively sponsored by the Castle, namely, William Corbet (the *Hibernian Telegraph*) and W. P. Carey (the *General Evening Post*). Ibid., 18. See also Inglis, *The Freedom of the Press*, 62–68. It should be noted that Carey, a one-time United Irishman, acted as a witness against William Drennan before the establishment of the newspaper, negating his value as an informer.

104. On the United Irish efforts on this front, see Inglis, *Freedom of the Press in Ireland*, 89–108; Curtin, *The United Irishmen*, 174–227. The literary output of the United Irish papers is surveyed in Thuente, *Harp Re-Strung*, 89–123.

105. The turbulent history of the newspaper's encounters with the law are recounted in Gillian O'Brien, '"Spirit, Impartiality and Independence": The *Northern Star*, 1792–1797', *Eighteenth-Century Ireland*, 13 (1998), 7–23. For the development of its distribution network across the northern counties, see Brian MacDonald, 'Distribution of the *Northern Star*', *Ulster Local Studies*, 18 (1997), 54–68.

106. Cited in Inglis, *Freedom of the Press*, 93.

107. See Mary Helen Thuente, '"The Belfast Laugh": The Context and Significance of United Irish Satires', in Smyth, *Revolution, Counter-Revolution and Union*, 67–82.

108. Quoted in Inglis, *Freedom of the Press*, 104.

109. Quoted in Thuente, *Harp Re-Strung*, 116.

110. Inglis, *Freedom of the Press*, 89–91.
111. See Curtin, *The United Irishmen*, 228–231, 240–245; Nancy Curtin, 'Symbols and Rituals in United Irish Mobilisation', in Gough and Dickson, *Ireland and the French Revolution*, 68–82.
112. Jacqueline R. Hill, 'National Festivals, the State and "Protestant Ascendancy" in Ireland, 1790–1829', *Irish Historical Studies*, 24 (1984), 30–51.
113. See the example quoted in Allan Blackstock, '"The Invincible Mass": Loyal Crowds in Mid-Ulster, 1795–6', in Eoin Magennis and Peter Jupp (eds), *Crowds in Ireland, c.1720–1920* (London: Palgrave Macmillan, 2000), 105. This article provides an important overview of this topic.
114. The 1798 Rebellion has been the subject of a vast academic and popular literature in recent years, prompted by its bicentenary. For some trenchant remarks on the achievements and limitations on this flurry of reconsideration, see Ian McBride, 'Reclaiming the Rebellion: 1798 in 1998', *Irish Historical Studies*, 31 (1999), 395–410; Thomas Bartlett, 'Why the History of the 1798 Rebellion Has yet to Be Written', *Eighteenth-Century Ireland*, 15 (2000), 181–190; Tom Dunne, *Rebellions: Memoir, Memory and 1798* (Dublin: Lilliput Press, 2004), 115–148.
115. The following sketch draws heavily on Thomas Bartlett, Kevin Dawson, and Dáire Keogh, *The 1798 Rebellion: An Illustrated History* (Dublin: Roberts Reinhart, 1998), 148–174.
116. On events in Dublin, see Tommy Graham, 'Dublin's Role in the 1798 Rebellion', in Póirtéir, *The Great Irish Rebellion*, 58–71.
117. This estimate of membership derives from Tommy Graham, 'The Transformation of the Dublin Society of United Irishmen into a Mass-Based Revolutionary Organization, 1791–6', in Thomas Bartlett, David Dickson, Dáire Keogh, and Kevin Whelan (eds), *1798: A Bicentenary Perspective* (Dublin: Four Courts Press, 2003), 136.
118. See L. M. Cullen, 'The United Irishmen: Problems and Issues in the 1790s' and Trevor McCavery 'Reformers, Reactionaries and Revolutionaries: Opinion in North Down and the Ards in the 1790s', both in *Ulster Local Studies*, 18 (1997), 7–27 and 69–94, respectively. See also L. M. Cullen, 'The Political Structures of the Defenders', in Gough and Dickson, *Ireland and the French Revolution*, 117–138; Trevor McCavery, '"As the Plague of Locusts came in Egypt": Rebel Motivation in North Down' in Bartlett et al., *1798 Rebellion*, 212–225.
119. See Daniel Gahan, 'Class, Religion and Rebellion: Wexford in 1798', in Smyth (ed.), *Revolution, Counter-Revolution and Union*, 83–98.
120. See Harman Murtagh, 'General Humbert's Futile Campaign', in Bartlett et al., *1798 Rebellion*, 174–187; Marianne Elliott, *Partners in Revolution: The United Irishmen and France* (New Haven: Yale University Press, 1982), 214–240.
121. For reflections on the quiescence of Munster, see David Dickson, 'Smoke without

social mixing and, 262; book, 263–264, 536n72; Hell Fire, 276–277; reciprocity and, 278; aesthetics and, 282

Coates, Hosea, 294

Coercion, toleration and, 496n93

Coffee, 223, 249–250

Coffeehouses, 223, 225, 228–230, 262, 293, 527nn76,77,80, 528n98; social aspect of, 209–210, 231–232; performances at, 210; alcohol and, 226, 528n89; legal business in, 229; culture of, 231–232; clientele of, 232, 245–246; of Limerick, 237; provincial, 237–238; social mixing and, 245; soldiers and, 245; violence and, 246–247; politics and, 248, 250

Coins, 199–200

Colbert's Circulating Library, 219–220

Colclough, Vesey, 349

A Collection of the Most Celebrated Irish Tunes (Neale and Neale), 143, 308

College Green, 297, 350, 364

College of Surgeons, 213

Collins, Arthur, 272

Collins, Thomas, 434

Colonial territories, 385

Colonisation, 3

Commercial civilisation, 328–329

Commercial equality, 382, 567n168

Commission of Overtures, 30

Committee of Commerce, 254

Committee of Merchants, 295, 296

Communal rights, 378

Communication, 210, 465, 514n70

Communion, 30, 35, 48, 51–52

Community, 328, 370, 376–380, 535n50, 536n72

A Concise Account of the Material Events and Atrocities which Occurred in the Late Rebellion (Musgrave), 417–418

Confederate Wars, 382

Confession, 11, 20; Christian, 23; legal restrictions of, 24; orthodoxy and, 29; of faith, 36; Church of Ireland and, 97; of Catholicism, 106, 112; patriotism and, 255; divide in, 325, 459; secular leadership for, 364; civility and, 462; kingship and, 462. *See also* Westminster Confession of Faith

Confessionalism, 14

Confraternity of Our Blessed Lady of Mount Carmel, 263

Connolly, Katharine, 166

Connor, Bernard, 148–156

Conquest, rights and, 84

Conscience, 25, 28, 32, 34–35, 72, 98, 423, 425, 485n41, 489n137

Considerations on Agriculture (Rye), 187

Constitution, 296, 319; Grand National Convention, 345–348, 350–351, 355, 356, 368, 379–380, 402; principles of, 349; volunteer movement and, 370; Molyneux on, 383; privilege and, 383–384; England and, 389, 393; design of, 390; rights and, 391; separation of powers, 391; development of, 393; change of, 398; mixed, 408

Conventions, 351–357

Convert Rolls, 116

Convulsionnaires, 147

Conynham, William Burton, 254

Cooley, Thomas, 295

Coombe, William, 277

Cooperation, politeness and, 278–281

Cork, 163, 188, 233, 238, 397, 439

Corkery, Daniel, 459

Cork Hill, 225

Cork Library, 233

Corn, 191

Corruption, 194, 201, 214, 350, 369, 387, 424, 569n211, 586n26

Cosmopolitanism, 7

Council of Arminum, 55

Council of Nicaea, 55, 101–102

Counter-Enlightenment, 4, 10

Counter-public sphere, 13, 233, 248, 250–251, 460

Counter-Reformation Catholicism, 3

County Kildare, 406

County Wexford, 406

Covenanters, 464

Cox, Richard, 141

Cox, Walter, 435

Craghead, Robert, 511n13

Creation, 73, 93, 99

Cromp, John, 298

Cross-confessional socialisation, 13

Crow Street, 218–219

Cuffe, John, 240

Cultural conflict, 430–437

Cultural empathy, society and, 557n170

Cultural intolerance, 578n91

Cultural liminality, 138

Cultural production, 430–432, 433

Cultural sensibility, 179

Culture: Anglicanism and, 128–129, 133, 143; Gaelic, 143; of theatre, 210, 234–237; of coffeehouses, 231–232; of associations, 256; of improvement, 285; politics and, 309, 311, 435–436, 577n87; organic theory of, 430; United Irishmen and, 430–432, 434, 436, 577nn89,90, 578n91; empiricism and, 433; popular, 436; of Dublin, 528n98; indigenous, 578n91

Cumberland, Duke of, 444–445

Cuming, Duncan, 54

Curragh, 437

Curry, John, 297, 298, 317–318, 319, 544n224

Custom House, 296, 545n253

Dalton, John, 272

Dame Street, 217–218

Dance, 178–179, 240

Death, 152

Debates, 227, 228

Deborah Dobson (fictional character), 335

Decency, 69, 279

Declaratory Act of 1720, 6, 330, 370, 378, 383

Decorum, 172, 279, 342–343

De Coverley, Roger, 169

Defenders, the, 443–444, 446

Deism, 16, 37, 154–155, 274

Delamain, Lawrence, 179

Delany, Patrick, 222

Democracy, 5, 7, 401, 408

Demosthenes, 212–213

Denmark, 78–80, 494n72

Denny, Arbella, 291

De Paul, Eustace, 213

Depravity of man, 24–28, 39–40, 147

Dermody, Thomas, 221

Dermott, Laurence, 252, 270, 274, 275–276

Derry, 60–61, 235–236

Desart, Baron, 240

Descartes, René, 8, 126

'Description of Sunday Evening Spent in a Coffeehouse in the City of Dublin' (Anketell), 232–233

Despotism, 410, 419, 423, 469

Devil, 94

Devonshire, Duke of, 284

The Diaboliad (Coombe), 277

Dialectics, 9

Dickson, William Steel, 353, 373

Discourse addressed to Magistrates and Men in Authority occasioned by the Enormous Licence and Irreligion of the Times (Berkeley), 95

Disease, 149, 163–164, 290

Disorderly conduct, 13

Dissenting community, 536n72

A Dissertation on the Principles of Human Eloquence (Leland), 323

Dissertations on the Ancient History of Ireland (O'Conor), 328

Divine intervention, 129

Divine will, 24

Divinity, 19, 92–93

Dixon, Thomas, 420

Dobbs, Arthur, 162, 203–205, 521n199

Dobbs, Francis, 354, 357, 369–370, 381, 559n31

Donegal, 116

Dopping, Anthony, 107

Doria, Andrew, 368, 369, 371, 564n101

Dorset, Duke of, 212, 550n32

Dowling, Vincent, 220

Drennan, William, 237, 263, 304, 390, 392, 394, 430, 568n206, 569n211; on Catholicism, 388–389; on politics, 391; medical background of, 393; United Irishmen and, 424, 575n62, 579n103; patriotism and, 431; letter to MacTier, 445; on volunteer movement, 568n201; trial of, 575n62

Drogheda, 163, 300

Drought, 163

Drought, Thomas, 354

Droz, Jean-Pierre, 224

Druidic theology, 329–330

Dublin: Presbyterianism and, 38, 225; poetry and, 133–134; beggars in, 161; bread riot in, 163; neighborhoods, 224–225; public sphere in, 224–233, 528n98; fashion, 230; theatre in, 242; United Irishmen and, 437; mortality rates in, 511n17; culture of, 528n98

Dublin Castle, 193, 212, 312–314, 315

Dublin Corporation, 294, 295, 299, 433, 569n224

Dublin Directory, 218, 226

Dublin Florists' Club, 253, 254

The Dublin Guide, 293

Dublin Home Rule assembly, 463

Dublin Intelligence, 223

Dublin Mercury, 210, 248

Dublin ministers, 46

Dublin Society, 254–262, 285, 312, 433, 534n16, 535nn43,47,50, 536n60, 547n285

Dublin Society of Surgeons, 213

Duchal, James, 46

Duelling, 246–247, 279

Duigenan, Patrick, 214–215

Dun, Patrick, 213

Dungannon Convention, 346, 351, 357

Duty, 49, 50, 203–204, 217, 444, 485n42

Economic development, 16

Economic voluntarism, 261

Economy, 161; social order and, 167; politeness and, 186; improvement and, 187; meltdown of, 198; children and, 206; failure of, 318; principles of, 319; neo-mercantilist, 382; human development and, 389. *See also* Political economy; Poverty

Edgeworth, Maria, 221, 464–466, 468, 472, 586nn22,26,31

Edgeworth, Richard, 237

Education, 426; standards of, 13; morality and, 43; rhetoric and, 173; habit and, 174; politeness and, 175, 515n93; improvement and, 196–197, 285–286; reform of, 197; art, 285; Catholicism and, 287; civility and, 287; women and, 287; principles of, 393; speech and, 514n68. *See also* Schools

Elegance, 177–178, 515n87

Elements of Mineralogy (Kirwan), 258
Elements of the Irish Language (Mac Cruitín), 141
Elizabeth (Queen), 469–470
Elocution, 175
Eloquence, reason and, 173
Elphin, 85
Emigration, Presbyterianism and, 511n13
Emlyn, Thomas, 54–58, 489n139
Emmet, Thomas Addis, 424
Emotions, 223, 310, 330–337, 468
Empiricism, 9, 12, 14, 409; Presbyterianism and, 24, 33; Boyse and, 39–40; Hutcheson and, 43–45; Belfast Society and, 46; Anglicanism and, 63, 85, 105, 133; God and, 77; of Connor, 149–150, 153, 155; improvement and, 189; of Rye, 189; agriculture and, 189–190, 543n219; Dublin Society and, 257–258; penal code and, 322; rationalism and, 344, 443; methodology of, 381; of Woodward, 400; loyalists and, 406–407, 447; FitzGibbon and, 416–417; of Musgrave, 420–422, 575n50; culture and, 433; labour and, 433; Edmund Burke and, 449, 451–452
England, 385–386; Ireland and, 2, 472, 588n58; urban centres of, 4; civil war in, 25; religion in, 71; landlords move to, 168; trade of, 202; Constitution and, 389, 393
English House of Lords, 6
English language, 141, 307, 521n197
English Privy Council, 113, 299, 313, 346, 365, 483n6
The Enlightenment (Ferrone), 478n36
Enniscorthy, 438
Equality, 83–84, 382, 407, 423, 567n168
Essai sur les moeurs (Voltaire), 2

Essay Concerning Human Understanding (Locke), 42, 172
An Essay on Spirit (Clayton), 97, 101, 499n154
An Essay on the Trade and Improvement of Ireland (Arthur Dobbs), 203
Essay on Toleration, or Plea for Liberty of Conscience (O'Leary), 18–19
An Essay towards a Natural, Experimental, and Medicinal History of the Mineral Waters of Ireland (Rutty), 289
Ethics (de Paul), 213
Ethics, chivalry and, 453–454
Ethnicity, religion and, 111
Euclid, 391
Europe, 3–4, 385
Evangelium Medici (Connor), 153
Evil, 389
Exchequer Street, 220
Existence, 90, 92, 99
De Existentia Dei (Michael Moore), 126, 128
'Expedients for Peace', 28–33, 48
Exportation, 198, 204
Exshaw, Edward, 224
Extension, 89–90
External spirits, 93

Fairs, 167, 178, 239, 240
Faith: communities, 11; ceremonies and, 15; human reason and, 15; God and, 18–19; error in, 19; mind and, 19; confession of, 36; essential and inessential articles of, 50–51, 59; of Emlyn, 54, 489n139; reasonableness of, 85–94; state and, 86; Berkeley and, 93–94; heresy and, 98; freedom and, 102; Trinity and, 102; public sphere and, 130–131, 321–322; pragmatic, 493n44. *See also* Religion; Westminster Confession of Faith

Family, 364–365, 487n79, 558n172

Famine, 163–167, 188

Farmers, 190, 289, 384

Farming, 2

Faroe, 78

Farther Considerations for the Improvement of the Tillage in Ireland (Pierson), 191

Fashion, 17, 95–96, 150–151, 178, 230, 455

Fast days, Catholic Church and, 165–166

Faulkner, George, 433–434

Faulkner's Dublin Journal, 284

Ferguson, Victor, 46

Ferrone, Vincenzo, 7, 478n36

Fideism, 62, 72, 102, 493n44

Fidelity, marriage and, 335

Field, John, 285

filí, 117, 502n41

Fires, 163

Fishamble Street, 218, 219, 286

Fishing, 384

Fitzgerald, Edward, 434, 437

Fitzgerald, John, 142

Fitzgerald, Thomas Judkin, 439

Fitzgerald, William, 281

FitzGibbon, John, 413, 414–417, 422

Fitzwilliam, Earl, 412–413

Flood, Henry, 245, 346, 348, 351

Flooding, 163

Food riots, 161

Food supply, 187–188

Foras Feasa ar Éirinn (Foundation of the History of Ireland), 142

Foreign demons, 137

Foreign goods, 17

Foreign luxury, 208

Foreign markets, 202

Fornication, 278

Foster, Yelverton, 401–402

Foundling Hospital, 290–291

Four Courts, 545n253

Fox, Charles James, 410, 424, 572n16

Frailty, improvement and, 285–293

France, 4, 351, 449, 455

Franco-Jacobite alliance, 108

Franquefort, Lieutenant, 247

Freedom, 102, 385–386, 388–389, 392, 407, 410

Freemasons, 13, 254, 262, 303, 443; origin of, 270; Society of, 270; lodges of, 270–272, 445–447, 538n115, 539n117; Grand Lodge, 271; Catholicism and, 271–274; Protestantism and, 272; membership, 273; Speculative, 273; free thinking and, 273–274; annual parade of, 274; calendar of, 274; levels of, 274; rituals of, 274, 540n150; ranks of, 275; structure of, 275; Bible and, 275–276; Genesis and, 276; God and, 276; Hell Fire Clubs, 276–278; Rebellion and, 445–447; United Irishmen and, 445–447; civil society and, 447; autonomy of, 539n147; public sphere and, 540n147, 582n144

Freethinking, 9, 23, 262, 459–460; speculative, 12, 23; fear of, 36, 37, 105; threat of, 58; Anglicanism and, 62–63, 105; Christianity and, 88; Synge and, 88; Berkeley and, 94, 97; prejudice and, 96; spectrum of Enlightenment and, 157; rituals of, 270–278; Freemasons and, 273–274

Free trade, 370, 382–385, 394, 521n199, 566n164, 567n168

Free will, God and, 73

French, John, 362

French civilisation, 454–455

French Revolution, 250, 405, 407, 408, 417, 432, 445, 448–457, 577n89

Frezell, John, 228

Friendly Brothers of St Patrick, 279–281

Friendship, 69, 180, 280–281
Fundamental Laws of the Friendly Brothers
    of St Patrick, 280–281
Funen, 78
Furly, Benjamin, 8

Gaelic culture, 143
Gaelic patronage system, 144
Gaelic poetry, 307, 310
Gaelic saints, 137
Gaelic scholarship, 325
Gaels, 134, 137
Gallagher, Owen, 226, 298–299
Gallantry, 168, 337, 392, 453, 454, 456,
    557n171
Gallican concillarism, 125
Galt, William, 263
Gambling, 240, 246
Gandon, James, 296, 545n253
Gardiner, Luke, 364, 367
Garrick, David, 334
Gaulstown House, 220
Geminianui, Franseco, 218
Gender, volunteer movement and, 392,
    569n211
General Committee, 269
General Grand Knot, 281
General Synod, 29–30
Genesis, 276
Genoa, 564n101
Gentleman's and Citizen's Almanack, 291
Geographic determinism, art and, 185
George I (King), 26, 198
George II (King), 27, 132, 261, 313
George III (King), 27, 298, 302, 360,
    410–411, 462, 547n287
George's Lane, 217
Gibbons, Luke, 578n91
Giffard, John, 433–434, 437, 440, 444
Giffard, William, 437

'Gile na Gile' (Ó Rathaille), 119
Gillen, Ultán, 476n14
Ginkel, Godert de, 62, 108
Glorvina (fictional character), 467–469
Gluttony, 168
God, 7, 478n36; existence of, 7, 93, 126,
    156; faith and, 18–19; judgements of, 19;
    power of, 19; behaviour and, 24; grace
    of, 24, 37; conscience and, 25, 28,
    34–35; Trinity and, 25; subscribers and,
    36; Hutcheson and, 44–45; will of, 46,
    50, 52, 63, 73, 86; Jesus Christ and,
    54–57, 98–100; Scholasticism and, 62;
    war and, 62, 104; reason and, 72; Swift
    on, 72, 73, 493n44; benevolence of, 73;
    creation and, 73, 99; free will and, 73;
    War of the Two Kings and, 74;
    empiricism and, 77; Berkeley on,
    92–94; fear of, 97; Clayton on, 98,
    102–103; Image of, 100; suffering and,
    104, 144; rationalism and, 105; Michael
    Moore and, 128; human beings and,
    129; Catholicism and, 144; distance
    from, 144–148; Jansenism and, 147;
    Connor on, 153; knowledge and, 269;
    Freemasons and, 276; happiness and,
    319; Arthur O'Connor on, 425; Russell
    on, 429; individual relationship with,
    493n44
Godwin, William, 185
Goldsmith, Oliver, 337, 339–343,
    557nn170,171
Goodall, James, 421
The Good Old Way Examined (Malcome),
    36–37, 48–49
Gospels, 15, 100
Goths, 79
Government, 369, 377–378, 414, 426
'Grace Nugent', 143
Graduate tax, 214

Grafton, Lord, 26

Grain prices, 417

Grammar, 134, 141

Grand Lodge, 271, 444–445

Grand National Convention, 345–348,
350–351, 355, 356, 368, 379–380, 402

Grattan, Henry, 346, 367, 374, 375,
401–402, 410, 412–413, 424, 465,
572n16

Greek, 127, 215

Gregg, James, 238

Grierson, Constantia, 222

Griffin, Michael, 557n170

Griffith, Amyas, 354

Guatimozin, 381–382, 567n180

Guild of Merchants and Corporation, 413

Gulliver's Travels (Swift), 60, 63–72,
492n36

Habermas, Jürgen, 480n52

Habit, education and, 174

Haceldama, 131, 505n96

Haliday, Samuel, 46

Hamilton, Francis, 247

Hamilton, Myrton, 236

Handel, George Frideric, 284, 542n194

Hanoverian accession, 27–28

Hansard, John, 266

Happiness, 43, 170, 183, 203–204, 319,
429, 478n36

Harrington, 1st Earl of (William
Stanhope), 257

Harris, Walter, 287–289

Hartley, Travers, 294

Harvest, 161–163, 314, 470

Hawkers, tax on peddlers and, 265

Hay, John, 233

Hayden, Margaret, 291

Hayes, Daniel, 277

Hayley, William, 155–156

Heaven, 18

Hebrew language, 100, 127

Hell Fire Clubs, 276–277

Helsham, Thomas, 222

Hely-Hutchinson, John, 123, 179,
214–216, 515n92

Henry II, 81–82, 301, 470

Henry III, 383

Henry IV, 392

Henry VIII, 83

Heresy, 425; Arianism and, 36, 37, 55, 71;
Malcome and, 47; of Emlyn, 56–57;
Swift and, 71; punishment for, 86;
morality and, 95; Clayton and, 97–98,
103; faith and, 98; opinions and, 98; as
virtue, 98; Lateran Council and, 419;
Musgrave and, 419. *See also* Emlyn,
Thomas

Hervey, Frederick, 348, 362, 363, 372

Heterodoxy, 4, 38, 53–54, 58, 95, 100, 104,
127, 146, 156

Hibernia Anglicana (Richard Cox), 141

Hibernian Antiquarian Society, 254,
285–286, 323, 547n285, 552n68

Hibernian Journal, 220

'Hibernicus's Letters' (Arbuckle), 224, 226

Hickson, Robert, 246

Higgins, Francis, 249, 434

High Church Tories, 27

High Dutch, 495n72

High Enlightenment, 12

Historical dynamic, 8–9

Historical Memoirs of the Irish Bards
(Walker), 221

Historical painting, 183

*An Historical Poem in Honour of the Loyal
Society of Journeymen Shoemakers*
(Ashton), 292

History, 129, 141–142, 369, 389–390, 451,
454

History of England (Hume), 1–2

History of Ireland from the Invasion of Henry II (Leland), 323

History of Poland (Connor), 149

Hoadley, John, 315

Hobbes, Thomas, 86, 88, 161–162, 172

Hoey, James, 219, 230, 248

Hogan, Owen, 299

Holland, 8, 386

Hollister, William, 219

Holmes, Richard, 511n40

Holy Ghost, 25

Holy Trinity. *See* Trinity

Honesty, 339

Honeycomb, William, 169

Honour, 339, 558n172

Hope Circulating Library, 220

Horatio (fictional character), 467–469

Horn, Pamela, 518n137

Horse racing, 240

Hortatio ad studium linguae Graecae et Hebraicae (Michael Moore), 127

Hospital for the Incurables, 216, 244, 292

Hospitality, 223, 328

Houlton, Dr, 236–237

House of Commons, 351, 365

Houyhnhnms (fictional horses), 69–70

Howard, Gorges Edmond, 192–194

Human beings: autonomy of, 92, 429; existence and, 92; spirit and, 92; philosophy and, 112, 147; God and, 129; clubs and, 262; as basic unit of analysis, 459. *See also* Individual; Man

Human capacity, 46, 59

Human condition, 268

Human development, 389, 450

Humanism, 478n36

Humanity: understanding and, 7–8, 19, 478n36; divinity and, 19; Presbyterianism and, 24–28; morality

and, 39; weakness of, 40, 381; rationalism and, 52; in *Gulliver's Travels*, 67; matter and, 89; sensory range of, 89–92; treatment of, 208; duty and, 217; emotions and, 223

Human nature, 35, 39–40, 49, 194, 391

Humbert, General, 438

An Humble Inquiry into the Scripture Account of Jesus Christ: Or A Short Argument concerning his Deity and Glory according to the Gospel (Emlyn), 54–57

An Humble Proposal for Obtaining His Majesty's Royal Charter to Incorporate a Society for Promoting Christian Knowledge among the Poor Natives of the Kingdom of Ireland (Maule), 264–265

Humble Remonstrance for the Repeal of the Laws Against the Roman Catholics, 317–318

Hume, David, 1–2, 263–264, 323, 391

Humphrey, Sir, 169

Hunting clubs, 239–240, 530n138

Hurling, 240–241

'The Hurling at Mohurry', 240

Husbandry, 191, 193, 194

Hussey, Thomas, 417

Hutcheson, Francis, 23, 41–45, 161–162, 179–180, 226, 487nn79,89, 516n97

Hutchinson, Robert, 238

Iceland, 78

Ideas, 90–93, 258

Identity, 504n69

Ignorance, 399

Image of God, 100

Imagination, 92, 176, 325

Imagined community, 328

Immaterialism, 89–91

Imperial aspect, 5

Imperialism, 383, 567n165

Imports, 200, 204, 249–250, 329, 382

Improvement, 12–13, 170; conditions of
life, 170; political economy and, 186;
agriculture and, 186–190, 194, 518n137;
theorising, 186–197; economy and, 187;
politics and, 187; empiricism and, 189;
rationalism and, 195, 409; state and,
195–196; education and, 196–197,
285–286; Catholicism and, 204–205;
refinement and, 207; Swift on, 207–208;
politeness and, 208; culture of, 285;
frailty and, 285–293; social activism and,
287; innovation and, 399; religion and,
518n138. See also *Modest Proposal*

Inanimate objects, 180

Incorporated Society for Promoting
English Protestant Schools in Ireland,
265–270

In Defence of the Enlightenment
(Todorov), 478n36

India, 588n58

Indigenous cultures, 578n91

Individual: Belfast Society and, 50; truth
seeking of, 52; sentiment and, 343;
autonomy, 451; beliefs and, 460;
relationship with God, 493n44; society
and, 523n4. *See also* Human beings; Man

Individuality, 451

Industrial developments, 204

Industry, 426

Inflation, harvest and, 314

Innocence, 177

Innovation, 398–399

*Inquiry in the Origins and Nature of the
Wealth of Nations* (Adam Smith),
382–383

*Inquiry into the Original or Our Ideas of
Beauty and Virtue* (Hutcheson), 42, 44,
179, 487n79

*An Inquiry into the Real and Imaginary
Obstructions to the Acquisition of the
Arts in England* (James Barry), 185

Inquisition, 32

Insurrection Act, 431, 440

Integrity, 324

Intellectual autonomy, 269

Intellectual expression, 309

Intellectual freedom, 102

Intellectual life, 124, 125, 459

Intuitive thought process, 9

Iredell, Francis, 511n13

Ireland: England and, 2, 472, 588n58;
history of, 3, 20; intellectual history of,
3, 7; children as metaphor for, 392–393.
See also Church of Ireland

Irenic Presbyterianism, 37–46

Irish clerics, 125, 475n8, 504n69

Irish Colleges, 125

Irish Hospitality (Shadwell), 242

Irish House of Lords, 365

Irish-language manuscripts, 133–136, 142

Irish Melodies (Thomas Moore), 467, 469,
470, 586n33

Irish Privy Council, 298, 302

Irish Rebellion (Temple), 76

Irish Republican Army, 462

Irish students, 504n69

Irish Treasury Board, 411

Irreligion, 88, 95–96, 127, 274

'Is Fada Liom Oíche Fhírfhliuch'
(Ó Rathaille), 121–122

Israel, Jonathan, 8, 479n44

Italian Circulating Library, 233

Ivers, Peter, 253

Ivory, Thomas, 285

Jackson's Circulating Library, 220

Jacobite parliament, 107

Jacobite rebellion, 212

Jacobite risings, 364

Jacobites, 60–62

Jacobitism, Catholicism and, 113

James I (King), 2

James II (King), 11–12, 27, 60–61, 101, 156,
    574n47; Protestantism and, 74–75, 77,
    107–108; Roman Catholicism and,
    74–75; Jacobite parliament and, 107;
    Nicholas Browne and, 121; Moore and,
    126; Nary and, 131–132

James III (King), 363

Jansenism, 125, 144, 147–148, 509n162

Jansensius, 146

Jason Quirk (fictional character), 465–466

Jaucourt, Louis chevalier de, 2

Jebb, Frederick, 381–385, 387–388, 391, 394

Jehovah, 99

Jesus Christ, 32, 35, 47–49, 54–57, 97–100,
    103, 123

John III (King), 148, 151

John Lord Marquis of Normandy, 151

Johnson, John, 379–380

Johnson, Philip, 441

Johnson, Robert, 567n180

Johnson, Samuel, 184, 221, 337

Jolly, Henry, 246–247

Jones, Nicholas, 247

Joshua, John Pim, 294

Journeymen Tailors, 292–293

Joy, Francis, 233

Joy, Henry, 408, 409, 435

Joyce, Patrick, 281

Jurisprudence, 451

Keane, John, 523n4

Kelly, Edward, 226, 243–245

Kelly, Hugh, 334–337, 555n120, 558n172

Kelly, James, 241, 565n134, 569n224

Kenmare, Viscount, 347

Kenney, John, 280

Kerwin, Patrick, 247

Kildare, 237

Kildare, Earl of, 266

Kildare Knot, 280, 281

Kildare Street Club, 254

Kilfeather, Siobhán, 574n50

King, William, 73–74, 77, 574n47

Kingship, confession and, 462

Kingsland, Viscount, 271

Kirkpatrick, James, 47–48

Kirwan, Richard, 258

Knot, 279–280

Knots of the Friendly Society of St
    Patrick, 303

Knowledge, 42, 84, 91, 269

Knox, Thomas, 442–443

Labour, 428, 433, 576n75

Lachrymæ academicæ (Duigenan), 214–215

Lament for Art O'Leary (Ní Chonaill),
    358–361, 562n70

Landlords, 165–168, 200–201, 206, 348,
    586n26

Land redistribution, 427

Land reform, 427

Lane, Richard, 238

Languages: Hebrew, 100, 127; Oriental,
    100; Irish, 133–136, 142, 307, 308;
    English, 141, 307, 521n197; rhetoric,
    171–173; decorum and, 172; modern,
    215; poetry and, 307; Charlotte Brooke
    on, 307–308; translations, 310;
    Phoenician, 324; translators, 325; of
    privilege, 403; nature of, 466; music
    and, 587n33. See also Poetry

Laputa (fictional island), 67–68

Lateran Council, 419

Latin, 215

Latitudinarianism, 85–88, 105

Law, John, 17

Laws: rule of law, 2; marriage, 25–26; of
    Jesus Christ, 32; natural, 40, 84,
    147–148; in New Testament, 48; of
    polity, 116, 501n35; civil, 126; moral,
    126; Mosaic, 127; refinement and,
    325–326; power of, 389–390; tithe
    and, 399–400; democracy and, 401;
    martial, 441; history and, 451, 454;
    Presbyterianism and, 483n13; Roman
    Catholicism and, 538n108
Lawson, John, 172, 174
Lectures Concerning Oratory (Lawson), 172
Lectures on Elocution (Thomas Sheridan),
    174
Legal rights, 400
Legislation, 83, 201, 318, 547n275
Legitimacy, 132, 210, 327, 369, 448
Leinster, 108, 163
Leland, Thomas, 212, 323–328, 330
Lens, Peter, 94
Leskean Cabinet, 258
'Letter from the Quidnuncs at St James
    Coffee-House and the Mall' in
    London, and addressed to 'their
    brethren at Lucas's Coffee-House', 230
Letters of Orellana, an Irish Helot
    (Drennan), 388–390, 393–394, 430–431,
    568n201, 569n218
The Letters of Owen Roe O'Nial (Pollack),
    381
'Letters on the British Constitution'
    (William Bruce and Joy), 407–409
Letters on the English Nation (Voltaire), 2
Letter to the Dilettanti Society (James
    Barry), 184
Letter to the Dublin Society (Madden),
    254–256, 259, 534n16
*A Letter to the People of Ireland, on the
    Present Situation of the Country*
    (Russell), 427–428, 432

Lewis, Richard, 226, 293
Libertine societies, 276–278
Licentiousness, 41, 95, 336–337
Lilliputians (fictional characters), 64–67,
    71
Limerick, 237, 439
Limerick, Viscount, 297–298
Linen industry, 314
Linguistics, 134
A List of the Absentees of Ireland (Prior),
    200
Litchfield, John, 238
Literature, 309, 434–435. *See also* Poetry
Lloyd, Sylvester, 144–147
Locke, John, 8, 15, 42, 88, 90, 172, 495n81,
    576n75
London, 5–6, 381
Louisa Mildmay (fictional character),
    334–337
Louis XIV, 60, 81, 108
Love, 40–41, 333, 340, 487n79, 569n216
Love, Walter D., 547n285
Love à la Mode (Macklin), 337–339
Low Church, 85
Loyalists: empiricism and, 406–407, 447;
    politics of, 406–407, 423; rationalism
    and, 423; United Irishmen and,
    447–448
Loyalty, privilege and, 346
Lucan House, 221
Lucas, Charles, 226, 294, 532n177
Lust, 341
Luttrell, Simon, 277
Luxury, 17, 194–195, 200, 208, 329, 346,
    353
Lying-In Hospital, 216–217
Lynch, Patrick, 432
Lynch, William, 134
Lynegar, Charles, 139–140
Lyster, Christopher, 350

Macarell, John, 294

MacCarthy, Justin, 108

MacCarthy clan, 121–122

Mac Craith, Aindrias, 123, 133

Mac Cruitín, Aobh Buidhe, 135, 140–141

Mac Domhnaill, Seán Clárach, 109–110

Mackay, Miss (actress), 218

MacKenna, Theobald, 304

Macklin, Charles, 337–339, 342

MacLaughlin, Cathal, 337

MacNamara, Daniel, 299

Macpherson, James, 553n74

MacSarcasm (fictional character), 338–339

MacTier, Samuel, 445

Madden, Samuel, 214, 254–256, 259, 534nn15,16,24

Magan, Francis, 434

Magdalen Asylum, 291

Magdalen House (fictional house), 335–336

Magill, Robert Hawkins, 229

Magistrates, power of, 19

Mahoney, Clarke, 272

Mahoney, Keane, 272

Maizeaux, Pierre des, 8

Major, Dorothy, 311–312

Malcome, John, 34–35, 47–49

Malebranche, 497n115

Malton, James, 226

Man, 7–8, 18; depravity of, 24–28, 39; subscribers and, 36; reason and, 43; equality and, 83–84; rights of, 84, 423, 430; science of, 157. See also Human beings; Humanity; Individual

Manhood, 69

Manners, 337–343, 454

Mannin, James, 285

Mansergh, Danny, 559n31

Manufacturing, 202, 384

Marlow (fictional character), 339–342

Marriage: Anglicanism and, 25–26; laws, 25–26; Presbyterianism and, 26, 366, 367, 563n95; women and, 332, 555n111; love and, 333; fidelity and, 335; sentiments and, 337–338, 339; Protestantism and, 366, 563n95; mixed, 367

Marsh, Narcissus, 219

Martial law, 441

Martin, Robert, 246–247

Marx, Karl, 576n75

Mary (Queen), 317, 469

Masons. See Freemasons

Master of the Revels, 212

Masturbation, 278

Materialism, 155, 207

Materialist philosophy, 89–90

Mathematics, 392

Matter, 89–91

Maule, Henry, 264–265, 268

Mayor, Lord, 218

McCarthy, Charles, 272

McCormack, W. J., 569n224

McDermott, Anthony, 294, 298

Meath, Earl of, 218

Meath Hospital, 291

Medico-Philosophical Society, 289–290

Meditation, 47

Memoirs of a Magdalen (Hugh Kelly), 334–337, 555n120

Memoirs of Captain Rock (Thomas Moore), 459, 464, 469–472, 587nn43,47

Memoirs of Miss Sidney Bidulph (Frances Sheridan), 331–334, 554n106, 555n111

Memoirs of the Different Rebellions in Ireland from the Arrival of the English (Musgrave), 420

Men of letters, 456

Mercantilism, 6, 13, 198, 202, 293–297

Mercier Hospital, 216

The Merry Fellow or Entertaining Magazine, 230
Mervyn, Arthur, 247
Messiah (Handel), 284, 542n194
Metaphysica genralis (Baron), 213
Metaphysics, 126, 319
Mezeer, Luke, 228
Michael (Archangel), 103
Military, 6, 370, 448
Militia, 371–372, 444
Militia Act, 561n61
Miller, Hannah, 238
Miller, James, 315
Mind, 19, 92–93
Ministers, 30, 33–34, 214, 400
Minor, Jenny, 311
Miss Burchell (fictional character), 332–334
Miss Hardcastle (fictional character), 339–342
Missionaries, of Catholicism, 115
Miss Neville (fictional character), 339–340
Modernisation, 3, 7, 463
Modest Proposal (Swift), 162, 206–209
Moira House, 221
Molesworth, Robert, 78–81, 220, 494nn71,72
Molyneux, William, 78, 81–82, 84, 383, 495n81
Monaghan militia, 440
Monarchy, 408, 448–449, 453
Money, 199–201, 534n24
Money bill crisis, 311–315, 550nn30,33
Monks of the Screw, 382
Montpellier, 144–145
Moore, Baron, 166
Moore, John, 355–356
Moore, Michael, 125–128
Moore, Roger, 326
Moore, Sean, 5

Moore, Thomas, 459, 464, 467, 469–472, 586n33, 587nn43,47
Morality: Presbyterianism and, 25, 28; religion and, 28; Boyse and, 39; humanity and, 39; Hutcheson and, 42–43; education and, 43; good and evil, 44; natural good, 44; autonomy of, 59; truth and, 62; Blasters and, 95; heresy and, 95; Nary and, 129; youth and, 129; refinement and, 169–170, 513n50; politeness and, 170; art and, 183, 185, 194; opinions and, 196; trade and, 203; civility and, 210; associations and, 278; women and, 287, 543n210; volunteer movement and, 354; feeling and, 386; people and, 428
Moral law, 126
Mornington, Lord, 284
Morris, Abraham, 359–361
Mosaic law, 127
Mosse, Bartholomew, 213, 216–217, 292
Mr Arnold (fictional character), 331–334, 557n172
Mr Hardcastle (fictional character), 340–341, 342
Mulligan, Peter, 134
Multiplier effect, poverty and, 199
Munster, 108, 117, 161, 363, 397, 439, 500n6, 502n40, 511n17
Murphy, Laughlin, 277
Musgrave, Richard, 417–422, 445, 574nn47,48,50, 575n55
Music, 143, 432, 468, 578n94, 587n33
Musical Academy, 219
Musical and Charitable Society, 143
Muskerry Constitutional Society, 359
Mysticism, 9

Naas, 421
Nagle, Nano, 287

Nary, Cornelius, 106, 129–132, 508n146

National Assembly, 450–451, 453, 456

National bank, 195

National debt, 313, 549n24

National identity, 463, 466

National independence, 407

National Journal, 435

National partiality, 390

National society, 195

Natural good, 44

Natural law, 40, 84, 147–148

Natural phenomena, 153–154

Natural rights, 53, 317, 402, 403, 406, 412, 415, 426, 571n245

Nature, 93, 176, 194

Neal, John, 143, 283

Neal, William, 143, 283–284

Neale, John, 308

Neale, William, 308

Necker, Jacques, 455

Nelson, Henry, 292–293, 544n235

Neophilosophers, 301

Nevin, Thomas, 46

Newcastle, Duke of, 162–163

Newcombe, William, 563n94

New congregations, 29

Newenham, Edward, 366

New History of the World (Nary), 129

New Light theology, 36, 485n42

A New Poem on the Ancient and Loyal Society of Journey-Men Tailors (Nelson), 292–293

New Ross, 439

Newspapers, 210, 223–224, 233–234, 248–249, 532nn177,180

New Testament, 15, 46, 48, 100, 103, 147

Nice Council, 36

Nicene Creed, 102

Ní Chonaill, Eibhlín Dubh, 358–362, 562n70

Nickson, Christina, 214–215

Nielson, Samuel, 434

Nobility, 201, 265, 279, 295–296

Nomism, 486n63

Non-governmental institutions, 523n4

Non-subscribers: ministers as, 30, 34; Synods and, 30, 31–33; Belfast Society, 36; orthodoxy and, 37, 486n63; prominent, 46; Jesus Christ and, 47–49; Presbyterianism and, 49; rethinking, 59

Nordic myth, 324–325, 552n74

North, Frederick, 364

Northern Star, 250, 435, 440

Nugent, Colonel, 247

Nugent, Robert, 271

Oaths: of abjuration, 114, 130; of supremacy, 114; of allegiance, 130, 132, 205, 297, 319, 362–363, 364, 367; public, 130, 464; of United Irishmen, secret, 443; fad, 583n152

Obedience, religion and, 35, 80

Objects, 89–92

Ó Bruadair, Dáibhí, 110

Observations on the Popery Laws (Curry and O'Conor), 317

O'Connell, Daniel, 472, 588n58

O'Connor, Arthur, 424–427, 430, 432, 440, 576n65

O'Connor, Dermot, 134, 507n137

O'Conor, Charles, 221, 297, 304, 317, 323, 327–330, 362, 363

Ó Dábhoireann, Uilliam an Chreatháin, 374

Ó Dálaigh, Seaghán, 164–165

Ó Dálaigh, Séamus, 374–375

Odensee, 79

Ó Dornín, Peadar, 133

O'Flaherty, Roderick, 81

'Of the Scythian or Celtic Nations'
    (O'Conor), 329
Ogle, George, 347, 350
Ó Gormáin, Muiris, 221
Ogygia (Roderick O'Flaherty), 81
O'Halloran, Sylvester, 290
Old Testament, 46, 103
O'Leary, Arthur, 18–20, 358–361,
    562n70
Ó Mathúna, Donnchadh Caoch, 112
Ó Míocháin, Thomás, 375
Ó Neachtain, Seán, 135–140
Ó Neachtain, Tadhg, 133, 134–136,
    141–143, 164
O'Neale, Cormuck, 76
O'Neill, Owen Roe, 381
'On Imagining a Friend had Treated the
    Author with Indifference' (Barber), 222
'On Love to Our Neighbour' (Boyse), 38
Ontology, 50
Opinions, 98, 196
Orange Lodge 132, 236
Orange Order, 436, 441, 443–445, 446
Ó Rathaille, Aogán, 110–111, 118–125
Oriental languages, 100
Original sin, 147, 509n162
Orlando Faulkland (fictional character),
    332, 334
Orpen, Francis, 238
Orpen, Susanna Maria Frances, 238
Orr, William, 431, 440
Orthodoxy: power and, 19; confession
    and, 29; Synods and, 33; non-
    subscribers and, 37, 486n63; ratio-
    nalism and, 52; Belfast Society and, 58;
    determination of, 86; Christianity and,
    98; Clayton and, 102, 104; public
    sphere and, 216
Ossian texts, 553n74
Oulart Hill, 438

Ould, Fielding, 213
Ouzel Galley Society, 293–294
Owensen, Robert, 218
Owenson, Sydney, 464, 467–469, 472

Paddy's Resource, 432
Pain, power and, 181
Painting, 183, 186
Palaeosophers, 301
Papal authority, 106, 395–396
Papists, 18, 380
Parents, 207
Paris, Irish clerics in, 475n8
Parliament, 6, 81; unification of, 312,
    549n20; reform of, 316, 368, 413;
    duration of, 348; corruption in, 350;
    representing the people, 368–380;
    independence of, 378; ministers and,
    400; Whig Party in, 410
Parliament Street, 228
Parsons, Richard, 277
Partnership, 450
Pasley, Thomas, 237
Passion, 178, 182, 326, 335, 342
'Patrick Sarsfield', 143
Patriotism, 353; agriculture and, 192;
    money and, 202; progress and, 207;
    confession and, 255; Dublin Society
    and, 261, 536n60; politics and, 300,
    547n275; volunteer movement and,
    354–355, 371; Drennan and, 431
Patriot party, 330, 345–346, 367, 375, 376,
    403
Patronage, 344, 349, 410–411, 423
Peddlers, tax on hawkers and, 265
Peep O'Day Boys, 444
Pelham, Thomas, 345
Penal code, 19, 112–117, 205, 263, 317,
    414–415, 515n81; origin of, 113; targets
    of, 113; oath of abjuration, 114, 130;

Penal code *(continued)*
oath of supremacy, 114; failure of, 116; loopholes in, 116; psychological pressure from, 117, 156; Articles of Limerick and, 130; Nary and, 130–131; social structure and, 131; repeal of, 273; challenging, 318, 551n51; War of the Two Kings and, 320, 322; ratification of, 320–321; Arthur Browne on, 322; empiricism and, 322; conversion to Catholicism and, 357–358; family relations in, 364–365; natural rights and, 412; wrongs of, 412; contradictory nature of, 501n32

Pensions, 348

People, 379–380, 396, 428, 568n201

Perception, 89–93

Perceval, Martha, 221

Perceval, Robert, 301

Persecution, 75

Personality, politeness and, 341

Personal Persuasion no Foundation for Religious Obedience (Malcome), 47

Persuasion, 51–52

Phiippics (Demosthenes), 212–213

Phillips, William, 218

A Philosophical Enquiry into the Origin of our Ideas of the Sublime and Beautiful (Edmund Burke), 179–180, 454

Philosophical Transactions, 188

Philosophy, 3, 89–90, 112, 147, 330, 392

Phoenician language, 324

Physico-Historical Society, 254, 287–289

Physiocratic theory, 428

Pierson, Samuel, 189–193

Pike, Joseph, 294

Pilkington, Laetitia, 222, 277

Pillaging, 2

Pim, Joseph, 294

Pinkerton, John, 553n74

Pitt, Moses, 81

Pitt, William, 297, 410–411, 412, 462

Plain Arguments in Defence of the People's Absolute Dominion over the Constitution (Peter Burrowes), 345, 376

Playhouse, regional, 212

Pleasure, 42, 44, 93, 104, 181, 182

Ploughing fields, 190–192

Plunkett, Richard, 326

Pococke, Richard, 253

Poems Moral and Descriptive (Dermody), 221

Poetry, 108–111, 500n6; Catholicism and, 111; of *filí*, 117, 502n41; of Munster, 117, 502n40; of Ulster, 117, 502n40; beauty in, 118–120; *aisling* genre of, 118–125; Scholasticism poetics, 118–128; poets as shamans, 121; ambiguity in expression of, 122; as defiance, 122; Jesus Christ in, 123; sex and, 123; Trinity in, 123; prophecy in, 124; Dublin and, 133–134; English, 185–186; Gaelic, 307, 310; language and, 307; songs and, 308; emotions and, 310; power of bards, 325; politics and, 374–375, 503n54; of United Irishmen, 431–432. *See also* Languages

Poles, 150–151, 153

Politeness, 12; behaviour and, 170, 171, 176, 207; morality and, 170; education and, 175, 515n93; speech and, 175; fashion and, 178; virtue and, 178; economy and, 186; improvement and, 208; cooperation and, 278–281; personality and, 341; elegance and, 515n87

Political economy, 12, 170, 384; Scottish school of, 17–18, 482n67; improvement and, 186; aesthetics and, 197; Irish school of, 197–206; writers of, 198. *See also* Economy

Political Enlightenment, 8, 10, 13–14, 308, 343–344, 461

Political philosophy, 392

Politics: religion and, 20, 95; Catholicism and, 112, 387, 388–389; art and, 185, 518n129; improvement and, 187; public sphere and, 247–248, 344, 523n5, 532n177; coffeehouses and, 248, 250; newspapers and, 248–249, 532nn177,180; theatre and, 249, 314–316, 532n187, 550n30; alcohol and, 250; civil society and, 260, 448, 460; Dublin Society and, 260; patriotism and, 300, 547n275; Royal Irish Academy and, 302–303; culture and, 309, 311, 435–436, 577n87; intellectual expression and, 309; relationships and, 309; corruption and, 369; poetry and, 374–375, 503n54; privilege and, 378–380, 394, 403; Drennan on, 391; rights and, 391, 400–401, 463; vocabulary of, 400; of United Irishmen, 406; of loyalists, 406–407, 423; violence and, 424, 441–442; legitimacy and, 448; monarchy and, 448–449; sentiment and, 454; Whig, 513n44

Pollock, Joseph, 382, 385–388, 391, 394, 568n197

Ponsonby, John, 298, 311–312, 412

Ponsonby, W. B., 413

Popery, 113, 116, 132, 205, 363, 419

Population, 206–207, 312

Portaferry Literary Society, 263

Porter, James, 434–435

Portraiture, 183

Potatoes, 519n150

Potts, James, 434

Pouget, François, 144

Poverty, 161–162, 187, 194, 198, 400, 521n199; multiplier effect and, 199;

alcohol and, 289; wealth and, 428; in France, 449

Powell, Martyn, 533n5

Power, John, 238

Poynings's law, 6, 108, 346, 352, 378

Pragmatic faith, 493n44

Prayers, 47

Pre-Christian era, 129, 324, 327, 328

Précis du Siècle de Louis XV (Voltaire), 2–3

Prejudice, 96–98, 173, 190, 324, 396, 399, 429, 449–450

Presbyterianism, 12; rationalism and, 23–24, 77; empiricism and, 24, 33; five basic tenets of, 24; depravity of man and, 24–28; humanity and, 24–28; in British Isles, 25; morality and, 25, 28; Scottish, 25; Catholicism and, 26; children of, 26; marriage and, 26, 366, 367, 563n95; Protestantism and, 26, 28; public sphere and, 26; scriptural interpretation and, 29; subscribers and, 36; Irenic, 37–46; Dublin and, 38, 225; non-subscribers and, 49; tolerance and, 53; toleration and, 53; Arianism and, 156; Dublin Society and, 259; in Ulster, 263, 396; volunteer movement and, 366, 404; army of, 374; false consciousness of, 420; intellectual life of, 459; laws and, 483n13; polite, 485n42; emigration and, 511n13. *See also* Synods

Presbytery of Antrim, 29, 30, 32, 484n27

The Present State of the Church of Ireland (Woodward), 395, 398

The Present State of the Tillage in Ireland Considered (Pierson), 189–190

The Press, 435

Pride, 70–72, 177

Priestcraft, 15

Primary ideas, 90

Prince of Wales, 410–411

The Principles of Human Knowledge (Berkeley), 88, 90–91

Prior, Thomas, 200–203, 521n198

Privacy, in urban environments, 522n2

Private judgement, 31, 47, 49, 485n41

Private sphere, 101, 209, 452

Privilege, 444; public sphere and, 245; in Articles of Limerick, 322; loyalty and, 346; of voting, 378; politics and, 378–380, 394, 403; of citizenship, 380; people and, 380; constitution and, 383–384; Church of Ireland and, 394; rights and, 400–401, 461; language of, 403; vocabulary of, 403; volunteer movement and, 403; United Irishmen and, 578n91

Proceedings of the Royal Dublin Society, 221

Profession de Foy (Barnewall), 147

Propaganda war, 445

Property rights, 113–114, 349, 365, 368, 376, 428, 464, 576n75

Prophecy, 124, 504n64

A Proposal for the General Encouragement of Learning in Dublin College (Madden), 214

Proposal for the Universal Use of Irish Manufactures (Swift), 198

Protestant Ascendancy, 395–396, 400–401, 414, 462, 466, 569n224, 573n32

The Protestant Catechism, 267

Protestantism, 3; Catholicism and, 18, 74–76, 80, 107–108, 244–245, 373–374; Presbyterianism and, 26, 28; dissenters of, 27; Boyse's definition of, 38; infallibility and, 49; James II and, 74–75, 77, 107–108; elections within, 115; Freemasons and, 272; slavery and, 345; reform movement and, 348;

marriage and, 366, 563n95; Newenham and, 366; volunteer movement and, 380; progress of, 396; Roman Catholicism and, 417–418; English and, 521n197

Protestant principle, 31

Provincial public sphere, 233–241, 530n134

Public health, 250

Public oaths, 130, 464

Public opinion, 423

Public speaking, 174, 175

Public sphere, 12–13, 207; counter-public sphere, 13, 233, 248, 250–251, 460; Presbyterianism and, 26; private and, 101, 209; faith, 130–131, 321–322; of Social Enlightenment, 211; state and, 211, 316; theatre and, 212; orthodoxy and, 216; unofficial, 220–224; women of, 221–223; after War of the Two Kings, 223; literary, 223–224; in Dublin, 224–233, 528n98; provincial, 233–241, 530n134; social mixing, 241–247; privilege and, 245; politics and, 247–248, 344, 523n5, 532n177; origin of, 293, 523n5; administration of, 303; private sphere and, 452; elite and, 522n2; Madden and, 534n24; Freemasons and, 540n147, 582n144; volunteer movement and, 559n32; spirit, 569n216. *See also* Bookshops; Clubs; Coffeehouses; Taverns

Pue's Occurrences, 240–241, 284

Pufendorf, Samuel, 213, 266–267

Purcell, John, 304

Pursell, Joseph, 291

Putland, John, 253, 254

Quakerism, 37, 38, 289–290, 464

The Querist (Berkeley), 16–18, 161, 170

Quesnelle, 146
Quidnuncs, 230

Racism, 578n91
Radical Enlightenment (Israel), 479n44
Radicalism, 402, 408–409, 424, 427–429,
    442, 444, 460, 532n179
Ranelagh, 219
Rape, 277
Rationalism, 9, 12, 14, 20, 23, 392;
    Presbyterianism and, 23–24, 77;
    scriptural interpretation and, 24, 33;
    Boyse and, 39; Hutcheson, 42–43;
    humanity and, 52; orthodoxy and, 52;
    scholasticism and, 59; Berkeley and, 85,
    94; God and, 105; Descartes and, 126;
    Catholicism and, 144, 377; of Connor,
    153, 155; improvement and, 195, 409;
    Dublin Society and, 257–258; optimism
    of, 334; empiricism and, 344, 443;
    rights and, 393; volunteer movement
    and, 394; United Irishmen and, 406;
    loyalists and, 423; Russell and, 429;
    superstition and, 430; republicanism
    and, 447; self-interest and, 454;
    agriculture and, 543n219
Raymond, Anthony, 141–143, 508n146
Reading practices, 430
Reading societies. *See* Book clubs
Reason, 15, 43, 50, 52, 69, 72, 92, 173,
    369
Rebellion (1641). *See* Ulster Rising
Rebellion (1798), 3, 14, 309, 420;
    beginning of, 437; regions of, 437–439;
    psychological impact of, 439; violence
    of, 439, 581n124; Freemasons and,
    445–447; conditions of, 447; casualties
    of, 581n124
Recusants, 18
Red Book of the Exchequer, 383

Refinement: morality and, 169–170,
    513n50; War of the Two Kings and, 171;
    ethos of, 171–179; of taste, 176; beauty
    and, 180; improvement and, 207;
    hunting clubs and, 239–240, 530n138;
    laws and, 325–326; false, 329
'Reflections on the Common Systems of
    Morality' (Hutcheson) 23
Reflections on the Revolution in France
    (Edmund Burke), 448–457
Reform bill, 351, 392
Reformed Churches, 39
Reform movement, 345–348, 351
Regency crisis, 410
Relationships, 309, 335, 493n44
Relief Act of 1737, 26
Religion, 330; heterodoxy, 4; rejection of
    orthodoxies, 4; Enlightenment and, 7–8,
    478n37; politics and, 20, 95; morality
    and, 28; harm done by, 34; obedience
    and, 35, 80; in England, 71; Molesworth
    and, 80–81; irreligion, 88, 95–96, 127,
    274; Berkeley on fashion and, 95–96;
    ethnicity and, 111; Gaels and, 137; War of
    the Two Kings and, 156; art and, 185;
    suffering and, 205; book clubs and, 264;
    freedom and, 388–389; civil society and,
    450; redefining, 460; secularism and,
    460, 480n52; improvement and, 518n138;
    volunteer movement and, 565n134;
    rituals and, 584n3
Religious anarchy, 36, 53
Religious Enlightenment, 8, 10, 11–12,
    156–158, 211, 460
Religious law, 31
*Religious Obedience Founded on Personal
    Persuasion* (Abernethy), 34, 51
Religious persecution, 423
Reliques of Irish Poetry (Brooke,
    Charlotte), 307, 310

Renaissance, 478n38

Repeal Act, 373

Repeal Bill, 412

Repression, of emotions, 334

Republicanism, 346, 353, 407, 424, 447

Revelation, 15

Revolution, slavery and, 409

Reynolds, James, 300

Reynolds, Joshua, 184

Rhetoric, 171–173

Richard I, 82

Richardson, Samuel, 331

Rightboy movement, 394–395, 397, 400, 444, 570n224, 570n231

Rights: natural, 53, 317, 402, 403, 406, 412, 415, 426, 571n245; conquest and, 84; of man, 84, 423, 430; property, 113–114, 349, 365, 368, 376, 428, 464, 576n75; communal, 378; universal, 378–379, 406, 426; constitution and, 391; human nature and, 391; politics and, 391, 400–401, 463; rationalism and, 393; language of, 400; legal, 400; privilege and, 400–401, 461; vocabulary of, 403; common sense and, 407; equality and, 423; civil, 471

Riots, 161, 163, 226, 243–244, 331, 444

Rituals, 270–278, 540n150, 584n3

Roberts, William, 238

Robertson, John, 18

Robertson, William, 263–264, 323

Robinson, Richard, 233

Roderick O'Connor (Shadwell), 242–243

Rogers, Patrick, 568n197

Roman Catholicism, 32, 38, 347–348, 377; James II and, 74–75; Clayton and, 102–103; Pope and, 113; principles of, 130; legitimacy and, 132; breeding and, 206; Protestantism and, 417–418;

atheism and, 419–420; laws and, 538n108. *See also* Catholicism

Roman Empire, 329

Rosse, Earl of, 277

Rothe regiment, 108

Rotunda complex, 219, 225

Rowe, Nicholas, 244

Rowland, Samuel, 238

Royal Academy, 184–185

Royal Charter, 261, 269, 302, 303

Royal College of Physicians, 213

Royal Exchange building, 295

Royal Irish Academy, 254, 260–261, 300–304

Royal Society, 188

Rule of law, 2

Rundle, Thomas, 267–268

Rural societies, 237–238, 530n134

Russell, Thomas, 427–429, 432

Rutland Square, 217

Rutty, John, 289–290

Ryder, Thomas, 234–235

Rye, George, 187–189

Sackville Mall, 216

Sages, prophecy and, 504n64

Saint Bartholomew's Day massacre, 2

Saints, 24

Salon, 223

Salvation, 35, 48, 50, 146, 478n36

Sampson, William, 434–435

Sanderson, Robert, 213

Santry, Lord, 277

Sarsfield, Patrick, 62

Satan, 103

Satanic society, 277

Scholasticism, 9, 33–37, 106, 156; worldview of, 24; Calvinist, 29; reliance on, 49; scriptural interpretation and,

51; rationalism and, 59; God and, 62; poetics of, 118–128; intellectual life and, 124; Aristotle and, 127; Nary and, 129; Irish-language manuscripts and, 133–136; Connor and, 152; Catholicism and, 157; solidarity and, 263–270

School for Scandal (Richard Brinsley Sheridan), 307

Schools, 266–267, 537n84

Science, 157, 480n51

Scotland, 4

Scottish Enlightenment, 4–5, 389

Scribal activity, 133–135, 144

Scriptural interpretation, 24, 29, 33, 49–51, 56

Sculpture, 186

Scythians, 324

Seanchas, 134

Secondary ideas, 90

Sectarianism, 14, 463–464

Secularisation, 8

Secularism, religion and, 460, 480n52

Self-consciousness, 514n68

Self-defense, 88

Self-governance, 84

Self-interest, 42, 454, 482n67

Selfishness, 38–39

Self-love, 44

Self-preservation, 181–182

Senses, 89–92, 99, 180

Sentimentalism, 555n120

Sentiments, 330–338, 342–343, 454

A Series of Letters Addressed to the Volunteers, 401

1788 foundation, 220

Seven Years' War, 298

Sex and Sexuality, 123, 333, 341, 359

Shadwell, Charles, 212, 242–243

Shame, 335

Shandon Charity School, 264

Shaw, John, 238

Shelborne, Earl of, 286

Sheridan, Charles Francis, 413

Sheridan, Frances, 331, 337, 554n106

Sheridan, Richard Brinsley, 307, 413, 557n171

Sheridan, Thomas, 174, 222, 226, 285–286, 514nn68,70, 527n80, 550n32, 557n171; civility and, 175; Edward Kelly and, 243–245; exile of, 315

She Stoops to Conquer (Goldsmith), 337, 339–343, 557n170

Shils, Edward, 523n4

Sidney Bidulph (fictional character), 331–333, 334, 554n106, 555n111

Sieyès, Emmanuel, 576n75

Simson, John, 41

Sincerity, 339, 342–343

Sir Callaghan O'Brallaghan (fictional character), 338–339, 340

Sir Condy (fictional character), 465–467

Sir Harry Hastings (fictional character), 335–336

Sir Robert Harold (fictional character), 334–336

Sir Theodore (fictional character), 338

Skinkwin, Austin, 238

Slavery, 150, 345, 386, 409, 470, 521n198

Slowey, Desmond, 557n171

Small, Stephen, 564n101

Smith, Adam, 17, 382–383, 517n113

Smith, Charles, 287–289

Smock-Alley, 212, 218, 227, 245, 315, 331

Sociability, 8

Social activism, 287

Social appearance, sentiments and, 342

Social boundaries, love and, 340

Social cohesion, 209

Social consequences, of volunteer movement, 354

Social control, 337, 406

Social empathy, 40

Social engineering, 323

Social Enlightenment, 8, 10, 12, 16, 158, 170, 209, 211, 250–251, 316, 381, 460–461

Social life, 209

Social mixing, 235, 241–247, 262, 354, 531n151

Social order, 121, 167, 309, 441–442, 460

Social radicalism, 427–428

Social rank, 342–343

Social structure, penal code and, 131

Social tolerance, 40

Social venues, 12–13

Society: art and, 183; national, 195; leaders of, 265; state and, 265, 454; holistic vision of, 343; luxury and, 353; as contract, 450; individual and, 523n4; cultural empathy and, 557n170. See also Civil society

Society for the Reformation of Manners, 171

Society of Artists in Dublin, 254

Society of Arts, 183

Society of Freemasons, 270

Society of Journeymen Smiths, 292

Society of the Charitable Instruction, 287

Society of United Irishmen, 442–443

Socinians, 16, 35, 37

Sodality of the Blessed Virgin Mary, 263

Soil type, 188–189

Soldiers, 245–246

Solidarity, scholasticism and, 263–270

Some Scattered Pieces upon Agriculture (Howard), 192–193

Some Thoughts on the General Improvement of Ireland (Anonymous), 195–197

Songs, 308, 578n94

'Song XLII', 252

Soul, 151–152, 177. See also Spirit

Sound doctrine, 37

Southwell, Edward, 246

Sovereignty, 521n197

Sparks, Luke, 218

The Spectator (Addison and Steele), 171–172

Spectrum of Enlightenment, 9, 23, 58, 157

Speculative Freemasons, 273

Speech, 174–175, 514n68

Spinoza, Benedict, 8

Spirit, 91–93, 99, 152

Spiritual authority, 480n52

Spiritual existence, 99

Spoken word, 174, 514n70

Staged manners, 337–343

Stair Éamoin Uí Chléire (Seán Ó Neachtain), 136–140

Stanhope, William. See Harrington, 1st Earl of

The Star, 431

State: Synods and, 33; faith and, 86; church and, 97, 462; improvement and, 195–196; power of, 196; money and, 200; public sphere and, 211, 316; Dublin Society and, 260; society and, 265, 454; resurrection of, 311–316; dishonesty of, 323; legitimacy of, 327; wisdom and beauty of, 390; conscience and, 489n137

The State of Ireland (Arthur O'Connor), 424–425, 432

State of the Protestants of Ireland (King), 74, 76

Steele, Richard, 171–172

Steevens, Richard, 291

Stereotypes, 338

Steuart, James, 17

Stevenson, James, 228

Stewart, A. T. Q., 3

St Nicholas Hospital, 291

Stone, George, 97, 312, 313, 315

St Patrick's Hospital, 216, 292

St Patrick's Purgatory, 116

Strettell, Edward, 294

Strugglers Club, 443

St Stephen's Green, 169, 221

Subjective realism, 43

Sublime, 179–182, 454

Subscribers, 33–37, 41–42, 50, 489n137

Sub-Synods, 29, 30

Subversion, 8, 13

Suffering, 104, 144, 205, 554n106

Supernatural, 153–155

Superstition, 3, 4, 20, 116, 377, 390, 430, 455, 471, 475n8

Supreme Council of the Inquisition, 146

Survivor guilt, 575n50

Sutton, Patrick, 373

Sweden, 79

Swift, Jonathan, 60, 63–73, 162, 198, 206–209, 220, 222, 292, 492n36, 493n44, 523n5

Swiney, Eugene, 233

Switzerland, 386

Sympathy, 182, 517n113

Synge, Edward, 85–88, 105, 132, 496nn90,91,93,94

Synods, 28–30, 31–34, 50–51

Szirtes, George, viii

Táin Bó Cuailnge, 133

Talbot, James, 267

Talbot, Richard. See Tyrconnell, 1st Earl of

Tandy, James Napper, 402, 433

Taste, 176–178

Taverns, 223, 227, 229–230, 245, 262, 282, 293

Tax, 195, 201, 214, 265

Technology, 6

Temple, John, 76, 574n47

Terror, 181

Terry, Henry, 238

Test Act, 299

Test clause, 366

'Testimony of Conscience' (Swift), 72

Theatre, 254; culture of, 210, 234–237; public sphere and, 212; rising demand for, 217; riots, 226, 243–244; social mixing and, 241–242, 531n151; in Dublin, 242; women and, 244, 531n162; didactic understanding of, 249; politics and, 249, 314–316, 532n187, 550n30; elite and, 550n30; viceregal command performances, 550n30

Theatre Royal, 217, 218, 234

Theatrical Booth, 217

Theology, 28, 36, 41, 49, 329–330, 485n42

Theory of sensibility, 178, 335

Thinking, 91

Thomas Street, 227

Thought processes, 9

Thoughts, awareness and, 91

Thoughts on the Conduct and Continuation of the Volunteers of Ireland (Anonymous), 373

Three Dialogues (Berkeley), 88

Thurles and Moate, 163

Tickell, John, 286

Tighe, Mary, 221

Tighe, William, 433

Tillage, 189–192

Tipperary, 439

Tithe, 394–400, 417, 471, 511n13, 570n231

Todd, Janet, 554n106

Todorov, Tzvetan, 478n36

'To Dr Richard Helsham upon My Recovery from a Dangerous Fit of Sickness' (Barber), 222

Toland, John, 8, 15–16, 20

Tolerance, 5, 7, 40, 42, 53, 58

Toleration, 132, 205; granting, 18–19; Presbyterianism and, 53; Catholicism and, 88, 496n93; legal, 319; benevolence of, 387; coercion and, 496n93

Toleration Act, 26

Tone, Theobald Wolfe, 405, 412, 423

Tony Lumpkin (fictional character), 340

Topography, 287–289

Tories, 198

Torture, 86

Townsend, Lord, 344, 532n177

Trade, 249–250; balance of, 198–199, 200; of England, 202; morality and, 203; free, 370, 382–385, 394, 521n199, 566n164, 567n168; restrictions, 378; slavery and, 521n198

Traditionalists, 47

Trail, James, 268–269

Transactions of the Royal Irish Academy, 303

Translators, 325

Transparency, 534n24

Treason, 130

A Treatise of Midwifery (Ould), 213

Treatise on Tolerance (Voltaire), 2

Treaty of Altona, 79

Treaty of Limerick, 60, 112, 490n2

The Tribune (Arbuckle), 167–170, 172

The Tricks of the Town Laid Open (Anonymous), 242

Trimleston, Baron, 298

Trinitarians, 100, 102

Trinity, 25, 35–36, 71–72, 102, 123

Trinity College, 126, 139–140, 172, 212, 213, 216, 256, 304, 413

Troy, John Thomas, 10

Trust, 13, 70

Truth, 52, 62, 175

Truth seeking, of individual, 52

Tuam, 85

Tudor, Jane, 285

Twiss, Richard, 227

Two Treatises of Government (Locke), 495n81

Tyrconnell, 1st Earl of (Richard Talbot), 76

Ulster, 117, 351; rule of law in, 2; poetry of, 117, 502n40; industry of, 162; Presbyterianism in, 263, 396

Ulster Rising, 1–2, 88, 326, 406, 418, 574n47

Understanding, 7–8, 19, 42, 91, 172, 478n36

Unigenitus, 147

The Union Star, 435

United Irishmen, 10, 222, 250, 402, 404, 418, 476n14; politics of, 406; rationalism and, 406; government and, 414; FitzGibbon and, 416; public opinion and, 423; Drennan and, 424, 575n62, 579n103; radicalism and, 424; republicanism and, 424; violence and, 424, 441, 470; extremes of, 427; culture and, 430–432, 434, 436, 577nn89,90, 578n91; poetry of, 431–432; music and, 432; propaganda of, 432; Dublin and, 437; yeomanry and, 442–447; secret oaths of, 443; Freemasons and, 445–447; loyalists and, 447–448; privilege and, 578n91

United Irish movement, 413, 423, 434–435

United Irish Rising, 405, 461

United Society of Pill Lane, 443

United States, 351, 386

Universal Circulating Library, 219–220

Universalism, 515n81

Universal rights, 378–379, 406, 426

Universe, imagination and, 92
University of Dublin, 107
University of Paris, 125–126
Urban environment, privacy in, 522n2
Usher, James, 176–178, 515n81
Usher's Quay, 50–51
Ussher, James, 9
Utility, 175, 318

Vallancey, Charles, 285
Vanburgh, John, 243
Vandals, 79
Verger, Thomas, 169
Vesey, Elizabeth, 221
Vice, 4–5, 44, 70, 96, 173
Victoria (Queen), 588n58
Vindication of a Sermon (Synge), 132
*Vindication of the Histories of the Old and
    New Testaments* (Clayton), 100, 103
*Vindication of the Presbyterian Ministers of
    the North of Ireland* (Kirkpatrick),
    47–48
Vinegar Hill, 438
Violante, Madame, 217–218
Violence, 168, 405; coffeehouses and,
    246–247; duelling, 246–247, 279; social
    mixing and, 246–247; interpersonal,
    278–279; passion and, 326, 342;
    radicalism and, 408–409, 460; politics
    and, 424, 441–442; United Irishmen
    and, 424, 441, 470; of Rebellion, 439,
    581n124; symbolic, 441; military and,
    448; intracommunal, 466
Virtue, 69; civic, 11, 392, 406; of
    Christianity, 31; Hutcheson and, 43, 44;
    heresy as, 98; rhetoric and, 173; second
    nature and, 174; politeness and, 178;
    wealth and, 198; shame and, 335;
    private, 387; public, 387; Dublin
    Society and, 535n50

Voltaire, 2–3, 315
Volunteer convention, 352, 387
Volunteer movement, 14, 211, 248, 273,
    309, 345, 348, 460–461; ambitions of,
    346; Catholicism and, 352, 371–373,
    376, 404, 405, 565nn125,134; youth and,
    353; morality and, 354; social conse-
    quences of, 354; social mixing and, 354;
    women and, 354; patriotism and,
    354–355, 371; uniforms of, 355–356,
    560n47; calendar of, 356; meetings of,
    356–357, 561nn56,57; civil society and,
    357; Presbyterianism and, 366, 404;
    constitution and, 370; militia and, 371;
    return of, 371–372; idealisation of, 372;
    political views of, 372; citizenship and,
    376; community and, 376; capacity of,
    379; division within, 380; Protestantism
    and, 380; dogmas of, 381; free trade
    and, 382, 566n164; decline of, 391;
    gender and, 392, 569n211; rationalism
    and, 394; desirability of continuing,
    401; Enlightenment and, 401–404;
    administrative structure of, 402; ban
    of, 402; radicalism and, 402, 442,
    532n179; implosion of, 403; privilege
    and, 403; conflict and, 404; structural
    pressure of, 442; public sphere and,
    559n32; Militia Act and, 561n61;
    religion and, 565n134; Drennan on,
    568n201
Vota, Father, 152
Voting, 348, 378
Vulgate Bible, 127

Wadding, Luke, 9
'The Wake of William Orr' (Drennan),
    431
Walker, Joseph Cooper, 221
Walpole, Robert, 163

Walsh, Francis, 134

Walzer, Michael, 523n4

War, 62, 84, 104

War of the Two Kings, 11–12, 105, 140,
148, 461; death toll in, 62; God and,
74; Anglicanism and, 81; Catholicism
and, 106, 345; social order and, 121;
Nary's counternarrative on, 131; religion
and, 156; refinement and, 171; public
sphere after, 223; duelling and, 279;
penal code and, 320, 322. *See also*
Articles of Limerick

Warren, Robert, 238

Warrin, Hugh, 233

Waterford, 234–235, 288, 417

Watson, Robert, 247

Watts, Richard, 219

Wealth, 194, 198, 204, 381, 428

Weapons, Catholicism and, 415

Webster, William, 397–398

Welsh, Andrew, 233

West, Benjamin, 184

West, Robert, 285

West Connaught, 81

Westminster Confession of Faith, 9, 24,
25, 28, 31; Synods and, 33–34; worldview of, 35; Hutcheson and, 45;
pessimism of, 49; schism created by,
49; Emlyn and, 58. *See also* Non-
subscribers; Subscribers

Westmorland, 414

Westropp, Thomas, 238

Wexford, 163, 418, 438

Wexford Bridge massacre, 420–422, 438

Whaley, Thomas ('Buck'), 277

Wheat, 191–192

Whelan, Kevin, 577n87

Whigs, 198, 381, 389, 567n165; Party, 401,
410; Club, 407, 410; republicanism

and, 407; death of, 407–413; British,
410; implosion of, 413; disintegration
of, 442; politics, 513n44

White, Daniel, 238

White, Thomas, 238

Whiteboys, 358, 361, 414, 415, 420,
444

The Whole Duty of Man (Pufendorf), 213,
266–267

Whyte, Samuel, 287

Whyte, Thomas, 282–284

Wide Streets Commission, 295

The Wild Irish Girl (Owenson), 464,
467–469

Will, spirit and, 91, 92

William (King), 316–317, 321

William III (King), 12, 60, 61, 79, 156,
559n32

Williamites, 61–62, 78, 81, 85, 102–103

William of Orange, 108

Williams, James, 219

Wills, Elizabeth, 238

Wilson, Peter, 228

Wilson, William, 226

Wilson's Almanack, 290

Wine, 168

Winstanley, John, 231–232

Witchcraft, 115

Woffington, Peg, 221, 315–316

Wollstonecraft, Mary, 185

Women, 327, 569n211; Berkeley and, 17;
of fashion, 17; beggars, 162; of public
sphere, 221–223; theatre and, 244,
531n162; charity and, 287, 543n210;
education and, 287; morality and, 287,
543n210; marriage and, 332, 555n111;
volunteer movement and, 354; suffering
of, 554n106

Wood Street congregation, 42, 53

Woodward, Richard, 395, 397–400,
     571n245, 573n32
Woollen Act, 383
Wordplay, 138, 140, 171
Worsdale, James, 277
Worth, Edward, 219
Wyse, Thomas, 259, 298

Yahoos (fictional characters), 68–70
Yeomanry, United Irishmen and, 442–447
Young Irelanders, 463
Youth, 95, 129, 353, 569n216

Zealand, 78

The Wiley Handbook of the Psychology
of Mass Shootings

The Wiley Handbook of the Psychology of Mass Shootings

Edited by

Laura C. Wilson

WILEY Blackwell

This edition first published 2017
© 2017 John Wiley & Sons, Inc.

Registered Office
John Wiley & Sons, Ltd, The Atrium, Southern Gate, Chichester, West Sussex, PO19 8SQ, UK

Editorial Offices
350 Main Street, Malden, MA 02148-5020, USA
9600 Garsington Road, Oxford, OX4 2DQ, UK
The Atrium, Southern Gate, Chichester, West Sussex, PO19 8SQ, UK

For details of our global editorial offices, for customer services, and for information about how to apply for permission to reuse the copyright material in this book please see our website at www.wiley.com/wiley-blackwell.

The right of Laura C. Wilson to be identified as the author of the editorial matter in this work has been asserted in accordance with the UK Copyright, Designs and Patents Act 1988.

Library of Congress Cataloging-in-Publication Data

Names: Wilson, Laura, 1984– author.
Title: The Wiley handbook of the psychology of mass shootings / Laura C. Wilson.
Other titles: Handbook of the psychology of mass shootings
Description: Hoboken : Wiley-Blackwell, 2016. | Series: Wiley clinical psychology handbooks | Includes index.
Identifiers: LCCN 2016021189| ISBN 9781119047933 (hardback) |
    ISBN 9781119047896 (epdf) | ISBN 9781119047926 (epub)
Subjects: LCSH: Mass shootings–Psychological aspects. | Murderers–Psychology. |
    BISAC: PSYCHOLOGY / Psychopathology / General.
Classification: LCC HM866 .W55 2016 | DDC 364.152/34019–dc23
LC record available at https://lccn.loc.gov/2016021189

A catalogue record for this book is available from the British Library.

Cover image: Gettyimages/Mimi Haddon

Set in 10.5/13pt Galliard by SPi Global, Pondicherry, India

Printed and bound in Malaysia by Vivar Printing Sdn Bhd

10 9 8 7 6 5 4 3 2 1

Contents

Notes on Contributors   vii

Preface   xv

Part I   Background on Mass Shootings   1

1   Challenges to the Empirical Investigation of Mass Shootings   3
Andrew J. Smith and Michael Hughes

2   The Patterns and Prevalence of Mass Public Shootings
in the United States, 1915–2013   20
Grant Duwe

3   Explaining Mass Shootings: Types, Patterns, and Theories   36
James Alan Fox and Jack Levin

Part II   The Psychology of Perpetrators   57

4   The Development of Rampage Shooters: Myths and Uncertainty
in the Search for Causes   59
Benjamin Winegard and Christopher J. Ferguson

5   Biosocial Perspective of Proactive Aggression: Applications
to Perpetrators of Mass Shootings   77
Jonathan Waldron and Angela Scarpa

6   The Challenge of Predicting Dangerousness   96
Sara Chiara Haden

Part III   The Role of Media in the Aftermath of Mass Shootings   115

7   The Influence of Media on Public Attitudes   117
Jaclyn Schildkraut and H. Jaymi Elsass

8   Social Media and News Coverage as Vicarious Exposure   136
Carolyn R. Fallahi

9   The Role of Technology in Expressions of Grief   153
     Kenneth A. Lachlan

10   The Impact of Journalism on Grieving Communities   170
     Henna Haravuori, Noora Berg, and Mauri Marttunen

Part IV   Psychological Considerations for Impacted Individuals   189

11   Mental Health Outcomes Following Direct Exposure   191
     Laura C. Wilson

12   Psychosocial Functioning Within Shooting-Affected Communities:
     Individual- and Community-Level Factors   210
     Heather Littleton, Julia C. Dodd, and Kelly Rudolph

13   Postdisaster Psychopathology Among Rescue Workers
     Responding to Multiple-Shooting Incidents   229
     Geoff J. May and Carol S. North

14   Distress Among Journalists Working the Incidents   247
     Klas Backholm

Part V   Clinical Interventions for Impacted Individuals   265

15   Empirically Based Trauma Therapies   267
     Thea Gallagher, Natalie G. Gay, Anu Asnaani,
     and Edna B. Foa

16   Public Relief Efforts From an International
     Perspective   293
     Kari Dyregrov, Atle Dyregrov, and Pål Kristensen

17   Mental Health Service Utilization Following Mass Shootings   312
     Andrew J. Smith, Katharine Donlon Ramsdell,
     Michael F. Wusik, and Russell T. Jones

18   Resiliency and Posttraumatic Growth   331
     Andrea M. Despotes, David P. Valentiner, and Melissa London

Part VI   Prevention, Ethics, and Future Directions   351

19   Threat Assessment and Violence Prevention   353
     Dewey Cornell and Pooja Datta

20   Ethical Conduct of Research in the Aftermath of Mass Shootings   372
     Elana Newman, Chelsea Shotwell Tabke, and Betty Pfefferbaum

21   Future Directions   388
     Danny Axsom

Index   401

Notes on Contributors

Anu Asnaani, Ph.D., is an Assistant Professor of Clinical Psychology in Psychiatry at the Center for the Treatment and Study of Anxiety. Dr. Asnaani received her Bachelor of Science degree in Psychology and her Doctoral degree in Clinical Psychology from Boston University. Her current interests include understanding how diversity influences emotion regulation, improving treatment outcome, and effectively increasing dissemination of empirically supported treatments for PTSD and other anxiety disorders. Dr. Asnaani specializes in cognitive-behavioral treatment.

Danny Axsom is an Associate Professor of Psychology at Virginia Tech. He researches topics at the intersection of social and clinical psychology, including the social psychology of trauma. This has included the study of adjustment and coping with sexual assault on college campuses, as well as responses to the mass shooting at Virginia Tech. He received his Ph.D. from Princeton University, and is a member of the editorial board of the *Journal of Experimental Social Psychology*.

Klas Backholm is an Associate Professor of Media and Communication at the Swedish School of Social Science, University of Helsinki, Finland. His main research areas are crisis psychology and mass communication. He is currently working with projects focusing on journalists' psychological wellbeing after crisis-related work assignments, and on best practices for how to include technical innovations such as tools for verification of web-based content into crisis-related journalistic work processes.

Noora Berg, M.Soc.Sci., is currently a postgraduate student at the National Institute for Health and Welfare, Department of Health, Mental Health Unit in Helsinki, Finland.

Dewey Cornell is a forensic clinical psychologist and Professor of Education who holds the Bunker Chair in the Curry School of Education at the University of Virginia. He is the author of more than 200 publications in psychology and education. His clinical work and research concerns the prevention of violence and bullying, the assessment of school climate, and the development of threat assessment practices in schools.

Pooja Datta is a graduate researcher and doctoral candidate in Clinical and School Psychology in the Curry School Education at the University of Virginia. Her research focuses on the prevention of violence and bullying, as well as school climate factors associated with bystander behavior, perception of staff support, and dating violence.

Andrea M. Despotes, B.A., J.D., is a clinical psychology student at Northern Illinois University. Her research examines the psychological consequences of trauma and risk factors for development of PTSD. Specifically, her work focuses on the potential relationships between and among attentional control, mindfulness, dACC function, and posttraumatic growth.

Julia C. Dodd is a doctoral student in Clinical Health Psychology at East Carolina University in Greenville, North Carolina, and is currently completing her predoctoral internship at the Charles George VA Medical Center in Asheville, NC. Her primary research interests are in the intersection of trauma and reproductive health issues, including infertility, sexual risk behaviors, and sexual dysfunction.

Grant Duwe is the Director of Research and Evaluation for the Minnesota Department of Corrections. Dr. Duwe is the author of the book *Mass Murder in the United States: A History* (2007), and he has written more than 40 articles that have been published in peer-reviewed academic journals such as *Criminology*, *Criminology and Public Policy*, *Criminal Justice and Behavior*, and *Sexual Abuse: A Journal of Research and Treatment*. He is currently a visiting fellow with the Bureau of Justice Statistics and is a nonresident scholar within Baylor University's Institute for Studies of Religion.

Atle Dyregrov, Professor, Ph.D, is head of professional issues at the Center for Crisis Psychology in Bergen, Norway and Professor of Clinical Psychology at the University of Bergen, Norway. Dr. Dyregrov is the author of numerous publications, journal articles, and more than 15 books. He has conducted research on various subjects relating to bereavement, trauma, and disaster. He is one of the founding members of the European Society for Traumatic Stress Studies and the Children and War Foundation.

Kari Dyregrov, Professor, Ph.D, is research leader at the Center for Crisis Psychology in Bergen, Norway and Professor at the Faculty of Health and Social Sciences at Bergen University College. She has conducted research on traumatic bereavement for 20 years and has led the research on the bereaved after the terror killings in Norway on July 22, 2011. She initiated The Norwegian Association for Suicide Bereaved, and has written many publications (e.g., *Effective Grief and Bereavement Support*, *After the Suicide*).

H. Jaymi Elsass is Lecturer in the School of Criminal Justice at Texas State University. Her primary research interests include episodic violent crime, moral panics, fear of crime, and juvenile delinquency. She is the coauthor of *Mass Shootings: Media, Myths, and Realities* and has published in *American Journal of Criminal Justice*, *Crime, Law and Social Change*, *Security Journal*, and *Criminology, Criminal Justice, Law & Society*, as well as several edited volumes.

Carolyn R. Fallahi graduated from the University of Missouri with her Ph.D. in Counseling Psychology. She specialized in the treatment of children in the areas of addiction, sexual abuse, psychiatric disorders, and learning differences. Currently, Dr. Fallahi is the chair of the Department of Psychological Science and works for Student Disability Services at Central Connecticut State University. Dr. Fallahi's research interests include the teaching of psychology, rejection sensitivity, vicarious exposure to trauma, and substance use.

Christopher J. Ferguson is a Professor in the Psychology Department at Stetson University in Florida. He has published numerous research articles related to the etiology of violent crime with a particular focus on media effects. He is a fellow of the American Psychological Association and also received an Early Career Scientist award from Division 46 (Media Psychology and Technology) of the APA. In addition to his academic work, he has published a novel, *Suicide Kings*. He lives in Orlando with his wife and son. His work can be followed at ChristopherJFerguson.com.

Edna B. Foa, Ph.D., is a Professor of Clinical Psychology in Psychiatry at the University of Pennsylvania and Director of the Center for the Treatment and Study of Anxiety. Her research activities have included the formulation of theoretical frameworks for understanding the mechanisms underlying anxiety disorders, the development of targeted treatments, and elucidating treatment mechanisms that can account for their efficacy. Dr. Foa has published 18 books, over 350 articles and book chapters, and her work has been recognized with numerous awards and honors.

James Alan Fox is the Lipman Family Professor of Criminology, Law and Public Policy at Northeastern University. With specializations in homicide and statistical methods, he has written 18 books, including *Extreme Killing*, *The Will to Kill*, and *Violence and Security on Campus*. He has published widely in both scholarly and popular outlets, and, as a member of its Board of Contributors, his column appears regularly in *USA Today*.

Thea Gallagher is a clinical faculty member at the Center for the Treatment and Study of Anxiety (CTSA) in the Perelman School of Medicine at the University of Pennsylvania. Dr. Gallagher completed her Psy.D. in Clinical Psychology at Philadelphia College of Osteopathic Medicine. At the CTSA,

Dr. Gallagher currently coordinates the OCD treatment study, is a study therapist, and serves as the CTSA media coordinator. Clinically, Dr. Gallagher specializes in a range of cognitive behavioral therapies.

Natalie G. Gay, B.A., graduated from the University of Pennsylvania with a degree in Psychology. As an undergraduate student she conducted marketing research for the Philadelphia Flyers and upon graduation worked for the Greater Philadelphia Chamber of Commerce. She intends to pursue a doctoral degree in Clinical Psychology, and is interested in the underlying neurobiological and cognitive mechanisms of PTSD.

Sara Chiara Haden, Ph.D., is an Associate Professor at Long Island University in Brooklyn. She completed her doctoral degree in Clinical Psychology at Virginia Tech in 2007. Her research focuses on risk and protective factors that impact the cycle of violence, outcomes associated with exposure to community violence, and how body awareness is implicated in traumatic experiences. Dr. Haden is a licensed psychologist in New York and primarily treats sex offenders and mentally ill offenders.

Henna Haravuori, M.D., Ph.D., is an adolescent psychiatrist and works as a senior researcher at the National Institute for Health and Welfare, Department of Health, Mental Health Unit in Helsinki, Finland and as a clinical teacher of Adolescent Psychiatry at the University of Helsinki and Helsinki University Hospital in Helsinki, Finland.

Michael Hughes, Professor of Sociology at Virginia Tech. His research focuses on mental health, racial attitudes, racial identity, and cultural choice. He has served as president of the Southern Sociological Society and editor of the *Journal of Health and Social Behavior*. Recent articles appeared in *Social Psychology Quarterly*, *Society and Mental Health*, and *Psychological Trauma: Theory, Research, Practice, and Policy*. With Carolyn J. Kroehler he is author of *Sociology: The Core*, 11th ed. (2013).

Russell T. Jones is a Professor of Psychology at Virginia Tech as well as the Founder and Director of the trauma program entitled: Recovery Effort After Child and Adult Trauma. He is also a clinical psychologist who specializes in clinical child and adult psychology and trauma psychology. His research targets the topic of child and adult stress and coping. He also studies coping with common stressful life events, as well as major traumas (i.e., natural, technological, and mass violence). He is an often-sought-out speaker on the topic of trauma and its impact on a variety of target populations including children, adults, first responders, as well as those impacted by school shootings.

Pål Kristensen, Ph.D., is a researcher and clinical psychologist. He is currently working at the Center for Crisis Psychology in Bergen, Norway on a study mapping the long-term mental health effect of loss of a family member or close friend in the 2011 terror attack on Utøya Island. His expertise and research interests concern bereavement and mental health following sudden, unexpected, and/or violent death, preventive interventions following loss, and treatment of prolonged grief disorder.

Kenneth A. Lachlan, Ph.D., Michigan State University, 2003, is an Associate Professor in the Department of Communication at the University of Connecticut, and the editor of *Communication Studies*. His research interests include crisis and risk communication, new media technologies, and the use of media to mitigate negative emotional experiences.

Jack Levin is Professor Emeritus and Codirector of Northeastern University's Brudnick Center on Violence and Conflict. He has authored or coauthored more than 30 books and 150 articles, most in the areas of murder and hate crime. Dr. Levin has received awards from the American Sociological Association, Society for the Study of Social Problems, Eastern Sociological Society, and the Association of Clinical and Applied Sociology. He has given presentations on multiple murder to numerous professional and community organizations in countries around the world.

Heather Littleton is an Associate Professor in the Department of Psychology at East Carolina University in Greenville, North Carolina. Her research focuses on the role of social cognitive variables in posttrauma adjustment, including following sexual assault and mass shootings. In addition, she is interested in the development of online interventions for trauma survivors. Dr. Littleton's work has been funded by the National Institute of Mental Health and the National Science Foundation.

Melissa London, M.A., is a doctoral clinical psychology student at Northern Illinois University. She will be completing her predoctoral internship at the Veterans Affairs Palo Alto Health Care System. Her research program on trauma psychology emphasizes risk and resiliency factors for psychological consequences of trauma. Specifically, she has focused on the role of cognitive and emotion regulation processes as well as cultural variation in response to and during recovery from trauma.

Mauri Marttunen, M.D., Ph.D., is a psychiatrist and an adolescent psychiatrist, research professor and head of the Mental Health Unit at the National Institute for Health and Welfare, Department of Health in Helsinki, Finland and a Professor of Adolescent Psychiatry at the University of Helsinki and Helsinki University Hospital in Helsinki, Finland.

Geoff J. May, M.D., is an investigator at the VA Center of Excellence in Research on Returning War Veterans in Waco, Texas and Assistant Professor of Psychiatry and Behavioral Sciences at the College of Medicine at Texas A&M University Health Science Center. He is examining changes in the brain's physiology in response to trauma, and electrophysiological treatments for PTSD and traumatic brain injury, including transcranial magnetic stimulation and EEG biofeedback.

Elana Newman, Ph.D., is the McFarlin Chair of Psychology, University of Tulsa, Research Director of the Dart Center for Journalism and Trauma, Codirector of the University of Tulsa Institute of Trauma, Adversity and Injustice, and a past president of the International Society of Traumatic Stress Studies. Dr. Newman specializes in understanding and intervening to prevent or treat trauma-related conditions and training different professionals to develop appropriate skills to effectively work with people suffering from trauma-related problems.

Carol S. North, M.D., M.P.E., serves as Medical Director of the Altshuler Center for Education & Research at Metrocare Services in Dallas, Texas. She holds The Nancy and Ray L. Hunt Chair in Crisis Psychiatry and is Professor of Psychiatry at The University of Texas Southwestern Medical Center in Dallas, Texas. For more than a quarter century, Dr. North has conducted federally funded research into disaster mental health, including four studies of multiple-shooting incidents.

Betty Pfefferbaum, M.D., J.D., is the George Lynn Cross Research Professor in the Department of Psychiatry and Behavioral Sciences at the University of Oklahoma College of Medicine. Dr. Pfefferbaum specializes in understanding and intervening to prevent and treat the impact of mass disasters, mass crime, and terrorism on children.

Katharine Donlon Ramsdell, doctoral student in Clinical Psychology at Virginia Tech, is presently completing her clinical internship at Duke University Medical Center in Durham, North Carolina. Her research interests are broadly within the field of traumatic stress and have centered on exploring factors associated with coping and resilience following mass trauma events as well as posttraumatic outcomes of pediatric injury.

Kelly Rudolph is a doctoral student in Clinical Health Psychology at East Carolina University in Greenville, North Carolina. Her primary research interests are the role of social cognitive variables in predicting sexual risk behavior in college women, as well as trauma recovery among victims of interpersonal traumas including sexual assault.

Angela Scarpa received her Ph.D. in Clinical Psychology from the University of Southern California. She is currently an Associate Professor of Psychology at Virginia Tech, Founder and Codirector of the Virginia Tech Autism Clinic, and Director of the VT Center for Autism Research. She is a licensed clinical psychologist with specialized training in individual and group behavioral and cognitive-behavioral therapy for children, families, and adults. Her general interest is in developmental psychopathology, with emphases on traumatic stress, neurodevelopmental conditions, and antisocial/aggressive behavior.

Jaclyn Schildkraut is an Assistant Professor of Public Justice at the State University of New York (SUNY) at Oswego. Her research interests include school shootings, homicide trends, mediatization effects, and crime theories. She is the coauthor of *Mass Shootings: Media, Myths, and Realities* and has published in *Homicide Studies, American Journal of Criminal Justice, Fast Capitalism, Criminal Justice Studies, Crime, Law and Social Change,* and *Criminology, Criminal Justice, Law & Society,* as well as several edited volumes.

Andrew J. Smith is a Ph.D. candidate in Clinical Psychology at Virginia Tech specializing in trauma, neuropsychology, and quantitative methods. His research interests are broadly focused on posttraumatic adaptation, with published studies among survivors of mass-violence, combat, disasters, brain injury, and stroke. He currently teaches abnormal and developmental psychology, holds a research position at a local VA medical center, and will begin his clinical internship in the Salt Lake City VA Healthcare System in 2016.

Chelsea Shotwell Tabke is a Clinical Psychology doctoral student at The University of Tulsa. She previously earned her Masters in Forensic Psychology from John Jay College of Criminal Justice. Chelsea is specializing in the study and treatment of traumatic stress with veterans and substance-abusing women. Current areas of interest are the relationship between and treatment of trauma, substance abuse, and criminal behavior.

David P. Valentiner is a Professor of Psychology and a core faculty member in the APA-Accredited Ph.D. program in Clinical Psychology at Northern Illinois University. His research examines cognitive and emotional factors underlying the development and maintenance of anxiety and stress conditions, development of anxiety conditions during adolescence, and recovery from such conditions during treatment and natural recovery.

Jonathan Waldron earned a Ph.D. in Clinical Psychology from Virginia Tech. His research focuses on social psychophysiological phenomena related to violence, victimization, and trauma. Specifically, he is interested in the interplay between psychological constructs (e.g., interpersonal problems, trauma, empathy, aggression) and the corresponding physiological variables associated with these constructs. He believes that clinical interventions can utilize physiological measures as both an outcome measure and as a direct means of manipulation.

Laura C. Wilson, Ph.D., is an Assistant Professor in the Department of Psychological Science at the University of Mary Washington. She earned a Ph.D. in Clinical Psychology (Virginia Tech) and M.A. in General/Experimental Psychology (The College of William & Mary). Her main area of research and clinical expertise is posttrauma functioning, particularly in survivors of mass trauma (e.g., mass shootings, terrorism, combat) or sexual violence.

Benjamin Winegard is an Assistant Professor at Carroll College in Montana. In addition to the evolutionary roots of violence he is active in researching the evolution of men's social behavior, political correctness, and sacred values, evidence-based approaches to social problems, and the dramatic story of human progress. He is fascinated by all aspects of human behavior and enjoys reading history, economics, psychology, biology, current events, and other disciplines that he has no business opining about.

Michael F. Wusik, doctoral student in Clinical Psychology at Virginia Tech, is presently completing his clinical internship at the VA Maryland Healthcare System in Baltimore, Maryland. His research interests are focused around self-handicapping, avoidance coping, and social psychological factors that contribute to approach and avoidance behaviors in the clinical setting.

Preface

I am often asked, "What led you to study mass shootings?" The answer is simple: "I am a Virginia Tech Hokie." With this response, most people instantly understand my connection to the topic. I am a psychologist with expertise in trauma, who also happens to be a proud graduate of the close-knit community of Virginia Tech located in Blacksburg, Virginia. The university is well known for its academic excellence, football team, unique school colors, and beautiful campus. In April 2007, it also became known for one of the deadliest shootings by a single perpetrator on U.S. soil. I, like so many impacted individuals, was left asking questions: "Why did this happen? Why did the shooter open fire on innocent victims? How do we help those affected by the shooting? How do we prevent the next shooting?" It is these questions, and dozens more, that drive this line of research.

At the time of publication, this book was the only known psychology reference work dedicated exclusively to the study of mass shootings. This may come as a surprise given the immense media and political attention mass shootings have received in the past 15 years. However, one thing that is apparent across the chapters in this volume is that mass shootings are an underresearched area within the field of psychology. This book contains the available empirical evidence, as presented by the foremost authorities in the field, to inform the reader on our current knowledge-base and identify gaps in the literature to guide future studies.

The chapters in this book are topically broad, and the contributors represent numerous fields (e.g., communication, criminal justice, criminology, psychiatry, psychology, sociology) and countries (e.g., Finland, Norway, United States). The material is presented in six sections. The first section, "Background on Mass Shootings," introduces the topic by identifying many of the challenges associated with this area of study, the prevalence and key features of such incidents, and explanations for mass shootings. The second section, "The Psychology of Perpetrators," discusses developmental and psychobiological features of mass shooters, and issues related to predicting dangerousness. The next section, "The Role of Media in the Aftermath of Mass Shootings," focuses on media as a means of influencing the public, a form of exposure, a medium for grief, and potential source of stress for grieving communities. The fourth section, "Psychological Considerations for Impacted Individuals," covers the wide range of individuals who are affected by mass shootings and details issues related to psychopathology. The fifth section, "Clinical Interventions for Impacted Individuals," includes information related to individual- and community-level clinical response, barriers to care for survivors, and resiliency and posttraumatic growth in the aftermath of mass shootings. The final section, "Prevention, Ethics, and Future Directions," covers a range of topics related to assessing for and reducing violence, conducting ethical research, and considerations for future directions.

There are a few additional comments that are necessary to properly orient the reader to this book. First, for the purpose of consistency, a mass shooting is defined in this book as an incident in which a gun was used to kill four or more victims. This definition was chosen because it is the most commonly used in the field and identifies boundaries for the material to be covered within this book. I acknowledge that this definition is controversial and flawed, specifically because of the restrictions on the number of victims and type of weapon. This will be further discussed in the first section of this volume. Second, although this book presents a breadth of information from a wide range of perspectives, the one thing that will not appear among these pages is the names of the shooters who have perpetrated mass shooting incidents. I made this request so that this book does not contribute to the notoriety that many shooters seek. Third, the contributors and I would like to acknowledge those who have participated in the research that made this reference book possible. In the aftermath of tragedy, many members of impacted communities have volunteered to share their stories in order to assist us in furthering our understanding of these incidents and improving the support we can provide to impacted individuals in the future. We thank you!

This book is being published at a time when society is demanding answers to how to predict mass killings and there is a heated debate about how to reduce gun violence. The violent nature of mass shootings elicits visceral and emotional responses from society, and empirically based knowledge and recommendations are often overlooked. In order to identify and enact best practices before, during, and after mass shootings, science must play a central role. I encourage policy makers to seek consultation from researchers who can offer guidance on science-driven policies and legislation. I urge researchers to conduct high-quality research (e.g., diverse samples and events, longitudinal designs) on this understudied topic, disseminate findings, and advocate for empirically based policy changes. This volume, as a compilation of the scientific progress that has been made thus far, is certainly a step in the right direction towards better understanding the nature of mass shootings, identifying potential avenues for the prevention of future incidents, and utilizing effective postevent response. I hold great hope that, with continued empirical and theoretical work, we will continue to ask robust research questions and apply what we have learned with the aim of better understanding these incidents.

Laura C. Wilson

Part I

Background on Mass Shootings

1
Challenges to the Empirical Investigation of Mass Shootings
Andrew J. Smith and Michael Hughes

The literature on the psychological consequences of mass shootings has grown rapidly in recent years. Studies have proliferated as independent researchers have addressed acute problems of trauma and recovery following mass shootings in schools, colleges, workplaces, and communities, and we have learned much about how the trauma of a mass shooting affects people (see Lowe & Galea, 2015; Shultz et al., 2014; Wilson, 2014). However, a number of issues and problems have emerged that pose challenges for researchers in this area. In this chapter we examine four core questions that reflect these challenges: What is a mass shooting? What are the outcomes in studies of the psychological effects of mass shootings, and how are they measured? What processes link mass shootings to psychological outcomes? What features of study design pose challenges for theoretical progress in understanding how exposure to mass shootings affects psychological functioning?

What Is a Mass Shooting?

The term *mass shooting* is more a term of convenience than a scientific concept. Both words that make up the term are problematic. How many victims qualify as a *mass*? The word *mass* means a large amount or number of something, but the lower bound for defining a *mass* in studies of *mass shootings* is typically no more than four (e.g., Wilson, 2014; see also Bjelopera, Bagalman, Caldwell, Finklea, & McCallion, 2013), which is not a mass in the conventional sense. The word *shooting* indicates that a firearm has been used to kill or injure victims. Common sense indicates that a *shooting* is experienced as disturbing or traumatic to victims and observers. However, this restriction is limiting if our interest is in events with fatalities and/or injuries that have serious psychological consequences. Similar acts using other means such as explosives, machete and knife attacks, and intentional vehicle homicides are also traumatic and disturbing (Fox & Levin, 2015).

Thus, a focus on shootings may in some ways be too narrow. But without further qualification, it may also be too broad. Assuming that we mean that a mass shooting involves some number of people who have been killed or injured using firearms, do we mean any such incident (Fox & Levin, 2015)? Do we include gang-related violence, robberies, and homicide-suicides that occur in private residences? An additional issue relates to whether our assessment of the magnitude of an event should be based only on the numbers of victims shot fatally. Nekvasil, Cornell, and Huang (2015) reconceptualize the phenomenon as a multiple casualty homicide, and argue that single homicides with more than one victim (i.e., wounded or injured survivors) qualify for our attention as well.

There is no straightforward solution to determining what to include under the mass shooting umbrella. The underlying issue is that the way analysts define a mass shooting largely depends on the function that the concept serves in the project to which it is applied. For example, in their Congressional Research Service Report, Bjelopera and colleagues (2013) define public mass shootings as "incidents occurring in relatively public places, involving four or more deaths – not including the shooter(s) – and gunmen who select victims somewhat indiscriminately. The violence in these cases is not a means to an end such as robbery or terrorism" (p. 4). This definition is in line with the purpose of the report to provide the U.S. Congress with a basis for discussion and debate about a form of violence that may not be adequately addressed by current legislation and policy. The number of fatalities required in this definition of public mass shootings was based on a definition of mass murder that the FBI presented in a report on serial murder (Federal Bureau of Investigation, 2008).[1] Arbitrariness in the number of fatalities in the definition of mass shootings is underscored by recent legislation passed by the U.S. Congress stating that "the term 'mass killings' means 3 or more killings in a single incident'" (Investigative Assistance for Violent Crimes Act of 2012, 2013, p. 126 STAT. 2435).

Researchers have also been inconsistent and have used several cutoffs from two to four shooting-caused casualties to define mass shootings (Nekvasil et al., 2015). In their study of nearly 19,000 homicide incidents from 2005 to 2010, Nekvasil and colleagues (2015) compare the effectiveness of cutoffs of two, three, four, and five or more victims, concluding: "It seems likely that no specific cutoff for number of victims is sufficient to identify a meaningfully distinct form of homicidal violence" (p. 8).

We can conclude that there is no fixed or universally accepted definition of a mass shooting. Definitions of mass shootings do not vary greatly, but all contain ad hoc and arbitrary elements that may affect research outcomes and thus our understanding of mass shootings prevention, prediction, and intervention innovation. This is also true of the definition used in the present volume: a gun violence incident that results in four or more victim deaths. Is there any rationale for settling, however provisionally, on this definition? We think that there is, and that the rational has two parts.

First, the focus on gun violence captures a large majority of multiple casualty homicides. Recent evidence demonstrates that the primary weapon used in more than four out of five such incidents is a firearm, and as the number of victims increases, the likelihood that a firearm was used increases monotonically (Nekvasil et al., 2015). A firearm was the primary weapon used in nearly 95% of multiple casualty homicides with six or more victims. Because shooting incidents are, by far, the most prevalent form of multiple homicide, they are more available for study than other incidents, and they provide evidence for understanding the vast majority of mass homicides that occur. Nonetheless, it is likely that as this tragic literature grows, studies will address an increasing diversity of research problems and theoretical issues, and researchers should be attentive to hypotheses about whether and how different forms of mass homicide may have different psychological outcomes.

Second, the likelihood that homicide is experienced as traumatic is higher in events involving higher casualty rates (e.g., four or more casualties). The dose-response model (Dohrenwend & Dohrenwend, 1974; March, 1993), to be discussed later in this chapter, predicts that the onset and severity of pathogenesis increases as the severity of the traumatic exposure increases. Accordingly, if researchers wish to study incidents that can be properly characterized as traumatic, then shooting incidents with four victim fatalities are more likely to qualify than incidents involving fewer casualties.

Notwithstanding this dose-response-based logic, it is important for researchers to remember that the cutoff of four fatalities is in common use not because of its potential to be pathogenic, but because it was the previous existing standard (Fox & Levin, 2015) endorsed by the FBI (Bjelopera et al., 2013; Federal Bureau of Investigation, 2008) for use in law enforcement and policy making. While the definition of a mass shooting offered in the present volume (i.e., four or more casualties resulting from gun violence) is useful, there are three reasons for believing that it can distort the knowledge base if applied consistently and rigidly:

1   The question remains open as to whether four or more fatalities is a meaningful cutoff to differentiate a traumatizing incident from one that is more benign.
2   There is no empirically supported or obvious reason why a fatal attack with a firearm would have more or qualitatively different psychological consequences than a life-threatening attack, fatal or not, with a knife, a machete, a blunt object, an explosive, a vehicle, an airplane, or any other weapon or object capable of inflicting serious injuries.
3   Unless we examine life-threatening attacks that result in zero fatalities, we cannot know whether fatal attacks are distinctly traumatogenic.

In short, there is no clear scientific justification for building a literature on traumatic homicides that is largely limited to shooting incidents with four or more fatalities until research provides convincing evidence that psychological responsiveness is dependent on the numbers of victims, that it matters whether victims have been killed or only injured, and that at least four victims are required in order for an event to be experienced as distinctly traumatic by victims and survivors. Researchers should look beyond the standard definition of mass shootings and, where possible, should define research problems that probe the extent of its usefulness.

What Are the Outcomes in Studies of the Psychological Effects of Mass Shootings?

Most psychological research on those exposed to mass shootings focuses on predicting posttraumatic stress reactions following the events, particularly posttraumatic stress disorder (PTSD) or posttraumatic stress symptoms (PTSS).[2] Researchers have also examined a number of other outcomes, including psychological distress, depressive symptoms, anxiety symptoms, grief, personal efficacy, and quality of life.

Posttraumatic stress disorder (PTSD)

PTSD is a pattern of symptoms that follows exposure to a traumatic event, differentiated from other psychological disorders by the externally derived nature of its etiology. The diagnostic criteria for PTSD are described in the *Diagnostic and Statistical Manual of Mental Disorders* (DSM) published by the American Psychiatric Association. The DSM has gone through five editions and two revisions, including DSM-III (American Psychiatric Association, 1980), DSM-III-R (American Psychiatric Association, 1987), DSM-IV (American Psychiatric Association, 1994), DSM-IV-TR (American Psychiatric Association, 2000), and DSM-5 (American Psychiatric Association, 2013).

Though PTSD has been controversial (McNally, 2003), and the diagnostic criteria have been revised several times since its first inclusion in DSM-III in 1980, the core elements have been relatively consistent across DSM revisions. The original diagnosis required that a person display symptoms from three symptom clusters (i.e., re-experiencing [intrusive recollections], avoidance/numbing, hyper-arousal; McNally, 2003) following exposure to a traumatic event, and that the symptoms cause clinically significant distress or impairment.

PTSD is most reliably diagnosed through the administration of structured diagnostic interviews conducted by trained interviewers, such as the Anxiety Disorders Interview Schedule IV (Brown & Barlow, 2014) and the Clinician-Administered PTSD Scale for DSM-5 (Weathers et al., 2013). Such an approach allows the probing of answers and clinical judgment by a trained interviewer, both of which increase the reliability of diagnoses. Self-report measures of PTSD that are administered by questionnaire have also been developed (e.g., Davidson et al., 1997; Foa, Cashman, Jaycox, & Perry, 1997; Kilpatrick, Resnick, Saunders, & Best, 1989; Norris & Hamblen, 2004; see Orsillo, 2001). These measures mimic a clinical interview in that the respondent is asked survey questions, either by a lay interviewer or in paper and pencil format, that tap the criteria that make up the PTSD diagnosis.

Posttraumatic stress symptoms (PTSS)

Diagnosing respondents by clinical interview in large studies is time-consuming and costly. In order to mitigate these problems, researchers have developed PTSS indices consisting of items that tap symptoms in some or all PTSD symptom clusters (e.g., Brewin et al., 2002; Foa, Riggs, Dancu, & Rothbaum, 1993; Kubany, Leisen, Kaplan, & Kelly, 2000; see also Norris & Hamblen, 2004; Orsillo, 2001). Most studies of the psychological consequences of mass shootings have used PTSS as the primary outcome. Data using these indices can be analyzed as dimensional measures (i.e., continuous variables) or, with the addition of a cutoff point defining a high level of posttraumatic stress (e.g., Hughes et al., 2011), as a dichotomy. However they are administered and operationalized, PTSS indices measure severity of symptoms on a continuum. They are not indicators of PTSD. Making a PTSD diagnosis requires not a particular number of symptoms, but a particular combination of symptoms from each symptom cluster, along with clinical significance.

PTSD diagnostic measures and PTSS continuous measures differ in several important ways. First, PTSS indices measure self-reported symptoms of post-traumatic stress, rather than whether a respondent meets the clinical criteria for PTSD. Second, dimensional indicators typically tap symptoms whether or not they are clinically significant (i.e., cause distress or impairment). Third, diagnostic interviews administered by trained mental health professionals in standardized format allow for clinical judgment that includes probes to clarify the meaning of answers, whereas dimensional assessments, which are typically administered in self-report questionnaire format, do not. Fourth, establishing a cutoff point on a continuous indicator of PTSS to define PTSD cases is not equivalent to a diagnosis of PTSD by a trained clinician. When research subjects evaluated for PTSD using cutoff points on a dimensional indicator are also separately diagnosed by clinical interviewers, there are often respondents with PTSD in clinical interviews who score below the cutoff point on the dimensional measure (false-negative), and there are respondents without PTSD in the clinical interview who score above the cutoff on the dimensional measure (false-positive). Those who have developed these dimensional assessments have worked to keep these errors in an acceptable range (e.g., Brewin et al., 2002; Foa et al., 1997), but they have not eliminated them, and the results of studies using PTSS measures should always be interpreted with these limitations in mind.

Psychological distress, depression, and anxiety

Less commonly, mass shootings researchers have examined outcomes other than PTSD and PTSS that can occur in the wake of traumatic events, including distress (e.g., Smith, Donlon, Anderson, Hughes, & Jones, 2015), depression (e.g., Vicary & Fraley, 2010), anxiety (e.g., Grills-Taquechel, Littleton, & Axsom, 2011), and grief (e.g., Smith, Abeyta, Hughes, & Jones, 2015). As is the case with measures of PTSS discussed above, distress, depression, and anxiety indices provide measures of symptom severity rather than clinical diagnoses. Whereas clinical cut-offs/norms for determining levels of severity for depression (Beck, Steer, & Brown, 1996) and distress (Kessler et al., 2002) are available, as measures of psychopathology, these measures share the same strengths and limitations as reviewed above for PTSS compared to PTSD.

Grief reactions

Grief is a normal psychological outcome that is likely to occur among people who were involved in social relationships with those killed in mass shootings. Feelings of loss, yearning, heartache, anger, and depression, along with disruptions in self-concept and confusion about one's place in the world are typical grief reactions. Normal grief subsides within a few weeks or months, but sometimes grief is persistent, causes significant distress, and is disabling. Complicated grief (Prigerson et al., 1995) and prolonged grief (Prigerson et al., 2009) are two similar ways this has been conceptualized. Using dimensional indices of grief symptoms, researchers have found prolonged grief among children (Nader, Pynoos, Fairbanks, & Frederick, 1990) and college students (Smith, Abeyta, et al., 2015) in the aftermath of mass shootings. Pathological grief has never been defined as a mental disorder in the DSM, but the recent DSM-5 (American Psychiatric Association, 2013) includes proposed criteria for persistent complex bereavement disorder, a prolonged and debilitating pattern of grief, in an appendix as a condition for further study.

Recent innovations in grief theory beyond the uni-dimensional and pathology-based complicated grief literature should be considered in future mass shootings studies and interventions. Specifically, multidimensional grief theory proposes that adaptive and maladaptive grief reactions may occur along three underlying, interrelated dimensions, including separation distress, existential/identity distress, and circumstance-related distress (Kaplow, Layne, Saltzman, Cozza, & Pynoos, 2013). The first two dimensions (i.e., separation-related distress, existential/identity-related distress) share some similarities with prior conceptualizations of grief.

Circumstance-related distress, on the other hand, is a reaction to traumatogenic elements embedded within the circumstances of a death, which are often violent and gruesome, involve human agency (e.g., malicious intent or negligence) or may involve intense pain, suffering, or progressive physical deterioration (Kaplow et al., 2013). Because of their very nature, mass shootings are theorized to contain causal risk factors (Layne, Steinberg, & Steinberg, 2014) for circumstance-related distress, particularly among people who were emotionally close to those who were killed (Pynoos, 1992). Under these conditions, circumstance-related distress may center on such aspects as the potential preventability of the event, malicious intent of the shooter(s), last moments (e.g., terror and suffering among victims; being unable to care for the victims in their last moments), gruesome injuries, and/or desires for revenge (Kaplow et al., 2013). Given that many of the reactions extend beyond the formal DSM-5 PTSD criteria, future research on mass shootings may consider multidimensional grief as a useful framework for understanding the broad spectrum of personal reactions to losses often consequent to mass shootings, including dual sets of reactions (e.g., traumatic stress and grief) arising from the interplay of traumatic stress exposure and bereavement (Pynoos, 1992).

What Processes Link Mass Shootings to Outcomes?

Most perspectives on how mass shootings affect psychological functioning are grounded in the dose-response model (Dohrenwend & Dohrenwend, 1974; McNally, 2003; Wilson, 2014). According to the model, the greater the exposure to traumatic conditions, the worse the psychological impact will be. The dose-response model provides the basis for the diagnosis of PTSD through the assumption that exposure to a traumatic event produces the symptom patterns characteristic of the disorder. The dose-response model adds the simple notion that as exposure increases, so too does the negative response.

Exposure

The literature on mass shootings generally assumes that greater direct or indirect exposure to a mass shooting influences the onset and severity of psychopathology (Norris, 2007; Wilson, 2014). Less clear are the kinds of exposures that lead to negative outcomes. Exposure characteristics that define the initial requirements for a PTSD diagnosis (i.e., Criterion A) have been altered in each edition of the DSM, an evolution that demonstrates how the field of traumatic stress has wrestled with the question: "What qualifies as traumatic exposure?" DSM-III considered traumatic exposure as "a recognizable stressor that would evoke significant symptoms of distress in almost anyone" (American Psychiatric Association, 1980, p. 238). DSM-III-R indicated that a traumatic event is "outside the range of usual human experience" and "markedly distressing to everyone" (American Psychiatric Association, 1987, p. 250). DSM-IV required that the "person experienced, witnessed, or was confronted with an event or events that involved actual or threatened death or serious injury or a threat to the physical integrity of self or others" and that the reaction "involved intense fear, helplessness, or horror" (American Psychiatric Association, 1994, 427–428[3]).

The definition of a traumatic event in the DSM-5 is considerably more restrictive, defining a traumatic event as "exposure to actual or threatened death, serious injury, or sexual violence in one (or more) of the following ways: (1) Directly experiencing the traumatic event(s), (2) witnessing in-person the event(s) as it occurred to others, (3) learning that the traumatic event(s) occurred to a close family member or close friend (in cases of actual or threatened death of a family member or friend, event(s) must have been violent or accidental), or (4) experiencing repeated or extreme exposure to aversive details of the traumatic event(s)" (American Psychiatric Association, 2013, p. 271). The DSM-5 specifically excludes previously considered forms of exposure through media (e.g., TV, radio, movies, pictures) unless such exposure is work related.

Direct and indirect exposure

The majority of the research on mass shootings has been done using the more expansive trauma definitions in the DSM-III, DSM-III-R, and DSM-IV, allowing investigators to look across a range of exposures in testing the dose-response model and to examine both direct and indirect exposure (e.g., DSM-5 excluded media exposure; Fallahi & Lesik, 2009; Haravuori, Suomalainen, Berg, Kiviruusu, & Marttunen, 2011). Direct exposure is experiencing an event first-hand by being a victim or by observing the event in person (e.g., being wounded, seeing others being killed or wounded, or observing the physical consequences and human suffering of others in the event aftermath; for a more in-depth understanding of direct exposure see Chapter 11 in this volume). Indirect exposure is experiencing consequences, depictions, and other elements of the event without being physically present at the site of the traumatic event (e.g., knowing someone who was killed or injured in a shooting, observing activities that unfold during or after a shooting [SWAT team response], or experiencing the event through media).

Research has sought to examine the impacts of both kinds of exposure on outcomes. For example, early research conducted following sniper attacks at an elementary school in 1984 examined associations between two exposure parameters – physical proximity to the shooting epicenter (i.e., direct exposure) and social proximity (e.g., closeness) to the deceased (i.e., indirect exposure) – and outcomes. This research revealed a dose-response relationship between physical proximity to the shooting epicenter (interpreted as increasing direct life threat) and PTSS symptoms both cross-sectionally (Pynoos, Frederick, et al., 1987) and longitudinally (Nader et al., 1990), as well as a dose-response relation between social proximity to the deceased child and longitudinal grief reactions (Nader et al., 1990; Pynoos, Nader, Frederick, Gonda, & Stuber, 1987). Subsequent mass shootings research has also made distinctions between direct and indirect exposure (e.g., Littleton, Axsom, & Grills-Taquechel, 2009). Review of the broad mass-disaster literature suggests that both direct and indirect forms of exposure are relevant to the study of mental health outcomes (see Neria, Nandi, & Galea, 2008).

Mediators and moderators

While influential early studies of traumatic stress straightforwardly applied the dose-response model (Nader et al., 1990; Pynoos, Frederick, et al., 1987; Pynoos, Nader, et al., 1987), more recent research emphasizes pre- and posttraumatic factors that may moderate or mediate the dose-response relationship (see Brewin, Andrews, & Valentine, 2000; Layne, Warren, Watson, & Shalev, 2007; Ozer, Best, Lipsey, & Weiss, 2003; Silverman & La Greca, 2002). If an association between two variables depends on the level of a third variable, that third variable is a moderator. If the effect of one variable on another is due to a third variable that intervenes between them, then that third variable is a mediator (Baron & Kenny, 1986; see also Wheaton, 1985).

Studies of mass shootings do not usually examine moderation and/or mediation of events themselves, as suggested by Baron and Kenny (1986), because most studies of mass shootings collect data only from those who were exposed to the shooting, and thus exposure to the event is a constant. Studies limited to those exposed to traumatic conditions can provide suggestive evidence that can be interpreted by the logic of mediation or moderation (e.g., Bomyea, Risbrough, & Lang, 2012; Littleton, Grills-Taquechel, & Axsom, 2009; Schwarz & Kowalski, 1992). In addition, studies of those exposed to shootings can examine whether event characteristics (e.g., event type, exposure severity) are mediated or moderated by other factors (Brewin et al., 2000; Ozer et al., 2003). However, it is important to understand that in order to establish whether the effect of exposure itself is mediated or moderated by other factors, one must first estimate the effect of exposure, and that requires a sample of people who have not been exposed. Because most studies of mass shootings include data only from exposed respondents, and not from a comparison group, control group, or group of otherwise unexposed respondents, the ability of researchers to examine mediation and moderation of exposure is often seriously limited.

Challenges in Research Design
and Theoretical Development

A number of theoretical frameworks have been applied to explain the effects of mass shootings, but little progress has been made in developing an integrative theory for how mass shootings cause psychological outcomes in survivors. Recent meta-analytic findings highlight the problem of lack of replication and the difficulty estimating aggregate effect-sizes in the current mass shootings literature (see Wilson, 2014). Most researchers studying mass shootings have focused on specific theoretical or applied questions, but they have not typically investigated alternate hypotheses in ways that could lead to a more comprehensive understanding of how traumatic experiences lead to pathogenic outcomes. The result is a collection of well-executed but theoretically disconnected studies that emphasize, for example, (1) peritraumatic processes (Kumpula, Orcutt, Bardeen, & Varkovitzky, 2011); (2) conservation of resources (Littleton, Axsom, et al., 2009); (3) social network interactions and coping appraisals (Smith, Donlon, et al., 2015); (4) emotion regulation (Bardeen, Kumpula, & Orcutt, 2013); (5) core belief alterations (Grills-Taquechel et al., 2011; Smith, Abeyta, et al., 2015); (6) gene-environment interaction influence on postshootings PTSS (Mercer et al., 2012).

Five other factors limit theoretical innovation and development in the mass shootings literature. First, sampling problems limit the generalizability of the findings in mass shooting studies. Specifically, mass shootings survivor samples are typically composed of respondents within a limited age range (e.g., children, adolescents, or emerging adults in the wake of shootings in schools or colleges). There have been some studies of shootings in places other than schools (e.g., Cafeteria shootings in Kileen, TX; North, Smith, & Spitznagel, 1994, 1997), allowing for examination of the effects of shootings on people at different points in the life course. However, because studies are not typically based on systematically collected and theoretically relevant data from adequate numbers of people of different ages, researchers who would like to consider developmental differences must make interpretations based on studies of different events, in different contexts, with different variables, and demographically different respondents.

Second is the related problem of there being few longitudinal studies of the psychological consequences of mass shootings. Without long-term follow-up research, and without consideration of developmental timing of events on long-term functioning, the effects of mass shootings cannot be fully known. For example, without following up with respondents who experience shootings during their college years, it is unclear whether such traumatic experiences impair the development of intimate relationships across the lifespan as argued on the basis of cross-sectional studies (e.g., Layne, Pynoos, & Cardenas, 2001). One notable strength in the mass shootings literature is the prospective studies made possible by ongoing research studies started prior to shooting events that have allowed researchers to add a focus on pre- to postshooting functioning changes (e.g., Bardeen et al., 2013; Littleton, Axsom, et al., 2009).

Third, although some early psychological research on the effects of shootings employed clinical interviews (Pynoos, Nader, et al., 1987), the majority of studies in this literature rely solely on the use of self-reports of symptom inventories that provide continuous measures of PTSS, distress, depression, anxiety, and/or grief reactions. As a result, our knowledge of how trauma affects psychological outcomes is shaped to an unknown degree by problems of response bias and other measurement errors known to affect self-report measures (e.g., Podsakoff, MacKenzie, Lee, & Podsakoff, 2003). Reasons for this measurement strategy are based largely on challenges that are involved in conducting postshooting research: clinical interviews are expensive, time-consuming, and intrusive during a sensitive posttraumatic time in communities affected by mass shootings, compared to cheaper, less intrusive, easier-to-administer self-report surveys. Nonetheless, without more studies that employ clinical interviews, and more studies that include explicit validation of self-report measures, our knowledge of how traumatic events affect psychological functioning is and will remain limited.

Fourth, due to the dominance of the dose-response model, studies in the mass shootings literature typically include some form of exposure (e.g., physical proximity to shootings, social proximity to shootings, direct vs. indirect exposure, perceived peritraumatic threat) as part of model testing. However, many different operational definitions of exposure have been used in studies of mass shootings. In addition, it is not always clear why certain exposure features have been selected by researchers and others ignored. Research is needed to develop an empirically supported typology of exposure to guide researchers to design studies with comparable measures. Shootings and exposure contexts vary across a number of dimensions, as do the characteristics, backgrounds, social networks, and life circumstances of survivors and bystanders. It is unlikely that exposure has the same effects in every case, and thus, as noted above, it is important to investigate how shooting characteristics and victim characteristics moderate and/or mediate various kinds of exposure. We will be unable to understand these processes in a theoretically coherent way unless there is some consistency in the operational definitions of exposure.

Fifth, publication of null findings are nonexistent in the mass shootings literature, and thus, there is little systematic knowledge about variables and interventions that *do not* work (see Hopewell, Loudon, Clarke, Oxman, & Dickersin, 2009). This problem is linked to the issue of consistent operational definitions. Unless researchers can be fairly certain that they are investigating the same kinds of exposure as others have, then the meaning of a null result is ambiguous. A null finding could be theoretically significant and mean that some form of exposure has no impact in certain situations or among certain kinds of victims, but it could just as well have little or no theoretical signifi-cance and simply mean that different operational definitions of exposure lead to different findings in different studies.

Conclusions

Our review of challenges in the study of mass shootings leads to three broad conclusions. First, previously applied definitions and frameworks may be too limiting and may stunt progress in understanding how shootings affect out-comes. Defining a mass shooting as a gun violence incident with four or more fatalities is clearly useful, but until we know that the restrictions built into the definition are meaningful in defining an incident that is distinctively trau-matogenic, researchers should be wary of applying it in a rigid way. Similarly, defining psychopathological outcomes in terms of the DSM-5 definition of PTSD severely limits researchers to a narrow range of exposure, and in addition, restricts the definition of psychopathology to a single monotonic response. As an outcome, it is important that PTSD is understood for epide-miological, clinical policy and planning, and legal purposes. But unless it can be shown that exposures that violate PTSD Criterion A are truly not associ-ated with negative psychological outcomes, and that subclinical symptom-atology has little or no impact on psychological adjustment following a trauma, researchers interested in developing a full understanding of the impact of mass shootings should avoid the strict application of the PTSD diagnosis in their research designs.

Second, unless there is some consistency in the theoretical and operational definitions of key concepts, it will be difficult to make any theoretical progress. Although there seems to be some consensus on the meaning and operational definitions of the key outcomes in mass shootings research, the same cannot be said for exposure. Without an empirically grounded consensus on how to conceptualize and measure exposure, it will be difficult to build a body of findings that promotes the development and testing of theoretically produc-tive hypotheses. This is also true of key factors hypothesized to mediate and moderate the effects of exposure. If each researcher conceptualizes and mea-sures these factors differently, the results may be interesting and provocative without being theoretically informative.

Third, most studies of mass shootings have been designed quickly in the aftermath of events that no one could have predicted. With little time to plan, researchers have used procedures that could be implemented in a short period of time, have relied on samples that were relatively easy to collect in schools and colleges, and have employed data collection instruments with measures that were close at hand. In addition, while there have been prospective studies done with respondents already recruited for studies with another purpose, there have been few longitudinal studies that could investigate issues of how traumatic events affect people going through different developmental stages in the life course. Researchers need to broaden the scope of their studies to examine more kinds of victims over longer periods of time. In addition, in view of the likelihood of future traumatic shooting incidents, some researchers should do prospective planning so that they are ready and able to do theoretically productive study when the opportunity arises.

Considering the frequency of mass shootings over the past three decades (Bjelopera et al., 2013), it is an unfortunate reality that the incidence of mass shootings is unlikely to significantly decline. Thus, social scientists will have opportunities to investigate these future traumatic shooting incidents and to add to a growing body of empirical evidence on how they affect the psychological adjustment among victims, bystanders, and those in their social networks. Although replication is important, it is also critical to generate knowledge that takes us beyond what we already know, and to do so in ways that facilitate the development of theoretical approaches that can complement and build upon one another in the service of promoting individual and community recovery.

Notes

1 The FBI (Federal Bureau of Investigation, 2008) defined mass murder as "(a) number of murders (four or more) occurring during the same incident, with no distinctive time period between the murders. These events typically involved a single location, where the killer murdered a number of victims in an ongoing incident" (p. 8).
2 For an overview of measures and issues in the assessment of PTSD and PTSS see http://www.ptsd.va.gov/professional/assessment/overview/index.asp
3 Criterion A is the same in the two versions of the DSM-IV.

References

American Psychiatric Association. (1980). *Diagnostic and statistical manual of mental disorders* (3rd ed.). Washington, DC: Author.

American Psychiatric Association. (1987). *Diagnostic and statistical manual of mental disorders* (revised 3rd ed.). Washington, DC: Author.

American Psychiatric Association. (1994). *Diagnostic and statistical manual of mental disorders* (4th ed.). Washington, DC: Author.

American Psychiatric Association. (2000). *Diagnostic and statistical manual of mental disorders* (revised 4th ed.). Washington, DC: Author.

American Psychiatric Association. (2013). *Diagnostic and statistical manual of mental disorders* (5th ed.). Washington, DC: Author.

Bardeen, J. R., Kumpula, M. J., & Orcutt, H. K. (2013). Emotion regulation difficulties as a prospective predictor of posttraumatic stress symptoms following a
mass shooting. *Journal of Anxiety Disorders, 27*(2), 188–196. doi:10.1016/j.
janxdis.2013.01.003

Baron, R. M., & Kenny, D. A. (1986). The moderator–mediator variable distinction in
social psychological research: Conceptual, strategic, and statistical considerations.
Journal of Personality and Social Psychology, 51(6), 1173–1182.

Beck, A. T., Steer, R. A., & Brown, G. K. (1996). *Manual for Beck Depression Inventory-II.*
San Antonio, TX: Psychological Corporation.

Bjelopera, J. P., Bagalman, E., Caldwell, S. W., Finklea, K. M., & McCallion, G.
(2013). *Public mass shootings in the United States: Selected implications for federal
public health and safety policy.* Congressional Research Service. Retrieved from
http://fas.org/sgp/crs/misc/R43004.pdf

Bomyea, J., Risbrough, V., & Lang, A. J. (2012). A consideration of select pretrauma factors as key vulnerabilities in PTSD. *Clinical Psychology Review, 32*(7),
630–641.

Brewin, C. R., Andrews, B., & Valentine, J. D. (2000). Meta-analysis of risk factors for
posttraumatic stress disorder in trauma-exposed adults. *Journal of Consulting and
Clinical Psychology, 68*(5), 748–766. doi:10.1037/0022-006X.68.5.748

Brewin, C. R., Rose, S., Andrews, B., Green, J., Tata, P., McEvedy, C., ... Foa, E. B.
(2002). Brief screening instrument for post-traumatic stress disorder. *British
Journal of Psychiatry, 181*, 158–162. doi:10.1192/bjp.181.2.158

Brown, T., & Barlow, D. (2014). *Anxiety and Related Disorders Interview Schedule for
DSM-5 (ADIS-5). Clinician Manual.* New York, NY: Oxford University Press.

Davidson, J. R., Book, S. W., Colket, J. T., Tupler, L. A., Roth, S., David, D., ...
Feldman, M. E. (1997). Assessment of a new self-rating scale for post-traumatic
stress disorder. *Psychological Medicine, 27*(1), 153–160.

Dohrenwend, B. S., & Dohrenwend, B. P. (1974). *Stressful life events: Their nature and
effects.* Oxford, UK: John Wiley & Sons.

Fallahi, C. R., & Lesik, S. A. (2009). The effects of vicarious exposure to the recent
massacre at Virginia Tech. *Psychological Trauma: Theory, Research, Practice, and
Policy, 1*, 220 230. doi:10.1037/a0015052

Federal Bureau of Investigation. (2008). *Serial murder: Multi-disciplinary perspectives
for investigators.* Washington, DC: Department of Justice.

Foa, E. B., Cashman, L., Jaycox, L., & Perry, K. (1997). The validation of a self-report
measure of posttraumatic stress disorder: The Posttraumatic Diagnostic Scale.
Psychological Assessment, 9(4), 445.

Foa, E. B., Riggs, D. S., Dancu, C. V., & Rothbaum, B. O. (1993). Reliability and
validity of a brief instrument for assessing post-traumatic stress disorder. *Journal of
Traumatic Stress, 6*(4), 459–473.

Fox, J. A., & Levin, J. (2015). Mass confusion concerning mass murder. *The
Criminologist, 40*(1), 8–11.

Grills-Taquechel, A. E., Littleton, H. L., & Axsom, D. (2011). Social support,
world assumptions, and exposure as predictors of anxiety and quality of life
following a mass trauma. *Journal of Anxiety Disorders, 25*, 498–506. doi:10.1016/j.
janxdis.2010.12.003

Haravuori, H., Suomalainen, L., Berg, N., Kiviruusu, O., & Marttunen, M. (2011). Effects of media exposure on adolescents traumatized in a school shooting. *Journal of Traumatic Stress, 24*(1), 70–77.

Hopewell, S., Loudon, K., Clarke, M. J., Oxman, A. D., & Dickersin, K. (2009). Publication bias in clinical trials due to statistical significance or direction of trial results. *Cochrane Database of Systematic Reviews, 1*(1), 1–29.

Hughes, M., Brymer, M., Chiu, W., Fairbank, J., Jones, R., Pynoos, R., … Kessler, R. (2011). Posttraumatic stress among students after the shootings at Virginia Tech. *Psychological Trauma: Theory, Research, Practice, and Policy, 3*, 403–411. doi:10.1037/a0024565

Investigative Assistance for Violent Crimes Act of 2012, 6 U.S.C. (2013). Retrieved from http://www.gpo.gov/fdsys/pkg/PLAW-112publ265/pdf/PLAW-112publ265.pdf

Kaplow, J. B., Layne, C. M., Saltzman, W. R., Cozza, S. J., & Pynoos, R. S. (2013). Using Multidimensional Grief Theory to explore effects of deployment, reintegration, and death on military youth and families. *Clinical Child and Family Psychology Review, 16*(3), 322–340.

Kessler, R. C., Andrews, G., Colpe, L. J., Hiripi, E., Mroczek, D. K., Normand, S. L., … Zaslavsky, A. M. (2002). Short screening scales to monitor population prevalences and trends in non-specific psychological distress. *Psychological Medicine, 32*(6), 959–976.

Kilpatrick, D. G., Resnick, H. S., Saunders, B. E., & Best, C. L. (1989). *The national women's study PTSD module.* Charleston, SC: National Crime Victims Research and Treatment Center, Department of Psychiatry & Behavioral Sciences, Medical University of South Carolina.

Kubany, E. S., Leisen, M. B., Kaplan, A. S., & Kelly, M. P. (2000). Validation of a brief measure of posttraumatic stress disorder: The Distressing Event Questionnaire (DEQ). *Psychological Assessment, 12*(2), 197.

Kumpula, M. J., Orcutt, H. K., Bardeen, J. R., & Varkovitzky, R. L. (2011). Peritraumatic dissociation and experiential avoidance as prospective predictors of posttraumatic stress symptoms. *Journal of Abnormal Psychology, 120*(3), 617–627.

Layne, C. M., Pynoos, R. S., & Cardenas, J. (2001). Wounded adolescence: School-based group psychotherapy for adolescents who have sustained or witnessed violent interpersonal injury. In M. Shafii & S. Shafii (Eds.), *School violence: Assessment, management, prevention* (pp. 163–186). Washington, DC: American Psychiatric Publishing.

Layne, C. M., Steinberg, J. R., & Steinberg, A. M. (2014). Causal reasoning skills training for mental health practitioners: Promoting sound clinical judgment in evidence-based practice. *Training and Education in Professional Psychology, 8*, 292–302.

Layne, C. M., Warren, J. S., Watson, P. J., & Shalev, A. Y. (2007). Risk, vulnerability, resistance, and resilience. In M. J. Friedman, T. M. Keane, & P. A. Resick (Eds.), *Handbook of PTSD: Science and practice.* New York, NY: Guilford Press.

Littleton, H. L., Axsom, D., & Grills-Taquechel, A. E. (2009). Adjustment following the mass shooting at Virginia Tech: The roles of resource loss and gain. *Psychological Trauma: Theory, Research, Practice, and Policy, 1*(3), 206–219.

Littleton, H., Grills-Taquechel, A., & Axsom, D. (2009). Resource loss as a predictor of posttrauma symptoms among college women following the mass shooting at Virginia Tech. *Violence and Victims, 24,* 669–686. doi:10.1891/0886-6708.24.5.669

Lowe, S., & Galea, S. (2015). The mental health consequences of mass shootings. *Trauma, Violence, & Abuse.* Advance online publication. doi:10.1177/1524838015591572

March, J. S. (1993). What constitutes a stressor? The "Criterion A" issue. In J. R. T. Davidson & E. B. Foa (Eds.), *Posttraumatic stress disorder: DSM-IV and beyond* (pp. 37–54). Arlington, VA: American Psychiatric Publishing.

McNally, R. J. (2003). Progress and controversy in the study of posttraumatic stress disorder. *Annual Review of Psychology, 54*(1), 229–252.

Mercer, K. B., Orcutt, H. K., Quinn, J. F., Fitzgerald, C. A., Conneely, K. N., Barfield, R. T., ... Resler, K. J. (2012). Acute and posttraumatic stress symptoms in a prospective gene×environment study of a university campus shooting. *Archives of General Psychiatry, 69,* 89–97. doi:10.1001/archgenpsychiatry.2011.109

Nader, K., Pynoos, R. S., Fairbanks, L., & Frederick, C. (1990). Children's PTSD reactions one year after a sniper attack at their school. *American Journal of Psychiatry, 147*(11), 1526–1530.

Nekvasil, E. K., Cornell, D. G., & Huang, F. L. (2015). Prevalence and offense characteristics of multiple casualty homicides: Are schools at higher risk than other locations? *Psychology of Violence, 15,* 236–245. doi:10.1037/a0038967

Neria, Y., Nandi, A., & Galea, S. (2008). Post-traumatic stress disorder following disasters: A systematic review. *Psychological Medicine, 38,* 467–480. doi:10.1017/S0033291707001353

Norris, F. H. (2007). Impact of mass shootings on survivors, families, and communities. *PTSD Research Quarterly, 18,* 1–7.

Norris, F. H., & Hamblen, J. L. (2004). Standardized self-report measures of civilian trauma and PTSD. In J. P. Wilson, T. M. Keane, & T. Martin (Eds.), *Assessing psychological trauma and PTSD* (pp. 63–102). New York, NY: Guilford Press.

North, C. S., Smith, E. M., & Spitznagel, E. L. (1994). Posttraumatic stress disorder in survivors of a mass shooting. *American Journal of Psychiatry, 151*(1), 82–88.

North, C. S., Smith, E. M., & Spitznagel, E. L. (1997). One-year follow-up of survivors of mass shooting. *American Journal of Psychiatry, 154,* 1696–1702.

Orsillo, S. M. (2001). Measures for acute stress disorder and posttraumatic stress disorder. In M. M. Antony & S. M. Orsillo (Eds.), *Practitioner's guide to empirically based measures of anxiety* (pp. 255–307). New York, NY: Kluwer Academic/Plenum.

Ozer, E. J., Best, S. R., Lipsey, T. L., & Weiss, D. S. (2003). Predictors of posttraumatic stress disorder and symptoms in adults: A meta-analysis. *Psychological Bulletin, 139*(1), 3–36.

Podsakoff, P. M., MacKenzie, S. B., Lee, J. Y., & Podsakoff, N. P. (2003). Common method biases in behavioral research: A critical review of the literature and recommended remedies. *Journal of Applied Psychology, 88*(5), 879.

Prigerson, H. G., Horowitz, M. J., Jacobs, S. C., Parkes, C. M., Aslan, M., Goodkin, K., ... Maciejewski, P. K. (2009). Prolonged grief disorder: Psychometric validation of criteria proposed for DSM-V and ICD-11. *PLoS Medicine, 6*(8), 917.

Prigerson, H. G., Maciejewski, P. K., Reynolds, C. F., III, Bierhals, A. J., Newsom, J. T., Fasiczka, A., ... Miller, M. (1995). Inventory of Complicated Grief: A scale to measure maladaptive symptoms of loss. *Psychiatry Research*, *59*, 65–79. doi:10.1016/0165-1781(95)02757-2

Pynoos, R. S. (1992). Grief and trauma in children and adolescents. *Bereavement Care*, *11*(1), 2–10.

Pynoos, R. S., Frederick, C., Nader, K., Arroyo, W., Steinberg, A., Eth, S., ..., Fairbanks, L. (1987). Life threat and posttraumatic stress in school-age children. *Archives of General Psychiatry*, *44*(12), 1057–1063.

Pynoos, R. S., Nader, K., Frederick, C., Gonda, L., & Stuber, M. (1987). Grief reactions in school age children following a sniper attack at a school. *Israel Journal of Psychiatry and Related Sciences*, *24*(1–2), 53–63.

Schwarz, E. D., & Kowalski, J. M. (1992). Personality characteristics and posttraumatic stress symptoms after a school shooting. *The Journal of Nervous and Mental Disease*, *180*(11), 735–736.

Shultz, J. M., Thoresen, S., Flynn, B. W., Muschert, G. W., Shaw, J. A., Espinel, Z., ... Cohen, A. M. (2014). Multiple vantage points on the mental health effects of mass shootings. *Current Psychiatry Reports*, *16*(9), 1–17.

Silverman, W. K., & La Greca, A. M. (2002). Children experiencing disasters: Definitions, reactions, and predictors of outcomes. In A. M. La Greca, W. K. Silverman, E. M. Vernberg, & M. C. Roberts (Eds.), *Helping children cope with disasters and terrorism* (pp. 11–33). Washington, DC: American Psychological Association

Smith, A. J., Abeyta, A., Hughes, M., & Jones, R. T. (2015). Persistent grief in the aftermath of mass violence: The predictive roles of posttraumatic stress symptoms, self-efficacy, and disrupted worldview. *Psychological Trauma: Theory, Research, Practice, and Policy*, *7*, 179–186. doi:10.1037/tra0000002

Smith, A. J., Donlon, K., Anderson, S. R., Hughes, M., & Jones, R. T. (2015). When seeking influences believing and promotes posttraumatic adaptation. *Anxiety, Stress, & Coping*, *28*, 340–356. doi:10.1080/10615806.2014.969719

Vicary, A. M., & Fraley, R. C. (2010). Student reactions to the shootings at Virginia Tech and Northern Illinois University: Does sharing grief and support over the internet affect recovery? *Personality and Social Psychology Bulletin*, *36*, 1555–1563. doi:10.1177/0146167210384880

Weathers, F. W., Blake, D. D., Schnurr, P. P., Kaloupek, D. G., Marx, B. P., & Keane, T. M. (2013). *The Clinician-Administered PTSD Scale for DSM-5 (CAPS-5)*. National Center for PTSD. Retrieved from www.ptsd.va.gov.

Wheaton, B. (1985). Models for the stress-buffering functions of coping resources. *Journal of Health and Social Behavior*, *26*(4), 352–364.

Wilson, L. C. (2014). Mass shootings: A meta-analysis of the dose-response relationship. *Journal of Traumatic Stress*, *27*, 631–638. doi:10.1002/jts.21964

2

The Patterns and Prevalence of Mass Public Shootings in the United States, 1915–2013

Grant Duwe

The 1960s marked the onset of a crime wave in the United States that did not begin to subside until the 1990s. The property crime rate nearly tripled in size from 1960 to 1990, while the violent crime rate in 1990 was roughly five times higher than it was 30 years earlier (Federal Bureau of Investigation, 1960, 1990). Over the past 20 years, however, crime has been on the decline. Perhaps most notably, the homicide rate in 2011 was about half of what it was in 1991 (Federal Bureau of Investigation, 1991, 2011).

Mass murder is an extreme form of violence that is, in some ways, an outlier within the broader context of crime. It may be tempting, therefore, to assume that mass killings not only defy explanation, especially from mainstream criminological theories, but also bear few similarities with crime in general. But the evidence shows that, similar to homicide and crime in general, the 1960s also marked the onset of a mass murder wave in the United States (Duwe, 2004, 2007). This wave was not unprecedented, however, as mass murder rates were just as high during the 1920s and 1930s (Duwe, 2004, 2007). And, once again, consistent with trends in homicide and crime in general, mass murder rates have generally been on the decline since the 1990s (Duwe, 2012).

Existing research on mass murder suggests the two waves during the twentieth century were qualitatively different (Duwe, 2004, 2007). The first one during the 1920s and 1930s was comprised mainly of familicides and felony-related massacres, which, then as now, are less likely to receive widespread news coverage. In contrast, the second mass murder wave contained a greater number of mass public shootings, which have long attracted intense interest and concern (Duwe, 2000, 2004).

There has been substantial debate about how to define mass public shootings, including factors such as the motivation behind the event and the number of casualties. In this chapter, I define mass public shootings as incidents that

The Wiley Handbook of the Psychology of Mass Shootings, First Edition. Edited by Laura C. Wilson.
© 2017 John Wiley & Sons, Inc. Published 2017 by John Wiley & Sons, Inc.

occur in the absence of other criminal activity (e.g., robberies, drug deals, gang "turf wars") in which a gun was used to kill four or more victims at a public location (Duwe, Kovandzic, & Moody, 2002). Prior to 1965, there had been relatively few mass public shootings in the United States. The frequency with which these incidents occurred, however, accelerated rapidly during the last third of the twentieth century (Duwe, 2007). The number of mass public shootings per decade grew from 13 during the 1970s to 30 in the 1980s, peaking with 37 in the 1990s. From 2000 to 2013, there were 53 mass public shootings in the United States.

In this chapter, I trace the history of mass public shootings in the United States by examining 160 cases that occurred between 1915 and 2013. Given that there has been increasing discussion of whether mass public shootings have recently been on the rise, I begin by delineating trends in their prevalence. Next, I focus on the patterns of mass public shootings by reporting incident, victim, and offender characteristics. But before describing the prevalence and patterns of mass public shootings in the United States, I provide a brief description of the dataset I used for this chapter.

Mass Public Shooting Dataset

Much of the data on the 160 cases are drawn from my previous research on mass killings that occurred in the United States between 1900 and 1999 (Duwe, 2004, 2007). In this research, I used the FBI's Supplementary Homicide Reports (SHR) to anchor my search for data on mass murders. It is important to acknowledge that the SHR data have flaws. As I have noted previously (e.g., Duwe, 2000, 2004), there is an underreporting problem with the SHR since it is a voluntary program involving law enforcement agencies across the country. Moreover, the SHR data contain a number of coding errors. Nevertheless, because the SHR contains incident, victim, and offender information on most murders committed in the United States since 1976, it is an invaluable source of data on homicides, mass murders, and, more narrowly, mass public shootings.

Still, the information provided by the SHR is limited. For example, the SHR does not record whether the homicide occurred in a public location or the number of wounded victims. Therefore, I have also relied on news accounts as a source of data on mass killings. More specifically, after using the SHR to identify when and where mass murders have occurred, I have searched online newspaper databases to collect additional information not included within the SHR. In using this triangulated data collection approach, I have been able to not only identify cases not reported to the SHR but also to correct errors in the SHR data.

After pioneering this methodology in my prior research on mass killings (Duwe, 2000, 2004, 2007; Duwe et al., 2002), others have since adopted the same approach in their own data collection efforts. For example, reporters from *USA Today* relied on the SHR and news reports as sources of data in the series of articles they published on mass killings (Overberg, Upton, & Hoyer, 2013). More recently, the Congressional Research Service (CRS; 2014) used the same process to collect data on mass shootings.[1]

For the cases that occurred between 1976 and 2013, I used the triangulated SHR-news report data collection strategy. Further, for cases occurring within this timeframe, but especially those that have taken place since 2000, I also relied on data collected by the CRS (2014). As a result, the dataset I used for this chapter is more accurate and complete than the datasets I have used in prior publications on mass public shootings (Duwe, 2012, 2013, 2014). Overall, during the 1976–2013 period, a little more than 1,000 mass murders occurred in the United States. Of these, 125 were mass public shootings.

Because the SHR did not become a valuable source of data until it underwent a major revision in 1976 (Riedel, 1999), I relied on the *New York Times* index to locate news accounts on mass murders that occurred between 1900 and 1975 (Duwe, 2000, 2004). During this 76-year period, I found news reports on 260 mass killings (Duwe, 2004). Of these incidents, 35 were mass public shootings, which brings the total to 160 for the 1900–2013 period.

Mass Public Shootings in Context

It is worth emphasizing that mass public shootings are a rare type of mass murder, which is itself a rare form of violence. In my previous work, I have defined mass killings as incidents in which four or more victims are murdered within a 24-hour period (Duwe, 2000, 2004, 2007). Since 1900, there have been more than 1,300 mass murders in the United States. But since 1976, when more complete data have been available, there have been a little more than 1,000, which amounts to an average of 28 mass murders each year. During the same period of time in the United States, there have been, on average, approximately 14,200 homicides per year. As a result, mass murders make up a mere 0.2% of all homicide incidents. But due to the greater number of victims per incident, mass killings account for roughly 1% of all homicide victims each year (Duwe, 2007).

As noted above, there were 125 mass public shootings in the United States from 1976 to 2013. Given that there were more than 1,000 mass murders during this same 34-year period, mass public shootings account for a little more than 12% of all mass killings. Familicides are by far the most common form of mass murder, making up nearly 45% of all mass killings since 1976. Familicides most often involve a male head of the household killing his partner (i.e., spouse, ex-spouse, fiancée), their children, relatives, or some combination of these. Felony-related massacres are the second most common type of mass murder, comprising roughly one quarter of all mass killings since 1976. These incidents typically involve a small group of young men who commit mass murder during a robbery.

The Prominence of Mass Public Shootings in the Social Construction of Mass Murder

Although rare, even within the context of mass killings, mass public shootings are often thought to define the essence of mass murder. As I noted above, mass public shootings generally capture extensive attention from the news media, and this has been true since the beginning of the twentieth century (see Chapters 7–10 for more on the role of the media following mass shootings). In a previous study, I examined the factors that predicted greater news coverage for 495 mass murders that took place in the United States between 1976 and 1996 (Duwe, 2000). The "body count," both in terms of wounded and killed victims, had the greatest impact on the extent to which the news media reported a mass murder. As shown later, the 160 mass public shootings had, on average, more than six fatal victims and nearly five wounded victims per incident, which are both greater in comparison to mass murders in general.

But the larger number of victims killed and wounded is not the only reason mass public shootings are the most newsworthy mass killings. Mass public shootings are also more likely to involve stranger victims than other mass murders. As I indicated in the 2000 study:

> massacres were even more tragic when strangers were killed. These incidents conjure up images of random violence because the slaughter of strangers connotes an indiscriminate selection of victims. As a result, a sharp distinction is drawn between victims and offenders: Victims are depicted as blameless or virtuous, whereas offenders are characterized as evil, crazy, and less than human. Moreover, the seemingly random selection of victims broadens the news interest by conveying the impression that anyone could be a victim of a mass killing. (Duwe, 2000, p. 391)

Mass public shootings are also, by their very definition, highly visible acts of violence. The results from my 2000 study showed, for example, that publicly occurring mass killings were significantly more newsworthy than those which took place in a residential setting. Again, I note that publicly occurring mass murders

> usually involved a number of people who witnessed and survived the attack, which gave the news media the means to deliver a fascinating firsthand account to the audience, allowing them to vicariously experience the horror of the event.

In addition, the audience is generally more apt to identify with the victims of these incidents, for they were killed simply because they were in the wrong place at the wrong time. (Duwe, 2000, p. 391)

More so than other mass murders, mass public shootings tend to be exceptionally newsworthy because they are "riveting, emotionally evocative incidents" that epitomize "news as theater – a morality play involving pure, innocent victims and offenders who seemingly went 'berserk' in a public setting" (Duwe, 2000, p. 391).

The extensive news coverage given to mass public shootings, especially in relation to other mass killings, has helped influence perceptions about the typical mass murder (Duwe, 2005). Because mass public shootings may involve, as we shall see later, individuals with mental health difficulties who use guns to carry out an attack at a public location, such as a school or the workplace, mass murder has been constructed as a problem involving gun control, workplace violence, school shooting, and, most recently, mental health. Given that perceptions help shape policy recommendations in the aftermath of such events, proposals to reduce mass killings have often focused on gun laws, school and workplace policies, and mental health reform.

Trends in the Prevalence of Mass Public Shootings

Amid the wave of publicity, interest, and concern following a mass public shooting, there are often attempts to promote better understanding by explaining and interpreting the incident within a broader context. To that end, the news media frequently interview "experts," who offer their views about the type of individual who commits this type of violence (i.e., a "profile" of a mass murderer), whether mass murders or, more narrowly, mass public shootings are on the rise, and what can be done in the future to prevent their occurrence. In a later section, I will describe the incident, victims, and offender characteristics of the 160 mass public shootings examined in this chapter. In the present section, however, I will present data on trends in the prevalence of mass public shootings.

Whether mass public shootings have recently been on the rise has been a matter of some debate. Often relying on the list of cases compiled by Mother Jones, some have argued that mass public shootings have become more frequent in the past 5–10 years (Follman, 2013). Others, including myself, have claimed that mass public shootings have not been on the rise. As I recently wrote, however, the truth is a little more complicated (Duwe, 2014).

But before delving more fully into this debate, it is worth first taking a look at long-term trends in the prevalence of mass public shootings. In my research on mass murder, which examines cases from 1900 to the present, the first mass public shooting in the twentieth century likely occurred in 1915 in Brunswick, Georgia in which a real estate dealer and prominent businessman used a shotgun to kill 6 and wound 32 more.[2] The offender had recently become involved in litigation in the local courts after losing a considerable amount of money in real estate transactions. He had had a number of dealings with Harry Dunwoody, a prominent attorney and local politician, who had been mayor of Brunswick at one time and had served in the Georgia legislature as a representative and as a senator.

Blaming Dunwoody for his financial losses, the offender began his attack at noon by killing Dunwoody in his office. He then went into the street and began to shoot at the crowd that gathered in response to the initial shotgun blasts. A few people were hit with stray bullets a couple of blocks away. After getting shot once, E. C. Butts, an attorney, went to a hardware store, grabbed a pistol, and started firing at the offender. Nearly 30 minutes after the offender had started his rampage, Butts hit him with a lethal shot ("Kills five," 1915).

Following this case, there was an additional mass public shooting in 1918 and two more in the late 1920s. During the 1930s, there were at least nine mass public shootings in the United States. One of these occurred on December 16, 1935, in Los Angeles, California when a 44-year-old male killed six coworkers and wounded one more. The offender had been employed by the Works Progress Administration (WPA), a New Deal initiative launched by Franklin Delano Roosevelt to help provide work for the unemployed during the Great Depression. He had been employed by the WPA for about a year to work on a project aimed at constructing a large sewer. Fired several days before the attack due to his inability to handle the water buckets, the offender returned to exact revenge on those he held responsible.

Workplace mass murderers are often paranoid and blame others for their employment problems. Indeed, when he was apprehended by the police after the shootings, the offender said, "I told those fellows last Friday I was coming to get them, and I did. They have been persecuting me for a year and that foreman wouldn't let me work on that job. But I fixed them up all right. If you only understood the whole thing, you wouldn't blame me for what I did. I know them all and I was going to clean them out" ("Slays 4 WPA men," 1935).

Following eight mass public shootings during the 1940s, there were only three cases that occurred in the United States between 1950 and 1965. As Fox and Levin (2011) have observed, 1966 marked the beginning of a mass murder wave, for that was the year in which massacres were committed weeks apart from each other in Chicago and Austin, and each was dubbed the "Crime of the Century" (Duwe, 2007). Killing 16 and wounding 30 more at the University of Texas, the attack in Austin was, at that time, the worst mass public shooting in American history. The Austin case proved to be a bellwether for the overall increase in mass public shootings over the past 50 years. In the

50 years prior to the Austin mass murder, there had been 24 mass public shootings. In the 50 years since that time, there have been 135.

When we look at trends in the prevalence of mass public shootings, particularly since the 1960s, a few points are worth making. First, although catastrophic, mass public shootings are, fortunately, very rare. Even when we focus on the past 50 years, wherein mass public shootings have been more common, we see an average of fewer than three cases per year. The average increases to four per year when we focus on the past 25 years, but the point remains that mass public shootings occur infrequently.

Second, when we assess prevalence trends over time, it is necessary to account for changes in the size of the population. When we try to determine whether crime (or certain types of crime such as murder) is up or down, we generally rely on a per capita measure (e.g., rate per 100,000 residents) that adjusts for population growth. In 2011, the number of murders in the United States (14,612 murders) was roughly the same as it was in 1969 (14,760 murders). Yet, given there were about 110 million more people living in the United States in 2011 (approximately 311 million) than in 1969 (approximately 201 million), the 2011 murder rate (4.7 per 100,000) is more than 35% lower than the 1969 rate (7.3 per 100,000).

Perhaps because mass public shootings are such a rare phenomenon, public debate over whether they have increased has seldom taken population growth into account. But in addition to looking at the total number of cases each year (or each month, decade, etc.), it is critical that we adjust for changes in the size of the U.S. population when assessing trends in the prevalence of mass public shootings. Due to the infrequency with which mass public shootings occur, I calculated the annual rate per 100 million of the U.S. population, as opposed to the rate per 100,000 commonly used to measure crime trends, for the 1960–2013 period (see Figure 2.1).

In addition to the annual rates per 100 million depicted in Figure 2.1, I present data on the total number of cases and the average rate per decade. As I indicated earlier in this chapter, the number of cases per decade steadily increased over the last four decades of the twentieth century, peaking at 37 during the 1990s. While the number of cases dropped slightly to 35 during the 2000s, 18 mass public shootings have already occurred during the first 4 years of the 2010s.

When we look at the rate data, we also see that rates climbed consistently from the 1960s through the 1990s. Even though more cases occurred during the 2000s than during the 1980s, the latter has a higher rate (1.27 vs. 1.18) due to a smaller U.S. population. The average annual rate for the first 4 years of the 2010s (1.44), is similar in size to, albeit a little higher than, the rate for the 1990s (1.41).

So, have mass public shootings recently been on the rise? The claims about a recent increase are valid, but only if we restrict our focus to the period of time

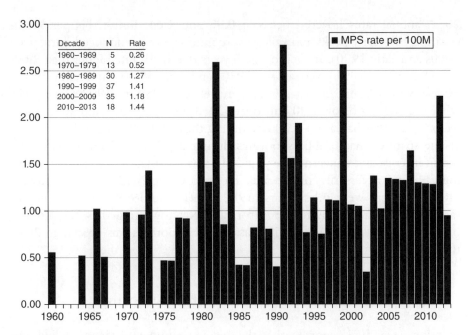

Figure 2.1 Mass public shooting rate per 100 million, 1960–2013.

since the mid-1990s. As rates of crime and violence began to fall in the latter half of the 1990s, mass public shootings rates also decreased. From 1994 to 2004, the average annual rate was 1.12. For the 2005–2013 period, however, the rate was 1.41, which represents a 26% increase.

But when we go farther back in time, rates for either the 2010–2013 or 2005–2013 periods look less remarkable. For example, the average annual rate for the 1988–1993 period was 1.52, which is similar to the rate observed for the 2007–2012 period (1.51). If we look at the 9-year time period from 1985 to 1993, we see an average rate of 1.20, which is less than the 1.41 rate for the 2005–2013 period. Yet, if we examine rates from 1980 to 1993, the annual average was 1.39, which is greater than the 1.26 average for the 2000–2013 period.

Compared to the dip in the mass public shooting rate from 1994 to 2004, there has been an uptick since 2005. But within the broader context, rates since 2005 have been similar to what we observed during the 1980s and early 1990s. It is worth remembering, however, that the increased frequency of mass public shootings during the late 1980s and early 1990s was a major catalyst in securing passage of the 1994 Federal Assault Weapons Ban (Duwe, 2005), which ultimately expired in 2004.

Although overall rates for the two periods are similar, there is at least one notable difference. Aside from 2012, annual rates for the 2005–2013 period were relatively consistent. For example, with the exception of the 2.23 rate in

2012, annual rates hovered between 0.95 and 1.64 during this period. In contrast, the yearly peaks and valleys were much more pronounced during the 1980s and early 1990s. In fact, of the 5 years that had a rate higher than 2.00, 3 (1982, 1984, 1991) were in the 1980s and early 1990s. Moreover, of the 10 years with rates higher than 1.50, 7 were between 1980 and 1993. Conversely, while the rate was below 1.00 only once (2013) between 2005 and 2013, there were 6 years that had a sub-1.00 rate during the 1980–1993 period.

The spate of mass public shootings during 2012 galvanized much of the recent interest and concern. The year 2012 was notable for mass public shootings, but not necessarily for the rate. To be sure, the 2012 rate was relatively high, but there were other years (1982, 1991, and 1999) that had higher rates. Rather, due largely to the Aurora and Newtown tragedies, the number of victims killed and wounded in mass public shootings was greater in 2012 than in any previous year.

The Patterns of Mass Public Shootings

In prior research, I reported that the average number of victims killed and wounded in 909 mass murders from 1900 to 1999 was 5.4 and 4.0, respectively (Duwe, 2007). As noted earlier, the carnage is, on average, greater for mass public shootings. In Table 2.1, which presents descriptive statistics on the 160 mass public shootings, the average number of victims killed was 6.5 and the average number wounded was 4.9.

The vast majority of mass public shooters act alone. Mass public shootings, like the one committed at Columbine, are relatively rare. Of the 160 cases, 153 (96%) were carried out by a lone offender.

School shootings have captured much of the recent attention focused on mass killings. As shown in Table 2.1, 14 of the cases (9%) could be classified as school shootings. Part of the reason for the relatively low percentage of school shootings among mass public shootings in general is due to the fact that very few occurred prior to the late 1990s. Historically, workplace shootings have been more prevalent, accounting for 31% of the cases. The remaining 60% fall into the "other" category, which includes cases such as the 2012 Aurora shooting or the 2011 attack carried out in Tucson, Arizona.

With the exception of one female offender, who committed a workplace shooting in California in 2006, all of the mass public shooters have been male. Nearly two thirds have been white, whereas roughly one fifth have been African-American. The average age among mass public shooters is 35. Nearly 80% were under the age of 45 at the time of the attack.

While not all mass public shooters have a history of mental illness, a little more than 60% had been either diagnosed with a mental disorder or demonstrated signs of serious mental illness prior to the attack. This rate is more than

Table 2.1 A description of mass public shootings.

Metrics		
Average number killed	6.47	
Average number wounded	4.89	
Number of offenders	*Number*	*Percentage*
Single offender	153	95.6
Multiple offenders	7	4.4
Type		
School	14	8.8
Workplace	50	31.2
Other	96	60
Gender		
Male	159	99.4
Female	1	0.6
Race/ethnicity		
White	101	63.1
African-American	30	19.6
American Indian	1	0.6
Asian	10	6.3
Hispanic	11	6.9
Missing	7	4.4
Age categories		
Younger than 25	37	23.1
25–34	40	25
35–44	46	28.8
45–54	15	9.4
55 and older	10	6.3
Missing	12	7.5
Mental illness		
Yes	97	60.6
Paranoid schizophrenia	61	59.8
Mood disorder (depression)	33	32.4
Other mental illness	8	7.8
Unknown	63	39.4
Precipitating event		
Yes	107	66.9
Unknown	53	33.1
Threats (verbal or written)		
Yes	49	30.6
No or unknown	111	69.4
Outcome		
Arrested	74	46.3
Suicide	60	37.5
Killed by police/civilians	26	16.1
Total	160	

three times higher than the 12-month prevalence rate of any mental illness among adults and about 15 times higher than that for serious mental illness (Substance Abuse and Mental Health Services Administration, 2013). Of these mentally ill mass public shooters, roughly one third sought or received mental health care prior to the attack. As shown in Table 2.1, paranoid schizophrenia has been the most common mental disorder, followed by depression.

Perhaps as a consequence of the relatively high rate of mental illness and, more narrowly, paranoid schizophrenia, mass public shooters often believe they have been persecuted. For the vast majority of mass public shooters, the attack is an act of vengeance against those whom the shooter holds responsible for his or her perceived mistreatment. Because mass public shooters generally feel as though others are out to get them, it is perhaps unsurprising that they are often distrustful and socially isolated, which may help explain why they are frequently characterized as "loners" (Duwe, 2007).

Contrary to popular perception that these offenders "just snap," mass public shootings are usually preceded by a great deal of planning and deliberation. As mass public shooters ruminate over the idea of exacting revenge and begin devising plans for their attack, they sometimes communicate threats either verbally or in writing. As shown in Table 2.1, at least 31% made some form of violent threats beforehand. Even though mass public shooters often spend weeks, months or years contemplating the attack, roughly two thirds experience a traumatic event – typically the loss of a job or an important relationship – that ultimately precipitates the violence.

When mass public shooters carry out the attack, they are more likely to target strangers than other mass murderers (Duwe, 2007). After the shootings, more than half of mass public shooters commit suicide or force others (mostly police) to kill them. The rate of suicidal behavior among mass public shooters is nearly double the rate for other mass killers and more than 10 times higher than that observed for homicide offenders in general (Duwe, 2007).[3] The high suicide rate may be due to the fact that many mass public shooters are tormented individuals who want to put an end to their life of pain and misery, but only after evening the score with those who were, in their minds, the sources of that pain and misery.

Conclusion

In this chapter, I presented evidence that the incidence of mass public shootings began to increase in the mid-1960s. Following higher rates of mass public shootings during the 1980s and early 1990s, rates were lower from the mid-1990s to the mid-2000s. Since 2005, mass public shooting rates have been similar to what they were in the 1980s and early 1990s. Moreover, the data suggest that mass public shooters, on average, have a history of mental health difficulties, are suicidal, and are socially isolated males who make violent threats and have suffered the loss of an important relationship or recently experienced failure at work or school.

Implicit to the debate over recent trends in the prevalence of mass public shootings is whether their incidence and/or severity can be reduced. This debate has, for the most part, focused on gun laws. Both sides of the gun control issue have argued that tightening or loosening firearms laws would reduce mass public shootings. The available evidence, however, suggests that neither approach would likely have much impact. For example, when the incidence of mass public shootings began to increase during the 1980s and 1990s, rates of gun ownership were relatively stable (Duwe, 2007). On the other hand, results from a previous study I coauthored indicate that right-to-carry-concealed firearms laws do not have a significant deterrent effect on mass public shootings (Duwe et al., 2002).

With the surge in mass public shootings, especially since the 1980s, school and workplace policies have gradually evolved to better address threats and manage risk. While violent threats directed at classmates or coworkers are generally taken more seriously now, that has not always been the case. For example, on September 1, 1989, a disgruntled employee committed a workplace shooting at the Standard Gravure plant in Louisville, Kentucky, killing 8 and wounding 12. When Standard Gravure's employees heard gunfire that morning, they knew the offender had returned to make good on the violent threats he had been expressing for months (Holmes & Holmes, 1992). Before an offender killed five of his former coworkers in Florida in 1996, he had repeatedly threatened them by promising, "If you mess with my job, I will take you out" ("Florida Killer," 1996).

Since the 1990s, particularly after the Columbine incident, many schools and workplaces have adopted a series of security measures to reduce the incidence or severity of shootings, including the implementation of procedures for reporting and assessing threats that arise. Over the past decade, a number of school and workplace shooting plots appear to have been thwarted because threats were promptly reported to authorities. While it is difficult to know with certainty whether these foiled plots would have resulted in mass murder had the threats been ignored, it is possible that the greater overall vigilance towards threats has reduced, at least to some degree, the incidence of mass public shootings.

Mental health reform is another area that has recently come to the fore in the debate over mass public shootings. As we have seen, mass public shooters have a relatively high rate of serious mental illness, when compared to the general population. Of these mentally ill mass public shooters, a little more than one third sought or received mental health care prior to the attack. To be sure, some may cite this as evidence of mental health treatment's ineffectiveness. After all, there are well-known examples in which mass public shooters had received treatment but nevertheless went on to commit mass murder. While improvements can almost certainly be made in the assessment of risk and treatment of those who come to the attention of mental health care professionals, the rate of untreated serious mental illness points to what is perhaps a bigger problem – a high treatment gap among mass public shooters. Indeed, roughly two thirds of the mentally ill mass public shooters did not receive the care they needed. A gap of this magnitude, however, is merely consistent with research showing higher rates of untreated serious mental illness for males (who have committed nearly all of the mass public shootings in this country) compared to females (Pattyn, Verhaeghe, & Bracke, 2015) and, more broadly, for the United States relative to most other Western countries (Kohn, Saxena, Levav, & Saraceno, 2004).

The calls for changes in gun laws, heightened security at schools and workplaces, and mental health reform have, to some extent, been rooted in the idea that mass public shootings have been on the rise. Because problems demand solutions, these proposals stand a better chance of being implemented when the problem – in this case, mass public shootings – is claimed to be increasing or getting worse. But the effort to call greater attention to the putatively growing threat of mass public shootings obscures evidence that may (or may not) be helpful in identifying ways to reduce this type of violence. That is, trying to understand why mass public shootings have recently increased, even if only modestly, may not be the best question to ask. Rather, what truly needs explaining is why the 1950–1965 period had fewer mass public shootings than any other time during the past 100 years. Similarly, why was the rate lower during the 1994–2004 period than at any other time during the past 40 years?

Determining why mass public shootings dropped during these two periods may shed light on whether it is possible to curb this type of violence in the future. The most recent dip in the mass public shooting rate started at about the same time that crime in general began to fall. The late 1990s and early 2000s also coincided with a bustling economy, a rising prison population, increases in the number of police, a fading crack cocaine epidemic, the aging of the baby boomers beyond their peak crime years and, perhaps most interestingly, a federal ban on assault weapons. As with crime in general, assault weapons are seldom used in mass killings or, even more specifically, mass public shootings (Duwe, 2007). Moreover, what little research exists on the assault weapons ban suggests it had a minimal short-term impact on gun violence (Koper & Roth, 2001, 2002). Nevertheless, the question of whether the assault weapons ban had an effect on the incidence and/or severity of mass public shootings has yet to be answered empirically.

As the public debate continues over whether mass public shootings have increased and what can be done to prevent their occurrence or reduce their severity, an important fact remains that bears repeating – mass public shootings are, fortunately, very rare. Emphasizing their rarity does not diminish the enormous impact they have on perceptions of public safety. Nor does it alter the fact that mass public shootings are rather costly to society. It has been estimated, for example, that one murder costs society somewhere between

$9 million and $17 million (Cohen & Piquero, 2009; DeLisi et al., 2010; McCollister, French, & Fang, 2010). When we consider that the average number of victims killed in a mass public shooting is 6.5, the average monetary cost to society is, at a minimum, anywhere between $59 and $111 million. Moreover, given that the average number of victims wounded – often very seriously – in mass public shootings is 5, the societal cost is likely millions more per incident. Thus, regardless of whether mass public shootings have been on the rise, they warrant attention and scrutiny simply due to the devastating impact one incident can have at the individual, local, and national levels.

Still, the infrequency with which they occur makes it very challenging to accurately predict who will commit a mass public shooting or to develop policies designed to reduce their incidence or severity (see Chapter 6 for more on the prediction of dangerousness). As Fox and DeLateur (2014) rightly point out, it is unrealistic to assume that any of the policy proposals that have been advanced would, individually or collectively, prevent a catastrophic shooting from ever taking place in the future. But these proposals, if implemented, could have a broader impact on crime, including violent offending. At the same time, it is worth remembering that long-term trends in the prevalence of mass murder tend to mirror those for crime and violence. The broad social forces or policies that are effective in reducing crime may thus have a similar, albeit less direct, effect on mass public shootings.

Notes

1 In both instances, I shared the mass murder dataset I had assembled as well as the methods I used in constructing the dataset with *USA Today* and CRS staff.
2 In my 2007 book, I briefly review some mass murders that took place prior to 1900 in the United States. In this admittedly superficial review, I did not identify any cases that fit the description of a mass public shooting. This is not to say that the 1915 Brunswick case is the nation's first mass public shooting, or even the first one in the twentieth century. Rather, the Brunswick case is simply the oldest mass public shooting I have been able to identify.
3 We also see a similarly high rate of suicidal behavior among mass murderers who kill their families. In contrast, the offenders in felony-related massacres seldom commit suicide or force others to kill them. The rate of suicidal behavior in felony-related mass killings is similar to that observed among homicides in general.

References

Cohen, M. A., & Piquero, A. R. (2009). New evidence on the monetary value of saving a high risk youth. *Journal of Quantitative Criminology, 25,* 25–49.
Congressional Research Service. (2014). Unpublished mass public shooting dataset.

DeLisi, M., Kosloski, A., Sween, M., Hachsmeister, E., Moore, M., & Drury, A. (2010). Murder by numbers: Monetary costs imposed by a sample of homicide offenders. *The Journal of Forensic Psychiatry & Psychology, 4*, 501–513.

Duwe, G. (2000). Body-count journalism: The presentation of mass murder in the news media. *Homicide Studies, 4*, 364–399.

Duwe, G. (2004). The patterns and prevalence of mass murder in twentieth-century America. *Justice Quarterly, 21*, 729–761.

Duwe, G. (2005). A circle of distortion: The social construction of mass murder in the United States. *Western Criminology Review, 6*, 59–78.

Duwe, G. (2007). *Mass murder in the United States: A history.* Jefferson, NC: McFarland & Company.

Duwe, G. (2012, July 21). Horrifying but rare. *Ottawa Citizen.* Retrieved from http://www.ottawacitizen.com/opinion/op-ed/Horrifying+rare/6967082/story.html

Duwe, G. (2013, January 3). Seven mass shootings in 2012 most since 1999: Recognizing warning signs key to prevention. *The Washington Times.* Retrieved from http://www.washingtontimes.com/news/2013/jan/3/seven-mass-shootings-in-2012-most-since-1999-recog/

Duwe, G. (2014, October 28). The truth about mass public shootings. *Reason.com.* Retrieved from http://reason.com/archives/2014/10/28/the-truth-about-mass-public-shootings

Duwe, G., Kovandzic, T., & Moody, C. (2002). The impact of right-to-carry concealed firearms laws on mass public shootings. *Homicide Studies, 6*, 271–296.

Federal Bureau of Investigation. (1960). *Crime in the United States, 1960.* Washington, DC: United States Department of Justice.

Federal Bureau of Investigation. (1990). *Crime in the United States, 1990.* Washington, DC: United States Department of Justice.

Federal Bureau of Investigation. (1991). *Crime in the United States, 1991.* Washington, DC: United States Department of Justice.

Federal Bureau of Investigation. (2011). *Crime in the United States, 2011.* Washington, DC: United States Department of Justice.

Florida killer said victims were racists, policy say. (1996, February 11). *New York Times,* pp. 37.

Follman, M. (2013, January 31). Why mass shootings deserve deeper investigation. *Boston.com.* Retrieved from http://www.boston.com/news/source/2013/01/op-ed_why_mass.html

Fox, J. A., & DeLateur, M. J. (2014). Mass shootings in America: Moving beyond Newtown. *Homicide Studies, 18*, 125–145.

Fox, J. A., & Levin, J. (2011). *Extreme killing: Understanding serial and mass murder.* Thousand Oaks, CA: Sage.

Holmes, R. M., & Holmes, S. T. (1992). Understanding mass murder: A starting point. *Federal Probation, 56*, 53–60.

Kills five, wounds 20, and is himself slain. (1915, March 7). *New York Times,* pp. 1, 5.

Kohn, R., Saxena, S., Levav, I., & Saraceno, B. (2004). The treatment gap in mental health care. *Bulletin of the World Health Organization, 82*, 858–866.

Koper, C. S., & Roth, J. A. (2001). The impact of the 1994 Federal Assault Weapon Ban on gun violence outcomes: An assessment of multiple outcome measures and some lessons for policy evaluation. *Journal of Quantitative Criminology*, *17*, 33–74.

Koper, C. S., & Roth, J. A. (2002). The impact of the 1994 Federal Assault Weapon Ban on gun markets: An assessment of the short-term primary and secondary market effects. *Journal of Quantitative Criminology*, *18*, 239–266.

McCollister, K. E., French, M. T., & Fang, H. (2010). The cost of crime to society: New crime-specific estimates for policy and program evaluation. *Drug and Alcohol Dependence*, *108*, 98–109.

Overberg, P., Upton, J., & Hoyer, M. (2013, December 3). USA Today research reveals flaws in mass-killing data. *USA Today*. Retrieved from http://www.usatoday.com/story/news/nation/2013/12/03/fbi-mass-killing-data-inaccurate/3666953/

Pattyn, E., Verhaeghe, M., & Bracke, P. (2015). The gender gap in mental health service use. *Social Psychiatry and Psychiatric Epidemiology*. Advance online publication. doi:10.1007/s00127-015-1038-x

Riedel, M. (1999). Sources of homicide data. In M. D. Smith & M. A. Zahn (Eds.), *Studying and preventing homicide: Issues and challenges* (pp. 31–48). Thousand Oaks, CA: Sage.

Slays 4 WPA men after he loses job. (1935, December 17). *New York Times*, p. 1.

Substance Abuse and Mental Health Services Administration. (2013). *Results from the 2012 National Survey on Drug Use and Health: Mental Health Findings*, NSDUH Series H-47, HHS Publication No. (SMA) 13-4805. Rockville, MD: Substance Abuse and Mental Health Services Administration.

3

Explaining Mass Shootings

Types, Patterns, and Theories

James Alan Fox and Jack Levin

The literature of abnormal psychology features a plethora of case studies analyzing the backgrounds and mindsets of individuals who slaughter family members, massacre coworkers, or kill indiscriminately (e.g., Abrahamsen, 1973; Lunde, 1976; Macdonald & Mead, 1968). Indeed, much of the conventional wisdom concerning mass murder was for years grounded in some of the most extreme and bizarre cases, especially those for which mental health professionals were consulted or asked to testify in criminal trials invoking the insanity defense.

By contrast, researchers in criminology and criminal justice have long all but ignored the topic (for notable exceptions see Duwe, 2007; Levin & Fox, 1985). Some may have regarded mass murder as merely a special form of homicide, explainable by the same theories applied to more commonplace incidents and not deserving of special treatment. Others may have conceded multiple homicide to be largely a psychiatric phenomenon, perpetrated by individuals who suffer from profound mental disorders, and therefore, best understood with theories of psychopathology.

Still other criminologists may have assumed that such incidents were not only aberrational, but so rare as to be unworthy of extensive empirical research, despite the fact that there were, on average, more than two mass killings a month in the United States. That posture has changed in the past few years, however, especially in 2012 when two of the most horrific massacres occurred. The moral panic and sense of urgency surrounding mass murder, and mass shootings in particular, have been fueled by various claims that they are reaching epidemic proportions. For example, the Mother Jones news organization, having assembled a database of public mass shootings from 1982 through 2012, reported a surge in incidents and fatalities, including a spike in and record number of casualties in 2012 (Follman, Pan, & Aronsen, 2013).

In advance of any attempt to measure trends in mass shootings and the reported increase, we must settle on a working definition of such violent

The Wiley Handbook of the Psychology of Mass Shootings, First Edition. Edited by Laura C. Wilson.
© 2017 John Wiley & Sons, Inc. Published 2017 by John Wiley & Sons, Inc.

episodes. Regrettably there has been considerable disagreement over the inclusion criteria of what constitutes a mass shooting, leading to confusion concerning patterns and trends.

As discussed in Chapter 1 of this Handbook, there has been some debate over the minimum body count in defining mass murder. We prefer to maintain the once standard minimum of at least four people killed, not counting the perpetrator. The most contentious disagreement among researchers surrounds the criteria for what constitutes a massacre. For example, many researchers have narrowly defined mass murder as those events that occur in public places by an assailant who kills his targets at random. As a result, these scholars eliminate from consideration, for example, robberies shrouded by executing all witnesses. The same holds true for gang-related murders, even though their victims are killed in a violent manner similar to more random acts that involve killing individuals while they shop, sit in a classroom, or go to a cinema.

Several studies of mass murder (e.g., Cohen, Azrael, & Miller, 2014; Follman et al., 2013) have also excluded family annihilations, even those with double-digit death tolls, ostensibly because they occur in a private setting where nonfamily members can feel safe from violence. Another possible reason is more psychological; many people believe they can anticipate and control what happens in their own homes and thus are more unnerved about crimes committed by strangers than by intimates.

Trends in Mass Shootings

It is important to note, at the outset, that the reported increase in mass murder, and particularly mass shootings, only holds for the highly restricted class of cases identified by Mother Jones – specifically, random shootings in public places not involving robbery. Conversely, an analysis of mass shootings that includes all types of incidents drawn from the FBI's Supplementary Homicide Reports (SHR) ranging from 1976 to 2012 fails to show an increase (see Fox & DeLateur, 2014).

Without minimizing the pain and suffering of the hundreds who have been victimized in recent attacks, the facts say that there has been no rise in mass shootings and certainly no epidemic. What is abundantly clear from the full array of mass shootings is the significant volatility in the annual counts. There have been several points in time when journalists have speculated about a possible epidemic in response to a flurry of high-profile shootings. Yet, these speculations have always proven to be premature when subsequent years reveal more moderate levels. The year 1991, for example, saw a 35-year-old gunman kill 23 people at a cafeteria in Killeen, Texas and a disgruntled graduate student murder five at the University of Iowa, along with other sensationalized incidents. The surge in mass killings that year was so frightening that a rumor spread throughout the nation that there would be a mass murder at a college campus in the Northeast on Halloween (Farrish, 1991). Fortunately, October 31 came and went without anything close to a massacre taking place.

Although the SHR is the most consistent and long-term source of data on multiple victim homicide, it certainly has issues in terms of accuracy. Some cases are missing because of noncompliant reporting agencies. Also, some small jurisdictions have inappropriately included all of their homicides for the year in one record, making it appear as if there had been one incident with multiple victims.

A team of analysts at *USA Today* methodically verified each and every SHR mass murder incident, those by gunfire as well as those involving other weapons of mass murder destruction (e.g., knife), from 2006 onward, and filled in missing cases based on news reports (Overberg, Hoyer, Upton, Hansen, & Durkin, 2013). Unfortunately, extending the data verification and augmentation further back would have been especially challenging. These data, although limited to a decade time frame, show no increase in mass killing, and mass shootings in particular.

Finally, with the attention on mass shootings largely driven by the debate over gun control, it is important not to lose sight of the many incidents (i.e., nearly one third of the mass murders reflected in the SHR) that involve weapons other than firearms (e.g., knife). However, consistent with the theme of this Handbook, we will analyze and discuss only mass shootings with four or more victims killed.

Characteristics of Mass Shootings

Although it does not span as long a time frame as other databases, including the Mother Jones collection and the SHR, the *USA Today* database of mass shootings features a high level of completeness (i.e., case inclusion) and accuracy (i.e., data quality). These data, therefore, offer an unparalleled opportunity to explore the characteristics of mass shootings as well as the offenders and victims involved. From 2006 through 2014, there were 200 incidents in which at least four people were murdered, involving a total of 246 assailants. Overall, 15% of the shooting sprees were perpetrated by more than one individual, while nearly three quarters of felony-related massacres (typically murders to cover-up robbery or other criminal enterprise) involved two or more accomplices. Finally, the 200 mass shootings claimed the lives of 1,009 victims, in total, not counting perpetrators who committed suicide or were killed by the police or a bystander.

This pool of incidents, offenders, and victims is certainly ample for deriving a clear picture of patterns, even though only 9 full years of data are available. The nature of the crime has not changed dramatically in recent decades, as analyses of the somewhat flawed SHR data would suggest (see Fox & Levin, 2015).

Table 3.1 displays the overall counts of cases, offenders, and victims for each of the years since 2006. Not only do the figures fail to reflect the reported increase over time, the trajectory, albeit short-term, is actually downward. Of course, the discrepancy between this short-term trend and the rise in cases reported by others, such as Mother Jones, may be due to the difference between examining all mass shootings (as we do here) as opposed to only those cases that meet some criteria for a more or less random, public massacre. In fact, as shown in Table 3.2, half of the cases in the *USA Today* database are family annihilations, typically committed behind closed doors, not in public spaces where bystanders may be targeted. Still, the 35 public massacres in this database are spread over the 9-year time frame with no apparent trajectory. Noteworthy as well is that since the six episodes occurring in 2012, which included the Aurora cinema shooting and the Sandy Hook school massacre, the number of public slaughters has diminished.

Table 3.1 Counts of incidents, offenders and victims.

Year	Incidents	Offenders	Victims
2006	24	34	112
2007	20	23	120
2008	27	41	125
2009	24	30	130
2010	19	28	89
2011	24	24	115
2012	20	22	123
2013	24	24	112
2014	18	20	83
Total	200	246	1009

Table 3.2 Case counts by incident type.

Year	Family	Felony	Public	Other	Total
2006	7	5	4	7	23
2007	8	2	3	7	20
2008	12	5	5	5	27
2009	15	2	4	3	24
2010	11	2	2	4	19
2011	17	1	4	2	24
2012	8	3	6	3	20
2013	9	4	4	4	21
2014	11	1	3	3	18
Total	98	25	35	38	196

Table 3.3 Region of occurrence by incident type.

| | Incident type | | | | |
Region	Family	Felony	Public	Other	Total
Northeast	3%	16%	14%	11%	8%
Midwest	26%	40%	17%	34%	28%
South	50%	40%	23%	34%	41%
West	21%	4%	46%	21%	24%
Total	*100%*	*100%*	*100%*	*100%*	*100%*
Count	*98*	*25*	*35*	*38*	*196*

Table 3.3 displays a breakdown of incidents by geographic region. Over 40% of the mass shootings occurred in the Southern states, which may relate to the region's lenient gun restrictions and high level of gun ownership. However, this percentage is only slightly higher than the 37% of U.S. population residing in the South. The Midwest is considerably overrepresented, with 28% of mass shootings occurring there but a population that is only 17% of the nation. This may have much to do with the high unemployment rates that hit this region hard during those years. The Northeast had only 8% of the massacres, well below the 18% of population that resides there. Finally, 24% of mass shootings occurred in the West, which is in line with its 23% share of the U.S. population.

There are some significant differences in the geographic patterns across the incident types (χ^2 (9) = 27.302, $p < .001$). The overrepresentation of the South is even greater among family massacres, which may in part be a function of larger family sizes so that the victim threshold of four would be more easily met and therefore the event would be considered a mass murder. Also, even though the total count is relatively small, the West had nearly half the public shootings. Public massacres often involve an assailant who moved west as a last chance for success, yet ultimately had to confront the difficult reality of continued failure. Many of these cases end with the dispirited perpetrator taking his or her own life. In fact, over half of the family massacres and public shootings result in suicide. This is in sharp contrast to felony-related cases in which almost none of the offenders commit suicide. Rather, they consider murder as a necessary cover-up for survival and the opportunity to enjoy the profits derived from their crimes.

Demographic characteristics of the assailants, specifically age, sex, and race, are presented in Table 3.4, where there are some significant differences in these distributions across the incident types. As shown, those who target family members tend to be older than single-victim murderers, reflecting the prevalence of middle-age men slaughtering their romantic partners (or ex-romantic partners) and their children. This is also true of assailants who commit mass

Table 3.4 Offender characteristics by incident type.

Characteristic	Family	Felony	Public	Other	Total
	Incident type				
Average number of perpetrators	1.1	2.2	1.0	1.4	1.3
Age					
Under 18	3%	8%	3%	0%	3%
18–29	32%	58%	37%	52%	43%
30–49	56%	34%	51%	46%	49%
50 and up	9%	0%	9%	2%	6%
Total	*100%*	*100%*	*100%*	*100%*	*100%*
Count	*101*	*53*	*35*	*46*	*235*
Sex					
Male	94%	94%	94%	94%	94%
Female	6%	5%	6%	6%	6%
Total	*100%*	*100%*	*100%*	*100%*	*100%*
Count	*102*	*56*	*35*	*47*	*240*
Race					
White	50%	11%	63%	33%	39%
Black	31%	66%	14%	44%	39%
Hispanic	13%	20%	9%	8%	13%
Other	7%	4%	14%	15%	9%
Total	*100%*	*100%*	*100%*	*100%*	*100%*
Count	*91*	*55*	*35*	*39*	*220*

murder in a public place (including their current or former workplace), often following a prolonged history of frustration and failure. By contrast, felony-related incidents involve perpetrators who tend to be under the age of 30, consistent with the age pattern of felons, in general. Overall, these differences in age distribution are significant (χ^2 (9) = 21.832, $p < .01$).

Differences in gender distribution across incident type are virtually non-existent (χ^2 (3) = 0.05, $p = .997$). Of course, men predominate in all categories of mass murder, constituting almost 95% of the assailants. This is consistent with murder as a whole, as men represent 90% of murderers. But, among mass killers the gender ratio is even more uneven. Men tend to be far more comfortable with firearms, and more apt to see them as a means to resolve their grudges against others or society.

In terms of race, whites and blacks constitute equal shares of assailants (i.e., each just below 40%), with Hispanics and other races (i.e., primarily Asians) each representing around 10%. The race patterns diverge significantly by incident type, however (χ^2 (9) = 44.940, $p < .001$). Half of the family killings are perpetrated by whites, while two thirds of the felony-related cases implicate black offenders.

Table 3.5   Victim characteristics by incident type.

	Incident type				
Characteristic	*Family*	*Felony*	*Public*	*Other*	*Total*
Average number of victims	4.6	4.5	7.7	4.2	5.0
Age					
Under 18	42%	22%	13%	15%	27%
18–29	19%	39%	28%	38%	27%
30–49	23%	19%	24%	41%	26%
50 and up	17%	20%	34%	7%	21%
Total	*100%*	*100%*	*100%*	*100%*	*100%*
Count	*439*	*110*	*270*	*159*	*978*
Sex					
Male	44%	53%	51%	62%	50%
Female	56%	47%	49%	38%	50%
Total	*100%*	*100%*	*100%*	*100%*	*100%*
Count	*450*	*112*	*270*	*161*	*993*
Race					
White	54%	35%	71%	54%	56%
Black	22%	47%	3%	32%	21%
Hispanic	17%	13%	12%	12%	14%
Other	7%	5%	14%	2%	8%
Total	*100%*	*100%*	*100%*	*100%*	*100%*
Count	*358*	*85*	*210*	*132*	*785*

The characteristics of victims slain in mass shootings are displayed in Table 3.5, across the various incident types. As shown, the average death toll from mass shootings was 5.0 victims, although public massacres averaged as many as 7.7 victims. In part this reflects the larger pool of potential victims typically present in public places, but is also skewed upward by a few exceptionally deadly events, including shootings at Virginia Tech in 2007 (32 deaths) and at Sandy Hook (26 deaths) in 2012.

The demographic patterns among victims are largely a function of the offender characteristics discussed above, reflecting the fact that mass killers generally do not select their victims at random, but usually target particular people for specific reasons.

The age breakdown among victims is fairly evenly spread across the four age groups, but not so in all situations (χ^2 (9) = 148.314, $p < .001$). In family massacres, children represent 42% of those killed, owing to the generational composition of families, including extended kin. The gender split among victims is exactly even overall, and close to even within all categories of incident type. The differences across these categories are significant (χ^2 (3) = 16.283, $p < .001$), but mostly due to the large sample size.

Finally, the racial composition of victims differs significantly by type of incident (χ^2 (9) = 101.135, $p < .001$). The majority of victims in family massacres are white, while the majority in felony-related incidents are black. These figures are relatively close to the racial make-up of perpetrators, consistent with the usual intraracial pattern observed in homicide. The racial distribution of victims killed in public shooting sprees is quite different from the other types of incidents. The large representation of white victims (over 70%) reflects the demographic make-up of Americans at most schools, shopping malls, restaurants, and other public locations.

A Typology of Mass Shootings

As in most of the social and behavioral sciences, researchers often struggle to create typologies or taxonomies to help explain behavior. When a heterogeneous phenomenon, such as mass murder, is addressed as a singular concept, it can be difficult to make sense of widely differing patterns of behavior.

Of course, the goal of creating mutually exclusive classifications is virtually impossible. The motivation-based typology we propose, not unlike other typologies before it, contains an unavoidable degree of overlap among its categories (e.g., a power-obsessed pseudocommando who massacres his coworkers to avenge perceived mistreatment at the workplace).

Power

The thirst for power and control has inspired many mass shooters, particularly the so-called pseudocommando killers who typically dress in battle fatigues and embrace symbols of power, including military-style rifles (Dietz, 1986). Yet the motive of power and control also encompasses what earlier typologies have termed the "mission-oriented killer" (Holmes & Holmes, 1994), whose crimes are designed to further a cause. Through killing, the perpetrator claims an attempt to rid the world of filth and evil, such as by killing marginalized groups. The larger his body count, the better he feels about himself. Having been regarded as weak and powerless in the past, he finally has the upper hand. He is the one who decides who lives and who dies.

In May 2014, a 22-year-old man killed 6 and injured 14 others in and around the California town of Isla Vista, in proximity to the campus of the University of California at Santa Barbara. The assailant blamed women and the men with whom they had relationships for his lack of appeal to members of the opposite sex and his continuing virginity. In his rambling 107,000 word manifesto, he wrote about feeling inferior compared to "all of those guys who walked around with beautiful girls." Women must be punished for rejecting him, he wrote, and popular men must be punished for enjoying their lives while he suffered "in lonely virginity."

By the age of 17, the perpetrator had already believed that his destiny in life was "to rise to power." He often fantasized about becoming powerful and inflicting pain and suffering on the men and women who had wronged him. "I will be a God," he wrote. After arming himself and waiting for the optimal moment to attack, he finally got what he had wanted. His new sense of power can be seen by him saying "Who's the alpha male now, bitches?"

Revenge

Many mass shootings are motivated by revenge against specific individuals or groups of people, or society at large. Most commonly, the murderer seeks to get even with people he knows – such as his estranged romantic partner and all of their children or the boss and all of his or her employees.

In discussing family homicide, Frazier (1975) described the concept of "murder by proxy," in which victims are chosen because they are identified with a primary target for revenge. Thus, a man might slaughter all of his children because he sees them as an extension of his romantic partner or ex-partner. In 1987, for example, an Arkansas man massacred his entire family, including his grandchildren, to avenge rejection by his wife and an older daughter with whom he had an incestuous relationship.

Frazier's concept of "murder by proxy" can be generalized to crimes outside the family setting, particularly in the workplace or in schools. In 1986, for example, a disgruntled letter carrier murdered 14 fellow postal workers in Edmond, Oklahoma, in an effort to eliminate everyone who he associated with his boss and the post office generally. The assailant in the 2012 Sandy Hook massacre was also apparently motivated by revenge. This 20-year-old had nothing against the first graders he killed, but they seem to have been proxies for his classmates who had tormented him years earlier when he was a student there.

These crimes involve specific victims (or proxies) who are chosen for specific reasons. Some revenge multiple killings, however, are motivated by a grudge against an entire category of individuals, typically defined by race or gender, if not all of humankind, who are viewed as responsible for the killer's difficulties in life (Levin & McDevitt, 2002).

In December 1989, for example, a 25-year-old man who blamed feminists for all of his failures in life, methodically executed 14 female engineering students at the University of Montreal. He specifically chose the engineering school where he would find women in roles traditionally controlled by men.

Loyalty

At least a few mass shooters are inspired to kill by a confused sense of love and loyalty – a desire to save their loved ones from misery and hardship. Certain family massacres involve what Frazier (1975) described as "suicide by proxy."

Typically, a husband/father is despondent over the fate of the family unit and takes not only his own life but also those of family members, in order to protect them all from pain and suffering.

In January 2009, for example, a husband and wife lost their jobs as medical technicians at a local hospital in West Los Angeles. Unable to pay their mortgage and deeply in debt, they gave up any hope of finding another job that would allow them to take care of their five young children. Out of desperation and a misguided sense of love, the unemployed husband/father fatally shot his wife and children, and then took his own life. His suicide note read: "We don't want to leave our children with a stranger."

In certain dangerous cults, there exists a desire for loyal disciples to be seen as obedient to their charismatic leader. In an extreme case, a large number of men, women, and children, most relocating from California to the jungles of Guyana, were the victims of murder/suicide in November 1978 at the hands of a 47-year-old paranoid leader. Convinced that the federal government was out to destroy his cult, he demanded that his followers drink cyanide-laced Flavor-Aid. Many waited obediently in line to commit suicide. For those who refused, however, the deranged cult figure had his assistants shoot them to death. In total, 913 men, women, and children lost their lives, many by gunfire.

Profit

Some mass murders are committed purely or partially for the sake of financial gain. They are designed to eliminate witnesses to a crime, often a robbery. For example, in February 2008, a man who pretended to be delivering goods to the stores at a shopping center in a suburb of Chicago was able to gain entry into a Lane Bryant clothing outlet. His purpose was actually to commit robbery. At gunpoint, he took six eyewitnesses – four customers, a part-time employee, and a store manager – to the back of the store, where they were shot. Only the part-time worker survived his injuries. The killer's identity was never determined.

Terror

A few mass homicides are, in fact, terrorist acts in which the perpetrators hope to send a message through violence. Some seek to change national policy; others attempt to eliminate a perceived enemy, either political or religious. They issue a more general warning that similar acts of terror can be expected to occur in the future.

In January 2015, for example, the offices of *Charlie Hebdo*, a satirical newspaper in Paris, France, was the site of a mass shooting perpetrated by two brothers who later identified themselves as belonging to a radical Islamic organization in Yemen.

Their motive was to stop cartoonists from depicting the Prophet Muhammad in a negative light. The gunmen shot to death 12 people and injured another 11.

Hate crimes are often also acts of terrorism in which a particular category of people is targeted. In August 2012, a 40-year-old Army veteran who identified as a white supremacist invaded a Sikh temple outside of Milwaukee and opened fire on the congregation inside. When the dust had settled, seven people had been shot to death including the killer. Not unlike many other Americans, the gunman might have mistaken Sikh Indians – based on their beards, turbans, and skin color – for Muslims. It is just as possible, however, that the perpetrator, the long-time leader of a white-power band named End Apathy, hated all nonwhite members of society.

Explaining Multiple Murder

It has long been popular among laypeople and professionals alike to seek the genesis of multiple murder within the psyche of the assailant. The more extreme the bloodshed and the more bizarre the motivation, the more apt we are to assume that the murderer is driven by compulsions symptomatic of some profound mental illness. However, theories and concepts to explain aspects of multiple homicide have emphasized the influence of environmental factors located in the family, economy, and society. Searching for variables associated with the most violent criminal behavior, researchers have investigated such factors as social learning, structural strain and frustration, everyday opportunities for victimization, as well as elements of self-control.

Social learning

Some individuals develop a propensity to kill from what they learn during their interactions with others. Early on, Sutherland (1939) proposed that criminal behavior is a result of associations with close friends and family member who reinforce positive attitudes toward criminality (as opposed to associations with those promoting more conventional attitudes). Decades later, Akers (2000) expanded this by recognizing that the influence of people who hold positive attitudes toward criminality varies depending on the frequency, duration, intensity, and priority of the interactions. Moreover, social learning is stronger when individuals perceive they are likely to be rewarded rather than punished for their criminal behavior. Akers also suggested that respected individuals often serve as role models for the initiation of criminality.

As recognized by Akers, not all of social learning comes from face-to-face relationships. Media images of infamous murderers have also served as role models for mass killers (Levin & Madfis, 2009). In July 2011, a Norwegian hate-monger took the lives of 77 people first by bombing a building in central

Oslo, and then by gunning down dozens of young people at a nearby summer camp of the Labour Party's youth wing. The killer's 1,500-page manifesto contained entire sections taken verbatim from the writings of Unabomber Theodore Kaczinski (Madfis & Levin, 2012).

Similarly the April 1999 Columbine massacre served as inspiration for several school rampage shooters (Larkin, 2007). In April 2002, for example, a 19-year-old man shot to death 13 teachers, 2 students, and 1 police officer in Erfurt, Germany. Police later discovered newspaper articles on his home computer about the two students who killed 12 schoolmates and a teacher at Columbine (Bondü & Scheithauer, 2010).

Strain Theory

In 1957, Robert Merton suggested that American culture stresses economic success without also emphasizing the opportunities necessary for attaining it. Members of society are urged to succeed economically even though many lack access to the structural means for improving their socioeconomic status. As a result, some Americans "innovate"; they act outside of conventional rules and seek to "get ahead" through criminal behavior.

In January 1993, for example, seven employees of Brown's Chicken Restaurant in Palatine, Illinois, were shot to death by two assailants who first robbed the fast-food restaurant. Using murder as a cover-up worked well, at least for some period of time. It took nearly nine years for the perpetrators to be apprehended.

Robbery is not the only strain-implicated motivation for mass murder. Some individuals who feel they have suffered profound economic failure seek to punish family members or coworkers whom they blame for their miseries. On December 26, 2000, for example, a 42-year-old employee of Edgewater Technology in Wakefield, Massachusetts killed seven coworkers after learning that his wages were to be garnished by the IRS through an arrangement with the company. Blaming his dire financial position on certain offices of the company, the vengeful gunman selectively targeted only those in the payroll and human resources departments.

Taking a broader view than Merton, Robert Agnew (1992) proposed his General Strain Theory whereby a range of negative experiences in social relationships at home, school, work, or in the neighborhood can lead to frustration, anger and, ultimately, to criminal behavior. Agnew identified several sources of strain, including the failure to achieve positively valued goals, the loss of social status, and the gap between aspirations and achievements.

Agnew's view of strain can help to explain why certain students would participate in a school rampage. Their successes are typically self-evaluated based not on the accumulation of money or excellent grades but on their popularity with peers. Rather than being accepted, almost all of them had been routinely bullied, humiliated, or ignored by their schoolmates (Kimmel & Mahler, 2003; Larkin, 2007; Newman, 2007). Leary, Kowalski, Smith, and Phillips (2003) determined that chronic rejection of the shooters was present in at least 13 of the 15 school shooting cases they examined (Levin & Madfis, 2009).

Strain was clearly represented in the biography of the student at Virginia Tech who, in April 2007, committed mass murder on his campus. After migrating to the United States from South Korea, he was diagnosed with a severe anxiety disorder as well as depression. He also was pitifully shy and spoke English with a difficult-to-understand accent. Into the eighth grade, he was ignored by most students and bullied by others. His sense of rejection grew throughout his youth, leading up to his decision while a senior at Virginia Tech to get his revenge. Just weeks before graduation, he shot to death 32 students and faculty on campus.

Routine Activity Theory

Cohen and Felson's (1979) Routine Activity Theory suggests that everyday situations which provide opportunities for being victimized present more important causal factors than such social-economic conditions as poverty and inequality. For understanding mass murder, this aspect of routine activity may be particularly important. According to Cohen and Felson, appropriate targets must be available, effective guardians must be absent, and the perpetrators must be motivated to commit the offense.

Rampage shooters may be influenced in their choice of victims by elements of routine activity. They may be drawn to lecture halls, classrooms, theaters, and auditoriums in which large numbers of potential victims are congregated and literally under their gun.

In July 2012, a 25-year-old man made an Aurora, Colorado cinema his venue for amassing a large body count. His performance as a graduate student in neuro-science at the University of Colorado had deteriorated so sharply that he decided to leave school. Apparently wanting to maximize the carnage in response to what must have been a profoundly frustrating academic experience, he chose to open fire at a crowded midnight showing of a Batman film. According to Lott (2012), the perpetrator may also have been attracted to this particular venue because it was the only cinema in the state of Colorado where firearms were explicitly banned, assuring him of being the only one packing heat. Before the smoke cleared, 12 members of the audience were killed and 70 more were wounded.

Control Theory

According to Hirschi's (1969) Control Theory, attachment to conventional individuals and institutions tends to immunize human beings from committing violent offenses. Freud (1910) long ago argued that the presence of a superego ensures that an individual will grow up having enough self-control to refrain from committing acts of extreme violence, including murder, even if he or she feels capable of avoiding punishment by the state.

When an individual lacks the internal controls, it becomes even more important that they reside in a network of significant others who are able to limit the propensity for violence. Many people refrain from engaging in violent behavior because they fear losing their relationships with others – family, friends, and peers. However, those who lack strong social ties may also lack the motivation to become law-abiding citizens. It is the person who has nothing to lose – who lacks attachments to others, does not make commitments to conventional behavior, and fails to adopt a belief in the moral appropriateness of the law – who is most likely to commit murderous acts.

Gottfredson and Hirschi (1990) emphasized the importance of parental love, supervision, and consistent discipline in the formation of self-control. Moreover, as noted by Sampson and Laub (1993), the ability of individuals to develop connections through stable informal bonds may protect them from committing criminal acts, including the most violent forms of homicides.

Certain mass murderers have exhibited a profound deficit with respect to social control. In April 2012, for example, a 43-year-old former student at Oikos University in Oakland, California opened fire on campus, killing seven and injuring another three. The South Korean native had relocated to the United States as a child. At the time of the attack, he was living in Oakland, apart from his family members. His mother had died a year earlier, one of his brothers remained in Virginia, and his second brother had recently been killed in an automobile accident. When he was expelled from the college, he was alone in what he saw as an exceptionally hostile environment. Any conventional forces that might have encouraged him to obey the law and reject violence were missing from his everyday life.

Biological predisposition

There may have been practical reasons for behavioral scientists over the past few decades to search for the roots of violent behavior in the social environment – namely, that the environment was amenable to both empirical investigation and intervention. In contrast, biological factors that might have been responsible for criminal behavior were regarded as fixed characteristics often beyond the reach of researchers and also not susceptible to change. There seemed to be little value in studying something that could not be modified.

Recently, however, behavioral scientists have broadened their research perspective by turning their attention to biological bases for criminal behavior, especially involving the perpetrator's brain. This recent increase in focus on the biological bases is largely due to the development of powerful imaging technologies that have made it possible to view detailed images of the human brain and to trace activity along its neural pathways. For the first time, researchers were able to investigate the structure and functions of the brain in relation to criminal violence.

Biological factors likely play a role in the etiology of mass shooters. In December 1983, a 41-year-old Ohioan was down on his luck, enough so that he and his wife left their hometown of Massillon and relocated to San Ysidro, California – a suburb of San Diego. Only months after taking a job as a security guard, he was fired. Angry at the world, he grabbed his rifle, shotgun, pistol, and hundreds of rounds of ammunition and told his wife he was "going hunting for humans." The determined gunman walked to the local McDonald's restaurant, where he opened fire on employees and customers inside. Before the SWAT team fatally shot the assailant, he had killed 21 people, most of whom were Latino children.

Not unlike so many other mass shooters, the McDonald's gunman seemed to fit a profile in which social and psychological factors played a key role. He had been chronically depressed, recently fired, and socially isolated by virtue of his move thousands of miles from family and friends. Moreover, he had access to firearms and knew how to use them.

According to Raine (2014), however, the perpetrator also may have been biologically predisposed to extreme aggression. Upon autopsy, a sample of his hair revealed extremely toxic levels of lead and cadmium commonly found in industrial workplaces and linked by research to violent behavior. For many years, the mass killer had worked as a welder where he would have been exposed routinely to toxic metals.

Some neurologists and a growing number of psychiatrists theorize that many violent individuals have incurred severe injury to the limbic region of the brain resulting from profound or repeated head trauma, typically during childhood. Psychiatrist Dorothy Lewis and neurologist Jonathan Pincus, for example, examined a group of murderers on Florida's death row and found that they all showed signs of neurological irregularities (see Lewis, Pincus, Feldman, Jackson, & Bard, 1986).

There is considerable evidence that severe head trauma can have potentially dire effects on behavior, such as inducing violent outbursts, learning disabilities, and epilepsy. According to Allely, Minnis, Thompson, Wilson, and Gillberg (2014), at least 10% of all mass killers have suffered head trauma. Although hardly approaching a majority, these figures are much higher in individuals who display extreme forms of violence than in the general population.

Recent findings support the value to behavioral scientists of including variations in brain structure and function, in addition to other biological mechanisms, when they attempt to explain the development of extreme violence. At the same time, the biological approach does not preclude examining the environment for causal factors in the etiology of murderous behavior. Indeed, there is also evidence that elements of the brain change in response to changes in the environment.

Moreover, those individuals who have experienced a neurodevelopmental issue may have also suffered problematic environmental risk factors, such as parental divorce, abuse, or major surgery as children. There is a complex inter-action between neurodevelopmental and environmental adversities which together can predispose an individual to become a mass killer. Of course, such a predisposition, even when strong, does not constitute predestination. No matter what and how strongly biological and environmental forces impact life choices, most individuals are able to remain morally and criminally responsible for their actions. See Chapter 5 for a more thorough discussion of the biological bases of the perpetration of mass shootings.

Discussion and Conclusion

Whatever the trends in multiple murder, the public perception is that these inci-dents are on the rise. To a great degree, this widespread belief is based on the extensive and expanded media exposure devoted to multiple murder. Aided by modern satellite technology, cable networks are able to provide marathon cov-erage of mass shootings even as the drama is still unfolding. Moreover, televised news and entertainment shows often feature biographical sketches of serial and mass murderers, capitalizing on the public's fascination with these high-profile criminals. Because of media overexposure, multiple murder can easily seem ubiquitous. See Chapter 7 for a more in-depth discussion of the impact of the media on the public's attitudes following mass shootings.

Fueled by dubious claims of an epidemic, the excessive and undue attention given to multiple murderers is often defended by citing a desire to understand the genesis of multiple homicide in order to identify would-be killers and inter-vene preventively. Although laudable, the expectation that we can avert carnage through scientifically guided prediction is misguided.

There are, of course, certain characteristics that are fairly typical among multiple murderers, including the demographic profile of white males often of middle age. Moreover, supported by the theories on causation, there are common patterns in the backgrounds of multiple murderers, such as head injury and childhood trauma, and key indicators, such as animal abuse and obsession with violent entertainment. However, because all these characteris-tics are somewhat prevalent in the general population, early identification is as challenging as finding a few needles in a massive haystack.

In the aftermath of multiple murder, it is easy to isolate warning signs that were apparently overlooked or ignored by family, friends, and even mandated reporters. These presumed telltale warning signs are actually yellow flags that turn red only after the blood has spilled. Hindsight is 20/20, whereas prediction is plagued by the exceptionally low base rate of multiple murder. See Chapter 6 for more on the difficulties associated with predicting dangerousness.

The distinction between troubled and troublesome is particularly important in dealing with warning signs. Once a distraught individual has become so angry that they make plans to kill a large number of victims, it is – in most cases – too late to intervene effectively. Most of the numerous grudge-holding individuals never commit a mass murder (Stone, 2015). While an individual is troubled but not yet troublesome, however, it may still be possible to intervene effectively with support and encouragement in order to improve the quality of life for a child who hates going to school but has not yet decided to get even.

Contrary to the widely held view, at least among laypeople, rather few mass killers suffer from schizophrenia or serious mental illness. Indeed, psychotic thinking tends to be found in purely random mass shootings, which are relatively rare. Not unlike millions of other Americans, mass murderers are far more apt to suffer from chronic depression stemming from repeated frustration. They are ill-equipped to deal with the stresses of daily life.

It would be a fitting legacy of mass murder if mental health services were expanded and improved. However, greater access to treatment options may not necessarily reach the few individuals on the fringes who turn a school, a shopping mall, or a movie theater into their own personal war zone. With their tendency to externalize blame and consider themselves as victims of mistreatment, mass murderers believe the problem resides in others, not themselves (Knoll, 2012). If urged or even coerced to seek counseling, the would-be mass murderer would likely resist angrily to the suggestion that something is wrong with him or her. He or she desires fair treatment, not psychological treatment (Fox & Levin, 2015).

In the aftermath of high-profile mass shootings, political leaders often rally to address the needs of the mentally ill. Unfortunately, this timing tends to stigmatize the vast majority of people who suffer from mental illness as if they too are mass murderers in waiting (see Barry, McGinty, Vernick, & Webster, 2013). However, no clear relationship between psychiatric diagnosis and mass murder has been established (Busch & Cavanaugh, 1986; Dietz, 1986; Taylor & Gunn, 1999).

The sudden initiative to aid individuals with psychological difficulties may be the right thing to do but for the wrong reason. For example, during an April 8, 2013 speech in Hartford, Connecticut delivered months after the Sandy Hook school shooting, President Barack Obama (Kliff, 2013) urged Congress to respond: "We need to help people struggling with mental health problems get the treatment they need *before it is too late*" (italics added). Our viewpoint is different: We should endeavor to help the mentally ill out of concern for their wellbeing, not just because we are worried about the wellbeing of those they might kill (Swanson, 2008).

References

Abrahamsen, D. (1973). *The murdering mind*. New York, NY: Harper & Row.

Agnew, R. (1992). Foundation for a general strain theory of crime and delinquency. *Criminology*, *30*, 47–88.

Akers, R. L. (2000). *Criminological theories: Introduction, evaluation, and application*. Los Angeles, CA: Roxbury.

Allely, C. S., Minnis, H., Thompson, L., Wilson, P., & Gillberg, C. (2014). Neurodevelopmental and psychosocial risk factors in serial killers and mass murderers. *Aggression and Violent Behavior*, *19*, 288–301.

Barry, C. L., McGinty, E. E., Vernick, J. S., & Webster, D. W. (2013). After Newtown – public opinion on gun policy and mental illness. *New England Journal of Medicine*, *368*, 1077–1081.

Bondü, R., & Scheithauer, H. (2010). Preventing severe targeted school violence. In W. Heitmeyer, H. G. Haupt, A. Kirschner & S. Malthaner (Eds.), *Control of violence*. New York, NY: Springer.

Busch, K. A., & Cavanaugh, J. L. (1986). The study of multiple murder: Preliminary examination of the interface between epistemology and methodology. *Journal of Interpersonal Violence*, *1*, 5–23.

Cohen, A. P., Azrael, D., & Miller, M. (2014, October 15). Rate of mass shootings has tripled since 2011, Harvard research shows. *Mother Jones*. Retrieved from http://www.motherjones.com/politics/2014/10/mass-shootings-increasing-harvard-research

Cohen, L. E., & Felson, M. (1979). Social change and crime rate trends: A routine activity approach. *American Sociological Review*, *44*, 588–608.

Dietz, P. E. (1986). Mass, serial, and sensational homicides. *Bulletin of the New York Academy of Medicine*, *62*, 477–491.

Duwe, G. (2007). *Mass murder in the United States: A history*. Jefferson, NC: McFarland & Company.

Farrish, K. (1991, October 30). Rumor of Halloween mass murder no treat. *Hartford Courant*. Retrieved from http://articles.courant.com/1991-10-30/news/0000210189_1_rumor-halloween-night-mass-murders

Follman, M., Pan, D., & Aronsen, G. (2013, February 27). A guide to mass shootings in America. *Mother Jones*. Retrieved from http://www.motherjones.com/politics/2012/07/mass-shootings-map

Fox, J. A., & DeLateur, M. J. (2014). Mass shootings in America: Moving beyond Newtown. *Homicide Studies*, *18*, 125–145.

Fox, J. A., & Levin, J. (2015). *Extreme killing: Understanding serial and mass murder*. Thousand Oaks, CA: Sage Publications.

Frazier, S. (1975). Violence and social impact. In J. C. Schoolar & C. M. Gaitz (Eds.), *Research and the psychiatric patient*. New York, NY: Brunner/Mazel.

Freud, S. (1910). The origin and development of psychoanalysis. *American Journal of Psychology*, *21*, 196–218.

Gottfredson, M. R., & Hirschi, T. (1990). *A general theory of crime*. Stanford, CA: Stanford University Press.

Hirschi, T. (1969). *Causes of delinquency.* Berkeley, CA: University of California Press.

Holmes, R. M., & Holmes, S. (1994). *Murder in America.* Newbury Park, CA: Sage.

Kimmel, M. S., & Mahler, M. (2003). Adolescent masculinity, homophobia, and violence. *American Behavioral Scientist, 46,* 1439–1458.

Kliff, S. (2013, April 9). Obama budget includes $235 million in new mental health spending. *Washington Post.* Retrieved from http://www.washingtonpost.com/blogs/wonkblog/wp/2013/04/09/exclusive-obama-budget-includes-235-million-in-new-mental-health-spending/

Knoll, J. L. (2012). Mass murder: Causes, classification, and prevention. *Psychiatric Clinics of North America, 35,* 757–780.

Larkin, R. W. (2007). The Columbine legacy: Rampage shootings as political acts. *American Behavioral Scientist, 52,* 1309–1326.

Leary, M. R., Kowalski, R. M., Smith, L., & Phillips, S. (2003). Teasing, rejection, and violence: Case studies of the school shootings. *Aggressive Behavior, 29,* 202–214.

Levin, J., & Fox, J. A. (1985). *Mass murder: America's growing menace.* New York, NY: Plenum.

Levin, J., & Madfis, E. (2009). Mass murder at school and cumulative strain: A sequential model. *American Behavioral Scientist, 52,* 1227–1245.

Levin, J., & McDevitt, J. (2002). *Hate crimes revisited.* Boulder, CO: Westview.

Lewis, D. O., Pincus, J. H., Feldman, M., Jackson, L., & Bard, B. (1986). Psychiatric, neurological, and psychoeducational characteristics of 15 death row inmates in the United States. *American Journal of Psychiatry, 143,* 838–845.

Lott, J. R. (2012, September 10). Did Colorado shooter single out Cinemark Theater because it banned guns? *FoxNews.com.* Retrieved from http://www.foxnews.com/opinion/2012/09/10/did-colorado-shooter-single-out-cinemark-theater.html

Lunde, D. P. (1976). *Murder and madness.* San Francisco, CA: San Francisco Book Company.

Macdonald, J. M., & Mead, M. (1968). *Homicidal threats.* Springfield, IL: CC Thomas.

Madfis, E., & Levin, J. (2012). School rampage in international perspective. In N. Böeckler, P. Seeger, P. Heitmeyer, & W. Sitzer (Eds.), *School shootings as a topic of research.* New York, NY: Springer.

Merton, R. K. (1957). *Social theory and social structure.* Glencoe, IL: Free Press.

Newman, K. S. (2007). *Rampage: The social roots of school shootings.* New York, NY: Basic Books.

Overberg, P., Hoyer, M., Upton, J., Hansen, B., & Durkin, E. (2013, December 3). Behind the bloodshed: The untold story of America's mass killings. *USA Today.* Retrieved from http://usatoday30.usatoday.com/news/nation/mass-killings/index.html#title

Raine, A. (2014). *The anatomy of violence: The biological roots of crime.* New York, NY: Vintage Books.

Sampson, R. J., & Laub, J. H. (1993). *Crime in the making: Pathways and turning points through life.* Cambridge, MA: Harvard University Press.

Stone, M. H. (2015). Mass murder, mental illness, and men. *Violence and Gender, 2,* 51–86.

Sutherland, E. H. (1939). *Principles of criminology* (3rd ed.). Philadelphia, PA: Lippincott.

Swanson, J. W. (2008) Preventing the unpredicted: Managing violence risk in mental health care. *Psychiatric Services, 59,* 191–193.

Taylor, P. J., & Gunn, J. (1999). Homicides by people with mental illness: Myth and reality. *The British Journal of Psychiatry, 174,* 9–14.

Part II
The Psychology of Perpetrators

4

The Development of Rampage Shooters
Myths and Uncertainty in the Search for Causes

Benjamin Winegard and Christopher J. Ferguson

In the days leading up to the shooting, the 14-year-old female shooter told half a dozen peers that she planned to "get" her former boyfriend and his friend at Spanaway Junior High School (McCarthy, 1985). On the fateful day, she retrieved a .22 caliber semiautomatic rifle from her parent's home and brought it to school underneath a blanket. She confronted the two boys outside of the gym – both were members of the wrestling team. One of the boys stepped in front of the other to prevent her from shooting, but she shot both from close range and they succumbed to their wounds. The girl fled and roamed the community for nearly two hours before returning to the school where she killed herself. It was November 26, 1985 (Brown & Balter, 1985).

This girl was not a known disciplinary problem, described rather as quiet, friendly, and something of a practical joker. She was also a perfectionist who obsessed over grades and school activities (McCarthy, 1985). In the lead-up to the shooting, her grades slipped, she lost the race for vice president of the student body, and her "boyfriend" seemed uninterested in having a serious relationship – even though the "breakup" took place 6 weeks before the shooting. This lonely 14-year-old girl, desperate, slit her wrists, either in a suicide attempt, a cry for help, or both. She also visited the school counselors where she discussed her feelings of insecurity (Brooks, 1985).

This case, like many tragic cases of mass shootings, is perplexing, poignant, and disturbing. This 14-year-old girl seems similar in every way to many thousands of teenaged girls who suffer similar insecurities, breakups, and suicidal thoughts. What made her different?

Given the ubiquity of today's media and a few recent high-profile mass shootings, it is not surprising that the study of such shootings is surging in psychology, sociology, education, and related disciplines. Nor is it surprising

The Wiley Handbook of the Psychology of Mass Shootings, First Edition. Edited by Laura C. Wilson.
© 2017 John Wiley & Sons, Inc. Published 2017 by John Wiley & Sons, Inc.

that mass shooting coverage in the media has exploded with Twitter and other social media platforms providing "live coverage" of such shootings when they occur. One potentially important area of study is the developmental trajectory of mass shooters. Are there reliable developmental factors that allow us to predict who will become a mass shooter and who will simply suffer their mental duress and trauma without causing others harm?

This chapter will demonstrate that there are no reliable predictors. Mass shootings are such astonishingly rare, idiosyncratic, and multicausal events that it is impossible to explain why one individual decides to shoot his or her classmates, coworkers, or strangers and another does not. The most that can be offered are some vague generalizations: Shooters tend to be male; to suffer from mental illness; to have experienced recent social loss (romantic relationship or otherwise); to be sensitive to perceived slights and injustices; and many were influenced explicitly by previous shootings (Cullen, 2013; Larkin, 2009, 2013). While this might seem unduly pessimistic, we note on the positive side that there are some promising typologies of school and mass shooters that seem worth exploring and expanding upon. And, more importantly, many of the factors, such as violent media and video games, that are popularly assumed to lead to school shootings probably do not.

In this chapter, we first summarize previous research on the developmental antecedents and psychological traits of mass shooters. We next present a tentative model of violence and utilize it as a tool to account for the complex causal network that leads to mass shootings. Finally, we document some popular causal explanations of the development of mass shooters and detail that these should be treated with skepticism. Indeed, if our only contribution in this chapter is to convince the reader that we do not currently, and may not ever, possess the knowledge to make explicable the introductory case, this chapter will have served a useful purpose.

Previous Research on Mass Shooters

Conclusive evidence on mass shooting perpetrators is understandably difficult to come by. First, such shootings are rare, resulting in a very small initial population of perpetrators. Second, most mass shooters die during their crimes, either killed by law enforcement or suicide. Third, those perpetrators who do survive are scattered across multiple state or federal prisons, or forensic hospitals, with minimal access to outside scholars. Thus, psychological research on perpetrators often relies on "psychological autopsies" based on police reports and accounts of witnesses or surviving family members.

The most comprehensive early report on mass shootings was conducted in 2002, and focused specifically on shootings occurring at schools. Conducted by the United States Secret Service and Department of Education (Vossekuil, Fein,

Reddy, Borum, & Modzeleski, 2002), this report compiled several dozen psychological autopsies of past school shooters going back decades, including interviews with some who were still alive. Perhaps most striking in the results of this report was that no true "profile" of perpetrators emerged. Some common assumptions, such as the perpetrators came from broken homes, were heavy consumers of violent media, or were victims of extreme bullying, were not supported by the available evidence. Perpetrators did tend to view themselves as victims of perceived injustices (real or imagined), often had long-standing issues with anger, rage or resentment, and tended to display evidence of chronic mental health issues, although these often went unidentified or untreated prior to the shootings. The best preventative indication of mass shootings was not the development of a "profile" that could be used to screen and identify individuals far in advance of a shooting, but rather taking seriously and reporting to authorities vocalized threats by potential shooters.

Several other scholars have conducted post-hoc analyses of shooting events. Lankford's (2013) analysis compared U.S. shooters to suicide terrorists and concluded that there were more similarities than differences between these groups. Fox and DeLateur (2014) also recently reviewed the literature on mass shootings and identified several myths that commonly develop about these events. These myths included false beliefs that mass shooting incidents are more common now than in the past, perpetrators "snap" suddenly when they commit their crimes, and exposure to violent media plays a causal role in such shootings (See Chapter 3).

Langman (2009) examined the case histories of 10 school shooters and concluded that they fit into three general categories. Traumatized shooters tended to come from difficult family backgrounds where they were subjected to intense abuse. Psychotic shooters had long-term difficulties with paranoia and psychosis-based disorders, such as schizophrenia or schizotypal personality disorder. Lastly, psychopathic shooters, like psychotic shooters, came from intact homes without abuse but displayed a profound lack of empathy. Langman (2013) has more recently updated his database to include 35 shooters and found that the threefold typology is applicable to the newly added cases. While Langman's approach is a valuable discussion point, we note that, like all approaches, it has several limitations. First, it is built upon only a small number of cases ($n = 35$). Second, as Langman noted, most individuals who have experienced any of the core features of the three categories (i.e., abuse, psychosis, or psychopathy) do not commit mass shootings. Lastly, categorical systems tend to emphasize the differences between shooters rather than find similarities between them.

One caution regarding mass shooting events is that these incidents are nationally traumatic and extremely high profile, which can lead to pseudoscientific public statements that support specific political agendas. Typically this takes the form of politicians demanding "studies" (often by national scientific bodies where they control the funding appropriations) while making clear, in advance, what results they wish the "study" in question to yield.

One remarkable example occurred after the 2012 Sandy Hook shooting in which a 20-year-old male killed 20 children and 6 adult faculty and staff at an elementary school in Connecticut. Because of the shooter's age, it was speculated that he might have been a frequent player of violent video games (e.g., KCCI, 2012). However, the official investigation report ultimately concluded that he was fonder of nonviolent games, such as *Dance, Dance Revolution*, than violent games (State's Attorney for the Judicial District of Danbury, 2013).

The shooting resulted in several calls for "research" into the alleged link between violent video games and gun violence, with the politicians who were calling for such research making it clear they intended to use it to attack the video game industry. Most of these efforts ultimately failed. However, one congressman, Frank Wolf, managed to persuade the National Science Foundation (NSF) to produce a dubious report on youth violence. Wolf was a very powerful member of Congress who chaired, among other things, the committee that oversaw funding for the NSF. Following the Sandy Hook shooting, Wolf asked the NSF to produce a report on youth violence. The NSF agreed and included as authors in that report two media scholars with a history of promoting exaggerated views linking media to extreme behavioral change. No scholars skeptical of media effects were invited to participate to balance out the report (Ferguson, 2014).

The NSF report eagerly linked video games and other violent media to mass shootings. To do so, the report selectively referenced mass shootings where perpetrators had played video games but ignored those that did not. The report also selectively reported research linking video games to aggression, while failing to report a single study, despite the existence of many, suggesting that violent video games or other media may not be linked to violence (Subcommittee on Youth Violence, 2013). The only exception was a 2008 meta-analysis by criminologist Joanne Savage that the NSF authors falsely claim linked violent media to violent crime even though Dr. Savage came to the opposite conclusion (Savage & Yancey, 2008). The report failed to mention that many mass shooters, young and old, did not consume violent video games or other violent media, nor did they mention any of the many studies that have contradicted their conclusions (Vossekuil et al., 2002). This example highlights the hazards of mixing politics, moral panics, the need for certainty, and science.

Difficulties in Identifying a Developmental Pathway

It appears that mass shooters tend to reach a remarkably consistent endpoint, marked by the combination of mental illness, psychopathic traits, severe depression, and resentment toward perceived injustices (Ferguson, Coulson, & Barnett, 2011). This endpoint appears to be reasonably similar to suicide terrorists (Lankford, 2013). However, the developmental path to this endpoint remains, largely, mysterious.

This is, in part, because violent behavior is partly innate, and even adaptive under some extreme circumstances, but can be brought forth in maladaptive ways through genetic predispositions coupled with a nearly infinite array of environmental stressors. How these stressors impact individuals is idiosyncratic. For much of the twentieth century, it was thought that violence was a purely learned behavior, and this view continues to cause much confusion in discussions of mass shootings. We do not mean to suggest that learning is irrelevant to violence, rather that simplistic imitative learning is unlikely to be the core feature of violence. Rather, violence is a complex process arising from genetic predispositions, immediate family and peer influences, mental resiliency, and environmental stressors. Diathesis-stress models of violence, such as the catalyst model (Ferguson et al., 2008), suggest that both genetic predispositions and a harsh early environment most likely contribute to the development of personalities which are more prone to aggression and violence than others. Indeed, this basic observation has been well-supported in previous literature (e.g., Caspi et al., 2002).

Development of this aggressive personality results in an array of potential responses to external stimuli. Aggressive personalities are more likely to lean toward aggressive responses, but these can still be restrained by the brain's impulse control device, the prefrontal cortex, which is involved in foreseeing consequences and restraining maladaptive impulses. This impulse control device can, in turn, break down under some circumstances, including brain injury, but may also function less efficiently when more external stress is applied to the individual.

This model explicitly indicates that forces that have direct impact on the developing child are far more likely to be influential than peripheral forces (Figure 4.1). This comes most into play when assessing potential factors, such as media violence, which have little direct impact on a developing child's world

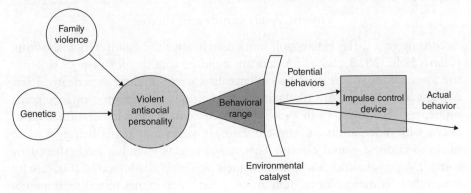

Figure 4.1   A catalyst model for violent antisocial behavior.

and, thus, are too distal to influence the developmental path to violence. That is to say, the developing child's mind treats real stimuli differently from that in a fictional universe.

This model tends to work well in understanding the developmental pathways toward most violent crimes, which are often linked to stress, abuse and neglect, depression, peer delinquency, and brain damage to the frontal lobes. However, with mass shootings, although some elements, such as stress and antisocial personality are present, there is less of a clear link to family abuse or neglect. Regardless, the presence of "grievance collecting" elements in most shooters may provide a key. Mass shooters typically view themselves as victimized and react disproportionately to such perceived grievances (Knoll, 2010b). It may be that mass shooters lack resiliency to perceived slights, neglect, or bullying that would have far less impact on developmentally typical individuals. The resultant lack of hope and feeling of social isolation thus become the element of abuse or neglect, which is a key feature of the catalyst model.

This process is consistent with those described in the most detailed case studies of shooters, and with broader research that suggests shooters delight in the fantasy of taking vengeance and in teaching their victims a lesson (Klein, 2005; Knoll, 2010a). In one case, a 30-year-old woman with a history of debilitating mental illness nursed grievances against nearly everyone she came into contact with, especially her ex-husband (Browner, 1988). Eventually, her desire to get even with her ex-husband and others who had wronged her led to a convoluted and almost nonsensical plan of revenge. In the course of her ill-conceived plan, this woman ended up shooting and killing a random 8-year-old boy and seriously wounding five others at a school in Winnetka, Illinois (Kaplan, Papajohn, & Zorn, 1990).

Purported Causal Factors That Are Not Supported

Violent video games and media

According to a 2013 Harris poll immediately after the Sandy Hook shooting (Harris Polls, 2013), 58% of Americans believed that the portrayal of violence in video games was related to violence in society. Polling Americans a few months later, Przybylski (2014) found an even split in opinions on video game influences. However, both polls also documented clear generational influences, with older adults and those unfamiliar with video games being far more likely to endorse causal effects. This causal effects view has been shared by some TV personalities and pundits, such as Dr. Phil McGraw (2007), who stated that "common sense" tells anyone that video games mixed with mental illness and rage lead to an explosive cocktail, as the "suggestibility is too high."

Interestingly, the National Rifle Association executive vice president, Wayne LaPierre, also agreed with this sentiment, when after the Sandy Hook shooting he asserted that violent video games were part of a "callous, corrupt, and corrupting shadow" industry that sows violence "against its own people" (Oremus, 2012). Perhaps more surprisingly, some scholars have echoed these alarmist pronouncements, comparing the relation of media violence and real-life aggression to the link between smoking and lung cancer (Strasburger & Grossman, 2001; Strasburger, 2007; Strasburger, Jordan, & Donnerstein, 2010). Other scholars have implicated violent video games as a contributing factor in mass shootings (Anderson & Dill, 2000).

Despite such assertions, there is no evidence to support the claim that violent video games are causally related to serious aggression, such as mass homicides and school shootings (Ferguson, 2008). In fact, there is minimal evidence that violent video games increase low-level aggression within the laboratory (Ferguson, 2007; Hall, Day, & Hall, 2011).

Several meta-analyses have been conducted on potential video game influences on milder aggression, relying particularly on studies involving WEIRD (i.e., Western, Educated, Industrialized, Rich, and Democratic) participants (Henrich, Heine, & Norenzayan, 2010). These meta-analyses have come to conflicting conclusions about potential effects. Two meta-analyses (Anderson et al., 2010; Greitemeyer & Mügge, 2014) came to the conclusion that violent games can have small but significant influences on mild aggression. However, both of these meta-analyses have been identified as problematic. Anderson et al. (2010) excluded numerous null studies from their analyses, resulting in spuriously high effects. Publication bias was also evident, but unreported, particularly in the "best practice" experimental studies (the majority of which were the authors' own studies), where effect size and sample size correlated $r = -.503$ ($p = .007$), which is a potential indication of p-hacking and avoidance of null results. Greitemeyer and Mügge (2014) appear to have numerous fundamental problems with their meta-analysis, including the inclusion of studies with no violent/nonviolent control group, the inclusion of studies multiple times in a single analysis, the violation of homogeneity assumptions, and sloppy extraction of effect sizes. The authors also suggested that "neutral" studies agreed with causationists more than skeptics, but achieved this result by including numerous studies by causationists (including coauthors on Anderson et al., 2010) as if they were "neutral."

Two other meta-analyses were more skeptical of video game influences. Sherry (2007) concluded that the weak effects seen were likely due to methodological shortcomings of the studies, which have been widespread. Sherry (2007) also noted that evidence that video games have more influence than other media due to their interactive nature was absent. Ferguson (in press), which focused on samples of children and adolescents, found little evidence of harmful effects for video games on aggression or mental health issues. Further, studies in the Ferguson (in press) meta-analysis that employed citation bias (only citing research that supported the author's own views) were more likely to find effects than those that did not.

Other scholars have noted that correlational relationships are not observed between violent game consumption and violent crime or bullying over time in the United States, nor between game consumption and crime cross-nationally (Markey, Markey, & French, in press). Markey et al. (in press) also observed that releases of popular violent video games, such as the Grand Theft Auto series, is followed by immediate declines in violence, suggesting a causal effect related to declined societal violence. The authors explain this as a function of routine activities theory in which popular video games occupy the time of young males who might otherwise have engaged in violence.

However, such data are correlational and we do not intend to assert a causal link. Although correlation does not equal causation, absence of correlation is good evidence for absence of causation. Causal advocates often defend against this inconvenient data by noting that violence is multidetermined. We certainly agree that violence is multidetermined, but this counter explanation fails for three reasons. First, noting that violence is multidetermined does not mean video games need be one of those causes. Second, causationists often argue, on one hand, for violent games having dramatic impact on a par with smoking and lung cancer, causing up to 30% of societal violence (e.g., Strasburger, 2007), or being akin to global warming or Holocaust denial (e.g., Strasburger, Donnerstein, & Bushman, 2014). Yet when faced with inconvenient correlational data, whether from individual studies or from real-world data (e.g., Breuer Vogelgesang, Quandt, & Festl, in press; von Salisch, Vogelgesang, Kristen, & Oppl, 2011), such data are dismissed. Comparisons to smoking/lung cancer and global warming also are problematic, since the correlational data in those cases clearly are in the direction expected by causationist arguments (lung cancer increases in smokers; global warming has increased along with pollutant emissions.)

A third problem with the dismissal of societal crime data is that many scholars who dismiss current crime data either used them when crime rates were rising in the 1980s, or eagerly sift about for crime data that appear to support causal beliefs. One recent curious argument suggests well-established crime data should be ignored in favor of teen gun injury data from the Centers for Disease Control (Bushman, Romer, & Jamieson, 2015). They suggest that gun injuries among teens can be used to infer gun violence rates by teens. However, the CDC data appear to be unreliable, with wild fluctuations from one year to the next. Further, why infer teen gun violence rates from CDC injury data, when teen gun violence data from the Bureau of Justice Statistics (2013) already document a declining trend?

When it comes to mass shootings, belief in a link between these events and video games is a clear product of confirmation bias. When shooters are older males (or more rarely, females), little attention is paid to video games. That is to say, few pundits or scholars take the time to point out that these older shooters did not play violent video games. Yet, video games are eagerly raised as an issue for young male shooters. This confirmation bias appears to intuitively capitalize on base rate behaviors. Because violent game play is ubiquitous among young males in the population, yet rare for older males, it is not surprising that young male shooters often played violent games. However, some cases of young male shooters, such as Sandy Hook or Virginia Tech, were found in official investigation reports to have little relation to violent games. Yet these exonerations often receive far less media attention than the initial speculation about video game influences.

Bad homes

Home life is the risk factor that laypeople blame most for mass shootings. In a 2001 Gallup poll (Moore, 2001), 92% of respondents asserted that home life, including relationship with parents, was "very/extremely" important in causing school shootings. Scholarly research on mass shooters has demonstrated that family-level variables, such as a lack of supervision, troubled relationships, and sexual/physical abuse, are significant risk factors that present themselves in mass shooters (Verlinden, Hersen, & Thomas, 2000; Langman, 2009). However, the Secret Service Report on school shootings (Vossekuil et al., 2002) noted that a majority of shooters (63%) came from two-parent families and case study research reveals that many shooters come from typical households (Cullen, 2009; Gibson, 1999; Langman, 2009, 2013). For example, the home life of the Sandy Hook shooter, while not idyllic, was far from abusive. The Sandy Hook shooter's mother was doting and his socioeconomic status was above average (Griffin & Kovner, 2013a). Many of the issues that the family encountered were due to the shooter's mental illness which placed strain on his mother (Griffin & Kovner, 2013b). The duress in the household appears to have been caused by the shooter rather than the parents, which is perhaps not uncommon, especially among adolescent shooters.

As the Sandy Hook case illustrates, assessing the impact of home life on the developmental trajectory of shooters is extremely difficult. The Red Lake shooter, for another example, suffered a traumatic childhood which included his father committing suicide after a standoff with the police and his mother suffering permanent brain damage from a car accident. It is tempting to grant causality to such traumatic events and to "explain" the shooter's behavior by reference to his or her upbringing. But this simply invites the question of why hundreds of thousands of children who suffer similar or worse trauma do not commit heinous crimes as adolescents or adults (Widom, 1989). More disconcerting, many studies that assess the impact of home environment on subsequent outcomes (behavioral or mental) are not genetically informed and therefore are incapable of demonstrating causality (Harris, 2007). When genetically informed studies are conducted, the family environment (or "shared environment" in behavioral genetic parlance) usually accounts for minimal variation in outcomes (Bouchard, 2004; Boutwell & Beaver, 2010; Wright, Beaver, Delisi, & Vaughn, 2008).

As we have illustrated above, the thread that seems to unite mass shooters is mental illness and perceived grievances. There is now a voluminous literature on the genetics of the mental pathologies that have been identified as prevalent in shooters (e.g., psychopathy, borderline personality, schizophrenia, bipolar, depression) and all of these disorders have a strong heritable component with little impact of shared environment (e.g., Bornovalova et al., 2013; Distel et al., 2008; Frick, Ray, Thornton, & Kahn, 2014; Larsson, Andershed, & Lichenstein, 2006; Lichtenstein et al., 2009; Viding, Jones, Paul, Moffitt, & Plomin, 2008).

Although these results do not disprove the hypothesis that the home environment is an important causal factor in the genesis of mass shooters, they do suggest that skepticism is appropriate. It is worth noting that gene x environment interactions (GxE) may be one way in which the home environment exerts an influence on individuals who are particularly vulnerable to specific environmental stimuli (Kim-Cohen et al., 2006; see Figure 4.1). From this perspective, some individuals may be more vulnerable than others to traumatic events that occur in the household. Out of this subset, a very few are traumatized to the point where, in conjunction with other factors, they commit serious acts of violence (Caspi et al., 2002). This seems to be a plausible hypothesis and one worth exploring in greater detail. Currently, attempts to replicate GxE interaction studies have had limited success and GxE studies suffer from confounds that limit the conclusions one can draw from them (Duncan & Keller, 2011; Keller, 2014). However, there is little evidence that the home environment is a crucial causal factor and there is much evidence that it is irrelevant in the majority of mass shootings (Langman, 2013).

Bullying

Of all the purported factors that have been offered to explain mass shootings, especially at schools, bullying is the one that probably resonates as the most plausible and understandable to laypeople. According to the above mentioned Gallup poll (Moore, 2001), 62% of respondents thought bullying and teasing were "very/extremely" important as causal factors in school shootings. Most individuals can think of a time in their lives when they were bullied, teased, or harassed, and many have the memories of such incidents seared into their brains. Thus, it is not surprising that bullying is believed by many scholars and laypeople to be a major contributing factor in shootings. This belief is seemingly well grounded by careful case study research that has demonstrated that the majority of school shooters were the victims of malicious bullying and teasing, especially pertaining to their sexuality and perceived lack of masculine traits (Kimmel & Mahler, 2003; Klein, 2012; Leary, Kowalski, Smith, & Phillips, 2003). Nevertheless, many shooters were not bullied and/or were themselves bullies (Langman, 2009; Meloy, Hempel, Mohandie, Shiva, & Gray, 2001). The 2013 Arapahoe High School shooter, for example, blamed teasing that occurred in elementary school for his subsequent psychological and anger issues, but was seen by others as a mercurial and difficult bully who was exceedingly arrogant (McCauley, 2014). Similarly, Cullen (2009) does not view the evidence as supporting that the Columbine shooters were bullied to any significant degree. Rather, Cullen views one of the shooters as a psychopath and the other as a seriously depressed individual seeking love, connection, and meaning.

Overall, researchers have found that bullying (defined as repetition, rejection, and unequal power) is surprisingly common, with some estimates that over 50% of students (ages 12–15 years) have been verbally bullied at least once in the past 2 months and 85–95% of LGBT and students with disabilities have experienced bullying (Swearer, Espelage, Vaillancourt, & Hymel, 2010; Wang, Iannotti, & Nansel, 2009). Other research estimates that bullying is less frequent, but still common, with estimates between 11 and 20% (Olweus, 2012; Salmivalli, 2010). There is strong evidence that both bullying and being a victim of bullying can lead to psychological and somatic distress including depression, self-harm, and, in extreme cases, suicidal ideation, and possibly suicide (Fekkes, Pijpers, & Verloove-Vanhorick, 2004; Hinduja & Patchin, 2010; Lereya et al., 2013). There is also an association between being a bully and antisocial outcomes later in life, but some controversy about whether being a victim of bullying leads to antisocial outcomes (Bender & Lösel, 2011; Ttofi, Farrington, & Lösel, 2012). Fortunately, we note, bullying incidents among youth appear to be declining, along with other forms of youth violence – although data on bullying have only been kept for approximately the past decade (Finkelhor, Turner, Ormrod, & Hamby, 2010; National Center for Education Statistics, 2015).

These facts, combined with case studies of shooters, seem to implicate bullying as a risk factor in school and other mass shootings. However, the case for bullying as a significant contributing factor in the developmental sequence of mass shooters is not as strong as it seems. It is difficult to explain how bullying could be an important cause of shootings when at least one fifth of all adolescents have been victims of bullying and only a miniscule fraction even contemplate shooting their peers. A counter to this argument is that any risk factor, whether mental illness or obsession with violence and weapons, leads only very rarely to a shooting. However, it is also the case that bullies and victims are not random individuals. For example, victims of bullying are likely to suffer from internalizing disorders, to lack social skills, and to be isolated; bullies are likely to be externalizers who possess negative views of their school and community; and bully-victims (e.g., individuals who bully others and also report being bullied) are likely to be comorbid internalizers/externalizers who are socially rejected (Cook, Williams, Guerra, Kim, & Sadek, 2010). Because internalizing and externalizing problems are highly heritable, it is not surprising that bullying and victimization run in families (Allison, Roeger, Smith, & Isherwood, 2014; Ball et al., 2008).

To the extent that being a victim of bullying (or being a bully) interacts with other salient environmental phenomena and risk factors to create a heightened sense of alienation, rejection, and marginalization, it is possible that it contributes to mass and, especially, school shootings (Newman, 2013). We view it as more likely that it is a strong sense of injustice, desire for revenge and glory, and marginalization that is causally operative and that bullying or victimization simply serve as noncausal indicators that are often correlated with relevant factors, such as possessing low status, lacking social skills, having a mental illness, and being socially marginalized (Larkin, 2009). That said, we view bullying as worthy of much more study and scrutiny and find it more plausible as a causal factor than either violent video games and media or bad homes.

Conclusion

Mass shootings are extremely rare, traumatic, and little-understood events (Duwe, 2004; Shultz, Cohen, Muschert, & de Apodaca, 2013). However, because mass shootings can seemingly occur in any place (e.g., school, home, workplace) and at any time, they cause trauma and panic. Unfortunately, even with hundreds of scholars pouring through archives and official reports from well-funded agencies, we know very little about mass shooters. There does not seem to be a universal profile nor is there a typical shooter (Langman, 2013; Vossekuil et al., 2002). This should not be taken to mean that there are not general traits shared by mass shooters. Almost all of the shooters that have been studied in detail were male, exhibited evidence of mental illness, and perceived that they were treated unjustly in some way, whether metaphysically (e.g., by an unjust universe) or specifically by peers (Ferguson et al., 2011; Klein, 2005; Knoll, 2010a). Unfortunately, these general traits are also present in many hundreds of thousands of adolescents and adults who never harm another person.

It is arguably more important to dispel widely held myths about shooters than to proffer another imperfect typology or speculate about the causes of mass shootings. This might guard against harmful policies or scapegoating. As we have documented, there is little evidence to support the widely held belief that mass shooters are produced by "broken" homes or inattentive parents. In this chapter, we have also argued that excessive focus on bullying or violent media may lead to ineffectual policies. In conclusion, we urge caution and modesty among scholars and policy makers when examining potential explanations for mass shootings.

References

Allison, S., Roeger, L., Smith, B., & Isherwood, L. (2014). Family histories of school bullying: Implications for parent-child psychotherapy. *Australasian Psychiatry, 22,* 149–153.

Anderson, C. A., & Dill, K. E. (2000). Video games and aggressive thoughts, feelings, and behavior in the laboratory and in life. *Journal of Personality and Social Psychology, 78,* 772–790.

Anderson, C. A., Shibuya, A., Ihori, N., Swing, E. L., Bushman, B. J., Sakamoto, A., … Saleem, M. (2010). Violent video game effects on aggression, empathy, and prosocial behavior in Eastern and Western countries: A meta-analytic review. *Psychological Bulletin, 136,* 151–173. doi:10.1037/a0018251

Ball, H. A., Arseneault, L., Taylor, A., Maughan, B., Caspi, A., & Moffitt, T. E. (2008). Genetic and environmental influences on victims, bullies and bully-victims in childhood. *Journal of Child Psychology and Psychiatry, 49,* 104–112.

Bender, D., & Lösel, F. (2011). Bullying at school as a predictor of delinquency, violence and other anti-social behaviour in adulthood. *Criminal Behaviour and Mental Health, 21,* 99–106.

Bornovalova, M. A., Huibregtse, B. M., Hicks, B. M., Keyes, M., McGue, M., & Iacono, W. (2013). Tests of a direct effect of childhood abuse on adult borderline personality disorder traits: A longitudinal discordant twin design. *Journal of Abnormal Psychology, 122,* 180–194.

Bouchard, T. J. (2004). Genetic influence on human psychological traits: A survey. *Current Directions in Psychological Science, 13,* 148–151.

Boutwell, B. B., & Beaver, K. M. (2010). The intergenerational transmission of low self-control. *Journal of Research in Crime and Delinquency, 47,* 174–209.

Breuer, J., Vogelgesang, J., Quandt, T., & Festl, R. (in press). Violent video games and physical aggression: Evidence for a selection effect among adolescents. *Psychology of Popular Media Culture.*

Brooks, K. (1985, December 10). A tragic lesson: Community agonizes over causes of teen slayings/suicide. *The Seattle Times.* Retrieved from http://nl.newsbank.com/

Brown, C. E., & Balter, J. (1985, November 27). 3 die as teen romance sours. *The Seattle Times.* Retrieved from http://nl.newsbank.com/

Browner, M. (1988, June 6). Mad enough to kill: Driven by an insane rage, a young woman turns her guns on 8-year-old and wounds an entire community. *People, 29.* Retrieved from http://www.people.com/people/archive/article/0,20099121,00.html

Bureau of Justice Statistics. (2013). *Firearm violence, 1993–2011.* Retrieved from http://bjs.gov/content/pub/pdf/fv9311.pdf

Bushman, B., Romer, D., & Jamieson, P. (2015). Distinguishing hypotheses from hyperbole in studies of media violence: A comment on Markey et al. *Human Communication Research, 41,* 174–183.

Caspi, A., McClay, J., Moffitt, T. E., Mill, J., Martin, J., Craig, I. W., … Poulton, R. (2002). Role of genotype in the cycle of violence in maltreated children. *Science, 297,* 851–854.

Cook, C. R., Williams, K. R., Guerra, N. G., Kim, T. E., & Sadek, S. (2010). Predictors of bullying and victimization in childhood and adolescence: A meta-analytic investigation. *School Psychology Quarterly, 25*, 65–83.

Cullen, D. (2009). *Columbine*. New York: Twelve.

Cullen, D. (2013, September 17). Let's stop naming mass shooters in our reporting. *BuzzFeed*. Retrieved from http://www.buzzfeed.com/davecullen/stop-naming-mass-shooters-in-reporting#.eiYa9MLNND

Distel, M. A., Trull, T. J., Derom, C. A., Thiery, E. W., Grimmer, M. A., Martin, N. G., … Boomsma, D. I. (2008). Heritability of borderline personality disorder features is similar across three countries. *Psychological Medicine, 38*, 1219–1229.

Duncan, L. E., & Keller, M. C. (2011). A critical review of the first 10 years of candidate gene-by-environment interaction research in psychiatry. *American Journal of Psychiatry, 168*, 1041–1049.

Duwe, G. (2004). The patterns and prevalence of mass murder in twentieth-century America. *Justice Quarterly, 21*, 729–761.

Fekkes, M., Pijpers, F. I., & Verloove-Vanhorick, S. P. (2004). Bullying behavior and associations with psychosomatic complaints and depression in victims. *The Journal of Pediatrics, 144*, 17–22.

Ferguson, C. J. (2007). Evidence for publication bias in video game violence effects literature: A meta-analytic review. *Aggression and Violent Behavior, 12*, 470–482.

Ferguson, C. J. (2008). The school shooting/violent video game link: Causal relationship or moral panic? *Journal of Investigative Psychology and Offender Profiling, 5*, 25–37.

Ferguson, C. J. (2014). Violent video games, mass shootings and the Supreme Court: Lessons for the legal community in the wake of recent free speech cases and mass shootings. *New Criminal Law Review, 17*, 553–586.

Ferguson, C. J. (in press). Do angry birds make for angry children? A meta-analysis of video game influences on children's and adolescents' aggression, mental health, prosocial behavior and academic performance. *Perspectives on Psychological Science*.

Ferguson, C. J., Coulson, M., & Barnett, J. (2011). Psychological profiles of school shooters: Positive directions and one big wrong turn. *Journal of Police Crisis Negotiations, 11*, 141–158.

Ferguson, C. J., Rueda, S., Cruz, A., Ferguson, D., Fritz, S., & Smith, S. (2008). Violent video games and aggression: Causal relationship or byproduct of family violence and intrinsic violence motivation? *Criminal Justice and Behavior, 35*, 311–332.

Finkelhor, D., Turner, H., Ormrod, R., & Hamby, S. (2010). Trends in childhood violence and abuse exposure: Evidence from 2 national surveys. *Archives of Pediatric and Adolescent Medicine, 164*, 238–242.

Fox, J., & DeLateur, M. (2014). Mass shootings in America: Moving beyond Newtown. *Homicide Studies, 18*, 125–145. doi:10.1177/1088767913510297

Frick, P. J., Ray, J. V., Thornton, L. C., & Kahn, R. E. (2014). Can callous-unemotional traits enhance the understanding, diagnosis, and treatment of serious conduct problems in children and adolescents? A comprehensive review. *Psychological Bulletin, 140*, 1–57.

Gibson, G. (1999). *Gone boy: A walkabout*. New York: Anchor Books.

Greitemeyer, T., & Mügge, D. O. (2014). Video games do affect social outcomes: A meta-analytic review of the effects of violent and prosocial video game play. *Personality and Social Psychology Bulletin*, *40*, 578–589. doi:10.1177/0146167213520459

Griffin, A., & Kovner, J. (2013a, February 17). Raising Adam Lanza. *The Hartford Courant*. Retrieved from http://www.courant.com/news/connecticut/newtown-sandy-hook-school-shooting/hc-raising-adam-lanza-20130217,0,5614292,full.story

Griffin, A., & Kovner, J. (2013b, June 30). Adam Lanza's medical records reveal growing anxiety. *The Hartford Courant*. Retrieved from http://articles.courant.com/2013-06-30/news/hc-adam-lanza-pediatric-records-20130629_1_nancy-lanza-adam-lanza-danbury-hospital

Hall, R. C., Day, T., & Hall, R. C. (2011). A plea for caution: Violent video games, the Supreme Court, and the role of science. *Mayo Clinic Proceedings*, *86*, 315–321.

Harris, J. R. (2007). *No two alike: Human nature and human individuality*. New York: W. W. Norton.

Harris Polls. (2013). Majority of Americans see connection between video games and violent behavior in teens. Retrieved from http://www.harrisinteractive.com/NewsRoom/HarrisPolls/tabid/447/mid/1508/articleId/1160/ctl/ReadCustom%20Default/Default.aspx

Henrich, J., Heine, S. J., & Norenzayan, A. (2010). The weirdest people in the world? *Behavioral and Brain Sciences*, *33*, 61–83.

Hinduja, S., & Patchin, J. W. (2010). Bullying, cyberbullying, and suicide. *Archives of Suicide Research*, *14*, 206–221.

Kaplan, J., Papajohn, G., & Zorn, E. (1990). *Murder of innocence: The tragic life and final rampage of Laurie Dann, "The schoolhouse killer."* New York: Warner.

KCCI. (2012). Expert: Parents talk to your kids about video games. Retrieved from http://www.kcci.com/news/central-iowa/Expert-Parents-talk-to-your-kids-about-video-games/-/9357080/17823232/-/qb6hq4/-/index.html

Keller, M. C. (2014). Gene x environment interaction studies have not properly controlled for potential confounders: The problem and the (simple) solution. *Biological Psychiatry*, *75*, 18–24.

Kim-Cohen, J., Caspi, A., Taylor, A., Williams, B., Newcombe, R., Craig, I. W., & Moffitt, T. E. (2006). MAOA, maltreatment, and gene–environment interaction predicting children's mental health: New evidence and a meta-analysis. *Molecular Psychiatry*, *11*, 903–913.

Kimmel, M. S., & Mahler, M. (2003). Adolescent masculinity, homophobia, and violence random school shootings, 1982–2001. *American Behavioral Scientist*, *46*, 1439–1458.

Klein, J. (2005). Teaching her a lesson: Media misses boys' rage relating to girls in school shootings. *Crime, Media, Culture*, *1*, 90–97.

Klein, J. (2012). *The bully society: School shootings and the crisis of bullying in America's schools*. New York: New York University Press.

Knoll, J. L. (2010a). The "pseudocommando" mass murderer: Part I, the psychology of revenge and obliteration. *Journal of the American Academy of Psychiatry and the Law Online*, *38*, 87–94.

Knoll, J. L. (2010b). The "pseudocommando" mass murderer: Part II, the language of revenge. *Journal of the American Academy of Psychiatry and the Law Online, 38,* 263–272.

Langman, P. (2009). Rampage school shooters: A typology. *Aggression and violent behavior, 14,* 79–86.

Langman, P. (2013). Thirty-five rampage school shooters: Trends, patterns, and typology. In N. Bockler, T. Seager, P. Sitzer, & W. Heitmeyer (Eds.), *School shootings: International research, case studies, and concepts for prevention* (pp. 131–156). New York: Springer.

Lankford, A. (2013). A comparative analysis of suicide terrorists, and rampage, workplace and school shooters in the United States from 1990 to 2010. *Homicide Studies.*

Larkin, R. W. (2009). The Columbine legacy rampage shootings as political acts. *American Behavioral Scientist, 52,* 1309–1326.

Larkin, R. W. (2013). Legitimated adolescent violence: Lessons from Columbine. In N. Bockler, T. Seager, P. Sitzer, & W. Heitmeyer (Eds.), *School shootings: International research, case studies, and concepts for prevention* (pp. 159–176). New York: Springer.

Larsson, H., Andershed, H., & Lichtenstein, P. (2006). A genetic factor explains most of the variation in the psychopathic personality. *Journal of Abnormal Psychology, 115,* 221–230.

Leary, M. R., Kowalski, R. M., Smith, L., & Phillips, S. (2003). Teasing, rejection, and violence: Case studies of the school shootings. *Aggressive Behavior, 29,* 202–214.

Lereya, S. T., Winsper, C., Heron, J., Lewis, G., Gunnell, D., Fisher, H. L., & Wolke, D. (2013). Being bullied during childhood and the prospective pathways to self-harm in late adolescence. *Journal of the American Academy of Child & Adolescent Psychiatry, 52,* 608–618.

Lichtenstein, P., Yip, B. H., Björk, C., Pawitan, Y., Cannon, T. D., Sullivan, P. F., & Hultman, C. M. (2009). Common genetic determinants of schizophrenia and bipolar disorder in Swedish families: A population-based study. *The Lancet, 373,* 234–239.

Markey, P. M., Markey, C. N., & French, J. E. (in press). Violent video games and real world violence: Rhetoric versus data. *Psychology of Popular Media Culture.*

McCarthy, K. (1985, December 4). No one took girl's threats seriously. *Associated Press.* Retrieved from http://nl.newsbank.com/

McCauley, K. (2014). Investigative Report Arapahoe High School Case #CT13-44545. Retrieved from https://schoolshooters.info/sites/default/files/official_report_karl_pierson.pdf

McGraw, P. (2007). Virginia Tech massacre: Interview with Larry King Live. Retrieved from http://transcripts.cnn.com/TRANSCRIPTS/0704/16/lkl.01.html

Meloy, J., Hempel, A. G., Mohandie, K., Shiva, A. A., & Gray, B. T. (2001). Offender and offense characteristics of a nonrandom sample of adolescent mass murderers. *Journal of the American Academy of Child & Adolescent Psychiatry, 40,* 719–728.

Moore, D. W. (2001, April 5). Americans look to parents to stop school shootings. *Gallup.* Retrieved from http://www.gallup.com/poll/1828/americans-look-parents-stop-school-shootings.aspx

National Center for Education Statistics. (2015). Measuring student safety: Bullying rates at school. Retrieved from http://nces.ed.gov/blogs/nces/post/measuring-student-safety-bullying-rates-at-school

Newman, K. S. (2013). Adolescent culture and the tragedy of rampage shootings. In N. Bockler, T. Seager, P. Sitzer, & W. Heitmeyer (Eds.), *School shootings: International research, case studies, and concepts for prevention* (pp. 55–77). New York: Springer.

Olweus, D. (2012). Cyberbullying: An overrated phenomenon? *European Journal of Developmental Psychology, 9,* 520–538.

Oremus, W. (2012, December 21). In kindergarten killer, the video game the NRA blamed for school shootings, everyone has a gun. *Slate.* Retrieved from http://www.slate.com/blogs/future_tense/2012/12/21/kindergarten_killers_nra_s_wayne_lapierre_blames_violent_video_games_for.html

Przybylski, A. (2014). Who believes electronic games cause real-world aggression? *Cyberpsychology, Behavior and Social Networking, 17,* 228–234.

Salmivalli, C. (2010). Bullying and the peer group: A review. *Aggression and Violent Behavior, 15,* 112–120.

Savage, J., & Yancey, C. (2008). The effects of media violence exposure on criminal aggression: A meta-analysis. *Criminal Justice and Behavior, 35,* 772–791.

Sherry, J. (2007). Violent video games and aggression: Why can't we find links? In R. Preiss, B. Gayle, N. Burrell, M. Allen, & J. Bryant, (Eds.) *Mass media effects research: Advances through meta-analysis* (pp. 231–248). Mahwah, NJ: L. Erlbaum.

Shultz, J., Cohen, A. M., Muschert, G. W., & de Apodaca, R. F. (2013). Fatal school shootings and the epidemiological context of firearm mortality in the United States. *Disaster Health, 1,* 1–18.

State's Attorney for the Judicial District of Danbury. (2013). *Report of the State's Attorney for the Judicial District of Danbury on the Shootings at Sandy Hook Elementary School and 36 Yogananda Street, Newtown, Connecticut on December 14, 2012.* Danbury, CT: Office of the State's Attorney Judicial District of Danbury.

Strasburger, V. C. (2007). Go ahead punk, make my day: It's time for pediatricians to take action against media violence. *Pediatrics, 119,* e1398-e1399.

Strasburger, V. C., Donnerstein, E., & Bushman, B. J. (2014). Why is it so hard to believe that media influence children and adolescents? *Pediatrics, 133,* 571–573.

Strasburger, V. C., & Grossman, D. (2001). How many more Columbines? What can pediatricians do about school and media violence? *Pediatric Annals, 30,* 87–94.

Strasburger, V. C., Jordan, A. B., & Donnerstein, E. (2010). Health effects of media on children and adolescents. *Pediatrics, 125,* 756–767.

Subcommittee on Youth Violence. (2013). *Youth violence: What we need to know.* Washington, DC: National Science Foundation.

Swearer, S. M., Espelage, D. L., Vaillancourt, T., & Hymel, S. (2010). What can be done about school bullying? Linking research to educational practice. *Educational Researcher, 39,* 38–47.

Ttofi, M. M., Farrington, D. P., & Lösel, F. (2012). School bullying as a predictor of violence later in life: A systematic review and meta-analysis of prospective longitudinal studies. *Aggression and Violent Behavior, 17,* 405–418.

Verlinden, S., Hersen, M., & Thomas, J. (2000). Risk factors in school shootings. *Clinical Psychology Review, 20*, 3–56.

Viding, E., Jones, A. P., Paul, J. F., Moffitt, T. E., & Plomin, R. (2008). Heritability of antisocial behaviour at 9: Do callous-unemotional traits matter? *Developmental Science, 11*, 17–22.

von Salisch, M., Vogelgesang, J., Kristen, A., & Oppl, C. (2011). Preference for violent electronic games and aggressive behavior among children: The beginning of the downward spiral? *Media Psychology, 14*, 233–258. doi:10.1080/15213269.2011.596468

Vossekuil, B., Fein, R. A., Reddy, M., Borum, R., & Modzeleski, W. (2002). *The final report and findings of the safe school initiative: Implications for the prevention of school attacks in the United States.* Washington, DC: U.S. Secret Service and U.S. Department of Education.

Wang, J., Iannotti, R. J., & Nansel, T. R. (2009). School bullying among adolescents in the United States: Physical, verbal, relational, and cyber. *Journal of Adolescent Health, 45*, 368–375.

Widom, C. S. (1989). The cycle of violence. *Science, 244*, 160–166.

Wright, J., Beaver, K., Delisi, M., & Vaughn, M. (2008). Evidence of negligible parenting influences on self-control, delinquent peers, and delinquency in a sample of twins. *Justice Quarterly, 25*, 544–569.

5

Biosocial Perspective of Proactive Aggression

Applications to Perpetrators of Mass Shootings

Jonathan Waldron and Angela Scarpa

"To […] decide whether there is a force in nature that causes crime, we must abandon the sublime realms of philosophy and even the sensational facts of the crime itself and proceed instead to the direct physical and psychological study of the criminal, comparing the results with information on the healthy and the insane" (Lombroso, 1876, p. 43). The Italian psychiatrist Cesare Lombroso's words about what predicted violent behavior seem obvious today, but at the time, they were revolutionary. His research and writings, documented in *L'Uomo Delinquente* (*The Criminal Man*), are some of the earliest works highlighting the need to examine the role of biology in understanding predictors of violence. Lombroso examined the physical bodies of criminals, documenting characteristics from head circumferences to the distance between toes. While his claims have mostly been discredited, Lombroso suggested that to understand violent perpetration, one must examine the "physical and psychological study of the criminal" (p. 43).

This chapter seeks to examine biological and psychosocial variables, and how these factors may interact to inform our understanding of the proactive aggression seen in perpetrators of mass shootings. We will begin with an overview of several theories, including the biosocial model and its relationship to violence. We discuss various functional subtypes of aggression and how the biosocial model may help us understand proactive aggression. We finally suggest how the biosocial model can be used to understand mass shooting perpetration and offer suggestions for researchers

The Wiley Handbook of the Psychology of Mass Shootings, First Edition. Edited by Laura C. Wilson.
© 2017 John Wiley & Sons, Inc. Published 2017 by John Wiley & Sons, Inc.

Biology and Aggression

Historically, biological predictors of violence have largely been ignored, and other theories, such as sociological theories (see Collins, 2009), have received much of the attention. Sociological theories emphasize learning principles and contexts, among other variables, in order to understand violent perpetration. Within the past few decades, the biological determinants of violence have once again become a focus of research (see Lorber, 2004; Scarpa & Raine, 2007) and researchers have begun questioning purely sociological theories. It should be noted that this is not a suggestion that sociological theories of violence are not informative. But, prior studies conducted on the biology of violence indicate it would be ill-advised to ignore the role of biological risk and protective factors.

Much of the early research during the biological resurgence involved animal aggression studies, which found promising results identifying biological indices of aggression (Moyer, 1976). Animal studies, however, were limited in their generalization to human behavior. Still, the need to examine how biology affects aggression was recognized. As one scholar wrote, "What seems no longer tenable at this juncture is any theory of human behavior which ignores biology and relies exclusively on sociocultural learning. Most scientists have been wrong in their dogmatic rejection and blissful ignorance of the biological parameters of our behavior" (van den Berghe, 1974, p. 779).

Biology clearly influences human aggression, antisocial tendencies, and criminal behavior (see Raine, 2013). While a full review of aggression antecedents is beyond the scope of this chapter, some biological factors that have been demonstrated include cardiac (Lorber, 2004; Ortiz & Raine, 2004; Portnoy & Farrington, 2015), electrodermal (Lorber, 2004), nutritional (Siegel & McCormick, 2006), hormonal (Raine, 2002), neurobiological (Rowe, 2001), and genetic (DiLalla, 2002) contributions. Importantly, these factors have been found to predict or increase the likelihood of aggression, but are not absolute determinants of aggression.

Cardiac measures, particularly resting heart rate, appear to be the best replicated biological correlate of aggression and antisocial behavior (Ortiz & Raine, 2004). Therefore, it will be of particular focus in this chapter. Several meta-analyses have found resting heart rate to be significantly related to antisocial behavior (Ortiz & Raine, 2004; Portnoy & Farrington, 2015), aggression and conduct problems, but not psychopathy (Lorber, 2004). Overall, the findings provide strong support of a relationship between heart rate and aggression, with a few minor differences based on the type of externalizing problems (e.g., psychopathy).

The cardiac-aggression relationship is important to point out, because arousal levels may serve to exacerbate or mitigate aggressive behaviors, beyond other difficulties a person may have (Ortiz & Raine, 2004). Higher heart rate may serve to protect individuals from engaging in aggressive behavior. For example, Stadler and colleagues (2008) examined the relationship between heart rate and treatment outcome in children diagnosed with disruptive behavior disorders. Those with a higher resting heart rate had lower aggression compared to those with lower resting heart rate. Furthermore, resting heart rate was the only significant predictor of treatment outcome among these children.

On the other hand, a persistent low level of cardiac arousal indicated by low resting heart rate may exacerbate aggression. This theory, called the under-arousal theory (Eysenck, 1997), proposes that chronic low heart rate is extremely unpleasant. Subsequently, individuals engage in stimulating behaviors to increase arousal so that this discomfort is reduced. This may include stimulating behaviors such as skydiving, drag racing, or simply avoiding boring tasks. Relevant to this chapter, this unpleasant state of low arousal may lead an individual to become aggressive or violent (Raine, Venables, & Mednick, 1997; Wilson & Scarpa, 2014), which could include mass murder.

While this is not an exhaustive review of all studies that have examined the full range of biological predictors of aggression, it provides evidence that biology does play a role in understanding an individual's risk for becoming violent. Further, certain factors (e.g., high resting heart rate) may attenuate the risk for acting violently toward others, while other factors (i.e., low resting heart rate) may heighten the risk. Moreover, as further reviewed below, social context cannot be understood in the absence of biological context and vice versa.

Biosocial Model

Biology influences but does not determine aggression. This is an important distinction for scientists, policy makers, and laypersons to remember. It is imperative that researchers examine multiple factors that contribute to violence and aggression, and, more importantly, the interaction between these different variables. Aggression is a very complex and multiply determined construct based on a variety of risk and protective factors that interact throughout development (Raine, 2002; Scarpa & Raine, 2007).

The biosocial theory is one model that attempts to explain aggression through a synergistic approach. The biosocial theory posits that to fully understand violence, one must examine the interaction between biological and social variables (Raine, Brennan, Farrington, & Mednick 1997). These variables influence the risk for violent perpetration by either increasing or decreasing the likelihood of the behavior occurring. Thus, the model allows for a level of plasticity in that the variables that predict aggression alter each other and influence the likelihood of violence. Crime can be a sequelae of biology and social factors alone, but the interaction among these variables also determines violence.

There are several studies that support this theory (see Raine, 2002; Rudo-Hutt et al., 2011 for full reviews). Raine, Brennan, Mednick, and Mednick (1996), for example, found that crime rates were higher in individuals who evidenced both biological and psychosocial risk factors than individuals with only social (i.e., poverty/unstable family environments) or biological (i.e., early life neuromotor problems) risk. Moffitt and colleagues (1997) found that those with higher blood serotonin levels who also came from a conflicted family were three times more likely to be aggressive at age 21 than men with only the serotonin or social risk factors. These findings emphasize how combinations of both social and biological risk factors can increase violence risk.

Brennan and colleagues (1997) examined the role of heart rate and skin conductance reactivity as protective factors in men. The researchers divided the participants into four groups: criminals with criminal fathers, criminals with noncriminal fathers, noncriminals with criminal fathers, and noncriminals with noncriminal fathers. Thus, having a criminal father can be viewed as a social risk factor, while having a noncriminal father was considered a social protective factor. Physiological reactivity was measured during an orienting paradigm. Results showed that noncriminals with criminal fathers had the most elevated skin conductance and heart rate reactivity compared to the other groups. Similar results have been found in other studies (e.g., Raine, Venables, & Williams, 1995), suggesting that increased arousal protects individuals from engaging in crime, even when they are faced with social risk.

Vagal tone, a parasympathetic index of cardiac activity, has been found to interact with sociological factors to predict aggressive behavior. In one study, low vagal tone in the context of parent's drinking problems (i.e., a social risk) increased externalizing problems over time (El-Sheikh, 2005). Higher respiratory sinus arrhythmia (RSA), another measure of vagal tone, protected boys who experienced maltreatment (i.e., a social risk) from engaging in aggressive behaviors (Gordis, Feres, Olezeski, Rabkin, & Trickett, 2010). Further, in girls, an interaction was found between RSA and skin conductance. Low RSA worsened the link between child maltreatment and aggression, but only when skin conductance reactivity was also low. When RSA was low, but skin conductance was high, this link was no longer significant.

Other cardiac studies find interesting results related to the environment. In one study, resting heart rate was assessed in 11-year-old males and females (Wadsworth, 1976). As expected based on the underarousal theory (Eysenck, 1997), low resting heart rate predicted criminal convictions later in life for males. Interestingly, when differences based on home stressors (i.e., intact families versus divorced/separated families) were examined, the connection between low resting heart rate and convictions only held in those with intact homes. In another similar study, murderers were found to have prefrontal glucose metabolism deficits (Raine, Buchsbaum, & LaCasse, 1997). Using the same sample and dividing them based on psychosocial deprivation (i.e., low deprived homes vs. high deprived homes), results showed that murderers who came from "good" homes showed reduced prefrontal functioning, compared to those who had deprived backgrounds (Raine, Stoddard, Bihrle, & Buchsbaum, 1998). Although Raine and Venables (1984) found that low resting heart rate was found in individuals with antisocial behavior, the connection between low resting heart rate and antisocial behavior only occurred in those from higher socioeconomic backgrounds. Similar results have been found in multiple different countries and through various biological indices (see Raine, 2013 for review).

The question therefore arises: What explains violent behavior when the individual's environment is relatively stable, healthy, and safe? We would think these individuals are less likely to engage in violent behavior. An interpretation of these findings is the "social push theory" (Raine & Venables, 1984). According to this theory, biological risk factors for violence (e.g., cardiac underarousal) are more influential in situations of low social risk (e.g., high socioeconomic status, intact homes) when compared to high social risk (e.g., low socioeconomic status, broken homes). That is, social criminogenic factors may "push" people towards antisocial behavior. We might expect a person from a lower socioeconomic status, less stable home or violent neighborhood, for example, to engage in antisocial behaviors or to be more aggressive; sometimes they need to in order to survive. But in the absence of that social push, when a person from an affluent area or stable home engages in violent or antisocial behaviors, biological factors likely play a more important role. Bear in mind that it is not to say that biological and social factors are not at work in all these situations, but instead that the differential influence of each type of influence needs to be considered.

While the biosocial theory is promising in helping elucidate factors that contribute to aggression, it is not without its methodological and ethical issues, and a number of critiques have been noted (Raine, 2013; Walters & White, 1989). Some have argued, for example, that biosocial researchers overemphasize biological factors at the detriment of important social variables. Further, the samples (e.g., murderers) examined may not generalize to the general population. Others have suggested that biosocial theories may be racist and classist because of the focus on biological variables and how these might be attributed to certain races and classes (Gabbidon, 2007). Moreover, there is the fear that a focus on biological factors may lead to an increase in stigma or, on the other side of the argument, that criminals may be exonerated due to their physical attributes.

Nevertheless, there is a lot of promise in the biosocial model and it could help explain the development of aggressive tendencies. The biosocial theory stresses the importance of multiple influences on behavior and is supported by a substantial literature base that has examined developmental psychopathology.

Aggression Functional Subtypes: Proactive and Reactive

As with many legal terms related to homicide (e.g., first-degree murder vs. voluntary manslaughter), aggression is usually viewed as having two distinct functions based on the motivation behind the act (Raine et al., 2006). Reactive, also known as impulsive or emotional aggression, is characterized by responding to provocation, frustration or threat with aggression and is considered a loss of control in the moment (Meloy, 1997; Moyer, 1976; Raine, Meloy, et al., 1998). It is often described as hot-tempered, as it has its roots in the frustration-aggression model.

Proactive, otherwise known as premeditated or instrumental aggression, is usually nonemotional, controlled, and purposeful in nature. This type of aggression is meant to intimidate and is usually goal-oriented. It is often described as cold-tempered. It has its roots in the social learning theory (Bandura, 1973) under the pretense that aggression is operantly and vicariously learned. Further, proactive aggression is related to the assumption that violent behavior will result in positive outcomes (Crick & Dodge, 1996). The person may have learned that violence leads to good things for them.

These two functional subtypes are important to distinguish for a variety of reasons. First, the theoretical rationales for these types of aggression differ, as well as the motivations behind why aggression occurs. Second, the developmental backgrounds related to reactive and proactive aggression are thought to differ. Reactive aggression is related to unpredictable environments, harsh parenting styles, and abuse (Dodge, Lochman, Harnish, Bates, & Pettit, 1997). Proactive aggression, on the contrary, is more often seen in children with stable home environments and supportive parents (Poulin & Dishion, 2000).

Third, each functional type of aggression is differentially associated with various externalizing and internalizing problems. Proactive aggression is more likely to be related to externalizing problems, such as delinquency, while reactive aggression tends to be associated with internalizing difficulties like depression and anxiety (Brendgen, Vitaro, Tremblay, & Lavoie, 2001; Card & Little, 2006; Fite, Raine, Stouthamer-Loeber, Loeber, & Pardini, 2010; Scarpa, Haden, & Tanaka, 2010). For example, Vitaro, Gendreau, Tremblay, and Oligny (1998) examined both functional types of aggression in 12-year-old boys from low socioeconomic backgrounds. They found that proactive aggression predicted greater conduct problems and oppositional behaviors at age 15. Further, reactive aggression actually lessened the relationship between proactive aggression and delinquent behaviors. Other studies have found similar findings (e.g., Fite et al., 2010), suggesting that proactive aggression is related to more disruptive behavior problems.

Finally, the biological profiles of the functional types of aggression may be different. Proactive aggression tends to be related to baseline biological arousal levels, while reactive aggression is more closely tied to biological reactivity

(Hubbard et al., 2002; Scarpa et al., 2010; Scarpa, Tanaka, & Haden, 2008). Specifically, those high in proactive aggressive behaviors tend to have low baseline arousal and very little physiological changes during provocation. Those with higher reactive aggressive behaviors usually have increased physiological arousal at baseline and more extreme changes during provocation.

Evidence for these biological differences in proactive and reactive aggressive has been found through a number of studies. In one, higher cortisol reactivity was linked to reactive, but not proactive, aggression (Lopez-Duran, Olson, Hajal, Felt, & Vazquez, 2009). Cortisol is known as a stress hormone, and greater reactivity reflects heightened arousal. In one of the only brain studies to look at the distinctions between functional aggression subtypes, murderers were classified as reactive or proactive killers based upon the murder for which they were charged (Raine, Meloy, et al., 1998). The reactive murderers (e.g., crimes of passion) tended to have lower left and right prefrontal functioning and greater right hemisphere subcortical limbic activity compared to noncriminal controls. The proactive murderers (e.g., serial killers), conversely, had prefrontal activation that was extremely similar to controls. Yet, the proactive murderers also had heightened right subcortical limbic activity, just like the reactive murderers. This subcortical limbic region is believed to shape emotions and aggression. The researchers suggested that both functional types of murderers were predisposed to aggression through greater activation in the subcortical limbic areas; proactive murderers, however, had the prefrontal regulatory capacity to engage in aggression in more controlled ways. More research is needed to fully understand differences between these functional types of aggression.

Biosocial Perspective and Proactive Aggression

Despite evidence suggesting that there are two main functional types of aggression, and substantial support for the biosocial model of violence perpetration, there is a dearth of studies that have examined these empirical areas conjointly. This prevents important questions from being answered when researchers fail to examine functional subtypes or fail to consider the interaction of biological and social influences. Below, we highlight some of the studies that have examined proactive aggression using a biosocial framework.

Only a few studies have examined genetic and social influences related to proactive aggression. This is in spite of a critique on the lack of research in this area (DiLalla, 2002). In one study, genetic effects accounted for 41% of the variance of proactive aggression in 6-year-olds twins (Brendgen, Vitaro, Boivin, Dionne, & Perusse, 2006), while environmental effects accounted for the remaining variance. In another study, proactive and reactive aggression were examined in a sample of twins and triplets between the ages of 9 and 10

(Baker, Raine, Liu, & Jacobson, 2008). In boys, proactive aggression had a heritability estimate of 50% while reactive aggression had a heritability estimate of 38%. The researchers proposed that reactive aggression may be largely due to environmental influences, while proactive aggression may be related more to genetic influences.

The underarousal theory can inform our study of proactive aggression based on the biosocial perspective. Scarpa and colleagues (2008) examined how community violence (i.e., a social risk) might interact with the biological variable of heart rate to predict different kinds of aggression. Community violence victimization was positively related to proactive aggression, but only when children had low resting heart rates. Community violence exposure was related to less proactive aggression when children had high resting heart rates. Most importantly, no main effects were found between community violence exposure and resting cardiac measures, suggesting that the interaction between biological and social factors was related to aggression, not either of these factors alone.

In another study, Murray-Close and Rellini (2012) examined women with and without a history of sexual abuse (i.e., a social risk). Proactive and reactive relational aggression were measured along with heart rate reactivity during a social stress task. Analyses demonstrated that blunted heart rate reactivity was related to proactive relational aggression in women with a history of sexual abuse, but not in women without a history of abuse. Women with a history of abuse and high heart rate activity were less likely to engage in proactive aggression, suggesting heart rate may serve to protect those with a social risk.

Wilson and Scarpa (2014) examined the role of resting heart rate and sensation seeking in predicting proactive aggression. Sensation seeking is a social risk factor that is related to engaging in stimulating activities in order to increase arousal. Direct effects showed that in college students, sensation seeking was positively associated with proactive aggression, while resting heart rate was not significant. However, once the interaction between heart rate and sensation seeking was entered, only the interaction was significant. Low resting heart rate was associated with greater proactive aggression, but only in those with low sensation seeking. Thus, this study supported the social push theory.

Some studies show how biological, social, and aggressive variables shift across time. In a longitudinal study of twins, Tuvblad, Raine, Zheng, and Baker (2009) examined twin pairs at ages 9 and 10. Twins were followed up again a few years later. Reactive and proactive aggression were measured at each time point. At ages 9–10, shared environment explained approximately 25% of the variance for both forms of aggression, while heritability explained 26% of the variance in reactive aggression and 32% of the variance in proactive aggression. At ages 11–14, heritability explained approximately 50% of the variance for both forms of aggression (Baker et al., 2008), while shared environment explained 15% of the variance in reactive aggression and 8% of the variance in proactive aggression. This suggests that the social and environmental influences reduced over time, while biological components were more persistent. Interestingly, reactive aggression decreased across time, but there were no significant changes in proactive aggression.

Other studies, however, do not support the biosocial theory and its relation to proactive aggression. Crozier and colleagues (2008) examined interactions between social processing, cardiac activity, and different forms of aggression in teenagers. They found no differences in resting heart rate based on the functional types of aggression. Portnoy and Farrington (2015) completed a meta-analysis examining resting heart rate and aggression. They found that the functional type of aggression did not moderate the resting heart rate and antisocial behavior relationship. They noted that very few studies examined the two functional types of aggression separately. Further, they did not examine a biosocial model.

Proactive and reactive aggression seem to be related to different physiological factors. For example, proactive aggression seems to be more related to genetic influences (Baker et al., 2008; Brendgen et al., 2006) and some studies find evidence of heart rate differences between the functional types (Murray-Close & Rellini, 2012; Scarpa et al., 2008). While there are mixed findings related to cardiac activity (Crozier et al., 2008; Portnoy & Farrington, 2015), these results may be due to methodological differences. More work is needed to understand the ways biology and social variables interact to predict proactive aggression.

Mass Shooters and Proactive Aggression: A Biosocial Framework

Can the biosocial theory be applied in explaining mass shootings? It is difficult to discuss explanations for the violence seen during mass shootings because little is known about mass shooters (Bjelopera, Bagalman, Caldwell, Finklea, & McCallion, 2013) and no known studies have examined a biosocial model in this population. We know that mass shooters are almost always male, and this may relate to gender differences observed in the functional subtypes of aggression (Baker et al., 2008; Tuvblad et al., 2009). However, beyond gender, little is known. Part of the difficulty arises because the perpetrators often commit suicide or are killed by police (Declercq & Audenaert, 2011; Mullen, 2004). Nevertheless, it is important to demonstrate how this model may be applied to mass shooters because it may inform future prevention and intervention work. Further, biological and social variables have already been utilized in court cases following crimes, and as discussed previously in this chapter, we know this theory is fairly informative in predicting certain kinds of violence (Feigenson, 2006).

The distinction between proactive and reactive aggression is relevant when discussing mass shootings, as the perpetrators generally engage in proactive aggression and lack emotion (Langman, 2009a; Meloy, 1997). Nonetheless, emotional turmoil usually does occur in the perpetrator; in fact, mass shooters typically experience frustration and feel provoked in some form, whether real or imagined, before the shootings happened (Declercq & Audenaert, 2011; Karpf & Karpf, 1994; Meloy, 1997). For example, one of the perpetrators in the Columbine shootings on April 20, 1999 (Cullen, 2009; Langman, 2009b), the perpetrator of the Luby's shooting on October 16, 1991 (Karpf & Karpf, 1994), and the perpetrator of the Virginia Tech shootings on April 16, 2007 (Langman, 2009b) were all described as having extreme emotional disturbances leading up to the shooting.

The mass shooting events themselves, however, are usually carefully thought out and deliberate in nature (Langman, 2009a). That is, there is usually a great amount of forethought, planning, and practice. The Columbine perpetrators planned their attacks for months and had even developed several stages for their murders (Cullen, 2009). During the Luby's shooting, the perpetrator displayed extreme emotions (e.g., shouting) when he first began his killing spree, but then became methodological and precise in his mannerisms (e.g., shooting people in the head, allowing others to live; Karpf & Karpf, 1994). These incidents were purposeful and controlled and the perpetrators often lacked emotion as the acts were committed.

This same pattern of unemotionality and deliberate forethought can be seen in several case studies of mass shooters. Meloy (1997), for example, noted a case where the perpetrator killed three people, including his estranged wife, and wounded several others on April 30, 1995. The perpetrator had previously purchased a rifle and seemed polite to others before the shooting occurred. During the actual shooting, eyewitnesses stated that the perpetrator "walked with a look of confidence like he has accomplished what he had come to do" and seemed to "not look scared or startled" (p. 327), suggesting low arousal levels and controlled emotions in the moment. Further, the perpetrator was seen surveying the parking lot prior to the incident by parking his vehicle at the highest point, and later returned to this same location during the actual shooting in order to have a clearer view of his targets. The perpetrator purchased several guns of various calibers, using the lower caliber on unarmed victims and using the high-powered assault weapons on police officers. Further, the perpetrator had taken the time to shave his head and put on a specific outfit. These descriptions very much portray someone engaged in premeditated acts of violence.

In another case study which utilized official court records and a clinical assessment, the perpetrator shot five individuals in their home (Declercq & Audenaert, 2011). While the perpetrator was frustrated and isolated at some points, the shootings were very carefully planned and executed. For example, the perpetrator had a passive accomplice, practiced shooting, and tried to develop a way to catch empty shells. Further, the shooting was made to look like a robbery, rather than a targeted shooting.

Based on the profiles noted above, it seems that mass shootings are typically characterized by proactive aggression. However, interactions of biological and social risk factors have not been studied in these profiles. In the case study by Meloy (1997), some social variables were clearly noted. For example, the perpetrator and his wife had separated, his wife was engaged in an affair, a restraining order was placed against the perpetrator, and the perpetrator no longer had custody of his son. All these factors suggest the man was coming from an unstable and broken home, which have been previously noted to exacerbate criminality in empirical studies by Raine and colleagues (1996). While biological factors could not be measured, Meloy (1997) compiled evidence from several witnesses that indicated the perpetrator seemed to have low levels of arousal and very controlled emotions while killing.

Social factors, such as employment or interpersonal loss, often precede mass shootings (Mullen, 2004); yet social risks do not always precede the event. For example, one of the perpetrators of the Columbine shootings was thought to come from an authoritarian home, while the other came from a more supportive home (Cullen, 2009). Still, there may have been additional internal social risk factors, such as depression or psychopathic tendencies. Again, these alone are not enough to predict who will become mass shooters.

Based upon the aforementioned research on biological risks for aggression and violence, it is important to consider that biology also may play a role in mass shooting incidents. The perpetrator in the University of Texas at Austin shootings on August 1, 1966 was found to have a "glioblastoma multiforme" (Governor's Committee, 1966, p. 7) on the right temporo-occipital lobe, which may have contributed to his behavior. Further, it was reported that he also experienced a great deal of personal stress, including having his parents separate, prior to the shootings. Could the combined influences of these risk factors have compelled this individual to commit mass murder? We will never know, but it does raise a number of possibilities that should be considered.

As mentioned, no known studies have examined a biosocial framework to predict mass shootings. However, there are many reports detailing psychosocial factors after mass shooting incidents. We suggest here that biological factors and the interactions between variables also should be considered in these profiles. Not only could this help us in understanding why the mass shooting occurred, but it could also help predict future risks for mass shooting. Mass shooters may have a very different profile compared to other criminals, including other types of murderers. For example, we know that certain personality types are related to different biological profiles and susceptibility to aggression (Lorber, 2004).

Based upon the biosocial theory, we urge that researchers incorporate as many social and biological variables as possible in their studies of violence and mass shootings. Gordis and colleagues (2010), for example, found that the interaction between maltreatment history and physiology in predicting aggression risk differed between boys and girls. The biosocial framework can help us understand how and why people aggress by examining interactions between variables. The implication is that important information on mass shootings can be gained if researchers expand their current research and incorporate a biosocial framework that also includes various functions of aggression, particularly proactive aggression.

Implications

In sum, there is now a large body of evidence supporting a biosocial framework for violence, including the social push theory that might explain why individuals from a less vulnerable social environment may engage in violence. Further, some researchers have incorporated a biosocial framework to examine proactive aggression, which is believed to be applicable to mass shooting incidents. In light of these findings, we offer some suggestions to help policy makers, researchers, and the public make informed decisions regarding the understanding of mass shooting.

Developmental prevention is one area that has particular promise based on biosocial theories (Rocque, Welsh, & Raine, 2012). This form of prevention involves interventions that target risk and protective factors in order to mitigate aggression, including proactive aggression. This could include both social and biological factors. Biosocial approaches have been touted as being one of the most effective approaches to violence prevention (Raine, 2002), with some arguing that "prevention approaches can potentially suppress genetic expression of risk factors by, for example, favorable family environment" (Fishbein, 2000, p. 101). It would be amazing to think that we may be able to intervene well before an incident occurs.

Given that individuals who are underaroused may be more likely to engage in proactive aggression due to discomfort, safe stimulating activities could be offered to the individual to help mitigate their increased risk for aggression. Individuals could also be taught to select safer, yet arousing activities. This might take the form of afterschool programming or athletics. These programs may be doubly (should we even say multiplicatively) beneficial. Such afterschool programming may also provide a buffer against the social risk while at the same time providing the biological changes needed in those at risk for underarousal. For example, afterschool programs could provide "economically disadvantaged children with cognitively stimulating and enriching experiences that their parents are unlikely to provide at home" (Duncan & Magnuson, 2004, p. 105).

While Duncan and Magnuson (2004) focused specifically on engagement that was cognitively arousing, the same rationale could be applied to biologically arousing activities.

Parenting programs also offer some promise in preventing criminal activity, which could include mass shootings. For example, the Nurse-Family Partnership program involved different groups, with one group of parents receiving nurse visits during pregnancy only, one group receiving nurse visits during pregnancy and the first 2 years of life, and one group with no nurse visits at all (Olds, Henderson, Chamberlin, & Tatelbaum, 1986; Olds et al., 1998). Caregivers who received postnatal nurse visits had significantly lower reports of engaging in child abuse. This was especially true for mothers who were poorer, unmarried, or teenagers. The nurses informed the mothers about pre- and postnatal care, development, and nutrition (i.e., a biological variable). When children were followed up as teenagers, those who had mothers in the treatment condition had committed fewer violent and criminal offenses. Considering what we know about the biosocial model, including the bidirectional influences of social factors on biology, this particular program likely influenced all factors from the model to temper hostility.

Another highly encouraging experimental study involved comparing 3-year-old children in a 2-year enrichment nursery school intervention to 3-year-olds in a control group (Raine et al., 2001). The enrichment program involved cognitive enhancement, nutrition and hygiene management, field trips, medical aid, social-emotional development, home visits, remedial components, parental involvement, and transitional help. Skin conductance and electroencephalogram (EEG) reactivity were measured in response to various stimuli, such as an orienting tone, speech and a neuropsychological test, at age 3 and then again at age 11. Those in the enrichment program showed, when compared to the control group, increased skin conductance amplitudes, quicker skin conductance rise and recovery times, as well as slow-wave EEG at rest and during a neuropsychological test that assessed selective and sustained attention. This study demonstrated that early enrichment impacted long-term biological processes related to arousal and information processing.

Additionally, these programs do not have to be time-consuming to be effective. Conrod, Castellanos-Ryan, and Strang (2010) examined the effectiveness of a coping skills program in teenagers with higher levels of impulsive or sensation-seeking behaviors. Those in the intervention group had two 90-minute sessions where problem-solving and cognitive behavioral therapy techniques were taught. Those who received the intervention were less likely to try drugs and used fewer drugs 2 years later.

The knowledge we have about differences based on functional aggression subtypes may also prove helpful. In younger individuals, both functional subtypes of aggression seem to be more related to social and environmental influences (Tuvblad et al., 2009). At this age, prevention could focus more on social variables with a particular emphasis on reactive aggression. As people age, parental styles may need to change and parents need to be aware that proactive aggression increases with age. More permissive parenting is linked to more proactive aggression, as parents are not modeling appropriate behavior or demonstrating consistent consequences in response to inappropriate behavior (Brendgen et al., 2001). By being more mindful of this change in functional aggression types, others could help model appropriate behavior as a way to mitigate violence risk. Additionally, prior research has demonstrated changes in reactive and proactive aggression across time. Early identification of those who are more reactive may help prevent these individuals from becoming proactively aggressive later.

Of course, as there are those that disagree with the biosocial model, there are also those who disagree with biological treatments. Raine (2013) highlights some of these controversies. Some fear that biology may be exploited and that people identified as being at risk for violent perpetration may be unfairly treated or even stigmatized. For example, a child may come from an affluent family and have low resting heart rate. Should we do something in order to prevent the possibility of proactive aggression? If we identify somebody that already has high rates of proactive aggression, should work be done to examine biological indices? Clearly, there are a lot of individuals who may have risk factors, but most will not engage in extreme violence, such as a mass shooting.

Although we currently do not, and likely will never, have a full understanding of the biological or social influences that contribute to mass shootings, prior research and existing theories certainly can inform us. As presented in this chapter, the distinction between nature and nurture is artificial. Biology does not exist without social factors influencing it; and social factors do not exist without biology influencing them. An understanding of the individual and behavior cannot be limited to expectations based on one factor or another. More work is needed to examine multiple biological and social factors to help understand mass violence.

Conclusions

Biosocial perspectives of mass shooting perpetration offer potentially useful findings in regard to the identification of those at risk of mass murder. In particular, we need to consider the interaction effects. Biologically based researchers could do a better job of examining the social factors at play; concurrently, social scientists would be remiss for ignoring the role of possible biological determinants. Moreover, aggression researchers are urged to recognize and take into account the functional subtypes of aggression and their biosocial origins.

Will these theories be able to detect every person at risk of committing a mass shooting? Of course not. However, biosocial models may help to identify those most at risk, whether through social, biological, or some interaction of these variables. This identification of multiple risks could lead to a better understanding of what prompts proactive aggression, and perhaps could lead to better mechanisms of pinpointing those most in danger of engaging in mass shootings. Intervention programs could then be implemented that specifically address the needs of these individuals and may help to mitigate the social and biological risk factors. By combining efforts across the various empirical foci, we will ideally have a better understanding of why individuals become mass shooting perpetrators and may be able to better intervene.

References

Baker, L. A., Raine, A., Liu, J., & Jacobson, K. C. (2008). Differential genetic and environmental influences on reactive and proactive aggression in children. *Journal of Abnormal Child Psychology, 36,* 1265–1278. doi:10.1007/s10802-008-9249-1.

Bandura, A. (1973). *Aggression: A social learning analysis.* Englewood Cliffs, NJ: Prentice-Hall.

Bjelopera, J. P., Bagalman, E., Caldwell, S. W., Finklea, K. M., & McCallion, G. (2013). Public mass shootings in the United States: Selected implications for federal public health and safety policy. Washington, DC: Congressional Research Service.

Brendgen, M., Vitaro, F., Boivin, M., Dionne, G., & Perusse, D. (2006). Examining genetic and environmental effects on reactive versus proactive aggression. *Development Psychology, 42,* 1299–1312.

Brendgen, M., Vitaro, F., Tremblay, R. E., & Lavoie, F. (2001). Reactive and proactive aggression: Predictions to physical violence in different contexts and moderating effects of parental monitoring and caregiving behavior. *Journal of Abnormal Child Psychology, 29,* 293–304.

Brennan, P. A., Raine, A., Schlusinger, F., Kirkegaard-Sorenson, L., Knop, J., Hutchings, B., … Mednick, S. A. (1997). Psychophysiological protective factors for male subjects at high risk for criminal behavior. *American Journal of Psychiatry, 154,* 853–855.

Card, N. A., & Little, T. D. (2006). Proactive and reactive aggression in childhood and adolescence: A meta-analysis of differential relations with psychosocial adjustment. *International Journal of Behavioral Development, 30,* 466–480.

Collins, R. (2009). *Violence: A micro-sociological theory.* Princeton, NJ: Princeton University Press.

Conrod, P. J., Castellanos-Ryan, N., & Strang, J. (2010). Brief, personality-targeted coping skills interventions and survival as a non-drug user over a 2-year period during adolescence. *Archives of General Psychiatry, 67,* 85–93.

Crick, N. R., & Dodge, K. A. (1996). Social information-processing mechanisms in reactive andproactive aggression. *Child Development, 67,* 993–1002.

Crozier, J. C., Dodge, K. A., Fontaine, R. D., Lansford, J. E., Bates, J. E., Petit, G. S., & Levenson, R. W. (2008). Social information processing and cardiac predictors of adolescent antisocial behavior. *Journal of Abnormal Psychology, 117,* 253–267. doi:10.1037/0021-843X.117.2.253

Cullen, D. (2009). *Columbine.* New York, NY: Twelve.

Declercq, F., & Audenaert, H. (2011). A case of mass murder: Personality disorder, psychopathology and violence mode. *Aggression and Violent Behavior, 16,* 135–143.

DiLalla, L. F. (2002). Behavior genetics of aggression in children: Review and future directions. *Developmental Review, 22,* 593–622.

Dodge, K. A., Lochman, J. E., Harnish, J. D., Bates, J. E., & Pettit, G. S. (1997). Reactive and proactive aggression in school children and psychiatrically impaired chronically assaultive youth. *Journal of Abnormal Psychology, 106,* 37–51.

Duncan, G. J., & Magnuson, K. (2004). Individual and parent-based intervention strategies for promoting human capital and positive behavior. In P. Lindsay Chase-Lansdale, K. Kiernan, & R. J. Friedman (Eds.), *Human development across lives and generations: The potential for change* (pp. 93–135). New York, NY: Cambridge University Press.

El-Sheikh, M. (2005). Does poor vagal tone exacerbate child maladjustment in the context of parental problem drinking? A longitudinal examination. *Journal of Abnormal Psychology, 114,* 735–741. doi:10.1037/0021-843X.114.4.735.

Eysenck, H. J. (1997). Personality and the biosocial model of antisocial and criminal behavior. In A. Raine, P. Brennan, D. P. Farrington, & S. A. Mednick (Eds.), *Biosocial bases of violence* (pp. 21–38). New York, NY: Plenum.

Feigenson, N. (2006). Brain imaging and courtroom evidence: On the admissibility and persuasiveness of fMRI. *International Journal of Law in Context, 2,* 233–255.

Fishbein, D. (2000). The importance of neurobiological research to the prevention of psychopathology. *Prevention Science, 1,* 89–106.

Fite, P. J., Raine, A., Stouthamer-Loeber, M., Loeber, R., & Pardini, D. A. (2010). Reactive and proactive aggression in adolescent males: Examining differential outcomes 10 years later in early adulthood. *Criminal Justice and Behavior, 37,* 141–157.

Gabbidon, S. L. (2007). *Criminological perspectives on race and crime.* New York, NY: Routledge.

Gordis, E. B., Feres, N., Olezeski, C. L., Rabkin, A. N., & Trickett, P. K. (2010). Skin conductance reactivity and respiratory sinus arrhythmia among maltreated and comparison youth: Relations with aggressive behavior. *Journal of Pediatric Psychology, 35,* 547–558. doi:10.1093/jpepsy/jsp113

Governor's Committee and Invited Consultants. (1996). Report to the governor: Medical aspects Charles J. Whitman catastrophe.

Hubbard, J. A., Smithmyer, C. M., Ramsden, S. R., Parker, E. H., Flanagan, K. D., Dearing, K. F., … Simons R. F. (2002). Observational, physiological, and self-report measures of children's anger: Relations to reactive versus proactive aggression. *Child Development 73,* 1101–1118.

Karpf, J., & Karpf, E. (1994). *Anatomy of a massacre.* Waco, TX: WRS Publishing.

Langman, P. (2009a). Rampage school shooters: A typology. *Aggression and Violent Behavior, 14,* 79–86. doi:10.1016/j.avb.2008.10.003

Langman, P. F. (2009b). *Why kids kill: Inside the minds of school shooters.* New York, NY: Palgrave Macmillan

Lombroso, C. (1876). Edition I. In M. Gibson & N. H. Rafter (Trans.), *Criminal minds.* Durham, NC: Duke University Press.

Lopez-Duran, N. L., Olson, S. L., Hajal, N. J., Felt, B. T., & Vazquez, D. M. (2009). Hypothalamic pituitary adrenal axis functioning in reactive and proactive aggression in children. *Journal of Abnormal Child Psychology, 37,* 169–182.

Lorber, M. F. (2004). Psychophysiology of aggression, psychopathy, and conduct problems: A meta-analysis. *Psychological Bulletin, 130,* 531–552.

Meloy, J. R. (1997). Predatory violence during mass murder. *Journal of Forensic Science, 42,* 326–329.

Moffitt, T. E., Caspi, A., Fawcett, J. W., Brammer, G. L., Raleigh, M., Yuwiler, A., & Silva, P. A. (1997). Whole blood serotonin and family background relate to male violence. In A. Raine, P. A. Brennan, D. P. Farrington, & S. A. Mednick (Eds.), *Biosocial bases of violence* (pp. 231–249). New York, NY: Plenum Press.

Moyer, K. (1976). *The psychobiology of aggression.* New York, NY: Harper & Row.

Mullen, P. E. (2004). The autogenic (self-generated) massacre. *Behavioral Sciences & the Law, 22,* 311–323.

Murray-Close, D., & Rellini, A. H. (2012). Cardiovascular reactivity and proactive and reactive relational aggression among women with and without a history of sexual abuse. *Biological Psychology, 89,* 54–62.

Olds, D., Henderson, C. R., Chamberlin, R., & Tatelbaum, R. (1986). Preventing child abuse and neglect: A randomized trial of nurse home visitation. *Pediatrics, 78,* 65–78.

Olds, D., Henderson, C. R., Cole, R., Eckenrode, J., Kitzman, H., Luckey, D., ... Powers, J. (1998). Long-term effects of nurse home visitation on children's criminal and antisocial behavior: 15-year follow-up of a randomized controlled trial. *Journal of the American Medical Association, 280,* 1238–1244.

Ortiz, J., & Raine, A. (2004). Heart rate level and antisocial behavior in children and adolescents: A meta-analysis. *Journal of the American Academy of Child and Adolescent Psychiatry, 43,* 154–162.

Portnoy, J., & Farrington, D. P. (2015). Resting heart rate and antisocial behavior: An updated systematic review and meta-analysis. *Aggression and Violent Behavior, 22,* 33–45.

Poulin, F., & Dishion, T. J. (2000). The peer and family experiences of proactively and reactively aggressive pre-adolescents. Paper presented at the biennial meeting of the Society for Research on Adolescence, Chicago, IL.

Raine, A. (2002). Annotation: The role of prefrontal deficits, low autonomic arousal, and early health factors in the development of antisocial and aggressive behavior in children. *Journal of Child Psychology and Psychiatry, 43,* 417–434.

Raine, A. (2013). *The anatomy of violence: The biological roots of crime.* New York, NY: Pantheon Books.

Raine, A., Brennan, D., Farrington, D., & Mednick, S. (1997). *Biosocial bases of violence.* New York, NY: Plenum.

Raine, A., Brennan, O., Mednick, B., & Mednick, S. A. (1996). High rates of violence, crime, academic problems, and behavioral problems in males with both early neuromotor deficits and unstable family environments. *Archives of General Psychiatry, 53,* 544–549.

Raine, A., Buchsbaum, M., & LaCasse, L. (1997). Brain abnormalities in murderers indicated by positron emission tomography. *Biological Psychiatry, 42,* 495–508.

Raine, A., Dodge, K. A., Loeber, R., Gatzke-Kopp, L., Lynam, D., Reynolds, C.,…. Liu, J. (2006). The reactive-proactive aggression questionnaire: Differential correlates of reactive and proactive aggression in adolescent boys. *Aggressive Behavior, 32,* 159–171.

Raine, A., Meloy, J. R., Bihrle, S., Stoddard, J., LaCasse, L., & Buchsbaum, M. S. (1998). Reduced prefrontal and increased subcortical brain functioning assessed using positron emission tomography in predatory and affective murderers. *Behavioral Sciences and the Law, 16,* 319–332.

Raine, A., Stoddard, J., Bihrle, S., & Buchsbaum, M. (1998). Prefrontal glucose deficits in murderers lacking psychosocial deprivation. *Neuropsychiatry, Neutropsychology, & Behavioral Neurology, 11,* 1–7.

Raine, A., & Venables, P. H. (1984). Tonic heart rate level, social class and antisocial behavior in adolescents. *Biological Psychology, 18,* 123–132.

Raine, A., Venables, P. H., Dalais, C., Mellingen, K., Reynolds, C., & Mednick, S. A. (2001). Early education and health enrichment at age 3–5 years is associated with increased autonomic and central nervous system arousal and orienting at age 11 years: Evidence from the Mauritius Child Health Project. *Psychophysiology, 38,* 254–266.

Raine, A., Venables, P. H., & Mednick, S. A. (1997). Low resting heart rate at age 3 years predisposes to aggression at age 11 years: Evidence from the Mauritius child health project. *Journal of the American Academy of Child and Adolescent Psychiatry, 36,* 1457–1464. doi:10.1097/00004583-199710000-00029

Raine, A., Venables, P. H., & Williams, M. (1995). High autonomic arousal and electrodermal orienting at age 15 years as protective factors against crime development at age 29 years. *American Journal of Psychiatry, 152,* 1595–1600.

Rocque, M., Welsh, B. C., & Raine, A. (2012). Biosocial criminology and modern crime prevention. *Journal of Criminal Justice, 40,* 306–312. doi:10.1016/j.jcrimjus.2012.05.003

Rowe, D. (2001). *Biology and crime.* Los Angeles, CA: Roxbury Press.

Rudo-Hutt, A., Gao, Y., Glenn, A., Peskin, M., Yang, Y., & Raine, A. (2011). *Biosocial interactions and correlates of crime.* Retrieved from http://repository.upenn.edu/neuroethics_pubs/90

Scarpa, A., Haden, S. C., & Tanaka, A. (2010). Being hot-tempered: Autonomic, emotional, and behavioral distinctions between childhood reactive and proactive aggression. *Biological Psychology, 84,* 488–496.

Scarpa, A., & Raine, A. (2007). Biosocial bases of violence. In D. J. Flannery, A. T. Vazsonyi, & I. Waldman (Eds.), *The Cambridge handbook of violent behavior* (pp. 447–462). Cambridge, UK: Cambridge University Press.

Scarpa, A., Tanaka, A., & Haden, S. C. (2008). Biosocial bases of reactive and proactive aggression: The roles of community violence exposure and heart rate. *Journal of Community Psychology, 36,* 969–988. doi:10.1002/jcop.20276

Siegel, L. J., & McCormick, C. (2006). *Criminology in Canada: Theories, patterns, and typologies* (3rd ed.). Toronto, Canada: Thompson.

Stadler, C., Grassmann, D., Fegert, J., Holtmann, M., Poustka, F., & Schmeck, K. (2008). Heart rate and treatment effect in children with disruptive behavior disorders. *Child Psychiatry and Human Development, 39*, 299–309, doi:10.1007/s10578-007-0089-y.

Tuvblad, C., Raine, A., Zheng, M., & Baker, L. A. (2009). Genetic and environmental stability differs in reactive and proactive aggression. *Aggressive Behavior, 35*, 437–452.

van den Berghe, P. L. (1974). Bringing the beast back in: Towards a biosocial theory of aggression. *American Sociological Review, 39*, 777–788.

Vitaro, F., Gendreau, P. L., Tremblay, R. E., & Oligny, P. (1998). Reactive and proactive aggression differentially predict later conduct problems. *Journal of Child Psychology and Psychiatry, 39*, 377–385.

Wadsworth, M. E. J. (1976). Delinquency, pulse rate and early emotional deprivation. *British Journal of Criminology, 16*, 245–256.

Walters, G., & White, T. (1989). Heredity and crime: Bad genes or bad research. *Criminology, 27*, 455–486.

Wilson, L. C., & Scarpa, A. (2014). Aggressive behavior: An alternative model of resting heart rate and sensation seeking. *Aggressive Behavior, 40*, 91–98. doi:10.1002/ab.21504

6

The Challenge of Predicting Dangerousness

Sara Chiara Haden

Controlling violence is a public health issue. Arguably each violent act impacts a lot of people – the perpetrator, survivor(s), family members, witnesses, and those who hear about it. Risk assessment, or predicting the likelihood that someone will become violent, is one of the most controversial topics within the intersection of behavioral science and the law. Most mental health professionals in both inpatient and outpatient settings regularly perform acute risk assessments of their patients during intakes, diagnostic evaluations, treatment planning, and discharge. The implications of these predictions are significant and can impact risk aversion policies, sanctions for "dangerous" persons, as well as consequences for mental health professionals who make false negative errors. To predict an individual's dangerousness is a powerful ability. But, is it even possible to correctly identify these individuals?

Despite the significant implications of violence risk assessment for those individuals assessed, the predictor (i.e., clinician), and society at large, there are several barriers to its utility. Also, the literature on predicting dangerousness is vast, contradictory, and empirically limited. One can find nearly every form of literature from clinical anecdotes to program evaluation studies describing how violence risk assessments should be performed. Some researchers focus on empirically determined correlates of violence, while others stress less rigorous psychodynamic formulations. This presents a challenge for clinicians identifying the most relevant factors in a violence risk assessment. Unfortunately, there is no consensus about how to best assess dangerousness.

In this chapter, three primary challenges of violence risk assessment are highlighted. First, I review the definitions of violence and its relationship to dangerousness. Second, I review the evolution of violence risk assessment – describing the characteristics of violence risk assessment and the accuracy of these assessments. Third, I review the vast number of correlates we use to predict dangerousness. Every incident of a mass shooting is distinct and predicting the likelihood that someone will be dangerous is difficult. Yet, we may be able to

The Wiley Handbook of the Psychology of Mass Shootings, First Edition. Edited by Laura C. Wilson.
© 2017 John Wiley & Sons, Inc. Published 2017 by John Wiley & Sons, Inc.

apply existing theories and previous empirical work to improve our under-standing of who commits such horrific acts of violence.

Challenge #1: The Question of Dangerousness

One of the primary challenges related to predicting dangerousness is the question clinicians are asked to answer. The question is not and should not be "Is this person dangerous?" This is decided by a yes or no response. Rather, relative risk is assessed quite narrowly and the question might be rephrased "What is the relative likelihood that this person may commit a specific violent act within a specific time frame?" The answer to this question is not as simple – and considers the nature of the risk (i.e., high, medium, or low), a specified time frame, and the context (e.g., inpatient hospitalization, incarceration). Risk assessment also determines an individual's risk of harm to self or others. Violence prediction varies by context and it is important to appreciate that not all methods of risk assessment will address every question. For example, threat assessment in the workplace may ask an entirely different kind of question (Stock, 2007).

Early on, Shah (1975), the director of the Center for Studies of Crime and Delinquency at the National Institute of Mental Health, argued that the law should not ask mental health professionals to predict dangerousness because the dangerousness criteria contradicted a clinician's commitment to the welfare of people with mental illness. When a clinician is asked to predict violence, it also needs to be recognized that there are political consequences that might influence answering the question posed. In fact, clinicians are more inclined to classify someone as dangerous as there is no liability if a client predicted to be dangerous is later confined or released (Melton, Petrila, Poythress, & Slobogin, 1997). When the assessment of dangerousness became more widespread, Shah later went on to call for improvements in its prediction, emphasizing that a clinician's ability to predict future violence depended on a myriad of factors.

Despite the question that is asked when the issue of dangerousness is assessed, the process used can certainly lead to a yes/no response. In 2003, Virginia began requiring a named structure violent assessment tool with a cutoff score specified by law for Sexually Violent Predator (SVP) cases. This means that if someone is above the cutoff score, then the person is deemed violent. Popular tools include the Rapid Risk Assessment of Sexual Offender Recidivism (RRASOR; Hanson, 1997) and STATIC-99 (Hanson & Thornton, 2000). Both tests are actuarial, focus on static variables (discussed at length in the fol-lowing section), and provide a yes/no response to the question of dangerous-ness. Certainly, these assessment results are easy for the courts to understand and subsequently impose.

Dangerousness is a legal concept. Clinicians cannot measure it directly, but may be able to tap an outcome of it, such as the propensity for future violent behavior. Comments on dangerousness are offered and, in turn, affect our understanding of the term – "dangerousness to others," "dangerousness to self," "criminal act," "homicidal or suicidal," and so forth. Oftentimes, "danger" refers to physical harm to other persons. The American Psychiatric Association (1983) defines a dangerous person as "a person [who] is likely in the near future to cause physical injury or physical abuse to another person or substantial damage to another person's property" (p. 673). There is also no universally accepted definition of "violence." Does it always involve physical contact? Understandably, the lack of clear and consistent guidelines on what constitutes risk influences the clinician's task. In fact, there are no guidelines to turn to for definitions of dangerousness in case law (Monahan & Shah, 1989).

Challenge #2: The Evolution of Violence Prediction

It is important to appreciate that the process of assessing dangerousness is inherently different from other predictive tasks clinicians may be asked to do (Litwack, 2001). Individuals deemed to be at greater risk are often treated differently than those not. In fact, many of those individuals whose risk is assessed will never be released into the community (Melton et al., 1997), arguably limiting the ability to even evaluate the validity of those assessments.

Historically, risk assessments distinguished "actuarial" from "clinical" methods. Meehl (1954) initially characterized actuarial methods as systemized and resulting in a probability statement. These forms of assessments tend to use strict decision rules and cutoff scores – like the RRASOR and STATIC-99 described earlier. Clinical methods create hypotheses about future behavior and are less focused on a fixed defined probability statement. Typically this dichotomy has also been viewed as either involving a "structured" or "unstructured" process, underscoring the difference in the very nature of these methods. Moreover, these methods tend to rely on different types of risk factors – either "static" (i.e., variables that cannot change) or "dynamic" variables (i.e., those that can change). However, Monahan (2003) argued that this dichotomy is not useful because many actuarial methods do not ignore clinical judgment and even require clinical skill to administer. Rather, risk assessment may be viewed on a *continuum* from completely unstructured (e.g., purely clinical risk assessment) to completely structured (e.g., purely actuarial method). Both ends of the continuum and where they meet are reviewed, along with evidence of their disputed effectiveness.

The pure "clinical" end of the risk assessment continuum

Primarily clinical methods of risk assessment include either unstructured or structured clinical opinion. For both types, clinicians are presumably educated on and have experience in predicting violence. The risk factors of focus in such a method stem from one's prior clinical experience and theoretical orientation. They are combined to generate a professional, albeit subjective, judgment of an individual's likelihood of dangerousness. The hallmarks of the clinical method are that it relies on the clinician's expertise and measures the probability of risk for a specific individual. It is not driven by empirical work and there are no rules about what aspects of the individual are collected. While the structured clinical opinion approach is considered to be more uniform than unstructured clinical opinion, and predictions are deemed more accurate when one is more confident (Douglas & Ogloff, 2003), these primarily clinical forms of risk assessment lack validity, reliability, and accountability (Stock, 2007).

Unfortunately the unimpressive ability of clinicians to accurately predict dangerousness has been well-documented (e.g., Monahan, 1984; Otto, 1992), with error rates ranging from 44% to 85%. While we prefer not to admit that clinicians are vulnerable to the same cognitive pitfalls as our patients, dangerousness estimates are affected by our inherent cognitive biases (Krauss & Sales, 2001). The fundamental attribution error biases risk assessments when clinicians incorrectly perceive a patient's behavior as being due to traits rather than states – potentially even more so when clinicians have actually received more training in these assessments. This means that when a clinician is assessing a criminal's dangerousness, the very nature of the context (e.g., violent criminal in prison) affects the clinician's assessment of the person's capacity for future dangerous behavior. Certainly clinicians know that people who engage in a behavior are not always going to engage in it again and they can appreciate that many behaviors will only be expressed under certain conditions. Even mass murderers will not kill under any circumstance. Unfortunately, our own stereotypes of a dangerous individual can lead to inaccurate risk assessment decisions.

Clinical risk assessment also fails to consider base rates of violence when estimating an individual's risk of violence. Persistent acts of violence are actually committed by a small proportion of the offender population – 50% of crimes are committed by 5–6% of offenders (Farrington, Ohlin, & Wilson, 1986). Predicting a very low-frequency event (e.g., mass murder) is quite difficult and errors will be made (Yang, Wong, & Coid, 2010). As many scholars in the field point out (e.g., Monahan, 1984), the error rate of false positives will be high since many people are going to wrongly be deemed violent when a low frequency event is being predicted. Moreover, in the case of risk assessment of offenders who have committed violent crimes in the past, the saliency and recency effect of that previous violent act leads clinicians to readily select evidence that supports the likelihood that the individual will offend again and to more easily ignore evidence that disconfirms it (Melton et al., 1997). In light of these cognitive practices, practitioners are likely to overpredict violence when performing clinical assessments of risk (Monahan et al., 2001).

Therefore, for the above reasons, evidence consistently fails to support the effectiveness of purely clinical methods of violent risk assessment. However, one of the primary issues with this form of risk assessment may be our confusion regarding what "clinical judgment" actually constitutes. Westen and Weinberger (2004) argue that "clinical judgment" in violence risk assessment does not stop at clinicians' observations and inferences, but these observations and inferences can then be aggregated using a structured measure discussed in a later section. The opposite end of the risk assessment continuum is a purely nonclinical method.

The pure "actuarial" end of the risk assessment continuum

Actuarial methods of risk assessment were inspired by methods used by insurance agencies (Roffey & Kaliski, 2012). Such assessment tools are said to require no clinical expertise and the information that they rely on could be gleaned from a chart review of one's history. For example, the RRASOR (Hanson, 1997) is considered an empirically derived actuarial tool to assess adult male sex offenders' increased risk based on only four items – (1) offender's age less than 25 years, (2) presence of prior offenses, (3) victim(s) unrelated to the offender, and (4) presence of male victim(s). In fact, this particular measure has consistently discriminated between recidivists and nonrecidivists with effect sizes as high as 1.11 (i.e., using a sample of sex offenders with mental retardation as measured with criteria from the Diagnostic and Statistical Manual for Mental Disorder-IV (American Psychiatric Association, 2000; Harris & Tough, 2004). Risk factors in pure actuarial assessment are preselected, weighted, statistically determined, and the individual assessed is compared to a norm-based reference group. A number is provided that represents the number of characteristics the patient satisfies, which determines which group the individual is most representative of – either the dangerous or nondangerous group (Harris, Rice, & Quinsey, 1993). The process is transparent, discrete, and precise. However, the nuances that characterize the score are ignored and certainly do not address risk management issues. The heterogeneity within each group is not elaborated on for simplicity's sake. Therefore individuals in the "dangerous" group may be quite different from one another but the score does not tell us how these individuals are different.

In terms of their accuracy, empirical studies have overwhelmingly supported the actuarial/structured/static method over the clinical/unstructured/dynamic methods (e.g., Grove, Zald, Lebow, Snitz, & Nelson, 2000; Meehl, 1954). In fact, in their 1998 American Psychological Association publication, Quinsey, Harris, Rice, and Cormier (1998) argued for the full replacement of the clinical method with the actuarial method. In their book elaborating on the Violence Risk Appraisal Guide (VRAG; Harris et al., 1993) measure, they stated that actuarial measures are "too good and clinical judgment too poor to risk contaminating the former with the latter" (Quinsey et al., 1998, p. 171). They cautioned clinicians that, while ultimately it may make sense to adjust decisions based on actuarial methods, clinicians have taken advantage of the adjustments and overused clinical opinions when assessing dangerousness.

In fact, the support for pure actuarial methods is often noted to be impressive (see Gottfredson, 1987; Loza & Dhaliwal, 1997). In a meta-analysis of 118 prediction studies of risk assessment for sex offenders, actuarial measures (predicting sexual or violent recidivism) were superior to all other methods (Hanson & Morton-Bourgon, 2009). In the prediction of sexual recidivism, the median effect size of actuarial measures was 0.74 compared to 0.44 for unstructured professional judgments. For predicting violent recidivism the median effect size was 0.79 for actuarial methods and 0.30 for unstructured professional judgment. The accuracy of four actuarial instruments predicting violent recidivism in four samples of sex offenders was demonstrated with receiver operating characteristic (ROC) curve areas,[1] with a value of .84 for the VRAG (Harris et al., 2003), suggesting an extremely high predictive accuracy and a large effect size.

A recent "state of the art" assessment, multimodel actuarial risk assessment, uses the Iterative Classification Tree method which allows multiple diverse combinations of risk factors to characterize different groups – appreciating the different combinations of risk factors from different "models" (Banks et al., 2004). Based on the Classification Tree approach applied to data mining, group membership is predicted in classes of multiple variables. The software is still new but the prediction ability is considered to be superior as it evaluates several different models of violence simultaneously (Skeem et al., 2004). Unlike the original actuarial method, the multimodal actuarial method provides a number of discrete classifications to consider and may address the original concerns about the failure of actuarial approaches to appreciate the heterogeneity of individuals within group. It does not require any clinical judgment and involves multiple models of predicting dangerousness. Although initial findings seem encouraging, additional research on its effectiveness is necessary.

By its very definition, purely actuarial methods of violence risk assessment do not consider "clinical judgment." This leads to one of its most significant flaws – the failure to consider case-specific information. All that matters in the actuarial method is the individual's score on the predetermined risk factors. Thus someone is classified as dangerous even if the conditions under which the individual expresses dangerous behavior are quite unique. "Equations tend to be inflexible" (Melton et al., 1997, p. 284). Moreover, we cannot ignore the false positive error rates in these statistical approaches. Early on, Cocozza and Steadman (1974) reported a 66% false positive error rate with actuarial methods (of course this is compared to an 85% false positive error rate with purely clinical techniques). Even Melton et al. (1997) state that the research on the effectiveness of actuarial methods has not fully supported that these methods are indeed superior to clinical methods. In a review by Litwack (2001), he outlined arguments against Quinsey et al.'s (1998) position, stating numerous reasons why actuarial assessments of dangerous can never truly substitute clinical assessment.

The middle of the continuum

Guided clinical judgment, also referred to as adjusted actuarial assessment, constitutes the middle of the risk assessment continuum and includes structured professional judgment (SPJ), anamnestic approaches, and actuarial risk assessment. Each of these methods to some extent emphasizes both empirically validated risk factors and clinical inferences and observations (Hanson, 1998).

SPJ focuses on empirically derived behavior that is related to violence, including variables in one's history and current triggers (Guy, Packer, & Warnken, 2012). Assessments can be individualized and contextualized and the evaluator can apply discretion. It is also appreciated that an individual's score can change – one's risk of engaging in dangerous behavior is dynamic. Each variable is scored and equally considered in the final scoring of the individual's dangerousness. There is no discrete grouping of dangerous or nondangerous. The most well-researched measure of this kind is the Historical, Clinical, Risk Management-20 (HCR-20) (Webster, Eaves, Douglas, & Wintrup, 1995) which includes 20 risk factors in three domains: historical (e.g., previous violence, psychopathy), clinical (e.g., negative attitudes, active symptoms of a major mental illness), and risk management (e.g., treatment noncompliance, plans lack feasibility). The HCR-20 Version 2 has been empirically validated in a number of studies assessing violence risk (e.g., Bloom, Webster, Hucker, & De Freitas, 2005). In their meta-analysis, Yang and colleagues (2010) compared nine risk assessment tools in 28 independent studies from 1999 to 2008. They found that the HCR-20 Version 2 and the Offender Group Reconviction Scale (designed for use by probation officers; Copas & Marshall, 1998) had the largest effect sizes, although they did not believe that the difference between the HCR-20 and the other instruments was clinically significant. The HCR-20 Version 3 was recently developed and, among changes to the names of the risk factors and content of some of the items, one of the primary changes was that the item ratings was revised to be nominal (N = Not Present, P = Possibly or Partially Present, or Y = Present) compared to the former numeric classification for items. In a study of the HCR-20 Version 3 in 56 offenders and 50 civil psychiatric patients, Version 3 significantly predicted violence at 4 to 6 weeks and 6 to 8 months as did Version 2, suggesting that both versions accurately predicted future violence (Strub, Douglas, & Nicholls, 2014).

The anamnestic approach to risk assessment involves a detailed examination of an individual's violence history – applying behavior analytic strategies to each act of violence (Melton et al., 1997). The interview hinges on each violent event – questioning the preceding and subsequent thoughts, feelings, behaviors, the violent act itself, as well as any individuals involved and other relevant information. It is tailored to the individual and focuses on how the individual's past might influence the way in which they might behave in the future. If we assume that their behavior will be repeated, then relying on patterns of violence might inform under what conditions violence will be perpetrated. Heilbrun, Yasuhara, and Shah (2010) note how this approach can descriptively convey relevant risk factors that can be linked to an individual's intervention plan. Unfortunately this specific approach lacks research. Further, risk factors can be subject to change and are quite individualized in this context.

Actuarial-forensic risk assessment is an actuarial method that is adjusted based on contextual factors. While, to the author's knowledge it has hardly been a researched form of risk assessment, there is a need for this form of risk assessment. For example, Urbaniok et al. (2007) compared an actuarial model of recidivism in a sample of offenders who have been sanctioned (i.e., sanction sample) to a sample of violent or sexual offenders who have been sentenced (i.e., verdict sample) in Zurich, Switzerland. They found that risk factors for violence differed between the groups and none of the actuarial assessments considered the context. While both samples were more likely to recidivate if their victims were strangers, the verdict sample was more likely to if there was a history of alcohol/drug abuse and less likely to when there was a relationship with the victim. The sanction sample was more likely to recidivate if they lived in a foster home prior to age 15 and had Swiss citizenship but less likely to recidivate if delusional symptoms were present at the time of the offense or they were married. Unfortunately, while risk factors are clinically modified and there is an appreciation of the function of the risks in the particular context, a major weakness of this method is that it provides an idiosyncratic interpretation that is perhaps not generalizable. It is unclear if the multimodel actuarial risk assessment described previously might be able to consider contexts as the actuarial-forensic method might suggest.

Challenge #3: Correlates of Dangerousness

This final section will review the factors that have been empirically tested and related to dangerous behavior. As previously discussed, there has been an important distinction established between the nature of these variables. Static variables refer to factors that cannot change; they are fixed. Often these variables are in one's past (e.g., history of violations), a characteristic of a crime that was committed (e.g., male victim), or stable characteristics of the person (e.g., biological sex). Many of the strict actuarial risk assessment methods tend to rely on static variables. Dynamic variables refer to variables that can change. Of course, some may seemingly be stable (e.g., an antisocial attitude), while others are acute (e.g., access to gun). Also some of these dynamic variables may be assessed in a dynamic way (i.e., how missing a scheduled appointment is related to a history of violating release conditions; Conroy & Murrie, 2007). Those risk assessments that are in the middle of the continuum tend to consider both types of variables when predicting dangerousness. In fact, some researchers have eschewed the static/dynamic dichotomy and focused on dispositional, historical, and contextual factors (Melton et al., 1997) or, on the HCR-20 – historical, clinical, and risk management factors.

Empirically supported correlates of violence

Violence risk assessment must explicitly consider empirically supported risk and protective factors. Of course the nature of the assessment might limit one's access to these factors, but when one does have access to this information, failing to identify how these empirically supported variables predict dangerousness is perhaps unethical.

Table 6.1 includes a list of the replicated individual variables linked to future violence. The list is not meant to be exhaustive as there are a myriad of factors that predict violent behavior. Presently, there is no standard measure that includes all of these empirically supported correlates. The list is divided into five categories: (1) demographic, (2) clinical, (3) historical, (4) present person, and (5) present contextual.

Demographic factors While these variables, which are characteristics of the individual, may be the easiest to identify, the mechanisms explaining why they are related to violent behavior remain unclear. Some demographic factors (e.g., race, marital status, socioeconomic status) have been significantly related to violence but their empirical support is not as strong as it is for age and biological sex. Younger age has been repeatedly linked to violence propensity. There is also evidence that as individuals age they slowly disengage from violent behavior. In fact, the age-crime curve shows that the prevalence of offending increases from late childhood, peaks during 15 to 19 years of age, and then declines starting in the early twenties (Farrington, 1986). Notably, the younger the person is, the more time the person has to commit a violent act (Harris et al., 1993).

Male sex has also been consistently related to increased dangerousness. Of course most of the research on risk assessment has been conducted exclusively with male populations. Some studies that have reviewed sex differences in risk factors like antisocial personality disorder (ASPD) and psychopathy have found that both are more frequent in males than females (Cale & Lilienfeld, 2002). Certainly the population of male offenders is 14 times that of female offenders (Guerino, Harrison, & Sabol, 2011). However, there still needs to be more work on sex differences in dangerousness.

Table 6.1 Empirically supported correlates of violence.

Demographic factors	
Younger age	Farrington (1986); Harris et al. (1993)
Sex (men)	Cale and Lilienfeld (2002); Guerino et al. (2011)
Clinical factors	
Psychopathy	Douglas et al. (2006)
Past/current substance abuse	Dowden and Brown (2002); Swanson et al. (1990)
Antisocial personality disorder	Bonta et al. (1998); Robins (1993)
Historical factors	
Supervision violation/poor treatment compliance	Bonta et al. (1996)
Past history of violent behavior	Bonta et al. (1998)
Arrest history/juvenile delinquency	Wolfgang et al. (1972)
Present person factors	
Anger	Caspi et al. (1994); Knight and Prentky (1990); Novaco (1994)
Impulsiveness	Monahan et al. (2001)
Negative affect	Douglas and Skeem (2005)
Antisocial attitudes	Gendreau et al. (1997); Mills, Kroner, and Hemmati (2004)
Present contextual factors	
Neighborhood	Monahan et al. (2001)
Social support	Webster et al. (1995)
Weapon availability	Berkowitz and LePage (1967)
Victim availability	Felson and Steadman (1983)

Clinical factors This group of correlates includes variables that are typically assessed by clinicians. The research on the link between major psychosis and violence, while often mentioned, is still unclear and therefore not included in Table 6.1. Some studies have found that the risk of violence is indeed higher among people diagnosed with a psychiatric disorder who are experiencing active psychotic symptoms (e.g., Swanson, Holzer, Ganju, & Jono, 1990); other research has reported that such symptoms can be linked to lower levels of violence (e.g., Estroff & Zimmer, 1994). It has been argued that the link between mental illness and violence may be based on an illusory correlation (i.e., perceiving a relationship between the two even when no relationship exists; Walters, 1992).

Psychopathy refers to the construct defined by Robert Hare and colleagues on the Psychopathy Checklist – Revised (PCL-R; Hare, 2003), consisting of interpersonal/affective personality traits and socially deviant behavior. It has reliably been related to violent recidivism (see Douglas, Vincent, & Edens,

2006 for a review). Notably it is also a factor considered on many risk assessment instruments (e.g., VRAG, HCR-20, and ICT). In the manual, Hare (2003) states that the PCL-R requires considerable "clinical judgment."

Substance abuse (past and present) is another factor positively related to dangerousness. Dowden and Brown (2002) reported that drug and alcohol abuse were consistently linked to recidivism. In fact, Swanson and colleagues (1990) reported that substance abuse also strengthened the relationship between mental disorder and criminal behavior. Substances affect inhibition and may contribute to poor self-regulation and a greater propensity to act when feeling triggered by a situation.

ASPD is also considered to predict dangerousness (Bonta, Law, & Hanson, 1998) and is part of the criteria that are embedded in the PCL-R. Some studies have found that ASPD explains the link between major psychoses and criminal behavior (Robins, 1993). By its very definition (American Psychiatric Association, 2013), someone who meets criteria for ASPD is more likely to engage in reckless behavior that harms others.

Historical factors These variables are typically the focus of strict actuarial measures – static characteristics stemming from a person's past behaviors. Supervision violation and poor treatment compliance are related to the failure to comply with prescribed conditions and include not following treatment guidelines, escaping from custody, or violating any probationary requirements. This factor has been related to violent recidivism (Bonta, Harman, Hann, & Cormier, 1996). Many violence risk assessment tools consider this factor, including the VRAG and HCR-20.

A past history of violent behavior is considered in nearly all violence risk assessment – even unstructured interviews. It has been firmly established as one of the strongest risk factors in numerous studies (see Bonta et al., 1998) and is also included in most actuarial assessment measures. The amnestic approach to risk assessment focuses on processing each violent incident from an individual's past. Of course, the context of past violence must be considered when it is used to predict dangerousness.

Arrest history and juvenile delinquency are inevitably related to one's past history of violence and younger age variables as well. There is also evidence that as the number of arrests increases, rearrest is nearly inevitable (e.g., 80% chance of rearrest with four or more arrests; Wolfgang, Figlio, & Sellin, 1972).

Present person factors This group of variables taps features of the person and involves current states. For most of these variables, valid and reliable methods of measurement exist. Anger is a variable in several violence risk assessment measures and has been well supported in the empirical literature and linked to violent behavior among offenders (e.g., Caspi et al., 1994) and psychiatric patients (Novaco, 1994). In fact, research with sex offenders demonstrated that rapists reported experiencing anger immediately prior to the commission of rape (Knight & Prentky, 1990). Interestingly, anger did not differentiate between violent and nonviolent recidivism in a sample of incarcerated male offenders (Loza & Loza-Fanous, 1999). Perhaps the method of assessing anger is inadequate when trying to reliably predict violent behavior.

Impulsivity speaks to self-regulation deficits and, depending on how it is measured, may be classified as a trait rather than a state. Certainly impulsivity involves a cognitive component – in fact the nonplanning dimension of impulsivity has been identified as a risk factor (Monahan et al., 2001). It is also considered in many of the risk assessment measures and other risk factors (e.g., ASPD, psychopathy). Traditionally, individuals who perceive an event as confrontational may respond without thinking – albeit violently – if they have difficulties inhibiting their responses. The individual lacks control over their feelings, behaviors, and thoughts. Impulsive aggression (versus premeditated aggression) is typically related to greater destruction.

Negative affect includes anger but is more generally applied to aversive mood states beyond anger, including sadness, disgust, fear, guilt, nervousness, contempt, and so forth (Watson, Clark, & Tellegen, 1988). Negative affect can be associated with greater impulsivity and substance use, as well as increased problems with one's social networks. Douglas and Skeem (2005) reported that negative affect (among other variables) is a critical dynamic variable that predicts violent behavior.

Antisocial attitudes are procriminal beliefs that support risk-taking behaviors. In their meta-analysis, Gendreau, Grant, Leipciger, and Collins (1979) found that antisocial attitude has the strongest link to criminal conduct – as well as prison misconduct (Gendreau, Goggin, & Law, 1997). Borne out of this literature, the Measure of Criminal Attitudes and Associates (MCAA; Mills, Kroner, & Forth, 2002) was developed to assess antisocial behavior and when given to incarcerated males significantly predicted violent recidivism (Mills, Kroner, & Hemmati, 2004).

Present contextual factors This group of variables involves characteristics of an individual's current environment. One's neighborhood can be a powerful predictor of violent behavior – generally studied in relation to the discharge of patients from mental health facilities. The MacArthur Study (Monahan et al., 2001) showed that individuals who resided in neighborhoods with increased poverty had the highest violence risk. Indeed, there are areas where violence is more common.

The impact of social support on violence risk depends on the nature of the support as well as the individual's perception of it. Individuals who have a social network that supports criminal attitudes and behaviors display greater violent behavior. Many risk assessment measures consider whether or not the individual has a social network (or problems with their social network). Presumably, individuals who perceive support from others that is not procriminal will be less inclined to engage in violent behavior.

Another contextual factor that is not considered in most risk assessment measures is the availability of a weapon. When there is a weapon present, the risk of perpetrating violence is heightened. In fact, the "weapons effect" posits that just seeing a gun can lead to more aggression (Berkowitz & LePage, 1967). This has implications for one's home and neighborhood. It is important to consider this relatively simple yet potent risk factor when performing a violence risk assessment.

Of course, it goes without saying that violence is more likely to occur when there are victims available. Individuals who do not discriminate between victims (e.g., a child molester who has both familial and nonfamilial victims) are more likely to recidivate. There are also commonalities among survivors of violent crime that cannot be ignored. Felson and Steadman (1983) found that homicide victims were overwhelmingly intoxicated, aggressive in some way towards the murderer, and threatened to use or used a weapon prior to their murder. Moreover, when someone else was present supporting the perpetrator, the violence tended to be much greater (Felson, Ribner, & Siegel, 1984).

The Challenge Continues

In Mossman's (2000) commentary of "accurate" predictions of violence, he highlighted that if we assume 1 in 1,000 people will kill and use a test that is 95% accurate in identifying potential killers, out of the 1,000 people, 95 will be accurately classified. However, if we assessed 10,000 people, 495 would be incorrectly classified. Mossman also reminded us that accurately classifying dangerous people is not the same as correctly identifying them. He argued that when dealing with a low base rate event, the method used for prediction needs to be nearly foolproof to be useful. Today, there is no such method.

Out of the many challenges that remain in the field of predicting dangerousness, one more needs to be mentioned. Oftentimes, clinicians who are making predictions about violence have not been trained on risk assessment and rely on cognitive biases when they attempt to predict dangerousness (Krauss & Sales, 2001). Unfortunately, there is no standard of training in dangerousness assessment (Borum, 1996). However, as Krauss and Sales (2001) point out – predictive accuracy may not be improved if appropriate training was available. Despite this, clinicians who perform violence risk assessment must be informed of its empirical literature, as well as its relationship to testimony about dangerousness. While risk communication and risk management are beyond the scope of this review, comprehensive training in risk assessment methods is necessary.

While clinicians continuously assess a patient's risk to inform treatment, it is rare for them to routinely employ empirically grounded psychometrically strong risk assessment measures. In fact, even board-certified forensic psychologists do not routinely use risk assessment measures (Archer, Buffington-Vollum, Stredny, & Handel, 2006). Practicing clinicians perceive dynamic, behavioral variables as more relevant in their assessment of violence than research-based variables (Elbogen, Mercado, Scalora, & Tomkins, 2002). Relatedly, despite the multiple findings that the Rorschach's (i.e., a projective test) relationship to violence is invalid and should not be admissible in court (see Lilienfeld, Wood, & Garb, 2000), it is still used in so-called "risk assessments." This can also be said for the Minnesota Multiphasic Personality Inventory (MMPI; Melton et al., 1997). Unfortunately, when clinicians rely on these types of measures they miss a more comprehensive and – perhaps accurate – assessment of an individual's risk of engaging in dangerous behaviors.

Can we predict who will commit the next mass shooting? This question might require a yes or no response, but it is clear from a review of the literature that it is impossible to provide a simple answer. Violent behavior is complex – as are our ways of predicting its occurrence. Mass shootings are undoubtedly extreme events and we are compelled to pay attention to them as they shake our society's sense of safety. As much as we would like to predict a person's likelihood of perpetrating a mass shooting, the bottom line is that we cannot 100% of the time predict anyone's extreme behavior. There is no proven formula for predicting behavior – especially a low base rate behavior such as mass shootings. However, we can use existing theories of violence risk assessment and prior empirical evidence to inform clinicians and aid them in making decisions.

Note

1   ROC curve areas are created based on an analytical technique similar to a cost-benefit analysis that plots the true positive rate against the false positive rate of a measure to compute a binary outcome. ROC analyses provide the probability of detecting group membership. ROC curve areas close to 1.00 indicate a highly sensitive measure.

References

American Psychiatric Association. (1983). Guidelines for legislation on the psychiatric hospitalization of adults. *American Journal of Psychiatry, 140*, 672–679.
American Psychiatric Association. (2000). *Diagnostic and statistical manual of mental disorders* (4th ed., text rev.). Washington, DC: Author.

American Psychiatric Association. (2013). *Diagnostic and statistical manual of mental disorders* (5th ed.). Washington, DC: Author.

Archer, R. P., Buffington-Vollum, J. K., Stredny, R. V., & Handel, R. W. (2006). A survey of psychological test use patterns among forensic psychologists. *Journal of Personality Assessment, 87*, 84–94.

Banks, S., Robbins, P. C., Silver, E., Vesselinov, R., Steadman, H. J., Monahan, J., … Roth, L. (2004). A multiple-models approach to violence risk assessment among people with mental disorder. *Criminal Justice and Behavior, 31*, 324–340.

Berkowitz, L., & LePage, A. (1967). Weapons as aggression-eliciting stimuli. *Journal of Personality and Social Psychology, 7*, 202–207.

Bloom, H., Webster, C., Hucker, S., & De Freitas, K. (2005). The Canadian contribution to violence risk assessment: History and implications for current psychiatric practice. *The Canadian Journal of Psychiatry, 50*(1), 3–11.

Bonta, J., Harman, W. G., Hann, R. G., & Cormier, R. B. (1996). The prediction of recidivism among federally sentenced offenders: A re-validation of the SIR scale. *Canadian Journal of Criminology, 38*, 61–79.

Bonta, J., Law, M., & Hanson, K. (1998). The prediction of criminal and violent recidivism among mentally disordered offenders: A meta-analysis. *Psychological Bulletin, 123*, 123–142.

Borum, R. (1996). Improving the clinical practice of violence risk assessment: Technology, guidelines and training. *American Psychologist, 51*, 945–956.

Cale, E. M., & Lilienfeld, S. O. (2002). Histrionic personality disorder and antisocial personality disorder: Sex-differentiated manifestations of psychopathy? *Journal of Personality Disorders, 16*, 52–72.

Caspi, A., Moffitt, T. E., Silva, P. A., Stouthamer-Loeber, M., Krueger, R. F., & Schmutte, P. S. (1994). Are some people crime-prone? Replication of the personality–crime relationships across countries, genders, race, and methods. *Criminology, 32*, 163–195.

Cocozza, J., & Steadman, H. (1974). Some refinement in the measurement and prediction of dangerous behaviour. *American Journal of Psychiatry, 131*, 1012–1014.

Conroy, M. A., & Murrie, D. C. (2007). *Historical overview of risk assessment, in forensic assessment of violence risk: A guide for risk assessment and risk management.* Hoboken, NJ: John Wiley & Sons, Inc.

Copas, J., & Marshall, P. (1998). The offender group reconviction scale: A statistical reconviction score for use by probation officers. *Applied Statistics, 47*, 159–171.

Douglas, K. S., & Ogloff, J. R. (2003). Multiple facets of risk for violence: The impact of judgmental specificity on structured decisions about violence risk. *International Journal of Forensic Mental Health, 2*(1), 19–34.

Douglas, K. S., & Skeem, J. (2005). Violence risk assessment: Getting specific about being dynamic. *Psychology, Public Policy and Law, 11*, 347–383.

Douglas, K., Vincent, G., & Edens, J. (2006). Psychopathy and aggression. In C. J. Patrick (Ed.), *Handbook of psychopathy* (pp. 533–554). New York, NY: Guilford Press.

Dowden, C., & Brown, S. L. (2002). The role of substance abuse factors in predicting recidivism: A meta-analysis. *Psychology, Crime & Law, 8*, 1–22.

Elbogen, E. B., Mercado, C. C., Scalora, M. J., & Tomkins, A. J. (2002). Perceived relevance of factors for violence risk assessment: A survey of clinicians. *International Journal of Forensic Mental Health*, *1*, 37–47.

Estroff, S., & Zimmer, C. (1994). Social networks, social support, and violence among persons with severe, persistent mental illness. In J. Monahan & H.S. Steadman (Eds.), *Violence and mental disorder: Developments in risk assessment* (pp. 259–295). Chicago, IL: University of Chicago Press.

Farrington, D. P. (1986). Age and crime. In M. Tonry and N. Morris (Eds.), *Crime and justice: An annual review of research* (Vol. 7) (pp. 189–250). Chicago, IL: University of Chicago Press.

Farrington, D. P., Ohlin, L. E., & Wilson, J. Q. (1986). *Understanding and controlling crime*. New York, NY: Springer.

Felson, R. B., Ribner, S. A., & Siegel, M. S. (1984). Age and the effect of third parties during criminal violence. *Sociology and Social Research*, *68*, 452–462.

Felson, R. B., & Steadman, H. J. (1983). Situational factors in disputes leading to criminal violence. *Criminology*, *21*, 59–74.

Gendreau, P., Goggin, C. E., & Law, M. A. (1997). Predicting prison misconducts. *Criminal Justice and Behavior*, *24*, 414–431.

Gendreau, P., Grant, B. A., Leipciger, M., & Collins, C. (1979). Norms and recidivism rates for the MMPI and selected experimental scales on a Canadian delinquent sample. *Canadian Journal of Behavioural Science*, *11*, 21–31.

Gottfredson, S. D. (1987). Statistical and actuarial considerations. In F. N. Dutile & C. H. Foust (Eds.), *The prediction of criminal violence* (pp. 71–81). Springfield, IL: Charles C. Thomas.

Grove, W. M., Zald, D. H., Lebow, B. S., Snitz, B. E., & Nelson, C. (2000). Clinical versus mechanical prediction: A meta-analysis. *Psychological Assessment*, *12*, 19–30.

Guerino, P., Harrison, P. M., & Sabol, W. J. (2011). *Prisoners in 2010*. NCJ 236096. Washington, DC: U.S. Department of Justice, Bureau of Justice Statistics. Retrieved from http://www.bjs.gov/content/pub/pdf/p10.pdf

Guy, L. S., Packer, I. K., & Warnken, W. (2012). Assessing risk of violence using structured professional judgment guidelines. *Journal of Forensic Psychology Practice*, *12*(3), 270–283.

Hanson, R. K. (1997). *The development of a brief actuarial scale for sex offender recidivism* (User Report No. 1997-04). Ottawa, Canada: Department of the Solicitor General of Canada.

Hanson, R. K. (1998). What do we know about sex offender risk assessment? *Psychology, Public Policy, And Law*, *4*(1), 50–72.

Hanson, R. K., & Morton-Bourgon, K. E. (2009). The accuracy of recidivism risk assessments for sexual offenders: A meta-analysis of 118 prediction studies. *Psychological Assessment*, *21*(1), 1–21.

Hanson, R. K., & Thornton, D. (2000). Improving risk assessments for sex offenders: A comparison of three actuarial scales. *Law and Human Behavior*, *24*, 119–136.

Hare, R. D. (2003). *The Hare Psychopathy Checklist – Revised* (2nd ed.). Toronto, Canada: Multi-Health Systems.

Harris, G. T., Rice, M. E., & Quinsey, V. L. (1993). Violent recidivism of mentally disordered offenders: The development of a statistical prediction instrument.
Criminal Justice and Behaviour, 20, 315–335.

Harris, G. T., Rice, M. E., Quinsey, V. L., Lalumière, M. L., Boer, D., & Lang, C.
(2003). A multisite comparison of actuarial risk instruments for sex offenders.
Psychological Assessment, 15(3).

Harris, A. J. R., & Tough, S. E. (2004). Should actuarial risk assessments be used with
sex offenders who are intellectually disabled? *Journal of Applied Research in
Intellectual Disabilities, 17*, 235–241.

Heilbrun, K., Yasuhara, K., & Shah, S. (2010). Violence risk assessment tools: Overview
and critical analysis. In R. K. Otto & K. S. Douglas (Eds.), *Handbook of violence
risk assessment. International perspectives on forensic mental health* (pp. 1–17). New
York, NY: Routledge.

Knight, R. A., & Prentky, R. A. (1990). Classifying sexual offenders: The development
and corroboration of taxonomic models. In W. L. Marshall, D. R. Laws, & H. E.
Barbaree (Eds.), *The handbook of sexual assault: Issues, theories and treatment of the
offender* (pp. 27–52). New York, NY: Plenum.

Krauss, D., & Sales, B. (2001). The effects of clinical and scientific expert testimony on
juror decision-making in capital sentencing. *Psychology, Public Policy, and Law, 7*,
267–310.

Lilienfeld, S. O., Wood, J. M., & Garb. H. N. (2000). The scientific status of projective
techniques. *Psychological Science in the Public Interest, 1*, 27–66.

Litwack, T. R. (2001). Actuarial versus clinical assessments of dangerousness. *Psychology,
Public Policy, and Law, 7*(2), 409–443.

Loza, W., & Dhaliwal, G. K. (1997). Psychometric evaluation of the Risk Appraisal
Guide (RAG): A tool for assessing violent recidivism. *Journal of Interpersonal
Violence, 12*, 779–793.

Loza W., & Loza-Fanous, A. (1999). Anger and prediction of violent and non-violent
offender's recidivism. *Journal of Interpersonal Violence, 14*, 1014–1029.

Meehl, P. E. (1954). *Clinical versus statistical prediction: A theoretical analysis and a
review of the evidence.* Minneapolis, MN: University of Minnesota.

Melton, G., Petrila, J., Poythress, N., & Slobogin, C. (1997). *Psychological evaluations
for the courts: A handbook for mental health professionals and lawyers* (3rd ed.). New
York, NY: Guilford Press.

Mills, J. F., Kroner, D. G., & Forth, A. E. (2002). Measures of Criminal Attitudes and
Associates (MCAA): Development, factor structure, reliability, and validity.
Assessment, 9, 240–253.

Mills, J. F., Kroner, D. G., & Hemmati, T. (2004). The Measures of Criminal Attitudes
and Associates (MCAA): The prediction of general and violent recidivism.
Criminal Justice and Behavior, 31, 717–733.

Monahan, J. (1984). The prediction of violent behavior: Toward a second generation
of theory and policy. *American Journal of Psychiatry, 141*, 10–15.

Monahan, J. (2003). Violence risk assessment. *Handbook of Psychology, 6*(26), 27–540.

Monahan, J., & Shah, S. A. (1989). Dangerousness and commitment of the mentally
disordered in the United States. *Schizophrenia Bulletin, 15*(4), 541–553.

Monahan, J., Steadman, H. J., Silver, E., Appelbaum, P. S., Robbins, P. C., Mulvey, E. P.,... Banks, S. (2001). *Rethinking risk assessment: The MacArthur study of mental disorder and violence*. Oxford, UK: Oxford University Press.

Mossman, D. (2000). Commentary: Assessing the risk of violence – Are "accurate" predictions useful? *Journal of the American Academy of Psychiatry and the Law, 28*, 272–281.

Novaco, R. W. (1994). Anger as a risk factor for violence among the mentally disordered. In J. Monahan & H. J. Steadman (Eds.), *Violence and mental disorder: Developments in risk assessment* (pp. 21–59). Chicago, IL: University of Chicago Press.

Otto, R. K. (1992). Prediction of dangerous behavior: A review and analysis of "second-generation research. *Forensic Reports, 5*, 103–133.

Quinsey, V. L., Harris, G. T., Rice, M. E., & Cormier, C. A. (1998). *Violent offenders: Appraising and managing risk*. Washington, DC: American Psychological Association.

Robins, L. N. (1993). Childhood conduct problems, adult psychopathology and crime. In S. Hodgins (Ed.). *Mental disorder and crime* (pp. 173–193). Newbury Park, CA: Sage.

Roffey, M., & Kaliski, S. Z. (2012). To predict or not to predict – that is the question. *African Journal of Psychiatry, 15*(4), 227–233.

Shah, S. A. (1975). Dangerous and civil commitment of the mentally ill: Some public policy considerations. *American Journal of Psychiatry, 132*, 501–505.

Skeem, J., Mulvey, E., Appelbaum, A., Banks, S., Grisso, T., Silver, E., & Robbins, P. (2004). Identifying subtypes of civil psychiatric patients at high risk for violence. *Criminal Justice & Behavior, 31*, 392–437.

Stock, H. V. (2007). Workplace violence: Advances in consultation and assessment. In A. M. Goldstein (Ed.), *Forensic psychology: Emerging topics and expanding roles* (pp. 511–549). Hoboken, NJ: Wiley.

Strub, D. S., Douglas, K. S., & Nicholls, T. L. (2014). The validity of Version 3 of the HCR-20 violence risk assessment scheme amongst offenders and civil psychiatric patients. *International Journal of Forensic Mental Health, 13*(2), 148–159.

Swanson, J. W., Holzer, C. E., Ganju, V. K., & Jono, R. F. (1990). Violence and psychiatric disorder in the community: Evidence from the Epidemiologic Catchment Area surveys. *Hospital and Community Psychiatry, 41*, 761–770.

Urbaniok, F., Endrass, J., Rossegger, A., Noll, T., Gallo, W. T., & Angst, J. (2007). The prediction of criminal recidivism. *European Archives of Psychiatry & Clinical Neuroscience, 257*(3), 129–134.

Walters, G. D. (1992). *Foundations of criminal science*. New York, NY: Praeger.

Watson, D., Clark, L. A., & Tellegen, A. (1988). Development and validation of brief measures of positive and negative affect: The PANAS Scales. *Journal of Personality and Social Psychology, 54*, 1063–1070.

Webster, C. D., Eaves, D., Douglas, K. S., & Wintrup, A. (1995). *The HCR-20 scheme: The assessment of dangerousness and risk*. Burnaby, Canada: Simon Fraser University and British Columbia Forensic Psychiatric Services Commission.

Westen, D., & Weinberger, J. (2004). When clinical description becomes statistical prediction. *American Psychologist, 59*, 595–613.

Wolfgang, M. E., Figlio, R. M., & Sellin, T. (1972). *Delinquency in a birth cohort.* Chicago, IL: University of Chicago Press.

Yang, M. S., Wong, C. P., & Coid, J. (2010). The efficacy of violence prediction: A meta-analytic comparison of nine risk assessment tools. *Psychological Bulletin, 136* (5), 740–767.

Part III

The Role of Media
in the Aftermath of Mass
Shootings

The Influence of Media
on Public Attitudes

Jaclyn Schildkraut and H. Jaymi Elsass

When it comes to public attitudes about mass shootings, the media are key in shaping these beliefs. Assuming the role of "moral entrepreneurs," as Becker (1963) refers to those individuals in an agenda-setting capacity, media producers are able to generate significant public concern about these events, including purported causes for why shootings occur, how to protect oneself against such an attack, and how often such incidents take place. Since most individuals never will be directly affected by a mass shooting event, media outlets serve as their main source of information (Graber, 1980; Surette, 1992). This information has significant bearing on public beliefs about mass shootings.

In order to understand the media's influence on such attitudes, it is imperative to consider the media's agenda-setting capabilities. Additionally, understanding the prevalence of news coverage devoted to mass shootings is important in determining how such an agenda is shaped and which events are given priority. Discussion also is offered regarding two key causal factors of mass shootings – gun control and mental health – and the subsequent shifts in public opinion. Such judgments may act as impetuses for change in the form of legislative responses to these events (Schildkraut & Hernandez, 2014; Soraghan, 2000). Finally, consideration is given to how public attitudes about mass shootings translate into other far-reaching impacts, such as perceived risks of victimization and fear of crime.

The Role of the Media in Agenda Setting

The mass media play an important role in society as they define and shape issues and events rather than just reflecting what is occurring in society (Barak, 1994; Gans, 1979). In a commentary on how the media contribute to the social construction of crime, Sacco (1995) notes that

The Wiley Handbook of the Psychology of Mass Shootings, First Edition. Edited by Laura C. Wilson.
© 2017 John Wiley & Sons, Inc. Published 2017 by John Wiley & Sons, Inc.

The ways in which the news media collect, sort, and contextualize crime reports help to shape public consciousness regarding which conditions need to be seen as urgent problems, what kinds of problems they represent, and, by implication, how they should be resolved. (p. 141)

This process, known as agenda setting, enables the mass media to highlight particular attributes of a story that call attention to, and lend support for, claims made by individuals in positions of power or influence (Entman, 2007; McCombs, 1997; McCombs & Shaw, 1972; Weaver, 2007). The process of agenda setting focuses on how objects or issues are portrayed in the media and the amount of importance assigned to each object's particular attributes (McCombs, 1997; Surette, 1992; Weaver, 2007). Additionally, this process is concerned with the relationship between the media and the audience as opposed to how the media interact with social institutions (e.g., the government) to determine which issues are of increased saliency (McCombs & Shaw, 1972).

According to McCombs (1997), one of the main goals of agenda setting is to achieve consensus among the public about the importance of a particular issue, and the media are instrumental in generating this agreement. By high-lighting certain stories as important (or, perhaps more accurately, as more important than others), news producers call attention to issues that either may directly or indirectly affect a particular community (Barak, 1994; McCombs, 1997; Reese, 2007). Over time, as more coverage is allocated to a particular issue, the saliency of that issue for the public likely increases, and eventually becomes a priority for the public's agenda (McCombs, 1997; Reese, 2007). Policies aimed at addressing the issue also can be pushed as part of the agenda (Entman, 2007). As Cohen (1963) notes, the media "may not be successful much of the time in telling people what to think, but it is stunningly successful in telling people what to think *about*" (p. 13).

Rarely, however, does the news or public agenda focus on more than a few key issues at a time (McCombs, 1997). This limited focus stems from the fact that few issues are able to command the consensus needed to maintain saliency (McCombs, 1997). Most often, the media focus on those issues that are the most serious or atypical in nature (Barak, 1994; Sacco, 1995) or those that threaten society's perceived stability (Gans, 1979), such as mass shoot-ings. At the same time, this limited focus allows for a more complete, full-bodied discussion to take place in both the public and media forums. When an issue is of perceived importance, the media agenda is impacted as the demand for information increases (Scheufele & Tewksbury, 2007). Accordingly, how the mass media portray such issues impacts the way in which the public perceives and understands them (Barak, 1994; Scheufele & Tewksbury, 2007).

Prevalence of Media Coverage of Mass Shootings

When word of a mass shooting breaks, media producers are quick to provide live, continuous coverage, often straight from the scene. Such a practice first was evident during the 1999 Columbine High School shooting, when CNN aired six uninterrupted hours of coverage from Littleton (Muschert, 2002). Additionally, in the first week after the shooting, 53 stories, totaling nearly four hours of airtime, were broadcast on the three major news networks – ABC, CBS, and NBC (Maguire, Weatherby, & Mathers, 2002). In fact, these stations devoted no less than half of their nightly news airtime to stories about Columbine, and in the year following the shooting, over 300 individual stories were broadcast (Robinson, 2011). By comparison, 13 other school shootings that had occurred within the same time period garnered just slightly more coverage than Columbine when all of their stories were combined (Maguire et al., 2002).

Shootings occurring in later years followed this "breaking coverage" pattern. On the day of the 2007 Virginia Tech shootings, network news stations devoted 60% of their airtime to covering the story (Pew Research Center for the People & the Press, 2007a). Similarly, 76% of cable news airtime was allocated to coverage of the shootings (Pew Research Center for the People & the Press, 2007a). In fact, despite typical daily viewership of approximately 450,000 and 900,000 on CNN and Fox News, respectively (Garofoli, 2007), audience sizes surged to 1.4 million and 1.8 million viewers for these same networks on the day of the shootings (Pew Research Center's Project for Excellence in Journalism, 2006). For three continuous days following the 2012 Sandy Hook Elementary School shooting, broadcasts on cable news networks, including CNN and Fox News, were live from Newtown (Applebome & Stetler, 2012; Askar, 2012). The networks' coverage of the shootings translated into high levels of viewership (between 2 and 3 million viewers per hour), with one show – Wolf Blitzer's *The Situation Room* (CNN) – rated second among adult audiences aged 18 to 49 (Kondolojy, 2012).

Such pervasive coverage is not limited to the television format; the newspaper medium also is prone to focus on mass shootings in its coverage. In the year following Columbine, approximately 10,000 articles were published in the nation's 50 largest newspapers (Newman, 2006). Of these, 170 appeared in *The New York Times* alone in the first 30 days after the event (Chyi & McCombs, 2004; Muschert & Carr, 2006; Schildkraut & Muschert, 2014). Local coverage via *The Denver Post* was more than triple *The New York Times* in the quantity of articles – over 600 stories about Columbine were posted during the first 30 days (Schildkraut, 2014). During the same time frame following Sandy Hook, *The New York Times* published 130 articles (Schildkraut, 2014; Schildkraut & Muschert, 2014). High levels of coverage also were devoted to shootings occurring outside of primary and secondary schools, including attacks at Virginia Tech in 2007, Fort Hood in 2009, a Tucson, Arizona political function in 2011, and an Aurora, Colorado movie theater in 2012 (Schildkraut, 2014).

With ever-advancing technology, newsmakers have begun to incorporate newer source formats into their production strategies to supplement the more traditional forms of media. This practice first was witnessed after Virginia Tech, when cell phone footage of the shooting, taken by a student and later uploaded through CNN's iReport feature, was aired by multiple news stations (Kellner, 2008; Schildkraut, 2012; Wigley & Fontenot, 2009). By that evening, the clip had received more than 1 million views (Stanley, 2007). Companion websites for cable news networks are also used regularly to augment television coverage and attract larger audiences. On the day of the Virginia Tech shootings, 108.8 million users logged on to MSNBC's website (Garofoli, 2007), compared to the average rate of 400,000 unique daily page views (TheWebStats.com, 2011).

Still, despite their inherent sensational nature, not all mass shootings garner the same amount of coverage (Schildkraut, 2014; Schildkraut, Elsass, & Meredith, 2015). The Columbine shooting is the archetypal event to which all other similar incidents are compared (Altheide, 2009; Kalish & Kimmel, 2010; Larkin, 2007, 2009; Muschert, 2007; Muschert & Larkin, 2007), primarily because it is perceived as the first of its kind. To date, no other incident, including Sandy Hook, has eclipsed the coverage of this earlier event (Schildkraut, 2014; Schildkraut & Muschert, 2014). Sandy Hook, in its own right, garnered considerable media attention as a result of the newsworthiness of the victims due to their young age. Sorenson, Manz, and Berk (1998) have noted that homicides in which victims are "white, in the youngest and oldest age groups, women, of high socioeconomic status, killed by strangers" (p. 1514) are seen as more newsworthy, and those killed in the Sandy Hook shooting embodied these characteristics.

In a separate examination, Schildkraut, Elsass, and Meredith (2015) found that the more victims, particularly fatalities, associated with an event, the more likely that shooting is to receive more prominent coverage (e.g., more articles, greater word counts). Those shootings occurring in the West, thus in closer proximity to Columbine, also received more coverage than those taking place in different regions of the country (Schildkraut, Elsass, & Meredith, 2015). The timing of events, with one shooting occurring in close temporal proximity to another, can also affect coverage patterns, particularly if the latter is considered less newsworthy than the prior incident. Such disparities in coverage have been observed following shootings at Heritage High School in Conyers, Georgia just 1 month after Columbine; Northern Illinois University in 2008, nearly 10 months after Virginia Tech; and a Sikh temple in Oak Creek, Wisconsin in 2012, only 2 weeks after Aurora.

The Gun Control Versus Right to Carry Debate

In the aftermath of mass shootings, one of the major issues at the center of the discourse is the debate between gun control and the right to carry. Proponents of gun control measures argue that tighter regulations will reduce the occurrence of mass shootings (Kleck, 2009; Schildkraut & Muschert, 2013; Schildkraut, Elsass, & Muschert, 2016; Wallace, 2015). Those on the opposite side of the debate advocate that the presence of armed citizens may stop future shooters and save lives (Kleck, 2009; Schildkraut & Muschert, 2013; Schildkraut et al., in press; Wallace, 2015). Much of the debate between these two camps takes place via the media. In fact, among the most commonly discussed causal factors of mass shootings, guns typically are the most frequently referenced (Schildkraut, 2014; Schildkraut & Muschert, 2013; Schildkraut et al., in press).

Public opinion with regard to the gun control debate has been shown to be influenced by the occurrence of mass shootings. A year after the 1999 shooting at Columbine High School, the Pew Research Center for the People & the Press (2000) found that support for gun control was at an all-time high – 66% of respondents approved stricter regulations, while just 29% favored protection of owners' rights (Carlson & Simmons, 2001; Connelly, 1999; Saad, 1999; Smith, 2002). In the following years, however, support for control measures began to wane while simultaneously increasing for gun rights (Pew Research Center for the People & the Press, 2014). The second highest peak for support was found just after the 2007 Virginia Tech shootings, with 60% of respondents favoring stricter regulations (Pew Research Center for the People & the Press, 2014). Other shootings, however, such as those at a political rally in Tucson, Arizona (Madison, 2011; Pew Research Center for the People & the Press, 2011) and an Aurora, Colorado movie theater (Blumenthal, 2012; Pew Research Center for the People & the Press, 2012a), failed to significantly impact the public's attitudes towards either side of the debate. Following the shooting at Sandy Hook Elementary School, support for gun control measures increased, albeit slightly (just 2% in one poll) from the Aurora massacre 5 months earlier (Pew Research Center for the People & the Press, 2012a; Saad, 2012a). Two years after Newtown, however, support for gun rights eclipsed support for regulation measures, due in part to the growing public perceptions that firearms are beneficial in protecting people from becoming crime victims (Doherty, 2015; Pew Research Center for the People & the Press, 2014).

In the wake of these events and in response to the subsequent reactions from the public, legislators are tasked to "do something" in order to address the perceived threat of future mass shootings. While the public often is torn on whether new laws should be passed or existing ones enforced (Pew Research

Center for the People & the Press, 2000; Saad, 2012a; Wozniak, 2015), many politicians opt for the former solution. Within 1 year of Columbine, over 800 pieces of legislation at both the state and federal levels related to firearms were introduced; only about 10% of these were enacted into law (Schildkraut & Hernandez, 2014; Soraghan, 2000). Following the December 2012 shooting at Sandy Hook, 23 bills aimed at gun control measures were introduced at the federal level alone in the first 75 days (Schildkraut, 2014). The state of New York also passed one of the most comprehensive gun control packages following the shooting (Hernandez, Schildkraut, & Elsass, 2015; "NYSAFE Act Gun Reform," n.d.).

Most often, the reform measures for firearms related to mass shootings focus on several key areas. One such area is what has been termed "the gun show loophole" (Kleck, 2009; Schildkraut & Hernandez, 2014), which refers to the ability to sell or transfer firearms between unlicensed private parties (Wintemute, 2013). Even though the public overwhelmingly supports background checks at gun shows (Saad, 2012a), such measures have failed to be implemented. After it was determined that three of the firearms used by the Columbine perpetrators were purchased at a gun show by one of their friends (neither shooter was of age to legally possess them at the time of the purchase), focus on closing this loophole appeared to be at an all-time high, even though the legislation had originally been introduced over a year earlier (Kleck, 2009; Schildkraut & Hernandez, 2014). While the state of Colorado did enact a law that made straw purchases such as this illegal (Soraghan, 2000), attempts to regulate background checks at a national level failed each time they were introduced (Schildkraut & Hernandez, 2014). Still, proposed measures aimed at strengthening background checks are often supported by public opinion, usually at a higher rate than other proposed regulations (Barry, McGinty, Vernick, & Webster, 2013; Carlson & Simmons, 2001; Doherty, 2015; McGinty, Webster, Vernick, & Barry, 2013; Wozniak, 2015).

Another key area of reform is the attempt to limit the type of weapons that civilians can own. According to Gallup public opinion polls, since the 1960s, the public consistently has opposed banning ownership of handguns by anyone other than law enforcement (Pew Research Center for the People & the Press, 2012c; Saad, 2012a). Most efforts to regulate firearms typically focus on assault weapons, even though they are used in just a fraction of these incidents (Fox & DeLateur, 2014; Mayors Against Illegal Guns, 2013). These guns characteristically resemble military weapons and often employ a semiautomatic firing mechanism, meaning that cartridges are automatically loaded into the firing position after each single shot without further action from the shooter (Kleck, 2009). Advocates of banning such weapons argue that their mechanisms allow for individuals to fire rounds more rapidly (Kleck, 2009). It is important to note, however, that the semiautomatic element is not solely limited to assault weapons. Many handgun models also bear this feature.

In 1994, Congress passed the Violent Crime Control and Law Enforcement Act, more commonly known as the Federal Assault Weapons Ban (AWB), which declared that it is "unlawful for a person to manufacture, transfer, or possess a semiautomatic assault weapon" (18 U.S.C. §§ 921–922). A list of 19 different firearms were banned under the act, and it contained a list of criteria to determine whether or not a gun constituted an assault weapon and thereby was prohibited (18 U.S.C. §§ 921–922; Singh, 1999). The ban, however, contained a sunset provision, meaning that it only was effective for 10 years before it would have to be renewed (Singh, 1999). Congress failed to reaffirm the legislation and it expired on September 13, 2004. Since its termination, a number of attempts to reinstitute federal regulations on such weapons have been introduced, but have not passed through Congress.

The effectiveness, or perhaps lack thereof, may have had an impact on public opinion related to such legislation. One of the weapons used in Columbine – the IntraTec Tec DC-9 – was illegal under the AWB, which was effective at the time of the shooting. The State of Connecticut also had an assault weapons ban in place at the time of Sandy Hook, but it is unclear whether the Bushmaster rifle used as the primary firearm in the shooting was prohibited at the time. Since the introduction of the AWB, public support for such a measure has subsided, dropping as much as 25% in some polls (Doherty, 2015). When support for such regulation is garnered, it typically is higher among nongun owners (Barry et al., 2013; McGinty, Webster, Vernick, & Barry, 2013; Wozniak, 2015). In some instances, opposition for a ban outweighs its support (Pew Research Center for the People & the Press, 2012b; Saad, 2012a). Further, as Fox and DeLateur (2014) note, the AWB had virtually no effect on the number of mass murders occurring, again potentially contributing to public perceptions of its ineffectiveness.

Another argument related to assault weapons is their ability to accept larger magazines, or more specifically, hold more bullets (Kleck, 2009). By limiting the number of rounds a clip will hold, this would force the shooter to have to reload more frequently, thereby creating opportunities for other individuals to either engage them or escape (Best, 2013; Kleck, 2009). Under the AWB, magazines capable of holding more than 10 rounds were considered to be large capacity and were prohibited for civilian-used firearms (Kleck, 2009; Schildkraut & Hernandez, 2014). This provision expired with the ban. Yet as Kleck (2009) and others have noted, such attempts to regulate the size of ammunition clips may be largely irrelevant as many mass shooters use multiple guns and magazines. Still, by and large, members of the public support proposed limitations on magazine capacities (Barry et al., 2013; Doherty, 2015; McGinty, Webster, Vernick, & Barry, 2013; Pew Research Center for the People & the Press, 2012c; Saad, 2012a). Such support, however, has failed to translate into enacted legislation, even after the Aurora movie theater shooter was found to have used a 100-round drum magazine (Dao, 2012).

A concern for many of the measures discussed here is that they regulate the masses, many of whom are responsible, law-abiding gun owners, in an attempt to prevent a statistically rare attack. What is more problematic with this line of thinking is that there are a number of issues with how the shooters are acquiring their firearms. For example, the shooters at Virginia Tech, Tucson, and Aurora used firearms in the attacks that were purchased legally in that the perpetrators passed all of the necessary background checks (even though they should have been excluded from such approvals due to mental health issues, as discussed in the next section). Others, such as the Thurston High School (1998) and Sandy Hook shooters, had free-range access to firearms that were purchased legally by a member of their family. A third group of shooters, including the 11-year-old and 13-year-old perpetrators of the 1998 Westside Middle School shooting in Jonesboro, Arkansas, acquire their weapons by theft (Kleck, 2009; Schildkraut & Hernandez, 2014). In all three scenarios, any of the proposed measures discussed here would have been largely ineffective. Still, the way in which the media frame the issue of gun violence after mass shootings has had a considerable impact on public attitudes about these events and the weapons that are used.

Mental Health and Mass Shooters

Aside from gun control, the mental health status of the perpetrators also often is called into question when determining why the shootings occurred. While this "usual suspect" routinely makes its way into the public discourse after such an event (Schildkraut, 2014; Schildkraut & Muschert, 2013; Schildkraut et al., 2016), it has been especially predominant in three key cases – Virginia Tech (2007), Tucson (2011), and Sandy Hook (2012). Following each of these shootings, information surfaced that each of the perpetrators had a long documented history of mental health issues. The Virginia Tech shooter suffered from major depressive disorder and selective mutism, an extreme form of social anxiety (Virginia Tech Review Panel [VTRP], 2007). The Tucson shooter, who killed 6 and wounded 13 others, including Congresswoman Gabrielle Giffords, had a history of schizophrenia and other psychological difficulties (Gassen & Williams, 2013). The Sandy Hook shooter had been diagnosed with Asperger's syndrome, a high functioning form of autism, at an early age (Hernandez et al., 2015).

In response to these events, a number of legislative measures were proposed, aimed at addressing the perceived dangerousness of individuals with mental health concerns (Hernandez et al., 2015; Schildkraut & Hernandez, 2014). A number of these proposals linked the issues of gun control and mental health, and centered on keeping firearms away from those who are mentally ill (Barry et al., 2013; McGinty, Webster, Vernick, & Barry, 2013). Support for this proposal is common among both gun owners and nonowners alike, regardless of political party ideology (McGinty, Webster, Vernick, & Barry, 2013).

Following the Virginia Tech shooting, for example, the investigation revealed that in December 2005, less than two years before the attack, the shooter had been involuntarily committed after threatening a fellow student (VTRP, 2007). The shooter was found to be mentally ill, refused to voluntarily seek treatment, and posed an imminent danger to himself and others, all of which are grounds for inpatient counseling. Regardless, he only was ordered to participate in outpatient treatment and he never followed up to receive these services (Bonnie, Reinhard, Hamilton, & McGarvey, 2009; VTRP, 2007). The shooter's detention at the behavioral health facility was never reported to the state's background check system as was mandated. This ultimately created the opportunity for him to legally acquire the firearms used in the shooting (Schildkraut & Hernandez, 2014). He purchased two guns, 30 days apart (in accordance with Virginia's required waiting period), with proof of residency and a photo ID (Roberts, 2009).

In the immediate aftermath of the shooting, then-Governor Timothy Kaine signed an executive order requiring the immediate reporting of any individual who had been deemed a danger to themselves or others to all relevant databases (Schildkraut & Hernandez, 2014). Similar legislation aimed at improving reporting was enacted in 12 other states (Brady Campaign Press Release, 2011). At the national level, President Bush signed into law the NICS Improvement Amendments Act in early 2008 (H.R. 2640, 2007; Schildkraut & Hernandez, 2014). The law was designed to require more frequent records updates, improve the speed of reporting, and promote better coordination between state and federal agencies (NICS Improvement Amendments Act, 2007; Schildkraut & Hernandez, 2014). Additionally, approximately $1.3 billion in federal funding was allocated to facilitate the establishment or updating of reporting systems at the state level (NICS Improvement Amendments Act, 2007; Schildkraut & Hernandez, 2014). In the first 5 years after the shooting, however, just $50 million was appropriated to make such improvements (Brady Campaign Press Release, 2011).

Similar concerns over mental health and mass shooters were prevalent after the Sandy Hook shooting, fueled by the revelation that the gunman had a long-standing diagnosis of Asperger's syndrome. Even though individuals with this diagnosis rarely are violent – approximately 2% of patients have exhibited aggressive behaviors towards people outside of their own family and no single individual has been found to use a weapon during a confrontation (Harmon, 2012) – the need for response filled the national discourse. Within the first year after the shooting, a number of recommendations were made to address mental health concerns in the United States (The White House, 2013). Just prior to the 1-year anniversary of the shooting, the Obama Administration pledged $100 million to increase services for individuals with mental health concerns

(Fox, 2013). Despite such funding, and in spite of budget cuts nationwide, most of the changes related to mental health care were seen at the state level. It was difficult, if not impossible, to discern if such changes were in response to Sandy Hook or the passage of the ObamaCare law that coincided with the shooting (Hernandez et al., 2015).

Regardless of advances made in the United States to reduce the stigmatization of mental illness, the introduction of such a concern into the discourse about mass shootings can affect public opinion as it relates to this particular issue. Following both the Tucson and 2013 Washington, DC, Navy Yard shootings, the failure of the mental health system to identify dangerous individuals was blamed in polls more than both access to firearms and violent media (Newport, 2011; Pew Research Center for the People & the Press, 2011; Saad, 2013). A similar trend also was evident after the Virginia Tech shooting (Pew Research Center for the People & the Press, 2007b). In one study, McGinty, Webster, and Barry (2013) found that individuals who consumed media coverage of a mass shooting were more likely to hold negative beliefs about individuals with mental illness. Such attitudes not only may impact support for policies (McGinty, Webster, & Barry, 2013), but also people's reactions to mass shootings more broadly. Wilson, Ballman, and Buczek (in press) similarly found that the way in which mental health is framed in news articles can influence public attitudes about mass shooters and the broader issue itself.

Perceptions of Safety and Fear of Crime

As noted at the outset of this chapter, the media serve as the primary source of information about mass shootings for the public, as most individuals never will directly experience such an incident. Nearly 95% of the population relies on the media for information pertaining to crime more generally (Graber, 1980; Surette, 1992). While upwards of 50% of news coverage typically is devoted to stories about crime (Maguire et al., 2002; Pollak & Kubrin, 2007; Surette, 1992), due to space and time constraints, the most serious and violent incidents receive the majority of attention (Chermak, 1995; Graber, 1980; Gruenewald, Pizarro, & Chermak, 2009; Mayr & Machin, 2012). Even still, not all events will be covered, and of those that are, they may not garner equitable amounts of coverage (Chermak, 1995; Gruenewald et al., 2009; Schildkraut, Elsass, & Meredith, 2015). Further, by focusing on only the most severe or extreme cases, the media give audiences a distorted understanding about crime (Barak, 1994; Maguire et al., 2002; Robinson, 2011).

Beyond influencing public opinion about issues such as gun control and mental health, the media coverage of mass shootings has a number of additional impacts on individuals' perceptions of such events. The amount of coverage and the way in which the stories are framed can affect how people perceive their likelihood of becoming a victim of a mass shooting or heighten their fear of crime in general. It is important to note that nearly all of the research conducted on fear of and perceived likelihood of crime following mass shootings has focused specifically on school shootings. Given the similarities between school shootings and mass shootings more generally, however, these findings can likely be extrapolated to the public more broadly. Public opinion polls also have been used to capture some of these perceptions.

Mass shootings have been shown to elicit perceptions that one's likelihood of victimization in such an event is higher than it actually is. Following Columbine, for example, Gallup found that more than 6 in 10 respondents (66–68%) agreed that there was some likelihood a similar event could happen in their own community (Gillespie, 2000; Saad, 2012b). This increased to 73% agreement following the 2005 shooting at a high school in Red Lake, Minnesota (Saad, 2012b). Interestingly, following the Sandy Hook shooting, only 52% of respondents expressed the belief that a similar attack could happen (Saad, 2012b). Further, respondents who were female, white, from the eastern region of the United States, and those living in suburban communities were more likely to report such agreement (Saad, 2012b). In the wake of the 2007 Virginia Tech shootings, college students also were likely to perceive that similar attacks could happen again (Fallahi, Austad, Fallon, & Leishman, 2009).

The problem with these perceptions of risk is that they are highly disproportionate to one's actual statistical likelihood of being a victim of a mass shooting. In the six school years preceding Columbine (1992/1993 through 1997/1998), researchers found that there were 226 deaths attributable to school shootings (Bernard, 1999; Donohue, Schiraldi, & Ziedenberg, 1998). In the same time frame, over 50 million students were enrolled in more than 80,000 schools across the nation (Sanchez, 1998). Therefore, the likelihood of any of those students falling victim to a school shooting was less than .00005%. These same students were significantly more likely to be struck by lightning (Bernard, 1999; Donohue et al., 1998), which in itself is a rare occurrence.

Despite the statistical unlikelihood of one becoming the victim of a mass shooting, people still remain fearful of such a possibility. Perceived risk of victimization and fear of crime are separate constructs, yet they often are used interchangeably (Warr, 2000; Warr & Stafford, 1983). Researchers contend that fear actually is caused by one's perceptions of one's risk of victimization (Warr, 2000; Warr & Stafford, 1983). Additionally, Ferraro (1995) elaborates that perceived risk is cognitive, while fear of crime is emotional. Most academic studies examining perceptions of mass shootings have focused on fear of crime.

Following Columbine, Addington (2003) reported that students expressed being more fearful at school after the shooting as compared to prior to the attack. Similarly, Brener, Simon, Anderson, Barrios, and Small (2002) found that students were more fearful after the shootings and, as a result, were more likely to avoid attending school. Fallahi and colleagues (2009) found that the more students consumed media coverage of the Virginia Tech shootings, the more fearful they reported of being attacked. Kaminski, Koons-Witt, Thompson, and Weiss (2010) found that both the Virginia Tech and the Northern Illinois University shootings increased fear of crime on campus, being murdered, and being attacked with a weapon.

Not all reactions specifically are related to a particular event. Instead, such perceptions may be attributable to the phenomenon of mass shootings more generally. Schildkraut, Elsass, and Stafford (2015) examined reactions to school shootings in the context of moral panics. They found that college students with greater fear of personal victimization (e.g., being murdered or attacked with a weapon) expressed more punitive attitudes towards school shooters (Schildkraut, Elsass, & Stafford, 2015). Those respondents who were more fearful also were more likely to believe that these events were occurring more frequently than they actually were and were more likely to subscribe to the idea of a moral panic over school shootings (Schildkraut, Elsass, & Stafford, 2015). In a separate study, Elsass, Schildkraut, and Stafford (2014) examined the role of media consumption in attitudes about school shootings. They found that social media usage, and Twitter in particular, led to greater beliefs that school shootings were a major problem in the United States (Elsass et al., 2014). In sum, this body of literature indicates that members of the general public hold disproportionate beliefs about mass shootings and that these attitudes are driven largely in part by the media coverage of such events.

Conclusion

Mass shootings have the ability to elicit considerable media attention, which translates into high levels of viewership. After the Columbine shooting, over 90% of people reported following the shooting either fairly or very closely (Pew Research Center for the People & the Press, 1999). In fact, the shooting was the top story of the year and the third most closely followed event behind the 1992 Rodney King verdict and the 1996 TWA airline crash (Pew Research Center for the People & the Press, 1999). Sandy Hook also was highly followed, with 87% of people reporting they paid close attention to the coverage (Saad, 2012b). Other mass shooting events, including Thurston High School (1998), Westside Middle School (1998), Virginia Tech, and Fort Hood (2009), garnered considerable interest from media audiences (Pew Research Center for the People & the Press, 2007a, 2009).

Beyond the issues discussed in this chapter, broader implications exist for media coverage of mass shootings. Some specific events, such as the Sandy Hook shooting, have been perceived as reflecting broader issues within society ("Washington Post-ABC News Poll," n.d.). Others, including Virginia Tech, Tucson, and Aurora, are perceived to be isolated acts of troubled individuals

("Washington Post-ABC News Poll," n.d.). Regardless of which stance a person takes, the media has been shown to have a strong influence on public attitudes regarding mass shootings. Accordingly, researchers must continue to examine both the coverage itself and its effects on consumers to understand the full impact of these events on society.

References

Addington, L. A. (2003). Students' fear after Columbine: Findings from a randomized experiment. *Journal of Quantitative Criminology, 19*(4), 367–387.

Altheide, D. L. (2009). The Columbine shooting and the discourse of fear. *American Behavioral Scientist, 52*(10), 1354–1370.

Applebome, P., & Stetler, B. (2012, December 16). Media spotlight seen as a blessing, or a curse, in a grieving town. *The New York Times*. Retrieved from http://www.nytimes.com/2012/12/17/business/media/newtown-has-mixed-feelings-about-the-media-horde-in-its-midst.html?ref=media&_r=0

Askar, J. G. (2012, December 17). TV coverage of Sandy Hook shootings draws heavy criticism: Reporting considered invasive, exploitative and sensationalized. *Deseret News*. Retrieved from http://www.deseretnews.com/article/865568947/In-context-where-TV-coverage-of-Sandy-Hook-shootings-fell-short.html?pg=all

Barak, G. (1994). Media, society, and criminology. In G. Barak (Ed.), *Media, process, and the social construction of crime: Studies in newsmaking criminology* (pp. 3–45). New York, NY: Garland Publishing.

Barry, C. L., McGinty, E. E., Vernick, J.S., & Webster, D. W. (2013). After Newtown – public opinion on gun policy and mental illness. *New England Journal of Medicine, 368*(12), 1077–1081.

Becker, H. S. (1963). *Outsiders: Studies in the sociology of deviance*. New York, NY: Free Press.

Bernard, T. (1999). Juvenile crime and the transformation of juvenile justice: Is there a juvenile crime wave? *Justice Quarterly, 16*(2), 337–356.

Best, J. (2013, June 16). How should we classify the Sandy Hook killings? Retrieved from http://reason.com/archives/2013/06/16/the-politics-of-gun-violence

Blumenthal, M. (2012, July 24). Gun control polls show longterm decline in support, despite Columbine bump. *Huffington Post*. Retrieved from http://www.huffingtonpost.com/2012/07/20/gun-control-polls-aurora-shooting_n_1690169.html

Bonnie, R. J., Reinhard, J. S., Hamilton, P., & McGarvey, E. L. (2009). Mental health system transformation after the Virginia Tech tragedy. *Health Affairs, 28*(3), 793–804.

Brady Campaign Press Release. (2011, January 7). One million mental health records now in Brady background check system. *BradyCampaign.org*. Retrieved from http://bradycampaign.org/media/press/view/1336/

Brener, N. D., Simon, T. R., Anderson, M., Barrios, L. C., & Small, M. L. (2002). Effect of the incident at Columbine on students' violence- and suicide-related behaviors. *American Journal of Preventive Medicine, 22*(3), 146–150.

Carlson, D. K., & Simmons, W. W. (2001, March 6). Majority of parents think a school shooting could occur in their community. *Gallup.* Retrieved from http://www.gallup.com/poll/1936/Majority-Parents-Think-School-Shooting-Could-Occur-Their-Community.aspx

Chermak, S. M. (1995). *Victims in the news: Crime and the American news media.* Boulder, CO: Westview Press.

Chyi, H. I., & McCombs, M. E. (2004). Media salience and the process of framing: Coverage of the Columbine school shootings. *Journalism and Mass Communication Quarterly, 81*(1), 22–35.

Cohen, B. C. (1963). *The press and foreign policy.* Princeton, NJ: Princeton University Press.

Connelly, M. (1999, August 26). Public supports stricter gun control laws. *The New York Times.* Retrieved from http://partners.nytimes.com/library/national/082699poll-watch.html

Dao, J. (2012, July 23). Aurora gunman's arsenal: Shotgun, semiautomatic rifle, and, at the end, a pistol. *The New York Times.* Retrieved from http://www.nytimes.com/2012/07/24/us/aurora-gunmans-lethal-arsenal.html

Doherty, C. (2015, January 9). A public opinion trend that matters: Priorities for gun policy. *Pew Research Center: FactTank.* Retrieved from http://www.pewresearch.org/fact-tank/2015/01/09/a-public-opinion-trend-that-matters-priorities-for-gun-policy/

Donohue, E., Schiraldi, V., & Ziedenberg, J. (1998, July). *School house hype: School shootings and the real risks kids face in America.* Washington, DC: Justice Policy Institute. Retrieved from http://www.justicepolicy.org/uploads/justicepolicy/documents/98-07_rep_schoolhousehype_jj.pdf

Elsass, H. J., Schildkraut, J., & Stafford, M. C. (2014). Breaking news of social problems: Examining media consumption and student beliefs about school shootings. *Criminology, Criminal Justice, Law & Society, 15*(2), 31–42.

Entman, R. M. (2007). Framing bias: Media in the distribution of power. *Journal of Communication, 57*(1), 163–173.

Fallahi, C. R., Austad, C. S., Fallon, M., & Leishman, L. (2009). A survey of the perceptions of the Virginia Tech tragedy. *Journal of School Violence, 8*(2), 120–135.

Ferraro, K. F. (1995). *Fear of crime: Interpreting victimization risk.* Albany, NY: State University of New York Press.

Fox, J. A., & DeLateur, M. J. (2014). Mass shootings in America: Moving beyond Newtown. *Homicide Studies, 18*(1), 125–145.

Fox, L. (2013, December 10). Sandy Hook anniversary leads White House to invest $100 million in mental health system. *U.S. News and World Report.* Retrieved from http://www.usnews.com/news/articles/2013/12/10/sandy-hook-anniversary-leads-white-house-to-invest-100-million-in-mental-health-system

Gans, H. J. (1979). *Deciding what's news: A study of CBS Evening News, NBC Nightly News, Newsweek, and Time.* New York, NY: Pantheon Books.

Garofoli, J. (2007, April 20). New-media culture challenges limits of journalism ethics. Retrieved from http://articles.sfgate.com/2007-04-20/news/17242016_1_new-media-traditional-media-traditional-news-sources/3

Gassen, S. G., & Williams, T. (2013, March 27). Before attack, parents of gunman tried to address son's strange behavior. *The New York Times.* Retrieved from http://

www.nytimes.com/2013/03/28/us/documents-2011-tucson-shooting-case-gabrielle-giffords.html

Gillespie, M. (2000, April 20). One in three say it is very likely that Columbine-type shootings could happen in their community. *Gallup*. Retrieved from http://www.gallup.com/poll/2980/One-Three-Say-Very-Likely-ColumbineType-Shootings-Could.aspx

Graber, D. A. (1980). *Crime news and the public*. Chicago, IL: University of Chicago Press.

Gruenewald, J., Pizarro, J., & Chermak, S. (2009). Race, gender, and the newsworthiness of homicide incidents. *Journal of Criminal Justice, 37*(3), 262–272.

Harmon, A. (2012, December 18). Fearing a stigma for people with autism. *The New York Times*. Retrieved from http://www.nytimes.com/2012/12/18/health/fearing-a-stigma-for-people-with-autism.html

Hernandez, T. C., Schildkraut, J., & Elsass, H. J. (2015). *The Sandy Hook Elementary School shooting and changes in mental health legislation: A review of the evidence*. Manuscript submitted for publication.

Kalish, R., & Kimmel, M. (2010). Suicide by mass murder: Masculinity, aggrieved entitlement, and rampage school shootings. *Health Sociology Review, 19*(4), 451–464.

Kaminski, R. J., Koons-Witt, B. A., Thompson, N. S., & Weiss, D. (2010). The impacts of Virginia Tech and Northern Illinois University shootings on the fear of crime on campus. *Journal of Criminal Justice, 38*(1), 88–98.

Kellner, D. (2008). Media spectacle and the "Massacre at Virginia Tech". In B. Agger & T.W. Luke (Eds.), *There is a gunman on campus* (pp. 29–54). Lanham, MD: Rowan & Littlefield Publishers.

Kleck, G. (2009). Mass shootings in schools: The worst possible case for gun control. *American Behavioral Scientist, 52*(10), 1447–1464.

Kondolojy, A. (2012, December 17). *Friday night cable ratings: 'Gold Rush' wins night + Sandy Hook news coverage, 'Jungle Gold', 'Duck Dynasty', 'Friday Night Smackdown' & more*. Retrieved from http://tvbythenumbers.zap2it.com/2012/12/17/friday-cable-ratings-gold-rush-wins-night-sandy-hook-news-coverage-jungle-gold-duck-dynasty-friday-night-smackdown-more/162164/

Larkin, R. W. (2007). *Comprehending Columbine*. Philadelphia, PA: Temple University Press.

Larkin, R. W. (2009). The Columbine legacy: Rampage shootings as political acts. *American Behavioral Scientist, 52*(9), 1309–1326.

Madison, L. (2011, January 20). Poll: Americans remain split on gun control. *CBS News*. Retrieved from http://www.cbsnews.com/news/poll-americans-remain-split-on-gun-control/

Maguire, B., Weatherby, G. A., & Mathers, R. A. (2002). Network news coverage of school shootings. *The Social Science Journal, 39*(3), 465–470.

Mayors Against Illegal Guns. (2013). Analysis of recent mass shootings. Retrieved from http://libcloud.s3.amazonaws.com/9/56/4/1242/1/analysis-of-recent-mass-shootings.pdf

Mayr, A., & Machin, D. (2012). *The language of crime and deviance: An introduction to critical linguistic analysis in media and popular culture*. London: Continuum International Publishing Group.

McCombs, M. E. (1997). Building consensus: The news media's agenda-setting roles. *Political Communication, 14*(4), 433–443.

McCombs, M. E., & Shaw, D. L. (1972). The agenda-setting function of the mass media. *The Public Opinion Quarterly, 36*(2), 176–187.

McGinty, E. E., Webster, D. W., & Barry, C. L. (2013). Effects of news media messages about mass shootings on attitudes towards persons with serious mental illness and public support for gun control policies. *American Journal of Psychiatry, 170*(5), 494–501.

McGinty, E. E., Webster, D. W., Vernick, J. S., & Barry, C. L. (2013). Public opinion on proposals to strengthen U.S. gun laws: Findings from a 2013 survey. In D. W. Webster & J. S. Vernick (Eds.), *Reducing gun violence in America: Informing policy with evidence and analysis* (pp. 239–258). Baltimore, MD: The Johns Hopkins University Press.

Muschert, G. W. (2002). *Media and massacre: The social construction of the Columbine story.* (Unpublished doctoral dissertation). University of Colorado at Boulder, Boulder, CO.

Muschert, G. W. (2007). The Columbine victims and the myth of the juvenile super-predator. *Youth Violence and Juvenile Justice, 5*(4), 351–366.

Muschert, G. W., & Carr, D. (2006). Media salience and frame changing across events: Coverage of nine school shootings, 1997–2001. *Journalism and Mass Communication Quarterly, 83*(4), 747–766.

Muschert, G. W., & Larkin, R. W. (2007). The Columbine High School shootings. In S. Chermak & F.Y. Bailey (Eds.), *Crimes and trials of the century* (pp. 253–266). Westport, CT: Praeger.

Newman, K. S. (2006). School shootings are a serious problem. In S. Hunnicutt (Ed.), *School shootings* (pp. 10–17). Farmington Hills, MI: Greenhaven Press.

Newport, F. (2011, January 24). Americans link gun laws, mental health to mass shootings. *Gallup.* Retrieved from http://www.gallup.com/poll/145757/Americans-Link-Gun-Laws-Mental-Health-Mass-Shootings.aspx

NICS Improvement Amendments Act of 2007, H.R. 2640, 110th Cong., 1st Sess. (2007).

"NYSAFE Act Gun Reform." (n.d.). Retrieved from https://www.governor.ny.gov/nysafeact/gunreform

Pew Research Center for the People & the Press. (1999, December 28). Columbine shooting biggest news draw of 1999. Retrieved from http://www.people-press.org/1999/12/28/columbine-shooting-biggest-news-draw-of-1999/

Pew Research Center for the People & the Press. (2000, April 19). A year after Columbine public looks to parents more than schools to prevent violence. Retrieved from http://www.people-press.org/2000/04/19/a-year-after-columbine-public-looks-to-parents-more-than-schools-to-prevent-violence/

Pew Research Center for the People & the Press. (2007a, April 25). Widespread interest in Virginia Tech shootings, but public paid closer attention to Columbine. Retrieved from http://people-press.org/report/322/widespread-interest-in-virginia-tech-shootings

Pew Research Center for the People & the Press. (2007b, April 23). Little boost for gun control or agreement on causes. Retrieved from http://www.people-press.org/2007/04/23/little-boost-for-gun-control-or-agreement-on-causes/

Pew Research Center for the People & the Press. (2009, November 11). Fort Hood shootings top interest, coverage. Retrieved from http://www.people-press.org/2009/11/11/fort-hood-shootings-top-interest-coverage/

Pew Research Center for the People & the Press. (2011, January 19). No shift toward gun control after Tucson shootings. Retrieved from http://www.people-press.org/2011/01/19/no-shift-toward-gun-control-after-tucson-shootings/

Pew Research Center for the People & the Press. (2012a, July 23). Colorado shootings capture public's interest. Retrieved from http://www.people-press.org/2012/07/23/colorado-shootings-capture-publics-interest/

Pew Research Center for the People & the Press. (2012b, December 17). Public divided over what Newtown signifies. Retrieved from http://www.people-press.org/2012/12/17/public-divided-over-what-newtown-signifies/

Pew Research Center for the People & the Press. (2012c, December 20). After Newtown, modest change in opinion about gun control. Retrieved from http://www.people-press.org/2012/12/20/after-newtown-modest-change-in-opinion-about-gun-control/

Pew Research Center for the People & the Press. (2014, December 10). Growing public support for gun rights. Retrieved from http://www.people-press.org/2014/12/10/growing-public-support-for-gun-rights/

Pew Research Center's Project for Excellence in Journalism. (2006, March 13). Cable TV audience: 2006 annual report, Fox News vs. CNN. Retrieved from http://www.journalism.org/node/507

Pollak, J. M., & Kubrin, C. E. (2007). Crime in the news: How crimes, offenders and victims are portrayed in the media. *Journal of Criminal Justice and Popular Culture, 14*(1), 59–83.

Reese, S. D. (2007). The framing project: A bridging model for media research revisited. *Journal of Communication, 57*(1), 148–154.

Roberts, J. (2009, February 11). Gun used in rampage traced to Va. Shops. *CBS News.* Retrieved from http://www.cbsnews.com/2100-500690_162-2695059.html

Robinson, M. B. (2011). *Media coverage of crime and criminal justice.* Durham, NC: Carolina Academic Press.

Saad, L. (1999, April 23). Public views Littleton tragedy as sign of deeper problems in country. *Gallup.* Retrieved from http://www.gallup.com/poll/3898/public-views-littleton-tragedy-sign-deeper-problems-country.aspx

Saad, L. (2012a, December 27). Americans want stricter gun laws, still oppose bans. *Gallup.* Retrieved from http://www.gallup.com/poll/159569/americans-stricter-gun-laws-oppose-bans.aspx

Saad, L. (2012b, December 28). Parents' fear for children's safety at school rises slightly. *Gallup.* Retrieved from http://www.gallup.com/poll/159584/parents-fear-children-safety-school-rises-slightly.aspx

Saad, L. (2013, September 20). Americans fault mental health system most for gun violence. *Gallup.* Retrieved from http://www.gallup.com/poll/164507/americans-fault-mental-health-system-gun-violence.aspx

Sacco, V. F. (1995). Media constructions of crime. *Annals of the American Academy of Political and Social Science, 539*, 141–154.

Sanchez, R. (1998, May 23). Educators pursue solutions to violence crisis; as deadly sprees increase, schools struggle for ways to deal with student anger. *The Washington Post*. Retrieved from http://pqasb.pqarchiver.com/washingtonpost/

Scheufele, D. A., & Tewksbury, D. (2007). Framing, agenda setting, and priming: The evolution of three media effects models. *Journal of Communication, 57*(1), 9–20.

Schildkraut, J. (2012). The remote is controlled by the monster: Issues of mediatized violence and school shootings. In G. W. Muschert & J. Sumiala (Eds.), *School shootings: Mediatized violence in a global age* (pp. 235–258). Bingley, U K: Emerald Publishing Group.

Schildkraut, J. (2014). *Mass murder and the mass media: An examination of the media discourse on U.S. rampage shootings, 2000–2012*. (Unpublished doctoral dissertation). Texas State University, San Marcos, TX.

Schildkraut, J., Elsass, H. J., & Meredith, K. (2015). *Mass shootings and the media: Why all events are not created equal*. Manuscript submitted for publication.

Schildkraut, J., Elsass, H. J., & Muschert, G. W. (2016). Satirizing mass murder: What many think, yet few will say. In L. Eargle and A. Esmail (Eds.), *Gun Violence in American Society: Crime, Justice, and Public Policy* (pp. 233–255). Lanham, MD: University Press of America.

Schildkraut, J., Elsass, H. J., & Stafford, M. C. (2015). Could it happen here? Moral panic, school shootings, and fear of crime among college students. *Crime, Law and Social Change, 63*(1), 91–110.

Schildkraut, J., & Hernandez, T. C. (2014). Laws that bit the bullet: A review of legislative responses to school shootings. *American Journal of Criminal Justice, 39*(2), 358–374.

Schildkraut, J., & Muschert, G. W. (2013). Violent media, guns, and mental illness: The three ring circus of causal factors for school massacres, as related in media discourse. *Fast Capitalism, 10*(1). Available at http://www.uta.edu/huma/agger/fastcapitalism/10_1/schildkraut10_1.html

Schildkraut, J., & Muschert, G. W. (2014). Media salience and the framing of mass murder in schools: A comparison of the Columbine and Sandy Hook school massacres. *Homicide Studies, 18*(1), 23–43.

Singh, R. (1999). Gun politics in America: Continuity and change. *Parliamentary Affairs, 52*(1), 1–18.

Smith, T. W. (2002). Public opinion about gun policies. *The Future of Children, 12*(2), 154–163.

Soraghan, M. (2000). Colorado after Columbine: The gun debate. *State Legislatures, 26*(6), 14–21.

Sorenson, S. B., Manz, J. G., & Berk, R. A. (1998). News media coverage and the epidemiology of homicide. *American Journal of Public Health, 88*(10), 1510–1514.

Stanley, A. (2007, April 17). Deadly rampage and no loss for words. Retrieved from http://www.nytimes.com/2007/04/17/us/17tvwatch.html?ref=us

Surette, R. (1992). *Media, crime, and criminal justice: Images and reality*. Pacific Grove, CA: Brooks/Cole Publishing Company.

TheWebStats.com. (2011). MSNBC.com. Retrieved from http://www.thewebstats.com/msnbc.com

The White House. (2013). Now is the time: The President's plan to protect our children and our communities by reducing gun violence. Washington, DC: The White House. Retrieved from http://www.whitehouse.gov/sites/default/files/docs/wh_now_is_the_time_full.pdf

Virginia Tech Review Panel. (2007). *Mass shootings at Virginia Tech April 16, 2007: Report of the review panel.* Arlington, VA: Governor's Office of the Commonwealth of Virginia. Retrieved from http://www.governor.virginia.gov/TempContent/techpanelreport.cfm

Wallace, L. (2015). Responding to violence with guns: Mass shootings and gun acquisition. *The Social Science Journal, 52*(2), 156–167.

Warr, M. (2000). Fear of crime in the United States: Avenues for research and policy. In D. Duffee (Ed.), *Measurement and analysis of crime: Criminal justice 2000.* Washington, DC: US Department of Justice, Office of Justice Programs.

Warr, M., & Stafford, M. (1983). Fear of victimization: A look at the proximate causes. *Social Forces, 61*(4), 1033–1043.

"Washington Post-ABC News poll." (n.d.). *Washington Post Politics.* Retrieved September 4, 2013 from http://www.washingtonpost.com/wp-srv/politics/polls/postabcpoll_20121216.html

Weaver, D. H. (2007). Thoughts on agenda setting, framing, and priming. *Journal of Communication, 57*(1), 142–147.

Wigley, S., & Fontenot, M. (2009). Where media turn during crises: A look at information subsidies and the Virginia Tech Shootings. *Electronic News, 3*(2), 94–108.

Wilson, L. C., Ballman, A. D., & Buczek, T. J. (in press). News content about mass shootings and attitudes towards mental illness. *Journalism & Mass Communication Quarterly.*

Wintemute, G. J. (2013). Comprehensive background checks for firearm sales: Evidence from gun shows. In D. W. Webster & J. S. Vernick (Eds.), *Reducing gun violence in America: Informing policy with evidence and analysis* (pp. 95–108). Baltimore, MD: The Johns Hopkins University Press.

Wozniak, K. H. (2015). Public opinion about gun control post-Sandy Hook. *Criminal Justice Policy Review.* doi:10.1177/0887403415577192

8

Social Media and News Coverage as Vicarious Exposure

Carolyn R. Fallahi

Research on the etiology of posttraumatic stress disorder (PTSD) has uncovered several biological, psychological, and social factors that contribute to both its development and maintenance. The severity of symptoms of PTSD is determined in large part by the degree of exposure to a traumatic stressor (Besser, Zeigler-Hill, Weinberg, Pincus, & Neria, 2015). For example, experiencing a violent crime firsthand – no matter the type – places an individual at greater risk for symptoms of PTSD than more indirect exposure. However, in the twenty-first century, modern technology has contributed an additional component or method by which individuals may experience trauma. From worldwide terrorist attacks and natural disasters to local crime and violence, everyday television, newspapers, radio, and the Internet provide millions of individuals and communities with a stream of play-by-play coverage of any and all types of trauma (Swenson & Henkel-Johnson, 2003). At any given moment of the day, viewers are able to tune in and receive the latest reports of these events and media stories. With this increase in information about traumatic events readily available at one's fingertips, psychologists have investigated the potential deleterious effects of vicarious or secondhand exposure to trauma (Pearlman & MacIan, 1995). Information on the effects of vicarious exposure should also be readily available to mental health workers and parents alike, allowing guidance and recommendations to reduce the unintended symptoms associated with exposure. This chapter provides a review of both direct and indirect exposure to trauma, with special attention to the effects of vicarious exposure to media coverage of school shootings.

Even though the impact of vicarious exposure has been addressed within the psychological literature, only a few studies have investigated and can attest to the effect of such exposure following the unparalleled and unique situation of a mass shooting. The ability and tendency to replay and rewatch graphic scenes on news networks have led to viewers' and community members' widely held beliefs that mass shootings are not only prevalent but are also likely to occur at

The Wiley Handbook of the Psychology of Mass Shootings, First Edition. Edited by Laura C. Wilson.
© 2017 John Wiley & Sons, Inc. Published 2017 by John Wiley & Sons, Inc.

one's own neighborhood school, mall, or movie theater (Lawrence & Mueller, 2003). In fact, a direct relationship exists between the level of violence and consequent media coverage of mass shootings: A greater level of violence seen during a particular event translates into more widespread coverage of that particular event within the news. In other words, a higher degree of media coverage on major networks is observed when the incident is more violent (Maguire, Weatherby, & Mathers, 2002). Similarly, vicarious exposure to this type of media coverage increases risk for symptoms of PTSD, exacerbates current symptoms, as well as increases the likelihood of prolonged distress in individuals and communities recovering from these incidents (Jemphrey & Berrington, 2000). The effects of direct exposure to trauma are well-documented; however, the influence of indirect exposure through media is less well known and warrants further study (Swenson & Henkel-Johnson, 2003).

Direct Exposure to Trauma

Direct exposure to a traumatic incident has been found to significantly increase risk for PTSD symptoms (Kim et al., 2009). Many well-documented events in history have produced survivors with symptoms of trauma. The terrorist attacks occurring on September 11, 2001 (9/11) is the quintessential example. Those survivors who directly experienced trauma were at risk for acute stress disorder (ASD) and PTSD. Galea et al. (2003) examined the prevalence of probable PTSD in the general population in New York City during the first 6 months following the 9/11 attacks. They found that immediately following the incident, 7.5% of their sample met the criteria for probable PTSD and that number declined to 0.6% 6 months later. Furthermore, several other studies show the impact of firsthand and secondhand exposure as an occupational hazard. Police, mental health workers, and medical personnel, all of whom worked with the victims of 9/11, were also considered to be at risk for the development of ASD and PTSD.

More specific to the topic of this chapter, several studies have documented the effects of direct exposure to mass shootings. The April 16, 2007 shooting at Virginia Polytechnic Institute and State University (more commonly known as Virginia Tech) was associated with high levels of PTSD in over 15% of respondents on an evaluation administered 4 months following the incident. Higher levels of PTSD symptoms were found in those respondents who were unable to confirm the safety of friends or those with a close friend killed (Hughes et al., 2011). Similarly, following the November 7, 2007 shooting at Jokela High School in Finland, Suomalainen, Haravuroi, Berg, Kiviruusu, and Marttunen (2010) found that direct exposure to the trauma, being older, and being female were associated with more severe PTSD symptoms. For more information on the effects of direct exposure to mass shootings, please refer to Chapter 11.

As discussed in relevant research, individuals who have survived trauma are more likely to demonstrate negative stress reactions including psychological and behavioral changes (Galea et al., 2002; Schlenger et al., 2002; Schuster et al., 2001) and they may meet the criteria for ASD and/or PTSD based on the fifth edition of the *Diagnostic and Statistical Manual of Mental Disorders* (DSM-5; American Psychiatric Association, 2013). Specifically, PTSD became an official American Psychiatric Association (APA) classification in DSM-III (American Psychiatric Association, 1980) and, in this edition, it emphasized trauma – experiences that are so horrific that they would cause most victims to develop a negative reaction, as opposed to more ordinary stressors (Friedman, 2014). In subsequent publications of the DSM, this requirement or definition of trauma has been the source of controversy (Shally-Jensen, 2013). Within the psychiatric community, concern over the restricted definition of trauma (e.g., perceived as life threatening) led to concerns about missing serious symptoms because the event did not rise to this threshold. Other critics worried about the overuse of the PTSD diagnosis. DSM-IV-TR (American Psychiatric Association, 2000) broadened the types of exposure, including both direct and indirect, and relied on a more subjective standard – highlighting that a person "perceived" harm (Scott, 2015). In the DSM-5 (American Psychiatric Association, 2013), exposure to a traumatic event continues to be required for the diagnosis; but a negative emotional reaction to trauma experienced vicariously through media exposure no longer satisfies Criterion A, unless the exposure is related to one's work (American Psychiatric Association, 2013; Friedman, 2014; Tasman, Kay, Lieberman, First, & Riba, 2015). The removal of vicarious exposure through media from the DSM-5 criteria emphasized that research has not shown a high prevalence of PTSD from that type of exposure (Friedman, 2013, 2014; Zoellner, Bedard-Gilligan, Jun, Marks, & Garcia, 2013).

Indirect Exposure to Trauma or Vicarious Trauma

Vicarious trauma, occasionally termed secondary trauma (Pearlman & Saakvitne, 1995; Regehr, Hemsworth, Leslike, Howe, & Chau, 2004) or secondary traumatic stress (Rogers, 2013), is the response to witnessing violence indirectly. Vicarious trauma has been studied in many different areas, including professionals exposed to trauma based on their career, as well as the more controversial line of research examining vicarious trauma associated with media exposure to violence.

Vicarious trauma has been often used in response to professionals who work extensively with trauma patients. In this type of exposure, the therapist does not experience the trauma firsthand, but nonetheless, manifests symptoms similar to PTSD, which include reexperiencing of the trauma, avoidance of anything that reminds the person of the trauma, alterations in mood, psychological numbing, and hyper-arousal. Secondary exposure as the result of hearing stories of trauma patients can lead to symptoms that are chronic, influence both thoughts and emotions, as well as cause a negative shift in cognitive schemas (Pearlman & Saakvitne, 1995; Regehr et al., 2004). These symptoms are similar to PTSD, but are considered at a lesser intensity.

Secondary trauma can affect social workers, psychologists, and counselors (McCann & Pearlman, 1990; Zosky, 2013), especially when working with very high stress cases such as childhood sexual abuse (Sommer & Cox, 2005). Aparicio, Michalopoulos, and Unick (2013) and Sommer and Cox (2005) discovered that social workers exposed to trauma by virtue of listening to the traumatic histories of their clients experienced both affective and cognitive symptoms. Similarly, McMann and Pearlman (1990) and Zosky (2013) found that helping professionals who work with clients with trauma experience long-term effects on their mental health, relationships, and worldview (Arnold, Calhoun, Tedeschi, & Cann, 2005). Evidence for such long-term effects can be seen in a study by Sexton (1999), who showed that vicarious traumatization results from the accumulation of listening to many clients in multiple therapy situations. This accumulation of experiences may lead to symptoms that include PTSD, anxiety, depression, loss of hope, concerns about control and safety, and substance use (Pearlman & Saakvitne, 1995; Vlahov et al., 2002). Furthermore, Lugris (2001) found that a therapist's previous experience with trauma, sexual history, and perceived social support influenced the experience of symptoms of hyper-arousal and severity of cognitive distortions. Other careers also have this risk in which exposure to chronic trauma is a hazard of the job (Regehr et al., 2004). Fields potentially at risk for vicarious exposure to trauma include journalists (See Chapter 14; McMahon, 2001), police personnel (See Chapter 13; Brown, Fielding, & Grover, 1999), and teachers (Auger, Seymour, & Roberts, 2004).

Vicarious Exposure to Media Violence

Other forms of indirect or vicarious exposure that have been studied include media violence or violent programming, such as videogames, movies, and television shows, which may also result in a plethora of negative symptoms (Cantor, 2000). The study of vicarious exposure through the media chronicles various psychological reactions, including lower-intensity PTSD symptoms as the result of watching trauma unfold on television, the Internet, and other media outlets (Ben-Zur, Gil, & Shamshins, 2012). As an example, exposure to media violence historically has been correlated with an increase in behavioral problems, the formation of aggressive scripts in memory, and hostile attributional biases (Huesman, Moise-Titus, Podolski, & Eron, 2003). Some research has also suggested a link between heavy viewing of media violence and later aggression (Bushman & Anderson, 2001; Paik & Comstock, 1994), an increase in negative mood states (Caprara, Renzi, Amolini, D'Imperio, & Travaglia, 1984), and aggressive behaviors and emotions (Anderson et al., 2003). Children who are exposed to high levels of media violence display higher levels of real-world violence and aggression (Huesmann & Taylor, 2006). However, it should be noted that Huesmann and Taylor (2006) conclude that the relationship between media violence and aggression or "real-world" violence is complex, with several variables contributing, which include the type of violence, the amount of exposure, and several characteristics of the individual (e.g., age, gender, intelligence, level of aggressiveness) as well as social influences, such as socioeconomic status, influence of the neighborhood, and parental influence.

Several studies examining the connection between viewing traumatic events in the media and children's stress reactions have documented a relationship between TV viewing and PTSD symptoms (Pfefferbaum et al., 2000; Pfefferbaum et al., 2001). In one study, Pfefferbaum (2001) surveyed over 2,000 middle-school children following the 1995 Oklahoma City bombing and found that strong emotional reactions to the incident and high television exposure were predictive of more PTSD symptomatology. In fact, the effects of this trauma were so intense that they were still apparent 7 weeks after the bombing (Pfefferbaum et al., 2001). In another study on the Oklahoma City bombing, Pfefferbaum, Seale, Brandt, Doughty, and Rainwater (2003) examined PTSD reactions in children who belonged to a community 100 miles away from the bombing and found that both media exposure and print exposure were associated with ongoing PTSD reactions in 88 sixth-graders.

Similar results were found in the Ben-Zur et al. (2012) study of the frequency of exposure to media coverage of the 9/11 terrorist attacks and subsequent levels of posttraumatic symptoms and distress. Other researchers studying the 9/11 coverage discovered that, as media viewing increased in the first seven days following the terrorist attack, so did the potential for probable PTSD (Ahern, Galea, Resnick, & Vlahov, 2004). Also, those who watched the most coverage of 9/11 (i.e., people in the highest third of viewing) showed 2.32 times greater odds for probable PTSD as compared with people in the lowest third of viewing. Schuster et al. (2001) conducted a national study to examine the reactions of adults and their children to the 9/11 terrorist attacks. They found that 44% of their sample exhibited at least one symptom of PTSD. Furthermore, a notable observation, 34% of the sample restricted their children's television viewing, understanding the potential negative consequences of allowing their children unrestricted television viewing of the attacks. Finally, Swenson and Henkel-Johnson (2003) examined reactions to the 9/11 attacks in a college community and found that 76% demonstrated one or more symptoms of PTSD and 32% reported three or more symptoms 3 months after the attack. The most common symptoms reported included hyper-vigilance, anxiety, and apprehension about the future.

Even what may be considered to be more positive images of 9/11 displayed through media yielded similar results. Saylor, Cowart, Lipovsky, Jackson, and Finch (2003) showed evidence of this perhaps unexpected outcome when they surveyed 179 students who were indirectly exposed to media coverage approximately one month after the 9/11 attacks. They showed that both negative and positive images (e.g., heroic images of 9/11) were significantly related to an increase in PTSD symptoms.

In another study examining students enrolled in a class about dream interpretation, Propper, Stickgold, Keeley, and Christman (2007) saw that every hour of television viewing of the attacks on New York City was associated with increased dream content related to 9/11. The authors concluded that dream content changed due to the traumatizing effects of the television exposure. Furthermore, these findings may show that the repeated viewing of horrific images could result in increased levels of stress and trauma in the general population. In another study on the effects of 9/11 on a college community, Swenson and Henkel-Johnson (2003) found that both faculty/staff and students showed symptoms of PTSD with heavy viewing of 9/11 coverage, with faculty and staff showing more severe symptoms.

Media Coverage of Mass Shootings

Just as the media responds to other traumatic events, in the case of mass shootings, news networks approach broadcasting with avid interest and ample coverage. Specific to mass shootings, however, the intense media coverage has led to an increase in the level of fear of violence in seemingly safe locations, such as schools and restaurants, due to frequent dramatizations of the potential threat of mass shootings within the community (Burns & Crawford, 1999). Rogers (2013) noted that the media coverage allowed the world to witness images of the Newtown murders and other highly covered tragedies, leading to concern that these tragedies could occur close to home.

Similar to the coverage of the terrorist attacks of 9/11, graphic images of mass shootings, such as the 2007 Virginia Tech tragedy, were replayed in the media for weeks following the incident (Fallahi & Lesik, 2009). On April 20, 1999, two students killed 12 students and 1 teacher and wounded 21 others prior to committing suicide at Columbine High School in Littleton, Colorado. Consistent with the broadcasting of other tragic events, the images of this tragedy were aired continuously (Addington, 2003). With that said, however, a key difference for this event could be noted. While we might expect violence in a war zone, traumatizing images of school-aged victims struck fear into communities' hearts and cultivated a concern for the safety of schools, a longtime considered safe place to send our children. In a similar vein, Roe-Berning and Straker (1997) found that as exposure to trauma increased, perceived invulnerability decreased in the case of both direct and indirect trauma. In other words, the campus – which at one time served as a safe haven for students and faculty alike – was now a reminder of the possibility of violent attacks directed towards innocent victims at any given moment. Under this current state of fear, feelings of vulnerability or a lack of protection permeated the school community.

On April 16, 2007, a 23-year-old student murdered 32 people and wounded 25 others prior to committing suicide at Virginia Tech in Blacksburg, Virginia. The media coverage was extensive. Fallahi and Lesik (2009) examined the response of students at a large state university in the northeast following the tragedy at Virginia Tech. They hypothesized and found a relationship between vicarious exposure through the news media and acute stress symptoms. As previously stated, acute stress symptoms are similar to symptoms of PTSD, but occur in the first few weeks of an exposure to a trauma.

In their study, 145 female and 167 male participants from undergraduate and graduate psychology courses estimated the number of hours they spent viewing news coverage of the Virginia Tech shootings, including both TV and Internet viewing. These participants were then assessed again approximately three weeks after the incident had occurred and were asked to rate their own symptoms of depression, anxiety, and stress (ranging from "not at all" to "very much so"). Self-ratings of ASD symptoms were obtained as extracted from the DSM-IV-TR (American Psychiatric Association, 2000). They included:

- Intrusive thoughts: experiencing thoughts associated with the case.
- Sleep disturbance: experiencing sleep disturbance – for example, trouble falling asleep, trouble staying asleep at night, and sleeping longer than usual.
- Appetite disturbance: experiencing either an increase or decrease in appetite.
- Nightmares: experiencing nightmares.
- Fear: increasing feelings of fear that something like the Virginia Tech case could either happen again somewhere else or at this university.
- Stomach upset: experiencing gastrointestinal distress – for example, upset stomach and butterflies in your stomach.
- Depressive symptoms: experiencing a sad or down mood.
- Symptoms of suicide: experiencing an increase in suicidal ideation.
- Disorganization: feeling disorganized, confused, and "in a daze."
- Alcohol and drugs: an increase in alcohol or drug use.
- Replaying the event: reliving the trauma of the Virginia Tech case involuntarily.
- Anger: experiencing symptoms of anger.
- Guilt: experiencing symptoms of guilt.

The authors were able to conclude that an increase in TV/Internet viewing of the Virginia Tech case often coincided with an increased likelihood of experiencing acute symptoms of intrusive thoughts, sleep disturbance, distraction, fear, stomach upset, depression, disorganization, replaying of the event, and symptoms of anger. The probability of experiencing acute symptoms of intrusive thoughts, sleep and appetite disturbance, distraction, fear, stomach disturbance, and anger were less than 9% for media viewing of 10 hours and ranged from 30% to 62% for 40 hours of exposure to the case. For suicide, disorganization, and replaying, the probability of experiencing acute symptoms was less than 3% for 10 hours of media exposure and ranged from 3.55% to 10.73% for 40 hours of exposure. Furthermore, through this study, researchers found that, for each additional hour watched of the Virginia Tech shootings media coverage, the odds of experiencing acute symptoms increased from 1.48 to 3.20, depending on the symptoms. Finally, they also found that female participants responded with more symptoms of fear as compared to males in the sample. This study improved upon past research by allowing for the prediction of the probability of experiencing acute symptomatology as the result of vicarious exposure to violence. In another way, this study allowed researchers to quantify the magnitude of the relationship (Fallahi & Lesik, 2009).

Similar to the aforementioned research, other studies focusing on both adults and children who have been exposed to mass shootings have also delineated the potential psychological aftermath of vicarious exposure to trauma for both individuals and communities. Addington (2003) found that a slight fear of victimization at school increased following the Columbine shootings. In one such study about the community, Palinkas, Prussing, Reznik, and Landsverk (2012) found that, in an analysis of two separate school shootings occurring at different high schools in San Diego County, higher incidences of PTSD at the community level were yielded as a result.

What We Know About Vicarious Exposure to Trauma

Based on previous research, a number of variables are recognized and considered predictive of the severity of symptoms resulting from vicarious exposure to trauma. They include the following.

Media coverage

Early studies examining children's media consumption initially focused on the amount of television viewing (Pfefferbaum et al., 2013). What was concluded from this research was that the more time spent watching information about tragedies being reported, discussed, or interpreted in news reports as well as other media outlets, the more significant the subsequent symptoms of trauma (Fallahi & Lesik, 2009).

Symptoms persist

Holmes, Creswell, and O'Connor (2007) examined London children who had watched television coverage of the 9/11 attacks. They found that the children experienced symptoms immediately after viewing television coverage, as well as experienced ongoing PTSD symptoms at 2 and 6 months after the event, showing that acute symptoms may place individuals at risk of more long-term and persistent difficulties.

Prior history of trauma-related problems and/or other psychiatric problems

While individuals in the general population may be at increased risk of developing ASD or PTSD after directly experiencing a traumatic event, a few subgroups are even more likely to experience symptoms depending on their mental health history. Specifically, a history of PTSD or other trauma-related difficulties places children, adolescents, and adults at increased risk for problems associated with both direct and vicarious exposure to trauma (Regehr et al., 2004). In addition, Maercker and Mehr (2006) hypothesized that media reports may lead to retraumatization of those victims already suffering trauma, which would only serve to impede their recovery.

Although Maercker and Mehr (2006) pointed to the potential for retraumatization, Rosen, Tiet, Cavella, Finney, and Lee (2005) maintained a slightly different conclusion based on their study. They sought to evaluate whether or not patients suffering from PTSD perceived their ongoing functioning to be impaired by the 9/11 attacks and subsequent events, whether or not patients' functioning changed significantly from predisaster levels, and how the amount of exposure to media coverage predicted changes in their functioning over time. In contrast to previous research pointing to the possible negative outcomes of high-volume vicarious exposure, this study led researchers to conclude that this association may reflect the negative social effects of isolative television viewing habits rather than retraumatization. Despite a lack of an increase in distress, half of the patients attributed problems in functioning to 9/11 and its aftermath, especially those participants who viewed more 9/11 media coverage (Rosen et al., 2005).

With a prior history of trauma, Gil-Rivas, Silver, Holman, McIntosh, and Poulin (2007) point to an additional risk of such individuals to exhibit further symptoms. In their study, a nationally representative group of adults and their adolescent children in a geographically distant location were examined. It was discovered that both adolescents' acute stress reactions as well as their prior mental health history were often associated with PTSD. Similarly, in a study examining the mental health response to 9/11, almost 40% of those receiving clinical treatment for the traumatic event had a preexisting PTSD and/or other emotional and psychiatric diagnosis (Pfefferbaum et al., 2013). Therefore, it may be difficult to distinguish between the onset of new symptoms, and an exacerbation of past symptoms following vicarious exposure to trauma. This is a well-known phenomenon that clinicians often witness. As an example, although the effects of exposure to trauma often decrease with time, one notable exception evidenced in relevant literature is the media effects on those previously diagnosed with PTSD or who have subclinical PTSD (van der Kolk, 1994; Wolfe, Erickson, Sharkansky, King, & King, 1999). For many individuals in this subgroup as well as others without a history of mental health problems, high exposure to violent media coverage may lead to physiological arousal, which can stimulate trauma-related memories and reinforce the meaning of those events, thereby increasing the chances of subclinical PTSD or ASD becoming PTSD.

High exposure to violent media is not limited to those with a history of diagnosis. Rather, television, radio, Internet, and other media outlets facilitate such viewing for people with various mental health backgrounds living around the world. When speaking to the sheer number of viewers of the 9/11 attacks, a rough approximation contends that at least 100,000 people witnessed first-hand the 9/11 events while millions of others watched the horrific scenes through the media (Yehuda, 2002). Specifically, Yehuda (2002) quantified the impact of the World Trade Center attack in terms of those who experienced the event directly and those who watched the media accounts of the attack. She suggests that 35% of the people who were directly involved with the attack developed symptoms of PTSD. In addition, those who watched coverage of the event developed symptoms as well. Specifically, the longer the exposure to media coverage of the event, the more likely people are to develop symptoms of PTSD. However, vicarious exposure to traumatic events through the media may yield a greater possibility of negative effects for those with a preexisting psychiatric diagnosis.

Sex

Perhaps in contrast to Rosen et al. (2005), Pesci (2000) found that higher levels of vicarious exposure to the Oklahoma City bombing were associated with higher reported levels of distress and symptoms of PTSD. However, another subgroup came into the foreground as possessing an even greater potential for symptoms: Children and adult females were more likely to report internalizing and externalizing symptoms of distress compared to adult males.

Age

Not surprisingly, the subgroups of children and adolescents are at greater risk for the effects of traumatization compared to adults. The reasons for this can be attributed to cognitive and emotional development, such as the development of coping mechanisms. Trauma-related stress reactions are more likely among children and adolescents whose coping mechanisms and cognitive and affective development have yet to prepare them to withstand the psychological pressures of traumatic victimization (Clark & Miller, 1998; Finkelhor & Kendall-Tackett, 1997). Additionally, children and adolescents often do not have the cognitive and verbal abilities to express the affect attached to witnessing or experiencing traumatic events (Yule, Perrin, & Smith, 2001). Therefore, children and adolescents tend to perceive traumatic events idiosyncratically (Urman, Funk, & Elliott, 2001) or 'child-specific' (Ahmad, Sofi, Sundelin-Wahlsten, & von Knorring, 2000, p. 240), thereby compounding psychological and emotional turmoil and setting the stage for such anxieties to be embedded, or comorbid, with other psychiatric disorders such as depression, somatization disorder, chemical abuse, or panic disorder (Bolton, O'Ryan, Udwin, Boyle, & Yule, 2000).

Conclusion

In 2013, the DSM-5 was published and includes a revised list of criteria for the diagnosis of PTSD, excluding vicarious exposure to media from the classification. This change reflects the APA's belief that vicarious exposure to media does not cause symptoms severe enough to yield the diagnosis of PTSD. However, even though mental health professionals can no longer technically diagnose PTSD and ASD from vicarious exposure, children and adults alike may experience significant symptoms and distress from secondhand exposure to traumatic events. In fact, mental health professionals are acutely aware of the toll that vicarious exposure can take on the development and the exacerbation of symptoms in their clients. For mental health professionals interested in prevention, it would be helpful to know the threshold of hours of media viewing associated with the development of acute symptoms. Further, with the current lack of longitudinal research available on this topic, mental health professionals do not maintain an understanding of the duration of symptoms or the long-term impact of violent media exposure. Fallahi and Lesik (2009) concluded that following a traumatic event, it would be prudent to ask clients about their exposure to and viewing of high-profile media events as a routine part of any assessment.

More research is needed to be able to understand the effects of vicarious exposure to trauma. Much of the literature has traditionally focused on correlational and self-report data. Specifically, when participants are asked about their symptoms, they are self-reporting both their symptoms and the number of hours they have viewed high-profile cases, without objective corroboration. Fallahi and Lesik (2009) also point out that without a pretest measure of

PTSD, we are limited in our understanding of whether or not there is a causal inference that media exposure resulted in the development of ASD or PTSD symptoms. In addition, the majority of the literature on vicarious exposure has also centered around terrorist attacks and/or natural disasters. The literature examining mass shootings is sparse and arguably unique, leading members of the community to fear that their neighborhoods and communities may be at risk (Lawrence & Mueller, 2003). As we continue to study the effects of vicarious exposure to trauma in both children and adults, it will be crucial to develop guidelines for both psychological practitioners as well as those psychologists working to advise newscasters on the potential negative effects of violent media (Fallahi & Lesik, 2009).

Acknowledgment

Thank you to Sara R. Fallahi for her editorial assistance.

References

Addington, L. A. (2003). Students' fear after Columbine: Findings from a randomized experiment. *Journal of Quantitative Criminology, 19*, 367–387. doi:10.1023/B:JOQC.0000005440.11892.27

Ahern, J., Galea, S., Resnick, H., & Vlahov, D. (2004). Television images and probable posttraumatic stress disorder after September 11: The role of background characteristics, event exposures, and perievent panic. *Journal of Nervous and Mental Disease, 192*(3), 217–226. doi:10.1097/01.nmd.0000116465.99830.ca

Ahmad, A., Sofi, M. A., Sundelin-Wahlsten, V., & von Knorring, A. L. (2000). Reliability and validity of a child-specific cross-cultural instrument for assessment Posttraumatic Stress Disorder. *European Child and Adolescent Psychiatry, 9*(4), 235–243. doi:10.1007/s007870070032

American Psychiatric Association. (1980). *Diagnostic and statistical manual of mental disorders* (3rd ed.). Washington, DC: Author.

American Psychiatric Association. (2000). *Diagnostic and statistical manual of mental disorders* (4th ed., text rev.). Washington, DC: Author.

American Psychiatric Association. (2013). *Diagnostic and statistical manual of mental disorders* (5th ed.). Washington, DC: Author.

Anderson, C. A., Berkowitz, L., Donnerstein, E., Huesmann, L. R., Johnson, J. D., Linz, D., ... Wartella, E. (2003). The influence of media violence on youth. *Psychological Science in the Public Interest, 4*(3), 81–110. doi:10.1111/j.1529-1006.2003.pspi_1433.x

Aparicio, E., Michalopoulos, L. M., & Unick, G. J. (2013). An examination of the psychometric properties of the Vicarious Trauma Scale in a sample of licensed social workers. *Health & Social Work, 38*(4), 199–206. doi:10.1093/hsw/hlt017

148 *Carolyn R. Fallahi*

Arnold, D., Calhoun, L. G., Tedeschi, R., & Cann, A. (2005). Vicarious posttraumatic growth in psychotherapy. *Journal of Humanistic Psychology, 45,* 239–263. doi:10.1177/0022167805274729

Auger, R., Seymour, J., & Roberts, W., Jr. (2004). Responding to terror: The impact of September 11 on K-12 schools and schools' responses. *Professional School Counseling, 7,* 222–230.

Ben-Zur, H., Gil, S., & Shamshins, Y. (2012). The relationship between exposure to terror through the media, coping strategies and resources, and distress and secondary traumatization. *International Journal of Stress Management, 19*(2), 132–150. doi:10.1037/a0027864

Besser, A., Zeigler-Hill, V., Weinberg, M., Pincus, A. L., & Neria, Y. (2015). Intrapersonal resilience moderates the association between exposure-severity and PTSD symptoms among civilians exposed to the 2014 Israel–Gaza conflict. *Self and Identity, 14*(1), 1–15. doi:10.1080/15298868.2014.966143

Bolton, D., O'Ryan, D., Udwin, O., Boyle, S., & Yule, W. (2000). The long-term psychological effects of a disaster experienced in adolescence: II: General psychopathology. *Journal of Child Psychology and Psychiatry, 41,* 513–523. doi:10.1111/1469-7610.00636

Brown, J., Fielding, J., & Grover, J. (1999). Distinguishing traumatic, vicarious and routine operational stressor exposure and attendant adverse consequences in a sample of police officers. *Work and Stress, 13*(4), 312–325. doi:10.1080/02678379950019770

Burns, R., & Crawford, C. (1999). School shootings, the media, and public fear: Ingredients for a moral panic. *Crime, Law and Social Change, 32,* 147–168. doi:10.1023/A:1008338323953

Bushman, B., & Anderson, C. (2001). Media violence and the American public. Scientific facts versus media misinformation. *American Psychologist, 56,* 477–489. doi:10.1037/0003-066X.56.6-7.477

Cantor, J. (2000). Media violence. *Journal of Adolescent Health, 27*(2), 30–34. doi:10.1016/S1054-139X(00)00129-4

Caprara, G. B., Renzi, P., Amolini, P., D'Imperio, G., & Travaglia, G. (1984). The eliciting cue value of aggressive slides reconsidered in a personological perspective. The weapons effect and irritability. *European Journal of Social Psychology, 14,* 313–322. doi:10.1002/ejsp.2420140306

Clark, D. B., & Miller, T. W. (1998). Stress response and adaptation in children: Theoretical models. In T. W. Miller (Ed.), *Children of trauma: Stressful life events and their effects on children and adolescents* (pp. 3–29). Madison, CT: International Universities Press.

Fallahi, C. R., & Lesik, S. A. (2009). The effects of vicarious exposure to the recent massacre at Virginia Tech. *Psychological Trauma: Theory, Research, Practice, and Policy, 1*(3), 220–230. doi:10.1037/a0015052

Finkelhor, D., & Kendall-Tackett, K. (1997). A developmental perspective on the childhood impact of crime, abuse, and violence victimization. In D. Cicchetti & S. L.Toth (Eds.), *Developmental perspectives of trauma: Theory, research, and intervention* (pp. 1–32). New York, NY: University of Rochester Press.

Friedman, M. J. (2013). Finalizing PTSD in DSM-5: Getting here from there and where to go next. *Journal of Traumatic Stress, 26,* 548–556. doi:10.1002/jts.21840

Friedman, M. J. (2014). A brief history of the PTSD diagnosis. *PTSD: National Center for PTSD.* Retrieved from http://www.ptsd.va.gov/professional/PTSD-overview/ptsd-overview.asp

Galea, S., Ahern, J., Resnick, H., Kilpatrick, D., Bucuvalas, M., Gold, J., & Vlahov, D. (2002). Psychological sequelae of the September 11 terrorist attacks in New York City. *New England Journal of Medicine, 346,*982–987. doi:10.1056/NEJMsa013404

Galea, S., Vlahov, D., Resnick, H., Ahern, J., Susser, E., Gold, J., ... Kilpatrick, D. (2003). Trends of probable post-traumatic stress disorder in New York City after the September 11 terrorist attacks. *American Journal of Epidemiology, 158*(6), 514–524. doi:10.1093/aje/kwg187

Gil-Rivas, V., Silver, R. C., Holman, E. A., McIntosh, D. N., & Poulin, M. (2007). Parental response and adolescent adjustment to the September 11, 2001 terrorist attacks. *Journal of Traumatic Stress, 20,* 1063–1068. doi:10.1002/jts.20277

Holmes, E. A., Creswell, C., & O'Connor, T. G. (2007). Post-traumatic stress symptoms in London school children following September 11th 2001: Peri-traumatic reactions and intrusive imagery. *Journal of Behaviour Therapy and Experimental Psychiatry, 38,* 474–490. doi:10.1016/j.jbtep.2007.10.003

Huesmann, L. R., Moise-Titus, J., Podolski, C., & Eron, L. D. (2003). Longitudinal relations between children's exposure to TV violence and their aggressive and violent behavior in young adulthood: 1977–1992. *Developmental Psychology, 39,* 201–221. doi:10.1037/0012-1649.39.2.201

Huesmann, L. R., & Taylor, L. D. (2006). The role of media violence in violent behavior. *Annual Review of Public Health, 27,* 393–415. doi:10.1146/annurev.publhealth.26.021304.144640

Hughes, M., Brymer, M., Chiu, W. T., Fairbank, J. A., Jones, R. T., Pynoos, R. S., ... Kessler, R. C. (2011). Posttraumatic stress among students after the shootings at Virginia Tech. *Psychological Trauma: Theory, Research, Practice, and Policy, 3*(4), 403–411. doi:10.1037/a0024565

Jemphrey, A., & Berrington, E. (2000). Surviving the media: Hillsborough, Dunblane and the press. *Journalism Studies, 1,* 469–483. doi:10.1080/14616700050081786

Kim, B., Kim, J., Kim, H., Shin, M., Cho, S., Choi, N. H., & ... Yun, M. (2009). A 6-month follow-up study of posttraumatic stress and anxiety/depressive symptoms in Korean children after direct or indirect exposure to a single incident of trauma. *Journal of Clinical Psychiatry, 70*(8), 1148–1154. doi:10.4088/JCP.08m04896

Lawrence, R., & Mueller, D. (2003). School shootings and the man-bites-dog criterion of newsworthiness. *Youth Violence and Juvenile Justice, 1*(4), 330–345. doi:10.1177/1541204003255842

Lugris, V. M. (2001). Vicarious traumatization in therapists: Contributing factors, PTSD symptomatology, and cognitive distortions. *Dissertation Abstracts International, 61,* 5571.

Maercker, A., & Mehr, A. (2006). What if victims read a newspaper report about their victimization? A study on the relationship to PTSD symptoms in crime victims. *European Psychologist, 11*, 137–142.

Maguire, B., Weatherby, G. A., & Mathers, R. A. (2002). Network news coverage of school shootings. *The Social Science Journal, 39*, 465–470. doi:10.1016/S0362-3319(02)00201-X

McCann, I. L., & Pearlman, L. A. (1990). Vicarious traumatization: A framework for understanding the psychological effects of working with victims. *Journal of Traumatic Stress, 3*(1), 131–149. doi:10.1007/BF00975140

McMahon, C. (2001). Covering disaster: A pilot study into secondary trauma for print media. Journalists reporting on disaster. *Australian Journal of Emergency Management, 16*(2), 52–56.

Paik, H., & Comstock, G. (1994). The effects of television violence on antisocial behavior: A meta-analysis. *Communication Research, 21*, 516–546. doi:10.1177/009365094021004004

Palinkas, L. A., Prussing, E., Reznik, V. M., & Landsverk, J. A. (2012). The San Diego East County school shootings: A qualitative study of community-level Post-traumatic stress. *Prehospital and Disaster Medicine, 19*(1), 113–121.

Pearlman, L. A., & MacIan, P. S. (1995). Vicarious traumatization: An empirical study of the effects of trauma work on trauma therapists. *Professional psychology: Research and Practice, 26*, 558–565. doi:10.1037/0735-7028.26.6.558

Pearlman, L. A., & Saakvitne, K. W. (1995). *Trauma and the therapist: Countertransference and vicarious traumatization in psychotherapy with incest survivors.* New York, NY: W. W. Norton.

Pesci, M. (2000). The Oklahoma City bombing: The relationship among modality of trauma exposure, gender, and posttraumatic stress symptoms in adolescents. *Dissertation Abstracts International, 60*, 4902.

Pfefferbaum, B. (2001). The impact of the Oklahoma City bombing on children in the community. *Military Medicine, 12*(Suppl), 49–50.

Pfefferbaum, B., Nixon, S. J., Tivis, R. D., Doughty, D. E., Pynoos, R. S., Gurwitch, R. H., & Foy, D. W. (2001). Television exposure in children after a terrorist incident. *Psychiatry: Interpersonal and Biological Processes, 64*, 202–211. doi:10.1521/psyc.64.3.202.18462

Pfefferbaum, B., Seale, T. W., Brandt Jr., E. N., Doughty, D. E., & Rainwater, S. M. (2003). Media exposure in children one hundred miles from a terrorist bombing. *Annals of Clinical Psychiatry, 15*(1), 1–8. doi:10.3109/10401230309085664

Pfefferbaum, B., Seale, T. W., McDonald, N. B., Brandt Jr., E. N., Rainwater, S. M., Maynard, B. T., ... & Miller, P. D. (2000). Posttraumatic stress two years after the Oklahoma City bombing in youths geographically distant from the explosion. *Psychiatry, 63*(4), 358–370.

Pfefferbaum, B., Weems, C., Scott, B., Nitiéma, P., Noffsinger, M., Pfefferbaum, R., & ... Chakraburtty, A. (2013). Research methods in child disaster studies: A review of studies generated by the September 11, 2001, terrorist attacks; the 2004 Indian Ocean tsunami; and hurricane Katrina. *Child & Youth Care Forum, 42*(4), 285–337. doi:10.1007/s10566-013-9211-4

Propper, R. E., Stickgold, R., Keeley, R., & Christman, S. D. (2007). Is television traumatic? Dreams, stress, and media exposure in the aftermath of September 11, 2001. *Psychological Science, 18*(4), 334–340. doi:10.1111/j.1467- 9280.2007.01900.x

Regehr, C., Hemsworth, D., Leslike, B., Howe, P., & Chau, S. (2004). Predictors of post-traumatic distress in child welfare workers: A linear structural equation model. *Children and Youth Services Review, 26,* 331–346. doi:10.1016/j.childyouth.2004.02.003

Roe-Berning, S., & Straker, G. (1997). The association between illusions of invulnerability and exposure to trauma. *Journal of Traumatic Stress, 10*(2), 319–327. doi:10.1002/jts.2490100212

Rogers, D. (2013, January 23). Secondary traumatic stress in the general public following disasters: A personal experience. *Policy Research Associates.* Retrieved from http://www.prainc.com/secondary-traumatic-stress-in-the-general-public-following-disasters-a-personal-experience/

Rosen, C., Tiet, Q., Cavella, S., Finney, J., & Lee, T. (2005). Chronic PTSD patient's functioning before and after September 11 attacks. *Journal of Traumatic Stress, 18,* 781–784.

Saylor, C. F., Cowart, B. L., Lipovsky, J. A., Jackson, C., & Finch, A. J. (2003). Media exposure to September 11 elementary school students' experiences and posttraumatic symptoms. *American Behavioral Scientist, 46*(12), 1622–1642. doi:10.1177/0002764203254619

Schlenger, W. E., Caddell, J. M., Ebert, L., Jordan, K., Rourke, K. M., Wilson, D., ... Kulka, R. A. (2002). Psychological reactions to terrorist attacks: Findings from the national study of Americans' reactions to September 11. *Journal of the American Medical Association, 288,* 581–588. doi:10.1001/jama.288.5.581

Schuster, M. A., Stein, B. D., Jaycox, L. H., Collins, R. L., Marshall, G. N., Elliott, M., ... Berry, S. A. (2001). A national survey of stress reactions after the September 11, 2001, terrorist attacks. *New England Journal of Medicine, 345,* 1507–1512. doi:10.1056/NEJM200111153452024

Scott, C. L. (2015). *DSM-5 and the law: Changes and challenges.* New York, NY: Oxford University Press.

Sexton, L. (1999). Vicarious traumatisation of counsellors and effects on their workplaces. *British Journal of Guidance & Counselling, 27*(3), 393–403. doi:10.1080/03069889900760341

Shally-Jensen, M. (2013). *Mental health care issues in America: An encyclopedia.* Santa Barbara, CA: ABC-CLIO.

Sommer, C. A., & Cox, J. A. (2005). Elements of supervision in sexual violence counselors' narratives: A qualitative analysis. *Counselor Education and Supervision, 45*(2), 119–134. doi:10.1002/j.1556–6978.2005.tb00135.x

Suomalainen, L., Haravuori, H., Berg, N., Kiviruusu, O., & Marttunen, M. (2010). A controlled follow-up study of adolescents exposed to a school shooting. *European Psychiatry, 26*(8), 490–497. doi:10.1016/j.eurpsy.2010.07.007.

Swenson, D. X., & Henkel-Johnson, J. (2003). A college community's vicarious stress reaction to September 11th terrorism. *Traumatology, 9*(2), 93–105. doi:10.1177/153476560300900203

Tasman, A., Kay, J., Lieberman, J. A., First, M. B., & Riba, M. B. (2015). *Psychiatry* (4th ed.). Oxford, UK: Wiley-Blackwell.

Urman, M. L., Funk, J. B., & Elliott, R. (2001). Children's experiences of traumatic events: The negotiation of normalcy and difference. *Clinical Child Psychology and Psychiatry, 6,* 403–424. doi:10.1177/1359104501006003009

Van der Kolk, B. (1994). The body keeps the score: Memory and the evolving psychobiology of post traumatic stress. *Harvard Review of Psychiatry, 1*(5), 253–265. doi:10.3109/10673229409017088

Vlahov, D., Galea, S., Resnick, H., Ahern, J., Boscarino, J. A., Bucuvalas, M., … Kilpatrick, D. (2002). Increased use of cigarettes, alcohol, and marijuana among Manhattan, New York, residents after the September 11th terrorist attacks. *American Journal of Epidemiology, 155,* 988–996. doi:10.1093/aje/155.11.988

Wolfe, J., Erickson, D. J., Sharkansky, E. J., King, D. W., & King, L. A. (1999). Course and predictors of posttraumatic stress disorder among Gulf War veterans: A prospective analysis. *Journal of Consulting and Clinical Psychology, 67*(4), 520–525. doi:10.1037/0022-006X.67.4.520

Yehuda, R. (2002). Post-traumatic stress disorder. *New England Journal of Medicine, 346,* 108–114. doi:10.1056/NEJMra012941

Yule, W., Perrin, S., & Smith, P. (2001). Traumatic events and post-traumatic stress disorder. In W. K. Silverman, P. A. Treffers, W. K. Silverman, & P. A. Treffers (Eds.), *Anxiety disorders in children and adolescents: Research, assessment and intervention* (pp. 212–234). New York, NY: Cambridge University Press.

Zoellner, L. A., Bedard-Gilligan, M. A., Jun, J. J., Marks, L. H., & Garcia, N. M. (2013). The evolving construct of Posttraumatic Stress Disorder (PTSD): DSM-5 criteria changes and legal implications. *Psychological Injury and Law, 6*(4), 277–289. doi:10.1007/s12207-013-9175-6

Zosky, D. L. (2013). Wounded healers: Graduate students with histories of trauma in a family violence course. *Journal of Teaching in Social Work, 33*(3), 239–250. doi: 10.1080/08841233.2013.795923

9

The Role of Technology in Expressions of Grief

Kenneth A. Lachlan

Mass shootings and other acts of purposeful large-scale destruction are increasingly capturing the attention of the general public. These graphic, visceral events inflict tremendous emotional and psychological damage on survivors, and on the family members and loved ones of the deceased. At the same time, media coverage of these events may be partially responsible for promoting emotional distress among onlookers both near and far, and continual consumption of news coverage related to such events may play a key role in psychological health (See Chapter 8).

This naturally leads to the examination of the role of technology in grieving and coping behaviors following mass shootings. The current chapter explores what is known about the role of both traditional media and new media technologies in managing grief and traumatic events. It begins by examining the literature concerning linear media, new media technologies, and traumatic events. It goes on to explore the role of interactive technologies in social support and online grieving, making an argument for their superiority as a mediated solution for grieving and the experience of loss without reliving post-traumatic stress disorder (PTSD)-inducing stimuli. Finally, it examines what is known specifically about mass shootings in terms of the effective use of new technologies in managing grief, and provides anticipated findings and suggestions for future research based on our knowledge of other literatures.

Stress, Dependencies, and Reliance on Media Technology

High-consequence events that induce grief and suffering, such as mass shootings and other purposeful mass casualty incidents, create a sense of uncertainty and unrest not typically associated with other patterns of media technology use. Weick (1995) and other scholars have identified this phenomenon as the "cosmology episode," when the world has been cast into

The Wiley Handbook of the Psychology of Mass Shootings, First Edition. Edited by Laura C. Wilson.
© 2017 John Wiley & Sons, Inc. Published 2017 by John Wiley & Sons, Inc.

uncertainty and individuals experience tremendous confusion and suffering. Following this shift, a fundamental compulsion exists to restore things to some type of rational order and closure. This drives a need to consume information and/or share information with others, in order to arrive at a less noxious state of mind. This basic drive to acquire and share information likely drives those affected to use different types of mediated technologies and the utility of these technologies in ratifying the cosmology episode leads to greater reliance upon them in the future for this purpose. It also forces us to critically examine the roles of both linear (i.e., television and radio) and interactive media technologies (e.g., social media such as Facebook and Twitter) in managing the psychological consequences associated with traumatic events, such as mass shootings. One useful theoretical framework for understanding these functions is the media dependency theory (Ball-Rokeach, 1973; Ball-Rokeach & DeFleur, 1976).

As a paradigm, media dependency theory (Ball-Rokeach, 1973; Ball-Rokeach & DeFleur, 1976) suggests that, in the absence of other resources, people are dependent on information acquired through technology to learn details, model behavior, and make sense of their surroundings. With limited access to a stress-inducing event, it is likely that mediated information sources are the primary source of information used in evaluating circumstances and deciding upon courses of action. In the event of a mass shooting this is likely to be the case, as those directly involved will have been evacuated from the scene, while those affected in a secondhand manner are unlikely to place themselves at the scene of the event. As people perceive a particular technology or outlet as functional and effective in solving problems, making decisions, or experiencing affective relief, they become increasingly dependent on that particular medium. Due to the perceived utility, that medium or outlet will subsequently exert additional persuasive power over them.

At the same time, there is likely to be great variability in media dependency based on the person and circumstance. Media dependencies may be heavily influenced by individual-level variables, such as personality, access to resources and locations, and degree of involvement in the event (DeFleur & Ball-Rokeach, 1989). For instance, those with a propensity toward information seeking may gravitate toward news outlets, as opposed to entertainment media. At the same time, audiences can only use the technologies to which they have access, and may not choose to seek information if the matter at hand is not perceived as relevant. Given that mass shootings tend to be perceived as events that involve dire consequences, and that those concerned will not likely have direct access to the scene, it is important to assess the roles of different technologically mediated solutions in the grief and suffering experienced after mass shootings, and to assess the extent to which audiences may rely on these technologies.

It is not difficult to see how these dependencies may play out in terms of high-risk events, such as mass shootings. Media dependency scholars, including Ball-Rokeach (1973), have argued that the perception that one has lost control over their surroundings, in the context of a high-consequence event, will produce especially strong motivation towards consuming information. Ambiguity will motivate those affected to become more dependent on technologically mediated information, and those impacted will be driven toward consuming information from sources they consider trustworthy and/or effective. It is likely the case that the affective needs and desire for grieving and closure associated with mass shootings will also be affected by media dependencies, and that those outlets found most effective in coping with grief and anxiety will be turned to again and again.

This assumption is not unlike the findings offered in the aftermath of other high-consequence events. Contemporary theorizing on uncertainty management and communication would posit that in the event of environmental risks that are of high probability and pose threats to life and property, people tend to seek out specific, technology-mediated information pertaining to the outcomes in question (Brashers et al., 2000). For decades, this body of research has offered more or less the same argument: that news media can be relied upon for the acquisition of information and for vicarious affect expression. This opportunity to experience affect and to identify with others allows the viewer to engage in coping and experience a reduction in the level of anxiety induced by the event (see Lachlan & Spence, 2014; Perse, Nathanson, & McLeod, 1996).

By the same token, this assumption is based on research that was conducted before the advent of social media. It is unclear whether these previously demonstrated results would apply to social media because this technology provides two-directional opportunities for the sharing of information and for giving and receiving social support. It may be the case that the grieving and vicarious affective responses associated with social media more closely resemble real-life social support. It is apparent that future research should compare the effectiveness of linear and interactive media in the processes of social support and grief since these mediated interactions may more closely resemble interpersonal ones.

Compounding this need for investigation is the high-stress nature of mass shootings and similar events. Under conditions of extreme duress and trauma it may be the case that these dependencies form very quickly. Those either directly or indirectly affected by such events may make fast decisions concerning the technological solutions they use in the management of grief and trauma, and will likely stick to those outlets and resources as the crisis unfolds. It is also likely that the medium through which they were first alerted of the event will continue to play a strong role in how all subsequent information is evaluated (Lachlan, 2013).

Media Use and Trauma: Vicarious Grief and Deleterious Effects

As suggested above, media dependency theory and the need to reduce uncertainty may drive audiences to seek mediated information in order to cope with their grief. At the same time, there may be deleterious effects associated with these patterns of media consumption. The following section provides an overview of what is known about the relationship between using traditional media to cope with high-stress situations, and its subsequent impact on emotional functioning and stress reactions. The extant literature is somewhat mixed in terms of the functionality of linear media in expressing grief vicariously and engaging in coping behaviors.

Some empirical evidence supports the notion that traditional media consumption may lead people to effectively cope with grief and tragedy. Following the September 11 terrorist attacks, for example, one study found that the most common means of coping was following the news through television and radio, and that the most effective means of coping in the immediate aftermath was the obtainment of information (DeRoma et al., 2003). This makes sense, given that seeing and hearing the accounts of others who are experiencing grief or trauma following a large-scale event may help individuals make sense of confusing and upsetting situations (Weick, 1995). Further, under these circumstances, formal leaders and others who are seen as credible and of goodwill can help the public to understand how to interpret and cope with the event and with the information that is presented (Seeger, Venette, Ulmer, & Sellnow, 2002; Spence et al., 2005).

Despite these few studies demonstrating support for the utility of media following traumatic events, the research on linear media as a coping mechanism in the aftermath of tragedy overwhelmingly suggests compound, negative effects associated with increased media exposure. While this research is not directly centered on mass shootings, these studies have implications for our understanding of the problems associated with the use of linear media in grieving and coping with traumatic loss. Numerous studies, for example, have offered data positing that children viewing coverage of the Oklahoma City bombings and September 11 terrorist attacks were more likely to develop depression and anxiety symptoms than those who did not view this information (Green, 1991; Hoven et al., 2004; Saylor, Cowart, Lipovsky, Jackson, & Finch, 2003; Terr et al., 1999). These studies included samples of children living near New York City following September 11 (Hoven et al., 2004) and samples of children living far from the city, suggesting that these disruptive patterns may be evident in those impacted both directly and indirectly by the tragedy (Saylor et al., 2003).

Similar findings have been found in adult samples, leading numerous researchers to claim that television coverage of highly tragic events may in and of itself constitute a type of exposure to trauma (Ahern, Galea, Resnick, & Vlahov, 2004). Adults who reported viewing more television images of the September 11 terrorist attacks were more likely to report PTSD symptoms 4 months after the attack (Ahern et al., 2004). Ahern et al. (2002) offered additional data that supported heightened depression symptoms among those exposed to high levels of news coverage of terror activity. All in all, these findings suggest that media exposure to a terrifying event, such as a mass shooting, can lead to negative emotional responses, even among those not directly involved (Galea et al., 2003; Liverant, Hofmann, & Litz, 2004). These responses have also manifested in the form of behavioral outcomes (e.g., use of alcohol, cigarettes, and marijuana) that have been associated with PTSD symptomology following large-scale tragedies (Vlahov et al., 2002).

The capacity for mediated communication to induce or magnify PTSD symptoms is particularly alarming when coupled with the expected symptoms that accompany the experience – vicariously or otherwise – of a mass shooting. Numerous studies have found that individuals involved in mass shooting incidents are at risk of PTSD (see Norris, 2007; Orcutt, Miron, & Sligowski, 2014). For example, following the 2007 Virginia Tech shooting, Hughes and colleagues (2011) reported that over 15% of students indicated some degree of PTSD symptoms 3 months later; among those most strongly affected by the shooting, a reduction in self-efficacy and skewed perception of the frequency of such events were identified as contributing factors to this distress. Scarpa and colleagues (2014) offer more evidence of PTSD symptoms among Virginia Tech students, faculty, and alumni. In their study of the impact of mediated interpersonal exchanges, it was found that medium of transmission was relatively unimportant, but the nature of the information exchanged was; "conveyance," or the sharing of factual information through electronic media, was positively related to subsequent PTSD symptoms.

Furthermore, public media involvement may serve to exacerbate these PTSD symptoms (See Chapter 10). Following a school shooting in Jokela, Finland, students who had given firsthand reports to media were more likely to experience greater PTSD symptoms at a later date than those who had not recounted the story (Haravuori, Suomalainen, Berg, Kiviruusu, & Marttunen, 2011). In this same study, the authors also found evidence of a double-dose effect – students who survived the shooting reported greater levels of PTSD after reliving the experience through repeated exposure to media coverage of the event. It may also be the case that specific patterns of information processing and coping tendencies play a role in how mediated information concerning a mass shooting contributes to the proliferation of ongoing psychological distress and difficulties. For example, Nolen-Hoeksema (2000) and others have argued that some individuals are prone to think repetitively about experiences they perceive as traumatic, emotionally arousing, or difficult to understand. As a result, individuals predisposed to this maladaptive coping style may focus the majority of their attention on reliving the negative emotions and consequences of an event, as opposed to seeking solutions to the disturbance in question. Those inclined to ruminate may then be more likely to experience long-term psychological or emotional distress associated with the tragedy, and this may lead to acute, diagnosable depressive disorders (Nolen-Hoeksema & Morrow, 1991; Nolen-Hoeksema, Parker, & Larson, 1994).

The research on coping and its relationship with mediated information concerning tragedy also reveals stark gender differences that are worth considering. This research largely suggests that women are more likely than men to engage in rumination when dealing with information that is traumatic or emotionally distressing (Nolen-Hoeksema & Girgus, 1994; Nolen-Hoeksema, Larson, & Grayson, 1999). Mak, Hu, Zhang, Xiao, and Lee (2009) add further evidence of gender differences in individuals' responses to upsetting information by examining neural activity in men and women who were exposed to highly positive, negative, and neutral images. The results suggested that imagery evoking negative emotions were more likely to drive women toward affective and emotion-focused strategies to reduce negative emotions, while males exposed to the same stimuli were more likely to use cognitive strategies. This is consistent with past research suggesting that men and women may differ in their responses to unpleasant stimuli and that there may be underlying differences between the sexes in terms of their propensity towards emotional recall and affective processing (see Cahill, 2006; Collignon et al., 2010; Seavey, Katz, & Zalk, 1975). In all, this suggests that the use of linear media as a means of coping with grief may be especially problematic for women, as the imagery presented may have greater capacity to induce ruminative thought patterns that contribute to PTSD and other stress-related disorders.

Social Media as an Alternative to Vicarious Grieving

Another key concern with the use of linear media as a method of vicarious grieving is its propensity toward isolating those in need. Regardless of the source, past research has supported that social support plays an important role in managing grief and dealing with trauma. A significant body of research suggests that social support from peers, caregivers, and those perceived to be similar to oneself can be effective in reducing psychological distress associated with traumatic events (Bonanno, Brewin, Kaniasty, & La Greca, 2010; Masten & Obradovic, 2008; Paul et al., 2015). Across this literature, social support has been demonstrated to be an effective tool in the reduction of grief and PTSD symptoms (Ellis, Nixon, & Williamson, 2009; La Greca, Silverman, Lai, & Jacard, 2010). At the same time, deficiencies in these social support mechanisms have been connected to increased psychological distress (Burton, Stice, & Seeley, 2004).

Given the problems associated with the use of traditional linear media (e.g., reliving the event), it is beneficial that there are other technologically mediated outlets for dealing with grief. Recent advances in interactive media allow for connections and interactions that more closely resemble face-to-face social support. Although seeking to make sense of mass shootings through the processing of linear media may contribute to greater psychological distress, there are emerging technological solutions that have been found to be effective in managing stress and grief by more closely mirroring interpersonal social support.

While there is extensive research in the communication and psychology literatures on the use of new media technologies for social support, scant research has specifically examined the intersection of online social support, interactive media technologies, and grieving. While these studies were not designed specifically to examine grief in the aftermath of a mass shooting, they offer valuable insight into the types of uses and responses we might expect under the circumstances. Walter, Hourizi, Moncur, and Pitsillides (2011) offer numerous arguments concerning cultural changes that impact the importance of news media and social media technologies in the mourning and grieving process. Among these, they argue that in recent years grieving and mourning in the Western world has shifted toward a model involving the celebration of the lives of the deceased individual. In this model, social media sites like Facebook offer the bereaved a chance to relive the life and experiences of the deceased, along with any shared experiences they may have had with the individual. In terms of face-to-face memorializing, the authors note that social media can also be used to coordinate these more traditional mourning and celebration rituals, or serve as an outlet for streaming the event, thus breaking down geographical barriers regarding attendance (Pitsillides, Katsikides, & Conreen, 2009).

Another important consideration offered by Walter and colleagues (2011) concerns the distinction between grief-specific and non-grief-specific websites in memorializing the deceased. Since the mid-1990s, text-based memorial sites have been available that allow individuals to express grief and mourn the departed. These sites often revolve around those who have been lost to a particular ailment or condition, such as cancer, AIDS, or substance abuse. Those participating in the community therefore begin with some degree of commonality, and it is widely accepted that one may mourn someone they did not know if they feel this sense of connectedness.

However, interactions also occur on websites (e.g., social media) that were not specifically designed with mourning in mind. Social media sites allow individuals who may not have previously known each other to share experiences and impressions of the deceased. This leads to the formation of relationships despite having no previous commonality except their knowledge of the person they are grieving. Walter and colleagues (2011) argue that these relationships are typically short-lived, given that they constitute "weak ties" (see Granovetter, 1973) and are situationally construed.

At the same time, the notion of the "weak tie" through social media has come under increased scrutiny in recent years. Recent research has indicated that bonds and relationships formed through social media may be every bit as meaningful and influential as those formed through face-to-face interactions, and research evidence suggests that this may be especially true in instances in which bonding involves the overcoming of emotional or psychological obstacles (see Ledbetter et al., 2011). It stands to reason, that in the context of mass shootings, the spontaneously formed social networks designed to grieve the deceased may develop into more stable, long-term communities dedicated to making sense of the loss and preventing similar incidents in the future.

Given the potential for people to form strong and meaningful social bonds through social media, the underlying psychological processes behind their use become an important consideration in our understanding of their utility in managing grief following mass shootings. Carroll and Landry (2010) offer important insights into our understanding of grief and bereavement and its connection to social media. They argue that, at least in contemporary American society, the goal of bereavement appears to be to create a sense of normalcy and a return to everyday life as quickly as possible. In this context, online social support and grief, such as those driven by Facebook and social media, become an important resource for those experiencing a tragedy, given that the mediums have the capability to memorialize the deceased quickly and across temporal and geographic separation. In this sense, social media sites allow the bereaved to construct a biography of the deceased using timelines and photographs, and both memorialize and celebrate the importance of that individual in their lives (Walter, 2006). It is also noteworthy that these practices are not dissimilar to grieving rituals practiced in other non-western cultures; writing on the Facebook or Myspace wall of a deceased person may facilitate grieving in a similar manner to behavioral gestures commonplace in the everyday lives of those grieving in African or Asian cultures, such as an extra place setting at the dinner table (Debatty, 2007).

In their ethnographic exploration of roughly 200 postings on the Myspace walls of deceased individuals, Carroll and Landry (2010) reported five common themes. First and most common is that of an overt expression of grief; nearly half of the posts they identified contained some expression of missing the individual, mourning their loss, or wishing that they rest in peace. Perhaps more interesting from a psychological perspective are the other themes that emerged. Myspace users were also likely to use the medium to express praise or admiration for the deceased individuals, often in the form of expressions of appreciation for those they impacted. Related to this is an acknowledgment of expertise; the authors also found that users would post requests for advice and guidance on the walls of the deceased, both as a request for help and as a tacit acknowledgment of the expertise and guidance the individual provided while they were alive. Other common themes included biographic or narrative accounts of shared experiences, and statements regarding the values for which the deceased individuals stood. All in all, the data provide a picture of the content that individuals post on the walls of the deceased, and provide a glimpse into how these individuals grieved. Well beyond simple expressions of grief and bereavement, the content reveals the ongoing psychological presence of the deceased in the minds of those choosing to post on their walls, and to some extent the utility of social media in facilitating grieving.

Arthur (2009) and others also note the importance of storytelling as a means of commemoration and grief following tragedies of significant scale. Numerous scholars have argued that the telling, listening, and sharing of commonly held experiences are basic components of the healing process. Arthur (2009) argues that commemoration through social media is not so much a form of collective memory, as it does not engender a uniform remembrance of the tragedy in question. Rather, it can be better categorized as a place of *collected memory*, a place where people can create a repository of pictures, stories, and shared experiences that individual mourners may pick and choose from in satisfying their needs for grieving and closure. These types of online commemorations, such as those associated with the September 11 terrorist attacks and natural disasters, can serve to solidify and even create new communities of those affected by the same tragedy (Hess, 2007; Recuber, 2012).

Such online repositories of information that users can tailor to their specific needs may be instrumental in the grieving process. One example of the use of new media technologies for grieving, social support, and collected memory in the specific context of a mass shooting can be found in the aftermath of the 2007 Virginia Tech shooting. Mastrodicasa (2008) reported that, in the aftermath of the shooting, more than 500 individual Facebook groups were created related to the shooting. These included tributes, social support groups, groups dedicated to discussion of gun control and mental health issues, general information concerning the event, and others. More specifically, the Facebook group "VT Unite," a forum dedicated to providing social support to grieving students, gained over 50 members within 24 hours of the shooting (Mastrodicasa, 2008; Read, 2007). As a matter of policy, Facebook froze the accounts of those who perished in the Virginia Tech shooting until they were contacted by a loved one or next of kin; after reopening the account, friends and loved ones reported finding comfort in visiting the pages and photo albums of those who had lost their lives in the shooting (Hortobagyi, 2007).

It should also be noted that traditional blogging sites, which were still popular in the late 2000s, played an important role in managing grief online following the Virginia Tech shooting; numerous student affairs organizations used these online web journals to field questions and inquiries regarding support for students, as well as an exchange of ideas about the management of student issues should a similar shooting take place on their campus. Palen and colleagues (2010) argued that in a broader sense, the Virginia Tech shooting marked the dawn of the use of both traditional blogging and microblog services (e.g., Twitter) in the management of crises and disasters. They offer that, related to the grieving process, individuals need to engage in sense making following a tragedy of such magnitude. They also note that during the Northern Illinois University shooting several years later, students and other members of the campus community once again returned to these blogging resources, though with an apparent degree of increased caution and sensitivity given users' greater awareness of the public, masspersonal nature of these interactions (Palen & Vieweg, 2008).

Masspersonal Communication and Dialogue

This leads to the consideration of another manner in which social media may be valuable as a technologically mediated technique for dealing with grief – the notion of "masspersonal" communication. In a short time, social media platforms, such as Facebook and Twitter, have emerged as central resources in making sense of the world. These platforms not only allow individual users to engage in direct dialogues with each other, but enable them to broadcast these interactions to a larger follower group. These conversations can be retrieved or viewed by others anonymously, or indexed using particular hashtags or keyword searches. As such, one can instantly find and trace dialogue between other users that are perceived as similar in some way.

Extended to the role of social media in expressions of grief and tragedy, it is easy to see how the observation of the dialogue of others may be beneficial to those suffering loss. The notion of "masspersonal" communication has been used to describe the blurring of lines between interpersonal and mediated communication (O'Reilly & Battelle, 2009; Westerman, Spence, & Van Der Heide, 2012), and scholars have offered that the illusion of dialogues or the perception of dialogue between others may be of some comfort to those experiencing stressful circumstances. Given that people may be drawn to media (whether linear or interactive) for affective needs, it may be the case that the observation of dialogue between others experiencing grief can, by itself, prove therapeutic and provide some sense of closure. On social media platforms, individual users can choose their own level of involvement; one does not necessarily need to become involved in the conversation if they are not comfortable doing so, or they can choose to gradually open up and disclose at a pace they find comfortable given the psychological stress they are experiencing. At the same time, the observation of others may help those experiencing grief feel as though they are not alone, and this itself may aid in the grieving process. This capability of social media for "masspersonal" information sharing allows social media users to both consume and create content, and may help lead to shared understanding among those both participating in and observing the dialogue in question (Lachlan, Spence, Lin, & Del Greco, 2014).

Regardless of the level of involvement chosen by the user, research evidence indicates that social media is becoming an increasingly important resource for mourning and for experiencing emotionally distressing events. Over six decades of research on the uses and gratifications of electronic media indicates that mediated technologies, coupled with interpersonal interactions, are critical resources for individuals experiencing crises (Bracken, Jeffres, Neuendorf, Kopfman, & Moulla, 2005; Deutschman & Danielson, 1960; Greenberg, 1964; Spitzer & Spitzer, 1965).

Among social media platforms, Twitter in particular has emerged as a timely and important resource for the management of large-scale crises (Armstrong & Gao, 2010; Sutton, Palen, & Shklovski, 2008; Westerman et al., 2014). Numerous studies have suggested that the capacity for Twitter to provide real-time updates and continual coverage of events like mass shootings, as they unfold, is perceived as a key advantage that the medium presents for those trying to make sense of highly uncertain and traumatic circumstances. Further, emergency management agencies are beginning to recognize the utility of the medium in addressing the emotional and psychological concerns of those affected by mass crises and disasters (Kavanaugh et al., 2011). This utility is magnified by the capacity of the medium to provide updates in almost real time, given a perception that traditional media outlets do not provide updates fast enough during developing situations that may be highly equivocal (Sutton et al., 2008).

Twitter's ability to offer fast, continual updates to those experiencing psychological distress stems from the formal features of the medium. Twitter can be used to link to URLs and other web resources, and the character limits of the medium may be less restrictive than is often assumed; while tweets are limited to 140 characters, it is easy to link to more detailed accounts of an incident. In terms of what Tweets are likely to be retweeted and contribute to a broader sense of community among those affected by tragedy, several studies offer data positing that a tweet is more likely to receive "serial transmission" if it contains a URL, as this heuristic is relied upon by users under trying circumstances to identify information that is more complete or more relevant to the issue at hand (Suh, Hong, Pirolli, & Chi, 2010). Further research posits that the very circumstances surrounding crisis and tragedy may contribute to the likelihood of serial transmission, as these circumstances produce a degree of motivation not found under conventional tweeting circumstances (Hughes & Palen, 2009). In sum, under circumstances of extreme duress, Twitter may emerge as a supplement to linear media, and the advantages offered by Twitter are those concerning first alerts, affective support, and engendering a sense of community among users, while linear media are more likely to be relied upon for informational updates, instructions, data, and behavioral recommendations (Jin & Liu, 2010; Lachlan et al., 2014; Liu, Jin, & Austin, 2013; Palen et al., 2010).

While little is known specifically about the role of social media in the management of grief following mass shootings, it is not difficult to extrapolate from the extant research on social media and social support. It is likely the case that new media technologies have the potential to provide a stable, interactive environment for the expression of grief. The findings from the literature on online social support would suggest that small, closed online communities have the capacity for offering social support that is every bit as effective as, if not more effective than, face-to-face support groups.

Conclusions

Evidence from a long history of research in the fields of communication and psychology points to the use of media technologies in grieving and in managing real-life events that induce suffering, confusion, and ambiguity. While much of this research has focused on natural disasters, it is not difficult to see how much of what has been learned from these studies informs our understanding of mass shootings. Further, a small number of studies specifically examining mass shootings shed light on these underlying processes.

We can be fairly certain that those affected by tragedies like mass shootings will have a strong desire to obtain information, both in order to make sense of highly equivocal circumstances and to mourn the loss of others as the details surrounding the incident come to light. Social media and commemorative websites may allow those adversely affected to experience grief, share experiences, and to storytell in a manner that allows them to find closure and move forward without necessarily reliving the trauma in question. Social media may also be effective in creating a sense of community, and in galvanizing those who share a collective sense of suffering as a result of the shooting. Future research should attempt to apply these expectations specifically to the context of media use and effects following mass shootings, in order to verify their plausibility in this specific, applied context. It may also be beneficial to investigate the possibility of negative effects associated with the use of social media under these circumstances. While most of the extant research has examined social media and its role in providing social support during crises, we should not consider it a panacea, and future research should examine whether or not the negative consequences associated with linear media use and rumination play out in the context of social media.

References

Ahern, J., Galea, S., Resnick, H., Kilpatrick, D., Bucuvalas, M., Gold, J., & Vlahov, D. (2002). Television images and psychological symptoms after the September 11 terrorist attacks. *Psychiatry, 65,* 289–300.

Ahern, J., Galea, S., Resnick, H., & Vlahov, D. (2004). Television images and probable posttraumatic stress disorder after September 11. *The Journal of Nervous and Mental Disease, 192,* 217–226.

Armstrong, C. L., & Gao, F. (2010). Now tweet this: How news organizations use Twitter. *Electronic News, 4,* 218–235.

Arthur, P. (2009). Trauma online: Public exposure of personal grief and suffering. *Traumatology, 15,* 65–75.

Ball-Rokeach, S. J. (1973). From pervasive ambiguity to a definition of the situation. *Sociometry, 38,* 378–389.

Ball-Rokeach, S. J., & DeFleur, M. L. (1976). A dependency model of mass-media effects. *Communication Research, 1,* 3–21.

Bonanno, G. A., Brewin, C. R., Kaniasty, K., & La Greca, A. M. (2010). Weighing the costs of disaster: Consequences, risks, and resilience in individuals, families, and communities. *Psychological Science in the Public Interest, 11,* 1–49. doi:10.1177/1529100610387086

Bracken, C. C., Jeffres, L., Neuendorf, K. A., Kopfman, J., & Moulla, F. (2005). How cosmopolites react to messages: America under attack. *Communication Research Reports, 22,* 47–58.

Brashers, D. E., Neidig, J. L., Haas, S. M., Dobbs, L. K., Cardillo, L. W., & Russell, J. A. (2000). Communication in the management of uncertainty: The case of persons living with HIV or AIDS. *Communication Monographs, 67,* 63–84.

Burton, E., Stice, E., & Seeley, J. R. (2004). A prospective test of the stress-buffering model of depression in adolescent girls: No support once again. *Journal of Consulting and Clinical Psychology, 72,* 689–697.

Cahill, L. (2006). Why sex matters for neuroscience. *Nature Reviews Neuroscience, 7,* 477–484.

Carroll, B., & Landry, K. (2010). Logging on and letting out: Using online social networks to grieve and mourn. *Bulletin of Science Technology & Society, 30,* 341–349.

Collignon, O., Girarda, S., Gosselina, F., Saint-Amoura, D., Leporea, F., & Lassondea, M. (2010). Women process multisensory emotion expressions more efficiently than men. *Neuropsychologia, 48,* 220–225.

Debatty, R. (2007, March). Ashes to ashes, data to dust. *Art Review,* p. 130.

DeFleur, M. L., & Ball-Rokeach, S. (1989). *Theories of mass communication* (5th ed.). White Plains, NY: Longman.

DeRoma, V., Saylor, C., Swickert, R., Sinisi, C., Marable, T. B., & Vickery, P. (2003). College students' PTSD symptoms, coping, and perceived benefits following media exposure to 9/11. *Journal of College Student Psychotherapy, 18,* 49–64.

Deutschman, P. J., & Danielson, W. A. (1960). Diffusion of knowledge of a major news story. *Journalism Quarterly, 37,* 345–355.

Ellis, A. A., Nixon, R. D. V., & Williamson, P. (2009). The effects of social support and negative appraisals on acute stress symptoms and depression in children and adolescents. *British Journal of Clinical Psychology, 48,* 347–361. doi:10.1348/01446 6508x401894

Galea, S., Vlahov, D., Resnick, H., Ahern, J., Susser, E., Gold, J., … Kilpatrick, D. (2003). Trends of probable post-traumatic stress disorder in New York City after the September 11 terrorist attacks. *American Journal of Epidemiology, 158,* 514–524.

Granovetter, M. (1973). The strength of weak ties. *American Journal of Sociology, 78,* 1360–1380.

Green, B. L. (1991). Evaluating the effects of disasters. *Psychological Assessment, 3,* 538–546.

Greenberg, B. S. (1964). Diffusion of news of the Kennedy assassination. *Public Opinion Quarterly, 28,* 225–231.

Haravuori, H., Suomalainen, L., Berg, N., Kiviruusu, O., & Marttunen, M. (2011). Effects of media exposure on adolescents traumatized in a school shooting. *Journal of Traumatic Stress, 24,* 70–77.

Hess, A. (2007). In digital remembrance: Vernacular memory and the rhetorical construction of web memorials. *Mass Communication & Society, 29,* 812–830.

Hortobagyi, M. (2007, May 8). Slain students' pages to stay on Facebook. *USA Today.* Retrieved from http://www.usatoday.com/news/nation/2007-05-08-facebook-vatech_N.html

Hoven, C. W., Duarte, C. S., Wu, P., Erickson, E. A., Musa, G. J., & Mandell, D. J. (2004). Exposure to trauma and separation anxiety in children after the WTC attack. *Applied Developmental Science, 8,* 172–183.

Hughes, A. L., & Palen, L. (2009). Twitter adoption and use in mass convergence and emergency events. *International Journal of Emergency Management, 6,* 248–260.

Hughes, M., Brymer, M., Chiu, W. T., Fairbank, J. A., Jones, R. T., Pynoos, R. S., ... Kessler, R. C. (2011). Posttraumatic stress among students after the shootings at Virginia Tech. *Psychological Trauma: Theory, Research, Practice, and Policy, 3,* 403–411.

Jin, Y., & Liu, B. F. (2010). The blog-mediated crisis communication model: Recommendations for responding to influential external blogs. *Journal of Public Relations Research, 22*(4), 429–455.

Kavanaugh, A., Fox, E. A., Sheetz, S., Yang, S., Li, L. T., Whalen, T., ... Xie, L. (2011, June). Social media use by government: From the routine to the critical. *Proceedings of the 12th Annual International Conference on Digital Government Research.* College Park, MD.

Lachlan, K. A. (2013). Risk assessment and negative affect: Examining compliance gaining in the context of major crises and disasters. In C. Liberman (Ed.), *Casing persuasive communication* (pp. 345–356). Dubuque, IA: Kendall-Hunt.

Lachlan, K. A., & Spence, P. R. (2014). Does message placement influence risk perception and affect? *Journal of Communication Management, 18*(2), 122–130.

Lachlan, K. A., Spence, P. R., Lin, X., & Del Greco, M. (2014). Screaming into the wind: Examining the volume and content of tweets associated with Hurricane Sandy. *Communication Studies, 65*(5), 500–518.

La Greca, A. M., Silverman, W. K., Lai, B., & Jacard, J. (2010). Hurricane-related exposure experiences and stressors, other life events, and social support: Concurrent and prospective impact on children's persistent posttraumatic stress symptoms. *Journal of Consulting and Clinical Psychology, 78,* 794–805. doi:10.1037/a0020775

Ledbetter, A. M., Mazer, J. P., DeGroot, J. M., Meyer, K. R., Mao, Y., & Swofford, B. (2011). Attitudes toward online social connection and self-disclosure as predictors of Facebook communication and social closeness. *Communication Research, 38,* 27–53.

Liu, B. F., Jin, Y., & Austin, L. L. (2013). The tendency to tell: Understanding publics' communicative responses to crisis information form and source. *Journal of Public Relations Research, 25,* 51–67.

Liverant, G. I., Hofmann, S. G., & Litz, B. T. (2004). Coping and anxiety in college students after the September 11th terrorist attacks. *Anxiety, Stress, and Coping, 17,* 127–139.

Mak, A. K. Y., Hu, Z. G., Zhang, J. X. X., Xiao, Z., & Lee, T. M. C. (2009). Sex-related differences in neural activity during emotion regulation. *Neuropsychologia, 47,* 2900–2908. doi:10.1016/j.neuropsychologia.2009.06.017

Masten, A. S., & Obradovic, J. D. (2008). Disaster preparation and recovery: Lessons from research on resilience in human development. *Ecology and Society, 13,* 9.

Mastrodicasa, J. (2008). Technology use in campus crisis. *New Directions for Student Services, 124,* 37–53.

Nolen-Hoeksema, S. (2000). The role of rumination in depressive disorders and mixed anxiety/depressive symptoms. *Journal of Abnormal Psychology, 109,* 504–511.

Nolen-Hoeksema, S., & Girgus, J. S. (1994). The emergence of gender differences in depression during adolescence. *Psychological Bulletin, 115,* 424–443.

Nolen-Hoeksema, S., Larson, J., & Grayson, C. (1999). Explaining the gender difference in depressive symptoms. *Journal of Personality and Social Psychology, 77,* 1061–1072.

Nolen-Hoeksema, S., & Morrow, J. (1991). A prospective study of depression and posttraumatic stress symptoms after a natural disaster: The 1989 Loma Prieta earthquake. *Journal of Personality and Social Psychology, 61,* 115–121.

Nolen-Hoeksema, S., Parker, L. E., & Larson, J. (1994). Ruminative coping with depressed mood following loss. *Journal of Personality and Social Psychology, 67,* 92–104.

Norris, F. H. (2007). Impact of mass shootings on survivors, families and communities. *PTSD Research Quarterly, 18,* 1–7.

Orcutt, H. K., Miron, L. R., & Sligowski, A. V. (2014). Impact of mass shootings on individual adjustment. *PTSD Research Quarterly, 25,* 1–9.

O'Reilly, T., & Battelle, J. (2009, June 1). Web squared: Web 2.0 five years on. Retrieved from http://assets.en.oreilly.com/1/event/28/web2009_websquared-whitepaper.pdf

Palen, L., Anderson, K., Mark, G., Martin, J., Sicker, D., Palmer, M., & Grunwald, D. (2010). A vision for technology-mediated support for public participation and assistance in mass emergencies and disasters. *Proceedings of the Association for Computing Machinery-BCS Visions of Computer Science Conference* (pp. 1–12). Edinburgh, UK: Association for Computing Machinery.

Palen, L., & Vieweg, S. (2008). Emergent, widescale online interaction in unexpected events: Assistance, alliance and retreat. *Proceedings of the Association for Computing Machinery Conference on Computer Supported Cooperative Work* (pp. 117–126). San Diego, CA: Association for Computing Machinery.

Paul, L. A., Felton, J. W., Adams, Z. W., Welsh, K., Miller, S., & Ruggiero, K. J. (2015). Mental health among adolescents exposed to a tornado: The influence of social support and its interactions with sociodemographic characteristics and disaster exposure. *Journal of Traumatic Stress, 28*, 1–8.

Perse, E., Nathanson, A. I., & McLeod, D. M. (1996). Effects of spokesperson sex, public announcement appeal, and involvement on evaluations of same-sex PSAs. *Health Communication, 8*, 171–189.

Pitsillides, S., Katsikides, S., & Conreen, M. (2009). *Digital death*. Paper presented at the International Federation for Information Processing Working Group 9.5, Athens, Georgia.

Read, B. (2007, April 17). Virginia Tech student's Facebook group offers a way to grieve. *Chronicle of Higher Education*. Retrieved from http://chronicle.com/wiredcampus/article/2007/virginia-tech-students-facebook-group-offers-away-to-grieve

Recuber, T. (2012). The presumption of commemoration: Disasters, digital memory banks, and online collective memory. *American Behavioral Scientist, 56*, 531–549.

Saylor, C. F., Cowart, B. L., Lipovsky, J. A., Jackson, C., & Finch, A. J., Jr. (2003). Media exposure to September 11: Elementary school students' experiences and posttraumatic symptoms. *American Behavioral Scientist, 46*, 1622–1642.

Scarpa, A., Sheetz, S. D., Wilson, L. C., Waldron, J. C., Patriquin, M. A., & Jones, R. T. (2014). Posttraumatic stress symptoms after the 2007 shootings at Virginia tech: Form and function of communication about the events. *Journal of Critical Incident Analysis, 4*, 1–20.

Seavey, C., Katz, P., & Zalk, S. (1975). Baby X: The effect of gender labels on adult responses to infants. *Sex Roles, 1*, 103–109.

Seeger, M. W., Vennette, S., Ulmer, R. R., & Sellnow, T. L. (2002). Media use, information seeking, and reported needs in post crisis contexts. In B. S. Greenberg (Ed.), *Communication and terrorism* (pp. 53–63). Cresskill, NJ: Hampton Press.

Suh, B., Hong, L., Pirolli, P., & Chi, E. H. (2010). Want to be retweeted? Large scale analytics on factors impacting retweet in Twitter network. *Proceedings of the Institute of Electrical and Electronics Engineers International Conference on Social Computing* (pp. 177–184). Minneapolis, MN: Institute of Electrical and Electronics Engineers.

Spence, P. R., Westerman, D., Skalski, P. D., Seeger, M., Ulmer, R. R., Venette, S., & Sellnow, T. L. (2005). Proxemic effects on information seeking after the 9/11 attacks. *Communication Research Reports, 22*, 39–46.

Spitzer, S. P., & Spitzer, N. S. (1965). Diffusion of the news of the Kennedy and Oswald deaths. In B. S. Greenberg & E. B. Parker (Eds.), *The Kennedy assassination and the American public: Social communications in crisis* (pp. 99–111). Stanford, CA: Stanford University Press.

Sutton, J., Palen, L., & Shklovski, I. (2008, May). Backchannels on the front lines: Emergent uses of social media in the 2007 Southern California wildfires. *Proceedings of the 5th International Association for Information Systems for Crisis Response and Management Conference*. Washington, DC: International Association for Information Systems for Crisis Response and Management.

Terr, L. C., Bloch, D. A., Michel, B. A., Shi, H., Reinhardt, J. A., & Metayer, S. (1999). Children's symptoms in the wake of Challenger: A field study of distant-traumatic effects and an outline of related conditions. *American Journal of Psychiatry, 156*, 1536–1544.

Vlahov, D., Galea, S., Resnick, H., Ahern, J., Boscarino, J. A., Bucuvalas, J. G., ... Kilpatrick, D. (2002). Increased use of cigarettes, alcohol, and marijuana among Manhattan, New York, residents after the September 11th terrorist attacks. *American Journal of Epidemiology, 155*, 988–996.

Walter, T. (2006). A new model of grief: Bereavement and biography. *Mortality, 1*, 8.

Walter, T., Hourizi, R., Moncur, W., & Pitsillides, S. (2011). Does the internet change how we die and mourn? An overview. *OMEGA – Journal of Death and Dying, 64*, 275–302.

Weick, K. E. (1995). *Sensemaking in organizations*. Thousand Oaks, CA: Sage.

Westerman, D., Spence, P. R., & Van Der Heide, B. (2012). A social network as information: The effect of system generated reports of connectedness on credibility on Twitter. *Computers in Human Behavior, 28*, 199–206.

10

The Impact of Journalism on Grieving Communities

Henna Haravuori, Noora Berg, and Mauri Marttunen

The roles of journalists and news media institutions are complex during and after accidents and disasters (Newman & Shapiro, 2014). One of the obligations of journalists and photographers is to witness and report about events that are of interest to a large number of people. Although reporters may be among the first ones on the scene, their role is different from rescue personnel. At times this may be confusing to survivors and professionals working at the scene, as well as to the journalists themselves (Englund, Forsberg, & Saveman, 2014; Newman & Shapiro, 2014). News reports can be essential in communicating necessary information to local communities about how to promote safety and can initiate the mobilization of necessary resources (Newman & Shapiro, 2014). Later the media coverage becomes more versatile and the media have a role in selecting what and how information is presented to the general population. Further, journalists have their own guiding principles and work ethics. Privacy and confidentiality are highly valued principles to both journalists and health care professionals, but journalists also have to balance the public's right and desire to know details about events (Newman & Shapiro, 2014).

Following crises, such as mass shootings, the media adopt an approach called the *crisis mode of communication* (Sumiala & Hakala, 2010). Media organizations shift into full alert as scheduled programs are cancelled and all their energy is geared towards covering the one subject. Television has been the central medium of communication for decades until more recently, as the Internet has gained a crucial role with both professional and amateur-produced news, and social media applications (Sumiala & Hakala, 2010).

When Kay, Reilly, Connolly, and Cohen (2010) studied news coverage in a small community after a homicide, they found the following and potentially harmful key themes about how the media impacted the grieving community: alienation from the community, anger at the media's public construction of the community, intrusion on community life, intrusion on the private processes of grief, and the triggering of renewed feelings of loss and grief. Media presence and coverage is expected by some survivors, and therefore they may not react to it in either a positive or negative way (Englund et al., 2014). On the other hand, there have been several situations where the presence of journalists at crisis sites and the subsequent news broadcasts were regarded as highly disturbing. In the present chapter, we will discuss the roles of the media and the field of journalism in recovery after traumatic events, in general and through particular examples of mass shootings.

Mediatizing or Stigmatizing?

Throughout the history of mass shootings, the media and the field of journalism have gone through tremendous changes, which are still continuing to evolve. In the 1960s, the University of Texas tower sniper attack was conveyed to the public through traditional communication channels, such as television, radio, and print media (Shultz, Muschert, Dingwall, & Cohen, 2013). In 1999, when the Columbine High School shooting occurred, the Internet was starting to gain more users, but news content was still mainly produced and spread by professional journalists. When the Jokela High School and Kauhajoki School shootings occurred in 2007 and 2008, respectively, the Internet was more widely used as a source for news but social media applications were just starting to gain popularity in the field of communications. By the time the Sandy Hook Elementary School shooting happened in 2012, social media had established its pivotal role as a primary form of communication. This change has meant that information is not merely conveyed from the top downward (i.e., from journalists to citizens), but also that anyone can create, distribute, and share news.

The media have an undeniable impact on social and cultural life (Sumiala & Hakala, 2010). Krotz (2009) has defined mediatization as "a historical, ongoing, long-term process in which more and more media emerge and are institutionalized … the process whereby communication refers to media and uses media so that media in the long run increasingly become relevant for the social construction of everyday life, society and culture as a whole" (p. 24). Media extend the natural limits of human communication, provide a substitution for social activities and social institutions, blend in with different nonmedia activities in social life, and operators and organizations from the different sectors of society accommodate to the media logic (Hakala, 2012; Sumiala & Hakala, 2010). For example, parents and students repeatedly talked about the media when asked about the social consequences of the Columbine High School shooting (Hawkins, McIntosh, Silver, & Holman, 2007). Media provide a unique way to experience crises and disasters, including involvement in activities such as mourning and grief, and can help activate recovery and resilience (see Chapter 9 for more on the role of technology in grief).

Following mass shootings, the victims are categorized in the media as deceased victims, injured victims, eyewitnesses, the bereaved, and mediated victims (Hakala, 2012). Injured victims that have minor or no physical traumas are usually targeted by journalists as firsthand sources of information while they are not of high priority in first-aid triage (Hakala, 2012). In the mediatization of victims, there is a great need for personalized stories. Journalists seek survival stories that provide clues for understanding and explaining the event (i.e., meaning making; Hakala, 2012). Mediatization of the crisis helps those not directly affected (i.e., outsiders) to understand the incident and participate in collective mourning (Sumiala & Hakala, 2010). There may be social media or Internet communities for grieving and memorializing the victims (see Chapter 9). Although this process certainly has an important role (e.g., expressing grief, communicating information), it also results in the loss of the victims' privacy.

After the Jokela High School shooting, the media coverage of the incident was very distressing for the surviving students because the media tried to blend into the students' nonmedia activities (Hakala, 2012). Their private emotions of shock, fear, sorrow, distress, and grief were invaded and exploited without invitation or permission (Raittila, Koljonen, & Väliverronen, 2010). Victims' stories were publicized in the media (Hakala, 2012). In addition to this example, there are several mass shooting cases where journalists and the continuous news flow sensationalized the grief in ways that even the involved individuals could not identify with (Hawkins et al., 2007; Jemphrey & Berrington, 2000).

Survivors' stories are shared in the mediatized world. But, how does it impact survivors themselves? One hypothesis is that news coverage retraumatizes survivors and impedes recovery. The opposing hypothesis is that news reports provide social recognition for survivors and are one form of positive support that may aid in recovery (Maercker & Mehr, 2006). Additionally, the public's perceptions of the survivors may be influenced by the picture that the media paint. Survivors may be portrayed as heroes or become stigmatized as vulnerable people, both potentially harming the survivor's sense of self (Libow, 1992). Perceived social acknowledgment is the survivor's experience of reactions from society, and can be distinguished as general positive acknowledgment (recognition), general negative acknowledgment (disapproval), and familial recognition/disapproval (Maercker & Mehr, 2006). Negative aspects of social acknowledgment have been found to increase posttraumatic stress symptoms (PTSS) among crime victims, at least in the short term (Maercker & Mehr, 2006). In addition, crime victims' reactions have been found to be significantly more negative (e.g., feelings of exposure and anger) when the content of the report is inaccurate. Maercker and Mehr (2006) concluded that individuals with lower psychological wellbeing may be retraumatized to a certain extent when they become the focus of the news coverage.

Mediatized Grief

While loss and grief are essential parts of human life, the grief work that is assumed to be required for recovery is not a clear concept (Bonanno & Kaltman, 1999). There have been theoretical models for *stages* and *phases of grief*, and a notion for a need to "work through" grief. However, there is little empirical support for this concept (Bonanno & Kaltman, 1999; Falconer, Sachsenweger, Gibson, & Norman, 2011). Bonanno and Kaltman (1999) suggested that models of grief and bereavement could be based on the theories of cognitive stress, attachment, social-functional approach to emotion, and trauma. They concluded that bereavement consists of four interacting components: the context of the loss, the continuum of subjective meanings associated with the loss, the changing representations of the lost relationship over time, and the role of coping and emotion-regulation processes. The meaning of a loss and the meaning-making process have quite different nuances after a traumatic event (Bonanno & Kaltman, 1999).

Grief is not only an intrapersonal experience, but also a broader phenomenon that impacts families, friends, and communities (see Chapter 12 for more on the impact on communities). Throughout history, societies and cultures have had a variety of customs and rituals that foster grief (Falconer et al., 2011; Sacre, 2013). The media, media culture, and new digital means of social interactions have changed the mourning rituals (Pantti & Sumiala, 2009). The roles of the media are complex: The media not only observe and report on these rituals but affect how the ritual is performed and experienced, how it is interpreted by the public, and how public reactions and emotions are managed (Pantti & Sumiala, 2009). Rituals performed through the media may promote a community's sense of social cohesion and shared values, while as a downside may exacerbate divisions between conflicting groups within a community (Pantti & Sumiala, 2009). What is emphasized and framed has an impact on not only individual-level but also community-level meaning making of the event, what should be remembered or dealt with as a collective trauma, and whether there is an obligation to forgive (Margalit, 2002).

Framing

Framing refers to the ways individuals, groups, and societies communicate and make social constructions about reality (Goffman, 1974). Said another way, framing is the process of making interpretations about social phenomena. Journalists frame news by selection, emphasis, exclusion, and elaboration of information (Muschert, 2009). Previously drawn frames define future frames and can even influence the course of events. In mass shooting incidents, the media do not merely report facts but actively take part in framing the event

(Ryan & Hawdon, 2008). Mass shootings attract the media's attention widely and some studies have examined the media's role in determining the discourse and perceptions of the event (see Chapter 7 for more on how media influence public beliefs). Through various processes some frames become more widely recognized than others and eventually a dominant frame is formed. It becomes the community's collective understanding of the tragedy (Hawdon, Oksanen, & Räsänen, 2012).

Studies have found that the media change the frames over time when covering mass shootings. For example, in the aftermath of the Columbine High School shooting, the published news was first framed to concentrate on what happened, and then widened to cover societal issues, such as gun laws and afterschool care (Chyi & McCombs, 2004; Muschert, 2009).

It has been very common in the American media to focus on the victims' lives. Meanwhile, some victims are more interesting than others to the media. In school shooting incidents, the focus has often been on heroic educators and innocent children (Schildkraut & Muschert, 2014). The media's framing process also depends on cultural factors. For example, the victim focus is rare in Finland and instead the news tends to focus on the perpetrators (Hawdon, Oksanen, & Räsänen, 2012).

The Role of Social Solidarity and How Journalism Affects It

Community can be understood as a multidimensional concept that includes dimensions of space, sentiment, and social structure (Campbell, 2000). Space refers to the geographic location and infrastructure of the community. Sentiment is the psychological attachment and emotional bond the members have with their community. Social structure refers to the social networks within the community (Hawdon & Ryan, 2011). An unexpected crime, such as a mass shooting, might affect all of these aspects of a community (see Chapter 12).

The unity of a community can be measured through levels of social solidarity, which can be defined in many ways and is sometimes referred to as social integration or cohesion. It can be seen as an umbrella term for positive interactions with others (Sorokin, 1947, 1954), feelings of togetherness, responsibility for others (Wilde, 2007), mutual social support, and sense of community (Nurmi, Räsänen, & Oksanen, 2011). Social solidarity can be manifested through several actions, such as providing help, willingness to discuss and express affect, and participation in public events. When an unexpected and violent crime occurs in a community, its social solidarity is tested. This is important because perceived social solidarity is associated with less distress after tragic events (Hawdon, Räsänen, Oksanen, & Ryan, 2012). This is no surprise since the association between social relations and wellbeing is widely recognized (House, Landis, & Umberson, 1988). It has been argued that people with fewer social contacts suffer from poorer mental health while larger social networks and stronger social relations are associated with better mental health (Fuhrer, Stansfeld, Chemali, & Shipley, 1999).

Two opposing arguments have been suggested about a violent crime's impact on a community's sense of solidarity. Several studies have suggested that social solidarity increases in a community after a tragedy, particularly right after the incident (Hawdon, Räsänen, et al., 2012). This perception was introduced by Émile Durkheim at the end of the nineteenth century (Durkheim, 1893/1997) and many contemporary studies have reached similar conclusions when examining mass shootings. The frame of solidarity is promoted when the media concentrate on reporting about community acts, information on the victims, and use community members as informants (Hawdon, Oksanen, & Räsänen, 2012). Other studies have suggested that a violent crime weakens the community's integration and sense of solidarity, and increases fear of crime and distrust among the community members (Lewis & Salem, 1986). For example, the news of a mass shooting might increase insecurity in the community since the media might enhance fears of the event reoccurring (Vuori, 2016).

Studies on mass shootings have observed indications of both increases and decreases in solidarity. In the case of the Virginia Tech shooting, solidarity first increased by 18% and slowly decreased after 6 months but never returned to the initial level (Hawdon, Ryan, & Agnich, 2010). In Finland, comparison of the incidents in Jokela and Kauhajoki revealed differences between the two communities (Nurmi et al., 2011). Jokela resembled Virginia Tech with numerous expressions of solidarity after the incident. However, this increase in solidarity might not have occured if the event had not been seen as affecting the community collectively (Ryan & Hawdon, 2008). This was the case in Kauhajoki, where expressions of solidarity were not seen since the community did not define the attack as targeting them collectively because the victims and perpetrator were not originally from the community (Hawdon, Oksanen, & Räsänen, 2012).

Increased solidarity might be harmful if, as a result, some groups are left out (Nurmi et al., 2011). In the cases of Virginia Tech and Jokela, social solidarity was perceived as a protective factor. But, in Jokela, increased solidarity eventually led to conflict and social guilt (Hawdon, Oksanen, & Räsänen, 2012; Hawdon, Räsänen, et al., 2012). A tragic event can cause polarization in many ways. Those who have been directly exposed to the event might feel that those who were not directly impacted do not understand how they feel. Previous studies have suggested that perceived social solidarity does not increase among the severely exposed in the same way that it does among other members of the community (Hawdon & Ryan, 2011; Vuori, 2016). For example, polarization occurred between the youths and adults in Jokela (Nurmi et al., 2011). The media can cement these barriers between groups by framing controversies between them. Spencer and Muschert (2009) reported on a controversy framed by the media following the Columbine shooting. The news covered the creation of spontaneous memorials in Columbine, especially 15 wooden crosses that were put up for the deceased, including the perpetrators. Spencer and Muschert (2009) described how the media framed a controversy around the two crosses for the perpetrators and established opposing opinions regarding the positioning of memorials for the perpetrators among the victims. Current evidence suggests that forces of social integration and disintegration might occur simultaneously in a community after a tragedy (Vuori, 2016).

One of the themes in the media is often the question of "who is to blame?" It has been recognized that based on the social causes perspective, communities tend to be blamed for mass shootings because they failed to see signs beforehand (Schildkraut & Muschert, 2013). For example, school subculture was heavily blamed after the Columbine High School shooting, although this occurred in the absence of a factual basis (Schildkraut & Muschert, 2013). Towns or communities may become synonymous with the mass shooting event that happened there. Whole communities and its members then have to work hard to maintain their true identities and not to let the tragic event define who they are or should be (Sacre, 2013).

Media Invading Community

There are several key media actions and journalist behaviors after mass shootings that should be highlighted. One of them is the speed of media production. Journalists arrive at the scene quickly and start to publish about the events while the facts are still unraveling. There are examples where the media rushed into communities while the mass shooting incident was still unresolved, and police and rescue operations were ongoing (e.g., Columbine, Jokela). When there is high pressure to publish, the accuracy of the news stories lags behind. The second feature is the overwhelming number of media representatives, who often remain in the community for long periods of time (Hawkins et al., 2007; Jemphrey & Berrington, 2000; Kitch & Hume, 2007; Raittila et al., 2010; Walsh-Childers, Lewis, & Neely, 2008). Third, many of the journalists use indiscreet ways to collect information for their stories, although most journalists follow their ethical code and are sensitive to the victims' needs. If authorities are slow in media reporting, the pressure to get stories from firsthand eye witnesses increases. Open conflict between journalists/media and the community may evolve.

After the school shooting in Dunblane, Scotland in 1996, there was an agreement among journalists to be discreet, not interview bereaved families immediately, and not cover funerals, which is atypical for the British press (Jemphrey & Berrington, 2000). However, most news reporters requested interviews later.

The Columbine High School shooting received worldwide media attention. The suburban town was filled with reporters and media equipment. The students and parents interviewed in the study by Hawkins et al. (2007) reported that the media actions were intrusive. Journalists knocked on doors and asked for interviews nonstop for almost two weeks. Furthermore, cameras followed grieving families to their homes. Photographing and filming the grieving and requests for interviews were relentless in places like the memorial for the victims. While in some cases, early news reports can help to piece together the details of the event and how to proceed, media intrusion is often perceived as harmful in the long term. This is especially true of inaccurate and exaggerated news content (Hawkins et al., 2007).

A documentary film by Moritz (2003) discussed how journalists, students, and community members viewed the news coverage of the Columbine incident. The conflict between the media and the community was long-lasting, while there were attempts to ease the tension (e.g., coordinating meetings with school officials and journalists). Even the journalists themselves found it difficult to do their job because of the presence of so many media personnel (i.e., the media circus). One perceptive narrative stated that the media personnel themselves became trauma triggers, reminding the traumatized and grieving community members of the event. The importance of accurate news reporting was stressed while recognized as hard to achieve due to the constant pressure to publish new content.

In a study by Walsh-Childers et al. (2008) it was concluded that journalists were a stressor for the survivors, family members, and community members following the 2007 Virginia Tech shooting. Unfortunately, the university located the media vehicles and equipment in the parking lot across from the inn on campus, where bereaved families were directed to go. It was impossible for the family members and students to avoid direct contact with the media. Three types of media actions were observed: journalists behaving badly, media mob, and journalists displaying compassion. Intrusive attempts to get interviews from injured students and families who had experienced a loss occurred frequently early on. The coverage was also perceived as negative and aggressive towards the school, as the media searched for someone to blame. Conversely, there were also notions of positive interactions with journalists. For example, many of them were sincerely concerned for interviewees' needs and did not aggressively push for interviews or live broadcasts (Walsh-Childers et al., 2008).

When the news broke about the Jokela High School shooting there were dozens of journalists on the scene within a half an hour, filming and photographing the escaping students and school workers. Phone calls and text messages were sent by some reporters to students who had been rescued or were still waiting to be rescued within the school building. The youths of Jokela reported intrusive attempts by journalists to obtain interviews and photographs, and students indicated it was particularly distressing when they were photographed even after they asked journalists not to. The news broke first online, and then on television and in printed news. Interestingly, Internet communities identified the probable perpetrator while the police operation was still ongoing (Investigation Commission of the Jokela School Shooting, 2009; Raittila et al., 2008; Raittila et al., 2010).

The official information released by the authorities was lacking for a long time in the case of the Jokela shooting, so the reporters felt pressure to gather information from those directly involved. It was especially problematic when the journalists conducted interviews with minors without informing their parents. There was no preparation and no safeguards in place to protect the students. Instead, the students were in the same location near the school as the journalists (Investigation Commission of the Jokela School Shooting, 2009; Raittila et al., 2008; Raittila et al., 2010).

The youths of the Jokela community collected a petition questioning the actions of the media. The questions raised were whether it was appropriate behavior to follow people entering and leaving the Crisis Centre, to find out personal details about the perpetrator, victims, or their families, to secretly photograph or listen to grieving people, and to try to enter homes. The youths felt that their crisis and grief were not respected by the media. The conflict was so severe that there was open hostility toward journalists (Investigation Commission of the Jokela School Shooting, 2009).

The students expressed a desire for empathy from the journalists during interviews. "How are you feeling?" types of questions felt inappropriate and naïve in contrast to being asked about the facts in the immediate aftermath. After giving interviews many students reported that they regretted or felt shame about the interview, and that it took time away from their recovery. As a consequence of agreeing to give interviews, some adolescents were shunned by their peer groups. Yet, some of the young people recognized that the journalists were just doing their job (Raittila et al., 2008).

The Kauhajoki School shooting happened less than a year after the Jokela incident. However, the actions of the media and the news content were noticeably different from the Jokela incident. First, there had been ongoing discussions with members of the media about work standards and ethics. When reporters arrived at remote Kauhajoki, there was no access to the scene. Information by the authorities was given fast and was updated regularly. There was little emotive content in the news at first. In fact, reporters and photographers were criticized for being too discreet. However, more dramatic news content emerged as time elapsed. Journalists were reportedly less aggressive in Kauhajoki when seeking interviews. Yet some students reported constant knocking on their doors and receiving phone calls and text messages requesting interviews (Investigation Commission of the Kauhajoki Shooting, 2010; Raittila et al., 2010).

Coverage on victims was very sensitive or was avoided altogether after the Kauhajoki tragedy. It is customary that names of the victims are not published immediately in Finland after accidents. Finnish journalists mainly avoided contact with the bereaved families. However, a foreign tabloid newspaper reporter visited six mourning families. Unfortunately, several of these visits occurred before police had confirmed the death of the family member. This behavior was viewed as inappropriate by the Finnish journalists (Investigation Commission of the Kauhajoki School Shooting, 2010; Raittila et al., 2010).

Contact With Journalists and Survivors' PTSS

The impact of how victims and survivors are approached by journalists has been one of the main concerns in this area of the literature. The possibility of revictimization or exacerbation of traumatic reactions is recognized within the ethical and practical guidelines that have been developed for journalists covering catastrophes (e.g., Simpson, 2006; see www.dartcenter.org).

A traumatic event weakens our feelings of security and sense of control, and uncontrollable media intrusions may contribute to this sense of violation and lack of control (Libow, 1992; Wilms, 2007). The interviewee may be in shock and may not understand that they are giving an interview. Further, the interviewee does not have control over how the interview material is used afterwards.

The extent and effects of contact with journalists among mass shooting survivors have been quantitatively studied after a few incidents. Findings are evaluated here from the Jokela and Kauhajoki School shootings in 2007 and 2008, respectively. Four months after the incidents, 231 middle and high schools students from Jokela (ages 13–19) and 189 vocational school and polytechnic school students from Kauhajoki (ages 15–30) reported on their perceptions of their contact with journalists, and their recovery and wellbeing (Haravuori, Suomalainen, Berg, Kiviruusu, & Marttunen, 2011; Haravuori, Suomalainen, & Marttunen, 2011; Haravuori et al., 2012). In addition, a Norwegian study on the survivors of the 2011 Utøya Island terrorist attack is reviewed. Following this event, media participation was studied for a longer period of time, since media coverage was intense for several months following the attack, and again at the time of the trial (Thoresen, Jensen, & Dyb, 2014). Interviews were conducted with 285 survivors 14–15 months after the attack.

Journalists and reporters reached a majority of the survivors in all three incidents. However, the proportions who gave interviews differed between the groups. Journalists asked 63% of the Jokela students about the events and 60% of the approached students answered the journalists' questions. Those approached by the journalists were older and more severely exposed to the events (Haravuori, Suomalainen, Berg, et al., 2011). In Kauhajoki, 58% of the students were asked about the events and 21% of them answered the questions. Again, more severely exposed students were approached more often (Haravuori, Suomalainen, & Marttunen, 2011). In Kauhajoki, the majority of the students were evacuated to one location and they were informed about the possibility of journalists asking for a comment and about their choice to not answer. The previous conflict between journalists and the Jokela community most likely influenced journalists' behaviors in Kauhajoki, but it is unclear how these differences in behaviors may have impacted Kauhajoki students (Raittila et al., 2010).

Students were asked an open question about "how did the reporter or reporters approach you?" The answers were grouped into three categories: positive (e.g., respectfully, politely), neutral (e.g., just approached, asked permission to interview), and negative (e.g., intrusively, boldly, attacked, took photos or interviewed after refusal). In Jokela, 17% of the students reported that reporters approached them in a positive way, 51% in a neutral way, and 32% in a negative way. In Kauhajoki, 6% reported being approached in a positive way, 65% in a neutral way, and 29% in a negative way. Age and sex did not affect the way the students perceived being approached. Those more severely exposed in Kauhajoki were more likely to report being approached in a positive way than other students (Haravuori, Suomalainen, & Marttunen, 2011).

Those who gave an interview were asked to further evaluate how it affected their wellbeing. About three out of four Jokela students perceived that giving an interview did not affect their condition, one fifth reported that their condition worsened, and 9% reported that they felt better after giving an interview. About one third of Kauhajoki students perceived that giving an interview worsened their condition, 61% reported that it did not have an effect, and 7% reported that they felt better afterwards. In both instances, students with PTSS were more likely to report that giving an interview worsened their condition (Haravuori, Suomalainen, & Marttunen, 2011).

Contact with journalists was analyzed as students who were (1) not approached, (2) approached and refused an interview, and (3) approached and interviewed. Among the surviving Jokela students, those who were approached and interviewed by reporters had higher levels of PTSS than those who were not approached (Haravuori, Suomalainen, Berg, et al., 2011). Conversely, symptoms did not differ between those who refused to be interviewed and those who were not approached by reporters. This was the case also when confounding factors, like sex and exposure severity, were included in the analyses.

The Finnish samples were also analyzed together and showed that being approached by a reporter compared to not being approached had an odds ratio

(OR) of 2.0 (95% CI [1.1, 3.6]), indicating higher levels of PTSS, even when factors like age, sex, study group, and level of exposure were controlled. Students who were interviewed compared to not approached were found to have an OR of 2.6 (95% CI [.3, 5.3]) for high levels of PTSS. Being approached but having refused an interview did not have a significant effect. These findings suggested that being approached and interviewed by journalists had an effect on posttraumatic distress in traumatized adolescents independent of their exposure level and demographic factors (Haravuori, Suomalainen, & Marttunen, 2011).

In the Norwegian study, a vast majority of the survivors (94%) were approached by reporters and most (88%) participated in interviews (Thoresen et al., 2014). The frequency of being approached by the media did not significantly differ based on age and in fact most of the young survivors (i.e., 91% of those between 13 and 16 years of age) were contacted by media. However, older students were more likely to be interviewed than younger students. Being approached by the media was appraised as negative or very negative by 11% of the sample, both positive and negative by 64% of the sample, and positive or very positive by 26% of the sample. Females were more likely to report negative appraisals of being approached. Media participation was perceived as quite a bit or extremely distressing among 13% of the survivors and 11% reported that they regretted participating in an interview. Older age groups reported that participation was more stressful.

Media participation among the Norwegian survivors was categorized as being (1) interviewed about the terror, (2) interviewed about the trial, or (3) contributing their own texts. None of these variables were related to posttraumatic stress reactions (Thoresen et al., 2014). But, because such a large proportion of survivors were approached by the media this association could not be properly analyzed. Appraisals of media participation as distressing and regretting participation were associated with greater levels of posttraumatic stress reactions when adjusted for demographics, social support, and feelings of being let down. Only the association of posttraumatic stress reactions and the perception of media participation as distressing remained significant after adjusting all media-related variables for each other and for the aforementioned variables. Positive appraisals of media participation were not found to be associated with posttraumatic stress reactions. The authors concluded that it could either be that media participation was more distressing for those with higher symptom levels, or that negative experiences with media participation increased symptom levels. Also, the Norwegian sample was composed of politically active young people, who may be more willing to take part in public discourse, some of them had received media training, and the survivors were described mainly in sympathetic ways in the media.

Before these three survivor samples, the effect of being interviewed on PTSS had been hypothesized to exist but had not yet been studied in samples of sufficient size in quantitative studies. The findings among the Finnish samples, which included adolescent and young adult participants, were quite similar. One exception is that the proportion of survivors that did not give an interview was larger after the incident in Kauhajoki. Further, the vast majority of the Utøya Island terrorist attack survivors were contacted by the media. Generally, being approached by journalists and giving interviews was associated with higher levels of PTSS. The results also suggested an independent effect irrespective of the participants' levels of exposure. The Norwegian study demonstrated an association between the perception of media participation as distressing and posttraumatic stress reactions providing clues to possible mediating factors. Yet, most participants across the three studies reported neutral perceptions of their interactions with journalists.

Impact of News Coverage on PTSS Among Survivors and Surviving Communities

The association between disaster news coverage and psychological symptoms (e.g., PTSS, anxiety, depressive symptoms) has been observed in several studies after various incidents, across different age groups, and even in individuals without direct connection to the incident. It has been postulated that these reactions are observed among those who are prone to symptomatology beforehand (Otto et al., 2007). See Chapter 8 for a more indepth discussion of the media as a form of vicarious exposure.

Children and adolescents are known to view considerable hours of newscasts of catastrophic events (Pfefferbaum et al., 2001). Children directly involved in the Oklahoma City bombing (1995) watched more of the newscasts than children without a direct connection to the event (Pfefferbaum et al., 1999). In a study of 3,200 middle and high school students in Oklahoma City, 67% of the students (73% of the bereaved) reported that most or all of their television viewing was bombing-related 7 weeks after the bombing. They also had the highest level of hyperarousal symptoms (Pfefferbaum et al., 1999). Television exposure explained more of the variance in PTSS than physical or emotional exposure in 2,000 Oklahoma middle school students 7 weeks after the event (Pfefferbaum et al., 2001). Similarly, there was an association between viewing intense images and probable posttraumatic stress disorder and depression among Manhattan residents who were directly affected by the 9/11 terrorist attacks (Ahern et al., 2002).

The news was widely followed through different media outlets among the surviving students of Jokela High School. Television was the most frequently (94%) followed media. Students also reported frequent use of the Internet (84%), newspapers (78%), and radio (approximately 50%; Haravuori, Suomalainen, Berg, et al., 2011). Following the news coverage was perceived to have no effect on one's condition or feelings in half of the participants, 15% reported feeling better, and one third reported feeling worse. However, there was no association with the severity of exposure and the reported effects of news coverage on feelings. But, females reported feeling worse more often than males. When Jokela students were compared to students from a distant school, the Jokela students were more likely to report feeling worse after following the news (Haravuori, Suomalainen, Berg, et al., 2011).

The news broadcasts and postings were also widely followed through different media outlets among the Kauhajoki students (Haravuori, Suomalainen, & Marttunen, 2011). Television was the most frequently (92%) followed media. Students also reported frequent use of the Internet, newspapers, and the majority also listened to radio (88%). The local radio station was one of the first news outlets to broadcast information about the event. Following the news was reported to have no effect on one's condition or feelings in one third of the answers, 15% reported feeling better, and as many as half reported feeling worse (Haravuori, Suomalainen, & Marttunen, 2011).

If the students followed a greater number (at least 3–4) of media outlets they were more likely to report feeling worse afterwards than those who followed fewer. Jokela students who followed a higher number of media outlets were observed to also have higher PTSS but this effect attenuated when other confounding factors were taken into account (Haravuori, Suomalainen, Berg, et al., 2011). When a combined sample of Jokela and Kauhajoki students was studied, an effect of following more news outlets on PTSS was observed (Haravuori, Suomalainen, & Marttunen, 2011). Exposure to television and newspaper coverage of the event was associated with PTSS, while exposure to radio and Internet were not (Haravuori, Suomalainen, & Marttunen, 2011). Print media has been found to be more strongly associated with PTSS than broadcast media in at least one previous study (Pfefferbaum et al., 2003). We can only speculate on the reasons for this, because one would expect that following the Internet requires intentional effort like print media and permits repeated exposure to potentially disturbing images and text. One hypothesis could be that in some cases social online communities may provide protective peer support.

A sample of San Diego East County residents were interviewed after two separate school shootings happened within the same school district within a month in 2001 (Palinkas, Prussing, Reznik, & Landsverk, 2004). The study included 85 participants 6 months after the incidents. Of those interviewed, 53% reported intrusive reminders of the trauma associated with intense media coverage and subsequent rumors, hoaxes, and threats, 45% reported avoidance symptoms, 31% reported hypervigilance symptoms, and 27% reported other types of psychological symptoms. The two most common responses given were intense anger at the media for constantly reminding them of what they had experienced and efforts to avoid similar reminders in conversations.

Conclusions

The fields of journalism and the media have intriguing and complex roles in the aftermath of mass shootings. Aspects of the event, such as the recovery process and the victims, are mediatized thoroughly. How the media portray individuals and communities after mass shootings has a direct impact on them. The sheer masses of reporters evading the community may be perceived as distressing, not to mention the indiscreet and harassing ways some journalists use to get comments from the survivors and bereaved.

National and international news reporters and published news sources have been observed to be more intrusive and unauthentic towards the grieving (Jemphrey & Berrington, 2000). This may be because the local media and newsroom personnel may be among the personally affected and grieving. They are reporting about an incident that happened to their community, and they are responsible to both their profession and community. These were argued to be among the factors associated with successful student online journalism after the Virginia Tech shooting (Moritz & Kwak, 2009). Student journalists published versatile material from inside sources; and they managed to do it in a professional and sensitive way that served their own community.

Authorities, like police and health care professionals, should prepare for interactions with the media in crisis situations, while journalists should continue to evaluate and discuss their work guidelines and ethics in relation to working with vulnerable survivors and grieving families (Newman & Shapiro, 2014). It is recommended that authorities inform the masses efficiently and effectively, and media personnel report accurately and respectfully. This approach would best serve individuals and communities as they find help, support, and comfort in times of crisis and would enable them to utilize existing and new media resources.

References

Ahern, J., Galea, S., Resnick, H., Kilpatrick, D., Bucuvalas, M., Gold, J., & Vlahov, D. (2002). Television images and psychological symptoms after the September 11 terrorist attacks. *Psychiatry, 65,* 289–300.

Bonanno, G. A., & Kaltman, S. (1999). Toward an integrative perspective on bereavement. *Psychological Bulletin, 125,* 760–776.

Campbell, C. (2000). Social structure, space and sentiment: Searching for common ground in sociological conceptions of community. In D. Chekki (Ed.), *Research in community sociology* (pp. 21–57). Greenwich, CT: JAI Press.

Chyi, H. I., & McCombs, M. E. (2004). Media salience and the process of framing: Coverage of the Columbine school shootings. *Journalism and Mass Communication Quarterly, 81,* 22–35.

Durkheim, É. (1997). *The division of labor in society* (W. D. Halls, Trans.). New York, NY: The Free Press. (Original work published in 1893.)

Englund, L., Forsberg, R., & Saveman, B. I. (2014). Survivors' experiences of media coverage after traumatic injury events. *International Emergency Nursing, 22,* 25–30.

Falconer, K., Sachsenweger, M., Gibson, K., & Norman, H. (2011). Grieving in the internet age. *New Zealand Journal of Psychology, 40,* 79–88.

Fuhrer, R., Stansfeld, S. A., Chemali, J., & Shipley, M. J. (1999). Gender, social relations and mental health: Prospective findings from an occupational cohort (Whithall II study). *Social Science and Medicine, 48,* 77–87.

Goffman, E. (1974). *Frame analysis: An essay on the organization of experience.* Cambridge, MA: Harvard University Press.

Hakala, S. (2012). The mediatized victim: school shootings as distant suffering. In G. W. Muschert, & J. Sumilala (Eds.), *Studies in media and communications: Vol. 7. School shootings: Mediatized violence in a global age* (pp. 255–278). Bingley, UK: Emerald Books.

Haravuori, H., Suomalainen, L., Berg, N., Kiviruusu, O., & Marttunen, M. (2011). Effects of media exposure on adolescents traumatized in a school shooting. *Journal of Traumatic Stress, 24,* 70–77.

Haravuori, H., Suomalainen, L., & Marttunen, M. (2011). Effects of media exposure on posttraumatic reactions. *Psychiatria Fennica, 42,* 32–48.

Haravuori, H., Suomalainen, L., Turunen, T., Berg, N., Murtonen, K., & Marttunen, M. (2012). [*Students exposed to the school shootings at Jokela and Kauhajoki – recovering and received support and care. Final report of a two-year follow-up study.*]. Helsinki, Finland: National Institute for Health and Welfare.

Hawdon, J., Oksanen, A., & Räsänen, P. (2012). Media coverage and solidarity after tragedies: The reporting of school shootings in two nations. *Comparative Sociology, 11,* 1–30.

Hawdon, J., Räsänen, P., Oksanen, A., & Ryan, J. (2012). Social solidarity and wellbeing after critical incidents: Three cases of mass shootings. *Journal of Critical Incident Analysis, 3,* 2–25.

Hawdon, J., Ryan, J., & Agnich, L. (2010). Crime as a source of solidarity: A research note testing Durkheim's assertion. *Deviant Behavior, 31,* 679–703.

Hawdon, J., & Ryan, J. (2011). Social relations that generate and sustain solidarity after a mass tragedy. *Social Forces, 89,* 1363–1384.

Hawkins, N. A., McIntosh, D. N., Silver, R. C., & Holman, E. A. (2007). Early responses to school violence. A qualitative analysis of students' and parents' immediate reactions to the shooting at Columbine High School. *Journal of Emotional Abuse, 4,* 197–223.

House, J. S., Landis, K. R., & Umberson, D. (1988). Social relationships and health. *Science. New series, 241,* 540–545.

Investigation Commission of the Jokela School Shooting. (2009). *Jokela School shooting on 7 November 2007 – report of the investigation commission.* Helsinki, Finland: Ministry of Justice Publications.

Investigation Commission of the Kauhajoki School Shooting. (2010). *Kauhajoki School shooting on 23 September 2008 – report of the investigation commission.* Helsinki, Finland: Ministry of Justice Reports and Guidelines.

Jemphrey, A., & Berrington, E. (2000). Surviving the media: Hillsborough, Dunblane and the press. *Journalism Studies, 1*, 469–483.

Kay, L., Reilly, R. C., Connolly, K., & Cohen, S. (2010). Help or harm? Symbolic violence, secondary trauma and the impact of press coverage on a community. *Journalism Practice, 4*, 421–438.

Kitch, C., & Hume, J. (2007). *Journalism in a culture of grief.* New York, NY: Routledge.

Krotz, F. (2009). Mediatization: A concept with which to grasp media and societal change. In K. Lundby (Ed.), *Mediatization: Concepts, changes, consequences* (pp. 21–40). New York, NY: Peter Lang.

Lewis, D., & Salem, G. (1986). *Fear of crime: Incivility and the production of social problem.* New Brunswick, NJ: Transaction Books.

Libow, J. A. (1992). Traumatized children and the news media: Clinical considerations. *American Journal of Orthopsychiatry, 62*, 379–386.

Maercker, A., & Mehr, A. (2006). What if victims read a newspaper report about their victimization? A study on the relationship to PTSD symptoms in crime victims. *European Psychologist, 11*, 137–142.

Margalit, A. (2002). *The ethics of memory.* Cambridge, MA: Harvard University Press.

Moritz, M. (Writer & Producer). (2003). *Covering Columbine* (Motion picture). Boulder, CO: University of Colorado at Boulder School of Journalism.

Moritz, M. J., & Kwak, S. (2009). Students as creators and consumers of e-news: The case of Virginia Tech. In K. Prasad (Ed.), *E-Journalism new media and news media* (pp. 209–224). New Delhi, India: B. R. Publishing.

Muschert, G. W. (2009). Frame-changing in the media coverage of a school shooting: The rise of Columbine as a national concern. *Social Science Journal, 46*, 164–170.

Newman, E., & Shapiro, B. (2014). Clinicians and journalists responding to disasters. *Journal of Child and Adolescent Psychopharmacology, 24*, 32–38.

Nurmi, J., Räsänen, P., & Oksanen, A. (2011). The norm of solidarity: Experiencing negative aspects of community life after a school shooting tragedy. *Journal of Social Work, 12*, 300–319.

Otto, M. W., Henin, A., Hirshfeld-Becker, D. R., Pollack, M. H., Biederman, J., & Rosenbaum, J. F. (2007). Posttraumatic stress disorder symptoms following media exposure to tragic events: Impact of 9/11 on children at risk for anxiety disorders. *Journal of Anxiety Disorders, 21*, 888–902.

Palinkas, L. A., Prussing, E., Reznik, V. M., & Landsverk, J.A. (2004). The San Diego East County School shootings: A qualitative study of community-level posttraumatic stress. *Prehospital and Disaster Medicine, 19*, 113–121.

Pantti, M., & Sumiala, J. (2009). Till death do us join: Media, mourning rituals and the sacred centre of the society. *Media, Culture & Society, 31*, 119–135.

Pfefferbaum, B., Nixon, S. J., Tivis, R. D., Doughty, D. E., Pynoos, R. S., Gurwitch, R. H., & Foy, D. W. (2001). Television exposure in children after a terrorist incident. *Psychiatry, 64*, 202–211.

Pfefferbaum, B., Nixon, S. J., Tucker, P. M., Tivis, R. D., Moore, V. L., & Gurwitch, R. H. … Geis, H. K. (1999). Posttraumatic stress responses in bereaved children after the Oklahoma City bombing. *Journal of the American Academy of Child and Adolescent Psychiatry, 38*, 1372–1379.

Pfefferbaum, B., Seale, T. W., Brandt, E. N., Jr., Pfefferbaum, R. L., Doughty, D. E., & Rainwater, S. M. (2003). Media exposure in children one hundred miles from a terrorist bombing. *Annals of Clinical Psychiatry, 15*, 1–8.

Raittila, P., Johansson, K., Juntunen, L., Kangasluoma, L., Koljonen, K., & Kumpu, V. … Väliverronen, J. (2008). [*Media coverage of Jokela school shooting.*]. Tiedotusopin laitoksen julkaisuja A 105. Finland: University of Tampere Journalism Research and Development Centre.

Raittila, P., Koljonen, K., & Väliverronen, J. (2010). *Journalism and school shootings in Finland 2007–2008*. Tampere, Finland: Tampere University Press.

Ryan, J., & Hawdon, J. (2008). From individual to community: The "framing" of 4–16 and the display of social solidarity. *Traumatology, 14*, 43–52.

Sacre, S. (2013). Effects of mass homicide on communities. In K. Gow & M. Celinski (Eds.), *Mass trauma: Impact and recovery issues* (pp. 95–109). Hauppauge, NY: Nova Science Publishers.

Schildkraut, J., & Muschert, G. W. (2013). Violent media, guns, and mental illness: The three ring circus of causal factors for school massacres, as related in media discourse. *Fast Capitalism, 10*(1). Retrieved from http://www.uta.edu/huma/agger/fastcapitalism/10_1/schildkraut10_1.html

Schildkraut, J., & Muschert, G. W. (2014). Media salience and the framing of mass murder in schools: A comparison of the Columbine and Sandy Hook massacres. *Homicide Studies, 18*, 23–43.

Shultz, J. M., Muschert, G. W., Dingwall, A., & Cohen, A. M. (2013). The Sandy Hook Elementary School shooting as tipping point – "This time is different." *Disaster Health, 1*, 65–73.

Simpson, R. (2006). *Covering violence: A guide to ethical reporting about victims and trauma*. New York, NY: Columbia University Press.

Sorokin, P. A. (1947). *Society, culture, and personality*. New York, NY: Harper and Brothers.

Sorokin, P. A. (1954). *The ways and power of love*. Boston, MA: Beacon Press.

Spencer, J. W., & Muschert, G. W. (2009). The contested meaning of the crosses at Columbine. *American Behavioral Scientist, 52*, 1371–1386.

Sumiala, J., & Hakala, S. (2010). Crisis: Mediatization of disaster in the Nordic media sphere. In T. Broddason, U. Kivikuru, B. Tufte, L. Weibull, & H. Østbye (Eds.), *The Nordic countries and the world. Perspectives from research on media communication* (pp. 361–378). Göteborg, Sweden: Nordicom.

Thoresen, S., Jensen, T. K., & Dyb, G. (2014). Media participation and mental health in terrorist attack survivors. *Journal of Traumatic Stress, 27*, 639–646.

Vuori, M. (2016). Revisiting local responses to mass violence. *Journal of Risk Research, 19*, 515–532.

Walsh-Childers, K., Lewis, N., & Neely, J. (2008). *Twice victimized: Lessons from the media mob at Virginia Tech*. Paper presented at the annual meeting of the Association for Education in Journalism and Mass Communication, Chicago, IL. Retrieved from http://citation.allacademic.com/meta/p271879_index.html

Wilde, L. (2007). The concept of solidarity: Emerging from the theoretical shadows? *British Journal of Politics and International Relations, 9*, 171–181.

Wilms, I. A. (2007). "Die Schüsse nach den Schüssen" oder das Medientrauma von Erfurt. *Psychotherapie Forum, 15*, 179–182.

Part IV

Psychological Considerations for Impacted Individuals

11
Mental Health Outcomes Following Direct Exposure
Laura C. Wilson

Exposure to traumatic events has consistently been found to increase survivors' risk for a myriad of adverse emotional, cognitive, behavioral, and physical health outcomes (see Norris, Friedman, & Watson, 2002; Norris, Friedman, Watson, Byrne, Diaz, & Kaniasty, 2002; Schnurr & Green, 2004 for reviews). These posttrauma difficulties have been found to range from mild transient stress reactions to persistent and debilitating psychopathology (Norris, Friedman, Watson, Byrne, et al., 2002). Although almost all individuals (i.e., 89.7%) will experience at least one traumatic event during their lifetime, only a small percentage of the population reports clinically significant levels of symptomatology as a result of exposure to traumatic events (e.g., 12-month prevalence rate of 4.7% for posttraumatic stress disorder (PTSD); Kilpatrick et al., 2013). In fact, many survivors display surprising levels of resiliency, or adaptation to stress, following traumatic events. For example, Norris, Tracy, and Galea (2009) found that approximately one half of individuals exposed to a terrorist attack never experienced more than mild distress. The heterogeneity observed among survivors has generated great interest among psychologists wanting to better understand the effects of trauma exposure on survivors' short- and long-term psychological functioning. The focus of this chapter will be on individuals' mental health functioning following direct exposure to mass shootings.

To review the literature on the mental health outcomes associated with direct exposure to mass shootings, several topics will be addressed. First, I will comment on the state of the literature and the implications of these issues as they relate to this chapter. Second, I will discuss the controversy of how to define exposure and how this applies to mass shooting survivors. Third, I will examine how individuals' levels of exposure to a mass shooting may impact their risk for psychopathology. Next, I will consider whether mass shootings may be associated with greater risk for psychological difficulties when compared to other types of trauma. Fifth, I will identify and discuss the types of psychopathology

The Wiley Handbook of the Psychology of Mass Shootings, First Edition. Edited by Laura C. Wilson.
© 2017 John Wiley & Sons, Inc. Published 2017 by John Wiley & Sons, Inc.

survivors typically experience. Lastly, I will examine factors that may help explain the heterogeneity observed among survivors. Due to space constraints, this chapter cannot serve as a comprehensive review of the literature. Rather, my goal is to highlight the key features of the literature base and identify areas that future research should further expand on.

State of the Literature

Prior to discussing the available literature on mental health outcomes in individuals impacted by mass shootings, it is first necessary to highlight three key features of the literature. These issues should be kept in mind when reading the discussion below because these observations about the state of the literature may influence the interpretation of the findings or the implications of the conclusions.

First, the trauma literature, as a whole, would be best described as a series of case studies (Norris, Friedman, Watson, Byrne, et al., 2002). That is, the majority of published articles on trauma have examined particular events that each have unique characteristics that make it difficult to generalize beyond that specific event and the examined population. In these situations, meta-analyses and systematic literature reviews are often recommended because, as aggregates of the literature, these types of methodologies provide more generalizable conclusions. For example, many of the mass shooting articles have been written about the Virginia Tech shooting, which occurred on April 16, 2007 (e.g., Hughes et al., 2011; Littleton, Axsom, & Grills-Taquechel, 2011; Vicary & Fraley, 2010). As Virginia Tech was the deadliest mass shooting in the United States to date (Hughes et al., 2011), it is difficult to determine whether the results obtained from that particular population and event would apply to survivors of other mass shootings. Unfortunately, there is a lack of meta-analyses and systematic reviews within this area of the literature. There is only one known meta-analysis, which examined the dose-response relationship in mass shooting survivors (i.e., Wilson, 2014). Therefore, the mass shooting literature is almost exclusively a series of case studies and this should be kept in mind when considering the findings discussed here.

Second, in comparison to other types of trauma (e.g., sexual assault, combat, natural disasters), mass shootings are relatively understudied and less is known about the mental health consequences of these incidents. This can be illustrated by a systematic literature search that was conducted for the purposes of this chapter. The search used PsycINFO and PubMED, and the keywords included *mass murder, mass shooting, mass violence, mass trauma, mass casualty, school shooting, school violence,* and *shooting,* cross-referenced with *posttraumatic stress disorder, acute stress disorder, trauma symptoms, posttraumatic stress symptoms,* and *stress reactions.* The search was limited to peer-reviewed journal articles published in English.

Using this search procedure, 142 total unique citations were identified and reviewed for potential inclusion. Articles were deemed relevant if they were empirical articles that examined PTSD in the aftermath of a mass shooting in a sample of individuals who satisfied the DSM-5 PTSD Criterion A (American Psychiatric Association, 2013), which will be discussed below in greater detail. Only a total of 16 articles were identified as meeting these criteria. Furthermore, many of these articles examined duplicate samples. For example, 4 of these 16 articles relied on the same group of participants exposed to a mass shooting in a Luby's restaurant in Killeen, Texas on October 16, 1991 (i.e., North, Smith, & Spitznagel, 1994, 1997; North, Spitznagel, & Smith, 2001; North, McCutcheon, Spitznagel, & Smith, 2002). The 16 articles identified in this search focused on only five mass shootings (i.e., Falun, Sweden on June 11, 1994; Jokela High School in Jokela, Finland on November 7, 2007; Luby's restaurant in Killeen, Texas on October 16, 1991; Northern Illinois University in DeKalb, Illinois on February 14, 2008; Virginia Tech in Blacksburg, Virginia on April 16, 2007). It is shocking that so few studies were located in this search and that only a total of five mass shootings were examined in the identified articles.

Third, the prior research that has been conducted in this area has included a wide range of exposure types. Although most studies have included participants who would be characterized as experiencing direct exposure (e.g., heard gunfire, saw people injured), these participants are often lumped in with a larger group of people who distally experienced the event (e.g., were on campus) or reported no connection to the event. For example, Littleton, Axsom, and Grills-Taquechel (2011) indicated that 30% of participants experienced severe direct exposure (e.g., in one of the buildings where the shootings occurred), 45% of participants experienced moderate direct exposure (e.g., were on campus), and 25% of participants did not report direct exposure to the event. However, Littleton, Axsom, and Grills-Taquechel (2011) reported prevalence rates of probable PTSD for the entire sample. Due to the nature of the literature, it is difficult to differentiate the impact of direct exposure from distal or an absence of exposure. Because of the overall dearth of studies focused on the impact of direct exposure on survivors, this review will have to rely heavily on literature that is based on participants with more indirect experiences (see Chapter 12 for a more thorough discussion of the impact of mass shootings on communities).

Overall, limited research has been dedicated to examining the mental health outcomes associated with exposure to mass shootings, and these studies have focused on a few particular events and included a wide range of exposure types. The discussion presented here is therefore limited by the small and homogenous literature base that would most accurately be described as a series of case studies. Regardless of the identified issues with the available empirical evidence, the information discussed here provides a basis for researchers and clinicians to better understand the psychological consequences observed within those individuals directly impacted by mass shootings.

Definition of Exposure

When examining posttrauma outcomes following mass shootings, another key issue to consider is how to define "exposure." It is apparent that individuals would meet the definition of exposure if they directly witnessed the event in person, such as seeing others be injured or killed, hearing gunfire, or if they were injured themselves. However, it is less clear whether an individual would meet the definition of exposure if they learned about details of the event through another person or watched extensive TV coverage of the event. Before discussing the mental health outcomes associated with exposure to a mass shooting, it is necessary to define "exposure."

In the trauma literature, direct exposure is often defined based on the stressor criterion (i.e., Criterion A) of the PTSD diagnosis, as listed in the *Diagnostic and Statistical Manual of Mental Disorders* (DSM; American Psychiatric Association, 2013). This criterion defines trauma exposure as actual or threatened death, serious injury, or sexual violence through direct exposure, witnessing the event in person, learning that a relative or close friend was exposed to the event, or extreme exposure to aversive details of the event not including through media or television (American Psychiatric Association, 2013). However, Criterion A has been a source of substantial controversy since it was first introduced (e.g., Brewin, Lanius, Novac, Schnyder, & Galea, 2009; Kilpatrick, Resnick, & Acierno, 2009; Weathers & Keane, 2007a, 2007b). For example, prior studies have found evidence of distress in individuals who report forms of exposure that do not meet this definition (e.g., TV coverage). Based on a nationwide study, 17% of the U.S. population endorsed PTSD symptoms 2 months following the September 11 terrorist attacks even though only a small fraction of the population would have met the DSM-5 definition of exposure (i.e., Criterion A; Silver, Holman, McIntosh, Poulin, & Gil-Rivas, 2002). Similar results have been demonstrated following other mass violence incidents and disasters, such as the Oklahoma City bombing (Pfefferbaum et al., 2002) and the Challenger explosion (Terr, Bloch, Michel, Shi, Reinhardt, & Metayer, 1999). Findings such as these are often cited as evidence that Criterion A may be too restrictive since individuals who are geographically distant from and have no personal ties to a traumatic event may still display PTSD symptoms or other forms of stress reactions (e.g., depression).

Exposure in this chapter will be broadly defined as personally witnessing or having a strong personal tie to, or exposure to, graphic and upsetting details about a mass shooting. This definition was chosen because forms of exposure that do not satisfy Criterion A have been found to be associated with event-related symptomatology following mass shootings. Fallahi and Lesik (2009) found a significant positive association between the amount of TV viewed following the Virginia Tech shooting and PTSD symptoms in college students at a geographically distant university. Although many experts may argue that TV coverage should not be considered trauma exposure, previous research suggests that some individuals may present with clinically significant levels of distress stemming from images and details they were exposed to through TV coverage of mass shootings. Additionally, low levels of exposure to mass shootings have been linked to heightened levels of distress (Orcutt, Miron, Seligowski, 2014). For example, Hughes et al. (2011) found that following the Virginia Tech shooting one of the strongest predictors of PTSD was an inability to confirm the safety of friends. Finally, due to the aforementioned limitations of the literature, this broad definition was necessary to allow some freedom in the empirical evidence that is applicable to this chapter.

Although some individuals' experiences during or following a mass shooting may not fit the typical definition of trauma exposure, they may still report psychological symptoms and their difficulties could warrant clinical intervention. For example, Vicary and Fraley (2010) found that nearly 75% of students at Virginia Tech and Northern Illinois University who participated in their study endorsed significant psychological distress (e.g., PTSD, depression) 2 weeks after the shootings that occurred at these schools. Although there is heated debate about the definition of trauma exposure and whether a diagnosis of PTSD is appropriate for someone who does not satisfy Criterion A, empirical evidence suggests that the impact of mass shootings on mental health extends beyond the survivors who directly witness the event (Norris, 2007). With this in mind, the mental health impact of a wide range of exposure types should be considered when working with individuals in the aftermath of mass shootings.

Dose-Response Relationship

A third topic to consider is how individuals' levels of exposure to a mass shooting may differentially impact their mental health outcomes. Perhaps the most frequently discussed theory describing the relationship between level of exposure and posttrauma functioning is called the dose-response relationship (Dohrenwend & Dohrenwend, 1974). According to this theory, a greater dose of trauma (i.e., level of exposure) will be associated with greater risk for the development of posttrauma psychopathology (Bowman & Yehuda, 2004). For example, an individual who directly witnessed a mass shooting in person (e.g., saw the shooter, was physically injured) will be at greater risk of experiencing psychological difficulties than an individual who learned that the event happened to a loved one.

The dose-response relationship originated in the DSM-III (American Psychiatric Association, 1980), which stated that "the severity, duration, and proximity of an individual's exposure to the traumatic event are the most important factors affecting the likelihood of developing this disorder" (p. 426). As can be seen in the excerpt from DSM-III, the level of direct exposure an individual experiences can be conceptualized in a number of ways, including physical distance, social connection, temporal duration, number of exposures, degree of life threat, and extent of physical injury. Additionally, based on this conceptualization, an individual's level of exposure is considered central to understanding the development and maintenance of psychopathology.

Although many studies have found support for this theory in a wide range of trauma populations, such as disaster survivors (e.g., Furr, Comer, Edmunds, & Kendall, 2010), military veterans (e.g., Brewin, Andrews, & Valentine, 2000) and crime victims (e.g., Brewin et al., 2000), the dose-response relationship has been a source of great contention. Most notably, several studies have failed to find evidence of this relationship (e.g., Ehlers, Mayou, & Bryant, 1998; Uranso et al., 1999). Furthermore, even when studies find support for the dose-response relationship, the results often support other predictors (e.g., preexisting mental health issues) as more informative in understanding individuals' risk for posttrauma psychopathology (Bowman, 1997). Therefore, the utility of the dose-response theory in understanding trauma survivors' risk of developing posttrauma psychopathology has been questioned and therefore may not be as useful as was once thought.

Although the level of exposure an individual experiences during a trauma has historically been cited as one of the most informative predictors for understanding their risk of psychopathology, this claim has been challenged. This question was examined in a recent meta-analysis investigating the dose-response theory in terms of predicting PTSD symptoms following mass shootings (Wilson, 2014). This meta-analysis included 13 independent effect sizes and found an overall significant weighted mean effect size of $r = .19$. This result suggests that as an individual's level of exposure to a mass shooting increased, their risk for event-related PTSD symptoms significantly increased. This supports the dose-response theory. Because the effect size was only small to medium in magnitude, the finding also indicated that although the level of event exposure was a significant predictor, it was not adequate as the sole predictor of PTSD symptoms. Therefore, it is essential that additional factors, such as pretrauma (e.g., preexisting mental health issues), peritrauma (e.g., dissociation) and posttrauma (e.g., social support) influences, be considered when understanding survivor mental health outcomes following mass shootings (Ozer, Best, Lipsey, & Weiss, 2003). Findings related to these additional influences will be discussed below.

Despite the limitations of the dose-response model, a survivor's level of exposure to a mass shooting can still be used to guide mental health intervention because, on average, greater exposure is associated with significantly greater risk of posttrauma difficulties (Wilson, 2014). Delivering mental health services in the aftermath of disasters can pose quite a challenge for professionals. Emergency management coordinators and crisis response teams often have to make quick decisions when coordinating and allocating mental health services, and typically have access to limited information. In such situations, the level of exposure within a population can be used as an initial, but imprecise, measure of risk for psychopathology until more thorough individualized assessment can be completed.

Type of Trauma

When discussing mental health in the aftermath of mass shootings, a fourth feature to examine is whether or not this type of trauma is associated with unique psychological consequences. As previously mentioned, the majority of trauma survivors do not develop long-lasting persistent psychopathology (Breslau, 2009). On the other hand, prior research suggests that mass shooting survivors may be at greater risk of mental health difficulties when compared to other types of trauma (e.g., natural disasters; Norris, Friedman, & Watson, 2002; Norris, Friedman, Watson, Byrne, et al., 2002). After accounting for other event and participant characteristics, Norris and colleagues (Norris, Friedman, & Watson, 2002; Norris, Friedman, Watson, Byrne, et al., 2002) found that mass violence (e.g., mass shooting, bombing) was associated with more severe impairment than natural and technological disasters. Specifically, 67% of mass violence survivors were identified as being severely or very severely impaired. Conversely, only 39% of technology disaster survivors and 34% of natural disaster survivors were either severely or very severely impaired. Interestingly, none of the mass violence survivors identified in the literature review conducted by Norris, Friedman, Watson, Byrne, et al. (2002) reported minimal or transient impairment, and the majority of individuals identified in the moderate impairment category were those who only experienced indirect exposure. Thus, prior research suggests that direct exposure to a mass shooting often leads to serious psychological difficulties (Norris, 2007) and mass shootings may be associated with greater posttrauma difficulties when compared to other types of trauma (Norris, Friedman, & Watson, 2002).

The greater risk of posttrauma difficulties among mass shooting survivors is further supported when prevalence rates of psychopathology following mass shootings are compared to other types of trauma. Substantial research has demonstrated that, on average, less than 10% of trauma survivors develop PTSD (Breslau, 2009; Kessler, Berglund, Demler, Jin, & Walters, 2005). Conversely, Norris (2007) reported that studies have demonstrated prevalence rates ranging from 10 to 36% for PTSD among mass shooting survivors. A recent study found that although a large percentage of individuals following a mass shooting were either resilient (46.1%) or displayed short-term stress reactions (41.1%), approximately 12% reported persistent PTSD (Miron, Orcutt, & Kumpula, 2014). This is slightly higher than the average prevalence of PTSD among trauma survivors as a whole (Breslau, 2009). Even though the majority of evidence suggests that individuals exposed to mass shootings are typically resilient or only display transient stress reactions, this type of traumatic event may be associated with greater risk for persistent symptomatology when compared to other forms of trauma (e.g., natural disasters, technological disaster).

If prior research suggests that mass shooting survivors are at increased risk of persistent and debilitating psychological difficulties, then this leads to the question of "why?" Trauma survivors, across all types of trauma, are susceptible to a wide range of negative beliefs, including self-blame, hopelessness, and overestimation of danger (Briere & Scott, 2006). It has been proposed that the heightened risk of posttrauma difficulties among those impacted by mass shootings is because of the unique characteristics of this type of event. Specifically, these incidents are purposeful and malicious acts, the incident is perceived as random and unpredictable, and victims tend to be indiscriminately selected (Briere & Elliott, 2000; Carlson & Dalenberg, 2000; Norris, Friedman, & Watson, 2002). These unique characteristics of mass shootings may be associated with greater feelings of hopelessness and have more detrimental effects on survivors' cognitions (e.g., just world belief, survivor guilt) than other types of trauma (Norris, Friedman, & Watson, 2002). These maladaptive thoughts and negative beliefs in turn increase risk for psychopathology (Dalgleish, 2004).

The heightened risk of mental health issues that stems from the unpredictable and malicious nature of these events should be kept in mind by those individuals charged with delivering mental health services in the immediate and long-term aftermath of mass shootings. Depending on the situation and the patients' needs, treatment goals may need to be tailored to address the maladaptive thoughts that may be contributing to psychological difficulties. Issues related to clinical intervention following mass shootings will be further discussed in Part V of this book. Despite the fact that mass shooting survivors may be at increased risk of posttrauma mental health difficulties due to the unique characteristics of this type of event, it is important to remember that only a minority of survivors will experience long-term distress (Miron et al., 2014).

Mental Health Outcomes

A fifth issue relevant to the study of posttrauma functioning is to identify the types of short- and long-term difficulties that survivors typically experience. It should be noted that trauma can impact any aspect of an individual's functioning, including physical health (e.g., immune functioning, cardiovascular health; see Schnurr & Green, 2004; D'Andrea, Sharma, Zelechoski, Spinazzola, 2011 for reviews), sleep (see Harvey, Jones, & Schmidt, 2003 for a review), sexual functioning (see De Silva, 2001 for a review), and attention (Aupperle, Melrose, Stein, & Paulus, 2012). For the purposes of this chapter, mental health symptoms and psychological disorders will be the focus. Regardless, it should be kept in mind that many of the devastating consequences of trauma (e.g., sense of emptiness, disruption in trust, decline in spirituality) may not be sufficiently captured by the diagnostic criterion of psychological disorders (Briere & Scott, 2006). This is important for clinicians to consider because their patients' difficulties may not be adequately detected with structured assessment tools or be accurately described with diagnostic labels. The key to consider is whether or not the patient is reporting distress and/or impairment as a result of their exposure to a mass shooting. The adverse consequences of mass shootings extend far beyond what will be discussed in this chapter.

PTSD is the most consistently observed psychological disorder following mass shootings (North et al., 1994). It has been demonstrated that only a small percentage of those impacted by mass shootings deny having any symptoms of PTSD (i.e., 3.4%; North et al., 1994). Although almost all mass shooting survivors endorse experiencing some level of psychological difficulties in the immediate aftermath of the event, the majority of them do not report persisting or debilitating psychopathology. North and colleagues (1994) found that 20.3% of male participants and 28.8% of female participants were new cases of PTSD following exposure to a mass shooting. Although PTSD is the most commonly reported disorder, individuals impacted by mass shootings also report other forms of psychopathology. Specifically, North and colleagues (1994) found that 6.9% of male participants and 11.3% of female participants reported a new psychological diagnosis other than PTSD (e.g., major depression disorder, substance use) after exposure to a mass shooting. In this chapter, emphasis will be placed on PTSD symptoms in the aftermath of mass shootings because it is the most commonly endorsed disorder.

The aforementioned systematic review conducted for the purposes of this chapter used key terms related to mass shootings and PTSD, and yielded 16 relevant studies. Of the 16 studies, 14 reported prevalence rates of probable Acute Stress Disorder (ASD) or PTSD among individuals impacted by a mass shooting. Within the first month following the examined mass shootings, the prevalence rates of probable ASD ranged from 26% (North et al., 2002) to 64% (Vicary & Fraley, 2010). From 2 to 6 months following the mass shootings, the prevalence of probable PTSD ranged from 15.4% (Hughes et al., 2011) to 28% (Littleton, Axsom, and Grills-Taquechel, 2011). From 7 months to 1 year following the mass shootings, the prevalence of probable PTSD ranged from 11.4% (Kumpula, Orcutt, Bardeen, & Varkovitzky, 2011) to 27% (Littleton, Axsom, and Grills-Taquechel, 2011). North and colleagues (North et al., 2001; North et al., 2002) found that the prevalence of probable PTSD 3 years following a mass shooting was approximately 18 to 19%. Overall, the findings of the systematic literature review suggested that the prevalence rates of PTSD following mass shootings decreased with time and many individuals who initially met criteria for ASD or PTSD did not report persisting long-term difficulties at a later time. A similar impact of time on prevalence rates has been observed in other trauma populations (Norris, Friedman, & Watson, 2002). As previously discussed, these results also confirm that mass shooting survivors may be at heightened risk of PTSD compared to other trauma populations (i.e., less than 10% of trauma survivors develop PTSD; Breslau, 2009; Kessler et al., 2005).

Substantial prior research demonstrates that trauma increases survivors' risk for many psychological disorders beyond PTSD (Brewin et al., 2009). These post-traumatic mental health responses have been found to include but are not limited to depression, anxiety (e.g., panic, generalized anxiety, specific phobia), somatization (e.g., conversion disorder), substance use, and dissociation (Briere & Scott, 2006; Fullerton & Ursano, 2005). Similar to other types of trauma, an array of mental health outcomes other than PTSD have been found in survivors of mass shootings. But, these difficulties have received substantially less attention in the literature than the more common diagnosis of PTSD.

Because fewer studies have examined non-PTSD disorders, it is difficult to present conclusions based on the literature base. However, a few specific studies can be referenced that point to the increased risk for non-PTSD psychological diagnoses in survivors of mass shootings. These previous studies suggest that mass shooting survivors may endorse a wide range of symptoms and diagnoses, including but not limited to depression (e.g., Johnson, North, & Smith, 2002; Littleton, Axsom, and Grills-Taquechel, 2011; North et al., 1994; Vicary & Fraley, 2010), substance use (e.g., Johnson et al., 2002; North et al., 1994; Suomalainen, Haravouri, Berg, Kiviruusu, & Marttunen, 2011), panic disorder (e.g., Johnson et al., 2002; North et al., 1994), generalized anxiety disorder (e.g., North et al., 1994), and overall psychiatric distress (e.g., Suomalainen et al., 2011). North et al. (1994) found that besides PTSD, the most commonly reported mental health issue among female mass shooting survivors was depression and among male mass shooting survivors was substance use. In general, PTSD is the primary mental health outcome examined and observed in the aftermath of mass shootings. However, the limited available evidence suggests that mass shooting survivors are at increased risk of a plethora of psychological difficulties, similar to those observed in other trauma populations.

Predictors of Mental Health Outcomes

A final area of investigation to consider is predictors of mental health outcomes among survivors. Because not all trauma survivors develop persistent post-trauma mental health difficulties (Friedman, Keane, & Resick, 2007), studies have been dedicated to elucidating this observed heterogeneity by examining demographic characteristics (e.g., gender, age), pretrauma predictors (e.g., prior trauma history, prior psychopathology), peritrauma factors (e.g., level of exposure, peritraumatic dissociation), and posttrauma influences (e.g., coping strategies, social support; see Brewin et al., 2000; DiGangi et al., 2013; Ozer et al., 2003) that may help account for these individual differences. These studies suggest that the etiology of posttrauma disorders, such as PTSD and depression, is very complex and multifaceted. Because greater emphasis has been placed on PTSD and a larger literature base is available, the discussion of predictors of mental health outcomes following mass shootings will focus on PTSD. The results of the previously mentioned systematic literature review that yielded 16 relevant articles will be referenced in this discussion.

Demographic characteristics

Previous studies examining numerous types of trauma have found that demographic variables, such as gender and socioeconomic status, are risk factors for the development of PTSD (Brewin et al., 2000). In the systematic literature search of articles examining PTSD following mass shootings, 11 articles assessed how the demographic characteristics of the samples were related to PTSD. The following demographic factors were not significantly related to PTSD: age (i.e., Bardeen, Kumpula, & Orcutt, 2013; Kumpula et al., 2011; Littleton, Kumpula, & Orcutt, 2011; Mercer et al., 2012; North et al., 1997; North et al., 2002; Suomalainen et al., 2011), year in school (i.e., Mercer et al., 2012), years of education (i.e. North et al., 1997; North et al., 2002), marital status (i.e., North et al., 1997; North et al., 2002), socioeconomic status (i.e. Suomalainen et al., 2011), and living arrangements (i.e., Suomalainen et al., 2011). Four articles reported that race and ethnicity were not significantly related to PTSD (i.e., Bardeen et al., 2013; Kumpula et al., 2011; Mercer et al., 2012; North et al., 1997; North et al., 2002). Conversely, one study found that African American participants reported significantly lower risk of PTSD and Asian American participants reported significantly greater risk of PTSD (Littleton, Kumpula, & Orcutt, 2011). Seven articles provided information on gender differences related to PTSD. Six of these seven articles found that women reported significantly greater PTSD than men (i.e., Hughes et al., 2011; North et al., 1994, 1997; North et al., 2001; Suomalainen et al., 2011; Vicary et al., 2010), which is consistent with the trauma literature as a whole (Tolin & Foa, 2006).

Pretrauma factors

Research has suggested that many variables that were once thought of as out-comes of trauma (e.g., coping style) are in fact preexisting risk factors that increase survivors' likelihood of developing PTSD (DiGangi et al., 2013). In the systematic literature search, eight articles examined the relationship between pretrauma factors and postshooting PTSD. The factors examined in the literature can be grouped into three categories: coping strategies, preshooting trauma/stress, and a history of psychopathology.

Coping strategies   Coping refers to any cognitive or behavioral strategy used to manage stressful situations (Folkman & Lazarus, 1980; Lazarus & Folkman, 1984). Individuals who reported emotion regulation difficulties (Bardeen et al., 2013) or experiential avoidance (Kumpula et al., 2011) prior to the shooting were more likely to report postshooting PTSD.

Preshooting trauma   Littleton, Kumpula, and Orcutt (2011) and Kumpula et al. (2011) found that preshooting trauma/stress was significantly related to greater PTSD. Conversely, Mercer et al. (2012) reported that there was no significant relationship between preshooting trauma and post-shooting PTSD.

Preshooting psychopathology   Three articles reported a positive correlation bet-ween preshooting PTSD and postshooting PTSD (Bardeen et al., 2013; Kumpula et al., 2011; Sewell, 1996). Conversely, North and colleagues (1994) reported that preshooting PTSD was not significantly related to post-shooting PTSD.

Five articles examined other types of psychopathology (e.g., anxiety, depression). Littleton, Axsom, and Grills-Taquechel (2011), North et al. (1994, 1997), and Sewell (1996) found that at least one type of non-PTSD preshooting psychopathology was positively related to postshooting PTSD. Conversely, Littleton, Kumpula, and Orcutt (2011) found that preshooting depression and anxiety were not significantly related to postshooting PTSD.

Peritrauma factors

Some evidence suggests that peritraumatic influences, such as peritraumatic emotions and dissociation, are the strongest predictors of PTSD (Ozer et al., 2003). Twelve articles were identified in the systematic literature search that discussed the relationship between peritrauma factors and postshooting PTSD. The peritrauma factors in the literature can be grouped into two categories: exposure level and dissociation.

Exposure   Nine articles found that exposure was significantly correlated with PTSD (Bardeen et al., 2013; Fergus, Rabenhorst, Orcutt, & Valentiner, 2011; Hughes et al., 2011; Kumpula et al., 2011; Littleton, Kumpula, & Orcutt, 2011; Mercer et al., 2012; Stephenson, Valentiner, Kumpula, & Orcutt, 2009; Suomalainen et al., 2011; Vicary et al., 2010). Sewell (1996) found that exposure was slightly positively correlated, albeit not statistically significant, with PTSD at 1 week, but was not related to PTSD at 3 months. North et al. (1997) reported that exposure was not significantly correlated with PTSD at 6 to 8 weeks or 1 year postshooting.

Peritraumatic dissociation   One article found that dissociation during the shooting was significantly positively correlated with PTSD at both 27 days and 35 weeks postshooting (Kumpula et al., 2011).

Posttrauma factors

Because most studies are cross-sectional, posttrauma factors are among the most commonly examined variables in terms of survivor psychopathology. Fifteen articles discussed the relationship between posttrauma factors and postshooting PTSD. These factors can be grouped into the following categories: coping strategies, social support, elapsed time, physiology/genetics, and psychopathology/symptomatology.

Coping strategies   Two articles found that emotion regulation difficulties and maladaptive coping following the shooting were significantly associated with greater postshooting PTSD (Bardeen et al., 2013; Littleton, Axsom, & Grills-Taquechel, 2011). Greater experiential avoidance and reduced trauma processing were significantly associated with greater postshooting PTSD (Kumpula et al., 2011; Sewell, 1996). North et al. (2001) found that using logic to cope was associated with significantly lower levels of postshooting PTSD, whereas assimilation, or the integration of the event into the person's cognitive schemas, was not related to PTSD.

Social support   Suomalainen and colleagues (2011) found a significant negative correlation between social support and postshooting PTSD, but failed to find a significant relationship between perceived mental support from a non-guardian adult and PTSD. North and colleagues (2001) found that seeking out the support of others was significantly associated with reduced PTSD at 1 month, but not at 1 year or 3 years. Three articles found that social support was not significantly related to postshooting PTSD (Mercer et al., 2012; North et al., 1994; Sewell, 1996).

Elapsed time   Vicary et al. (2010) and Bardeen et al. (2013) found that PTSD significantly reduced in severity with time following the mass shooting.

Physiology/genetics   Fergus et al. (2011) found that heart rate, skin conductance, and cortisol levels measured during a writing and reading task about the shooting were not significantly related to PTSD at 8.8 weeks postshooting. Mercer et al. (2012) found that STin2 and 5-HTTLPR serotonin transporter genotypes were not significantly related to PTSD at 3.2 weeks postshooting. However, Rs25531 and 5-HTTLPR multimarker genotypes were significantly related to PTSD at 3.2 weeks postshooting.

Psychopathology   North and colleagues (1997) found that postshooting psychopathology, not including PTSD, was significantly positively associated with postshooting PTSD at 6 to 8 weeks and 1 year. Whereas, North and colleagues (2002) found that postshooting comorbid psychopathology was not significantly related to postshooting PTSD at 3 years.

Three articles found that PTSD immediately following the shooting was significantly positively correlated with long-term PTSD (Kumpula et al., 2011; Littleton, Axsom, and Grills-Taquechel, 2011; Littleton, Kumpula, & Orcutt, 2011). Three articles found that postshooting depression symptoms were significantly positively correlated with postshooting PTSD (Larsson, 2000; Littleton, Axsom, and Grills-Taquechel, 2011; North et al., 1994). Whereas Littleton, Kumpula, and Orcutt (2011) found that postshooting depression symptoms were not significantly correlated with PTSD. Three articles found that postshooting anxiety was significantly positively correlated with postshooting PTSD (Larsson, 2000; Littleton, Axsom, D., & Grills-Taquechel, 2011; Littleton, Kumpula, & Orcutt, 2011).

Somatic/physical concerns (Larsson, 2000; Stephenson et al., 2009), social dysfunction (Larsson, 2000; Stephenson et al., 2009), insomnia (Larsson, 2000), and cognitive concerns (Stephenson et al., 2009) were significantly positively correlated with postshooting PTSD. Conversely, alcohol use was not significantly positively correlated with postshooting PTSD (North et al., 1994).

Summary of predictors of mental health outcomes

Prior research has consistently demonstrated a large amount of variability among mass shooting survivors, with the majority of individuals reporting either resiliency or transient distress (Miron et al., 2014). Numerous factors have been examined as potential explanations for this heterogeneity. Overall, a review of the literature suggests that survivor gender, level of exposure, and pre- and postshooting psychopathology are among the strongest predictors of PTSD in the aftermath of mass shootings. Although little empirical evidence is available assessing whether these factors can help account for variability in other forms of psychopathology (e.g., depression, panic) following mass shootings, it can be assumed that these findings likely generalize to the development and maintenance of non-PTSD psychological disorders.

Conclusion

Based on the review of the literature presented here, several conclusions emerge. First, survivors of mass shootings tend to report resiliency or mild transient stress reactions. Although most survivors report experiencing a few symptoms that are consistent with those seen in cases of ASD or PTSD, the symptoms typically do not meet full criteria for a diagnosis and dissipate within a few weeks of the shooting. Second, a wide range of experiences and levels of exposure to a mass shooting can lead to trauma-related symptomatology, such as watching extensive TV coverage or an inability to confirm the safety of friends. Individuals who do not meet Criterion A of the PTSD diagnostic criteria may still report distress and impairment, and clinical intervention may be appropriate. Third, although there are a lot of similarities in the mental health outcomes of survivors of mass shootings and other types of trauma, the available empirical evidence suggests that mass shootings may be associated with heightened risk of posttrauma psychopathology due to the unique characteristics of these events. Overall, clinicians are encouraged to complete a thorough assessment to consider all potential factors that may be contributing to the onset and maintenance of their patients' difficulties. Furthermore, it is recommended that researchers include a wide range of predictors when attempting to understand survivor outcomes. It is often falsely assumed that individuals who are directly exposed to traumatic events are inevitably at high risk of posttrauma difficulties or that individuals with low levels of exposure will not report distress. Individual differences, such as pretrauma psychopathology, may help researchers and clinicians better predict each survivor's level of risk for persisting symptomatology.

With these key findings in mind, a larger issue emerged from the reviewed literature. Overall, there is a dearth of information about mass shootings, particularly the impact of direct exposure, which has resulted in a lack of empirical evidence related to the mental health consequences of this type of incident. Few articles have been written, and these articles have examined a limited number of mass shootings and have focused mostly on PTSD. This chapter should serve as a call for additional research aimed at better understanding the effects of mass shootings on mental health and how to best support the survivors.

Acknowledgment

I would like to thank Kari Gent from the University of Mary Washington for assisting me as an independent coder for the systematic literature review discussed in this chapter.

References

American Psychiatric Association. (1980). *Diagnostic and statistical manual of mental disorders* (3rd ed.). Washington, DC: Author.

American Psychiatric Association. (2013). *Diagnostic and statistical manual of mental disorders* (5th ed.). Washington, DC: Author.

Aupperle, R. L., Melrose, A. J., Stein, M. B., & Paulus, M. P. (2012). Executive function and PTSD: Disengaging from trauma. *Neuropharmacology, 62,* 686–694.

Bardeen, J. R., Kumpula, M. J., & Orcutt, H. K. (2013). Emotion regulation difficulties as a prospective predictor of posttraumatic stress following a mass shooting. *Journal of Anxiety Disorders, 27,* 188–196.

Bowman, M. (1997). *Individual differences in posttraumatic response: Problems with the adversity-distress connection.* Mahwah, NJ: Erlbaum.

Bowman, M. L., & Yehuda, R. (2004). Risk factors and adversity-stress model. In G. M. Rosen (Ed.), *Posttraumatic stress disorders: Issues and controversies* (pp. 15–38). Chichester, UK: Wiley.

Breslau, N. (2009). The epidemiology of trauma, PTSD, and other posttrauma disorders. *Trauma, Violence, & Abuse, 10,* 198–210.

Brewin, C. R., Andrews, B., & Valentine, J. D. (2000). Meta-analysis of risk factors for posttraumatic stress disorder in trauma-exposed adults. *Journal of Consulting and Clinical Psychology, 68,* 748–766.

Brewin, C. R., Lanius, R. A., Novac, A., Schnyder, U., & Galea, S. (2009). Reformulating PTSD for DSM-V: Life after Criterion A. *Journal of Traumatic Stress, 22,* 366–373.

Briere, J., & Elliott, D. M. (2000). Prevalence, characteristics, and long-term sequelae of natural disaster exposure in the general population. *Journal of Traumatic Stress, 13,* 661–679.

Briere, J., & Scott, C. (2006). *Principles of trauma therapy.* Thousand Oaks, CA: Sage.

Carlson, E. B., & Dalenberg, C. J. (2000). A conceptual framework for the impact of traumatic experiences. *Trauma, Violence, and Abuse: A Review Journal, 1,* 4–28.

D'Andrea, W., Sharma, R., Zelechoski, A. D., & Spinazzola, J. (2011). Physical health problems after single trauma exposure: When stress takes root in the body. *Journal of American Psychiatric Nurses Association, 17,* 387–392.

Dalgleish, T. (2004). Cognitive approaches to posttraumatic stress disorder: The evolution of multirepresentational theorizing. *Psychological Bulletin, 130,* 228–260.

De Silva, P. (2001). Impact of trauma on sexual functioning and sexual relationships. *Sexual and Relationship Therapy, 16,* 269–278.

DiGangi, J. A., Gomez, D., Mendoza, L., Jason, L. A., Keys, C. B., & Koenen, K. C. (2013). Pretrauma risk factors for posttraumatic stress disorder: A systematic review of the literature. *Clinical Psychology Review, 33,* 728–744.

Dohrenwend, B. S., & Dohrenwend, B. P. (1974). *Stress life events: Their nature and effects.* New York, NY: Wiley.

Ehlers, A., Mayou, R. A., & Bryant, B. (1998). Psychological predictors of chronic posttraumatic stress disorder after motor vehicle accidents. *Journal of Abnormal Psychology, 107,* 508–519.

Fallahi, C. R., & Lesik, S. A. (2009). The effects of vicarious exposure to the recent massacre at Virginia Tech. *Psychological Trauma: Theory, Research, Practice, and Policy, 1*, 220–230.

Fergus, T. A., Rabenhorst, M. M., Orcutt, H. K., & Valentiner, D. P. (2011). Reactions to trauma research among women recently exposed to a campus shooting. *Journal of Traumatic Stress, 24*, 596–600.

Folkman, S., & Lazarus, R. S. (1980). An analysis of coping in a middle-aged community sample. *Journal of Health and Social Behavior, 21*, 219–239.

Friedman, M. J., Keane, T. M., & Resick, P. A. (2007). PTSD: Twenty-five years of progress and challenges. In M. J. Friedman, T. M Keane, & P. A. Resick (Eds.), *Handbook of PTSD: Science and practice* (pp. 3–18). New York, NY: The Guilford Press.

Fullerton, C. S., & Ursano, R. J. (2005). Psychological and psychopathological consequences of disasters. In J. J. Lopez-Ibor, G. Christodoulou, M. Maj, N. Sartorius, & A. Okasha (Eds.), *Disasters and mental health* (pp. 13–36). Chichester, UK: Wiley.

Furr, J. M., Comer, J. S., Emunds, J. M., & Kendall, P. C. (2010). Disasters and youth: A meta-analytic examination of posttraumatic stress. *Journal of Consulting and Clinical Psychology, 78*, 765–780.

Harvey, A. G., Jones, C., & Schmidt, D. A. (2003). Sleep and posttraumatic stress disorder: A review. *Clinical Psychology Review, 23*, 377–407.

Hughes, M., Brymer, M. J., Chiu, W. T., Fairbank, J. A., Jones, R. T., Pynoos, R. S., … Kessler, R. C. (2011). Posttraumatic stress among students after the shootings at Virginia Tech. *Psychological Trauma: Theory, Research, Practice, and Policy, 3*, 403–411.

Johnson, S. D., North, C. S., & Smith, E. M. (2002). Psychiatric disorders among victims of a courthouse shooting spree: A three-year follow-up study. *Community Mental Health Journal, 38*, 181–194.

Kessler, R. C., Berglund, P., Demler, O., Jin, R., & Walters, E. E. (2005). Lifetime prevalence and age of onset distributions of DSM-IV disorders in the National Comorbidity Survey Replication. *Archives of General Psychiatry, 62*, 593–602.

Kilpatrick, D. G., Resnick, H. S., & Acierno, R. (2009). Should PTSD criterion A be retained? *Journal of Traumatic Stress, 22*, 374–383.

Kilpatrick, D. G., Resnick, H. S., Milanak, M. E., Miller, M. W., Keyes, K. M., & Friedman, M. J. (2013). National estimates of exposure to traumatic events and PTSD prevalence using DSM-IV and DSM-5 criteria. *Journal of Traumatic Stress, 26*, 537–547.

Kumpula, M. J., Orcutt, H. K., Bardeen, J. R., & Varkovitzky, R. L. (2011). Peritraumatic dissociation and experiential avoidance as prospective predictors of posttraumatic stress symptoms. *Journal of Abnormal Psychology, 120*, 617–627.

Larsson, G. (2000). Dimensional analysis of the Impact of Event Scale using structural equation modeling. *Journal of Traumatic Stress, 13*, 193–204.

Lazarus, R. S., & Folkman, S. (1984). *Stress, appraisal, and coping.* New York, NY: Springer.

Littleton, H., Axsom, D., & Grills-Taquechel, A. E. (2011). Longitudinal evaluation of the relationship between maladaptive trauma coping and distress: Examination following the mass shooting at Virginia Tech. *Anxiety, Stress & Coping: An International Journal, 24,* 273–290.

Littleton, H., Kumpula, M., & Orcutt, H. (2011b). Posttraumatic symptoms following a campus shooting: The role of psychosocial resource loss. *Violence and Victims, 26,* 461–476.

Mercer, K. B., Orcutt, H. K., Quinn, J. F., Fitzgerald, C. A., Conneely, K. N., Barfield, R. T., ... Ressler, K. J. (2012). Acute and posttraumatic stress symptoms in a prospective gene × environment study of a university campus shooting. *Archives of General Psychiatry, 69,* 89–97.

Miron, L. R., Orcutt, H. K., & Kumpula, M. J. (2014). Differential predictors of transient stress versus posttraumatic stress disorder: Evaluating risk following target mass violence. *Behavior Therapy, 45,* 791–805.

Norris, F. H. (2007). Impact of mass shootings on survivors, families and communities. *PTSD Research Quarterly, 18*(3), 1–7.

Norris, F. H., Friedman, M. J., & Watson, P. J. (2002). 60,000 disaster victims speak: Part II. Summary and implications of the disaster mental health research. *Psychiatry: Interpersonal and Biological Processes, 65,* 240–260.

Norris, F. H., Friedman, M. J., Watson, P. J., Byrne, C. M., Diaz, E., & Kaniasty, K. (2002). 60,000 disaster victims speak: Part I. An empirical review of the empirical literature, 1981–2001. *Psychiatry: Interpersonal and Biological Processes, 65,* 207–239.

Norris, F. H., Tracy, M., & Galea, S. (2009). Looking for resilience: Understanding the longitudinal trajectories of response to stress. *Social Science & Medicine, 68,* 2190–2198.

North, C. S., McCutcheon, V., Spitznagel, E. L., & Smith, E. M. (2002). Three-year follow-up of survivors of a mass shooting episode. *Journal of Urban Health, 79,* 383–391.

North, C. S., Smith, E. M., & Spitznagel, E. L. (1994). Posttraumatic stress disorder in survivors of a mass shooting. *American Journal of Psychiatry, 151,* 82–88.

North, C. S., Smith, E. M., & Spitznagel, E. L. (1997). One-year follow-up of survivors of a mass shooting. *The American Journal of Psychiatry, 154,* 1696–1702.

North, C. S., Spitznagel, E. L., & Smith, E. M. (2001). A prospective study of coping after exposure to a mass murder episode. *Annals of Clinical Psychiatry, 13,* 81–87.

Orcutt, H. K., Miron, L. R., & Seligowski, A. V. (2014). Impact of mass shootings on individual adjustment. *PTSD Research Quarterly, 25,* 1–9.

Ozer, E. J., Best, S. R., Lipsey, T. L., & Weiss, D. S. (2003). Predictors of posttraumatic stress disorder and symptoms in adults: A meta-analysis. *Psychological Bulletin, 129,* 52–73.

Pfefferbaum, B., Seale, T. W., McDonald, N. B., Brandt, E. N., Rainwater, S., Maynard, B. T., ... Miller, P. D. (2002). Posttraumatic stress two years after the Oklahoma City bombing in youths geographically distant from the explosion. *Psychiatry, 63,* 358–370.

Schnurr, P. P., & Green, B. L. (2004). *Trauma and health: Physical health consequences of exposure to extreme stress.* Washington, DC: American Psychological Association.

Sewell, Kenneth, W. (1996). Constructional risk factors for a post-traumatic stress response after a mass murder. *Journal of Constructivist Psychology, 9*, 97–107.

Silver, R. C., Holman, E. A., McIntosh, D. N., Poulin, M., & Gil-Rivas, V. (2002). National longitudinal study of psychological responses to September 11. *The Journal of the American Medical Association, 288*, 1235–1244.

Stephenson, K. L., Valentiner, D. P., Kumpula, M. J., & Orcutt, H. K. (2009). Anxiety sensitivity and posttrauma stress symptoms in female undergraduates following a campus shooting. *Journal of Traumatic Stress, 22*, 489–496.

Suomalainen, L., Haravouri, H., Berg, N., Kiviruusu, O., & Marttunen, M. (2011). A controlled follow-up study of adolescents exposed to a school shooting: Psychological consequences after four months. *European Psychiatry, 26*, 490–497.

Terr, L. C., Bloch, D. A., Michel, B. A., Shi, H., Reinhardt, J. A., & Metayer, S. (1999). Children's symptoms in the wake of the Challenger: A field study of distant-traumatic effects and an outline of related conditions. *American Journal of Psychiatry, 156*, 1536–1544.

Tolin, D. F., & Foa, E. B. (2006). Sex differences in trauma and posttraumatic stress disorder: A quantitative review of 25 years of research. *Psychological Bulletin, 132*, 959–992.

Uranso, R. J., Fullerton, C. S., Epstein, R. S., Crowley, B., Kao, T. C., Vance, K., ... Baum, A. (1999). Acute and chronic posttraumatic stress disorder in motor vehicle accident victims. *The American Journal of Psychiatry, 156*, 589–595.

Vicary, A. M., & Fraley, R. C. (2010). Student reactions to the shootings at Virginia Tech and Northern Illinois University: Does sharing grief and support over the internet affect recovery? *Personality and Social Psychology Bulletin, 36*, 1555–1563.

Weathers, F. W., & Keane, T. M. (2007a). The criterion A problem revisited: Controversies and challenges in defining and measuring psychological trauma. *Journal of Traumatic Stress, 20*, 107–121.

Weathers, F. W., & Keane, T. M. (2007b). The crucial role of Criterion A: A response to Maier's commentary [Comment]. *Journal of Traumatic Stress, 20*, 917–919.

Wilson, L. C. (2014). Mass shootings: A meta-analysis of the dose-response relationship. *Journal of Traumatic Stress, 27*, 631–638.

12

Psychosocial Functioning Within Shooting-Affected Communities

Individual- and Community-Level Factors

Heather Littleton, Julia C. Dodd, and Kelly Rudolph

Recent research following mass shooting events has examined not only those individuals directly exposed to or affected by the violence (see Chapter 11), but also the impact of the shooting on the whole community. In addition, there is growing awareness that mass shooting events may not only affect individuals' levels of adjustment, but may also affect community identity, solidarity, and overall functioning. Indeed, it has been argued that events such as mass shootings are best thought of as communal traumas, leaving whole communities affected in their wake (Littleton, Grills-Taquechel, & Axsom, 2009; North & Pfefferbaum, 2002). As a result, it is imperative that both research and intervention focus on the whole community to adequately capture the impact of such events and develop programs to improve outcomes among all members of affected communities.

It is in this spirit that we review the literature regarding the impact of mass shootings on the community. In this chapter, we will first review literature regarding the prevalence of adjustment difficulties among individuals in mass-shooting-affected communities. Emerging research supports that a number of individuals with less severe or even no direct exposure to a mass shooting event may experience adjustment difficulties, including anxiety, depression, and posttraumatic stress disorder (PTSD) symptoms, and, further, that chronic adjustment difficulties can develop. Next, we will discuss predictors of adjustment difficulties following mass shootings including the role of preshooting vulnerability, shooting-related exposure and loss, appraisals of shooting-related threat, and postshooting experiences. Then, we will discuss the possibility that mass shooting events may represent opportunities for

The Wiley Handbook of the Psychology of Mass Shootings, First Edition. Edited by Laura C. Wilson.
© 2017 John Wiley & Sons, Inc. Published 2017 by John Wiley & Sons, Inc.

positive changes in individuals' functioning. Finally, we will review research regarding how the community itself may be altered by a mass shooting including changes in community solidarity, identity, and sense of safety within the community.

Throughout this chapter we will primarily review research conducted following four mass shooting events. We chose to focus on these events as the preponderance of work on the broader impact of mass shootings has focused on these four incidents. Two of these mass shooting events, the Virginia Tech (VT) campus shooting and the Northern Illinois University (NIU) campus shooting, occurred on college campuses in the United States, and two occurred in Finland, one at a high school (i.e., Jokela shooting) and one on a college campus (i.e., Kauhajoki shooting). All four events involved a lone, well-armed gunman, resulted in multiple fatalities, and were perpetrated by a current or former student (i.e., member of the affected community).

The VT campus shooting occurred on April 16, 2007 and involved a currently enrolled student. The incident occurred over the course of several hours in two campus buildings; students were on lockdown on campus as well as in the small town where the campus was situated. The gunman first shot two people in a campus dormitory, and later entered a classroom building, chained the doors, and went through multiple classrooms firing upon students and faculty who were trapped inside, before finally taking his life. By the end of the incident, 32 individuals had been killed by the gunman and another 25 individuals were wounded, making it the most deadly mass shooting in U.S. history at that time (Associated Press, 2007; Littleton, Grills-Taquechel, & Axsom, 2009). The NIU campus shooting occurred on February 14, 2008 and involved a former student who opened fire on a class in a large lecture hall. Five students were killed in the shooting and an additional 21 individuals were wounded before the shooter took his life. The entire campus was placed on lockdown during the shooting event (CNN, 2008; Miron, Orcutt, & Kumpala, 2014). The Jokela high school shooting in Finland occurred on November 7, 2007 and involved a current student who shot and killed six students as well as the school nurse and principal. During the incident, students and staff were barricaded in classrooms for several hours while the gunman roamed the school building and attempted to set the school on fire; he later took his own life. The incident marked the first mass shooting in Finland (CNN, 2007; Nurmi, 2012). The Kauhajoki shooting took place on September 23, 2008 at Seinäjoki University and involved a current student who entered a classroom building and shot his classmates, killing nine students and a faculty member and wounding two other individuals. During the shooting incident, he also set multiple fires on campus and was at large for several hours after the campus was evacuated before taking his own life (Associated Press, 2009; Nurmi, 2012).

Prevalence of Adjustment Problems in Mass Shooting-Affected Communities

Historically, research on adjustment following mass shooting incidents had focused on those individuals directly exposed (e.g., Norris, 2007). In contrast, more recent research has documented the existence of adjustment difficulties among individuals throughout the affected community. Much of this work has evaluated immediate and distal PTSD symptoms and probable PTSD diagnoses among affected individuals. This research has supported that a sizable percentage of individuals in shooting-affected communities experience PTSD symptoms in the near term. For example, Suomalainen, Haravuori, Berg, Kiviruusu, and Marttunen (2011) conducted a study of 231 students attending Jokela High School at the time of the shooting, finding that 53% of female students and 28% of male students reported PTSD symptoms 4 months after the shooting. In addition, 27% of female students and 7% of male students endorsed sufficient symptoms to support a probable PTSD diagnosis. Similarly, in a representative sample of 4,639 VT students who were assessed 3 months postshooting, 23.2% of women and 9.9% of men met criteria for probable PTSD (Hughes et al., 2011). Orcutt and colleagues were conducting a longitudinal study of sexual victimization among women at NIU at the time of the campus shooting and followed these women over the course of 3 years postshooting primarily via online surveys, with the first survey administered within 3 weeks of the shooting incident (Orcutt, Bonanno, Hannan, & Miron, 2014). Of the 812 eligible women, 691 completed the initial near-term postshooting survey with 42% reporting symptoms consistent with a probable diagnosis of PTSD (Miron et al., 2014). Similarly, in a sample of 36 individuals indirectly exposed to a mass shooting in a high-rise office building in San Francisco (e.g., in the building at the time of the shooting, saw SWAT team responding to the shooting), 33% met the *Diagnostic and Statistical Manual of Mental Disorders* (DSM-IV) criteria for acute stress disorder 8 days postshooting (Classen, Koopman, Hales, & Spiegel, 1998).

Research regarding the extent to which PTSD symptoms persist in the longer term postshooting is mixed. In their study of NIU women, Miron and colleagues (2014) found that 11.9% of women reported symptoms consistent with a diagnosis of probable PTSD at 8 months postshooting (as compared to the 42% who reported symptoms in the first several weeks postshooting). Additionally, when they examined PTSD symptom trajectories 3 years postshooting, they found that 8.2% of individuals exhibited a symptom pattern of persistent moderate PTSD symptoms and 1.8% displayed a symptom pattern of persistent severe PTSD symptoms (Orcutt et al., 2014). Like Orcutt and colleagues, Littleton and colleagues were conducting a study of the impact of sexual victimization on college women's adjustment at the time of the VT campus shooting, and followed these women via online surveys at 2 months, 6 months, and 1 year postshooting, with a total of 363 of the original 843 women completing at least one of the postshooting surveys (Littleton, Axsom, & Grills-Taquechel, 2011; Orcutt & Littleton, 2010). In their study, persistent elevations in PTSD symptoms were more common, with 28% of women experiencing probable shooting-related PTSD at 2 months postshooting, 23% at 6 months, and 27% at 1 year postshooting (Littleton, Axsom, & Grills-Taquechel, 2011).

In contrast to the findings supporting that PTSD symptoms are elevated in the near term postshooting and remain elevated for a percentage of individuals in the long term, extant research supports that general anxiety and depression symptoms are unlikely to increase for most in the near term. For example, in the previously mentioned sample of 368 VT women, Littleton, Axsom, and Grills-Taquechel (2011) identified that 19% of the sample met the criteria for probable depression 2 months postshooting. The prevalence of depression rose at 6 months to 22% and rose again at 1 year postshooting, with 24% endorsing probable depression. However, the overall prevalence of depression across assessments was similar to the level of preshooting depression. There also were few overall changes in general anxiety symptoms at 2 months and 6 months postshooting (Grills-Taquechel, Littleton, & Axsom, 2011). However, it should be noted that a more recent analysis of symptom trajectories over time in this sample found that while the majority of participants did not experience increased symptoms postshooting, 23% experienced a sharp increase in anxiety at 2 months postshooting, with this group continuing to display elevated anxiety at 1 year postshooting. With regards to depression trajectories, 13% experienced a sharp increase in depression after the shooting, although their overall depression symptoms decreased by 1 year postshooting. In addition, another 10% showed delayed stress reactions, initially reporting modest depression postshooting which then increased at 6 months postshooting and continued to increase at 1 year postshooting (Mancini, Littleton, & Grills, 2016).

Thus, overall research on postshooting adjustment among members of affected communities supports that PTSD symptoms are a common response in the near term and a portion of affected individuals will experience significant PTSD symptoms in the longer term, although how frequently such symptoms persist may vary. In contrast, most individuals do not experience significant increases in depression and general anxiety, although some individuals do appear to develop increased symptoms, with a minority of these individuals developing persistent distress or experiencing delayed stress reactions.

Predictors of Adjustment Problems Among Individuals Affected by a Mass Shooting

Given that a number of individuals within communities affected by mass shootings will experience short-term and persistent adjustment difficulties, it is imperative to understand the factors that are associated with adjustment problems among these individuals. Research investigating such predictors has elucidated the potential role of preshooting vulnerability factors, shooting-related exposure and loss, shooting-related appraisals of threat, as well as a number of postshooting factors in predicting adjustment both in the immediate aftermath of the shooting as well as longer term. Additionally, several studies have included both prospective and longitudinal designs, as well as been informed by theoretical models developed for understanding adjustment following highly stressful and traumatic events.

Several studies have supported the role of pretrauma vulnerability factors in influencing adjustment following mass shootings. For example in Littleton and colleagues' research following the VT campus shooting, both preshooting psychological distress (i.e., depression and anxiety symptoms) and preshooting social support were related to worse adjustment postshooting both in the near and longer term. Further, preshooting distress and social support were related to both postshooting general distress and shooting-related PTSD symptoms. However, it should be noted that, in general, the size of these relationships was in the small to medium-sized range (Grills-Taquechel et al., 2011; Littleton, Axsom, & Grills-Taquechel, 2009; Littleton, Grills-Taquechel, & Axsom, 2009). Finally, while having a history of sexual trauma prior to the shooting was unrelated to adjustment both prior to the shooting and in the near term, women with sexual trauma histories reported significantly higher levels of both depression symptoms and shooting-related PTSD symptoms at 1 year post-shooting (Littleton, Grills-Taquechel, Axsom, Bye, & Buck, 2012). Similarly, in Orcutt and colleagues' longitudinal study of women affected by the NIU campus shooting, preshooting general distress, PTSD symptomology, and severity of prior trauma exposure all predicted immediate postshooting PTSD. In contrast, only severity of preshooting trauma exposure predicted persistence of PTSD at 8 months postshooting (Miron et al., 2014).

Several studies have also investigated the impact of level of shooting exposure on adjustment. In general, results have found that exposure is related to adjustment among those with the highest levels of direct exposure. For example, in a linear growth mixture model study of women's PTSD symptoms over the course of 3 years following the NIU shooting, Orcutt and colleagues (2014) found that those who evidenced a pattern of resiliency were less likely to report severe direct exposure to the shooting, such as seeing the gunman fire on someone, than individuals who demonstrated either a pattern of shooting-related distress followed by recovery or chronic shooting-related PTSD symptomology. Additionally, shooting-related exposure was related to risk for persistent PTSD at 8 months postshooting (Miron et al., 2014). Similarly, Suomalainen and colleagues (2011) in their study of students attending Jokela High School at the time of the shooting found that students who reported the highest level of exposure to the shooting (e.g., students who reported their life was in danger, saw the gunman fire on someone) were more likely to report clinically elevated PTSD symptoms. Additionally, Hughes and colleagues (2011) found in their representative sample of over 4,000 VT students that direct exposure to the shooting (e.g., seeing fleeing students) was associated with an odds ratio of between 1.4 and 1.7 of reporting elevated shooting-related PTSD symptoms. In contrast, Littleton and colleagues found that exposure was generally only weakly related to postshooting adjustment, although it should be noted that their sample of VT women did not include individuals with more severe direct exposure to the shooting (Grills-Taquechel et al., 2011; Littleton, Axsom, & Grills-Taquechel, 2009).

Additionally, loss of a loved one in the shooting (e.g., friend, significant other) has been found to be related to postshooting adjustment in some investigations, but not others. Hughes and colleagues (2011) found that loss of someone close in the shooting was associated with an odds ratio of 3.6 for experiencing elevated PTSD symptoms, and loss of a friend or acquaintance was associated with an odds ratio of 1.9 for risk for PTSD among VT students. In contrast, Littleton, Axsom, and Grills-Taquechel (2009) found that reported loss of a friend in the VT shooting was unrelated to any postshooting adjustment variable. Hughes and colleagues (2011) noted that in their sample, a very high percentage of individuals reported that they were close to a victim as compared to the percentage of the student body killed (9.1% of participants reported being close to someone killed whereas only 0.4% of the students were killed). Littleton, Axsom, and Grills-Taquechel (2011) similarly found that nearly 30% of participants reported that they lost a friend in the VT shooting incident. Hughes and colleagues (2011) speculated that the shared experience of the campus shooting served to increase perceived closeness to the victims. However, it also seems plausible that the experience of heightened distress following the shooting could have served to increase students' perceptions of personal loss due to the shooting and thus increased perceived closeness to the victims.

In contrast to the somewhat mixed findings for more objective measures of shooting-related exposure and loss, subjective appraisal of threat or danger to oneself or loved ones has been associated with adjustment difficulties post-shooting. For example, Hughes and colleagues (2011) found that a reported inability to get in touch with friends during the VT shooting incident was associated with a 2.5 increased odds of experiencing elevated PTSD symptoms 4 months postshooting. Similarly, in a linear growth mixture modeling analysis of women's anxiety symptoms in the year following the VT shooting, Mancini and colleagues (2016) found that women who demonstrated a pattern of persistent distress (i.e., continued elevated anxiety symptoms over 1 year) following the shooting were more likely than women demonstrating a resilient trajectory to report that they believed their own life and/or that of their friends and loved ones were in danger during the shooting. Finally, Miron and colleagues (2014) found that women's reports of dissociative symptoms during the NIU shooting predicted both immediate postshooting PTSD symptoms and persistence of PTSD symptom at 8 months postshooting.

Several studies have also examined the relationship of postshooting factors to adjustment postshooting, often drawing on extant theoretical models of adjustment following stressful or traumatic experiences. One such theoretical model that has been applied to explain postshooting adjustment is the conservation of resources (COR) model (Hobfoll & Lilly, 1993). Briefly, this theory posits that highly stressful events are likely to have an impact on functioning to the extent to which such events are associated with loss of valued resources, which is defined as "objects, personal characteristics, conditions, or energies that are valued in their own right, or that are valued because they act as conduits to the achievement or protection of valued resources" (Hobfoll, 2001, p. 339). Loss of resources is posited to be particularly detrimental to adjustment both because individuals must invest further resources to regain what is lost and because initial loss increases vulnerability to further loss (Hobfoll & Lilly, 1993). Although a mass shooting may not result in tangible losses for most indirectly exposed individuals, individuals may still be vulnerable to loss of intrapersonal (e.g., sense of life direction, optimism) and interpersonal (e.g., intimacy with loved ones) resources. Supporting this model's assertions, Littleton and colleagues found that women who reported loss of intra- and interpersonal resources in the immediate aftermath of the VT shooting experienced more PTSD symptoms and general distress 6 months postshooting (Littleton, Axsom, & Grills-Taquechel, 2009; Littleton, Grills-Taquechel, Axsom, 2009). Further, lower social support and greater psychological distress preshooting predicted postshooting resource loss, suggesting that such individuals may be more vulnerable to resource loss. Finally, participants' initial resource loss postshooting significantly predicted their reports of further resource loss 6 months postshooting, supporting the supposition that initial loss increases risk for future resource loss. Similarly, among women exposed to the NIU shooting, Littleton, Kumpula, and Orcutt (2011) found that initial postshooting resource loss predicted PTSD symptoms at 8 months postshooting after controlling for demographics, preshooting trauma history, shooting exposure, and initial postshooting distress and PTSD symptoms.

Another posttrauma variable that has been examined is individuals' coping behaviors. Littleton, Axsom, and Grills-Taquechel (2011) examined the relationship between both general distress and PTSD in association with women's shooting-related coping strategies following the VT shooting. Specifically, using structural cross-lagged regression, they examined the relationship between postshooting adjustment and use of shooting-related avoidance coping over 1 year. In this study, they drew on Snyder and Pulvers' (2001) model of coping with stressful events which posits that individuals rely on avoidant coping strategies, such as engaging in emotional and behavioral avoidance and withdrawing from others, when they appraise a stressful event as exceeding their coping resources. Reliance on these strategies is then posited to lead to a number of negative outcomes over time including persistent distress, rumination about the stressor and one's inability to manage it, and eventual demoralization (Snyder & Pulvers, 2001). The results supported that both shooting-related PTSD and general distress (i.e., depression and anxiety symptoms) predicted avoidance coping. Shooting-related coping in turn predicted general distress at 1 year postshooting, but not 1 year postshooting PTSD symptoms. They posited that avoidance coping may be particularly predictive of the demoralization and depression that occurs over time in individuals experiencing PTSD, rather than directly fueling PTSD symptomology. In contrast, the reexperiencing and arousal symptoms of PTSD may lead to continued appraisals that one is unable to manage one's trauma-related distress and thus result in continued reliance on avoidance coping (Littleton, Axsom, & Grills-Taquechel, 2011).

In a similar vein, Orcutt and colleagues examined the role of difficulties with engaging in strategies to manage negative emotions more generally as a predictor of adjustment following the NIU shooting (Bardeen, Kumpala, & Orcutt, 2013). Using a cross-lagged panel design, they found that pre-shooting PTSD symptomology predicted immediate postshooting emotion regulation difficulties. Further, immediate postshooting emotion regulation difficulties predicted PTSD symptoms 8 months postshooting, although immediate postshooting PTSD symptoms did not predict emotion regulation difficulties at 8 months. For general distress, a similar pattern emerged with the exception that preshooting emotion regulation difficulties did not predict immediate postshooting general distress (Bardeen et al., 2013). In interpreting these findings, they argued that pretrauma emotion regulation difficulties may have led to more threatening appraisals of the shooting, as well as more negative appraisals of one's coping resources, which led to a reliance on avoidance coping strategies to manage the shooting (Bardeen et al., 2013). The fact that emotion regulation difficulties predicted general distress in the longer term is also consistent with the notion that reliance on ineffective avoidance coping leads to demoralization and depression over time.

Two longitudinal investigations following the VT shooting also supported the importance of disruptions in worldview after the shooting as a predictor of adjustment difficulties. These studies drew from the shattered assumptions framework of Janoff-Bulman (1989) who theorized that traumatic events threaten individuals' basic beliefs about themselves and the world (e.g., the extent to which people and the world are seen as benevolent and good, the extent to which the self has value). Further, she and others argue that being able to successfully reconcile this threat is necessary for positive posttrauma adjustment (Janoff-Bulman, 1989; Resick & Schnicke, 1992). Supporting this framework, Smith, Abeyta, Hughes, and Jones (2015) found that students' appraisals that the shooting had a negative impact on their personal worldview predicted severity of grief symptoms at 1 year postshooting among those who had lost a close friend in the shooting. Further, experiencing increased PTSD symptoms at 3 months postshooting predicted disruptions in worldview 1 year postshooting. Smith and colleagues (2015) argued that their findings supported the idea that PTSD symptoms may interfere with adaptive coping and cognitive processing of a traumatic experience via multiple routes, including undermining coping self-efficacy. Indeed, coping self-efficacy at 3 months postshooting also predicted perceived disruptions in worldview at 1 year postshooting (Smith et al., 2015). Additionally, Littleton and colleagues (2012) found that less belief in benevolence at 2 months postshooting mediated the relationship between having a sexual trauma history and experiencing shooting-related PTSD and general distress at 1 year. They posited that it is the challenge to one's worldview and resources presented by multiple traumatic experiences (i.e., experiencing childhood sexual abuse and/or rape as well as the shooting) which enhance vulnerability to worse adjustment outcomes following multiple traumas, as opposed to viewing these adjustment differences as the result of a simple accumulation of symptoms (Littleton et al., 2012). Indeed, women with sexual trauma histories reported similar levels of PTSD and depression symptoms as women without such histories at 2 months postshooting, whereas at 1 year postshooting the PTSD symptoms of sexual trauma victims remained elevated and their depressive symptoms increased, while both types of symptoms decreased for women without sexual trauma histories (Littleton et al., 2012).

Finally, research following the VT, NIU, and the Jokela high school shootings confirm the importance of social support, particularly from family, in predicting postshooting adjustment (Grills-Taquechel et al., 2011; Miron et al., 2014; Suomalainen et al., 2011). Additionally, as mentioned previously, Littleton, Axsom, and Grills-Taquechel (2009) found that preshooting social support was predictive of lower levels of resource loss postshooting, suggesting that one way social support may relate to adjustment is in protecting individuals from such loss. This is consistent with models emphasizing social support's role in promoting subjective wellbeing and adaptive coping, which could then serve to reduce risk for resource loss (Cohen & Wills, 1985; Flannery, 1990; Littleton, 2010). The finding regarding the importance of family support in promoting better adjustment (e.g., Grills-Taquechel et al., 2011: Suomalainen et al., 2011) could in part reflect the developmental level of the individuals exposed (i.e., high school students and primarily freshman college students). Additionally, family support may have been particularly important because students' family members were likely not directly affected by the shootings in the same way as participants' other sources of support, such as their friends, who likely also attended the same school or university (Grills-Taquechel et al., 2011).

Improvements in Adjustment Following a Mass Shooting

Interestingly, a more recent analysis of adjustment trajectories among VT women conducted by Mancini and colleagues (2016) found that, for some individuals, rather than leading to increased adjustment difficulties, a mass shooting incident may instead lead to improvements in individuals' adjustment, likely due in part to the outpouring of social support and increased community solidarity that can accompany such events. Specifically, in their linear growth mixture modeling study of adjustment patterns 1 year post-shooting, they identified a group of approximately 7 to 13% of women who reported *elevated* distress *prior* to the shooting who then experienced improvements in their depression and anxiety symptoms from pre- to postshooting, with a pattern of increasing improvement in symptoms from 2 months to 1 year postshooting. Suggesting that social support and solidarity promote such improvements, those who experienced symptom improvements reported a large and significant increase in social support postshooting when compared to individuals' whose social support did not change or only slightly increased. Similarly, they reported more gains in interpersonal resources at each post-shooting assessment than all other groups. They hypothesized that for some individuals who were experiencing psychological distress prior to the shooting the incident represented an opportunity to utilize resources/experiences available (e.g., that of a shared painful experience, mutual helping behaviors among community members) to reduce their own distress and enhance their wellbeing (Mancini et al., 2016). Thus, this adjustment pattern was distinct from resilience (i.e., individuals who are not distressed prior to a traumatic event and maintain their positive adjustment) and posttraumatic growth (i.e., individuals who experience perceived growth/gains after experiencing increased distress/struggle after a trauma).

Broader Community Changes Following a Mass Shooting

As alluded to in the previous section, mass shootings may also lead to community-level changes in multiple domains. Most of the research examining these processes has focused on changes in social solidarity following shooting events, including the positive and negative consequences of these changes. Some studies have also examined influences on, and the impact of, alterations to the community's identity now that it is linked to a mass shooting event. Finally, a few studies have examined influences on community perceptions of safety following the shooting.

Following a mass shooting event, there frequently is an increase in social solidarity within the affected community. Social solidarity has been defined as "a positive way of relating to others in interaction, or as feelings of togetherness and responsibility for others" and as "a broad conception underlining mutual social support and sense of community" (Nurmi, Räsänen, & Oksanen, 2011, p. 303). The idea that social solidarity increases after a community tragedy is not new; indeed, the origins of this idea can be traced back to Émile Durkheim (1893), who first suggested that following a crime, especially a shocking or particularly violent crime, the collective community comes together to reestablish and reinforce the community norms that have been violated (Räsänen, Hawdon, Näsi, & Oksanen, 2014). Since that early observation, multiple studies have documented this rise in solidarity following community-level traumatic events, such as natural disasters, terrorist attacks, and mass shootings (Kaniasty & Norris, 2004).

This increase in social solidarity among affected communities can be enormously beneficial following a tragedy, such as a mass shooting, as it provides increased social support, tangible resources, and optimism to a community in need. Indeed, researchers investigating the effects of three mass shootings – the two school shootings in Finland as well as a 2007 mall shooting in Nebraska where eight individuals were killed and three were injured – found that stronger perceptions of social solidarity in the community were associated with increased emotional wellbeing and decreased depressive symptoms both immediately after the shooting and 13 and 18 months later (Hawdon, Räsänen, Oksanen, & Ryan, 2012). Researchers in this study also measured and controlled for individuals' perceived levels of general support (e.g., support from friends, family) and were thus able to identify a unique contribution of perceived social solidarity over and above general social support.

Although there are clear and undeniable benefits to the rise in social solidarity after a mass shooting, researchers have also documented a "dark side of solidarity" (Hawdon et al., 2012, p. 5). Specifically, community members may feel pressure to participate in shared mourning and collective expressions of unity, even if they themselves are experiencing different emotional reactions (Nurmi et al., 2011). Individuals who perceive themselves as coping differently than the "norm" may experience feelings of guilt and isolation that they are not feeling what social messages say they "should" be feeling. Similarly, members of the community may differ in how they define and think about the shooting incident. As time passes, differences in readiness to "move on" from the shooting may create tensions among members of the community. Nurmi and colleagues (2011) observed that this was the case in the Jokela community after the mass shooting. Kaniasty and Norris (2004) agree that "People's needs, wishes, and their ways of coping [after a mass trauma] may collide and augment the experience of stress" (p. 206). Additionally, some affected communities may develop a feeling of "us against them," where they view outsiders with distrust and suspicion, and believe that those who are not members of the community will be unable to understand what they are feeling or what they need (Nurmi et al., 2011).

Within the community, tensions may also exist between those who were directly affected (e.g., observed the shooting, lost a loved one) and those who were more indirectly affected (Nurmi et al., 2011). Conflict may arise in cases where lawsuits are brought against an organization following the shooting, such as in the case of the VT shooting (du Lac, 2013). Aside from the obvious division of those involved or not involved in the lawsuit, some community members may feel that legal action is justified while others may view it as inappropriate or capitalizing on tragedy (Kelly, 2014). Similarly, members of the community may experience conflict regarding distribution of resources allocated to aid community recovery. As an example, in the months after the VT shooting, approximately $7 million was donated to the Hokie Spirit Memorial Fund (Hincker, 2007). Disagreements as to the most appropriate means of distributing this money (e.g., directly to victims' families, to university scholarships/endowments, to campus preparedness and emergency alarm system) eventually led to the appointment of Kenneth Feinberg, the Special Master of the federal September 11th Victim Compensation Fund, to manage distribution of the funds (Hincker, 2007). Kaniasty and Norris (2004) observe that inequitable distribution of resources following a disaster or community tragedy is one of the quickest ways for a community to lose its high postdisaster solidarity and subsequently turn to conflict. All of these different frictions and tensions – differing emotional reactions, readiness to move on, definitions of the trauma, levels of exposure to the shooting, beliefs about ongoing litigation, and views about the allocation of resources – have the potential to develop into conflict and division as members of the community attempt to heal from the shooting. Thus, initial solidarity may be short-lived and instead greater divisions may occur among community members over time.

Indeed, it is likely inevitable that the increase in the social solidarity that occurs in a community following a mass shooting will decline. It has been theorized that in general social solidarity peaks immediately after a shooting. It remains elevated for approximately six months postshooting and then gradually returns to preshooting levels (Räsänen et al., 2014). This gradual withdrawal of social support and resources can feel like a betrayal to members of the community who still perceive a need for help, and can counteract some of the positive benefits of receiving the social support in the first place. This surge and subsequent decline of social support and solidarity is delineated in the social support deterioration deterrence (SSDD) model and has been applied to a variety of disasters (Kaniasty & Norris, 2004). However, initial high levels of support and assistance following a tragedy can serve a protective role against the subsequent decline in social support, resulting in the eventual social support disruptions having a less severe impact on wellbeing if it is preceded by high helping and solidarity (Kaniasty & Norris, 2004).

Another way mass shootings can influence communities is through the effect on the community's collective identity. For better or worse, after such a violent and salient tragedy, community names often become synonymous with the shooting. Thus, in many cases, the community's identity becomes indelibly linked with the tragedy that occurred there. In some cases this altered identity can be embraced as part of the increase in social solidarity following a shooting, as in the case of the "Today, we are all Hokies" (i.e., expressing solidarity through identifying with Virginia Tech's mascot, the Hokie bird) phrase that was frequently used following the VT shooting (e.g., Grossman, 2007). In these cases, the altered communal identity can be seen as a source of strength, resilience, and optimism in overcoming a tragedy. In fact, admission applications to Virginia Tech were higher in the year after the shooting than the previous year and have remained high since the shooting (Johnson, 2011), suggesting that Virginia Tech's identity was not harmed by the tragedy, but rather the shooting event was incorporated as something they had overcome as a community. Alternatively, the association with a mass shooting event can become a source of shame and guilt for these communities. In the case of the Jokela school shooting, community members reported feeling stigmatized by their association with Jokela and embarrassed to tell outsiders where they resided (Nurmi et al., 2011). In extensive interviews with community leaders in Jokela, these leaders reported concerns that outsiders would not be able to understand their experiences. In fact, they noted that fewer Jokela youth left the community to attend vocational or high school in the year after the shooting, and indicated this may be evidence of members of the community isolating themselves and withdrawing from outsiders (Nurmi et al., 2011). Whether community identity is altered in a positive or stigmatized manner likely depends on many different factors, including preexisting characteristics (e.g., closeness of the community, size, geographic isolation), characteristics of the shooting, posttrauma factors (e.g., portrayal of the event and community by the media; see Chapter 7), political response, and other external influences (Nurmi, 2012). Demonstrating how these processes can occur, Nurmi (2012) identified that in the case of the two school shootings in Finland, one community (Jokela) was characterized as a victim of the tragedy and received an outpouring of support and solidarity, while the other community (Kauhajoki) was characterized as simply a site where a tragedy took place. Before the shooting, Jokela was described as "a close-knit community, both geographically and socially" (Nurmi, 2012, p. 17), but warm and inclusive of new people. Conversely, Kauhajoki was described as larger, more isolated, with a strong regional identity, and more distrustful of outsiders. The shooter in Jokela was a youth from that town, and his victims were similarly locals; however, in Kauhajoki the shooter was an "outsider" who moved there to attend the university, and many of his victims were also originally from elsewhere (Vuori, Hawdon, Atte, & Räsänen, 2013). The preexisting differences and characteristics of the shooting events, as well as factors such as media portrayal and timing (with Jokela representing the first school shooting in Finland's history), may have contributed to differential effects on community identity following these shootings.

Additionally, for some communities, feelings of collective guilt may arise due to beliefs that the community should have somehow predicted and intervened to avert the shooting. For example, one leader of the Jokela community commented after the shooting, "A lot of times when something like this happens, people want to find out whose fault it is. So maybe it's a kind of ... shared feeling of guilt" (Nurmi et al., 2011, p. 314). School shootings in particular lead to this type of questioning and either direct or indirect attributions of blame, as the shooter is often a member of the community and thus the violence appears to emerge from and occur within the community. Kaniasty and Norris (2004) point out that "To protect their own conceptions of justice and deservingness, people may stigmatize and reject the victims both as individuals and as a collective" (p. 217). In these ways, members of the affected community may experience blame and stigmatization following a mass shooting that could become incorporated into their new postshooting collective identity.

One of the most visible changes to a community following a mass shooting, which may in part emerge from concerns about the community's inability to prevent the shooting, is a change in security protocols, reflecting altered perceptions of safety within the community. After such a tragedy, communities tend to react by implementing new policies and procedures designed to increase safety and prevent future similar crimes. After the VT shooting, for example, the university spent approximately $11.4 million in safety and security updates, such as an increased police force and new alarm systems (Johnson, 2012). These increased security measures are likely reflective of a desire of community members to increase feelings of safety following the violation of safety assumptions inherent in a mass shooting event. Interestingly, one study examined the effects of social solidarity on safety concerns – specifically fear of a future shooting – following the Finland school shootings, and found a significant negative relationship between perceptions of social solidarity and fear of a shooting reoccurrence; that is, perceptions of solidarity were protective against fears of another shooting occurring (Räsänen et al., 2014). However, this relationship was no longer significant at 18 months postshooting, suggesting that this relationship declines over time, likely related to the decrease in social solidarity. Solidarity may be protective against loss of safety perception because individuals who have high trust in their neighbors and their community may be less likely to believe that another terrible crime can occur there, or to believe that a member of their community could perpetrate such an act. Alternatively, if individuals have strong feelings of trust and unity in their community, they may not believe that the shooter's mentality was the fault of the community, and thus may not feel that their community is at risk of reoccurrence. This high solidarity may also serve as a reminder of all of the positive aspects of their community, helping them to preserve their preshooting view.

Another study of individuals following the shootings in Finland found that the reverse appears to be true as well; just as strong solidarity predicts low fear of a shooting reoccurrence, community fear of another school shooting weakened perceived solidarity in the community (Hawdon, Räsänen, Oksanen, & Vuori, 2014). However, this effect was only found in Jokela, and not in Kauhajoki. Researchers hypothesized this might be because the citizens of Jokela identified more strongly with the shooting incident since the shooter was a member of their own community, and thus there was more fear that another shooting would indicate that something must be seriously wrong with the community. However, after the second shooting in Kauhajoki, school shootings were considered a national problem in Finland, and so there was less focus on Kauhajoki as giving rise to the shooter's behaviors (Hawdon et al., 2014). Thus, it is clear that a shooting event can have a significant impact on the affected community in multiple areas of functioning, with a mix of potential positive and negative outcomes.

Conclusions

To conclude, a growing body of literature supports that a sizable percentage of individuals in mass shooting affected communities will experience distress including PTSD symptoms in the immediate aftermath. For a portion of these individuals, these adjustment problems will persist and can be accompanied by other forms of distress, such as depressive symptomology. Not surprisingly, persistent adjustment problems are predicted by the interaction of preshooting vulnerability factors, shooting-related exposure, appraisals of the shooting event, and postshooting experiences. In addition to affecting individual adjustment, the occurrence of a shooting event can lead to community-level changes including increased social solidarity, changes in community identity, and changes in perceptions of safety within the community. Finally, for at least some individuals the positive community changes that occur in the immediate aftermath of a mass shooting can represent an opportunity for improvement in adjustment.

Given the unfortunate reality that mass shooting events are likely to continue to occur in our society, there is a need to utilize this information to more comprehensively intervene in affected communities. This includes intervention at the individual level with those at risk for, or experiencing, persistent distress (see Chapter 15), as well as at the community level to promote adaptive solidarity and positive community identity (see Chapter 16). Work in these areas is necessary to improve individual and community resilience and recovery following such tragedies.

References

Associated Press. (2007, April 28). Va. Tech wounded may heal slowly. Retrieved from www.nytimes.com/aponline/AP-Virginia-Tech-The-Wounded.html

Associated Press. (2009, September 24). Gunman kills 10 in attack at a school in Finland. Retrieved from www.nytimes.com/2008/09/24/world/europe/24finland.html

Bardeen, J. R., Kumpula, M. J., & Orcutt, H. K. (2013). Emotion regulation difficulties as a prospective predictor of posttraumatic stress symptoms following a mass shooting. *Journal of Anxiety Disorders, 27,* 188–196. doi:10.1016/j.janxdis.2013.01.003

Classen, C., Koopman, C., Hales, R., & Spiegel, D. (1998). Acute stress disorder as a predictor of posttraumatic stress symptoms. *The American Journal of Psychiatry, 155,* 620–624. doi:10.1176/ajp.155.5.620

Cohen, S., & Wills, T. A. (1985). Stress, social support, and the buffering hypothesis. *Psychological Bulletin, 98,* 310–357. doi:10.1037/0033-2909.98.2.310

CNN. (2007, November 8). Finland in mourning after fatal school shooting. Retrieved from www.cnn.com/2007/WORLD/europe/11/08/school.shooting/index.html

CNN. (2008, February 14). 6 shot dead, including gunman, at Northern Illinois University. Retrieved from www.cnn.com/2008/US/02/14/university.shooting/

du Lac, J. F. (2013, October 31). Va. Supreme Court overturns verdict in wrongful death suit against Virginia Tech. *The Washington Post.* Retrieved from www.washingtonpost.com/local/va-supreme-court-overturns-verdict-in-wrongful-death-suit-against-virginia-tech/2013/10/31/047864ac-423c-11e3-a751-f032898f2dbc_story.html

Durkheim, É. (1893). *The division of labor in society.* New York, NY: The Free Press.

Flannery, R. B., Jr. (1990). Social support and psychological trauma: A methodological review. *Journal of Traumatic Stress, 3,* 593–611. doi:10.1002/jts.2490030409

Grills-Taquechel, A. E., Littleton, H. L., & Axsom, D. (2011). Social support, world assumptions, and exposure as predictors of anxiety and quality of life following a mass trauma. *Journal of Anxiety Disorders, 25,* 498–506. doi:10.1016/j.janxdis.2010.12.003

Grossman, C. L. (2007, April 17). 'Today, we are all Hokies' on Facebook. *USA Today.* Retrieved from usatoday30.usatoday.com/tech/webguide/internetlife/2007-04-17-facebook_N.htm

Hawdon, J., Räsänen, P., Oksanen, A., & Ryan, J. (2012). Social solidarity and wellbeing after critical incidents: Three cases of mass shootings. *Journal of Critical Incident Analysis, 3,* 2–25.

Hawdon, J., Räsänen, P., Oksanen, A., & Vuori, M. (2014). Social responses to collective crime: Assessing the relationship between crime-related fears and collective sentiments. *European Journal of Criminology, 11,* 39–56. doi:10.1177/1477370813485516

Hincker, L. (2007, July 6). Administrator of 9/11 victim compensation fund to administer Hokie Spirit Memorial Fund distributions. *Virginia Tech News.* Retrieved from http://www.vtnews.vt.edu/articles/2007/07/2007-385.html

Hobfoll, S. E. (2001). The influence of culture, community, and the nested-self in the stress process: Advancing conservation of resources theory. *Applied Psychology: An International Review, 50,* 337–421. doi:10.1111/1464-0597.00062

Hobfoll, S. E., & Lilly, R. S. (1993). Resource conservation as a strategy for community psychology. *Journal of Community Psychology, 21,* 128–148.

Hughes, M., Brymer, M., Chiu, W. T., Fairbank, J. A., Jones, R. T., Pynoos, R. S., ... Kessler, R. C. (2011). Posttraumatic stress among students after the shooting at Virginia Tech. *Psychological Trauma: Theory, Research, Practice, and Policy, 3,* 403–411. doi:10.1037/a0024565

Janoff-Bulman, R. (1989). Assumptive worlds and the stress of traumatic events: Applications of the schema construct. *Social Cognition, 7,* 113–136. doi:10.1521/soco.1989.7.2.113

Johnson, J. (2011, December 13). Tragedy, scandal don't have to define a school, experts say. *The Washington Post.* Retrieved from www.washingtonpost.com/local/education/tragedy-scandal-dont-have-to-define-a-school-experts-say/2011/12/09/gIQAiRJ6rO_story.html

Johnson, J. (2012, April 13). Report: Virginia Tech massacre cost $48.2 million. *The Washington Post.* Retrieved from http://www.washingtonpost.com/blogs/campus-overload/post/report-virginia-tech-massacre-cost-482-million/2012/04/13/gIQAdDmxET_blog.html

Kaniasty, K., & Norris, F. H. (2004). Social support in the aftermath of disasters, catastrophes, and acts of terrorism: Altruistic, overwhelmed, uncertain, antagonistic, and patriotic communities. In R. J. Ursano, A. E. Norwood, & C. S. Fullerton (Eds.), *Bioterrorism: Psychological and public health interventions* (pp. 200–222). Cambridge, UK: Cambridge University Press.

Kelly, C. (2014, February 4). Mass shooting lawsuits can serve purpose. *The Hartford Courant.* Retrieved from http://articles.courant.com/2014-02-04/news/hc-op-fresh-talk-kelly-mass-shooting-lawsuits-usef-20140204_1_columbine-lawsuits-erin-peterson-julia-pryde

Littleton, H. L. (2010). The impact of social support and negative disclosure reactions on sexual assault victims: A cross-sectional and longitudinal evaluation. *Journal of Trauma & Dissociation, 11,* 210–227. doi:10.1080/15299730903502946

Littleton, H., Axsom, D., & Grills-Taquechel, A. E. (2009). Adjustment following the mass shooting at Virginia Tech: The roles of resource loss and gain. *Psychological Trauma: Theory, Research, Practice, and Policy, 1,* 206–219. doi:10.1037/a0017468

Littleton, H., Axsom, D., & Grills-Taquechel, A. E. (2011). Longitudinal evaluation of the relationship between maladaptive trauma coping and distress: Examination following the mass shooting at Virginia Tech. *Anxiety, Stress, and Coping, 24,* 273–290. doi:10.1080/10615806.2010.500722

Littleton, H. L., Grills-Taquechel, A. E., & Axsom, D. (2009). Resource loss as a predictor of posttrauma symptoms among college women following the mass shooting at Virginia Tech. *Violence and Victims, 24,* 669–686. doi:10.1891/0886–6708.24.5.669

Littleton, H. L., Grills-Taquechel, A. E., Axsom, D., Bye, K., & Buck, K. S. (2012). Prior sexual trauma and adjustment following the Virginia Tech campus shootings: Examination of the mediating role of schemas and social support. *Psychological Trauma: Theory, Research, Practice, and Policy, 4,* 578–586. doi:10.1037/a0025270

Littleton, H., Kumpula, M., & Orcutt, H. (2011). Posttraumatic symptoms following a campus shooting: The role of psychosocial resource loss. *Violence and Victims, 26,* 461–476. doi:10.1891/0886–6708.26.4.461

Mancini, A., Littleton, H. L., & Grills, A. E. (2016). Can people benefit from acute stress? Social support, psychological improvement, and resilience following the Virginia Tech campus shootings. *Clinical Psychological Science, 4,* 401–417. doi:10.1177/2167702615601001

Miron, L. R., Orcutt, H. K., & Kumpala, M. J. (2014). Differential predictors of transient stress versus posttraumatic stress disorder: Evaluating risk following targeted mass violence. *Behavior Therapy, 45,* 791–805. doi:10.1016/j.beth.2014.07.005

Norris, F. H. (2007). Impact of mass shootings on survivors, families, and communities. *PTSD Research Quarterly, 18,* 1–7.

North, C. S., & Pfefferbaum, B. (2002). Research on the mental health effects of terrorism. *JAMA, 288,* 633–636. doi:10.1001/jama.288.5.633

Nurmi, J. (2012). Making sense of school shootings: Comparing local narratives of solidarity and conflict in Finland. *Traumatology, 18,* 16–28. doi:10.1177/1534765611426787

Nurmi, J., Räsänen, P., & Oksanen, A. (2011). The norm of solidarity: Experiencing negative aspects of community life after a school shooting tragedy. *Journal of Social Work, 12,* 300–319. doi:10.1177/1468017310386426

Orcutt, H. K., Bonanno, G. A., Hannan, S. M., & Miron, L. R. (2014). Prospective trajectories of posttraumatic stress in college women following a campus mass shooting. *Journal of Traumatic Stress, 27,* 249–256. doi:10.1002/jts.21914

Orcutt, H., & Littleton, H. (2010). Implementing and managing a quick-response research project: Advice from researchers responding to the tragedies at Virginia Tech and Northern Illinois University. *Traumatic Stress Points, 24,* 5–6.

Räsänen, P., Hawdon, J., Näsi, M., & Oksanen, A. (2014). Social solidarity and the fear of risk: Examining worries about the recurrence of a mass tragedy in a small community. *Sociological Spectrum, 34,* 338–353. doi:10.1080/02732173.2014.917248

Resick, P. A., & Schnicke, M. K. (1992). Cognitive processing therapy for sexual assault victims. *Journal of Consulting and Clinical Psychology, 60,* 748–756. doi:10.1037/0022–006X.60.5.748

Smith, A. J., Abeyta, A. A., Hughes, M., & Jones, R. T. (2015). Persistent grief in the aftermath of mass violence: The predictive roles of posttraumatic stress symptoms, self-efficacy, and disrupted worldview. *Psychological Trauma: Theory, Research, Practice, and Policy, 7,* 179–186. doi:10.1037/tra0000002

Snyder, C. R., & Pulvers, K. M. (2001). Dr. Seuss, the coping machine, and "Oh, the Places You'll Go." In C. R. Snyder (Ed.), *Coping with stress: Effective people and processes* (pp. 3–29). Oxford, UK: Oxford University Press.

Suomalainen, L., Haravuori, H., Berg, N., Kiviruusu, O., & Marttunen, M. (2011). A controlled follow-up study of adolescents exposed to a school shooting: Psychological consequences after four months. *European Psychiatry, 26,* 490–497. doi:10.1016/j.eurpsy.2010.07.007

Vuori, M., Hawdon, J., Atte, O., & Räsänen, P. (2013). Collective crime as a source of social solidarity: A tentative test of a functional model for responses to mass violence. *Western Criminology Review, 14,* 1–15.

13

Postdisaster Psychopathology Among Rescue Workers Responding to Multiple-Shooting Incidents

Geoff J. May and Carol S. North

Despite some evidence to suggest that the prevalence of multiple shootings in the United States may be increasing (Ali & North, 2016), little is yet known about the psychological health of rescue workers after such disasters. Rescue workers called to respond to these events may include police, security guards, emergency medical service (EMS) workers, and firefighters. Police may be especially prone to trauma exposure in response to mass shooting scenarios because they may be endangered by gunfire aimed at them by the shooter(s).

Only one study has focused on professional responders to mass shooting incidents. This study used the Impact of Event Scale to collect self-report posttraumatic symptom data in 140 police, fire, medical, and mental health responders to a mass shooting at an elementary school (Sloan, Rozensky, Kaplan, & Saunders, 1994). The responder groups did not differ from one another in numbers of reported symptoms. A greater number of hours worked was significantly associated with higher intrusion and avoidance scores immediately after the disaster, and these relationships persisted 6 months later. Time pressure to perform duties was associated with avoidance but not intrusion scores at baseline, but these relationships were no longer present at 6 months. No other predictors of posttraumatic stress symptoms at baseline or follow-up were found.

No known published studies specifically focused on rescue workers responding to mass shootings have provided data based on full diagnostic assessments of psychiatric disorders. Although not exclusively focused on rescue workers, North and colleagues did include first responders in some of their research following four shooting incidents and collected full diagnostic data from their participants (See North & King, 2009). Survivors who were not rescue workers,

The Wiley Handbook of the Psychology of Mass Shootings, First Edition. Edited by Laura C. Wilson.
© 2017 John Wiley & Sons, Inc. Published 2017 by John Wiley & Sons, Inc.

will be referred to as "civilians" in this chapter. Soon after these incidents, 19% of the survivors in the combined sample obtained from the four studies, which included first responders and civilians, were diagnosed with posttraumatic stress disorder (PTSD) related to the shooting, and 32% had a postdisaster psychiatric disorder. At 3 years the proportion with current shooting-related PTSD had dropped to 12%, and only 23% had any current psychiatric disorder. Although rescue workers were included in two of these four studies, their data were not presented separately from the civilians of the disasters, who represented the majority of the samples (North, McCutcheon, Spitznagel, & Smith, 2002; North, Smith, & Spitznagel, 1994, 1997).

Because no other data from studies focusing on rescue workers responding to shooting incidents are available in the published literature, additional inferences can only be drawn from a review of the literature on rescue workers responding to other types of incidents, rescue workers studied without reference to a specific incident, and comparative studies of different types of rescue workers in a variety of situations. Studies of rescue workers responding to mass casualty incidents have generally investigated other types of disasters such as terrorist attacks, earthquakes, and hurricanes. Although it has been posited that man-made disasters and particularly intentionally caused incidents, such as mass shootings, may lead to worse mental health consequences than natural disasters (Norris et al., 2002), research on disaster survivors by North and colleages found that when the analysis controlled for magnitude of the disaster (i.e., number of fatalities), disaster-related PTSD prevalence was not associated with disaster type (North, Oliver, & Pandya, 2012).

Some studies have compared postdisaster psychopathology among different types of rescue workers. A study of rescue and recovery workers who assisted at the World Trade Center disaster site after the September 11, 2001 (9/11) attacks in New York City used the PTSD Symptom Checklist to approximate diagnostic criteria for PTSD. The prevalence of "probable" PTSD identified by this method was significantly lower in police (8%) compared to firefighters (14%) and EMS personnel (17%; Perrin et al., 2007). Few studies other than those investigating the 9/11 attacks have compared different types of rescue/recovery workers in response to the same disaster because most disasters (e.g., fires, mass shootings, structural collapses) historically have attracted predominantly one type of responder.

An exceptionally large meta-analysis by Norris et al. (2002) concluded that disaster rescue and recovery workers demonstrated greater "remarkable resilience" compared to other disaster survivors (p. 207). A diagnostic study using a fully structured diagnostic interview (i.e., Diagnostic Interview Schedule) that examined male firefighters who served as rescue and recovery workers in the Oklahoma City bombing found disaster-related PTSD in 13%. The incidence of PTSD in the firefighters and the level of functional impairment was significantly lower than in directly exposed male bombing survivors

(23%; North, Tivis, McMillen, Pfefferbaum, Cox, et al., 2002). The fire-fighters had a higher postdisaster prevalence of alcohol use disorder (24%) compared to civilians, but almost all of this difference could be attributed to preexisting disorders (47%); that is to say, there was almost no inci-dent alcohol use disorder following the disaster (North, Tivis, McMillen, Pfefferbaum, Cox, et al., 2002). The firefighter responders who screened positive for alcohol use disorder had lower levels of functioning compared to their colleagues (North, Tivis, McMillen, Pfefferbaum, Spitznagel, et al., 2002). Vanishingly few studies of rescue workers in any type of disaster have used a full diagnostic assessment interview of postdisaster psychiatric disor-ders. The importance of using diagnostic instruments rather than symptom scales is demonstrated in one multiple-shooting study using a structured diagnostic interview that found an abundance of posttraumatic stress symp-toms but very few individuals with PTSD (Johnson, North, & Smith, 2002).

Studies of rescue workers not selected based on their response to a disaster have examined prevalence rates of psychopathology. A comprehensive systematic review of 28 studies reporting on 40 samples with a total of 20,424 rescue workers with diverse trauma response histories using many different PTSD measures (Berger et al., 2012) found the current prevalence of PTSD to be 10%. Conversely, PTSD prevalence in those with a history of response to a natural disaster was 17%, which was not significantly different from the rate of those with no disaster response history ($p = .07$). However, ambulance personnel had significantly greater PTSD (15%) compared to major disaster responders who were firefighters (7%) or police (5%; $p = .04$ in both comparisons).

One study examined Canadian police officers selected not for disaster response but for experience of a trauma sustained in the routine course of duty. Using a structured diagnostic interview (i.e., Clinician Administered PTSD Scale), this study found that 7% of trauma-exposed officers had developed PTSD in relation to the event they identified as the most traumatic (Martin, Marchand, & Boyer, 2009). Another study of police officers found that most had been exposed to duty-related trauma; using a symptom measure to assess PTSD, this study found a 6% prevalence within 3 months of duty-related trauma exposure and a total of 7% by 12 months (Carlier, Lamberts, & Gersons, 1997). A prevalence study of German firefighters not selected relative to any particular incident found that 29% scored positive on a symptom screener for current alcohol problems (Boxer & Wild, 1993).

The above literature review demonstrates that very little study has been done to characterize postdisaster psychopathology among rescue workers respond-ing to mass shooting incidents, although information from studies of broader populations is available. Extrapolation of findings from other studies that com-bine rescue workers with civilians, however, cannot explain how rescue workers might differ from civilians in their psychopathology related to exposure to mass shooting incidents. Additionally, inconsistencies in the sampling of disaster workers, the types of disasters examined, assessment of trauma exposures, and measurement of psychopathology have further obfuscated attempts to understand disaster responder mental health. Findings from this broader body of work, however, faintly suggest that rescue workers may experience less PTSD than directly exposed disaster survivors, and that firefighter responders may have alcohol use disorders endemic within the profession that may be largely unrelated to disaster trauma exposures.

This review has demonstrated that little information is available from full diagnostic assessment data in studies of rescue workers specifically after mass shootings, and such studies are needed to understand the prevalence of disaster-related psychopathology in this population. To build on the reviewed literature, this article presents combined data from two studies of rescue workers responding to multiple-shooting incidents and civilians of these incidents using structured diagnostic instruments for assessment of psychiatric disorders in relation to the disasters. The consistent methods in the two studies permitted merging of the data for the analysis presented in this chapter.

Methods

The data for the current analyses were collected following two multiple-shooting incidents as part of two previous studies. The data were originally published without separate presentation of the findings from the rescue workers and civilians in the samples. One of the incidents was a cafeteria shooting in 1991 in Killeen, Texas that left 24 dead and another 20 injured (North et al., 1994). The other incident was a courthouse shooting in 1992 in Clayton, Missouri that resulted in one fatality and five injuries (Johnson et al., 2002). As a general principle in this book, a mass shooting is defined as one in which four or more people are killed, which fits the cafeteria incident in Killeen, but not the courthouse incident in Clayton. However, we feel the data are still relevant for the purposes of this chapter, particularly in light of the overall lack of prior research on this topic.

For the Killeen cafeteria massacre study, a systematic sample of directly exposed survivors was originally recruited from a list of all individuals who were present at the shooting, with an 82% participation rate, including a sample of 16 rescue workers and 107 civilians ($n = 123$). For the Clayton courthouse study, a volunteer sample of directly exposed survivors was recruited, including 8 rescue workers and 71 civilians ($n = 79$). All but two of the 24 total rescue workers in the combined sample from both incidents were male. Because it has been well documented that civilian women (Norris et al., 2002) as well as female police officers (Bowler et al., 2012) are more likely than their male counterparts to be emotionally affected by trauma, and because the rescue workers in this study were almost all men, the sample for this analysis was restricted to men for adequate comparison of rescue workers with civilians. The final sample ($n=88$) for these analyses included a total of 22 male rescue workers and 66 male civilians (14 rescue workers and 46 civilians in Killeen, and 8 rescue workers and 20 civilians in Clayton).

Study participants were interviewed 6 to 8 weeks after the disaster, and follow-up interviews were conducted at approximately 1 year postdisaster, with a 93% follow-up participation rate. No differences in follow-up attrition were found between the rescue workers and the civilians.

All participants were interviewed using the Diagnostic Interview Schedule for DSM-III-R (DIS-III-R; Robins, Helzer, Cottler, & Goldring, 1989) and the Disaster Supplement (Robins & Smith, 1983). These interviews provided data on demographics, exposure to trauma in the disaster, personal perceptions of the disaster, role in the disaster (type of rescue worker, civilian), lifetime pre-disaster and postdisaster psychiatric disorders, and psychosocial interventions and treatment received.

Data are summarized and presented as counts, percentages, means, and standard deviations. Categorical variables were compared using Fisher's exact tests, and continuous variables were compared using Welch t tests.

Results

Table 13.1 lists the demographic characteristics of the combined sample at baseline. The sample consisted largely of nonminorities who were in their late thirties, with 2 years of college education. Almost all were employed, and two thirds were married at the time of the shooting. The only significant demographic difference between the rescue workers and civilians was that the rescue workers were slightly younger. Most (82%, $n=18$) of the rescue workers were police officers, and the remaining few consisted of EMS workers (9%, $n=2$) and security guards (9%, $n=2$). Because the EMS workers and security guards were

Table 13.1 Demographic characteristics of the sample.

	Rescue workers (n = 22)	Civilians (n = 66)	Total sample (n = 88)
Years of age: mean (*SD*)	37.7 (6.2)*	39.9 (13.9)*	38.6 (12.6)
Nonwhite ethnic group: % (n)	5 (1)	18 (12)	15 (13)
Years of education: mean (*SD*)	14.2 (1.4)	14.4 (2.3)	14.4 (2.1)
Currently employed: % (n)	100 (22)	96 (63)	97 (85)
Currently married: % (n)	68 (15)	70 (46)	69 (61)

Note: * Significant difference between groups ($p<0.02$, Welch Two Sample t-test).

Table 13.2 Disaster experience.

	Rescue workers (n = 22) % (n)	Police (n = 18) % (n)	Security/ EMS (n = 4) % (n)	Civilians (n = 66) % (n)
Disaster trauma exposure				
On scene during shooting	36 (8)***	44 (8)**	0 (0)**	89 (59)
Witness to shooting	27 (6)*	33 (6)	0 (0)	56 (37)
Witness to aftermath only	68 (15)***	61 (11)***	100 (4)**	11 (7)
Saw others hurt or killed	91 (20)*	89 (16)	100 (4)	67 (44)
Personally injured	9 (2)	6 (1)	25 (1)	27 (18)
Perceptions of incident				
Felt personally harmed by incident	18 (4)	6 (1)	75 (3)*	26 (17)
Felt overwhelmed by incident	73 (16)	83 (15)	25 (1)*	80 (53)
Perceived risk of dying	14 (3)***	17 (3)**	0 (0)	60 (38)

Note: Compared to civilians, *$p \le .05$, **$p \le .01$, ***$p \le .001$.

few in number and similar to one another but different from the police officers in their disaster experience, predisaster history and postdisaster psychopathology, the EMS workers and security guards were combined to create a separate group consisting of four participants for the subsequent analyses. To illustrate the effects of this small group on the sample, they are presented both separately and in combination with police (i.e., rescue workers).

Table 13.2 presents data on disaster trauma exposure and perceptions of the event by study subgroups. Only about one fourth of the rescue workers directly witnessed the shooting, but two thirds were at the scene during the aftermath and virtually all of them witnessed seriously injured or dead people. Very few rescue workers were injured. In contrast, most of the civilians were present during the shooting, and one fourth of them were injured. These group differences in exposure are thus consistent with findings that most of the civilians but few of the rescue workers believed they might die in the incident. In particular, compared to civilians, a higher proportion of security officers and EMS workers reported that they felt personally harmed, and a lower proportion of security officers and EMS workers reported that they felt overwhelmed by the incident.

Table 13.3 provides predisaster and postdisaster prevalence rates of psychiatric disorders by subgroup, as assessed at the baseline interviews. Because very few postdisaster disorders other than PTSD, major depression, and alcohol and drug use disorders were observed, only these selected diagnoses are presented. The disaster-related prevalence of PTSD was 17% and the postdisaster prevalence of

Table 13.3 Psychiatric disorders at baseline.

	Rescue workers (n =22) % (n)	Police (n =18) % (n)	Security/ EMS (n =4) % (n)	Civilians (n =66) % (n)
PTSD				
Lifetime predisaster prevalence	14 (3)	18 (3)	0 (0)	3 (2)
Disaster-related prevalence	14 (3)	11 (2)	25 (1)	18 (12)
Incidence	14 (3)	11 (2)	25 (1)	18 (12)
Major depression				
Lifetime predisaster prevalence	9 (2)	11 (2)	0 (0)	2 (1)
Postdisaster prevalence	9 (2)	6 (1)	25 (1)	3 (2)
Incidence	9 (2)	6 (1)	25 (1)	2 (1)
Alcohol use disorder				
Lifetime predisaster prevalence	33 (7)	18 (3)*	100 (4)*	44 (29)
Postdisaster prevalence	10 (2)	0 (0)	50 (2)	17 (11)
Incidence	0 (0)	0 (0)	0 (0)	3 (2)
Drug use disorder				
Lifetime predisaster prevalence	10 (2)	6 (1)	25 (1)	13 (8)
Postdisaster prevalence	0 (0)	0 (0)	0 (0)	0 (0)
Incidence	0 (0)	0 (0)	0 (0)	0 (0)

Note: Compared to civilians, *$p \le .05$.

major depression was 5% in the combined sample of rescue workers and survivors. One third (33%) of the combined sample had any postdisaster disorder (27% of rescue workers and 35% of civilians). There were no significant differences between the rescue worker and survivor groups in prevalence of any or all of these disorders either before or after the disaster. Among 18 individuals who developed disaster-related PTSD as measured either at index or follow-up, 8 (56%) were in current remission from PTSD at follow-up.

The postdisaster prevalence of alcohol use disorder for the combined sample was 15%, with no significant difference between rescue workers and civilians. New (incident) alcohol use disorders were rare after the shooting episodes, and none occurred among rescue workers. The predisaster prevalence of alcohol use disorder was 41% in the combined samples. Police officers had significantly lower, and security and EMS workers had significantly higher, lifetime predisaster prevalence of alcohol use disorder compared to civilians. Although 11% of the sample met predisaster drug use disorder criteria, no postdisaster drug use disorder was found.

Table 13.4 Mental health treatment and psychological interventions.

	Rescue workers (n = 22) % (n)	Police (n = 18) % (n)	Security/ EMS (n = 4) % (n)	Civilians (n = 66) % (n)
Formal mental health treatment	18 (4)	22 (4)	0 (0)	36 (24)
Delivered by:				
Mental health professional	5 (1)*	6 (1)	0 (0)	30 (20)
Psychiatrist	0 (0)	0 (0)	0 (0)	5 (3)
Other mental health professional	5 (1)*	6 (1)	0 (0)	26 (17)
Religious pastor/ chaplain	9 (2)	11 (2)	0 (0)	6 (4)
Family doctor	5 (1)	6 (1)	0 (0)	2 (1)
Psychological intervention	82 (18)***	89 (16)***	50 (2)	38 (25)
Debriefing	73 (16)***	78 (14)***	50 (2)	35 (23)
Support group	59 (13)***	67 (12)***	25 (1)	12 (8)

Note: Compared to civilians, *p < .05, ***p < .001.

The rescue workers and civilians received different types of interventions and treatment (see Table 13.4). Fewer than one in five rescue workers received formal mental health treatment, but more than one third of civilians received formal mental health treatment. Most mental health treatment received by civilians was provided by mental health professionals who were not psychiatrists. Most of the rescue workers participated in an informal psychological intervention: nearly three fourths in psychological debriefing and more than half in support groups. Few civilians received these interventions.

Disaster-related PTSD was not associated with any demographic variable, membership in any rescue worker category, perceived risk of dying in the disaster, seeing people hurt or killed, having family or friends who were hurt or killed, or predisaster lifetime psychopathology.

Discussion

This study provided new information about rescue workers responding to multiple-shooting incidents through comparison of 22 rescue workers with 66 civilians who were present during the shootings, in a combined dataset from two separate studies that used similar research methods. The rescue workers resembled the civilians demographically. However, the disaster-related trauma exposures of the rescue workers and civilians differed. Most of the rescue workers witnessed the aftermath and carnage of the dead and the wounded, but few were endangered during the shooting. In contrast, most of the civilians were directly exposed to the violence and many of them were injured. Despite these differences in disaster trauma exposures, both groups had a similar prevalence of disaster-related PTSD and other disorders. Postdisaster major depression was infrequent. New (incident) alcohol use disorders were rare, and no rescue workers developed an alcohol use disorder after the disaster.

A chief strength of this dataset is the collection of the data using a fully structured diagnostic instrument. The study obtained detailed information on disaster-related trauma exposure. The samples were very small, however, and almost all of the rescue workers responding to the shooting incidents were police, yielding insufficient statistical power to compare police and other rescue workers. Also, firefighters were not represented in this sample of rescue workers. Information about temporally remote predisaster periods may have been subject to recall bias. Unfortunately, the naturalistic, observational design of this study did not allow for meaningful investigation into effects of the treatment and other interventions in association with psychosocial outcomes because of potential confounding of severity of psychopathology with seeking treatment and outcomes (i.e., individuals with more severe psychopathology likely received treatment, and individuals with more difficulties would be expected to have more difficulties over time).

The slight but nonsignificant overrepresentation of preexisting PTSD among rescue workers compared to civilians likely reflects the years of exposure to trauma in their professions. Compared to civilians, police officers had a significantly lower prevalence and other rescue workers had a significantly higher prevalence of predisaster alcohol use disorders. It is possible that police may be distinct from other rescue workers with a generally lower predilection for alcohol use disorder, and other rescue workers (EMS and security workers in this sample) may have a relatively higher predilection to alcohol use disorder.

The findings from this study differ from a methodologically similar study of rescue and recovery workers comprised of firefighters responding to the Oklahoma City bombing. The firefighter rescue workers in the Oklahoma City bombing study had significantly less bombing-related PTSD and significantly more lifetime alcohol use disorder (almost all preexisting) compared to bombing survivors. In contrast, the largely police-comprised rescue worker sample in the current study did not have significantly less PTSD or significantly more alcohol use disorder compared to the civilians of the shooting.

Because similar methods were used in these studies, other factors must have contributed to these differences, such as differences between police and firefighter rescue workers, differences between bombing or multiple-shooting incidents, or other variables associated with the specific disasters. If the differences lie with the rescue worker population, it might reflect greater posttraumatic resilience and proclivity toward alcohol use disorders among firefighter rescue workers and lack of posttraumatic resilience without alcohol proclivity among police officer rescue workers, compared to civilians of the same incidents. Although 100% of the EMS and security workers had lifetime alcohol use disorder, the small number ($n = 4$) in this group reduces confidence in this finding. In contrast with the findings of Perrin et al. (2007), which found that police have a lower rate of PTSD when compared to that of firefighters or EMS workers, the current study demonstrates that police have PTSD liability comparable to that of both EMS workers and to previously reported liability in firefighters after the Oklahoma City bombing (North, Tivis, McMillen, Pfefferbaum, Spitznagel, et al., 2002). Other studies comparing and contrasting different rescue worker groups have been so few, have used very different methodological designs, and have yielded inconsistent results. The main conclusion can only be that studies must be conducted with rigorous and consistent methods so that definitive findings can be obtained and meaningful comparisons made.

In multiple-shooting incidents, not only are the individuals who are targeted at risk for PTSD, but also the rescue workers. This especially applies to police who may become engaged in a shootout with the perpetrator(s) and thus also have the experience of being a target, which might confer greater risk for PTSD compared to other responders. In this study, very few rescue workers reported having been involved in the active shooting. In other mass shooting incidents in which responders are endangered by gunfire, however, the incidence of PTSD related to the event might be higher. Although the study of the Oklahoma City firefighters suggested that they were less vulnerable to PTSD than survivors of the direct bomb blast, response to a shooting incident in which they are targeted might place disaster responders at equal or greater risk compared to civilians. The current study could not examine this possibility because of the low numbers of responders who were engaged in the gunfire.

In the current analyses, rescue workers and civilians differed in how their mental health needs were addressed after the shooting incidents. The rescue workers received relatively little formal mental health treatment compared to the civilians. Only 4 of the 22 rescue workers in this study received any formal treatment for mental health problems (only one by a mental health professional), even though more than one fourth received a diagnosis of a postdisaster psychiatric disorder. The treatment disparity between the rescue workers and civilians was not consistent with the similar postdisaster prevalence rates of PTSD, major depression, and alcohol use disorder found in these two groups. However, far more of the rescue workers compared to civilians had participated in informal psychological interventions, especially psychological debriefings.

Other disaster studies have confirmed the low proportions of rescue workers who received psychiatric treatment in the current study. In a sample of utility workers who were deployed to the site of the 9/11 attacks on the World Trade

Center in New York City, of 174 workers who accepted a referral for mental health treatment based on a diagnosis of PTSD, major depressive disorder, panic disorder, generalized anxiety disorder, or significant difficulty in role functioning during a psychological evaluation, 58% did not attend a single treatment session (Jayasinghe et al., 2005). Among rescue workers who responded to a plane crash, 15% obtained psychiatric treatment in the 13 months after the disaster, and another 17% reported needing such care but not getting it (Fullerton, Ursano, & Wang, 2004).

In a study of firefighters who served as rescue and recovery workers in the Oklahoma City bombing and received structured diagnostic assessments, 38% of a sample of male firefighters had a postdisaster psychiatric disorder, but only 16% received psychiatric treatment, representing well under half of the proportion with a postdisaster disorder (North, Tivis, McMillen, Pfefferbaum, Spitznagel, et al., 2002). In contrast, a study of directly exposed male and female survivors of the Oklahoma City bomb blast studied by the same group with similar research methods found that 45% had a postdisaster psychiatric disorder, and 41% received formal mental health treatment. Previously, it has been observed that disaster workers may be less likely than others to receive treatment (Jayasinghe et al., 2005).

Data from the combined samples in the current analyses suggest that treatment utilization overall was not as abundant as the need (with a one-third prevalence of psychiatric disorders yet fewer than one fourth receiving mental health treatment). A focused examination of the rescue workers revealed that very few received psychiatric treatment.

Several studies have reported data on debriefings received by rescue workers. A study of 181 firefighters responding to the Oklahoma City bombing found that 92% participated in "mandatory" workplace debriefings (North, Tivis, McMillen, Pfefferbaum, Cox, et al., 2002). Of 105 police officers who responded to a plane crash, 44% participated in debriefing (Carlier, Lamberts, Van Uchelen, & Gersons, 1998). Of a sample of 243 police officers exposed to various traumas, 35% had received debriefing (Carlier, Voerman, & Gersons, 2000). In a sample of 202 police officers exposed to a suicide on the job, 20% utilized counseling or debriefing by a peer or clergy (Lukaschek, Baumert, & Ladwig, 2011). Taken together, the findings of all of these studies suggest that more rescue workers generally receive debriefing than professional mental health treatment.

Because there is little to no systematic literature on the psychiatric treatment of rescue workers, knowledge about treatment of this population must draw from the treatment literature for general populations, with unknown applicability to rescue workers. A vast literature documents the strength of the evidence accumulated from research on psychotherapy and pharmacotherapy in the treatment of PTSD (Berg et al., 2007), major depressive disorder, (Gelenberg et al., 2010), and alcohol use disorder (Kleber et al., 2007).

Rescue workers, who have been characterized in general as not wanting to talk about their emotions (McGhee, 2014) may prefer medication to psychotherapy; alternatively, those with objections to psychopharmacology can instead choose psychotherapeutic options.

Psychological debriefing has become widespread as a workplace intervention for first responders, EMS workers, and military service members (Nash & Watson, 2012), while it is rarely used in more general populations. Psychological debriefing was not designed to treat or prevent PTSD or other trauma-related psychopathology (Regel, 2007), and has not been demonstrated to be effective as such (Forneris et al., 2013; Kearns, Ressler, Zatzick, & Rothbaum, 2012). Part of the reason for the popularity of psychological debriefings among emergency responders is that this intervention skirts the known problems of stigma against psychiatric treatment that are well known in this population (Dudek, 1999; Loo, 1986; Miller, 2008; Sloan et al., 1994). Participants in debriefings report finding it subjectively helpful (Bisson, Jenkins, Alexander, & Bannister, 1997; Lee, Slade, & Lygo, 1996; Magyar & Theophilos, 2010; Regel, 2007). However, it has been shown to lead to short-term increases in posttraumatic stress symptom severity (Carlier et al., 2000; Kearns et al., 2012). Its use as a sole intervention may deprive individuals with PTSD or other postdisaster psychopathology from needed mental health services that might benefit them. The findings from the current study validate this concern: Almost all of the rescue workers, who had similar prevalence of postdisaster psychopathology compared to civilians, received debriefing, but very few received psychiatric care; in contrast, few civilians received debriefing, but many more received formal mental health treatment.

Additional caveats have been presented in recent years to the use of psychological debriefing. One is that participation in debriefings should not be made mandatory (Rose, Bisson, Churchill, & Wessely, 2002). Individuals with PTSD by definition have considerable avoidance and numbing reactions, which are conceptualized as arising from an inability to cope with prominent intrusion and hyperarousal symptoms (Foa, Riggs, & Gershuny, 1994; Thompson & Waltz, 2010). It follows that individuals with prominent avoidance and numbing responses might have difficulties participating in an intervention focused on an overwhelming trauma that they have recently experienced and may find this intervention in itself to be further traumatizing (Rose et al., 2002). Consistent with this possibility, research has demonstrated that PTSD symptoms may increase in the short term after participation in debriefing (Carlier et al., 2000; Kearns et al., 2012). Other concerns expressed about psychological debriefing are that single sessions may be insufficient or even detrimental, and that follow-up is important for identifying individuals needing additional treatment (Nash & Watson, 2012; Regel, 2007). It is thus advisable to identify individuals with high levels of distress or psychopathology already apparent in the early postdisaster phases and refer them to further assessment and/or treatment rather than including them in debriefing activities (Forneris et al., 2013; Nash & Watson, 2012).

In practice, however, debriefings have routinely been administered regardless of participants' readiness to confront intrusive memories, and without follow-up (Nash & Watson, 2012). The sanctioned substitution of psychological debriefing for formal treatment in the workplace may serve to send a message that only this intervention is needed, further discouraging rescue workers from receiving psychiatric services.

The data presented in this analysis of rescue workers responding to multiple-shooting incidents demonstrated evidence of mental health needs, little utilization of formal psychiatric care, and a reliance on informal psychological interventions. These findings indicate a need to refocus resources to provide treatment for individuals with psychiatric disorders, for whom brief psychological interventions are insufficient and possibly even harmful. A recent systematic review (North & Pfefferbaum, 2013) provided a framework to guide disaster mental health response and direct individuals, including rescue workers, to appropriate interventions. This disaster mental health framework is composed of three main functions: identification of cases, stabilization and triage to appropriate care, and provision of mental health services.

Conceptually, this disaster mental health framework indicates that psychiatric diagnosis is a necessary first step for identification of need for care (preceded by screening if the burden of numbers is prohibitory of full diagnostic assessment of all individuals). Addressing postdisaster distress through psychological interventions can be helpful for most people affected by disasters, especially in the early postdisaster time frame. Individuals diagnosed with trauma-related psychiatric disorders, however, need referral to appropriate treatment. The findings in the current study suggest that following this framework would have resulted in the referral of a higher proportion of rescue workers with psychiatric disorders to treatment services than to psychological debriefings not meant for treating psychiatric illness.

The findings that rescue workers in this study had higher lifetime prevalence and a similar postdisaster prevalence of alcohol use disorder compared to civilians in these time frames suggest the need for assessment for alcohol use disorders and their treatment in this population. This recommendation is not just in the context of disaster because of the finding that alcohol use disorders are specific to this population rather than to disaster; clearly, there is no need to wait for a disaster to intervene. The relatively low prevalence of alcohol use disorder in police compared to other rescue workers in this study and other studies suggests that firefighters, security guards, and EMS workers may especially benefit from this intervention, but further study is needed to verify these results.

There are several known barriers to utilization of disaster mental health services by rescue workers. One is perceived stigma associated with carrying a psychiatric diagnosis and receiving treatment. There is a culture of "machismo" (Egan, 2001), promoting attitudes that rescue workers in general may feel a need to represent themselves as pillars of strength. In this context, mental illness may be viewed as evidence of weakness and inability to cope, implying lack of fitness for duty. A logical extension of these views is that to avoid being branded as being weak of character or incompetent for the rescue worker line of work, mental health professionals must be avoided. There exists a lore that police officers wish to avoid being branded as having psychological problems not only because their peers and superiors will see them as weak, but also because they fear that being labeled with a psychiatric diagnosis could limit promotion opportunities, get them fired, or end their career (McGhee, 2014; Royle, Keenan, & Farrell, 2008).

Potential threats to confidentiality may occur with provision of mental health services at the workplace where others can observe the employee receiving care, and with processing of insurance or billing claims for psychiatric care through the place of employment. Concern about loss of confidentiality understandably provides a strong disincentive for rescue workers to seek mental health treatment and to be open in self-disclosure in treatment (Taube & Elwork, 1990). Studies are needed to accurately document the magnitude of the perception of this risk among rescue workers and the factors that lead to these perceptions. General recommendations to all employers for protection of confidentiality of rescue workers can be made, and subsequent assessment can be carried out to determine if employers have indeed provided adequate protections and to reassess the degree of nonparticipation in mental health services among those in need.

Perception that mental illness is incurable can result in continuing stigma associated with mental illness even after it is successfully treated (Bolton, 2003;Thornicroft, 2006). Ironically, treatment can help rescue workers come to the realization that seeking treatment requires the very strength of character that is valued in their profession. A cultural shift to view mental illness as a normal and treatable response to stress will help to reduce the stigma that currently impedes treatment (Royle et al., 2008).

Yet another barrier to psychiatric care for rescue workers is lack of access to adequate services. The availability of specialists in evidence-based trauma-focused therapy is limited, especially in rural areas. Telemedicine could provide one potential means of overcoming this shortage of specialists, as suggested by a pilot study of prolonged exposure therapy for combat veterans. In this study, PTSD improved significantly with both in-person therapy and telehealth treatment, and the two methods of treatment delivery were equivalent in symptom outcomes (Tuerk, Yoder, Ruggiero, Gros, & Acierno, 2010).

Conclusions

Data on rescue workers responding to multiple-shooting incidents are virtually nonexistent; the current small study of 22 rescue workers is the only such study providing full diagnostic assessment data that exists. The datasets that were used for the analyses in the current study were small and lacking in representation of broad disciplines of rescue workers. The collective research conducted to date on rescue worker mental health has lacked sufficient numbers and systematic methods needed to combine and compare samples to provide firm conclusions and definitively inform policy and practice. This lack of knowledge is even more acute for the specific subpopulation of disaster rescue workers. Only so much can be extrapolated from research on rescue workers in other settings to apply to rescue workers responding to mass shootings. Further studies with method-ological rigor are needed, using instruments that assess full diagnostic criteria for psychiatric disorders. In addition to PTSD, major depressive disorder and alcohol use disorder are prevalent and warrant assessment in research studies. Both predisaster and postdisaster morbidity data should be obtained as well as detailed exposure data that can be classified according to currently existing criteria for PTSD.

Once sufficient data on the mental health sequelae of mass shootings on rescue workers become available from epidemiological, naturalistic, and obser-vational studies, future research will need to develop and test interventions and treatments specific to this population. Although much work remains to be done, the rescue workers who come to the aid of mass shooting survivors deserve the best treatment we have to offer.

References

Ali, O. M., & North, C. S. (2016). Survivors of mass shooting incidents: The response of mental health. In *Encyclopedia of mental health* (2nd ed.). Oxford, UK: Elsevier.

Berg, A., Breslau, N., Goodman, S., Lezak, M., Matchar, D., Mellman, T., ... Geller, A. (2007). *Treatment of PTSD: An assessment of the evidence*: Washington, DC: National Academies Press.

Berger, W., Coutinho, E. S., Figueira, I., Marques-Portella, C., Luz, M. P., Neylan, T. C., ... Mendlowicz, M. V. (2012). Rescuers at risk: A systematic review and meta-regression analysis of the worldwide current prevalence and correlates of PTSD in rescue workers. *Social Psychiatry Psychiatric Epidemiology, 47*(6), 1001–1011. doi:10.1007/s00127-011-0408-2

Bisson, J. I., Jenkins, P. L., Alexander, J., & Bannister, C. (1997). Randomised con-trolled trial of psychological debriefing for victims of acute burn trauma. *The British Journal of Psychiatry, 171*(1), 78–81.

Bolton, J. (2003). Reducing the stigma of mental illness. *Student British Medical Journal, 11*, 104.

Bowler, R. M., Harris, M., Li, J., Gocheva, V., Stellman, S. D., Wilson, K., ... Cone, J. E. (2012). Longitudinal mental health impact among police responders to the 9/11 terrorist attack. *American Journal of Industrial Medicine, 55*(4), 297–312. doi:10.1002/ajim.22000

Boxer, P. A., & Wild, D. (1993). Psychological distress and alcohol use among fire fighters. *Scandinavian Journal of Work, Environment & Health*, 121–125.

Carlier, I. V., Lamberts, R. D., & Gersons. B. P. (1997). Risk factors for posttraumatic stress symptomatology in police officers: A prospective analysis. *Journal of Nervous and Mental Disorders, 185*(8), 498–506.

Carlier, I. V., Lamberts, R. D., Van Uchelen, A. J., & Gersons, B. P. (1998). Disaster-related post-traumatic stress in police officers: A field study of the impact of debriefing. *Stress and Health, 14*(3), 143–148.

Carlier, I. V., Voerman, A. E., & Gersons. B. P. (2000). The influence of occupational debriefing on post-traumatic stress symptomatology in traumatized police officers. *British Journal of Medical Psychology, 73*(1), 87–98.

Dudek, B. (1999). [Prevention of detrimental effect of traumatic effect in the workplace]. *Medycyna Pracy, 50*(6), 571–579.

Egan, P. (2001). *The perception of the desirability of instituting peer: Critical incidence stress debriefing within a local municipal fire and rescue service* (Unpublished master's thesis). University of Cape Town, South Africa.

Foa, E. B., Riggs, D., & Gershuny, B. (1994). Arousal, numbing, and intrusion. *American Journal of Psychiatry, 152*, 116–120.

Forneris, C. A., Gartlehner, G., Brownley, K. A., Gaynes, B. N., Sonis, J., Coker-Schwimmer, E., ... Woodell, C. L. (2013). Interventions to prevent post-traumatic stress disorder: A systematic review. *American Journal of Preventative Medicine, 44*(6), 635–650.

Fullerton, C. S., Ursano, R. J., & Wang, L. (2004). Acute stress disorder, posttraumatic stress disorder, and depression in disaster or rescue workers. *American Journal of Psychiatry, 161*(8), 1370–1376.

Gelenberg, A. J., Freeman, M. P., Markowitz, J. C., Rosenbaum, J. F., Thase, M. E., Trivedi, M. H., ... Fawcett, J. A. (2010). Practice guideline for the treatment of patients with major depressive disorder, third edition, *American Journal of Psychiatry, 167*(10), 1.

Jayasinghe, N., Spielman, L., Cancellare, D., Difede, J., Klausner, E., & Giosan, C. (2005). Predictors of treatment utilization in world trade center attack disaster workers: Role of race/ethnicity and symptom severity. *International Journal of Emergency Mental Health, 7*(2), 91.

Johnson, S. D., North, C. S., & Smith, E. M. (2002). Psychiatric disorders among victims of a courthouse shooting spree: A three-year follow-up study. *Community Mental Health Journal, 38*(3), 181–194.

Kearns, M. C., Ressler, K. J., Zatzick, D., & Rothbaum, B. O. (2012). Early interventions for PTSD: A review. *Depression and Anxiety, 29*(10), 833–842.

Kleber, H. D., Weiss, R. D., Anton Jr, R. F., George, T. P., Greenfield, S. F., Kosten, T. R., ... & Reiger, D. (2007). Treatment of patients with substance use disorders, American Psychiatric Association. *American Journal of Psychiatry, 164*(4 Suppl.), 5–123.

Lee, C., Slade, P., & Lygo, V. (1996). The influence of psychological debriefing on emotional adaptation in women following early miscarriage: A preliminary study. *British Journal of Medical Psychology, 69*(1), 47–58.

Loo, R. (1986). Post-shooting stress reactions among police officers. *Journal of Human Stress, 12*(1), 27–31. doi:10.1080/0097840X.1986.9936763

Lukaschek, K., Baumert, J., & Ladwig, K. H. (2011). Behaviour patterns preceding a railway suicide: Explorative study of German Federal Police officers' experiences. *BioMed Central Public Health, 11*, 620. doi:10.1186/1471-2458-11-620

Magyar, J., & Theophilos, T. (2010). Review article: Debriefing critical incidents in the emergency department. *Emergency Medicine Australasia*, *22*(6), 499–506.

Martin, M., Marchand, A., & Boyer, R. (2009). Traumatic events in the workplace: Impact on psychopathology and healthcare use of police officers. *International Journal of Emergency Mental Health*, *11*(3), 165–176.

McGhee, T. (2014, June). Police officers struggle with PTSD, but treatment can bring stigma. *The Denver Post*.

Miller, L. (2008). Stress and resilience in law enforcement training and practice. *International Journal of Emergency Mental Health*, *10*(2), 109–124.

Nash, W. P., & Watson, P. J. (2012). Review of VA/DOD clinical practice guideline on management of acute stress and interventions to prevent posttraumatic stress disorder. *Journal of Rehabilitation Research and Development*, *49*(5), 637.

Norris, F. H., Friedman, M. J., Watson, P. J., Byrne, C. M., Diaz, E., & Kaniasty, K. (2002). 60,000 disaster victims speak: Part I. An empirical review of the empirical literature, 1981–2001. *Psychiatry*, *65*(3), 207–239.

North, C. S., & King, R. V. (2009). Eyewitness to mass murder: Findings from studies of four multiple shooting episodes. In Y. Neria (Ed.), *Mental health and disasters* (pp. 497–507). New York, NY: Cambridge University Press.

North, C. S., McCutcheon, V., Spitznagel, E. L., & Smith, E. M. (2002). Three-year follow-up of survivors of a mass shooting episode. *Journal of Urban Health*, *79*(3), 383–391. doi:10.1093/jurban/79.3.383

North, C. S., Oliver, J., & Pandya, A. (2012). Examining a comprehensive model of disaster-related posttraumatic stress disorder in systematically studied survivors of 10 disasters. *American Journal of Public Health*, *102*(10), e40–48. doi:10.2105/AJPH.2012.300689

North, C. S., & Pfefferbaum, B. (2013). Mental health response to community disasters: A systematic review. *JAMA*, *310*(5), 507–518.

North, C. S., Smith, E. M., & Spitznagel, E. L. (1994). Posttraumatic stress disorder in survivors of a mass shooting. *American Journal of Psychiatry*, *151*(1), 82–88.

North, C. S., Smith, E. M., & Spitznagel, E. L. (1997). One-year follow-up of survivors of a mass shooting. *American Journal of Psychiatry*, *154*(12), 1696–1702.

North, C. S., Tivis, L., McMillen, J. C., Pfefferbaum, B., Cox, J., Spitznagel, E. L. ... Smith, E. M. (2002). Coping, functioning, and adjustment of rescue workers after the Oklahoma City bombing. *Journal of Traumatic Stress*, *15*(3), 171–175.

North, C. S., Tivis, L., McMillen, J. C., Pfefferbaum, B., Spitznagel, E. L., Cox, J., ... Smith, E. M. (2002). Psychiatric disorders in rescue workers after the Oklahoma City bombing. *American Journal of Psychiatry*, *159*(5), 857–859.

Perrin, M. A., DiGrande, L., Wheeler, K., Thorpe, L., Farfel, M., & Brackbill, R. (2007). Differences in PTSD prevalence and associated risk factors among World Trade Center disaster rescue and recovery workers. *American Journal of Psychiatry*, *164*(9), 1385–1394. doi:10.1176/appi.ajp.2007.06101645

Regel, S. (2007). Post-trauma support in the workplace: The current status and practice of critical incident stress management (CISM) and psychological debriefing (PD) within organizations in the UK. *Occupational and Environmental Medicine (London, England)*, *57*(6), 411–416.

Robins, L. N., Helzer, J. E., Cottler, L., & Goldring, E. (1989). *NIMH Diagnostic Interview Schedule, Version III-Revised*. St. Louis, MO: Washington University.

Robins, L. N., & Smith, E. M. (1983). *The Diagnostic Interview Schedule/Disaster Supplement*. St. Louis, MO: Washington University.

Rose, S. C., Bisson, J., Churchill, R., & Wessely, S. (2002). Psychological debriefing for preventing post traumatic stress disorder (PTSD). *Cochrane Database of Systematic Reviews, 2*, 1–47 doi:10.1002/14651858.CD000560

Royle, L., Keenan, P., & Farrell, D. (2008). Issues of stigma for first responders accessing support for post traumatic stress. *International Journal of Emergency Mental Health, 11*(2), 79–85.

Sloan, I. H., Rozensky, R. H., Kaplan, L., & Saunders, S. M. (1994). A shooting incident in an elementary school: Effects of worker stress on public safety, mental health, and medical personnel. *Journal of Trauma Stress, 7*(4), 565–574.

Taube, D. O., & Elwork, A. (1990). Researching the effects of confidentiality law on patients' self-disclosures. *Professional Psychology: Research and Practice, 21*(1), 72.

Thompson, B. L., & Waltz, J. (2010). Mindfulness and experiential avoidance as predictors of posttraumatic stress disorder avoidance symptom severity. *Journal of Anxiety Disorders, 24*(4), 409–415.

Thornicroft, G. (2006). *Shunned: Discrimination against people with mental illness*. Oxford, UK: Oxford University Press.

Tuerk, P. W., Yoder, M., Ruggiero, K. J., Gros, D. F., & Acierno, R. (2010). A pilot study of prolonged exposure therapy for posttraumatic stress disorder delivered via telehealth technology. *Journal of Traumatic Stress, 23*(1), 116–123.

14

Distress Among Journalists Working the Incidents

Klas Backholm

Suddenly occurring large-scale crises, such as mass shootings, are at the heart of the news (Brayne, 2007). Journalists immediately start covering the unfolding events, and are expected to rapidly create products for several media platforms. A journalist's job description in a crisis differs from other crisis occupational groups on several levels. For example, journalists are the only group present at a crisis scene with a main work description that does not focus on handling the actual crisis, but rather to inform the public about what has happened (Englund, 2008; Newman, Shapiro, & Nelson, 2009). In addition, while first responders and other rescue personnel often deal with emergencies on a regular basis, most journalists are only sporadically exposed to crisis-related assignments (Smith, Newman, & Drevo, 2015). Journalistic work related to crises is not limited to only those journalists who are present at the crisis scene. The work description may also include combinations of tasks and settings, such as carrying out tasks from one's office or doing interviews elsewhere with individuals indirectly affected by the event (Weidmann & Papsdorf, 2010). To understand how journalists may be affected psychologically by large-scale incidents, such as a mass shooting, one must have insight into the occupation-specific conditions and expectations related to news reporting following crisis events.

The Assignment

To date, a limited number of research publications have focused on the impact of mass shootings on journalists' psychological health. Therefore, to be able to provide an adequate description of mental health-related issues among journalists who work potentially traumatic events, I have chosen to also include information based on other forms of large-scale crises in this chapter. I will also illustrate the included content by presenting examples from our research on the

---

The Wiley Handbook of the Psychology of Mass Shootings, First Edition. Edited by Laura C. Wilson.
© 2017 John Wiley & Sons, Inc. Published 2017 by John Wiley & Sons, Inc.

mass shootings that occurred in Jokela and Kauhajoki in Finland in 2007–2008, as well as the terrorist attack that involved a shooting at Utöya Island and bombing in central Oslo, Norway in 2011.

Several studies that used a qualitative approach have provided descriptions of the journalistic tasks that are carried out, and the emotions provoked, during an ongoing mass shooting or other type of large-scale crisis (Backholm, Moritz, & Björkqvist, 2012; Berrington & Jemphrey, 2003; Englund, 2008; Idås, 2013; Raittila, Koljonen, & Väliverronen, 2010). When the first pieces of information about an unfolding event reach a news office, a well-oiled machine is set in motion. In the first minutes, several processes are initiated. In parallel with the news desks investigating the details of what is happening, coordinating editors identify available journalists and assign tasks to those who are at the office at that moment. Individual journalists assess the relevance and the status of the tasks they were carrying out before they heard about the crisis, and decide whether they can postpone the tasks and focus on the new assignment or not. The journalists' physiological arousal is quickly heightened, and the individual, as well as the collective news office, adjusts to what has suddenly changed from an ordinary to a hectic day at the office. Although sudden, this adjustment is not unexpected, as most journalists see crisis-related work as a potential part of their work description (Brayne, 2007; Simpson & Coté, 2006).

Journalists differ in how they compare their crisis-related work to everyday routines. According to some, crisis-related assignments are just a more extreme version of their typical work activities. The same tasks are carried out in both cases, but crises involve some unique contextual factors, such as more demanding time constraints and increased difficulty in reaching interviewees. These factors require increased professional focus. Others see crisis-related assignments as very different from their everyday work. During crises, a journalist may need to consider specific aspects of journalism practice that are irrelevant in their everyday work. For example, one may need to approach victims and make a decision about whether this person is a reliable witness or not. Also, journalists may need to take into account their own level of risk because they could potentially witness grotesque details while carrying out work tasks (Brayne, 2007; Englund, 2008; Hughes, 2012; Raittila et al., 2010; Simpson & Coté, 2006). In other words, a journalist will need to rely on their previous experience from everyday work to be able to carry out their work in a demanding situation – but will also need to apply specific journalistic principles which are unique to an assignment of this type.

As mentioned above, the sudden change from an ordinary to a hectic day at the office may cause a heightened level of physical and psychological stress among the workers. Journalists have often referred to the heightened level of arousal in a crisis as going into "hyper mode" or switching into "autopilot" (Backholm et al., 2012; Englund, 2008; Idås, 2013). This "autopilot" may lead journalists to focus entirely on the assignment, feel a high level of physical alertness, experience a sense of detachment from reality, forget basic needs such as eating, and suppress personal emotions to be able to continue to work while faced with distressing details about a crisis.

The term "autopilot" may not be ideal, as it can be interpreted as a person who is not in control of themselves. Conversely, it reflects the journalist's professional ability and readiness to suddenly change into a more extreme work mode. Idås (2013) described the combined functions of focusing entirely on the task and distancing oneself from the emotional distress provoked by any gruesome details of the crisis as a professional shield that allows the journalist to get the job done.

Journalists have described how, in most cases, the professional shield or "autopilot" is in place and continues to protect them from emotional distress until the assignment is over (Englund, 2008; Idås, 2013). When the high level of assignment-related stress is reduced, often co-occurring with the journalist physically leaving the crisis scene or office setting, personal emotions may emerge. In a study conducted with journalists who worked at the scene or indirectly with the Jokela school shooting in Finland ($n = 196$; Backholm & Björkqvist, 2012), 126 participants chose to describe their general "thoughts or feelings" after working the incident. A majority focused on describing work-related tasks or the overall nature of the assignment by mentioning that they were on "autopilot" or operated like a robot.

Distress in the immediate aftermath of the assignment may take on varying forms, including combinations of general sadness or anxiety, empathy for the victims, occupation-related guilt, crying, fear, shock, dissociation, anger, or overwhelming fatigue. In contrast, some journalists report only mild or complete lack of distress in the aftermath of a crisis (Backholm & Idås, 2015; Brayne, 2007; Englund 2008; Simpson & Coté, 2006; Newman et al., 2009). In the aforementioned study of journalists from the Jokela school shooting in Finland (Backholm & Björkqvist, 2012), 43% of the participants reported negative emotions, such as feelings of fear, sadness or anxiety, in the direct aftermath of the event. A couple of journalists mentioned that the assignment did not provoke any reactions, and a select few described positive reactions, such as reporting that the case was rewarding from a journalistic viewpoint. In another study based on semistructured interviews with 28 journalists who worked the scene during either the Jokela incident or the Kauhajoki shooting in Finland in 2008, roughly 50% of the participants reported short-term distress (Backholm et al., 2012).

Although most of the reactions described above are experienced as negative and discomforting at the time, they should not necessarily be interpreted as early signs of a long-lasting psychological diagnosis caused by direct or indirect exposure to the crisis. On the contrary, for most people, their reactions in the aftermath of a crisis should be seen as part of a normal healing process of trying to understand the meaning and impact of the sudden and unexpected event. In addition, individual differences affect how potentially traumatic experiences are processed. Journalists who do not experience distress in the immediate aftermath of an assignment should therefore not be automatically labeled as avoiding or suppressing their feelings, as the person may have interpreted the assignment as a low-risk situation (Backholm & Björkqvist, 2012; Bryant, 2004; Idås, 2013; Norris & Slone, 2014). Later in this chapter, I will return in more detail to the occupational risk factors for long-term psychological impairment that may occur during and in the direct aftermath of a crisis.

Although short-term distress in journalists mainly seems to occur after an assignment is over, there are some descriptions in the literature of how the professional shield, or "autopilot," can be disrupted during an ongoing assignment. When this happens, journalists' stress levels may increase to such a degree that they can no longer distance themselves from the emotional impact of the crisis. As a consequence, overwhelming exhaustion, lack of energy, or related difficulties may appear (Backholm, 2012; Idås, 2013). In turn, their ongoing work tasks may suffer, at least momentarily. This type of disruption of the professional shield has seldom been described in detail or been empirically investigated. Thus, there is a lack of detailed information about its exact causes and relevant contexts.

However, one factor that has been described as a disruption by some journalists who worked either the Jokela or Kauhajoki school shootings in Finland (Backholm, 2012; Idås, 2013) or the tsunami in Asia in 2004 (Idås, 2010) was ethical dilemmas. Such dilemmas can be defined as an inner conflict between the journalistic requirements of the assignment and feelings of empathy for those directly affected by the crisis. These journalists reported that they experienced dilemmas when they went beyond their own personal norms for ethically acceptable behavior in the line of work, usually due to requirements set by the editorial office or other factors beyond their control.

For example, a journalist who worked the Kauhajoki shooting described how he was ordered by his superiors to visit the home of a friend of the perpetrator and ask this person for an interview. An elderly woman answered the door and declined to participate. A few hours after the visit to the home, the journalist's editorial office informed him that the friend was actually one of those killed in the shooting. As the reporter strongly believed that "death knocks" (i.e. visiting the homes of victims' families to ask for interviews) was a form of unethical journalism, this turn of events caused a severe disruption in the journalist's professional shield and resulted in a strong emotional reaction during the ongoing assignment (Backholm et al., 2012). As will be described in greater detail below, such ethical dilemmas may not only cause acute distress, but can also increase the risk for long-term psychological difficulties.

Long-Term Psychological Impairment in Journalists

The first scientific publication on long-term psychological distress among journalists was published as late as 1994 (Freinkel, Koopman, & Spiegel, 1994; Simpson & Coté, 2006). Feinstein (2006), who published the first study on war correspondents' occupational health, argued that the reason trauma-related mental health among journalists was not examined until then was a reflection of the expectation of journalistic objectivity. Journalists were expected to objectively report on crises and to not include subjective opinions. As a result, a journalist should not be psychologically affected by the event.

During the past two decades, studies on trauma and journalism have continuously added to the collective knowledge base. Although we now have a relatively solid foundation of empirical information about several central issues related to the psychological impact of trauma on journalists, the generalizability of these studies is questionable and our knowledge is limited because of the types of crises examined, sample inclusion criteria, time periods used for data collection, and sample sizes (Aoki, Malcolm, Yamaguchi, Thornicroft, & Henderson, 2013; Backholm, 2012; Smith et al., 2015). Subsequently, the conclusions presented below, although informative, should be interpreted with caution.

Posttraumatic stress disorder (PTSD) has been the psychological disorder of focus in most studies examining the impact of crisis-related work among journalists (Smith et al., 2015). In the fifth edition of the *Diagnostic and Statistical Manual of Mental Disorders* (DSM-5), a diagnosis of PTSD requires that an individual was exposed to a traumatic stressor either directly (e.g., physically witnessing an event) or indirectly (e.g., hearing that the event happened to a close relative). Related to the topic of this chapter, exposure to extreme details, including through media, does satisfy this criterion, when it is work-related. Furthermore, the individual must report symptoms that span four categories. These symptom domains include intrusion symptoms (i.e., when the trauma is reexperienced in a sudden and involuntary manner), avoidance of reminders of the trauma, changes in cognition and mood, and alterations in physiological arousal or reactivity (e.g., hyper-vigilance, aggression, self-destructiveness; American Psychiatric Association, 2013; Miller, Wolf, & Keane, 2014). The symptoms must persist for at least one month and be severe enough to lead to significant impairment and distress. Estimates of lifetime PTSD in nonjournalist general population studies in Europe and North America usually range from 1 to 9% (American Psychiatric Association, 2013; Blanco, 2011; Kilpatrick et al., 2013).

In the aftermath of mass shootings or other crisis-related assignments, a small subgroup of journalists develops PTSD. However, the majority of journalists report few long-term psychological difficulties. In a review of 11 studies, the prevalence of PTSD among journalists who had worked crises was between 0.0 and 33.0% (Aoki et al., 2013). Smith et al. (2015) found evidence of similar figures, which ranged from 4.3 to 35.0%, in their review of 15 studies. However, when studies were excluded if they included subjects with chronic exposure to severe stressors (e.g., war correspondents) the documented prevalence rates were lower.

Some studies on journalistic work during and after mass shootings have included PTSD prevalence figures. In a sample of journalists who worked the Norwegian terrorist attack in 2011 ($n = 375$), during which almost half of the group ($n = 144$) was on the scene either in Oslo or at Utöya, 9% had probable PTSD (Idås & Backholm, 2016). Similarly, 12% of journalists who worked the Jokela school shooting in Finland in 2007 ($n = 196$) reported symptoms severe enough to be suggestive of PTSD (Backholm & Björkqvist, 2012). A majority of the journalists in this sample (86%) were only indirectly exposed to the unfolding crisis and had not worked at the crisis scene.

When it comes to the prevalence of PTSD, it is important to remember that the figures presented above represent the small group of journalists who had severe reactions to the crisis and met full criteria for the disorder. There are some journalists who would best be described as experiencing partial or subsyndromal PTSD (i.e., experiencing some symptoms but not meeting the full diagnostic criteria; Friedman, Resick, Bryant, & Brewin, 2011). These journalists are important to consider because they may need postassignment organizational support or mental health care services. However, as the prevalence of partial PTSD has seldom been reported in journalist samples, we know very little about this subgroup.

PTSD is not the only type of psychological impairment that may occur following work-related exposure to a traumatic event. In nonjournalist trauma samples, at least one comorbid diagnosis is the rule rather than the exception (see Blanco, 2011 for review of epidemiological studies). According to the DSM-5, 80% of people with PTSD have a second mental disorder (American Psychiatric Association, 2013). The main comorbid disorders include depression, somatization, anxiety, and substance abuse (Reardon, Brief, Miller, & Keane, 2014).

Other forms of psychological difficulties have also been studied in journalist samples, either as disorders that co-occur with PTSD or as the main outcome disorder following potentially traumatic assignments. Such types of impairment include depression (Feinstein, Owen, & Blair, 2002; McMahon, 2001; Teegen & Grotwinkel, 2001; Weidmann, Fehm, & Fydrich, 2008), general psychological distress (Feinstein, 2013; Feinstein, Audet, & Waknine, 2013; Weidmann & Papsdorf, 2010), substance abuse (Feinstein, 2013; Feinstein & Starr, 2015), and burnout (Backholm & Björkqvist, 2010; Dworznik, 2008; Thoresen, 2007). However, to date, there is not enough evidence to be able to identify any conclusive prevalence rates for specific comorbid disorders following trauma in journalist samples (Aoki et al., 2013), or to identify patterns of comorbidity relevant for journalists working mass shootings.

Risk Factors for Psychological Impairment in Journalists

Despite an overall lack of empirical evidence, the available research has revealed several factors that increase the risk for long-term psychological impairment in journalist samples. Again, the following overview of risk factors should be interpreted with caution as the current knowledge about this occupational group is limited due to the relatively small number of studies, inclusion of varying types of samples, and a wide range of definitions of distress across the studies. Some of the most extensive meta-analyses of risk factors for PTSD in nonjournalist samples have been provided by Brewin, Andrews, and Valentine (2000) and Ozer, Best, Lipsey, and Weiss (2003). Many of the same factors that predict PTSD in general population samples have been found among journalists. Such factors include previous exposure to traumatic situations and use of avoidant coping strategies when faced with life stressors. In addition, a number of factors have been demonstrated that reflect the unique tasks and contexts relevant for journalistic work. Occupation-specific risk factors include the journalist's previous experience with crisis-related assignments, as well as the conflict of being a working journalist and an empathic fellow citizen. Below, central risk factors for psychological distress are divided into subgroups based on whether the factors are present before the crisis assignment (i.e., preassignment risk factors), occur during the crisis (i.e., peri-assignment factors), or happen after the assignment (i.e., postassignment factors).

Preassignment risk factors

Some of the personality and cognitive risk factors observed in nonjournalist samples (e.g., neuroticism, aggressive temperament, avoidant coping strategies) have also been related to long-term psychological functioning in journalists (Marais & Stuart, 2005; Smith, 2008). For example, in a sample of South African news journalists ($n=50$), Marais and Stuart (2005) found that those who had a more hostile or aggressive temperament reported more severe PTSD symptoms. Smith (2008) studied whether coping style was related to psychological distress in a sample of American news journalists ($n=167$) and found that participants who avoided dealing with problems reported higher levels of PTSD symptoms and general psychological distress.

The number of years working as a journalist seems to affect the severity of PTSD symptoms in several ways. Being an inexperienced journalist (Backholm & Idås, 2015; Teegen & Grotwinkel, 2001) or a very experienced journalist

(Newman, Simpson, & Handschuh, 2003; Simpson & Boggs, 1999) have both been found to enhance the individual's risk for more severe impairment. It has been suggested that inexperienced journalists have underdeveloped work skills and thus may be more vulnerable when carrying out crisis-related assignments. Conversely, very experienced colleagues may suffer from accumulative experiences of potentially traumatic events during their careers.

The everyday pressure and requirements in the newsroom may in themselves also affect personal wellbeing, regardless of years of experience as a journalist. Studies have shown that a higher level of everyday stress at one's workplace is related to more psychological distress after working a crisis assignment (Hatanaka et al., 2010; Smith, 2008; Weidmann & Papsdorf, 2010). In a sample of news journalists from Germany, Austria, and Switzerland ($n=81$), Weidmann and Papsdorf (2010) combined measures of environmental stressors in the workplace, interpersonal problems at work, time pressure, workload, job demands, and freedom at the workplace into a work stress score, and found that more everyday work stress was related to more severe distress within two of the PTSD symptom categories (i.e., intrusion and avoidance symptoms).

Greater previous exposure to traumatic events in one's personal life has been linked to greater levels of journalists' PTSD symptoms, as well as other forms of distress (e.g., depression and burnout; Backholm & Björkqvist, 2010; McMahon, 2005; Newman et al., 2003; Pyevich, Newman, & Daleiden, 2003; Weidmann et al., 2008; Weidmann & Papsdorf, 2010). Working a crisis that is closely reminiscent of the journalist's personal life may increase the risk for postassignment impairment. For example, being a journalist from the affected region or being a parent to children roughly the same age as the crisis victims may be associated with more distress after the assignment. Berrington and Jemphrey (2003) found that among journalists who worked the Dunblane mass shooting in Scotland in 1996, those who had young family members reported more emotional distress after the assignment. The same was true for journalists who worked the scene of the two Finnish school shootings in 2007–2008. The shootings were the first incidents of this type to occur in the country, and journalists who had children reported that they experienced distressing intrusive thoughts about their children's future in relation to the "new unsafe school environment" (Backholm & Björkqvist, 2012; Backholm et al., 2012).

In some studies, greater exposure to previous crisis-related assignments has been linked to greater distress (Browne, Evangeli, & Greenberg, 2012; Marais & Stuart, 2005; Newman et al., 2003; Pyevich et al., 2003; Simpson & Boggs, 1999), while other studies have not found a relation (Backholm & Björkqvist, 2010; Dworznik, 2008; Smith, 2008). These mixed findings may be explained by the fact that journalistic work during crises may take on varying forms, as stated above. For example, some journalists may be directly exposed to the unfolding event, while others carry out their work from a distance. Thus, focusing on the number or range of previous assignments without detailed information about the nature of the exposure may not be the most fruitful approach.

Peri-assignment risk factors

Studies focusing on work in extreme crisis scenarios, such as war or ongoing conflict zones, have shown that more severe exposure during the assignment is linked to more severe psychopathology symptoms (e.g., PTSD, depression, substance abuse; Feinstein et al., 2002; Feinstein, 2013; Feinstein & Starr, 2015). Also, studies in nonconflict settings that have included measurements of the nature and intensity of the assignment (e.g., the number of gruesome details a journalist is exposed to, whether the journalist was directly threatened, attacked, or injured during the assignment; Pyevich, 2001) have shown that more severe events are associated with increased risk of PTSD, depression, and burnout (Backholm & Björkqvist, 2010; Dworznik, 2008; Idås, 2011; Smith, 2008; Thoresen, 2007). Because journalists who work mass shootings may be exposed to a wide range of gruesome details, (e.g., reporting details of a large number of victims, learning that some of the victims were young, directly witnessing deceased or injured), the nature of this crisis subtype may be especially harmful for journalists, particularly for those at the scene of the event.

The "gruesomeness" of an assignment has often been measured in terms of the journalist's level of exposure to details while at the scene of the unfolding crisis. As previously mentioned, the first requirement for a diagnosis of PTSD in the DSM-5 (American Psychiatric Association, 2013) is the stressor criterion. This requirement states than an individual must experience a traumatic event through direct exposure, witnessing the event, indirect exposure by learning the event happened to someone close to them, or repeated/extreme exposure to aversive details of the event via electronic media, television or pictures, as long as this exposure is work-related. Therefore, for a journalist, exposure to a traumatic event may include viewing recorded material, such as pictures or videos from the crisis. A few studies with journalists have examined varying subtypes of indirect exposure. More frequent exposure to video footage of violent events produced by other journalists or the public (e.g., video clips recorded with smart phones at the crisis scenes) have both been linked to greater levels of PTSD symptoms and other forms of psychological impairment (Feinstein et al., 2013; Weidmann & Papsdorf, 2010).

Related to this, current journalistic work with mass shootings often includes using several social media platforms in addition to more traditional types of information sources to monitor the crisis, to gauge the public's view of the crisis, and to identify eye witnesses or other potential participants for one's media products (Silverman, 2014). The challenges related to journalists' social media usage during crises have been identified in the ongoing European

Researching Social Media and Collaborative Software Use in Emergency Situations (RESCUE) project. The journalists and communication experts who are participating in this project have pinpointed several sources of stress, which include problems related to identifying relevant content among the vast amounts of information posted on social media platforms during a crisis and being able to verify the trustworthiness of the identified information (Hornmoen et al., 2015). These results have been replicated in other studies (Bae Brandtzaeg, Luders, Spangenberg, Rath-Wiggins, & Folstad, 2016), but it is premature to conclude whether this stress may be a risk factor for long-term psychological impairment among journalists. However, the initial evidence indicates that the amount of time journalists spend monitoring user-generated content may affect their wellbeing (Feinstein et al., 2013). This suggests that monitoring events that have a high impact on social media, such as mass shootings, is also a risk factor for long-term psychological impairment. The possible effect of the information and interaction between journalists and the public in social media platforms during mass shootings and similar crises needs to be taken into consideration in future studies on journalists and trauma.

As stated in the section above about the journalist's professional shield, this protective function may be disrupted during an assignment, which may lead to greater stress and difficulties while carrying out work tasks. Studies on long-term impairment have shown that greater peri-assignment distress is associated with increased risk for subsequent long-lasting impairment among journalists (Backholm, 2012; Englund, 2008; Hatanaka et al., 2010; Idås, 2013). In a sample of Japanese journalists ($n=270$), Hatanaka and colleagues (2010) found that peri-assignment symptoms (e.g., dissociation, sleeplessness, digestive problems) predicted more severe PTSD symptoms.

Hatanaka et al. (2010) also investigated whether occupation-specific problems during an assignment (i.e., factors that may disrupt the professional shield) were related to greater levels of PTSD among journalists who worked at the scene of the crisis ($n=179$). In this study, the problems they examined included how difficult it was to complete the assignment and the number of complaints received about the coverage. The results revealed that as the number of problems increased, the journalists reported more long-term impairment. A study conducted with news journalists who worked the terrorist attack in Norway in 2011 ($n=371$; Backholm & Idås, 2015) included journalists who had either worked the bomb explosion in the capital of Norway or a mass shooting at a youth camp on the island of Utöya. This study examined occupation-specific problems during the assignment in a slightly different way by focusing on ethical dilemmas, which were unexpected events that forced a journalist to break their norms for ethically acceptable journalistic behavior (Backholm, 2012; Idås, 2010). The results revealed that those with greater exposure to ethical dilemmas also reported more severe PTSD symptoms 8–9 months after the incident.

Postassignment risk factors

Risk factors for long-term psychological impairment should not be limited to only those occurring before or during a possibly traumatic event. Posttrauma factors, such as contextual circumstances or the development of certain event-related traits in those affected, may also increase risk for PTSD (Vogt, King, & King, 2014). Contextual circumstances are factors related to the external situation. For example, the explanation of the cause of the crisis is left unidentified or affected individuals receive low levels of peer support. Event-related traits are internal factors in an affected person, and may include negative thoughts (e.g., shame, guilt) or unhealthy behaviors related to how one handled the incident. Few studies with journalism samples have included measures of such factors, but there is some evidence that posttrauma factors are important to consider in journalist samples.

One factor that may affect journalists' wellbeing after working crises is the public debate and criticism related to journalistic work and ethics. The public view of the crisis is, to a large degree, dictated by how the event is portrayed in mass media (see Chapter 7 for more on the impact of media on the public's attitudes). Unaffected citizens gather their information about an event via mass and social media, as well as personal communication with their peers. In turn, these individuals share select parts of this information via their own social media networks. This information gathering and forwarding process is based on an underlying expectation that journalists will provide the public with a trustworthy and broad picture of the unfolding event (Brayne, 2007; Coombs, 2015; Falkheimer & Olsson, 2015; Muschert, 2007).

However, the journalistic work carried out during the event may also become the outspoken focus of the public debate, especially if the work is not in line with the underlying public expectations. For example, rumors of unethical journalism may cause a public debate about journalism ethics in the crisis aftermath, no matter if the rumor can be verified or not. This debate may also expand from the case in question to a more general criticism against journalistic work during and after a crisis. One such example was the debate following the Finnish mass shooting in Jokela in 2007. A group of young adults started a mass petition on the web to highlight what they experienced as unethical journalistic behavior at the crisis scene. As a result, a majority of Finnish media organizations updated their internal ethical codes of conduct. However, identifying the actual journalists that carried out unethical tasks during the shooting proved to be difficult (Raittila et al., 2010).

Public criticism against crisis-related journalism may also be instigated simply because of the vast amount of overall coverage of the event in national or regional media. This public reaction may take varying forms. For example, following the mass shooting at Utøya Island, Norway in 2011, two out of three Norwegians ($n = 802$) and approximately half of Norwegian journalists

($n = 637$) thought the media coverage was too extensive (Aarebrot & Maeland, n.d.). During the trial following the attack, some newspaper stands in Norway chose to not display front covers of newspapers that showed pictures of the perpetrator, and Facebook groups demanded boycotts against newspapers (Brurås, 2011).

The criticism of the coverage has in some studies been proposed as a risk factor for psychological distress in journalists. In the aftermath of the Jokela school shooting in Finland, some journalists (28 %) indicated that the criticism against their trade provoked by the online mass petition caused short-term negative emotions. The journalists indicated that the public expects them to cover the incident, but criticize them when they do. They reported that their reactions included anger, frustration, and a strong need to defend their own or colleagues' work (Backholm & Björkqvist, 2012). However, it is difficult to compare the impact of public criticism when examining different types of crises because the content and dynamics of the criticism depend on the nature of the event. Furthermore, it is still unclear how this factor contributes to long-term psychological impairment in journalists. Due to the nature of the event (e.g., occur in public places, result in mass casualties), mass shootings result in massive media attention. The risk of negative public reactions about journalistic practices may in these cases be particularly damaging – especially if the main target group of the shooting is children or young adults. Therefore, journalists who work mass shootings may be at greater risk of becoming targets of criticism.

In addition to identifying posttrauma risk factors, some studies with journalist samples have investigated how the postassignment development of specific individual traits may affect long-term symptoms of distress. Pyevich et al. (2003) found that American newspaper journalists ($n = 906$) with greater previous exposure to potentially traumatic assignments tended to develop more negative posttrauma cognitive schemas, and in turn, more severe PTSD symptoms. The results revealed that more negative cognitive beliefs mediated the relationship between previous trauma exposure and PTSD.

Another factor that has been investigated as a possible mediator in the relationship between crisis-related assignments and PTSD in journalist samples is guilt. Browne et al. (2012) found that more severe trauma-related guilt mediated the association between a greater amount of previous work with crises and greater PTSD symptoms in 50 British news journalists. In a study on the coverage of the Norwegian terrorist attack ($n = 371$; Backholm & Idås, 2015), a similar pattern was found. Journalists who had experienced more ethical dilemmas during their assignment also experienced more postassignment guilt (e.g., having been too intrusive towards those directly affected), as well as more long-term psychological distress in the form of PTSD symptoms.

Thus, although defined somewhat differently between studies, the development of posttrauma negative cognitions seems to be relevant for long-term psychological functioning. This is consistent with previous research with trauma victims (Dalgleish, 2004; Kubany & Watson, 2003; Lee, Scragg, & Turner, 2001). The development of negative cognitions is also one of the symptoms of PTSD based on the DSM-5 diagnostic criteria (American Psychiatric Association, 2013). Therefore, the possible causes of guilt and other relevant negative cognitions warrant further scholarly attention, preferably in studies with a longitudinal research design.

Resilience in Journalists

The main focus of this chapter has been on the possible negative mental health consequences of crisis work in journalists. However, as mentioned above, most journalists report few psychological difficulties after working a mass shooting or other type of potentially traumatic assignment (Newman et al., 2009). Therefore, a discussion of resilience, or the ability to overcome adversity or stress (Rutter, 2006), is warranted. As stated by Bonnano (2004), factors that promote resilience in an occupational group exposed to a potentially traumatic event should not be limited to only "the opposite" of risk factors, but rather other factors should also be included.

Few studies with journalists have included factors that promote resilience. But of the few factors that have been examined, one of the most commonly included is the level of social support the journalist receives following the assignment, either from family, friends, or colleagues. Studies with varying types of journalist samples have generally found evidence of the positive effects of having a well-functioning social network (Aoki et al., 2013; Newman et al., 2003; Thoresen, 2007; Weidmann et al., 2008), with a few exceptions (e.g., Hatanaka et al., 2010). The types of support provided by different individuals may vary. For example, family and friends know the person outside of the occupational role, and therefore can provide support that reflects the journalist's personal needs. Colleagues likely have more insight into the occupation-specific challenges and how the assignment in question was experienced by the journalist. Therefore, they are able to provide profession-focused social support after the assignment (Brayne, 2007; Idås, 2013).

Another factor that may support resilience among journalists, which is related to workplace social support and recognition, is the level of personal satisfaction a journalist experiences with their products. For journalists, being pleased with how one managed or completed specific tasks or the final media products may reflect a more general feeling of having actively contributed to a positive outcome following a crisis (Newman et al., 2009). This could be seen as the opposite of experiencing ethical dilemmas, but should perhaps not be limited to dilemmas only. For example, Hatanaka et al. (2010) constructed a scale reflecting level of achievement during coverage, consisting of items such as positive feedback from the public. They, however, did not find any relation between the scale and levels of impairment among the 270 participating journalists. Marais and Stuart ($n = 50$; 2005) did, on the other hand, find that those journalists who perceived that they could handle the demands related to crisis-related work had lower levels of posttrauma distress. Clearly, broadening the scope of future research beyond focusing on risk factors would be relevant for the knowledge in the area of journalism and trauma.

Conclusions

To conclude, several key findings and general comments should be highlighted regarding our current knowledge base about psychological impairment in journalists who work mass shootings. First, journalists who work mass shootings or other types of crises may react strongly to what they experience in their line of work. However, in most cases, journalists are able to carry out the tasks at hand and typically do not develop severe long-term trauma-related psychological disorders. Second, to understand distress and resilience among journalists who work crises, we need to understand the specific occupational challenges (e.g., ethical dilemmas) relevant to journalists and mass media. Third, due to the type of event (e.g., large number of victims, grotesque details), mass shootings may be associated with heightened risk for psychological distress in journalists – but we need additional future research before we can draw any final conclusions. Fourth, to promote wellbeing and resilience among journalists, workplaces and organizations need to more directly address crisis-related challenges and dilemmas by providing statements on expected behavior and ethically acceptable ways of carrying out work tasks during crisis-related assignments. Fifth, news organizations need to strive to create a workplace climate where mental health services are readily available and usage of these services is encouraged and rewarded.

References

Aarebrot, F., & Maeland, P. A. (n.d.). *For mye mediedekning av 22. juli, synes to av tre nordmenn* [Too much media coverage of July 22, say two out of three Norwegians]. Retrieved from http://www.mynewsdesk.com/material/pressrelease/749946/download?resource_type=resource_attached_pdf_document

American Psychiatric Association. (2013). *Diagnostic and statistical manual of mental disorders* (5th ed.). Washington, DC: Author.

Aoki, Y., Malcolm, E., Yamaguchi, S., Thornicroft, G., & Henderson, C. (2013). Mental illness among journalists: A systematic review. *International Journal of Social Psychiatry, 59*, 377–390. doi:10.1177/0020764012437676

Backholm, K. (2012). *Work-related crisis exposure, psychological trauma and PTSD in news journalists.* (Unpublished doctoral thesis). Åbo Akademi University, Åbo, Finland.

Backholm, K., & Björkqvist, K. (2010). The effects of exposure to crisis on well-being of journalists: A study on crisis-related factors predicting psychological health in a sample of Finnish journalists. *Media, War & Conflict, 3,* 138–151. doi:10.1177/1750635210368309

Backholm, K., & Björkqvist, K. (2012). Journalists' emotional reactions after working with the Jokela school shooting incident. *Media, War & Conflict, 5,* 175–190. doi:10.1177/1750635212440914

Backholm, K., & Idås, T. (2013, June). *Ethical dilemmas as a predictor for PTSD in news journalists working with large-scale violence.* Paper presented at the 13th European Conference on Traumatic Stress, Bologna, Italy.

Backholm, K., & Idås, T. (2015). Ethical dilemmas, work-related guilt, and posttraumatic stress reactions in news journalists working with the terror attack in Norway 2011. *Journal of Traumatic Stress, 28,* 142–148. doi:10.1002/jts.22001

Backholm, K., Moritz, M., & Björkqvist, K. (2012). US and Finnish journalists: A comparative study of roles, responsibilities and emotional reactions to school shootings. In G. W. Muschert & J. Sumiala (Eds.), *School shootings: Mediatized violence in a global age* (pp. 143–162). Bingley, UK: Emerald. doi:10.1108/S2050-2060(2012)0000007011

Bae Brandtzaeg, P., Luders, M., Spangenberg, J., Rath-Wiggins, L., & Folstad, A. (2016). Emerging journalistic verification practices concerning social media. *Journalism Practice, 10,* 323–342. doi:10.1080/17512786.2015.1020331

Berrington, E., & Jemphrey, A. (2003). Pressures on the press: Reflections on reporting tragedy. *Journalism, 4,* 225–248. doi:10.1177/146488490342005

Blanco, C. (2011). Epidemiology of PTSD. In D. J. Stein, M. J. Friedman, & C. Blanco (Eds.), *Post-traumatic stress disorder* (pp. 49–74). Chichester, UK: Wiley-Blackwell.

Bonnano, G. A. (2004). Loss, trauma and human resilience. Have we underestimated the human capacity to thrive after extremely aversive events? *American Psychologist, 59,* 20–28. doi:10.1037/0003-066X.59.1.20

Brayne, M. (2007). *Trauma & journalism. A guide for journalists, editors & managers.* Retrieved from http://dartcenter.org/sites/default/files/DCE_JournoTrauma Handbook.pdf

Brewin, C., Andrews, B., & Valentine J. D. (2000). Meta-analysis of risk factors for posttraumatic stress disorder in trauma-exposed adults. *Journal of Consulting and Clinical Psychology, 68,* 748–766. doi:10.1037/0022-006X.68.5.748

Browne, T., Evangeli, M., & Greenberg, N. (2012). Trauma-related guilt and post-traumatic stress among journalists. *Journal of Traumatic Stress, 25,* 207–210. doi:10.1002/jts.21678

Brurås, S. (2011). *Media ethics in the coverage of the Breivik attacks.* Retrieved from http://svein-b.blogspot.fi/p/media-ethics-in-coverage-of-breivik.html

Bryant, R. A. (2004). Assessing acute stress disorder. In J. P. Wilson & T. M. Keane (Eds.), *Assessing psychological trauma and PTSD* (2nd ed.) (pp. 45–60). New York, NY: Guilford Press.

Coombs, W. T. (2015). *Crisis communication. Planning, managing, and responding* (4th ed.). Thousand Oaks, CA: Sage.

Dalgleish, T. (2004). Cognitive approaches to posttraumatic stress disorder: The evolution of multirepresentational theorizing. *Psychological Bulletin, 130,* 228–260. doi:10.1037/0033-2909.130.2.228

Dworznik, G. J. (2008). *The psychology of local news: Compassion fatigue and posttraumatic stress in broadcast reporters, photographers, and live truck engineers.* (Unpublished doctoral dissertation). Kent State University, Kent, OH.

Englund, L. (2008). *Katastrofens öga. En studie av journalisters arbete på olycksplats [The eye of the disaster. A study of journalists' work at accident scenes and disaster sites].* (Unpublished doctoral thesis). University of Gothenburg, Gothenburg, Sweden.

Falkheimer, J., & Olsson, E. (2015). Depoliticizing terror: The news framing of the terrorist attacks in Norway, 22 July 2011. *Media, War & Conflict, 8,* 70–85. doi:10.1177/1750635214531109

Feinstein, A. (2006). *Journalists under fire: The psychological hazards of covering war.* Baltimore, MD: John Hopkins University Press.

Feinstein, A. (2013). Mexican journalists and journalists covering war: A comparison of psychological wellbeing. *Journal of Aggression, Conflict and Peace Research, 5,* 77–85. doi:10.1108/17596591311313672

Feinstein, A., Audet, B., & Waknine, E. (2013). Witnessing images of extreme violence: A psychological study of journalists in the newsroom. *Journal of the Royal Society of Medicine Open, 5,* 1–7. doi:10.1177/2054270414533323.

Feinstein, A., Owen, J., & Blair, N. (2002). A hazardous profession: War, journalists, and psychopathology. *American Journal of Psychiatry, 159,* 1570–1575. doi:10.1176/appi.ajp.159.9.1570

Feinstein, A., & Starr, S. (2015). Civil war in Syria: The psychological effects on journalists. *Journal of Aggression, Conflict and Peace Research, 7,* 57–64. doi:10.1108/JACPR-04-2014-0119

Freinkel, A., Koopman, C., & Spiegel, D. (1994). Dissociative symptoms in media eyewitnesses of an execution. *American Journal of Psychiatry, 151,* 1335–1339.

Friedman, M. J., Resick, P. A., Bryant, R. A., & Brewin, C. R. (2011). Considering PTSD for DSM-5. *Depression & Anxiety, 28,* 750–769. doi:10.1002/da.2076

Hatanaka, M., Matsui, Y., Ando, K., Inoue, K., Fukuoka, Y., Koshiro, E., & Itamura, H. (2010). Traumatic stress in Japanese broadcast journalists. *Journal of Traumatic Stress, 23,* 173–177. doi:10.1002/jts.20496

Hornmoen, H., Backholm, K., Frey, E., Ottosen, R., Reimerth, G., & Steensen, S. (2015, July). *Key communicators' perceptions on the use of social media in risks and crises.* Paper presented at the International Association for Media and Communication Research Conference, Montreal, Canada.

Hughes, S. (2012, December 17). *Newton shootings: Interviewing traumatised children.* Retrieved from http://www.bbc.co.uk/blogs/collegeofjournalism/entries/e0ffafd2-aa6c-38ee-a2ee-992b2549bedb

Idås, T. (2010). *Journalistene og tsunamien: Ekstreme inntrykk – men dilemmaene stresset mest [Journalists and the tsunami: Extreme exposure – but the dilemmas caused distress].* (Unpublished master's thesis). University of Oslo, Oslo, Norway.

Idås, T. (2011, October). *Journalistene som dekket terror* [The journalists who covered terror]. Paper presented at the biannual Gull- og Gråsteinkonferensen, Oslo, Norway.

Idås, T. (2013). *Krevende oppdrag. Hvordan mestre stress [Demanding assignments. How to handle stress]*. Oslo, Norway: Cappelen Damm.

Idås, T., & Backholm, K. (2016, May). *Risk and resilience among journalists covering potentially traumatic events*. Poster presented at the UNESCO Research Conference on the Safety of Journalists, Helsinki, Finland.

Kilpatrick, D. G., Resnick, H. S., Milanak, M. E., Miller, M. W., Keyes, K. M., & Friedman, M. J. (2013). National estimates of exposure to traumatic events and PTSD prevalence using *DSM-IV* and *DSM-5* criteria. *Journal of Traumatic Stress*, *26*, 537–547. doi:10.1002/jts.21848

Kubany, E. S., & Watson, S. B. (2003). Guilt: Elaboration of a multidimensional model. *Psychological Record*, *53*, 51–90.

Lee, D. A., Scragg, P., & Turner, S. (2001). The role of shame and guilt in traumatic events: A clinical model of shame-based and guilt-based PTSD. *British Journal of Medical Psychology*, *74*, 451–466. doi:10.1348/000711201161109

Marais, A., & Stuart, A. D. (2005). The role of temperament in the development of posttraumatic stress disorder amongst journalists. *South African Journal of Psychology*, *35*, 89–105.

McMahon, C. (2001). Covering disaster: A pilot study into secondary trauma for print media journalists reporting on disaster. *Australian Journal of Emergency Management*, *16*(2), 52–56.

McMahon, C. (2005, September). *Journalists and trauma: The parallel worlds of post-traumatic growth and posttraumatic stress*. Paper presented at the annual The Australian Psychological Conference Society, Melbourne, Australia.

Miller, M. W., Wolf, E. J., & Keane, T. M. (2014). Posttraumatic stress disorder in *DSM-5:* New criteria and controversies. *Clinical Psychology: Science and Practice*, *21*, 208–220. doi:10.1111/cpsp.12070

Muschert, G. W. (2007). Research in school shootings. *Sociology Compass*, *1*, 60–80. doi:10.1111/j.1751–9020.2007.00008.xRB

Newman, E., Shapiro, B., & Nelson, S. (2009). Journalism and media during disasters. In Y. Neria, S. Galea, & F. H. Norris (Eds.), *Mental health and disasters* (pp. 291–301). New York, NY: Cambridge University Press.

Newman, E., Simpson, R., & Handschuh, D. (2003). Trauma exposure and post-traumatic stress disorder among photojournalists. *Visual Communication Quarterly*, *10*, 4–13. doi:10.1080/15551390309363497

Norris, F. H., & Slone, L. B. (2014). The epidemiology of trauma and PTSD. In M. J. Friedman, T. M. Keane, & P. A. Resick (Eds.), *Handbook of PTSD. Science and Practice* (2nd ed.) (pp. 100–120). New York, NY: Guilford Press.

Ozer, E. J., Best, S. R., Lipsey, T. L., & Weiss, D. S. (2003). Predictors of posttraumatic stress disorder and symptoms in adults: A meta-analysis. *Psychological Bulletin*, *129*, 52–73. doi:10.1037/1942–9681.S.1.3

Pyevich, C. M. (2001). *The relationship among cognitive schemata, job-related traumatic exposure, and PTSD in journalists*. (Unpublished doctoral dissertation). University of Tulsa, Tulsa, OK.

Pyevich, C. M., Newman, E., & Daleiden, E. (2003). The relationship among cognitive schemas, job-related traumatic exposure, and posttraumatic stress disorder in journalists. *Journal of Traumatic Stress, 16*, 325–328. doi:10.1023/A:1024405716529

Raittila, P., Koljonen, K., & Väliverronen, J. (2010). *Journalism and school shootings in Finland 2007–2008.* Tampere, Finland: Tampere University Press.

Reardon, A. F., Brief, D. J., Miller, M. W., & Keane, T. M. (2014). Assessment of PTSD and its comorbidities in adults. In M. J. Friedman, T. M. Keane, & P. A. Resick (Eds.), *Handbook of PTSD. Science and practice* (2nd ed.) (pp. 369–390). New York, NY: Guilford Press.

Rutter, M. (2006). Implications of resilience concepts for scientific understanding. *Annals of the New York Academy of Sciences, 1094*, 1–12. doi:10.1196/annals.1376.002

Silverman, C. (Ed.). (2014). *Verification handbook. A definitive guide to verifying digital content for emergency coverage.* Maastricht, Netherlands: European Journalism Centre.

Simpson, R. A., & Boggs, J. G. (1999). An explanatory study of traumatic stress among newspaper journalists. *Journalism and Communication Monographs, 1*, 1–26. doi:10.1177/152263799900100102

Simpson, R., & Coté, W. (2006). *Covering violence: A guide to ethical reporting about victims and trauma.* New York, NY: Columbia University Press.

Smith, R. (2008). Trauma and journalism: Exploring a model of risk and resilience. (Unpublished doctoral dissertation). University of Tulsa, Tulsa, OK.

Smith, R., Newman, E., & Drevo, S. (2015, July 1). *Covering trauma: Impact on journalists.* Retrieved from http://dartcenter.org/content/covering-trauma-impact-on-journalists

Teegen, F., & Grotwinkel, M. (2001). Traumatic exposure and post-traumatic stress disorder of journalists: An internet-based study. *Psychotherapeut, 46*, 169–175.

Thoresen, S. (2007). *Mestring og stress hos innstspersonell og journalister mobilisert til Tsunamikatastrofen [Coping and stress in rescue personnel and journalists involved in the Tsunami disaster].* Oslo, Norway: Nasjonalt kunnskapssenter om vold og traumatisk stress.

Vogt, D. S., King, D. W., & King, L. A. (2014). Risk pathways for PTSD. In M. J. Friedman, T. M. Keane, & P. A. Resick (Eds.), *Handbook of PTSD. Science and practice* (2nd ed.) (pp. 146–165). New York, NY: Guilford Press.

Weidmann, A., Fehm, L., & Fydrich, T. (2008). Covering the tsunami disaster: Subsequent post-traumatic and depressive symptoms and associated social factors. *Stress and Health, 24*, 129–135. doi:10.1002/smi.1168

Weidmann, A., & Papsdorf, J. (2010). Witnessing trauma in the newsroom: Posttraumatic symptoms in television journalists exposed to violent news clips. *Journal of Nervous & Mental Disease, 198*, 264–271. doi:10.1097/NMD.0b013e3181d612bf

Part V

Clinical Interventions
for Impacted Individuals

15
Empirically Based Trauma Therapies

Thea Gallagher, Natalie G. Gay, Anu Asnaani, and Edna B. Foa

Posttraumatic stress disorder (PTSD) is a psychiatric disorder that is associated with significant adverse health and life consequences. Researchers have found PTSD to be the most prevalent *Diagnostic and Statistical Manual of Mental Disorders* (DSM) diagnosis following traumas of mass shootings, terrorist attacks, and large-scale acts of violence (Breslau, 2001; Hughes et al., 2011; North, Smith, & Spitznagel, 1994). North, McCutcheon, Spitznagel, and Smith (2002) conducted a three-year follow-up study examining prevalence rates of psychopathology in survivors of a mass shooting incident in Texas. Consistent with the PTSD literature, they found that rates of PTSD were most prevalent 1 month after the shooting and decreased over time. However, those who did not recover reported increased symptoms over time, emphasizing how crucial it is to provide evidence-based treatments to individuals who do not recover naturally. Fortunately, treatment research from the past three decades has yielded significant advances in the psychotherapeutic and psychopharmacological interventions for PTSD. Specifically, there is compelling evidence that cognitive-behavioral therapies (CBTs) and selective serotonin reuptake inhibitors (SSRIs) are effective in reducing PTSD symptomology, with treatment gains from CBT maintained at follow-ups of a year or more (see Taylor et al., 2003).

Researchers and clinicians determine the value of a given PTSD treatment primarily through the use of randomized control trials (RCTs). RCTs are designed to demonstrate that the observed outcomes of a specific treatment can be attributed to that specific treatment rather than to extraneous variables such as expectancy (Kraemer, 2004). Evidence-based treatments for PTSD include Prolonged Exposure Therapy (PE; Foa, Rothbaum, Riggs, & Murdock, 1991; Foa, Dancu, et al., 1999; Foa et al., 2005), Cognitive Processing Therapy (CPT; Resick & Schnicke, 1993), Eye Movement Desensitization and Reprocessing (EMDR; Rothbaum, Astin, & Marsteller, 2005), and sertraline and paroxetine, both of which are SSRIs (Ahearn,

The Wiley Handbook of the Psychology of Mass Shootings, First Edition. Edited by Laura C. Wilson.
© 2017 John Wiley & Sons, Inc. Published 2017 by John Wiley & Sons, Inc.

Juergens, Cordes, Becker, & Krahn, 2011). While there is a dearth of RCTs specifically focusing on individuals with PTSD from mass shootings, results from a recent meta-analysis indicate that the type of trauma experienced (e.g. combat/terror, childhood sexual abuse, sexual assault, natural disaster) did not affect treatment response to PTSD-specific treatments (Powers, Halpern, Ferenschak, Gillihan, & Foa, 2010).

In this chapter, we will discuss psychosocial treatments first, and then we will describe pharmacological interventions for PTSD. We will start with PE, discussing its theoretical basis, empirical support, and key treatment components. We will do the same for CPT and EMDR. Following the discussion of CBTs for PTSD, we present a case study to illustrate how treatment can be applied to individuals with PTSD from a mass shooting incident, using PE as the sample treatment approach. Lastly, we will briefly discuss the empirical support for SSRIs as a pharmacological treatment approach for PTSD.

Prolonged Exposure Therapy

Theoretical basis

PE is an evidence-based CBT proven to be a reliable and safe intervention for individuals with PTSD (van Minnen, Harned, Zoellner, & Mills, 2012). PE is based on the Emotional Processing Theory (EPT) developed by Foa and Kozak (1985, 1986). This theory suggests that emotions such as fear are encoded in memory in the form of cognitive networks. Fear networks are hypothesized to contain three important types of information: (1) information about the feared stimuli or situation; (2) information about the person's response to the feared stimuli or situation; and (3) information about the meaning of the feared stimuli and the consequent response (Foa & Kozak, 1986).

Foa, Steketee, and Rothbaum (1989) and Foa and Cahill (2001) posited that the fear networks of individuals with PTSD differ from the fear networks of individuals with other anxiety disorders in several key ways. First, the fear network of individuals with PTSD is larger, because it contains a greater number of erroneous or inaccurate connections between stimulus, response, and meaning elements. Second, the network is more easily activated by stimulus, response, or meaning elements. Third, the affective and physiological response elements of the networks are more intense. Accordingly, stimuli reminiscent of the traumatic experience activate the fear network and prompt states of high sympathetic arousal (e.g., increased heart rate and blood pressure, sweating, muscle tension), retrieval of fear-related memories (e.g., intrusive memories, dissociative flashbacks), intense feelings of fear and anxiety, and fear-related behavioral acts (e.g., avoidance or escape behaviors, hypervigilant behaviors).

According to PE, the mechanisms of therapeutic recovery are activation of the fear network and incorporation of disconfirming information (Cahill & Foa, 2007). Persistent avoidance of trauma-related stimuli prevents the activation of the fear structure and the incorporation of information that disconfirms the expected harm. Thus, the principal aim of PE is to facilitate new learning by helping patients confront trauma-related thoughts, memories, feelings, objects, and activities in a safe environment (Foa, Huppert, & Cahill, 2006).

Empirical support

Numerous RCTs comparing PE to a waitlist control group or an active treatment condition, like CPT or EMDR, indicate that PE is effective in reducing PTSD symptoms (see Cahill, Rothbaum, Resick & Follette, 2009). Studies have shown that PE leads to significantly greater pre- to posttreatment reductions in PTSD symptomatology when compared to waitlist (e.g., Foa et al., 1991; Foa, Dancu, et al, 1999; Keane, Fairbank, Caddell, & Zimering, 1989; Resick, Nishith, Weaver, Astin, & Feuer, 2002; Rothbaum et al., 2005), supportive counseling (Bryant, Moulds, Guthrie, Dang, & Nixon, 2003; Schnurr et al., 2007), relaxation (Marks, Lovell, Noshirvani, Livanou, & Thrasher, 1998; Taylor et al., 2003; Vaughan et al., 1994), and treatment as usual (Asukai, Saito, Tsuruta, Ogami, & Kishimoto, 2008; Cooper & Clum, 1989; Nacasch et al., 2011).

Often, individuals with PTSD present with additional psychiatric and physical health problems, and PE has demonstrated efficacy with a number of common comorbid disorders, including alcohol dependence (Foa et al., 2013), borderline personality disorder (Harned, Pantalone, Ward-Ciesielski, Lynch, & Linehan, 2011), depression (Hagenaars, Van Minnen, & Hoogduin, 2010), psychosis (van den Berg et al., 2015), and mild to moderate traumatic brain injury (Sripada et al., 2013). Furthermore, PE often reduces or improves secondary features associated with PTSD, such as depression, guilt, and social functioning (Foa, Dancu, et al., 1999; Keane, Marshall, & Taft, 2006; Rauch et al., 2010).

In summary, there is sufficient evidence from RCTs to justify the widespread, routine use of PE for individuals with PTSD and concurrent depressive and anxiety symptoms. Given the large evidence base for PE, prestigious psychological and governmental institutions have identified PE as a first-line treatment for individuals suffering from PTSD (i.e., American Psychiatric Association [APA], 2004; International Society for Traumatic Stress Studies [ISTSS], see Cahill et al., 2009; Department of Veterans Affairs/Department of Defense [VA/DoD], 2010).

Treatment overview

Typically, PE sessions are 90 minutes in length, and a full course of the treatment lasts 10 to 15 sessions. PE is comprised of three main components, as well as two minor components. The core components of PE are "in vivo" exposure, which refers to real-life interaction with trauma reminders, "imaginal" exposure, which refers to the patient's revisiting of the trauma memory, and processing of imaginal exposure, which is the time where patients reevaluate negative trauma-related cognitions about themselves, others, and the world. The other components of PE include training in controlled breathing and psychoeducation about the nature of trauma reactions and the rationale for exposure therapy (Foa, Hembree, & Rothbaum, 2007).

Detailed treatment approach

Session 1   The first session entails exploration of the effects of the traumatic experience and the subsequent development of PTSD with the patient. In addition, the therapist provides the rationale underlying PE and the processes by which it reduces PTSD symptoms. The therapist explains to the patient that their posttrauma difficulties are maintained primarily by two factors: avoidance of thinking or talking about the trauma and avoidance of situations, people, places, and so forth that are trauma reminders. The therapist explains that avoidance helps by decreasing distress or anxiety in the short run, but it maintains PTSD symptoms in the long run. Specifically, avoidance of thinking about the trauma prevents the individual from processing the traumatic memory, organizing it, and gaining present perspective about it. The second factor that maintains PTSD is unrealistic, negative perceptions about oneself as "entirely incompetent" and the world as "entirely dangerous." These perceptions are further maintained by avoidance, since avoidance does not allow patients to experience any disconfirmation of such negative beliefs.

After discussing the rationale for PE, the therapist conducts an interview to acquire information about trauma history, identify the most distressing trauma memory (which will be the focus of the imaginal exposure), and identify the beginning and end points of the trauma for imaginal exposure. This first session then ends with breathing retraining and assignment of homework.

Session 2   Session 2 begins with a discussion about the common reactions to trauma, which helps to normalize the patient's symptoms and other reactions they have had since the trauma. This is followed by rationale for in vivo exposure and generating a list of situations and objects that the patient avoids because they are related to the trauma. These are ordered in a hierarchy from the least distressing to the most distressing, on a scale ranging from 0 to 100, according to the patient's assessment of the amount of distress they would feel when confronting these avoided situations. This list is used by the patient and the therapist to select the in vivo assignments for homework each week, ensuring that items selected for homework generate at least a moderate level of distress. The patient is instructed to remain in the avoided situation until their distress level decreases by about half.

Session 3   At Session 3, the therapist introduces the rationale for imaginal exposure, followed by the patient's first imaginal exposure in session. Specifically, the patient is asked to recount the traumatic memory that was selected in Session 1 for about 30–45 minutes, repeatedly within this time frame if necessary. The narrative is audiotaped, and homework includes listening to the recording daily. Imaginal exposure is followed by processing this exercise, with the patient and therapist discussing the experience of revisiting the trauma and any feelings or insights that may have emerged during the imaginal exposure.

Sessions 4–5   Sessions 4 and 5 of PE are identical to Session 3 with the exception that the rationale for imaginal exposure is not presented in these sessions.

Sessions 6–9   From Session 6 onward, imaginal exposure is conducted for about 30–45 minutes, followed by a time of processing. During these sessions, however, "hotspots" are targeted, which refer to parts of the trauma that have been identified as the most *currently* distressing parts of the trauma memory for the patient. These "hot spots" are introduced after the client has had a few imaginal sessions where they have experienced habituation to less distressing parts of the memory.

Session 10   At the final session, the therapist has the patient recount the entire memory for about 20–30 minutes, pulling all of the parts of the memory back together. The patient is therefore able to narrate the newly organized memory. When the patient is finished, the therapist provides encouragement to the patient, and also asks the patient to identify the difference between this final retelling as compared to the initial imaginal exposure. The patient is prompted to describe what differences they notice in how they feel now as compared to how they felt after doing it for the first time, accompanied by reviewing what they have learned in the course of PE, what has changed or improved, and what they need to continue to work on in order to maintain their gains.

To summarize, PE for PTSD is an extensively validated and effective treatment. Therapy is goal-oriented, time-limited, and focused on the present. It begins with a thorough assessment of the symptoms of PTSD, and then addresses these symptoms through exposures. In the majority of cases, patients who have completed a course of PE have learned how to better manage their PTSD symptoms, understanding that avoidance leads to continued fear, and therefore facing the trauma and trauma reminders promotes recovery and mastery.

Cognitive Processing Therapy

Theoretical basis

CPT is another evidence-based CBT designed specifically to treat PTSD and comorbid symptoms (Resick & Schnicke, 1992). The underlying theory serving as a basis of CPT, the cognitive trauma theory of PTSD, posits that avoidance and problematic appraisals of the trauma lead to the onset and maintenance of PTSD (Resick & Schnicke, 1993). The authors assert that therapy should target two main "stuck points," or patterns of thinking, that interfere with natural recovery. The first stuck point is assimilation and the second is overaccommodation.

Resick and Schnicke (1993) explain that assimilation occurs when individuals try to make sense of their traumatic experience by incorporating it into previously held beliefs about the self, others, and the world. Overaccommodation occurs when an individual modifies an existing schema inaccurately or by overgeneralizing. In treatment, biased beliefs about the cause or meaning of the event (assimilation) and overgeneralized beliefs about the self, others, or the world (overaccommodation) are directly challenged and modified, leading to a reduction in the emotions (e.g. guilt, anger, shame) that are manufactured by erroneous beliefs. Adaptive reconciliation of the trauma with one's beliefs and cognitions facilitates the reduction of natural emotional reactions (e.g. fear, horror, grief) to the trauma, as well. A principal goal of CPT is to help patients integrate new information with previously existing cognitive schemas in a more context-specific, adaptive way.

Empirical support

While PE has the most evidence to support its efficacy, CPT has also amassed considerable evidence supporting its efficacy in reducing PTSD and related symptoms (e.g., Owens, Pike, & Chard, 2001; Resick, Williams, Suvak, Monson, & Gradus, 2012; Sobel, Resick, & Rabalais, 2009). Preliminary research findings demonstrated that receiving a course of CPT improves PTSD symptoms significantly more than a waitlist control group (Resick & Schnicke, 1992). Later studies report that CPT fairs well compared to active treatment conditions, as well. For example, Resick et al. (2002) compared CPT and PE among female rape victims, and the results of the trial showed no statistical differences between CPT and PE on the primary outcome variables of PTSD and depressive symptoms.

As mentioned previously, PTSD can often co-occur with other diagnoses and mental health symptoms. Fortunately, research studies measuring the effects of CPT on PTSD symptoms in individuals with comorbid diagnoses report that those individuals are still able to improve. Individuals with comorbid depression (Liverant, Suvak, Pineles, & Resick, 2012; Resick et al., 2002), borderline personality features (Clarke, Rizvi, & Resick, 2008), traumatic brain injury (TBI; Chard, Schumm, McIlvain, Bailey, & Parkinson, 2011), and alcohol use disorder (Kaysen et al., 2014) show equivalent gains in CPT compared to those without comorbid disorders. Moreover, CPT has demonstrated efficacy in reducing symptoms of depression, guilt, generalized anxiety, and social adjustment (Monson et al., 2006; Resick et al., 2008), and has been associated with improvements in physical health (Galovski, Monson, Bruce, & Resick, 2009).

Since the hallmark component of CPT is cognitive restructuring, Rizvi, Vogt, and Resick (2009) investigated cognition (i.e., level of education, intelligence, age) and mood state (i.e., anger, guilt, depression) factors that are associated with PTSD and their impact on treatment outcome. These variables were hypothesized to affect the ability to adopt new ways of thinking, with the premise that negative mood states may interfere with the processing of traumatic memories. The study demonstrated that level of education, intelligence, and age did not affect treatment efficacy for the entire sample. While these cognitive factors did not affect an individual's ability to improve, several factors (i.e., younger age, lower intelligence, higher trait anger) were related to treatment drop-out. Perhaps counterintuitively, individuals with higher baseline depression and guilt reported more improvement in PTSD symptomatology at posttreatment, and there were no significant effects of anger on posttreatment outcomes. These findings support the conclusion that individuals with various cognitive abilities and mood states can participate in cognitive restructuring and reap the benefits of CPT.

As an important note about the current protocol for CPT, Resick et al. (2008) conducted an RCT dismantling the components of CPT. The results of the study indicated that a CPT protocol with cognitive restructuring and without exposure is as effective as the full CPT protocol that includes an exposure component. Thus, the new version of the CPT protocol omits the impact statement and focuses on cognitive restructuring. The new protocol is referred to as CPT-C and is being more widely tested, but the majority of treatment efficacy findings for CPT use the original protocol.

As with PE, CPT has garnered significant evidence for its efficacy and, therefore, is regarded as a gold-standard treatment for PTSD. CPT, like PE, is endorsed by APA (2004), ISTSS (Cahill et al., 2009), and VA/DoD (2010).

Treatment overview

A full course of CPT can be done individually with a therapist or in a group setting. Individual CPT consists of 12 therapy sessions that last 50–60 minutes. Group-delivered CPT consists of the same number of sessions; however, each session lasts 90 minutes. The first session consists of psychoeducation, which informs the patient of common reactions to trauma and teaches the patient about therapy. In the second session, the patient writes their impact statement. The impact statement is the patient's interpretation of the traumatic event (which serves as an exposure) and is used later in therapy to identify "stuck points" (i.e., distorted beliefs and problematic cognitions). Throughout the subsequent sessions of treatment, the therapist works with the client to challenge their maladaptive self-statements and to modify their extreme beliefs. Examples of common cognitive distortions include concern around the meaning of the trauma (e.g., "I must have deserved this because bad things don't happen to good people"), the meaning of symptoms resulting from the experience (e.g., "If I were stronger then I would be able to get over this"), the perceived negative reactions of other people (e.g., "People will judge my decisions and think that this is my fault"), and beliefs about future vulnerability to negative events (e.g., "The world is unsafe"; Iverson, King, Cunningham, & Resick, 2015).

The therapist facilitates recovery in session, and also assigns worksheets for homework that reinforce what is being learned in therapy. To measure changes in maladaptive thoughts occurring in the context of PTSD, several commonly used tools are administered at multiple points throughout CPT, including the Trauma and Attachment Belief Scale (TABS; Pearlman, 2003), the Posttraumatic Cognitions Inventory (PTCI; Foa, Ehlers, Clarke, Tolin, & Orsillo, 1999), and the World Assumption Scale (WAS; Janoff-Bulman, 1989). Cognitive distortions are thought to increase and maintain PTSD symptoms largely by increasing avoidance behavior (Dunmore, Clark, & Ehlers, 1999; Ehlers & Clark, 2000; Foa, Ehlers, et al., 1999) and, therefore, CPT is designed to explore and correct maladaptive beliefs resulting as a consequence of the trauma.

Detailed treatment approach

Below is an outline of the CPT treatment manual as is currently used in VA hospitals (Resick, Monson, & Chard, 2014).

Session 1   In Session 1, the therapist works to build rapport with the patient while also educating him/her about the symptoms of PTSD and depression. The therapist should make an effort during this session to normalize any perceived anxiety on the part of the patient. The therapist provides a rationale for the treatment based on the cognitive conceptualization of PTSD. Any questions the patient might have during this session should be answered and the patient should be assured of the robust nature of the treatment. Another goal of Session 1 is to lay out the course of treatment. The therapist spends time discussing treatment compliance with the patient, and should assess the patient's level of motivation and willingness to engage in the treatment. At the end of the session the patient is asked to write, before the next session, one page on why they thought this traumatic event occurred (i.e., impact statement) as well as read the handout on "stuck points." In addition, the therapist asks the patient to offer any feedback or reactions to the session. Any apprehension and/or concerns should be normalized and the patient should be praised for their bravery of taking this step towards recovery.

Session 2   In Session 2, the therapist asks the patient to read their impact statement. The patient and therapist discuss the identified stuck points, which might focus on topics like self-blame and shame. The therapist reviews the patient's

PTSD symptoms and reiterates the theory behind CPT. A-B-C worksheets, which focus on the interaction between thoughts, emotions, and behaviors, are introduced. The homework assigned is the completion of one A-B-C worksheet a day, with one involving the worst trauma.

Session 3 In Session 3, the A-B-C homework is reviewed and stuck points discussed, with some focus placed on assimilation. The event is reviewed in session, and the patient is assisted in labeling thoughts and emotions connected to the events. The therapist begins to use Socratic questioning to help the patient begin to look more closely at the accuracy of their beliefs about the trauma, especially as connected to topics such as self-blame and guilt. The therapist asks questions such as "what do you mean when you say you're to blame?," "what would you say to your best friend if they were in your shoes?," and "what would it mean if you gave up that belief?" The patient is asked to complete another A-B-C worksheet, and the homework of writing the trauma account is assigned.

Session 4 During the next session, the therapist asks the patient to read their trauma account out loud with emotional expression. The therapist identifies certain stuck points as the patient reads aloud, and utilizes more Socratic questions to help the patient challenge their self-blame. The therapist asks the patient questions and makes statements like, "help me understand how a provocative outfit means that you were asking to be raped." The therapist talks with the patient about the difference between responsibility and blame, which is where the patient may have trouble differentiating. The patient should begin to understand that they were not completely to blame, but they might be struggling to shake the feeling that they were responsible for this. At the end of the session, the patient is instructed to rewrite their trauma memory, and is encouraged to read it daily along with completing the A-B-C sheets daily.

Session 5 In this session, the patient is asked by the therapist to read the newest trauma account aloud and identify differences between the first and second account. The patient is asked more Socratic questions to continue to challenge the self-blame/guilt that they might continue to endorse. The therapist continues cognitive therapy on stuck points for the trauma event. The Challenging Questions worksheet, which helps the patient challenge maladaptive and problematic beliefs, is introduced at the end of this session and it is explained so that the patient can complete it for homework. The patient is asked to challenge one stuck point daily using the worksheet. The patient is also instructed to continue to read the trauma account daily.

Session 6 In this session, the therapist reviews the Challenging Questions worksheet that the patient has completed for homework. The therapist continues with cognitive strategies to help the patient to challenge stuck points. The therapist introduces the Patterns of Problematic Thinking worksheet and this is explained and assigned for homework. The goal of this worksheet is to have the patient identify problematic thinking patterns. It is assigned to help the patient shift to utilizing Socratic questioning themselves, and should help them to be more supportive of themselves. The trauma account is only reread if the account needed to be reassigned and if it is clinically relevant to read it in session.

Session 7   During this session, the patient and therapist review the Patterns of Problematic Thinking worksheet, and the Challenging Beliefs worksheet with a trauma example is introduced. The Safety Module is also introduced, which helps the patient to discuss safety beliefs that were disrupted or confirmed by the trauma. The patient should be able to see how the trauma influenced his/her beliefs about safety, trust, power/control, esteem, and intimacy, which ultimately influenced his/her behaviors/avoidance. The Challenging Beliefs worksheet helps to challenge these safety beliefs. The homework assigned is to identify stuck points daily, including a safety stuck point with the Challenging Beliefs worksheet. The Safety Module is assigned for reading. The patient should continue reading the trauma accounts if they still have strong emotions about them.

Session 8   During this session, the patient and therapist review the Challenging Beliefs worksheet and the Trust Module is introduced. Stuck points to self-trust and other-trust are explored, as these are both places where a patient might feel unresolved and distressed. For homework, the patient is encouraged to use the Challenging Beliefs worksheet for these trust stuck points. The patient is asked to continue to read the trauma if there is still distress associated with the recounting of the trauma memory.

Session 9   In this session, the Challenging Beliefs worksheet for trauma-related-stuck points is reviewed and the therapist works to generate alternative beliefs with the patient. The module on Power/Control is introduced and these beliefs are explored as related to self and others. The patient continues to practice challenging beliefs with the Challenging Beliefs worksheet.

Session 10   During this session, the therapist helps the patient to gain a balanced view of power/control using the Challenging Beliefs worksheet. Anger issues are also addressed at this session. The module on Esteem is introduced and the assignment for receiving compliments and engaging in pleasurable activities is assigned. The patient is also instructed to challenge stuck points daily, with one relating to esteem issues using the Challenging Beliefs worksheet.

Session 11   Homework reviewed in this session focuses on discussing the patient's reactions to behavioral assignments, such as giving and receiving compliments and engaging in pleasurable activities. The patient and therapist discuss how it was for the patient to accept compliments and to do things that make him/her happy. The therapist helps the patient to identify and challenge esteem issues and assumptions. The Intimacy module is introduced and the patient is encouraged to identify stuck points, with one that relates to intimacy issues, and confront them using the Challenging Beliefs worksheet. The patient is also asked to write a final impact statement about what it means that they were raped.

Session 12 During this session, the therapist helps the patient identify and challenge any intimacy issues/assumptions, and any remaining stuck points. The patient is asked to read their final impact statement. The therapist reads the original impact statement and differences are compared. The patient should be able to see that their perception of the trauma has completely changed. The therapist involves the patient in reviewing the course of treatment and patient progress. The therapist encourages the patient to continue with behavioral assignments and continue to use the skills they have learned moving forward.

CPT helps patients to process distressing thoughts and memories through cognitive restructuring and helps patients to gain a greater understanding of their traumatic events. By utilizing the skills acquired in this therapy, patients learn where they have become "stuck" in their processing of traumatic events. CPT helps individuals with PTSD to see how the experience of their trauma has changed the way they interpret the world, themselves, and others. Ultimately, the goal is for patients to be able to make new meaning of their traumatic memories, and move forward in their lives with new insight.

Eye Movement Desensitization and Reprocessing

Theoretical basis

EMDR was developed as a short-term, efficacious treatment designed for individuals who are symptomatic following a traumatic experience (Shapiro, 1995, 1996). The original paradigm explaining this therapeutic approach has been revised, and EMDR is now guided by the adaptive information processing (AIP) model, which theorizes how the brain intrinsically processes information and stores memories (Solomon & Shapiro, 2008). AIP posits that there is a physiological information-processing system in place to process new information and organize and store that new information into preexisting memory networks containing related thoughts, images, and emotions (Shapiro & Maxfield, 2002). According to AIP, traumatic memories left insufficiently processed become the basis of distorted thoughts and maladaptive behaviors and reactions

(Shapiro, 2007). In an explanation of the theory and therapeutic components of EMDR, Shapiro and Forrest (2001) assert that the primary goal of EMDR is to facilitate processing of the trauma memory with the underlying hypothesis that processing will facilitate corrections in distorted thoughts and maladaptive behaviors. One of this therapy's distinguishing characteristics is its use of bilateral physical stimulation, such as side-to-side eye movements, alternating hand taps, or alternating auditory tones while the person undergoing treatment is mentally focusing on aspects of various life experiences.

During EMDR, the therapist guides the client through 30-second, dual-stimulation exercises using bilateral eye movements, tones, or taps while the client focuses on the target disturbing experience and then on any related negative thoughts, associations, and body sensations. The AIP model suggests that these dual-attention exercises disrupt the client's stored memory of the trauma to facilitate an elimination of negative beliefs, emotions, and somatic symptoms associated with the memory as it connects with more adaptive information stored in the memory network. Although it would be oversimplistic to assume that one mechanism of action is responsible for EMDR effects, Cahill, Carrigan, and Frueh (1999) state that there is little evidence that eye movements have any impact on standardized, psychometric or physiological outcome measures.

Empirical support

Empirical evidence supports findings of treatment gains in EMDR relative to no treatment control conditions for individuals with PTSD, depressive, and anxiety symptoms (Bisson & Andrew, 2005; Carlson, Chemtob, Rusnak, Hedlund, & Muraoka, 1998; Rothbaum, 1997). However, while several RCTs have found comparable gains in EMDR compared to an active treatment condition (e.g., Devilly & Spence, 1999; Rothbaum et al., 2005; Taylor et al., 2003), it is important to interpret the findings carefully and cautiously. Noted by Bisson and Andrew (2005), a portion of the empirical evidence in support of EMDR does not meet the standards set forth by Foa and Meadows (1997) in which researchers and clinicians should evaluate the methodology of PTSD treatment studies. In a recent meta-analysis, it was mentioned that a large proportion of support comes from studies where the sample size is small, the fidelity for the comparison treatment condition is less stringent than the fidelity of the EMDR condition, and the protocol, specifically the number of EMDR sessions in a full course of treatment, varies (Bisson & Andrew, 2005).

Nevertheless, there is evidence that EMDR is as effective in reducing PTSD symptoms as several active treatment conditions, such as the combination of stress inoculation training and PE (Lee, Gavriel, Drummond, Richards, & Greenwald, 2002) and the combination of exposure and cognitive restructuring (Power et al., 2002). Evidence suggests that EMDR improves secondary symptoms of trauma, such as depression, dissociative symptoms, and state anxiety (Rothbaum et al., 2005).

As with PE and CPT, EMDR has sufficient evidence to be supported by APA (2004), ISTSS (Cahill et al., 2009), and VA/DoD (2010).

Treatment overview

There are eight phases of EMDR, with Phases 3 through 8 repeated in most sessions. During the first phase, which can last one or two sessions, the therapist collects the patient's trauma history and a treatment plan is developed. The treatment plan includes the specific targets on which to use EMDR (e.g. past and present sources of distress, skills training). Phase 2, lasting between one and four sessions, aims to build the relationship between the therapist and client, set treatment goals and expectations, and familiarize or educate the patient on their symptoms. This phase marks the beginning of skill-based training where patients learn skills that will help them with emotion regulation, impulse control, and general functioning. Phases 3 through 8 involve invoking, processing, and reevaluating the distressing traumatic event(s). EMDR sessions usually range from 50 to 90 minutes in length and a full course of EMDR can be completed in a few sessions or over a period of months based on the individual patient's needs and presenting traumas (Shapiro, 2001).

The eight stages of EMDR as described by Shapiro (2001, 2002) are explained below.

Phase 1 In the first phase of treatment, the therapist takes a full history, which includes gathering information about the patient's trauma, and discusses treatment planning with the patient. The therapist also spends time evaluating the patient's readiness for EMDR. The therapist chooses appropriate trauma memories as the foci (i.e., "targets") for treatment, such as disturbing memories, related historical events, current scenarios that cause distress, and imaginal structures for positive actions in the future. The EMDR treatment plan addresses both the trauma-specific memories and present reminders of the event. These are extrapolated upon in this phase of treatment.

Phase 2 In the second phase of treatment, which is a preparation or stabilization phase, the therapist and the patient work on building rapport, and the therapist provides a rationale for EMDR. The focus is placed on helping the patient build on and utilize personal resources, such as safety, affect management, and self-control before they can address the traumatic memory.

Phase 3 In this phase, the patient begins to process the traumatic memory with a structured clinician-directed assessment of the sensory, cognitive, and affective components connected to the incident. The patient is asked to identify a distressing memory related to the trauma, identify an irrational negative belief associated with this memory, choose a desired positive belief, and rate the validity of the positive thought when paired with the trauma memory using a 7-point Validity of Cognition (VOC) scale, where 1 "feels completely false" and 7 "feels completely true." The patient then is asked to combine the image associated with the traumatic memory with the negative belief and rate their Subjective Unit of Disturbance (SUD) level using a 10-point scale, as well as identify any physical sensations related to the trauma along with their bodily location (e.g., racing heart). After this, the patient might identify the emotions of fear and confusion. The intensity of these emotions as well as other emotions experienced during the reactivation of the trauma memory would be assessed using SUD ratings.

Phase 4   During this stage of treatment, the patient is asked to think of the trauma image, the negative belief, and the bodily reactions associated with the trauma memory. The therapist moves their fingers from side to side, approximately 12 inches in front of the patient's face, while the patient tracks the fingers with their eyes for 15 or more seconds. The therapist can also use auditory tones or hand claps in lieu of eye movements. After the set of eye movements, the therapist stops and asks the patient to let go of the memory, inhale deeply, and asks, "what do you get now?" Following each set of eye movements, the therapist guides the patient as to what to attend to next, which is generally the new material (e.g., image, thought, sensation, emotion). The goal is to support cognitive and/or emotional change. If the patient seems blocked, the therapist may need to intervene with the patient more.

Phase 5   After the patient identifies a SUD rating reduction as far as possible toward zero (i.e., no distress), the positive cognition from Phase 4 is again measured using the VOC scale. The patient is directed to think of the target image while silently rehearsing the positive cognition. Another set of eye movements is conducted, followed by another assessment of the validity of the positive thought. The cycle is repeated until the VOC level climbs as far as possible towards 7 (completely valid).

Phase 6   In this phase, the patient is asked to label any signs of body discomfort or tension while focusing on the negative image and the positive belief. If the patient endorses the aforementioned, this is taken as a sign that the trauma processing is incomplete. Any negative sensations are targeted for processing until the tension dissipates.

Phase 7   This stage focuses on assessing whether the memory has been processed fully and, if not, relaxation or visualization can be used to help a patient reach closure if they are still feeling activated by the memory. The patient is asked to keep a journal of feelings, thoughts, and dreams in between sessions along with applying the coping skills learned.

Phase 8 Phase 8 is defined by reevaluation, where each session that follows the initial session incorporates an assessment of whether the treatment goals have been attained and maintained. Novel trauma-related material that emerges during the course of treatment may be discussed. Sessions are scheduled as needed to help the patient to continue to focus on trauma memories, current triggers, and coping skill acquisition and consolidation.

EMDR utilizes various elements of many effective therapies to maximize the effect of treatment. EMDR integrates these different psychotherapies into a standardized set of procedures and clinical protocols that have been found to be effective for the treatment of PTSD. The treatment focuses on processing historical events, current incidents that cause distress, and future experiences that will require different responses from the patient. EMDR can be effectively used to treat a range of complaints that accompany distressing life events.

Detailed Case Example

In order to more fully exemplify the application of an empirically supported treatment for PTSD, a detailed case example is provided below. PE is chosen as the sample treatment approach, with discussion around how this treatment was used to address PTSD symptoms in a woman who had witnessed a mass shooting at a grade school.

Ms. A is a 27-year-old Caucasian woman who was a teacher at a school during a school shooting. She lived alone at the time of the shooting but after the shooting, she developed PTSD symptoms subsequently leading to most of her nights being spent at her parents' house.

Ms. A's trauma involved hearing gunshots fired in her school, followed by screams of children. During the shooting, she instructed her third-grade students to follow the protocol set in place for a school shooting, and her classroom was not entered by the assailant. After she was told that it was safe to leave the classroom, she took her students out of the building. During the entire event, Ms. A was able to stay calm and ultimately lead her students to safety. She didn't incur any physical injuries as a result of this event. After the shooting, the school was closed for a couple of weeks, and before school sessions resumed, she noticed an increase in anxiety and fear when she realized that she would have to go back to teach. The first day that school resumed, she felt extremely anxious while driving to school and was unable to get out of her car to enter the building. She is presently on a leave of absence from her teaching position, as she was not able to enter the school building. The catalyst for seeking treatment was the fear that she might not be able to teach again.

Ms. A has been feeling more depressed and isolated for the past 3 months, as those are the months that she has not been able to teach, and she has been finding that she is spending more time alone in her room at her parent's house, and not spending much time with friends or colleagues. She has noticed that she is becoming increasingly avoidant of crowds, being alone in her apartment, the school itself, movies or news that references school shootings and any Facebook posts about the event or from other teachers she used to work with. Ms. A stated that her fears had continued to increase since the shooting, and her domains of avoidance were also extending to crowded places or any reminders of that day. She was experiencing frequent intrusive thoughts about the details of the shooting, and the noises she heard, and was experiencing intense emotional distress when reminded of it. Ms. A was also avoiding any thoughts or situations that triggered the memories of the shooting, and she was continuing to experience flashbacks from that day. She also reported having nightmares of the event, accompanied by significant sleep disturbance.

Ms. A had no prior trauma history, and she had no prior psychiatric history or treatment history. She denied any prior or present alcohol or drug abuse at the time of her initial evaluation. She decided to seek help after 3 months of avoidance of school and school-related reminders. The initial evaluation found that Ms. A had moderately severe PTSD, and met criteria for no other diagnoses.

In formulating the treatment plan for Ms. A, the therapist took into account the index trauma (i.e., the school shooting) and helping Ms. A to return to her life as a teacher, which she was completely avoiding. Therefore, imaginal exposure focused on the shooting, where the beginning of the imaginal exposure was hearing the children's screams, followed by shots fired, and ended with exiting the building. Her in vivo exposure hierarchy included items such as going to crowded places, sleeping at home alone, and progressed to looking at pictures of the school, visiting the school, and reading news articles about the shooting.

During the imaginal processing, it became apparent that Ms. A had felt helpless during the shooting. She had always been able to solve the problems that arose in her life, and she was considered by many to be competent in many areas. She had won "teacher of the year" awards in the past, and felt a great sense of responsibility towards her students. She commented several times, "I really thought we were all going to die, and I thought he was going to kill my students." She also felt guilt and shame at the fact that she did not die, or incur any injuries, while other teachers had. She stated that she blamed herself for not being able to recover from this event, and she expressed anger and frustration towards herself and her inability to "get over it and get back in the classroom."

Ms. A displayed appropriate emotional engagement with the trauma memory during her imaginal exposures. She initially reported high distress (SUDS) levels, and showed progressive habituation of distress between and during sessions. Her affect was congruent with her self-report levels. She engaged in productive processing in the latter part of sessions where she would verbalize feelings of guilt, shame, fear, and responsibility. She was able to wrestle with these themes, and came to new realizations such as "I did the best I could, considering the circumstances." During her sessions she also came to realizations such as "bad things happen sometimes that you can't control" and "it is hard for me to understand how some people can want to hurt other people." The patient began to accept that the shooting was a tragic event that was out of her control, and that she did the best she could to deal with it in the moment. She also came to realize that the world can be sometimes dangerous, but it is not always. There was quite a significant shift during treatment in her negative views of herself, the future, and the world, a view that began in response to the shooting.

Ms. A was highly motivated, worked hard in her therapy, was compliant with homework assignments, and practiced the skills she learned in treatment in between sessions. The treatment produced a significant reduction in Ms. A's PTSD symptoms, and she began to engage in her activities of daily living as she had been able to before the trauma. By the end of treatment, she had plans to begin teaching again in a few weeks after the summer was over. Assessments were conducted before, during, and after treatment, up to a year following therapy. Ms. A's PTSD severity decreased by 80% from pre- to post-treatment, and a year after treatment the severity had declined by 90%. She continued to maintain her treatment gains. Two years after treatment, her therapist received an email from her, informing her she had started an annual race/fundraiser in honor of the victims of the shooting. She indicated that this was a sign to her that she had successfully moved forward in her life in spite of such a tragedy.

Selective Serotonin Reuptake Inhibitors

Evidence from multisite RCTs has established support for pharmacotherapy as another first-line treatment for PTSD. Specifically, the U.S. Food and Drug Administration (FDA) approved sertraline and paroxetine as pharmacological treatments of choice for PTSD (Friedman & Davidson, 2014). Both sertraline (brand name: Zoloft) and paroxetine (brand names: Pexeva, Paxil) are SSRIs that work by increasing the neurotransmitter serotonin in the synaptic cleft (therefore increasing brain activity stimulated by serotonergic stimulation) by inhibiting its reuptake. Data on several important RCTs are summarized below.

RCTs have demonstrated that SSRIs are safe, well-tolerated, and effective treatments for PTSD in contrast to placebo and can produce remission in 30% of study participants (e.g., Brady et al., 2000; Davidson, Rothbaum, van der Kolk, Sikes, & Farfel, 2001; Londborg et al., 2001; Marshall, Beebe, Oldham, & Zaninelli, 2001; Tucker & Trautman, 2000). SSRIs meet four independent clinical practice guidelines: (1) reduce reexperiencing, avoidant, and arousal symptoms; (2) produce clinical global improvement; (3) are effective treatments for comorbid disorders, such as depression and panic; and (4) reduce associated symptoms like irritability and impulsivity (Friedman & Davidson, 2014). Additionally, Londborg et al. (2001) conducted an open-label study that showed remission rates increased from 30 to 55% when sertraline treatment was extended from 12 to 36 weeks. This implies that some nonresponders to acute treatment will respond to continued treatment. Unfortunately, discontinuation of sertraline and fluoxetine (but not paroxetine) was associated with a relapse of PTSD symptoms after several months of treatment discontinuation (Davidson, Pearlstein, et al., 2001; Davidson et al., 2005; Martenyi, Brown, Zhang, Prakash, & Koke, 2002; Rapaport, Endicott, & Clary, 2002). Since these early studies, there have been further RCTs with SSRIs. Based on several reviews, paroxetine, sertraline, and fluoxetine produce statistically significant improvements in PTSD symptoms compared to placebo (Friedman, Davidson, & Stein, 2009; Stein & Ipser, 2011; Stein, Ipser, & Seedat, 2006; Youngner, Rothbaum, & Friedman, 2014).

In spite of this empirical support, however, a number of studies have failed to show any difference compared to placebo (e.g., Brady et al., 2005; Davidson et al., 2006; Friedman, Marmar, Baker, Sikes, & Farfel, 2007; Martenyi, Brown, & Caldwell, 2007; Shalev et al., 2012; Tucker et al., 2001). This inconsistency is perhaps due to the heterogeneity of PTSD, as well as the presence of a clinically significant response to placebo. Furthermore, while four of six clinical practice organizations for PTSD (i.e., APA, 2004; Australian Centre for Posttraumatic Mental Health, 2013; ISTSS, see Cahill et al., 2009; VA/DoD, 2010) recommend SSRIs as first-line monotherapy for PTSD, there are two regulating bodies that do not recommend SSRIs. The first is the Institute of Medicine (IOM; 2012), which excluded a number of studies considered by other organizations because of more stringent criteria regarding methodology and data-analytic strategies. The other organization is the United Kingdom's National Institute for Health and Clinical Excellence (NICE; 2005), which included unpublished studies and did not consider results with an effect size under 0.5 as a positive trial.

To better understand how SSRI monotherapy can be used to treat PTSD, a few small studies have tested whether adjunctive pharmacotherapy might benefit CBT partial responders. Simon and colleagues (2008) randomized PE partial responders (after eight sessions) to PE continuation with and without paroxetine (vs. placebo) augmentation. There was no benefit to the addition of

SSRI treatment. However, two small studies suggest that the reverse design is effective, with partial responders to sertraline showing significant improvement when SSRI treatment was augmented with PE (Otto et al., 2003; Rothbaum et al., 2006).

Unfortunately, there have been no new FDA-approved medications for over 10 years, especially ones designed to target the specific pathophysiology of PTSD. Since large-scale pharmacology trials are expensive, researchers and pharmaceutical companies need to work in conjunction to advance research in a more economical fashion. If the mechanisms of change of existing medications can be better understood, and if a specific medication aimed at correcting the pathophysiological abnormalities associated with PTSD is developed, then, perhaps, psychopharmacology can be a more effective and equivalent first-line option for treatment of PTSD as compared to the efficacious psychotherapies described previously.

Conclusion

PE, CPT, and EMDR have been found to be effective in targeting and reducing symptoms in patients who have been diagnosed with PTSD. These three empirically supported psychosocial treatments have also been found to effectively improve overall functioning in PTSD patients and to help patients maintain treatment gains over time. While SSRIs can be helpful, the effects of the medication have not been shown to last after discontinuation. The evidence-based therapies reviewed in this chapter are recommended for the treatment of individuals with PTSD to improve their functioning and reduce disability associated with the disorder. Victims of mass shootings are at greater risk of suffering from PTSD, and having such evidence-based treatments for providers to implement with these patients is important for effective clinical practice.

References

Ahearn, E. P., Juergens, T., Cordes, T., Becker, T., & Krahn, D. (2011). A review of atypical antipsychotic medications for posttraumatic stress disorder. *International Clinical Psychopharmacology*, *26*(4), 193–200.

American Psychiatric Association. (2004). Practice guideline for the treatment of patients with acute stress disorder and posttraumatic stress disorder. *American Journal of Psychiatry*, *161*(Suppl 11), 1–31.

Asukai, N., Saito, A., Tsuruta, N., Ogami, R., & Kishimoto, J. (2008). Pilot study on prolonged exposure of Japanese patients with posttraumatic stress disorder due to mixed traumatic events. *Journal of Traumatic Stress*, *21*(3), 340–343.

Australian Centre for Posttraumatic Mental Health. (2013). *Australian guidelines for the treatment of acute stress disorder & posttraumatic stress disorder*. Melbourne,

Victoria: Australian Government National Health and Medical Research Council. Retrieved from http://phoenixaustralia.org/wp-content/uploads/2015/03/Phoenix-ASD-PTSD-Guidelines.pdf

Bisson, J., & Andrew, M. (2005). Psychological treatment of post-traumatic stress disorder (PTSD) (Review). *The Cochrane Library, 3*(1).

Brady, K., Pearlstein, T., Asnis, G. M., Baker, D., Rothbaum, B., Sikes, C. R., & Farfel, G. M. (2000). Efficacy and safety of sertraline treatment of posttraumatic stress disorder: A randomized controlled trial. *Journal of the American Medical Association, 283*(14), 1837–1844.

Brady, K. T., Sonne, S., Anton, R. F., Randall, C. L., Back, S. E., & Simpson, K. (2005). Sertraline in the treatment of co-occurring alcohol dependence and posttraumatic stress disorder. *Alcoholism: Clinical and Experimental Research, 29*(3), 395–401.

Breslau, N. (2001). The epidemiology of posttraumatic stress disorder: What is the extent of the problem? *Journal of Clinical Psychiatry, 62*, 16–22.

Bryant, R. A., Moulds, M. L., Guthrie, R. M., Dang, S. T., & Nixon, R. D. (2003). Imaginal exposure alone and imaginal exposure with cognitive restructuring in treatment of posttraumatic stress disorder. *Journal of Consulting and Clinical Psychology, 71*(4), 706–712.

Cahill, S. P., Carrigan, M. H., & Frueh, B. C. (1999). Does EMDR work? And if so, why? A critical review of controlled outcome and dismantling research. *Journal of Anxiety Disorders, 13*(1), 5–33.

Cahill, S. P., & Foa, E. B. (2007). Psychological theories of PTSD. In M. J. Friedman, T. M. Keane, & Resick, P. A. (Eds.), *Handbook of PTSD: Science and practice* (2nd ed., pp. 55–77). New York, NY: Guildford Press.

Cahill, S., Rothbaum, B. O., Resick, P. A., & Follette, V. M. (2009). Cognitive-behavioural therapy for adults. In E. Foa, T. Keane, M. Friedman, & J. Cohen (Eds.), *Effective treatments for PTSD: Practice guidelines from the International Society for Traumatic Stress Studies* (pp. 139–223). New York, NY: Guilford Press.

Carlson, J. G., Chemtob, C. M., Rusnak, K., Hedlund, N. L., & Muraoka, M. Y. (1998). Eye movement desensitization and reprocessing (EDMR) treatment for combat-related posttraumatic stress disorder. *Journal of Traumatic Stress, 11*(1), 3–24.

Chard, K. M., Schumm, J. A., McIlvain, S. M., Bailey, G. W., & Parkinson, R. B. (2011). Exploring the efficacy of a residential treatment program incorporating cognitive processing therapy-cognitive for veterans with PTSD and traumatic brain injury. *Journal of Traumatic Stress, 24*(3), 347–351.

Clarke, S. B., Rizvi, S. L., & Resick, P. A. (2008). Borderline personality characteristics and treatment outcome in cognitive-behavioral treatments for PTSD in female rape victims. *Behavior Therapy, 39*(1), 72–78.

Cooper, N. A., & Clum, G. A. (1989). Imaginal flooding as a supplementary treatment for PTSD in combat veterans: A controlled study. *Behavior Therapy, 20*(3), 381–391.

Davidson, J. R., Payne, V. M., Connor, K. M., Foa, E. B., Rothbaum, B. O., Hertzberg, M. A., & Weisler, R. H. (2005). Trauma, resilience and saliostasis: Effects of treatment in post-traumatic stress disorder. *International Clinical Psycho-pharmacology, 20*(1), 43–48.

Davidson, J., Pearlstein, T., Londborg, P., Brady, K. T., Rothbaum, B., Bell, J., ... Farfel, G. (2001). Efficacy of sertraline in preventing relapse of posttraumatic stress disorder: Results of a 28-week double-blind, placebo-controlled study. *American Journal of Psychiatry, 158*(12), 273–281.

Davidson, J., Rothbaum, B. O., Tucker, P., Asnis, G., Benattia, I., & Musgnung, J. J. (2006). Venlafaxine extended release in posttraumatic stress disorder: A sertraline- and placebo-controlled study. *Journal of Clinical Psychopharmacology, 26*(3), 259–267.

Davidson, J. R., Rothbaum, B. O., van der Kolk, B. A., Sikes, C. R., & Farfel, G. M. (2001). Multicenter, double-blind comparison of sertraline and placebo in the treatment of posttraumatic stress disorder. *Archives of General Psychiatry, 58*(5), 485–492.

Department of Veterans Affairs/Department of Defense. (2010). VA/DoD clinical practice guideline for the management of post-traumatic stress. Retrieved from http://www.healthquality.va.gov/guidelines/MH/ptsd/cpg_PTSD-FULL-201011612.pdf

Devilly, G. J., & Spence, S. H. (1999). The relative efficacy and treatment distress of EMDR and a cognitive-behavior trauma treatment protocol in the amelioration of posttraumatic stress disorder. *Journal of Anxiety Disorders, 13*(1), 131–157.

Dunmore, E., Clark, D. M., & Ehlers, A. (1999). Cognitive factors involved in the onset and maintenance of posttraumatic stress disorder (PTSD) after physical or sexual assault. *Behaviour Research and Therapy, 37*(9), 809–829.

Ehlers, A., & Clark, D. M. (2000). A cognitive model of posttraumatic stress disorder. *Behaviour Research and Therapy, 38*(4), 319–345.

Foa, E. B., & Cahill, S. P. (2001). Psychological therapies: Emotional processing. In N. Smelser & P. B. Bates (Eds.), *International encyclopedia of social and behavioral sciences*. Oxford, UK: Elsevier.

Foa, E. B., Dancu, C. V., Hembree, E. A., Jaycox, L. H., Meadows, E. A., & Street, G. P. (1999). A comparison of exposure therapy, stress inoculation training, and their combination for reducing posttraumatic stress disorder in female assault victims. *Journal of Consulting and Clinical Psychology, 67*(2), 194–200.

Foa, E. B., Ehlers, A., Clark, D. M., Tolin, D. F., & Orsillo, S. M. (1999). The Posttraumatic Cognitions Inventory (PTCI): Development and validation. *Psychological Assessment, 11*(3), 303–314.

Foa, E. B., Hembree, E. A., Cahill, S. P., Rauch, S. A., Riggs, D. S., Feeny, N. C., & Yadin, E. (2005). Randomized trial of prolonged exposure for posttraumatic stress disorder with and without cognitive restructuring: Outcome at academic and community clinics. *Journal of Consulting and Clinical Psychology, 73*(5), 953–964.

Foa, E., Hembree, E., & Rothbaum, B. (2007). *Prolonged exposure therapy for PTSD: Emotional processing of traumatic experiences: Therapist guide.* New York, NY: Oxford University Press.

Foa, E. B., Huppert, J. D., & Cahill, S. P. (2006). Emotional processing theory: An update. In B. O. Rothbaum (Ed.), *Pathological anxiety: Emotional processing in etiology and treatment* (pp. 3–24). New York, NY: Guilford Press.

Foa, E. B., & Kozak, M. J. (1985). Treatment of anxiety disorders: Implications for psychopathology. In M. J. Tuma, A. Hussain & J. D. Maser (Eds.), *Anxiety and the anxiety disorders* (pp. 421–452). Hillsdale, NJ: Lawrence Erlbaum Associates.

Foa, E. B., & Kozak, M. J. (1986). Emotional processing of fear: Exposure to corrective information. *Psychological Bulletin, 99*(1), 20–35.

Foa, E. B., & Meadows, E. A. (1997). Psychosocial treatments for posttraumatic stress disorder: A critical review. *Annual Review of Psychology, 48*, 449–480.

Foa, E. B., Rothbaum, B. O., Riggs, D. S., & Murdock, T. B. (1991). Treatment of posttraumatic stress disorder in rape victims: A comparison between cognitive-behavioral procedures and counseling. *Journal of Consulting and Clinical Psychology, 59*(5), 715–723.

Foa, E. B., Steketee, G., & Rothbaum, B. O. (1989). Behavioral/cognitive conceptualizations of post-traumatic stress disorder. *Behavior Therapy, 20*(2), 155–176.

Foa, E. B., Yusko, D. A., McLean, C. P., Suvak, M. K., Bux, D. A., Oslin, D., … Volpicelli, J. (2013). Concurrent naltrexone and prolonged exposure therapy for patients with comorbid alcohol dependence and PTSD: A randomized clinical trial. *The Journal of the American Medical Association, 310*(5), 488–495.

Friedman, M. J., & Davidson, J. R. T. (2014). Pharmacotherapy for PTSD. In M. J. Friedman, T. M. Kean, & P. A. Resick (Eds.). *Handbook of PTSD: Science and practice* (2nd ed., pp. 482–501). New York, NY: Guilford Press.

Friedman, M. J., Davidson, J. R. T., & Stein, D. J. (2009). Psychopharmacology for adults. In E. B. Foa, T. M. Kean, M. J. Friedman, & J. A. Cohen (Eds.), *Effective treatments for PTSD: Practice and guidelines for the International Society for Traumatic Stress* (2nd ed., pp. 245–278). New York, NY: Guilford Press.

Friedman, M. J., Marmar, C. R., Baker, D. G., Sikes, C. R., & Farfel, G. M. (2007). Randomized, double-blind comparison of sertraline and placebo for posttraumatic stress disorder in a Department of Veterans Affairs setting. *Journal of Clinical Psychiatry, 68*(5), 711–720.

Galovski, T. E., Monson, C., Bruce, S. E., & Resick, P. A. (2009). Does cognitive–behavioral therapy for PTSD improve perceived health and sleep impairment? *Journal of Traumatic Stress, 22*(3), 197–204.

Hagenaars, M. A., van Minnen, A., & Hoogduin, K. A. (2010). The impact of dissociation and depression on the efficacy of prolonged exposure treatment for PTSD. *Behaviour Research and Therapy, 48*(1), 19–27.

Harned, M. S., Pantalone, D. W., Ward-Ciesielski, E. F., Lynch, T. R. & Linehan, M. M. (2011). The prevalence and correlates of sexual risk behaviors and sexually transmitted infections in outpatients with borderline personality disorder. *The Journal of Nervous and Mental Disease, 199*, 832–838.

Hughes, M., Brymer, M., Chiu, W. T., Fairbank, J. A., Jones, R. T., Pynoos, R. S., … Kessler, R. C. (2011). Posttraumatic stress among students after the shootings at Virginia Tech. *Psychological Trauma: Theory, Research, Practice, and Policy, 3*(4), 403–411.

Institute of Medicine. (2012). *Treatment of posttraumatic stress disorder: An assessment of the evidence.* Washington, DC: The National Academies Press.

Iverson, K. M., King, M. W., Cunningham, K. C., & Resick, P. A. (2015). Rape survivors' trauma-related beliefs before and after cognitive processing therapy:

Associations with PTSD and depression symptoms. *Behaviour Research and Therapy, 66,* 49–55.

Janoff-Bulman, R. (1989). Assumptive worlds and the stress of traumatic events: Applications of the schema construct. *Social Cognition, 7*(2), 113–136.

Kaysen, D., Schumm, J., Pedersen, E. R., Seim, R. W., Bedard-Gilligan, M., & Chard, K. (2014). Cognitive processing therapy for veterans with comorbid PTSD and alcohol use disorders. *Addictive Behaviors, 39*(2), 420–427.

Keane, T. M., Fairbank, J. A., Caddell, J. M., & Zimering, R. T. (1989). Implosive (flooding) therapy reduces symptoms of PTSD in Vietnam combat veterans. *Behavior Therapy, 20*(2), 245–260.

Keane, T. M., Marshall, A. D., & Taft, C. T. (2006). Posttraumatic stress disorder: Etiology, epidemiology, and treatment outcome. *Annual Review of Clinical Psychology, 2,* 161–197.

Kraemer, H. C. (2004). Statistics, placebo response, and clinical trial design in psychopharmacology. In A. F. Schatzberg & C. B. Nemeroff (Eds.), *The American psychiatric publishing textbook of psychopharmacology* (pp. 173–183). New York, NY: American Psychoanalytic Association.

Lee, C., Gavriel, H., Drummond, P., Richards, J., & Greenwald, R. (2002). Treatment of PTSD: Stress inoculation training with prolonged exposure compared to EMDR. *Journal of Clinical Psychology, 58*(9), 1071–1089.

Liverant, G. I., Suvak, M. K., Pineles, S. L., & Resick, P. A. (2012). Changes in posttraumatic stress disorder and depressive symptoms during cognitive processing therapy: Evidence for concurrent change. *Journal of Consulting and Clinical Psychology, 80*(6), 957–967.

Londborg, P. D., Hegel, M. T., Goldstein, S., Goldstein, D., Himmelhoch, J. M., Maddock, R., ... Farfel, G. M. (2001). Sertraline treatment of posttraumatic stress disorder: Results of 24 weeks of open-label continuation treatment. *The Journal of Clinical Psychiatry, 62*(5), 325–331.

Marks, I., Lovell, K., Noshirvani, H., Livanou, M., & Thrasher, S. (1998). Treatment of posttraumatic stress disorder by exposure and/or cognitive restructuring: A controlled study. *Archives of General Psychiatry, 55*(4), 317–325.

Marshall, R. D., Beebe, K. L., Oldham, M., & Zaninelli, R. (2001). Efficacy and safety of paroxetine treatment for chronic PTSD: A fixed-dose, placebo-controlled study. *American Journal of Psychiatry, 158*(12), 1982–1988.

Martenyi, F., Brown, E. B., & Caldwell, C. D. (2007). Failed efficacy of fluoxetine in the treatment of posttraumatic stress disorder: Results of a fixed-dose, placebo-controlled study. *Journal of Clinical Psychopharmacology, 27*(2), 166–170.

Martenyi, F., Brown, E. B., Zhang, H., Prakash, A., & Koke, S. C. (2002). Fluoxetine versus placebo in posttraumatic stress disorder. *Journal of Clinical Psychiatry, 63*(3), 199–206.

Monson, C. M., Schnurr, P. P., Resick, P. A., Friedman, M. J., Young-Xu, Y., & Stevens, S. P. (2006). Cognitive processing therapy for veterans with military-related posttraumatic stress disorder. *Journal of Consulting and clinical Psychology, 74*(5), 898–907.

Nacasch, N., Foa, E. B., Huppert, J. D., Tzur, D., Fostick, L., Dinstein, Y., ... Zohar, J. (2011). Prolonged exposure therapy for combat-and terror-related posttraumatic stress disorder: A randomized control comparison with treatment as usual. *Journal of Clinical Psychiatry, 72*(9), 1174–1180.

National Institute for Health and Care Excellence. (2005). *Post-traumatic stress disorder (PTSD): The management of PTSD in adults and children in primary and secondary care.* London, UK: Gaskell and the British Psychological Society. Retrieved from http://www.nice.org.uk/guidance/cg26/evidence/cg26-posttraumatic-stress-disorder-ptsd-full-guideline-including-appendices-1132

North, C. S., McCutcheon, M. V., Spitznagel, E. L., & Smith, E. M. (2002). Three-year follow-up of survivors of a mass shooting episode. *Journal of Urban Health, 79*(3), 383–391.

North, C. S., Smith, E. M., & Spitznagel, E. L. (1994). Posttraumatic stress disorder in survivors of a mass shooting. *American Journal of Psychiatry, 151*(1), 82–88.

Otto, M. W., Hinton, D., Korbly, N. B., Chea, A., Ba, P., Gershuny, B. S., & Pollack, M. H. (2003). Treatment of pharmacotherapy-refractory posttraumatic stress disorder among Cambodian refugees: A pilot study of combination treatment with cognitive-behavior therapy vs sertraline alone. *Behaviour Research and Therapy, 41*(11), 1271–1276.

Owens, G. P., Pike, J. L., & Chard, K. M. (2001). Treatment effects of cognitive processing therapy on cognitive distortions of female child sexual abuse survivors. *Behavior Therapy, 32*(3), 413–424.

Pearlman, L. A. (2003). *Trauma and attachment belief scale.* Los Angeles, CA: Western Psychological Services.

Power, K., McGoldrick, T., Brown, K., Buchanan, R., Sharp, D., Swanson, V., & Karatzias, A. (2002). A controlled comparison of eye movement desensitization and reprocessing versus exposure plus cognitive restructuring versus waiting list in the treatment of post-traumatic stress disorder. *Clinical Psychology & Psychotherapy, 9*(5), 299–318.

Powers, M. B., Halpern, J. M., Ferenschak, M. P., Gillihan, S. J., & Foa, E. B. (2010). A meta-analytic review of prolonged exposure for posttraumatic stress disorder. *Clinical Psychology Review, 30*(6), 635–641.

Rapaport, M. H., Endicott, J., & Clary, C. M. (2002). Posttraumatic stress disorder and quality of life: Results across 64 weeks of sertraline treatment. *Journal of Clinical Psychiatry, 63*(1), 59–65.

Rauch, S. A., Favorite, T., Giardino, N., Porcari, C., Defever, E., & Liberzon, I. (2010). Relationship between anxiety, depression, and health satisfaction among veterans with PTSD. *Journal of Affective Disorders, 121,* 165–168.

Resick, P. A., Galovski, T. E., Uhlmansiek, M. O. B., Scher, C. D., Clum, G. A., & Young-Xu, Y. (2008). A randomized clinical trial to dismantle components of cognitive processing therapy for posttraumatic stress disorder in female victims of interpersonal violence. *Journal of Consulting and Clinical Psychology, 76*(2), 243.

Resick, P. A., Monson, C. M., & Chard, K. M. (2014). *Cognitive processing therapy: Veteran/military version: Therapist and patient materials manual.* Washington, DC: Department of Veterans Affairs.

Resick, P. A., Nishith, P., Weaver, T. L., Astin, M. C., & Feuer, C. A. (2002). A comparison of cognitive-processing therapy with prolonged exposure and a waiting condition for the treatment of chronic posttraumatic stress disorder in female rape victims. *Journal of Consulting and Clinical Psychology, 70*(4), 867.

Resick, P. A., & Schnicke, M. K. (1992). Cognitive processing therapy for sexual assault victims. *Journal of Consulting and Clinical Psychology, 60*(5), 748.

Resick, P. A., & Schnicke, M. (1993). *Cognitive processing therapy for rape victims: A treatment manual.* Newbury Park, CA: Sage.

Resick, P. A., Williams, L. F., Suvak, M. K., Monson, C. M., & Gradus, J. L. (2012). Long-term outcomes of cognitive–behavioral treatments for posttraumatic stress disorder among female rape survivors. *Journal of Consulting and Clinical Psychology, 80*(2), 201.

Rizvi, S. L., Vogt, D. S., & Resick, P. A. (2009). Cognitive and affective predictors of treatment outcome in cognitive processing therapy and prolonged exposure for posttraumatic stress disorder. *Behaviour Research and Therapy, 47*(9), 737–743.

Rothbaum, B. O. (1997). A controlled study of eye movement desensitization and reprocessing in the treatment of posttraumatic stress disordered sexual assault victims. *Bulletin-Menninger Clinic, 61*, 317–334.

Rothbaum, B. O., Astin, M. C., & Marsteller, F. (2005). Prolonged exposure versus eye movement desensitization and reprocessing (EMDR) for PTSD rape victims. *Journal of Traumatic Stress, 18*(6), 607–616.

Rothbaum, B. O., Cahill, S. P., Foa, E. B., Davidson, J. R. T., Compton, J., Connor, K. M., Hahn, C. (2006). Augmentation of sertraline with prolonged exposure in the treatment of posttraumatic stress disorder. *Journal of Traumatic Stress, 19*(5), 625–638.

Schnurr, P. P., Friedman, M. J., Engel, C. C., Foa, E. B., Shea, M. T., Chow, B. K., ... & Bernardy, N. (2007). Cognitive behavioral therapy for posttraumatic stress disorder in women: A randomized controlled trial. *Journal of the American Medical Association, 297*(8), 820–830.

Shalev, A. Y., Ankri, Y., Israeli-Shalev, Y., Peleg, T., Adessky, R., & Freedman, S. (2012). Prevention of posttraumatic stress disorder by early treatment: Results from the Jerusalem Trauma Outreach and Prevention study. *Archives of General Psychiatry, 69*(2), 166–176.

Shapiro, F. (1995). *Eye movement desensitization and reprocessing: Basic principles, protocols, and procedures.* New York, NY: Guilford Press.

Shapiro, F. (1996). Eye movement desensitization and reprocessing (EMDR): Evaluation of controlled PTSD research. *Journal of Behavior Therapy and Experimental Psychiatry, 27*(3), 209–218.

Shapiro, F. (2001). *EMDR basic principles and protocols.* New York, NY: Guilford Press.

Shapiro, F. (2002). EMDR and the role of the clinician in psychotherapy evaluation: Towards a more comprehensive integration of science and practice. *Journal of Clinical Psychology, 58*(12), 1453–1463.

Shapiro, F. (2007). EMDR, adaptive information processing, and case conceptualization. *Journal of EMDR Practice and Research, 1*(2), 68–87.

Shapiro, F., & Forrest, M. S. (2001). *EMDR: Eye movement desensitization and reprocessing.* New York, NY: Guilford Press.

Shapiro, F., & Maxfield, L. (2002). Eye movement desensitization and reprocessing (EMDR): Information processing in the treatment of trauma. *Journal of Clinical Psychology, 58*(8), 933–946.

Simon, N. M., Connor, K. M., Lang, A. J., Rauch, S., Krulewicz, S., LeBeau, R. T., ... Pollack, M. H. (2008). Paroxetine CR augmentation for posttraumatic stress disorder refractory to prolonged exposure therapy. *Journal of Clinical Psychiatry*, *69*(3), 400–405.

Sobel, A. A., Resick, P. A., & Rabalais, A. E. (2009). The effect of cognitive processing therapy on cognitions: Impact statement coding. *Journal of Traumatic Stress*, *22*(3), 205–211.

Solomon, R. M., & Shapiro, F. (2008). EMDR and the adaptive information processing model potential mechanisms of change. *Journal of EMDR Practice and Research*, *2*(4), 315–325.

Sripada, R. K., Rauch, S. A., Tuerk, P. W., Smith, E., Defever, A. M., Mayer, R. A., ... Venners, M. (2013). Mild traumatic brain injury and treatment response in prolonged exposure for PTSD. *Journal of Traumatic Stress*, *26*(3), 369–375.

Stein, M. B., & Ipser, J. C. (2011). Pharmacotherapy of PTSD. In D. J. Stein, M. J. Friedman, & C. Blanco (Eds.), *Post-traumatic stress disorder* (pp. 149–162). New York, NY: Wiley.

Stein, M. B., Ipser, J. C., & Seedat, S. (2006). Pharmacotherapy for posttraumatic stress disorder (PTSD). *Cochrane Database of Systematic Reviews* (*1*): CD002795.

Taylor, R. S., Thordarson, D. S., Maxfield, L., Fedoroff, I. C., Lovell, K., & Ogrodniczuk, J. (2003). Comparative efficacy, speed, and adverse effects of three PTSD treatments: Exposure therapy, EMDR, and relaxation training. *Journal of Consulting and Clinical Psychology*, *71*, 330–338.

Tucker, P., & Trautman, R. (2000). Understanding and treating PTSD: Past, present, and future. *Bulletin of the Menninger Clinic*, *64*(3), A37–A51.

Tucker, P., Zaninelli, R., Yehuda, R., Ruggiero, L., Dillingham, K., & Pitts, C. D. (2001). Paroxetine in the treatment of chronic posttraumatic stress disorder: Results of a placebo-controlled, flexible-dosage trial. *Journal of Clinical Psychiatry*, *62*(11), 860–868.

van den Berg, D. P., de Bont, P. A., van der Vleugel, B. M., de Roos, C., de Jongh, A., van Minnen, A., & van der Gaag, M. (2015). Prolonged exposure vs eye movement desensitization and reprocessing vs waiting list for posttraumatic stress disorder in patients with a psychotic disorder: A randomized clinical trial. *Journal of the American Medical Association*, *72*, 259–267.

van Minnen, A., Harned, M. S., Zoellner, L., & Mills, K. (2012). Examining potential contraindications for prolonged exposure therapy for PTSD. *European Journal of Psychotraumatology*, *3*.

Vaughan, K., Armstrong, M. S., Gold, R., O'Connor, N., Jenneke, W., & Tarrier, N. (1994). A trial of eye movement desensitization compared to image habituation training and applied muscle relaxation in post-traumatic stress disorder. *Journal of Behavior Therapy and Experimental Psychiatry*, *25*(4), 283–291.

Youngner, C. G., Rothbaum, B. O., & Friedman, M. J. (2014). Posttraumatic stress disorder. In G. O. Gabbard (Ed.), *Gabbard's treatments of psychiatric disorders* (5th ed., 479–503). Arlington, VA: American Psychiatric Publishing.

16

Public Relief Efforts From an International Perspective

Kari Dyregrov, Atle Dyregrov, and Pål Kristensen

The grief and the longing will always be present as long as I live. I will always have him with me. I miss Ben every second and I think very often of him ... I have little energy, lack concentration; I read documents at work for the third time and I wonder if I've understood what they say. I know I am different to before July 22; I am quite sure about that. I have poorer concentration, and I have a lower energy level ... I struggled a lot with sleep problems, but during the last three to four months, I have improved a great deal.

(The mother of an 18-year-old boy shot at Utøya)

In all my nightmares, Karen is taken away from me in one form or another ... it is not happening in a particular place, there are different places. She may show up smiling, then someone drags her away from me, and the closer I get, the further away she goes. I get very scared when I have these nightmares, and sometimes I manage to wake up immediately, while other times I am aware that I have nightmares, but I cannot wake up ... At night I cannot sleep well, because I am tired, and it is such a vicious circle in a way. I cannot rest in the body ...

I had to see the place, because I spoke to Karen on the phone just before she was shot. She cried on the phone, she was scared, and in a way, she knew she would not survive. She asked me what she should do, and I told her, "You must hide, Karen" ... She said she had no place to hide anymore, and she had wet feet, and she froze. She was very scared; she was crying so much ... I asked her to hang up so that she could hide ... "But mom" she repeated, "I have no place to hide anymore." I said, "Karen you must find a place" – and so she hung up on me. When I came to Utøya, I saw that she was right. She had had no place to hide, it was an open place, and I think I gave her the dumbest advice I could have given ... I spoke with Karen at 18.28 [6:28 p.m.] ... and the murderer was detained at 18.34 [6:34 p.m.].

(The mother of a 15-year-old girl shot at Utøya)

The Wiley Handbook of the Psychology of Mass Shootings, First Edition. Edited by Laura C. Wilson.
© 2017 John Wiley & Sons, Inc. Published 2017 by John Wiley & Sons, Inc.

The Terror Killings of July 22, 2011

The terror killings were the deadliest onslaught in Norway since World War II, in what has been a largely peaceful country. First, the Norwegian-born ultra-conservative terrorist detonated a 950-kilogram car bomb close to several government buildings in the city of Oslo, killing 8 people and severely injuring 10. Just before the bomb went off, the terrorist drove to Utøya, a small island outside of Oslo, where approximately 550 adolescents and young adults were attending a youth political summer camp for the Norwegian Labor Party. Dressed as a police officer, he lied his way onto a small ferry and crossed to the island. Here, he chased the youngsters all over the island for 1 hour and 20 minutes (between the hours of 5:09 and 6:33 p.m.) with the aim of killing as many as possible. Although the youths attempted to hide, he hunted them and shot them in their hiding places and as they fled, including killing some as they tried to swim to safety. Many wounded individuals who played dead were killed when the terrorist checked his victims for vital signs. During the shooting, many of the desperate – and later murdered – youths were in contact with their shocked parents or siblings via their mobile phones. Their desperate family members tried to comfort them or advise them to flee from the terrorist before they eventually lost contact with them. Before the terrorist was arrested, he had killed 69 individuals, mainly of a young age ($M = 21$ years old, ranging from 15 to 51 years old), at close range. In addition, 56 persons were taken to the hospital with injuries that ranged from minor to severe wounds.

The perpetrator was caught alive and a lengthy trial was started 9 months after the incident and lasted 2 months. He was sentenced to 21 years of preventive detention. The event was the main media story for more than a year in Norway, and not a day went by without pictures or stories appearing in newspapers, on the radio or on TV. Furthermore, the Norwegian population took part in a wide range of memorial events in the aftermath of the terror.

The killings on Utøya resulted in approximately 210 parents and siblings losing a child or a sibling. In addition, others lost their partners, parents, other relatives (e.g., uncles, aunts, cousins), or close friends. Thus, this incident directly impacted a large group of individuals.

Present Chapter

As part of a book on mass shootings that incorporates a wide range of topics, this chapter could have dealt with many important issues connected to the Norwegian terror events. Although much help was provided to the survivors, both those who were in the government buildings and those who survived the event at Utøya, we have chosen to focus on the psychosocial follow-up offered to bereaved family members following the Utøya killings. This group was large and the hardest hit in terms of loss. It can be argued that they were provided the most help and support, and are the group of victims about whom the authors possess special expertise.

It is also important for us to comment on the nature of the events that occurred on July 22, 2011. As has been discussed in great detail in other chapters in this book (see Chapters 1–3), the terms "mass murder" and "mass shooting" can be defined in a number of ways. There is no doubt that the events that happened in Norway on that day should be considered mass murder, given the large number of individuals who were killed. In addition, many definitions require that the incident occur in a public place and both events on July 22, 2011 would satisfy this requirement. Furthermore, the second event on Utøya Island involved a firearm and therefore would meet that criterion of the mass shooting definition. The main area of controversy for this event in relation to these definitions involves the motive. Specifically, the assailant was motivated by his political and religious beliefs, and therefore it is classified as a terrorist attack. However, as was discussed by Fox and Levin in Chapter 3, a motivation-based typology approach to understanding mass shootings would classify the event on Utøya Island as a mass shooting motivated by terror. Regardless, the point of this chapter is to offer a discussion of the psychosocial follow-up provided to bereaved individuals in Norway following a mass murder incident and provide an international perspective on intervention following mass violence incidents that is applicable to mass shootings. The authors of this chapter represent various professional backgrounds (i.e., sociology and psychology), and have decades of research and clinical experience working with the bereaved in the aftermath of traumatic losses. Furthermore, we have been involved in the planning and execution of follow-up programs for the Norwegian health authorities, including disasters that occurred prior to the events of July 22, 2011. In addition, we are conducting a longitudinal research project on the bereaved from this terror event. In this chapter, we draw on our previous and present clinical and research experience.

We first present the history of the development of the Norwegian practice of psychosocial follow-up after critical incidents. Thereafter, the public Norwegian psychosocial follow-up programs that were initiated after the terror attack of July 22, 2011 are sketched out, followed by a discussion of data derived from brief evaluations. The chapter concludes with some basic issues concerning follow-up after unnatural death.

The Development of Psychosocial Follow-Up for the Bereaved in Norway

Prior to the 1980s, crisis psychology and psychosocial follow-up were unknown concepts to the Norwegian population. Conversely, in the past three decades, the field of crisis psychology has been developing in Norway. Psychosocial follow-up involves comprehensive and need-related assistance. This includes early crisis (e.g., counseling, medication), psychological (e.g., information, cognitive therapy, trauma-specific treatment techniques), social (e.g., mobilization/advice on social networks), practical (e.g., help with care responsibilities), economic (e.g., help with support schemes/subsidies), legal (e.g., legal settlement, inheritance or insurance matters), forensic (e.g., help with rights about autopsy), and religious (e.g., religious counseling, advice from priests or religious groups) interventions.

In the early 1980s, Atle Dyregrov, one of the founders of the Center for Crisis Psychology (CCP), argued for the establishment of emergency teams to provide psychosocial follow-up after large-scale disasters (Dyregrov, A., 1983). He also asserted that crisis teams should be formed to offer psychosocial intervention after single traumatic deaths (Dyregrov, A., 1985). At that time, these ideas fell on deaf ears among health bureaucrats and politicians in Norway. Nonetheless, there were many signs of enthusiasts' hard work with victims after traumatic deaths in local communities. Research has supported the importance of helping communities impacted by traumatic deaths, and gradually the health authorities have taken more responsibility in providing psychosocial follow-up for the bereaved after these types of losses. Thus, there has been a gradual development of public psychosocial follow-up after crises and catastrophes in Norway, for which there are several plausible explanations.

In 1997–1998, the CCP explored how local communities responded to the bereaved after violent deaths (Dyregrov, K., 2002). While we have documented a variety of practices, four major strategies for psychosocial assistance after traumatic deaths were identified among 321 (71%) local communities in Norway. These were: (1) the "prevention strategy" (i.e., early intervention and follow-up), (2) the "treatment strategy" (i.e., intervention after diagnosis), (3) the "ignorance strategy" (i.e., no intervention due to lack of awareness of problems and/or priority), and (4) the "de-medicalization strategy" (i.e., no intervention out of desire to not interfere with and medicalize grief reactions). It is likely that these strategies, which seem to be based on explicit ideologies, also exist in varying degrees and forms in many Western countries today (Dyregrov, K., 2004).

It is documented internationally that the bereaved often ask for help from professionals, social networks, and peers in the wake of traumatic losses (Dyregrov, K., & Dyregrov, A., 2008; Levin, 2004; Price, Jordan, Prior, & Parkes, 2011; Wilson & Clark, 2005). Parallel to the research revealing the great variation in public assistance for the bereaved after traumatic losses, the first nationwide research project on the bereaved was conducted by the CCP. This research documented a distinct discrepancy between the need for help and the help received, as reported by both the helpers and the bereaved (Dyregrov, K., 2002). When asked to describe the ideal form of public help, the bereaved highlighted the following: immediate outreach help from trained personnel, information about the event and reactions that may arise, help for bereaved children, and the opportunity to meet with others who have experienced similar losses. Because many individuals isolated themselves or lacked the necessary energy, they asked for active outreach from helpers. In addition, the bereaved stressed that if they turned down help shortly after the traumatic loss, offers of help should be respectfully repeated over time. They asked for systems that provided automatic contact from professional teams, stability and continuity in support, competent helpers, and help that was flexible and individually tailored (Dyregrov, K., & Dyregrov, A., 2008).

Emerging international and national studies have shown a high prevalence of anxiety, depression, trauma and complicated grief reactions, and impairment in daily functioning in the bereaved after unnatural deaths (Dyregrov, K., 2003; Li, Precht, Mortensen, & Olsen, 2003; Stroebe, Schut, & Stroebe, 2007). Increased mortality has been documented among those bereaved after unnatural deaths compared to natural deaths (Li et al., 2003), as well as other negative health consequences which are indicated by the presence of symptoms and illnesses (e.g. cancer), and the use of medical services (Stroebe et al., 2007). In addition, individuals bereaved following unnatural deaths stemming from natural disasters demonstrate similar difficulties (Kristensen, Weisæth, & Heir, 2012). For young people, their age, closeness to the event, loss of close persons, lack of support at school, and complex family dynamics are predictors of psychopathology, somatic complaints, behavioral difficulties, and absenteeism from school in the aftermath of terror (Norris et al., 2002). Due to such research, there has been an increasing understanding that those bereaved after unnatural deaths need more assistance than has previously been acknowledged or provided. The increasing knowledge about the risks of developing mental and physical health problems after unnatural deaths has likely contributed to a gradual shift from a strategy of late intervention (i.e., waiting until symptoms arise) to a more active preventative strategy for follow-up.

The gradual shift towards listening more to the "users" of healthcare services has contributed to the development of the follow-up model, making the services more in line with the needs and wishes of the bereaved. In the Norwegian Directory of Health's report "User Involvement in the Mental Health Field" (Report IS-1315, 2006), a user is defined as "a person who makes use of relevant services in one form or another." User involvement is defined as "the users' influence on the development of services" (p. 7) and it is established that "user involvement implies that the public services utilize the users' experience and knowledge to provide the best possible help" (p. 8).

Due to Norway being a self-declared welfare state, laws and regulations have emerged over the years, leading to the follow-up model that was initiated after the terror of July 22, 2011. In 2000, a law was enacted that paved the way for plans to ensure reliable services during crises and war. This has increased the preparedness and response in local communities for those bereaved after large-scale events. Nonetheless, for many years, more systematic help initiatives were utilized only when more than one family was affected. In the wake of the tsunami in South East Asia in 2004, in which 84 Norwegians lost their lives, a new trend was implemented whereby general practitioners were asked to contact and follow up with the bereaved and the survivors. Thereafter, the "Comprehensive National Health and Social Preparedness Plan" was enacted in 2007, and the "Guideline for Psychosocial Interventions in Crises, Accidents and Disasters" was launched in August 2011 (Report IS-1810, 2011) and revised in 2015. These guidelines aim at securing high-quality and appropriate psychosocial follow-up after crises and disasters. Also in 2011, the authorities launched the "Guidelines for Follow-Up after Suicide," signaling an interest in providing help to the bereaved following single-incident traumatic deaths.

Key Governmental Relief Efforts After the Terror of July 22, 2011

This section will cover the key interventions that were offered to the bereaved who lost their children, siblings, parents, and partners at Utøya (for a full overview see Report IS-1984E, 2011). We will review the relief efforts by discussing (a) the information and support center, (b) the national memorials, (c) the proactive model for help in local communities, (d) the visits to the site of death, (e) the weekend gatherings for the bereaved families, and (f) the seminars for school managers and teachers.

Information and support center

In line with previous experiences (Weisæth, 2004), local health authorities established an information and support center at Sundvolden Hotel close to Utøya, immediately after the terror attacks. Thus, from the early evening of July 22, 2011, emergency healthcare was in place. A sympathetic setting with food, refreshments, and privacy rooms was provided for the family members of those individuals who were at Utøya. In the reception center, the bereaved could access help from doctors, psychiatrists, psychologists, nurses, a chaplain, and an imam. There was a fair amount of chaos and a lack of preplanned structure in operating the center, and the local authorities did the best they could. Volunteers and personnel on duty managed to rapidly coordinate and offer services that helped serve the influx of survivors, survivors' family members, and the bereaved (Dyregrov, A. et al., 2012). The center's personnel assisted the family members and, together with police, provided information regularly. Gradually, only the family members of those unaccounted for remained at the center. It took approximately a week before all the people who were killed were identified. The functioning of the information and support center has not been formally evaluated.

Memorials

On July 25, 3 days after the terror killings, a national memorial service was arranged in the capital of Oslo and broadcasted live on all three of the major television networks. Famous artists performed, the Norwegian Prime Minister, the King of Norway, and the Mayor of Oslo gave speeches, and the Norwegian Royal Family and Scandinavian royalty attended to pay their last respects to the deceased. On the same day, the citizens of Oslo showed their sympathy for the victims when more than 200,000 participated in a procession with red roses (the symbol of the political party of the murdered youths) raised in the air. All around the country, actions demonstrating sympathy and support were performed during the subsequent weeks (e.g. support concerts, parades). Although many of the bereaved did not partake in memorials due to their grief or because they were still searching for their loved ones, they valued the support and warmth that was shown by the entire population. There were government officials (i.e., ministers) present at all 77 of the funerals following the terror, and they were all covered by the Norwegian government-owned radio and television public broadcasting company.

The proactive model for psychosocial follow-up

On July 22, 2011, the Ministry of Health and Social Care Services assigned the Norwegian Directorate of Health (NDH) to coordinate and secure follow-up for families directly affected by the terror. To inform the services, the NDH established a liaison forum and an expert group to provide advice within the municipalities and the occupational health service.

Through the crisis teams in the municipalities, the health authorities decided to enact a more proactive model for follow-up than previously adopted by local authorities following disasters. The primary features of the model are described in a report by the NDH (Report IS-1984E, 2011). The main aim of the follow-up model was to secure contact and continuity between the bereaved and the health and support services. Another aim was to ensure regular assessment of social support and the need for further actions. To fulfill the aims of reaching out to individuals who needed help, either in the short or the longer term, certain principles were implemented. To ensure that everyone was offered help, the follow-up was proactive and systematic. This was secured through the assignment of a coordinator to work with every family, who preferably had either healthcare or social/educational qualifications. This person initiated contact with the family and offered a personal meeting within the first weeks after the terror killings. If the families turned down the offer at first contact, the coordinator was to repeat the offer later. The coordinator was told to maintain frequent contact initially (weekly), and thereafter adapt to the needs of the family. In the meetings (or phone calls), the contact would assess for the need of and then offer support.

If specialist medical or psychological treatment became necessary, they would refer to an appropriate provider and arrange for the services. The follow-up by the family coordinator was designed to last at least one year.

Based on questionnaires and in-depth interviews, the CCP has evaluated how helpful the bereaved found the follow-up model in the local communities. Compared to those in previous Norwegian studies, the bereaved after the 2011 terror attack expressed a greater need for help and were given more comprehensive and proactive community services (Dyregrov, K., Kristensen, Johnsen, & Dyregrov, A., 2015) than those bereaved by single-incident traumatic deaths (Dyregrov, K., 2002, 2003; Dyregrov, K., Berntsen, & Silviken, 2014). Nearly all the bereaved reported a significant need for help after the terror killings, and during the first year and a half almost all the parents (94%) and siblings (97%) had received help from a range of professionals (Dyregrov, K., Kristensen, Johnsen, & Dyregrov, 2015). The helpers most commonly accessed were psychologists/psychiatrists, general practitioners/medical doctors, the police, family counselors, and teachers/the school. Although psychologists/psychiatrists and general practitioners were the professional groups with which most of the parents and siblings had been in contact, they were also the group of helpers that the family members reported that they wish they had had more contact with. Half of the parents had been contacted by a crisis team, whereas others had been contacted by other groups of healthcare providers. Only a small minority of the bereaved felt that they had lacked help after their loss. Few parents reported that they lacked help for their children, and in line with the bereaved perceiving less need for help over time, they also reported that the relief measures provided to them had been gradually reduced. Despite the fact that 25% of the bereaved reported that the public support services appeared strained and experienced barriers to receiving help, a large majority praised the help that had been provided.

In general, those bereaved after the Utøya terror perceived the community proactive follow-up model as a step in the right direction. As many as 75% stated that, to a large extent or a fairly large extent, they were satisfied with the help received through the community health services. This is a huge improvement compared to the satisfaction of the bereaved with the community follow-up after suicide, accidents, and sudden infant deaths (SIDS) in 1998 (Dyregrov, K., 2002) and 2009 (Dyregrov, K., Bernsten, et al., 2014). Only 34% and 33%, respectively, reported satisfaction at those times.

There may be several reasons why the bereaved after Utøya were more satisfied. First, helpers were more active and initiated contact with families. In addition, families were given a contact person who provided continuity and maintained contact during the follow-up. Second, many of the bereaved received comprehensive and need-related help, and many received help from psychologists and general practitioners, which in previous studies were the most missed and requested types of help. Third, assistance after July 22, 2011 was even offered to the children who were impacted by the event, which was not the case in previous studies. Fourth, the termination of help took place later in time than previously reported by the bereaved, securing better long-term follow-up.

A father who lost his 17-year-old daughter at Utøya explains why this follow-up model was important to his family:

> The Crisis Team came to our cabin where we had escaped after the terror, and saw that we were surrounded by a huge social network. They talked with us for some time and found out how we managed. Then they informed us that they would be there for us for whatever need we would have in the days to come – and thereafter they retreated nicely and quietly into the background. It was *very important*, yes … to know that we had something to fall back on if something happened.

In line with what the bereaved have reported in previous studies and with what was included in the follow-up model after July 22, 2011, more than 80 bereaved parents and siblings stressed the most vital aspects of the follow-up:

- Make contact and offer help.
- Repeat the contact if someone refuses at first.
- Give the bereaved a contact person who can ensure continuity in the support services.
- Make sure the follow-up includes all those biologically or psychologically close to the deceased.
- Base the help on competence and communicate it with empathy.
- Be flexible and listen to what the bereaved need, but take charge when necessary.
- At an early stage, provide the bereaved with clear information about how the death happened, about normal grief reactions, about what will happen next, and where they can receive help.
- Repeat the information.
- Help the bereaved establish contact with a psychologist and/or other necessary professionals.
- Help the bereaved get in contact with others who have experienced the same kind of loss.
- The school and workplace should offer accommodations without the bereaved having to ask.

Visits to the site of death

As has been the tradition for the past three decades in Norway (Kristensen, Tønnessen, Weisæth, & Heir, 2012), the professional expert team of the NDH recommended that the bereaved families be offered the opportunity to visit

Utøya and see the site of death. A total of 360 family members, representing 60 of the deceased, visited Utøya on the first collective visit on August 19, 2011. Thereafter, the authorities arranged four more collective visits (on October 1, 2011, and on the first, second, and third anniversaries of the terror), where an unknown number of the bereaved and survivors, and their families, (re)visited the island. In addition, a significant proportion of the bereaved visited Utøya on their own.

The authorities planned the visit in great detail and organized several caretaking efforts before the first visit in August 2011. Besides cleaning the facilities and having flowers available for every family, a letter was sent to the bereaved families ahead of the visit. In the letter, they received information on what to expect, advice on ritualizing their visit, and how to care for accompanying children. Each family was allowed to bring 10 individuals, including their contact person from their local community if they wanted. Health teams were available on the island.

Two police officers from the National Criminal Investigation Service Norway (KRIPOS) and a volunteer from the Red Cross escorted each family, one by one, to the place where their loved ones had been killed. On the site, the police showed them where the deceased was found and answered questions that the family had about the deaths. Each family was allowed time and space alone at their site (many victims died at the same place), and they were accompanied by qualified personnel with expertise in dealing with such situations. This allowed the bereaved to have a dignified and supported experience. Flowers were available for all to take with them to the site, and memorials had been set up in nearby buildings. Because many had to wait for a while before they could visit "their" site, a large tent was set up with activities for children and food/drink services. Here, the Minister of Health and the Police Director also gave speeches.

In a separate venue, away from but still close to the island, personal effects had been washed and arranged on tables with white tablecloths, which were labeled for each of the deceased. The bereaved who wished to could visit this venue, whereby the police and civil defense had created a very respectful environment. They could take the personal effects of their loved one home if they wanted. Importantly, the families could spend as much or little time at Utøya as they wanted (Kristensen, Dyregrov, & Dyregrov, 2015; Report IS-1984E, 2011).

In a self-report study examining bereaved parents' and siblings' experiences of visiting Utøya, nearly two thirds reported that visiting the site of death was both beneficial and a burden, and one third reported that it had only been beneficial. The most commonly reported benefits were an existential/emotional need to see the site, and an increased cognitive clarity about what had happened. Some reported that visiting the site had reduced ruminations and misinterpretations about the circumstances of the death. The most burdensome aspect of the visit was an activation of trauma and grief reactions (Kristensen et al., 2015). Although visiting the site of death can be stressful, it is our conclusion that the benefits outweigh the burdens. Thus, we recommend that bereaved families be provided the opportunity to visit the site of death after terror events. Such visits can be particularly important for persons who are struggling with complicated grief reactions, such as avoidance of the reality of the death and/or maladaptive grief-related ruminations. However, adequate and thorough preparations are necessary before such collective visits are conducted.

Weekend gatherings

In addition to the help from local communities, the Utøya-bereaved families were offered weekend gatherings by the Norwegian health authorities. The aim of the gatherings was to increase the recognition, understanding, and normalization of grief reactions. In addition, help and advice on how to mobilize social support, cope using psycho-educational methods, and how to live with grief were key objectives.

The NDH gave the CCP the task of developing a plan and a program for providing collective support, and to lead the professional work during these gatherings. In order to deal with more than 250 bereaved, a large and competent organization was needed. Therefore, the gatherings were coordinated within a temporary organization with the NDH as the host responsible for all the practical arrangements, while the CCP set up and designed the professional content of the program in collaboration with other institutions that have worked with traumatic grief. The professional program was outlined in manuals for group leaders for each weekend. The manual for the first weekend contained the philosophy of the program, outlined how to structure the small groups, and described important aspects of how to run the groups. All of the group leaders were selected from institutions familiar with running groups for the bereaved (i.e., CCP, Modum Bad, Ahus Hospital). Regardless of their previous experience with groups, we deemed it important to outline the special issues that were involved in this work. It was stressed that the group work would be different from usual grief groups because the nature of the killings and the magnitude of the event were unprecedented in Norway. A separate manual was developed for group leaders who worked with the young bereaved.

Four weekend gatherings were held in a hotel at 4, 8, 12, and 18 months after the mass killing. In total, 182, 224, 232, and 217 parents and siblings (including stepparents, stepsiblings, and partners of adult children) took part, respectively (Dyregrov, A., Dyregrov, K., Straume, & Grønvold Bugge, 2014; Report IS-1984E, 2011). At each gathering, four group meetings were conducted, each lasting for 1.5 hours, with a total of 16 group sessions occurring across all four gatherings (Dyregrov, A., Dyregrov, K., Straume, & Grønvold Bugge, 2014). In addition, the Red Cross established an activity program for children and adolescents outside of the hours the youngsters spent in the program.

The family gatherings consisted of plenary and parallel sessions, small group meetings, activities for children and adolescents, and informal meeting times. In the small groups (10–12 persons), participants were divided by relational status to the deceased. The weekends usually started on a Friday afternoon with a welcome session and introductions. Each gathering followed the same sequence: a welcome address from the organizers (NHD), a welcome from a representative of the National Support Group, and an introduction to the professional content by the CCP (Dyregrov, A., Dyregrov, K., Straume, & Grønvold Bugge, 2014). The plenary sessions focused on closely defined themes designed to promote self-awareness, normalize experiences, and teach the participants about reaction patterns and coping. The topics that were covered during the sessions with adults were:

- The event, the time that had passed before the first weekend gathering, and the passing of anniversaries.
- Living with grief, differences within the family, and how to support each other.
- How to be a parent (caring capacities) and how to cope with children's grief.
- Challenges with social networks, work and school, and family communication.
- How to optimize social support.
- Advice for parents on young people and issues related to school.
- How to deal with the media and preparation for the court case.
- Reactions to the verdict and the commission report.
- Passing the 1-year mark and commemoration rituals.
- Future perspectives and grief over time.
- Self-help methods.

Importantly, the bereaved received extensive self-help advice and learned how to:

- Restrict the time they think about the deceased and set aside a specific time to approach the loss.
- Make use of imagery techniques to reduce intrusive memories and fantasies.
- Make use of distraction and behavioral activation methods to control attention and improve daily functioning.
- Make use of thought-stopping techniques coupled with setting aside time to approach their grief.
- Learn to monitor and control internal dialogue.
- Take part in social activities to regain their social capacity.
- Use "therapeutic rituals" to limit or end parts of their grief.

- Write letters to their lost loved one where they expressed everything they never had a chance to say or do, ask for forgiveness for things said or done that they regretted.
- "Ask" the dead person for advice or think about what they would have said.
- Give themselves permission to grieve less.
- Seek help if there is no increase in the hours and days where things seem a little better.
- Use sleep techniques and sleep hygiene to improve sleep. (Dyregrov, A., Dyregrov, K., Straume, & Grønvold Bugge, 2014)

A special program was in place for children and adolescents, which was similar in content to the adult program but adjusted for age. Besides talking with other bereaved youngsters, the program contained child-appropriate activities, including arts and sports. The program had more concrete activities than the adult program (e.g., cards for identifying feelings and recognizing grief, use of drawings for smaller children, writing tasks for older children/adolescents). The themes covered in the group sessions included how they learned about what happened, their thoughts and feelings about the killings, the funeral, the media coverage, what had helped them, how best to cope with everyday life, family and social networks, the grief of their parents, school issues, what they had learned, and hopes for the future.

As the CCP had been greatly involved with the program, the NDH undertook the evaluation of the weekend gatherings. They found the response from the participants almost overwhelming with more than 90% reporting that they found the gatherings extremely or very helpful and none who found them counterproductive or unnecessary. The small group sessions were found to be especially helpful by the bereaved, who reported that they had trusted the professional leaders and felt safe to share thoughts and feelings. The participants particularly emphasized the usefulness of being with others who had experienced a loss similar to themselves and having their experience validated (Dyregrov, A., Dyregrov, K., Straume, & Grønvold Bugge, 2014). One parent expressed this in a note to the NDH:

> It is intense to go so deeply into one's feelings and experiences related to what happened on July 22nd, but so good to find that I am taken seriously and that I can be with others who lost their loved ones in the same manner as me. I really feel that these gatherings help me in my grief process. I feel stronger and better prepared to handle the future.

Some of the bereaved stated the importance of the firm – but gentle – structure of the gatherings, and commented on the necessity of them being led by people not affected by the terror. During the gatherings, they felt that their experiences and reactions were validated and normalized, they could access information (e.g., self-help methods), and be helped to integrate their loss. Being with the other bereaved, establishing new ties, and discussing their future challenges assisted them in establishing new life goals. By experiencing the comfort of being with others in "the same" situation, the bereaved found that the gatherings contributed to their resilience and aided them on their way towards a new future (Dyregrov, A. et al., 2014; Rutten et al., 2013).

Seminars for school managers and teachers

Because more than 500 school students survived the terror, the Norwegian Directorate for Education and Training arranged two seminars for schools that each lasted 2 days and included students who were directly involved (i.e., bereaved, survivors). The seminars took place 4 and 8 months after the terror. The aim was to increase awareness and knowledge about the problems that the bereaved or survivors of Utøya might face in the aftermath of the terror, and connect the school leaders/teachers by forming a national discussion network. Through increased knowledge, the teachers became more capable of recognizing problems, and offered support and care to prevent dropouts and minimize learning difficulties among affected schoolchildren.

The seminars consisted of plenary lectures and group work, and specialists from several fields (e.g., education, psychology, sociology, law) covered themes such as:

- Why organize a nationwide school network?
- Cooperation between home and school.
- Flexibility to adapt schooling for affected students within existing school laws and regulations.
- The need for special attention on posttraumatic stress, grief, and school functioning.
- What schools can do to help with school-related difficulties.
- Relevant questions concerning the trial.
- Sharing of experiences locally and regionally.
- Issues related to regulatory practices, especially absences, grading, and testing.
- Sharing of informational resources through websites and written materials.
- Advice given to parents and young people at national and regional gatherings concerning reactions, social support, media, the trial, coping, and so forth.
- How the trial may impact the students and how to handle this in the classroom.
- Questions for the panel of lecturers.

School materials and advice were developed for school personnel, and information was disseminated via websites (Schultz, Langballe, & Raundalen, 2014). A practical step-by-step procedure was recommended for communicating with students, and guidelines were made available to teachers about how to protect students during the lengthy televised trial (Raundalen, Schultz, & Langballe, 2012).

How Are the Bereaved Today?

All previous knowledge has attested that serious and longstanding problems and reduced quality of life could be expected for a high percentage of closely bereaved persons after the terror killings, which constituted the largest national tragedy since World War II for Norway. Therefore, there has been a tremendous determination and effort on the part of the Norwegian authorities to try to minimize the burdens of the many bereaved persons. Nonetheless, in our longitudinal research project on parents, siblings, and close friends bereaved at Utøya, we documented very strong grief and trauma reactions (Dyregrov, K., Dyregrov, A., & Kristensen, 2014; Johnsen, Laberg, Matthiesen, Dyregrov, A., & Dyregrov, K., 2015). Further, the decrease in symptoms and functional impairment for parents and siblings more than three years after the terror killings appears to be occurring rather slowly (Dyregrov, K., Kristensen, & Johnsen, 2015; Kristensen et al., 2015). How can we understand this in light of the huge relief efforts conducted?

There are a number of plausible explanations for the slow recovery. Above all, it may be connected to the extreme nature of the event, imposing a huge burden on, and especially strong trauma and grief reactions in, the bereaved. Second, the bereaved who we are studying are the population most at risk of suffering after traumatic deaths (e.g., parents losing a young child to sudden, unnatural, and violent death). In addition, the bereaved themselves pointed out that grief processing was put on hold for more than a year due to the fact that they had to deal with the media coverage of the events, the trial and conviction of the perpetrator, the commission report, and other related events (Dyregrov, K., Dyregrov, A., & Kristensen, 2014). The bereaved have been surrounded by almost constant reminders, even beyond the first year following the terror. Thus, the recovery may continue, but at a slower pace than has been previously documented in response to other events (Bonanno, Westphal, & Mancini, 2011).

Although we know that the bereaved are very satisfied with the help they have received, we do not know whether the quality or amount of professional help has been optimal for their difficulties. Furthermore, considering the probability that many would need grief and trauma therapy after such an event, and considering the great variation in professional competence in the field, there were some deficits in the help provided. In line with suggestions from the bereaved, the proactive model for follow-up can be improved by increasing the helpers' competence, improving the "chemistry" between the helpers and the bereaved, and increasing the duration of follow-up (Dyregrov, K., Kristensen, Johnsen, & Dyregrov, A., 2015). Finally, there is a possibility that the bereaved would have been far worse off without all the help measures that were initiated. Our conclusion as to how the measures worked is associated with many questions and uncertainties, which should – preferably – have been answered through efficacy studies. Although efficacy studies are both necessary and desirable, these types of studies on follow-up for those bereaved after large-scale terror pose major ethical and practical challenges. Even so, we have to find ways to evaluate the effectiveness of complex help measures, such as those used after the terror attack in Norway on July 22, 2011.

What Will the Future Bring?

In agreement with one of the bereaved fathers, we would argue that the terror shootings were "a large-scale experiment in the consequence of unprecedented brutality, the consequences of which Norway could not foresee. The authorities had to take this into account when they decided on short- and long-term follow-up, and they could not underestimate what relief measures it would take." Although many preventive measures have been set in place for the bereaved, we cannot know the effects of these measures, or how they will influence reactions over time. We hope that all the assistance efforts have minimized the burdens, and that the future will become brighter – although the bereaved will have to live with their loss:

> I hope to go forward … Yes, I've noticed that life goes forward, very slowly … but especially when I start to think about what Tom will never experience … but also not seeing him again … The pain of not having him around has not decreased the last two years, whatsoever; it has become worse, really. However, I think that it has something to do with the fact that grief was put on hold for over a year, which might have delayed our reactions compared to others who may have had less noise around a death. It is getting better, but surely not very much better. But it's got to be better in the future.
>
> (The father of a 21-year-old man shot at Utøya)
>
> I will certainly not be a paternal grandfather for sure … I think I will miss Eric my entire life … I'm thinking of what could have been, he was the most irreplaceable boy for us, he was so nice as a guy, so I'm going to (voice cracking) be reminded

of that my whole life. I think the last person I come to think of when I myself die will be Eric. I think that longing will be the last feeling I have ... when I myself die. I will not be scared, I'm just going to feel a sense of privation, I think.

(The father of a 15-year-old boy shot at Utøya)

References

Bonanno, G. A., Westphal, M., & Mancini, A. D. (2011). Resilience to loss and potential trauma. *Annual Review of Clinical Psychology, 7*, 511–535.

Dyregrov, A. (1983). Katastrofepsykologi II. Psykososial katastrofeintervensjon [Psycho-social intervention after disasters]. *Tidsskrift for Norsk Psykologforening, 20*, 194–202.

Dyregrov, A. (1985). Krisehjelpsteam [Crisis help-team]. *Tidsskrift for Norsk Psykologforening, 22*, 206–210.

Dyregrov, A., Dyregrov, K., Straume, M., & Grønvold Bugge, R. (2014). Weekend family gatherings for bereaved after the July 22, 2011 killings in Norway. *Scandinavian Psychologist, 1*, e8. doi:10.15714/scandpsychol.1.e8

Dyregrov, A., Straume, M., Grønvold Bugge, R., Dyregrov, K., Heltne, U., & Hordvik, E. (2012). Psykososialt katastrofearbeid etter 22. juli [Psycho-social disaster work after July 22]. *Tidsskrift for Norsk Psykologforening, 49*, 666–669.

Dyregrov, K. (2002). Assistance from local authorities versus survivors' needs for support after suicide. *Death Studies, 26*, 647–669.

Dyregrov, K. (2003). *The loss of child by suicide, SIDS, and accidents: Consequences, needs and provisions of help.* (Unpublished doctoral dissertation). University of Bergen, Norway.

Dyregrov, K. (2004). Strategies of professional assistance after traumatic deaths. Empowerment or disempowerment? *Scandinavian Journal of Psychology, 45*, 179–187.

Dyregrov, K., Berntsen, G., & Silviken, A. (2014). Needs and barriers for professional help – a qualitative study of bereaved in Sámi areas. *Suicidology Online, 5*, 47–58.

Dyregrov, K., & Dyregrov, A. (2008). *Effective grief and bereavement support: The role of family, friends, colleagues, schools and support professionals.* London, UK: Jessica Kingsley Publishers.

Dyregrov, K., Dyregrov, A., & Kristensen, P. (2014). Traumatic bereavement and terror: The psychosocial impact on parents and siblings 1.5 years after the July 2011 terror-killings in Norway. *Journal of Loss and Trauma.* doi:10.1080/15325 024.2014.957603.

Dyregrov, K., Kristensen, P., & Johnsen, I. (2015). Etterlatte foreldre, partnere, søsken og venner etter Utøya-drapene 22.07.2011. Oppsummering av forskningsprosjekt – 3¼ år etter. Minirapport III [Bereaved parents, partners, siblings and friends after the Utøya killings 22.07.2011. Summary of the research project – 3¼ years after. Mini Report III]. Bergen, Norway: Senter for Krisepsykologi.

Dyregrov, K., Kristensen, P., Johnsen, I., & Dyregrov, A. (2015). The psycho-social follow-up after the terror of July 22nd 2011 as experienced by the bereaved. *Scandinavian Psychologist, 2*, e1. doi:10.15714/scandpsychol.2.e1 DOI:10.15714/scandpsychol.2.e1#_blank

Johnsen, I., Laberg, J. C., Matthiesen, S. B., Dyregrov, A., & Dyregrov, K. (2015). Psychosocial functioning after losing a close friend in an extreme terror incident. *Scandinavian Psychologist, 2*, e1. doi:10.15714/scandpsychol.2.e1 DOI:10.15714/scandpsychol.2.e1#_blank

Kristensen, P., Dyregrov, K., & Dyregrov, A. (2015). Det er både helt grusomt og godt på samme tid. Etterlatte foreldre og søskens opplevelse av besøk til Utøya etter terrorangrepet 22.07.11 ["It feels both awful and good at the same time": Bereaved parents and siblings experiences of visiting Utøya Island after the terrorist attack 22.07.11]. *Tidsskrift for Norsk Psykologforening, 52*, 6, 486–496.

Kristensen, P., Tønnessen, A., Weisæth, L., & Heir, T. (2012). Visiting the site of death: Experiences of the bereaved after the 2004 Southeast Asian tsunami. *Death Studies, 36*, 462–476.

Kristensen, P., Weisæth, L., & Heir, T. (2012). Bereavement and mental health after sudden and violent losses: A review. *Psychiatry: Interpersonal and Biological Processes, 75*, 1, 76–97.

Levin, B. G. L. (2004). Coping with traumatic loss: An interview with the parents of TWA 800 crash victims and implications for disaster mental health professionals. *International Journal of Emergency Mental Health, 1*, 25–31.

Li, J., Precht, D. H., Mortensen, P. B., & Olsen, J. (2003). Mortality in parents after death of a child in Denmark: A nationwide follow-up study. *The Lancet, 361*(1), 1–5.

Norris, F. H., Friedman, M. J., Watson, P. J., Byrne, C. M., Diaz, E., & Kaniasty, K. (2002). 60,000 disaster victims speak: Part I. An empirical review of the empirical literature, 1981–2001. *Psychiatry: Interpersonal and Biological Processes, 65*, 3, 207–239.

Price, J., Jordan, J., Prior, L., & Parkes, J. (2011). Living through the death of a child: A qualitative study of bereaved parents' experiences. *International Journal of Nursing Studies, 48*, 1384–1392.

Raundalen, M., Schultz, J-H., & Langballe, Å. (2012). *Suggestions for how Norwegian teachers can protect students during the 22 July terror trial in Oslo, 2012.* Oslo, Norway: Center for Crisis Psychology & NKVTS.

Report IS-1315. (2006). *Brukermedvirkning – psykisk helsefeltet. Mål, anbefalinger og tiltak i Opptrappingsplan for psykisk helse [User interaction – the mental health field. Objectives, recommendations and measures of the National Programme for Mental Health].* Oslo, Norway: The Norwegian Directorate of Health.

Report IS-1810. (2011). *Guidelines for psychosocial follow-up after crisis, accidents and disasters.* Oslo, Norway: The Norwegian Directorate of Health.

Report IS-1984E. (2011). *Learning for better emergency preparedness. The medical response to the terrorist incidents of July 22nd 2011.* Oslo, Norway: The Norwegian Directorate of Health.

Rutten, B. P. F., Hammels, C., Geschwind, N., Menne-Lothmann, C., Pishva, E., Schruers, K., ... Wichers, M. (2013). Resilience in mental health: Linking psychological and neurobiological perspectives. *Acta Psychiatrica Scandinavica*, *128*, 3–20.

Schultz, J-H., Langballe, Å., & Raundalen, M. (2014). Explaining the unexplainable: Designing a national strategy on classroom communication concerning the 22 July attack in Norway. *European Journal of Psychotraumatology*, *5*, 1–5. doi:10.3402/ejpt.v5.22758

Stroebe, M., Schut, H., & Stroebe, W. (2007). Health outcomes of bereavement. *Lancet*, *370*, 1960–1973.

Weisæth, L. (2004). Preventing after-effects of disaster trauma: The information and support centre. *Prehospital and Disaster Medicine*, *19*, Special Issue 01, 86–89.

Wilson, A., & Clark, S. (2005). *South Australian Suicide Postvention Project. Report to Mental Health Services*. Adelaide, Australia: Department of Health.

17
Mental Health Service Utilization Following Mass Shootings

Andrew J. Smith, Katharine Donlon Ramsdell, Michael F. Wusik, and Russell T. Jones

Epidemiological research conducted in the wake of disasters has demonstrated low rates of mental health (MH) treatment service utilization and high rates of treatment drop-out among those in need of MH services. For example, following Hurricane Katrina, only 18% of people with newly onset disorders and 46% of those with serious difficulties sought MH treatment (Wang et al., 2007). Among survivors of a fire-related disaster, 44% of those in need of MH services sought them (van der Velden, Yzermans, Kleber, & Gersons, 2007). Research conducted following the September 11 terrorist attacks (9/11) reported that 36% of individuals with probable posttraumatic stress disorder (PTSD) sought services (Stuber, Galea, Boscarino, & Schlesigner, 2006). Moreover, among those who do seek MH treatment, high levels of treatment drop-out have been observed (e.g., 60% drop-out rate among Hurricane Katrina survivors who sought MH treatment; Wang et al., 2007). These findings highlight a need to further understand factors and mechanisms that create barriers to care in the wake of mass disasters.

A number of studies and reviews have focused on three dimensions that drive health care utilization in the wake of disasters: (a) predisposing characteristics (e.g., socioeconomic status), (b) enabling resources (e.g., social support), and (c) need (both perceived and evaluated; see review by Rodriguez & Kohn, 2008). These studies have largely been based on Andersen's (1995) behavioral model of health care utilization, providing important insight into factors that correlate with MH service utilization and/or barriers to utilization. Beyond Andersen's model, MH care utilization following mass shootings – as well as individual and community recovery – is influenced by interactions among individual survivors, survivors' social networks, purveyors of MH interventions, and community/societal response to disasters.

Examining interactions among these dimensions may prove helpful in understanding how often individuals seek needed services, mechanisms that drive seeking or nonseeking, and the extent to which MH services effectively meet individual and community treatment needs. Thus, in addition to reviewing and summarizing evidence derived from research that has employed Andersen's (1995) health care utilization model, this chapter explores possible mechanisms that determine MH service utilization related to intraindividual, interpersonal, and sociocontextual factors. By merging what is known from research built on Andersen's model with modern theories of posttraumatic resilience (see Bonanno & Burton, 2013; Maercker & Horn, 2012), the current approach intends to inform future directions and innovation in MH care efficacy following mass shootings. Notably, a review of the literature yielded only one study that examined barriers to MH service utilization specifically following mass shootings (see Schwarz & Kowalski, 1992). As such, the current chapter draws from the disaster literature as a whole. Throughout the chapter, please refer to Table 17.1 for a review of the literature on MH utilization in the wake of disasters.

The Behavioral Model of Health Services

Predisposing characteristics

Demographic characteristics (e.g., age, gender, race, education, income, marital status) are the most frequently examined factors in association with postdisaster MH service use, and findings vary by context. Regarding age, among New York City residents following 9/11, being younger predicted more MH service use (Boscarino, Adams, & Figley, 2004), whereas among other disaster samples (e.g., Manhattan residents following 9/11, Hurricane Katrina survivors) middle-aged survivors were more likely than younger or older to seek MH services (Boscarino, Galea, Ahern, Resnick, & Vlahov, 2002; Wang et al., 2007). Being younger has predicted increased informal help seeking (e.g., help from family, friends, neighbors) across several disaster contexts (Adams, Ford, & Dailey, 2004; Goto, Wilson, Kahana, & Slane, 2002), whereas being older has predicted more formal help seeking (e.g., help from psychologist, physician, psychiatrist, MH counselor; Goto et al., 2002).

Research has also demonstrated that women utilize more postdisaster MH services than men (Boscarino et al., 2002; Tucker, Pfefferbaum, Jeon-Slaughter, Garton, & North, 2014; van der Velden et al., 2007). Women may seek more informal support than men (Adams et al., 2004; Goto et al., 2002), whereas in some cultures and contexts men may be more likely than women to seek formal services (Goto et al., 2002). With regard to marital status, findings vary by context. Specifically, 9/11 and fire-disaster research showed that not being

Table 17.1 Postdisaster mental health treatment seeking and utilization: Organized by Andersen's (1995) behavioral health model of treatment utilization.

Study	Disaster type	Predisposing factors	Enabling/disabling factors	Need
Adams et al., 2004	September 11 terrorist attacks (2001)	**More formal MH service use:** • Close relationship with victim **More informal MH service use:** • Age = younger adult • Gender = female	**More formal MH service use:** • Received informal help **More informal MH service use:** • Received formal help	**More formal MH service use:** • Sleep disturbance • Increased postdisaster smoking/drinking **More informal MH service use:** • 1+ problems (e.g., worry)
Boscarino, Adams, et al., 2004	September 11 terrorist attacks (2001)	**More MH service use:** • Age = younger		**MH service use:** • Panic attack during disaster • PTSD • Depression • Greater exposure to disaster epicenter
*Boscarino et al., 2005	September 11 terrorist attacks (2001)	**Factors associated with MH service use:** • Race • Had a regular doctor		**Factors associated with MH service use:** • Panic attack during disaster **More MH service use:** • Greater exposure to disaster
Boscarino, Galea, et al., 2004	September 11 terrorist attacks (2001)	**Factors associated with service use:** • 4+ lifetime traumatic events • 2+ stressful life events in 12 months prior to disaster • Race **More MH service use:** • Education = graduate degree		**Factors associated with service use:** • PTSD • Depression **More MH service use:** • Increased alcohol use after disaster • Depression

Study	Disaster	Findings
Boscarino et al., 2002	September 11 terrorist attacks (2001)	**More MH service use:** • Panic attack during event
Ford et al., 2006	September 11 terrorist attacks (2001)	**More MH service use:** • Age = 45–64 years • Gender = female • 4+ lifetime traumatic events • 2+ stressful life events in 12 months prior to disaster **More MH service use:** • 1+ poor physical health days per month • 1+ poor MH days per month
Goto et al., 2002	Miyake Island volcanic eruption (2000)	**More MH service use:** • Nondisabled • Nonsmoker • Current drinker • Marital status = single • Employed • No increase in smoking since disaster **More formal MH service use:** • Age = older • Gender = male **More informal MH service use:** • Age = younger • Gender = female **More MH service use:** • Higher PTSD and depression severity related to more seeking with physicians, not with psychologists or MH professionals
*Stuber et al., 2006	September 11 terrorist attacks (2001)	**More MH service use:** • MH services prior to disaster • Income above $30k • Had a regular doctor • MH problem prior to disaster • Being in worse physical health **Reasons for not using MH services:** • Cost too high • Lack of knowledge • Stigma • Time constraints • Lack of trust in MH system • Fear discussing the disaster **Reasons for not using MH services:** • Perceive others need care more than oneself • Perception that oneself and/or social network can provide necessary support

(continued on p. 316)

Table 17.1 (*Continued*)

Study	Disaster type	Predisposing factors	Enabling/disabling factors	Need
Tucker et al., 2014	Oklahoma City bombing (1995)	**More MH service use:** • Gender = female • Injury or hospitalization		**More MH service use:** • PTSD • Depression
van der Velden et al., 2007	Dutch fireworks disaster (2000)	**More MH service use:** • Gender = female • Marital status = single • Immigrant status • Previous MH service utilization • Predisaster psychological problems	**More MH service use:** • Having private insurance • Being relocated after disaster	**More MH service use:** • Comorbid PTSD, anxiety, and depression symptoms
*Wang et al., 2007	Hurricane Katrina (2005)	**More MH service use:** • Age = middle age, 40–59 • Marital status = being married at some point in the lifespan • Owning one's home without a mortgage • Race • Education = low or high levels of education	**More MH service use:** • Having health insurance **Reasons for not using MH services despite need for services:** • Lack of available services • Lack of transportation • Lack of financial means • Inconvenience • Stigma • Ineffectiveness of treatment	**Reasons for not using MH services despite need for services:** • Low need (thinking problem was not severe or would resolve on its own) • Desire to handle problem by oneself

		More MH service use:	More MH service use:
*Wang et al., 2008	Hurricane Katrina (2005)	• Race	• Having health insurance
			Reasons for failing to initiate or continue MH services among participants with MH problems:
			• Lack of available services
			• Lack of financial means
			• Stigma
			• Ineffectiveness of treatment

Note: * Assessed barriers to care.

married was associated with more MH service use (Ford, Adams, & Dailey, 2006; van der Velden et al., 2007), whereas "being married at any point in the lifespan" was associated with more post-Hurricane Katrina service use (Wang et al., 2007).

Previous research has suggested that ethnic minorities may be less likely than whites to use services (Boscarino, Adams, Stuber, & Galea, 2005; Boscarino, Galea et al., 2004; Wang et al., 2007, 2008). However, in the Dutch fire-disaster sample, holding immigrant status was associated with more MH service use (van der Velden et al., 2007). More education was associated with increased postdisaster MH service use following both 9/11 and Hurricane Katrina (Boscarino, Galea et al., 2004; Wang et al., 2007). However, post-Hurricane Katrina research revealed a less-than-simple relationship between education and MH service use (Wang et al., 2007). Specifically, more MH service use occurred among those with low (e.g., less than high school degree) and high (e.g., college degree) education levels, and less among those with middle education levels (e.g., high school degree). Interestingly, only one study has demonstrated income as a predictor of postdisaster MH service utilization (Stuber et al., 2006). Other factors associated with more postdisaster MH service use include being employed and nondisabled (Ford et al., 2006), as well as owning a home (Wang et al., 2007).

Additionally, increased postdisaster MH service use was associated with more severe trauma history (i.e., experiencing four or more traumatic events), recent history of stressful events (Boscarino et al., 2002), and having a closer social relationship with a disaster victim (Adams et al., 2004). MH service use prior to disaster, predisaster MH problems, being in worse physical health, being injured or hospitalized, and having a regular doctor have promoted more MH service seeking across several postdisaster contexts (Boscarino et al., 2005; Stuber et al., 2006; Tucker et al., 2014; van der Velden et al., 2007).

Enabling and disabling characteristics

The studies that have specifically focused on barriers to care post-9/11 (Stuber et al., 2006) and post-Hurricane Katrina (Wang et al., 2007, 2008) provide the most comprehensive findings associated with factors that enable and disable MH service use. Wang and colleagues (2007, 2008) found that lack of available services, lack of transportation, lack of financial means, inconvenience, fear of stigma, and perceived ineffectiveness of treatment were reasons for not using MH services despite having a perceived need for such services. In the wake of 9/11, Stuber and colleagues (2006) identified the following reasons for not seeking services: cost too high, lacking knowledge about how to get help, fear of stigma, time constraints, lack of trust in MH professionals, and fear of discussing the disaster. Conversely, having health insurance promoted MH service use across various disasters samples (Wang et al., 2007, 2008; van der Velden et al., 2007). Further, Adams and colleagues (2004) demonstrated a possible reciprocal enabling relationship showing that receiving informal help may lead to more formal help seeking, and vice versa. Whereas income has only been supported as a predictor of MH service in one known postdisaster study (Stuber et al., 2006), perception of cost and/or perceived lack of financial means have been supported as barriers to care among disaster survivors (Stuber et al., 2006; Wang et al., 2007, 2008).

Need

Need is recognized as the strongest indicator of MH services use (Andersen, 1995; Parslow & Jorm, 2000). Ample data suggest that a variety of psychopathology-related factors increase MH service use (e.g., PTSD, depression, comorbid disorders; Boscarino, Adams, et al., 2004; Boscarino, Galea, et al., 2004; Tucker et al., 2014; van der Velden et al., 2007). Some research has demonstrated that in the acute aftermath of a disaster, neither PTSD nor depression predicted MH service use (Boscarino et al., 2002). Other research has supported that having any mental or physical health concerns, lower self-esteem (Boscarino, Adams, et al., 2004), and increased postdisaster alcohol use (Boscarino, Galea, et al., 2004) were associated with more service use (Ford et al., 2006).

Peri-traumatic factors and experiences have also been found to be associated with MH service use. Following 9/11, research demonstrated that higher exposure (e.g., being in closer physical proximity) was associated with (Boscarino, Adams, et al., 2004) and predicted (Boscarino et al., 2005) more MH service use. Additionally, having had a panic attack during the 9/11 terrorist attacks was associated with more postdisaster MH service use (Boscarino, Adams, et al., 2004; Boscarino et al., 2005; Boscarino et al., 2002).

The barriers to care identified in research conducted following both 9/11 (Stuber et al., 2006) and Hurricane Katrina (Wang et al., 2007) provide important details associated with "need" based factors involved in MH service use. Participants in post-9/11 research reported perceptions that "others need care more than oneself" and "oneself or one's social network can provide adequate support" as reasons for not seeking MH services (Stuber et al., 2006). Wang and colleagues (2007) reported the following need-based reasons: thinking problems were not severe or would resolve on their own, and desire to handle the problem by oneself.

Factors and Mechanisms That May Confer Barriers to MH Service Use

Intraindividual considerations

The most common reasons that participants endorse for not seeking MH treatment involve attitudinal barriers and low perceived need (Andrade et al., 2000). Additionally, posttrauma psychopathology and phenomenology may be involved in survivors' treatment-seeking decisions following mass shootings (Schwarz & Kowalski, 1992). The following subsections focus on the roles of trauma-induced psychopathology, MH literacy, and attitudinal factors (e.g., stigma) in the process of MH service use following mass shootings.

Psychopathology PTSD is the most widely studied MH outcome in the wake of mass shootings. Hughes and colleagues (2011) demonstrated that 15% of the students sampled in the wake of the Virginia Tech shootings had probable PTSD. Individuals with current symptoms of PTSD, particularly those related to avoidance and reexperiencing symptoms, may be less likely to seek treatment. Evidence and clinical observation indicate that the anticipation of having to confront memories and traumatic reminders may lead individuals with PTSD to avoid seeking treatment (Schwarz & Kowalski, 1992). This may be evident in survivors who have a perceived need for service, yet decide not to seek services due to "fear of discussing the disaster" (Stuber et al., 2006).

A byproduct of traumatic experiences, particularly amid disasters caused by human-malice, is that survivors may begin to view the world as dangerous, unpredictable, and inherently unsafe (Janoff-Bulman, 1989). Following the Virginia Tech shootings, individuals who perceived a lack of control over their outcomes were at greater risk for psychological distress (Grills-Tacquechel, Littleton, & Axsom, 2011), with maintenance of disrupted worldviews leading to more severe psychological outcomes (Smith, Abeyta, Hughes, & Jones, 2015). It is reasonable to suggest that the existential, negative worldview that can follow exposure to mass violence is involved in inhibiting individuals from seeking needed services, although this facet of MH service seeking is yet to be directly tested.

MH literacy The broad MH literature draws an association between low MH literacy and decreased help seeking (Wright, Wright, Perry, & Foote-Ardah, 2007). The concept of MH literacy refers to "knowledge and beliefs about mental disorders which aid in their recognition, management, or prevention" (Jorm et al., 1997, p. 183), and is characterized by five factors: (1) the ability to recognize specific disorders or psychological distress, (2) knowledge about risk factors and causes, (3) knowledge about interventions, including self-help and professional, (4) attitudes that lead to recognition and help-seeking behaviors, and (5) knowledge about how to attain MH resources (Jorm et al., 1997).

Many people may fail to seek help for psychological distress because, although they recognize personal distress, they may not consider their symptoms to be out of the realm of "normal" (Gulliver, Griffiths, & Christensen, 2010). In community surveys, underrecognition of psychological disorders is common (e.g., Dahlberg, Waern, & Runeson, 2008; Wang et al., 2007). For example, an Australian national survey of mental disorders revealed that only one third of participants were able to accurately recognize PTSD symptoms when presented with vignettes that described fictional people portraying actual PTSD symptoms (Reavley & Jorm, 2011).

MH literacy has also been linked to MH treatment-seeking barriers and is predicated on beliefs that individuals can manage symptoms on their own and that treatment is unnecessary (Jorm et al., 2006). Indeed, following both 9/11 and Hurricane Katrina, many individuals who considered seeking MH treatment did not do so because they believed they could handle the problem on their own (Stuber et al., 2006; Wang et al., 2007) or that symptoms would diminish over time (Wang et al., 2007, 2008).

Having a higher degree of MH literacy is also associated with having experience with predisaster MH treatment services. This notion is indirectly supported by mass disaster research that shows that individuals with premorbid MH problems may be more likely to receive formal MH services after a disaster (van der Velden et al., 2007; Stuber et al., 2006). Perhaps previous MH service use results in survivors being better informed about psychological wellbeing and service availability.

Stigma   The disaster literature supports stigma as a primary barrier (Stuber et al., 2006; Wang et al., 2007, 2008), perhaps by influencing beliefs about the helpfulness of treatment and the likelihood that individuals will seek treatment (see Yap, Wright, & Jorm, 2011). Self-stigmatizing beliefs center on attitudes that people with MH vulnerabilities and needs are incompetent (Corrigan, 2004). Recent epidemiological survey research (e.g., Yap et al., 2011) demonstrates an association between stronger "beliefs that mental disorders are a sign of weakness" and "less favorable attitudes towards professional MH help seeking." Higher levels of stigma promote lower perceived need for treatment among those who have MH difficulties, which in turn leads to nonuse of needed MH services (Schomerus et al., 2012). These findings elucidate possible attitudinal barriers that underlie low levels of postdisaster MH service use (e.g., perceptions that "one does not need services" or that "services are ineffective"; Wang et al., 2007).

As noted above, barriers research identifies beliefs regarding "desire to/ability to manage MH symptoms on my own" as a prominent factor in MH services utilization (Stuber et al., 2006; Wang et al., 2007). Further, this idea has been linked to MH literacy with the possibility of having stigma-related implications. For example, individuals who express higher levels of MH stigma within their personal belief systems prefer to manage MH difficulties on their own (Griffiths, Crisp, Jorm, & Christensen, 2011). Additionally, Jorm and colleagues (2006) reported that individuals who do not believe that their symptoms represent a true underlying condition may believe that MH difficulties can be managed through willpower and that professional help is unnecessary. These same individuals, who maintain underlying beliefs that "MH difficulties are a sign of weakness," may go on to malign those who do seek treatment.

Interpersonal considerations

Social network dynamics are critically important to recognizing and understanding treatment need and seeking following large-scale disasters. Postdisaster trauma theory (Kaniasty & Norris, 1995) and empirical evidence (Brewin, Andrews, & Valentine, 2000) highlight perceptions of social support availability and receipt of tangible aid from one's social network as particularly important predictors of MH outcomes. Considering that very little research to date has examined social network dynamics in relation to MH treatment seeking, a good starting point for understanding such dynamics can be gained through research that has focused on understanding sources of social support (e.g., formal vs. informal support seeking). For example, following the Virginia Tech shootings, seeking of social support among informal social networks enabled postshootings recovery through its influence on perceptions of social support availability and self-efficacy (Smith, Donlon, Anderson, Hughes, & Jones, 2015).

Studies conducted following the terrorist attack on Utøya Island, Norway and the Estonia ferry disaster of 1994 demonstrated that disaster survivors often perceived that others cannot truly understand disaster experiences, and that this may be a major barrier to accessing needed informal social support (Thoresen, Jensen, Wentzel-Larsen, & Dyb, 2014; Arnberg, Hultman, Michel, & Lundin, 2013). These findings are consistent with Thoits (2011), who suggested that social support drawn from fellow trauma survivors can be powerful during the coping process through means of shared intimate knowledge of a coexperienced disaster. These findings are perhaps also commensurate with post-9/11 research that demonstrated that a high proportion of participants (43%) who sought emotional support via informal social networks (e.g., friends, family) reported feeling unable to divulge thoughts and feelings due to fear that it would make social network members uncomfortable (Stein et al., 2004), which also harkens conceptual overlap with social constraints theory. Social constraints are defined as any social interaction causing the trauma survivor to feel unsupported, misunderstood, alienated, and/or unable to disclose traumatic experiences (Lepore & Revenson, 2007). Increased social constraints decrease the likelihood of trauma disclosure, thereby decreasing cognitive processing (Lepore, 2001). This may lead survivors to feel stigmatized and isolated, and may keep them from accessing needed MH services.

Sociocontextual considerations

In the wake of mass violence, it is common to see communities rally together to foster collective support and healing. For example, "WE ARE VIRGINIA TECH" became a rallying cry among the Virginia Tech community following the shootings. Similarly, following the Boston Marathon bombings, "BOSTON STRONG" became as much a community identity as it did a statement of encouragement.

Durkheim (1964) suggested that crime (and, to extrapolate, community trauma) has the power to bring together a community. Additionally, Collins (2004) suggested that crime communally experienced holds the power to increase social solidarity. Although community solidarity efforts and campaigns are enacted as a means of building cohesion and enabling survivor recovery/resiliency, polarizing effects can occur that increase barriers to MH service use. The following sections delve into possible pros and cons of such sociocontextual campaigns that may have complex, polarizing effects that can promote and/or deter help seeking and resilience. See Chapter 12 for a more thorough discussion of the impact of mass shootings on communities.

Sociocontextual factors involved in enhancing recovery and help seeking   The common understanding that community solidarity campaigns are a recovery-enabling mechanism is partially justified in the literature. For example, increases in solidarity following a traumatic event relate to enhanced pride, resolve, feelings of support, and physical health (Hawdon, Räsänen, Oksanen, & Ryan, 2012; Savage & Russell 2005; Smith & Christakis, 2008). Strengthened social networks as the result of increased solidarity have the power to mitigate the negative effects of a traumatic event via suppression of maladaptive coping and provision of needed physical and emotional resources that promote resilience (Cohen, 2004). Further, community solidarity and social support following a traumatic experience can ameliorate feelings of helplessness and meaninglessness in victims (Walsh, 2007). The literature clearly details a number of benefits associated with increased community and social network solidarity in the enablement of postmass violence recovery.

Sociocontextual factors involved in deterrence of recovery and help seeking   Evidence also speaks to less-than-positive outcomes that can be incurred in disaster-affected communities. The social support deterioration deterrence model (Kaniasty & Norris, 1995) was developed in light of the realities that communities and individual perceptions of social support can deteriorate in the wake of disaster, providing theory and evidence for how survivors frequently experience a sense of disillusionment with the support they receive. Support can be experienced as ineffective, inadequate, or disappointing. Conversely, even when support adequately meets the needs of survivors, individuals may view tangible support as finite and time restricted. In turn, longitudinal erosion of perception of support availability may confer barriers to MH service seeking and utilization that coincides with a decline in expectation for support efficacy and increased interpersonal withdrawal, leading individuals to be less likely to seek help.

Despite the enablement that can occur through increased community solidarity, campaigns can inadvertently increase stigma and decrease treatment-seeking behavior. Strength-based campaigns that advertise a "resilient community" comprised of "resilient individuals" may be empowering for those who feel resilient, while simultaneously disempowering and/or alienating those struggling with MH difficulties, physical health consequences, and traumatic loss. Nurmi, Räsänen, and Oksanen (2011) examined the negative aspects of community solidarity following a shooting incident in Jokela, Finland and found that increased perceptions of community social solidarity led to increased perceived social stigmatization. It seems that as the Jokela community reshaped its identity in the wake of disaster, individual community members struggled to identify themselves within the new posttrauma community. Individual community members were less likely to report being from Jokela when talking with outsiders. "Us" (i.e., those directly exposed to the trauma) versus "them" (i.e., those who were not directly exposed to the trauma) divisions, lack of trust, and alienation grew over time. These findings can be extrapolated to MH service seeking, because MH service providers who were considered "outsiders" may be viewed as less trustworthy in the eyes of the most directly affected (and perhaps most in need) survivors. This suggests the potential power of support that would come from within rather than from outside disaster-affected communities.

Conclusions

This chapter examined the current literature on MH service utilization and barriers to care in the aftermath of disasters. In this chapter we (a) summarized the literature derived from Andersen's (1995) three-factor behavioral health care model, and (b) extended the literature via introducing intraindividual, interpersonal, and sociocontextual mechanisms that may underlie MH service use and barriers following mass shootings.

The most direct implications of this chapter can be drawn from research that assessed why disaster survivors do not seek MH services, even when they perceived need for such services. Postdisaster research demonstrates the following participant reasons for not using MH services despite having a need: cost, lack of available services and/or knowledge of services, time constraints, lack of trust in the system, fear of discussing the disaster, lack of transportation, lack of financial means, inconvenience, fear of stigma, and perceived ineffectiveness of treatment (Stuber et al., 2006; Wang et al., 2007, 2008).

Each of these reasons for not seeking services despite having a need for help should be considered by those charged with assisting survivors in accessing care. For example, given that cost was consistently reported as a barrier to treatment, creative solutions may be applied. The juxtaposition between the lack of evidence for income as a predictor of MH service use (Stuber et al., 2006) and the perception of cost/perceived lack of financial means as a consistent predictor of MH service use (Stuber et al., 2006; Wang et al., 2007, 2008) suggests several possibilities for ameliorating the impact of this barrier. Perhaps public relations and marketing campaigns can clearly and precisely articulate actual costs of MH services in mass disaster environments, and in doing so, reduce any cost-related uncertainty among survivors. Additionally, considering that health insurance is associated with more MH service seeking in the wake of disasters (van der Velden et al., 2007; Wang et al., 2007, 2008), the introduction of affordable healthcare through recent legislation may influence future help-seeking behavior. The need for strong collaboration between MH advocates, practitioners, and policy makers is of primary importance (Harris, Lieberman, & Marans, 2007).

Another approach to managing postmass shootings MH treatment barriers involves consideration of the role of MH service literacy and attitudes towards MH services. By attending to groups who may not be as MH literate or who maintain more negative beliefs about MH services, clinicians and researchers may have more success in the recruitment and enrollment of these people into MH treatment and research studies. Further, campaigns focused on increasing public awareness of common postdisaster MH difficulties (e.g., PTSD, depression, meaning and motivation difficulties, grief) may not only increase knowledge of available services, but may also reduce stigma through education that normalizes these difficulties. Information that is easy to access and understand may improve literacy and reduce stigma in a manner that encourages MH treatment utilization.

Very few studies have sought to understand the enabling facets of Andersen's (1995) model. Studies that examine social support and MH treatment seeking within formal versus informal networks (Adams et al., 2004; Goto et al., 2002) provide an important starting point for understanding enabling factors. Research that examines informal networks may carry cost-effective implications for reaching large groups of people in the wake of disasters by promoting support structures that naturally occur in communities. Evidence suggests that a possible reciprocal, enabling relationship exists wherein one's initial informal support-seeking efforts may bolster formal MH service seeking and, in turn, promote healthier continued support seeking in informal networks (Adams et al., 2004). Continued empirical and theoretical attention should be paid to enabling dynamics such as these.

Although the Anderson (1995) model has served as a benchmark for identifying treatment-seeking behavior for approximately two decades, future research aimed at understanding barriers to care and resilience among trauma-affected communities may be bolstered by social psychology applications of understanding social network dynamics in the wake of disasters. For example, empirical applications of social constraints theory (Lepore, 2001; Lepore & Revenson, 2007; Ozer & Weinstein, 2004), social support deterioration deterrence model (Kaniasty & Norris, 1995), social acknowledgement theory (Maercker & Muller, 2004), and social cognitive theory (e.g., Smith, Donlon, et al., 2015) may provide fruitful inroads to understanding enabling facets of social network and sociocontextual interactions that may drive intraindividual responses and facilitate or deter seeking MH treatment services.

Sociocontextual implications are also important to consider. Ample evidence suggests that community cohesion and solidarity can be bolstered in response to mass violence (e.g., Hawdon & Ryan, 2011; Shrum, 2007). However, little is known about how strength-based campaigns, which are initiated with good intentions to combat vulnerability and increase solidarity, may adversely affect those who have been impacted by mass violence. For example, a majority of survivors may experience strength-based community solidarity campaigns as a source of protection from an increased sense of vulnerability and existential crises (see Pyszczynski, Solomon, & Greenberg, 2003). However, those who feel vulnerable rather than strong in the wake of mass violence may experience community-wide solidarity efforts as stigmatizing and alienating in a manner that drives them away from help seeking and communal healing. Notwithstanding the powerful effects and intentions of community resiliency and solidarity campaigns, more attention should be devoted to understanding unintended consequences that result in the alienation of those who are struggling to adapt to life after mass shootings.

References

Adams, M. L., Ford, J. D., & Dailey, W. F. (2004). Predictors of help seeking among Connecticut adults after September 11, 2001. *Research and Practice, 9,* 1596–1602. doi:10.2105/AJPH.94.9.1596

Andersen, R. M. (1995). Revisiting the behavioral model and access to medical care: Does it matter? *Journal of Health and Social Behavior, 36,* 1–10.

Andrade, L., Caraveo-Anduaga, J. J., Berglund, P., Bijl, R., Kessler, R. C., Demler, O., ... & Wittchen, H. U. (2000). Cross-national comparisons of the prevalences and correlates of mental disorders. WHO International Consortium in Psychiatric Epidemiology. *Bulletin of the World Health Organization, 78,* 413–426.

Arnberg, F. K., Hultman, C. M., Michel, P. O., & Lundin, T. (2013). Fifteen years after a ferry disaster: Clinical interviews and survivors' self-assessment of their experience. *European Journal of Psychotraumatology, 4,* 1–9. doi:10.3402/ejpt.v4i0.20650

Bonanno, G. A., & Burton, C. L. (2013). Regulatory flexibility an individual differences perspective on coping and emotion regulation. *Perspectives on Psychological Science, 8*, 591–612. doi:10.1177/1745691613504116

Boscarino, J. A., Adams, R. E., & Figley, C. R. (2004). Mental health service use 1-year after the World Trade Center disaster: Implications for mental health care. *General Hospital Psychiatry, 26*, 346–358. doi:10.1016/j.genhosppsych.2004.05.001

Boscarino, J. A., Adams, R. E., Stuber, J., & Galea, S. (2005). Disparities in mental health treatment following the World Trade Center Disaster: Implications for mental health care and health services research. *Journal of Traumatic Stress, 18*, 287–297. doi:10.1002/jts.20039

Boscarino, J. A., Galea, S., Adams, R. E., Ahern, J., Resnick, H., & Vlahov, D. (2004). Mental health service and medication use in New York City after the September 11, 2001, terrorist attack. *Psychiatric Services, 55*, 274–283.

Boscarino, J. A., Galea, S., Ahern, J., Resnick, H., & Vlahov, D. (2002). Utilization of mental health services following the September 11th terrorist attacks in Manhattan, New York City. *International Journal of Emergency Mental Health, 4*, 143–155.

Brewin, C. R., Andrews, B., & Valentine, J. D. (2000). Meta-analysis of risk factors for posttraumatic stress disorder in trauma-exposed adults. *Journal of Consulting and Clinical Psychology, 68*, 748–766. doi:10.1037/0022-006X.68.5.748

Cohen, S. (2004). Social relationships and health. *American Psychologist, 59*, 676–684.

Collins, R. (2004). Rituals of solidarity and security in the wake of terrorist attacks. *Sociological Theory, 22*, 53–87. doi:10.1111/j.1467-9558.2004.00204.x

Corrigan, P. (2004). How stigma interferes with mental health care. *American Psychologist, 59*, 614–625. doi:10.1037/0003-066X.59.7.614

Dahlberg, K. M., Waern, M., & Runeson, B. (2008). Mental health literacy and attitudes in a Swedish community sample: Investigating the role of personal experience of mental health care. *BMC Public Health, 8*, 8. doi:10.1186/1471-2458-8-8

Durkheim, E. (1964). *The division of labor in society.* New York, NY: The Free Press/ Simon & Schuster.

Ford, J. D., Adams, M. L., & Dailey, W. F. (2006). Factors associated with receiving help and risk factors for disaster-related distress among Connecticut adults 5–15 months after the September 11th terrorist incidents. *Social psychiatry and psychiatric epidemiology, 41*, 261–270.

Goto, T., Wilson, J. P., Kahana, B., & Slane, S. (2002). PTSD, depression and help-seeking patterns following the Miyake Island volcanic eruption. *International Journal of Emergency Mental Health, 4*, 157–172.

Griffiths, K. M., Crisp, D. A., Jorm, A. F., & Christensen, H. (2011). Does stigma predict a belief in dealing with depression alone? *Journal of Affective Disorders, 132*, 413–417. doi:10.1016/j.jad.2011.03.012

Grills-Taquechel, A. E., Littleton, H. L., & Axsom, D. (2011). Social support, world assumptions, and exposure as predictors of anxiety and quality of life following a mass trauma. *Journal of Anxiety Disorders, 25*, 498–506. doi:10.1016/j.janxdis.2010.12.003

Gulliver, A., Griffiths, K. M., & Christensen, H. (2010). Perceived barriers and facilitators to mental health help-seeking in young people: A systematic review. *BMC Psychiatry, 10*, 113. doi:10.1186/1471-244X-10-113

Harris, W. W., Lieberman, A. F., & Marans, S. (2007). In the best interests of society. *Journal of Child Psychology and Psychiatry, 48*, 392–411.

Hawdon, J, Räsänen, P, Oksanen, A., & Ryan, J. (2012). Social solidarity and wellbeing after critical incidents: Three cases of mass shootings. *Journal of Critical Incident Analysis, 3*, 2–25.

Hawdon, J., & Ryan, J. (2011). Social relations that generate and sustain solidarity after a mass tragedy. *Social Forces, 89*, 1363–1384. doi:10.1093/sf/89.4.1363

Hughes, M., Brymer, M., Chiu, W., Fairbank, J., Jones, R., Pynoos, R., ... & Kessler, R. (2011). Posttraumatic stress among students after the shootings at Virginia Tech. *Psychological Trauma: Theory, Research, Practice, and Policy, 3*, 403–411. doi:10.1037/a0024565

Janoff-Bulman, R. (1989). Assumptive worlds and the stress of traumatic events: Applications of the schema construct. *Social Cognition, 7*, 113–136. doi:10.1521/soco.1989.7.2.113

Jorm, A. F., Kelly, C. M., Wright, A., Parslow, R. A., Harris, M. G., & McGorry, P. D. (2006). Belief in dealing with depression alone: Results from community surveys of adolescents and adults. *Journal of Affective Disorders, 96*, 59–65. doi:10.1016/j.jad.2006.05.018

Jorm, A., Korten, A.E., Jacomb, P. A., Christensen, H., Rodgers, B., & Pollitt, P. (1997). Mental health literacy: A survey of the public's ability to recognize mental disorders and their beliefs about the effectiveness of treatment. *Medical Journal of Australia, 166*, 182–186. doi:10.1192/bjp.177.5.396

Kaniasty, K., & Norris, F. H. (1995). Mobilization and deterioration of social support following natural disasters. *Current Directions in Psychological Science, 4*, 94–98. doi:10.1111/1467- 8721.ep10772341

Lepore, S. J. (2001). A social-cognitive processing model of emotional adjustment to cancer. In A. Baum & B. L. Andersen (Eds.), *Psychosocial interventions for cancer* (pp. 99–116). Washington, DC: American Psychological Association.

Lepore, S. J., & Revenson, T. A. (2007). Social constraints on disclosure and adjustment to cancer. *Social and Personality Psychology Compass, 1*, 313–333. doi:10.1111/j.1751-9004.2007.00013.x

Maercker, A., & Horn, A. B. (2012). A socio-interpersonal perspective on PTSD: The case for environments and interpersonal processes. *Clinical Psychology and Psychotherapy, 6*, 1–17. doi:10.1111/j.1751-9004.2007.00013.x

Maercker, A., & Muller, J. (2004). Social acknowledgement as a victim or survivor: A scale to measure a recovery factor of PTSD. *Journal of Traumatic Stress, 17*, 345–351.

Nurmi, J., Räsänen, P., & Oksanen, A. (2011). The norm of solidarity: Experiencing negative aspects of community life after a school tragedy. *Journal of Social Work, 11*, 1–20. doi:10.1177/1468017310386426

Ozer, E. J., & Weinstein, R. S. (2004). Urban adolescents' exposure to community violence: The role of support, school safety, and social constraints in a school-based sample of boys and girls. *Journal of Clinical Child and Adolescent Psychology, 33*, 463–476. doi:10.1207/s15374424jccp3303_4

Parslow, R. A., & Jorm, A. F. (2000). Who uses mental health services in Australia? An analysis of data from the National Survey of Mental Health and Wellbeing.

The Australian and New Zealand Journal of Psychiatry, 34, 997–1008. doi:10.1046/j.14401614.2000. 00839.x

Pyszczynski, T., Solomon, S., & Greenberg, J. (2003). *In the wake of 9/11: The psychology of terror.* Washington, DC. American Psychological Association.

Reavley, N. J., & Jorm, A. F. (2011). Recognition of mental disorders and beliefs about treatment and outcome: Findings from an Australian national survey of mental health literacy and stigma. *Australian and New Zealand Journal of Psychiatry, 45,* 947–956. doi:10.3109/00048674.2011.621060

Rodriguez, J. J., & Kohn, R. (2008). Use of mental health services among disaster Survivors. *Current Opinion in Psychiatry, 21,* 370–378.

Savage, A., & Russell, L. A. (2005). Tangled in a web of affiliation: Social support networks of dually diagnosed women who are trauma survivors. *Journal of Behavioral Health Services & Research, 32,* 199–215.

Schomerus, G., Auer, C., Rhode, D., Luppa, M., Freyberger, H. J., & Schmidt, S. (2012). Personal stigma, problem appraisal and perceived need for professional help in currently untreated depressed persons. *Journal of Affective Disorders, 139,* 94–97. doi:10.1016/j.jad.2012.02.022

Schwarz, E. D., & Kowalski, J. M. (1992). Reluctance to utilize mental health services after a disaster. *The Journal of Nervous and Mental Disease, 180,* 767–772.

Shrum, W. (2007). Hurricane stories, from within. *Social Studies of Science, 37,* 97–102.

Smith, A. J., Abeyta, A., Hughes, M., & Jones, R. T. (2015). Persistent grief in the aftermath of mass violence: The predictive roles of posttraumatic stress symptoms, self-efficacy, and disrupted worldview. *Psychological Trauma: Theory, Research, Practice, and Policy, 7,* 179–186. doi:10.1037/tra0000002

Smith, A. J., Donlon, K., Anderson, S. R., Hughes, M., & Jones, R. T. (2015). When seeking influences believing and promotes posttraumatic adaptation. *Anxiety, Stress, & Coping, 28,* 340–356. doi:10.1080/10615806.2014.969719

Smith, K. P. & Christakis, N. A. (2008). Social networks and health. *Annual Review of Sociology, 34,* 405–429. doi:10.1146/annurev.soc.34.040507.134601

Stein, B. D., Elliott, M. N., Jaycox, L. H., Collins, R. L., Berry, S. H., Klein, D. J., & Schuster, M. A. (2004). A national longitudinal study of the psychological consequences of the September 11, 2001 terrorist attacks: Reactions, impairment, and help-seeking. *Psychiatry: Interpersonal and Biological Processes, 67,* 105–117.

Stuber, J., Galea, S., Boscarino, J. A., & Schlesinger, M. (2006). Was there unmet mental health need after the September 11, 2001 terrorist attacks? *Social Psychiatry and Psychiatric Epidemiology, 41,* 230–240.

Thoits, P. A. (2011). Mechanisms linking social ties and support to physical and mental health. *Journal of Health and Social Behavior, 52,* 145–161. doi:10.1177/0021146510395592

Thoresen, S., Jensen, T. K., Wentzel-Larsen, T., & Dyb, G. (2014). Social support barriers and mental health in terrorist attack survivors. *Journal of Affective Disorders, 156,* 187–193.

Tucker, P., Pfefferbaum, B., Jeon-Slaughter, H., Garton, T. S., & North, C. S. (2014). Extended mental health service utilization among survivors of the Oklahoma City Bombing. *Psychiatric Services, 65,* 559–562.

van der Velden, P. G., Yzermans, C. J., Kleber, R. J., & Gersons, B. P. R. (2007). Correlates of mental health services utilization 18 months and almost 4 years post-disaster among adults with mental health problems. *Journal of Traumatic Stress*, *20*, 1029–1039. doi:10.1002/jts.20273

Walsh, F. (2007). Traumatic loss and major disasters: Strengthening family and community resilience. *Family Process*, *46*, 207–227.

Wang, P., Gruber, M., Powers, R., Schoenbaum, M., Speier, A., Wells, K., & Kessler, R. (2007). Mental health service use among Hurricane Katrina survivors in the eight months after the disaster. *Psychiatric Services*, *58*, 1403–1411. doi:10.1111/j.1545-5300.2007.00205.x

Wang, P., Gruber, M., Powers, R., Schoenbaum, M., Speier, A., Wells, K., & Kessler, R. (2008). Disruption of existing mental health treatments and failure to initiate new treatment after Hurricane Katrina. *American Journal of Psychiatry*, *165*, 34–41.

Wright, E. R., Wright, D. E., Perry B. L., & Foote-Ardah, C. (2007). Stigma and the sexual isolation of people with serious mental illness. *Social Problems*, *54*, 78–98. doi:10.1525/sp.2007.54.1.78

Yap, M., Wright, A., & Jorm, A. (2011). The influence of stigma on young people's help- seeking intentions and beliefs about the helpfulness of various sources of help. *Social Psychiatry and Psychiatric Epidemiology*, *46*, 1257–1265.

18

Resiliency and Posttraumatic Growth

Andrea M. Despotes, David P. Valentiner, and Melissa London

Prior research regarding the consequences of mass shootings, as well as trauma more broadly, has focused on the development of pathology, particularly Posttraumatic Stress Disorder (PTSD). However, recently there has been increased recognition that trauma reactions are more complex than previously thought (Bryant, 2015) and may include aspects that are positive (Tedeschi & Calhoun, 2004). Facilitating healthy outcomes following mass shootings requires not only that we understand maladaptive adjustment following trauma, but also that we develop a more nuanced appreciation of recovery.

We begin this chapter with a brief overview of the typical response to experiences of trauma, highlighting the diagnostic bias toward pathologizing such responses. Next, we describe the information-processing model, which has had a dominant influence in past research on recovery from trauma, and examine its neurobiological underpinnings. With this background, we then summarize the literature regarding resilience, highlighting its essence as a dynamic process that leads to psychologically healthy outcomes. Lastly, we describe recent efforts to examine response to trauma through the lens of posttraumatic growth, an approach that has been enriching the way that researchers and clinicians think about response to trauma. We hope this chapter helps foster constructive responses to mass shootings.

De-Pathologizing Responses to Trauma

Some researchers have noted that examining responses to trauma, such as a mass shooting, through the lens of PTSD is problematic because it pathologizes trauma reactions (Brewin, Lanius, Novac, Schnyder, & Galea, 2009). For individuals exposed to severe trauma, the prototypical response pattern is for symptoms to develop immediately (or within days or weeks) after the trauma,

The Wiley Handbook of the Psychology of Mass Shootings, First Edition. Edited by Laura C. Wilson.

and then gradually decline over time (Bonanno & Mancini, 2012). Studies undertaken with respect to mass shootings support the view that a majority of individuals impacted by the shooting will naturally recover, returning to pre-shooting symptom levels within months of the trauma (Orcutt, Bonanno, Hannan, & Miron, 2014). These studies suggest that the normative response to trauma involves the presence of some psychological difficulties immediately following the event and that the processing of trauma happens spontaneously (Morina, Wicherts, Lobbrecht, & Priebe, 2014; Orcutt et al., 2014). However, the *Diagnostic and Statistical Manual of Mental Disorders, Fifth Edition* (American Psychiatric Association, 2013) classifies PTSD symptoms that occur within 3 days of (and lasting up to a month after) a traumatic experience as Acute Stress Disorder. Therefore, the field identifies psychological difficulties following trauma as a psychological disorder. See Chapter 11 for more on psychopathology following exposure to a mass shooting.

Because posttrauma symptoms are normal and natural, the primary research question might be more appropriately framed as one of "offset" rather than "onset." That is, why do symptoms resolve for some individuals but not for others (Valentiner, Foa, Riggs, & Gershuny, 1996)?

Information-Processing Models of PTSD

There are several related information-processing models of PTSD that are derived from information-processing theory, which provides an explanation for natural recovery from trauma, as well as for symptom reduction as a result of exposure-based psychotherapies (Foa, Steketee, & Rothbaum, 1989; Litz & Keane, 1989; Thrasher, Dalgleish, & Yule, 1994). In general, these models propose that a traumatic event, such as a mass shooting, confronts the individual with new information that is highly consequential. If the new information contradicts information that is already stored in memory, integration of the new information into memory may be problematic. Symptoms of numbing and avoidance might be viewed as attempts to cope with the problematic information, whereas blame, guilt, intrusions, and reexperiencing symptoms can be viewed as attempts to reconcile the trauma with pretrauma memories. The unprocessed trauma memory is easily activated and results in high levels of fear and arousal until the trauma information is reconciled with pretrauma memories.

Natural recovery following trauma and successful PTSD treatment can be viewed as different paths to achieving the revision of beliefs that ultimately enables resolution of inconsistencies between trauma-related information and pretrauma memories. Treatment approaches influenced by information-processing models include Prolonged Exposure Therapy (Foa, Hembree, & Rothbaum, 2007; Foa, Rothbaum, Riggs, & Murdock, 1991), Cognitive

Processing Therapy (Resick, Nishith, Weaver, Astin, & Feuer, 2002), and Cognitive Therapy for PTSD (Ehlers, Clark, Hackmann, McManus, & Fennell, 2005), all of which are viewed as highly effective (see Stein, Cloitre, et al., 2009, for a review). A central theme of these approaches is that, as trauma-related information and pretrauma memories are integrated, a new understanding is developed and retained in memory, resulting in the resolution of PTSD symptoms. See Chapter 15 for more on empirically supported trauma therapies.

Also consistent with information-processing models of PTSD and effective treatment approaches, Janoff-Bulman and Frantz (1997) proposed that the experience of trauma challenges an individual's basic assumptions about the world, the self, and/or people. The authors argued that trauma recovery processes (whether natural or through treatment) involve "meaning making," or the development of a new system of fundamental beliefs. This development of a new belief system is often viewed as the reconciliation of trauma information with an individual's pretrauma memories (Resick et al., 2002), as posited by information-processing approaches. As discussed further below, meaning making may also be related to resilience and posttraumatic growth.

Neurobiology of PTSD

Recent progress in our understanding of the neurological structures associated with PTSD converges with the information-processing models. This convergence suggests some new lines of inquiry related to resilience and posttraumatic growth.

Shin, Rauch, and Pitman (2006) proposed that three brain regions are particularly important for understanding PTSD. First, PTSD is associated with hyperactivation of the amygdala, often viewed as the emotion center of the brain. High levels of activation in the amygdala are associated with heightened fear (Pissiota et al., 2002; Rauch et al., 1996; Shin et al., 2004). The amygdala plays a central role in threat assessment and, in cooperation with the second brain region (i.e., hippocampus) identified by Shin et al. (2006), is centrally involved in fear conditioning.

The amygdala and hippocampus appear to mediate the development of initial PTSD symptoms. Trauma activates the amygdala and the hippocampus encodes the experience. For a day or so following the trauma, the hippocampus rapidly replays the trauma and consolidates (i.e., stores) it in memory. Activation of the amygdala accompanies and facilitates this consolidation process, and is triggered by recall of the trauma.

A third brain region, the medial prefrontal cortex (mPFC) becomes involved later and appears to be important in the resolution of symptoms. Activity of the amygdala and of the mPFC have an inverse relationship – activation of the amygdala (such as that underlying a strong fear response) is associated with low levels of activation of the mPFC, whereas deactivation of the amygdala is associated with higher levels of activation in the mPFC.

When a trauma is remembered, the amygdala is reactivated. Successful inhibition of symptoms depends on activation of the mPFC to deactivate the amygdala. Activation of the mPFC appears to reflect the learning that takes place as symptoms resolve, either spontaneously or via successful treatment. For the new learning (and resulting deactivation of the amygdala) to be lasting, the hippocampus must then update the trauma memory – a process called reconsolidation. We speculate that these changes in the mPFC are the neurobiological underpinnings of belief change that takes place during natural recovery and effective treatment.

A fourth brain region, the dorsal anterior cingulate cortex (dACC), is in close communication with the mPFC. High levels of activation and inefficient functioning of the dACC appear to be risk factors for developing PTSD (Shin et al., 2009; Shin et al., 2011). What is known about the dACC (see Etkin, Egner, & Kalisch, 2011) suggests that it is involved in searching for and creating new meaning of the trauma. As meaning making is seen as important for the symptom reduction that occurs during natural recovery and successful treatment following trauma (Resick et al., 2002), we speculate that the dACC may be of particular relevance to the topics of resilience and/or posttraumatic growth.

Recent Developments in "Fear Erasure": Unknown Implications for Meaning Making and Posttraumatic Growth

The acute response to stress and the subsequent pattern of arousal, avoidance, reexperiencing, and disorganization of mood is normal and natural (Morina et al., 2014; Orcutt et al., 2014). Consistent with this view, attempts to intervene early, such as by using critical incident stress debriefing, appear to be counterproductive and potentially harmful (see Szumilas, Wei, & Kutcher, 2010, for a review). Also consistent with this view, pharmacological interventions that interfere with or attenuate the acute stress response lead to higher levels of PTSD, and interventions that facilitate or enhance the acute stress response generally lead to lower levels of PTSD (see Steckler & Risbrough, 2012, for a review).

However, recent developments in "fear erasure" suggest that PTSD symptoms might also be resolved without the development of new meaning through actively processing the traumatic experience (Brunet et al., 2008; Gamache, Pitman, & Nader, 2012; Schiller et al., 2010). To understand this emerging literature, consider the aforementioned process of reconsolidation, whereby the hippocampus updates (or reconsolidates) the trauma memory after the trauma is recalled. When new meaning has developed, including meaning that serves an inhibitory function, that new meaning is encoded in the trauma memory. Reconsolidation preserves the fear-activating part of the memory, and potentially updates the memory with new meaning that deactivates fear. However, it appears possible to interfere with reconsolidation both pharmacologically (Brunet et al., 2008; Gamache et al., 2012) and by adapting commonly used psychotherapy procedures (Schiller et al., 2010), with the result that the fear-activating part of the trauma memory is erased, although the declarative memory of the trauma remains intact. This type of resolution of trauma without development of inhibitory learning (and the meaning-making that putatively accompanies it) may sometimes occur spontaneously (Weems et al., 2014). The potential role of this phenomenon with respect to resilience and posttraumatic growth, or perhaps in undermining posttraumatic growth, has not been examined.

Resilience

With that background, we turn to the concept of resilient responses to mass shootings and other traumatic events. In lay terms, resilience denotes the ability to adjust easily to change; thus, a resilient object regains its original shape after being bent or compressed, and a resilient person recovers readily from illness, depression, or adversity ("Resilience," n.d.). The psychological construct of resilience is less clearly defined, however. In the context of response to a traumatic stressor, resilience has been conceptualized as: (1) the presence of internal or external protective factors (and/or the absence of risk factors), (2) positive outcome (i.e., lack of psychopathology), and (3) a process of adaptation (Dutton & Greene, 2010). In the discussion that follows, we discuss protective factors that appear to confer resilience, as well as a conception of resilience as a process in which the dynamic relationship among protective factors over time ultimately leads to adaptive outcomes. See Chapter 11 for a discussion of risk factors associated with the development of psychopathology following trauma.

Protective Factors Conferring Resilience

Various individual characteristics, both psychological (Connor & Davidson, 2003; Dutton & Greene, 2010) and biological (Charncy, 2004), as well as social elements (Dutton & Greene, 2010), have been identified as factors protecting individuals from maladaptive responses to trauma. Psychological characteristics that have been found to confer better adjustment following trauma generally include hardiness, altruism, self-esteem, internal locus of control, and ego defense (Agaibi & Wilson, 2005). Connor and Davidson (2003) proposed that resilience following crime victimization is found in individuals who are oriented towards goals, are tenacious, trust their instincts, see themselves as adaptable, perceive that they can control their lives, and have spiritual beliefs.

In the mass shooting context, there is specific support for the association of adaptive responses to trauma with self-esteem and internal locus of control. In a study surrounding the 2007 Virginia Tech shootings, Grills-Taquechel, Littleton, and Axsom (2011) found that world assumptions regarding positive self-worth after the shootings predicted less anxiety and greater quality of life postshooting. Furthermore, greater posttrauma beliefs in randomness were associated with greater emotional anxiety, particularly for high exposure subjects, whereas greater beliefs in self-controllability following the shooting were associated with lower physiological anxiety for high exposure (but not low exposure) participants.

Additionally, studies have revealed potential links between biological processes and resilience following an experience of trauma. In particular, the following broad biological domains have been implicated in whether or not an experience of trauma results in the development of PTSD or depression: (1) structural and functional neural plasticity of the brain, (2) emotional reactivity (e.g., startle reflex), (3) neuroendocrine function, (4) lack of symmetry between brain hemispheres, and (5) immune function focused on hypothalamic-pituitary-adrenal axis dysregulation (Dutton & Greene, 2010). Moreover, certain endogenous compounds appear to be related to resilient responses to acute stress (see Charney, 2004; Dutton & Greene, 2010, for reviews).

Finally, the tendency to develop PTSD symptoms following trauma is moderately heritable (Stein, Jang, Taylor, Vernon, & Livesley, 2014). This heritability of risk for PTSD might be explained by associations between psychological factors related to resilience and genes linked to the 5-HTTLPR serotonin transporter (Stein, Campbell-Sills, & Gelernter, 2009). In the context of the 2008 Northern Illinois University campus shooting, Mercer et al. (2012) examined genetic risk factors among females and found that the combination of two genetic polymorphisms (5-HTTLPR and rs25531) was associated with increased posttrauma symptoms about one month after the shooting. Although multiple studies have implicated genes associated with the serotonin system, overall the genetic risk is not yet well understood.

Certain aspects of communities and social networks also have proven to be important protective factors in traumatic circumstances (Dutton & Greene, 2010; Norris & Stevens, 2007). In particular, "community resilience" has been fostered in groups that (1) provide trustworthy information and effective communication; (2) are competent and economically developed; and (3) facilitate connections between survivors and natural social supports such as family and friends (Norris & Stevens, 2007). Related to these observations, Hobfoll, Watson, et al. (2007) recommended fostering safety and calmness, efficacy and hope, and connectedness as key features in designing effective interventions following mass traumas (Dutton & Greene, 2010).

Resilience as Adaptive Process

In contrast to viewing resilience as a collection of protective factors, Bonanno (2012) defines resilience as a "stable trajectory of healthy functioning in response to a clearly defined event" (p. 753). In so doing, he distinguishes it from both internal and external protective factors measured at a single point in time, and rejects the characterization of resilience as an absence of psychopathology (or an "average" level of adjustment) following trauma as overly simplistic. Instead, based on studies that examine subpopulations of trauma survivors with distinct patterns of responding, Bonanno and colleagues (Bonanno, 2004, 2005; Bonanno & Mancini, 2012) argue that resilience should be conceptualized as one of several possible processes of adaptation that unfolds in the wake of a potentially traumatic event.

Such studies have identified four prototypical patterns of response to extreme stress: (1) *chronic disruption*, involving severe disruption to normal functioning soon after the trauma and periodically for an extended period thereafter; (2) *delayed response*, in which a mild to moderate dysfunctional initial response to a traumatic stressor is followed by more severe dysfunction in the long term; (3) *gradual recovery*, characterized by moderate to severe disruption soon after an acute stressor, with gradual reduction in symptomology in the years following the trauma; and (4) *resilience*, characterized by functioning at or near pretrauma levels for the long term following exposure, although there may be brief, mild impairment in functioning shortly following the traumatic experience (e.g., Bonanno, 2004, 2005). Of these four prototypical trajectories, resilient responding is the most common (Bonanno, 2005).

Orcutt et al. (2014) examined symptom trajectories in response to the February 14, 2008 shooting at Northern Illinois University as part of a study that is noteworthy not only because of the mass shooting context, but also because certain pretrauma symptom measures were available, allowing for an examination of the immediate change in symptoms due to the mass shooting event. Orcutt and colleagues (2014) identified four trajectories of symptoms, though somewhat different than the four trajectories identified by Bonanno (2004). Most of the participants (65%) fit a resilience pattern, with no significant symptoms over the study period (about 2.5 years posttrauma). Compared to the other trajectories, this "minimal impact–resilience" trajectory was associated with lower levels of exposure, less prior trauma history, and more adaptive emotion regulation strategies 1 month trauma.

The second largest group of participants (25%) in the Orcutt et al. (2014) study fit a "high impact–recovery" trajectory, showing minimal symptoms preshooting, moderate symptoms at the 1-month postshooting assessment and returning to a minimal symptom level at the 7-month postshooting and subsequent assessments. The third largest group of participants (8%) fit a "moderate impact–moderate symptoms" trajectory, showing moderate symptoms preshooting, high levels of symptoms at the 1-month postshooting assessment, and a return to moderate symptoms at the 7-month and subsequent assessments. A small portion of the sample (2%) fit the fourth trajectory, characterized as a "chronic dysfunction" trajectory, showing high symptom levels throughout the study period, including at the preshooting assessment.

As noted above, other studies of symptom trajectories over time (e.g., Bonanno & Mancini, 2012) have identified that a small number of individuals respond to trauma with a delayed reaction, showing modest initial symptoms (if any) that worsen significantly at a later time. No delayed onset trajectory was evident in the Orcutt et al. (2014) study.

Caution should be exercised when using these proportions to estimate responses to other mass shooting events, as the Orcutt et al. (2014) study did not include any males and contextual factors (such as severity of exposure) likely affected the number of individuals impacted by the shooting and the duration of symptoms. Overall, however, the results of the Orcutt et al. (2014) study support the view that a majority of individuals impacted by mass shootings will be minimally affected and naturally recover, returning to preshooting symptom levels within months of the trauma.

Posttraumatic Growth

Related to the concept of resilience is the construct of posttraumatic growth. Whereas resilience is characterized by maintaining a stable equilibrium following a traumatic experience (Bonanno, 2004), posttraumatic growth has been heralded as a potential positive psychological outcome of trauma that is profound and transcends pretrauma functioning (Tedeschi & Calhoun, 2004).

There is no broadly accepted definition of posttraumatic growth. A prominent view conceptualizes it as a deeper appreciation of life, coupled with recognition of enhanced intra- and interpersonal relationships that can result from reconstructing a belief system that has been shattered by trauma (Tedeschi & Calhoun, 2004). This perspective is partly based on the idea that trauma challenges survivors' fundamental beliefs (i.e., that the world is benevolent and meaningful, that the self is worthy) and thereby motivates them to reevaluate such beliefs (Janoff-Bulman, 2010) in light of deeper understandings regarding life's fragility and their own strength after having persevered through adversity. As observed by Jayawickreme and Blackie (2014), others have characterized posttraumatic growth as: (1) an increase in psychological wellbeing (Linley & Joseph, 2004); (2) a form of positive personality change resulting from restructuring one's life narrative (Pals & McAdams, 2004), or (3) a two-faceted construct encompassing both illusions of self-enhancement to relieve distress in the short term and functional coping mechanisms that lead to constructive change in the long term (Hobfoll, Hall, et al., 2007; Maercker & Zoellner, 2004).

Most of the research regarding posttraumatic growth has operationalized the construct using the Posttraumatic Growth Inventory (PTGI; Tedeschi & Calhoun, 1996), a 21-item self-report scale encompassing the following five dimensions of growth: greater appreciation for life, warmer and more intimate relationships, enhanced sense of personal strength, recognition of new life possibilities, and spiritual development (Jayawickreme & Blackie, 2014). Numerous studies have confirmed the five-factor structure of posttraumatic growth (Brunet, McDonough, Hadd, Crocker, & Sabiston, 2010; Morris, Shakespeare-Finch, Rieck, & Newbery, 2005; Taku, Cann, Calhoun, & Tedeschi, 2008), with one such analysis also finding acceptable fit for a structure comprised of one higher-order construct having five first-order domains (Linley, Andrews, & Joseph, 2007). However, a recent review of cross-cultural research on posttraumatic growth indicated that the factor structure of posttraumatic growth may be culture-dependent, embodying between two and five factors depending on the population examined (Weiss & Berger, 2010). A review of findings using the PTGI and similar measures provides a starting point for our evaluation of the status of the research on posttraumatic growth.

Predictors of Posttraumatic Growth

The possibility that the often-tragic consequences of trauma might be counterbalanced by constructive benefits has engendered a significant amount of research into the nature and correlates of posttraumatic growth. Studies indicate that gender has a small to moderate effect on the level of growth perceived by individuals, with women reporting higher levels of growth than men (Helgeson, Reynolds, & Tomich, 2006; Vishnevsky, Cann, Calhoun, Tedeschi, & Demakis, 2010). In particular, two meta-analyses examining the effect of gender found a small effect of female gender ($r = .08$, $p < .001$; Helgeson et al., 2006) and a small to moderate effect of female gender ($g = .27$, 95% CI [.21, .32]; Vishnevsky et al., 2010), respectively.

Investigations into the relationship between posttraumatic growth and personality traits have yielded inconsistent results. The initial validation studies of the PTGI indicated that posttraumatic growth was related to four of the five primary personality domains (all except neuroticism; Tedeschi & Calhoun, 1996), and a more recent meta-analysis confirmed a lack of relationship between growth and neuroticism (Helgeson et al., 2006). Furthermore, in two separate meta-analyses, posttraumatic growth was moderately related to optimism (Helgeson et al., 2006; Prati & Pietrantoni, 2009), albeit with relatively small effect sizes. However, in other studies, optimism was unrelated to posttraumatic growth (Lowe, Manove, & Rhodes, 2013; Park, Cohen, & Murch, 1996), although, in one such study, postevent growth scores were predictive of the change in level of optimism between time 1 (preevent) and time 2 (postevent; Park et al., 1996). Similarly, more recent work has failed to discern a relationship between growth and either openness or agreeableness (Garnefski, Kraaij, Schroevers, & Somsen, 2008; Zoellner, Rabe, Karl, & Maercker, 2011). Despite some inconsistencies, posttraumatic growth has generally been found to have modest associations with personality in expected ways.

Other factors that have exhibited a moderate relationship with growth include various forms of coping (with religious coping and positive reappraisal coping producing the largest effect sizes), social support, and spirituality (Helgeson et al., 2006; Prati & Pietrantoni, 2009). The subjective nature of the threat posed by trauma also appears to be an important determinant of posttraumatic growth (Helgeson et al., 2006; Linley & Joseph, 2004). Moreover, posttraumatic growth has been positively associated with centrality of the traumatic event to the life and/or identity of the traumatized person (Blix, Birkeland, Hansen, & Heir, 2015) and disruption in core beliefs (Cann, Calhoun, Tedeschi, Kilmer, et al., 2010). In a recent study examining the effect of core beliefs, rumination, and perceived stressfulness of the traumatic event, reexamination of core beliefs was the strongest predictor of posttraumatic growth (Taku, Cann, Tedeschi & Calhoun, 2015). Notably, these research findings regarding the relationship between core beliefs and posttraumatic growth are reminiscent of the emphasis on meaning making and revision of pretrauma beliefs under information-processing models of PTSD recovery.

Lastly, Tedeschi and Calhoun (2004) have proposed that posttraumatic growth results from constructive cognitive processing of trauma, which they refer to as deliberate rumination. Deliberate rumination consists of repetitive thoughts that are directed toward problem-solving or making sense of the event (Cann et al., 2011; Tedeschi & Calhoun, 2004), as contrasted with unconstructive rumination or brooding, which consists of repetitive thoughts that are automatic and intrusive. Although both deliberate and intrusive rumination have demonstrated positive associations with PTSD symptoms, deliberate rumination has consistently demonstrated positive associations with posttraumatic growth (Cann, Calhoun, Tedeschi, & Solomon, 2010; Cann et al., 2011; Stockton, Hunt, & Joseph, 2011; Taku et al., 2015), whereas the relationship between intrusive rumination and posttraumatic growth has been less consistent (Cann, Calhoun, Tedeschi, & Solomon, 2010; Taku et al., 2015).

Relationship of Posttraumatic Growth to Psychological Outcomes

Some have assumed that posttraumatic growth implies an enhanced level of functioning as compared to the pretrauma state (Zoellner & Maercker, 2006). Instead, posttraumatic growth is a complex construct that is distinct from psychological wellbeing (Tedeschi & Calhoun, 2004). Accordingly, posttraumatic growth can coexist with PTSD symptoms, and it should not be viewed as residing at one end of a continuum of responses to trauma, with PTSD symptoms at the other end (Zoellner & Maercker, 2006).

Tedeschi and Calhoun (2004) assert that the transformative quality of posttraumatic growth results, in part, from the extreme emotion involved in processing a crisis. Consistent with this view, there is evidence indicating that, to a certain extent, higher levels of trauma and posttraumatic distress are associated with greater posttraumatic growth. Several studies have found a curvilinear relationship between posttraumatic growth and trauma/symptom severity (Dekel, Mandl, & Solomon, 2011; Shakespeare-Finch & Lurie-Beck, 2014), such that moderate levels of trauma were associated with the greatest levels of posttraumatic growth. These studies suggest that posttraumatic growth increases with trauma severity and resulting symptomology up to a point, after which it begins to erode.

Despite the aforementioned results, research findings regarding the relationship between posttraumatic psychological adjustment and posttraumatic growth have not been uniform. A meta-analysis of 87 cross-sectional studies found that posttraumatic growth was unrelated to anxiety, quality of life, and global distress (Helgeson et al., 2006). In the same analysis, posttraumatic growth was positively correlated with positive wellbeing and negatively associated with depression, despite the fact that it also was positively related to intrusive/avoidant thoughts about the stressor, a key symptom of PTSD. In contrast, Zoellner and Maercker (2006) reported that the majority of cross-sectional studies have found no significant relationship between posttraumatic growth, and symptoms of PTSD and depression. Lastly, a more recent meta-analysis found a significant positive relationship between posttraumatic growth and PTSD symptoms ($r = .315$, $p < .001$; Shakespeare-Finch & Lurie-Beck, 2014).

In contrast to the previously mentioned findings based on cross-sectional studies, longitudinal studies tend to show a positive, albeit small, association between perceived posttraumatic growth and psychological adjustment (Zoellner & Maercker, 2006), such that higher posttraumatic growth reported at the time of a first assessment predicted decreases in PTSD and depression symptoms at the time of a second assessment. This difference in findings between cross-sectional and longitudinal studies may indicate that posttraumatic growth reflects a process that occurs following trauma exposure rather than a personal characteristic or a discrete trauma outcome. It may take time follow-ing an experience of trauma for perceived posttraumatic growth to be trans-lated into healthier psychological outcomes.

The notion that posttraumatic growth represents a distinct pattern of responding to trauma is supported by the literature. In a meta-analysis of 87 cross-sectional studies, time elapsed since trauma of more than two years was positively related to greater positive wellbeing and lower depression, whereas time elapsed since trauma of less than two years was positively related to anxiety and global distress (Helgeson et al., 2006). Just as resilience appears to reflect one of a number of distinct patterns of response to trauma characterized by a relatively rapid return to baseline functioning (Bonanno, 2012), posttraumatic growth may reflect a separate posttraumatic adjustment process involving high levels of PTSD symptoms in the period shortly after the traumatic event, with gradual resolution of symptoms over time associated with reaching a new and different functional equilibrium. This idea could explain the inconsistent find-ings observed in the cross-sectional literature.

The idea that posttraumatic growth is a process that contributes to better psychological adjustment over time was tested recently in the mass shooting context. In a longitudinal study, Miron, Orcutt, and Kumpula (2014) examined the relationship between posttraumatic growth approximately one month after the 2008 shooting at Northern Illinois University and probable PTSD reported either acutely (at about one month postshooting) or both acutely and 8 months following the shooting. Contrary to expectations, posttraumatic growth soon after the shooting event predicted contemporaneous probable PTSD as well as probable PTSD 8 months following the shooting. This unexpected result may be attributable to the length of time elapsed between data collections. That is, consistent with the findings of Helgeson et al. (2006) above, the 8-month time frame that elapsed between the shooting event and distal measurement of PTSD symptoms in Miron et al. (2014) may have been too short to detect an effect. In addition, like many studies of posttraumatic growth, Miron et al. (2014) used the PTGI to measure posttraumatic growth. Frazier and colleagues (2009) have argued that the PTGI measures *perceived* posttraumatic growth, rather than actual growth, and that perceived posttraumatic growth is more akin to positive reinterpretation coping than it is a reflection of actual, positive post-traumatic change. Because positive reinterpretation coping and PTSD symp-toms both vary with the severity of trauma, the results obtained by Miron et al. (2014) may reflect that, at 8 months following the shooting, the trauma resolution process was at a relatively early stage in which the coping aspects of posttraumatic growth mask its salutary effects.

This interpretation of the results in Miron et al. (2014) is in line with certain alternative conceptualizations of posttraumatic growth. For example, Zoellner and Maercker (2006) posit that perceived posttraumatic growth (such as mea-sured by the PTGI) may encompass both motivated positive illusions, which tend to be associated with psychological distress, and transcendent aspects, which relate to positive psychological adjustment. Similarly, Hobfoll, Hall, et al. (2007) suggest that measures of perceived growth initially may represent cognitive attempts to reduce the impact of trauma, but true posttraumatic growth (which they term "action-focused" growth) follows only after a survivor has converted growth-related cognitions into practice. As such, Miron et al. (2014) highlight the need for more longitudinal studies of posttraumatic growth, over longer periods of time (Anusic & Yap, 2014; Jayawickreme & Blackie, 2014).

Related to the idea of action-focused posttraumatic growth, system justification theory (Blasi & Jost, 2006; Jost & Banaji, 1994) has some interesting implications. System justification theory proposes that believing that the status quo is fair serves protective psychological functions for the individual, even when the status quo results in social or economic injustice (e.g., discrimination) and works against the individual's own interests. Confidence that the status quo is inherently just is one type of pretrauma belief that might be challenged by an experience of trauma. If recovery from trauma reflects a revision or reaffirmation of pretrauma beliefs that has been converted into practice, the associated actions could challenge or buttress the status quo, respectively. Thus, for mass shooting traumas, beliefs regarding gun rights and gun control, balancing security and privacy, and attitudes toward individuals with mental illness may come to the fore (Kaminski, Koons-Witt, Thompson, & Weiss, 2010; Kleck, 2009; McGinty, Webster, & Barry, 2013), and individuals' processing of such traumas may serve as a call to social or political action with respect to such beliefs.

We speculate that the process of reconciling a mass shooting with protective pretrauma beliefs is not only an individual process. To the degree that such beliefs are shared, reconciliation also takes place through public dialogue, social and political action, and cultural change.

Conclusions

Disrupted functioning in the immediate wake of a trauma is normal, and finding equilibrium is a process that takes time. Current recommendations are to allow exposed individuals to regulate their own utilization of intervention services, rather than requiring or strongly encouraging use of such services.

There is evidence that certain individual characteristics are associated with greater likelihood of resilient responses to trauma. Further, some studies indicate that distinct subpopulations of trauma survivors may exist, with each exhibiting its own characteristic trauma response pattern. After a mass shooting event, a minority of individuals in the environment are likely to have difficulties initially. A small number of these individuals will experience more persistent symptoms. Recovery for some may involve changing important personal beliefs. This process may involve religious and social communities, and include actions that foster social, political, and cultural change. Dialogue in public forums may reflect some individuals' attempts to cope with, recover from, and grow after the shooting event, and has the potential to affect the recovery of others.

Behavioral scientists have a responsibility to examine psychological functioning following mass shooting events. Studies of mass shooting trauma can improve public policy and community response, increase our understanding of how individuals can respond positively, and reduce some of the suffering. Exposed individuals may find participation in trauma-related research to be rewarding, possibly giving meaning to difficult experiences they may have had (see Chapter 20 for more on research participation following mass shootings; Fergus, Rabenhorst, Orcutt, & Valentiner, 2011). Findings from that research may help us to address psychological functioning not only after mass shootings, but also in the wake of other types of trauma.

References

Agaibi, C. E., & Wilson, J. P. (2005). Trauma, PTSD, and resilience: A review of the literature. *Trauma, Violence, and Abuse, 6,* 195–216. doi:10.1177/1524838005277438

American Psychiatric Association (2013). *Diagnostic and statistical manual of mental disorders* (5th ed.). Washington, DC: Author.

Anusic, I., & Yap, S. C. (2014). Using longitudinal studies to understand post-traumatic growth. *European Journal of Personality, 28,* 332–361. doi:10.1002/per.1970

Blasi, G., & Jost, J. T. (2006). System justification theory and research: Implications for law, legal advocacy, and social justice. *California Law Review, 94*(4), 1119–1168.

Blix, I., Birkeland, M. S., Hansen, M. B., & Heir, T. (2015). Posttraumatic growth and centrality of event: A longitudinal study in the aftermath of the 2011 Oslo bombing. *Psychological Trauma: Theory, Research, Practice, and Policy, 7*(1), 18–23. doi:10.1037/tra0000006

Bonanno, G. A. (2004). Loss, trauma, and human resilience: Have we underestimated the human capacity to thrive after extremely aversive events? *American Psychologist, 59,* 20–28. doi:10.1037/0003-066X.59.1.20

Bonanno, G. A. (2005). Resilience in the face of potential trauma. *Current Directions in Psychological Science, 14*(3), 135–138.

Bonanno, G. A. (2012). Uses and abuses of the resilience construct: Loss, trauma, and health-related adversities. *Social Science & Medicine, 74*(5), 753–756. doi:10.1016/j.socscimed.2011.11.022

Bonanno, G. A., & Mancini, A. D. (2012). Beyond resilience and PTSD: Mapping the heterogeneity of responses to potential trauma. *Psychological Trauma: Theory, Research, Practice, and Policy, 4*(1), 74. doi:10.1037/a0017829

Brewin, C. R., Lanius, R. A., Novac, A., Schnyder, U., & Galea, S. (2009). Reformulating PTSD for DSM-V: Life after Criterion A. *Journal of Traumatic Stress, 22*(5), 366–373. doi:10.1002/jts.20443

Brunet, J., McDonough, M. H., Hadd, V., Crocker, P. R., & Sabiston, C. M. (2010). The Posttraumatic Growth Inventory: An examination of the factor structure and invariance among breast cancer survivors. *Psycho-Oncology, 19*(8), 830–838. doi:10.1002/pon.1640

Brunet, A., Orr, S. P., Tremblay, J., Robertson, K., Nader, K., & Pitman, R. K. (2008). Effect of post-retrieval propranolol on psychophysiologic responding during subsequent script-driven traumatic imagery in post-traumatic stress disorder. *Journal of Psychiatric Research, 42*(6), 503–506.

Bryant, R. A. (2015). Post-traumatic stress disorder: Biological dysfunction or social construction? In D. Bhugra & G. S. Malhi (Eds.), *Troublesome disguises: Managing challenging disorders in psychiatry* (pp. 140–152). Hoboken, NJ: John Wiley & Sons.

Cann, A., Calhoun, L. G., Tedeschi, R. G., Kilmer, R. P., Gil-Rivas, V., Vishnevsky, T., & Danhauer, S. C. (2010). The Core Beliefs Inventory: A brief measure of disruption in the assumptive world. *Anxiety, Stress & Coping, 23*(1), 19–34.

Cann, A., Calhoun, L. G., Tedeschi, R. G., & Solomon, D. T. (2010). Posttraumatic growth and depreciation as independent experiences and predictors of well-being. *Journal of Loss and Trauma, 15*(3), 151–166. doi:10.1080/15325020903375826

Cann, A., Calhoun, L. G., Tedeschi, R. G., Triplett, K. N., Vishnevsky, T., & Lindstrom, C. M. (2011). Assessing posttraumatic cognitive processes: The Event Related Rumination Inventory. *Anxiety, Stress, and Coping, 24*(2), 137–56. doi:10.1080/10615806.2010.529901

Charney, D. S. (2004). Psychobiological mechanisms of resilience and vulnerability: Implications for successful adaptation to extreme stress. *American Journal of Psychiatry, 161*, 195–216.

Connor, K. M., & Davidson, J. R. (2003). Development of a new resilience scale: The Connor-Davidson resilience scale (CD-RISC). *Depression and Anxiety, 18*(2), 76–82. doi:10.1002/da.10113

Dekel, S., Mandl, C., & Solomon, Z. (2011). Shared and unique predictors of post-traumatic growth and distress. *Journal of Clinical Psychology, 67*(3), 241–252. doi:10.1002/jclp.20747

Dutton, M. A., & Greene, R. (2010). Resilience and crime victimization. *Journal of Traumatic Stress, 23*(2), 215–222. doi:10.1002/jts.20510

Ehlers, A., Clark, D. M., Hackmann, A., McManus, F., & Fennell, M. (2005). Cognitive therapy for post-traumatic stress disorder: Development and evaluation. *Behaviour Research and Therapy, 43*(4), 413–431. doi:10.1016/j.brat.2004.03.006

Etkin, A., Egner, T., & Kalisch, R. (2011). Emotional processing in anterior cingulate and medial prefrontal cortex. *Trends in Cognitive Sciences, 15*(2), 85–93.

Fergus, T. A., Rabenhorst, M. M., Orcutt, H. K., & Valentiner, D. P. (2011). Reactions to trauma research among women recently exposed to a campus shooting. *Journal of Traumatic Stress, 24*(5), 596–600. doi:10.1002/jts.20682

Foa, E. B., Hembree, E. A., & Rothbaum, B. O. (2007). *Prolonged exposure therapy for PTSD: Emotional processing of traumatic experiences, therapist guide.* New York, NY: Oxford University Press.

Foa, E. B., Rothbaum, B. O., Riggs, D. S., & Murdock, T. B. (1991). Treatment of posttraumatic stress disorder in rape victims: A comparison between cognitive-behavioral procedures and counseling. *Journal of Consulting and Clinical Psychology, 59*(5), 715.

Foa, E. B., Steketee, G., & Rothbaum, B. O. (1989). Behavioral/cognitive conceptu-alizations of post-traumatic stress disorder. *Behavior Therapy, 20*(2), 155–176.

Frazier, P., Tennen, H., Gavian, M., Park, C., Tomich, P., & Tashiro, T. (2009). Does self-reported posttraumatic growth reflect genuine positive change? *Psychological Science, 20*(7), 912–919. doi:10.1111/j.1467-9280.2009.02381.x

Gamache, K., Pitman, R. K., & Nader, K. (2012). Preclinical evaluation of reconsolida-tion blockade by clonidine as a potential novel treatment for posttraumatic stress disorder. *Neuropsychopharmacology, 37*(13), 2789–2796.

Garnefski, N., Kraaij, V., Schroevers, M. J., & Somsen, G. A. (2008). Posttraumatic growth after a myocardial infarction: A matter of personality, psychological health, or cognitive coping? *Journal of Clinical Psychology in Medical Settings, 15*, 270–277. doi:10.1007/s/1088-008-913-5

Grills-Taquechel, A. E., Littleton, H. L., & Axsom, D. (2011). Social support, world assumptions, and exposure as predictors of anxiety and quality of life following a mass trauma. *Journal of Anxiety Disorders, 25*(4), 498–506. doi: 10.1016/j.janxdis.2010.12.003

Helgeson, V. S., Reynolds, K. A., & Tomich, P. L. (2006). A meta-analytic review of benefit finding and growth. *Journal of Consulting and Clinical Psychology, 74*(5), 797. doi:10.1037/0022-006X.74.5.797

Hobfoll, S. E., Hall, B. J., Canetti-Nisim, D., Galea, S., Johnson, R. J., & Palmieri, P. A. (2007). Refining our understanding of traumatic growth in the face of terrorism: Moving from meaning cognitions to doing what is meaningful. *Applied Psychology: An International Review, 56*(3), 345–366. doi:10.1111/j.1464-0597.2007.00292.x

Hobfoll, S. E., Watson, P., Bell, C. C., Bryant, R. A., Brymer, M. J., Friedman, M. J., ... Ursano, R. J. (2007). Five essential elements of immediate and mid-term mass trauma intervention: Empirical evidence. *Psychiatry, 70*, 283–315.

Janoff-Bulman, R. (2010). *Shattered assumptions: Towards a new psychology of trauma.* New York, NY: Simon & Schuster.

Janoff-Bulman, R., & Frantz, C. M. (1997). The impact of trauma on meaning: From meaningless world to meaningful life. In M. J. Power & C. R. Brewin (Eds.), *The transformation of meaning in psychological therapies: Integrating theory and prac-tice* (pp. 91–106). Hoboken, NJ: John Wiley & Sons.

Jayawickreme, E., & Blackie, L. E. (2014). Post-traumatic growth as positive person-ality change: Evidence, controversies and future directions. *European Journal of Personality, 28*(4), 312–331. doi:10.1002/per.1963

Jost, J. T., & Banaji, M. R. (1994). The role of stereotyping in system-justification and the production of false consciousness. *British Journal of Social Psychology, 33*(1), 1–27.

Kaminski, R. J., Koons-Witt, B. A., Thompson, N. S., & Weiss, D. (2010). The impacts of the Virginia Tech and Northern Illinois University shootings on fear of crime on campus. *Journal of Criminal Justice, 38*(1), 88–98. doi:10.1016/j.jcrimjus.2009.11.011

Kleck, G. (2009). Mass shootings in schools: The worst possible case for gun control. *American Behavioral Scientist, 52*(10), 1447–1464.

Linley, P. A., Andrews, L., & Joseph, S. (2007). Confirmatory factor analysis of the Posttraumatic Growth Inventory. *Journal of Loss and Trauma, 12*(4), 321–332. doi:10.1080/15325020601162823

Linley, P. A., & Joseph, S. (2004). Positive change following trauma and adversity: A review. *Journal of Traumatic Stress, 17*(1), 11–21. doi:10.1023/B:JOTS. 0000014671.27856.7e

Litz, B. T., & Keane, T. M. (1989). Information processing in anxiety disorders: Application to the understanding of post-traumatic stress disorder. *Clinical Psychology Review, 9*(2), 243–257. doi:10.1016/0272-7358(89)90030-5

Lowe, S. R., Manove, E. E., & Rhodes, J. E. (2013). Posttraumatic stress and posttraumatic growth among low-income mothers who survived Hurricane Katrina. *Journal of Consulting and Clinical Psychology, 81*(5), 877. doi:10.1037/a0033252

Maercker, A., & Zoellner, T. (2004). The Janus face of self-perceived growth: Toward a two-component model of posttraumatic growth. *Psychological Inquiry, 15,* 41–48.

McGinty, E. E., Webster, D. W., & Barry, C. L. (2013). Effects of news media messages about mass shootings on attitudes toward persons with serious mental illness and public support for gun control policies. *American Journal of Psychiatry, 170*(5), 494–501. doi:10.1176/appi.ajp.2013.13010014

Mercer, K. B., Orcutt, H. K., Quinn, J. F., Fitzgerald, C. A., Conneely, K. N., Barfield, R. T.,... Ressler, K. J. (2012). Acute and posttraumatic stress symptoms in a prospective gene × environment study of a university campus shooting. *Archives of General Psychiatry, 69*(1), 89–97. doi:10.1001/archgenpsychiatry.2011.109

Miron, L. R., Orcutt, H. K., & Kumpula, M. J. (2014). Differential predictors of transient stress versus posttraumatic stress disorder: Evaluating risk following targeted mass violence. *Behavior Therapy, 45*(6), 791–805. doi:10.1016/j. beth.2014.07.005

Morina, N., Wicherts, J. M., Lobbrecht, J., & Priebe, S. (2014). Remission from posttraumatic stress disorder in adults: A systematic review and meta-analysis of long term outcome studies. *Clinical Psychology Review, 34*(3), 249–255. doi:10.1016/j. cpr.2014.03.002

Morris, B. A., Shakespeare-Finch, J., Rieck, M., & Newbery, J. (2005). Multidimensional nature of posttraumatic growth in an Australian population. *Journal of Traumatic Stress, 18,* 575–585. doi:10.1002/jts.20067

Norris, F. H., & Stevens, S. P. (2007). Community resilience and the principles of mass trauma intervention. *Psychiatry, 70,* 320–328.

Orcutt, H. K., Bonanno, G. A., Hannan, S. M., & Miron, L. R. (2014). Prospective trajectories of posttraumatic stress in college women following a campus mass shooting. *Journal of Traumatic Stress, 27*(3), 249–256. doi:10.1002/jts.21914

Pals, J. L., & McAdams, D. P. (2004). The transformed self: A narrative understanding of posttraumatic growth. *Psychological Inquiry, 15*(1), 65–69.

Park, C. L., Cohen, L. H., & Murch, R. L. (1996). Assessment and prediction of stress-related growth. *Journal of Personality, 64,* 71–105. doi:10.1111/j.1467-6494.1996. tb00815.x

Pissiota, A., Frans, Ö., Fernandez, M., von Knorring, L., Fischer, H., & Fredrikson, M. (2002). Neurofunctional correlates of posttraumatic stress disorder: A PET symptom provocation study. *European Archives of Psychiatry and Clinical Neuroscience, 252*(2), 68–75. doi:10.1007/s004060200014

Prati, G., & Pietrantoni, L. (2009). Optimism, social support, and coping strategies as factors contributing to posttraumatic growth: A meta-analysis. *Journal of Loss and Trauma, 14*(5), 364–388. doi:10.1080/15325020902724271

Rauch, S. L., van der Kolk, B. A., Fisler, R. E., Alpert, N. M., Orr, S. P., Savage, C. R., … Pitman, R. K. (1996). A symptom provocation study of posttraumatic stress disorder using positron emission tomography and script-driven imagery. *Archives of General Psychiatry, 53*(5), 380–387. doi:10.1001/archpsyc.1996.01830050014003

Resick, P. A., Nishith, P., Weaver, T. L., Astin, M. C., & Feuer, C. A. (2002). A comparison of cognitive-processing therapy with prolonged exposure and a waiting condition for the treatment of chronic posttraumatic stress disorder in female rape victims. *Journal of Consulting and Clinical Psychology, 70,* 867–879.

Resilience. (n.d.). In *Merriam-Webster's online dictionary* (11th ed.). Retrieved from http://www.merriam-webster.com/dictionary/resilience

Schiller, D., Monfils, M. H., Raio, C. M., Johnson, D. C., LeDoux, J. E., & Phelps, E. A. (2010). Preventing the return of fear in humans using reconsolidation update mechanisms. *Nature, 463*(7277), 49–53.

Shakespeare-Finch, J., & Lurie-Beck, J. (2014). A meta-analytic clarification of the relationship between posttraumatic growth and symptoms of posttraumatic distress disorder. *Journal of Anxiety Disorders, 28*(2), 223–229. doi:10.1016/j.janxdis.2013.10.005

Shin, L. M., Bush, G., Milad, M. R., Lasko, N. B., Brohawn, K. H., Hughes, K. C., … Pitman, R. K. (2011). Exaggerated activation of dorsal anterior cingulate cortex during cognitive interference: A monozygotic twin study of posttraumatic stress disorder. *American Journal of Psychiatry, 168*(9), 979–985.

Shin, L. M., Lasko, N. B., Macklin, M. L., Karpf, R. D., Milad, M. R., Orr, S. P., … Pitman, R. K. (2009). Resting metabolic activity in the cingulate cortex and vulnerability to posttraumatic stress disorder. *Archives of General Psychiatry, 66*(10), 1099–1107.

Shin, L. M., Orr, S. P., Carson, M. A., Rauch, S. L., Macklin, M. L., Lasko, N. B., … Pitman, R. K. (2004). Regional cerebral blood flow in the amygdala and medial prefrontal cortex during traumatic imagery in male and female Vietnam veterans with PTSD. *Archives of General Psychiatry, 61*(2), 168–176.

Shin, L. M., Rauch, S. L., & Pitman, R. K. (2006). Amygdala, medial prefrontal cortex, and hippocampal function in PTSD. *Annals of the New York Academy of Sciences, 1071*(1), 67–79.

Steckler, T., & Risbrough, V. (2012). Pharmacological treatment of PTSD – established and new approaches. *Neuropharmacology, 62*(2), 617–627.

Stein, D. J., Cloitre, M., Nemeroff, C. B., Nutt, D. J., Seedat, S., Shalev, A. Y., … Zohar, J. (2009). Cape Town consensus on posttraumatic stress disorder. *CNS Spectrums, 14*(1 Suppl. 1), 52–58.

Stein, M. B., Campbell-Sills, L., & Gelernter, J. (2009). Genetic variation in 5HTTLPR is associated with emotional resilience. *American Journal of Medical Genetics Part B: Neuropsychiatric Genetics, 150*(7), 900–906. doi:10.1002/ajmg.b.30916

Stein, M. B., Jang, K. L., Taylor, S., Vernon, P. A., & Livesley, W. J. (2014). Genetic and environmental influences on trauma exposure and posttraumatic stress disorder symptoms: A twin study. *American Journal of Psychiatry, 159*(10), 1675–1681.

Stockton, H., Hunt, N., & Joseph, S. (2011). Cognitive processing, rumination, and posttraumatic growth. *Journal of Traumatic Stress, 24*(1), 85–92.

Szumilas, M., Wei, Y., & Kutcher, S. (2010). Psychological debriefing in schools. *Canadian Medical Association Journal, 182*(9), 883–884.

Taku, K., Cann, A., Calhoun, L. G., & Tedeschi, R. G. (2008). The factor structure of the Posttraumatic Growth Inventory: A comparison of five models using confirmatory factor analysis. *Journal of Traumatic Stress, 21*(2), 158–164.

Taku, K., Cann, A., Tedeschi, R. G., & Calhoun, L. G. (2015). Core beliefs shaken by an earthquake correlate with posttraumatic growth. *Psychological Trauma: Theory, Research, Practice, and Policy.* Advance online publication. doi:10.1037/tra0000054

Tedeschi, R. G., & Calhoun, L. G. (1996). The Posttraumatic Growth Inventory: Measuring the positive legacy of trauma. *Journal of Traumatic Stress, 9*(3), 455–471.

Tedeschi, R. G., & Calhoun, L. G. (2004). Posttraumatic growth: Conceptual foundations and empirical evidence. *Psychological Inquiry, 15*(1), 1–18.

Thrasher, S. M., Dalgleish, T., & Yule, W. (1994). Information processing in posttraumatic stress disorder. *Behaviour Research and Therapy, 32*(2), 247–254.

Valentiner, D. P., Foa, E. B., Riggs, D. S., & Gershuny, B. S. (1996). Coping strategies and posttraumatic stress disorder in female victims of sexual and nonsexual assault. *Journal of Abnormal Psychology, 105*(3), 455.

Vishnevsky, T., Cann, A., Calhoun, L. G., Tedeschi, R. G., & Demakis, G. J. (2010). Gender differences in self-reported posttraumatic growth: A meta-analysis. *Psychology of Women Quarterly, 34*(1), 110–120.

Weems, C. F., Russell, J. D., Banks, D. M., Graham, R. A., Neill, E. L., & Scott, B. G. (2014). Memories of traumatic events in childhood fade after experiencing similar less stressful events: Results from two natural experiments. *Journal of Experimental Psychology: General, 143*(5), 2046.

Weiss, T., & Berger, R. (2010). Posttraumatic growth around the globe: Research findings and practice implications. In T. Weiss & R. Berger (Eds.), *Posttraumatic growth and culturally competent practice: Lessons learned from around the globe* (pp. 189–195). Hoboken, NJ: John Wiley & Sons. doi:10.1002/9781118270028.ch14

Zoellner, T., & Maercker, A. (2006). Posttraumatic growth in clinical psychology – A critical review and introduction of a two component model. *Clinical Psychology Review, 26*(5), 626–653.

Zoellner, T., Rabe, S., Karl, A., & Maercker, A. (2011). Post-traumatic growth as outcome of a cognitive-behavioural therapy trial for motor vehicle accident survivors with PTSD. *Psychology and Psychotherapy: Theory, Research and Practice, 84*(2), 201–213.

Part VI

Prevention, Ethics, and Future Directions

19
Threat Assessment and Violence Prevention
Dewey Cornell and Pooja Datta

Behavioral threat assessment has emerged over the past two decades as a specialized form of risk assessment concerned with the immediate risk posed by an individual who has threatened to commit an act of violence (Borum, Fein, Vossekuil, & Berglund, 1999; Meloy, Hart, & Hoffman, 2014). A typical threat assessment begins when an individual is reported to have threatened to harm someone or engaged in threatening behavior. A threat assessment team then gathers information to determine whether the person poses a serious risk of violence. Many individuals might threaten violence as an expression of frustration or anger, but lack genuine intent to harm someone. Others might be capable of violence, but the threat could be ameliorated through counseling, conflict mediation, or another intervention that resolves the underlying problem. In the most extreme cases, there may be a very serious threat that requires law enforcement intervention to prevent an imminent attack.

The shift from an initial assessment phase to an intervention phase depends on the seriousness of the threat and the nature of the underlying problem or conflict. For this reason, threat assessment might be described more accurately as threat management and regarded as a problem-solving approach to violence prevention. There are many different threat management strategies, ranging from a simple apology to conflict resolution, counseling to psychiatric hospitalization, and a firm warning by authorities to arrest and criminal charges. In all cases, the overarching goal is to prevent violence by responding to the problem or concern that led to the threatening behavior with an appropriately calibrated risk reduction plan.

Basic Principles

Threat assessment is a relatively new and evolving field of practice that is guided by some general principles. First among these principles is the recognition that there is no single profile or type of individual who threatens and subsequently

---

commits a violent act (Randazzo et al., 2006). Threat assessment must be distinguished from a profiling approach that seeks to identify violent individuals through a checklist of warning signs or psychological characteristics. Prospective profiling as a means of predicting who will commit a violent act has been widely criticized as an inaccurate process prone to many false positive cases (Sewell & Mendelsohn, 2000). As the FBI's profiling experts concluded, "Trying to draw up a catalogue or 'checklist' of warning signs to detect a potential school shooter can be shortsighted, even dangerous. Such lists, publicized by the media, can end up unfairly labeling many nonviolent students as potentially dangerous" (O'Toole, 2000, p. 2). The heterogeneity of individuals who commit violent acts, in combination with the diversity of environmental factors that could provoke or inhibit violence, render a profiling approach impractical and unrealistic.

A second principle is that there is a critical distinction between making a threat and posing a threat (Randazzo et al., 2006; Vossekuil, Fein, Reddy, Borum, & Modzeleski, 2002). Many individuals make threatening statements that they have no intention of carrying out. Threats may be expressions of anger or sarcasm, and they may represent hyperbole or rhetoric rather than a genuine intent to harm (Cornell & Sheras, 2006). Some threats may be intended to frighten or intimidate, with no intent to follow through on the threatened action (Calhoun & Weston, 2009). A threat assessment team is concerned with identifying the subset of individuals who pose a threat because they have the motivation and the means to carry out their threat. The team should investigate whether the person has acquired weapons, developed a plan, recruited assistance, or engaged in some other preparation to act. Virtually anyone might make a threat, if sufficiently frustrated, but only a small proportion of individuals will take actions that pose a threat.

Conversely, someone can pose a threat without making a threat. A person who is determined to carry out a violent act might refrain from expressing a threat in order to avoid detection, but these cases are relatively rare in comparison to the vast majority of persons who communicate their intentions to harm someone before carrying out an attack (O'Toole, 2000; Vossekuil et al., 2002). The U.S. Secret Service study of school shootings found that many of the students had not directly threatened their intended target, although typically they communicated threats to third parties such as friends or classmates (Vossekuil et al., 2002). The FBI study of school shootings referred to the "leakage" of the individual's intentions through behaviors and statements that reflect an interest in carrying out a violent act (O'Toole, 2000). In Germany, a school shooting prevention program was designed specifically to train teachers to identify leakage of violent intentions among their students and to refer them for a threat assessment (Leuschner et al., in press).

A third principle of threat assessment is that a violent attack is not a spontaneous act committed by someone who has "just snapped" (Randazzo et al., 2006).

Although a fight might erupt unexpectedly between two individuals having an argument, mass shootings and other acts of targeted violence are almost always preceded by planning and preparation. Case studies document that individuals contemplate and ruminate, then eventually plan and prepare to carry out the violent attack over a period of weeks, months, or longer (Fein & Vossekuil, 1998; Vossekuil et al., 2002). The importance of this principle is that there is an opportunity for prevention during the time period when a would-be aggressor is preparing to attack.

Pathways to violence

Cornell and Sheras (2006) contended that there are three main pathways to violence that should be considered in a threat assessment. These pathways reflect differences in the motivation and psychological functioning of violent individuals that would be obscured if compared to a single profile or set of warning signs. Several case examples of mass shootings illustrate the opportunities for intervention using a threat assessment approach.

The first and most common pathway to violence involves an act of instrumental violence for personal gain, such as robbery or sexual assault. These acts are most often committed by individuals with an antisocial background, and a history of prior violence and criminal behavior. They tend to affiliate with other like-minded individuals and may be involved in gangs. Their acts of aggression may be motivated by drug dealing, stealing, or another predatory goal. They may have a psychopathic personality characterized by dishonesty, narcissism, and lack of empathy for others. Because these individuals have considerable experience with fighting and other aggressive behaviors, and lack inhibitions against harming others, they have a propensity to use violence in many different situations and with little provocation. For this reason, they may display both reactive and instrumental aggression, although what distinguishes them from other aggressive individuals is their proclivity to engage in instrumental aggression (Cornell et al., 1996). Instrumental violent offenders are not likely to commit a suicidal mass shooting, but could engage in a more instrumental mass shooting against a rival group, such as a gang.

One example of a mass homicide involving gang members was the 2015 shoot-out between rival bike gangs in Waco, Texas. According to news reports, five rival biker gangs congregated at a restaurant to resolve turf and recruitment disputes (Holley, Freedom du Lac, Berman, & Madigan, 2015). Even though this case does not appear to involve a planned act of violence, it occurred in the context of a feud in which the individuals anticipated the potential for violence and came armed with guns and knives. An argument beginning in the restroom escalated into a fight in which nine individuals were killed and 18 injured from gunshot and stab wounds (Fernandez, Kovaleski, & Montgomery, 2015).

A more typical instrumental homicide may occur in the context of a planned robbery. For example, in 2015 one or more robbers invaded a home in Washington, DC held three family members and a housekeeper hostage for 19 hours, and tortured a 10-year-old boy in order to coerce the father into obtaining $40,000 in cash. The assailant(s) then killed the hostages and set the home on fire (Leshan, 2015). These behaviors suggest the actions of a psychopathic individual engaged in predatory, instrumental violence in pursuit of personal gain.

A second, conflict, pathway involves individuals who commit acts of reactive or hostile violence that is less motivated by instrumental gain than by revenge or retaliation. They are often embroiled in an emotional conflict or dispute that they cannot tolerate, and perceive themselves as victims of bullying, harassment, or some other unfair treatment that justifies taking action against others. These conflicts can arise in diverse circumstances, such as a student bullied at school, an employee mistreated by a supervisor, or a person rejected by a romantic interest. The perceived injustice and mistreatment may be grossly exaggerated and the person may develop a generalized resentment of other people or society in general. Individuals with a fragile self-esteem and wounded narcissism may experience the conflict as so demeaning and shameful that they see a dramatic act of violence as the only way to retaliate for their sense of injury.

One example of a conflict-related mass shooting is the 2014 case of a 22-year-old in Isla Vista, California who killed six persons and injured 14 others before he killed himself (Lovett & Nagourney, 2014). According to a law enforcement report (Brown, 2015), the shooter had been shy and anxious in childhood and had symptoms of Asperger's syndrome. He was variously diagnosed with Pervasive Developmental Disorder and Autism, and received mental health treatment and medication throughout his adolescence and until his death. He wrote a 137-page manifesto describing many frustrations and disappointments in life, although his primary motivation appears to have been intense anger that he was unable to find a girlfriend and resentment that women seemed to prefer other young men whom he deemed to be less intelligent and attractive than himself. The shooter decided to carry out a "Day of Retribution," and purchased handguns and practiced for months before his attack. Immediately before carrying out his attack, he uploaded a video to YouTube and sent emails to family members and friends expressing his anger at being rejected by women and describing his plans for revenge. His statements on the video were angry and extreme, but were delivered in a calm and coherent manner with no evidence of delusions or formal thought disorder.

The third pathway to violence is a psychotic pathway traversed by individuals with a severe mental disorder, such as schizophrenia or bipolar disorder. In a psychotic state, they are guided by delusions and/or auditory hallucinations that justify their actions. One example is the 2007 shooting at Virginia Tech, where a 23-year-old student killed 32 people and wounded 17 others before killing himself (Virginia Tech Review Panel, 2007; Virginia Tech Review Panel Addendum, 2009). The shooter raised concern in middle school when he wrote an essay expressing his admiration for the two high school students who carried out the Columbine shooting. He was notably withdrawn and anxious, and often refused to speak at school. He was identified as severely emotionally disturbed, but obtained good grades and displayed no aggressive behavior in high school. In college, he continued to be shy and withdrawn, and aspired to be a writer. His creative writing instructors repeatedly expressed concern about his odd behavior in class, his readily apparent anger, and his preoccupation with violence in his writings. University authorities sent him for a mental health assessment after several incidents in which he appeared to be stalking female classmates and he was hospitalized overnight after he made a suicidal statement to his roommates. In his final semester before graduation, he purchased handguns and began practicing at a local shooting range. In the week before his attack he made anonymous bomb threats and tested the response of authorities to a chained door. He also made a video manifesto containing angry, rambling statements in which he compared himself to Jesus Christ and described his actions as a heroic act of retaliation against wealthy, materialistic persons who had tormented and tortured him. There was disagreement about his psychological diagnosis, but the video manifesto contained statements suggesting persecutory and grandiose delusions consistent with paranoid schizophrenia.

Several studies of juvenile homicide offenders support these three pathways to violence (Cornell, 1990; Cornell, Benedek, & Benedek, 1987; Greco & Cornell, 1992). The relatively low number of homicide offenders with psychotic disorders (Meloy, Hempel, Mohandie, Shiva, & Gray, 2001) makes it a difficult group to study, despite the high media profile of some specific cases. Many other studies contrast two groups, omitting the psychotic group. For example, multiple studies have supported a distinction between affective/reactive aggression and predatory/proactive aggression (e.g., Cornell et al., 1996; Dodge, Lochman, Harnish, Bates, & Pettit, 1997). This distinction is also frequently mentioned during the analysis of criminal offenders (Hanlon, Brook, Stratton, Jensen, & Rubin, 2013; Meloy, 2006). Although the distinction between reactive and proactive aggression is compelling, threat assessment teams should not assume that offenders engage in only one form of aggression. Both forms of aggression are present in the most severe violent offenders (Blais, Solodukhin, & Forth, 2014; Marsee, Frick, Barry, Kimonis, & Aucoin, 2014). Cornell and colleagues (1996) observed that psychopathy was associated with both instrumental and reactive violence, whereas nonpsychopathic offenders tended to commit reactive crimes.

Threat Assessment as a Form of Risk Assessment

There is debate about the distinction between threat assessment and risk assessment. Although the terms are sometimes used interchangeably, there is growing agreement that threat assessment is a specialized form of risk assessment that has important distinguishing characteristics (Meloy et al., 2014). Risk assessments are typically conducted for the purposes of making a decision about someone's release from institutional care (Monahan, 2010) or incarceration (Otto & Douglas, 2011). In many risk assessments, the anticipated act of violence may be unknown, there is no specific target or intended victim, and the timeframe for violence is open-ended. A risk assessment may be aimed at determining someone's generalized lifetime risk of violence, but threat assessment is concerned with whether someone will carry out a certain threatened act toward a particular victim in the near future. When the risk of violence is judged to be too high, a decision is made to continue the individual's confinement. The determination of a threshold or cut-off point for these decisions is not easily established and rests in part on value judgments about the degree of risk that is deemed tolerable.

Although threat assessments are more narrowly focused and situational than conventional risk assessments, this simple distinction generates a number of complications. Risk assessments tend to rely on instruments developed to predict violence whereas threat assessments place more emphasis on interventions to prevent violence. Because a conventional risk assessment has an open-ended, long-term time frame, there is less attention to situational factors and the individual's current mental state, plans, or intentions. Instead, risk assessments tend to rely on an actuarial approach based on scoring the presence or absence of static risk factors, such as the person's gender, previous violence, and criminal history. This approach has led to the development of quantitative risk assessment instruments such as the Violence Risk Appraisal Guide (VRAG; Quinsey, Harris, Rice, & Cormier, 2006).

Risk assessment instruments can be divided between those that rely on an actuarial formula to determine risk and those that encourage the clinician to make professional judgments that are guided by the instrument but also consider additional information not included in the list of risk factors (Reddy et al., 2001). The value of clinical judgment has been actively debated for more than 60 years (Meehl, 1954), with some authorities more recently recommending a synthesized view (Falzer, 2013; Monahan & Skeem, 2014). Examples of widely used structured clinical judgment instruments are the Historical, Clinical Risk management-20 (HCR-20; Douglas, Hart, Webster, & Belfrage, 2013) and the Structured Assessment of Violence Risk in Youth (SAVRY; Borum, Bartel, & Forth, 2006).

Because threat assessment is concerned with a specific and potentially imminent threat, there is much more emphasis on taking action to prevent violence. In the immediate context of threat assessment, the individual's mental state and current behavior are central concerns. In many cases a potential victim can be identified and can be advised on actions to reduce risk rather than aggravate or provoke the aggressor. Much of the risk assessment literature is concerned with identifying a fixed set of predictors that can be measured in a sample of subjects, ignoring individual variation and idiosyncratic factors. This simplification is necessary for data collection and statistical analyses, but unrealistic for prevention purposes because it ignores potentially important information that is specific to the individual case and does not factor in the effects of interventions. For these reasons, professional judgment is considered an essential component of threat assessment (Borum et al., 2006). See Chapter 6 for more about predicting dangerousness.

Violence Prevention Versus Prediction

One common objection to threat assessment is that violence is too difficult to predict and therefore threat assessment is futile. This objection rests on the erroneous assumption that prevention requires prediction. Decades of research has found that professionals are only moderately successful in identifying individuals who subsequently commit serious acts of violence (Fazel, Singh, Doll, & Grann, 2012). However, the unpredictability of violence in individual cases does not mean violence cannot be prevented on a larger scale. There are obvious examples in the public health field of prevention programs that have saved lives from individually unpredictable causes (Mozaffarian, Hemenway, & Ludwig, 2013). For example, motor vehicle accidents occur unexpectedly and seem unpredictable, but there is ample evidence that traffic safety laws, driver training, and well-designed cars reduce the rate of accidents. Another example is the public health campaign to reduce tobacco smoking that has saved millions of lives. By identifying risk factors like smoking, prevention programs can have widespread effects without knowledge of which individuals have been saved. The American Psychological Association (2013) report on gun violence recommended a similar application of prevention principles to address violence.

Prevention is conceptualized as occurring on three levels (O'Connell, Boat, Warner, 2009). The first level is primary or universal prevention, which includes efforts to address the underlying environmental conditions and general factors that lead to the negative outcome, such as a disease, injury, or in this case, violence. Universal interventions are aimed at the general population. The secondary or selective level is aimed at individuals who are deemed to be at risk for the negative outcome, and the tertiary or indicated level is for those who already demonstrate the negative outcome and are in need of treatment to prevent recurrence or worsening.

Threat assessment can be regarded as a method of identifying the appropriate level of prevention needed for a specific individual. For example, an employee who threatens a coworker could need different interventions depending on the seriousness of their threat. If the threat was an overstatement made in a moment of frustration that ended in a retraction and apology, the appropriate intervention might be to remind the employee of the company policy regarding aggressive behavior. If the individual continued to feel angry or frustrated with this coworker, then conflict resolution or perhaps a reassignment of work responsibilities might be appropriate. Finally, if the threat assessment team identified the individual as someone with a history of violence who has continued to engage in threatening behavior and might pose a risk of violence, it would be important to engage law enforcement authorities and consider stronger actions to prevent a violent outcome. Some typical actions include mandating a period of mental health counseling, and if necessary, suspending the individual from employment.

True violence prevention efforts must begin well before there is a gunman in the parking lot. Violence prevention can begin at a primary level by helping families to raise healthy, well-adjusted children who are less prone to violence. Primary prevention can also be aimed at improving school and community services, so that all youth receive the benefits of good education, health care, and freedom from crime. Secondary prevention can ameliorate risk factors for violence that range from behavioral problems, bullying, and mental disorders, to social and economic disadvantages that are the seedbed for criminal violence.

Prevention of gun violence

Of special concern is the prevention of gun violence, which accounts for the majority of homicides and mass killings in the United States (Nekvasil, Cornell, & Huang, 2015). There is now substantial evidence supporting several key prevention strategies (Webster, 2015). One secondary prevention strategy that appears modestly successful is the restriction of firearm sales to high-risk individuals, such as individuals who are under a domestic violence protection order or those hospitalized because they are deemed to be a threat to themselves or others. Both strategies reduce firearm violence, even though such individuals could evade detection by purchasing a firearm from a private dealer or at a gun show (Webster & Wintemute, 2015). The limitation of this approach is that only a small proportion of gun violence can be attributed to persons under a domestic violence restraining order or hospitalized for mental illness. Moreover, federal laws that might prevent gun violence more successfully have legal loopholes and are weakly enforced, making them relatively ineffective (Webster & Wintemute, 2015).

One especially promising tertiary prevention strategy is the "special deterrence" approach developed as part of Boston's highly successful Operation

Ceasefire (Braga & Weisburd, 2015). This program brought together law enforcement, social services, and a number of community groups to focus on a group of gangs that accounted for the majority of youth homicide in the city. Ironically, this strategy included explicit threats by law enforcement that gun violence would result in severe consequences, accompanied by outreach services offered by other agencies. This strategy seems to have worked in 9 of 10 cities where it has been tried (Braga & Weisburd, 2012).

Applications of Threat Assessment

Threat assessment is applied across a wide range of settings and circumstances, and contextual factors introduce variations in how the method is applied. A brief review of the different applications of threat assessment will elucidate some of the features that distinguish it from traditional risk assessment.

Threats aimed at public figures

The U.S. Secret Service made substantial contributions to the concept of threat assessment through its Exceptional Case Study Project, which examined 83 persons known to have attacked or planned to attack prominent public officials and celebrities (Fein & Vossekuil, 1998). The study provided three key conclusions. First was that there was no profile of "the assassin," and that would-be assassins were best identified by behaviors indicating planning and preparation to carry out an attack. Second, most assassins were not motivated by serious mental illness, but were acting to bring attention to a problem or grievance. Third, direct threats against the intended victims did not increase the likelihood that the individual would make an attack, although the majority of individuals communicated their thoughts or plans to family members, friends, or other associates. The report noted that often the individual had experienced a major life disappointment, such as loss of a relationship or a financial setback that triggered feelings of shame and depression. The report recommended that a threat assessment should include a detailed interview with the individual and development of a management plan to monitor and redirect the individual.

Threats against government officials are extraordinarily common and have resulted in numerous attacks worldwide. A high proportion of attacks are committed by persons with mental illness who may have delusional ideas about their target (Hoffmann, Meloy, & Sheridan, 2014). Perhaps the most famous and influential case in mental health law involved a woodturner who believed that the Tory party was persecuting him and in 1843 he attempted to assassinate the British prime minister and mistakenly killed his secretary Edward Drummond (Dalby, 2006). Many individuals testified at his trial that they knew of the perpetrator's hostility toward the government and his irrational conviction that the government was somehow injuring him. The perpetrator's acquittal as not guilty by reason of insanity led to the development of legal standards for insanity widely used in England and the United States (Packer, 2009).

A more contemporary case is that of a man who, in 2011, attempted to assassinate Arizona Congresswoman Gabrielle Giffords and in the process shot 19 persons, killing six. The shooter was diagnosed with paranoid schizophrenia (Serrano, 2011). This case in particular reflects the need for community-based threat assessment teams that could be a resource for family members and friends to seek help. According to an Anti-Defamation League (2012) report, the shooter's online writings and videos expressed numerous paranoid ideas about the government, such as the belief that the government was brain-washing people by "controlling grammar." Many of his writings were disjointed and illogical. According to police records, his parents had been highly concerned about his angry and irrational behavior (Orr, 2013). His father had confiscated the shooter's shotgun and repeatedly disabled his car to prevent him from leaving the house.

Although mental illness is linked to violence in some high-profile cases, systematic examination of a wider sample of cases reveals other patterns. Many individuals who threaten government officials or the public at large are motivated by political or ideological beliefs (Fein & Vossekuil, 1997, 1999). The 2013 Boston Marathon bombing that killed three people and injured approximately 264 others is an example (Majority Staff of the Committee on Homeland Security, 2014). In this case, two Chechen brothers were moti-vated by extremist Islamic beliefs to carry out a mass attack on U.S. citizens. Currently, there is intensive research on identifying individuals whose political or ideological beliefs would motivate them to commit mass murder; Meloy and Mohandie (2014, p. 388) described these individuals as "violent true believers."

Workplace threats

Violence in the workplace is another arena for threat assessment. For example, threat assessments may be conducted when an employee with a grievance has threatened a coworker or supervisor. When the threat involves an employee, the threat assessment team has leverage to work with the individual to resolve the threat. In such cases, the threat assessment team not only evaluates the risk of violence, it also looks for ways to respond to the employee's concerns and, if possible, resolve them (Calhoun & Weston, 2009; Miller, 1999; Nicoletti & Spooner, 1996). The team may work in collaboration with the employee's supervisors and might advise them to refrain from actions that would aggravate the situation, such as taking punitive action against the employee, and encourage interactions that might de-escalate the situation and facilitate reconciliation.

There is no more effective way to prevent a threatened act of violence than to address the source of the frustration and anger underlying the threat. This is a good example of how threat assessment has evolved from a focus on prediction of violence in more traditional forms of risk assessment to an emphasis on prevention of violence.

Stalking

In cases that take place outside of an institutional setting, the threat assessment team has more limited opportunities for intervention. Stalking presents an especially difficult challenge for threat assessment. The threat assessment team may have little access to the threatening individual and may lack the leverage to engage them in an assessment if the stalking behavior is not taking place in the context of a workplace or school. The motives for stalking also may make it difficult to resolve the individual's conflict or problem. In cases of intimate partner violence, the person may refuse to accept that a former partner no longer wants to be in a relationship. In these cases, much of the threat assessment is focused on assessing the individual's risk of violence and there are a variety of specialized risk assessment instruments to assist the team (Kropp & Cook, 2014).

A report by the National Center for Victims of Crime (2002) provides specific guidance on threat assessment in stalking cases. The guidelines encourage gathering as much information as possible about the victim and the suspect. For example, the guidelines recommend evaluating whether the stalker has a military background, uses others to monitor the victim, and has contacted or threatened the victim's family or friends. The team should also inquire about the victim's degree of fear and apprehension and whether they have obtained a restraining order against the stalker (National Center for Victims of Crime, 2002).

Threat assessment in schools

After the 1999 shooting at Columbine High School in Colorado, reports by the FBI (O'Toole, 2000) and U.S. Secret Service and Department of Education (Fein et al., 2002) recommended that schools adopt a threat assessment approach to violence prevention. Although most school authorities and educators were unfamiliar with threat assessment at the time, it has become widely recognized as a valuable school practice (Cornell, 2014, 2015). In schools, a threat assessment is most often concerned with understanding why a student (or someone else associated with the school) made a threat or engaged in threatening behavior. A school-based threat assessment team gathers information and then develops appropriate interventions that address the underlying problem or concern that motivated the threat.

The key dilemma in school-based threat assessment is to avoid overreacting to the common day-to-day threats that are not serious while not underreacting to more serious threats. School-age children and youth engage in a great deal of verbal aggression, and may make threats simply as an expression of anger or frustration. A survey of 4,400 high school students found that approximately 12% reported being threatened with harm by another student in the past 30 days (Nekvasil & Cornell, 2012). Nearly three quarters did not believe the threat was serious and only about one quarter reported the threat to school authorities. Similarly, acts of physical aggression, harassment, and bullying are much more common in schools than in the adult workplace. According to the Youth Risk Behavior Survey, 20% of female and 18% of male high school students nationwide reported being bullied at school in the past 12 months (Centers for Disease Control and Prevention, 2014). Sixteen percent of boys and 8% of girls in grades 9–12 reported being in a physical fight at school during the previous 12 months (Robers, Kemp, & Truman, 2013).

Serious acts of violence are rare in schools. According to the National Crime Victimization Survey, the annual rate of serious violent crime (i.e., robbery, forcible rape, aggravated assault) is approximately 3.5 incidents per 1,000 students (Robers et al., 2013). The media attention given to school homicides suggests there is an epidemic, but in fact the rate is extraordinarily low. In the 10-year period from 2001 to 2011, there were 200 homicides of school-age children in U.S. schools, an average of about 20 per year (Robers et al., 2013). Although 20 homicides is a tragic and unacceptable amount, it means that in the nation's 120,000 schools, the average school will have a student homicide every 6,000 years (120,000 ÷ 20).

A comparison of homicides across locations is important information for a threat assessment team, because there may be a tendency to overestimate the risk of a student committing a shooting at school (Cornell, 2006). A study using the FBI's National Incident-Based Reporting System (NIBRS) examined the prevalence of homicides, including mass shootings, across 37 states over a 6-year period (Nekvasil et al., 2015). The most common locations for homicides were residences, which accounted for approximately half of all incidents, regardless of the number of victims. Even homicide incidents with six or more victims occurred much more frequently in residences (48.9%) than roads (14.4%), parking lots (10.0%), or restaurants (11.1%), which were the next most common locations. Schools (K-12 schools, colleges, and universities were grouped together) accounted for just 1.1% of the homicide incidents with six or more victims, and less than 1% of the incidents with fewer victims. Schools and religious institutions were the safest locations identified in the study.

Many school authorities have devised threat assessment systems for their school or adapted systems from the literature (e.g., O'Toole, 2000; Van Dreal, 2011; Van Dyke & Schroeder, 2006; Vossekuil et al., 2002). The Virginia Student Threat Assessment Guidelines (Cornell & Sheras, 2006) was developed in 2002 based on reports from the FBI (O'Toole, 2000) and Secret Service and U.S. Department of Education (Vossekuil et al., 2002), as well as research conducted in Virginia public schools. The Virginia threat assessment model is described in a 145-page manual (Cornell & Sheras, 2006) and presents a seven-step decision tree to guide school-based teams through a process of evaluating the threat, quickly resolving transient threats that are deemed not serious, and focusing more resources on substantive (i.e., serious) threats. A typical threat assessment team consists of a school administrator (e.g., principal or assistant principal), counselor, psychologist, social worker, and resource officer (e.g., law enforcement officer).

There is considerable research supporting the Virginia threat assessment model. Two field tests demonstrated that school-based teams could carry out threat assessments in a practical, efficient manner without violent outcomes (Cornell et al., 2004; Strong & Cornell, 2008). Almost all students were returned to school and few received long-term suspensions or transfers to another school. Another study found that staff training in threat assessment lowered concern about school shootings and decreased support for zero-tolerance discipline (Allen, Cornell, Lorek, & Sheras, 2008). Two quasi-experimental controlled studies found that schools using the Virginia Guidelines experienced lower suspension rates and less bullying, and their students reported greater willingness to seek help for threats of violence (Cornell, Gregory, & Fan, 2011; Cornell, Sheras, Gregory, & Fan, 2009). A randomized control study of 40 schools found that students who made threats of violence in schools using the Virginia Guidelines were much more likely to receive counseling services and less likely to be suspended or transferred to a different school than in the control schools (Cornell, Allen, & Fan, 2012). In 2013, the Virginia Student Threat Assessment Guidelines was recognized as an evidence-based practice in the National Registry of Evidence-Based Programs and Practices (NREPP; 2013).

A statewide examination found that secondary schools using the Virginia Guidelines recorded fewer school suspensions than other schools, controlling for school size, the percentage of low income students, and the percentage of minority students (JustChildren & Cornell, 2013). A promising finding was that suspension rates were lower for both white and black students in schools using the Virginia Guidelines, and the lower rate for black students substantially reduced the racial disparity in long-term suspensions. In 2013, Virginia legislation mandated that all its public schools establish threat assessment teams; a statewide evaluation of this system is under way (Cornell et al., 2015).

Conclusions

In conclusion, threat assessment represents an evolutionary step forward in the practice of violence risk assessment. Unlike conventional risk assessment that typically measures static risk factors to predict the long-term risk of violence with no specific target, a threat assessment is concerned with an immediate threat of violence towards an identified target. Consequently, threat assessment places greater emphasis on situational and dynamic risk factors, and uses them to develop a prevention plan. Threat assessment has been applied to specialized problems, such as the protection of public figures, acts of terrorism, and domestic violence. Threat assessment teams have been established in institutional settings, such as businesses and schools, but can also be used at a community level. Analyses of mass murder cases reveal many opportunities where a threat assessment approach might have been effective. However, much more research is needed to develop threat assessment practices and validate their effectiveness as violence prevention strategies.

References

Allen, K., Cornell, D., Lorek, E., & Sheras, P. (2008). Response of school personnel to student threat assessment training. *School Effectiveness and School Improvement, 19*, 319–332.

American Psychological Association. (2013). *Gun violence: Prediction, prevention, and policy.* Retrieved from http://www.apa.org/pubs/info/reports/gun-violence-prevention.aspx

Anti-Defamation League. (2012). *The mindset of Jared Lee Loughner.* Retrieved from http://www.adl.org/assets/pdf/combating-hate/The-Mindset-Of-Jared-Lee-Loughner.pdf

Blais, J., Solodukhin, E., & Forth, A. E. (2014). A meta-analysis exploring the relationship between psychopathy and instrumental versus reactive violence. *Criminal Justice and Behavior, 41*, 797–821. doi:10.1177/0093854813519629

Borum, R., Bartel, P., & Forth, A. (2006). *SAVRY: Structured Assessment of Violence Risk in Youth: Professional manual.* Lutz, FL: Psychological Assessment Resources.

Borum, R., Fein, R., Vossekuil, B., & Berglund, J. (1999). Threat assessment: Defining an approach for evaluating risk of targeted violence. *Behavioral Sciences & the Law, 17*, 323–337. doi:10.1002/(SICI)1099-0798(199907/09)17:3<323::AID-BSL349>3.0.CO;2-G

Braga, A. A., & Weisburd, D. L. (2012). The effects of focused deterrence strategies on crime: A systematic review and meta-analysis of the empirical evidence. *Journal of Research in Crime and Delinquency, 49*, 323–358. doi:10.1177/0022427811419368

Braga, A. A., & Weisburd, D. L. (2015). Focused deterrence and the prevention of violent gun injuries: Practice, theoretical principles, and scientific evidence. *Annual Review of Public Health, 36*, 55–68. doi:10.1146/annurev-publhealth-031914-122444

Brown, B. (2015). *Isla Vista mass murder: May 23, 2014. Investigative summary.* Santa Barbara County Sheriff's Office, Santa Barbara, CA. Retrieved from Santa Barbara County Sheriff Office's website http://www.sbsheriff.us/documents/ISLAVISTAINVESTIGATIVESUMMARY.pdf

Calhoun, F. S., & Weston, S. W. (2009). *Threat assessment and management strategies: Identifying howlers and hunters.* Boca Raton, FL: CRC Press.

Centers for Disease Control and Prevention (2014). Youth Risk Behavior Surveillance System (YRBSS). Retrieved from http://www.cdc.gov/healthyyouth/yrbs/index.htm

Cornell, D. (1990). Prior adjustment of violent juvenile offenders. *Law and Human Behavior, 14*, 569–578.

Cornell, D. (2006). *School violence: Fears versus facts.* Mahwah, NJ: Lawrence Erlbaum.

Cornell, D. (2014). Best practices in threat assessment in schools. In A. Thomas and P. Harrison (Eds.), *Best practices in school psychology* (6th ed.; pp. 259–272). Bethesda, MD: National Association of School Psychologists.

Cornell, D. (2015). Student threat assessment. In R. H. Witte and S. Mosley-Howard (Eds.), *Mental health practice in today's schools: Current issues and interventions* (pp. 379–398). New York, NY: Springer.

Cornell, D., Allen, K., & Fan, X. (2012). A randomized controlled study of the Virginia Student Threat Assessment Guidelines in grades K-12. *School Psychology Review, 41*, 100–115.

Cornell, D., Benedek, E., & Benedek, D. (1987). Juvenile homicide: Prior adjustment and a proposed typology. *American Journal of Orthopsychiatry, 57*, 383–393.

Cornell, D., Gregory, A., & Fan, X. (2011). Reductions in long-term suspensions following adoption of the Virginia Student Threat Assessment Guidelines. *Bulletin of the National Association of Secondary School Principals, 95*, 175–194.

Cornell, D., Maeng, J., Huang, F., Burnette, A., Datta, P., & Heilbrun, A. (2015). *Threat assessment in Virginia schools: Technical report of the Threat Assessment Survey for 2013–2014.* Charlottesville, VA: Curry School of Education, University of Virginia.

Cornell, D., & Sheras, P. (2006). *Guidelines for responding to student threats of violence.* Longmont, CO: Sopris West.

Cornell, D., Sheras, P., Gregory, A., & Fan, X. (2009). A retrospective study of school safety conditions in high schools using the Virginia Threat Assessment Guidelines versus alternative approaches. *School Psychology Quarterly, 24*, 119–129.

Cornell, D., Sheras, P. Kaplan, S., McConville, D., Douglass, J., Elkon, A., ... Cole, J. (2004). Guidelines for student threat assessment: Field-test findings. *School Psychology Review, 33*, 527–546.

Cornell, D. G., Warren, J., Hawk, G., Stafford, E., Oram, G., & Pine, D. (1996). Psychopathy in instrumental and reactive violent offenders. *Journal of Consulting and Clinical Psychology, 64*, 783–790.

Dalby, J. T. (2006). The case of Daniel McNaughton: Let's get the story straight. *American Journal of Forensic Psychiatry, 27*, 17–32.

Dodge, K. A., Lochman, J. E., Harnish, J. D., Bates, J. E., & Pettit, G. S. (1997). Reactive and proactive aggression in school children and psychiatrically impaired chronically assaultive youth. *Journal of Abnormal Psychology, 106*, 37–51. doi:10.1037/0021-843X.106.1.37

Douglas, K. S., Hart, S. D., Webster, C. D., & Belfrage, H. (2013). *HCR-20: Assessing risk for violence (Version 3).* Burnaby, Canada: Mental Health, Law, and Policy Institute, Simon Fraser University.

Falzer, P. R. (2013). Valuing structured professional judgment: Predictive validity, decision-making, and the clinical-actuarial conflict. *Behavioral Sciences & the Law, 31*, 40–54.

Fazel, S., Singh, J. P., Doll, H., & Grann, M. (2012). Use of risk assessment instruments to predict violence and antisocial behavior in 73 samples involving 24,827 people: Systematic review and meta-analysis. *BMJ*, 345. doi:10.1136/bmj. e4692

Fein, R. A., & Vossekuil, B. V. (1997). *Preventing assassination: Secret Service Exceptional Case Study Project.* Retrieved from https://www.ncjrs.gov/pdffiles1/ Photocopy/167224NCJRS.pdf

Fein, R. A., & Vossekuil, B. V. (1998). *Protective intelligence and threat assessment investigations: A guide for state and local law enforcement officials.* July, 1998. Retrieved from http://www.secretservice.gov/ntac/PI_Guide.pdf

Fein, R. A., & Vossekuil, B. V. (1999). Assassination in the United States: An operational study of recent assassins, attackers, and near-lethal approachers. *Journal of Forensic Sciences, 44,* 321–333. Retrieved from http://www.secretservice.gov/ ntac.htm

Fein, R. A., Vossekuil, B., Pollack,W. S., Borum, R., Modzeleski,W., & Reddy, M. (2002). *Threat assessment in schools: A guide to managing threatening situations and to creating safe school climates.* Washington, DC: U.S. Secret Service and U.S. Department of Education.

Fernandez, M., Kovaleski, S. F., & Montgomery, D. (2015, May 19). Mass roundup of bikers in Waco shootout tests limits of court system. *The New York Times.* Retrieved from http://www.nytimes.com/2015/05/20/us/waco-texas-biker-shooting.html

Greco, C., & Cornell, D. (1992). Rorschach object relations of adolescents who committed homicide. *Journal of Personality Assessment, 59,* 574–583.

Hanlon, R. E., Brook, M., Stratton, J., Jensen, M., & Rubin, L. H. (2013). Neuropsychological and intellectual differences between types of murderers: Affective/impulsive versus predatory/instrumental (premeditated) homicide. *Criminal Justice and Behavior, 40,* 933–948. doi:10.1177/0093854813479779

Hoffman, J., Meloy, J. R., & Sheridan, L. (2014). Contemporary research on stalking, threatening, and attacking public figures. In J. R. Meloy & J. Hoffmann (Eds.), *The international handbook of threat assessment* (pp. 160–177). New York, NY: Oxford University Press.

Holley, P., Freedom du Lac, J., Berman, M., & Madigan, T. (2015, May 17). Police say 170 arrested in deadly biker gang shootout at Texas restaurant. *The Washington Post.* Retrieved from http://www.washingtonpost.com/news/post-nation/wp/ 2015/05/17/shootout-among-rival-biker-gangs-in-texas-restaurant-kills-9/

JustChildren, & Cornell, D. (2013). *Prevention v. punishment: Threat assessment, school suspensions, and racial disparities.* Legal Aid Justice Center, Charlottesville, VA. https://www.justice4all.org/wp-content/uploads/2013/12/UVA-and-JustChildren-Report-Prevention-v.-Punishment.pdf

Kropp, P. R., & Cook, A. N. (2014). Intimate partner violence, homicide, and stalking. In R. Meloy & J. Hoffman (Eds.), *The international handbook of threat assessment* (pp. 178–194). Oxford Press.

Leshan, B. (2015, May 20). $40K delivered to home, boy tortured before DC murder, fire. *WUSA 9.* Retrieved from http://www.wusa9.com/story/news/local/ 2015/05/20/savopoulis-10-year-old-boy-tortured-before-murders-and-fire-in-dc/27643991/

Leuschner, V., Fiedler, N., Schultze, M., Ahlig, N., Göbel, K. Sommer, F., ... Scheithauer, H. (in press). Prevention of targeted school violence by responding to students' psychosocial crises: The NETWASS Program. *Child Development*.

Lovett, I., & Nagourney, A. (2014, May 24). Video rant, then deadly rampage in California town. *The New York Times*. Retrieved from http://www.nytimes.com/2014/05/25/us/california-drive-by-shooting.html

Majority Staff of the Committee on Homeland Security. (2014). *The road to Boston: counterterrorism challenges and lessons from the Marathon bombings*. March, 2014. Retrieved from https://homeland.house.gov/sites/homeland.house.gov/files/documents/Boston-Bombings-Report.pdf

Marsee, M. A., Frick, P. J., Barry, C. T., Kimonis, E. R., & Aucoin, K. J. (2014). Profiles of the forms and functions of self-reported aggression in three adolescent samples. *Development and Psychopathology, 26*, 705–720.

Meehl, P. E. (1954). *Clinical vs. statistical prediction*. Minneapolis, MN: University of Minnesota Press.

Meloy, J. R. (2006). Empirical basis and forensic application of affective and predatory violence. *Australian and New Zealand Journal of Psychiatry, 40*, 539–547. doi:10.1080/j.1440–1614.2006.01837.x

Meloy, J. R., Hart, S. D., & Hoffman, J. (2014). Threat assessment and threat management. In J. R. Meloy & J. Hoffman (Eds.), *The international handbook of threat assessment* (pp. 3–17). New York: Oxford University Press.

Meloy, J. R., Hempel, A. G., Mohandie, K., Shiva, A. A., & Gray, B. T. (2001). Offender and offense characteristics of a nonrandom sample of adolescent mass murderers. *Journal of the American Academy of Child & Adolescent Psychiatry, 40*, 719–728.

Meloy, J. R., & Mohandie, K. (2014). Assessing threats by direct interview of the violent true believer. In J. R. Meloy & J. Hoffmann (Eds.), *The international handbook of threat assessment* (pp. 388–395). New York, NY: Oxford University Press.

Miller, L. (1999). Workplace violence: Prevention, response, and recovery. *Psychotherapy: Theory, Research, Practice, Training, 36*, 160–169. http://doi.org/10.1037/h0087694

Monahan, J. (2010). The classification of violence risk. In R. Otto and K. Douglas (Eds.), *Handbook of violence risk assessment* (pp. 187–198). New York, NY: Routledge.

Monahan, J., & Skeem, J. L. (2014). The evolution of violence risk assessment. *CNS Spectrums, 19*, 419–424.

Mozaffarian, D., Hemenway, D., & Ludwig, D. S. (2013). Curbing gun violence: Lessons from public health successes. *JAMA: Journal of the American Medical Association, 309*, 551–552. doi:10.1001/jama.2013.38

National Center for Victims of Crime. (2002, April). *Creating an effective stalking protocol*. Retrieved from http://www.victimsofcrime.org/docs/src/creating-an-effective-stalking-protocol.pdf?sfvrsn=2

National Registry of Evidence-Based Programs and Practices. (2013). *Virginia student threat assessment guidelines*. Retrieved from http://www.nrepp.samhsa.gov/ViewIntervention.aspx?id=263

Nekvasil, E. K., & Cornell, D. G. (2012). Student reports of peer threats of violence: Prevalence and outcomes. *Journal of School Violence, 11*, 357–375. doi:10.1080/15388220.2012.706764

Nekvasil, E., Cornell, D., & Huang, F. (2015). Prevalence and offense characteristics of multiple casualty homicides: Are schools at higher risk than other locations? *Psychology of Violence*. Online first publication. doi:10.1037/a0038967

Nicoletti, J., & Spooner, K. (1996). Violence in the workplace: Response and intervention strategies. In G. R. VandenBos & E. Q. Bulatao (Eds.), *Violence on the job: Identifying risks and developing solutions* (pp. 267–282). Washington, DC: American Psychological Association.

O'Connell, M. E., Boat, T. Warner, K. E. (2009). *Preventing mental, emotional, and behavioral disorders among young people: Progress and possibilities.* Washington, DC: National Academies Press.

Orr, B. (2013, March 27). Newly released Jared Lee Loughner file reveals chilling details. *CBS News.* Retrieved from http://www.cbsnews.com/news/newly-released-jared-lee-loughner-files-reveal-chilling-details/

O'Toole, M. E. (2000). *The school shooter: A threat assessment perspective.* Quantico, VA: National Center for the Analysis of Violent Crime, Federal Bureau of Investigation. Retrieved from http://www.fbi.gov/stats-services/publications/school-shooter

Otto, R. K., & Douglas, K. S. (Eds.). (2011). *Handbook of violence risk assessment.* New York, NY: Routledge.

Packer, I. K. (2009). *Evaluation of criminal responsibility.* New York, NY: Oxford University Press.

Quinsey, V. L., Harris, G. T., Rice, M. E., & Cormier, C. A. (2006). *Violent offenders: Appraising and managing risk* (2nd ed.). Washington, DC: American Psychological Association.

Randazzo, M. R., Borum, R., Vossekuil, B., Fein, R., Modzeleski, W., & Pollack, W. (2006). Threat assessment in schools: Empirical support and comparison with other approaches. In S. R. Jimerson & M. J. Furlong (Eds.), *The handbook of school violence and school safety: From research to practice* (pp. 147–156). Mahwah, NJ: Erlbaum.

Reddy, M., Borum, R., Berglund, J., Vossekuil, B., Fein, R., & Modzeleski, W. (2001). Evaluating risk for targeted violence in schools: Comparing risk assessment, threat assessment, and other approaches. *Psychology in the Schools, 38*, 157–172.

Robers, S., Kemp, J., & Truman, J. (2013). *Indicators of school crime and safety: 2012* (NCES 2013-036/NCJ 241446). National Center for Education Statistics, U.S. Department of Education, and Bureau of Justice and Statistics, Office of Justice Programs, U.S. Department of Justice. Washington, DC.

Serrano, R. A. (2011, May 26). Loughner ruled unfit for trial. *Los Angeles Times.* Retrieved from http://articles.latimes.com/2011/may/26/nation/la-na-loughner-sanity-20110526

Sewell, K., & Mendelsohn, M. (2000). Profiling potentially violent youth: Statistical and conceptual problems. *Children's Services: Social Policy, Research, & Practice, 3*, 147–169.

Strong, K., & Cornell, D. (2008). Student threat assessment in Memphis City Schools: A descriptive report. *Behavioral Disorders, 34*, 42–54.

Van Dreal, J. (2011). *Assessing student threats: A handbook for implementing the Salem-Keizer system.* Lanham, MD: Rowman & Littlefield Education.

Van Dyke, R. B., & Schroeder, J. L. (2006). Implementation of the Dallas threat of violence risk assessment. In S. Jimerson & M. Furlong (Eds.), *Handbook of school safety and school violence* (pp. 603–616). Mahwah, NJ: Lawrence Earlbaum.

Virginia Tech Review Panel. (2007). *Mass shootings at Virginia Tech, April 16, 2007. Report of the review panel.* Retrieved from http://www.vtreviewpanel.org/report/index.html

Virginia Tech Review Panel Addendum. (2009). *Mass shooting at Virginia Tech: Addendum to the report of the review panel.* November, 2009. Retrieved from http://scholar.lib.vt.edu/prevail/docs/April16ReportRev20091204.pdf

Vossekuil, B., Fein, R., Reddy, M., Borum, R., & Modzeleski, W. (2002). *The final report and findings of the Safe School Initiative: Implications for the prevention of school attacks in the United States.* Washington, DC: U.S. Secret Service and U.S. Department of Education.

Webster, D. W. (2015). Commentary: Evidence to guide gun violence prevention in America. *Annual Review of Public Health, 36,* 1–4. http://doi.org/10.1146/annurev-publhealth-031914-122542

Webster, D. W., & Wintemute, G. J. (2015). Effects of policies designed to keep firearms from high-risk individuals. *Annual Review of Public Health, 36,* 21–37. doi:10.1146/annurev-publhealth-031914-122516

20

Ethical Conduct of Research in the Aftermath of Mass Shootings

Elana Newman, Chelsea Shotwell Tabke, and Betty Pfefferbaum

Mass shootings are complex and confusing situations that pose many methodological challenges for researchers who aim to promote knowledge that may help future impacted communities. Advancing scholarship about mass shootings requires multidisciplinary knowledge and a commitment to ethical decision-making. While the knowledge base is growing, the literature on ethical decision-making while conducting such research is limited. In fact, only one study has investigated individuals' reactions to participating in a study following a mass shooting (Fergus, Rabenhorst, Orcutt, & Valentiner, 2011). Given this lack of specific information on the ethical conduct of research about mass shootings, this chapter will primarily draw on information from the literature on the ethics of human subjects research related to trauma as a whole.

There is no consensus on how to define "mass shooting" among researchers (Shultz et. al., 2014). For the purposes of this chapter, we will define mass shooting as a mass murder conducted with a firearm. According to the Federal Bureau of Investigation, a mass murder is an incident in which four or more people are killed in a single incident, with no distinctive temporal separation between the murders (Morton & Hilts, 2008). The discerning characteristic that defines this "mass" event is the qualification that the murders occurred during a single time period. This stipulation qualitatively differentiates "mass" events from "spree" or "serial" events, which require a distinctive "cool down" period between the murders. This definition is not perfect, particularly in its distinction between "mass" and "spree" shootings (see Chapters 1–3 for more information on the definition of mass shooting), but for the purposes of exploring issues related to ethical research this definition should suffice as it focuses on interpersonal violence that involves multiple victims. Given this

The Wiley Handbook of the Psychology of Mass Shootings, First Edition. Edited by Laura C. Wilson.
© 2017 John Wiley & Sons, Inc. Published 2017 by John Wiley & Sons, Inc.

definition, this review relies on evidence and scholarship about ethical research practice in the aftermath of mass disasters, terrorism, and interpersonal violence. While many of these events share similarities (e.g., multiple victims, bystanders, impact on family members, the need for coordinated responses, coverage in the news), mass shootings may be distinct in numerous ways. For example, naturally caused mass disasters lack the interpersonal element of mass shootings. Also, while terrorism is designed to intentionally elicit fear, panic, and behavior change in the public (Terrorism, 2012), such reactions may be a byproduct of mass shootings, but are not necessarily the key causal motivation. Yet, despite critical differences among these traumatic events, the overall similarities can serve as a basis to describe ethical issues in the conduct of research on mass shootings. Moreover, a recent meta-analysis of responses to trauma-focused research participation found no differences between participants who had experienced either sexual or nonsexual trauma (Jaffe, DiLillo, Hoffman, Haikalis, & Dykstra, 2015), which further justifies our ability to rely on the general scholarship related to ethical research practice in the field of trauma.

This review is predicated on the assumption that researchers who study mass shootings are well-intentioned practitioners who seek to answer essential questions in ways that are methodologically and ethically sound. With respect to ethical research practice, researchers and regulatory bodies must consider and weigh the ethical principles of autonomy/respect for persons, beneficence and nonmaleficence, and justice (National Commission for the Protection of Human Subjects of Behavioral Research [National Commission], 1979). Broadly speaking, respect for persons involves regard for the autonomy and capabilities of individuals to make informed decisions about research participation. In addition, it involves protecting those with diminished autonomy while still allowing them the freedom to enact choices within their capabilities. Beneficence aims to maximize the potential benefits and minimize the potential harms of research participation. Potential harm is evaluated by examining the probability of costs, such as inconvenience and discomfort, as well as the probability of long-lasting psychological or physical harm. Justice requires equitable selection of participants such that those who undertake the burden of research should be those who are likely to benefit. Thus, the foundational principles of autonomy, beneficence, and justice guide ethical decision-making during the process of conducting research.

Although ethical decision-makers are advised to balance these principles equally, it is difficult to operationalize each principle and equally weigh each concern. Further, given the complexities, these judgments are susceptible to human decision-making errors (Newman & Kaloupek, 2004). These errors may be heightened due to the intense reactions (e.g., anger, fear, disgust, grief, blame, curiosity) and various community and policy concerns (e.g., safety, gun violence, mental health, corrections practice, social class, poverty) that are evoked by mass shootings. In light of these issues, special care needs to be taken when interacting with those most proximal to the event (e.g., survivors and their families, bystanders, community members, perpetrators). The present chapter reviews the evidence base to offer recommendations on how to conduct ethically informed research. Most psychological research on mass shootings to date has involved noninvasive procedures – interviews, surveys, and physiological measures (e.g., cortisol, skin conductance) – where the risks were relatively low. Nevertheless, it is necessary to ensure that research promotes autonomy, is associated with a favorable benefit-cost ratio, and in some way benefits those who participate.

Overview of General Issues for Victims and Impacted Communities

The present chapter will examine ethical issues that are pertinent to research in the aftermath of mass shootings and relevant findings from research on trauma-affected populations. First, the issues of autonomy and respect will be discussed. Second, attention will be paid to the vulnerability, decisional capacity, and consent/assent of potential participants. Third, beneficence and nonmaleficence will be explored in terms of the benefits, risks, and confidentiality of potential participants. Fourth, the issue of justice will be discussed in the context of the burden that potential participants may carry, as well as the dissemination of the results of the study. Lastly, broader, overarching concerns will be examined.

Autonomy/respect for persons

Autonomy and respect as fundamental principles of research require that each person be given the respect, time, information, and opportunity to make independent decisions about their own research participation, within the limits of their own capabilities (National Commission, 1979). In the aftermath of mass shootings, it is vital to assure that the autonomy of survivors, bystanders, and the greater community is not violated. Mass shootings often generate fear, anger, confusion, and uncertainty among those directly and indirectly impacted by the events, which could increase the vulnerability of potential participants or exacerbate coercion. The vulnerability of research participants generally refers to a susceptibility to be misled, mistreated, or exploited by researchers (Levine, 2004; National Commission, 1979). Although vulnerability is not explicitly defined in federal regulations, the regulations do require extra protection of those considered vulnerable. Researchers must be mindful that survivors may be physically and/or psychologically injured, which may compromise their decision-making abilities. Mass shootings can violate the sense of self-efficacy and independence of those impacted by the events. Thus, research needs to be conducted in a way as to not take advantage of the victims feeling powerless and to not further foster any feelings of a lack of control.

With regard to autonomy, the major focus of ethical decision-making revolves around the potential participants' decisional capacity to consent to research. The consensus within the psychological literature is that decisional capacity is not impaired in survivors as a result of exposure to trauma, including those who subsequently develop posttraumatic stress disorder (PTSD). However, it should be noted that many individuals impacted by mass shootings may have other conditions or disorders that affect their ability to consent (e.g., severe head injury, acute psychosis). However, this body of literature is extremely flawed, since few published studies about decisional capacity among trauma survivors indicate if and how many participants were excluded due to concerns about conditions that would affect their ability to give consent, such as extremely low intelligence, psychosis, and/or head injury (Collogan, Tuma, Dolan-Sewell, Borja, & Fleischman, 2004). Clearly trauma survivors and those with PTSD do require care and attention, but as a class they do not appear to meet the definition of vulnerable groups in terms of decisional capacity (Collogan, Tuma, Dolan-Sewell, et. al., 2004; Newman & Kaloupek, 2004, 2009). Nevertheless, as with all research endeavors, specific individuals in the sample may have deficits that should be evaluated and considered using best practice guidance and tools (Appelbaum & Grisso, 2001).

Previous research has demonstrated that across several trauma-focused studies, most participants have indicated that they were treated with respect while participating in their respective research studies (e.g., Kassam-Adams & Newman, 2002; Newman, Willard, Sinclair, & Kaloupek, 2001; Widom & Czaja, 2005). In addition, available studies suggest that most adult and child participants in trauma-focused research indicate that they felt able to refuse to participate, to stop or skip questions, and to tell research staff when they did not like aspects of the research protocol (e.g., Hebenstreit & DePrince, 2012; Hurley & Underwood, 2002; Kassam-Adams & Newman, 2002, 2005; Ruzek & Zatzick, 2000). A minority, however, indicated that they did not feel able to refuse to participate initially (e.g., Ruzek & Zatzick, 2000). To counteract any coercive pressure a potential participant may experience due to feeling powerless or having a desire to help, it is important to stress the voluntary nature of the study to all participants in the aftermath of a mass shooting. It may also be useful to remind participants of the voluntary nature of the study throughout data collection. However, there is no empirical evidence as to whether this is effective in reducing any perceived coercion (Fontes, 2004).

With regards to survivors of mass disasters, another means of potential coercion relates to the issue of research versus clinical services because many survivors may mistakenly believe they are receiving therapeutic assistance when interacting with research personnel. It is imperative in the aftermath of mass disasters that participants understand that they are being approached for research and not clinical services (Collogan, Tuma, & Fleischman, 2004; Fleischman & Wood, 2002; Qureshi et. al., 2007). While there are no data to inform us on how often this misconception occurs with respect to mass shootings, particularly in research without an intervention component, practice recommendations include urging survivors to consult with family members prior to research participation and clearly stating the research question in the informed consent procedures (Collogan, Tuma, & Fleischman, 2004; Fleischman & Wood, 2002; Qureshi et. al., 2007). In the future, more studies need to assess the degree to which this is a problem in the aftermath of disasters, and specifically mass shootings.

Given that many mass shootings, especially school shootings, involve children, assent is a critical concern for researchers. Children cannot give legal consent, but the recommended practice is that all children be given an opportunity to assent to participate, to whatever degree is possible given their developmental age (Institute of Medicine, 2004). Fortunately, for researchers who present information in a developmentally appropriate way, the majority of children seem capable of understanding the voluntary nature of participation, as noted in pediatric traffic injury studies (e.g., Kassam-Adams & Newman, 2002, 2005). With respect to fully understanding the actual research aims and procedures, a small body of literature provides mixed evidence. A study conducted on peer provocation suggests that children 8 years of age and under may have difficulty understanding concepts of confidentiality and research tasks. In addition, children up to age 12 may struggle with understanding the aim of the research studies (Hurley & Underwood, 2002). On the other hand, a study of injured children found that 87% appraised the explanation of the study as accurate and 76% believed the study was confidential (Kassam-Adams & Newman, 2005). Thus, the evidence suggests that most children and adolescents who experience a mass shooting are able to make choices about whether to engage in research, when it is presented in a clear and developmentally appropriate fashion. However, they may not be able to comprehend all details of the studies. Overall, trauma-related studies show that participants tend to perceive that they were treated with respect, and self-report responses by both children and adults reveal that they are generally satisfied with the information and procedures involved in informed consent (Chu, DePrince, & Weinzierl, 2008; DePrince & Chu, 2008; Kassam-Adams & Newman, 2005; Newman et. al., 2001; Ruzek & Zatzick, 2000). Nevertheless, more empirical evidence is needed and ways to enhance participant comprehension of study designs, particularly child participants, should be pursued.

Finally, the issues involved in assuring autonomy for participants in research focused on perpetrators of mass shootings are complex. Opportunities for research with perpetrators of mass shootings are rare, largely due to the majority of perpetrators committing suicide or being killed by police during the event (Blair & Schweit, 2014). However, if the opportunity for research with apprehended perpetrators presents itself, there are a number of important factors to consider. Informed consent in criminal justice research is unique both before the trial and after prosecution. Prior to the trial, researchers studying perpetrators must be well-versed in the laws and reporting requirements (e.g., mandatory reporting requirements regarding abuse or future crimes) related to such work and must carefully communicate those as part of the consent process. For example, researchers need to be aware of and communicate to participants that the researchers themselves may be legally compelled to disclose information they gather from the perpetrator(s), should study information be relevant to the case (Jones, 2012; Lowman & Palys, 2001). Communication of this information is essential in informed consent procedures with perpetrators so that they are able to make an informed decision about participation.

As in the case of studying perpetrators of sexual violence, research of mass violence should not be used for the investigation of criminal cases (Jewkes, Dartnall, & Sikweyiya, 2012). Given that it is very difficult to assure that information shared during research will not be accessed for prosecution, research is not typically conducted at this time. However, if research is conducted, research teams need to be careful to avoid incriminating disclosure (Jewkes et. al., 2012). For instance, the methodology used may create circumstances in which perpetrators reveal information that incriminates them or implies their involvement in crimes. In this case, researchers should warn participants against providing too much detail, as well as the potential legal consequences of such disclosures should the researchers be subpoenaed (Jewkes et. al., 2012). After the trial and conviction, concerns about whether the person is able to volunteer to participate must be carefully considered. In addition to all the protection measures used for prisoners, as defined by Subpart C of the Code of Federal Regulations for the protection of human subjects (Department of Health and Human Services, 2009), consent must clarify that research participation will not affect the ways in which correctional authorities perceive the participants.

In conclusion, there is no evidence to suggest that persons who experience traumatic events or who suffer from PTSD as a result have deficits in their capacity to consent, although this has not been established specific to mass shootings. Most experts agree that it seems unlikely that decision-making capacity is impaired among survivors and witnesses of mass shootings. However, the base rates of exclusion for deficits related to decision-making capacity are seldom reported in trauma studies, so there is no systematic way to assess this issue. Similarly, the current evidence suggests that survivors and those with PTSD are not more susceptible to coercion or inability to appreciate the content of the consent process than other participants. Thus, evidence indicates that it is ill-advised to apply the broad category of vulnerability to trauma survivors or individuals with PTSD. Clearly trauma survivors and those with

PTSD do require care and attention, but as a class they do not appear to meet the definition of vulnerable groups (Collogan, Tuma, Dolan-Sewel, et. al., 2004). Nevertheless, those who study the psychological effects of mass trauma should strive to emphasize that the participants have the choice to participate or not, and provide clear explanations of the research questions and methods used throughout the recruitment and consent processes. Those who study mass shootings could contribute to the field by proactively collecting data about the efficacy of their recruitment and consent procedures. Furthermore, those who study perpetrators need to focus on assuring that consent is freely given and abide by all the special precautions and recommendations for obtaining consent from prisoners.

Beneficence and nonmaleficence

Research in general, and specifically in relation to mass shootings, can involve many potential benefits (e.g., empowerment, altruism, insight, feeling of satisfaction or value after participating), costs (e.g., inconvenience, boredom, time, minimal distress), and risks (e.g., injury, psychological discomfort, unwanted media attention; Newman & Kaloupek, 2004). Careful consideration of each of these potential benefits, costs, and risks can inform research designs and decisions to assure that the value of systematically gathering information does not exceed its costs.

Minimal risk   Much of the research literature has focused on the concept of trauma-related distress and whether it exceeds minimal risk. Minimal risk is when "the probability and magnitude of harm or discomfort anticipated in the research are not greater in and of themselves than those ordinarily encountered in daily life or during the performance of routine physical or psychological examinations or tests" (Department of Health and Human Services, 2009, p. 4). Most trauma researchers argue that the risk experienced during typical survey and interview studies about mental health after traumatic events satisfies the definition of minimal risk because any distress ensued by thinking about the events is no greater than distress encountered as a result of other daily reminders (e.g., news, reminders of loss; Becker-Blease & Freyd, 2006). Given the extensive news coverage of most mass shootings and the aftermath, most mental health surveys and interviews about the impact of the event are highly unlikely to exceed minimal risk, since the distress encountered should be no greater than that generated in daily life.

One study has focused on mass shootings in particular. In a study of 58 college students who were on a campus where a school shooting occurred, but not in the classroom where the event took place, participants wrote and read a narrative about their reactions to the shooting 6 weeks after the event. Using both objective (i.e., cortisol, heart rate, skin conductance) and subjective (i.e., self-report) measures, the authors assessed both subjective and objective distress. While those with PTSD symptoms had more subjective distress, but not objective distress, than those without symptoms, 85% indicated they would participate again if asked. No information was provided about the 15% who would not participate again. Thus, it appears that the majority of bystanders and witnesses experience tolerable distress when asked to think about their experiences during a mass shooting. This is consistent with existing research from other studies, which suggests that a small portion of participants experience some distress (e.g., McClinton Appollis, Lund, de Vries, & Mathews, 2015), both expected and unexpected, during trauma-related research. However, research studies indicate that this distress is not perceived as beyond minimal risk, it is manageable, it is not the same as regretting participating, and most respondents perceive the benefits as worth the emotional costs (Carter-Visscher, Naugle, Bell, & Suvak, 2008; Hebenstreit & DePrince, 2012; Jaffe et. al., 2015; McClinton et al., 2015; Verschuur, Spinhoven, van Emmerik, & Rosendaal, 2008). Some argue that the expression of mildly negative, but tolerable affect during research may represent the participants' emotional engagement in the research project rather than being an indicator of harm (Collogan, Tuma, Dolan-Sewell, et. al., 2004; Dyregov, Dyregrov, & Raundalen, 2000; Newman & Kaloupek, 2004). Nonetheless, as many as 24% of participants perceive their participation as more upsetting than they anticipated (Carlson et. al., 2003; Newman, Walker, & Gefland, 1999; Ruzek & Zatzick, 2000; Ybarra, Langhinrichsen-Rohling, Friend, & Diener-West, 2009). Therefore, the potential for harm needs to be communicated to participants and mitigated whenever possible. While distress may be minimal, it is prudent to create protocols in which the provision of mental health support is always available should a participant experience intense distress.

Confidentiality as a risk   Given that mass shootings result in a finite number of potential participants among the identifiable victims, direct witnesses, and perpetrator(s), threats to confidentiality of potential participants is particularly pronounced. Participants may be readily identified given the extensive public information available about many of those directly affected. Even if presented as group data, sharing certain information about mental health, social functioning, and social and economic class may place participants' confidentiality at risk. Researchers need to consider these factors ahead of time to develop a means of presenting the relevant information but also ensuring they protect the identities of the participants. In some cases, it may be wise to postpone the dissemination of results until information is amassed across a number of mass shootings so that research participants cannot be as easily identified.

In addition, researchers examining mass shooting may need to account for potential threats to confidentiality if criminal or civil proceedings are in process. In addition to presenting a potential obstacle to successful research recruitment, such legal proceedings might pose issues related to safeguarding confidentiality. Immediately de-identifying data and recording certain demographic information in separate files from sensitive information are all possible strategies to consider. The pursuit of a Certificate of Confidentiality might also be prudent, which will allow researchers to refuse to disclose identifying and sensitive information obtained in research to legal teams. However, there are two exceptions to the protection a Certificate of Confidentiality provides, the former of which is most relevant to mass shooting studies. Research teams would be required to comply with requests from the United States Government for the purpose of auditing or evaluating federally funded projects and with requests for information to ensure compliance with regulations of the Federal Food and Drug Administration (FDA; Check, Wolf, Dame, & Beskow, 2014). Overall, researchers should be judicious and employ all necessary measures to protect and ensure the confidentiality of potential participants whenever possible.

Justice

With respect to research, the principle of justice typically focuses on distributive justice, in that there is a fair allocation of the potential benefits and burdens of research so that no one group or class of participants bears disproportionate benefits or risks from the research (National Commission, 1979). Thus, the population from which research participants are recruited should match the groups that benefit from the potential results of the study. When applied to mass shooting research, the general justice issues focus on assuring that (1) the needs of mass shooting stakeholders are represented in research and (2) the research generated on mass shooting survivors benefits the needs of this group so they are not bearing the costs without the benefits. An additional aspect of justice could include procedural justice, the degree to which stakeholders influence the research agenda, and the questions and resources allocated to generating knowledge about the conditions affecting them.

Research burden   One of the challenges of conducting research on mass shootings and survivors of particular disasters relates to the finite number of directly affected individuals. After a mass shooting, there can be an influx of researchers, journalists, and other interested parties vying for access to the individuals and communities directly impacted by these events. Multiple researchers may attempt to access the same individuals, thus posing a burden to those coping with the aftermath of shootings. Moreover, there is potential that different teams may be studying the same research question, further amplifying research burden. While it is difficult to balance the need to protect the participants and the freedom of scholarship, strategies can be implemented that prioritize reducing research burden for potential participants. These strategies include coordination among different research teams and data sharing (Collogan, Tuma, & Fleischman,

2004). Furthermore, collaboration among Institutional Review Boards and/or the use of a centralized Institutional Review Board allows for greater oversight, monitoring, and gatekeeping related to research burden and can result in preventing research teams from duplicating studies (Collogan, Tuma, & Fleischman, 2004). Appropriate guidelines should be developed to make coordinated research and data sharing possible. In the case of certain episodes of terrorism, the director of the Office of Human Research Protections has issued a mandate to require that provisional review and approval of protocols use a centralized review panel consisting of local stakeholders and experts (Fleischman & Wood, 2002). However, the potential success of such approaches is uncertain. Following the 1995 Oklahoma City bombing, the Governor designated the University of Oklahoma Health Sciences Center (OUHSC) as the lead institution overseeing bombing-related research. The OUHSC Institutional Review Board organized to assist colleagues at other institutions, provide local oversight, serve as a research clearinghouse, and offer full expedited review to bombing-related studies. Of particular concern was the protection of participants and their referral to services if necessary (North, Pfefferbaum, & Tucker, 2002; Quick, 1998). No such mechanism was established in New York City following the September 11 attacks, which was a more catastrophic event in a much more complicated environment (Fleischman & Wood, 2002).

Dissemination The goal of the respective research study should inform the dissemination of the subsequent findings. If the goal of the research on mass shootings is to prevent these events from occurring in the future, then dissemination efforts should be undertaken to deliver study results back into the broader community (e.g., through television, Internet, news) to inform future prevention efforts. If the goal is to better inform or rehabilitate affected communities, researchers should disseminate findings through community resources (e.g., relaying information to community organizations, conducting presentations for community members). Lastly, if the goal of the research is to understand the impact on mental health, efforts should be undertaken to deliver study results to the mental health professionals who serve affected or involved communities (Fontes, 2004). Ultimately, the principle of justice prescribes that research on mass shootings should not only benefit the scientific community but also those who undertake the burden of this research. Thus, findings should be disseminated in a manner that benefits stakeholders.

Overarching Concerns

Especially in the context of mass shootings, the potential impact of the research question should be weighed in regard to how it will affect the community. In defining research goals for studies including disaster survivors, it has been suggested that the potential results should serve to promote the field for the greater good (Ferreira, Buttell, & Ferreira, 2015). This would conceptually combine both principles of beneficence and justice. As such, the purpose of the research needs to both advance science and have the potential to serve the currently affected community and future affected communities. Research on mass shootings should utilize the best methodology, integrate the most up-to-date theory and science, and promote new knowledge. While replication studies are essential for confirming or disconfirming the validity and generalizability of previous research findings, replication could needlessly repeat the same studies with the same samples at the potential expense of increasing participant burden (Cromer & Newman, 2011). For example, there comes a point at which some facts are evident from accumulated studies, such as there being a high likelihood that a percentage of mass shooting survivors will struggle with symptoms of anxiety, PTSD, and depression. Without the burden of unnecessarily replicating these findings, studies that address more sophisticated questions about mediators and moderators, course, and severity might take precedence. Additionally, the research team might anticipate ahead of time if the research question itself poses any potential harm to the community stakeholders should criminal proceedings emerge. Thus, the utility and context of the specific research question should be carefully considered.

Clearly there are many areas for potential future advancement. Given the lack of consensus about how mass shootings are defined (Shultz et. al., 2014), researchers need to characterize their findings in light of a specific definition, so that the research base can accrue in ways that acknowledge differences across studies and eventually a clear shared definition will be identified. Without this clarity, clear conclusions cannot be drawn. Much of the extant research has focused on individuals in the affected communities but community-level impact studies to understand the overall effect appear to be warranted (Muschert, 2007; see Chapter 12 for more on community-level difficulties). Schultz and colleagues (2014) have noted a lack of systematic examination of the psychological impact upon first responders including hospital-based personnel (see Chapter 13 for more on the mental health consequences in first responders). In addition, only a few studies exist focusing on the impact upon journalists covering these events (Backholm & Idås, 2015; see Chapter 14 for more on the psychological impact on journalists).Thus, there are many affected groups (e.g., funeral personnel, medical examiners) that require further attention. Additionally, more interdisciplinary research that integrates psychological, criminal, sociological, communication, and civic perspectives may advance our understanding of individual and community effects. Prevention, harm reduction, and intervention are important areas for research focus, both in terms of disaster behavioral health (Schultz et. al., 2014) and crime prevention.

Recently, survivors of nine different mass shootings issued a press release urging media to not name the shooter or promote their image (No Notoriety, 2015). This campaign notes that news reports may unintentionally foster mass murder given that certain types of mass killers are motivated by the desire for notoriety or fame. The degree to which a change in news practice is followed and effective in prevention is worthy of study (see Chapters 7–10 for more on the role of journalism in the aftermath of mass shootings). Moreover, the degree to which scholars should follow the same guidelines and make a deliberate effort to not contribute to the notoriety of individual perpetrators is an interesting and important question. Postponing the dissemination of results until enough information is gathered that the perpetrators involved in the research cannot be readily identified may mitigate this issue. In addition, as previously mentioned, the scope of dissemination should match the goal of the research.

Lastly, the responsibility of researchers to contextualize and comment on controversial social policy recommendations in light of research findings is an intriguing area of ethical practice. Mass shootings are highly publicized events that raise many societal concerns, especially around public safety, gun legislation, mental health policy, and criminal reform (see Chapter 4 for more on issues related to the development of mass shooters). For example, one of the debates that has ensued is the degree to which research on mass shootings should impact gun ownership policies. On the one hand, mass shootings represent a minority of firearm homicides (Schulz et. al., 2014), but on the other hand, they receive the most societal attention with respect to gun control issues. To what degree should researchers who study mass shootings raise this concern without trivializing the pain and importance associated with such events? Similarly, to what degree do researchers have a moral responsibility to weigh in on issues about firearm access and other evidence-informed policy recommendations about those who are dangerous or mentally ill (e.g., McGinty, et. al., 2014; Rosenberg, 2014)? These issues are extremely important and it is vital that researchers take an evidence-based approach to commenting on policy that accounts for the strengths and weaknesses of the existing evidence base.

Conclusions

Weisburd (2003) argues there is a moral imperative to conduct randomized trials in evaluating crime and justice interventions. We extend this argument and conclude that there is a moral imperative to use ethically sound methodology to answer all questions pertaining to mass shootings. From the existing evidence on other forms of violence and disasters, research can be conducted safely and ethically with participants affected by mass shootings, if carefully implemented. Further, there is an imperative for scholarship to move beyond simply replicating accepted knowledge to transform our ability to prevent mass shootings, mitigate the ill-effects among affected individuals, and promote effective community response.

Mass shootings are devastating events that can have far-reaching social and psychological consequences. In the face of conducting research after one of these events, researchers need to take appropriate steps to ensure they are acting ethically. Though there is only one study that has directly examined research practice after a mass shooting incident (Fergus et. al., 2011), the broader literature that has examined ethical research following trauma tells us that issues related to autonomy and respect, beneficence and nonmaleficence, and justice are of particular importance. Further, researchers have an ethical obligation to pursue understudied areas and use evidence accurately to help policy makers and citizens determine sensible policies related to controversial issues raised by mass shootings.

References

Appelbaum, P., & Grisso, T. (2001). *MacArthur competence assessment tool for clinical research (MacCAT-CR)*. Sarasota, FL: Professional Resource Press/Professional Resource Exchange.

Backholm, K., & Idås, T. (2015). Ethical dilemmas, work-related guilt, and posttraumatic stress reactions of news journalists covering the terror attack in Norway in 2011. *Journal of Traumatic Stress, 28*, 142–148. doi:10.1002/jts.22001

Becker-Blease, K., & Freyd, J. (2006). Research participants telling the truth about their lives: The ethics of asking and not asking about abuse. *American Psychologist, 61*, 218–226. doi:10.1037/0003-066X.61.3.218

Blair, J. P., & Schweit, K. W. (2014). *A study of active shooter Incidents, 2000–2013*. Texas State University and Federal Bureau of Investigation. Washington, DC: U.S. Department of Justice.

Carlson, E. B., Newman, E., Daniels, J. W., Armstrong, J., Roth, D., & Loewenstein, R. (2003). Distress in response to and perceived usefulness of trauma research interviews. *Journal of Trauma & Dissociation, 4*, 131–142. doi:10.1300/J229v04n02_08

Carter-Visscher, R. M., Naugle, A. E., Bell, K. M., & Suvak, M. K. (2008). Ethics of asking trauma-related questions and exposing participants to arousal-inducing stimuli. *Journal of Trauma & Dissociation, 8*, 27–55. doi:10.1300/J229v08n03_03

Check, D. K., Wolf, L. E., Dame, L. A., & Beskow, L. M. (2014). Certificates of confidentiality and informed consent: Perspectives of IRB chairs and institutional legal counsel. *IRB, 36*, 1–8.

Chu, A., DePrince, A., & Weinzierl, K. (2008). Children's perception of research participation: Examining trauma exposure and distress. *Journal of Empirical Research on Human Research Ethics, 3*, 49–51. doi:10.1525/jer.2008.3.1.49

Collogan, L. K., Tuma, F., Dolan-Sewell, R., Borja, S., & Fleischman, A. R. (2004). Ethical issues pertaining to research in the aftermath of disaster. *Journal of Traumatic Stress, 17,* 352–363.

Collogan, L. K., Tuma, F. K., & Fleischman, A. R. (2004). Research with victims of disaster: Institutional Review Board considerations. *IRB: Ethics & Human Research, 4,* 9–11. doi:10.2307/3563698

Cromer, L. D., & Newman, E. (2011). Commentary on research ethics in victimization studies: Widening the lens. *Violence against Women, 17,* 1536–1548.

Department of Health and Human Services Part 46 Protection of Human Subjects, 45 C.F.R. §§46.301–46.306 (2009).

DePrince, A., & Chu, A. (2008). Perceived benefits in trauma research: Examining methodological and individual difference factors in responses to research participation. *Journal of Empirical Research on Human Research Ethics, 3,* 35–47. doi:10.1525/jer.2008.3.1.35

Dyregrov, K., Dyregrov, A., & Raundalen, M. (2000). Refugee families' experience of research participation. *Journal of Traumatic Stress, 13,* 413–426.

Fergus, T. A., Rabenhorst, M. M., Orcutt, H. K., & Valentiner, D. P. (2011). Reactions to trauma research among women recently exposed to a campus shooting. *Journal of Traumatic Stress, 24,* 596–600. doi:10.1002/jts.20682

Ferreira, R. J., Buttell, F., & Ferreira, S. B. (2015). Ethical considerations for conducting disaster research with vulnerable populations. *Journal of Social Work Values & Ethics, 12,* 29–40.

Fleischman, A. R., & Wood, E. R. (2002). Ethical issues in research involving victims of terror. *Journal of Urban Health, 79,* 315–321.

Fontes, L. (2004). Ethics in violence against women research: The sensitive, the dangerous, and the overlooked. *Ethics & Behavior, 14,* 141–174.

Hebenstreit, C. L., & DePrince, A. P. (2012). Perceptions of participating in longitudinal trauma research among women exposed to intimate partner abuse. *Journal of Empirical Research on Human Research Ethics, 7,* 60–69. doi:10.1525/jer.2012.7.2.60

Hurley, J. C., & Underwood, M. K. (2002). Children's understanding of their research rights before and after debriefing: Informed assent, confidentiality, and stopping participation. *Child Development, 73,* 132–14.

Institute of Medicine. (2004). *The ethical conduct of clinical research involving children.* Washington, DC: The National Academy of Sciences.

Jaffe, A. E., DiLillo, D., Hoffman, L., Haikalis, M., & Dykstra, R. E. (2015). Does it hurt to ask? A meta-analysis of participant reactions to trauma research. *Clinical Psychology Review, 40,* 40–56. doi:10.1016/j.cpr.2015.05.004

Jewkes, R., Dartnall, E., & Sikweyiya, Y. (2012). *Ethical and safety recommendations for research on perpetration of sexual violence.* Medical Research Council. Retrieved from http://www.svri.org/EthicalRecommendations.pdf

Jones, J. A. (2012). Ethical considerations in criminal justice research: Informed consent and confidentiality. *Student Pulse.* Retrieved from http://www.studentpulse.com/a?id=674

Kassam-Adams, N., & Newman, E. (2002). The reactions to research participation questionnaires for children and for parents (RRPQ-C and RRPQ-P). *General Hospital Psychiatry, 24,* 336–342.

Kassam-Adams, N., & Newman, E. (2005). Child and parent reactions to participation in clinical research. *General Hospital Psychiatry, 27,* 29–35.

Levine, C. (2004). The concept of vulnerability in disaster research. *Journal of Traumatic Stress, 17,* 395–402. doi:10.1023/B:JOTS.0000048952.81894.f3

Lowman, J., & Palys, T. (2001). The ethics and law of confidentiality in criminal justice research: A comparison of Canada and the U.S. *International Criminal Justice Review, 11,* 1–33. doi:10.1177/105756770101100101

McClinton Appollis, T., Lund, C., de Vries, P. J., & Mathews, C. (2015). Adolescents' and adults' experiences of being surveyed about violence and abuse: A systematic review of harms, benefits, and regrets. *American Journal of Public Health, 105,* e31–45. doi:10.2105/AJPH.2014.302293

McGinty, E. E., Frattaroli, S., Appelbaum, P. S., Bonnie, R. J., Grilley, A., Horwitz, J., & ... Webster, D. W. (2014). Using research evidence to reframe the policy debate around mental illness and guns: Process and recommendations. *American Journal of Public Health, 104,* e22–e26. doi:10.2105/AJPH.2014.302171

Morton, R. J., & Hilts, M. A. (Eds.). (2008). *Serial murder: Multi-disciplinary perspectives for investigators.* National Center for the Analysis of Violent Crime, Federal Bureau of Investigation. Retrieved from http://www.fbi.gov/stats-services/publications

Muschert, G. W. (2007). Research in school shootings. *Sociology Compass, 1,* 60–80. doi:10.1111/j.1751-9020.2007.00008.x

National Commission for the Protection of Human Subjects of Behavioral Research. (1979). *The Belmont report: Ethical principles and guidelines for the protection of human subjects of research* (DHEW Publication No. OS 78-0012). Washington, DC: U.S. Government Printing Office.

Newman, E., & Kaloupek, D. (2004). The risks and benefits of participating in trauma-focused research studies. *Journal of Traumatic Stress, 17,* 383–394.

Newman, E., & Kaloupek, D. (2009). Overview of research addressing ethical dimensions of participation in traumatic stress studies: Autonomy and beneficence. *Journal of Traumatic Stress, 22,* 595–602. doi:10.1002/jts.20465

Newman, E., Walker, E. A., & Gefland, A. (1999). Assessing the ethical costs and benefits of trauma-focused research. *General Hospital Psychiatry, 21,* 187–196. doi:10.1016/S0163-8343(99)00011-0

Newman, E., Willard, T., Sinclair, R., & Kaloupek, D. (2001). The costs and benefits of research from the participants' view: The path to empirically informed research practice. *Accountability in Research, 8,* 27–47.

No Notoriety. (2015). Victims from nine mass shootings issue challenge to media [Press release]. Retrieved from http://nonotoriety.com/mediachallenge/

North, C. S., Pfefferbaum, B., & Tucker, P. (2002). Ethical and methodological issues in academic mental health research in populations affected by disasters: The Oklahoma City experience relevant to September 11, 2001. *CNS Spectrums, 7,* 580–584.

Quick, G. (1998). A paradigm for multidisciplinary disaster research: The Oklahoma City experience. *The Journal of Emergency Medicine, 16,* 621–630.

Qureshi, K. A., Gerson, R. R. M., Smailes, E. S., Raveis, V. H., Murphy, B., Matzner, G., & Fleischman, A. R. (2007). Roadmap for the protection of disaster research participants: Findings from the world trade center evacuation study. *Prehospital and Disaster Medicine, 22,* 486–493.

Rosenberg, J. (2014). Mass shootings and mental health policy. *Journal of Sociology & Social Welfare, 41,* 107–121.

Ruzek, J., & Zatzick, D. (2000). Ethical considerations in research participation among acutely injured trauma survivors: An empirical investigation. *General Hospital Psychiatry, 22,* 27–36.

Shultz, J. M., Thoresen, S., Flynn, B. W., Muschert, G. W., Shaw, J. A., Espinel, Z., & … Cohen, A. M. (2014). Multiple vantage points on the mental health effects of mass shootings. *Current Psychiatry Reports, 16,* 469. doi:10.1007/s11920-014-046

Terrorism, 18 U.S.C. §2331 (2012).

Verschuur, M. J., Spinhoven, P., van Emmerik, A. A. P., & Rosendaal, F. R. (2008). Participation in a trauma-focused epidemiological investigation may result in sensitization for current health problems. *Social Psychiatry & Psychiatric Epidemiology, 43,* 132–129.

Weisburd, D. (2003). Ethical practice and evaluation of interventions in crime and justice. The moral imperative for randomized trials. *Evaluation Review, 27,* 336–354.

Widom, C. S., & Czaja, S. J. (2005). Reactions to research participation in vulnerable subgroups. *Accountability in Research: Policies and Quality Assurance, 12,* 115–138.

Ybarra, M. L., Langhinrichsen-Rohling, J., Friend, J., & Diener-West, M. (2009). Impact of asking sensitive questions about violence to children and adolescents. *Journal of Adolescent Health, 45,* 499–507. doi:10.1016/j.jadohealth.2009.03.009

21

Future Directions

Danny Axsom

Rarely is the timeliness of a book so evident as in the case of mass shootings. In the latter half of 2015 alone, mass shootings occurred with a disturbing and numbing regularity – Charleston, South Carolina; Roseburg, Oregon; Paris; Colorado Springs, Colorado; San Bernadino, California. Considering just the United States, 26 mass shooting murders (four or more killed in a single incident, not including the shooter) were documented between January 23 and December 13 of 2015. If we define mass shootings more broadly to include four or more either killed or injured, 317 such incidents occurred during this time frame (Gun Violence Archive, 2015); in other words, there was an average of about one mass shooting per day.

In light of these events, this book is a timely and welcome addition to the literature. The chapters, collectively, provide a state-of-the-art snapshot of what we know about the prediction, consequences, and prevention of mass shootings, the media's role in covering them, and interventions for those impacted. Although in many cases what we know is frustratingly little, each chapter hints at promising research and policy implications for the future.

Here, I try to step back and offer some broader suggestions for future directions. The ideas in this chapter reflect my own disciplinary bias as a psychologist and, to some extent, as a social psychologist. However, in many ways psychology is uniquely situated for understanding the complex factors involved in mass shootings. As a "hub" science (Cacioppo, 2007), it intersects with both larger (e.g., sociology) and smaller (e.g., neuroscience) units of analysis, while maintaining a focus on the person. Psychology also has a long history of involvement in the study of traumatic life events (e.g., "shell shock," Myers, 1915; the 1942 Coconut Grove fire, Lindemann, 1944), as well as eclectic methods and a range of potentially relevant theories. My comments are organized around three central questions: (1) What is unique about mass shootings? (2) How can we minimize the impact of public mass shootings? (3) How can we minimize the likelihood of public mass shootings?

The Wiley Handbook of the Psychology of Mass Shootings, First Edition. Edited by Laura C. Wilson.
© 2017 John Wiley & Sons, Inc. Published 2017 by John Wiley & Sons, Inc.

What Is Unique About Mass Shootings?

The roll call of recent high-profile mass shootings noted above highlights their diverse nature. They vary, among other ways, by country (e.g., United States, France), setting (e.g., schools, clinics, churches, concert halls, government buildings, restaurants), number of shooters, and likely motive. What are the common threads that tie these events, and in what ways are mass shootings, collectively, unique among other forms of trauma? It would be surprising if reactions to mass shootings were completely unique, and, indeed, several chapters in this book note parallels with findings from the broader trauma literature – for example, the influence of prior traumatic experiences, degree of exposure to the shootings, social support, coping strategies, and worldview maintenance on subsequent adjustment. But we also know that different types of trauma vary in risk for development of posttraumatic stress disorder (e.g., sexual assault for women; Kessler, Sonnega, Bromet, Hughes, & Nelson, 1995). What then, compared to other traumatic events, is unique about mass shootings?

Mass shootings, as Smith and Hughes point out in Chapter 1, are a particular form of mass killing, which might also include bombings or knifings, for example. Mass killings, despite their seeming frequency, constitute only a small portion (about 1%) of all homicides in the United States (see Chapter 2). Though the majority of mass killings involve shooting, most mass shootings do not occur in public; public mass shootings amount to only about 12% of all mass killings. School shootings are rarer still, constituting only about 9% of all public mass shootings. Broad references to mass shootings, then, incorporate a wide range of events. Does it even make sense to refer to such a broad, heterogeneous category of killings?

Answering this question requires clarity in what is being studied. Yet, as one moves from chapter to chapter within this volume, the answer is not always clear or consistent. Chapter 2 discusses patterns of *public* mass shootings (including characteristics of shooters), but Chapter 3 offers explanations of mass shootings more generally, including incidents involving suicide (e.g., Guyana), familicide, and felonies (e.g., robbery). One consequence of these varying definitions is differing views on the role of mental illness (e.g., mental illness is a stronger influence in public mass shootings), motive (e.g., to eliminate witnesses in a felony), and number of shooters (e.g., single shooters are more common in public mass shootings). Chapter 4 then discusses "rampage shooters" but does not define initially what is meant by a mass shooting. Most of the examples provided are from *school* shootings, which, as noted above, are a small minority of public mass shootings. Wilson (Chapter 11) discusses mental health outcomes following direct exposure to mass shootings, but in reality the focus is on public mass shootings. Littleton et al. (Chapter 12) examine psychosocial functioning within "shooting affected communities," but focus largely on public mass shootings, mostly school-related. The title might also pertain to more common homicides; would anyone argue that Baltimore, for example, with well over 300 documented homicides in 2015, is not a shooting-affected community (Baltimore City Homicides/Murders, 2015)? May and North (Chapter 13) focus on rescue workers responding to "multiple shooting" events, but this term does not distinguish public from more common private mass shootings (e.g., killings occurring in a residence). The problem is not unique to this volume. Orcutt, Miron, and Seligowsk (2014), in a recent review of the impact of mass shootings on individual adjustment, define mass shootings as an individual acting alone with generally personal (compared to political) motivation, entering a densely populated space and killing as many people as possible. Limiting the review to single shooters seems odd, as it excludes such events as Columbine, one of the best-known public mass shootings of the modern era.

A related issue, noted by Smith and Hughes (Chapter 1), is how best to conceptualize *mass* shootings. Some use the FBI standard of four or more victims killed. But this seems arbitrary and, from a research, prevention, and intervention perspective, premature, given the current state of knowledge on these topics. Orcutt, Miron, et al. (2014), in their review of mass shootings, focus on multiple victims irrespective of the number killed, and so include shootings with one death and multiple injuries (e.g., the 1988 Winnetka, Illinois elementary school shooting). Norris (2007), in a previous review of the impact of mass shootings, likewise includes seven incidents that involved fewer than four victims killed.

These definitional and operational ambiguities make it difficult to compare "apples to apples." Future progress in our understanding of mass shootings will require more precision about the phenomenon of interest.

Broadly speaking, however, the most common ultimate referent throughout this book is public mass shootings. As Wilson notes (Chapter 11), what little evidence there is suggests that public mass shootings may be more traumatic than some other traumatic events. Likewise, Norris (2007) concluded that the effects of (public) mass shootings, versus other disasters, fell into the category of "severe" along a continuum of minimal, moderate, severe, and very severe. These conclusions are not surprising, given that public mass shootings are rare, random, intentional acts of violence that often occur in what are otherwise considered "safe" public spaces (e.g., schools) to ordinarily privileged people (at least in terms of violence exposure). Consequently, public mass shootings receive intense media exposure, which brings its own challenges (see Chapter 10).

However, reliable estimates about the effects of public mass shootings will require not only more studies, but more studies that sample the range of circumstances under which such shootings occur. Consider the events mentioned at the outset of this chapter. If we compare the range of public mass shootings with the range of *studied* public mass shootings, it becomes evident that our current understanding relies heavily on school shootings, especially on college campuses. The affected populations are likely to be younger, more educated, more white, wealthier, and healthier than the general population; this restricted range on demographic characteristics may be one reason factors such as age, socioeconomic status, and ethnicity are sometimes weak predictors of shooting outcomes. These samples also represent Western cultures. This book admirably extends the focus of mass shootings beyond the United States, but Finland and Norway share key characteristics with the United States; all are what Henrich, Heine, and Norenzayan (2010) refer to as WEIRD (predominantly Western, educated, industrialized, rich, and democratic). Henrich et al. cite numerous examples from psychology of findings generated from WEIRD samples that are moderated by culture. If we look beyond WEIRD cultures, what will we find? Despotes et al. (Chapter 18) note, for example, that the factor structure of the Posttraumatic Growth Inventory may be culture-dependent.

My comments should not be taken as a criticism of the work done to date. Studies of campus shootings have been largely done by researchers who work at these campuses, and have sometimes involved participants who were already undertaking other studies. This makes sense given the logistical, methodological, and ethical challenges of studying public mass shootings (see Chapter 20). We study not only what we feel compelled to study, but what we can study.

Going forward, as we move beyond the level of individual studies to make broader claims, attention to representativeness of the events being studied will be important. So will greater attention to the representativeness of samples. Wilson (Chapter 11) notes that, for understandable reasons, many studies of public mass shootings involve samples dominated by participants less directly impacted by the shootings. High postshooting distress among indirect victims is an important finding in its own right, but it leaves us with an incomplete picture. This range restriction in exposure to the shootings might also help explain the sometimes inconsistent relationships reported between exposure and subsequent outcomes (see Chapters 1, 11, 12).

Public mass shootings may also share certain similarities with other, seemingly related events. Consider the Boston Marathon bombing in 2013, which killed three and injured over 260; it was a rare, random, intentional act of violence in an otherwise safe public space. Or the 9/11 terrorist attacks in the United States. Going forward, comparing public mass shootings with other traumatic events that share a broader threat similarity may hold promise, perhaps via a meta-analysis. This will require articulating what exactly it is about these public traumas that make them uniquely challenging and worthy of attention.

How Can We Minimize the Impact of Public Mass Shootings?

Although mass shootings are horrific events, most people exposed to them eventually return to levels of functioning at or near where they were prior to the incident. This is a tribute to human strength, both individual and collective. It also usually occurs without the help of formal interventions. For those who pursue formal help, there is solid scientific evidence from randomized control trials (RCTs) that there are interventions (especially Prolonged Exposure [PE] and Cognitive Processing Therapy [CPT]) that work after trauma exposure (see Chapter 15). Though little of this research focuses specifically on individuals impacted by public mass shootings, there is every reason to think, given the underlying theoretical rationale for the treatments, that mass shooting survivors would also benefit.

Unfortunately, not everyone recovers, and those who do may take many months or years. Often people with demonstrable mental health needs choose not to seek or avail themselves of professional help, or drop out during treatment; this is especially true of ethnic minorities (see Chapter 17).

These patterns suggest a number of directions for future research and intervention; there is much more to be learned. Who, for example, is most vulnerable to the effects of public mass shootings, and who is likely to be most resilient? Prospective research designs, combined with advanced statistical techniques such as latent growth mixture modeling, are promising developments for understanding different response trajectories after trauma (Bonanno, Brewin, Kaniasty, & La Greca, 2010; Mancini, Littleton, & Grills, 2015; Orcutt, Bonanno, Hannan, & Miron, 2014; see Chapter 12). They allow for a more nuanced and multivariate understanding of subgroups of survivors, which will help identify those most at risk, and perhaps in need of professional help. Longitudinal designs also allow for better understanding of vexing questions that are difficult to assess cross-sectionally, such as the relationship between vicarious exposure through media and symptomatology (see Chapter 8), or between symptoms and posttraumatic growth (PTG; see Chapter 18).

For those who recover without professional help, how does this take place? As Bonanno et al. (2010) have noted, the impact of trauma usually depends on multiple risk and resilience factors, each of which might have a small to moderate effect, but the combination of which can be powerful. These factors can exist at multiple levels – the individual, their social network, and the larger community (see Chapter 12). Because most people cope with mass traumas without relying on professional help, understanding these informal systems of coping and recovery is essential.

The need for theory

Progress in understanding the impact of public mass shootings, as well as interventions that might help, will require better theoretical development going forward. As Smith and Hughes note in Chapter 1, the dominant conceptual approach has been a dose-response model, but they point to many of its flaws (see also Chapter 11 regarding exposure as a predictor). Other approaches discussed in the book include fear networks, resource conservation, world assumptions, social support deterioration, emotion regulation, and neurological factors (e.g., serotonergic stimulation). Though each is valuable, there seem to be common themes across the book that might be worth considering as broad ways of thinking about the trauma of public mass shootings.

The importance of meaning making

Mass shootings can pose an existential threat to our basic beliefs about ourselves, others, and the world. Terror Management Theory (Greenberg, Soloman, & Pyszczynski, 1997) and World Assumptions Theory (Janoff-Bulman, 1992) both place a central focus on this threat, as does CPT; meaning is one of three elements of Foa's Emotional Processing Theory (see Chapter 15). Shootings can also disrupt key relationships with others and interfere with central roles (e.g., parent, spouse, worker) that give our lives meaning. Recovery, then, can be seen in part as an attempt to make meaning out of something that has challenged or even shattered one's core beliefs.

This aligns with elements of PE and CPT, each of which emphasizes the importance of cognitive restructuring after trauma. Outside of therapy, other people (e.g., family, friends, reference groups) help provide us with understandings about why things happen, and validate whatever meanings we may adopt. Conflict over meaning is a way that others can be a source of further distress rather than comfort. Reexamination of core beliefs is an element of PTG (see Chapter 18), and can be seen in what Tedeschi and Calhoun (2004) refer to as deliberative rumination (e.g., sense making). Meaning making also aligns with religious coping and spirituality as coping styles related to PTG. Community rituals such as memorials and the social identity derived from a sense of cohesiveness can give meaning after public shootings (see Chapter 12). After the Virginia Tech shootings on April 16, 2007, the poet Nikki Giovanni's widely admired and reproduced convocation address the following day ended with "We will prevail, We will prevail, We will prevail, We are Virginia Tech." Finally, the meaning making lens is well suited for understanding one role that media can play after mass traumas. In addition to answering basic questions about what happened, media often examine why the event occurred, and in doing so can support or further challenge our attempt to make existential sense of the event (see Chapter 7). And "new media" such as Facebook and Twitter allow meaning making to occur in a more overtly interactive way.

The importance of uncertainty reduction

Mass shootings pose an epistemic as well as an existential threat. The uncertainty after public mass shootings can take many forms. For example, immediately, questions arise about one's own safety and the status of loved ones and friends; and subsequently, uncertainty arises about the nature, course, and appropriateness of one's emotions, about explanations for behavior during the shooting, or about altered role relationships. There is a long history in social psychology of uncertainty leading to heightened social influence (e.g., affiliation, social comparison; Schachter, 1959) as we attempt to understand ambiguous or frightening situations.

There is some overlap here, of course, with meaning making, and the therapy-assisted cognitive restructuring referred to above is sometimes about maladaptive ways that people may have reduced their uncertainty (e.g., illogical self-blame). Uncertainty reduction was an important goal in the comprehensive intervention in Norway after the Oslo bombing and Utøya shootings in July of 2011 (see Chapter 16), both immediately after the incident and continuing over time (e.g., provision of information to families about what happened and allowing them, if desired, a structured visit to the site of the killings). Uncertainty reduction is an ideal way to think about media effects, and about the role of technology. Both positive and negative effects of media exposure and use are noted in Chapters 7–10.

The importance of social relationships

Humans are fundamentally social creatures. Others are a key to our survival, as individuals and as a species; others provide material, psychological, and existential support. Thus, our connectedness to others is central to our existence (Baumeister & Leary, 1995). Public mass shootings can represent a threat to our social relations. And social relationships seem to play a key role in post-trauma adjustment, often for the better but sometimes for the worse.

Examples are numerous. Citing the broader trauma literature, Smith and Hughes (Chapter 1) note that social support facilitates cognitive processing, validates emotional reactions (see above regarding uncertainty reduction), and promotes both formal and informal help-seeking. The role of social support in postshooting adjustment is highlighted at several points in this book. Littleton et al. (Chapter 12) note that, in the Virginia Tech shootings, low preshooting social support predicted postshooting resource loss, which in turn predicted greater subsequent distress. Mancini et al. (2015), also examining the Virginia Tech shootings, reported that a subgroup of 7–13% of women exhibited elevated distress prior to the shootings, then improvement at 2 months that continued 1 year postshooting; one thing that characterized this group was a large increase in postshooting social support. One can speak of social competence in building and holding resources. Therefore, it is not surprising that Cognitive Processing Therapy includes skill development that helps people connect better to others, and to develop trust (see Chapter 15). The Norwegian comprehensive intervention described in Chapter 16 has an interesting social component, with a social support assessment and advice for maintaining and developing support, plus the formation of support groups composed exclusively of families who had also gone through the same bombing-shooting experience.

Chapter 9 discusses social media as a tool for utilizing (and building) social support in ways similar to more traditional face-to-face interactions. Social media can be used to organize postshooting memorial or remembrance events and to stream the events for people who cannot attend, and to create discussion and advocacy groups (e.g., about gun control and mental health after the Virginia Tech shootings). Community building seems especially important after a public mass shooting, which, as a violent, intentional trauma, may represent a unique threat to the fabric of the community. As noted in Chapter 12, emergent properties such as community solidarity may influence individual functioning. Finally, Rosen, Tiet, Cavella, Finney, and Lee (2005; described in Chapter 8) conclude that the association between vicarious trauma exposure through media and problems may "reflect the negative social effects of isolative television viewing habits rather than retraumatization."

Of course, social relationships can have a darker side. As discussed in Chapter 17, Lepore and Revenson's social constraints theory (Lepore & Revenson, 2007) highlights social interactions that "cause the trauma survivor to feel unsupported, misunderstood, alienated, and/or unable to disclose traumatic experiences." And the social support deterioration hypothesis (Kaniasty & Norris, 1995) points to how mass traumas can strain existing networks (e.g., helping others in chronic need can take a toll on the helper).

Taking the above perspectives into account, the impact of public mass shootings is likely to be minimized by naturally occurring processes and formal interventions that enable generative meaning making, reduce uncertainty, and protect or enhance positive social relationships. This analysis has a number of implications for future directions.

It suggests a greater focus on religion and spirituality, because these often intersect seamlessly with meaning making, uncertainty reduction, and social relationships.

It suggests the need for greater breadth in the populations chosen to be studied after public mass shootings; this might include ethnic minorities and non-WEIRD samples, because each may go about meaning making, uncertainty reduction, and relationship maintenance or building differently, or in a way that challenges our current, tentative understandings.

It suggests a greater focus on the role of work in coping with trauma, because jobs can provide structure and give meaning to our lives and serve as an important source of social relationships; work can also have a dark side, adding to the burdens people feel while attempting to cope with mass traumas. In some cases, of course, an individual's work places them in direct contact with public mass shootings, as in the case of police, rescue workers (see Chapter 13), and journalists (see Chapter 14). The unique challenges of these roles deserve more attention, for what they can tell us about both resilience and risk; there might also be better ways of training workers that could help buffer them in these difficult roles.

It suggests a closer look at other types of role performance around which meaning and social relationships are structured, such as parent or spouse.

It suggests that closer attention should be paid to the timing of interventions, considering their implications for the likely unfolding of meaning making, uncertainty reduction, and social relationships. Ill-timed interventions may be ineffective, or actually worsen functioning and stress (e.g., critical incident stress debriefing (CISD); see Wilson, 2011).

It suggests examining help-giving as well as help-receiving among those impacted by shootings, because assisting others can strengthen social relationships and enhance a sense of pride and meaning. For example, Chapter 15 describes a case study of an elementary school teacher struggling after a school shooting. Her successful recovery with the help of PE eventually leads her to organize a fundraising race to honor victims of the shooting. This illustrates help-giving, action-based meaning making, and, likely, enhanced social relationships (isolation was a problem while she was on leave from work after the shooting). This example is not unusual, as mass traumas typically offer many opportunities for individuals to help others. Help-giving is but one of many potential examples of incorporating findings and concepts from the field of positive psychology. It might also be thought of as an example of action-focused (compared to perceived) PTG (see Chapter 18). In a different vein, help-giving might also make it more likely that people will accept or seek help from others, including professionals, if one barrier to receiving help is a reluctance to become obligated to others, or a sense that one is uniquely needy. Of course, help-giving can have a dark side, as noted by the social support deterioration hypothesis. Understanding what moderates the effect of help-giving on outcomes after public mass shootings would be important.

The above considerations suggest three further methodological points. First, when possible, future research should strive to go beyond the exclusive use of self-report data, especially from a single source. Questions about perceived versus actual PTG, help-giving, and role performance are difficult to assess exclusively via self-report.

Second, in addition to more rigorous quantitative studies (e.g., with prospective designs that are adequately powered), the study of public mass shootings might benefit from greater use of rigorous qualitative research. Qualitative research can be especially useful for hypothesis generation, for illustrating boundary conditions of established claims, and for rich descriptive detail, all of which would be useful in this fledgling literature; theoretically informed qualitative research can also be used for hypothesis testing, of course. Qualitative research might also be helpful for studying shootings where literacy may be a concern, including in international settings, where self-report measures developed and normed in the United States, for example, would be of less value. To those who might think of qualitative research as simply a series of case studies, in many ways one can make the same argument about current quantitative studies of mass shootings (see Chapter 11). At this point in our understanding of public mass shootings, methodological hegemony is not warranted.

Third, future research on interventions should be mindful that RCTs represent the gold standard for determining treatment efficacy, and therefore should be incorporated whenever possible. Consider the Norwegian intervention described in Chapter 16. The intervention is admirable, remarkable really, in its comprehensiveness. Yet Dyregrov et al. note that very strong grief and trauma reactions persisted over time, along with functional impairment, suggesting the intervention was not very effective. They posit that this was because of the strong stressor (e.g., losing a child to a sudden, violent death) and the intense media coverage of the killer's trial and a subsequent commission report. They also note that outcomes might have been worse without the intervention. All this is certainly possible. But maybe the intervention simply was not very effective or even made functioning worse. Without a control group and random assignment, we do not know. The authors note the desirability of such studies but mention ethical and practical problems. We might consider that there is also an ethical issue in not doing an efficacy study. The Cambridge Somerville Youth Study conducted in the 1930s was a similarly impressive, well-intentioned, and comprehensive intervention, designed to reduce juvenile delinquency, but it failed (McCord, 1978), and actually made things worse (we know this because they did conduct a RCT). In the trauma field, CISD is another example of a prematurely tested intervention (Wilson, 2011).

A more strategic point is that the complexity of public mass shootings should encourage researchers to think about the merits of forming interdisciplinary teams (e.g., psychologists, sociologists, neuroscientists); for the study of public shootings in non-WEIRD populations, international interdisciplinary teams will be necessary.

How Can We Minimize the Likelihood of Public Mass Shootings?

It is easy to get discouraged about the prevention of mass shootings. They seem to occur with an alarming regularity. Moreover, efforts to identify predictors of such shootings, or to build profiles of shooters, are stymied by the problem of false positives. As Winegard and Ferguson note in Chapter 4, for every vague generalization such as the shooter having suffered a recent loss, experiencing a sense of injustice, or being a male under the age of 45, there are almost infinitely more nonshooters with this characteristic. To add to the complexity, predictors likely vary by type of mass shooting (e.g., mass shooting vs. public mass shooting vs. school shooting). And predictors may change over time. Malcolm Gladwell (2015) recently discussed the sociologist Mark Granovetter's theory that thresholds for acting change as more people do something. The idea is that many people might have the potential to commit a public mass shooting, but reservations or barriers put them below a threshold for acting on that potential. Each new shooting lowers the threshold. The explicit referencing by school shooters to previous school shootings seems to have grown after Columbine, with Virginia Tech often cited too. The implication is that predictors of past shootings, even if they were known, may not prevent future shootings.

Rather than throw our hands in the air in despair, the best approach is to recognize the inevitably poor utility of profiles and to look instead for more proximal indicators like whether someone has made a vocalized threat, regardless of whether they fit some broad profile. Chapter 4 notes the 2002 recommendation of the Department of Education that, for identifying school shooters, the best approach is not to screen and identify individuals far in advance, but to report vocalized threats to authorities, and to encourage others to do so. Cornell and Datta (Chapter 19) describe this approach as less about instruments of prediction and more about interventions with known threats. They note that while threats are not always known, often there is some indication or "leakage" beforehand. The focus is then on the subset of threats that might be carried out because the person has the motivation and means (e.g., has the person acquired a weapon, made a plan, engaged in other preparation?). In contrast to a popular conception of shooters simply "snapping," usually there is lots of planning. This creates opportunities for prevention, and is a more optimistic view of what we can do.

Some interventions described in these chapters, like programs to reduce bullying, or afterschool programs with physical activity, or intensive early interventions with parents (see Chapter 5), may not prevent mass shootings, but they are important in their own right because they reduce other negative outcomes. They bring to mind Cornell and Datta's statement (Chapter 19), "True violence prevention efforts must begin well before there is a gunman in the parking lot."

Going forward, efforts at prevention should also emphasize media education. In its roles of reducing uncertainty and of meaning making, the media, like the general public, seems to prefer quick, simple, "common-sense" answers. Unfortunately, as noted in Chapter 4, many of these answers, like violent video games or mental illness or bullying, do not hold up well as explanations of public mass shootings. As psychologists, we can do a better job of explaining to journalists where not to look, and why; we can also characterize more effective prevention efforts, like threat assessment, in ways that are easier to comprehend.

For the media's part, it should resist the temptation to be professional stenographers, simply reporting what some people purport to believe without consideration of the scientific evidence behind the claim. This is because, as Winegard and Ferguson point out in Chapter 4, public discussion of the causes of mass shootings is sometimes hijacked by those with other, broader agendas (e.g., gun regulation, media violence). Sometimes, calls to study x are in reality calls *not* to study y (e.g., video games instead of guns). Again, media education is essential, as a necessary, if not sufficient, answer to this problem.

Finally, when it comes to prevention of mass shootings, the Federal Government should treat the issue as a public health problem (vs. simply a criminal justice or civil liberties issue), and fully commit the tools of science to understanding and preventing the phenomenon. Haden, in Chapter 6, makes a similar point, as do Cornell and Datta in Chapter 19 and the American Psychological Association (2013) in its report on gun violence. This means, among other things, a serious examination of the role of gun availability in mass shootings. The answers ultimately obtained from such research may not be simple or directly translatable to policy; that is the way science works. But the failure to use the best tools of science to examine all plausible factors in mass shootings is unconscionable. We all deserve better.

References

American Psychological Association. (2013). *Gun violence: Prediction, prevention, and policy.* Washington, DC: American Psychological Association.

Baltimore City Homicides/Murders. (2015, December 18). Retrieved from http://chamspage.blogspot.com/2014/12/2015-baltimore-city-homicidesmurders.html

Baumeister, R. F., & Leary, M. R. (1995). The need to belong: Desire for interpersonal attachments as a fundamental human motivation. *Psychological Bulletin, 117,* 497–529.

Bonanno, G. A., Brewin, C. R., Kaniasty, K., & La Greca, A. M. (2010). Weighing the costs of disaster: Consequences, risk, and resilience in individuals, families, and communities. *Psychological Science in the Public Interest, 11*(1), 1–49.

Cacioppo, J. (2007, September 8). Psychology is a hub science. *APS Observer, 20*(8).

Gladwell, M. (2015, October 19). How school shootings catch on. The New Yorker.

Greenberg, J., Soloman, S., & Pyszczynski, T. (1997). Terror management theory of self-esteem and cultural worldviews: Empirical assessments and conceptual refinements. In M. P. Zanna (Ed.), *Advances in experimental social psychology* (Vol. 29, pp. 61–139). New York, NY: Academic Press.

Gun Violence Archive. (2015, December 18). Retrieved from http://www.gunviolencearchive.org/reports/mass-shooting

Henrich, J., Heine, S. J., & Norenzayan, A. (2010). The weirdest people in the world? *Behavioral and Brain Sciences, 33,* 61–8 3.

Janoff-Bulman, R. (1992). *Shattered assumptions.* New York, NY: Free Press.

Kaniasty, K., & Norris, F. H. (1995). Mobilization and deterioration of social support following natural disasters. *Current Directions in Psychological Science, 4,* 94–98. doi:10.1111/1467- 8721.ep10772341

Kessler, R. C., Sonnega, A., Bromet, E., Hughes, M., & Nelson, C. B. (1995). Posttraumatic stress disorder in the National Comorbidity Study. *Archives of General Psychiatry, 52,* 1048–1060.

Lepore, S. J., & Revenson, T. A. (2007). Social constraints on disclosure and adjustment to cancer. *Social and Personality Psychology Compass, 1,* 313–333. doi:10.1111/j.1751-9 004.2007.00013.x

Lindemann, E. (1944). Symptomatology and management of acute grief. *American Journal of Psychiatry, 101,* 141–148.

Mancini, A., Littleton, H., & Grills, A. (2015). Can people benefit from acute stress? Social support, psychological improvement, and resilience after the Virginia Tech campus shootings. *Clinical Psychological Science.* doi:10.1177/2167702615601001

McCord, J. (1978). A thirty-year follow-up of treatment effects. *American Psychologist, 33,* 284–289.

Myers, C. S. (1915). A contribution to the study of shell shock. *Lancet, 1,* 316–320.

Norris, F. (2007). Impact of mass shootings on survivors, families, and communities. *PTSD Research Quarterly, 18*(3), 1–7.

Orcutt, H. K., Bonanno, G. A., Hannan, S. M., & Miron, L. R. (2014). Prospective trajectories of posttraumatic stress in college women following a campus mass shooting. *Journal of Traumatic Stress, 27,* 1–8.

Orcutt, H. K., Miron, L. R., & Seligowski, A. V. (2014). Impact of mass shootings on individual adjustment. *PTSD Research Quarterly, 25,* 1–9.

Rosen, C., Tiet, Q., Cavella, S., Finney, J., & Lee, T. (2005). Chronic PTSD patient's functioning before and after September 11 attacks. *Journal of Traumatic Stress, 18,* 781–784.

Schachter, S. (1959). *The psychology of affiliation.* Stanford, CA: Stanford University Press.

Tedeschi, R. G., & Calhoun, L. G. (2004). Posttraumatic growth: Conceptual foundations and empirical evidence. *Psychological Inquiry, 15*(1), 1–18.

Wilson, T. D. (2011). *Redirect: The surprising new science of psychological change.* New York, NY: Little, Brown, & Company.

Index

A–B–C worksheets in prolonged exposure
therapy 275
action-focused posttraumatic growth 343
actuarial risk assessment 98, 100–2, 103,
106, 358
acute stress disorder (ASD) 199, 200, 205
media and 137, 138, 142, 144, 145,
146, 147
adaptive responses to trauma 336, 337–8
adjusted actuarial assessment 102
adjustment
in community, problems in 212–19
improvement of 219
predictors 212–13, 213–18
prevalence 212–13
posttraumatic growth and 341–2
adolescents
bereaved, Utöya and Oslo 305
vicarious exposure 145–6
see also entries under juvenile
adversity, resilience to see resilience
affective (emotional/impulsive/reactive)
aggression or violence 82–3, 83–4,
84–5, 85, 86, 90, 357
aftermath
ethics of research in 372–87
journalists in 258
distress 249–50
media in see media
afterschool programs 88–9
age
mass murderer 40–1
victims and survivors 42
mental health outcomes 201

mental health service utilization 313
vicarious exposure and 145–6
violence propensity 104
agenda setting by media 117–18
aggression 63
biological factors 50, 78–9, 80, 81,
82–3, 84–5, 87–8, 88–9, 90
functional subtypes 82–3, 83, 85, 89
proactive (premeditated/instrumental)
or 77–95, 355–6
reactive (emotional/impulsive/
affective) 82–3, 83–4, 84–5, 85, 86,
90, 357
alcohol use disorder, rescue workers 235
amygdala and PTSD 333, 334
anamnestic approach to risk
assessment 102–3
Andersen's (1995) behavioral model of
health service utilization 312,
314–16, 324, 325
anger in risk assessment 106–7
antisocial attitudes and behavior
cardiac measures and 78
catalyst model 63
in risk assessment 107
antisocial personality disorder (ASPD)
104, 106
anxiety 8, 213, 336
see also fear
Arapahoe High School (Centennial,
Colorado – 2013) 69
arousal levels see hyperarousal; underarousal
arrest history 106
Asperger's syndrome 124, 125, 356

The Wiley Handbook of the Psychology of Mass Shootings, First Edition. Edited by Laura C. Wilson.
© 2017 John Wiley & Sons, Inc. Published 2017 by John Wiley & Sons, Inc.

assailants *see* perpetrators
assassination 361–2
assent (consent) to research 375–8
assignments, crisis-related
    (journalists) 247–50
  previous 254–5
Aurora (Colorado – 2012) 28, 39, 48,
    120, 121, 123, 124, 128
Austin (Texas – 1966) 25, 26, 87
autonomy 374–7
autopilot, journalists on 248–9, 250
avoidance (as coping strategy) 216–17, 269
  therapy targeting 270

behavioral model of health service
    utilization 312, 313–19,
    324, 325
beneficence 374, 378–9
bereavement 160, 173
  Utøya and Oslo, public relief
    efforts 293–311
  see also mourning
biological factors
  perpetrators 49–51
    aggression 50, 78–9, 80, 81,
    82–3, 84–5, 87–8, 88–9, 90
  survivor resilience 336
  see also neurobiology
biological treatments 90
biosocial (biological and psychosocial)
    theory of proactive
    aggression 77–95
Blacksburg *see* Virginia Tech
blame
  media views on who is to
    blame 176, 177
  perpetrators 25, 43, 44, 47, 52
  see also self-blame
blogging sites 161–2
Boston (Massachusetts)
  Marathon bombings (2013) 323, 362,
    391
  Operation Ceasefire 360–1
brain and neurological factors 49–51
  see also prefrontal cortex
Brunswick (Georgia – 1915) 25
bullying 68–70

Canadian police officers 231
cardiac measures (incl. heart rate) and
    aggression 78–9, 80–1, 84–5

case studies
  mass shootings 86–7
  prolonged exposure therapy
    281–3, 396
  trauma literature as series of 192
catalyst model for violent antisocial
    behavior 63
causal/etiological/predisposing factors
    (mass shootings) 26–55, 59–95
  myths and uncertainties 59–76
Center for Crisis Psychology
    (CCP – Norway) 296, 300,
    303, 304, 305
Certificate of Confidentiality 380
Challenging Beliefs worksheet in prolonged
    exposure therapy 276, 277
Challenging Questions worksheet in
    prolonged exposure therapy 275
characteristics of mass shootings 38–43
Charlie Hebdo 45–6
Chicago (Illinois – 1966) 25
Chicago (Illinois – 2008) 45
children
  afterschool programs 88–9
  bereaved, Utøya and Oslo 305
  development 63–4
  as perpetrators 59
  vicarious exposure 145–6
    in media to violence 140, 156
  see also adolescents; educational institute
    shootings; juvenile delinquency
chronic disruption (in normal posttrauma
    function) 337
cingulate cortex, anterior 334
circumstance-related distress 8, 9
clinical factors, violence propensity 105,
    105–6
clinical risk assessment 98–100
CNN 119, 120, 211
coercion in research 375–6, 377
cognitive–behavioral therapies (CBTs) 267,
    268–77
cognitive processing of trauma,
    constructive 340
cognitive restructuring 273, 277,
    278, 393, 394
collective community
  collective guilt 223
  collective identity 222–3, 393
  collective unity 174, 220, 223–4
colleges *see* educational institute shootings

Columbine High School (Columbine, Colorado – 1999) 28, 31, 47, 69, 86, 87, 357, 363, 390, 398
  media coverage and 119, 120, 121, 122, 123, 127, 128, 141, 143, 171, 176, 177
communication
  crisis mode of 170
  masspersonal 162–4
community (surviving) 170–87, 210–28
  ethical issues (in general) 374–81
  impact of journalism on 170–87
  psychosocial functioning 210–28
  resilience 336
  solidarity 174–6, 219–24, 323, 395
confidentiality
  mental health services in workplace 242
  research and risks to 379–80
  see also disclosure
conflict
  in community 221
  violence associated with 356
consent to research 375–8
conservation of resources 216
constructive cognitive processing of trauma 340
context
  mass shootings in U.S. 22–3
  present contextual factors for violence propensity 105, 107–8
  responsibility of research to contextualize 383
control
  power and *see* power and control
  survivors' loss/lack of 179, 320, 375
control theory 48–9
Conyers, Heritage High School (Georgia – 1999) 120
coping (ability/strategies) 156, 158–9, 203, 216–18
  by avoidance *see* avoidance
  children and adolescents 146
  journalists 253
  posttraumatic growth and 339, 340, 342
  pretrauma 202
  work and 395
cosmology episode 153–4
crime (felony incl. robbery)
  case counts of felony incidents (U.S. 2006–2014) 39
  demographics

offenders 41
  victims 42
  fear *see* fear
  region of occurrence 40
  research in mass violence and investigation of criminal cases 377
  strain theory and 47
  violence for purposes of 355
    schools 364
crisis mode of communication 170
Crisis Team, Utöya 299, 300, 301
critical incident stress debriefing *see* debriefing
cultural life, media impact 171–2

dangerousness 96–114
  correlates 103–8
  predicting 96–114
  the question of 97–8
  see also violence
dataset in U.S. (1915–2013) 21–2
deaths *see* fatalities; homicides/killings/murder; loss; suicide
debriefing (psychological) 239–41, 334
  critical incident 334
  rescue workers 239–41
decisional capacity to consent to research 374, 375
definition of mass shooting 3–6, 14, 20–1, 22, 37, 232, 295, 372, 388
delayed response to traumatic stressor 337
delinquency, juvenile 106, 397
demographics
  impacted individuals
    mental health outcomes 201–2
    mental health service utilization 313–18
    rescue workers 233–4
    vicarious exposure 145–6
  of mass shooters 40–1
  violence propensity and 104–5
Denver Post 119
Department of Education 60–1, 363, 365, 398
de-pathologizing responses to trauma 331–2
dependency, media 153–4
depression 8, 200, 204, 213, 214, 217, 269, 272, 273
  journalists 252, 255
  mental health service use and 319

depression (*cont'd*)
  posttraumatic growth and 341, 342
  rescue workers 235
detection and identification and prediction
    (of those at risk of mass
    murder) 96–114, 258, 359–61
  evolution of 98–103
  theories and 87, 91
  warning signs 52–3, 354
  see also risk
developmental prevention 88
Diagnostic and Statistical Manual of Mental
    Disorders (DSM)
  grief reactions 8
  traumatic exposure 9–10, 138, 194, 196
    PTSD and 6–7, 138
dialogue (of others) 162–4
diathesis–stress models of violence 63
direct exposure (directly affected) 9,
    10–11, 137–8, 191–209, 214–15
  adjustment problems 214–15
  mental health outcomes 191–209
  rescue workers 229–46
  tensions between those indirectly
    affected and 221
Directorate of Health, Norwegian
    (NDH) 299, 301, 303, 305
disabling factors, mental health service
    utilization 314–17, 318–19
disclosure
  incriminating 377
  of perpetrator's name, urging media
    to refrain from 383
  see also confidentiality
disconfirming information 269
  ignoring evidence 99
disruption, chronic (in normal posttrauma
    function) 337
dissemination of research findings 381
dissociation, peritrauma 202, 203, 215–16
distress (psychological) 8
  circumstance-related 9
  existential/identity-related 8
  failing to seek help 321
  journalist 247–64
dose–response model 5, 9, 10, 11,
    13, 195–7
  moderators and mediators of 11
dream content and 9/11 attacks 141
drug abuse *see* substance abuse
drug therapy, PTSD 283–5

DSM *see* Diagnostic and Statistical Manual
    of Mental Disorders
Dunblane (Scotland – 1996) 176, 254
Dunwoody, Harry 25
Dyregrov, Atle, Norway killings and 296–7

educational institute shootings (schools/
    colleges/universities) 12
  previous/earlier reports 62
  prolonged exposure therapy, case
    study 281–3
  research on shootings at 398
    ethical aspects 378–9
  time trends (U.S. 1915–2013) 24, 28,
    31, 32
  see also school *and specific incidents*
emergency medical service (EMS)
    workers 229, 230, 233–4, 235,
    236, 237, 238, 240, 241
emotional (affective/impulsive/reactive)
    aggression or violence 82–3, 83–4,
    84–5, 85, 86, 90, 357
empathy
  journalists and 178, 250
  psychopaths lack of 61, 355
enabling factors, mental health service
    utilization 314–17, 318–19, 324
enrichment nursery school
    interventions 89
environmental factors 62
  aggression 83–4
  genetic factors interacting with 68
epidemiology/time trends, U.S. 20–35,
    37–43
Erfurt (Germany – 2002) 47
Esteem module in prolonged exposure
    therapy 276
Estonia ferry disaster (1994) 322
ethics 372–87
  media/journalists 176, 250, 256, 257,
    258, 259, 260, 383
  of research in aftermath 372–87
ethnicity *see* race and ethnicity
etiological factors *see* causal/etiological/
    predisposing factors
evidence-based treatments 267–77, 285
Exceptional Case Study Project 361
existential distress 8
existential threat 393
explanations for mass shootings
    (predominantly U.S.) 26–55, 59–95

exposure 9–11, 191–209
  adjustment problems and level
    of 212–15
  definition 194–5
  direct *see* direct exposure
  dose–response model *see* dose–response
    model
  imaginal 270–1, 282, 283
  indirect/secondary/vicarious *see*
    vicarious/indirect/secondary
    exposure
  journalists 247–64
  mental health outcomes 191–209
  minimizing impact of 391–7
  rescue workers 229–46
  see also prolonged exposure therapy
eye movement desensitization and
  reprocessing 277–81
eyewitnesses 86, 172

Facebook 154, 159, 160, 161, 162,
  258, 393
fame, desire for 383
family incidents (U.S. 2006–2014)
  case counts 39
  demographics
    offenders 41
    victims 41
  region of occurrence 40
family life (home life) 67–8, 87
  see also parenting
family members
  bereaved *see* bereavement
  support 218
    public relief efforts at Utøya and
      Oslo 293–311, 394
fatalities/deaths (victim)
  family members' visit to site of 301–3
  number
    in definition of mass shooting 4, 5,
      20–1, 22, 37, 232, 372, 388, 390
    news coverage and 130
  see also bereavement; homicides;
    loss; memorializing; mourning
FBI's Supplementary Homicide Reports
  (SHR) 21–2, 38
fear
  of crime
    media influence on 126–8
    of shooting recurrence 224
  erasure 334

networks, and prolonged exposure
  therapy 268–9
  see also anxiety
Federal Assault Weapons Ban/AWB
  (1994) 27, 123
Federal government 125–6, 399
felony *see* crime
financial compensation 221
financial gain, mass murder for 45
Finland
  shared characteristics of perpetrators with
    Norway and U.S. 391
  specific incidents *see* Jokela High School;
    Kauhajoki School
firearm violence *see* gun violence
firefighters 229, 230–1, 232, 237–8, 239
fluoxetine 284
Fort Hood (Killeen, Texas – 2009) 120,
  128
Fox News 119
framing 173–4
France (Paris – 2015), terrorism 45–6

gender (sex)
  mass murderers 28, 40–1, 85
  survivors and victims 42, 43
    mental health outcomes 201
    mental health service utilization 313
  vicarious exposure and 145
  violence propensity 104
  see also males
general strain theory 47–8
genetic (inherited/heritable) risk factors
  perpetrators 63, 68
    aggression 84
    environmental factors interacting
      with 68
    prevention approaches and suppression
      of 88
  PTSD 204, 336
geographical occurrence by incident type
  (2006-2014 in U.S.) 40
Germany, Erfurt (2002) 47
Giffords, Gabrielle 362
Giovanni, Nikki (poet) 393
government
  Federal 125–6, 399
  Norway killings and relief efforts
    of 298–307
  threats aimed at officials in
    361–2

grief 153–87
    community, impact of journalism on
        170–87
    management 155, 162–4, 173
    media and expressions of 153–69
    mediatized 173
    reactions to 8–9, 302–3
    vicarious 158–62
growth, posttraumatic *see* posttraumatic
        growth
guided clinical judgment 102
guilt and shame 222
    collective 223
    journalists 258
gun (firearm) violence 4–5, 66
    prevention (incl. gun control) 121–4,
        360–1, 399
        mental health concerns and 124–5
Guyana (Jonestown – 1978) 45

hate crimes 46
head trauma 50
health care
    behavioral model of utilization 312,
        313–19, 324, 325
    mental *see* treatment
heart rate and aggression 78–9, 80–1,
        84–5
help and support
    failing to seek 321, 396
    media role 156, 158–64, 164
    public efforts 293–311
        mental health services *see* treatment
        Utøya and Oslo 293–311, 394
    social 155, 158, 159, 161, 164, 203,
        218–22
    sociocontextual factors affecting seeking
        of 323–4
heritable factors *see* genetic risk factors
Heritage High School (Conyers,
        Georgia – 1999) 120
high impact–recovery trajectory 338
hippocampus 333, 334, 335
Historical Clinical, Risk Management-20
        (HCR-20) 102, 104, 106, 358
historical trends (time trends) in
        U.S. 20–35, 37–43
history (individual people's)
    of trauma-related problems prior to
        event 144–5
    violence propensity and relationship to
        105, 106

home life 67–8, 87
homework in prolonged exposure therapy
        270, 271, 274, 275, 276, 276–7
homicides/killings/murder (mass) 389
    juvenile 357
    by proxy 44
    social construction 23–4
    Waco, Texas (2015) 355
    see also fatalities
Hurricane Katrina (2005) 312, 313, 316,
        317, 318, 319, 321
5-hydroxytryptamine *see* serotonin
hyperarousal (high arousal levels)
    journalists 248, 251
    survivors 139, 182, 217, 240
hypoarousal (underarousal),
        perpetrators 79, 80, 81, 82–3, 84,
        86, 87, 88

identification, of those at risk of mass
        murder *see* detection
identity
    collective 222–3, 393
    of perpetrator, urging media to refrain
        from disclosing 383
identity distress 8
imaginal exposure 270–1, 282, 283
Impact of Event Scale 229
impulsive (affective/emotional/impulsive/
        reactive) aggression or violence
        82–3, 83–4, 84–5, 85, 86, 90, 357
impulsivity in risk assessment 107
incidents (2006-2014 in U.S.)
    case counts by types of 39
    counts by types 39
    geographical occurrence by types of 40
indirect exposure *see* vicarious exposure
information and support center, Norway
        killings 298–307
information-processing models of
        PTSD 332–3
inherited factors *see* genetic risk factors
injured victims, media targeting of 172
instrumental (proactive/reactive) aggression
        or violence 77–95, 355–6
interactive media 154, 155, 159, 164
Internet/online (incl. websites) 171
    Finnish shootings 178, 183
    memorializing 159
    see also media; social media
interpersonal factors affecting mental health
        service use 322–3

interventions *see* treatment
Intimacy module in prolonged exposure
    therapy 277
intraindividual factors affecting mental
    health service use 320–2
Isla Vista (California – 2014) 43, 356

jobs, advantages and disadvantages
    of 395
    see also workplace
Jokela High School (Finland – 2007) 324
    community psychosocial
        functioning 211, 212, 214, 218,
        220, 223, 224
    media and 137, 157–8, 171, 172, 175,
        177–8, 179–80, 182–3
    journalists 249, 250, 252, 257, 258
Jonestown (Guyana – 1978) 45
journalists and reporters 247–64
    approach to/contact with survivors 176,
        179–80
    distress 247–64
    ethics 176, 250, 256, 257, 258, 259,
        260, 383
    see also media and journalism
justice in research 374, 380–1
juvenile delinquency 106, 397
    see also adolescents
juvenile homicide offenders 357

Kauhajoki School (Finland – 2008) 171,
    175, 178–9, 180, 182, 183
    community psychosocial functioning
        183, 211, 222, 224
    media and 171, 175, 178–9, 180,
        182, 183
    journalists 248, 249, 250
Killeen, Texas (Luby's restaurant – 1991)
    37, 193, 232, 233
killings *see* homicides/killings/murder

law (legislation)
    gun control 121–4, 124–5, 360
    mental health 124–6
lawsuits 221
legal action 221
legislation *see* law
linear media 154, 155, 156, 158–9, 163
literacy, mental health 320–1, 325
longitudinal studies of impact 12, 15, 217,
    295, 307, 341, 342, 392
Los Angeles (California – 1935) 25

loss (of loved one) 173, 215
    writing letters to them 305
    see also bereavement; grief; mourning

McDonald's in San Ysidro
    (California – 1984) 50
males (men) 28
    protective factors, men 88
    violence propensity 104
    see also gender
mass, meaning of word 3
mass homicides/killings/murder *see*
    homicides/killings/murder
mass shooting, definition 3–6, 14, 20–1,
    22, 37, 232, 295, 372, 388
masspersonal communication 162–4
meaning of trauma, making 334–5, 393
media and journalism (incl. news and media
    technology) 115–87
    in aftermath 24, 115–87, 398–9
    community impact 170–87
    deleterious/negative effects 136,
        156–8, 164
    ethics 176, 250, 256, 257, 258, 259,
        260, 383
    not naming the perpetrator 383
    prevalence of coverage 119–20
    public attitudes/perception and the
        influence of 117–35, 172
    utility/supportive role 156, 158–64, 164
    vicarious exposure and 136–52
    dependency 153–4
    reliance on 153–5
    social *see* social media
    violence in, exposure to 64–7, 139–41
    see also journalists
medial prefrontal cortex, survivors 333–4
mediatizing 171–3
mediators and moderators of dose–response
    relationship 11
memorializing and remembrance 159,
    160, 172, 176, 299, 395
memory
    pretrauma 333, 334
    trauma 335
        cognitive processing therapy and
            275, 276
        eye movement desensitization and
            reprocessing and 278, 279, 280, 281
        prolonged exposure therapy and
            270, 271
    PTSD and 332

men *see* males
mental health (psychological health – of
      impacted persons) 189–264
   minimizing impact on 391–7
   outcomes 6–9, 189–264
      in direct exposure *see* direct exposure
      journalists 251–9
      longitudinal studies 12, 15, 217, 295,
         307, 341, 342, 392
      posttraumatic growth and 341–3
      predictors 201–5
      rescue workers 229–46
   pretrauma history of problems in *see*
      pretrauma/preshooting factors
   public figures threatened by people with
      problems of 361–2
   services and treatment *see* treatment
   see also trauma
mental status of perpetrators *see* psychology
Midwest, incident type (2006–2014) 40
minimal impact–resilience trajectory 338
minimal risk in research on impacted
      people 378–9
Miyake Island volcanic eruption 315
moderate impact–moderate symptoms
      trajectory 338
moderators and mediators of dose–response
      relationship 11
monetary compensation 221
moral panic 128
mortalities *see* fatalities; homicides/
      killings/murder; suicide
Mother Jones 24, 36, 37, 38, 39
mourning 159, 163, 172, 179
   rituals 173, 393
   see also bereavement; memorializing
MSNBC 120
multidimensional grief 8, 9
murder *see* homicides/killings/murder
MySpace 160

naming the perpetrator, urging media to
      refrain from 383
National Center for Victims of Crime
      report (2002) 363
National Crime Victimization Survey 364
National Instant Criminal Background
      Check System (NICS) Improvement
      Amendments Act (2007) 125
National Rifle Association (NRA) 65
National Science Foundation (NSF) 62

need for mental health services 319
negative affect in risk assessment 107
negative emotions 158
   journalists 249, 258
   management difficulties 217
neighborhood in risk assessment 107
neurobiology (brain)
   perpetrators 49–51
   PTSD 333–4
   see also prefrontal cortex
New York City (9/11; September 11,
      2001) terrorist attack 137, 140–1,
      141, 144, 145, 156, 157, 161, 182,
      194, 221, 230, 238–9, 312, 313,
      314, 315, 318, 319, 321, 332, 381,
      391
New York Times 22, 119
news *see* journalists; media *and specific
      media*
newspapers 119, 259
   Kauhajoki tragedy 119
   Utøya Island 259
NICS Improvement Amendments Act
      (2007) 125
9/11 (September 11, 2001) terrorist
      attack 137, 140–1, 141, 144, 145,
      156, 157, 161, 182, 194, 221, 230,
      238–9, 312, 313, 314, 315, 318,
      319, 321, 332, 381, 391
nonmaleficence 374, 378–9
Northeast states, incident type
      (2006–2014) 40
Northern Illinois University (NIU;
      DeKalb, Illinois – 2008) 336,
      337, 342
   adjustment problems 211, 212, 214,
      216, 217, 218
   media and 120, 128, 162
   mental health outcomes 193, 195
Norway, Oslo and Utöya killings (2011)
      46–7, 293–309, 322, 394, 397
   journalist distress 248, 252, 256, 257–8
   media and 179, 181, 182
   shared characteristics of perpetrators with
      Finland and U.S. 391
notoriety, desire for 383
null findings/studies 13, 65
numbers of victim deaths in definition of
      mass shooting 4, 5, 20–1, 22, 232,
      372, 388, 390
nursery school enrichment programs 89

Oak creek Sikh temple (Oak Creek, Wisconsin – 2012) 120
Oakland (California), Oikos University in (2012) 49
Obama, President, and his administration 52, 125–6
offenders *see* perpetrators
Oikos University in (Oakland, California – 2012) 49
Oklahoma City bombing (Oklahoma – 1995) 140, 145, 156, 182, 194, 230, 237, 238, 239, 316, 381
online *see* Internet
optimism and posttraumatic growth 340
Oslo and Utöya *see* Norway
outcomes
  processes linking mass shootings to 9–11
  psychological/mental health *see* mental health

Palatine (Illinois – 1993) 47
panic, moral 128
paranoid schizophrenia 30, 357, 362
parenting
  permissive 90
  programs 89
Paris (France – 2015), terrorism 45–6
paroxetine 283, 284
past history of violent behaviour 105, 106
patterns (in U.S.) 28–30
Patterns of Problematic Thinking worksheet in prolonged exposure therapy 276
peritrauma factors
  impact on mental health outcomes 202–3
    journalists 255–6
  impact on mental health service use 319
perpetrators/offenders/assailants
  counts (U.S. 2006–2014) 39
  ethics in research focused on 376–7
  naming, urging media to refrain from 383
  psychology *see* psychology
  typology 43–6
personal life, journalists 254
personality traits and posttraumatic growth 339–40
pharmacotherapy, PTSD 283–5
physiology and PTSD outcome 204

police 229, 230, 231, 232, 233–4, 237–8, 239, 241, 242
  Utøya 302
population size (U.S.) 26
posttraumatic factors
  adjustment problems 216–17
  as mental health outcome predictors 203–4
    journalists 257–9
posttraumatic growth 219, 334–5, 338–43
  definition 338–9
  psychological outcomes and 341–3
Posttraumatic Growth Inventory (PTGI) 339, 342
posttraumatic stress 153–4
  journalists as cause of 177
posttraumatic stress disorder (PTSD) 6–7, 193–205, 331–4, 336, 341, 342
  barriers to mental health service use 320, 321
  communities and 212–18
  information-processing models of 332–3
  journalists 251–9
  media influence 136–47, 157
  neurobiology 333–4
  posttraumatic growth and 341, 342
  posttraumatic stress symptoms vs 7
  rescue workers 230–2, 234–5, 236, 237–40, 242, 243
  research ethics and people with 377–8
  treatments for 267–92
posttraumatic stress symptoms (PTSS) and difficulties 7–8, 8, 179–83, 197
  media impacts 172, 179–83
posttraumatic symptoms 332
  persistence after vicarious exposure 155
  self-report of 7, 13
  trajectories over time 337–8
  see also posttraumatic stress symptoms
power and control 43–4
  worksheet in prolonged exposure therapy 276
predatory (instrumental/premeditated/proactive) aggression or violence 77–95, 355
prediction *see* detection and identification and prediction
predisposing factors
  mass shootings *see* causal/etiological/predisposing factors
  mental health service utilization 313–18

prefrontal cortex
  perpetrators 63, 80–1, 83
  survivors 333–4
premeditated (instrumental/predatory/
    proactive) aggression or
    violence 77–95, 355
present contextual factors, violence
    propensity 105, 107–8
present person factors, violence
    propensity 105, 106–7
pretrauma/preshooting factors (prior to
    incident) 202
  adjustment problems 214
  mental health issues 144–5, 202
    journalists 253–5
    rescue workers 234–5
    utilization of mental health services
      and 318
prevalence trends (U.S.) 24–8, 31
prevention (minimizing likelihood of
    violence and mass shootings)
    359–61, 397–9
  developmental 88
  future research 397–9
  warning signs in 52–3, 354
primary prevention 358, 359
proactive (instrumental/predatory/
    premeditated) aggression or
    violence 77–95, 355
proactive model of psychosocial follow-up,
    Norway killings 299–301
professional shield, journalists' 249,
    250, 256
profit, mass murder for 45
prolonged exposure therapy (PE) 268–71,
    285
  case study 281–3, 396
  combat veterans 242
prospective studies 12–13, 14
protective factors
  perpetration 80
    men 88
  survivor responses 335–7
proxy
  murder by 44
  suicide by 44
psychological health *see* mental health
psychology of perpetrators (incl.
    psychological/mental health
    and illness) 57–114
  media and 124–6

U.S. (patterns and prevalence
    considerations) 29, 30, 31–2, 36
psychopathy 104, 105–6, 355, 357
psychosis (psychotic illness) 61, 105,
    356–7, 375
psychosocial functioning in
    community 210–28
psychosocial therapies and
    follow-ups 268–82
  Utøya and Oslo bereaved persons
    295–8, 299–307
public attitudes/perceptions
  of journalists work and ethics 257
  media influence 117–35, 172
public figures, threats against 361–2
public health problems 359
  government treating mass shootings
    as 399
public incidents/mass shootings 388–99
  case counts 39
  demographics
    offenders 41
    victims 42
  future research 388–99
  region of occurrence 40

qualitative studies 396
quantitative studies 396

race and ethnicity
  assailant 41
  victims and survivors 42, 43
    mental health outcomes 201
    mental health service utilization 318
rampage shooters 48, 59–76
  development 59–76
randomized controlled trials (RCTs) as gold
    standard for treatment efficacy 397
Rapid Risk Assessment of Sexual Offender
    Recidivism (RRASOR) 97, 98, 100
rate data (U.S.) 26
  violent crime 364
reactive (emotional/impulsive/affective)
    aggression or violence 82–3, 83–4,
    84–5, 85, 86, 90, 357
reconsolidation 334, 334–5
recovery
  gradual 337
  sociocontextual factors affecting 323–4
Red Lake High School (Red Lake,
    Minnesota – 2005) 67, 127

reexperiencing *see* rumination

religion and spirituality 393, 395

reliving the experience/trauma *see* rumination

remembrance and memorializing 159, 160, 172, 176, 299, 395

replaying the experience/trauma *see* rumination

reporters *see* journalists

rescue workers, psychopathology 229–46

research 372–400
  in aftermath, ethics 372–87
  design, challenges 12–14
  dissemination of findings 381
  future directions 388–400

resilience 214, 335–7
  journalists 259
  protective factors conferring 335–7

respect for persons 374–7

revenge 44

risk (of committing violence incl. mass murder)
  assessment 96–114
    threat assessment as form of 353, 358–9
  detecting those at *see* detection

robbery *see* crime

routine activity theory 48

RRASOR (Rapid Risk Assessment of Sexual Offender Recidivism) 97, 98, 100

rs25531 polymorphism 204, 336

rumination (in reliving and replaying the experience/trauma) 142, 157–8, 217
  deliberate 340, 393

safety, media influence on perceptions of 126–8

Safety Module in prolonged exposure therapy 276

San Diego, California
  San Ysidro McDonald's shooting (1984) 50
  school shootings (2001) 143, 183

San Ysidro (California – 1984) 50

Sandy Hook Elementary School (Newtown, Connecticut – 2012) 39, 42, 44, 52, 54, 62, 64, 65, 67
  medial coverage 119, 120, 121, 122, 123, 124, 125, 126, 127, 128, 171

Santa Barbara, Isla Vista nearby to University of California at 43, 356

schizophrenia 52, 61, 124, 356
  paranoid 30, 357, 362

school(s)
  afterschool programs 88–9
  bullying 68–70
  shootings in *see* educational institute shootings
  threat assessment 363–5
  see also nursery school enrichment programs

school managers and teachers of Utöya, seminars for 306–7

Scotland, Dunblane (1996) 176, 254

secondary prevention 358, 359

Secret Service (U.S.) 60–1, 67, 354, 361, 363, 365

security guards 233–4, 241

security protocols, postshooting 223

selective serotonin reuptake inhibitors in PTSD 283–5

self-blame 198, 274, 275, 394

self-help, Utöya and Oslo bereaved family members 304–5

self-report 396
  bereaved persons experiences of visiting Utøya 302–3
  of traumatic symptoms 7, 13
  rescue workers 229

self-stigmatizing beliefs 321

separation-related distress 8

September 11 terrorist attacks (2001) 137, 140–1, 141, 144, 145, 156, 157, 161, 182, 194, 221, 230, 238–9, 312, 313, 314, 315, 318, 319, 321, 332, 381, 391

serotonin (5-HT; 5-hydroxytryptamine)
  selective serotonin reuptake inhibitors in PTSD 283–5
  transporter (5-HTTLPR) gene, PTSD and 204, 336
  violence risk and blood levels of 80

sertraline 283, 284, 285

sex *see* gender

sexual abuse/trauma (history of)
  perpetrators and 84, 139
  survivors and 214, 218, 373

shame *see* guilt and shame

shooting, meaning of word 3

Sikh temple in Oak Creek
        (Wisconsin – 2012) 120
skin conductance 80, 89
social and biological factors (biosocial
        theory) of proactive
        aggression 77–95
social constraints theory 322, 326, 395
social construction of mass murder 23–4
social learning 46–7
social life, media impact 171–2
social media 128, 136–52, 155, 171
    journalists and 255–6, 257
    supportive role (e.g. dealing with
        grief) 158–64, 164, 395
social networks 323, 326, 336
    mental health service use and 322
    violence risk and 108–9
social push theory 81, 84, 88
social solidarity 174–6, 219–24, 323, 395
social support 155, 158, 159, 161,
        164, 203, 218–22, 322, 323,
        394–5
    journalists 259
    in risk assessment 107–8
sociocontextual factors affecting mental
        health service use 322–3
socioeconomic status
    perpetrators 47, 67, 81, 104
    victims and survivors 120, 140, 201,
        312, 391
solidarity, social/community 174–6,
        219–24, 323, 395
Southern states, incident type
        (2006-2014) 40
Spanaway Junior High School (Spanaway,
        Washington – 1985) 59
spirituality and religion 393, 395
SSRIs (selective serotonin reuptake
        inhibitors) in PTSD 283–5
stalking 363
STATIC-99 97, 98
stigmatizing 42, 171–2, 222, 223,
        325, 326
    mental health issues 126
        as barrier to mental health service
            utilization 321–2, 324
        rescue workers 242
    see also self-stigmatizing beliefs
STin2 gene 204
storytelling 161, 164
strain theory 47–8

stress
    critical incident stress debriefing
        see debriefing
    perpetrators 63
    resilience to *see* resilience
    survivors/community etc. *see*
        posttraumatic stress; posttraumatic
        stress disorder; posttraumatic stress
        symptoms; trauma
    see also distress
Structured Assessment of Violence Risk in
        Youth (SAVRY) 358
structured professional judgment
        (SPJ) 102
stuck points in prolonged exposure
        therapy 272, 273, 274, 275,
        276, 277
substance abuse
    PTSD and 200, 252
    rescue workers 235
    violence and 106, 107
suicide 30, 40, 45, 59, 355
    by proxy 44
Sundvolden Hotel information and support
        center 298–307
supervision violation 106
Supplementary Homicide Reports (SHR),
        FBI's 21–2, 38
support *see* help and support
survivors (impacted persons/groups)
    arousal levels, high 139, 182, 217, 240
    control and its loss/lack 179, 275, 320
    journalist approaches to/contact
        with 176, 179–80
    psychological/mental health *see* mental
        health
    resilience *see* resilience
    sexual abuse/trauma and 214, 218, 373
    stress *see* posttraumatic stress;
        posttraumatic stress disorder;
        posttraumatic stress symptoms;
        trauma
    trauma *see* trauma
    violence (sense of) 179, 220, 223
    see also community; victims
symptoms, posttraumatic *see* posttraumatic
        symptoms
system justification theory 343

teachers of Utöya, seminars for 306–7
technology, media *see* media; social media

television (TV) coverage 119
  vicarious exposure via, and deleterious
      effects 140, 141, 143, 144, 145,
      156–7, 194, 195
    posttraumatic stress symptoms 182, 184
terrorism 45–6
tertiary prevention 359, 360–1
theories 36–55
  challenges to development of 12–14
  need for 392–3
therapy *see* treatment
threat
  assessment 353–71
    applications 361–5
    basic principles 353–4, 353–5
  posing vs making a 354
  posttraumatic growth and 340
Thurston High School (Springfield,
      Oregon – 1998) 124, 128
time
  adjustment over 342
  interventions and their timing 396
  posttraumatic stress disorder reducing
      over 204
  posttraumatic symptom trajectories
      over 337–8
  trends over, mass shootings in
      U.S. 20–35, 37–43
transformative quality of posttraumatic
      growth 341
trauma (psychological – and traumatic
      stress) 5, 331–49
  exposure to *see* exposure
  mediators and moderators 11
  memory *see* memory
  predisaster *see* pretrauma/preshooting
      factors
  reliving/replaying the *see* rumination
  responses to 331–49
    adaptive 336, 337–8
    de-pathologizing 331–2
  see also posttraumatic stress;
      posttraumatic stress disorder;
      posttraumatic stress symptoms
treatment/therapy/interventions
      (perpetrators – potential and actual)
  biological 90
  poor compliance with 106
treatment/therapy/interventions (victims
      and survivors), mental health
      265–330, 392

empirically-based 267–92
expanding and improving services 52
need for services 319
randomized controlled trials (RCTs) as
    gold standard for efficacy 397
rescue workers 236, 237, 238–42, 243
utilization of services 312–30
  barriers to 320–4, 324–5, 326
Trust Module in prolonged exposure
      therapy 276
Tucson, Arizona (2011) 28, 120, 121,
      124, 126, 128
twin studies, aggression 83, 84
Twitter 60, 128, 154, 162, 163, 393
typology of perpetrators 43–6

uncertainty, sense of 153–4
  reducing 156, 393–4, 395, 396, 398
underarousal, perpetrators 79, 80, 81,
      82–3, 84, 86, 87, 88
United States
  Department of Education 60, 363,
      365, 398
  epidemiology/time trends 20–35
  explanations for mass shootings 36–55
  Secret Service 60–1, 67, 354, 361,
      363, 365
  shared characteristics of perpetrators with
      Finland and Norway 391
unity, collective 174, 220, 223–4
universal (primary) prevention 358, 359
universities (in general) *see* educational
      institute shootings
University of California at Santa Barbara,
      Isla Vista nearby to 43, 356
University of Iowa (Iowa City,
      Iowa – 1991) 37
University of Oklahoma Health Sciences
      Center (OUHSC) 381
University of Texas at Austin (Austin,
      Texas – 1966) 25, 26, 87
USA Today 22, 28, 39
Utöya and Oslo (Norway – 2011) 46–7,
      179, 181, 182, 248, 252, 256,
      257–8, 293–309, 322, 394, 397

vagal tone 80
vicarious/indirect/secondary exposure
      (indirectly affected) 9, 10–11,
      136–52, 255
  grieving from 158–62

vicarious/indirect/secondary exposure
(indirectly affected) (*cont'd*)
  media role 136–52
  our knowledge about 143–6
  tensions between those directly affected
    and 221
victim(s) (incl. fatalities)
  availability in risk assessment 108
  categorizing by media 172
  counts (U.S. 2006-2014) 39
  ethical issues (in general) 374–81
  media influence on fear of becoming a
    126–8
  number in definition of mass shooting
    4, 5, 20–1, 22, 37, 232, 372,
    388, 390
  see also survivors
victimization
  media influence on public fear of
    126–8
  shooters viewing themselves as
    subjects of 64
video game violence 62, 64–7
violation
  supervision 106
  survivor sense of 179, 220, 223
violence (and violent attack) 64–7, 354–5,
    355–7
  catalyst model 63
  definition 98
  empirically supported correlates of 104
  gun *see* gun violence
  instrumental aggression or 77–95, 355–6
  media, exposure to 64–7, 139–41
  pathways to 355–7
  prediction *see* detection and identification
    and prediction
  predisposing and causative factors 63
  prevention *see* prevention
  risk of committing *see* risk
  threat of *see* threat
  video game 62, 64–7
  see also dangerousness
Violence Risk Appraisal Guide
    (VRAG) measure 100, 101,
    106, 358
Violent Crime Control and Law
    Enforcement Act (1994 – Federal
    Assault Weapons Ban) 27, 123

Virginia Student Threat Assessment
    Guidelines 364–5
Virginia Tech (VT; Blacksburg,
    Virginia – 2007) 48, 86, 192, 193,
    195, 320, 322, 323, 336, 357, 393,
    394, 395, 398
  community psychosocial
    functioning 211–23
  media coverage 86, 119, 120, 121, 124,
    125, 126, 127, 128, 137, 141,
    142–3, 157, 161, 175, 177, 184
  visit by family members to site of
    death 301–3
vulnerability of research participants 374

Waco, Texas (2015) 355
Wakefield, Massachusetts (2000) 47
warning signs
  detecting and dealing with 52–3, 354
  overlooking 52–3
weapon availability in risk assessment 108
websites *see* Internet
weekend gatherings of Utöya and Oslo
    bereaved family members 303–6
WEIRD (Western, Educated, Industrialized,
    Rich, and Democratic)
    participants 65, 391, 395
wellbeing, journalist effects on feelings
    of 180
Western states, incident type
    (2006–2014) 40
Westside Middle School (Jonesboro,
    Arkansas – 1998) 124, 128
Winnetka Elementary School (Winnetka,
    Illinois – 1988) 64, 390
work (job), advantages and disadvantages
    of 395
workplace 395
  confidentiality concerning mental health
    service provision in 242
  journalist stress in 254
  mass murders, history 25, 28, 31, 32
  threat assessment 362–3
World Trade Center (9/11; September 11,
    2001) terrorist attack 137, 140–1,
    141, 144, 145, 156, 157, 161, 182,
    194, 221, 230, 238–9, 312, 313,
    314, 315, 318, 319, 321, 332,
    381, 391